Lecture Notes in Computer Science 12254

More information about this series at http://www.springer.com/series/7407

Osvaldo Gervasi · Beniamino Murgante ·
Sanjay Misra · Chiara Garau ·
Ivan Blečić · David Taniar ·
Bernady O. Apduhan · Ana Maria A. C. Rocha ·
Eufemia Tarantino · Carmelo Maria Torre ·
Yeliz Karaca (Eds.)

Computational Science and Its Applications – ICCSA 2020

20th International Conference
Cagliari, Italy, July 1–4, 2020
Proceedings, Part VI

 Springer

Editors
Osvaldo Gervasi ⓘ
University of Perugia
Perugia, Italy

Sanjay Misra ⓘ
Chair- Center of ICT/ICE
Covenant University
Ota, Nigeria

Ivan Blečić ⓘ
University of Cagliari
Cagliari, Italy

Bernady O. Apduhan
Department of Information Science
Kyushu Sangyo University
Fukuoka, Japan

Eufemia Tarantino ⓘ
Polytechnic University of Bari
Bari, Italy

Yeliz Karaca ⓘ
Department of Neurology
University of Massachusetts
Medical School
Worcester, MA, USA

Beniamino Murgante ⓘ
University of Basilicata
Potenza, Potenza, Italy

Chiara Garau ⓘ
University of Cagliari
Cagliari, Italy

David Taniar ⓘ
Clayton School of Information Technology
Monash University
Clayton, VIC, Australia

Ana Maria A. C. Rocha ⓘ
University of Minho
Braga, Portugal

Carmelo Maria Torre ⓘ
Polytechnic University of Bari
Bari, Italy

ISSN 0302-9743   ISSN 1611-3349 (electronic)
Lecture Notes in Computer Science
ISBN 978-3-030-58816-8   ISBN 978-3-030-58817-5 (eBook)
https://doi.org/10.1007/978-3-030-58817-5

LNCS Sublibrary: SL1 – Theoretical Computer Science and General Issues

This Springer imprint is published by the registered company Springer Nature Switzerland AG
The registered company address is: Gewerbestrasse 11, 6330 Cham, Switzerland

Preface

These seven volumes (LNCS volumes 12249–12255) consist of the peer-reviewed papers from the International Conference on Computational Science and Its Applications (ICCSA 2020) which took place from July 1–4, 2020. Initially the conference was planned to be held in Cagliari, Italy, in collaboration with the University of Cagliari, but due to the COVID-19 pandemic it was organized as an online event.

ICCSA 2020 was a successful event in the conference series, previously held in Saint Petersburg, Russia (2019), Melbourne, Australia (2018), Trieste, Italy (2017), Beijing, China (2016), Banff, Canada (2015), Guimaraes, Portugal (2014), Ho Chi Minh City, Vietnam (2013), Salvador, Brazil (2012), Santander, Spain (2011), Fukuoka, Japan (2010), Suwon, South Korea (2009), Perugia, Italy (2008), Kuala Lumpur, Malaysia (2007), Glasgow, UK (2006), Singapore (2005), Assisi, Italy (2004), Montreal, Canada (2003), and (as ICCS) Amsterdam, The Netherlands (2002) and San Francisco, USA (2001).

Computational science is the main pillar of most of the present research, industrial and commercial applications, and plays a unique role in exploiting ICT innovative technologies. The ICCSA conference series has provided a venue for researchers and industry practitioners to discuss new ideas, to share complex problems and their solutions, and to shape new trends in computational science.

Apart from the general track, ICCSA 2020 also included 52 workshops in various areas of computational science, ranging from computational science technologies to specific areas of computational science, such as software engineering, security, machine learning and artificial intelligence, blockchain technologies, and of applications in many fields. We accepted 498 papers, distributed among 6 conference main tracks, which included 52 in workshops and 32 short papers. We would like to express our appreciation to the workshops chairs and co-chairs for their hard work and dedication.

The success of the ICCSA conference series in general, and of ICCSA 2020 in particular, vitaly depends on the support from many people: authors, presenters, participants, keynote speakers, workshop chairs, session chairs, Organizing Committee members, student volunteers, Program Committee members, Advisory Committee members, international liaison chairs, reviewers, and others in various roles. We take this opportunity to wholeheartedly thank them all.

We also wish to thank our publisher, Springer, for their acceptance to publish the proceedings, for sponsoring part of the Best Papers Awards, and for their kind assistance and cooperation during the editing process.

We cordially invite you to visit the ICCSA website http://www.iccsa.org where you can find all the relevant information about this interesting and exciting event.

July 2020

Osvaldo Gervasi
Beniamino Murgante
Sanjay Misra

Welcome to the Online Conference

The COVID-19 pandemic disrupted our plans for ICCSA 2020, as was the case for the scientific community around the world. Hence, we had to promptly regroup and rush to set in place the organization and the underlying infrastructure of the online event.

We chose to build the technological infrastructure using only open source software. In particular, we used Jitsi (jitsi.org) for the videoconferencing, Riot (riot.im) together with Matrix (matrix.org) for chat and asynchronous communication, and Jibri (github.com/jitsi/jibri) for live streaming sessions on YouTube.

Six Jitsi servers were set up, one for each parallel session. The participants of the sessions were helped and assisted by eight volunteer students (from the Universities of Cagliari, Florence, Perugia, and Bari), who assured technical support and smooth running of the conference proceedings.

The implementation of the software infrastructure and the technical coordination of the volunteers was carried out by Damiano Perri and Marco Simonetti.

Our warmest thanks go to all the volunteering students, to the technical coordinators, and to the development communities of Jitsi, Jibri, Riot, and Matrix, who made their terrific platforms available as open source software.

Our heartfelt thanks go to the keynote speakers: Yaneer Bar-Yam, Cecilia Ceccarelli, and Vincenzo Piuri and to the guests of the closing keynote panel: Mike Batty, Denise Pumain, and Alexis Tsoukiàs.

A big thank you goes to all the 454 speakers, many of whom showed an enormous collaborative spirit, sometimes participating and presenting in almost prohibitive times of the day, given that the participants of this year's conference come from 52 countries scattered over many time zones of the globe.

Finally, we would like to thank Google for letting us livestream all the events via YouTube. In addition to lightening the load of our Jitsi servers, that will allow us to keep memory and to be able to review the most exciting moments of the conference.

We all hope to meet in our beautiful Cagliari next year, safe from COVID-19, and finally free to meet in person and enjoy the beauty of the ICCSA community in the enchanting Sardinia.

July 2020

Ivan Blečić
Chiara Garau

Organization

ICCSA 2020 was organized by the University of Cagliari (Italy), University of Perugia (Italy), University of Basilicata (Italy), Monash University (Australia), Kyushu Sangyo University (Japan), and University of Minho (Portugal).

Honorary General Chairs

Antonio Laganà	Master-UP, Italy
Norio Shiratori	Chuo University, Japan
Kenneth C. J. Tan	Sardina Systems, UK
Corrado Zoppi	University of Cagliari, Italy

General Chairs

Osvaldo Gervasi	University of Perugia, Italy
Ivan Blečić	University of Cagliari, Italy
David Taniar	Monash University, Australia

Program Committee Chairs

Beniamino Murgante	University of Basilicata, Italy
Bernady O. Apduhan	Kyushu Sangyo University, Japan
Chiara Garau	University of Cagliari, Italy
Ana Maria A. C. Rocha	University of Minho, Portugal

International Advisory Committee

Jemal Abawajy	Deakin University, Australia
Dharma P. Agarwal	University of Cincinnati, USA
Rajkumar Buyya	The University of Melbourne, Australia
Claudia Bauzer Medeiros	University of Campinas, Brazil
Manfred M. Fisher	Vienna University of Economics and Business, Austria
Marina L. Gavrilova	University of Calgary, Canada
Yee Leung	Chinese University of Hong Kong, China

International Liaison Chairs

Giuseppe Borruso	University of Trieste, Italy
Elise De Donker	Western Michigan University, USA
Maria Irene Falcão	University of Minho, Portugal
Robert C. H. Hsu	Chung Hua University, Taiwan

Tai-Hoon Kim	Beijing Jaotong University, China
Vladimir Korkhov	Saint Petersburg University, Russia
Sanjay Misra	Covenant University, Nigeria
Takashi Naka	Kyushu Sangyo University, Japan
Rafael D. C. Santos	National Institute for Space Research, Brazil
Maribel Yasmina Santos	University of Minho, Portugal
Elena Stankova	Saint Petersburg University, Russia

Workshop and Session Organizing Chairs

Beniamino Murgante	University of Basilicata, Italy
Sanjay Misra	Covenant University, Nigeria
Jorge Gustavo Rocha	University of Minho, Portugal

Award Chair

| Wenny Rahayu | La Trobe University, Australia |

Publicity Committee Chairs

Elmer Dadios	De La Salle University, Philippines
Nataliia Kulabukhova	Saint Petersburg University, Russia
Daisuke Takahashi	Tsukuba University, Japan
Shangwang Wang	Beijing University of Posts and Telecommunications, China

Technology Chairs

| Damiano Perri | University of Florence, Italy |
| Marco Simonetti | University of Florence, Italy |

Local Arrangement Chairs

Ivan Blečić	University of Cagliari, Italy
Chiara Garau	University of Cagliari, Italy
Ginevra Balletto	University of Cagliari, Italy
Giuseppe Borruso	University of Trieste, Italy
Michele Campagna	University of Cagliari, Italy
Mauro Coni	University of Cagliari, Italy
Anna Maria Colavitti	University of Cagliari, Italy
Giulia Desogus	University of Cagliari, Italy
Sabrina Lai	University of Cagliari, Italy
Francesca Maltinti	University of Cagliari, Italy
Pasquale Mistretta	University of Cagliari, Italy
Augusto Montisci	University of Cagliari, Italy
Francesco Pinna	University of Cagliari, Italy

Davide Spano	University of Cagliari, Italy
Roberto Tonelli	University of Cagliari, Italy
Giuseppe A. Trunfio	University of Sassari, Italy
Corrado Zoppi	University of Cagliari, Italy

Program Committee

Vera Afreixo	University of Aveiro, Portugal
Filipe Alvelos	University of Minho, Portugal
Hartmut Asche	University of Potsdam, Germany
Ginevra Balletto	University of Cagliari, Italy
Michela Bertolotto	University College Dublin, Ireland
Sandro Bimonte	CEMAGREF, TSCF, France
Rod Blais	University of Calgary, Canada
Ivan Blečić	University of Sassari, Italy
Giuseppe Borruso	University of Trieste, Italy
Ana Cristina Braga	University of Minho, Portugal
Massimo Cafaro	University of Salento, Italy
Yves Caniou	Lyon University, France
José A. Cardoso e Cunha	Universidade Nova de Lisboa, Portugal
Rui Cardoso	University of Beira Interior, Portugal
Leocadio G. Casado	University of Almeria, Spain
Carlo Cattani	University of Salerno, Italy
Mete Celik	Erciyes University, Turkey
Hyunseung Choo	Sungkyunkwan University, South Korea
Min Young Chung	Sungkyunkwan University, South Korea
Florbela Maria da Cruz Domingues Correia	Polytechnic Institute of Viana do Castelo, Portugal
Gilberto Corso Pereira	Federal University of Bahia, Brazil
Alessandro Costantini	INFN, Italy
Carla Dal Sasso Freitas	Universidade Federal do Rio Grande do Sul, Brazil
Pradesh Debba	The Council for Scientific and Industrial Research (CSIR), South Africa
Hendrik Decker	Instituto Tecnológico de Informática, Spain
Frank Devai	London South Bank University, UK
Rodolphe Devillers	Memorial University of Newfoundland, Canada
Joana Matos Dias	University of Coimbra, Portugal
Paolino Di Felice	University of L'Aquila, Italy
Prabu Dorairaj	NetApp, India/USA
M. Irene Falcao	University of Minho, Portugal
Cherry Liu Fang	U.S. DOE Ames Laboratory, USA
Florbela P. Fernandes	Polytechnic Institute of Bragança, Portugal
Jose-Jesus Fernandez	National Centre for Biotechnology, CSIS, Spain
Paula Odete Fernandes	Polytechnic Institute of Bragança, Portugal
Adelaide de Fátima Baptista Valente Freitas	University of Aveiro, Portugal

Manuel Carlos Figueiredo	University of Minho, Portugal
Maria Celia Furtado Rocha	PRODEB–PósCultura, UFBA, Brazil
Chiara Garau	University of Cagliari, Italy
Paulino Jose Garcia Nieto	University of Oviedo, Spain
Jerome Gensel	LSR-IMAG, France
Maria Giaoutzi	National Technical University of Athens, Greece
Arminda Manuela Andrade Pereira Gonçalves	University of Minho, Portugal
Andrzej M. Goscinski	Deakin University, Australia
Sevin Gümgüm	Izmir University of Economics, Turkey
Alex Hagen-Zanker	University of Cambridge, UK
Shanmugasundaram Hariharan	B.S. Abdur Rahman University, India
Eligius M. T. Hendrix	University of Malaga, Spain, and Wageningen University, The Netherlands
Hisamoto Hiyoshi	Gunma University, Japan
Mustafa Inceoglu	EGE University, Turkey
Peter Jimack	University of Leeds, UK
Qun Jin	Waseda University, Japan
Farid Karimipour	Vienna University of Technology, Austria
Baris Kazar	Oracle Corp., USA
Maulana Adhinugraha Kiki	Telkom University, Indonesia
DongSeong Kim	University of Canterbury, New Zealand
Taihoon Kim	Hannam University, South Korea
Ivana Kolingerova	University of West Bohemia, Czech Republic
Nataliia Kulabukhova	Saint Petersburg University, Russia
Vladimir Korkhov	Saint Petersburg University, Russia
Rosa Lasaponara	CNR, Italy
Maurizio Lazzari	CNR, Italy
Cheng Siong Lee	Monash University, Australia
Sangyoun Lee	Yonsei University, South Korea
Jongchan Lee	Kunsan National University, South Korea
Chendong Li	University of Connecticut, USA
Gang Li	Deakin University, Australia
Fang Liu	AMES Laboratories, USA
Xin Liu	University of Calgary, Canada
Andrea Lombardi	University of Perugia, Italy
Savino Longo	University of Bari, Italy
Tinghuai Ma	Nanjing University of Information Science and Technology, China
Ernesto Marcheggiani	Katholieke Universiteit Leuven, Belgium
Antonino Marvuglia	Research Centre Henri Tudor, Luxembourg
Nicola Masini	CNR, Italy
Ilaria Matteucci	CNR, Italy
Eric Medvet	University of Trieste, Italy
Nirvana Meratnia	University of Twente, The Netherlands

Pablo Vanegas	University of Cuenca, Ecuador
Marco Vizzari	University of Perugia, Italy
Varun Vohra	Merck Inc., USA
Koichi Wada	University of Tsukuba, Japan
Krzysztof Walkowiak	Wroclaw University of Technology, Poland
Zequn Wang	Intelligent Automation Inc., USA
Robert Weibel	University of Zurich, Switzerland
Frank Westad	Norwegian University of Science and Technology, Norway
Roland Wismüller	Universität Siegen, Germany
Mudasser Wyne	SOET National University, USA
Chung-Huang Yang	National Kaohsiung Normal University, Taiwan
Xin-She Yang	National Physical Laboratory, UK
Salim Zabir	France Telecom Japan Co., Japan
Haifeng Zhao	University of California, Davis, USA
Fabiana Zollo	University of Venice, Italy
Albert Y. Zomaya	The University of Sydney, Australia

Workshop Organizers

Advanced Transport Tools and Methods (A2TM 2020)

| Massimiliano Petri | University of Pisa, Italy |
| Antonio Pratelli | University of Pisa, Italy |

Advances in Artificial Intelligence Learning Technologies: Blended Learning, STEM, Computational Thinking and Coding (AAILT 2020)

Valentina Franzoni	University of Perugia, Italy
Alfredo Milani	University of Perugia, Italy
Sergio Tasso	University of Perugia, Italy

Workshop on Advancements in Applied Machine Learning and Data Analytics (AAMDA 2020)

Alessandro Costantini	INFN, Italy
Daniele Cesini	INFN, Italy
Davide Salomoni	INFN, Italy
Doina Cristina Duma	INFN, Italy

Advanced Computational Approaches in Artificial Intelligence and Complex Systems Applications (ACAC 2020)

Yeliz Karaca	University of Massachusetts Medical School, USA
Dumitru Baleanu	Çankaya University, Turkey, and Institute of Space Sciences, Romania
Majaz Moonis	University of Massachusetts Medical School, USA
Yu-Dong Zhang	University of Leicester, UK

Affective Computing and Emotion Recognition (ACER-EMORE 2020)

Valentina Franzoni	University of Perugia, Italy
Alfredo Milani	University of Perugia, Italy
Giulio Biondi	University of Florence, Italy

AI Factory and Smart Manufacturing (AIFACTORY 2020)

Jongpil Jeong	Sungkyunkwan University, South Korea

Air Quality Monitoring and Citizen Science for Smart Urban Management. State of the Art And Perspectives (AirQ&CScience 2020)

Grazie Fattoruso	ENEA CR Portici, Italy
Maurizio Pollino	ENEA CR Casaccia, Italy
Saverio De Vito	ENEA CR Portici, Italy

Automatic Landform Classification: Spatial Methods and Applications (ALCSMA 2020)

Maria Danese	CNR-ISPC, Italy
Dario Gioia	CNR-ISPC, Italy

Advances of Modelling Micromobility in Urban Spaces (AMMUS 2020)

Tiziana Campisi	University of Enna KORE, Italy
Giovanni Tesoriere	University of Enna KORE, Italy
Ioannis Politis	Aristotle University of Thessaloniki, Greece
Socrates Basbas	Aristotle University of Thessaloniki, Greece
Sanja Surdonja	University of Rijeka, Croatia
Marko Rencelj	University of Maribor, Slovenia

Advances in Information Systems and Technologies for Emergency Management, Risk Assessment and Mitigation Based on the Resilience Concepts (ASTER 2020)

Maurizio Pollino	ENEA, Italy
Marco Vona	University of Basilicata, Italy
Amedeo Flora	University of Basilicata, Italy
Chiara Iacovino	University of Basilicata, Italy
Beniamino Murgante	University of Basilicata, Italy

Advances in Web Based Learning (AWBL 2020)

Birol Ciloglugil	Ege University, Turkey
Mustafa Murat Inceoglu	Ege University, Turkey

Blockchain and Distributed Ledgers: Technologies and Applications (BDLTA 2020)

Vladimir Korkhov   Saint Petersburg University, Russia
Elena Stankova   Saint Petersburg University, Russia
Nataliia Kulabukhova   Saint Petersburg University, Russia

Bio and Neuro Inspired Computing and Applications (BIONCA 2020)

Nadia Nedjah   State University of Rio de Janeiro, Brazil
Luiza De Macedo Mourelle State University of Rio de Janeiro, Brazil

Computer Aided Modeling, Simulation and Analysis (CAMSA 2020)

Jie Shen   University of Michigan, USA

Computational and Applied Statistics (CAS 2020)

Ana Cristina Braga   University of Minho, Portugal

Computerized Evidence Based Decision Making (CEBDEM 2020)

Clarice Bleil de Souza   Cardiff University, UK
Valerio Cuttini   University of Pisa, Italy
Federico Cerutti   Cardiff University, UK
Camilla Pezzica   Cardiff University, UK

Computational Geometry and Applications (CGA 2020)

Marina Gavrilova   University of Calgary, Canada

Computational Mathematics, Statistics and Information Management (CMSIM 2020)

Maria Filomena Teodoro   Portuguese Naval Academy, University of Lisbon, Portugal

Computational Optimization and Applications (COA 2020)

Ana Rocha   University of Minho, Portugal
Humberto Rocha   University of Coimbra, Portugal

Computational Astrochemistry (CompAstro 2020)

Marzio Rosi   University of Perugia, Italy
Cecilia Ceccarelli   University of Grenoble, France
Stefano Falcinelli   University of Perugia, Italy
Dimitrios Skouteris   Master-UP, Italy

Cities, Technologies and Planning (CTP 2020)

Beniamino Murgante	University of Basilicata, Italy
Ljiljana Zivkovic	Ministry of Construction, Transport and Infrastructure and Institute of Architecture and Urban & Spatial Planning of Serbia, Serbia
Giuseppe Borruso	University of Trieste, Italy
Malgorzata Hanzl	University of Łódź, Poland

Data Stream Processing and Applications (DASPA 2020)

Raja Chiky	ISEP, France
Rosanna VERDE	University of Campania, Italy
Marcilio De Souto	Orleans University, France

Data Science for Cyber Security (DS4Cyber 2020)

Hongmei Chi	Florida A&M University, USA

Econometric and Multidimensional Evaluation in Urban Environment (EMEUE 2020)

Carmelo Maria Torre	Polytechnic University of Bari, Italy
Pierluigi Morano	Polytechnic University of Bari, Italy
Maria Cerreta	University of Naples, Italy
Paola Perchinunno	University of Bari, Italy
Francesco Tajani	University of Rome, Italy
Simona Panaro	University of Portsmouth, UK
Francesco Scorza	University of Basilicata, Italy

Frontiers in Machine Learning (FIML 2020)

Massimo Bilancia	University of Bari, Italy
Paola Perchinunno	University of Bari, Italy
Pasquale Lops	University of Bari, Italy
Danilo Di Bona	University of Bari, Italy

Future Computing System Technologies and Applications (FiSTA 2020)

Bernady Apduhan	Kyushu Sangyo University, Japan
Rafael Santos	Brazilian National Institute for Space Research, Brazil

Geodesign in Decision Making: Meta Planning and Collaborative Design for Sustainable and Inclusive Development (GDM 2020)

Francesco Scorza	University of Basilicata, Italy
Michele Campagna	University of Cagliari, Italy
Ana Clara Mourao Moura	Federal University of Minas Gerais, Brazil

Geomatics in Forestry and Agriculture: New Advances and Perspectives (GeoForAgr 2020)

Maurizio Pollino	ENEA, Italy
Giuseppe Modica	University of Reggio Calabria, Italy
Marco Vizzari	University of Perugia, Italy

Geographical Analysis, Urban Modeling, Spatial Statistics (GEOG-AND-MOD 2020)

Beniamino Murgante	University of Basilicata, Italy
Giuseppe Borruso	University of Trieste, Italy
Hartmut Asche	University of Potsdam, Germany

Geomatics for Resource Monitoring and Management (GRMM 2020)

Eufemia Tarantino	Polytechnic University of Bari, Italy
Enrico Borgogno Mondino	University of Torino, Italy
Marco Scaioni	Polytechnic University of Milan, Italy
Alessandra Capolupo	Polytechnic University of Bari, Italy

Software Quality (ISSQ 2020)

Sanjay Misra	Covenant University, Nigeria

Collective, Massive and Evolutionary Systems (IWCES 2020)

Alfredo Milani	University of Perugia, Italy
Rajdeep Niyogi	Indian Institute of Technology, Roorkee, India
Alina Elena Baia	University of Florence, Italy

Large Scale Computational Science (LSCS 2020)

Elise De Doncker	Western Michigan University, USA
Fukuko Yuasa	High Energy Accelerator Research Organization (KEK), Japan
Hideo Matsufuru	High Energy Accelerator Research Organization (KEK), Japan

Land Use Monitoring for Sustainability (LUMS 2020)

Carmelo Maria Torre	Polytechnic University of Bari, Italy
Alessandro Bonifazi	Polytechnic University of Bari, Italy
Pasquale Balena	Polytechnic University of Bari, Italy
Massimiliano Bencardino	University of Salerno, Italy
Francesco Tajani	University of Rome, Italy
Pierluigi Morano	Polytechnic University of Bari, Italy
Maria Cerreta	University of Naples, Italy
Giuliano Poli	University of Naples, Italy

Machine Learning for Space and Earth Observation Data (MALSEOD 2020)

Rafael Santos	INPE, Brazil
Karine Ferreira	INPE, Brazil

Building Multi-dimensional Models for Assessing Complex Environmental Systems (MES 2020)

Marta Dell'Ovo	Polytechnic University of Milan, Italy
Vanessa Assumma	Polytechnic University of Torino, Italy
Caterina Caprioli	Polytechnic University of Torino, Italy
Giulia Datola	Polytechnic University of Torino, Italy
Federico dell'Anna	Polytechnic University of Torino, Italy

Ecosystem Services: Nature's Contribution to People in Practice. Assessment Frameworks, Models, Mapping, and Implications (NC2P 2020)

Francesco Scorza	University of Basilicata, Italy
David Cabana	International Marine Center, Italy
Sabrina Lai	University of Cagliari, Italy
Ana Clara Mourao Moura	Federal University of Minas Gerais, Brazil
Corrado Zoppi	University of Cagliari, Italy

Open Knowledge for Socio-economic Development (OKSED 2020)

Luigi Mundula	University of Cagliari, Italy
Flavia Marzano	Link Campus University, Italy
Maria Paradiso	University of Milan, Italy

Scientific Computing Infrastructure (SCI 2020)

Elena Stankova	Saint Petersburg State University, Russia
Vladimir Korkhov	Saint Petersburg State University, Russia
Natalia Kulabukhova	Saint Petersburg State University, Russia

Computational Studies for Energy and Comfort in Buildings (SECoB 2020)

Senhorinha Teixeira	University of Minho, Portugal
Luís Martins	University of Minho, Portugal
Ana Maria Rocha	University of Minho, Portugal

Software Engineering Processes and Applications (SEPA 2020)

Sanjay Misra	Covenant University, Nigeria

Smart Ports - Technologies and Challenges (SmartPorts 2020)

Gianfranco Fancello	University of Cagliari, Italy
Patrizia Serra	University of Cagliari, Italy
Marco Mazzarino	University of Venice, Italy
Luigi Mundula	University of Cagliari, Italy

| Ginevra Balletto | University of Cagliari, Italy |
| Giuseppe Borruso | University of Trieste, Italy |

Sustainability Performance Assessment: Models, Approaches and Applications Toward Interdisciplinary and Integrated Solutions (SPA 2020)

Francesco Scorza	University of Basilicata, Italy
Valentin Grecu	Lucian Blaga University, Romania
Jolanta Dvarioniene	Kaunas University of Technology, Lithuania
Sabrina Lai	University of Cagliari, Italy
Iole Cerminara	University of Basilicata, Italy
Corrado Zoppi	University of Cagliari, Italy

Smart and Sustainable Island Communities (SSIC 2020)

Chiara Garau	University of Cagliari, Italy
Anastasia Stratigea	National Technical University of Athens, Greece
Paola Zamperlin	University of Pisa, Italy
Francesco Scorza	University of Basilicata, Italy

Science, Technologies and Policies to Innovate Spatial Planning (STP4P 2020)

Chiara Garau	University of Cagliari, Italy
Daniele La Rosa	University of Catania, Italy
Francesco Scorza	University of Basilicata, Italy
Anna Maria Colavitti	University of Cagliari, Italy
Beniamino Murgante	University of Basilicata, Italy
Paolo La Greca	University of Catania, Italy

New Frontiers for Strategic Urban Planning (StrategicUP 2020)

Luigi Mundula	University of Cagliari, Italy
Ginevra Balletto	University of Cagliari, Italy
Giuseppe Borruso	University of Trieste, Italy
Michele Campagna	University of Cagliari, Italy
Beniamino Murgante	University of Basilicata, Italy

Theoretical and Computational Chemistry and its Applications (TCCMA 2020)

| Noelia Faginas-Lago | University of Perugia, Italy |
| Andrea Lombardi | University of Perugia, Italy |

Tools and Techniques in Software Development Process (TTSDP 2020)

| Sanjay Misra | Covenant University, Nigeria |

Urban Form Studies (UForm 2020)

| Malgorzata Hanzl | Łódź University of Technology, Poland |

Urban Space Extended Accessibility (USEaccessibility 2020)

Chiara Garau	University of Cagliari, Italy
Francesco Pinna	University of Cagliari, Italy
Beniamino Murgante	University of Basilicata, Italy
Mauro Coni	University of Cagliari, Italy
Francesca Maltinti	University of Cagliari, Italy
Vincenza Torrisi	University of Catania, Italy
Matteo Ignaccolo	University of Catania, Italy

Virtual and Augmented Reality and Applications (VRA 2020)

Osvaldo Gervasi	University of Perugia, Italy
Damiano Perri	University of Perugia, Italy
Marco Simonetti	University of Perugia, Italy
Sergio Tasso	University of Perugia, Italy

Workshop on Advanced and Computational Methods for Earth Science Applications (WACM4ES 2020)

Luca Piroddi	University of Cagliari, Italy
Laura Foddis	University of Cagliari, Italy
Gian Piero Deidda	University of Cagliari, Italy
Augusto Montisci	University of Cagliari, Italy
Gabriele Uras	University of Cagliari, Italy
Giulio Vignoli	University of Cagliari, Italy

Sponsoring Organizations

ICCSA 2020 would not have been possible without tremendous support of many organizations and institutions, for which all organizers and participants of ICCSA 2020 express their sincere gratitude:

Springer International Publishing AG, Germany
(https://www.springer.com)

Computers Open Access Journal
(https://www.mdpi.com/journal/computers)

IEEE Italy Section, Italy
(https://italy.ieeer8.org/)

Centre-North Italy Chapter IEEE GRSS, Italy
(https://cispio.diet.uniroma1.it/marzano/ieee-grs/
index.html)

Italy Section of the Computer Society, Italy
(https://site.ieee.org/italy-cs/)

University of Cagliari, Italy
(https://unica.it/)

University of Perugia, Italy
(https://www.unipg.it)

University of Basilicata, Italy
(http://www.unibas.it)

   Monash University, Australia
(https://www.monash.edu/)

Kyushu Sangyo University, Japan
(https://www.kyusan-u.ac.jp/)

University of Minho, Portugal
(https://www.uminho.pt/)

Scientific Association Transport Infrastructures, Italy
(https://www.stradeeautostrade.it/associazioni-e-organizzazioni/asit-associazione-scientifica-infrastrutture-trasporto/)

Regione Sardegna, Italy
(https://regione.sardegna.it/)

Comune di Cagliari, Italy
(https://www.comune.cagliari.it/)

Referees

A. P. Andrade Marina	ISCTE, Instituto Universitário de Lisboa, Portugal
Addesso Paolo	University of Salerno, Italy
Adewumi Adewole	Algonquin College, Canada
Afolabi Adedeji	Covenant University, Nigeria
Afreixo Vera	University of Aveiro, Portugal
Agrawal Smirti	Freelancer, USA
Agrawal Akshat	Amity University Haryana, India
Ahmad Waseem	Federal University of Technology Minna, Nigeria
Akgun Nurten	Bursa Technical University, Turkey
Alam Tauhidul	Louisiana State University Shreveport, USA
Aleixo Sandra M.	CEAUL, Portugal
Alfa Abraham	Federal University of Technology Minna, Nigeria
Alvelos Filipe	University of Minho, Portugal
Alves Alexandra	University of Minho, Portugal
Amato Federico	University of Lausanne, Switzerland
Andrade Marina Alexandra Pedro	ISCTE-IUL, Portugal
Andrianov Sergey	Saint Petersburg State University, Russia
Anelli Angelo	CNR-IGAG, Italy
Anelli Debora	University of Rome, Italy
Annunziata Alfonso	University of Cagliari, Italy
Antognelli Sara	Agricolus, Italy
Aoyama Tatsumi	High Energy Accelerator Research Organization, Japan
Apduhan Bernady	Kyushu Sangyo University, Japan
Ascenzi Daniela	University of Trento, Italy
Asche Harmut	Hasso-Plattner-Institut für Digital Engineering GmbH, Germany
Aslan Burak Galip	Izmir Insitute of Technology, Turkey
Assumma Vanessa	Polytechnic University of Torino, Italy
Astoga Gino	UV, Chile
Atman Uslu Nilüfer	Manisa Celal Bayar University, Turkey
Behera Ranjan Kumar	National Institute of Technology, Rourkela, India
Badsha Shahriar	University of Nevada, USA
Bai Peng	University of Cagliari, Italy
Baia Alina-Elena	University of Perugia, Italy
Balacco Gabriella	Polytechnic University of Bari, Italy
Balci Birim	Celal Bayar University, Turkey
Balena Pasquale	Polytechnic University of Bari, Italy
Balletto Ginevra	University of Cagliari, Italy
Balucani Nadia	University of Perugia, Italy
Bansal Megha	Delhi University, India
Barazzetti Luigi	Polytechnic University of Milan, Italy
Barreto Jeniffer	Istituto Superior Técnico, Portugal
Basbas Socrates	Aristotle University of Thessaloniki, Greece

Berger Katja	Ludwig-Maximilians-Universität München, Germany
Beyene Asrat Mulatu	Addis Ababa Science and Technology University, Ethiopia
Bilancia Massimo	University of Bari Aldo Moro, Italy
Biondi Giulio	University of Firenze, Italy
Blanquer Ignacio	Universitat Politècnica de València, Spain
Bleil de Souza Clarice	Cardiff University, UK
Blečić Ivan	University of Cagliari, Italy
Bogdanov Alexander	Saint Petersburg State University, Russia
Bonifazi Alessandro	Polytechnic University of Bari, Italy
Bontchev Boyan	Sofia University, Bulgaria
Borgogno Mondino Enrico	University of Torino, Italy
Borruso Giuseppe	University of Trieste, Italy
Bouaziz Rahma	Taibah University, Saudi Arabia
Bowles Juliana	University of Saint Andrews, UK
Braga Ana Cristina	University of Minho, Portugal
Brambilla Andrea	Polytechnic University of Milan, Italy
Brito Francisco	University of Minho, Portugal
Buele Jorge	Universidad Tecnológica Indoamérica, Ecuador
Buffoni Andrea	TAGES sc, Italy
Cabana David	International Marine Centre, Italy
Calazan Rogerio	IEAPM, Brazil
Calcina Sergio Vincenzo	University of Cagliari, Italy
Camalan Seda	Atilim University, Turkey
Camarero Alberto	Universidad Politécnica de Madrid, Spain
Campisi Tiziana	University of Enna KORE, Italy
Cannatella Daniele	Delft University of Technology, The Netherlands
Capolupo Alessandra	Polytechnic University of Bari, Italy
Cappucci Sergio	ENEA, Italy
Caprioli Caterina	Polytechnic University of Torino, Italy
Carapau Fermando	Universidade de Evora, Portugal
Carcangiu Sara	University of Cagliari, Italy
Carrasqueira Pedro	INESC Coimbra, Portugal
Caselli Nicolás	PUCV Chile, Chile
Castro de Macedo Jose Nuno	Universidade do Minho, Portugal
Cavallo Carla	University of Naples, Italy
Cerminara Iole	University of Basilicata, Italy
Cerreta Maria	University of Naples, Italy
Cesini Daniele	INFN-CNAF, Italy
Chang Shi-Kuo	University of Pittsburgh, USA
Chetty Girija	University of Canberra, Australia
Chiky Raja	ISEP, France
Chowdhury Dhiman	University of South Carolina, USA
Ciloglugil Birol	Ege University, Turkey
Coletti Cecilia	Università di Chieti-Pescara, Italy

Coni Mauro	University of Cagliari, Italy
Corcoran Padraig	Cardiff University, UK
Cornelio Antonella	Università degli Studi di Brescia, Italy
Correia Aldina	ESTG-PPorto, Portugal
Correia Elisete	University of Trás-os-Montes and Alto Douro, Portugal
Correia Florbela	Polytechnic Institute of Viana do Castelo, Portugal
Costa Lino	Universidade do Minho, Portugal
Costa e Silva Eliana	ESTG-P Porto, Portugal
Costantini Alessandro	INFN, Italy
Crespi Mattia	University of Roma, Italy
Cuca Branka	Polytechnic University of Milano, Italy
De Doncker Elise	Western Michigan University, USA
De Macedo Mourelle Luiza	State University of Rio de Janeiro, Brazil
Daisaka Hiroshi	Hitotsubashi University, Japan
Daldanise Gaia	CNR, Italy
Danese Maria	CNR-ISPC, Italy
Daniele Bartoli	University of Perugia, Italy
Datola Giulia	Polytechnic University of Torino, Italy
De Luca Giandomenico	University of Reggio Calabria, Italy
De Lucia Caterina	University of Foggia, Italy
De Morais Barroca Filho Itamir	Federal University of Rio Grande do Norte, Brazil
De Petris Samuele	University of Torino, Italy
De Sá Alan	Marinha do Brasil, Brazil
De Souto Marcilio	LIFO, University of Orléans, France
De Vito Saverio	ENEA, Italy
De Wilde Pieter	University of Plymouth, UK
Degtyarev Alexander	Saint Petersburg State University, Russia
Dell'Anna Federico	Polytechnic University of Torino, Italy
Dell'Ovo Marta	Polytechnic University of Milano, Italy
Della Mura Fernanda	University of Naples, Italy
Deluka T. Aleksandra	University of Rijeka, Croatia
Demartino Cristoforo	Zhejiang University, China
Dereli Dursun Ahu	Istanbul Commerce University, Turkey
Desogus Giulia	University of Cagliari, Italy
Dettori Marco	University of Sassari, Italy
Devai Frank	London South Bank University, UK
Di Francesco Massimo	University of Cagliari, Italy
Di Liddo Felicia	Polytechnic University of Bari, Italy
Di Paola Gianluigi	University of Molise, Italy
Di Pietro Antonio	ENEA, Italy
Di Pinto Valerio	University of Naples, Italy
Dias Joana	University of Coimbra, Portugal
Dimas Isabel	University of Coimbra, Portugal
Dirvanauskas Darius	Kaunas University of Technology, Lithuania
Djordjevic Aleksandra	University of Belgrade, Serbia

Duma Doina Cristina	INFN-CNAF, Italy
Dumlu Demircioğlu Emine	Yıldız Technical University, Turkey
Dursun Aziz	Virginia Tech University, USA
Dvarioniene Jolanta	Kaunas University of Technology, Lithuania
Errico Maurizio Francesco	University of Enna KORE, Italy
Ezugwu Absalom	University of KwaZulu-Natal, South Africa
Fattoruso Grazia	ENEA, Italy
Faginas-Lago Noelia	University of Perugia, Italy
Falanga Bolognesi Salvatore	ARIESPACE, Italy
Falcinelli Stefano	University of Perugia, Italy
Farias Marcos	National Nuclear Energy Commission, Brazil
Farina Alessandro	University of Pisa, Italy
Feltynowski Marcin	Lodz University of Technology, Poland
Fernandes Florbela	Instituto Politecnico de Bragança, Portugal
Fernandes Paula Odete	Instituto Politécnico de Bragança, Portugal
Fernandez-Sanz Luis	University of Alcala, Spain
Ferreira Ana Cristina	University of Minho, Portugal
Ferreira Fernanda	Porto, Portugal
Fiorini Lorena	University of L'Aquila, Italy
Flora Amedeo	University of Basilicata, Italy
Florez Hector	Universidad Distrital Francisco Jose de Caldas, Colombia
Foddis Maria Laura	University of Cagliari, Italy
Fogli Daniela	University of Brescia, Italy
Fortunelli Martina	Pragma Engineering, Italy
Fragiacomo Massimo	University of L'Aquila, Italy
Franzoni Valentina	Perugia University, Italy
Fusco Giovanni	University of Cote d'Azur, France
Fyrogenis Ioannis	Aristotle University of Thessaloniki, Greece
Gorbachev Yuriy	Coddan Technologies LLC, Russia
Gabrielli Laura	Università Iuav di Venezia, Italy
Gallanos Theodore	Austrian Institute of Technology, Austria
Gamallo Belmonte Pablo	Universitat de Barcelona, Spain
Gankevich Ivan	Saint Petersburg State University, Russia
Garau Chiara	University of Cagliari, Italy
Garcia Para Ernesto	Universidad del Pais Vasco, EHU, Spain
Gargano Riccardo	Universidade de Brasilia, Brazil
Gavrilova Marina	University of Calgary, Canada
Georgiadis Georgios	Aristotle University of Thessaloniki, Greece
Gervasi Osvaldo	University of Perugia, Italy
Giano Salvatore Ivo	University of Basilicata, Italy
Gil Jorge	Chalmers University, Sweden
Gioia Andrea	Polytechnic University of Bari, Italy
Gioia Dario	ISPC-CNT, Italy

Giordano Ludovica	ENEA, Italy
Giorgi Giacomo	University of Perugia, Italy
Giovene di Girasole Eleonora	CNR-IRISS, Italy
Giovinazzi Sonia	ENEA, Italy
Giresini Linda	University of Pisa, Italy
Giuffrida Salvatore	University of Catania, Italy
Golubchikov Oleg	Cardiff University, UK
Gonçalves A. Manuela	University of Minho, Portugal
Gorgoglione Angela	Universidad de la República, Uruguay
Goyal Rinkaj	IPU, Delhi, India
Grishkin Valery	Saint Petersburg State University, Russia
Guerra Eduardo	Free University of Bozen-Bolzano, Italy
Guerrero Abel	University of Guanajuato, Mexico
Gulseven Osman	American University of The Middle East, Kuwait
Gupta Brij	National Institute of Technology, Kurukshetra, India
Guveyi Elcin	Yildiz Teknik University, Turkey
Gülen Kemal Güven	Namk Kemal University, Turkey
Haddad Sandra	Arab Academy for Science, Technology and Maritime Transport, Egypt
Hanzl Malgorzata	Lodz University of Technology, Poland
Hegedus Peter	University of Szeged, Hungary
Hendrix Eligius M. T.	Universidad de Málaga, Spain
Higaki Hiroaki	Tokyo Denki University, Japan
Hossain Syeda Sumbul	Daffodil International University, Bangladesh
Iacovino Chiara	University of Basilicata, Italy
Iakushkin Oleg	Saint Petersburg State University, Russia
Iannuzzo Antonino	ETH Zurich, Switzerland
Idri Ali	University Mohammed V, Morocco
Ignaccolo Matteo	University of Catania, Italy
Ilovan Oana-Ramona	Babeş-Bolyai University, Romania
Isola Federica	University of Cagliari, Italy
Jankovic Marija	CERTH, Greece
Jorge Ana Maria	Instituto Politécnico de Lisboa, Portugal
Kanamori Issaku	RIKEN Center for Computational Science, Japan
Kapenga John	Western Michigan University, USA
Karabulut Korhan	Yasar University, Turkey
Karaca Yeliz	University of Massachusetts Medical School, USA
Karami Ali	University of Guilan, Iran
Kienhofer Frank	WITS, South Africa
Kim Tai-hoon	Beijing Jiaotong University, China
Kimura Shuhei	Tottori University, Japan
Kirillov Denis	Saint Petersburg State University, Russia
Korkhov Vladimir	Saint Petersburg University, Russia
Koszewski Krzysztof	Warsaw University of Technology, Poland
Krzysztofik Sylwia	Lodz University of Technology, Poland

Kulabukhova Nataliia	Saint Petersburg State University, Russia
Kulkarni Shrinivas B.	SDM College of Engineering and Technology, Dharwad, India
Kwiecinski Krystian	Warsaw University of Technology, Poland
Kyvelou Stella	Panteion University of Social and Political Sciences, Greece
Körting Thales	INPE, Brazil
Lal Niranjan	Mody University of Science and Technology, India
Lazzari Maurizio	CNR-ISPC, Italy
Leon Marcelo	Asociacion de Becarios del Ecuador, Ecuador
La Rocca Ludovica	University of Naples, Italy
La Rosa Daniele	University of Catania, Italy
Lai Sabrina	University of Cagliari, Italy
Lalenis Konstantinos	University of Thessaly, Greece
Lannon Simon	Cardiff University, UK
Lasaponara Rosa	CNR, Italy
Lee Chien-Sing	Sunway University, Malaysia
Lemus-Romani José	Pontificia Universidad Católica de Valparaiso, Chile
Leone Federica	University of Cagliari, Italy
Li Yuanxi	Hong Kong Baptist University, China
Locurcio Marco	Polytechnic University of Bari, Italy
Lombardi Andrea	University of Perugia, Italy
Lopez Gayarre Fernando	University of Oviedo, Spain
Lops Pasquale	University of Bari, Italy
Lourenço Vanda	Universidade Nova de Lisboa, Portugal
Luviano José Luís	University of Guanajuato, Mexico
Maltese Antonino	University of Palermo, Italy
Magni Riccardo	Pragma Engineering, Italy
Maheshwari Anil	Carleton University, Canada
Maja Roberto	Polytechnic University of Milano, Italy
Malik Shaveta	Terna Engineering College, India
Maltinti Francesca	University of Cagliari, Italy
Mandado Marcos	University of Vigo, Spain
Manganelli Benedetto	University of Basilicata, Italy
Mangiameli Michele	University of Catania, Italy
Maraschin Clarice	Universidade Federal do Rio Grande do Sul, Brazil
Marigorta Ana Maria	Universidad de Las Palmas de Gran Canaria, Spain
Markov Krassimir	Institute of Electrical Engineering and Informatics, Bulgaria
Martellozzo Federico	University of Firenze, Italy
Marucci Alessandro	University of L'Aquila, Italy
Masini Nicola	IBAM-CNR, Italy
Matsufuru Hideo	High Energy Accelerator Research Organization (KEK), Japan
Matteucci Ilaria	CNR, Italy
Mauro D'Apuzzo	University of Cassino and Southern Lazio, Italy

Mazzarella Chiara	University of Naples, Italy
Mazzarino Marco	University of Venice, Italy
Mazzoni Augusto	University of Roma, Italy
Mele Roberta	University of Naples, Italy
Menezes Raquel	University of Minho, Portugal
Menghini Antonio	Aarhus Geofisica, Italy
Mengoni Paolo	University of Florence, Italy
Merlino Angelo	Università degli Studi Mediterranea, Italy
Milani Alfredo	University of Perugia, Italy
Milic Vladimir	University of Zagreb, Croatia
Millham Richard	Durban University of Technology, South Africa
Mishra B.	University of Szeged, Hungary
Misra Sanjay	Covenant University, Nigeria
Modica Giuseppe	University of Reggio Calabria, Italy
Mohagheghi Mohammadsadegh	Vali-e-Asr University of Rafsanjan, Iran
Molaei Qelichi Mohamad	University of Tehran, Iran
Molinara Mario	University of Cassino and Southern Lazio, Italy
Momo Evelyn Joan	University of Torino, Italy
Monteiro Vitor	University of Minho, Portugal
Montisci Augusto	University of Cagliari, Italy
Morano Pierluigi	Polytechnic University of Bari, Italy
Morganti Alessandro	Polytechnic University of Milano, Italy
Mosca Erica Isa	Polytechnic University of Milan, Italy
Moura Ricardo	CMA-FCT, New University of Lisbon, Portugal
Mourao Maria	Polytechnic Institute of Viana do Castelo, Portugal
Mourão Moura Ana Clara	Federal University of Minas Gerais, Brazil
Mrak Iva	University of Rijeka, Croatia
Murgante Beniamino	University of Basilicata, Italy
Muñoz Mirna	Centro de Investigacion en Matematicas, Mexico
Nedjah Nadia	State University of Rio de Janeiro, Brazil
Nakasato Naohito	University of Aizu, Japan
Natário Isabel Cristina	Universidade Nova de Lisboa, Portugal
Nesticò Antonio	Università degli Studi di Salerno, Italy
Neto Ana Maria	Universidade Federal do ABC, Brazil
Nicolosi Vittorio	University of Rome, Italy
Nikiforiadis Andreas	Aristotle University of Thessaloniki, Greece
Nocera Fabrizio	University of Illinois at Urbana-Champaign, USA
Nocera Silvio	IUAV, Italy
Nogueira Marcelo	Paulista University, Brazil
Nolè Gabriele	CNR, Italy
Nuno Beirao Jose	University of Lisbon, Portugal
Okewu Emma	University of Alcala, Spain
Oluwasefunmi Arogundade	Academy of Mathematics and System Science, China
Oppio Alessandra	Polytechnic University of Milan, Italy
P. Costa M. Fernanda	University of Minho, Portugal

Parisot Olivier	Luxembourg Institute of Science and Technology, Luxembourg
Paddeu Daniela	UWE, UK
Paio Alexandra	ISCTE-Instituto Universitário de Lisboa, Portugal
Palme Massimo	Catholic University of the North, Chile
Panaro Simona	University of Portsmouth, UK
Pancham Jay	Durban University of Technology, South Africa
Pantazis Dimos	University of West Attica, Greece
Papa Enrica	University of Westminster, UK
Pardede Eric	La Trobe University, Australia
Perchinunno Paola	Uniersity of Cagliari, Italy
Perdicoulis Teresa	UTAD, Portugal
Pereira Ana	Polytechnic Institute of Bragança, Portugal
Perri Damiano	University of Perugia, Italy
Petrelli Marco	University of Rome, Italy
Pierri Francesca	University of Perugia, Italy
Piersanti Antonio	ENEA, Italy
Pilogallo Angela	University of Basilicata, Italy
Pinna Francesco	University of Cagliari, Italy
Pinto Telmo	University of Coimbra, Portugal
Piroddi Luca	University of Cagliari, Italy
Poli Giuliano	University of Naples, Italy
Polidoro Maria João	Polytecnic Institute of Porto, Portugal
Polignano Marco	University of Bari, Italy
Politis Ioannis	Aristotle University of Thessaloniki, Greece
Pollino Maurizio	ENEA, Italy
Popoola Segun	Covenant University, Nigeria
Pratelli Antonio	University of Pisa, Italy
Praticò Salvatore	University of Reggio Calabria, Italy
Previtali Mattia	Polytechnic University of Milan, Italy
Puppio Mario Lucio	University of Pisa, Italy
Puttini Ricardo	Universidade de Brasilia, Brazil
Que Zeli	Nanjing Forestry University, China
Queiroz Gilberto	INPE, Brazil
Regalbuto Stefania	University of Naples, Italy
Ravanelli Roberta	University of Roma, Italy
Recanatesi Fabio	University of Tuscia, Italy
Reis Ferreira Gomes Karine	INPE, Brazil
Reis Marco	University of Coimbra, Portugal
Reitano Maria	University of Naples, Italy
Rencelj Marko	University of Maribor, Slovenia
Respondek Jerzy	Silesian University of Technology, Poland
Rimola Albert	Universitat Autònoma de Barcelona, Spain
Rocha Ana	University of Minho, Portugal
Rocha Humberto	University of Coimbra, Portugal
Rocha Maria Celia	UFBA Bahia, Brazil

Rocha Maria Clara	ESTES Coimbra, Portugal
Rocha Miguel	University of Minho, Portugal
Rodriguez Guillermo	UNICEN, Argentina
Rodríguez González Alejandro	Universidad Carlos III de Madrid, Spain
Ronchieri Elisabetta	INFN, Italy
Rosi Marzio	University of Perugia, Italy
Rotondo Francesco	Università Politecnica delle Marche, Italy
Rusci Simone	University of Pisa, Italy
Saganeiti Lucia	University of Basilicata, Italy
Saiu Valeria	University of Cagliari, Italy
Salas Agustin	UPCV, Chile
Salvo Giuseppe	University of Palermo, Italy
Sarvia Filippo	University of Torino, Italy
Santaga Francesco	University of Perugia, Italy
Santangelo Michele	CNR-IRPI, Italy
Santini Francesco	University of Perugia, Italy
Santos Rafael	INPE, Brazil
Santucci Valentino	Università per Stranieri di Perugia, Italy
Saponaro Mirko	Polytechnic University of Bari, Italy
Sarker Iqbal	CUET, Bangladesh
Scaioni Marco	Politecnico Milano, Italy
Scorza Francesco	University of Basilicata, Italy
Scotto di Perta Ester	University of Naples, Italy
Sebillo Monica	University of Salerno, Italy
Sharma Meera	Swami Shraddhanand College, India
Shen Jie	University of Michigan, USA
Shou Huahao	Zhejiang University of Technology, China
Siavvas Miltiadis	Centre of Research and Technology Hellas (CERTH), Greece
Silva Carina	ESTeSL-IPL, Portugal
Silva Joao Carlos	Polytechnic Institute of Cavado and Ave, Portugal
Silva Junior Luneque	Universidade Federal do ABC, Brazil
Silva Ângela	Instituto Politécnico de Viana do Castelo, Portugal
Simonetti Marco	University of Florence, Italy
Situm Zeljko	University of Zagreb, Croatia
Skouteris Dimitrios	Master-Up, Italy
Solano Francesco	Università degli Studi della Tuscia, Italy
Somma Maria	University of Naples, Italy
Sonnessa Alberico	Polytechnic University of Bari, Italy
Sousa Lisete	University of Lisbon, Portugal
Sousa Nelson	University of Algarve, Portugal
Spaeth Benjamin	Cardiff University, UK
Srinivsan M.	Navodaya Institute of Technology, India
Stankova Elena	Saint Petersburg State University, Russia
Stratigea Anastasia	National Technical University of Athens, Greece

Šurdonja Sanja	University of Rijeka, Croatia
Sviatov Kirill	Ulyanovsk State Technical University, Russia
Sánchez de Merás Alfredo	Universitat de Valencia, Spain
Takahashi Daisuke	University of Tsukuba, Japan
Tanaka Kazuaki	Kyushu Institute of Technology, Japan
Taniar David	Monash University, Australia
Tapia McClung Rodrigo	Centro de Investigación en Ciencias de Información Geoespacial, Mexico
Tarantino Eufemia	Polytechnic University of Bari, Italy
Tasso Sergio	University of Perugia, Italy
Teixeira Ana Paula	University of Trás-os-Montes and Alto Douro, Portugal
Teixeira Senhorinha	University of Minho, Portugal
Tengku Izhar Tengku Adil	Universiti Teknologi MARA, Malaysia
Teodoro Maria Filomena	University of Lisbon, Portuguese Naval Academy, Portugal
Tesoriere Giovanni	University of Enna KORE, Italy
Thangeda Amarendar Rao	Botho University, Botswana
Tonbul Gokchan	Atilim University, Turkey
Toraldo Emanuele	Polytechnic University of Milan, Italy
Torre Carmelo Maria	Polytechnic University of Bari, Italy
Torrieri Francesca	University of Naples, Italy
Torrisi Vincenza	University of Catania, Italy
Toscano Domenico	University of Naples, Italy
Totaro Vincenzo	Polytechnic University of Bari, Italy
Trigo Antonio	Instituto Politécnico de Coimbra, Portugal
Trunfio Giuseppe A.	University of Sassari, Italy
Trung Pham	HCMUT, Vietnam
Tsoukalas Dimitrios	Centre of Research and Technology Hellas (CERTH), Greece
Tucci Biagio	CNR, Italy
Tucker Simon	Liverpool John Moores University, UK
Tuñon Iñaki	Universidad de Valencia, Spain
Tyagi Amit Kumar	Vellore Institute of Technology, India
Uchibayashi Toshihiro	Kyushu University, Japan
Ueda Takahiro	Seikei University, Japan
Ugliengo Piero	University of Torino, Italy
Valente Ettore	University of Naples, Italy
Vallverdu Jordi	University Autonoma Barcelona, Spain
Vanelslander Thierry	University of Antwerp, Belgium
Vasyunin Dmitry	T-Systems RUS, Russia
Vazart Fanny	University of Grenoble Alpes, France
Vecchiocattivi Franco	University of Perugia, Italy
Vekeman Jelle	Vrije Universiteit Brussel (VUB), Belgium
Verde Rosanna	Università degli Studi della Campania, Italy
Vermaseren Jos	Nikhef, The Netherlands

Contents – Part VI

**International Workshop on Computational Studies for Energy
and Comfort in Buildings (SECoB 2020)**

**International Symposium on Software Engineering Processes
and Applications (SEPA 2020)**

International Workshop on Scientific Computing Infrastructure (SCI 2020)

Virtual Testbed: Concept and Applications

Alexander Bogdanov[1], Alexander Degtyarev[1,2(✉)], Ivan Gankevich[1],
Vasily Khramushin[1], and Vladimir Korkhov[1,2]

[1] Saint Petersburg State University, Universitetskaya nab., 7-9,
199034 Saint Petersburg, Russia
{a.v.bogdanov,a.degtyarev,i.gankevich,
v.korkhov}@spbu.ru, khram@mail.ru
[2] Plekhanov Russian University of Economics, Stremyanny Lane, 36,
117997 Moscow, Russia

Abstract. In this paper the virtual testbed as a problem-solving environment is considered in different aspects. Fundamental questions for virtual testbed development are (1) characteristics of mathematical models and their interaction; (2) computational aspects and mapping of algorithms onto hardware; (3) information streams and data smanagement. The authors propose the concept of a virtual private supercomputer as a tool for virtual testbed computer environment. Examples of the implementation of the virtual testbed in different areas are given. The article summarizes achievements of the authors in the field of virtual testbed during last years.

Keywords: Virtual testbed · Virtual private supercomputer · Direct simulation · Big data

1 Introduction

The development of computer technology and information technology has stimulated the emergence of new mathematical models and numerical methods for solving complex problems over the past 20-30 years. The ability to solve complex problems in an increasingly complete and close to natural conditions formulation has led to the fact that the mathematical models have reached such a high degree of adequacy that they can often be used as a substitute for a physical experiment if the physics of the investigated phenomenon is fully understood. In the vast majority of cases of modeling and designing complex technical objects (ship, underwater vehicle, aircraft, automobile, turbine, etc.) this situation can be considered fair. Carrying out such an experiment using exclusively computer technology based on mathematical modeling can be considered as a virtual experiment, the cost of which is much lower than a physical experiment, and the range of possible conditions for its implementation is incomparably wider, since it allows the study of extreme and potentially dangerous situations in natural conditions. Thus, the concept of a "virtual testbed" emerged as a problem-oriented environment [1].

The emergence of this concept, in the first place, was associated with the need to consider increasingly complex models to study the behavior of dynamic objects that

O. Gervasi et al. (Eds.): ICCSA 2020, LNCS 12254, pp. 3–17, 2020.
https://doi.org/10.1007/978-3-030-58817-5_1

require the use of high-performance computing. Currently, the use of such types of computing tools requires the researcher to have more knowledge of the features of modern computing technologies. In many ways, this fact becomes an obstacle to their implementation, and as a result, a decrease in the effectiveness of research in various subject areas. The strong gap between the high level of "hardware" and the low level of its application has led to the emergence of a new concept for the use of information technology [2, 3].

When considering the elements of a virtual testbed, the study of complex technical objects requires the use of many models that describe various phenomena. Some of them are independent, and some of them depend on each other. Often the very nature of these applications precludes the possibility of their joint launch in a homogeneous computing environment. In real time, the simulation of all processes of complex objects that affect the final result of complex objects behavior cannot be organized on a single computing node just because it requires the adequate use of various computer resources, for example, high-performance computing, data processing, visualization, etc. Thus, in certain situations, it is necessary to interact parallel computing applications of different complexity and nature, databases, information assimilation, visualization of results, etc. So, the testbed is a complex of multi-level applications, which requires a distributed computing environment [4, 5]. Therefore, in the general case, the use of a heterogeneous computing environment is not the result of scientific experiments, but the only possible tool for implementing of a problem-oriented environment.

This article summarizes the research conducted by the authors over the past 15 years towards the development of the concept of virtual testbed. The references contain the main key works published in this direction.

2 Computational Aspects of Virtual Testbed

Under the accurate mathematical modeling (when nature of the phenomenon is well-known) of the functioning of an object and the possibility of its detailed description, modern computational tools make it possible to almost completely reproduce its behavior. Such an approach allows, in the overwhelming number of situations, to replace an expensive model experiment with a computational simulation. At the same time, a computational experiment is free from such disadvantages as scale effects, limited possibilities to reproduce external excitations, significant difficulties or the impossibility to study complex critical situations in a model experiment, etc. However, in order to computational experiment fully reproduces the real behavior of an object, it is necessary to have good models of the object dynamics and the external environment. These models include the fundamental laws of physics, such as the laws of conservation and the closing relations. For example, for technical objects like ships, aircrafts, cars, etc. we can consider just only three laws: conservation of mass, momentum and energy [6].

$$\frac{D\rho}{Dt} + \rho\left(\vec{\nabla} \cdot \vec{V}\right) = 0$$

$$\rho\frac{D\vec{V}}{Dt} = \rho\vec{f} + \vec{\nabla} \cdot \Pi_{ij} \tag{1}$$

$$\frac{\partial E_t}{\partial t} + \vec{\nabla} \cdot E_t\vec{V} = \frac{\partial Q}{\partial t} - \vec{\nabla} \cdot \vec{q} + \rho\vec{f} \cdot \vec{V} + \vec{\nabla} \cdot \left(\Pi_{ij} \cdot \vec{V}\right)$$

where ρ is density, $\vec{V}$ is velocity, $\vec{f}$ is force of potential nature per unit volume, Π_{ij} are components of stress tensor, E_t is total energy of unit volume, Q is heat dissipation of external sources, $\vec{\nabla} \cdot \vec{q}$ is heat losses due to thermal conductivity through the control surface per unit time. The third and fourth terms in the last equation correspond to the work of mass and surface forces.

In fact, there is no need to implement these laws in a computational experiment in the form of differential equations or other usual approaches. It is possible to use direct computer simulation with the corresponding fundamental laws applied to all the elementary objects in the space under consideration. This approach requires high-performance computer resources and mapping of the computational algorithms onto the hardware architecture.

Such attempts have been made for a long time, since it became clear that computer technology can really ensure the application of the Lagrange approach in describing the behavior of a continuous medium [7]. The development of this idea over the past 50 years has formed a fairly wide area of CFD, both based on various approaches to solving the Navier-Stokes equation (based on the second equation in (1)), and various particle methods that reproduce the Lagrange approach [7–10]. Currently, one of the most popular methods in this direction is SPH (smooth particle hydrodynamics) [9, 10]. However, all these approaches, ultimately, are based on the finite-difference representation of conservation laws (1), which include derivatives of at least second order. Due to the peculiarities of the conservation equations, their finite-difference analogues are solved using implicit numerical schemes. Such an approach reduces the solution of the problem to systems of linear equations of high dimension. It makes it possible to ensure the stability of the numerical implementation, but it is difficult to parallelize and does not provide step-by-step monitoring of each calculation cell.

At the same time, the development of continuum-particle methods based on the "large particle method" [8] leads to computational models of tensor mathematics with independent control of the state of each calculated cell-fluid particle, computational algorithms and functional logic of the synthesis of physical phenomena and processes for which is provided by parallel-running arithmetic-logic cores, which exactly corresponds to the development trends of computer technology at the request of graphic visualization of three-dimensional space phenomena and dynamic processes with them. It is the use of tensor algebra for direct modeling of physical phenomena and processes as part of generalized tensor mathematics that allows us to efficiently synthesize the hydrodynamic and geometric aspects of the computing process as a whole. This has long been understood in field theory. Such a program was outlined and brilliantly implemented for quantum gravity.

This approach makes it possible to implement direct numerical modeling of unsteady processes using explicit schemes [11–13]. It has an excellent historical analogue in the form of the calculus of fluxes of Isaac Newton.

Geometrical construction of spatial problem includes scalar, vector and tensor numerical objects. For description of large mobile elementary particles in a three-dimensional space we introduce two coordinate systems: an absolute one and a mobile local (associated with the particle) one (Fig. 1).

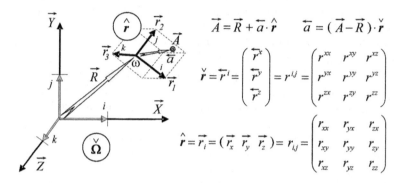

$$\vec{A} = \vec{R} + \vec{a} \cdot \hat{r} \qquad \vec{a} = (\vec{A} - \vec{R}) \cdot \check{r}$$

$$\check{r} = \vec{r}^i = \begin{pmatrix} \vec{r}^x \\ \vec{r}^y \\ \vec{r}^z \end{pmatrix} = r^{i,j} = \begin{pmatrix} r^{xx} & r^{xy} & r^{xz} \\ r^{yx} & r^{yy} & r^{yz} \\ r^{zx} & r^{zy} & r^{zz} \end{pmatrix}$$

$$\hat{r} = \vec{r}_i = (\vec{r}_x \ \vec{r}_y \ \vec{r}_z) = r_{i,j} = \begin{pmatrix} r_{xx} & r_{yx} & r_{zx} \\ r_{xy} & r_{yy} & r_{zy} \\ r_{xz} & r_{yz} & r_{zz} \end{pmatrix}$$

Fig. 1. Geometry of global space (Ω (with check)) and local basis (r (with hat)); i, j, k are unitary vectors in connected reference systems [12]

In this case, the continuum-corpuscular approach is constructed according to numerical first-order schemes with sequential difference integration of the laws of motion at conjugate stages with respect to the scalar argument - time. Separation of the stages of computations according to the total physical processes allows for end-to-end control and hybrid rearrangement of mathematical dependencies according to current estimates of the state of the simulated continuous medium, taking into account the intensity of the physical interaction of adjacent shell-cells as virtual numerical objects.

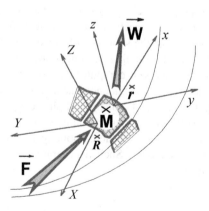

Fig. 2. Separation of calculation stages by physical processes.

Such a separation of calculations by physical stages allows us to divide a computational experiment into three successive stages [11–13]:

Stage 1 – Kinematic parameters are calculated for the centers of large fluid particles. For this purpose, the current source data at fixed nodes of Eulerian coordinates are used.

Stage 2 – Lagrange or large deformable fluid particles are involved in free motion. They redistribute the internal properties of the original Euler cells to adjacent space.

Stage 3 – Laws of conservation of mass and energy are consistent. This is achieved by deformation of shifted fluid particles. The next step is re-interpolation of characteristics of current in initial nodes of the fixed Euler computational mesh.

They are based on computational schemes of mixed Lagrange and Eulerian approaches. Idea of mixing of these two approaches is not new [14]. Approach proposed for the virtual testbed realization has advantages in combination with tensor mathematics and effective realization in code.

The formal construction of physical objects and operations in tensor mathematics leads to rigorous definitions for a kind of "model of the world" of computational hydromechanics illustrated on Fig. 2:

1) the continuum-corpuscular computational model of the "large particles" method in tensor notation reduces to a double linear difference interpolation of physical fields (instead of integrating second-order equations of motion).

2) the movement and interaction of large fluid particles are constructed in the operations of the multiplication, that is more consistent with the physics of spatial processes (there are no restrictions on the smallness of differential approximations).

3) the use of explicit numerical schemes and discrete numerical fields increase the efficiency of direct computational experiments, and do not exclude the possibility of checking the correctness, and, if necessary, using hybrid meshes to achieve adequate engineering results of direct numerical simulation.

3   Virtual Testbed as a Case for Big Data

As we considered in [15] a virtual testbed solves complex problems of modeling and working with big amount of data. The main aspects of a virtual testbed are the following:

- Computing machinery – hardware;
- Uniform information environment – GRID, middleware;
- Program repository – libraries;
- System integration – principles of testbed operation;
- Concept of real time systems.

Combining of all these components in one place makes it possible to organize such system in which all the accumulated data are linked to each other and used when necessary. For example, drawings of technical object created during design process are used in the future to implement the simulators. Training results of operators/navigators/ pilots in simulator are used for modification of the object. The data obtained as a result of direct simulation are used to form knowledge base of on-board intelligent system, etc. We see that this is a problem of Big Data.

However, the problem is the following. As we published earlier [16, 17], Big Data has different nature. In accordance with CAP theorem we divided it in 6 different types [16] (one of them is not implemented). In this classification [16, 17], our system belongs to the type characterized not so much by volume, as by heterogeneity and complex hierarchy. Here we are dealing with both data processing, and complex computations. In the first case, we should consider the data as a whole, in the second case, data are exchanged between different branches. At the same time, in the process of modeling, for example, it must be done at least twice – in preprocessing and postprocessing. As a result, we get a huge amount of heterogeneous data that change the original state of knowledge. With this data and knowledge it is necessary to work differently under different conditions.

The problem is that no software stack describes all classes. Analysis showed that existing Hadoop systems do not cover even 40% of all cases. Our class belongs to this exclusion and selecting tools for working with large amounts of data in this case is a separate task for the development team. Not infrequently, the architecture had to be drastically changed because of increased data loads and control of stored data was lost and the collection of statistics became more and more difficult. There is a need for a solution that allows not only to store all sorts of information with the ability to download from different sources but also has a set of tools to analyze the collected information. A data lake is a concept, an architectural approach to centralized storage that allows you to store all structured and unstructured data with the possibility of unlimited scaling. A data lake can store structured data from relational databases (rows and columns), semi-structured data (CSV, journals, XML, JSON), unstructured data (emails, documents, PDF files) and binary data (images, audio, video). Quite popular is the approach in which incoming data is converted into metadata. This allows you to store data in its original state, without special architecture or the need to know which questions you may need to answer in the future, without the need to structure the data and have various types of analytics - from dashboards and visualizations to big data processing, real-time analytics and machine learning to make the right decisions.

As a result of the analysis of existing solutions, the following functional modules were identified that are the most necessary and need to be developed in the universal solution:

- Storage for all data with the ability to create separate storage for hot/cold data, for ever-changing data or to handle fast streaming
- Security module
- Databases for structured data
- The module of tools for working with data (analysis, data engines, dashboards, etc.)
- Machine learning module
- Services for the development of add-ons, modifications and deployment of storage.

4 Virtual Private Supercomputer as a Tool for Virtual Testbed Organization

Handling massive amounts of data is commonplace for most modern scientific, engineering, and business applications. The Virtual testbed is a good example of a complex system encompassing a number of applications that represent its functional modules listed in the previous section. As these applications need to target a number of big data related challenges, while delivering expected results in a timely manner, they frequently pose large computing power requirements. In this context, High Performance Computing (HPC) becomes a key factor for speeding up data processing, while also enabling faster time to market, lower capital expenditures, and higher valued innovation. To this end, HPC solutions have traditionally taken advantage of cluster and datacenter infrastructures for running applications having those computing power requirements. In addition, practitioners have also been leveraging cloud computing resources for meeting HPC demands when available resources do not suffice. In fact, the pay-per-use cost model and resource elasticity makes cloud computing an interesting environment for HPC, which can be provided with instant availability and flexible scaling of resources, among other benefits.

In spite of the benefits of using cloud computing for HPC, a current approach has been the allocation of physical infrastructures in dedicated mode for fast HPC provisioning. Although convenient, it frequently leads to underutilized resources, e.g., an application may not fully utilize provided CPU and/or network resources. It also prevents dealing adequately with those applications whose resource demands grow beyond available capacity. Traditional virtualization technologies can help solving the problem but the overhead of both a) bootstrapping a virtual infrastructure for each application and b) sharing physical resources among several virtual instances might be significant. Boosting available physical resources by using cloud computing, in turn, has been hampered because of limited support for shifting HPC applications to the cloud. These issues hinder the wide adoption of cloud computing by the HPC community, thus becoming paramount to understand how one can perform smooth and effective migration of HPC applications to the cloud.

Traditional cloud-based solutions are oriented towards long running stateful services that are flexible in respect to consumed CPU and network load at a single timeframe. In turn, HPC applications are in essence batch processes that have clear input and output data requirements. Also, in most cases they are fine-tuned for stable computational environment settings and size. Thus, they significantly differ from cloud-based services in terms of possible management, i.e., their requirements can be quantified. The solution that brings together the flexibility of virtualized cloud-based computing environments and performance of traditional computing clusters is needed to create an application-centric distributed system that provides each application with a customized virtual environment with as much resources as the application needs or is allowed to use.

The Virtual Private Supercomputer [4, 18] is a universal environment for monitoring and managing a high-performance computing cluster, in the structure of which virtual elements are included. Virtual containers are application containers with various file systems, configuration of modules and software libraries. The tools for combining these elements located on different nodes of the cluster, as well as non-virtualized network equipment and other auxiliary devices and systems into a single system for general-purpose calculations, are the core part of the virtual supercomputer. The virtual supercomputer isolates the user from a number of technical limitations of computing devices using virtualization technologies, allowing users to vary the characteristics of computing elements and balance the workload. To create a personal computing environment with the specified characteristics, lightweight virtualization technologies are used primarily, which leads to minimal overhead, but allows users to create isolated virtual computing systems. The developed tools for managing a virtual supercomputer automate many processes, provide monitoring of node load and task execution, optimally select the right amount of resources based on application requirements and change it if necessary. The virtual supercomputer is designed to solve problems within the time period established by an individual user agreement, which is achieved by selecting and setting up an optimal set of middleware components for the task being solved. In general, the concept of a virtual supercomputer allows users to consolidate heterogeneous resources into a single complex that adapts to the solution of the problem from a computational point of view, taking into account individual requirements determined by the user agreement.

One of the main parts of the virtual supercomputer is a task scheduler for batch processing of data and a software interface to it, designed to develop distributed applications and, in particular, programs for parallel computing and parallel data processing. The scheduler ensures the smooth operation of such programs in the conditions of unpredictable technical (hardware) failures of the cluster computing nodes, by automatically re-executing parts of the task that were executed on failed nodes, on the remaining nodes. The performance of programs written using the provided software interface is not inferior to traditional technologies of parallel computing and running tasks on a cluster (MPI + PBS/SLURM), provided that the cluster nodes do not fail during calculations. Otherwise, the performance significantly exceeds analogues, since not the whole task is restarted, but only a small part of it.

To ensure fault tolerance, each task is divided into control objects - entities that describe the program execution logic. These objects are combined in a hierarchy, which is used to uniquely determine the restart point of the program without interrogating the cluster nodes involved in the calculations. All nodes of the cluster are also combined in a hierarchy used to evenly distribute the load. The calculations are carried out by creating a large number of control objects (one for each logical part of the task) and mapping their hierarchy to the hierarchy of cluster nodes. This mapping has an arbitrary form with the only condition that control objects directly connected to each other are either on the same cluster node or directly connected to each other.

Another major component of the virtual supercomputer is the system for automatic configuration of a distributed computing cluster based on virtualized resources in accordance with application requirements and implementation of a user and software interface to it [19]. One of the key parameters for launching tasks, for determining the value of which the software launch system is responsible, is the amount of required computing resources or cluster configuration. It includes the number of nodes, threads in each node, memory and communication speed between nodes. The user who starts the task and even the programmer who developed it cannot always determine the accuracy, which cluster configuration or the task will run faster or which configuration uses unreasonably many resources. Within the framework of the virtual supercomputer, a method for automated determination of the optimal cluster configuration, which is used in the developed of a system to launch computing tasks on virtualized resources, was designed and implemented [20, 21]. For users, a web interface is provided in which they can select an application, select computing resources and send a task to be performed. At the same time, all the details of creating and configuring computing resources and performing tasks can be hidden from the user. After completing the task, the software system will upload the output of the task to the user's cloud storage. Depending on the parameters of the task, the software system offers the user the optimal configuration of computing resources (the number of nodes, threads and memory) at which the task execution time will be minimal, or offers to explicitly enter the desired configuration. An API has also been developed for launching tasks, managing and monitoring cluster status based on open standard data exchange protocols.

5   Applications of Virtual Testbed Concept

Let us briefly review applications of developed concept in different directions.

5.1   Marine Virtual Testbed

This application served as a starting point for the development of a general concept for a virtual testbed. An attempt to create a modeling environment for marine objects in the mid-90s based on mathematical models of the behavior of marine objects, the external environment and their interaction, which were widespread at that time, was unsuccessful. The reason for the failure was both the features of the models and the inconsistency of approaches of specialists from various scientific fields: physics, hydrometeorology, and engineering research. The mathematical models for describing the behavior of marine objects were initially of a qualitative nature. This determined the approach in describing external perturbations as a harmonic wave of a given amplitude and frequency. Any complication of mathematical models, consisting in a more accurate description of the disturbing forces, was based on these assumptions [22]. As a result, the complexity of the mathematical description grew, it was no longer possible to obtain solutions of new mathematical models in any form, and it was impossible to use these complex models for direct simulation [23]. The latter is due, first of all, to the fact that the real windwave surface, which is the source of the ship's motion at sea, could not be inserted into any of the serious models developed at that time. They were all focused on the sine wave. On the other hand, there were also no models that could adequately reproduce the spatio-temporal fields of wind waves, due to their irregularity.

To create an integrated modeling environment for marine objects, it was necessary:

1. To develop models of the objects themselves and the external environment that allows direct simulation;

2. To develop approaches to link these heterogeneous models with each other so that the results of one model can serve as the initial data of another model;
3. To provide high performance collaboration of heterogeneous models in a distributed computing environment.

As these tasks were solved, the general concept of the virtual testbed was formed.

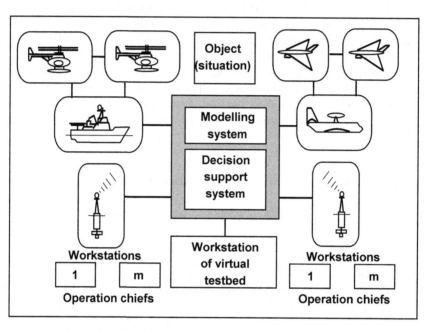

Fig. 3. Functional diagram of complex environment organization

Initially, a model of wind-wave perturbations was developed [24, 25, etc.]. In its final form, from the point of view of application to a virtual testbed, this model is given in [26, 27]. A number of works were carried out to increase the computational efficiency of this model [5, 28, 29, etc.]. This made it possible to develop models of direct simulation of the behavior and interaction of marine objects in the sea. In its final form, the marine virtual testbed is a highly efficient environment for modeling, studying critical situations, planning operational scenarios [30], data assimilation and storage [15] onto a database and a visualization system for results [31]. This virtual testbed became the prototype of a fully functional simulator with elements of a decision support system that provides the following functions:

- Collection and analysis of information about the current state of the facility and the environment, remote monitoring.
- Evaluation and coordination of joint actions of the facility, based on current conditions, with the goal of optimal solution of the general problem.

- Centralized decision support system (DSS) of operators of control systems of dynamic objects in non-standard situations, organization of information support for the interaction of decision makers in the management of ongoing operations.
- Computer modeling of possible scenarios for the development of the situation in order to choose the optimal strategy for managing the facilities of the complex.
- Centralized management of fully automated technical means.
- Document management and information accumulation in dynamic databases.

Schematically, these functions are shown in Fig. 3.

5.2   Knowledge Base Intelligence System Testing

The creation of a fully-functional marine virtual testbed makes it possible to conduct experiments in conditions that are impossible or extremely dangerous in full-scale or model experiments: extreme operating conditions and external influences, catastrophic development of emergency situations (capsizing, avalanche flooding of compartments with loss of buoyancy, etc.), tracking scenarios of joint actions of various technical objects (landing of an airplane/helicopter on the flight deck, mooring and transfer of cargo to the sea, etc.). The on-board decision support systems are called upon to make safe the operation of technical facilities in various conditions and the skill level of the crew. Any of these real-time systems are based on a complex of measuring equipment, processing of dynamic processes, a subsystem of mathematical modeling and a system of rules (knowledge base of an onboard intelligent system).

The formation of a hypothesis testing plan and the implementation of decisions in DSS is carried out on the basis of mathematical modeling data for the vessel dynamics scenarios in the considered extreme situation. The decision-making procedure includes assessing the minimum time for the implementation of the decision with an acceptable level of risk. Decision making is carried out in conditions of uncertainty and lack of time. In this case, there is a risk of incorrect operator actions. For intelligent operator support, fuzzy models are used in this situation. The specificity of such models consists in the use of fuzzy estimates and graph interpretation, which makes it possible to attribute the formation of operator actions to the number of combinatorial problems on graphs [1].

Modeling situations in the face of uncertainties, testing the knowledge base, and ensuring the fastest search for the optimal solution require a detailed recreation of the picture of the interaction between the dynamics of the object and the environment. In this sense, a virtual testbed can be considered as a tool for filling and testing the knowledge base [32].

5.3   Virtual Particle Accelerator

A virtual accelerator reflects the other side of the concept of a virtual testbed. Elementary particle physics is still not fully known. It is for this purpose that various accelerators are built. Each such installation costs a lot of money, requires a lot of effort, but most importantly, after its creation it cannot be used outside the range of parameters narrow enough for which it was designed. A striking example is the LHC.

Therefore, it is fundamentally important in the initial stages to conduct a comprehensive simulation of various components of the accelerator in order to create the optimal design. In particle accelerator physics the problem is that we cannot see what is going on inside the working machine. It is important to represent the space charge forces of beam a software based on analytical models for space charge distributions. For these purposes we need special algorithms for predictor-corrector method for beam map evaluation scheme including the space charge forces. It allows us to evaluate the map along the reference trajectory and to analyze beam envelope dynamics. Such Virtual Accelerator provides a set of services and tools of modeling beam dynamics in accelerators on distributed computing resources [33, 34].

5.4   Virtual Testbed for Financial Modeling

One of the typical spheres of "complex applications", i.e. computational tasks that deal with large amounts of significantly irregular information when the rate of input data subject to processing in a reasonably limited time varies by several orders, is financial mathematics. Finally, the end user to make a decision should have information in a comprehensible form. Such applications are characterized by the following factors.

- Tremendous number of end users (brokers)
- Large variety of heterogeneous sources of information
- Unpredictable moments of sudden data volume "explosion"
- Necessity to keep in mind as long prehistory as possible to make the prognoses more precise
- Limited time to make decisions, in practice in a real time manner

The current state and dynamics of changes in global financial system based on the financial markets play nowadays a significant role in the life of the world economic community. The financial markets are as active as never before. In modern electronic markets, stock prices may change several times within a few milliseconds. Participating traders (that can also be computers) have to evaluate the prices and react very quickly in order to get the highest profit, which requires a lot of computational effort. Information of huge volume received from a large variety of heterogeneous sources is then to be processed using properly adequate mathematical tools.

Over the years, increasingly sophisticated mathematical models and derivative pricing strategies have been developed, but their credibility was violated by the financial crisis of 2007–2010. Contemporary practice of mathematical finance has been subjected to criticism from such a notable figures within the field, as Nassim Nicholas Taleb in his book "The Black Swan" [35]. The book focuses on the extreme impact of certain kinds of rare and unpredictable events and humans' tendency to find simplistic explanations for these events retrospectively. Taleb claims that the prices of financial assets cannot be characterized by the simple models currently in use, rendering much of current practice at best irrelevant, and, at worst, dangerously misleading. Many mathematicians and applied fields scientists are now attempting to establish more effective theories and methods.

Generally speaking, the fundamental computational problem for adequate providing activity of the army of brokers consists in huge amount and large variety of input heterogeneous sources of information still drastically enlarged by archives' stored data, limited time to make decisions, in practice in a real time manner, and in unpredictable moments of sudden data volume "explosion". Just the case for a virtual testbed [36, 37].

6 Conclusion

Thus, the approach proposed for modeling wind and wave impacts on marine objects turned out to be amazingly effective for a wide range of problems of modeling complex technological and natural systems. It turns out that it is well suited for working with modern hybrid GPU-based calculators, as well as multi-threaded processors. New opportunities for it are opened by the Virtual Private Supercomputer paradigm described above and the approach to classification of Big Data. The combination of these tools allows you to create a flexible toolkit for creating virtual repositories oriented to work with a wide range of applied tasks.

Acknowledgments. The paper has been prepared within the scope of the project of St.Petersburg State University (id 51129503, 51129820) and partly supported by Russian Fund for Basic Research (grant N 17-29-04288).

Competing Interests. The authors declare that there is no conflict of interests regarding the publication of this paper.

References

1. Bogdanov, A., Degtyarev, A., Nechaev, Y.: Problems of virtual testbed development for complex dynamic processes modelling. In: Proceedings of International conference "Supercomputer systems and its applications" (SSA'2004), Minsk, Belorussia, in Russian. pp. 31–37 (2004)
2. Bogdanov, A., Degtyarev, A., Korkhov, V.: Desktop supercomputer: what can it do? Phys. Part. Nucleic. Lett. **14**(7), 985–992 (2017). https://doi.org/10.1134/S1547477117070032
3. Bogdanov, A., Degtyarev, A., Korkhov, V.: New approach to the simulation of complex systems. EPJ Web Conf. **108**, 01002 (2016). https://doi.org/10.1051/epjconf/201610801002
4. Bogdanov, A., Degtyarev, A., Korkhov, V., Gaiduchok, V., Gankevich, I.: Virtual supercomputer as basis of scientific computing. In: Horizons in Computer Science Research — New York: Nova Science Publishers. vol. 11, pp. 159–198 (2015)
5. Gankevich, I., Degtyarev A.: Model of distributed computations in virtual testbed. In: 9th International Conference on Computer Science and Information Technologies (CSIT 2013), Revised Selected Papers, 6710358. pp. 240–244 (2013). https://doi.org/10.1109/csitechnol.2013.6710358
6. Pletcher, R.H., Tannehill, J.C., Anderson, D.A.: Computational Fluid Mechanics and Heat Transfer, 3rd edn. CRC Press, Taylor&Francis Group (2013)
7. Alder, B., Fernbach, S., Rotenberg, M.: Methods in Computational Physics: Advances in Research and Applications. Fundamental Methods in Hydrodynamics, vol. 3. Academic Press, Cambridge (1964)
8. Belocerkovski, O.M., Davidov, Y.M.: Method of large particles in gas dynamics. Computational Experiment (1982) [in Russian]

9. Monaghan, J.J.: Smoothed particle hydrodynamics. Rep. Prog. Phys. **68**, 1703–1759 (2005)
10. Violeau, D.: Fluid Mechanics and the SPH Method: Theory and Applications. Oxford University Press, UK (2012)
11. Degtyarev, A., Khramushin, V.: Design and construction of computer experiment in hydrodynamics using explicit numerical schemes and tensor mathematics algorithms. Math. Mod. **26**(11), 4–17 (2014)
12. Degtyarev, A., Khramushin, V., Shichkina, Y.: Tensor methodology and computation geometry in direct computational experiments in fluid mechanics. AIP Conf. Proc. **1863**, 110006 (2017). https://doi.org/10.1063/1.4992291
13. Bogdanov, A., Khramushin, V.: Tensor arithmetic, geometric and mathematic principles of fluid mechanics in implementation of direct computational experiments. In: EPJ Web Conf. **108**, 02013 (2016). https://doi.org/10.1051/epjconf/201610802013
14. Hirt, C.W., Amsden, A.A., Cook, J.L.: An arbitrary Lagrangian-Eulerian computing method for all flow speeds. J. Comput. Phys. **135**, 203–216 (1997). https://doi.org/10.1016/0021-9991(74)90051-5
15. Degtyarev, A., et al.: Virtual testbed as a case for big data. CEUR Workshop Proc. **2267**, 58–64 (2018). eid = 2-s2.0-85060084592
16. Bogdanov, A., et al.: Big Data as the future of information technology. CEUR Workshop Proc. **2267**, 26–31 (2018). eid=2-s2.0-85060087168
17. Bogdanov, A., et al.: Is the Big Data the future of information technologies? In: The 20th Small Triangle Meeting on theoretical physics, pp. 15–28 (2019)
18. Gankevich, I., Korkhov, V., Balyan, S., Gaiduchok, V., Gushchanskiy, D., Tipikin, Y., Degtyarev, A., Bogdanov, A.: Constructing virtual private supercomputer using virtualization and cloud technologies. In: Murgante, B. (ed.) ICCSA 2014. LNCS, vol. 8584, pp. 341–354. Springer, Cham (2014). https://doi.org/10.1007/978-3-319-09153-2_26
19. Korkhov, V., Kobyshev, S., Krosheninnikov, A., Degtyarev, A., Bogdanov, A.: Distributed computing infrastructure based on dynamic container clusters. In: Gervasi, O. (ed.) ICCSA 2016. LNCS, vol. 9787, pp. 263–275. Springer, Cham (2016). https://doi.org/10.1007/978-3-319-42108-7_20
20. Kuchumov, R., Korkhov, V.: Fair resource allocation for running HPC workloads simultaneously. In: Misra, S. (ed.) ICCSA 2019. LNCS, vol. 11622, pp. 740–751. Springer, Cham (2019). https://doi.org/10.1007/978-3-030-24305-0_55
21. Kuchumov, R., Petrunin, V., Korkhov, V., Balashov, N., Kutovskiy, N., Sokolov, I.: Design and implementation of a service for cloud HPC computations. In: Gervasi, O. (ed.) ICCSA 2018. LNCS, vol. 10963, pp. 103–112. Springer, Cham (2018). https://doi.org/10.1007/978-3-319-95171-3_9
22. Lugovsky, V.V.: Nonlinear problems of seaworthiness. L.: Sudostroenie, pp. 236 (1966). (in Russian)
23. Belenky, V., Sevastianov, N.: Stability and Safety of Ships - Risk of Capsizing, 2nd edn. SNAME, 444 pp. (2007)
24. Bukhanovskii, A.V., Degtyarev, A.B., Lopatukhin, L.I., Rozhkov, V.A.: Probabilistic modeling of sea wave climate. Izv. Atmos. Ocean Phys. **34**(2), 235–239 (1998)
25. Boukhanovsky, A., Rozhkov, V., Degtyarev, A.: Peculiarities of computer simulation and statistical representation of time—spatial metocean fields. In: Alexandrov, V.N., Dongarra, J.J., Juliano, B.A., Renner, R.S., Tan, C.J.K. (eds.) ICCS 2001. LNCS, vol. 2073, pp. 463–472. Springer, Heidelberg (2001). https://doi.org/10.1007/3-540-45545-0_55
26. Degtyarev, A., Reed, A.: Synoptic and short-term modeling of ocean waves. Int. Shipbuild. Prog. **60**, 523–553 (2013). https://doi.org/10.3233/isp-130091

27. Degtyarev A.B.: New approach to wave weather scenarios modeling. In: Almeida Santos Neves M., Belenky V., de Kat J., Spyrou K., Umeda N. (eds) Contemporary Ideas on Ship Stability and Capsizing in Waves. Fluid Mechanics and Its Applications, vol. 97, pp. 599–617. Springer, Dordrecht (2011). https://doi.org/10.1007/978-94-007-1482-3_34

28. Degtyarev, A., Gankevich, I.: Hydrodynamic pressure computation under real sea surface on basis of autoregressive model of irregular waves. Phys. Part. Nuclei. Lett. **12**(3), 389–391 (2015). https://doi.org/10.1134/S1547477115030073

29. Bogdanov, A., Degtyarev, A., Nechaev, Y.: Parallel algorithms for virtual testbed. In: Proceedings of 5th International Conference Computer Science & Information Technologies (CSIT 2005), Erevan, pp. 393–398 (2005)

30. Degtyarev, A., Khramushin, V., Gankevich, I., Petriakov, I., Gavrikov, A., Grigorev, A.: Virtual testbed: ship motion simulation for personal workstations. In: Misra, S. (ed.) ICCSA 2019. LNCS, vol. 11622, pp. 717–728. Springer, Cham (2019). https://doi.org/10.1007/978-3-030-24305-0_53

31. Gavrikov, A., et al.: Real-time visualization of ship and wavy surface motions based on GPGPU computations. CEUR Workshop Proc. **2267**, 415–418 (2018)

32. Nechaev, Yu., Degtyarev, A., Boukhanovsky, A.: Complex situations simultation when testing intelligence system knowledge base. In: Alexandrov, V.N., Dongarra, J.J., Juliano, B. A., Renner, R.S., Tan, C.J.K. (eds.) ICCS 2001. LNCS, vol. 2073, pp. 453–462. Springer, Heidelberg (2001). https://doi.org/10.1007/3-540-45545-0_54

33. Kulabukhova, N., Bogdanov, A., Degtyarev, A.: Problem-solving environment for beam dynamics analysis in particle accelerators. In: Gervasi, O. (ed.) ICCSA 2017. LNCS, vol. 10408, pp. 473–482. Springer, Cham (2017). https://doi.org/10.1007/978-3-319-62404-4_35

34. Kulabukhova, N., et al.: Simulation of space charge dynamics on HPC. In: Proceedings of the 5th International Particle Accelerator Conference IPAC14, June 15–20, Dresden, Germany, pp. 1609-1611. JACoW (2014). https://doi.org/10.18429/jacow-ipac2014-tupri024

35. Taleb, N.N.: The black swan: the impact of the highly improbable. Random House Trade Paperback Edition, 2nd edn. pp. 446 (2010)

36. Bogdanov, A.V., Stepanov, E.A., Khmel, D.S.: Assessment of the dynamics of Asian and European option on the hybrid system. J. Phys. Conf. Ser. **681**(1), 012007 (2016). https://doi.org/10.1088/1742-6596/681/1/012007

37. Bogdanov, A.V., Bogdanov, S.A., Rukovchuk, V.P., Khmel, D.S.: Deep learning approach for prognoses of long-term options behavior. In: Misra, S. (ed.) ICCSA 2019. LNCS, vol. 11620, pp. 631–640. Springer, Cham (2019). https://doi.org/10.1007/978-3-030-24296-1_51

Virtual Testbed: Simulation of Air Flow Around Ship Hull and Its Effect on Ship Motions

Anton Gavrikov[ID], Alexander Degtyarev[ID], Denis Egorov[ID],
Ivan Gankevich[✉][ID], Artemii Grigorev[ID], Vasily Khramushin[ID],
and Ivan Petriakov[ID]

Saint Petersburg State University, 7-9 Universitetskaya Emb.,
St Petersburg 199034, Russia
{st047437,a.degtyarev,st047824,i.gankevich,st016177,
v.khramushin,st049350}@student.spbu.ru
https://spbu.ru/

Abstract. Strong wind causes heavy load on the ship in a seaway bending and pushing it in the direction of the wind. In this paper we investigate how wind can be simulated in the framework of Virtual testbed—a near real-time ship motion simulator. We propose simple model that describes air flow around ship hull with constant initial speed and direction which is based on the law of reflection. On the boundary the model reduces to the known model for potential flow around a cylinder, and near the boundary they are not equivalent, but close enough to visualise the effect of the hull on the flow. Then we apply this model to simulate air flow around real-world ship hull and conclude that for any real-world situation ship roll angle and ship speed caused by the wind is small to not cause capsizing, but large enough to be considered in onboard intelligent systems that determine real roll, pitch and yaw angles during ship operation and similar applications.

Keywords: Wind field · Law of reflection · Flow around cylinder · Uniform translational motion · OpenMP · OpenCL · GPGPU

1   Introduction

Ship motion simulation studies focus on interaction between the ship and ocean waves—a physical phenomena that gives the largest contribution to oscillatory motion—however, intelligent onboard systems require taking other forces into account. One of the basic functionality of such a system is determination of initial static ship stability parameters (roll angle, pitch angle and draught) from the recordings of various ship motion parameters, such as instantaneous roll, pitch

---

Supported by Saint Petersburg State University (grants no. 51129371 and 51129725) and Council for grants of the President of the Russian Federation (grant no. MK-383.2020.9).

O. Gervasi et al. (Eds.): ICCSA 2020, LNCS 12254, pp. 18–28, 2020.
https://doi.org/10.1007/978-3-030-58817-5_2

and yaw angles, and their first and second instantaneous derivatives (e.g. angular velocity and angular acceleration). During ship operation these initial static ship stability parameters deviate from the original values as a result of moving cargo between compartments, damaging the hull, compartment flooding etc. These effects are especially severe for fishing and military vessels, but can occur with any vessel operating in extreme conditions.

Intelligent onboard system needs large amount of synchronous recordings of ship motions parameters to operate, mainly angular displacement, velocity and acceleration and draught, but these parameters depend on the shape of the ship hull and obtaining them in model tests is complicated, let alone field tests. Field tests are too expensive to perform and do not allow to simulate particular phenomena such as compartment flooding. Model tests are too time-consuming for such a task and there is no reliable way to obtain all the derivatives for a particular parameter: sensors measure one particular derivative and all other derivatives have to be calculated by numerical differentiation or integration, and integration has low accuracy for time series of measurements [3]. The simplest way to obtain those parameters is to simulate ship motion on the computer and save all the parameters in the file for future analysis.

Arguably, the largest contribution to ship motion besides ocean waves is given by wind forces: air has lesser density than water, but air motion acts on the area of ship hull which may be greater than underwater area due to ship superstructure. Steady wind may produce non-nought roll angle, and thus have to be taken into account when determining initial static ship stability parameters. In this paper we investigate how wind velocity field can be simulated on the boundary and near the boundary of the ship hull. We derive a simple mathematical model for uniform translational motion of the air on the above-water boundary of the ship hull. Then we generalise this model to calculate wind velocity near the boundary still taking into account the shape of the above-water part of the ship hull. Finally, we measure the effect of wind velocity on the ship roll angle and carry out computational performance analysis of our programme.

2   Related Work

Studies on the effect of the wind on ship motions mostly focus on capsizing probability [2,4], whereas our work focuses on the direct effect of wind on ship motions and on how to incorporate ship roll angle change due to wind in onboard intelligent systems. As a result, we do not use probabilistic methods, but we use direct simulation of air flow.

Similar simulations can be performed in a wind tunnel [1] but in the case of onboard intelligent systems we need to gather a lot of statistical data to be able to tune the system for each ship hull shape. Performing large number of simulations in a wind tunnel is time-consuming and a computer programme is the most efficient option for this task.

3   Methods

3.1   Analytic Representation of Wind Velocity Field

Air motion without turbulence can be decomposed into two components: translational motion—air particles travel in the same direction with constant velocity, and circular motion—air particles travel on a circle. Translational motion describe sea breeze, that occurs on the shore on the sunrise and after the sunset. Circular motion describe storms such as typhoons and hurricanes. Translational motion is a particular case of circular motion when the radius of the circle is infinite. Due to the fact that the scale of circular motion is much larger than the size of a typical ship hull we consider only translational motion in this paper.

Since there is no rotational component, air flow is described by equations for irrotational inviscid incompressible fluid. In this context fluid velocity v is determined as a vector gradient ∇ of scalar velocity potential ϕ and continuity equation and equation of motion are written as

$$\Delta\phi = 0; \qquad v = \nabla\phi;$$
$$\rho\frac{\partial\phi}{\partial t} + \frac{1}{2}\rho|\nabla\phi|^2 + p + \rho g z = p_0. \tag{1}$$

Here p_0 is atmospheric pressure, g is gravitational acceleration, ρ is air density, p is pressure. We seek solutions to this system of equations for velocity potential ϕ. Continuity equation restricts the type of the function that can be used as the solution, and equation of motion gives the pressure for a particular velocity potential value.

Ship hull boundary is defined by a parametric surface S and surface normal n:

$$S = S(a, b, t) \qquad a, b \in A = [0, 1]; \qquad n = \frac{\partial S}{\partial a} \times \frac{\partial S}{\partial b}$$

The simplest parametric surface is infinite plane with constant normal. The computer model of a real ship hull is composed of many triangular panels with different areas and different orientations that approximate continuous surface. On the boundary the projection of wind velocity on the surface normal is nought:

$$\nabla\phi \cdot n = 0; \qquad r = S. \tag{2}$$

The solutions to the governing system of equations differ in how boundary is incorporated into them: in our model the boundary is taken into account by adding velocity of a reflected air particle in the solution. Velocity v_r of the particle that is reflected from the surface with surface normal n is given by the law of reflection (Fig. 1):

$$v_r = v - 2(v \cdot n)n. \tag{3}$$

When we add velocity of incident and reflected air particles we get a vector that is parallel to the boundary. As we move away from the boundary its impact on the velocity decays quadratically with the distance. The reason for using the law of reflection to describe air flow on the boundary is that the corresponding solution reduces to the known analytic solution for the potential flow around a cylinder (see Sect. 4.1). Quadratic decay term is borrowed from this known solution.

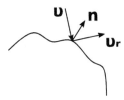

Fig. 1. The law of reflection diagram for incident and reflected air particle velocities v and v_r and surface normal n.

In the following subsections we describe the solution that we obtained for the velocity field *on* the boundary and *near* the boundary.

3.2   Uniform Translational Motion on the Static Body Surface

On the surface we neglect the impact of neighbouring panels on the velocity field on the ground that the real ship hull surface is smooth, i.e. neighbouring panels have approximately the same normals. This assumption does not hold for aft and bow of some ships, and, as a result, velocity field near these features has stream lines with sharp edges. We consider this effect negligible for the determination of roll angle caused by the wind, since the area of panels that distort wind field is small compared to the area of all other panels.

We seek solutions to the governing system of Eq. (1) with boundary condition (2) of the form

$$\phi = \boldsymbol{v} \cdot \boldsymbol{r} + C\left(\boldsymbol{v}_r \cdot \boldsymbol{r}\right); \qquad \boldsymbol{r} = (x, y, z),$$

Here $\boldsymbol{r}$ is spatial coordinate, C is the coefficient, and $\boldsymbol{v}_r$ is velocity of reflected air particle defined in (3). This solution is independent for each panel. Plugging the solution into boundary condition (2) gives

$$(\boldsymbol{v} + C\boldsymbol{v}_r) \cdot \boldsymbol{n} = 0,$$

hence

$$C = -\frac{\boldsymbol{v} \cdot \boldsymbol{n}}{\boldsymbol{v}_r \cdot \boldsymbol{n}} = 1$$

and velocity is written simply as

$$\boldsymbol{\nabla}\phi = \boldsymbol{v} + \boldsymbol{v}_r. \tag{4}$$

This solution satisfies continuity equation. It gives velocity only at the centre of each ship hull panel, but this is sufficient to calculate pressure and force moments acting on the ship hull.

3.3   Uniform Translational Motion Near the Static Body Surface

Near the surface there are no neighbouring panels, the impact of which we can neglect, instead we add reflected particle velocities for all the panels and decay the velocity quadratically with the distance to the panel. Here we can neglect panels surface normals of which has large angles with the wind direction for efficiency, but they do not blow up the solution.

We seek solutions of the form

$$\phi = \boldsymbol{v} \cdot \boldsymbol{r} + \iint_{a,b \in A} C \frac{\boldsymbol{v}_r \cdot \boldsymbol{r}}{1 + |\boldsymbol{r} - \boldsymbol{S}|^2} da\, db,$$

where $| \cdot |$ denotes vector length. Plugging the solution into boundary condition and assuming that neighbouring panels do not affect each other (this allows removing the integral) gives the same coefficient $C = 1$, but velocity vector is written differently as

$$\boldsymbol{\nabla}\phi = \boldsymbol{v} + \iint_{a,b \in A} \left(\frac{1}{s} \boldsymbol{v}_r - \frac{2}{s^2} \left(\boldsymbol{v}_r \cdot \boldsymbol{r} \right) \left(\boldsymbol{r} - \boldsymbol{S} \right) \right) da\, db; \qquad s = 1 + |\boldsymbol{r} - \boldsymbol{S}|^2. \quad (5)$$

Besides the term for reflected air particle velocity that decays quadratically with the distance to the panel, there is a term that decays quaternary with the distance and that can be neglected.

This solution reduces to the solution on the boundary when $\boldsymbol{r} = \boldsymbol{S}$ and takes into account impact of each panel on the velocity direction which decays quadratically with the distance to the panel.

4   Results

4.1   Verification of the Solution on the Example of Potential Flow Around a Cylinder

Potential flow around a cylinder in two dimensions is described by the following well-known formula:

$$\phi\left(r, \theta\right) = U r \left(1 + \frac{R^2}{r^2} \right) \cos\theta.$$

Here r and θ are polar coordinates, R is cylinder radius and U is x component of the velocity. Cylinder is placed at the origin. To prove that our solution on the boundary (4) reduces to this solution we write it in Cartesian form using polar coordinate identities

$$r = \sqrt{x^2 + y^2}; \qquad \theta = \arccos \frac{x}{\sqrt{x^2 + y^2}}.$$

Then in Cartesian coordinates the solution is written as

$$\phi(x, y) = U x \left(1 + \frac{R^2}{x^2 + y^2} \right)$$

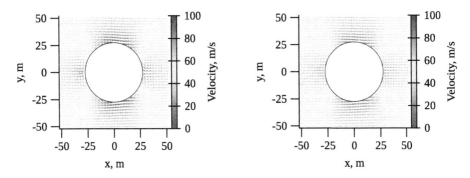

Fig. 2. Wind velocity fields for air flow around a cylinder: left—known solution (6), right—our solution (5).

and the velocity is written as

$$\boldsymbol{\nabla}\phi = \begin{bmatrix} U\left(R^2(y^2 - x^2) + (x^2 + y^2)^2\right) \\ -2R^2Uxy \end{bmatrix} / (x^2 + y^2)^2. \tag{6}$$

On the boundary $x^2 + y^2 = R^2$ and the velocity is written as

$$\boldsymbol{\nabla}\phi = \frac{2U}{R^2}\begin{bmatrix} y^2 \\ -xy \end{bmatrix}.$$

Now if we write surface normal as $\boldsymbol{n} = (x/R, y/R)$ and let $\boldsymbol{v} = (U, 0)$, our solution (4) quite surprisingly reduces to the same expression.

To reduce solution near the boundary (5) to the solution for potential flow around a cylinder, we let $s = |\boldsymbol{r}|^2/|\boldsymbol{S}|^2$ (here $\boldsymbol{r}$ is the radius vector in Cartesian coordinates). Then the solution is written as

$$\boldsymbol{\nabla}\phi = \boldsymbol{v} + \frac{1}{s}\boldsymbol{v}_r$$

and reduces to general form of the solution for potential flow around a cylinder given in (6).

We compared both solutions (see Fig. 2) for a cylinder with $R = 27.4429$, and discovered that maximum distance between velocity fields produced from both of them is 11% of the maximum velocity. Our formula shows slightly smaller decay near the boundary, but this problem cannot be solved by introducing coefficients. Perhaps, comparing our solution to the solution produced by CFD methods may shed light on which one is closer to the reality. On the ship hull boundary the solutions are equivalent.

4.2   Ship Roll Angle and Velocity

Wind causes non-nought force moment and force acting on a ship that bend and move the ship in the direction of the wind. This effect is stronger for the ships with large hull areas exposed to the wind, like fully-loaded containerships, but other ships are also affected.

We measured how wind speed affects Aurora's transversal velocity and roll angle. For that purpose we made wind blow directly in the starboard of the ship and varied wind speed. We stopped the experiment after 60 s and measured maximum roll angle and maximum transversal velocity. We have found that in order to produce 1° static roll angle we need wind speed of ≈35 m/s (Fig. 3), and wind with that speed makes the ship move in transversal direction with the speed of ≈0.2 m/s. We expect these numbers to be smaller for smaller ships.

We have found that the law of reflection (3) in its original form does not allow to calculate the effect of wind on the symmetric ship hull: it happens because the pressure on the leeward and windward side of the ship is the same—which is not the case for real-world phenomena where the pressure is different due to turbulence. To overcome this problem we introduce a coefficient α that controls reflection ratio:

$$v_r = v - 2\alpha \left(v \cdot n \right) n.$$

When $\alpha = 1$ this formula equals (3), when $\alpha = 0$ there is no reflection and the wind velocity does not change its direction near the ship hull. In our tests we used $\alpha = 0.5$. A better solutions would be to incorporate turbulence in the model which is one of the directions of future research.

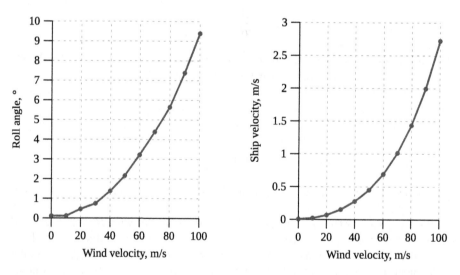

Fig. 3. Dependence of Aurora's roll angle on wind speed (left) and dependence of Aurora's transversal velocity on wind speed (right).

4.3   Computational Performance Analysis

We implemented solutions (4) and (5) in Virtual testbed wind solver. Virtual testbed is a programme for workstations that simulates ship motions in extreme conditions and physical phenomena that causes them: ocean waves, wind, compartment flooding etc.

We performed benchmarks for three ships: Diogen, Aurora and MICW. Diogen is a small-size fishing vessel, Aurora is mid-size cruiser and MICW is a large-size ship with small moment of inertia for the current waterline (Fig. 4). Ships in our database do not have superstructures, they have only hulls and compartments. The main difference between them that affects benchmarks is the number of panels into which the hull is decomposed. These numbers and sizes are shown in Table 1.

Table 1. Parameters of ship hulls that were used in the benchmarks.

	Diogen	Aurora	MICW
Length, m	60	126.5	260
Beam, m	15	16.8	32
Depth, m	15	14.5	31
No. of panels	4346	6335	9252

Benchmarks were performed using three workstations: DarkwingDuck, GPUlab, Capybara. DarkwingDuck is a laptop, GPUlab is a desktop workstation, and Capybara is a desktop with professional graphical accelerator server-grade processor (Table 2). All of the workstations are equipped with graphical accelerators that allow to greatly increase their performance.

Wind solver was written for both OpenMP and OpenCL to make use of graphical accelerator available on most modern workstations. The solvers use single precision floating point numbers. Benchmark results are presented in Table 3.

Table 2. Hardware configurations for benchmarks. For all benchmarks we used GCC version 9.1.0 compiler and optimisation flags `-O3 -march=native`.

Node	CPU	GPU	GPU GFLOPS	
			Single	Double
DarkwingDuck	Intel i7-3630QM	NVIDIA GT740M	622	
GPUlab	AMD FX-8370	NVIDIA GTX1060	4375	137
Capybara	Intel E5-2630 v4	NVIDIA P5000	8873	277

5   Discussion

Solution on the boundary (4) provides simple explanation of areas with the highest and lowest pressure for potential flow around a cylinder. At left-most and

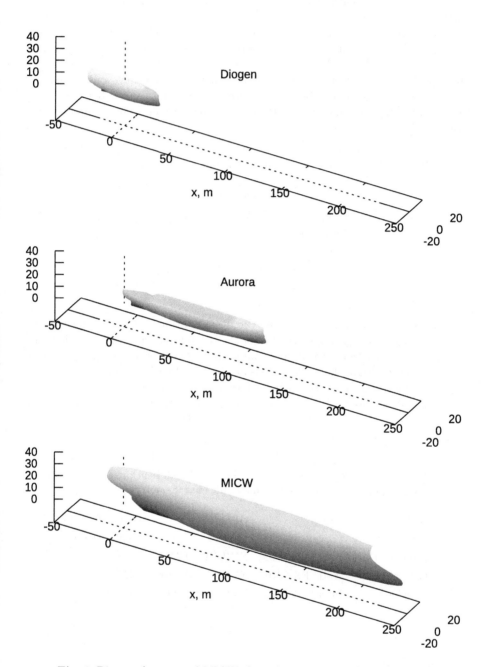

Fig. 4. Diogen, Aurora and MICW three-dimensional ship hull models.

Table 3. Performance benchmarks results. Numbers represent average time in milliseconds that is needed to compute wind field on the ship hull and near the ship hull.

Node	Diogen		Aurora		MICW	
	MP	CL	MP	CL	MP	CL
DarkwingDuck	114	14.00	164	16	314	29
GPUlab	62	1.35	90	2	175	3
Capybara	33	0.87	48	1	99	6

right-most points on the cylinder boundary (Fig. 2) velocity is nought because incident and reflected particle velocities have opposite directions and cancel each other out. At top-most and bottom-most points incident and reflected particle velocities have the same direction and total velocity is two times larger than the velocity of the flow.

In order to be compatible with the surface of any object, solution near the boundary (5) uses different term s than the solution for potential flow around a cylinder which makes reflected velocity term reach maximum value for the point on the boundary, and for the point near the boundary the solution includes reflected velocity vectors for each panel.

Wind speed of 35 m/s that we obtained in ship roll angle experiments matches hurricane with 14 m high waves on the Beaufort scale which would affect the ship more severely than the wind. The main reason for such a large value is that ships in our database do not have superstructures and hence the surface area affected by the wind is much smaller than in reality. Nevertheless, in intelligent onboard systems even small variations in static roll at less severe weather conditions have to be considered for the correct operation of the system.

The introduction of the coefficient α that controls reflection ratio is the simplest way of taking turbulence into account. $\alpha < 1$ increases the wind speed on the leeward side of the ship as a result of wind "going around" the ship hull. More sophisticated turbulence model would give more accurate results.

Performance benchmarks showed that performance of both OpenMP and OpenCL solvers increases from the least powerful (DarkwingDuck) workstation to the most powerful one (Capybara). In addition to this, performance of OpenCL is always better than of OpenMP by a factor of 16–58. Our solver uses explicit analytic formula to compute wind field and to compute wind field at each point iterates over all panels of the ship. All panels are stored and accessed sequentially and all points of wind field are stored sequentially and accessed in parallel, which makes the solver easy to implement in OpenCL and allows to achieve high performance on the graphical accelerator. Finally, as expected performance increases and the ratio between OpenCL and OpenMP performance decreases from the large-size to small-size ship. The only exception from the above-mentioned observations is the performance of OpenCL on Capybara for MICW hull. This behaviour requires further investigation.

6   Conclusion

This paper proposes a new simple mathematical model for wind field around the ship hull. On the ship hull boundary this model is equivalent to the known formula for potential flow around a cylinder. Near the boundary this model is close to this formula, but has slightly smaller decay. In both cases the model satisfies boundary conditions and continuity equation (conservation of mass), which makes it suitable for physical simulations. The main advantage of the model is its simplicity, the use of Cartesian coordinates and its applicability to bodies of any form, not just cylinders.

We applied this model to simulate ship motions under the effect of wind with constant speed and direction (and in the absence of all other effects except buoyancy force), and discovered that to get static roll angle of 1° we need wind speed of a hurricane (12 on the Beaufort scale). Also, simulation of ship motions due to wind is not possible without taking into account turbulence, but in the absence of turbulence model we used the simple coefficient that controls reflection ratio to adapt the model for this kind of simulation.

From the computational standpoint the proposed model shows high performance on modern processors as well as graphical accelerators due to linear memory access pattern and absence of synchronisation and data transfer between parallel processes. Using any up-to-date workstation is enough to perform real-world simulations.

Future work is to include stratification and circular motion in the model. Stratification—an increase of wind speed with height—is known phenomena in atmosphere which affects wind field around tall ships, and thus may improve accuracy of our solver. The motivation behind including circular motion is to better understand air motion around object and the fact that linear motion is a special case of it when the circle radius is infinite. Another possible direction of future work is to use more advanced turbulence model.

Acknowledgements. Research work is supported by Saint Petersburg State University (grants no. 51129371 and 51129725) and Council for grants of the President of the Russian Federation (grant no. MK-383.2020.9).

References

1. Andersen, I.M.V.: Wind loads on post-panamax container ship. Ocean Eng. **58**, 115–134 (2013). https://doi.org/10.1016/j.oceaneng.2012.10.008
2. Bulian, G., Francescutto, A.: A simplified modular approach for the prediction of the roll motion due to the combined action of wind and waves. Proc. Inst. Mech. Eng. Part M J. Eng. Marit. Environ. **218**(3), 189–212 (2004). https://doi.org/10.1243/1475090041737958
3. Kok, M., Hol, J.D., Schön, T.B.: Using inertial sensors for position and orientation estimation. Found. Trends Signal Process. **11**(1–2), 1–153 (2017). https://doi.org/10.1561/2000000094
4. Paroka, D., Ohkura, Y., Umeda, N.: Analytical prediction of capsizing probability of a ship in beam wind and waves. J. Ship Res. **50**(2), 187–195 (2016)

Virtual Testbed: Simulation of Ocean Wave Reflection from the Ship Hull

Ivan Petriakov⬡, Alexander Degtyarev⬡, Denis Egorov⬡,
Ivan Gankevich$^{(\boxtimes)}$⬡, Anton Gavrikov⬡, Artemii Grigorev⬡,
and Vasily Khramushin⬡

Saint Petersburg State University, 7-9 Universitetskaya Emb.,
St. Petersburg 199034, Russia
{st049350,st047824,st047437,st016177}@student.spbu.ru,
{a.degtyarev,i.gankevich,v.khramushin}@spbu.ru
https://spbu.ru/

Abstract. Diffraction and radiation forces result from the interaction between the ship hull and the moving fluid. These forces are typically simulated using added masses, a method that uses mass to compensate for not computing these forces directly. In this paper we propose simple mathematical model to compute diffraction force. The model is based on Lagrangian description of the flow and uses law of reflection to include diffraction term in the solution. The solution satisfies continuity equation and equation of motion, but is restricted to the boundary of the ship hull. The solution was implemented in velocity potential solver in Virtual testbed—a programme for workstations that simulates ship motions in extreme conditions. Performance benchmarks of the solver showed that it is particularly efficient on graphical accelerators.

Keywords: Ocean wave diffraction · Ocean wave radiation · Fluid velocity field · Law of reflection · OpenCL · OpenMP · GPGPU

1 Introduction

There are two mathematical models that describe rigid body motion and fluid particle motion: equations of translational and angular motion of the rigid body (Newton's Second Law) and Gerstner equations for ocean waves (which are solutions to linearised equations of motions for fluid particles). Usually, we use these models independently to generate incident ocean waves and then compute body motions caused by these waves. To measure the effect of still fluid on an oscillating rigid body (radiation forces) and the effect of fluid particles hitting the body (diffraction forces), we use added masses and damping coefficients—simplified formulae derived for small-amplitude oscillatory motion.

Supported by Saint Petersburg State University (grants no. 51129371 and 51129725) and Council for grants of the President of the Russian Federation (grant no. MK-383.2020.9).

But, what if we want to simulate large-amplitude rigid body motion with greater accuracy? There are two possible ways. First, we may use numerical methods such as Reynolds-Averaged Navier Stokes (RANS) method [5]. This method is accurate, can be used for viscous fluid, but not the most computationally efficient. Second, we may solve Gerstner equations with appropriate boundary condition and use the solution to compute both rigid body and fluid particle motion around it. This paper explores this second option. Similar approach was followed by Fenton in [1–3], but the distinctive feature of our approach is the use of law of reflection to derive analytic expressions for reflected waves and fluid particles.

2 Methods

2.1 Equations of Motions with a Moving Surface Boundary

An oscillating rigid body that floats in the water and experiences incident waves both reflects existing waves and generates new waves:

- fluid particles hit the body, causing it to move, and then reflect from it;
- moving body hits fluid particles and makes them move.

Both wave reflection and generation have the same nature—they are caused by the collision of the particles and the body—hence we describe them by the same set of formulae. Hereinafter we borrow the mathematical notation for Lagrangian description of the flow from [4].

In Lagrangian description of flow instantaneous particle coordinates $\boldsymbol{R} = (x, y, z)$ depend on particle positions at rest (independent initial coordinates) $\boldsymbol{\zeta} = (\alpha, \beta, \delta)$ and time t, i.e. $\boldsymbol{R} = \boldsymbol{R}(\alpha, \beta, \delta, t)$. Using this notation equation of motion (conservation of momentum) is written as

$$\boldsymbol{R}_{tt} + g\hat{z} + \frac{1}{\rho}\nabla_R p = 0, \tag{1}$$

where $\boldsymbol{R}$—particle coordinates, $\hat{z}$—unit vector in the direction of positive z, p—pressure, ρ—fluid density, g—gravitational acceleration. Continuity equation (conservation of mass) is written as

$$|\mathbb{J}| = 1, \qquad \frac{\partial}{\partial t}|\mathbb{J}| = 0, \qquad \mathbb{J} = \begin{bmatrix} x_\alpha & y_\alpha & z_\alpha \\ x_\beta & y_\beta & z_\beta \\ x_\delta & y_\delta & z_\delta \end{bmatrix}.$$

Multiplying both sides of (1) by $\mathbb{J}$ and noting that $\nabla_\zeta p = \mathbb{J}\nabla_R p$ gives

$$\mathbb{J}\boldsymbol{R}_{tt} + g\boldsymbol{\nabla}\left(\boldsymbol{R} \cdot \hat{z}\right) + \frac{1}{\rho}\boldsymbol{\nabla}p$$

Following [4] we seek solution to this equation in the form of a simultaneous perturbation expansion for position, pressure, and the vorticity function:

$$\boldsymbol{R} = \boldsymbol{R}_0 + \boldsymbol{R}_1 + \boldsymbol{R}_2 + \dots$$
$$p = p_a - \rho g\delta + p_1 + p_2 + \dots$$

Zeroth order terms are related to particles positions at rest:

$$\boldsymbol{R}_0 = \zeta$$
$$p_0 = p_a - \rho g \delta$$

First-order terms are solutions to linearised equation of motion and equation of continuity:

$$\boldsymbol{R}_{1tt} + g\boldsymbol{\nabla}\left(\boldsymbol{R}_1 \cdot \hat{z}\right) + \frac{1}{\rho}\boldsymbol{\nabla}p_1 = 0$$

$$\boldsymbol{\nabla} \cdot \boldsymbol{R}_1 = 0$$

We seek solutions of the form $\boldsymbol{R}_1 = \nabla w$ to make the flow irrotational. Plugging this form into the equations gives

$$\boldsymbol{\nabla}\left(w_{tt} + g w_\delta + p_1/\rho\right) = 0$$
$$\Delta w = 0 \tag{2}$$

The first equation denotes conservation of momentum (Newton's second law, equation of motion) and the second equation denotes conservation of mass (equation of continuity).

When we have no boundary condition we seek solutions of the form

$$w\left(\alpha, \beta, \delta\right) = \operatorname{Re} f(u, v) \exp\left(iu\alpha + iv\beta + k\delta - i\omega t\right), \tag{3}$$

where u and v are wave numbers. We plug (3) into continuity equation (2) where p_1 is constant and get $k = \sqrt{u^2 + v^2}$. That means that expression (3) is the solution to this equation when k is wave vector magnitude, i.e. w decays exponentially with increasing water depth multiplied by wave vector magnitude.

Then we plug (3) into equation of motion (2) and get $\omega^2 = gk$, which is dispersion relation from classic linear wave theory. That means that the expression is the solution to this equation when angular frequency depends on the wave number, i.e. waves of different lengths have different phase velocities.

Before solving this system of equations for an arbitrary moving surface boundary, we consider particular cases to substantiate the choice of the form of the solution.

We use $\operatorname{Re} \exp\left(iu\alpha + iv\beta + k\delta - i\omega t\right)$ to describe fluid particle potential. Here u and v are wave numbers, ω is angular frequency, and k is wave vector. This notation makes formulae short and is equivalent to the description that uses traditional harmonic functions. This notation allows for easy transition to irregular waves via Fourier transforms which are essential for fast computations. Such solutions will be studied in future work.

2.2   Stationary Surface Boundary

In this section we explore solutions stationary surface boundary in a form of infinite plane surface. On such a boundary the projection of particle velocity to the surface normal is nought. We write boundary conditions and corresponding solutions for different orientations of this boundary and then generalise these solutions to a parametric surface.

Infinite Wall. On a vertical surface the boundary condition is written as

$$\frac{d}{dt}\boldsymbol{\nabla} w \cdot \boldsymbol{n} = \frac{d}{dt}\frac{\partial}{\partial \alpha} w = 0; \qquad \alpha = \alpha_0; \qquad \boldsymbol{n} = \begin{bmatrix} 1 \\ 0 \\ 0 \end{bmatrix}.$$

Here we consider only α coordinate, the derivations for β are similar. The potential of incident fluid particle has the form

$$w\left(\alpha, \beta, \delta, t\right) = \exp\left(k\delta - i\omega t\right)\exp\left(iu\alpha + iv\beta\right).$$

Velocity vector of this particle is

$$\frac{d}{dt}\boldsymbol{\nabla} w = i\omega\left(\boldsymbol{d}_k + i\boldsymbol{d}_i\right)\exp\left(k\delta - i\omega t\right)\exp\left(iu\alpha + iv\beta\right);$$

$$\boldsymbol{d}_k = \begin{bmatrix} 0 \\ 0 \\ k \end{bmatrix}; \qquad \boldsymbol{d}_i = \begin{bmatrix} u \\ v \\ 0 \end{bmatrix}.$$

where $\boldsymbol{d}_i$ is horizontal incident wave direction and $\boldsymbol{d}_k$ is a vector that contains amplitude damping coefficient. (We use the vector instead of the scalar to shorten mathematical notation, otherwise we would have write a separate formula for vertical coordinate.) The law of reflection states that the angle of incidence equals the angle of reflection. Then the direction of reflected wave is[1]

$$\boldsymbol{d}_r = \boldsymbol{d}_i - \boldsymbol{d}_s = \boldsymbol{d}_i - 2\boldsymbol{n}\left(\boldsymbol{d}_i \cdot \boldsymbol{n}\right) = \begin{bmatrix} -u \\ v \\ 0 \end{bmatrix}.$$

We seek solutions of the form

$$w\left(\alpha, \beta, \delta, t\right) = \left[C_1 \exp\left(iu\alpha\right) + C_2 \exp\left(-iu\alpha\right)\right]\exp\left(k\delta - i\omega t\right)\exp\left(iv\beta\right). \qquad (4)$$

We plug this expression into the boundary condition and get

$$C_1 \exp\left(iu\alpha_0\right) - C_2 \exp\left(-iu\alpha_0\right) = 0,$$

hence $C_1 = C \exp(-iu\alpha_0)$ and $C_2 = -C \exp(iu\alpha_0)$. Constant C may take arbitrary values, here we set it to 1. Plugging C_1 and C_2 into (4) gives the final solution

$$w\left(\alpha, \beta, \delta, t\right) = \cosh\left(iu\left(\alpha_0 - \alpha\right)\right)\exp\left(k\delta - i\omega t\right)\exp\left(iv\beta\right).$$

There are two exponents in this solution with the opposite signs before horizontal coordinate α. These exponents denote incident and reflected wave respectively. The amplitude of the reflected wave does not decay as we go farther from the boundary, but decay only when we go deeper in the ocean. This behaviour corresponds to the real-world ocean waves.

---

[1] Initially, we included the third component of incident wave direction making the vector complex-valued, however, the solution blew up as a result of mixing real and imaginary parts in dot products involving complex-valued vectors. The problem was solved by reflecting in two dimensions which is intuitive for ocean waves, but not for particles.

Infinite Plate. On a horizontal surface the boundary condition is written as

$$\frac{d}{dt}\boldsymbol{\nabla} w \cdot \boldsymbol{n} = \frac{d}{dt}\frac{\partial}{\partial \delta} w = 0; \qquad \delta = \delta_0; \qquad \boldsymbol{n} = \begin{bmatrix} 0 \\ 0 \\ 1 \end{bmatrix}.$$

Analogously to wave direction we write vector form of the incident particle trajectory radius damping coefficient as $(0, 0, k)$, hence vector form of the reflected coefficient is $(0, 0, -k)$. We seek solutions of the form

$$w\left(\alpha, \beta, \delta, t\right) = \left[C_1 \exp\left(k\delta\right) + C_2 \exp\left(-k\delta\right)\right] \exp\left(-i\omega t\right) \exp\left(iu\alpha + iv\beta\right). \quad (5)$$

We plug this expression into the boundary condition and get

$$C_1 \exp\left(k\delta_0\right) - C_2 \exp\left(-k\delta_0\right) = 0.$$

Hence $C_1 = C\exp\left(-k\delta_0\right)$ and $C_2 = C\exp\left(k\delta_0\right)$. Constant C may take arbitrary values, here we set it to $1/2$. Plugging C_1 and C_2 into (5) gives the final solution

$$w\left(\alpha, \beta, \delta, t\right) = \cosh\left(k\left(\delta - \delta_0\right)\right) \exp\left(-i\omega t\right) \exp\left(iu\alpha + iv\beta\right).$$

There are two exponents in this solution with opposite signs before vertical coordinate δ. These exponents make the radius of the particle trajectories decay exponentially while approaching the boundary δ_0 (i.e. with increasing water depth). This is known solution from linear wave theory.

Infinite Panel. On an arbitrary aligned infinite surface the boundary condition is written as

$$\frac{d}{dt}\boldsymbol{\nabla} w \cdot \boldsymbol{n} = 0; \qquad \boldsymbol{n} \cdot \left(\boldsymbol{\zeta} - \boldsymbol{\zeta_0}\right) = 0,$$

where $\boldsymbol{\zeta_0}$ is the point on the boundary plane and the third component of the normal vector is nought: $\boldsymbol{n} = (n_1, n_2, 0)$, $|\boldsymbol{n}| = 1$. The direction of incident wave is $\boldsymbol{d_i} = (u, v, 0)$ and the direction of reflected wave is $\boldsymbol{d_r}$. We seek solutions of the form

$$\begin{aligned} w\left(\alpha, \beta, \delta, t\right) = &\, C_1 \exp\left(\left(i\boldsymbol{d_i} + \boldsymbol{d_k}\right) \cdot \boldsymbol{\zeta} - i\omega_1 t\right) \\ &+ C_2 \exp\left(\left(i\boldsymbol{d_r} + \boldsymbol{d_k}\right) \cdot \boldsymbol{\zeta} - i\omega_2 t\right). \end{aligned} \quad (6)$$

We plug this expression into the boundary condition and get

$$\left(i\boldsymbol{d_i} \cdot \boldsymbol{n}\right) C_1 + \left(i\boldsymbol{d_r} \cdot \boldsymbol{n}\right) C_2 \exp\left(-i\boldsymbol{d_s} \cdot \boldsymbol{\zeta_0}\right) = 0.$$

Here we substitute $\boldsymbol{d_r} \cdot \boldsymbol{n}$ with $-\boldsymbol{d_i} \cdot \boldsymbol{n}$ which is derived from the formula for $\boldsymbol{d_r}$. Hence, the boundary condition reduces to

$$C_1 - C_2 \exp\left(-i\boldsymbol{d_s} \cdot \boldsymbol{\zeta_0}\right) = 0.$$

Hence $C_1 = \frac{1}{2}\exp\left(-\frac{1}{2}i\boldsymbol{d}_s \cdot \boldsymbol{\zeta}_0\right)$ and $C_2 = \frac{1}{2}\exp\left(\frac{1}{2}i\boldsymbol{d}_s \cdot \boldsymbol{\zeta}_0\right)$. This solution reduces to the solution for the wall when $\boldsymbol{n} = (0, 0, 1)$.

In a computer programme it is more practical to set $C_1 = 1$ and $C_2 = \exp\left(i\boldsymbol{d}_s \cdot \boldsymbol{\zeta}_0\right)$: that way you have to integrate only the second term in the solution over all ship hull panels (see Sect. 3.1).

2.3   OpenCL Implementation

Solution for fluid velocity field was implemented in velocity potential solver in the framework of Virtual testbed. Virtual testbed is a programme for workstations that simulates ship motions in extreme conditions and physical phenomena that causes them: ocean waves, wind, compartment flooding etc. The main feature of this programme is to perform all calculations nearly in real time, paying attention to the high accuracy of calculations, which is partially achieved using graphical accelerators.

Virtual testbed uses several solvers to simulate ship motions. The algorithm for velocity potential solver is the following.

– First of all, we generate wavy surface, according to our solution and using wetted ship panels from the previous time step (if any).
– Second, we compute wetted panels for the current time step, which are located under the surface calculated on the previous step.
– Finally, we calculate Froude—Krylov forces, acting on a ship hull.

These steps are repeated in infinite loop. Consequently, wavy surface is always one time step behind the wetted panels. This inconsistency is a result of the decision not to solve ship motions and fluid motions in one system of equations, which would be too difficult to do.

Let us consider process of computing wavy surface in more detail. Since wavy surface grid is irregular (i.e. we store a matrix of fluid particle positions that describe the surface), we compute the same formula for each point of the surface. It is easy to do with C++ for CPU computation, but it takes some effort to efficiently run this algorithm with GPU acceleration. Our first naive implementation was inefficient, but the second implementation that used local memory to optimise memory loads and stores proved to be much more performant.

First, we optimised storage order of points making it fully sequential. Sequential storage order leads to sequential loads and stores from the global memory and greatly improves performance of the graphical accelerator. Second, we use as many built-in vector functions as we can in our computations, since they are much more efficient than manually written ones and compiler knows how to optimise them. This also decreases code size and prevents possible mistakes in the manual implementation. Finally, we optimised how ship hull panels are read from the global memory. One way to think about panels is that they are coefficients in our model, as array of coefficients is typically read-only and constant.

This type of array is best placed in the constant memory of the graphical accelerator that provides L2 cache for faster loads by parallel threads. However, our panel array is too large to fit in constant memory, so we simulated constant memory using local memory: we copied a small block of the array into local memory of the multiprocessor, computed sum using this block and then proceeded to the next block. This approach allowed to achieve almost 200-fold speedup over CPU version of the solver.

A distinctive feature of the local memory is that it has the smallest latency, at the same time sharing its contents between all computing units of the multiprocessor. Using local memory we reduce the number of load/store operations to global memory, which has larger latency. As far as global memory bandwidth remains a bottleneck, this kind of optimisation would improve performance. To summarise, our approach to write code for graphical accelerators is the following:

- make storage order linear,
- use as many built-in vector operations as is possible,
- use local memory of the multiprocessor to optimise global memory load and stores.

Following these simple rules, we can easily implement efficient algorithms.

3   Results

3.1   Diffraction

In the first experiment we use solution for infinite panel to simulate wave diffraction around Aurora's ship hull (see Fig. 1). In order to apply (6) to this problem we use smoothing kernel that accumulates influence of every panel on a particular point of ocean surface:

$$w = \sum_j K_j w_j; \qquad K_j = \frac{1}{1 + |\zeta - \zeta_0|^2}$$

Here w_j is solution (6) written for panel j, K_j is smoothing kernel, ζ_0 is the centre of the panel. In the centre of the panel $K_j = 0$ and far from the ship hull $K_j \to 0$.

In the experiment waves with amplitude 1 approach the ship from the aft. The results of the experiment are shown in Fig. 2. Near the aft waves change their direction to be tangent to the waterline curve, follow the curve to the bow, and then restore their original direction. The amplitude of waves near the hull is also increased.

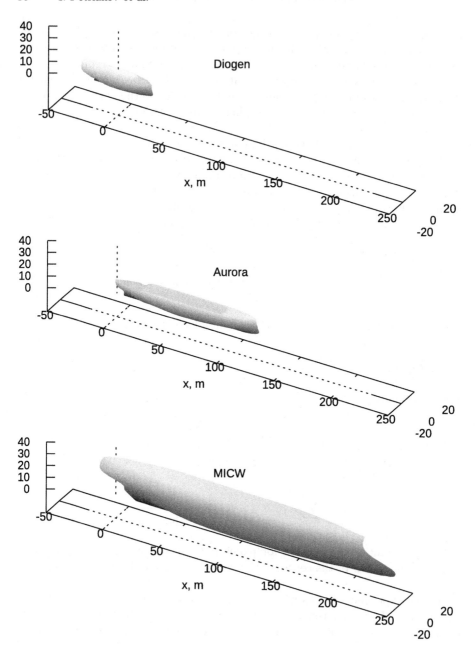

Fig. 1. Diogen, Aurora and MICW three-dimensional ship hull models.

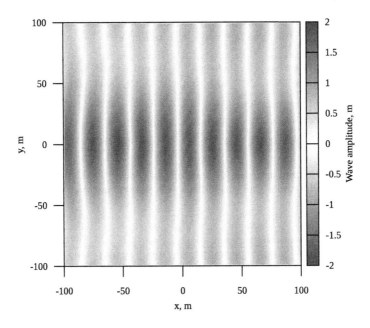

Fig. 2. Wave diffraction around Aurora's hull (the hull is not shown). Top view.

3.2   Performance Benchmarks

We implemented velocity potential solver using OpenMP for parallel computations on a processor and OpenCL for graphical accelerator. The solver uses single precision floating point numbers. Benchmark results are presented in Table 2.

We performed benchmarks for three ships: Diogen, Aurora and MICW. Diogen is a small-size fishing vessel, Aurora is mid-size cruiser and MICW is a large-size ship with small moment of inertia for the current waterline (Fig. 1). The main difference between the ships that affects benchmarks is the number of panels into which the hull is decomposed. These numbers are shown in Table 1.

Table 1. Parameters of ship hulls that were used in the benchmarks.

	Diogen	Aurora	MICW
Length, m	60	126.5	260
Beam, m	15	16.8	32
Depth, m	15	14.5	31
No. of panels	4346	6335	9252

Benchmarks were performed using three workstations: DarkwingDuck, GPUlab, Capybara. DarkwingDuck is a laptop, GPUlab is a desktop workstation, and Capybara is a desktop with professional graphical accelerator server-grade processor (Table 3).

Table 2. Performance benchmarks results. Numbers represent average time in milliseconds that is needed to generate waves with reflection.

Node	Diogen		Aurora		MICW	
	MP	CL	MP	CL	MP	CL
DarkwingDuck	5462	48	7716	41	7725	11
GPUlab	5529	11	8222	10	6481	3
Capybara	2908	16	2091	8	2786	4

Table 3. Hardware configurations for benchmarks. For all benchmarks we used GCC version 9.1.0 compiler and optimisation flags -O3 -march=native.

Node	CPU	GPU	GPU GFLOPS	
			Single	Double
DarkwingDuck	Intel i7-3630QM	NVIDIA GT740M	622	
GPUlab	AMD FX-8370	NVIDIA GTX1060	4375	137
Capybara	Intel E5-2630 v4	NVIDIA P5000	8873	277

4   Discussion

All the solutions obtained for various boundaries in this papre satisfy continuity equation and equation of motion, but they are all written for *plane* surface boundaries with different orientations. Typical ship hull three-dimensional model is represented by triangulated surface, and in the centre of each triangular panel fluid particle velocity vector does not depend on the surface normal of the other panels. So, the solution for plane surface boundary is enough to compute fluid velocity field directly *on* the surface boundary.

In order to generalise the solution for fluid velocity field *near* the surface boundary, we need to calculate weighted average of reflection terms of each underwater panel of the surface. Using inverse squared distance as the weight gives acceptable results in our experiments, but may not be appropriate in others.

It is not clear how much we have to increase wave amplitude near the boundary. One way to control the amplitude increase is to introduce the coefficient C into the reflection formula $d_r = d_i - C d_s$ and before reflection term in (6). When $C = 1$ the wave is fully reflected from the boundary and the amplitude is doubled, when $C = 0$ no reflection occurres and the amplitude does not change.

Performance benchmarks showed that graphical accelerator greatly improves performance of velocity potential solver. Linear memory access patterns and large amount of floating point operations make this solver an ideal candidate for running on a graphical accelerator, and these features are the result of deriving explicit solution for fluid motions near the ship hull boundary.

5   Conclusion

This paper proposes a new model for ocean wave diffraction near ship hull. This model uses law of reflection to simulate incident and reflected waves and fluid particle motion. Although, the solutions are written for infinite plane surfaces, they can be used to compute fluid velocity at the centre of each triangle of the triangulated ship hull surface and can be generalised to compute fluid velocity near the ship hull using weighted sum over all panels.

The model was implemented in Virtual testbed velocity potential solver and was found to be highly efficient on a graphical accelerator. Future work is to incorporate radiation into the model and compare the solution to existing empirical approaches.

Acknowledgements. Research work is supported by Saint Petersburg State University (grants no. 51129371 and 51129725) and Council for grants of the President of the Russian Federation (grant no. MK-383.2020.9).

References

1. Fenton, J.D.: Wave forces on vertical bodies of revolution. J. Fluid Mech. **85**(2), 241–255 (1978). https://doi.org/10.1017/S0022112078000622
2. Fenton, J.D.: A spectral method for diffraction problems. In: Proceedings of International Symposium on Waves - Physical and Numerical Modelling, pp. 961–970. The University of British Columbia, Vancouver (1994)
3. Fenton, J.D., et al.: Simulating wave shoaling with boundary integral equations. In: 11th Australasian Conference on Coastal and Ocean Engineering: Coastal Engineering a Partnership with Nature; Preprints of Papers, p. 71. Institution of Engineers, Australia (1993)
4. Nouguier, F., Chapron, B., Guérin, C.A.: Second-order Lagrangian description of tridimensional gravity wave interactions. J. Fluid Mech. **772**, 165–196 (2015). https://doi.org/10.1017/jfm.2015.179
5. Wackers, J., et al.: Free-surface viscous flow solution methods for ship hydrodynamics. Arch. Comput. Meth. Eng. **18**(1), 1–41 (2011). https://doi.org/10.1007/s11831-011-9059-4

A Modified Algorithm of Porting a Wave Motion

Alexander V. Bogdanov, Vladimir V. Mareev,
Nikita Storublevtcev$^{(\boxtimes)}$, Victor Smirnov, and Ivan Podsevalov

Faculty of Applied Mathematics and Control Processes, Saint-Petersburg State
University, 198504 Petergof, Saint-Petersburg, Russia
{bogdanov,map}@csa.ru, 100.rub@mail.ru

Abstract. The purpose of our work is to identify the key features of algorithms in porting codes for calculating of essentially nonlinear processes to a modern cluster of hybrid architecture. The KPI equation with a source term was numerically modeled to reveal the features of the occurrence of extreme waves. A methodology for the implementation of boundary conditions for the modified KPI equation was also proposed.

Keywords: High performance computing · CPU architectures · GPU · FPGA · Rogue wave · KPI

1 Introduction

One of the main challenges of computational physics is the high computational cost of any simulation sufficiently complex to be practically useful. With the continuous advancement of computer hardware, this problem is slowly but steadily solved. The highly parallel architecture of General-Purpose Graphical Processing Units (GPGPUs) lends itself well to the simulation of various processes, such as fluid dynamics.

Unlike previous works dedicated to porting of applications to a different software-hardware platform [16–18], in this paper we present a modified algorithm of porting, using a wave motion model based on heterogeneous generalized two-dimensional Kadomtsev–Petviashvili equation taking into account the new boundary conditions as an example.

2 The Problem

Extreme waves—frequently called "killer waves" ("rogue waves" or "freak waves")—are lone waves of at least 20-30 m in height, which unexpectedly arise in the ocean with otherwise little disturbance and have completely unpredictable and uncharacteristic behavior compared to other ocean waves [1–8].

The study of the generation of powerful waves, in particular, solitary, is carried out using numerical simulation. For this purpose, model partial differential equations are used. Some important information is obtained as a result of observations and experiments.

O. Gervasi et al. (Eds.): ICCSA 2020, LNCS 12254, pp. 40–50, 2020.
https://doi.org/10.1007/978-3-030-58817-5_4

In our previous analysis it was shown that the main problems in the numerical simulation of two-dimensional waves with the effects of an avalanche-like increase in amplitude are associated with changes in the type of equations in the transition from a continuum to a discrete analogue of the problem. In particular, the loss of full integrability or reduction in the number of conservation equations in a discrete problem is critical [14, 19]. As a result of this, a number of compensation mechanisms typical for nonlinear waves are destroyed, and effects called artifacts appear. Since these effects are most pronounced in completely integrable systems, the most "unpleasant" model with the maximum violation of the compensation conditions, namely KPI, was chosen for analysis.

Kadomtsev-Petviashvili equation $\left[u_t + 0.5(u^2)_x + \beta u_{xxx}\right]_x = \eta u_{yy}$ in regards to the function $u(x,y,t)$ is usually labeled as "KPI equation" and is considered at $t \geq 0$, $x,y \in (-\infty, \infty)$, $\beta, \eta > 0$. This equation is also called "unstable Kadomtsev-Petviashvili equation" or "focusing effect equation".

Earlier, for the two-dimensional KPI equation with growing solutions, a strategy for creating mesh methods was formulated and analyzed. When solving such problems numerically, the possibility of parallelizing programs using graphic processors was tested.

Using finite-difference approach for KPI equation calculation is not effective due to the presence of the mixed derivative u_{tx}.

Instead of the original equation KPI its integro-differential analogue is considered [16]:

$$u_t + 0.5\left(u^2\right)_x + \beta u_{xxx} = \eta S(x,y,t) + G(x,y) \qquad (1)$$

Equation (1) with respect to function $u(x,y,t)$ is considered in the domain $t \geq 0$, $x,y \in (-\infty, \infty)$, $\beta, \eta \geq 0$, $S(x,y,t) = \int_{-\infty}^{x} u_{yy}(x',y,t)dx'$; $G(x,y)$ is external source. Solution of the Eq. (1) is sought for initial distribution $u(x,y,0)$.

The continuous region of the equation KPI specification is replaced by a finite computational domain $[x_{\min}, x_{\max}] \times [y_{\min}, y_{\max}] \times [0,T]$. A uniform differential grid with time t and spatial coordinates x and y is set in the calculation area:

$$x_j = (j - j_0)\Delta x, j \in [1, M], x_{\min} = x_1, x_{\max} = x_M$$

$$y_k = (k - L/2)\Delta y, k \in [1, L], y_{\min} = y_1, y_{\max} = y_L$$

$$y_k = (k - L/2)\Delta y, k \in [1, L], y_{\min} = y_1, y_{\max} = y_L$$

$t^n = n\Delta t, n = 0, 1, 2, \ldots, T/\Delta t - 1$, with $\Delta x, \Delta y$ being spatial coordinates steps, Δt being time step, j_0 being the index corresponding to $x = 0$, $u[(j - j_0)\Delta x, (k - L/2)\Delta y, n\Delta t] = u_{j,k}^n$.

For (1) the approximation is performed using the central-difference operators.

$$u_{j,k}^{n+1} - u_{j,k}^n + \Delta t/(4\Delta x)\left(F_{j+1,k}^{n+1} - F_{j-1,k}^{n+1}\right) +$$
$$\beta \Delta t/(2\Delta x^3)\left(u_{j+2,k}^{n+1} - 2u_{j+1,k}^{n+1} + 2u_{j-1,k}^{n+1} - u_{j-2,k}^{n+1}\right) = \tag{2}$$
$$\Delta t\eta S_{j,k}^{n+1} + \Delta t G_{j,k}$$

The integral $S(x, y, t)$ is calculated by the trapezoid method, the integrand derivative u_{yy} is approximated by second order central differences:

$$\int\limits_{-\infty}^{x_j} u_{yy}dx' \approx \int\limits_{x_{min}}^{x_j} u_{yy}dx' \equiv S_{j,k}^n$$

$$S_{j,k}^n \approx \frac{\Delta t}{\Delta y^2}\left(u_{j,k-1}^{n+1} - 2u_{jk}^{n+1} + u_{j,k+1}^{n+1}\right).;$$

$$u_{yy} \approx \frac{u_{j,k-1}^n - 2u_{j,k}^n + u_{j,k+1}^n}{\Delta y^2} \tag{3}$$

The resulting system of difference equations (2) is reduced to the form:

$$a_j\Delta u_{j-2,k}^{n+1} + b_j\Delta u_{j-1,k}^{n+1} + c_j\Delta u_{j,k}^{n+1} + d_j\Delta u_{j+1,k}^{n+1} + e_j\Delta u_{j+2,k}^{n+1} = f_{j,k}^n \tag{4}$$

with $\Delta u_{j,k}^{n+1} = u_{j,k}^{n+1} - u_{j,k}^n$ and $F_{j,k}^{n+1} \equiv (u^2)_{j,k}^{n+1} = (u^2)_{j,k}^n + 2u_{j,k}^n\Delta u_{j,k}^{n+1} + O(\Delta t^2)$.

The boundary conditions KPI are used: $u_x = u_{xx} = 0$ along boundary lines x_1 and x_M, and $u_y = 0$ along the lines y_1 and y_L, $x_{min} = x_1$, $x_{max} = x_M$, $y_{min} = y_1$, $y_{max} = y_L$:

$$u_{-1,k}^n = u_{0,k}^n = u_{1,k}^n; u_{M+2,k}^n = u_{M+1,k}^n = u_{M,k}^n;$$

$$u_{j,0}^n = u_{j,1}^n; u_{j,L+1}^n = u_{j,L}^n$$

KPI solutions dampen proportionally to the square of distance $O[1/(x^2 + y^2)]$, which means that in practical calculations it is impossible to choose a sufficiently large area $[x_{min}, x_{max}] \times [y_{min}, y_{max}]$ to use uniform Dirichlet conditions.

The coefficients $a_j, b_j, c_j, d_j, e_j, f_j$ (4) are determined from relations for the derivatives. Difference scheme is an implicit linearized finite-difference scheme. Quasi-one-dimensional system is solved by the five-point sweep method. In some necessary cases, a flow correction procedure (FCT) is used [9].

A series of previous papers [10–16] was devoted to the numerical simulation of nonlinear KdVB and KPI type equations. In these papers, a difference scheme was chosen, its testing was carried out, and numerical results were obtained. Various methods for numerical solution of KPI were discussed in [13].

The main features of the difference scheme are illuminated in [12, 13, 15].

As an initial distribution is considered the ellipsoid of rotation:

$$u(x, y, 0) = \sigma \exp\left[-\omega\left(x^2/a_1^2 + y^2/b_1^2\right)\right], \tag{5}$$

where $\sigma > 0$, the volume $V_1 = \pi \sigma a_1 b_1 / \omega$, and a_1, b_1 being the half axis. A distribution of sources as an ellipsoid of rotation is chosen:

$$G(x, y) = c_2 \sqrt{1 - (x - x_0)^2/a_2^2 - (y - y_0)^2/b_2^2}, \tag{6}$$

with the volume $V_2 = 2\pi a_2 b_2 c_2 / 3$, and a_2, b_2, c_2 being the half axis, (x_0, y_0)—center of ellipsoid.

When calculating such an Eq. (1) by a finite-difference method in a bounded rectangular region, the integral S introduces a significant error in the solution. Because of the finite region of calculation, the integral S at the boundaries of the region does not tend to zero. In order to get rid of the distortion of the numerical solution, due to the reasons described above, the following procedure is proposed [19].

From the test results, several conclusions were drawn – the schema has sufficient resolution for areas of high gradient; the schema describes the process of formation and distribution of solitons with characteristic conservation very well; the scheme satisfactorily handles cases with initial distributions that are not entirely integrable; a more powerful hardware is needed to model long-term cases.

When calculating the equation system (4) with boundary conditions (5), the flow condition along the y axis are not implemented correctly, which leads to reflection condition.

To be able to correctly set the boundary condition of the flow type $u_y = 0$ at $y = y_{\min}$, $y = y_{\max}$ in the left part of Eq. (2) a small quantity is introduced, which can be called artificial convection over y: $-\varepsilon \cdot \text{sign}(u_y) u_y$, where the parameter $\varepsilon > 0$ and small enough ($\varepsilon \ll 1$), such as not to introduce significant error in the solution of the corresponding Eq. (1).

Instead of the integral $S(x, y, t)$, the function $P(y)$ is introduced:

$$\tilde{S}(x, y, t) = P(y) \cdot S(x, y, t),$$

where

$$P(y) = \begin{cases} 1, y \in [y_{\min} + \delta, y_{\max} - \delta] \\ h^-(y), y \in [y_{\min}, y_{\min} + \delta] \\ h^+(y), y \in [y_{\max} - \delta, y_{\max}] \end{cases}$$

For functions $h^-(y)$ and $h^+(y)$ fulfil the symmetry condition: $h^-(y_{\min} + y^*) = h^+(y_{\max} - y^*)$ at $y^* \in [0, \delta)$.

When choosing the finite function $P(y)$, and practically the function $h^+(y)$, there are two criteria:

The function $h^+(y)$ should monotonously decrease in the band adjacent to the upper boundary $y_{\max}$ (increase in the lower band for $y_{\min}$).

The derivative of function $h^-(y)$ and $h^+(y)$ at the boundaries $y_{\min}$ and $y_{\max}$ should be as small as possible.

During the choice of finite function $P(y)$ several different $h^+(y)$ functions were considered, in particular, sigmoid function, 3-rd degree spline, parabolas.

3 Porting Challenges

Model in question is represented by 7 matrices of equal size, which are operated upon by 4 main functions. Each matrix holds single-precision 32-bit floating-point values representing the wave height relative to the base ocean level.

Two functions also feature temporary data arrays, size of which can differ depending on the implementation. In the original algorithm for CPU, these arrays were equal to 1–4 rows of the main matrices. Some of this temporary data can be reduced or eliminated completely by usage of additional on-the-spot calculations, but some of is required for parallelization. Reduction in temporary data increases cache localization, which can have a positive influence on performance, but inhibits parallelization, for example, automated loop unwinding.

Matrices U_0 and U_1 represent the previous and current model states respectively. Since each subsequent model state depends on a previous one, we are forced to hold both in memory at all times. Matrix $P_{j,k}$ is responsible for boundary smoothing and contains coefficients from 0 to 1, with edge cells set at zero.

Matrix $G_{j,k} \equiv G(x_j, y_k)$ is the external perturbation matrix. Matrix $(U\_yy)_{j,k}$—is second derivative u_{yy} (3).

Matrix s_eta $\equiv S_{jk}^n$. Matrix $(U\_y)_{j,k}$—is first derivatives u_y in boundary conditions.

The original implementation was written in Fortran 95. OpenCL was chosen as the framework for the GPGPU porting process. Main reason for that choice was high degree of portability and low dependency from the host-side code language.

As was mentioned above, heterogeneous architecture of GPGPUs is a good fit for matrix operations, but not all functions of the model allow for complete cell-level parallelism, as each cell's value may be dependent on the adjacent ones. Additionally, some functions feature accumulation calculations on one or both axes, making full parallelization very difficult.

For example, the function implementing five-point tridiagonal matrix algorithm, can be roughly represented like this:

```
for k in 1..N-1{
for j in 2..M-2{
a[j+1] = F1(a[j-1], a[j], b[j-1], b[j], u0[j*, k], u_y[j, k], s_eta[j, k],
g[j, k])
b[j+1] = F2(a[j-1], a[j], b[j-1])
c[j+1] = F3(a[j-1], c[j-1], c[j], , u0[j*, k], u_y[j, k], s_eta[j,k], g[j,
k])
}
for j in M-3..0{
U`[j] = F4(U`[j+1], U`[j+2], a[j+1], b[j+1], c[j+1])
u[j,k] = u0[j,k] + U`[j]
}
}
```

Where j* - neighborhoods j, i.e. j − 1. j. j + 1; a, b, c and U' are temporary buffer matrices, F, G and H are simple linear functions, and U is the result. From this it is easy to see that column calculation is relatively independent, while row calculation includes forward and backward accumulation. In all other main functions, every element's value is dependent on the adjacent one. For example, an element with coordinates $[x, y]$ may rely on one at $[x + / - 1, y]$, and in the worst case require a simple additive accumulation.

Taking all of this into account, the main focus was made on the inter-column parallelization, which ended up being surprisingly straightforward, with very little code changes required. Five-point tridiagonal matrix algorithm implementation required buffer arrays for each row, which were allocated using private memory which for datasets of this size is automatically projected onto the global device memory, and as such does not require additional synchronization. This resulted in an expected increase of performance.

Next step was to implement the inter-row parallelism, at least in the trivial cases, such as calculation of U_yy and U_y matrices, which do not feature accumulation. This had significantly improved calculation times. This is most likely due to the memory block read optimization.

When calculating s_eta j-th row element depends on the intermediary results from j − 1-th element. In the original algorithm it was solved by allocating a temporary row s such that s[j] = s[j − 1] * F1(U_yy[j*, k]), after which s_eta was calculated as s_eta [j] = F2(s[j]). This approach is ill-suited for GPU, because cumulative addition is hard to parallelize and intermediary results have to be stored in global memory. Thankfully, it can be avoided by utilizing local memory − breaking the calculation of s into blocks, each calculating F1(U_yy[j*, k]) in parallel, after which the main thread performs the additive accumulation and immediately calculates F2(s[j]), and repeats the same for the next block. Despite the fact that F1 function is very simple in terms of calculation, this approach game a noticeable boost to performance. This is, most likely, due to the GPU architecture details − global memory access is much more efficient when reading a block of data in parallel, inside a single local group.

The last step was to improve the five-point tridiagonal matrix algorithm parallelization. In this case local memory would not help as there is simply not enough of it to contain all the required data. The solution was to create a single buffer matrix and utilize the comparatively large 4 Gb global memory space. Big memory usage is unpleasant, but acceptable if it solves a much larger problem of slow global memory access. Each matrix element is only dependent on the two previous ones, which allows us to store these two values in faster memory. This way, at the first stage of calculations, each iteration writes the data into global memory but does not read it, which allows the optimizer to perform a much faster asynchronous write. For subsequent iterations the same data is stored in private memory, which is fast for both write and read. At the second stage of calculations the intermediary data is only read from global memory, which avoid the need for additional synchronization. There was a risk that the intermediary data would not fit into the private memory, since it is very limited, but in practice there were no problems with it, and it provided a significant boost to performance.

4 Numerical Tests

The benchmarking platform specifications are as follows:
CPU AMD FX 8550 ~4 GHz
GPU AMD R9 380 ~970 MHz
For the testing purposes, the model size was limited to 960 by 640 cells, with 200 iterations, which equates to 0.01 s of simulation time. Benchmark results of different versions are presented in Table 1.

Table 1. Benchmark results

Version	Time (s)
CPU	28.683
GPU	1.355
GPU async	1.338
GPU 2d	0.304
GPU 2d async	0.302

As seen from the above Table 1, the simple inter-column parallelism increased the computation speed by ~20 times despite significantly lower GPU clock speed. Utilization of asynchronous kernel calls did provide an additional small boost to performance.

Inter-row parallelization of trivial functions cut down the total computation time by ~40%, while s_eta optimization improved it to ~50%. The last step brought it to a total of ~75% less compute time than a simple inter-column version, or about 90 times faster than the CPU version.

Unfortunately, it was impossible to showcase performance increase per core, as profiling software provided incoherent results.

5 Porting Results

An analysis of the results calculated with various finite functions showed that the most suitable for this initial distribution (5) are two functions: a spline of the 3rd order $h^+(\bar{y}) = 2\bar{y}^3 - 3\bar{y}^2 + 1$ and a parabola $h^+(\bar{y}) = \bar{y}^2 - 2\bar{y} + 1$, $\varepsilon = 0.01$.

Figure 1 shows visible effects of the interaction of propagating waves with the boundary $y = y_{min}$ and $y = y_{max}$. For this picture and for all furthers, the main numerical values of the parameters are the same: mesh is $800 \times 600(x \times y)$, $\Delta x = \Delta y = 0.1$, $\Delta t = 5 \cdot 10^{-5}$, $\beta = \eta = 1$. In our case it is $y_{min} = -31.9, y_{max} = 48$.

The Gaussian distribution (5) is taken with $\sigma = 10$, $a_1 = 2$, $b_1 = 3$, $\omega = 1.570796$.

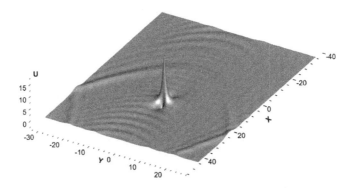

Fig. 1. The effects of the interaction of propagating waves without smoothing at $t = 8$.

Figure 2 gives a comparison of the smoothing effect for functions $h^+(\bar{y})$ for upper band: sigmoid function $h^+(\bar{y}) = 0.5[1 \pm \tanh(\bar{y}/2)]$. The width $\delta = 0,11 \cdot |y_{max} - y_{min}| = 6.6$ (11% from the width of the computational domain $|y_{max} - y_{min}|$).

The testing (Fig. 2) was conducted for the case with a rotation ellipsoid (6) source where $a_2 = 2, b_2 = 3, c_2 = 5$, i.e. $V_2 = 20\pi$. Grid: 800×600, $\Delta x = \Delta y = 0.1$, $\Delta t = 5 \cdot 10^{-5}$. $t = 14$, $\varepsilon = 0.01$ (Fig. 3).

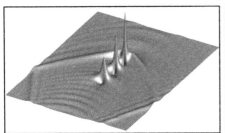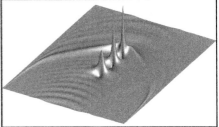

Fig. 2. Comparing the smoothing effect for functions $h^+(\bar{y})$ for upper band: sigmoid function (left) and parabola (right).

It is obvious that both functions give almost identical results (Fig. 4), but parabola gives better ones.

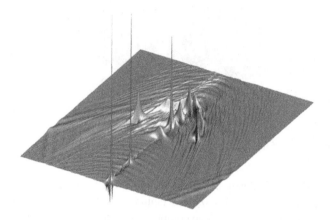

Fig. 3. External source. The effects of the interaction of propagating waves without smoothing at $t = 14$.

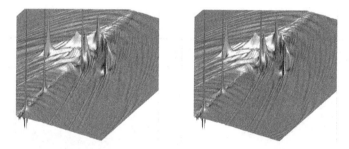

Fig. 4. External source. Comparing the smoothing effect for functions $h^+(\bar{y})$ for upper band: spline $h_3^+(\bar{y}) = 2\bar{y}^3 - 3\bar{y}^2 + 1$ (left) and parabola $h_4^+(\bar{y}) = \bar{y}^2 - 2\bar{y} + 1$ (right) at $t = 14$ and $\varepsilon = 0.01$.

6   Conclusion

The analysis of various numerical procedures for nonlinear equations describing the evolution of strong waves is carried out. An equation is chosen that is a generalization of the Kadomtsev-Petviashvili-I (KPI) equation, which shows the main part of the problems of the evolution of ocean waves and at the same time is the most difficult from the point of view of stability of the numerical algorithm. The solution of such problems reveals the features of various types of discretization.

Numerical analysis shows that the proposed approach solves at least those problems that are related to the complete integrability of the original model. A calculation method is proposed by introducing a smooth finite function and artificial convection. It works quite efficiently, at least for nonlinear equations with an infinite evolution domain. The proposed procedure showed acceptable accuracy. We managed not only to clearly demonstrate the effects of an avalanche-like increase in the amplitude of two-dimensional waves, but also to solve all the main problems leading to numerical errors, namely, the shift of the wave crest and the appearance of artifacts. Since the transition to more realistic models of "killer waves" is associated with a decrease in the number of restrictions in the transition to a discrete model, there is every reason to hope that our method there will be even more effective.

References

1. Kundu, A.: Tsunami and Nonlinear Wave, 316 pp. Springer Science & Business Media, Berlin (2007)
2. Todorov, M.D.: Nonlinear Waves: Theory, Computer Simulation, Experiment, 184 pp. Morgan & Claypool Publishers, San Rafael (2018)
3. Infeld, E., Rowlands, G.: Nonlinear Waves, Solitons and Chaos, 2nd edn, p. 406. Cambridge University Press, Cambridge (2000)
4. Zeytounian, R.K.: Theory and Applications of Nonviscous Fluid Flows, 295 pp. Springer Science & Business Media, Berlin (2012)
5. Yang, J.: Nonlinear Waves in Integrable and Non-integrable Systems, 430 pp. Society for Industrial and Applied Mathematics, Philadelphia (2010)
6. Feng, B.F., Mitsui, T.: A finite difference method for the Korteweg-de Vries and the Kadomtsev-Petviashvili equations. J. Comput. Appl. Math. **90**, 95–116 (1998)
7. Popov, S.P.: Numerical implementation of two-soliton solutions to the Kadomtsev-Petviashvili equation. Comput. Math. Math. Phys. **40**(10), 1447–1455 (2000)
8. Ayadi, M.: Numerical simulation of Kadomtsev–Petviashvili–Benjamin–Bona-Mahony equations using finite difference method. Appl. Math. Comput. **219**(24), 11214–11222 (2013)
9. Boris, J.P., Book, D.L.: Flux corrected transport I, SHASTA, a fluid transport algorithm that works. J. Comput. Phys. **11**, 38–69 (1973)
10. Bogdanov, A., Stankova, E., Mareev, V.: High performance algorithms for multiphase and multicomponent media. In: 14th Ship Stability Workshop, pp. 242–245, UTMSPACE, Malaysia (2014)
11. Bogdanov, Alexander V., Mareev, Vladimir V., Stankova, Elena N.: Hybrid approach perturbed KdVB equation. In: Gervasi, O., et al. (eds.) ICCSA 2015. LNCS, vol. 9158, pp. 331–341. Springer, Cham (2015). https://doi.org/10.1007/978-3-319-21410-8_26
12. Bogdanov, A., Mareev, V.: Numerical simulation perturbed KdVB equation. In: EPJ Web of Conferences [MMCP 2015 Stará Lesná, Slovakia, 2015], vol. 108, p. 02014 (2016)
13. Bogdanov, A.V., Mareev, V.V.: Numerical simulation KPI equation. In: Proceedings of the 15th International Ship Stability Workshop, 13–15 June, Stockholm, Sweden, pp. 115-117 (2016)
14. Bogdanov, A.V., Mareev, V.V.: Hybrid approach for nonlinear wave equation. In: AIP Conference Proceedings, Published by the American Institute of Physics (ICNAAM 2016), vol. 1863, 9–25 September 2016, Rhodes, Greece, p. 110005 (2017). 10.1063/1.4992290
15. Bogdanov, A.V., Mareev, V.V., Kulabukhova, N.V., Degtyarev, A.B., Shchegoleva, N.L.: Influence of external source on KPI equation. In: Gervasi, O. (ed.) ICCSA 2018. LNCS, vol. 10963, pp. 123–135. Springer, Cham (2018). https://doi.org/10.1007/978-3-319-95171-3_11

16. Stepanov, E., Khmel, D., Mareev, V., Storublevtcev, N., Bogdanov, A.: Porting the algorithm for calculating an asian option to a new processing architecture. In: Gervasi, O. (ed.) ICCSA 2018. LNCS, vol. 10963, pp. 113–122. Springer, Cham (2018). https://doi.org/10.1007/978-3-319-95171-3_10
17. Bogdanov, A., Storublevtcev, N., Mareev, V.: On porting of applications to new heterogeneous systems. In: Proceedings of the VIII International Conference "Distributed Computing and Grid-technologies in Science and Education" (GRID 2018), pp. 328–332 (2018)
18. Bogdanov, A.V., Mareev, V.V., Storublevtcev, N.: Algorithms for the calculation of nonlinear processes on hybrid architecture clusters. In: Proceedings of the VIII International Conference "Distributed Computing and Grid technologies in Science and Education" (GRID 2018), September 10-14 Dubna, Moscow region, Russia, RWTH Aahen University, pp. 333–336, ISSN 1613-0073 (2018)
19. Bogdanov, A.V., Mareev, V.V.: On some problems of the numerical implementation of nonlinear systems on example of KPI equation. In: EPJ Web of Conferences. Mathematical Modeling and Computational Physics 2019, vol. 226, Stara Lesha, Slovakia, p. 01003 (2020). https://doi.org/10.1051/epjconf/202022601003

Service-Oriented Petri Net Model

Oleg Iakushkin$^{(\boxtimes)}$

Saint-Petersburg University, 7/9 Universitetskaya nab., St. Petersburg 199034, Russia
o.yakushkin@spbu.ru

Abstract. In this paper, we consider the existing problems of colour stochastic Petri nets (CSPN) for modelling of systems of interconnected applications - services. The main issues that arise when modelling service applications and their interactions are as follows: support of composite types and indexed arrays, describing operations on top of them. It is also important to note the problem of using global time in model combinations – it is hard to describe different levels of abstraction. For example, to combine the network behaviour such as delays, duplication, and packet loss and its effects on business logic. To solve all of these problems, we propose a new model of a service-oriented Petri net (SOPN). It is built based on the stochastic Petri net (SPN) by adding some restrictions and extension components. We added tools for creating data structures, fundamental types such as integers, rational numbers, ordered arrays. The model presented in this paper provides the toolkit for creating complex atomic operations in terms of model-controlled time. Meanwhile, for all the new components and features transition to the basic SPN model is supported.

Keywords: Modelling · Petri net · Services · CSPN

1 Introduction

It is important to analyse the methods of problems solving using services in a distributed computing environment, and it is necessary to create a modelling apparatus that allows a comprehensive description of complex processes and to draw qualitative conclusions about the behaviour of the systems in question [2,7,8].

2 Problem at Hand

Service systems are characterised by characteristics that allow us to limit the space covered during the simulation. In this regard, we introduce several axioms.

Axiom 1: *In the service systems under consideration, only frequently recurring phenomena can be modelled using Bayesian networks, the modelling of the remaining events should be carried out unambiguously and decomposed into the logic of finite state machines.*

© Springer Nature Switzerland AG 2020
O. Gervasi et al. (Eds.): ICCSA 2020, LNCS 12254, pp. 51–66, 2020.
https://doi.org/10.1007/978-3-030-58817-5_5

The specifics of the systems justifies this assumption under consideration - service systems can be distinguished by a long term of continuous operation and cyclic processes of resolving the same type of user requests [4–6]. Such behaviour leads to the fact that most of the events of service systems are repeated many times by updating the probabilistic modelling of system events regardless of their primary source.

Axiom 2: *Objects that can be modified in the systems under consideration can be converted to the format of finite sets of real numbers.*

2.1   Inspecting Type Requirements

Let us inspect this assumption for fundamental programming types:

- Real number (including **int, float, double, long** etc.) $a = b/c$ can be represented as a set of $\{b, c\}$;
- A **string** of characters of a known size can be represented as $\{c_1, c_2, ... c_n\}$ where c_i is a character from a finite alphabet (represented as an integer)
- An **enum** is a straight set of integers by defenition
- If we know all of our application types we can create a set $\mathbb{T} = \{\tau_1, \tau_2, ...\tau_n\}$ that can be used to denote a set of pairs describing a type instance at hand - its current values v and type identifier i, $\tau = \{i, v\}$. Combinations of such pairs compose type instances and allow for complex types like **struct** and their nested versions.
- An indexed array such as **vector** or **List** can be described by pairs of integers $o_i = \{1, 2, ...N\}$ and their instance values so that array element would be a set $e = \{o_i, \tau\}$

Thus for complex types, we need integers and a way of their composition into sets.

2.2   Looking at SPN Capabilities

There are many works devoted to how Petri nets can be utilised to describe technological processes [9]. The concept of colours is often resorted to simplifying such descriptions. Colour is a special kind of label that can be unambiguously correlated with a specific value from a previously known set. Models CSPN, GCSPN retain the ability to switch from a model that uses colours to the original [1,12,13]. It is important to emphasise that the formalism of Petri nets involves the departure of labels in the transition one at a time [10,11].

In the framework of this paper, we will mostly adhere to the SPN definitions from [3,10]. Define the SPN by indicating the significant properties of this work.

Definition 1. *SPN building blocks:*

- *A finite set of places $P = \{p_1, p_2, ..., p_n\}$;*
- *A finite set of transitions $T = \{t_1, t_2, ..., t_n\}$;*

- *A subset of immediate transitions $E' \subset T$. An immediate transition fires the instant it becomes enabled, whereas a timed transition fires after a positive amount of time;*
- *A marking s is configuration $s = (s_1, s_2, ... s_n)$ of marks assigned to places $d_1, d_2, ... d_n$ respectfully. All possible markings compose a countably infinite set G;*
- *Sets $I(t), L(t), J(t) \subseteq D$ of normal input places, inhibitor input places, and output places, for each transition $t \in T$. We will call them places connected to transition t;*
- *A transitions $T(s)$ are enabled when $T(s) = \{t \in T : s_j \geq 1 \text{ for } d_j \in I(t) \text{ and } s_j = 0 \text{ for } d_j \in L(t)\}$. in other words when all connected inhibitor input places are empty and marks can be obtained from all connected normal places;*
- *The marking of an SPN changes when one or more enabled transitions fire. When a transition fires it removes at most one token from each of its input places and deposits at most one token in each of its output places;*
- *$T* \subseteq T(s)$, denote by $p(s', s, T*)$ the probability that the new marking is s' given that the marking is s and the transitions in the set $T*$ fire simultaneously;*
- *For each transition t the priority $\varrho(t)$ is defined as a finite, non-negative integer. Whenever transitions t and t' are in a conflict, meaning they can t fire simultaneously, the net behaves as if only one with highest priority fires.*

Criticism of Traditional SPNs. Two main problems arise to have capabilities of service model description:

- Creation of a transition as a function of the total number of marks, is not possible without creating special schematic solutions. Thus integers can not be used out of the box;
- If a transition is defined as timed and fires only after a certain time δ, it is hard to combine it with other transitions to gain predetermined time characteristics. Thus item grouping and combination requires additional support in terms of additional markings and places.

2.3   Task Definition

We need to create an extension set that would allow SPN users to create:

- Integers;
- Composable types;
- Operation combinations with fixed time characteristics;
- Composable groups fro pattern definition and reuse.

So we will get a modelling framework that allows users to:

- Create their type combinations;
- Create transitions that operate on such types;
- Combine network subsections into reusable patterns.

3 Our Solution - Service-Oriented Petri Net Model

First, we will suggest a set of restrictions that will simplify work with a network structure, keeping SPN compatibility. Then using graph notation of Petri networks [5]. We will create a set of extensions that solve our problem, having transparent convertibility to basic SPN. We call our solution Service-Oriented Petri Net Model (SOPN).

3.1 Core Extensions

Several main building blocks must be discussed to be capable of building complicated SOPN structures.

Probability Function for Each Transition. Let us reformulate the way we deal with state change probability $p(s', s, T*)$. Such approach generalises the way states change on a subset of T and a state s as a whole. This makes it hard to formulate the network in terms of transitions and places. One would like to define a set describing transition firing probability functions $\Gamma = \{\gamma_1, \gamma_2, ...\gamma_k\}$ for each transition in $T = \{t_1, t_2, ...t_k\}$. So that γ is by itself free from system configuration state s and is evaluated when a transition is enabled by $I(t)$ and $L(t)$. This is a restriction that reduces SPN modelling power, yet provides clarity to network definition from a practical system modelling standpoint.

Time as a Marking. Service systems are composed of indirection layers. Processes on such layers may have different time scales while doing similar operations. To solve such a problem, we make all time-related transactions dependent on network marking configuration s instead of abstract system time. We do it by adding a place-transition subsystem to the network and cause all timed transitions dependent on it.

A time counter is connected so that each transition in the system can to fire only when time transition is enabled. When time transition is enabled will be calling it a unit of time - a *tick*.

As you can see on Fig. 1 a transaction may require any integer amount of time before it will be enabled to fire from the *time* point of view.

Note that on Fig. 1 we depict actual transaction that shall be started after integer time m as a blue square.

Generalised Locking Strategy. Service-oriented programs need to allow transition compositions that can be executed in a single time step - like functions in programming composed of operation sets. Thus we had to create a locking extension that can see if a given transaction can start its execution and when it has finished it.

– A lock place with one mark thru a transition is connected to a "work" place. this transition is also connected to all "enablers" of all required transitions.

Levels

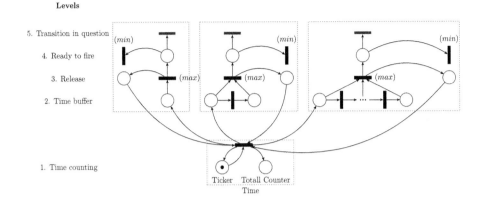

5. Transition in question

4. Ready to fire

3. Release

2. Time buffer

1. Time counting

Ticker Totall Counter
Time

Fig. 1. A time structure embedded into state configuration

- if a transition *is not enabled* that marks are collected, and transition did not fire.
- Otherwise transition logic fires. Now we can look at transition combination as a separate network, operating as one immediate transition.
- After all required operations finished execution and are ready to return results to output places we empty "done" places equipped with one mark and release the lock.

All locks are allowed to enable "work" no more than once in a time tick.

Thus we present (see Fig. 2) a lock logic extension that enables transition combination. Note that transition composition inputs are depicted as a blue rectangular and outputs as orange ones.

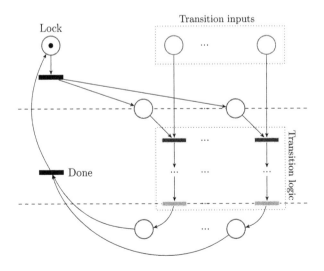

Fig. 2. A transition lock structure

Transition Composition. Generalised locking strategy enables us to create *functional transactions* that are composed of sets of operation transactions. In other words combination of a lock structure enabled for all such groups of trans-actions, that in essence depict functions, in combination with a global time clock allow us to define complex functions following SPN formalism. Such functions can be defined as $f(t, r, p, I)- > O$, where t is the required integer amount of time steps, r conveys function execution priority compared to others, I depicts input requirements (incoming transitions) and p show execution probability when all requirements are enabled, while O depicts output transition options. Note that any such *fuctional transition* is just an SPN graph with some nodes defined as *Inputs* and some defined as *Outputs*.

It is essential to be able to combine as many transitions into one as needed so that their combination can fire in a predictable amount of time (in one or more system ticks). So *fuctional transformations* can be combined allowing complicated behaviours.

When we can be assured that our *fuctional transition* is executed in a single *time step* we can start to reason about such transition as an SPN graph separated from its surroundings. It is important to note that all of such subgraph required inputs shall be *passed on to it* - locked or consumed so that other transitions will not be able to change them in parallel. Thus we can deal with *"all"* input place items as a form of *functional transition* requirement.

Copy and Move. A good examples of simple *functional transitions* are *"copy all inputs from one place to another"* and *"move all items from one place to another"*.

Fig. 3. *Functional transitions* to copy and move input

To replicate values between two nodes, a copy *functional transition*, that keeps all source items and clones them into output place is depicted in Fig. 3.

Its SPN implementation graph details can be found on Fig. 4. Here we depict:

- Input place is depicted by a blue circle (all of its inputs shall be frozen before this transition fires);
- Input transition by a blue rectangle which is enabled when the time, probability and general locks are enabled;
- Output place for all input place items as an orange circle;
- Output transition as an orange rectangle, so that transition would unlock the system when it has finished its execution.

Move implementation is similar Fig. 4.

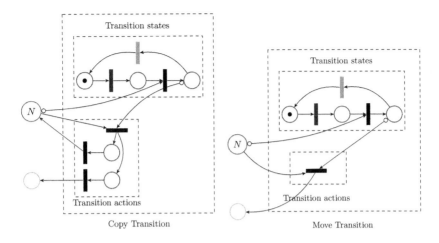

Fig. 4. Implementations of copy and move *functional transitions*

Condition Swithces. It is paramount to be capable of selecting an option depending on all items in a place. So we need a *functional transition* for a switch.

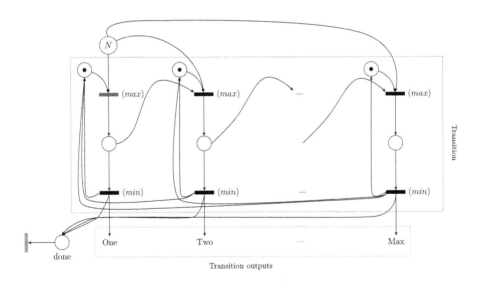

Fig. 5. A switch condition structure

In other words, it is essential to be able to switch depending on the input. An example of such a switch is presented in Fig. 5. We utilise priorities (in parenthesis near transitions) to prioritise transition activation and release the lock when a switch has selected a value. Note that this *condition switch* approach can be used to implement all kinds of behaviours, including inhibitor transitions for empty checking.

The main disadvantage of such graph is that to convey with SPN formalism it requires *fixed maximum input size of N*. Yet as it is an extension, such capacity can be set and fixed before SOPN network execution.

Functional Transition Composition. As we can copy parts of our SPN graphs and combine them we can create functions composed from sets of operations.

An example of *functional transaction* combination possibilities is shown on Fig. 6.

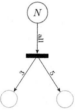

Fig. 6. A subnet operating on input and outputing a const value depending on it

Implementation is shown in detail here Fig. 7. As you can see we have a switch case leading to copy as preexisting *functional transactions*.

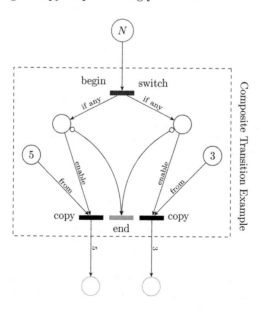

Fig. 7. A subnet operating on input and outputing a const value depending on it implemetation option

Theorem 1. *For any set F composed of functional transitions, if all of each of its outputs are reachable, all outputs of its combinations will also be reachable.*

Proof. Proof by contradiction: say not all of its outputs combinations are reachable. Then at least one of the transition nodes in a SOPN graph is newer reached. Yet we know that all of the graph building blocks, thus all nodes are reachable. This creates a contradiction. Therefore for any set F composed of *functional transitions*, if all of its outputs are reachable than all outputs of its combinations will also be reachable.

3.2 Integers

3.3 Integer Operations

On top of integers, we need to be able to perform a set of different mathematical operations. In this paper we present a basic set of integer operations such as $\{+, -, >, ==, <, *, /, \%\}$ in Fig. 8.

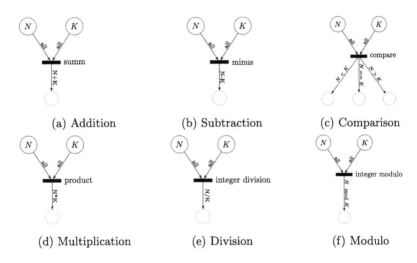

(a) Addition   (b) Subtraction   (c) Comparison

(d) Multiplication   (e) Division   (f) Modulo

Fig. 8. Basic math operations $+, -, >, ==, <, *, /, \%$

Addition and Subtraction. Basic mathematical operations such as addition and subtraction are depicted in Figs. 9, 11.

Compare. The comparison allows us to take two nodes with values N and K and to get any of the three results, namely $K == N$ or $K > N$ or $K < N$. As shown in Fig. 8c we deplete original places values thus sometimes copy operation may proceed as shown in implementation details here Fig. 12.

Transition states

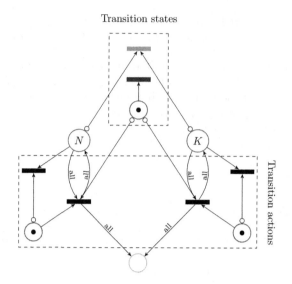

Fig. 9. An addition subnet

Multiplication, Division and Mod. Multiplication extension relies heavily on data copying and inhibitor connections as shown in Fig. 13. Division operation is relying on subtraction (see Fig. 14). Mod transition is heavily dependent on division (as shown in Fig. 14)

3.4   Nested Types

Arrays Extension. Complex types such as arrays with fixed length and operations on top of them can be implemented as a set of *functional transactions* on top of a group of places as shown on Fig. 15. Here we depict read operations, and others can be implemented similarly.

Nested Types Extension. We need a description of where the entire array, integer or some other combination of places set with *functional transitions* on top of them are located. So we present a notation for that: *type-place bonding*. Alike they do it in programs we have a separation of flow logic and memory management. SOPN user is managing a higher-level abstraction of places that are associated with type instances indirectly:

– For each place that will be handling complex types on SOPN network we have a unique integer address number - thus we call it a *holder place*;
– Each type is composed of its data places (on top of which functional transitions are defined) and a place that keeps its address, its *location Id*;
– Before simulation is executed maximum allowed type instance counts are defined;

Transition states

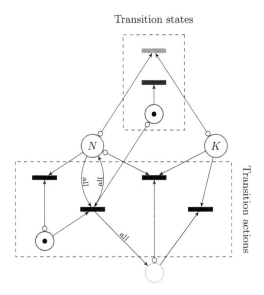

Fig. 10. A minus operation subnet

– When a transaction takes a type instance from one holder place to another, it changes instance location Id.

Thus SOPN user is working with a graph of type instances bound to places (similar to pointers). When a *functional transition* operation is activated, it changes or creates new cases not only by setting data, yet also by changing type location Id.

Structured Types. We have defined integers, arrays, timesteps and locking logic for basic colourless mark token types. Yet how to distinguish an array of *type A* from integer of *type B*? If we add colour to nodes using CSPN as a base, we can define a complex type structure like this:

```
struct data {
    int number;
    string text;
}
```

As a colorset like this: $data = \{int, \{int_1, ..., int_n\}\}$ where n is max array length, red color set would indicate integer type, blue color set would indicate a character type and green colorset would indicate fixed size character array type. Here colors will allow CSPN type conversion, separation and compatability operations, while SOPN extensions will allow *transition functions*, global time and locking operations, type-place bonding.

Transition states

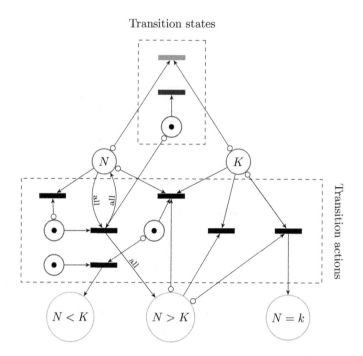

Fig. 11. A comparison transition

3.5   Modules

Portable types and operations on top of them provide a low-level abstraction for general logic description and RPC types. Yet, when it comes to a service-oriented network, it is paramount also to have interaction patterns that can describe services interactions with each other. Thus we present a *module* concept. A module is a SOPN subgraph that consists of places and transitions and can be easily replicated. It has publicly available transitions and places. Time inside of it can be scaled by all transitions time multiplication by a constant. An example of a module can be seen in Fig. 10.

Comparing Module Implementations. We will be calling a modules SOPN subgraph places connected to a module *public transitions* and that module's *public places - related* places. A configuration evolution distribution (CED) $O(s)- > s_o$ means that for any initial configuration s, of places *related* to a given module, we know what marks that will be placed into its *related* places. For different module implementations, the time t and probability p that any such transformation will happen and how long it will take can change. CED computation can usually be done if no external modifications will happen to the configuration of places *related* to a module, or a module locks interactions with external components while it is in operation.

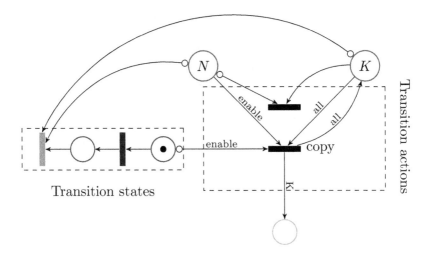

Fig. 12. An multiplication transition

Theorem 2. *If for a module its CED is known, module inner makings will not affect its behaviour while CED is not changed, and thus module inner graph can be changed in any way while it respects CED in SOPN graph.*

Proof. Proof by construction: say we know a CED of a module in SOPN graph, and another module - a SOPN subgraph with the same CED. Now if we replace one with another, its graph will change, yet as CED is not changed and thus SOPN graph will function as before concerning new module implementation timings and probabilities.

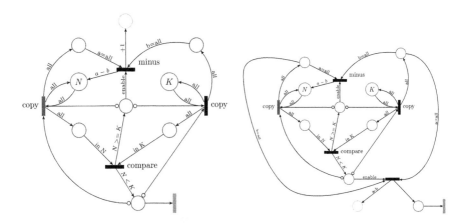

Fig. 13. A mod and division transition

Theorem 3. *A SOPN graph composed from a set G of modules with known CED will always have a CED related only to CEDs of its modules.*

Proof. Proof by construction: Now say we have a SOPN composed of modules with known CEDs. If we change any module implementation while keeping its CED for all other modules CED will not modify, only timings and probabilities will. So general SOPN graph system as a whole CED will not change. If we replace a *module* with a different CED public SOPN system, CED will change with it. Thus system CED is directly related to its modules CED.

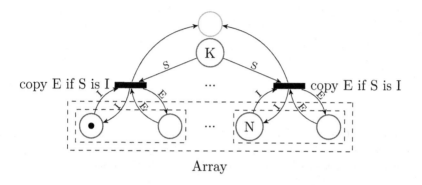

Fig. 14. Get element from array transition

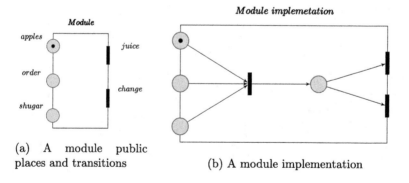

(a) A module public places and transitions

(b) A module implementation

Fig. 15. A module

So We can change modules with the same outputs yet different performance characteristics and perform implementation comparisons.

4   Conclusion

For formal modelling of the interaction of service systems, the ability to describe the interaction protocols of nodes is essential. This requires support for a set of seemingly simple data types: integers, floating-point numbers, enumerations, strings. However, existing implementations of Petri nets focusing on mathematical generality operate in terms of transferring units of information-labels from positions to transitions one at a time. This principle in their formal definitions also guides existing varieties of colour Petri nets such as CSPN and GCSPN. To solve the problem of describing service interactions, we developed a new model Service-Oriented Petri Net Model based on stochastic Petri nets described in this article. The main difference in our approach is the assumption of the known maximum sizes of the data types depicted in the model. Also, we use the method to determine the time in the form of a position-label pair specified inside the system.

Acknowledgement. The authors would like to acknowledge the Reviewers for the valuable recommendations that helped in the improvement of this paper.

References

1. El Akchioui, N., Dib, F., Lefebvre, D., Ncir, N., Sebbane, S., Leclercq, E.: About the fluifidication of SPN by CPN for complex dynamical systems: critical regions. Institute of Electrical and Electronics Engineers Inc. (2020)
2. Gischer, J.: Shuffle languages, petri nets, and context-sensitive grammars. Commun. ACM **24**(9), 597–605 (1981)
3. Haas, P.J.: Stochastic Petri Nets: Modelling, Stability Simulation. Springer, London (2006). https://doi.org/10.1007/b97265
4. Iakushkin, O.: Intellectual scaling in a distributed cloud application architecture: a message classification algorithm, pp. 634–637. Institute of Electrical and Electronics Engineers Inc. (2015)
5. Iakushkin, O.: Cloud middleware combining the functionalities of message passing and scaling control, vol. 108. EDP Sciences (2016)
6. Iakushkin, O., Grishkin, V.: Unification of control in P2P communication middleware: towards complex messaging patterns, vol. 1648. American Institute of Physics Inc. (2015)
7. Iakushkin, O., Sedova, O., Valery, G.: Application control and horizontal scaling in modern cloud middleware. In: Gavrilova, M.L., Tan, C.J.K. (eds.) Transactions on Computational Science XXVII. LNCS, vol. 9570, pp. 81–96. Springer, Heidelberg (2016). https://doi.org/10.1007/978-3-662-50412-3_6
8. Iakushkin, O., Shichkina, Y., Sedova, O.: Petri nets for modelling of message passing middleware in cloud computing environments. In: Gervasi, O., et al. (eds.) ICCSA 2016. LNCS, vol. 9787, pp. 390–402. Springer, Cham (2016). https://doi.org/10.1007/978-3-319-42108-7_30
9. Khetkarn, K., Vatanawood, W.: Formal modeling of priority queue using generalized stochastic petri nets, pp. 39–43. Association for Computing Machinery (2019)

10. Kordon, F., Linard, A., Paviot-Adet, E.: Optimized colored nets unfolding. In: Najm, E., Pradat-Peyre, J.-F., Donzeau-Gouge, V.V. (eds.) FORTE 2006. LNCS, vol. 4229, pp. 339–355. Springer, Heidelberg (2006). https://doi.org/10.1007/11888116_25
11. Liu, F., Heiner, M., Yang, M.: An efficient method for unfolding colored petri nets. In: Proceedings of the 2012 Winter Simulation Conference (WSC), pp. 1–12. IEEE (2012)
12. Ma, M., Xihou, S.J., Huang, J.G.: Study on hierarchical modeling and performance evaluation method about parallel automatic test system. J. Syst. Simul. **22**(12), 2779–2783+2787 (2010)
13. Ma, T., Pang, S., Zhang, W., Hao, S.: Virtual machine based on genetic algorithm used in time and power oriented cloud computing task scheduling. Intell. Autom. Soft Comput. **25**(3), 605–613 (2019)

Evolving Principles of Big Data Virtualization

Alexander Bogdanov[1], Alexander Degtyarev[1,3],
Nadezhda Shchegoleva[1(✉)], Valery Khvatov[2],
and Vladimir Korkhov[1,3]

[1] Saint Petersburg State University, St. Petersburg, Russia
{a.v.bogdanov,n.shchegoleva,v.korkhov}@spbu.ru
[2] DGT Technologies AG., Enschede, The Netherlands
valery.khvatov@gmail.com
[3] Plekhanov Russian University of Economics,
36, Stremyanny per, Moscow 117997, Russia
http://dgt.world/

Abstract. The fact that over 2000 programs exist for working with various types of data, including Big Data, makes the issue of flexible storage a quintessential one. Storage can be of various types, including portals, archives, showcases, data bases of different varieties, data clouds and networks. They can have synchronous or asynchronous computer connections. Because the type of data is frequently unknown a priori, there is a necessity for a highly flexible storage system, which would allow to easily switch between various sources and systems. Combining the concept of virtual personal supercomputer with the classification of Big Data that accounts for different storage schemes would solve this issue.

Keywords: Big Data · Data virtualization · Virtual personal supercomputer · Data network · Data marketplaces

1 Introduction

One of the advance computer paradigms is a virtual personal supercomputer [1]. Virtualization brings all computing objects, such as applications, computers, machines, networks, data and even services, to the ability to overcome physical limitations through a wide range of technologies, tools and methods, and provide significant operational advantages for the entire infrastructure. In an increasingly virtualized world, the most effective approach to data are structures that allow it to be virtualized. The well-known data virtualization approach complements the paradigm mentioned above. Big Data has a few features that must be considered when virtualizing them.

To understand the main problems of storage systems for Big Data, it's enough to notice that they arise when you have to match the type of Big Data, how the storage is connected to data servers, and finally, how to organize work with data. The most natural way to classify Big Data follows from Brewer's theorem and leads to six different types of data [2]. The use of cloud storage in addition to the traditional in-band and out-of-band connection allows to implement various ways of connecting storage with data servers, most often hybrid [3]. And finally, you can work with data through

© Springer Nature Switzerland AG 2020
O. Gervasi et al. (Eds.): ICCSA 2020, LNCS 12254, pp. 67–81, 2020.
https://doi.org/10.1007/978-3-030-58817-5_6

electronic archives, registers, databases, knowledge bases, streaming libraries, data lakes, data meshes, etc. Most often, a distributed system implements several ways of organizing such work.

Thus, the central problem for storage systems now is their flexibility. Now it's already obvious that to achieve flexibility it is most efficient to use virtualization. Gartner's report [4] gives such a definition of data virtualization - the federalization of queries to different data sources into virtual images, which are then used by applications or middleware to create analytical conclusions. However, with this head-on understanding of virtualization, the user will require a sufficiently high qualification and a lot of technical effort to achieve efficiency. The way out of this situation is considered intellectual virtualization [5]. The main idea of this approach is to organize the main part of calculations on remote resources, which are grouped to increase processing speed by data types and tools used. Despite the attractiveness of this approach, it is still quite difficult to implement, and in addition, on distributed systems, there is a problem of a decrease in processing speed due to the need to control errors in data combined into one pool (the situation is quite similar to the problem of a decrease in the speed of consensus processing in distributed ledgers) [6, 7].

It seems to us that a significant part of the problems can be solved if we use the paradigm of the Virtual Personal Supercomputer [8], which was developed for computing, but also used to build a framework for distributed ledgers [9]. The idea of this approach is to virtualize not only the processing itself, but also the entire field on which the processing is performed, namely the network, file system and shared memory. This allows you to create a single image of the operating environment, which simplifies the user's work and increases the processing speed. In this paper, we show how our approach allows us to create an ecosystem that combines the features of federated databases, data lakes, and data networks.

2   Approaches to Store Super Large Amounts of Data

Without context, data is essentially raw information. Information as the very concept means that data is woven into some context. However, even so, it is just material suitable for reporting. To be truly meaningful, data should be focused on business context or carry some functionality, thus becoming knowledge.

The recipient of data needs to pay attention to its sources. Another significant factor is the difference in data volume, especially noticeable for scientific endeavours. In the context of an IT environment, data's physical accessibility is just as important as its structure. The issues lie with the number of resources available to developers and the notable possibility of moving to the cloud to greatly simplify development and further support.

Data can further be divided into several categories. Chaotic data (Unstructured), organized data (Structured), and weakly structured data (Semi-Structured). Structured data follows a specific defined model, for example that of the database. Unstructured data does not and is most frequently stored in a binary format, such as image. Weakly structured data is textual and is stored according to some preset pattern. Weakly structured data can be found in files with extensions of .log, json, .xml. Unstructured data is much more common than semi-structured and structured types – by several factors in fact. Even though unstructured data can accumulate quickly and is hard to sort, it can carry vital information. Semi-structured data is much more popular though.

Modern data platforms possess almost uniform principal characteristics. They are centralized rather than decentralized, monolithic rather than modular, and have tightly coupled pipelined architecture that could only be managed by a group of highly skilled data engineers.

These platforms typically employ one of three ways to organize data storage:

1. Proprietary corporate data warehouses and business analytic platforms. These are very expensive solutions understood only by a small number of specialists. This small spread leads to their positive impact being severely underestimated in business settings.
2. Big Data ecosystems. These could also be called a Data Marketplace. They possess a data lake and are managed by a central team of specialized high-class engineers.
3. Previous Generation-based. These solutions are more or less similar to the previous generations, but slant towards streaming data. This ensures that data is available in real time. Kappa architecture is most frequently used (Fig. 1). Batch and streaming processing for data conversion that are frequently used are Kappa (Fig. 1). Batch and streaming processing for data conversion are combined within such platforms as Apache Beam. Other features often include fully managed cloud storage services, data pipeline mechanisms, and most recently machine learning platforms. It is obvious that such a data platform eliminates some of the key weaknesses of the previous ones. For instance, data is available in real-time and Big Data infrastructure is less expensive to maintain. However, other problems of the previous solutions remain unsolved.

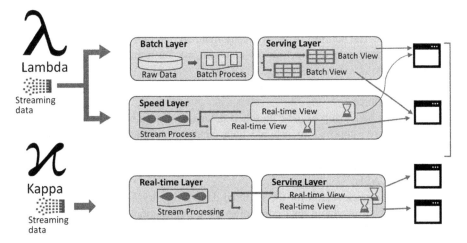

Fig. 1. Lambda and Kappa architectures.

Centralized data platform architectures often fail due to the following notable flaws:

- Inability to manage the consistent emergence of new information sources. As the availability of data increases, the capacity to utilize and organize it under the control of one centralized platform decreases.
- The requirements of building new associations within variously combined data leads to an ever-growing number of transformations. Their aggregates, projections, and slicings significantly increase response time. This has consistently been an issue and remains so even in modern data platform architectures.
- Accounting for the impact of previous data platform architecture generations, specialists distinguish several phases of data processing. The problem arises in relation to the structure of the teams that create and manage the platform. Some of them have high-class data engineers who understand the sources of data origin and how it is used to make decisions. Others are overwhelmed by specialists with extensive experience in technical work with Big Data, but without any knowledge of business and the subject area.

These problems can be resolved by an entirely new paradigm. Such is the distributed data network, an entirely new corporate architecture of a data platform.

To success in decentralizing the monolithic data platforms, our very understanding of data, its location, and ownership needs to shift ideologically. Instead of transferring data from domains to a common lake or central platform, domains should be the ones that house and maintain their datasets, preferably in accessible form. This implies in turn that data can be duplicated in different domains and converted to a form suitable for whichever domain required.

Within this system, the source domain data sets must be absolutely separate from the internal datasets of source systems. The very nature of domain datasets is radically different from internal data required for the operating systems to work. These are much larger in volume, are invariably synchronized facts, and change much less frequently than their respective systems, as business facts do not change so often. The actual underlying storage should be suitable for Big Data, but separate from existing operational databases. The datasets of the source domain are the most quintessential datasets and represent raw data at the time of creation, not customized or modeled for a particular client.

The domain-specific data platform should be able to easily restore these user data sets from the source.

In this case, ownership of the data sets is delegated from the central platform to the domains that are supposed to provide data cleaning, preparation, aggregation and maintenance, as well as the use of the data pipeline. The teams that manage the domains provide the ability to process their data to other specialists in the organization in the form of APIs.

To ensure a quick search for the required data, a registry must be implemented, a data catalog of all available data containing meta-information, such as their owners, source of origin, origin, samples of data sets, etc.

Note that a secure and manageable global control of access to data sets should be implemented. This requirement is mandatory, whether the architecture is centralized or not.

The proposed distributed data network [10] as a platform is focused on domains belonging to independent groups that have data processing engineers and data owners using a common data infrastructure as a platform for hosting, preparing and maintaining their data assets.

A mesh data network platform is a specially designed distributed data architecture with centralized management and standardization for interoperability that is provided by a common and consistent data self-service infrastructure.

Thus, a formal set of requirements can be generalized to form a virtual data model:

- Abstract representation of data in terms of the object model and its sections (rejection of a rigid structure due to a mesh data network).
- Differential confidentiality allowing to determine access parameters on the fly depending on the general role model.
- API-centering data management systems for loading data on demand.
- Refusal from strict separation of streaming and batch processing of data with the necessary switching on the fly, as a part of the implementation of the KAPPA architecture); building a feedback system based on a generalized metadata model.

3 Big Data Types

In [2] it was shown that the solution to this problem is should be based on new specification of Big Data types. This article proposed a method for determining the types of Big Data, the formation of ecosystems (software stacks) for different types of data, and substantiates the Data Lake concept.

Let's consider in more detail the data itself. We propose an approach based on the CAP theorem, albeit the theorem itself concerns distributed data storage, not the data itself. We can divide data into 6 classes (Error! Reference source not found.), however only 5 classes out of 6 potential are possible because PA-class cannot exist by itself, and modern corporate architectures are distributed - that is, divided - by default. Then we have the following data classes.

C – class (consistency): It is characterized by data that: agreed - this is a guarantee that simultaneous reading from different places will return the same value; that is, the system does not return outdated or conflicting data; stored in one place (usually); may not have backups (there is too much data to do backup for them); often analytical data with a short life span.

A – class (availability): It is characterized by data that: should always be available; can be stored in different places; have at least one backup or at least one other storage location; are important data, but do not require significant scaling.

CA – class: data must be consistent and accessible; potentially a monolithic system, without the possibility of scaling or scaling under the condition of instant exchange of information about the changed data between the master-slave nodes; there is no resistance to distribution, if scaling is provided for (branches), then each branch works with a relatively independent database.

In this case, the CA class is divided into 3 subclasses:

1) Big Data of large sizes that cannot be represented in a structured way or they are too large (stored in Data Lake or Data Warehouse): data has any format and extension (text, video, audio, images, archives, documents, maps, etc.); whole data collected, the so-called "raw data"; large data that is unreasonable to place in the database (unstructured data in the case of data warehouses); multidimensional data. Medical data that cannot be stored in tabular form (x-ray, MRI, DNA, etc.) are the example of this type.

2) Data of a specific format that can be represented in a structured form (biological data, DNA and protein sequences, data on a three-dimensional structure, complete genomes, etc.) characterized by multidimensional data; data must be analyzed and their sizes reach gigantic values. Medical and bioinformatics data that need to be searched and stored in a relational table with extensions of xml, json, etc. are the example of this type.

3) Other data well presented in relational databases which: have a clear structure or can be represented in the concept of a relational database; the size of the stored data does not matter (provided that lightweight objects or links to large objects are stored in the storage); transactional required;

"Raw" data, though not recommended (an exception - if the logs are stored), customer data, logs, clicks, weather statistics or business analytics, personal data, rarely updated, customer base, etc. are the example of this type.

CP – class It is characterized by data that: must be consistent and at the same time there is support for the distributed state of the system, which has the potential for scaling; structured, but can easily change their structure; must be presented in a slightly different format (graph, document), that is, data for social networks, geographic data and any other data that can be presented in the form of a graph; have a complex structure, because of which there is a potential need for storing files in a document-oriented format; they accumulate very quickly, so a distribution mechanism is needed; no permanent availability requirements.

Frequently recorded, rarely read statistics, as well as temporary data (web sessions, locks, or short-term statistics) stored in a temporary data store or cache are the example of this type.

PA – class: It is characterized by data that: should be available and at the same time there is high support for the distributed state of the system, which has the potential for scaling; have a complex structure, the potential need to store files in a different format with the ability to change the scheme without the need to transfer all the data to a new scheme (Cassandra); accumulate quickly.

This class is suitable for data that is historical in nature. The main task here is to store large amounts of data with the potential growth of this information every day, statistical and other processing of information online and offline in order to obtain certain information (for example, about the interests of users, mood in conversations, to identify trends and etc.).

Before determining the type of system, we must estimate the total system parameters (maximum number of users for simultaneous operation, the ability to scale services, the availability of personalized access), evaluate the project (having its own server capacity, cost comparison with the cost of building rental of services), evaluate time data access, query performance evaluation for cloud infrastructures, construct the automatic allocation system and send requests in a distributed database (Fig. 2).

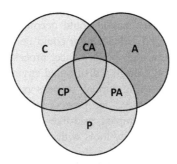

Fig. 2. Graphical representation of Big Data classes.

4 Virtual Supercomputer Solution

The virtual supercomputer is an idea of making a utility-centric computational environment with configurable computation and community characteristics based completely on virtualization technologies used in distributed systems. Such an environment permits flexible partitioning of available physical assets depending on software requirements and priorities of execution. Here we will present some of the widespread standards that must be adhered to while creating one. These concepts are beneficial for fixing problems of a large scale on a virtual supercomputer and some of them can be neglected for small-scale issues [5]:

- A virtual supercomputer is completely determined through its application programming interface (API) and this API must be unbiased of the platform. The API takes form of a high-level programming language. It is the only method to interact with the virtual supercomputer. Moreover, the API does not cover all of the functions of the scheduling system underlying the computer. It is just the means to avoid complications with integration and connection.
- The API of a virtual supercomputer supplies the functionality for seamless integration with other systems. Large-scale problems can be solved when various allotted systems cooperate effectively and their seamless interplay composes the dynamic hybrid distributed systems capable of extending capacity on a need basis. It can even be thought of a s method of scaling a virtual computer to solve problems that are too complicated for just one virtual supercomputer.
- Efficient data processing is achieved with the aid of the virtual supercomputer by distributing data among available nodes and be means of running small programs called queries – essentially on each host where the required data resides. This approach not only supports concurrent operations when running queries on each host, but also has the benefit of minimizing the transfers of data. It should be noted that in current implementations, these programs are not generic. They are parts of an algorithm and are designed specifically to fit the data model which the said

algorithm was initially developed. The shared interface of the virtual memory allows for the efficient processing of data located on any host. To summarize, the storage of large data sets is done by distributed databases, while the general-purpose programs required to process them are written in the virtual shared memory.

- Even using light-weight virtualization could become advantageous in regards to performance. Container-based virtualization could be a good choice for achieving the elusive balance between high performance, process isolation and control, and ease of administering the system in a distributed environment.
- Load balance is achieved using virtual processors with controlled clock rate, memory allocation, network access and process migration when possible.
- Virtual supercomputer uses complex grid-like security mechanisms, since it is possible to combine GRID security tools with cloud computing technologies.

To summarize, the virtual supercomputer is quintessentially an API that offers functions to run programs, work with data stored in a distributed database and to work with virtual shared memory in the application-centric manner based on application requirements and priorities.

5 Virtualizing Data

5.1 Generic Approaches

In the recent times there has been a significant growth in demand for operational access to data. The term "analytics on demand" has appeared to signify a very rapid data-informed business decision making process. Meanwhile, there is practically no time allocated for traditional processes of transforming and loading data as a result of this process. The situation is made more complex by the volume and speed of new data, which appears at a rate beyond the abilities of typical modern corporate infrastructures.

The most effective way to surpass these limitations is to have "virtualized data access". Data virtualization has appeared long ago and some of the older examples are datasets from relational data bases, NoSQL databases, Big Data platforms and even corporate applications, which allows for the creation of logical data storages that may be accessed through SQL, REST and etc. (Error! Reference source not found.). This grants access to data from a large number of distributed sources and various formats, without the requirement for the users to know where it is stored. This eliminates the necessity to move data or to allocate resources for its storage. Apart from greater effectiveness and faster data access, data virtualization may give the necessary basis for fulfilling the requirements of data management (Fig. 3).

Virtualization has three features that support the scalability and operational efficiency required for big data environments:

- Partitioning: sharing resources and moving to streaming data.
- Isolation: Transition to the object representation of data with reference to the domain model.
- Encapsulation: Logical storage as a single entity

Fig. 3. Data virtualization.

This solution changes the general approach to data in data access abstraction, semantic storage, real-time data access and decentralized security (Error! Reference source not found.) (Fig. 4).

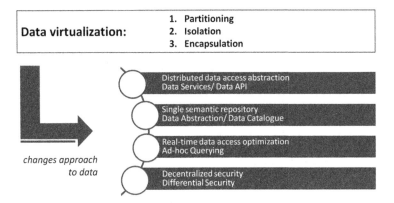

Fig. 4. Features of data virtualization.

Finding and training data processing engineers may be a slow process. **Meanwhile, the results may be suboptimal, if the data specialist does not understand** the business user requirements or is unaware of which methods should be used to accomplish the goals they set. Therefore, suppliers frequently develop analytic products that allow users to resolve these problems themselves.

The main problem lies in the fact that companies have often various data types in different formats, which are located on different systems and servers. A part of them is in the cloud, a part may be located on local services, and access to all of these is determined by varying security policies and practices.

To enable effective work there must be a way to collect disparate data from all of the organization's resources in to one place and represented in one precise way. To allow for unified data access, organizations typically perform a process known as transforming cloud data.

Transforming cloud data makes data of all formats and sources (both cloud and local ones) readable and accessible. However, there is a set of problems, which make data transformation a long, complicated, and frequently expensive task.

Many suppliers of data virtualization technologies force clients to transform data into their own format before it could be read and used. However, this process of data transformation may lead to data distortion or loss during this translation. Moreover, proprietary formats of many suppliers are incompatible with other technologies. Therefore, you face new problems of continuous integration due to the attachment to a certain supplier. As the data sizes rise, so does the volume of engineering that is required to control the different data sources to quickly fulfill requests.

A solution to these problems is data virtualization, which would create complete independences from the data source format. That means that data does not have to be replicated or transformed in some way. Instead of relying on complex and time-consuming data transformation and transfer processes, it would be more effective to use some business language that would allow the users to easily work with data.

Consequentially, there is a need for a solution that would intellectually virtualize all of the disparate data from various sources into a single unified representation. From there, different BI instruments could receive quick and consolidated answers to make business-decisions. Data is requested "as is", but users perceive it as a singular data storage.

Therefore, smart data virtualization is the new paradigm for controlling data. The "smart" virtualization of data resolves problems of scalability and productivity. Smart data virtualization platforms allow users to avoid large traffic volumes due to federative connections, which create a distributed cache that is optimized for the data platform. By avoiding unnecessary data transfers, the smart data virtualization allows for a more stable productivity of requests with far smaller resources required.

Meanwhile, it is necessary to implement work with different data sources: relationship databases (for example, Oracle, Teradata, Snowflake), file-based ones (CSV, JSON, XML, HDFS, S3), API-based ones (REST, HTML), and application-based ones (Salesforce, Workday, Service Now). This will allow for the use of practically any data: local, cloud, structured and unstructured without using ETL or transferring the data by hand.

At the same time, the virtualization platform must allow for even better productivity than native platforms that they work with, since the level of virtualization must correspond to or surpass the current solutions that they are replacing.

We must note that because data virtualization platforms are an intermediary software for analytic requests, it is necessary that the platform must integrate with the security structure of the enterprise.

All of the aforementioned challenges could be received using a virtual supercomputer.

5.2   Big Data Virtualization

Virtualization of Big Data through logical constructs and object access (the data themselves may be stored in different sources and be collected on request and/or be accessed (interpreted) at various trigger points (event-based integration)):

- Logical storage of data according to function is analogous to a traditional storage of data, with several exceptions. For a start, in a logical data warehouse (LDW) data is not stored, unlike in data storages where data is prepared, filtered, and placed.
- Logical abstraction and division: heterogeneous data sources may now easily interact through data virtualization.
- Differential confidentiality (intersecting access levels).

The fact that over 2000 programs exist for working with various types of data, including Big Data, makes the issue of flexible storage a quintessential one. Storage can be of various types, including portals, archives, showcases, data bases of different varieties, data clouds and networks. They can have synchronous or asynchronous computer connections. Because the type of data is frequently unknown a priori, there is a necessity for a highly flexible storage system, which would allow to easily switch between various sources and systems.

Combining the virtual personal supercomputer with the classification of Big Data that accounts for different storage would solve this issue.

5.3   Data Networks and Data Marketplaces

We looked at several important characteristics of modern data platforms: centralized, monolithic, and with rigid conveyor architecture controlled by a group of highly specialized data engineers.

There are three core approaches that should be noted within the classification of data storage.

The first is proprietary data storage. These storages and business analytics platforms are highly inflexible, very expensive solutions. Using them involves a small group of specialists, which leads to wasted potential that this storage may have had on the business operations.

The second is a Big Data ecosystem. It contains a data lake managed by a centralized team of highly specialized data engineers.

Finally, the third type is the data marketplace (Error! Reference source not found.). These solutions are similar to the first two, but lean towards streaming of data and real-time access to insight. Batch and streaming data conversion processes are combined through platforms like Apache Beam, Kappa architectures are used, as well as fully controllable cloud storage services, data conveyor mechanisms, and machine learning platforms.

Real-time analysis and expensive Big Data infrastructures are problems for the first two approaches, but not for the latter. If we are looking into the main problems of using a centralized data platform architecture, the following should be mentioned:

Continuous emergence of new data sources. The amount of data accessible is increasing at an exponential rate and the ability to use and reconcile this data under one platform's control is diminishing proportionally.

Organizations seek to combine data in different ways to reflect their fluid business environments and demands. This leads to an increasing number of data transformations, aggregates, projections, and slicing. The response time rises beyond acceptable levels, which is a problem faced even by modern data platform architectures.

When implementing data platform architectures, specialists are influenced by past architecture generations when identifying data processing stages. In particular, this is seen when structuring commands that create and control the platform. These specialists are mostly high-class data engineers, who understand data sources and the principles of using data to make decisions. Some specialists have great technical experience, but frequently lack the knowledge of business and areas of application.

The new paradigm for corporate data platform architectures is the decentralized data network, as it allows for the successful resolution of aforementioned problems. This paradigm requires a shift in the understanding of data, its location and belonging (Fig. 5).

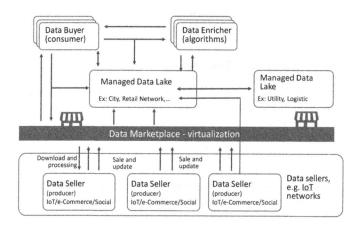

Fig. 5. Data marketplace.

Instead of transferring data from domains into lakes or from centrally owned platforms, there must be an easier way to store and service data, including duplicating data in different domains to allow greater flexibility in its transformation.

A recent example of such a decentralized platform for data storage is the DGT Network [11]. It creates a virtual data mesh, connecting different sources of data across corporate information borders into unified analytics accessed by authorized users in a manner conductive to differential confidentiality.

6   Big Data Virtualization Applications

Studies have shown that data marketplaces already offer several important advantages for companies seeking to put their data to effective work. One of these uses is the construction of ecosystems, best illustrated by the data marketplace powered by the DGT Network. DGT Network allows for horizontal integration by creating distinctive clusters of enterprise-operated nodes, which exchange data through a secure F-BFT Protocol and record it in a unified ledger (the Direct Acyclic Graph ledger). Even though this ledger serves as a "unified source of truth" for its participants, the differential anonymity protects corporate privacy of source data, while still allowing analytics to provide relevant insights to participants in real time.

Other advantages of data virtualization may include new monetization opportunities. One particular digital marketplace adds value to Europe's electric-automobile market by enabling data and transactional gateways for a diverse group of businesses, including charging-infrastructure providers, vehicle manufacturers, mobility-service players and others. These participants use customer habits and market trends as raw data that informs their dynamic pricing structures.

Many industries are beginning to embrace virtualization of Big Data within their operations. One example is the Data Marketplace launched by the IOTA Foundation as a proof of concept in 2017. IOTA initially launched an open-source distributed ledger that connects Internet of Things devices to process micro transactions in exchange for crypto currency. Unlike a blockchain, IOTA's distributed ledger – the IOTA Tangle does not group transactions in blocks, like a typical blockchain, but instead sees them as a stream of individual transactions entangled together through a relatively simple network algorithm – in order to participate, a node needs to perform a small amount of computational work to verify the two previous transactions. The IOTA Data Marketplace was designed to be a simplified platform that simulates how an IOTA-connected device is economically incentivized for sharing secure data over to a web browser. Despite its limited functionality as a Proof-of-Concept for the larger IOTA platform, the IOTA Data Marketplaces has been utilized by over 70 organizations, including Accenture, Bosch, KPMG, T-Mobile, Fujitsu, Philips, Tele2 and other organizations working with Internet of Things devices and sensors.

A study by McKinsey notes how highly applicable digital marketplaces are to IOT data as a field through combining data sets and data streams to ensure consistency, high quality, and security. As part of their research on the underutilization of IoT data by corporate enterprises, they note a typical example where one oil rig with 30,000 sensors examines only 1 percent of the data collected to detect and control anomalies, ignoring the greatest value that comes in predictive analytics and optimization. In this application, a dynamic data would harness that additional information by making both its sourcing and processing effective and inexpensive.

Some dynamic business models are especially adept at using Kappa Architecture and data virtualization. Uber, for example, uses data processing systems like Apache Link and Apache Spark to calculate real-time pricing, to enable optimized driver dispatching, and to minimize the fraud on their platform. With its widespread operations, Uber relies on this architecture to process data on a massive scale with exactly-once semantics. In order to backfill Uber's streaming pipeline, Uber has tested Kappa architecture through two of the most commonly used methods: relating data from Apache Hive to Kafka and backfilling as a batch job. Even though neither approach was found to be scalable enough for Uber's data velocity, they have found a solution by modeling their Hive connector as a streaming source in Spark Streaming.

7 Conclusion

Data virtualization is a method of organizing access to data without requiring the information about its structure or place in any particular information system.

The main goal is to simplify access and use of data by turning it into a service, essentially shifting the paradigm from storage to usage.

Previously, the task of using data was solved through integration into an intermediary storage system. It already had some elements of virtualization through data marts created by data producers. Now the data consumer is coming into the focus.

There are three core characteristics of virtualization that support scalability and operational effectiveness necessitated by Big Data environments. These include: portioning, which is the division of resources and a shift to streamed data; isolation, which is an object-oriented approach to data with domain application in mind; and encapsulation, keeping the logical storage as a singular object.

Data services and API change the way distributed information is accessed. Data abstraction forms from a single semantic repository. Access to data in real-time and ad-hoc querying are optimized. Finally, differential security and privacy are achieved. Data virtualization is more than just a modern approach, it is an entire new way of seeing data.

References

1. Bogdanov, A.: Private cloud vs personal supercomputer. In: Distributed Computing and GRID Technologies in Science and Education, pp. 57–59. JINR, Dubna (2012)
2. Bogdanov, A.V., Shchegoleva, N.L., Ulitina, I.V.: Database ecosystem is the way to data lakes. In: Proceedings of the 27th Symposium on Nuclear Electronics and Computing (NEC 2019), vol. 2507, pp. 147–152. Aahen University (2019)
3. Nemade, R., Nitsure, A., Hirve, P., Mane, S.B.: Detection of forgery in art paintings using machine learning. Int. J. Innov. Res. Sci. Eng. Technol. **6**(5), 8681–8692 (2017)
4. Menon, S., Beyer, M., Zaidi, E., Jain, A.: Market guide for data virtualization, 16 November 2018. ID: G00340606. https://www.gartner.com/en/documents/3893219/market-guide-for-data-virtualization
5. Gankevich, I., et al.: Constructing virtual private supercomputer using virtualization and cloud technologies. In: Murgante, B. (ed.) ICCSA 2014. LNCS, vol. 8584, pp. 341–354. Springer, Cham (2014). https://doi.org/10.1007/978-3-319-09153-2_26
6. Bogdanov, A., Degtyarev, A., Korkhov, V., Gaiduchok, V., Gankevich, I.: Virtual supercomputer as basis of scientific computing. In: Horizons in Computer Science Research, Chap. 5, vol. 11, pp. 159–198. NOVA Science Publishers (2015)

7. Bogdanov, A., Degtyarev, A., Korkhov, V.: New approach to the simulation of complex systems. In: EPJ Web of Conferences, vol. 108, pp. 1–12 (2016). Article number: 01002
8. Bogdanov, A., Degtyarev, A., Korkhov, V.: Desktop supercomputer: what can it do? Phys. Part. Nuclei Lett. **14**(7), 985–992 (2017). https://doi.org/10.1134/S1547477117070032. ISSN 1547-4771
9. Korkhov, V., Kobyshev, S., Degtyarev, A., Bogdanov, A.: Light-weight cloud-based virtual computing infrastructure for distributed applications and hadoop clusters. In: Gervasi, O. (ed.) ICCSA 2017. LNCS, vol. 10408, pp. 399–411. Springer, Cham (2017). https://doi.org/10.1007/978-3-319-62404-4_29
10. Zhamak, D.: How to move beyond a monolithic data lake to a distributed data mesh. https://martinfowler.com/articles/data-monolith-to-mesh.html
11. DGT, the decentralized enterprise platform. http://dgt.world/

On the Effectiveness of Using Various Machine Learning Methods for Forecasting Dangerous Convective Phenomena

E. N. Stankova[1]([⊠]) [iD], I. O. Tokareva[1], and N. V. Dyachenko[2] [iD]

[1] Saint-Petersburg State University,
7-9, Universitetskaya nab., St. Petersburg 199034, Russia
e.stankova@spbu.ru, tio_777@mail.ru
[2] Russian State Hydrometeorological University,
98, Malookhtinsky pr., St. Petersburg 195196, Russia
nat230209@yandex.ru

Abstract. The paper considers the possibility of thunderstorm forecasting using only dynamical and microphysical parameters of the cloud, simulated by the 1.5D model with further processing by machine learning methods. The problem of feature selection is discussed in two aspects: selection of the optimal values of time and height when and where the output model data are fixed and selection of fixed set of the most representative cloud parameters (features) among all output cloud characteristics. Five machine learning methods are considered: Support Vector Machine (SVM), Logistic Regression, Ridge Regression, boosted k-nearest neighbour algorithm and neural networks. It is shown that forecast accuracy of all five methods reaches values exceeding 90%.

Keywords: Machine learning · Support Vector Machine (SVM) · Logistic Regression · Ridge Regression · Boosted k-nearest neighbour algorithm · Neural networks · Numerical model of convective cloud · Weather forecasting · Thunderstorm forecasting

1 Introduction

In recent decades mathematicians and programmers are working hard to improve existing numerical weather forecasting models. Nowadays machine learning methods are considered to be one of the most promising tool of such improvement.

Machine learning (ML) is a class of artificial intelligence methods which do not try to solve a problem directly, but by training corresponding algorithms in the process of solution of many similar tasks.

Machine learning is used when:

- it is too complicated to compose system of the equations for a problem solution;
- the solution must be adapted to a new dataset;
- the solution needs to be scaled.

© Springer Nature Switzerland AG 2020
O. Gervasi et al. (Eds.): ICCSA 2020, LNCS 12254, pp. 82–93, 2020.
https://doi.org/10.1007/978-3-030-58817-5_7

Machine learning algorithms are divided into two groups: supervised and unsupervised learning algorithms. Classification and regression belongs to the first group, clustering to the second one.

Clustering (or cluster analysis) is the task of breaking down multiple objects into groups called clusters. Inside each group there should be "similar" objects, and objects of different groups should be as different as possible. The main difference between clustering and classification is that the list of groups is not clearly defined and is determined during the operation of the algorithm.

The classification problem is the task of assigning a sample to one of several pairwise disjoint sets.

Regression or regression analysis is a statistical method for studying the influence of one or more independent variables on a dependent variable.

The use of machine learning methods in meteorology is twofold. On the one hand, "pure" machine learning models are being developed, where certain atmospheric parameters are predicted on the basis of observational data obtained at meteorological stations, weather centers, etc. [1–3]. On the other hand, machine learning methods are used to verify models by establishing relationships between model forecasts and the actual meteorological situation [4, 5].

In our work, we used the so-called "hybrid" approach [6, 7], combining numerical simulation and machine learning methods to identify the dependence of dynamic, microphysical and electrical parameters of convective clouds. This kind of identification is quite important for forecasting thunderstorm with the help of the models which do not have the block describing electrical processes. It should be noted that Semi-empirical methods of Peskov, Yagudin, Reshetov, Lebedeva and others [8] are still used for operational forecasting of such dangerous phenomena as thunderstorms. These methods are based on the calculation of complex coefficients, which are functions of some cloud parameters, determined either using a synoptic map or using the aerological diagram. The use of modern numerical cloud models for the purpose of forecasting is limited, on the one hand, by the lack of computational resources that are required to implement, for example, modern three-dimensional models with a detailed description of the microphysical and electrical characteristics of the cloud. Such models describe with the greatest degree of detail the dynamic, microphysical and electrical processes in the clouds in all the complexity of their interaction and, therefore, should ensure the best quality of forecasts. However, their use is impossible for operational forecasting in small meteorological centers, due to the lack of the necessary computing power there. On the other hand, the use of models of lower dimensionality and lower functionality sets the problem of determining the likelihood of thunderstorm development only by analyzing the calculated values of the dynamic and microphysical characteristics of the cloud, which are the output of the models, as the latter do not have the block describing electrical processes.

Usage of the machine learning methods for establishing relationship between the output of the numerical model and the probability of thunderstorm, hail, heavy rain will provide effective tool for forecasting most dangerous convective phenomena.

Dangerous meteorological events are in the focus of research in the works [9, 10]. The authors suggested using neural networks to simulate the movement of typhoons, which are the developed tropical cyclones, usually formed in the northwestern Pacific

Ocean. Tropical cyclone intensity changes in the western North Pacific was predicted in [9] using the back-propagation neural network. In [10] a generative adversarial network (GAN) was used for prediction the tracks of typhoons using satellite images as inputs. The neural network was trained with the help of time series of satellite images of typhoons which occurred in the Korea Peninsula in the past.

We concentrate on forecasting only dangerous convective phenomena, mainly thunderstorms, using different machine learning algorithms. Discussion is provided of the most effective method for selection of model output data subsequently used as input for machine learning (features selection).

2 Convective Cloud Model

Modelling of a convective cloud has been conducted by using time dependent, one and a half dimensional (1.5-D) hydrodynamic model with a detailed description of microphysical processes. A cloud shape is simulated by two nested cylinders following the approach suggested by Asai and Kasahara [11]. Cloudy region is represented by the inner cylinder while the downdraft flow outside the cloud is represented by the outer cylinder.

Evolution of dynamical cloud characteristics is simulated by numerical solution of the system of partial differential equations. Buoyancy force, gravity, turbulence are taken into account as well as heat generation/consumption ejected during condensation/evaporation of water vapor and freezing/melting of cloud droplets. A vertical component of the velocity, temperature excess in the cloud, relative humidity, mixing ratio of water vapour, mixing ratio of water drops and cloud thickness are the main dynamical cloud characteristics simulated by the model.

Evolution of microphysical cloud characteristics in time and height is simulated by a numerical solution of the set of stochastic equations for mass distribution functions of cloud drops, columnar crystals, plate crystals, dendrites, snowflakes, graupel and frozen drops. The influence of the following processes is taken into account: nucleation, condensation, sublimation, coalescence, freezing, melting and breakup. Spectra of liquid and solid hydrometeors as well as liquid and ice content of a cloud are calculated with the help of distribution functions obtained earlier.

Transition from the continuous partial differential equations to the finite difference equations is conducted using forward-upstream scheme. Averaged value of the vertical velocity is obtained over two mesh points depending upon the sign of the vertical velocity value (positive or negative).

Though dynamical and microphysical processes develop simultaneously, it is not possible to calculate them in a single time step. The only solution is to split them in time using time-splitting method. Dynamical processes are calculated in the first half of the time step, and microphysical processes in the second half of the time step.

Radiosonde sounding data are used as an input or initial conditions for the model. Radiosonde soundings provide vertical distributions of environmental temperature and relative humidity. It is considered that all cloud characteristics with the exception of temperature and mixing ration of water vapour are equal to zero at the top and at the bottom boundaries of the cylinders. Impulses of temperature and velocity are set at the initial time moment to push the evolution of the simulated cloud.

The model is able to reproduce the whole cycle of cloud evolution if the conditions in the outer atmosphere is suitable for convection development. Besides, calculated values of cloud parameters allow predicting the probability of the development of such dangerous meteorological phenomena as thunderstorms, hails and rain storms.

Detailed description of the model can be found in [12–15].

Input data are collected with the help of integrated information system [16–18]. We need a significant amount of radiosonde soundings for obtaining sufficient training and test data set collections. This task is not a trivial one, as we have to integrate the data about the dangerous phenomenon occurrence and radiosonde data obtained in the place and at the time of the phenomenon observation. It should be mentioned that the problem has not been solved completely, as the collected test data sets appeared to be small enough for such machine learning algorithm as neural networks that resulted in changing of the structure to perceptron complex.

480 radiosonde soundings with and 196 soundings without phenomena have been collected. 220 soundings related to thunderstorms, 174 ones to heavy rains and 86 soundings to light rains. Different machine learning algorithms use different number of data as test and training data sets. For example, 416 records have been formed for neural networks, where 220 samples correspond to the presence of a dangerous convective phenomenon and 196 samples to its absence. The training set contains 333 samples and the test one contains 83 ones.

3 Algorithms for Data Formation and Preprocessing

Solution of machine learning problems require to find an unknown relationship between a known set of objects and a set of answers. In our case the fact of dangerous phenomenon occurrence can be considered as an answer, and the results of numerical modeling, can be considered as an object. Radiosonde sounding data are used as the model input.

The numerical parameters of the simulated clouds are chosen as object features. The numerical model of convective cloud simulates the whole cycle of natural cloud evolution consisting of three stages: stage of development, mature stage and dissipation stage. Moreover, the output results are produced on every time step of simulation and presents the data on every space step, that is on every 200 m. So the problem is what time step and what height should be chosen for taking the data for future use as object features.

We use three approaches for feature selection. The first one, described in detail in [4, 5, 19, 20] is used for the following machine learning algorithms: Support Vector Machine (SVM), Logistic Regression, Ridge Regression and boosted k-nearest neighbour algorithm.

The first approach assumes fixing the numerical parameters at the moment of maximum cloud development and at the height, where the maximum ratio of water droplets is observed. These time moment and height correspond to the mature stage of cloud evolution. Feature selection has been provided by using recursive feature elimination algorithm with automatic tuning of the number of features selected with cross-validation. As a result, the following 6 simulated cloud parameters have been chosen as the optimal features to be used for subsequent machine learning processing. These parameters are: the vertical component of the velocity, temperature excess in the cloud, relative humidity, mixing ratio of water vapor, mixing ratio of water drops and cloud thickness.

The second approach is used in the works [4, 5] to refine the results obtained with Support Vector Machine (SVM), Logistic Regression and Ridge Regression algorithms.

The second approach suggests:

- to use individual sets of features for each case of chosen time and height;
- to use the parameters obtained at the stages of cloud development and dissipation (time); and at the lower and the higher levels of maximum ratio of water droplets
- to use features, obtained during the whole cloud evolution in a single set of parameters.

Feature selection has been realized using the L1 regularization method (LASSO) to overcome model overfitting.

Five cases with the different values of time and height have been considered.

Case 1 corresponds to the same height and time (mature stage of cloud development, height of maximum ratio of water droplets). L1 regularization method provides the following cloud parameters, to be used as optimal features: vertical component of the velocity, horizontal velocity, temperature excess in the cloud, mixing ratio of water vapor, mixing ratio of water drops, overall density, pressure and cloud thickness.

Case 2 also corresponds by time to the mature stage of cloud development but the height is chosen to be 300 m lower than that chosen for the first case. In this case optimal features differ slightly from the first case. They are: horizontal velocity, temperature excess in the cloud, mixing ratio of water vapor, mixing ratio of water drops, overall density, pressure, maximum horizontal velocity that was achieved during the whole simulated cloud evolution.

Case 3 is similar to the case 2 but the height was chosen to be 300 m higher than that chosen for the Case 1. Obtained optimal features are as follows: vertical component of the velocity, temperature excess in the cloud, mixing ratio of water drops.

Case 4 corresponds to the stage of development, that is 5 min earlier than the time of the Cases 1–3. The height is the same as in the Case 1. Obtained optimal features are the same as in the Case 3 plus overall density and pressure.

Case 5 corresponds to the stage of dissipation, that is 15 min later than the time of the Cases 1–3. The height is the same as in the Case 1. Obtained optimal features are as follows: vertical component of the velocity, temperature excess in the cloud, mixing ratio of water drops, relative humidity, pressure, overall density, mixing ratio of water drops, hail and graupel.

The third approach for feature selection is used for neural network algorithm. The numerical parameters are fixed, similar to the first approach, at the moment of maximum cloud development and at the height, where the maximum ratio of water droplets is observed. The most significant features have been selected using the Recursive Feature Elimination method from the scikit-learn library [21] with Random Forest algorithm as an estimator. As a result, the following eight features have been chosen: mixing ratio of vapor and aerosol particles, relative humidity, density, temperature excess in the cloud over the temperature in the environment atmosphere, pressure, the vertical component of the velocity, temperature inside the cloud.

4 Forecast Accuracy Using Support Vector Machine (SVM), Logistic Regression and Ridge Regression Algorithms

Forecast accuracy amounts to 97.7%, 98.6% and 98.1% for Support Vector Machine, Logistic Regression and Ridge Regression correspondingly while using the first approach of data formation and preprocessing [4, 5]. Though looking very promising these results need to be checked and clarified.

For this purpose, the second approach is used for data formation and preprocessing with the same machine learning algorithms. It allows to investigate the influence of a cloud evolution stage upon the choice of cloud parameters and to check the accuracy of application of feature elimination method.

The results have been obtained using the Scikit-learn library [21]. They are presented in the Tables 1 and 2.

Table 1. Forecast accuracy of machine learning methods

Method	Case 1	Case 2	Case 3
Logistic Regression	93,7	94,6	93,2
Support Vector Machine	94,1	96,1	95,0
Ridge Regression	94,1	95,0	94,6

The analyses of the presented results shows that Logistic regression produces the lowest forecast accuracy in all Cases in comparison with the two other methods. SVM and Ridge Regression show approximately the same accuracy. Maximum accuracy has been obtained by SVM method in Case 2.

The choice of the time moment of cloud evolution does not influence much upon the forecast accuracy of the three methods. We may use the cloud parameters at any stage of its development. Influence of the height is more noticeable The best results have been achieved at the height which was 300 m lower than the height of the maximum mixing ratio of cloud droplets.

5 Forecast Accuracy Using Neural Network Algorithm

As it is written above the third approach of data formation and preprocessing is used for neural network algorithm. The data are normalized using the Standard Scaler method from the scikit-learn library, which converts the data to the standard normal distribution.

Table 2. Forecast accuracy of machine learning methods

Method	Case 4	Case 5
Logistic Regression	93,7	93,7
Support Vector Machine	94,1	93,7
Ridge Regression	93,7	94,6

We consider the only one type of the convective phenomenon, namely thunderstorm. The data set contains 416 records, including 220 samples corresponding to thunderstorm presence and 196 samples to its absence. Training data set contains 333 samples and the test one contained 83. Due to the small amount of data test set is used for validation.

We also create labels for each sample in the data set. Since there are only two cases, the presence and absence of the phenomenon, we can create one label per sample. But we decide to use two labels per sample, one for each case, mainly because we will need to divide the output variables of the neural network at some point. So there are two types of labels: "*target 1*" and "*target 2*". "*Target 1*" is equal to 1 and "*target 2*" is equal to zero in a case of a thunderstorm occurrence. "*Target 1*" is equal to 0 and "*target 2*" is equal to 1 in a case of a thunderstorm absence.

We investigate 3 types of perceptron structure: classical multi-layer perceptron (Fig. 1) and two types of complexes, consisting of single layer perceptron structures. The use of different perceptron structures is due to a small amount of data used as a training data set. In this case the use of the algorithms based on classical neural networks may be inefficient [22]. To avoid this the method described in [23] is used for increasing the efficiency of our neural network. The method involves separation of the set of input and output variables into several perceptrons (Fig. 2 and 3) with a simpler structure and then their combination into a single perceptron complex.

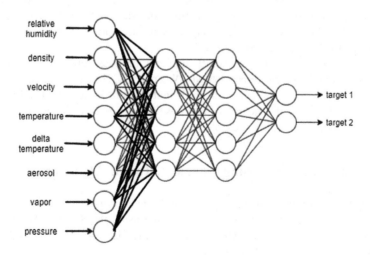

Fig. 1. Classical multi-layer perceptron

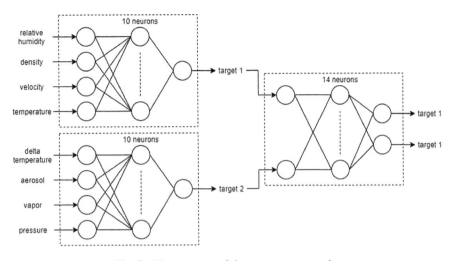

Fig. 2. Fist structure of the perceptron complex

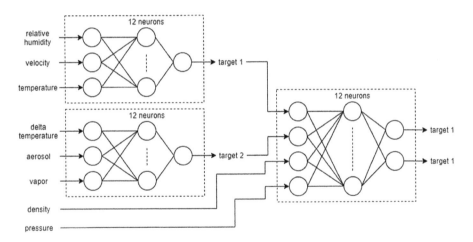

Fig. 3. Second structure of the perceptron complex

The network shown in Fig. 1 gives the highest accuracy value on the test data for a classical layer perceptron. This structure has been found experimentally and showed the accuracy of the trained network of 89.1%.

Perceptron complexes presented in Fig. 2 and 3 show the accuracy of 90.0% and 91.6% correspondingly.

Network design and all calculation are provided using Keras deep learning framework [24]. Networks are trained using Backpropagation. The hyperbolic tangent represents the activation function for all layers, Softmax is used as the output function.

The training algorithms for the perceptron complexes (Fig. 2 and 3) are different for the first level perceptrons and the resulting ones. The training and test data sets for the first level perceptron are constructed on the base of the initial data taking into account the input and output variables for each current perceptron. All the outputs are stored. The training and test data sets for the resulting perceptron have been constructed on the base of the initial data and the calculated output values of the first level perceptrons taking into account the input and output variables of the perceptron.

We also try to solve the problem of small data set using the approach proposed in [25]. The author suggests a cross-variation method for the problem solution. All the data are used as a training data set, except for one sample, which is used to test the network after training. Then this procedure is repeated so every sample is sequentially excluded from the initial data set. Thus, each sample can be considered as both training and test one. After receiving the loss values for all test samples, they are averaged and an assessment is got of the neural network testing. The disadvantages of this method are the need to repeat the training many times, which takes a considerable amount of time, as well as the possible inaccuracy of the estimates of individual sample losses due to the influence of the stochastic component of the learning process. As a result of applying this method the estimated accuracy of network is equal to 89.9%.

6 Discussion

In the paper we continue to examine the effectiveness of using various machine learning methods for forecasting dangerous convective phenomena. Table 3 illustrates the results obtained both in the previous works [4, 5, 20] and present paper. We have considered five machine learning methods: Support Vector Machine (SVM), Logistic Regression, Ridge Regression, boosted k-nearest neighbour algorithm and neural networks. The table contains the best accuracy which could be possible achieved independently of the feature selection methods and approaches of data formation.

Table 3. Maximum forecast accuracy of the five machine learning methods

Method	Forecast accuracy
Logistic Regression [4, 5]	98.6%
Support Vector Machine [4, 5]	97.7%
Ridge Regression [4, 5]	98.1%
Boosted k-nearest neighbour algorithm [20]	99.0%
Neural networks	91.6%

The table does not contain the results described in Sect. 4 of the present paper and shown in Tables 1 and 3 as the accuracy achieved with second approach of data formation and preprocessing is lower than the accuracy obtained with the help of the first approach. That means that the stage of cloud evolution is not crucial for the choice of the most representative cloud parameters (features).

As it can be seen from the Table 3 the best results are achieved using Boosted k-nearest neighbour algorithm [20], the worst results were achieved with the neural networks algorithms.

But all the obtained values of forecast accuracy should be treated as preliminary ones, as the data sets used are relatively small for machine learning methods.

In future the research should be focused on obtaining sufficient number of radio-sonde soundings with the corresponding model simulations for formation relevant data sets for training and testing.

For correct comparison, forecast accuracy of the different machine learning methods should be obtained by the same feature selection methods and the same approaches to data formation.

Besides the forecast accuracy all machine learning methods should be compared by their numerical performance. The method which will show the optimal combination of precision and performance should be recommended for the operational forecasting of the dangerous convective phenomena.

7   Conclusions

The possibility of thunderstorm forecasting is considered, based upon numerical modelling with the subsequent processing of the output data by machine learning methods.

The problem of feature selection is discussed in two aspects: selection of the optimal values of time and height when and where the output model data are fixed and selection of the most representative cloud parameters (features). The results obtained with the help of Support Vector Machine (SVM), Logistic Regression and Ridge Regression show low dependence of forecast accuracy upon the height and the time moment of the output data selection.

The possibility of using neural networks for forecasting dangerous convective phenomena is analysed. Neural networks with three different structures are considered. The best achieved accuracy equals to 91.6%.

Comparison of different machine learning methods is provided. It is shown that forecast accuracy of all five methods reaches values exceeding 90%.

The choice of the most effective method should be based upon the investigation of the performance of machine learning method on the training and testing data sets of a larger volume.

References

1. Information on https://www-03.ibm.com/press/us/en/pressrelease/49954.wss
2. Information on https://arnesund.com/2015/05/31/using-amazon-machine-learning-to-predict-the-weather/
3. Information on https://yandex.ru/company/technologies/meteum/

4. Stankova, E.N., Balakshiy, A.V., Petrov, D.A., Shorov, A.V., Korkhov, V.V.: Using technologies of OLAP and machine learning for validation of the numerical models of convective clouds. In: Gervasi, O., et al. (eds.) ICCSA 2016. LNCS, vol. 9788, pp. 463–472. Springer, Cham (2016). https://doi.org/10.1007/978-3-319-42111-7_36

5. Stankova, E.N., Balakshiy, A.V., Petrov, D.A., Korkhov, V.V.: OLAP technology and machine learning as the tools for validation of the numerical models of convective clouds. Int. J. Bus. Intell. Data Min. 14(1/2), 254–266 (2019)

6. Abramovich, K.G., et al.: Guide to forecasting meteorological conditions for aviation, Goskomgidromet, Moscow (1985). (in Russian)

7. Stankova, E.N., Grechko, I.A., Kachalkina, Y.N., Khvatkov, E.V.: Hybrid approach combining model-based method with the technology of machine learning for forecasting of dangerous weather phenomena. In: Gervasi, O., et al. (eds.) ICCSA 2017. LNCS, vol. 10408, pp. 495–504. Springer, Cham (2017). https://doi.org/10.1007/978-3-319-62404-4_37

8. Information on https://www.microsoft.com/en-us/research/wp-content/uploads/2016/11/KD D_2014_keynote_horvitz.pdf

9. Baik, J.-J., Paek, J.-S.: A neural network model for predicting typhoon intensity. J. Meteorol. Soc. Jpn. 78, 857–869 (2000). https://doi.org/10.2151/jmsj1965.78.6_857

10. Ruettgers, M., Lee, S., Jeon, S., You, D.: Prediction of a typhoon track using a generative adversarial network and satellite images. Sci. Rep. 9 (2019). Article number: 6057. https://doi.org/10.1038/s41598-019-42339-y

11. Asai, T., Kasahara, A.: A theoretical study of the compensating downward motions associated with cumulus clouds. J. Atmos. Sci. 24, 487–497 (1967)

12. Raba, N.O., Stankova, E.N.: Research of influence of compensating descending flow on cloud's life cycle by means of 1.5-dimensional model with 2 cylinders. In: Proceedings of MGO, vol. 559, pp. 192–209 (2009). (in Russian)

13. Raba, N., Stankova, E.: On the possibilities of multi-core processor use for real-time forecast of dangerous convective phenomena. In: Taniar, D., Gervasi, O., Murgante, B., Pardede, E., Apduhan, B.O. (eds.) ICCSA 2010. LNCS, vol. 6017, pp. 130–138. Springer, Heidelberg (2010). https://doi.org/10.1007/978-3-642-12165-4_11

14. Raba, N.O., Stankova, E.N.: On the problem of numerical modeling of dangerous convective phenomena: possibilities of real-time forecast with the help of multi-core processors. In: Murgante, B., Gervasi, O., Iglesias, A., Taniar, D., Apduhan, B.O. (eds.) ICCSA 2011. LNCS, vol. 6786, pp. 633–642. Springer, Heidelberg (2011). https://doi.org/10.1007/978-3-642-21934-4_51

15. Raba, N.O., Stankova, E.N.: On the effectiveness of using the GPU for numerical solution of stochastic collection equation. In: Murgante, B., et al. (eds.) ICCSA 2013. LNCS, vol. 7975, pp. 248–258. Springer, Heidelberg (2013). https://doi.org/10.1007/978-3-642-39640-3_18

16. Petrov, D.A., Stankova, E.N.: Use of consolidation technology for meteorological data processing. In: Murgante, B., et al. (eds.) ICCSA 2014. LNCS, vol. 8579, pp. 440–451. Springer, Cham (2014). https://doi.org/10.1007/978-3-319-09144-0_30

17. Petrov, D.A., Stankova, E.N.: Integrated information system for verification of the models of convective clouds. In: Gervasi, O., et al. (eds.) ICCSA 2015. LNCS, vol. 9158, pp. 321–330. Springer, Cham (2015). https://doi.org/10.1007/978-3-319-21410-8_25

18. Stankova, E.N., Petrov, D.A.: Complex information system for organization of the input data of models of convective clouds. Vestnik Saint-Petersburg Univ. Ser. 10, Appl. Math. Comput. Sci. Control Processes (3), 83–95 (2015). (in Russian)

19. Stankova, E.N., Ismailova, E.T., Grechko, I.A.: Algorithm for processing the results of cloud convection simulation using the methods of machine learning. In: Gervasi, O., et al. (eds.) ICCSA 2018. LNCS, vol. 10963, pp. 149–159. Springer, Cham (2018). https://doi.org/10.1007/978-3-319-95171-3_13

20. Stankova, E.N., Khvatkov, E.V.: Using boosted k-nearest neighbour algorithm for numerical forecasting of dangerous convective phenomena. In: Misra, S., et al. (eds.) ICCSA 2019. LNCS, vol. 11622, pp. 802–811. Springer, Cham (2019). https://doi.org/10.1007/978-3-030-24305-0_61
21. Information on http://scikit-learn.org/
22. Dudarov, S.P., Diev, A.N., Fedosova, N.A., Koltsova, E.A.: Simulation of properties of composite materials reinforced by carbon nanotubes using perceptron complexes. Comput. Res. Model. 7(2), 253–262 (2017)
23. Dudarov, S.P., Diev, A.N.: Neural network modeling based on perceptron complexes with small training data sets. Math. Methods Eng. Technol. 114–116 (2013)
24. Information on. https://keras.io/
25. Korobkova, S.V.: Problems of the effective approximation of multidimensional functions using neural networks. Bull. South. Fed. Univ. Tech. Sci. 58(3), 121–127 (2006). (in Russian)

Algorithm for Creating Massive Amounts of Unique Three-Dimensional Models and Materials from Rocks

Oleg Iakushkin$^{(\boxtimes)}$, Egor Budlov, Ekaterina Bainova, and Olga Sedova

Saint-Petersburg University, 7/9 Universitetskaya nab., St. Petersburg 199034, Russia
o.yakushkin@spbu.ru

Abstract. The article describes the algorithm for creating three-dimensional models of stones from their polygonal mesh and a prototype photo. This method extracts PBR textures from the source image of the object and makes them seamless. Then, using the Blender software, a UV scan of the model is built. At the next stage, the coordinates of the sweep seams are extracted, and the quality of the textures is improved. Then, the resulting textures are superimposed on the object following the UV scan. The result is a three-dimensional model of the object with the textures applied to it. Also, a program was implemented that allows you to perform the above actions with a click of a button, which makes the process of obtaining a finished model as simple as possible. Among other things, the model was successfully exported to other programs working with 3D graphics.

Keywords: Modelling · Archaeology · Photogrammetry · Object reconstruction

1 Introduction

Currently, one of the main tasks of 3D modelling is the creation of three-dimensional models of archaeological artefacts, which should take into account the shape, material and size of the object [20]. Also no less important is the problem of generating texture of an object from a photograph of its prototype. Since some objects can deteriorate even from exposure to sunlight and under the influence of climatic conditions, the creation of electronic copies will facilitate the task of preserving unique artefacts [14,16]. Creating three-dimensional digital copies of objects opens up several possibilities, such as:

- Detailed familiarization with art objects and various coloured artefacts without physical risk [15].
- Usage of the objects in research and historical reconstruction [4,13].
- Creating physical copies of objects [1].

O. Iakushkin—This research was partially supported by the Russian Foundation for Basic Research grant (project no. 17-29-04288).

O. Gervasi et al. (Eds.): ICCSA 2020, LNCS 12254, pp. 94–104, 2020.
https://doi.org/10.1007/978-3-030-58817-5_8

As a result of researching cultural and historical monuments, a set of information that describes them is formed. However, the data obtained during this process is usually not enough for precise reconstruction, and the work of reconstructing the model takes a lot of time and effort. Although modern technologies provide ways to create textures from an image [11] automatically, it is often necessary to make additional changes manually, which requires special skills. This work aims to facilitate the task of constructing volumetric models of archaeological finds and providing artists with tools to change these automatically generated textures manually.

2 Related Work

3D modelling has recently been one of the most intriguing and challenging fields in computer vision and graphics research. Some of the developments in this area are:

- modelling of stones from sketches.
- reconstruction of walls from generated stones [9].
- recreation of surfaces from video [18,19].
- building of continuous textures using pictures [10].

Although modern technologies provide the ability to create textures from an image [5,21] automatically, and research in this area continues [2,3], 3D models obtained using existing solutions often either require many input data, or do not look realistic, or require a significant amount of time to be spent on mastering the software and manual execution of all actions, which are serious drawbacks. Also, often there is a need to make further changes manually, which requires additional special skills.

(a) Image 1

(b) Image 2   (c) Image 3

Fig. 1. Input images

3   Problem Definition

Our task is to create an algorithm that allows getting a three-dimensional model of the desired object, while using a small amount of input data (Fig. 1), and to implement it as an automated system. Such a model in appearance should be close to the original. Despite the complexity of the task, the system should not require special knowledge from the user in the subject area (in particular, 3D modelling or archaeology). It should also satisfy the following requirements:

- High realism of the 3D model of the desired object obtained as a result of the program.
- High degree of system automation. The process of building a model should not require any additional actions from the user other than launching the program.
- High speed of execution. The time spent on the program should not be large, which will allow simulating large volumes of objects in a short time.
- Availability to make manual changes to the resulting model by the user to further increase realism.

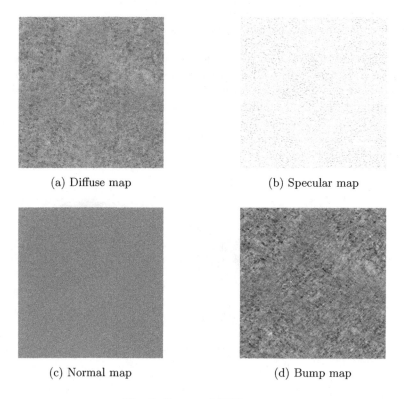

(a) Diffuse map   (b) Specular map

(c) Normal map   (d) Bump map

Fig. 2. Extracted PBR maps

4   Solution Method

The input data for the algorithm are an image of the object (photo, drawing, etc.) and its colourless model. Performing the following sequence of steps will allow us to get a realistic 3D model of the required object:

I. Extraction of PBR maps from the original image.
II. Improving the quality of the extracted maps.
III. Generation of a colourless model.
IV. UV-unwrapping of the model.
V. Creation of a scalable PBR material.
VI. Removal of seams.
VII. Export of the results.

4.1   Extraction of PBR Maps

Physically Correct Rendering (PBR) is a set of rendering rules that takes into account the behaviour of light in reality to create a realistic image. The extraction is performed with Python programming language using 'bitmap2material' algorithm. The results are illustrated on Fig. 2.

4.2   Improving the Quality

The resolution of the extracted PBR maps is quite low. We can improve it by increasing the size of the texture itself. It can be done by repeatedly placing the same texture a few times in a row and column (Fig. 3).

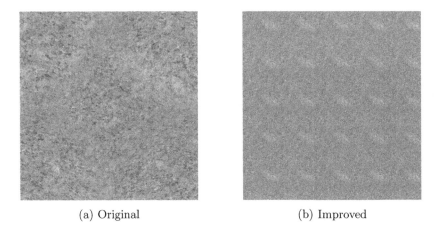

(a) Original   (b) Improved

Fig. 3. Diffuse map

4.3 Generation of a Colourless Model

For the 3D reconstruction process, we need information about the size and shape of the object. We can get them from a colourless 3D model. This task was already solved in another paper [8], so we are going to use the result in our work (Fig. 4).

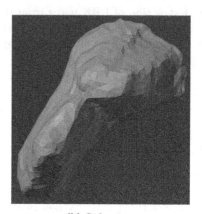

(a) Front view   (b) Side view

Fig. 4. Colourless model

4.4 UV-unwrapping

Now we need to project our 3D model to a 2D plane, which is called "UV-unwrapping". 'UV' here means two-dimensional coordinate system. It is the process of 'unfolding' a mesh so that we can create a 2D texture which fits the 3D object. This way, we can preserve the most important characteristics of the original object, such as its shape, size and connectivity [12]. In our work we used popular 3D-editor "Blender" [6,7,17]. Its advantage is that although this software is free and open, it provides a vast range of possibilities for working with various 2D and 3D objects.

1. Group faces of the object into several groups based on their normal vectors.
2. For each group, calculate its average normal vector and derive the orthogonal projection from projecting 3D faces to a 2D plane. Proportional weighting coefficients (based on sizes) are also used, so vectors of larger faces take priority.
3. Place each group on a rectangular (UV) area as compactly as possible.

The resulting UV scan was made using Blender smart UV project and is shown on Fig. 5. If necessary, it can also be scaled and rotated for better quality.

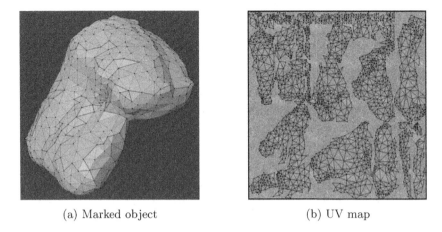

(a) Marked object   (b) UV map

Fig. 5. 2D unwrapping

4.5   Creation of the Material

The next stage is to create a single scalable material from the generated PBR maps. This process can be divided into several steps:

1. Create a new clean material and associate it with the object.
2. Enable usage of graphic schemes.
3. Create and connect a diagram.
4. Load the generated maps from phase I.

The resulting PBR material can be quickly applied to any number of models, which creates a possibility to model many objects of the same type in a short time.

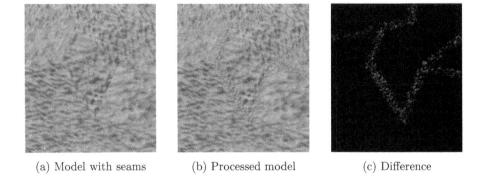

(a) Model with seams   (b) Processed model   (c) Difference

Fig. 6. Removal of seams

4.6   Removal of Seams

Although the model is now wrapped in texture, we can not call it completed yet. That is because we still have some visible seams on the model, which are not present on the prototype object. If we want the model look realistic, these seams should be removed. The following algorithm was used to camouflage the seams (each generated image should be of the same size as the original texture):

1. Create a black and white binary image with a black background and white lines along the edges of UV islands.
2. Calculate the average colour of texture.
3. Generate an image consisting of pixels having a random colour, where the colour of each pixel should differ from the average colour of the texture by several tints.
4. Create a binary image with random black and white pixels.
5. Use logical AND with images from steps 1 and 4.
6. Use the image from step 5 as a mask to combine original texture and image from step 3 (Fig. 6).

4.7   Export of the Results

The final step is to export the result to various other 3D editors (Fig. 7). Although Blender is quite practical and convenient to work with, it should be possible to export the generated texture. With this, artists will be able to use the software most suitable for their manual adjustments, and programmers will be able to work in the environment most familiar to them. In this paper, we used "Unreal Engine 4" – cross-platform development environment.

(a) Clean object   (b) Object with texture

Fig. 7. Model exported to Unreal Engine 4

5   Experiments

This algorithm was tested on various pairs of colourless models and photographs of stones (Fig. 8–9). Upon finishing all the steps, we get a completed 3D model. Although the resulting model already looks quite authentic, it is still ready for further manual improvements if necessary. Also, additional functional was created that allows to artificially break a generated model of a stone (Fig. 10).

Table 1. Execution time

Stage of the algorithm	Windows	Docker container
Extraction of main PBR maps	27 s	37 s
Extraction of additional shading map	70 s	134 s
Improving the quality of textures	0.5 s	0.8 s
UV unwrapping	0.7 s	1 s
Material creation	0.1 s	0.2 s
Removing seams on the model	0.1 s	0.2 s
Saving and exporting	16 s	38 s
Total runtime	114.4 s	211.2 s

The execution time of the algorithm is presented in Table 1. While the "extraction of PBR maps" part of the algorithm takes a lot more time than combining, we need to do it only once. After that, we can get a lot of differently shaped but similarly coloured objects fast. This will allow us to create a lot of 3D models of the same type in a short time.

   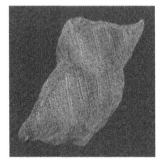

(a) Clean object   (b) Object with texture

Fig. 8. Sample 1

(a) Clean object   (b) Object with texture

Fig. 9. Sample 2

(a) Monolithic object   (b) Broken object

Fig. 10. Stone breaking

6   Conclusion

In this work, an algorithm was created that allows us to make a 3D model of the object from its real image and colourless model. It was implemented using Python programming language and 3D editor "Blender"[1]. The program itself can be run either as an extension for this software or independently in Docker container. This process was automatized and did not require any user actions until its completion. Further manual changes for better quality are also possible. The execution time is not too long, which allows us to create large amounts of unique three-dimensional models in a short time.

The main tasks of the future work are: further improving the quality of the resulting model, addition of texture styling tools in automatic mode and complete integration into a web-service format.

Acknowledgments. This research was partially supported by the Russian Foundation for Basic Research grant (project no. 17-29-04288).

---

[1] GitHub repository: https://github.com/8-lines/blender_PBR.

References

1. Anastasiadou, C., Vettese, S.: "From souvenirs to 3D printed souvenirs". Exploring the capabilities of additive manufacturing technologies in (re)-framing tourist souvenirs. Tour. Manag. **71**, 428–442 (2019)
2. Choy, C.B., Xu, D., Gwak, J.Y., Chen, K., Savarese, S.: 3D-R2N2: a unified approach for single and multi-view 3D object reconstruction. In: Leibe, B., Matas, J., Sebe, N., Welling, M. (eds.) ECCV 2016. LNCS, vol. 9912, pp. 628–644. Springer, Cham (2016). https://doi.org/10.1007/978-3-319-46484-8_38
3. Degtyarev, A., Iakushkin, O., Shvemberger, S.: Decomposition of the modeling task of some objects of archeological research for processing in a distributed computer system. Comput. Res. Model. **7**, 533–537 (2015)
4. Eve, S.: Augmenting phenomenology: using augmented reality to aid archaeological phenomenology in the landscape. J. Archaeol. Method Theory **19**, 582–600 (2012). https://doi.org/10.1007/s10816-012-9142-7
5. Fan, H., Su, H., Guibas, L.: A point set generation network for 3D object reconstruction from a single image. In: 2017 IEEE Conference on Computer Vision and Pattern Recognition (CVPR), pp. 2463–2471, July 2017
6. Hess, R.: The Essential Blender: Guide to 3D Creation with the Open Source Suite Blender. No Starch Press, San Francisco (2007)
7. Hess, R.: Blender Foundations: The Essential Guide to Learning Blender 2.5. Focal Press, Waltham (2013)
8. Iakushkin, O., Fatkina, A., Plaksin, V., Sedova, O., Degtyarev, A., Uteshev, A.: Reconstruction of stone walls in form of polygonal meshes from archaeological studies. In: Gervasi, O., et al. (eds.) ICCSA 2018. LNCS, vol. 10963, pp. 136–148. Springer, Cham (2018). https://doi.org/10.1007/978-3-319-95171-3_12
9. Iakushkin, O., Selivanov, D., Tazieva, L., Fatkina, A., Grishkin, V., Uteshev, A.: 3D reconstruction of landscape models and archaeological objects based on photo and video materials. In: Gervasi, O., et al. (eds.) ICCSA 2018. LNCS, vol. 10963, pp. 160–169. Springer, Cham (2018). https://doi.org/10.1007/978-3-319-95171-3_14
10. Iakushkin, O.O., Malevanniy, D.M., Degtyarev, A.B., Selivanov, D.A., Fatkina, A.I.: Texture generation for archaeological reconstructions. In: Proceedings of the VIII International Conference "Distributed Computing and Grid-Technologies in Science and Education", pp. 462–466 (2018)
11. Iakushkin, O., Budlov, E., Uteshev, A., Grishkin, V.: Automated creation of unique editable textures for three-dimensional models of archaeological artefacts. In: Misra, S., et al. (eds.) ICCSA 2019. LNCS, vol. 11622, pp. 752–760. Springer, Cham (2019). https://doi.org/10.1007/978-3-030-24305-0_56
12. Julius, W.: Developing a process for automating UV mapping and polygon reduction (2016)
13. Krokos, M., Dykes, T., Hassan, A., Croton, D., Gheller, C.: Interactive 3D visualization for theoretical virtual observatories. Mon. Not. R. Astron. Soc. **477**(2), 1495–1507 (2018). https://doi.org/10.1093/mnras/sty855
14. Liarokapis, F., Kouřil, P., Agrafiotis, P., Demesticha, S., Chmelík, J., Skarlatos, D.: 3D modelling and mapping for virtual exploration of underwater archaeology assets. ISPRS Int. Arch. Photogramm. Remote Sens. Spat. Inf. Sci. **XLII–2/W3**, 425–431 (2017)
15. Malevanniy, D., Sedova, O., Iakushkin, O.: Controlled remote usage of private shared resources via Docker and NoVNC. In: Misra, S., et al. (eds.) ICCSA 2019. LNCS, vol. 11622, pp. 782–791. Springer, Cham (2019). https://doi.org/10.1007/978-3-030-24305-0_59

16. Marques, L., et al.: Cultural heritage 3D modelling and visualisation within an augmented reality environment, based on geographic information technologies and mobile platforms. ACE: Archit. City Environ. **11**, 117–136 (2017)
17. Matsuyama, T., Nobuhara, S., Takai, T., Tung, T.: 3D Video and Its Applications. Springer, London (2012). https://doi.org/10.1007/978-1-4471-4120-4
18. Oleg, I., et al.: Position tracking in 3D space based on a data of a single camera. In: Misra, S., et al. (eds.) ICCSA 2019. LNCS, vol. 11622, pp. 772–781. Springer, Cham (2019). https://doi.org/10.1007/978-3-030-24305-0_58
19. Oleg, I., et al.: The architecture of the robot-finder based on SLAM and neural network. In: Misra, S., et al. (eds.) ICCSA 2019. LNCS, vol. 11622, pp. 761–771. Springer, Cham (2019). https://doi.org/10.1007/978-3-030-24305-0_57
20. Remondino, F., Campana, S.: 3D recording and modelling in archaeology and cultural heritage. BAR Int. Ser. **2598**, 111–127 (2014)
21. Remondino, F., El-Hakim, S., Girardi, S., Rizzi, A., Benedetti, S., Gonzo, L.: 3D virtual reconstruction and visualization of complex architectures - the 3D-arch project. Int. Arch. Photogramm. Remote Sens. Spat. Inf. Sci. **38** (2009)

KLT Bin Detection and Pose Estimation in an Industrial Environment

Aleksei Beloshapko[1](✉), Christian Knoll[2], Bilel Boughattas[3], and Vladimir Korkhov[1]

[1] Saint-Petersburg State University, 7/9 Universitetskaya nab.,
St. Petersburg 199034, Russia
beloshapko-alexey@rambler.ru, v.korkhov@spbu.ru
[2] Robert Bosch GmbH, Robert-Bosch-Campus 1, 71272 Renningen, Germany
Christian.Knoll@de.bosch.com
[3] University of Stuttgart, Postfach 10 60 37, 70049 Stuttgart, Germany
bilel.boughattas@gmail.com

Abstract. In order for Automated Guided Vehicles (AGV's) to handle KLT bins (Kleinladungsträger, Small Load Carrier) in a flexible way, a robust bin detection algorithm has to be developed. This paper presents a solution to the KLT bin detection and pose estimation task. The Mask R-CNN network is used to detect a KLT bin on color images, while a simple plane fitting approach is used to estimate its 5DoF position. This combination gives promising results in a typical use case scenario when the KLT bin is aligned with the camera view.

Keywords: KLT bin picking · Object detection · Instance segmentation · Pose estimation · Plane fitting · Industry 4.0

1 Introduction

A constant evolution of the information technologies brings changes to the industry. There is a huge trend for improving flexibility, transparency and automation of the production plants, which is a part of adoption of the Industry 4.0 paradigm. In particular, new technologies allow for better customization and flexibility of shop-floor production and logistics. Therefore, they loosen some of the restrictions imposed to allow for automation in the past, and generate a bulk of new tasks to be solved.

An integration of AGVs (Automated Guided Vehicles) for internal production plant logistics allowed a better flexibility in comparison to conveyors. However, these vehicles require smart software to perform the task of goods and material picking and delivery. One of the common ways to keep the workpieces and products is to use KLT bins (Kleinladungsträger, also known as a Small Load Carrier). This creates a task of a localization of such transport containers in an industrial environment in order to pick them.

© Springer Nature Switzerland AG 2020
O. Gervasi et al. (Eds.): ICCSA 2020, LNCS 12254, pp. 105–118, 2020.
https://doi.org/10.1007/978-3-030-58817-5_9

2   Related Work

The task of KLT bin detection has attracted little attention of researchers. In most applications where KLT bins are used, the software can assume its position to be fixed. This includes an extensively investigated task of "order picking", see [5, 9, 15] for an example.

This work is heavily related to [4], where the case of KLT bin detection with fisheye cameras is investigated. The main difference is the type of camera in use and a different use case scenario: in that work, the target distance to the KLT bin was assumed extremely small. In this work, we use a Color-Depth camera, and do not make any strict assumptions about KLT bin position.

Another attempt to solve this task was made by [14]. They concentrated on a particular case where the KLT bin is observed from the top, so that only edges of vertical sides of a bin are visible. They developed an algorithm based on KLT bin top edges detection, followed by a RANSAC-based procedure to choose the best hypothesis.

A related investigation was made by [20] to detect pallets in an industrial environment with range data only. The main idea was to use deep learning instead of classical computer vision approaches to detect the object of interest in a range data. We also use deep learning for object detection, and the neural networks in use are similar. However, we use the color image for object detection, and the range image is used for pose estimation only.

The task is also related to more general fields of research: object detection and object pose estimation.

2.1   Object Detection

In certain situations, the classical computer vision approach could be successfully applied for object detection. If the 3D shape of the object is known in advance, a shape matching algorithm like [8] can be applied. If the appearance of the object is known, then there is an option to use a keypoint feature matching approach like SURF [3] or ORB [23]. If the object does not have enough texture for feature matching, but has enough discriminative contours, then a 2D shape-based matching [28] can be applied.

However, a KLT bin lacks for 3D shape information as it consists of plane segments. In addition, no texture information is available. The contours of the object consist of straight lines, so in this sense a KLT bin is easily blended into an industrial environment. Thus, it is not possible to rely on some single aspect of object appearance. This leads us to the development of a detector that accepts the raw object image as the input. The use of machine learning methods is the most promising option that addresses these issues.

Nowadays the research on object detection on color and range images is largely driven by neural networks. In this work we use Mask R-CNN network [11] to perform KLT bin detection and segmentation. This solution avoids hardcoding the object appearance, but requires to collect a large training dataset instead. The network itself remains a state-of-the-art solution for instance segmentation tasks, but possibly could be optimized by using a more recent and optimized backbone classifier like EfficientNet [25].

2.2 Object Pose Estimation

There is a wide choice of methods for pose estimation. In this work, we rely on box shape of a KLT bin, thus using a plane segmentation and fitting approach [24] as a base algorithm. If a 3D shape matching algorithm was used for object detection, then the pose estimate could be obtained after an iterative closest-point refinement [29]. There are also a number of methods based on deep learning that handle the task of pose estimation, see [13,26,27].

3 The KLT Bin Detection and Pose Estimation Task

In this paper, we present an approach to KLT bin detection and pose estimation using a RGB-D camera [18]. We define three distinct scenarios that we handle:

1. Horizontal view case: The camera and the KLT bin are aligned and only the side part of the bin is visible
2. Vertical view case: The camera and the KLT bin are aligned and only the top part of the bin is visible
3. General view case: The camera and the KLT bin are not aligned so that more than one side of the bin is visible

The KLT bin and the camera are said to be aligned if the optical axis of the camera is almost parallel to some of the KLT bin sides (with tilt tolerance up to $5°$ of rotation). The aligned positions of a KLT bin are of the special interest for us, because these scenarios are a typical case in the industrial environment.

The task is to localize all the KLT bins in the 3D space that are visible to the camera. The task is solved in two stages: a KLT bin detection and a KLT bin pose estimation. The detection stage uses the Mask R-CNN network to process the color image and generate region proposals that contain KLT bins. The second stage processes point clouds that correspond to these regions and generates the pose estimates. The core algorithm for this is the RANSAC-based plane detection followed by a least-squares refinement. The pose estimation step is only performed for the aligned case. See Fig. 1 for an overview.

Fig. 1. Overview of the pipeline for KLT bin detection and pose estimation

4 KLT Bin Detection with Mask R-CNN

Our solution is based on the object detection capabilities of the Mask R-CNN [11] neural network. This network takes a color image as an input, and produces object bounding boxes alongside with their object segmentation masks and class labels. We modified the network to detect objects of only two classes: a KLT bin class and not-a-bin class (referred to as a "background" class). For each bounding box with KLT bin class label, we get a segmentation mask that we later use for pose estimation.

4.1 Mask R-CNN

The network itself consists of four major image processing stages, which are depicted in Fig. 2. The first step is to use a classification network in a fully-convolutional manner to generate a pyramid of feature maps. We use the ResNet-101 network [12] as a classification backbone. The second stage is to produce a set of rough bounding boxes that might contain an object using the top feature map of the pyramid. This is done with a Region Proposal Network [21]. At the third stage the location of generated bounding boxes is being refined. For each rough bounding box estimate, the network predicts deltas for top-left corner location and for box size. Finally, the last stage generates a class label and a segmentation mask for each of the refined object bounding box.

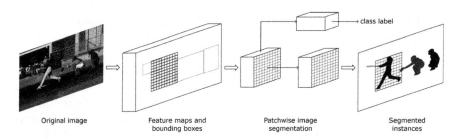

Fig. 2. The Mask-RCNN network pipeline [11]

4.2 Training Dataset

To train such a network, we created a training dataset for KLT bin instance segmentation. The raw data was obtained with Intel RealSense cameras (D415 and D435). The labeling was performed either manually, or based on color thresholding, or with a semi-automatic approach. Each labeled image went through our data augmentation pipeline to enlarge the training dataset and improve data variety.

Semi-automatic Labeling Procedure. The semi-automatic procedure was introduced to label a large amount of images with less effort than just manual labeling. The idea is to capture a video sequence of the object of interest and then use a surface reconstruction method to create a 3D mesh of the captured area. Then labeling of this 3D mesh is equivalent to labeling of the complete video sequence.

The procedure consists of 5 steps:

1. A Color-Depth video sequence of a KLT bin is captured
2. The video sequence is processed with a surface reconstruction method to produce a 3D mesh of the area and a camera relative pose estimate for each image frame
3. The 3D mesh labeling is performed
4. The labeled parts of the mesh are back-projected to each of the images of the sequence. This is possible with the corresponding camera pose estimates. The projection of a labeled part generates an object segmentation mask.
5. The resulting segmentation masks are refined for each image of the sequence.

At Step 1 a human captures a video sequence while going around an area with some KLT bins. It is better to make a complete circle, or a path with shortcuts to ensure loop closures at the reconstruction stage.

At Step 2, the depth images sequence is fed to some 3D surface reconstruction method. We used KinectFusion [17] and Open3D [6] for mesh generation. While KinectFusion is faster, it does not use loop closures, so it quickly accumulates a camera pose drift. Open3D reconstruction pipeline is completely offline, but uses loop closures to improve the quality of the mesh and the camera trajectory estimate. Therefore, KinectFusion is more suitable for short sequences, while Open3D is able to handle long image sequences, but takes more time to process.

At Step 3, one has to manually specify the parts of the mesh that belong to KLT bins. We used Meshlab [7] to simply crop out parts that are KLT bins. As this step is manual, the complete procedure is semi-automatic. To make the procedure fully automatic, one has to automate this particular step.

At Step 4, the KLT bin meshes are back-projected to the original images of the video sequences to form the segmentation masks. As for each image frame there is a camera pose estimate, the back-projection is done simply by projecting all mesh faces to the camera frame.

At Step 5, all the segmentation masks are refined via a Grab-cut based procedure. For this step we used an OpenCV implementation of the Grab-cut [22] algorithm. For each segmentation mask, the inner part of the region is treated as "sure-foreground", while the outer part as "sure-background". The area near the region boundary was treated as either "probably-foreground" or "probably-background". With this initialization, the Grab-cut algorithm was run for a single iteration on the color image. This step removes some specific artifacts of the segmentation, such as decimation effect due to the voxel-based nature of the mesh.

As a result, for each image in a video sequence the KLT bin segmentation masks are generated.

Data Augmentation Pipeline. The data augmentation primary target is to make a more representative dataset. Usually neural networks trained with the use of data augmentation are more robust to certain challenging situations. Our augmentation pipeline perform color augmentation image rotation and background substitution.

Color augmentation is performed along the hue axis. This ensures that the training dataset contains KLT bins of any color.

Random image rotation is performed in a standard way: the image is rotated in the image plane around its center. The complete rotation angle range of 360° is used.

After these three transformations are applied, the resulting KLT bin region is cut-and-pasted onto some other background image. This ensures background variation, as we captured the KLT bins images at just several background scenes.

4.3   Experiments

The training data consists of 11000 labeled images. 4200 of them are obtained with the semi-automatic labeling procedure, 6500 with background subtraction method and 300 were labeled manually. 10% of the semi-automatically labelled images were used for training as they are, while the rest went through the data augmentation pipeline, with each image producing 10 new ones. Thus, the final training data set had 106220 images with mask labels. See Fig. 3 for some training images samples.

The Mask R-CNN network was trained for 20 epochs. Each epoch had 1200 optimization steps with the batch size of 1. We used a 3-stage training scheme, where during the first two stages the ResNet weights were partially fixed. Batch Normalization [16] was used to regularize the network.

The test dataset consisted of 390 manually labeled images captured at 8 different scenes. See Fig. 4 for samples.

The mean Intersection over Union (IoU) metric is used to evaluate the quality of image segmentation. This metric is one of the standard ways to evaluate the image segmentation accuracy. The IoU metric has the value in range $[0, 1]$ and the value of 1 means perfect match of the prediction mask with the ground truth.

We also estimate the object detection performance with a confusion matrix. Object detection is implemented by prediction the image bounding boxes. This functionality is a part of the Mask R-CNN pipeline.

We estimate these three entries of the confusion matrix: the True Positive (TP) rate, the False Positive (FP) rate and the False Negative (FN) rate. The TP rate is the number of correct bounding box predictions divided by the number of bin bounding box predictions. The False Positive rate is the number of incorrect bounding box predictions divided by the total number of bin bounding box predictions. The False Negative rate is the number of ground truth bin regions that were not detected divided by the total number of ground truth bin regions.

This way the FP rate indicates the responses on the non-existent bin, while FN rate indicates real bins that were not detected. The sum of the True Positive and the False Positive rate is always 1.

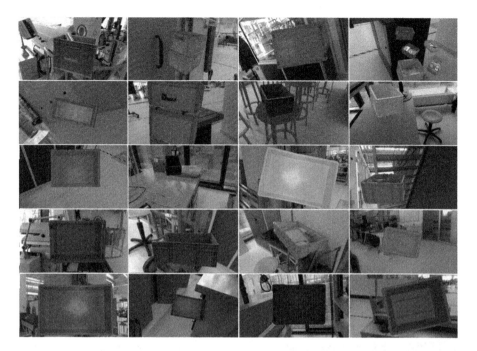

Fig. 3. Samples of images that were generated with a data augmentation pipeline and used to train the Mask R-CNN network for KLT bin detection

Fig. 4. Some examples of the test images. Left image relates to the vertical view scenario, the center image - to the horizontal view scenario, right image shows a general position case

Table 1 reports the results. It can be seen that Mask R-CNN handles well the vertical and general view cases, while failing a lot in the horizontal view case. A data inspection revealed that the majority of the detection misses belong to a single bin type that appears a lot in the test dataset, but does not in the training dataset. This indicates that the network works poorly on the bin types that were not trained. See Fig. 5 for an example of bin detection.

The histogram Fig. 6 shows the IoU metric value distribution across regions generated by the Mask R-CNN. Most of the detections fall in the range of 0.8–1.0, having few outliers.

Table 1. Evaluation of the Mask R-CNN network over test datasets

Test set	Total images	TP rate	FN rate	FP rate	mIoU
Vertical view	250	0.960	0.035	0.039	0.939
Horizontal view	160	0.989	**0.399**	0.010	0.919
General view	59	0.983	0.016	0.016	0.912

Fig. 5. An example of an image processed with the Mask R-CNN pipeline. The detected bin instances are labeled with a bounding box rectangle and painted with the predicted mask region. Note that the blue bin in the right part of the image is not detected (Color figure online)

5   KLT Bin Pose Estimation Using Plane Fitting

For the aligned use cases when only one side of a KLT bin is observed, its relative position can be estimated by fitting a plane into the KLT bin point cloud. See Fig. 7 for a KLT bin point cloud sample. This cloud can be generated out of the depth image and the segmentation provided by Mask R-CNN, assuming that camera intrinsic parameters are known.

To conduct the experiment, we used the implementation of the plane fitting algorithm from Point Cloud Library [24]. The method accepts a point cloud and does a RANSAC-based plane fitting followed by least-squares refinement. As a result, we obtain a plane center point and a normal vector estimate for each KLT bin region.

The accuracy of such approach is validated against another pose estimation method that relies on tracking of a fixed checkerboard pattern.

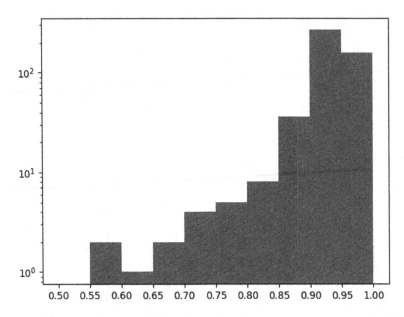

Fig. 6. A log-scale histogram of IoU metric values for the regions generated with Mask R-CNN on the test image set

Fig. 7. The image of a KLT bin over uniform background and the corresponding colored pointcloud captured by the RGB-D camera. Figure made with the Intel RealSense Viewer. (Color figure online)

5.1 Camera Pose Estimation via Charuco Marker Tracking

The ground truth for camera pose estimation is obtained with the Charuco marker [10] tracking approach. The Charuco marker is the planar checkerboard pattern with AruCo markers [2] inside the checkerboard cells. The advantage of using such a pattern instead of a regular checkerboard pattern is that it is less ambiguous when the pattern is partially occluded. When tracking a checkerboard pattern, it is usually required to have all checkerboard corners visible. The use of AruCo markers makes it possible to recover feature point correspondences even if some of the feature points are occluded.

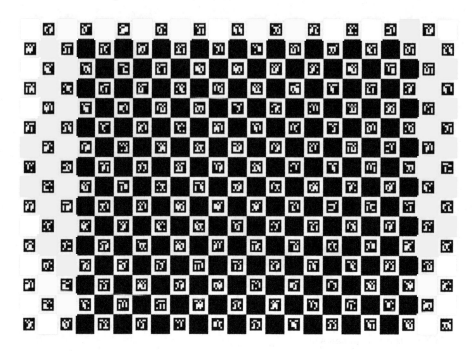

Fig. 8. The Charuco marker used for camera pose estimation

The use of the checkerboard pattern allows feature detection with subpixel accuracy. Having accurate correspondences between 3D marker points and their projections on the color image frame, it is possible to formulate a Perspective-n-Point problem [19], that could be solved by minimizing the feature point reprojection error. Given a sufficient number of points, this method achieves state-of-the-art accuracy [1].

We use a Charuco board with 24 × 17 cells. The checkerboard cell size is 51 mm, and each of the internal white cell contains an AruCo marker. AruCo marker dimensions is 0.8 times smaller than the hosting checkerboard cell. A total of 184 AruCo markers are in use. See Fig. 8.

The AruCo marker dictionary was generated with the procedure described in [10]. In short, we set a minimum hamming distance threshold between AruCo markers being equal to 3. Then we randomly sample the AruCo markers and add them to a dictionary if its distance to all markers in the dictionary is less than the threshold. This way, we obtain a collection of AruCo markers that have significant difference between each other.

Of course, the hamming distance threshold of 3 is quite a low requirement. This comes as a trade-off of having a large AruCo marker dictionary.

The KLT bin is placed directly on the Charuco marker, see Fig. 9.

Fig. 9. Sample images used to evaluate the pose estimation precision. Left and center - KLT bin side (horizontal) views, right - top (vertical) view

The KLT bin occludes some part of the marker, but the use of internal markers makes the corner identification still possible.

5.2 Experiments

We simulated three different scenarios: horizontal views on sides of a KLT bin and a vertical view, see Fig. 9. The camera was moved around being pointed to the KLT bin and capturing Color-Depth images. For each of such images, we obtain a full 6DoF pose with Charuco marker tracking approach.

For each of the images that have the pose estimated with sufficient accuracy, we run our KLT bin detection pipeline. First, Mask R-CNN network estimates the region of the image where the KLT bin appears. Second, the plane fitting is run on the part of point cloud that corresponds to that region. This way we obtain a center point and the normal vector of the KLT bin. Finally, the center point estimate is expressed in the global coordinate frame defined by the Charuco marker.

It has to be noted that the ChArUco pattern as a background creates an additional challenge for object detection and instance segmentation. This pattern is similar to bin regions as it also contains little texture information and a large amount of straight lines. This influences the segmentation accuracy, which in turn has an influence on the pose estimation accuracy.

We evaluate the precision bin centre estimates. To do so, we estimate a centroid point of all these estimates, and then compute the average deviation. Table 2 shows the details.

Table 2. KLT bin center point estimation precision evaluation. All precision values are given in meters

Scenario	Total images	Average center deviation	Max center deviation	Camera viewpoint variation	Max camera viewpoint shift
Side view #1	33	**0.0321**	0.105	0.2107	0.5938
Side view #2	29	**0.0316**	0.0876	0.2155	0.5488
Top view	193	**0.0360**	0.1490	0.1939	0.7082

Given these precision values, it is clear that the pipeline gives a rough position estimate of a bin. However, these evaluation conditions are more challenging than the typical use case, so we treat these precision estimates as an upper precision boundary.

6   Conclusion

The presented method can be applied for KLT bin detection and pose estimation in an industrial environment. The strong sides of the proposed solution is the flexibility of the bin detection algorithm that is based on machine learning techniques, along with the simplicity of the pose estimation approach.

The weak spots are the bin detection rate and the segmentation accuracy. The use case of a horizontal view on a KLT bin has to be additionally addressed. The direct way to reduce the False Negative rate is to populate the training dataset with more images of non-detected bins.

The plane fitting approach used for pose estimation is a simple and effective option, but it depends heavily on the region proposal accuracy generated by the neural network. One of the easiest way to improve pose estimation precision is to perform a time-based filtering with a Kalman filter. This is an option in the case when the camera trajectory is known. Another way is to introduce a more sophisticated pose estimation algorithm. The techniques based on machine learning could be the preference to avoid further constraints on the object appearance.

References

1. An, G.H., Lee, S., Seo, M.W., Yun, K.J., Cheong, W.S., Kang, S.J.: Charuco board-based omnidirectional camera calibration method. Electronics **7**, 421 (2018)
2. Babinec, A., Jurišica, L., Hubinský, P., Duchoň, F.: Visual localization of mobile robot using artificial markers. Procedia Eng. **96**, 1–9 (2014). https://doi.org/10.1016/j.proeng.2014.12.091
3. Bay, H., Tuytelaars, T., Van Gool, L.: SURF: speeded up robust features. In: Leonardis, A., Bischof, H., Pinz, A. (eds.) ECCV 2006. LNCS, vol. 3951, pp. 404–417. Springer, Heidelberg (2006). https://doi.org/10.1007/11744023_32
4. Beloshapko, A., Korkhov, V., Knoll, C., Iben, U.: Industrial fisheye image segmentation using neural networks. In: Misra, S., et al. (eds.) ICCSA 2019. LNCS, vol. 11622, pp. 678–690. Springer, Cham (2019). https://doi.org/10.1007/978-3-030-24305-0_50
5. Buchholz, D., Kubus, D., Weidauer, I., Scholz, A., Wahl, F.M.: Combining visual and inertial features for efficient grasping and bin-picking. In: 2014 IEEE International Conference on Robotics and Automation (ICRA), pp. 875–882 (2014)
6. Choi, S., Zhou, Q.Y., Koltun, V.: Robust reconstruction of indoor scenes. In: 2015 IEEE Conference on Computer Vision and Pattern Recognition (CVPR), pp. 5556–5565 (2015)
7. Cignoni, P., Callieri, M., Corsini, M., Dellepiane, M., Ganovelli, F., Ranzuglia, G.: MeshLab: an open-source mesh processing tool. In: Eurographics Italian Chapter Conference, vol. 1, pp. 129–136 (2008). https://doi.org/10.2312/LocalChapterEvents/ItalChap/ItalianChapConf2008/129-136

8. Drost, B., Ilic, S.: 3D object detection and localization using multimodal point pair features. In: 2012 Second International Conference on 3D Imaging, Modeling, Processing, Visualization Transmission, pp. 9–16 (2012)

9. Drost, B., Ulrich, M., Navab, N., Ilic, S.: Model globally, match locally: efficient and robust 3D object recognition. In: 2010 IEEE Computer Society Conference on Computer Vision and Pattern Recognition, pp. 998–1005 (2010)

10. Garrido-Jurado, S., Muñoz-Salinas, R., Madrid-Cuevas, F., Marín-Jiménez, M.: Automatic generation and detection of highly reliable fiducial markers under occlusion. Pattern Recogn. **47**, 2280–2292 (2014). https://doi.org/10.1016/j.patcog. 2014.01.005

11. He, K., Gkioxari, G., Dollár, P., Girshick, R.B.: Mask R-CNN. CoRR abs/1703.06870 (2017). http://arxiv.org/abs/1703.06870

12. He, K., Zhang, X., Ren, S., Sun, J.: Deep residual learning for image recognition. CoRR abs/1512.03385 (2015). http://arxiv.org/abs/1512.03385

13. Hodan, T., Haluza, P., Obdržálek, S., Matas, J., Lourakis, M.I.A., Zabulis, X.: T-LESS: an RGB-D dataset for 6d pose estimation of texture-less objects. CoRR abs/1701.05498 (2017). http://arxiv.org/abs/1701.05498

14. Holz, D., Behnke, S.: Fast edge-based detection and localization of transport boxes and pallets in RGB-D images for mobile robot bin picking. In: Proceedings of ISR 2016: 47st International Symposium on Robotics, pp. 1–8 (2016)

15. Holz, D., et al.: Active recognition and manipulation for mobile robot bin picking. In: Röhrbein, F., Veiga, G., Natale, C. (eds.) Gearing Up and Accelerating Cross-fertilization between Academic and Industrial Robotics Research in Europe. STAR, vol. 94, pp. 133–153. Springer, Cham (2014). https://doi.org/10.1007/978-3-319-03838-4_7

16. Ioffe, S., Szegedy, C.: Batch normalization: accelerating deep network training by reducing internal covariate shift. CoRR abs/1502.03167 (2015). http://arxiv.org/abs/1502.03167

17. Izadi, S., et al.: Kinectfusion: real-time 3D reconstruction and interaction using a moving depth camera. In: Proceedings of the 24th Annual ACM Symposium on User Interface Software and Technology, UIST 2011, New York, NY, USA, pp. 559–568. Association for Computing Machinery (2011). https://doi.org/10.1145/2047196.2047270.https://doi.org/10.1145/2047196.2047270

18. Keselman, L., Woodfill, J.I., Grunnet-Jepsen, A., Bhowmik, A.: Intel realsense stereoscopic depth cameras. CoRR abs/1705.05548 (2017). http://arxiv.org/abs/1705.05548

19. Lu, X.: A review of solutions for perspective-n-point problem in camera pose estimation. J. Phys. Conf. Ser. **1087**, 052009 (2018). https://doi.org/10.1088/1742-6596/1087/5/052009

20. Mohamed, I.S., Capitanelli, A., Mastrogiovanni, F., Rovetta, S., Zaccaria, R.: Detection, localisation and tracking of pallets using machine learning techniques and 2D range data. CoRR abs/1803.11254 (2018). http://arxiv.org/abs/1803.11254

21. Ren, S., He, K., Girshick, R.B., Sun, J.: Faster R-CNN: towards real-time object detection with region proposal networks. CoRR abs/1506.01497 (2015). http://arxiv.org/abs/1506.01497

22. Rother, C., Kolmogorov, V., Blake, A.: Grabcut-interactive foreground extraction using iterated graph cuts. In: ACM Transactions on Graphics (SIGGRAPH), August 2004. https://www.microsoft.com/en-us/research/publication/grabcut-interactive-foreground-extraction-using-iterated-graph-cuts/

23. Rublee, E., Rabaud, V., Konolige, K., Bradski, G.: ORB: an efficient alternative to SIFT or SURF. In: 2011 International Conference on Computer Vision, pp. 2564–2571 (2011)
24. Rusu, R., Cousins, S.: 3D is here: Point Cloud Library (PCL). In: IEEE International Conference on Robotics and Automation (ICRA 2011), May 2011. https://doi.org/10.1109/ICRA.2011.5980567
25. Tan, M., Le, Q.V.: EfficientNet: rethinking model scaling for convolutional neural networks. CoRR abs/1905.11946 (2019). http://arxiv.org/abs/1905.11946
26. Tremblay, J., To, T., Sundaralingam, B., Xiang, Y., Fox, D., Birchfield, S.: Deep object pose estimation for semantic robotic grasping of household objects. CoRR abs/1809.10790 (2018). http://arxiv.org/abs/1809.10790
27. Xiang, Y., Schmidt, T., Narayanan, V., Fox, D.: PoseCNN: a convolutional neural network for 6D object pose estimation in cluttered scenes. CoRR abs/1711.00199 (2017). http://arxiv.org/abs/1711.00199
28. Xu, X., Zhang, X., Han, J., Wu, C.: HALCON application for shape-based matching. In: 2008 3rd IEEE Conference on Industrial Electronics and Applications, pp. 2431–2434 (2008)
29. Zinsser, T., Schmidt, J., Niemann, H.: A refined ICP algorithm for robust 3-D correspondence estimation. In: Proceedings 2003 International Conference on Image Processing (Cat. No. 03CH37429), vol. 2, p. II-695 (2003)

Detection and Localization of Embedded Subtitles in a Video Stream

Grishkin Valery$^{(\boxtimes)}$ and Sene Jean

Saint-Petersburg State University, St.Petersburg 199034, Russia
v.grishkin@spbu.ru

Abstract. Videos with superimposed external subtitles constitute the major part of modern video content. However, there are quite a lot of diverse videos with embedded subtitles as well. In this regard, the problem arises of extracting and converting embedded subtitles into modern formats of external subtitles. Important steps in solving this problem are detection, localization, and binding of these subtitles to frames of the video stream. This paper proposes a method for detection and localization of embedded subtitles in video stream. The method is based on the search for static regions in the frames of the video stream and subsequent analysis of the connected areas inside them. Based on the results of this analysis, we determine whether a region belongs to the area of subtitles and localize text strings in the detected subtitles. The proposed method does not require large computational costs and can work in real time.

Keywords: Embedded subtitles · Subtitles localization · Image segmentation

1 Introduction

Currently, multimedia content makes up most of the information on the Internet. A significant part of this content are the videos superimposed with subtitles. Subtitles come in two varieties - external and embedded. External ones are contained in a separate file and are added by a video player software during playback. These subtitles can be easily replaced, edited or deleted if necessary, by appropriate actions with the subtitle file. Embedded subtitles are always displayed during video playback and are part of the video file. Thus, the task of localization and recognition of embedded subtitles is a task of image processing and can be solved by various relevant methods.

Embedded subtitles are text overlaid on video frames. At the same time, various text characters related to the displayed natural scene may also be present on the frames themselves. Thus, the text information contained in the frames of the video is divided into 2 types: the text located on the scene (Scene Text) and the text embedded from the outside source (Embedded Text). Subtitles are Embedded Text.

The Scene Text comes in great variety and variability. E.g. different frames of the video can have it written in several languages, being of different colors,

© Springer Nature Switzerland AG 2020
O. Gervasi et al. (Eds.): ICCSA 2020, LNCS 12254, pp. 119–128, 2020.
https://doi.org/10.1007/978-3-030-58817-5_10

fonts, sizes, orientations, and shapes. Quality of such text in the image cannot be guaranteed due to the shooting conditions and corresponding distortions—defocusing, poor lighting, shadows, blips, etc. In contrast, the Embedded Text on almost all frames of the video is presented in one language, normally is of the same size, font, and orientation. Image quality of the text is approximately the same for all frames—it has a high contrast and is well focused. In addition, the embedded text has temporal homogeneity—the frequency of text changes does not exceed a certain value, and for a certain period the text itself does not change nor does its position or orientation. These features make it possible to distinguish subtitles from a complex background, including the Scene Text, and to localize the position of subtitles by simpler methods than the ones used to detect and recognize text in the scene.

Traditional methods of localizing and recognizing text on images of video frames use one of three approaches. The first approach uses various classifiers from the area of sliding multi-scale windows. The second approach is based on applying classifiers to the static regions identified in the frame images. The third approach involves texture analysis of images.

In the first approach, each sliding window is tested for being part of a text segment. All windows classified as ones containing text are grouped into text regions according to certain rules. Then, one of the OCR classifiers is applied to each text region [1–3].

The second approach is much like the first but differs in the stage of finding a text region. In this case, the image is searched for static regions, each of which is checked for belonging to a text segment. Typically, in a static region, areas of uniform color or brightness are searched for by connected components analysis and then grouped together [4–6]. Connected areas that conform to certain constraints, such as size and shape, are then used as a basis for text extraction.

Texture-based analysis reveals periodic components in brightness or color, as well as in directions of the structures of text areas [7–9]. For texture features, one can use the results of applying various spectral transformations to the image. These transformations include Fourier transform, discrete cosine transform, and discrete multilevel wavelet transform. Texture analysis can be applied to the entire frame, as well as to sliding windows or static regions.

Recently, methods of deep learning have been in use to solve problems of localization and text recognition. In this case, text areas are treated as objects for segmentation. A pre-trained convolutional neural network is used to obtain a map of object segmentation. This map shows whether each pixel in the image belongs to a symbol, to a text area, or to another object [10,11]. Interconnected pixels of this map are marked as text candidates and are further detected as a character or as a text region. Many works [12,13] describe various architectures of convolutional neural networks that allow localization of individual characters and text regions, as well as text recognition in identified regions. It should be noted that great successes have been achieved in this approach. However, use of deep learning methods requires large training sets and sufficiently powerful computers; in addition, these methods cannot always work in real time. Therefore, using these methods for localization and recognition of subtitles is quite expensive in terms of performance and computing power.

In this work, we propose a method for localizing subtitles in a video stream which is based on the mentioned features of the embedded text. The method is based on the analysis of static regions of image frames, it does not require large computational costs and can work in real time.

2   The Method of Detection and Localization of Subtitles in a Video Stream

The essence of the method is the search for static regions in the frame images with a subsequent analysis of connected areas within these regions in order to determine whether the region belongs to the subtitle area. To that end, a background model is built over several frames of the video. Based on this model, a binary background image mask is generated. An analysis of connected components reveals static regions in this mask, some of which may include subtitles. Then, using heuristic rules, an analysis is made of the relationship of parameters of static regions, which reveals the affiliation of these region groups to subtitles. The structure of the method for detecting and localizing subtitles is shown in Fig. 1.

2.1   Preliminary Processing

At this stage, frames images are extracted from the video stream one by one. Each image of the frame, depending on the resolution of the original video stream, may decrease by 2 or 4 times. This is required in order to reduce frame processing time. The standard background subtraction procedure is applied to the resulting frames. For separating background and foreground objects, we propose to use a method based on a Gaussian mixture model (GMM). This model is based on the use of information about the color change of an image pixel on several frames [14]. Since the text in the subtitles does not change for several frames in a row, the subtitles belong to the background. Applying this method yields two binary frame image masks, which constitute the result of preprocessing. The second mask can be used to detect changes in the position of the subtitles or changes in the text itself. Before further processing, the resulting masks are subjected to a morphological image opening operation in order to eliminate possible high-frequency noise. Figure 2 shows the video frame and its background mask which has been obtained from 5 preceding frames.

2.2   Static Area Segmentation

First, the background mask is binarized using the adaptive threshold [15]. For static regions segmentation, the connected components search method is applied to the binary background mask. The result is a grayscale image in which the brightness of each pixel corresponds to the number of the static region to which

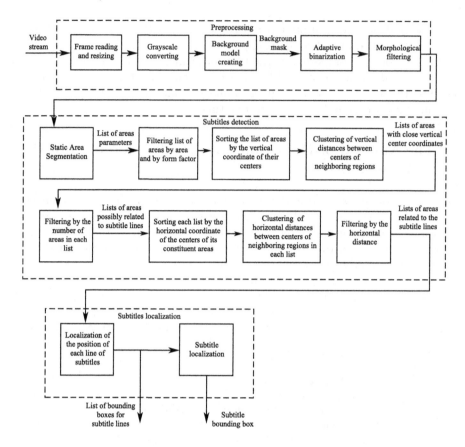

Fig. 1. The structure of the method for detecting and localizing subtitles.

Fig. 2. Preprocessing: a) the video frame; b) its background mask.

this pixel refers. In addition, segmentation process creates a list of these regions. Each interconnected region is described by a set of parameters. This set includes the coordinates of the center of the region, the area of the region, and the coordinates and sizes of the bounding rectangles. These parameters are then used for subtitle areas localization. Figure 3 shows the results of segmentation of static regions obtained using a binary background mask.

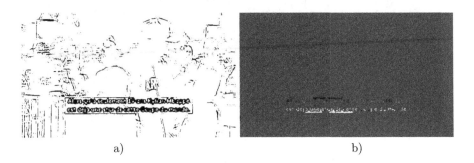

a)   b)

Fig. 3. Segmentation of static regions: a) the binary background mask; b) the static regions.

2.3   Detection and Localization of Subtitle Regions

At the first step, the list of regions obtained during segmentation is filtered by occupied area. Since the regions with subtitle symbols have a relatively small area, only regions having an area that lies in a certain range are included in the filtered list. The upper bound of the range is equal to the maximum possible size of a subtitle character area, while the lower bound depends on the size of small details in the frame image and on the interference. Any text character has a form factor which is defined as a height-to-width ratio of that character. For characters of the most common fonts, this ratio lies in a certain limited range. As such, the list is additionally filtered by a predefined range of form factors. Figure 4 shows the results of filtering static regions by area and by form factor.

Subtitles are lines of text located in a certain close area of the frame. Changes in their position are rather rare compared to the frame rate. Normally, text lines of subtitles are oriented horizontally. Therefore, a sign of the possible presence of subtitles is the concentration of the identified areas (possibly related to text characters) in some lines of the frame. In other words, the text line of the subtitle is displayed as a set of areas whose centers have approximately the same vertical Y-coordinate. Moreover, the distribution of horizontal X-coordinates of these centers should demonstrate a certain periodicity.

At the second step of the algorithm, the filtered list of regions is sorted by the vertical Y-coordinate of the centers of these regions. In this sorted list, differences between adjacent vertical coordinates $\{\Delta y_i = y_{i+1} - y_i\}$ are calculated. The resulting set of these differences is divided into two classes using the clustering procedure. Relatively small differences go to one class, while relatively large ones

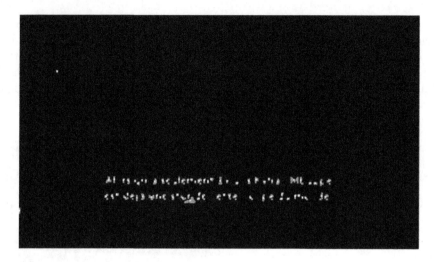

Fig. 4. The results of filtering static regions by area and by form factor. White dots indicate the location of the centers of the identified areas, presumably related to subtitles

go to the other class. The class with small differences supposedly includes areas with subtitle lines. The average value of this difference with some tolerance, say 2.5σ, sets the range of values for checking whether the area belongs to a text string in the vicinity of the vertical coordinate being checked. Next, the sorted list is scanned, with creating dedicated lists of areas having approximately the same vertical coordinates of their centers. Lists containing fewer elements than a predefined threshold, for example 5, are ignored in the subsequent steps of the algorithm. The number of lists remaining may likely match the number of text lines in subtitles. These lists are then checked to see whether the areas they contain belong to text lines of subtitles.

At the next step of the algorithm, we check whether the remaining lists of regions have any periodicity in the distances between the centers of the regions along the horizontal X-coordinate. In order to do this, like at the previous step, each list is sorted by the horizontal X-coordinate. Then we create a set of distances between the centers of regions in the horizontal direction $\{\Delta x_i = x_{i+1} - x_i\}$. A clustering procedure is also applied to the generated sets, which splits each set into two classes. Possible distances between characters are grouped in one class, and distances between words in a string are grouped in another class. Next, areas in each list are checked for being part of a subtitle line. If the range of distances in the first class is not too big, i.e., possible distances between the characters are approximately the same, then this list contains areas of the subtitle text string. In case of a large spread of distances, the assumption is that this list does not contain areas belonging to the subtitle line. If no periodicity is detected in any of these lists of regions, the assumption is again that the given frame does not contain subtitles. Figure 5 shows the lines with periodicity in horizontal distances between the centers of the regions.

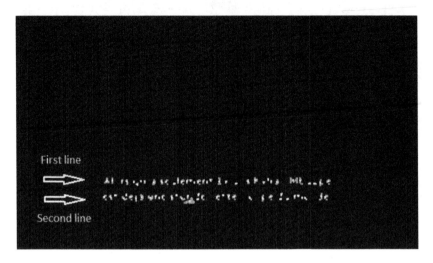

Fig. 5. The lines with periodicity in horizontal distances between the centers of the regions

After the lists of areas being part of the subtitle lines are identified, the search for the parameters of the bounding rectangles is performed, both for each detected text line and for the entire subtitle area. This search utilizes information about locations and sizes of local areas' bounding rectangles $\{x_i, y_i, w_i, h_i\}$ which can be found in lists corresponding to individual text lines of subtitles.

Here x_i, y_i are the coordinates of the upper left corner, and the w_i, h_i are the width and the height with a rectangle with index $i = 1, \ldots, N$, where N being the number of areas in the list. Figure 6 shows the areas and their bounding rectangles in the detected subtitle lines.

Since these lists have been ordered earlier by horizontal and vertical coordinates, the parameters X, Y, W, H of the bounding rectangle for the subtitle line are calculated as

$$X = \min(x_i),$$

$$Y = \min(y_i),$$

$$W = \max(x_i) - \min(x_i) + w_{x_{max}},$$

$$H = \max(y_i) - \min(y_i) + w_{y_{max}}.$$

Thus, each subtitle line is localized. The bounding rectangle for the entire subtitle area is defined in a similar way. Figure 7 shows bounding rectangles both for each detected subtitle line and for the entire subtitle area. The subtitle areas detected by the method are slightly smaller than the real areas, so we proportionally expand the calculated bounding rectangles by 5%. This allows you to more

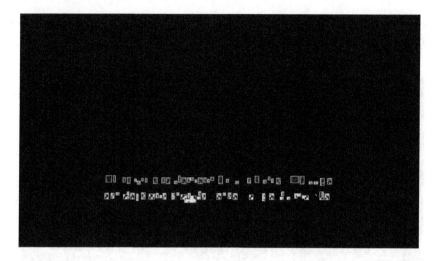

Fig. 6. The areas and their bounding rectangles in the detected subtitle lines.

accurately localize the area of subtitles. The localized image areas with subtitles are then passed on to the OCR system for recognition of the subtitle text.

a)   b)

Fig. 7. The bounding rectangles for subtitle lines and for the entire subtitle area : a) in the binary mask; b) in the the video frame.

3   Experimental Results

The proposed method for detecting and localizing embedded subtitles is implemented in C# using the EmguCV computer vision library with support for GPU platform computing. An experimental verification of the method was carried out on several videos containing embedded subtitles. The subtitles in these videos were in different parts of the frame, came in different sizes and colors, however had enough contrast. The results of localization of such subtitles are shown in Fig. 8. This figure also shows the results of processing a frame without subtitles,

Fig. 8. The results of localization of subtitles in the video stream : a), b) true subtitles localization; c) no subtitles; d) false localization text as subtitles

as well as false detection of subtitles in the frame where a text document is displayed. The throughput of the implemented method on a 2.5 GHz Intel Core i5 processor is 20 FPS without GPU support and about 46 FPS when using GPU tools. The resulting processing speed, even without using a GPU, allows you to process the video stream and extract embedded subtitles in real time.

4   Conclusion

This paper proposes a method for detection and localization of embedded subtitles in a video stream. The method is based on the search for static regions in the frames of the video stream and on the subsequent analysis of the connected areas inside these regions. Experimental results show the effectiveness of the proposed method and prove the possibility of its application in real time. However, if the video stream contains a long streak of frames displaying text documents, the method may erroneously detect text strings of these documents as subtitles. This drawback of the method can be eliminated by counting the total number of lines in the identified subtitle area and filtering this value by a given threshold.

References

1. Keechul, J., Kwang, K., Anil, J.: Text information extraction in images and video: a survey. Pattern Recogn. **37**(5), 977–997 (2004). https://doi.org/10.1016/j.patcog. 2003.10.012
2. Yin, X.-C., Zuo, Z.-Y., Tian, S., Liu, C.-L.: Text detection, tracking and recognition in video: a comprehensive survey. IEEE Trans. Image Process. **25**(6), 1–1 (2016). https://doi.org/10.1109/TIP.2016.2554321
3. Adam, C., et al.: Text detection and character recognition in scene images with unsupervised feature learning. In: 2011 International Conference on Document Analysis and Recognition (ICDAR), pp. 440–445. IEEE (2011). https://doi.org/ 10.1109/ICDAR.2011.95
4. Daehyun, K., Kwanghoon, S.: Static text region detection in video sequences using color and orientation consistencies. In: 19th International Conference on Pattern Recognition, ICPR 2008, pp. 1–4 (2008). https://doi.org/10.1109/ICPR. 2008.4761629
5. Satish, H., Suresh, V.: Character recognition of video subtitles. ICTACT J. Image Video Process. **07**(02), 1351–1356 (2016). https://doi.org/10.21917/ijivp. 2016.0196
6. Bahman, Z., Jingyue, C., Peter, W.: Instantaneously responsive subtitle localization and classification for TV applications. IEEE Trans. Consum. Electron. **57**(1), 274–282 (2011). https://doi.org/10.1109/TCE.2011.5735513
7. Felzenszwalb, P., Huttenlocher, D.: Pictorial structures for object recognition. Int. J. Comput. Vision **61**(1), 55–79 (2005). https://doi.org/10.1023/B:VISI. 0000042934.15159.49
8. Mishra, A., Alahari, K., Jawahar, C.V.: Unsupervised refinement of color and stroke features for text binarization. Int. J. Doc. Anal. Recogn. (IJDAR) **20**(2), 105–121 (2017). https://doi.org/10.1007/s10032-017-0283-9
9. Zhou, X., et al.: EAST: an efficient and accurate scene text detector. In: The IEEE Conference on Computer Vision and Pattern Recognition (CVPR) (2017)
10. Yao, C., Bai, X., Shi, B., Liu, W.: Strokelets: a learned multi-scale representation for scene text recognition. In: Proceedings of the IEEE Conference on Computer Vision and Pattern Recognition (CVPR), pp. 4042–4049 (2014)
11. Zhang, Z., Zhang, C., Shen, W., Yao, C., Liu, W., Bai, X.: Multi-oriented text detection with fully convolutional networks. In: Proceedings of the IEEE Conference on Computer Vision and Pattern Recognition (CVPR) (2016)
12. Busta, M., Neumann, L., Matas, J.: Deep textspotter: an end-to-end trainable scene text localization and recognition framework. In: 2017 IEEE International Conference on Computer Vision (ICCV), pp. 2223–2231. IEEE (2017). https:// doi.org/10.1109/ICCV.2017.242
13. Valery, G., Alexander, E., Oleg, I.: Localization of text in photorealistic images. In: Misra, S., et al. (eds.) ICCSA 2019. LNCS, vol. 11622, pp. 825–834. Springer, Cham (2019). https://doi.org/10.1007/978-3-030-24305-0_63
14. Horprasert, T., Harwood, D., Davis, L.S.: A statistical approach for real-time robust background subtraction and shadow detection. In: IEEE ICCV, vol. 99, pp. 1–19 (1999)
15. Chan, F.H.Y., Lam, F.K., Zhu, H.: Adaptive thresholding by variational method. IEEE Trans. Image Process. **7**(3), 468–473 (1998)

Distance Education Programs on the Example of Medical Education

A. A. Tikhomirova[1], A. V. Barmasov[1,2] ⓘ, A. M. Barmasova[1] ⓘ,
E. N. Stankova[1(✉)] ⓘ, and T. Yu. Yakovleva[3] ⓘ

[1] St. Petersburg State Pediatric Medical University under the Ministry of Health
of the Russian Federation, 2, Litovskaya ul., St. Petersburg 194100, Russia
tikhomirova@bk.ru, {a.barmasov,e.stankova}@spbu.ru,
abarmasova@yandex.ru
[2] St. Petersburg State University, 7-9, Universitetskaya nab.,
St. Petersburg 199034, Russia
[3] Russian State Hydrometeorological University, 98, Malookhtinsky pr.,
St. Petersburg 195196, Russia
yakovtat@yandex.ru

Abstract. This article is concerned with the use of distance education programs in medical education. The proposed approach includes the development of professionally oriented teaching, the use of multimedia lecture courses, the use of Learning Management Systems, webinars, etc.

Keywords: E-learning · Distance learning · Distance education technologies · Computer technology · Continuing medical education · Higher medical school · Multimedia lecture courses · Computer learning management system · Webinars · Teaching physics

1 Fundamentals of the Use of Distance Educational Technologies in Medical Education

The content of the training of future and current health care professionals is regulated by professional standards that guide the educational process towards the formation of stable knowledge, skills, and practical skills among students based on the results of studying a wide range of disciplines. This led to the emergence of a competency-based approach in medical education [1]. The scope of competence of employees is regulated by professional standards that define labour functions and labour activities.

There is a shortage of personnel in the Russian healthcare system, which will require significant time expenditures to overcome it. Therefore, the industry needs not just a quantitative increase in labour resources but also an increase in the quality of their training. Educational programs compiled on the basis of professional standards for medical specialties contain components aimed not only at improving knowledge, but also at increasing practical training for obtaining both medical and managerial skills.

Orientation to the formation of professional competencies dictates the need to use innovative pedagogical methods and technologies that can be implemented through

© Springer Nature Switzerland AG 2020
O. Gervasi et al. (Eds.): ICCSA 2020, LNCS 12254, pp. 129–141, 2020.
https://doi.org/10.1007/978-3-030-58817-5_11

distance learning (DL). At the present stage, it has proved its value and effectiveness as one of the most promising and rapidly developing forms of education.

Therefore, the Russian higher medical school today is also aimed at developing students' information competencies with the possibility of their full use upon completion of training. The use of e-learning and distance education technologies (DET) in the implementation of the educational process in medical universities of our country occurs within the framework of the global educational trend, but at the same time, there are features and limitations due to industry and national characteristics.

New definitions have appeared in the domestic legislative framework in the field of education: e-learning, distance educational technologies, electronic information educational environment.

E-learning is understood as the organization of the educational process using the information contained in the databases and used in the implementation of educational programs and the information processing technologies, technical means, as well as information and telecommunication networks that ensure the transmission of the specified information through communication lines, the interaction of educational process participants.

In the Federal Educational Standards of higher education, there has been a shift in emphasis on the cognitive process, the motivational component of students, since the effectiveness of this process is correlated with the cognitive activity of students.

Modern medical education should train and graduate not only professionals – professionals who are competitive in the medical services market but also creative people who can quickly adapt to changing conditions who can work independently, making decisions and taking responsibility for their actions.

Remote (distance) education technologies are educational technologies that are implemented mainly with the use of information and telecommunication networks with indirect (at a distance) interaction between students and teachers.

The strategic goal of DL is to provide the student with equal opportunities to receive education at any level at the place of residence or professional activity based on the use of information and communication technologies.

The advantages of DL include accessibility, modularity, a high degree of interactivity, dynamic access to information; the possibility of self-control; an active help system, multimedia presentation of information, the ability to study the material at an individual pace and repeated calls to it if necessary, increased motivation, high visibility, development in the learning process, lack of fear of making a mistake, choosing a personal educational path, confidentiality.

Specialists in the strategic problems of education in an environment of global informatization regard distance learning as an educational system of the 21st century. DL allows you to solve such a pressing contemporary problem as rapid information development, including in healthcare.

The electronic information and educational environment (EIEE) is a system that includes electronic information resources, electronic educational resources, and a set of information technologies, telecommunication technologies, appropriate technological means and ensuring that students learn the educational programs in full, regardless of their location. The example of typical EIEE – see Fig. 1.

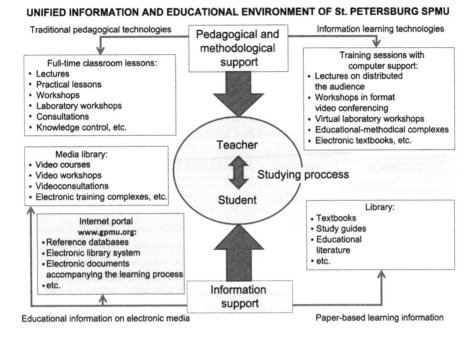

Fig. 1. Unified information and educational environment of St. Petersburg State Pediatric Medical University

World Federation for Medical Education (WFME) distinguishes two periods in the training of health care professionals: basic (undergraduate) education and postgraduate education.

The specifics of using DET in the training of medical workers is due to the fact that they can be used mainly in the implementation of theoretical training of students, therefore, within the existing periods of medical education, it is possible to distinguish the stages associated with the degree of integration of DET in them:

Stage 1: pre-university education, admission to the university (submission of documents, passing entrance examinations conducted by the university, a competition of certificates) can be implemented in full using distance technologies.

Stages 2 and 3: undergraduate and postgraduate studies can be implemented in a mixed form: theoretical courses, non-clinical disciplines, some sections of clinical disciplines, independent work using DET (for example, humanitarian, socio-economic and mathematical disciplines), the remaining disciplines in the traditional form characteristic of full-time education.

Stage 4: Continuing Medical Education (CME) involves the implementation of a well-established approach in which the educational program is modular in nature and the proportion of pre-school education in it is at least 50%. This allows you to significantly expand the possibilities of postgraduate education of medical specialists and implement the principles of the CRISIS Model, which is used in modern medicine and consists of six main components.

An acronym CRISIS means [2]:

Convenience – the convenience of training: the student of the course chooses the individual speed of the course, the place and time of training.
Relevance – relevance of the course content to the practitioner.
Individualization – individualization of training and the choice of modules that are most important for a particular student.
Self-assessment – the ability to self-test and obtain immediate results of verification tests and tasks, which allows you to pay attention to the most difficult topics for a particular listener.
Independent learning – independent learning in which the student plays the most active role.
Systematic approach – clearly structured programs and courses.

Distance learning systems provide users with a wide range of tools for implementing communication between participants in the educational process: chat, forum, blog, and conference. When creating educational content, you can use a variety of tools to solve problems of various complexity levels: from developing test tasks to creating complex multimedia courses. The students are remotely provided with methodological support; if necessary, they can communicate with the teacher in off-line and on-line modes. Also, group work can be implemented for course participants and partners to discuss, exchange views and information, present achievements through the communication capabilities of the Internet. A large amount of additional information is available to trainees remotely, which they can use during training on the course.

The control of learning outcomes is organized by the leading teacher and consultants at intermediate stages during the development by students of training materials and the final stage in the form of tests, presentations, creative assignments.

Moreover, DL is not an addition to the traditional education system, it is a special education technology based on high-quality methodological materials available regardless of the time and location of the student.

The introduction of DET leads to a change in the pedagogical paradigm: the central place in which is assigned to students, the main goal is to develop the ability to self-education; students play an active role in the educational process; the basis of the educational activity is the collaboration of the student and teacher, which entails a change in teaching methods, models of activity and the interaction of teachers and students.

DL allows you to plan, implement the educational process and manage it. Such an organization of the educational process most fully meets the global pedagogical practice in medical education, the principles of evidence-based medicine, the requirements of the standards for the provision of medical care and recommendations for the management of patients.

Specialists distinguish three organizational and technological forms of implementation of DET [3, 4].

Unit media – the use of any one training tool and channel of information transfer. The model is characterized by the use of primarily printed material as a means of training. There is practically no two-way communication, which brings this distance learning model closer to traditional distance learning.

Multimedia – the use of various teaching aids: printed material, computer programs for educational purposes on various media, audio, and video recordings, etc.

Hypermedia – a third-generation pre-release model using advanced information technologies with the dominant role of computer telecommunications [3, 4].

The international pedagogical community regards DET as a tool to eliminate the educational inequality of the inhabitants of geographically separated regions at the state level [5].

The use of e-learning and DET in the domestic higher medical school, on the one hand, is developing within the framework of world educational trends, on the other hand, it has a number of features and limitations related to industry and national specifics.

Assessing the Russian market of distance education services and e-learning, we can state the fact that it lags behind the world level, which is indirectly associated with the underdevelopment of the legislative framework, as well as the lack of a systematic approach in this area.

One of the advantages of using DET in the World is the ability at the state level to eliminate educational inequality for people living in different regions. Specialists subdivide consumers of e-learning into several categories:

- corporate consumers (organizations in which there is a need to regularly train personnel, for example, in a network of branches);
- educational organizations (state educational institutions and private companies providing educational services);
- individual consumers of e-learning.

Distance Learning Systems (DLS), in turn, are divided into:

- technological subsystems Learning Management Systems (LMS), Learning Content Management Systems (LCMS);
- subsystems of business processes that implement distance learning;
- personnel subsystems (teachers, students, specialists serving LMS).

From a strategic perspective, the development of LMS is seen as a transition to TMS (Talent Management Systems) that are aimed at the accumulation and development of human capital.

In our opinion, this transition in domestic health care is most consonant with the developing concept of CME within the framework of the paradigm "Education through the whole life".

The positive aspects of the use of DET in medical education with advanced training of health professionals include

- reduced time spent on training (no need to travel to the place of study, separation from medical practice for full-time attendance at classes);
- reduction of economic costs for the educational process (for travel, accommodation, classroom fees, teaching fees by reducing the number of teachers required);
- the opportunity to study at any time, regardless of the teacher;
- an increase in the quality of mastering educational material, the possibility of repeatedly acquainting oneself with it if necessary;

- easily implemented updating of training materials;
- transparency of the educational process;
- accessibility and efficiency of obtaining statistics on the educational process and its results.

In this case, we can talk about the formation of a transition from the traditional form of education "by necessity" to self-education "on-demand", that is, when there is a need for information, for example, in the case of a lack of clarity of the clinical picture when diagnosing a disease. In this case, the doctor himself acts as the customer of the necessary knowledge.

The situation is more complicated with the use of DET in the educational process of students of a medical university. To determine the degree of readiness of students to work with DLS by the specialists of the Department of Medical Informatics, St. Petersburg State Pediatric Medical University, a study was made of the level of students developing professional competencies regarding the use of information and communication technologies in educational activities after studying the discipline "Medical Informatics". 55 full-time students were interviewed by the face-to-face questioning method (20 people studying at the Faculty of Medicine and 35 people studying at the Faculty of Pediatrics).

The questionnaire contained the following questions

1. Do you know how to use a text editor?
2. Do you know how to use a spreadsheet editor?
3. Do you know how to use the means of creating presentations?
4. Do you use search engines in your independent work?
5. Do you use electronic library systems in your independent work?
6. Do you use the educational materials of the University's EIEE?

Each question suggested the following answer options: "yes", "find it difficult to answer" and "no".

The study showed that the vast majority of students answered positively to questions about the ability to use a text and spreadsheet editor (86.1% and 73.7%, respectively). Also, high affirmative answers (88.2%) were received on the question of the ability to use presentation creation tools. The use of search engines in independent work was indicated by 100% of respondents, but only 54.4% of them build complex search queries. The use of electronic library systems in independent work was confirmed by 58.6% of respondents. In the oral comments given by the examinees when filling out the questionnaire, it was noted that these skills are most in-demand when drawing up illustrative material in the learning process. 62.2% of the surveyed participants worked with educational materials of the University's EIEE.

At the same time, the study showed that among those who are able to build a complex search query (34.55% of all respondents), the percentage of affirmative answers to questions about the ability to use a text and spreadsheet editors and presentation creation tools was 100%. In addition, these persons were significantly more likely (93%) to use the educational materials of the University's EIEE independently, without additional tasks from teachers.

The study showed that the ability to build a complex search query in a search engine can be a marker of successful mastery of the subject "Medical Informatics" and readiness to use DET in teaching theoretical disciplines at a medical university. To confirm this hypothesis, two groups were identified: the first, which included students who answered positively to the question about the ability to build a complex search query in a search engine – 19 students, and the second group, who were difficult to answer this question – 33 students.

Students of the first group showed a positive attitude towards the subject, an understanding of the role of the formed competencies in further professional activities and a willingness to use elements of DL. Respondents in this group possessed all levels of declared skills. In the second group, a positive attitude towards the study of medical informatics also prevailed, but there was no understanding of the role of competences in further professional activity and the preference was expressed for the traditional full-time organization of classes. At the same time, 5 students (9.1% of the total composition) indicated a negative attitude to the subject.

Based on the results obtained, it can be said that for junior students of a medical university there is a problem of low demand for the use of DET, which is associated with a low level of motivation and a lack of understanding of the importance of the formation and development of competencies associated with the development of the studied disciplines. The authors attribute this to the lack of a sustainable skill in organizing and performing independent work.

2   Multimedia Lectures

Currently it is not enough to use only printed materials [6–12]. These printed publications should be supplemented with modern multimedia materials [13–15].

An important feature of the lecture courses is the combination of fundamental and profilization, which is manifested in the choice of priorities and examples of the application of physics in other fields of knowledge - in medicine, biology, geology, soil science, ecology, etc. [16].

Medical specialties (along with specialties that indirectly use medical and biological knowledge) occupy a special place among many natural science and Humanities disciplines that contain General physics in the educational process. All physiological processes occurring in the human and animal bodies are subject to physical laws. In addition, most diagnostic methods, like many therapeutic methods, are based on the use of physical phenomena and processes. Almost all medical equipment is based on physical principles and is actually a physical device. It can be argued that medicine largely uses the results of theoretical and experimental achievements in the field of physics [16].

It is possible to distinguish professionally-oriented questions in each of the sections of general physics – the main methods for determining physical quantities in medicine and biology; features of physical phenomena and processes in biology and medical practice; use in diagnostics and medical practice of physical phenomena, processes, devices (used in diagnostics and clinical practice); description of the principle of operation of modern medical devices [16].

The use of professionally-oriented physical tasks in the training of future doctors positively affects the results of students' training, contributes to the development of the creative personality of future specialists, and the formation of a student's value attitude to the medical profession. Therefore, future doctors need to know, for example, the main details of vision [17–19], proteins [20], photosynthesis [21], the influence of physical factors on the biosphere [22–25], and others [15].

The authors of this innovative approach to the development of educational and methodological support for teaching General physics to students of natural science areas of St. Petersburg State University, which consists in the profiling and interdisciplinarity of training courses, were nominated by the Academic Council of St. Petersburg State University for the Award of the Government of St. Petersburg for outstanding achievements in higher education in 2020.

Currently, it is very important to give medical students basic knowledge about telemedicine. The main goal of telemedicine is to provide medical services to remote patients who are far from medical centres and have limited access to medical services. Moreover, in the context of the COVID-19 pandemic, the widespread use of telemedicine has proven to be effective. In a situation where there are no reliable guidelines for the treatment of new diseases, consultation with specialists from medical centres becomes simply necessary. The technical basis of telemedicine is modern technologies for data transmission and reproduction, which allows video conferences and high-quality digital images to be transmitted over long distances in an effort to improve resuscitation care and speed up medical decisions [15, 26–28].

3   Learning Management Systems and E-Lab

Learning management systems (LMS) are used as a platform for creating, storing, and presenting various learning materials. The most popular LMS (Blackboard Learn and MOODLE) were considered by the authors earlier [16].

Blackboard Learn is a virtual learning environment and course management system developed by Blackboard Inc. It is Web server software that includes course management, a customizable open architecture, and a scalable design that allows it to integrate with student information systems and authentication protocols. Its main objectives are to add online elements to traditional face-to-face courses and develop fully online courses with few or no face-to-face meetings [16].

MOODLE (abbreviation for Modular Object-Oriented Dynamic Learning Environment) is a free and open-source learning management software system written in PHP and distributed under the GNU General public license. MOODLE is used for mixed learning, distance learning, and other e-learning projects in schools, universities, workplaces, and other sectors. With customizable management features, it is applicable for creating private websites with online courses for teachers and trainers to achieve learning goals. MOODLE allows you to expand and adapt learning environments using plug-ins from community sources [16].

LMS Blackboard Learn and LMS MOODLE promote effective independent work of students by providing access to electronic tutorials, manuals, by the realization of effective feedback to lecturers via interactive testing, video conferences, and on-line discussions [16]. Both distance learning systems were widely used in distance learning settings during the COVID-19 pandemic. Thus, Blackboard Learning has become the main distance learning system at St. Petersburg State University. In some cases, St. Petersburg State University also used MOODLE.

LMS MOODLE performed slightly better compared to LMS Blackboard Learn for our specific tasks in medical education. Thus, St. Petersburg State University, which initially preferred LMS Blackboard Learn, has recently started using LMS MOODLE along with this system. At the same time, it is difficult to distinguish the fundamental differences between these two systems for the purpose of medical education. Much is determined by the number of students, the financial capacity of the University, and the preferences of teachers and students.

In the context of distance learning during the COVID-19 pandemic at St. Petersburg State University and at St. Petersburg State Pediatric Medical University, real laboratory work in physics was performed by students remotely, and communication with the teacher was carried out via e-mail.

Another way to realize the idea of distance learning is the use of the informational infrastructure of a program instrumental complex for carrying out a laboratory practicum at the university (e-lab). This complex includes the instrumental part for carrying out real experiments with the available equipment, the program complex of virtual laboratory works and a document management system, enabling to produce the descriptions and reports on the laboratory practical works and to record student's progress and to estimate student's work appropriately [26].

4 Hypermedia

The continuous computerization of recent decades is changing the structure of information, the way it is used, and the nature of human thinking. Science is rapidly developing, interdisciplinary and transdisciplinary connections are emerging, and education is becoming more intensive, but this also creates new challenges. Education (thinking and textbooks) must be adapted, combining speed and flexibility with the stability and integrity of educational units. In this situation, digital educational information and the learning process itself acquire some hypertext (HT) characteristics with their pro et contra, which must be taken into account. We believe that the training course should be built around a minimalist core containing all the basic concepts, closed and self-contained, and surrounded by relatively independent HT-type structures with well-defined boundaries [29–31].

5 Conclusions

Modern medical education should be based on a global approach that emphasizes professional competence, activity, students' independence, and the ability to adapt to changing conditions of professional activity. The use of information and educational technologies and DET opens up new opportunities for the continuous training of health professionals and their retraining, making training more accessible.

Compliance with these fundamental principles will allow one to successfully assimilate training material, will contribute to the formation of a high level of intellectual and moral development of medical workers, and will ensure the specialist's competitiveness and its integration into the global professional process, mastery of communication methods and observance of bioethics rules.

The use of Web technologies in distance learning most fully meets the requirements for modern medical education and complements the existing model for training health workers.

The current set of educational services based on information and telecommunication technologies includes video lectures, webinars, distance learning courses, placement of training materials on Web sites, data exchange between tutors and students by e-mail, distance testing, etc.

The listed elements of educational content can be successfully used to organize independent work and test the knowledge of medical students in the study of theoretical disciplines.

The current need for high motivation for training and the availability of practical training makes the distance form of medical education at the present stage the most suitable for professional retraining of advanced training for specialists with a doctor's diploma.

Competition conditions in the market of medical educational services dictate high demands on the quality of the proposed educational programs and individual modules. The need for annual training of working health care professionals, which may require traveling to another region, is fraught with certain difficulties: the need for a competent replacement for the period of study, on duty, family circumstances. In this regard, it is advisable to use distance technologies to create training cycles that involve intramural and extramural modes of conduct, as well as individual remote modules.

The use of DET requires well-developed teaching materials from the creators of such courses. Moreover, the quality and success of pre-school education to a large extent depend on the effective organization, the quality of the materials used and the skill of the teachers involved in the educational process.

Undoubtedly, distance education is a self-education implemented within the framework of an educational institution, which can confirm the qualifications obtained with an appropriate education document. The specifics of preschool education is associated with the strengthening of the active role of the student in their own education with an increase in the volume of educational arrays and the heuristic component of the educational process due to interactive forms, multimedia training programs, and comfortable learning conditions.

After reviewing a number of available electronic resources and summarizing the practical teaching experience, both at the Department of Medical Informatics of the Pediatric University and at other educational institutions, the authors came to the conclusion that, despite the delay in the development of the Russian e-learning market compared to the world pace, future trends the use of e-learning and distance learning technologies in the educational process of medical universities coincide with global trends:

- mobile training;
- integration with social services (networks);
- development of Software as a Service (SAAS) solutions.

References

1. Gelman, V.Y., Tikhomirova, A.A.: Problems of IT Department in a Medical University. Educ. Sci. J. **19**(5), 153–165 (2017). https://doi.org/10.17853/1994-5639-2017-5-153-165. (in Russian)
2. Harden, R.M.: A new vision for distance learning and continuing medical education. J. Contin. Educ. Health Prof. **25**(1), 43–51 (2005)
3. Asaul, A.N., Kaparov, B.M.: Management of a higher educational institution in an innovative economy. In: Asaul, A.N. (ed.) Gumanistika, St. Petersburg, 280 p. (2007). (in Russian)
4. Malkov, V.V.: Survey of the methods of the realization of the remote educational technologies. Vestnik MGUP named after Ivan Fedorov. No. 1 (2015). (in Russian)
5. Tikhomirova, A.A.: The use of telemedicine technologies in the system of continuing medical education. Pediatrician. **8**(S1), M324–M325 (2017). (in Russian)
6. Barmasov, A.V., Kholmogorov, V.E.: Course of general physics for nature managers. In: Chirtsov, A.S. (ed.) Mechanics, BHV-St. Petersburg, St. Petersburg, 416 p. (2008, 2012). (in Russian)
7. Barmasov, A.V., Kholmogorov, V.E.: Course of general physics for nature managers. In: Bobrovsky, A.P. (ed.) Oscillations and Waves, BHV-St. Petersburg, St. Petersburg, 256 p. (2009, 2012). (in Russian)
8. Barmasov, A.V., Kholmogorov, V.E.: Course of general physics for nature managers. In: Bobrovsky, A.P. (ed.) Molecular Physics and Thermodynamics, BHV-St. Petersburg, St. Petersburg, 512 p. (2009, 2012). (in Russian)
9. Barmasov, A.V., Kholmogorov, V.E.: Course of general physics for nature managers. In: Bobrovsky, A.P. (ed.) Electricity, BHV-St. Petersburg, St. Petersburg, 448 p. (2010, 2013). (in Russian)
10. Barmasov, A.V., Barmasova, A.M., Struts, A.V., Yakovleva, T.Yu.: Dynamics of rigid body. In: Elements of the Theory and the Collection of Tasks. Publishing house of St. Petersburg State Pediatric Medical University, St. Petersburg, 28 p. (2012). (in Russian)
11. Barmasov, A.V., Barmasova, A.M., Struts, A.V., Yakovleva, T.Yu.: Processing of Results of Measurements of Physical Quantities. Publishing house of St. Petersburg State Pediatric Medical University, St. Petersburg, 92 p. (2012). (in Russian)
12. Nordling, C., Österman, J.: Physics handbook for science and engineering. In: Barmasov, A. V. (ed.) Authorized Translation from the English Language Edition, BHV-St. Petersburg, St. Petersburg, 528 p. (2011). (in Russian)
13. Bukina, M.N., Barmasov, A.V., Ivanov, A.S.: Modern teaching methods for the teaching general physics and mathematical processing of results of measurements of physical quantities. In: Modern Educational Technology in the Teaching Natural Sciences and the Humanities: Proceedings of the International Scientific-Methodical Conference, 27–29 May 2014, Mining University, St. Petersburg, 562 p. pp. 408–414 (2014). (in Russian)

14. Bukina, M.N., Barmasov, A.V., Lisachenko, D.A., Ivanov, A.S.: Modern methods of teaching physics and the concepts of modern natural science. In: Modern Educational Technologies in Teaching Natural-Scientific and Humane Disciplines: Proceedings of the II International Scientific-Methodical Conference on 09–10 April 2015. Mining University, St. Petersburg, 732 p., pp. 516–520 (2015). (in Russian)

15. Barmasova, A.M., Yakovleva, T.Yu., Barmasov, A.V., et al.: Multimedia lecture course on processing of results of measurements of physical quantities for students users. In: Spirin, G. G. (ed.) Abstracts of Scientific-Methodical Workshop on "The Physics in the Engineering Education System of the EurAsEC Member States" and the Meeting of Heads of Physics Departments of Technical Universities of Russia. The Scientific Seminar was Held from, 25–27 June 2007, Zhukovsky Air Force Engineering Academy, Moscow, 344 p., p. 42 (2007). (in Russian)

16. Stankova, E.N., Barmasov, A.V., Dyachenko, N.V., Bukina, M.N., Barmasova, A.M., Yakovleva, T.Yu.: The use of computer technology as a way to increase efficiency of teaching physics and other natural sciences. In: Gervasi, O., et al. (eds.) ICCSA 2016. LNCS, vol. 9789, pp. 581–594. Springer, Cham (2016). https://doi.org/10.1007/978-3-319-42089-9_41

17. Struts, A.V., Barmasov, A.V., Brown, M.F.: Methods for studying photoreceptors and photoactive molecules in biological and model systems: rhodopsin as a canonical representative of the seven-transmembrane helix receptors. Bulletin of St. Petersburg University. Series 4. Physics, Chemistry, No. 2, pp. 191–202 (2014). (in Russian)

18. Struts, A.V., Barmasov, A.V., Brown, M.F.: Spectral methods for study of the G-protein-coupled receptor rhodopsin. I. Vibrational and electronic spectroscopy. Opt. Spectrosc. 118 (5), 711–717 (2015). https://doi.org/10.1134/S0030400X15050240

19. Struts, A.V., Barmasov, A.V., Brown, M.F.: Spectral methods for study of the G-protein-coupled receptor rhodopsin. II. Magnetic resonance methods. Opt. Spectrosc. 120(2), 286–293 (2016). https://doi.org/10.1134/S0030400X16010197

20. Bukina, M.N., Bakulev, V.M., Barmasov, A.V., Zhakhov, A.V., Ishchenko, A.M.: Luminescence diagnostics of conformational changes of the Hsp70 protein in the course of thermal denaturation. Opt. Spectrosc. 118(6), 899–901 (2015). https://doi.org/10.1134/S0030400X15060065

21. Barmasov, A.V., Korotkov, V.I., Kholmogorov, V.Y.: Model photosynthetic system with charge transfer for transforming solar energy. Biophysics 39(2), 227–231 (1994)

22. Kholmogorov, V.Y., Barmasov, A.V.: The biosphere and physical factors. Electromagnetic fields and life. In: The Problems of Theoretical and Applied Ecology, RSHMU, St. Petersburg, 267 p., pp. 27–47 (2005). (in Russian)

23. Barmasov, A.V., Barmasova, A.M., Yakovleva, T.Yu.: The biosphere and the physical factors. Light pollution of the environment. In: Proceedings of the Russian State Hydrometeorological University, vol. 33, pp. 84–101 (2014). (in Russian)

24. Yakovleva, T.Yu., Barmasova, A.M., Barmasov, A.V.: The biosphere and the physical factors. Possible hazards of wide application of white LEDs. In: The World Science and Education in Contemporary Society: Collection of Scientific Works on Materials of the International Scientific-Practical Conference, 30 October 2014, Part III. OOO "AR-Consult", Moscow, pp. 42–50 (2014). (in Russian)

25. Barmasov, A.V., Barmasova, A.M., Yakovleva, T.Yu.: The biosphere and physical factors. The geomagnetic field. In: Modern Trends in the Development of Science and Technology, vol. 3–4, pp. 127–131 (2015). (in Russian)

26. Dyachenko, N.V., Barmasov, A.V., Stankova, E.N., Struts, A.V., Barmasova, A.M., Yakovleva, T.Yu.: Prototype of informational infrastructure of a program instrumentation complex for carrying out a laboratory practicum on physics in a university. In: Gervasi, O., et al. (eds.) ICCSA 2017. LNCS, vol. 10408, pp. 412–427. Springer, Cham (2017). https://doi.org/10.1007/978-3-319-62404-4_30

27. Bobrovsky, A.P., Dyachenko, N.V., Barmasov, A.V., et al.: Electronic lab for laboratory workshop on physics at the university. In: Interuniversity Collection of Scientific Works "Information Technologies and Systems: Management, Economics, Transport, Law, vol. 2 (20)/Ed. Doctor of Technical Sciences, Prof. Istomin E.P. – SPb: Andreevsky Publishing House LLC, 150 p., pp. 36–48 (2017). (in Russian)

28. Barmasov, A.V., Barmasova, A.M., Klikunova, K.A., Struts, A.V.: Medical electronics. Physical Methods in Medicine. SPb: Publishing house of SPbGPMU (2020, Prepared for publication). (in Russian)

29. Lisachenko, D.A., Barmasov, A.V., Bukina, M.N., Stankova, E.N., Vysotskaya, S.O., Zarochentseva, E.P.: Best practices combining traditional and digital technologies in education. In: Gervasi, O., et al. (eds.) ICCSA 2017. LNCS, vol. 10408, pp. 483–494. Springer, Cham (2017). https://doi.org/10.1007/978-3-319-62404-4_36

30. Barmasov, A.V., Barmasova, A.M., Stankova, E.N., Bukina, M.N., Lisachenko, D.A., Vysotskaya, S.O.: Modern approach to creating university learning courses: using network ideas for creating a hypertext (on example of courses on physics and concepts of modern science). In: Misra, S., et al. (eds.) ICCSA 2019. LNCS, vol. 11622, pp. 655–666. Springer, Cham (2019). https://doi.org/10.1007/978-3-030-24305-0_48

31. Barmasov, A.V., Barmasova, A.M., Bukina, M.N., et al.: The experience of combining traditional and computer technologies in the teaching of physics in higher education In: Modern Educational Technologies in the Training of Specialists for the Mineral Resource Complex: Proceedings of the III All-Russian Scientific Conference, 5–6 March 2020, Mining University, St. Petersburg, pp. 462–468 (2020). (in Russian)

The Impact of CPU Frequency Scaling on Power Consumption of Computing Infrastructures

Adriano M. Garcia[1]($\boxtimes$) [ID], Matheus Serpa[2] [ID], Dalvan Griebler[1] [ID], Claudio Schepke[3] [ID], Luiz G. L. Fernandes[1] [ID], and Philippe O. A. Navaux[2] [ID]

[1] Pontifical Catholic University of Rio Grande do Sul (PUCRS), Porto Alegre, RS, Brazil
adriano.garcia@edu.pucrs.br, dalvan.griebler@acad.pucrs.br,
luiz.fernandes@pucrs.br
[2] Informatics Institute, Federal University of Rio Grande do Sul (UFRGS), Porto Alegre, RS, Brazil
{msserpa,navaux}@inf.ufrgs.br
[3] Federal University of Pampa (UNIPAMPA), Alegrete, RS, Brazil
claudioschepke@unipampa.edu.br

Abstract. Since the demand for computing power increases, new architectures emerged to obtain better performance. Reducing the power and energy consumption of these architectures is one of the main challenges to achieving high-performance computing. Current research trends aim at developing new software and hardware techniques to achieve the best performance and energy trade-offs. In this work, we investigate the impact of different CPU frequency scaling techniques such as **ondemand**, **performance**, and **powersave** on the power and energy consumption of multi-core based computer infrastructure. We apply these techniques in PAMPAR, a parallel benchmark suite implemented in PThreads, OpenMP, MPI-1, and MPI-2 (spawn). We measure the energy and execution time of 10 benchmarks, varying the number of threads. Our results show that although **powersave** consumes up to 43.1% less power than **performance** and **ondemand** governors, it consumes the triple of energy due to the high execution time. Our experiments also show that the **performance** governor consumes up to 9.8% more energy than **ondemand** for CPU-bound benchmarks. Finally, our results show that PThreads has the lowest power consumption, consuming less than the sequential version for memory-bound benchmarks. Regarding performance, the **performance** governor achieved 3% of performance over the **ondemand**.

This research received funding from Coordenação de Aperfeiçoamento de Pessoal de Nivel Superior - Brasil (CAPES) - Finance Code 001, FAPERGS 01/2017-ARD project PARAELASTIC (N° 17/2551-0000871-5), FAPERGS 05/2019-PQG project PARAS (N° 19/2551-0001895-9), and Universal MCTIC/CNPq N° 28/2018 project SPARCLOUD (No. 437693/2018-0). It has also been supported by National Council for Scientific and Technological Development (CNPq) and Green Cloud project (2016/2551-0000 488-9), from FAPERGS and CNPq Brazil, program PRONEX 12/2014.

© Springer Nature Switzerland AG 2020
O. Gervasi et al. (Eds.): ICCSA 2020, LNCS 12254, pp. 142–157, 2020.
https://doi.org/10.1007/978-3-030-58817-5_12

Keywords: PAMPAR · CPU Frequency Governors · Power consumption

1 Introduction

Nowadays, governments are imposing limits on the power and energy consumption for supercomputing infrastructures [5]. The consequence is that different supercomputer manufacturers are making an effort to reduce this consumption [24]. The list of the world's most energy-efficient supercomputers called the Green500 [5] has been showing significant changes in the latest results. The USA and some countries in Europe that led the Top500 (the 500 most powerful supercomputers) are not reaching good positions in the Green500. However, that scenario has changed in the past two years. These countries have begun to make investments in Computational Science to improve the energy efficiency of their supercomputing infrastructures and now they lead the Green500 list [5]. Therefore, ways of reducing energy consumption without losing computational performance are widely discussed today.

Computer performance is the amount of useful work accomplished by a computer system [20]. This amount can be increased using parallel programming. To achieve performance with parallel programming, it is necessary to use different processing units to execute different parts of a program concurrently. However, a program does not run 100% in parallel. At a certain part of the execution, these parties need to communicate to exchange information. This happens at least once at the beginning and again at the end of the program. This communication can occur either through access to shared memory addresses or through the exchange of messages. The problem is that these communication operations can cause extra energy expenditure. While parallelism allows for increased program performance, the need for task-to-task communication can impact the power and energy consumption [23]. Thus, although parallelism allows performance gains, this can lead to higher power and energy consumption. This power and energy consumption grows mainly according to the number of processors that are used in parallel and the volume of communication among them. This increase may present a significant impact on the power and energy consumption of supercomputing infrastructures. On the other hand, the reduction in execution time allowed by the parallelization causes a decrease in the total energy consumption in some cases.

Parallelism techniques can be implemented in a program using Parallel Programming Interfaces (PPIs). Some PPIs are best suited for specific languages, platforms, and architectures. Some interfaces use memory to communicate among different parallel tasks for programs running on processors that share memory regions. For programs that will run on a distributed architecture, some PPIs do the communication through the exchange of messages, such as Message Passing Interface (MPI). In addition to these main features, several other factors and peculiarities of each PPI can impact the performance of a parallel program. One of these factors is the frequency of the processor, which is adjusted through different governors. These governors can prioritize performance or energy consumption. These governors can set the processor frequency at maximum (more performance) and minimum (more power savings).

As seen, many factors can impact the performance, power and energy consumption of parallel programs. It is necessary to understand better the role that different PPIs play when used with variations in processor frequency. With this understanding, it is possible to find the best trade-offs between performance, power and energy consumption. Contributing to this subject, this paper evaluates the power and energy consumption of different parallel programming interfaces using different CPU governors. We evaluate the behavior of the PPIs with the governor's ondemand, performance, and powersave. These governors were chosen because they can highlight the characteristics of the parallel applications. The goal of our work is to show the impact of different PPIs and applications on the power and energy consumption and performance varying the governor policies of the processor (ondemand, performance, and powersave) and find out how it is impacted according to specific application characteristics.

To achieve the goal, in this paper, we run the PAMPAR[1] suite [8] changing the governor settings. PAMPAR consists of 13 parallel benchmarks developed to evaluate the performance and energy consumption of PPIs. Despite the serial code, each benchmark is implemented using well-known PPIs in the Computational Science field, such as PThreads, OpenMP, MPI-1, and MPI-2 (dynamic process spawn). The authors of the suite ran experiments to measure the performance and energy consumption of PAMPAR benchmarks to estimate the power and energy consumption of the PPIs without regard to the CPU-enabled governor [9,10]. In this paper, we explore this gap.

The remainder of this work is organized as follows. In Sect. 2, we introduce the governors for frequency scaling and present more details about the benchmark selection. Section 3 shows how our experiments were structured and bring some information to a better understanding of the results. Section 4 discusses the results. The related works are discussed in Sect. 5 and, finally, Sect. 6 draws the final considerations and future works.

2   Background

2.1   CPU Frequency Scaling Governors

The CPU frequency scaling allows the operating system to increase or decrease the CPU frequency to save power [15]. CPU frequencies can be scaled automatically depending on the system load, in response to ACPI (Advanced Configuration and Power Interface) events, or manually by the user. CPU frequency scaling is implemented in the Linux kernel, and the infrastructure is called CPUFreq. Since kernel 3.4, the required modules are loaded automatically, and the ondemand governor is activated by default. However, other governors can be enabled, such as powersave, performance, userspace, or conservative. Each

---

[1] https://github.com/adrianomg/PAMPAR.

governor has its unique behavior, purpose, and suitability in terms of workload [18]. In this paper, we evaluate performance, power and energy consumption. In this way, we investigate the ondemand, performance, and powersave governors.

The ondemand is a dynamic governor that uses CPU load as a metric to select the CPU frequency. It measures the time elapsed between consecutive invocations of its worker routine and computes the fraction of that time in which the given CPU was not idle. This way, it can estimate the current CPU load. The ratio of the active time (non-idle) to the total CPU time is taken as an estimate of the load. In our work, this governor is attached to a policy shared by multiple CPUs, so the load is estimated for all of them, and the best result is used as the load estimate for the entire policy.

To achieve the highest possible clock frequency by the CPU, the governor performance can be enabled. Once enabled, the highest frequency will be set statically and will not change. It is indicated for cases in which the CPU will deal with a heavy workload or will be rarely idle, at least. That is because this particular governor is opposed to the power saving benefit.

Contrary to performance, the powersave governor forces the processor to use the lowest possible clock frequency. Once activated, the operation of this governor is similar to performance. However, in this case, the lowest frequency will be statically adjusted and will not change. Therefore, as expected, this particular governor offers maximum power savings, but at the cost of lower CPU performance.

2.2 Benchmark

The objective of this work is to investigate the impact of different CPU governors and PPIs on power and energy consumption. However, it is difficult to find a well-known benchmark suite that offers a diverse set of benchmarks implemented with several PPIs for general-purpose architectures. The most parallel suites do not offer a set of benchmarks representing diverse domains and fully parallelized in many PPIs (e.g., NPB, PARSEC, Rodinia, etc.). Most of them implement no more than a couple of PPIs or only small subsets in different PPIs, and these subsets do not always match the same benchmarks.

This way, we looked for any other benchmark suite that could be suitable for our goals. Thus, we found PAMPAR. It is a new parallel benchmark suite with 13 C/C++ benchmarks from many domains, such as physics, engineering, chemistry, image processing, pattern recognition, biological simulation, linear algebra, etc. The suite consists of 3 micro benchmarks, seven kernels, and three pseudo-applications. They were developed to establish a relationship between performance and energy consumption in embedded systems and general-purpose architectures [9]. The main factor that makes PAMPAR suitable for our work is that all benchmarks on the suite are parallelized in 4 PPIs: PThreads, OpenMP, MPI-1, and MPI-2. These PPIs are also the target of this work because they are the most widespread in the Computational Science field. Besides this, they are supported by most multicore based infrastructures, both embedded and general-purpose.

3   Methodology

The experiments were carried out on a computer equipped with 2 Intel® Xeon® Silver 4116 processors. Each processor has 12 physical cores operating at the 2.1 GHz frequency 3 GHz turbo frequency. Its memory system consists of three levels of cache: a 32 KB L1i and 32 KB L1d cache and a 1 MB cache L2 for each core. Level L3 has a 16.5 MB cache shared between all cores using Smart Cache technology. The main memory (RAM) is 96 GB in size and DDR4 technology. The operating system is Linux Debian kernel version 4.19.0-8 using GNU GCC 9.3 compiler with -O2 optimization flag, OpenMP 4.5, and OpenMPI 3.1.3. This machine represents a node in a large supercomputing infrastructure.

PAMPAR benchmark was used for the experiments. We selected the Medium workload class. This class includes 2048 × 2048 input matrices for benchmarks that use matrices, for instance. To increase the accuracy of experiments, the results presented in Sect. 4 are the average of 10 executions of each benchmark. The results graphs show the average energy consumption values and the 95% confidence intervals according to the Student's t-distribution [19]. During the experiments, the computer remained locked to ensure that other applications did not interfere with the results.

The benchmarks deployed with MPI-2 begin the execution with a single process. Then, this process (parent process) invokes new child processes that do not need to be identical to the parent. After creating a child process, it will belong to an intra-communicator, and the communication between parent and child will occur through this communicator.

The Intel® Performance Counter Monitor (PCM) 2.0 toolkit was used to measure energy consumption [13]. It has a tool to monitor the power states of the processor and DRAM memory. This way, the total energy consumption is the sum of the energy required by the DRAM modules and core domains (CPU and cache memories). For the execution time, the time in the beginning and the end of each benchmark's main function was measured using the GNU time library, and the difference of these values was used.

4   Results

4.1   Power and Energy Consumption

In this section, we present the energy consumption results of PAMPAR benchmarks and their PPIs impact over different governors for the CPUs. Figure 1, Table 1 and Fig. 2 show the results for different benchmarks. The figures are charts, where facets are different governors, and bars are the energy consumption in joules for each PPI. Each chart displays the results by benchmarks individually. These results refer to running using two, six, and twelve parallel threads/processes for each case. Also, a dashed horizontal line represents the sequential result of the respective benchmark.

In Fig. 1 and Table 1 are presented results for the CPU-bound benchmarks. The exception is DJ, JA, and MM benchmarks that are not fully CPU-bound, as they do a bit more memory access, but not enough to be classified as highly memory-bound. These results show that powersave governor consumes the triple of energy than ondemand and performance, on average. For all the results that present this behavior, this difference is reduced as the number of parallel tasks increases. However, since the execution time of performance and ondemand are low, they present higher power consumption results. Moreover, it shows that performance governor consumes 4.8% more energy than ondemand due to its high frequency used per core. For CPU-bound benchmarks using ondemand governor on this infrastructure, great power and energy consumption savings are not expected because this kind of application requires high computing power in most of its execution time.

Moreover, looking more closely at PPI behavior, it is possible to observe that ondemand has less impact on OpenMP and PThreads than MPI-1 and MPI-2. For OpenMP and PThreads the performance governor consumes 1.4% and 2.2% more energy, while for MPI-1 and MPI-2, it is 4.8% and 9.7%. The difference in these PPIs can be explained in the context of threads and processes. Threads are often a lighter type of process for the system, while processes are heavier. A thread shares with other threads its code area, data, and operating system resources. Because of this sharing, the operating system needs to deal with less scheduling costs and thread creation, when compared to context switching by processes—all of these factors impact performance and, consequently, on energy. Also, in a larger infrastructure using distributed processing, it would impact much more.

The DJ benchmark shows the highest energy savings using ondemand and performance over the powersave governor, about three times less. Using 12 threads, performance governor consumed 12.5% more energy for OpenMP than ondemand. We can also see that the tendency of powersave to consume triple the energy with two threads, is not confirmed with 12 threads, where the consumption does not reach double. For DFT and HA the performance energy consumption overhead varies from 2.7% to 5.1%. The MM presents an unusual behavior, that is, for this benchmark powersave governor consumes less than twice the energy consumed by ondemand and performance. We hypothesize that once this benchmark mixes computation with memory operations, which would execute in a low frequency, the ondemand governor takes a wrong decision, decreasing cores frequency when the maximum frequency would be more effective.

The DP benchmark using ondemand and performance governors show a different PThreads behavior regarding the other PPIs with low number of parallel tasks. With six and twelve threads, PThreads follows the pattern that is seen in most CPU-Bound benchmarks. However, using two threads, this consumption exceeds the consumption of other PPIs. The other three PPIs follow the

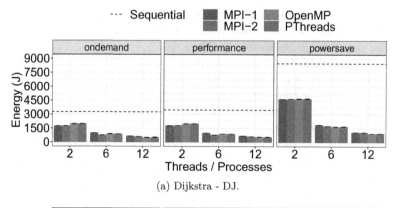

(a) Dijkstra - DJ.

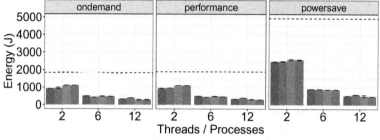

(b) Disc. Fourier Transf. - DFT.

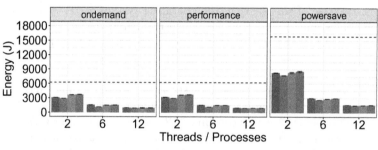

(c) Harmonic Sums - HA.

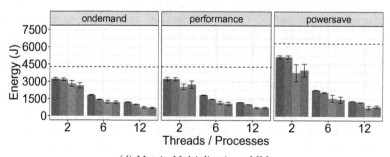

(d) Matrix Multiplication - MM.

Fig. 1. Energy consumption for CPU-bound benchmarks.

Table 1. Energy consumption for CPU-bound benchmarks (joules).

Threads/Processes		MPI-1		MPI-2		OpenMP		Pthreads	
		6	12	6	12	6	12	6	12
DP	Ondemand	402.27	265.15	360.08	369.75	319.62	170.74	341.62	211.31
	Performance	403.75	267.18	368.12	367.18	349.15	181.30	352.35	224.13
	Powersave	729.65	412.03	738.71	502.54	572.84	304.51	681.68	362.36
NI	Ondemand	236.80	161.16	253.27	266.56	207.56	122.93	189.58	112.40
	Performace	237.99	161.36	262.37	267.10	208.15	134.47	190.25	120.06
	Powersave	447.07	260.23	474.71	356.52	417.31	222.03	380.96	202.09
PI	Ondemand	415.34	268.92	382.37	380.02	387.84	218.55	387.76	229.41
	Performace	413.46	269.70	390.60	383.34	384.41	228.39	386.86	233.60
	Powersave	789.08	443.19	792.24	519.20	755.86	405.23	759.45	405.47

pattern by increasing the number of threads, where MPI-2 consumes less energy than MPI-1 and OpenMP. This behavior is not the same for performance and powersave.

Table 1 shows the results of energy consumption of DP, NI and PI benchmarks. They are three CPU-bound micro-benchmarks that perform simple iterative operations. We present the values in a table because the graphs were very similar for differences to be noticed. In this table it can be seen that ondemand and performance consumed almost the same amount of energy with MPI-1 and MPI-2. But OpenMP and PThreads showed differences between these two governors. In DP Pthreads with 6 threads, ondemenand consumed 3.2% less energy than the performance governor. Using 12 threads, performance consumed 6.2% more energy. Regarding NI OpenMP with 12 threads, performance consumed 9.8% more energy than ondemand. The powersave governor showed the same behavior seen in the previous benchmarks.

MM shows similar behavior to DP in performance and ondemand, but for both MPI PPIs. The consumption of these two PPIs grows at a higher rate than the other PPIs as the number of threads increases. The difference in this benchmark is that OpenMP also uses more power than both MPI PPIs. For two threads, the rate of increase is not as high as PThreads, but for six and twelve, it consumes the same or more. Also, using MPI-1 and MPI-2, this benchmark was the one that most approached the consumption of the sequential version among the CPU-Bound benchmarks.

In the memory-bound benchmarks (Fig. 2), it is possible to observe that ondemand has a high impact on Pthreads. For MPI-1, MPI-2, and OpenMP, performance governor consumes 1.8%, 2.7%, and 2.3% less energy, respectively, while for Pthreads, it consumes up to 14.3% less, which represents 27.8% of power increase. The GS and JA benchmarks show the highest energy consumption for MPI. On average, performance governor consumes 13.8% and 11.4% more power, respectively, while for other memory-bound benchmarks, it represents less than 7.2%. Powersave governor has almost the same behavior as for CPU-bound benchmarks. It consumes 43.1% less power than performance governor and 37.9% less than ondemand. It is expected, as memory-bound benchmarks consume most of its time in-memory operations and the workloads we use to fit into the infrastructure's cache memory. So these benchmarks generally do not need to access main memory, which would be more costly in terms of energy.

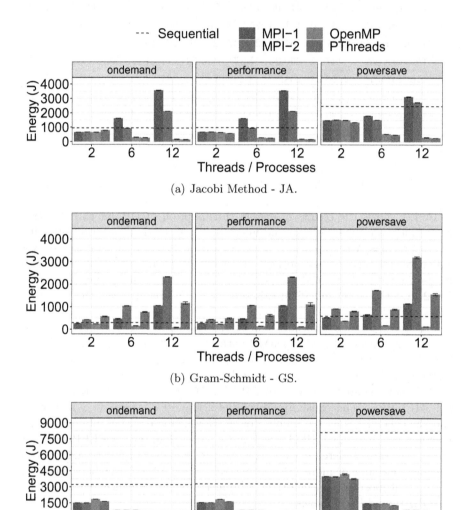

(a) Jacobi Method - JA.

(b) Gram-Schmidt - GS.

(c) Turing Ring - TR.

Fig. 2. Energy consumption for memory-bound benchmarks.

This way, the powersave takes advantage through the decrease in the CPU frequencies while these memory operations are done. The low power consumption by PThreads in memory-bound benchmarks does not represent that the total power consumed was lower in this PPI. As next section will show, the execution time and the energy consumption are higher than OpenMP. A low power consumption means that the benchmark consumed less energy over time, but that time was higher than OpenMP. It means that PThreads has a lower overhead caused by parallelization over OpenMP. In fact, for all memory-bound benchmarks, OpenMP uses about two and three times more memory than PThreads [9].

On the other hand, PThreads have approximately ten times more cache misses than other PPIs in memory-bound benchmarks [9]. In this way, the execution of PThreads takes more time, but the use of hardware in this period is less intense about the other PPIs, which implies in lower consumption of energy over time. This increase in execution time can be caused by busy waiting for PThreads.

JA and GS with OpenMP reach a high energy consumption with MPI. They are memory-bound benchmarks, so the overhead of communication and synchronization among threads begins to impact negatively. With MPI-1 and MPI-2, the results indicates that, despite the total energy, the power consumption are very similar to the results of CPU-bound benchmarks. The growth of power consumption as the number of parallel processes increases follows the same pattern previously observed. It is perceived that MPI-2 has a lower consumption than MPI-1 in most cases for both CPU and memory-bound. This small difference may be caused by dynamic process creation. This causes processes to be created later in MPI-2.

Another observed factor is that PThreads access less the memory system during synchronization. This means that for memory-bound programs parallelized using PThreads, this processor we used is a good choice since it provides considerable performance improvements at the same price in energy consumption. For CPU-bound programs, the power consumption for each PPI is very similar. The impact of particular characteristics of each communication model on the memory system is reduced as the benchmarks use more CPU.

4.2 Performance

Regarding performance, the benchmark showed similar behavior for the three governors across all CPU-bound benchmarks, and the same occurred for memory-bound benchmarks. Thus, we only present representative tests from HA, TR, and MM using twelve parallel threads/processes for the sake of space. They represent CPU-Bound (CPU-B), memory-bound (WMEM-B), and weakly memory-bound (WMEM-B) benchmarks, respectively. The results are presented in Fig. 3.

In CPU-bound benchmarks the governor performace achieved a maximum performance of only 3% over the ondemand. That happens because these benchmarks will run most of the time on the CPU. It means that the ondemand

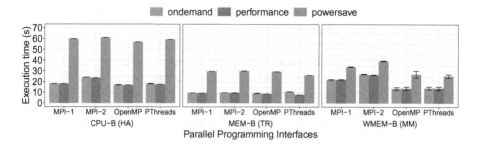

Fig. 3. Execution time using twelve parallel threads/processes.

governor can perform well because it will operate most of the time at the highest frequency. Regarding the powersave governor, it is possible to draw a relationship with the result of power and energy. The powersave consumed about three times the energy compared to other governors. The same behavior occurs the other way around with the execution time, which shows that powersave spends approximately the triple of the time running CPU-bound benchmarks.

The memory-bound benchmarks are represented by TR (MEM-B on Fig. 3). In this type of benchmark the ondemand governor does not perform as closely as performance for PThreads, as seen in CPU-bound benchmarks. This shows the impact that is switching on frequency levels causes each time a benchmark goes into memory operations. This pattern is seen in weakly memory-bound benchmarks, as well. MPI-2 presents the same behavior of CPU-bound benchmarks, with powersave spending around the triple of time to compute. What causes this behavior is the need for communication among threads by TR. In MPI-2, these communications go through an inter-communicator that links the main process with the dynamically created ones. It increases the cost of each communication operation. TR is characterized as one of the benchmarks that do most communication operations [16]. Each process does one communication operation for each element of the input vector. In our test case, that means 96 thousand exchange data operations using a 2048 × 2048 input matrix and twelve threads. Therefore, all these characteristics together causes the ondemand to lose performance over the performance governor. Regarding threads, it impacts more in PThreads than OpenMP, which uses directives to improve communication. For MPI-2, the need for an inter-communicator also impacts negatively.

For the last, MM is representing weakly memory-bound benchmarks (WMEM-B on Fig. 3). These benchmarks are weakly memory-bound because they spend most of their time on the CPU but still make a considerable amount of memory accesses. The other two benchmarks in this category are DJ and JA. DJ was not much affected by the change of governors and showed similar behavior to the CPU-bound benchmarks. That is because the DJ looks for paths between nodes in a sparse matrix and does not have to read and write for each value. MM, on the other hand, accesses three arrays to do read and write operations, needing to do more accesses than DJ. Thus, the matrix access pattern in the benchmark source code shows that MM has an access pattern that increases cache misses (by changing the j and k indexes). The overhead presented by MPI-1 and MPI-2 in this benchmark shows that the power governor did not increase execution time over the other two in MPI-2. In other PPIs, the difference was also much smaller compared to that seen in CPU-bound benchmarks. Therefore MM's pattern of memory access has had a significant impact on execution time with ondemand and performance governors.

The performance results show that the amount of memory access and communication operations are the biggest influences on the performance using different CPU governors. For benchmarks that do many memory-accesses, CPU governors do not define specific behavior and vary depending on how memory-bound the benchmark is. While ondemand and performance achieved almost 70% performance over powersave in CPU-bound and memory-bound benchmarks, for the weakly memory-bound benchmarks this performance gain is around 30%. Thus, using frequency scaling only on the CPU may not make much difference when using highly memory-bound benchmarks. To improve the performance of this type of benchmark through governors, it is necessary to balance the use of frequency scaling in memory. This scenario would probably change a lot if we used a larger supercomputing infrastructure. The MPI benchmarks would require to communicate through the network, which is a costly operation for the infrastructure.

5 Related Work

The impact of frequency scaling governors is widely discussed. However, few studies evaluate the performance, power and energy consumption of parallel benchmarks using different governors.

Dzhagaryan and Milenković [7] evaluated how the number of threads and frequency scaling impact the energy consumption of multicore based infrastructure. The authors used PThreads benchmarks from the PARSEC benchmark for the experiments. They concluded that for an Intel® Xeon® processor 1240 v2 a frequency between 2.8 and 3.0 GHz gives the best trade-off between performance, power and energy consumption.

Jiang C. [14] attempted to find a relationship between multicore processor frequency levels and application performance. The author tested a couple of benchmarks (PI Calculation and File Compression) with different workloads. However, he did not evaluate parallel benchmarks, which reduces the contribution of evaluating a multicore based infrastructure.

Ibrahim et al. [12] investigated the impact of dynamically scaling the frequency of compute nodes on the performance and energy consumption of a Hadoop cluster infrastructure. They ran the PUMA benchmark and another couple of distributed programs using different governors. The paper does not exploit parallelism.

Catalán et al. [3] evaluated the energy efficiency of dense linear algebra routines using low-power multicore processors and analyzed whether the potential energy reduction achieved when scaling the processor to operate at a low voltage compensates the cost of integrating a fault tolerance mechanism. The authors used matrix-vector and matrix-matrix multiplication kernels using the BLIS framework. The authors did not exploit TLP or different PPIs.

Teng et al. [17] propose a set of algorithms that use compile-time information to achieve energy efficiency by frequency scaling control at run-time. The authors concluded that in a power-saving configuration, the memory-intensive benchmarks achieved better performance over CPU-intensive.

Chadha and Gerndt [4] implemented an energy-aware tuning plugin for DVFS based on a neural network. This neural network was trained using various OpenMP, MPI, and hybrid benchmarks. The authors did not exploit TLP or PPIs. In our work, we evaluate the impact of each application's characteristics, but we also assess the impact of different PPIs on power, energy and performance.

Oliveira et al. [2] proposed an automatic and non-intrusive framework to optimize parallel applications implemented with OpenMP, at the static time, by selecting the ideal number of threads and CPU frequency level to execute each parallel region. This framework consists of an optimization algorithm based on a genetic algorithm that optimizes the trade-off between performance and energy consumption. For the experiments, the authors used eight benchmarks parallelized with OpenMP, five of them from the NAS Parallel Benchmarks. The paper does not exploit the impact of the characteristics of the benchmarks and evaluates only OpenMP.

Almatouq et al. [1] propose an optimization technique that balances performance and energy consumption by applying a joint control of core, resource, and frequency scaling. The technique was validated using benchmarks from the PARSEC benchmark. Although the benchmarks are evaluated individually, the authors did not exploit TLP or PPI characteristics.

It is assumed that execution time and energy consumption behave in a non-linear manner concerning frequency scaling. Based on that, Rauber and Rünger [21] proposed a scheduling process to independent tasks assignment and frequency scaling selection to improve efficiency. The experiments were done for the SPEC CPU benchmarks. The authors only exploited parallelism for independent sequential tasks.

Sheikh et al. [22] use genetic algorithms to find the best trade-offs for energy, performance, and temperature using a DVFS-based algorithm. The experiments were carried over five parallel benchmarks, and the authors evaluated the application characteristics and multiple TLP. However, they did not investigate the PPI impact on the computing infrastructure.

Marques et al. [6] investigated how multidimensional frequency scaling (CPU, RAM, and L2 cache) can improve Energy-Delay Product (EDP) in multicore embedded systems. They used nine parallel benchmarks from different benchmark suites, but do not mention any particular PPI.

Lorenzon et al. [16] ran the same benchmarks that make up the PAMPAR suite to find significant trade-offs between performance and energy in different architectures. The results showed that there is no single best case with higher performance and lower energy consumption. However, the author evaluated divided the benchmarks into CPU-bound and memory-bound and evaluated these two groups as if all the benchmarks were one, presenting unified results for each group. In this work, we evaluate each benchmark individually and also evaluate the impact of CPU governors.

All of the aforementioned related work evaluates the relationship between performance and power in multicore processors. However, the works which use parallel applications in experiments do not necessarily focus on exploring details of parallelism, such as varying the number of parallel threads or addressing a particular PPI. Nevertheless, none of them investigated the impact of using different PPIs. Also, some of them do not investigate the impact of each benchmark characteristics properly. In our work, we do an energy consumption assessment of 4 PPIs using 10 parallel benchmarks and varying the number of parallel threads/processes. We evaluated the impact of three different governors for frequency scaling and how these governors behaved according to the benchmarks and PPI characteristics.

6   Conclusions and Future Work

In this paper, we evaluated the power and energy consumption and performance of different CPU frequency scaling techniques such as `ondemand`, `performance`, and `powersave` on multicore based computer infrastructure. We applied the techniques in the PAMPAR parallel benchmark, a set of benchmarks to evaluate the performance and energy consumption of PPIs. We show the power and energy consumption of 10 benchmarks written in PThreads, OpenMP, MPI-1, and MPI-2, popular PPIs in the Computational Science area, varying the number of threads/processes and the CPU governors.

Our experimental results showed that the power and energy consumption has an increasing rate proportional to the number of threads/processes used in parallel. Moreover, we demonstrated that `powersave` consumes the triple of energy and up to 43.1% less power than `performance` and `ondemand` governors. The `performance` governor consumes 9.7% more power than `ondemand` for CPU-bound and 27.8% for memory-bound benchmarks. Another important factor to observe is that the way each benchmark communicates in MPI could make the power and energy consumption to be higher in large computing infrastructure. This impact shows up on the performance, as well. Benchmarks that do many memory-accesses or exchange data operations tend to reduce the performance gains with the `powersave` governor. Although these factors impact less on the `performance` and `powersave` governors, there is no trade-off between performance, energy, and power by using these governors because they are too strict for only one goal.

In the future, we intend to verify how the distribution of threads/processes to different cores and processors affects our experiments. Experiments using more nodes and a more extensive distributed supercomputing infrastructure would be necessary to improve the analysis over the MPI PPI. We also consider evaluating real-world benchmarks and other PPIs such as Intel TBB or UPC, for instance, the NAS Benchmarks [11].

References

1. Almatouq, M.: Performance and power optimization for multi-core systems using multi-level scaling. Ph.D. thesis, University of California, Irvine (2019)
2. De Oliveira, C.C., Lorenzon, A.F., Beck, A.C.S.: Automatic tuning TLP and DVFS for EDP with a non-intrusive genetic algorithm framework. In: 2018 VIII Brazilian Symposium on Computing Systems Engineering (SBESC), pp. 146–153, November 2018. https://doi.org/10.1109/SBESC.2018.00029
3. Catalán, S., Herrero, J.R., Quintana-Ortí, E.S., Rodríguez-Sánchez, R.: Energy balance between voltage-frequency scaling and resilience for linear algebra routines on low-power multicore architectures. Parallel Comput. **73**, 28–39 (2018)
4. Chadha, M., Gerndt, M.: Modelling DVFS and UFS for region-based energy aware tuning of HPC applications. In: 2019 IEEE International Parallel and Distributed Processing Symposium (IPDPS), pp. 805–814, May 2019. https://doi.org/10.1109/IPDPS.2019.00089
5. Dongarra, J., Meuer, H., Strohmaier, E.: Green500 Supercomputer, June 2019. https://www.top500.org/green500/. Accessed 28 June 2019
6. dos Santos Marques, W., de Souza, P.S.S., Lorenzon, A.F., Beck, A.C.S., Beck Rutzig, M., Diniz Rossi, F.: Improving EDP in multi-core embedded systems through multidimensional frequency scaling. In: 2017 IEEE International Symposium on Circuits and Systems (ISCAS), pp. 1–4, May 2017. https://doi.org/10.1109/ISCAS.2017.8050515
7. Dzhagaryan, A., Milenković, A.: Impact of thread and frequency scaling on performance and energy in modern multicores: a measurement-based study. In: Proceedings of the 2014 ACM Southeast Regional Conference, p. 14. ACM (2014)
8. Garcia, A.M.: Towards a Benchmark for Performance and Power Consumption Evaluation of Parallel Programming Interfaces. Master's thesis, Universidade Federal do Pampa (2016)
9. Garcia, A.M., Schepke, C., Girardi, A.: PAMPAR: a new parallel benchmark for performance and energy consumption evaluation. Concurrency and Computation: Practice and Experience (2019). https://doi.org/10.1002/cpe.5504
10. Garcia, A.M., Schepke, C., Girardi, A.G., da Silva, S.A.: A new parallel benchmark for performance evaluation and energy consumption. In: Senger, H., et al. (eds.) VECPAR 2018. LNCS, vol. 11333, pp. 188–201. Springer, Cham (2019). https://doi.org/10.1007/978-3-030-15996-2_14
11. Griebler, D., Löff, J., Mencagli, G., Danelutto, M., Fernandes, L.G.: Efficient NAS benchmark kernels with C++ parallel programming. In: 2018 26th Euromicro International Conference on Parallel, Distributed and Network-based Processing (PDP), pp. 733–740, March 2018
12. Ibrahim, S., Phan, T.D., Carpen-Amarie, A., Chihoub, H.E., Moise, D., Antoniu, G.: Governing energy consumption in Hadoop through CPU frequency scaling: an analysis. Future Gener. Comput. Syst. **54**, 219–232 (2016)
13. Intel: Intel Performance Counter Monitor - A better way to measure CPU utilization (2012). http://www.intel.com/software/pcm. Accessed 12 March 2019

14. Jiang, C.: System level power characterization of multi-core computers with dynamic frequency scaling support. In: 2012 IEEE International Conference on Cluster Computing Workshops, pp. 73–79. IEEE (2012)
15. Le Sueur, E., Heiser, G.: Dynamic voltage and frequency scaling: the laws of diminishing returns. In: Proceedings of the 2010 International Conference on Power Aware Computing and Systems, pp. 1–8 (2010)
16. Lorenzon, A.F., Cera, M.C., Schneider Beck, A.C.: Performance and energy evaluation of different multi-threading interfaces in embedded and general purpose systems. J. Signal Process. Syst. **80**(3), 295–307 (2014). https://doi.org/10.1007/s11265-014-0925-9
17. Lu, T., Pande, P.P., Shirazi, B.: A dynamic, compiler guided DVFS mechanism to achieve energy-efficiency in multi-core processors. Sustain. Comput.: Inform. Syst. **12**, 1–9 (2016)
18. Mittal, S.: A survey of techniques for improving energy efficiency in embedded computing systems. Int. J. Comput. Aided Eng. Technol. **6**(4), 440–459 (2014)
19. Ott, R.L., Longnecker, M.T.: An Introduction to Statistical Methods and Data Analysis. Nelson Education (2015)
20. Rauber, T., Rünger, G.: Parallel Programming: For Multicore and Cluster Systems. Springer, London (2010)
21. Rauber, T., Rünger, G.: A scheduling selection process for energy-efficient task execution on DVFS processors. Concurr. Comput.: Pract. Exp. **31**(19) (2019).https://doi.org/10.1002/cpe.5043
22. Sheikh, H.F., Ahmad, I., Arshad, S.A.: Performance, energy, and temperature enabled task scheduling using evolutionary techniques. Sustain. Comput.: Inform. Syst. **22**, 272–286 (2019). https://doi.org/10.1016/j.suscom.2017.10.002
23. Silveira, D.S., Moro, G.B., Cruz, E., Navaux, P.O., Schnorr, L.M., Bampi, S.: Energy consumption estimation in parallel applications: an analysis in real and theoretical models. In: XVII Simposio em Sistemas Computacionais de Alto Desempenho, pp. 134–145 (2016)
24. Solana, A.: Europe's greenest supercomputer: why energy-efficient HPC is on the rise (2019). https://www.zdnet.com/article/europes-greenest-supercomputer-why-energy-efficient-hpc-is-on-the-rise/. Accessed 14 June 2019

Performance Impact of IEEE 802.3ad in Container-Based Clouds for HPC Applications

Anderson M. Maliszewski[1,3](✉) ⓘ, Eduardo Roloff[1] ⓘ, Dalvan Griebler[2,3] ⓘ,
Luciano P. Gaspary[1] ⓘ, and Philippe O. A. Navaux[1] ⓘ

[1] Informatics Institute, Federal University of Rio Grande Do Sul (UFRGS),
Porto Alegre, Brazil
{ammaliszewski,eroloff,paschoal,navaux}@inf.ufrgs.br
[2] Pontifical Catholic University of Rio Grande do Sul (PUCRS), Porto Alegre, Brazil
dalvan.griebler@acad.pucrs.br
[3] Laboratory of Advanced Research on Cloud Computing (LARCC),
Três de Maio Faculty (SETREM), Três de Maio, Brazil

Abstract. Historically, large computational clusters have supported
hardware requirements for executing High-Performance Computing
(HPC) applications. This model has become out of date due to the high
costs of maintaining and updating these infrastructures. Currently, computing resources are delivered as a service because of the cloud computing
paradigm. In this way, we witnessed consistent efforts to migrate HPC
applications to the cloud. However, if on the one hand cloud computing
offers an attractive environment for HPC, benefiting from the pay-per-
use model and on-demand resource allocation, on the other, there are still
significant performance challenges to be addressed, such as the known
network bottleneck. In this article, we evaluate the use of a Network
Interface Cards (NIC) aggregation approach, using the IEEE 802.3ad
standard to improve the performance of representative HPC applications executed in LXD container based-cloud. We assessed the aggregation impact using two and four NICs with three distinct transmission
hash policies. Our results demonstrated that if the correct hash policy is
selected, the NIC aggregation can significantly improve the performance
of network-intensive HPC applications by up to ≈40%.

Keywords: Cloud computing · NIC aggregation · Bonding · LXD

1 Introduction

In recent years, consistent efforts have been made to migrate HPC applications to
cloud computing (CC). This approach is based mainly on the use of the characteristics of these environments, such as; pay-per-use model and access to a shared
pool of computing resources. Thus, when a request is made, resources are pro-
visioned on-demand in a scalable/elastic manner and released almost instantly
with minimal effort, requiring only a network connection to access [10]. However,
with the increasing adoption of CC, some challenges were also posed, including

© Springer Nature Switzerland AG 2020
O. Gervasi et al. (Eds.): ICCSA 2020, LNCS 12254, pp. 158–167, 2020.
https://doi.org/10.1007/978-3-030-58817-5_13

the virtualization impact, which presents an overhead due to its additional layer when compared to the native environment as well as the multi-tenants who share/compete for resources (*i.e.*, network interconnection) [6,9].

HPC applications used in clouds are often developed with the Message Passing Interface (MPI) standard to take advantage of the underlying distributed system. Since this type of workload typically handles large amounts of data, requiring high computing power, a key factor explored is how to speed up its performance, as this consequently reduces allocation costs. Such performance improvements can be made with both software and hardware optimization. On the hardware side, the network interconnection is pointed out by several studies as one of the main bottlenecks [11,13,14], because it is the central point of interconnection between servers, and thus also be shared between the processing of several flows originated from different cloud instances. In addition, another alternative is to allocate a faster cloud instance, which can increase overall performance, but theoretically also increases the cost.

In previous studies, we introduced our first Network Interface Cards (NIC) aggregation approach, which used bonding mode 0, also known as Balance Round Robin to improve network performance using a private cloud deployment [8] with LXD containers. The results highlighted that parallel applications with network-intensive patterns increased their performance by up to 38%. Thus, we argue that this approach could be employed by public cloud providers, taking advantage of existing hardware, increasing performance, and reducing costs. In this work, we make progress on the state-of-the-art by evaluating a different NIC aggregation approach which used the bonding mode 4, also known and specified as IEEE 802.3ad. We used 4 synthetic HPC applications, and executed them with two and four NICs aggregated, using three distinct hash policies (layer 2, layer 2 + 3, and layer3 + 4), and the environment without NICs aggregated (Regular TCP) as a baseline to the results. As far as we know, there is no other work in the literature that performs the same studies. With this assessment we provide the following contributions:

- A reproducible performance assessment of the IEEE 802.3ad NIC aggregation standard implemented with three distinct hash policies and two different numbers of aggregated NICs, relative to a baseline without aggregation, in container-based cloud deployments, evaluating their impact in the performance of representative synthetic high-performance applications.
- We demonstrate that the NIC aggregation approach deployed with the cloud instances can significantly improve the applications performance by up to $\approx 40\%$ when the correct transmission hash policy is selected.

The remainder of the paper is organized as follows. In Sect. 2, we present our methodology, concerning hardware/software specification, NIC aggregation, and transmission hash policies description, alongside as our private cloud deployment, benchmarks used, and the experimental setup. Next, in Sect. 3 we present the evaluation and discuss the obtained results. In Sect. 4 we cover some of the most prominent related works. Finally, in Sect. 5, we conclude the paper with some final remarks and prospective directions for future research.

2 Scope and Methodology

This Section describes the hardware/software specifications alongside with the NIC aggregation approach, in which the bonding mode 4 or 802.3ad and its different transmit hash policies are covered. Also, the private cloud management platform, benchmarks, and the experimental setup used to conduct the experiments are reported.

2.1 Hardware/Software Specifications

The computational environment which has supported our experiments was composed of four HP ProLiant server with identical hardware resources. Each one has two six-core AMD Opteron processor 2425 HE, 32 GB of RAM, 4 Intel Gigabit network interface cards (NICs) interconnected by a Gigabit Switch. The software specification has Ubuntu Server 18.04 64-bit (kernel 4.15.0–99) as the operating system (OS), MPI Open MPI 2.1.1 library, GCC/GNU Fortran compiler version 7.5.0. Besides, OpenNebula cloud manager was used with version 5.10.1 and the Ethernet Channel Bonding Driver with version 3.7.1. All softwares involved in the evaluation process were used with their last stable available version. The LXD instances were created using the LXC versions 3.0.3 and used the same OS, MPI wrapper, and GCC version as the physical servers.

2.2 NIC Aggregation

Also known as Link Aggregation (LA) or Bonding, it is a technique that combines several NICs into a logical link. It is commonly used to interconnect pairs of network devices (i.e., switches, routers, etc.) to improve bandwidth and resilience in a cost-effective way, by merely adding new links together with existing ones instead of replacing equipment [1,5]. The specific behavior of connected interfaces is based on the choice of a mode of use, among seven existing modes. Another equally important use of NIC aggregation is to fail over transparently. This is preferred for deployments where high availability is critical. The same idea can be further extended to provide a combination of increased bandwidth and transparent fail over with degraded performance in a NIC failure event.

In our approach, we used up to 4 NICs with the IEEE 802.3ad Dynamic link aggregation. This mode creates aggregation groups that share the same speed and duplex settings. The selection of the slave for outgoing traffic is made according to the transmission hash policy, which can be changed from the standard simple XOR policy using the xmit_hash_policy option. To compare the performance between hash policies, we evaluated three of them, which are the most used. They are described below.

- **Layer 2:** This policy uses XOR of hardware MAC addresses and packet type ID field to generate the hash. This algorithm will place all traffic to a particular network peer on the same slave.

– **Layer 2 + 3:** This policy uses a combination of layer2 and layer3 protocol information to generate the hash. Uses XOR of hardware MAC addresses and IP addresses to create the hash. If the protocol is IPv6, then the source and destination addresses are first hashed using ipv6_addr_hash. This algorithm will place all traffic to a particular network peer on the same slave. This policy is intended to provide a more balanced distribution of traffic than layer2 alone, especially in environments where a layer3 gateway device is required to reach most destinations.

– **Layer 3 + 4:** This policy uses upper layer protocol information, when available, to generate the hash. This allows for traffic to a particular network peer to span multiple slaves, although a single connection will not span multiple slaves. If the protocol is IPv6, then the source and destination addresses are first hashed using ipv6_addr_hash. For fragmented TCP or UDP packets and all other IPv4 and IPv6 protocol traffic, the source and destination port information are omitted. This algorithm is not fully 802.3ad compliant. A single TCP or UDP conversation containing both fragmented and unfragmented packets will see packets striped across two interfaces. This may result in out of order delivery. Most traffic types will not meet these criteria, as TCP rarely fragments traffic, and most UDP traffic is not involved in extended conversations. Other implementations of 802.3ad may or may not tolerate this noncompliance.

Limitations. Although NIC aggregating has the potential to improve performance, it also has implications for its usage. For example, all the configuration is done manually, the maximum number of aggregated physical links is limited to eight, and all network interfaces must operate at the same speed to be aggregated. Besides, the IEEE 802.3ad mode also imposes its request, which requires a switch with support to use this aggregation mode.

2.3   Private Cloud Deployment

In the deployment of the private cloud environment, we used the OpenNebula manager. It was chased because of being one of the most popular private cloud managers and by following our previous work [8]. Also, we deployed instances using the LXD containers because they use a lightweight virtualization. In the Fig. 1 is depicted the representation of our system. We used four servers, each one with four NICs connected to the same switch. NICs are them grouped into a logical link called bond 0 and bridged to the containers. OpenNebula manages the containers and create a cluster establishing the communication over the underlying bonded NICs.

2.4   Benchmarks

We conduct our evaluation using four HPC benchmarks (IS, FT, BT, and SP) from the Numerical Aerodynamic Simulation Parallel Benchmarks (NPB)

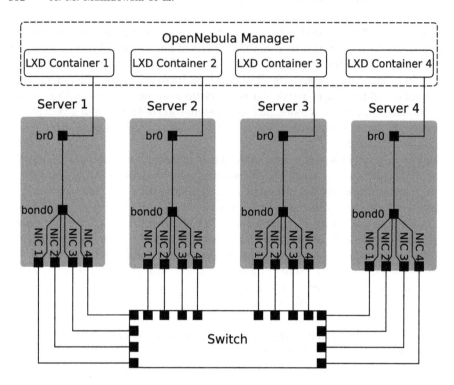

Fig. 1. High level representation of our system.

suite [2]. The NPB set, used with version 3.4, was designed to evaluate the performance of different hardware and software in HPC systems. In this paper, the NPB benchmarks were chosen based on our previous work, which demonstrated that these applications tend to benefit or get worse results when using the NIC aggregation approach. All NAS benchmarks were compiled with size C with -O3 flag, mpifort and mpicc for Fortran and C codes, and executed with 32 MPI processes (8 per node). Above is a short description of the NPB benchmarks. **IS** performs a sort of integer keys using a linear time Integer Sorting algorithm on computation of the key histogram. **FT** contains the computational kernel of a 3-D Fast Fourier Transform (FFT). **BT** and **SP** both apply variations of the Alternating Direction Implicit (ADI) approximate factorization technique to decouple solution of the x,y, and z-coordinate directions which results are 5×5 block-tridiagonal and scalar pentadiagonal, respectively [2,12].

2.5   Experimental Setup

We employ a reproducible research methodology [15], using R, Git, and a laboratory notebook. All data collected in this work is publicly available[1]. To guide the experiments execution, for the baseline (Regular TCP), each number of NICs aggregated (802.3ad-2NICs or 802.3ad-4NICs), and different transmit hash policy (layer2, layer2 + 3, and layer3 + 4) used, we generated an experiment design [7], totaling seven individual designs. Different designs were created due to the need to restart the underlying server when a different aggregation or transmission policy was applied. With the reboot process, we also made sure that there was no interference in the experiments related to various levels of cache (e.g., memory, processor instructions). The designs have 30 replications, where the five applications executed were randomized. The reported execution times measurements are averages of the replications, and the error bars were calculated considering a confidence level of 99.7%, assuming a Gaussian distribution.

3   Evaluation

Our performance evaluation results are shown in Fig. 2 for BT, SP, IS, and FT applications, each represented in an individual sub-figure. The execution times using the unit of time measurement in seconds is represented on the Y-axis using different scales. The name of the application is shown on the X-axis.

BT has improved its performance in ≈4.66% when executed using two NICs aggregated and in ≈12.52% when executed with four NICs aggregated with the layer 2 policy. On the other hand, when higher layers policies are used, the execution time was increased. For instance, using the layer 2 + 3 policy and 2 NICs aggregated, we can not stat a difference compared with the execution time of Regular TCP, because the error bars overlap. Using the same policy, but with four NICs, the times were improved in ≈6.30% compared to our baseline, but worse if compared to the layer 2 policy with 4 NICs. Using the higher layer policy (layer3 + 4), BT worsened its performance with 2 NICs in ≈5.87%, and improved in ≈5.18% with four NICs.

SP improved its performance in ≈2.78% with two NICs and ≈16.92% with four NICs aggregated, with the layer 2 policy. Similarly as BT, SP executed with 2 NICs with layer2 + 3 policy has no difference compared to the baseline and with 4 NICs improved ≈8.54%. Finally, with layer3 + 4 policy, SP with 2 NICs aggregated has worse results than the baseline in ≈10.90% and improved its performance in ≈4.83% with four NICs.

IS has a short execution time (less than 15 s for all number of NICs aggregated and policies). Layer 2 shows the best performance, with two NICs aggregated having improved its performance in ≈32.74% and with four NICs in ≈40.37%. With layer 2 + 3 policy the error bars of two interfaces aggregated have a range which stays in the same line as our baseline, so it can not be point out as improved or not. On the other hand, with four NICs in layer2 + 3 IS has improved its

---

[1] https://github.com/andermm/ICCSA-2020.

performance in ≈15.27%. Finally both two and four NICs aggregated with the layer 3 + 4 policy lost performance compared to the baseline, in ≈5.32% and ≈8.13%, respectively.

FT follows a similar pattern as other applications on layer 2 and layer 2 + 3. For instance, layer 2 with two NICs has improved its performance in ≈23.39% and with four NICs in ≈26.56%. Also, in layer 2 + 3 FT with two NICs has error bars overlapped with baseline and an improvement in ≈7.86% with four interfaces. Contrary to the other applications behaviour, FT improved its performance in both number of NICs aggregated using the policy 3 + 4, in ≈10.94% with two network interfaces and in ≈4.83% with four NICs. FT application is known to be Communication-Bound spending almost its entire execution doing MPI operations, with a slight portion of Computing. This application sends a considerable amount of small messages, which turns it latency-sensitive.

4   Related Work

Aggregation of NICs has been explored with different purposes and approaches using techniques such as bonding or MultiPath TCP (MPTCP) to improve performance. In our previous work [8], we focused on implementing NIC aggregation with network bonding mode 0 - balance round-robin. Our results highlighted the aggregation potential to improving the performance of HPC applications.

Watanabe et al. [16] investigated the impact of topology and link aggregation on a large-scale PC cluster with Ethernet. They performed several experiments High-Performance LINPACK Benchmark (HPL) using 4–6 NICs aggregated using a torus topology. Their results have shown that the performance can be significantly improved in overall HPC applications up to 650%. This would allow cloud infrastructure using commodity hardware to improve network performance without significant additional investments in hardware side.

Chaufournier et al. [4] created a comprehensive assessment of the feasibility of using MPTCP to improve the performance of data center and cloud applications. Their results showed that while MPTCP provides useful bandwidth aggregation, congestion prevention, and improved resiliency for some cloud applications, these benefits do not apply uniformly across all applications. Similarly, Wang et al. [17] evaluated the applicability of MultiPath TCP (MPTCP) to improve the performance of the MapReduce application. Its scenario explored the capabilities of GPUs and showed the impact of network bottlenecks on application performance. As a result, it demonstrated that the use of aggregation of network links reduced the data transfer time and improved the overall performance.

Rista et al. [3] created a methodology for evaluating performance measures such as bandwidth, throughput, latency and execution times for Hadoop applications. In the assessment, they also employed the Network Bonding 4 (IEEE 802.3ad) mode but mainly explored the benefits that aggregation brings with up to 3 instances simultaneously in LXC containers. As a result of, they achieved performance improvements by reducing application times in ≈33%. Although the results obtained are promising, the use of simultaneous instances, also known as

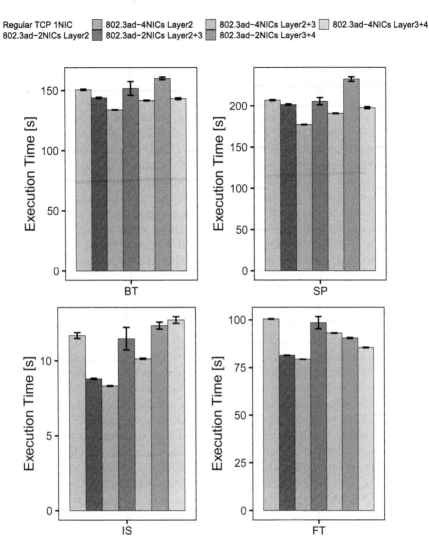

Fig. 2. Performance results of BT, SP, IS and FT applications executed using Regular TCP, two, and four NICs aggregated with bonding mode 4 - 802.3ad for Regular TCP as baseline, layer2, layer2 + 3, and layer3 + 4 transmission hash policies.

multi-tenant, does not apply to HPC applications, as these require that there is no competition for computational resources.

In contrast to the previous works, our evaluation focuses on applying/implementing NIC aggregation with network bonding mode 4 or IEEE 802.3ad to reduce the execution time of HPC applications. Differently for other works, our scenario covers HPC applications running on real-world cloud environments and assessing their performance with two and four NICs aggregated. Finally, we also evaluated different transmission hash policies algorithm to discover which of them offer the best performance.

5   Final Considerations and Future Work

This work sought to evaluate the performance of link aggregation in LXD instances with three different transmission hash policies in comparison with the baseline of a single network interface (Regular TCP). Considering that network interconnection can cause overhead for HPC applications executing in cloud environments, our goal was to evaluate an approach using NIC aggregation.

The results showed that our NIC aggregation approach integrated into the cloud improved the applications performance in the majority of the hash policies implementations. For instance, IS applications, which have a short execution time, improved its performance with four NICs aggregated in $\approx 40.37\%$. Other applications like BT and SP which have blocking MPI operations have not fully exploited NIC aggregation by the low network utilization. We can highlight a pattern that all applications followed, which is a significant gain of performance using the layer 2 policy, and a scalar loss of performance as hash policies that use higher layers are applied (i.e., layer 2 + 3 and layer 3 + 4). The only application that does not followed exactly this pattern is FT, which could improve its performance using layer 3 + 4 for both two and four NICs aggregated. This happens because of application characteristics, in which FT makes intensive use of the network, allowing it to improve its performance.

In addition, when comparing the use of two against four NICs aggregated, we can see a gain of performance on all applications using four NICs between any hash policy used. This shows the potential of NIC aggregation to improve the performance. In our experiences, we also can highlight that this implementation can be easily integrated into a ready-to-use cloud environment through the use of linux bridges. In future work we plan to: (I) compare the results obtained with the use of IEEE 802.3ad mode against the balanced round-robin mode, evaluated in our previous article [8]. (II) evaluate this approach with other virtualization technologies. (III) assess this environment with a wide range of real applications, considering more complicated scenarios (i.e real-time environments).

Acknowledgment. This work has been supported by the projects; 1) "GREEN-CLOUD: Computação em Cloud com Computação Sustentável" (#16/2551-0000 488-9) from FAPERGS and CNPq Brazil, program PRONEX 12/2014. 2) Coordenação de Aperfeiçoamento de Pessoal de Nível Superior - Brasil (CAPES) - Finance Code 001. 3) FAPERGS 01/2017-ARD project ParaElastic (N° 17/2551-0000871-5) and the Universal MCTIC/CNPq N° 28/2018 project SParCloud (No. 437693/2018-0). 4) BRICS Pilot Call 2016 project CloudHPC. 5) CNPq/MCTIC/BRICS-STI No 18/2016 Project Number 441892/2016-7. Finally, we thank the Três de Maio Faculty (SETREM) and the Laboratory of Advanced Research on Cloud Computing (LARCC), for providing access to computational infrastructure.

References

1. IEEE standard for information technology - local and metropolitan area networks - part 3: carrier sense multiple access with collision detection (CSMA/CD) access method and physical layer specifications-aggregation of multiple link segments. IEEE Std 802.3ad-2000, pp. 1–184 (2000)
2. Bailey, D., et al.: The NAS parallel benchmarks; summary and preliminary results. In: ACM/IEEE Conference on Supercomputing (SC), pp. 158–165 (1991)
3. Rista, C., Griebler, D., Maron, C.A.F., Fernandes, L.G: Improving the network performance of a container-based cloud environment for hadoop systems. In: 15th International Conference on High Performance Computing & Simulation (HPCS) (2017)
4. Chaufournier, L., Ali-Eldin, A., Sharma, P., Shenoy, P., Towsley, D.: Performance evaluation of multi-path TCP for data center and cloud workloads. In: ACM/SPEC International Conference on Performance Engineering, pp. 13–24 (2019)
5. Davis, T., et al.: Linux Ethernet Bonding (2011). https://www.kernel.org/doc/Documentation/networking/bonding.txt
6. Gupta, A., et al.: Evaluating and improving the performance and scheduling of HPC applications in cloud. IEEE Trans. Cloud Comput. (TCC) (2016)
7. Jain, R.: The Art of Computer Systems Performance Analysis: Techniques for Experimental Design, Measurement, Simulation, and Modeling. John Wiley & Sons Inc, Digital Equipment Corporation-Litleton, Massachusetts (1991)
8. Maliszewski, A.M., Vogel, A., Griebler, D., Roloff, E., Fernandes, L., Navaux, P.O.: Minimizing communication overheads in container-based clouds for HPC applications. In: IEEE Symposium on Computers and Communications (ISCC), pp. 1–6 (2019)
9. Mauch, V., Kunze, M., Hillenbrand, M.: High performance cloud computing. Future Gen. Comput. Syst. **29**(6), 1408–1416 (2013)
10. Mell, P., Grance, T., et al.: The NIST definition of cloud computing. Nat. Inst. Stand. Technol. (NIST) (2011)
11. Pretto, G.R., et al.: Boosting HPC applications in the cloud through JIT traffic-aware path provisioning. In: Misra, S., et al. (eds.) ICCSA 2019. LNCS, vol. 11622, pp. 702–716. Springer, Cham (2019). https://doi.org/10.1007/978-3-030-24305-0_52
12. Ramachandran, A., Vienne, J., Van Der Wijngaart, R., Koesterke, L., Sharapov, I.: Performance evaluation of NAS parallel benchmarks on Intel Xeon Phi. In: International Conference on Parallel Processing (ICPP), pp. 736–743 (2013)
13. Roloff, E., Diener, M., Gaspary, L.P., Navaux, P.O.A.: HPC application performance and cost efficiency in the cloud. In: Euromicro International Conference on Parallel, Distributed and Network-based Processing (PDP), pp. 473–477 (2017)
14. Sadooghi, I., et al.: Understanding the performance and potential of cloud computing for scientific applications. IEEE Trans. Cloud Comput. (TCC) **5**(2), 358–371 (2017)
15. Stanisic, L., Legrand, A., Danjean, V.: An effective Git and org-mode based workflow for reproducible research. ACM SIGOPS Oper. Syst. Rev. **49**(1), 61–70 (2015)
16. Watanabe, T., Nakao, M., Hiroyasu, T., Otsuka, T., Koibuchi, M.: Impact of topology and link aggregation on a PC cluster with ethernet. In: IEEE International Conference on Cluster Computing, pp. 280–285 (2008)
17. Wang, C., Yang, C., Liao, W., Chang, R., Wei, T.: Coupling GPU and MPTCP to improve hadoop/mapreduce performance. In: International Conference on Intelligent Green Building and Smart Grid (IGBSG), pp.1–6 (2016)

Collecting HPC Applications Processing Characteristics to Facilitate Co-scheduling

Ruslan Kuchumov[✉] and Vladimir Korkhov

Saint Petersburg State University, 7/9 Universitetskaya nab.,
St. Petersburg 199034, Russia
kuchumovri@gmail.com, v.korkhov@spbu.ru

Abstract. In this paper we describe typical HPC workloads in terms of scheduling theory models. In particular, we cover machine environments that are common for high performance computing (HPC) field, possible objective functions and available jobs characteristics. We also describe resources that are required by HPC applications and how to monitor and control their usage rates. We provide the basis for defining mathematical model for application resource usage and validate it on experimental data.

Keywords: High performance computing · Co-scheduling · Scheduling theory

1 Introduction

The broader goal of this research is to reduce queue wait time of high performance computing (HPC) applications in cluster schedulers by applying co-scheduling strategy. Co-scheduling allows to assign multiple applications that have different requirements for resources to a single cluster node that have enough resources to execute them simultaneously and without interference. For example, some applications that are only disk IO-intensive can be executed simultaneously with applications that only network-intensive as they are using completely different resources.

This strategy allows to improve resources utilization of a cluster and reduce wait of jobs in the queue as compared to the commonly used scheduling strategies where a node can execute a single application at a time. Now, a lot of attention in the scientific community is focused on the feasibility of this strategy, and in particular on practical aspects [11].

Since co-scheduling requires more information about jobs resource requirements that is used in a common scheduler (e.g. number of cores and time of computation) it's important to find out these jobs parameters and metrics and to collect them together in a mathematical model that can later be used for making scheduling decisions.

© Springer Nature Switzerland AG 2020
O. Gervasi et al. (Eds.): ICCSA 2020, LNCS 12254, pp. 168–182, 2020.
https://doi.org/10.1007/978-3-030-58817-5_14

Scheduling theory has emerged long before HPC field. Its main focus is to formalize scheduling problems and to apply different mathematical methods for creating schedules that are subject to certain constraints and the same time optimize the objective function.

In scheduling theory, models are distinguished by their notation, which consists of three fields usually denoted as α, β and γ. Each field may be a comma-separated list of words. The first field describes the machine environment, the second describes the task characteristics and constraints, and the last one – objective function. Later in this paper we will use term "job" as a model for HPC applications and "machine" as a modeling term for cluster computing node.

In classical theory, there are important assumptions [4] that may limit its applicability to the co-scheduling problem. At first, each job can be processed by at most one machine and each machine can process at most one job (operation). Second, job execution time does not change in time. Third, job execution time is known in advance. In the latest development of the scheduling theory at least one of these assumptions is changed.

In the problem of co-scheduling all of the propositions of classical scheduling theory are changed, which makes the problem of defining the model challenging. Moreover, from a practical point of view, there are also a lot of open questions.

Sharing a common resource between multiple applications without introducing some sort of contentions is not always possible. Additional information regarding job's resources consumption has to be collected and taken into account during scheduling. What makes matter worse is that required information is not easily available, it can not be provided by the user at the job submission stage, and it is not easy to obtain it by monitoring jobs behavior during its execution. There is a lot of work done already by scientific community on collecting such information by interpreting available metrics, such as hardware counters or operating system events.

In this paper we will focus instead on collecting and abstracting this information for defining a formal model.

The rest of this paper is organized as follows. In Sect. 2 we describe possible ways and their rationale for defining machine environment. In Sect. 3 we describe possible objective functions for the model. In Sect. 4 we describe which job characteristics from the scheduling theory are common in HPC. In Sect. 5 we expand on job resources characteristics that are relevant for co-scheduling and propose an abstraction for describing these resources. In Sect. 6 we validate our hypotheses from the previous section using benchmarks in cluster environments.

2 Machine Environments

Scheduling theory defines multiple different machine environments [10]. Machines are considered to process a single job or stay idle at any point in time.

There are three commonly used environments with parallel machines that are distinguished by job processing speed. The first one is identical machines, where all jobs are executed at the same rate. The second one is uniform machines, where machines have different processing speeds. The third one is the environment with unrelated machines, that is, the speed of processing of each job depends on the machine where it is being processed.

There are also environments with dedicated machines. In this case it is assumed that a job consists of multiple stages or operations which are performed on different machines. Each job must be executed on every machine. There are flow shop, open shop and job shop environments and their variation. In the flow shop each job must be processed in a specific order. In job shop each job may have a specific route for processing. In open shop there is no constrains to jobs processing routes.

In the environments above, it is assumed that machines are available continuously and do not have downtime. However, there are also environments that consider machines' non-availability periods.

In HPC systems, there are clusters with computational nodes that can process any job. These nodes are not dedicated and they can process any eligible job. Each node of a cluster consists of multiple CPU cores. Typical HPC job is a hierarchy of processes and threads, some processes can be executed on different nodes and may use cluster interconnect for its communications. Threads, on the other hand, are spawned by a process and can only be executed within a single node, as they share a common memory. Threads are assigned for execution at CPU cores by operating system scheduler. Usually, this scheduler implements some sort of fair-scheduling policy.

In order to model scheduling in HPC environment, we need to define machine environment and decide what to use as a machine. If we assume that cluster nodes can not be overcommitted with jobs, that is, each node can execute a single job at a time, then nodes can be used as machines in scheduling theory. This model can be applied to the commonly used cluster schedulers, that do not allow node overcommitting.

Since co-scheduling in HPC implies overcommiting nodes with multiple jobs, then they can not be represented by machine models in classical scheduling theory. As an alternative, CPU cores in each node can be modeled as machines, since they can not execute multiple threads simultaneously. But, this would introduce multiple layers of complexity. At first, CPU cores should be grouped into sets that represent each node. Then, jobs have to be defined as a hierarchy of processes and threads, where processes can be executed on different nodes and threads can only be within the CPU cores of the same node. Lastly, scheduling problems also become hierarchical: there is scheduling of processes between nodes and there is scheduling of threads between CPU cores. The last one is done by the operating system, but in this model definition its scheduling policy has to be considered.

Another alternative is to deviate from the classical scheduling theory and to model cluster nodes as machines but allow for execution of multiple jobs at any point in time. In this case, CPU cores can be modeled later as one of the resources.

If the cluster nodes are heterogeneous, then they can be modeled as a set of parallel machines. In a more general case, computing nodes may have different hardware, which results in different job execution speeds, so the model would be with uniform machines. In even more general case, hardware may have a different effect on each job (e.g. there can be different kinds of accelerators that are utilized by some jobs and not by others) which requires a more general model with unrelated machines.

In some cases, the network interconnect between computing nodes should be taken into account. For example, there can be different bandwidth and latency between nodes in the cluster depending on the relative position of nodes in the cluster. As a result, the job processing speed may depend on the position of assigned nodes within the network topology. Some models consider different network topologies in their machine environments [2].

3   Objective Functions

In scheduling theory there is a large variety of objective functions. For example, the makespan – completion time of the last job in the schedule, flowtime – the sum of completion times of all jobs, there are many due-dates related objective functions (e.g. lateness or tardiness). Sometimes job parameters in objective functions can be weighed (e.g. weighted completion times), weights can also be functions of job completion times. Some objective functions may not be regular. In some models multiple objective functions are used.

In HPC commonly considered objective functions can be classified into completion time related functions (makespan and flowtime), fairness objective functions and resource utilization objective function (e.g. cost of computation, power consumption).

4   Job Processing Characteristics

In the scheduling theory, each model may define multiple processing characteristics. These characteristics affect the set of feasible schedules and the process of decision making for constructing an optimal schedule. Below we discuss some of these characteristics that are relevant for describing applications in HPC field.

Precedence constraint is one of those characteristics. It implies that there is predecessor/successor constraint defined for each job forming a decency graph defined for a set of jobs. In the scheduling theory different special cases of these graphs are usually considered such as in-tree, out-tree and chain trees. In HPC it is common to have dependencies between applications, for example, when one application may require data files created by another application.

Sequence-dependent setup-time defines the amount of time the job has to wait before it can start its processing. This required time may be different for each job and for each machine where the job is being processed. In some models there may be setup-times families that do not require waiting time between jobs from the same families. In HPC applications may require transmission of large data files to the local disk storage or may require compilation for the local hardware architectures. These activities may take a long time and can be modeled as sequence-dependent setup-time.

Machine feasibility requires for each job to have a set of machines where it can be processed. There are usually special cases considered where feasibility sets are non-intersecting or nested. This requirement may appear in HPC when applications have specific requirements for the hardware environment where they are being processed. For example, some applications may require computing nodes with specific accelerators such as GPGPUs or FPGAs that may be located only on some nodes in the cluster.

When multiprocessor job characteristic is present in the model definition, it means that each job may require multiple machines at the same time for its processing. The number of machines is fixed. In HPC it is very common to have this requirement for distributed applications. Sometimes the special case of power of two number of machines is considered in the scheduling theory literature, which is also very common in HPC.

The alternative to having multiprocessor jobs is to have moldable and malleable jobs. Moldable jobs utilize as many machines as specified when the job is started and the set of these machines does not change during job processing. Malleable jobs allow to change the number of machines they are using during their processing. Similar to multiprocessor jobs moldable are common in HPC among distributed applications. Malleable jobs, on the other hand, are rare as implementing them would require additional scheduler-job negotiation protocol or would require jobs to be fault-tolerant.

There is also a large number of models which define resources and consider how applications may use them during their processing. For example, there are renewable resources (when usage in every time is constrained), non-renewable resources (when total consumption is constrained) and double-constrained resources (when both usage and consumption are constrained). In HPC applications also require resources, such as main memory, licenses, disk space, computation cost and so on. These resources may also be categorized into renewable, non-renewable and double-constrained categories. Below in the paper we describe some of the resources and provide some basis for the defined model.

5   Resource Usage Metrics

In this section we describe some resources that are commonly required by applications in HPC field. Some of these resources, like the number of computing nodes, do not change during application execution, others are constant and may change during the runtime. For the latest, we describe how to monitor those requirements in real time. Rates of usage of some of the resources can be changed either directly or indirectly affecting the application's execution time.

5.1   Required Number of Nodes

Applications that are commonly used in HPC are moldable and not malleable. When started they take in some form a list of nodes; processes can be started and after that, the number of nodes does not change. Some applications may be moldable, but they may require the number of nodes to be a power of two.

For MPI-based applications, that are very common in HPC, there are extension interfaces, such as PMIx [3] or MPI-FT [8], that allow to scale up or down the working application. There are also possibilities to migrate working MPI processes between nodes, such as BLCR [5] and CRIU [9]. It may change the number of nodes used by the application, but it would not change the number of MPI processes. As a result of migration, some nodes may be overcommitted with processes, but scaling up would not be possible.

Another option for scaling applications that support checkpoint restarts is to simply restart an application with a new number of nodes. In this case the application would continue from the latest checkpoint on a new nodes configuration.

In order for the application to be malleable for the number of nodes, it would have to be completely fault-tolerant. Some application-level HPC schedulers provide fault-tolerance: any node can be turned off and the application would continue working with the remaining nodes, when a new node is added the application would be using it as well.

Since all of these solutions require support from the application and are not completely transparent, they can not be taken into account for the general case.

Usually processing time of each application depends on the number of nodes. Some scheduling models take that into account and define some functional dependency. There are a lot of models of dependency between processing time and the number of nodes, usually linear and convex models are defined, some are more complicated and consider the diminishing returns on the number of nodes.

5.2   CPU Cores

Similar to the number of nodes, the number of threads in a running application can not be changed from the outside. Otherwise, it would require some sort of negotiation protocol between the application and the scheduler.

But unlike the number of nodes, the number of threads may change in the runtime. The application may spawn and terminate its threads, some threads may become idle for some time. This number of threads of the application can be observed as a function of time during application execution. In order to do so, it is sufficient to monitor the number of threads of the application and their states. Then, to count the number of required threads it is sufficient to count all active (runnable) threads.

Linux's procfs pseudo-filesystem provides information about the states of all threads. The thread, for example, maybe in the runnable state, indicating that it is waiting for its turn in the runqueue, it may be in interruptable sleeping state when it executes sleep instruction or waits for a lock or another event, it may in an uninterruptible sleep state when it is performing disk I/O operations or in any other state. To find out which threads belong to the same application we have placed its parent process before starting an application in a control group, this way the kernel reports children threads and processes identifiers when they are spawned.

This number of the running threads can be used as the required number of CPU cores in every time point. If this number is larger than the number of available CPU cores, then it means that some threads are ready to run, but they are waiting in run-queues for their turn. This number may also decrease when threads enter sleeping states, for example, when the are waiting on a lock or performing disk I/O operations.

In the ideal case, all of the runnable threads should run in parallel. For example, if they are performing inter-thread communications through the shared memory and they are assigned to the same CPU core, then the round trip time of these communications would include wait time in the queue. Besides that, over-committing would cause frequent context switching and possible cache invalidations, if threads are using different memory domains. Although it may introduce significant delays, changing the number of available CPU cores in runtime is possible.

Another metric related to the usage of CPU cores by the application is the number of executed instructions. This metrics depends on application behavior (i.e. which instruction applications execute), the hardware as different CPU architectures may have different speeds for the same instructions and on the way the application was compiled. There is also no simple way to control it directly on per-application basis. Nevertheless, we have found a use for it in our experiments as a measure of how application execution speed is affected by limits in other resources.

5.3 Memory Bus Bandwidth

Access to the main memory is shared between all CPU cores. In a simple case, each CPU core assesses memory through the same memory controller which communicates over the sequential bus with memory modules. Memory bandwidth of the bus is limited, and, in general, the communication frequency of the bus is lower than the clock frequency of CPU cores. As a result, a single CPU core may fully saturate memory bandwidth if it does not work with CPU caches effectively.

Because of that, memory bandwidth can be considered as a shared resource for the applications running on different CPU cores within the same computing node. When, for example, two applications that are capable of utilizing full memory bandwidth are scheduled together, they would interfere with each other and it would lead to the slowdown of their execution time.

For our purposes, we estimated memory throughput of the application with the number of cache misses at the last cache level. When cache miss happens at the last level, the memory controller accesses the main memory through the memory bus. The number of cache misses is provided by

CPU hardware counters and it can be periodically monitored by Linux kernel (PERF_COUNT_HW_CACHE_MISSES perf event). Clearly, this metric depends on cache configuration, and can not be reproduced on different hardware. Estimating the required memory bandwidth of an application in a portable, hardware-independent way is not trivial. The reason for that is multiple levels of memory caches. Some regions of the memory may be cached, and when an application is accessing these regions, the memory accesses may be satisfied from the cache without reaching the memory bus. Associative cache, memory prefetch and the fact that some caches are shared between CPU cores make estimation even harder. There are many research papers on this topic, e.g. [6].

The maximum memory bus bandwidth available to an application can not be controlled directly. Having bandwidth requirements for each application, the decision maker may schedule for simultaneous execution applications that together do not consume all available bandwidth. In case combined memory bus utilization of all applications reaches the maximum value, the performance of all applications would degrade, as memory accesses would take more time.

5.4   Network Bandwidth

For distributed applications that require multiple computation nodes and an interconnect network between them for communication, network bandwidth can be considered as another shared resource. Network bandwidth may be shared between applications not only when they are running on the same set of nodes, but also when their sets of nodes do not intersect and they are connected to the same switch with limited bandwidth. When all available bandwidth is utilized communication time between nodes would increase so as the total execution time of an application.

There are multiple ways to measure network throughput of each application. For example, network packets coming from the application may be marked, using control groups or iptables rules, and then counted by network filters. Another possible way is to create virtual network interfaces using network namespaces for each application and count the number received and transmitted bytes on these interfaces. For our purposes and as we work in an isolated environment, it was sufficient to count the number of bytes transmitted by the physical network interface.

Network bandwidth available to each application can be controlled directly using Linux kernel traffic control policies. Several different queuing disciplines allow to shape network traffic and change network bandwidth. For our purposes and environment it was sufficient to use HTB (Hierarchical Token Bucket) queuing discipline.

Network bandwidth can also be shared equally between all running applications using SFQ (Stochastic Fairness Queue). In this case, all available bandwidth would be shared between all applications that require network access. So, for example, when at some time point there is only one application that transmits data, it would receive all available bandwidth. We have described that in more detail in our previous paper [7].

5.5   Resource Usage Model

Assume that the aforementioned metrics of resource consumption are measured for each application in ideal conditions when no other application was running at the same time and interfering with the one being measured. Having these metrics along with application execution time is not sufficient for making decisions for co-scheduling. The reason for that is that when an application is sharing common resources with another application, its resource usage metrics may change from the one measured in the ideal conditions. They are likely to decrease in this case in co-scheduling conditions which would affect total execution time.

Regardless of available resource shares and other applications that are running simultaneously, the total amount of work performed by the application should not change from the ideal conditions. This total amount of work can be represented by the total amount of CPU instructions, the total number of bytes written and read from the memory and the total number of bytes transmitted and received through the network card.

Another characteristic of the application that is invariant to the changes of available rates is the sequence of instructions. For example, for every 10 executed instructions application may issue 1 instruction that causes LLC cache miss, or for every 10 Kb of received data, the application may execute 300 million instructions. As a result, ratios between resource rates stay constant regardless of resource limits. This assumption is applicable only to the time intervals when resource rates are constant or periodical with a very small period.

On a larger scale, an application may consist of multiple stages that have different resource rates and amounts of work. For example, these stages may include initialization, a loop of computation and data synchronizations followed by the output stage. In each of these stages application may perform a different amount of work at different rates, so resource rate limitations may have different effects of the duration of each stage.

Because of all of these features, we propose to describe resource consumption of an application as a sequence of low-resolution stages, where each stage is defined by the total amount of work that needs to be done and a function describing dependencies between resource usage rates. Using these parameters it is possible to estimate the total execution time of the application and its required resource rates depending of the resource limits.

Since during a single stage application may require multiple resources, its execution time may not depend linearly on resource limits, according to the Amdahl's law. For example, an application may perform 1 unit of work with one resource and another 1 unit of work with another resource per single time interval. If we increase the rate for one of the resources two times, the total amount of work during this interval would increase 1.5 times. Linear dependency is only possible when all of the resource rates are scaled at the same time, which is not feasible in real world as it would require controlling all of the activities of the application.

6 Experiments

To validate our resource model we have used benchmark applications from NAS Parallel Benchmarks suite [1], executed it with different resource constraints and monitored how they affect application behavior. There are two goals for performing these experiments. The first one is to show that an application performs a constant amount of work regardless of the limits on resource rates. The second one to show that dependencies between resource rates do not depend on resource limits.

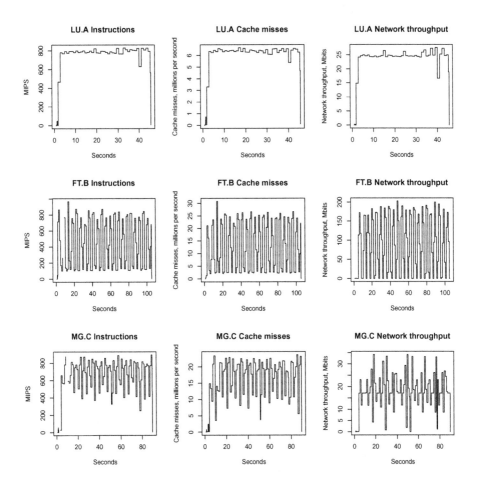

Fig. 1. Resource usage rates in every second of application run-time. For these applications resource rates are almost constant (LU) or periodical with a small period (FT and MG)

We have implemented a program for monitoring resource usage rates periodically (every 0.5 s). We have monitored the number of instructions per second (in millions per second), the memory bus throughput (in millions cache misses per second) and the network throughput (number of transmitted and received megabits per second). The technique for measuring these resources was described in the previous sections. Example of observed resource usage rates for some applications are shown in Fig. 1.

Applications in NAS Parallel Benchmark (NPB) suite solve mathematical problems that are commonly used in HPC applications. Among these tests are the following: CG (conjugate gradient), MG (Multi-Grid), FT (discrete 3D fast Fourier Transform), BT (Block Tri-diagonal solver), LU (Lower-Upper Gauss-Seidel solver) and UA (Unstructured Adaptive mesh). Sizes of these problems are distinguished by so-called classes and they are denoted by the last letter in the benchmark name ("A", "B", "C" and so on).

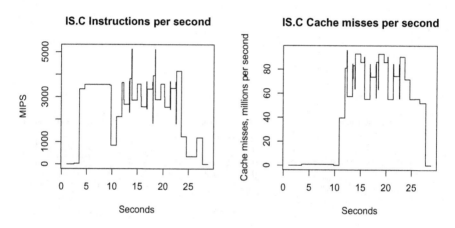

Fig. 2. In IS.C benchmark three stages can be noticed. The first one ends at 10th second, the second one ends at 22nd second.

For our goals, we have selected only the applications that have either constant resource usage rates or periodical rates with a small period. Some applications in NPB, have multiple stages with different rates (for example, IS.C in Fig. 2). As each stage would require a separate model, we have omitted such tests.

We have executed MPI versions of NPB on the 4-node cluster with 4 cores and have measured resource rates on one of them (the one that does not have MPI master process). For controlling memory bandwidth we have used HTB queening discipline in Linux traffic control.

In Table 1 and Fig. 3 you can see that for all tests there are linear dependencies between network transmission rates and the number of instructions and caches misses per second. R^2 values of linear regression for these parameters are close to 1. The total amount of transmitted (and received) bytes is constant and is not affected by the changes in network bandwidth.

The total number of instructions and cache misses is affected by the changes in network transmission rates. The possible explanation for that is when the

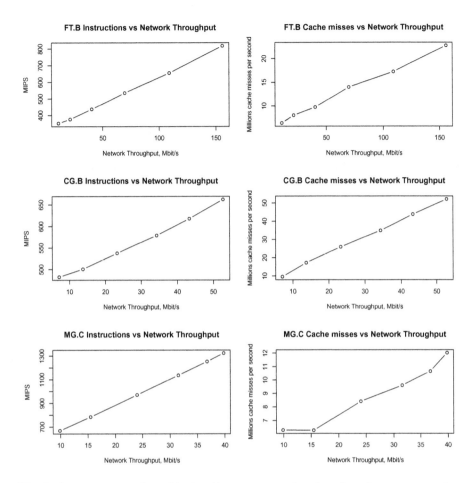

Fig. 3. An average number of instructions per second and cache misses per second as a function of the network throughput of an application.

Table 1. Per-benchmark results for MPI NPB tests. First two columns contains R^2 values for the number of instructions per second and memory bus throughput versus application's network throughput linear regression models. In the next columns there are absolute deviation from the mean value (in percents) of the number of transmitted bytes, executed instructions and cache misses.

	MIPS vs TP, R2	Misses vs TP, R2	TX Data, %	Instr., %	Misses., %
CG.B	0.9956	0.9985	0.3305	56.3411	10.8913
LU.A	0.9998	0.9620	0.2474	23.9812	24.9657
BT.A	0.9999	0.9789	0.6518	32.4141	39.5725
FT.B	0.9992	0.9955	0.5180	59.9892	47.1960
MG.C	0.9968	0.9929	0.4928	23.6905	10.0647

application is waiting for network data to be received or transmitted, it performs instructions in user-space which are counted in the total number. This may happen when a single thread waits for data on the socket in the system space and other threads wait for notification from this thread in the user-space.

In order to show that the total number of executed instructions and cache misses is also constant regardless of the constraints, we have executed OpenMP version of NPB applications. We have executed it on a single node with 4 cores. 2 cores of this node were used for running and measuring the test itself, other 2 cores were used to run workloads that differ in their intensity of memory bus communications. The reason for this approach is that memory bus bandwidth can not be controlled directly as, for example, network bandwidth, and we can affect it only by interacting with it.

For controlling memory bus bandwidth indirectly, we have used a synthetic test that allocates 512 Mb of memory in a loop, then accesses every 64th or 4096th byte of this memory and after that frees this memory. Such access pattern causes an allocation of physical memory pages and populating cache levels with cache lines from this memory, as the result available bandwidth for the test application decreases. We have also run multiple copies of this synthetic test to have a different effect on memory bus bandwidth of the application.

Table 2. Per-benchmark results for OpenMP NPB tests. First columns contains R^2 values for the number of instructions per second versus LLC cache misses linear regression model. In the next column there are absolute deviation from the mean value (in percents) of the number of executed instructions and cache misses.

	MIPS vs Cache misses, R2	Instr., %	Misses., %
CG.B	0.9999403	0.1745595	0.0883977
FT.B	0.9988642	0.0023119	0.7274650
LU.A	0.9554370	0.4167756	2.1089845
MG.B	0.6842153	0.0574678	8.9376413
UA.A	0.9879625	0.9258455	1.7547919

In Table 2 you can see that similar to the MPI version, in OpenMP version of NPB benchmarks there is a linear dependency between the number of cache misses and the number of executed instructions per second and R^2 values are close to 1 for all tests. Also, the total number of executed instruction and cache misses does not depend on the memory bus throughput of the application.

As mentioned previously, execution time has non-linear dependency from the resource usage rates. You can see in Fig. 4 that for network throughput the dependency is not linear, although for memory bus throughput this dependency is close to linear.

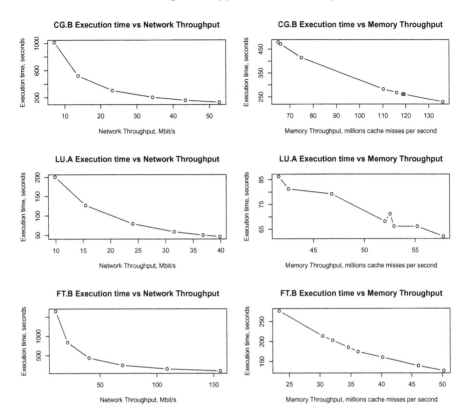

Fig. 4. Benchmark execution time as a function of the number of last level cache misses and network throughput

7   Conclusion

In this paper, we have described typical HPC workloads in terms of scheduling theory models. In particular, we have covered possible ways of defining machine environments in scheduling theory model to represent cluster environments in HPC field. We have also described which job processing characteristics from the scheduling theory can be applied for describing HPC applications.

We have covered different application's resource requirements such as the number of computing nodes, CPU cores, memory bandwidth and network bandwidth. We have described how to monitor them during application execution, how to control them when it is possible.

For these resources we have provided an abstraction based on the following propositions. The first one is that the total amount of consumed resource does not change regardless of resources usage rates. The second one is that relations between resource usage rates are linear and also do not change regardless of resource usage rates. Using these propositions it possible to describe application usage rate as a sequence of stages where each stage would be defined by the amount of consumed resources and relations between resource usage rates.

We have tested these propositions using NAS Parallel Benchmark tests in 4-node cluster and we have found these propositions are valid. For different resource constraints the total amount of consumed resources does not deviate from the mean value more than 1% and coefficient of determination for the linear model of resource rates is very close to 1.

Using this approach it is possible now to estimate application execution time as a function of resource constraints. This later would allow to make decisions by how much the applications may be constrained when they are scheduled together in a co-scheduling strategy.

Acknowledgements. Research has been supported by the RFBR grant No. 19-37-90138.

References

1. Bailey, D.H., et al.: The NAS parallel benchmarks. Int. J. Supercomput. Appl. **5**(3), 63–73 (1991)
2. Błażewicz, J., Ecker, K.H., Pesch, E., Schmidt, G., Sterna, M., Weglarz, J.: Handbook on Scheduling: From Theory to Practice. Springer, Heidelberg (2019). https://doi.org/10.1007/978-3-319-99849-7
3. Castain, R.H., Hursey, J., Bouteiller, A., Solt, D.: Pmix: process management for exascale environments. Parallel Comput. **79**, 9–29 (2018)
4. Gawiejnowicz, S.: Time-Dependent Scheduling. Springer, Heidelberg (2008). https://doi.org/10.1007/978-3-540-69446-5
5. Hargrove, P.H., Duell, J.C.: Berkeley lab checkpoint/restart (BLCR) for Linux clusters. In: Journal of Physics: Conference Series, vol. 46, p. 494. IOP Publishing (2006)
6. Haritatos, A.H., Papadopoulou, N., Nikas, K., Goumas, G., Koziris, N.: Contention-aware scheduling policies for fairness and throughput. Co-Sched. HPC Appl. **28**, 22 (2017)
7. Kuchumov, R., Korkhov, V.: Fair resource allocation for running HPC workloads simultaneously. In: Misra, S., et al. (eds.) ICCSA 2019. LNCS, vol. 11622, pp. 740–751. Springer, Cham (2019). https://doi.org/10.1007/978-3-030-24305-0_55
8. Louca, S., Neophytou, N., Lachanas, A., Evripidou, P.: MPI-FT: Portable fault tolerance scheme for MPI. Parallel Process. Lett. **10**(04), 371–382 (2000)
9. Pickartz, S., Eiling, N., Lankes, S., Razik, L., Monti, A.: Migrating LinuX containers using CRIU. In: Taufer, M., Mohr, B., Kunkel, J.M. (eds.) ISC High Performance 2016. LNCS, vol. 9945, pp. 674–684. Springer, Cham (2016). https://doi.org/10.1007/978-3-319-46079-6_47
10. Pinedo, M.: Scheduling: Theory, Algorithms, and Systems, vol. 5. Springer, Heidelberg (2012). https://doi.org/10.1007/978-1-4614-2361-4
11. Trinitis, C., Weidendorfer, J.: Co-scheduling of HPC Applications, vol. 28. IOS Press (2017)

An Analytical Computing Infrastructure for Monitoring Dynamic Networks Based on Knowledge Graphs

Igor Kulikov[1] , Gerhard Wohlgenannt[2] , Yulia Shichkina[1(✉)] ,
and Nataly Zhukova[3]

[1] Saint-Petersburg Electrotechnical University "LETI", Saint-Petersburg, Russia
i.a.kulikov@gmail.com, strange.y@mail.ru
[2] ITMO University, St. Petersburg, Russia
gwohlg@itmo.ru
[3] St. Petersburg Institute for Informatics and Automation of the Russian
Academy of Sciences, St. Petersburg, Russia
nazhukova@mail.ru

Abstract. Dynamic network monitoring systems are typically designed to solve a predefined number of tasks, new requirements lead to expensive development efforts and sometimes even require changes in the system architecture. Knowledge graphs are powerful and flexible tools for information integration and supported by a set of standardized vocabularies and languages (the "Sematic Web" toolset). In this work, we discuss the application of knowledge graphs to develop and analyze an analytical computing infrastructure for a dynamic network monitoring system. As a typical dynamic network, a multiservice telecommunication network is considered. The presented system combines static models of a telecommunication network and dynamic monitoring data and makes it possible to obtain complex analytical reports using SPARQL queries over the knowledge graph. Those reports are of crucial importance to network stakeholders for improving the network services and performance. First, we analyze problems solved by traditional monitoring systems, and identify the classes of problems such systems cannot solve. Then we propose an analytical monitoring system architecture based on knowledge graphs to address these classes of problems. We present the system structure and detailed descriptions of the ontological and mathematical models of the resulting knowledge graph. In order to test the architecture discussed, we create an example task of the analytical monitoring system and analyze system performance depending on the size of the knowledge graph. The results of the analysis are presented using a number of SPARQL queries.

Keywords: Knowledge graph · Dynamic network · Monitoring system · Ontology · Domain ontology · Semantic web

© Springer Nature Switzerland AG 2020
O. Gervasi et al. (Eds.): ICCSA 2020, LNCS 12254, pp. 183–198, 2020.
https://doi.org/10.1007/978-3-030-58817-5_15

1   Introduction

Dynamic network monitoring systems are designed for solving a known set of problems. New tasks are expensive to implement and often cannot be solved without architecture changes. We offer a more flexible system and data architecture.

As a typical dynamic network, a multiservice telecommunication network (TN) is considered. Telecom operators are in need of an analytical computing infrastructure to provide solutions for complex monitoring tasks, and changes in requirements and tasks. In this paper, we aim to

a) investigate the set of features of current monitoring solutions,
b) define a set of requirements for an analytical computing monitoring infrastructure,
c) propose an architecture and data model for solving the discussed problems,
d) create an example for a new task in this solution that provides dynamic modelling capabilities,
e) define the benefits for TN stakeholders.

1.1   Traditional Telecommunication Network Monitoring Systems

We first discuss the goals, features and components of traditional Telecommunication Network Monitoring Systems (TN-MS) in order to establish which functionality is lacking in traditional systems. TN-MS are described as data providers for network management systems [1]. There are three main goals for traditional telecommunication network monitoring systems [2]:

- network performance monitoring;
- emergency monitoring;
- user account monitoring.

These goals overlap with the functional areas of network management systems [3]. As mentioned in the goals of the paper, we first discuss the problems that traditional monitoring systems can solve (different monitoring systems can be compared regarding their ability to solve these problems) [3–5]:

1. Report generation based on the main indicators of network quality according to the Service-Level-Agreement (SLA);
2. Trend identification concerning the main network performance indicators;
3. Trend forecasting for the main network performance indicators;
4. Network topology analysis;
5. SNMP support;
6. Application of an agent-based monitoring model;
7. Event logging;
8. Message delivery support for different delivery methods.

All of these tasks are elements in the structure of goals for monitoring systems. A typical monitoring system contains the following components [6]:

- The main server, including the server software core, the DBMS, the subsystem for interacting with agents, the user notification subsystem, the graphical user interface, the report generation subsystem, and the event logging subsystem.
- Agents, including the agent software core, the server interaction subsystem, the configuration subsystem, the monitoring subsystem (including the monitoring of physical parameters, the operating system status, the network host status, and the application status).

Data models of traditional monitoring systems are designed based on network performance indicators according to the SLA. As a rule, systems existing today store their data in SQL databases. It should be noted that traditional systems do not solve the problem of analyzing the relationship between monitoring parameters, the network structure, the structures of available data, the distribution of access rights provided by services and applications, and user behavior. Such problems can be solved by the analytical computing infrastructure of the monitoring system.

1.2   Problem Definition

By analyzing of incoming requests statistic from the stakeholders of the TN of a major cable TV operator in North America, we identify the following groups of features not available in traditional monitoring systems:

- User classification based on different criteria taking into account both traditional monitoring data and data from other systems (e.g. data on billing, location, distribution of access rights, statistics on the use of services, applications, and data);
- Search for information associated with network elements such as metadata associated with data assets, services schedules, previous behavior statistic etc. (with information broken down by users, services, applications, and data);
- Analysis of user interests (and their changes);
- Streamlining the search for key causes of incidents;
- Dynamic control of telecommunication network parameters based on monitoring metrics, including metrics on user interests and activity.

This is not an exhaustive list; it can be expanded after a more detailed analysis of the needs of telecommunication network operators in monitoring data. The problems mentioned above can be solved by creating an analytical computing infrastructure built on both a single traditional monitoring system and group of monitoring systems.

2   Requirements for Ther Analytical Computing Infrastructure for Monitoring a Telecommunication Network

2.1   Use-Cases for the Introduction of an Analytical Monitoring System

Here we discuss how monitoring system data can be analyzed along with various static models of the telecommunication network and data on user behavior regarding the use of resources, services, and applications. Several use-cases divided into layers depending on the user groups are presented in Table 1.

Table 1. Analytical monitoring system scenarios

User role	Use-case
End-user (customer layer)	Monitoring current access restriction data
	Receiving personalized recommendations (offers of services and data for purchase)
	Improving the search service by taking into account the interests of the user when sorting search results
	Collecting geographic information and location data on user devices when providing services to the user
Network owners (business layer)	Monitoring information on user interests (for developing customized ads and giving personalized recommendations)
	Identification of target user groups for advertising purposes (analysis of statistics on user preferences)
	Generation of comprehensive analytical reports based on data from static network models and dynamic monitoring data
	Search for new semantic links between data from monitoring systems
	Two-way analysis of trends in various network performance indicators and their relationship with statistics on user behavior
Network operation (operations layer)	Instant search for the causes of problems encountered by users (expert search)

2.2   General Static and Dynamic Telecommunication Network Model Requirements

In order to solve analytical problems, it is necessary to combine a variety of static models of telecommunication networks that are available and add dynamic monitoring data. We suggest combining the following models and types of data:

1. Static models

   - Billing model;
   - Access permission model;
   - Network topology model;
   - Application hierarchy model;
   - Service hierarchy model;
   - Data model;

2. Dynamic data

- Data from traditional monitoring systems;
- Data from operational logs;
- Data on user activity.

The dynamic data needs to be connected with the static models.

2.3   Requirements for the Interaction Between a Static Model, Traditional Monitoring Data, and the Statistics on User Activity

In order for the analytical computing infrastructure to be able to solve the problems discussed, it is necessary to fulfill the following requirements for the structure of dynamic data and the interaction between these data and a static model:

- The data on the event being monitored should contain the following information:
  - event identifier;
  - time stamp;
  - event type identifier;
  - geographic information (if applicable);
  - a set of logical links between the event and the static network model.
- Events and network parameters that are fed into the analytical computing infrastructure of the monitoring system should be selected in such a way that they allow solving the problems at hand.
- Data flow parameters (data recording schedule, the number of monitoring parameters, methods and parameters for deleting obsolete data) need to be selected so that both the requirements for analytical reports are fulfilled and the desired performance is achieved (a system optimization issue connected with system design or configuration).

3   The Knowledge Graph as a Solution Core

3.1   The Knowledge Graph as a Core of the Solution

In general, using of knowledge graphs can support knowledge-driven applications and serve as a smart knowledge factory generating new knowledge. Knowledge graphs are used for both open-source projects (open knowledge graphs) and corporate ones (industrial knowledge graphs). Well-known open knowledge graphs are DBpedia [9], Google Knowledge Graph [10], YAGO [11], Wikidata [12]. Knowledge graphs provide an opportunity to expand our understanding of how knowledge can be managed on the Web and how that knowledge can be distinguished from more conventional Web-based data publication schemes such as Linked Data [24]. Standard problems solved by industrial knowledge graphs are for example [13]:

- Creating digital twins of real equipment.
- Risk management.
- Process monitoring.
- Operating services for sophisticated equipment.

In order to build the analytical computing infrastructure for monitoring a telecommunication network, we propose combining structural graph models of networks with dynamic data on network parameters and statistics on user activity in a single knowledge graph. This will allow making connections between monitoring data and the data from static network models as well as between different types of monitoring data (through semantic links within a single model). As a result, it will be possible to generate complex analytical reports that include data on both the network status and the links between different network processes.

We propose to represent the telecommunication network knowledge graph as an RDF (Resource Description Framework) graph, i.e. in "subject – predicate – object" triple format. In this configuration, a multitude of RDF statements form a directed graph with subjects and objects as nodes and links between them as edges [14, 15, 20, 21].

A telecommunication network provides users with services, which may include data transmission services (voice transmission or data transmission) or access to applications and/or data. Telecommunication networks are used by end users, business units of network operators, and owners. Each end user has access entitlements regarding services and data, and there can also be financial arrangements (billing). Communication channels can be different in both their physical properties (wired communication/optical communication/radio relay transmission) and bandwidth. A generalized model for monitoring a telecommunication network combines all of the components mentioned within a knowledge graph. The knowledge graph consists of mostly static structural models of the network, and of dynamic monitoring data that reflect user activity, services invocation, service performance statistics, errors, emergencies, and other events.

In contrast to traditional approaches, KGs make it possible to easily add new entity types to the model (static and dynamic), to use common domain ontologies to integrate external data, and to apply graph query languages for powerful search functionality.

The static component of the knowledge graph of a telecommunication network is based on the Telecommunications Service Domain Ontology (TSDO) [16]. Based on the architecture of the semantic services of telecommunication networks [17], the analytical computing infrastructure has the following layers:

- Semantic web-service based on Unified Service Architecture;
- Common Service Facilities and Value-added service Layer;
- Personalized Application.

The use of a generally accepted ontological model is critical for the subsequent integration of the analytical computing infrastructure for monitoring the telecommunication network with external applications and systems that deal with semantically linked data. The structure of the ontological model is shown in Fig. 1.

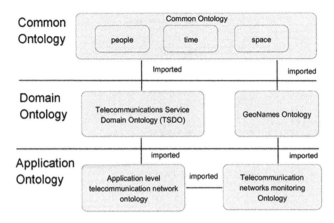

Fig. 1. The ontological model of the knowledge graph of the analytical computing infrastructure.

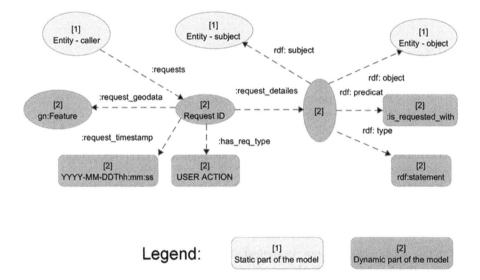

Fig. 2. The structure of the dynamic part of the knowledge graph.

The services and applications are described using the Web Ontology Language (OWL) model [22], which is compatible with the ontology presented [17]. In order to add geographic data to the model, the GeoNames ontology is imported at the level of domain ontologies [7].

3.2 Dynamic and Static Parts of the Model

The following KG sketches the design of the dynamic data model (Fig. 2):

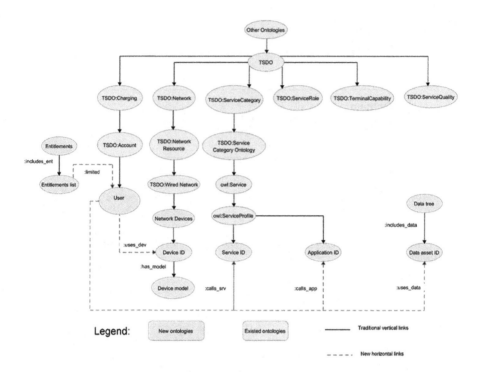

Fig. 3. The structure of the static part of the knowledge graph.

The static KG model is based on the ontological model shown in Fig. 1. The generalized hierarchy of the static model up to the application level (telecommunication network specialization) is shown in Fig. 3.

When designing the analytical computing infrastructure of a monitoring system, we start with the structural and ontological models of the static part of the knowledge graph. Next, the structure of dynamic data and the data arrival rate are defined.

3.3 The Architecture of the Analytical Computer Infrastructure Based on the Knowledge Graph

The block chart of the proposed analytical computing infrastructure based on the knowledge graph is presented in Fig. 4.

The proposed system consists of the following components:

1. The monitoring system core. The core includes:

- Application server accommodating the business logic for the performance of the whole system: schedule of interaction with other components, data bus, message exchange, file storage.
- Dynamic REST service supporting API for queries made by external systems.
- Set of adapters for querying data from external systems (monitoring, operator IT systems, etc.)

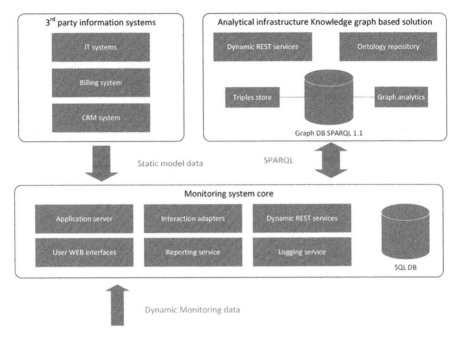

Fig. 4. The block chart of the analytical computing structure of a monitoring system based on the knowledge graph.

- Web interface for the system users and administrators.
- Reporting service which can represent reports in Web interface or send them to external consumers.
- System event logging service.
- SQL database designed to store monitoring dynamic data appropriate for storing in the system but inappropriate for placing in the knowledge graph.

2. Knowledge graph which includes:

- SPARQL 1.1 compliant RDF data storage. This component is the key element to the solution holding knowledge graph triples (static and dynamic components) and supporting the functions of adding/removing triples and searching in the RDF storage. The storage also includes a data analytics module. It stores both static and dynamic graph data connected by the common ontology.
- Ontology repository storing replicas of all ontological models the knowledge graph is based on. The delivered standards for data and ontology description: RDF [20], RDFS [21], OWL [22].
- Dynamic REST service supporting API for interaction with external systems, in particular, with the monitoring system core.

3. Operator IT systems supplying static data for the model used. Within the proposed monitoring system, the following operator IT systems are considered:

- The IT system for network infrastructure management supplies data on network topology, network devices, network services, network applications, accessible data, and access rights.
- The billing system supplies data on users, their devices, personal accounts, tariffs, and payments.
- The CRM systems supply data on the history of operator-user interaction.

3.4   Dynamic System Modeling

In order to evaluate performance, – we carried out tests to measure the speed of executing SPARQL queries depending on the size of the static and dynamic models of the knowledge graph, using the Metaphactory platform [8]. The parameters of the models that were analyzed and test results are presented in Table 2.

Table 2. Dynamic system modeling results

	Static data: Number of nodes: 100,000		
	Number of events		
	100,000	1,000,000	10,000,000
Request#1* execution time	1sec, 76ms	7sec, 683ms	1min, 49sec, 426ms
RDF data upload time, sec	21,8	198	2 542
	Static data: Number of nodes: 1,000,000		
	Number of events		
	100,000	1,000,000	10,000,000
Request#1* execution time, ms	2sec, 493ms	14sec, 188ms	2min, 1sec, 726ms
RDF data upload time, sec	95,5	283	2 712

*-Request#1 is defined below.

From the experiments, we can conclude that the analytical computing infrastructure for monitoring a telecommunication network based on a knowledge graph in the example presented has acceptable performance indicators if the knowledge graph has a size of 1 million nodes in the static network model and covers 10 million dynamic events.

Different approaches to optimizing the speed of query execution are described in [18] and [19].

4 Example Solution

4.1 Use-Case

The overall idea of the use case is to analyze service call frequency of end-users. This use-case has been chosen as example of analyzing dynamic data from different models and information systems.

Initial Data: A telecommunication network that provides services, applications, and sells access to content. The devices used are both stationary and mobile. When using services, data is generated about the period of use and the location of the device. In addition, emergencies happening to the operator's equipment are monitored taking into account geographic information.

Task: In this use case, we want to break down data on service call frequency by for following criteria:

- hours
- device models
- city districts

We want to overlay data on emergencies happening to the operator's network with data on service call frequency and break it down by the categories mentioned. This is not a regular task for the traditional TN-MS because the data to be analyzed is in different operator IT systems. Also, the available data in traditional TN-MS systems is aggregated and many initial data associations have been lost. This makes the use-case interesting and relevant, and it covers some of the discussed monitoring tasks.

4.2 The Knowledge Graph Model

To solve the problem, we propose the following KG model (Fig. 5).

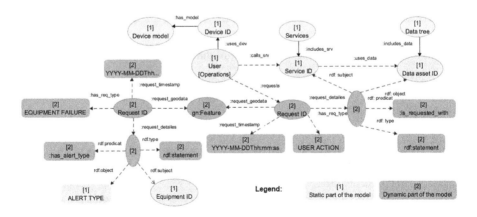

Fig. 5. The structure of the knowledge graph as an example of implementing the system.

4.3   SPARQL Requests/Responses

The application for generating an RDF/XML model of the knowledge graph, the RDF/XML model itself, and the SPARQL queries used in the paper are available on GitHub [23].

Below we provide a query and its response which limits the list of user's events by the following criteria:

- Date: 2020-02-01
- Event type: USER_ACTION
- Device model: Moto2k
- City district: <https://sws.geonames.org/8504951/>

SPARQL REQUEST #1:
PREFIX rdf: <http://www.w3.org/1999/02/22-rdf-syntax-ns#>
PREFIX rdfs: <http://www.w3.org/2000/01/rdf-schema#>
PREFIX xsd: <http://www.w3.org/2001/XMLSchema>
PREFIX my: <http://127.0.0.1/bg/ont/test1#>
*SELECT ***
WHERE
{
?Device my:has_the_device_model "Moto2k" .
?Device my:has_id ?Device_id .
?User my:uses_device ?Device_id .
?Request_ID my:request_timestamp ?Date .
FILTER contains(?Date, "2020-02-01") .
?Request_ID my:requests ?User .
?Request_ID my:has_req_type "USER_ACTION" .
?Request_ID my:request_geodata <https://sws.geonames.org/8504951/> .
?Request_ID my:request_detailes ?Detailes_ID .
?Detailes_ID rdf:subject ?Request_subject .
?Detailes_ID rdf:object ?Request_object .
}

The first rows of the response are shown in the Table 3.

Table 3. Response for the request #1

Device ID	User	Date	Request subject	Request object
D71	<http://127.0.0.1/User_71/>	2020-02-01T14:50:17	WatchTV	<http://127.0.0.1/Asset_7/>
D60	<http://127.0.0.1/User_60/>	2020-02-01T12:22:05	PPV	<http://127.0.0.1/Asset_4/>
D60	<http://127.0.0.1/User_60/>	2020-02-01T15:53:51	WatchTV	<http://127.0.0.1/Asset_10/>

The next SPARQL query (incl. result) retrieves equipment alerts for the following search criteria:

- Date: 2020-02-01
- Event type: EQUIPMENT_FAILURE
- City district: https://sws.geonames.org/8504951/

```
SPARQL REQUEST #2:
PREFIX rdf: <http://www.w3.org/1999/02/22-rdf-syntax-ns#>
PREFIX rdfs: <http://www.w3.org/2000/01/rdf-schema#>
PREFIX xsd: <http://www.w3.org/2001/XMLSchema>
PREFIX my: <http://127.0.0.1/bg/ont/test1#>
SELECT *
WHERE
{
 ?Request_ID my:request_timestamp ?Date .
 FILTER contains(?Date, "2020-02-01") .
 ?Request_ID my:has_req_type "EQUIPMENT_FAILURE" .
 ?Request_ID my:request_geodata <https://sws.geonames.org/8504951/> .
 ?Request_ID my:request_detailes ?Detailes_ID .
 ?Detailes_ID rdf:subject ?Request_subject .
 ?Detailes_ID rdf:object ?Request_object .
}
```

The first rows of the response are shown in the Table 4.

Table 4. Response for the request #2

Date	Request subject	Request object
2020-02-01T09:11:09	<http://127.0.0.1/Device_78/>	STB_out_of_memory
2020-02-01T03:40:33	<http://127.0.0.1/Device_94/>	STB_out_of_memory
2020-02-01T11:35:01	<http://127.0.0.1/Device_93/>	STB_out_of_memory
2020-02-01T22:00:01	<http://127.0.0.1/Device_18/>	STB_out_of_memory

Finally, we analyze the distribution of events for both user actions and equipment alerts. Request parameters:

- Date: 2020-02-01
- Event type: All event types
- Device model: All models
- City district: https://sws.geonames.org/8504951

```
SPARQL REQUEST #3:
PREFIX rdf: <http://www.w3.org/1999/02/22-rdf-syntax-ns#>
PREFIX rdfs: <http://www.w3.org/2000/01/rdf-schema#>
PREFIX xsd: <http://www.w3.org/2001/XMLSchema>
PREFIX my: <http://127.0.0.1/bg/ont/test1#>
SELECT *
WHERE
{
  ?Request_ID my:request_timestamp ?Date .
  FILTER contains(?Date, "2020-02-01") .
  ?Request_ID my:request_geodata <https://sws.geonames.org/8504951/> .
  ?Request_ID my:request_detailes ?Detailes_ID .
  ?Detailes_ID rdf:subject ?Request_subject .
  ?Detailes_ID rdf:object ?Request_object .
}
```

The first few results are shown in the Table 5.

Table 5. Response for the request #3

Date	Request_subject	Request_object
2020-02-01T14:13:54	WatchTV	<http://127.0.0.1/Asset_2/>
2020-02-01T14:03:46	nPVR	<http://127.0.0.1/Asset_7/>
2020-02-01T14:50:17	WatchTV	<http://127.0.0.1/Asset_7/>
2020-02-01T09:11:09	<http://127.0.0.1/Device_78/>	STB_out_of_memory

5 Conclusion

With the proposed analytical computing infrastructure for monitoring a telecommunication network (as a typical most complex dynamic network) based on a knowledge graph it is possible to combine different static network models in a single semantic model and add dynamic monitoring data to the system. The KG model allows to address new classes of problems that could be tackled using traditional monitoring systems. Further, the KG (based on ontologies as backbone) can be easily integrated with other systems based on semantic data models. In addition to solving new classes of monitoring tasks, telecom operators can more easily realize complex analytical monitoring solutions and a more flexible architecture in general. From the end-user's point of view, the operator can provide more personalized services. We discuss an example use case of an analytical problem of monitoring a telecommunication network. The example shows some of the benefits of analyzing dynamic monitoring data within a single knowledge graph. Test results show that such systems can process large amounts of data with acceptable performance. The suggested approach provides benefits when building an analytical monitoring infrastructure based on soft requirements and when the monitoring functionality needs to be extended in the future. KG technologies allow to create powerful tools for system analysis. Also, this approach can be used in different subject areas for dynamic objects modelling, e.g. natural phenomena. The base of this model can be built using already existed models of machine learning [25–27]. In future work, we will study which kinds problems such models can solve in more detail, and how to optimize links in the KG, and then create a full prototype of the solution with the discussed benefits.

Acknowledgment. To Metaphacts GmbH, Daimlerstrasse 36, 69190, Walldorf, Germany for the license to model knowledge graphs on the Metaphactory platform.

Funding. The research was funded by Russian Foundation for Basic Research (RFBR) according to the research projects #18-57-34001 and #19-07-00784.

References

1. Wong, E.: Network monitoring fundamentals and standards. Computer Science (2000). https://www.cse.wustl.edu/~jain/cis788-97/ftp/net_monitoring/index.html
2. Stallings, W.: SNMP, SNMPv2, and RMON Practical Network Management, 2nd edn. Addison-Wesley Professional Computing and Engineering (1996). A good general reference in basics of RMON
3. Apostolopoulos, T.K., Daskalou, V.C.: On the implementation of a prototype for performance management services. In: IEEE Symposium on Computers and Communications, pp. 57–63 (1995). A research paper on a prototype for management services
4. Stanford University: Network monitoring tools. Stanford University. http://www.slac.stanford.edu/xorg/nmtf/nmtf-tools.html
5. Comparison of network monitoring systems. https://en.wikipedia.org/wiki/Comparison_of_network_monitoring_systems
6. Natarov, A., Shirokii, A.: Next generation network monitoring systems—critical requirements and design. https://doi.org/10.15688/mpcm.jvolsu.2018.3.4
7. GeoNames ontology. http://www.geonames.org/ontology/documentation.html
8. Haase, P., Herzig, D.M., Kozlov, A., Nikolov, A., Trame, J.: metaphactory: a platform for knowledge graph management. Semant. Web **10**(6), 1109–1125 (2019)
9. DBpedia. https://wiki.dbpedia.org/about
10. Introducing the Knowledge Graph: things, not strings, 16 May 2012. http://googleblog.blogspot.com/2012/05/introducing-knowledge-graph-things-not.html
11. Suchanek, F.M., Kasneci, G., Weikum, G.: Yago: a core of semantic knowledge. In: WWW 2007: Proceedings of the 16th International Conference on World Wide Web, pp. 697–706, May 2007. https://doi.org/10.1145/1242572.1242667
12. Erxleben, F., Günther, M., Krötzsch, M., Mendez, J., Vrandečić, D.: Introducing wikidata to the linked data web. In: Mika, P., et al. (eds.) ISWC 2014. LNCS, vol. 8796, pp. 50–65. Springer, Cham (2014). https://doi.org/10.1007/978-3-319-11964-9_4
13. Hubauer, T., et al.: Use cases of the industrial knowledge graph at siemens. In: International Semantic Web Conference (P&D/Industry/BlueSky) (2018)
14. RDF primer. https://www.w3.org/TR/rdf-primer/
15. Farber, M., Ell, B., Menne, C., Rettinger, A., Bartscherer, F.: Linked data quality of DBPedia, Freebase, OpenCyc, Wikidata, and YAGO. Semantic Web J. (2016). http://www.scmantic-web-journal.net/contenv/linked-data-quality-dbpedia-freebase-opencyc-wikidata-and-yago. Accessed August 2016

16. Qiao, X., Li, X., Chen, J.: Telecommunications service domain ontology: semantic interoperation foundation of intelligent integrated services. In: Ortiz, J.H. (ed.) Telecommunications Networks - Current Status Future Trends, 30th March 2012. IntechOpen (2012). https://doi.org/10.5772/36794

17. Qiao, X., Li, X., You, T., Sun, L.: Semantic telecommunications network capability services. In: Domingue, J., Anutariya, C. (eds.) ASWC 2008. LNCS, vol. 5367, pp. 508–523. Springer, Heidelberg (2008). https://doi.org/10.1007/978-3-540-89704-0_35

18. Han, S., Zou, L., Yu, J.X., Zhao, D.: Keyword search on RDF graphs - a query graph assembly approach. In: CIKM 2017: Proceedings of the 2017 ACM on Conference on Information and Knowledge Management, pp. 227–236, November 2017. https://doi.org/10.1145/3132847.3132957

19. Zou, L., Özsu, M.T., Chen, L., Shen, X., Huang, R., Zhao, D.: gStore: a graph-based SPARQL query engine. VLDB J. 23(4), 565–590 (2014). https://doi.org/10.1007/s00778-013-0337-7

20. RDF. https://www.w3.org/RDF/

21. RDFS. https://www.w3.org/TR/rdf-schema/

22. OWL. https://www.w3.org/OWL/

23. GitHub repository link. https://github.com/kulikovia/ICSSA-2020

24. McCusker, J.: What is a knowledge graph? http://www.semantic-web-journal.net/content/what-knowledge-graph

25. Stankova, E.N., Balashiy, A.V., Petrov, D.A., Korkhov, V.V.: OLAP technology and machine learning as the tools for validation of the numerical models of convective clouds. Int. J. Bus. Intell. Data Min. 14(1/2), 254–266 (2019). https://doi.org/10.1504/IJBIDM.2019.096793. ISSN online 1743-8195, ISSN print 1743-8187

26. Stankova, E.N., Khvatkov, E.V.: Using boosted k-nearest neighbour algorithm for numerical forecasting of dangerous convective phenomena. In: Misra, S., et al. (eds.) ICCSA 2019. LNCS, vol. 11622, pp. 802–811. Springer, Cham (2019). https://doi.org/10.1007/978-3-030-24305-0_61

27. Stankova, E.N., Ismailova, E.T., Grechko, I.A.: Algorithm for processing the results of cloud convection simulation using the methods of machine learning. In: Gervasi, O., et al. (eds.) ICCSA 2018. LNCS, vol. 10963, pp. 149–159. Springer, Cham (2018). https://doi.org/10.1007/978-3-319-95171-3_13

International Workshop
on Computational Studies for Energy
and Comfort in Buildings (SECoB 2020)

Energy Performance of a Service Building: Comparison Between EnergyPlus and Revit

João Silva[1,2(✉)] ⓘ, José Brás[1,2] ⓘ, Ricardo Noversa[1,2] ⓘ,
Nelson Rodrigues[1,2] ⓘ, Luís Martins[2] ⓘ, José Teixeira[2] ⓘ,
and Senhorinha Teixeira[1] ⓘ

[1] ALGORITMI Centre, University of Minho, Guimarães, Portugal
st@dps.uminho.pt
[2] Mechanical Engineering and Resource Sustainability Centre (MEtRICs),
University of Minho, Guimarães, Portugal

Abstract. Currently, the energy consumption study in buildings is very important, since it is one of the sectors of activity where there is great potential to improve energy efficiency. On the market, there are several simulation software, and the aim of this work consists in conducting a comparison between two dynamic simulation software, EnergyPlus, and Revit, with respect to the results obtained of thermal loads and annual energy consumption of a service building.

In the simulation using EnergyPlus, an annual energy consumption of 442 MWh was obtained, that compares with 533 MWh when using Revit. Concerning the thermal loads in the sales area of the hypermarket, the simulation results for the thermal loads were the following: 761 kW for heating and 79 kW for cooling, versus 924 kW for heating and 86 kW for cooling when using the EnergyPlus and the Revit software, respectively. This discrepancy between the values obtained could be due to the limited selection of climatic files in Revit as well as the different definitions of the HVAC systems.

Keywords: Energy performance · Services building · Simulation

1 Introduction

One of the most important energy consumers in the European Union (EU) is the building sector. This sector is responsible for approximately 36% of CO_2 emissions and 40% of the final energy demands [1, 2]. In Portugal, the Building sector is responsible for around 30% of the final energy consumption and Araújo et al. [3] reported that 50% of this consumption can be reduced by using energy efficiency measures corresponding to 400 million tons of saved CO_2 emissions.

Therefore, buildings may provide an important opportunity to reduce energy consumption and thus to minimize the negative impacts on global warming. Consequently, great challenges to achieve the decarbonization agenda of the EU and make this sector energy efficient are occurring in the building sector.

For this purpose, the EU has implemented several Directives since 2002 and more recently the Directive 2010/31/EU on the energy performance of buildings and Directive 2012/27/EU on energy efficiency [2]. These set of Directives are important

© Springer Nature Switzerland AG 2020
O. Gervasi et al. (Eds.): ICCSA 2020, LNCS 12254, pp. 201–213, 2020.
https://doi.org/10.1007/978-3-030-58817-5_16

measures to phase out inefficient buildings. They are the major legislative and policy package in the EU, focusing on existing and new buildings and are usually referred to as the Energy Performance of Buildings Directive. Recently, one indication of these rules is the transformation of existing buildings into nearly zero-energy buildings, to be required by 2050.

Following the regulatory approach, to optimize and develop sustainable design and efficient energy analysis, several novel methods have been used [4]. Computer simulation tools are an effective method to analyze different systems such as manufacturing procedures, construction processes, and energy analysis [5, 6]. Building dynamic simulations play an important role in determining the optimal design variables since the building's response to these new features can be highly sensitive to local climate factors. The major tools in the building energy field are whole-building energy simulation programs that consider key performance indicators such as energy demand and costs [7]. De Boeck et al. [8] provide a recent literature review on improving the energy performance of residential buildings by the following topics: area of application and design variables, objectives and performance measures, type of analysis, solution methodology, software tools, case study location and type of building. There is a recent trend in more papers leading to energy objectives. However, the author recommended some important future research opportunities, based on imperfections of past studies, such as the specific trade-off between winter and summer energy consumptions that should be considered to find suitable energy efficiency solutions. Furthermore, the author highlighted the most applied tools in the literature and EnergyPlus is one of them.

Regarding this subject, energy analysis of buildings, some interesting review works present the capabilities, importance, and developments of this type of tool. For instance, Østergård et al. [9] reviewed the recent developments in both academia and in the commercial software industry that target challenges in building energy simulation. Based on this review, the authors proposed a simulation framework that facilitates proactive, intelligent and experience-based building simulation. Lopes et al. [10] recently provided an important literature review concerning energy efficiency policies and regulations for buildings, highlighting how the Brazilian labeling program can be improved compared to the Portugal and United States programs. Previously, in 2009, Pérez-Lombard et al. [11] analyzed the origin and the historic development of energy certification schemes in buildings along with the definition, scope and critical aspects of a building energy certificate. Other interesting works in this area are the works developed by Araújo et al. [3], Abela et al. [12] and Li et al. [13]. The first author analyzed the Portuguese thermal regulation for residential buildings and studied the influence of some parameters considered as important to the energy efficiency of buildings on energy performance and the energy certification rate. Abela et al. [12], in its turn, investigated if the current calculation methodologies in utilization for the generation of energy performance certification processes in the Mediterranean countries are appropriated. The authors analyzed different national methodologies from Cyprus, Italy, Malta, and Spain on four test case study dwellings. Finally, Li et al. [13] provided a review of the current energy performance certificate situations in the EU and discusses the direction of future improvements.

Shrivastava et al. [14] report a critical literature review of the solar water heating system simulation. This work presents a comparative analysis of popular simulation tools and their architecture from the perspective of TRNSYS. The author stated that this simulation software provided good agreement within error between 5 and 10%. Furthermore, the author recommends the simultaneous analysis of the same system on different programs to avoid bias results. The different programs and recent technology developments in Building Information Modeling (BIM) and Building Energy Modeling (BEM) were reviewed by Farzaneh et al. [15]. Garcia et al. [16] propose a new idea to facilitate the information exchange of BIM and BEM software applications under the support of open standard schemes.

In addition to these works, some authors investigated the energy performance and savings in specific applications. Sadeghifam et al. [17] examined the energy saving in building elements and how its interaction in conjunction with effective air quality factors can contribute towards an ultimate energy efficient design. These works were based on a typical house in Malaysia and the building was modeled using Revit software and then imported to EnergyPlus software to evaluate the best option in terms of energy savings.

Herrando et al. [18] established a systematic method to perform and analyze in detail the Energy Performance Certification of 21 Faculty Buildings located at the University of Zaragoza (Spain), according to the transposition of Directive 2010/31/EU. The results provided by this tool have been analyzed in detail to extract as much information as possible about the building's energy performance as well as to identify limitations of the software and propose potential improvements to shorten the difference between real and estimated energy consumption.

Gerrish et al. [19] evaluated the potential for the use of BIM as a tool to support the visualization and management of a building's performance.

Nizam et al. [20] presented a framework to estimate the embodied energy content within the BIM environment. This framework facilitated the incorporation of the embodied energy assessment procedure into an integrated building model for the design process by highlighting major contributors during different phases.

Shiel et al. [21] examined two different buildings and the influence of some parameters within a design stage on the predicted energy usage. However, as the majority of the BIM software programs do not provide the possibility to inform the actions that will improve the building energy performance and how much they will cost, Ruiz et al. [22] applied a new methodology to design the annual energy demand, life-cycle cost, and energy rating of a building.

In this way, the objective of this paper is to study the energy performance in a new service building in Portugal and to perform the same analysis using two different programs to avoid bias results as suggested by Srivastava et al. [14]. This is an important work to provide answers to very specific questions during design of the new building since with building energy simulation tools the energy performance can be evaluated and the influence of some key variables can be analyzed in an easy and fast way. Regarding this is added value, the owners of the service building will be able to see the building energy demand that is a consequence of what is being projected and what will be its cost and energy performance.

2 Case Study

The methodology used in this study to analyze the energy consumption in a service building is presented in this chapter. Firstly, the building, its main characteristics, and equipment are described. Then, the procedure used to analyze the energy performance using two different simulation tools is presented.

2.1 Building Description

Building. The building is located at São João da Madeira, in the district of Aveiro, Portugal. The building, still under construction, will be a hypermarket, consisting of three floors. The first floor, called Floor −1, is below ground level. This floor will have a technical space and a parking area. The second floor, identified as Floor 0, will mainly consist of the spaces affected by the commercial/sales area, where customers may access the services authorized by the hypermarket itself. Also, this floor will have technical spaces, warehouses, toilets, a coordination room, and a garage. The third floor, defined as Floor 1, will consist of a training room, a break room, changing rooms, toilets, and technical spaces.

The building will have a height of 12 m, presenting the main front oriented to the east, with east-west lighting. Figure 1 shows the orientation of the building and its rotation to the north. Considering that 0° refers to the north, it appears that the upper front is rotated by 26° to the northwest.

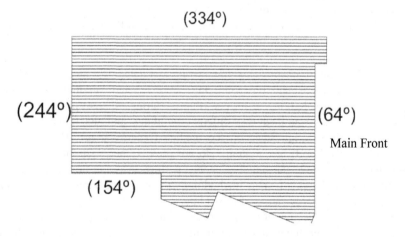

Fig. 1. Illustration of the building orientation plan.

HVAC Equipment. The air conditioning system will consist of three *Rooftop* units (heat pumps) inserted in the roof of the building, producing heating and cooling for the sales area. For the remaining climate zones, there are split units. As for the air renewal of the sales space, it will be provided by three rooftop units, through the mixture of fresh air from outside. The ventilation of the remaining spaces with permanent occupation will be ensured through an air handling unit (AHU) with energy recovery flow. Extraction and insufflation units were also accounted for in various areas, such as technical areas, bakery and kitchen, toilets, garage, and car park. Table 1 presents the characteristic of the proposed building's air conditioning system.

Table 1. Characteristic of the building's air conditioning system.

Zone	Equipment	Heating Power (kW)	Cooling Power (kW)	COP	EER
Locker room - men	*Split* MUPR-18	5.56	5.27	3.50	4.00
Locker room - women	Split MUPR-24	7.61	7.32	3.60	3.20
Training room		7.61	7.32	3.60	3.20
Restroom		7.61	7.32	3.60	3.20
Coordinator room		4.10	3.51	3.50	2.80
Cabinet		7.61	7.32	3.60	3.20
Sales area - access zone	*Rooftop* IPJ 160	36.79	37.32	3.62	3.20
Sales area - neutral zone	*Rooftop* IPJ 320	72.12	73.04	3.54	3.20

COP – Coefficient of performance
EER- Energy efficiency ratio

2.2   Simulation Study

The EnergyPlus is a robust energy simulation software with a high potential for simulation of the building energy consumption under different thermomechanical conditions. This open-source software is approved by the Portuguese Department of Energy and used worldwide. With excellent precision for radiant and convection heat fluxes between indoor and outdoor, HVAC systems performance, heat exchanges with all external surfaces, thermal comfort, natural, artificial and hybrid systems can be modeled through this software. The core of this energy simulation tool is a model of the building that is based on fundamental heat balance principles.

Regarding the Revit software, this software is essentially used for design and allows to perform some calculations, from structural to energetic analyzes. However, the analytical part of this software is still under development. Regarding the numerical procedure, this software is based on steady state for heating and cooling load calculation of non-residential buildings according to radiant time series calculation method, a simplified method based directly on a heat balance method.

The next subsections will present each of the needed tasks to perform the energy simulation with both tools.

3D Model. In order to perform energy simulations, the first step is to define the geometry of the building in question. Regarding the EnergyPlus software, for modeling purposes, the SketchUp software was used, and the final model was modeled through blocks, resulting in the definition of thirty-six spaces of which sixteen are defined as thermal zones. After the definition of the 3D model, represented in Fig. 2 a), with the characteristics of the surfaces and thermal zones, the model was exported to OpenStudio plugin that is connected to the EnergyPlus. This is a friendlier and simpler interface than working directly with EnergyPlus software.

Concerning the Revit model, the architecture of the building was initially imported from an AutoCAD program file. In this way, it allowed modeling the building with the best possible accuracy. However, an effort was taken in creating a model as close as possible to the one the developed with SketchUp, in order to minimize possible differences between the two software. Figure 2 b) presents the model developed with Revit software.

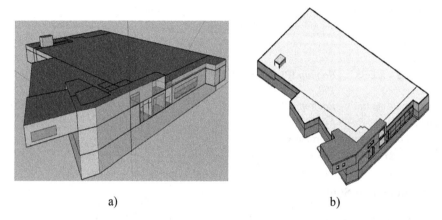

a)   b)

Fig. 2. Exterior view of the 3D building: a) EnergyPlus model and b) Revit model.

Input Data.

Climatic Zone. Climate data is one of the most important parameters in the thermal simulation of buildings. Through the CLIMAS-SCE software, the municipality in question was selected, obtaining information such as geographic coordinates, altitude, climatological statistics, among others. Figure 3 presents an overview of this information.

The selection of the climate file in Revit is quite different compared to OpenStudio. While in OpenStudio, a ".epw" file created using the spreadsheet provided by the SCE is imported, in Revit, it is not necessary to proceed with this import, because only the building geographical coordinates are introduced.

As expected, Revit does not have a library of climatic files for each location in the world, therefore, the software selects a location that has a climatic file closest to the location of the building coordinates defined. As there is no climatic file referring to São João da Madeira in Revit libraries, a climatic file from Porto, which is approximately 35 km away, was used.

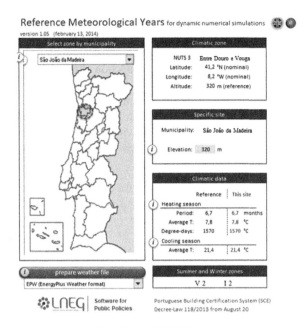

Fig. 3. Climas-SCE1.05 software.

Thermal Zones. The building is open every day of the week from 9 am to 8 pm. However, the profiles of the variables that characterize the use of the different thermal zones were defined, such as occupation, use of electrical equipment, lighting, ventilation, thermostats, metabolic rate, fans, among others, since they have different working periods. Correct determination of a profile requires defining its typical behavior on a day, defining the corresponding period (weekly, monthly, or yearly), as well as including possible constraints (holidays). The different periods were all defined individually in both energy programs.

The process of schedules definition in Revit is much more restrictive, compared to OpenStudio. While in OpenStudio it is possible to define an opening time for different periods of the week, month and year, in Revit it is only possible to define a time which is constant throughout the year. Since in a hypermarket the rate of equipment operation and occupancy is different on weekends than the rest of the week this is a significative simplification.

Constructive Solutions. EnergyPlus supports an online component library to define the properties of the various surfaces, considering the materials and their position in the building envelope. However, the user can customize and create its own constitution of the building elements. In the present work, several materials were created, defining their properties, to obtain the real constitution of all the building's envelope solutions. The constituent materials of walls, ground surfaces, roofs, and glass walls, were defined in terms of roughness, thickness, conductivity, density and specific heat. The procedure was the same as the Revit software. Table 2 presents the main material properties considered in energy simulation for both software.

Loads. The loads refer to the internal gains existing in the various thermal zones of the building. These gains are associated with the number of occupants, the power of electrical equipment and lighting. Thus, it is important to define these variables. Table 3 presents the number of occupants, as a function of the thermal zone, as well as the power of electrical and lighting equipment. Other types of loads associated with other areas were accounted for, such as the lighting in the outdoor area, parking lot and warehouses, the consumption of fans present in these areas, as well as the electric consumption of the elevator and escalators. Revit software provided the same capabilities as EnergyPlus and all this information was inserted in the same way.

Table 2. Material properties of the envelope surface.

	Thickness (m)	Conductivity (W/m.K)	Thermal Resistance ($(m^2.^{\circ}C)/W$)
Exterior wall	0.4	1.935	2.08
Interior wall	0.26	2.318	2.53
Exterior roof	0.12	156.04	2.50
Ground	0.38	7.24	1.45

Table 3. Loads defined in the energy simulation programs.

Zone	Number of persons	Light (W)	Electric equipment (W/m^2)
Sales area	403	21,026	13
Locker room	20	507	3
Training room	13	245	5
Rest room	12	136	5
Coordinator room	3	86	5
Cabinet	1	50	–
Escalator	1	1,334	–
Escalator	1	274	–
Stairs	1	274	–
Stairs	1	179	–
Circulation zone	1	274	–
Circulation zone	1	179	–
Circulation zone	1	274	–
Circulation zone	1	288	–
Bathroom	1	56	3

HVAC System. As for the building's HVAC system, it was necessary to create several systems that met the building's HVAC requirements. In EnergyPlus it is not possible to insert different HVAC systems for the same zone, so the three rooftop units were joined in one to acclimate the sales area. A system illustrated in Fig. 4, was created in this zone, consisting of a Coil Cooling DX Single Speed and a Coil Heating DX Single Speed, a diffuser, a thermostat and ventilation conditions were defined. Insufflation and exhaust fans were not included because they were accounted for equipment efficiency.

The operation of rooftops is controlled according to a thermostat which implements a temperature of air insufflation dependent on the heating or cooling thermal load to ensure a temperature setpoint temperature of 25 °C in summer and 21 °C in winter. In the present case, the air is inflated with a minimum value at 16 °C for summer and a maximum of 33 °C for winter. In the other air-conditioned spaces, identical systems were used, and heat recovery units were included.

Regarding Revit modeling, the creation of HVAC systems is not allowed, and it is only possible to select an HVAC system that belongs to the software libraries. Furthermore, it is not possible to change the characteristics of these HVAC systems. In this way, the Package Terminal Heat Pump system was used, which is the most identical system to a Rooftop.

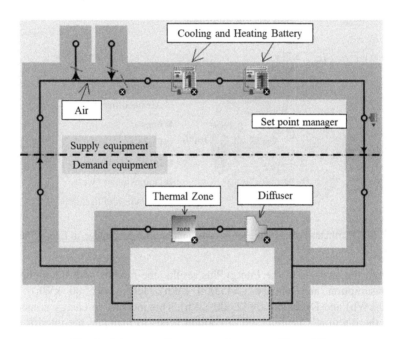

Fig. 4. Sales area climate control system at EnergyPlus.

3   Results and Discussion

In this section, the simulation results are presented and discussed. The two subsections concern the results of the energy consumption and thermal loads obtained with the two different simulation tools. Furthermore, an analysis of the differences between the two software is presented.

3.1   EnergyPlus Results

Initially, the annual energy consumptions obtained with the simulation tool are presented and, later, the daily ones. Daily consumptions refer to the two-day energy consumption of the climate file considered to have peak representative environmental conditions of the summer and winter periods. That is two days whose temperatures were the most extreme, in São João da Madeira, resulting in the selection of January 21 and August 22.

Figure 5 presents the distribution of annual energy consumption, and most of the consumption is due to lighting and air conditioning purposes, representing 66.5% of final consumption. Furthermore, it should be noted that regarding the different zones of the building, the sales area represented, in two typical day days of winter and summer season, energy expenses equivalent to 91% of the general consumption, becoming the most consuming thermal zone of the building.

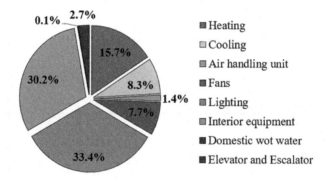

Fig. 5. Distribution of annual energy consumption as a percentage in EnergyPlus.

Through the analysis of the EnergyPlus results, the months with the highest electrical consumption are January (≈45,000 kWh), July (≈42,500 kWh), August (≈42,000 kWh) and December (≈42,000 kWh). This increase in energy consumption is due to the building's heating and/or cooling needs to maintain the interior temperature and ensure thermal comfort. The obtained results in the simulation regarding the heating and cooling section were increased by 5% since in the simulation linear thermal bridges were not considered.

3.2   Revit Results

Unlike EnergyPlus in Revit it is only possible to determine the annual energy consumption. With this software, the annual energy consumption of 533.5 MWh was obtained, with the main sector responsible for being the lighting sector (27.7%). Figure 6 presents the annual energy consumption of the building according to the main components.

Regarding the thermal loads and annual electricity consumption, the results obtained with the two simulation tools are quite different about the annual energy consumption. With EnergyPlus 442 MWh was obtained, while with Revit software 533 MWh was the annual energy consumption prediction. The thermal loads in the sales area of the hypermarket, in the simulation using EnergyPlus, the following maximum thermal loads in the sales area were obtained: 761 kW and 79 kW for heating and cooling, respectively. However, with Revit, 924 kW of heating and 86 kW of cooling were obtained.

This discrepancy is expected since Revit is not a software whose main functionality is the dynamic simulation, unlike EnergyPlus, but a software-oriented for design. The level of complexity of Revit compared with EnergyPlus is lower, which makes difficult to obtain a correct dynamic simulation of the building. The two limitations already pointed of the restriction in the definition of the climate file and the definition of the HVAC system, can difficult the right simulations.

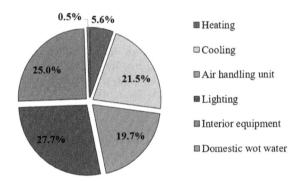

Fig. 6. Distribution of annual energy consumption as a percentage in Revit.

4 Conclusions

On the market, there are several building energy simulation software and EnergyPlus and Revit programs were selected to analyze the results obtained for thermal loads and annual energy consumption of a service building.

In the simulation using EnergyPlus, the annual energy consumption of 442 MWh was obtained, that compares with a value of 533 MWh when using Revit. Concerning the thermal loads, the simulation using EnergyPlus showed results for heating and cooling 10% lower when compared with the values predicted by the Revit software. This discrepancy between the values is mainly because Revit is very limited in the selection of climatic files and the definition of the HVAC systems.

However, it is important to emphasize in this work, independently of the characteristics of each software, the different options included and the influence on the results, this will be minimized depending on the user experience. This is nevertheless a characteristic of any simulation program. This aspect was noted in the present case study which has a simple air conditioning system and a diversified building, promoting the qualities of the EnergyPlus software.

Acknowledgments. The authors would like to express their gratitude for the support given by FCT within the R&D Units Project Scope UIDB/00319/2020 (ALGORITMI) and R&D Units Project Scope UIDP/04077/2020 (MEtRICs).

References

1. von Platten, J., Holmberg, C., Mangold, M., et al.: The renewing of energy performance certificates - reaching comparability between decade-apart energy records. Appl. Energy **255**, 113902 (2019)
2. Li, Y., Kubicki, S., Guerriero, A., Rezgui, Y.: Review of building energy performance certification schemes towards future improvement. Renew. Sustain. Energy Rev. **113**, 109244 (2019)
3. Araújo, C., Almeida, M., Bragança, L.: Analysis of some Portuguese thermal regulation parameters. Energy Build. **58**, 141–150 (2013)
4. Pacheco, R., Ordóñez, J., Martínez, G.: Energy efficient design of building: a review. Renew. Sustain. Energy Rev. **16**, 3559–3573 (2012)
5. Garwood, T.L., Hughes, B.R., Oates, M.R., et al.: A review of energy simulation tools for the manufacturing sector. Renew. Sustain. Energy Rev. **81**, 895–911 (2018)
6. Gao, H., Koch, C., Wu, Y.: Building information modelling based building energy modelling: a review. Appl. Energy **238**, 320–343 (2019)
7. Stevanović, S.: Optimization of passive solar design strategies: a review. Renew. Sustain. Energy Rev. **25**, 177–196 (2013)
8. De Boeck, L., Verbeke, S., Audenaert, A., De Mesmaeker, L.: Improving the energy performance of residential buildings: a literature review. Renew. Sustain. Energy Rev. **52**, 960–975 (2015)
9. Østergård, T., Jensen, R.L., Maagaard, S.E.: Building simulations supporting decision making in early design – a review. Renew. Sustain. Energy Rev. **61**, 187–201 (2016)
10. Lopes, A.C.P., Oliveira Filho, D., Altoe, L., et al.: Energy efficiency labeling program for buildings in Brazil compared to the United States' and Portugal's. Renew. Sustain. Energy Rev. **66**, 207–219 (2016)
11. Pérez-Lombard, L., Ortiz, J., González, R., Maestre, I.R.: A review of benchmarking, rating and labelling concepts within the framework of building energy certification schemes. Energy Build. **41**, 272–278 (2009)
12. Abela, A., Hoxley, M., McGrath, P., Goodhew, S.: An investigation of the appropriateness of current methodologies for energy certification of mediterranean housing. Energy Build. **130**, 210–218 (2016)
13. Li, Y., Kubicki, S., Guerriero, A., Rezgui, Y.: Review of building energy performance certification schemes towards future improvement. Renew. Sustain. Energy Rev. **113**, 109244 (2019)
14. Shrivastava, R.L., Kumar, V., Untawale, S.P.: Modeling and simulation of solar water heater: a TRNSYS perspective. Renew. Sustain. Energy Rev. **67**, 126–143 (2017)
15. Farzaneh, A., Monfet, D., Forgues, D.: Review of using building information modeling for building energy modeling during the design process. J. Build. Eng. **23**, 127–135 (2019)
16. Guzmán Garcia, E., Zhu, Z.: Interoperability from building design to building energy modeling. J. Build. Eng. **1**, 33–41 (2015)
17. Sadeghifam, A.N., Zahraee, S.M., Meynagh, M.M., Kiani, I.: Combined use of design of experiment and dynamic building simulation in assessment of energy efficiency in tropical residential buildings. Energy Build. **86**, 525–533 (2015)

18. Herrando, M., Cambra, D., Navarro, M., et al.: Energy performance certification of faculty buildings in spain: the gap between estimated and real energy consumption. Energy Convers. Manag. **125**, 141–153 (2016)
19. Gerrish, T., Ruikar, K., Cook, M., et al.: BIM application to building energy performance visualisation and management: challenges and potential. Energy Build. **144**, 218–228 (2017)
20. Nizam, R.S., Zhang, C., Tian, L.: A BIM based tool for assessing embodied energy for buildings. Energy Build. **170**, 1–14 (2018). https://doi.org/10.1016/j.enbuild.2018.03.067
21. Shiel, P., Tarantino, S., Fischer, M.: Parametric analysis of design stage building energy performance simulation models. Energy Build. **172**, 78–93 (2018)
22. Aparicio Ruiz, P., Guadix Martín, J., Salmerón Lissén, J.M., Sánchez de la Flor, F.J.: An integrated optimisation method for residential building design: a case study in Spain. Energy Build. **80**, 158–168 (2014)

Thermal Simulation of a Supermarket Cold Zone with Integrated Assessment of Human Thermal Comfort

Ricardo Noversa[1,2] ⓘ, João Silva[1,2] ⓘ, Nelson Rodrigues[1,2(✉)] ⓘ,
Luís Martins[2] ⓘ, José Teixeira[2] ⓘ, and Senhorinha Teixeira[1] ⓘ

[1] ALGORITMI Centre, University of Minho, Guimarães, Portugal
{nelson.rodrigues,st}@dps.uminho.pt
[2] Mechanical Engineering and Resource Sustainability Centre (MEtRICs),
University of Minho, Guimarães, Portugal

Abstract. This work seeks to analyze the thermal comfort of the occupants in a large building of Commerce and Services, integrating measures of assessment and energy efficiency promotion. The building is still in the construction phase and at its conclusion, will correspond to a supermarket located in the Central region of Portugal. For the evaluation of thermal comfort, Fanger's methodology was used, where the Predicted Mean Vote (PMV) and Predicted Percentage of Dissatisfied (PPD) were calculated based on a detailed analysis of the environmental variables. These are essential to obtain, namely, mean air velocity, mean radiant temperature, mean air temperature and relative humidity. The other crucial variables are the metabolic rate and the thermal clothing resistance. The simulations necessary for the thermal comfort assessment were performed in ANSYS Fluent, in order to minimize the energy consumption in the cold thermal zone of the building, the sales area with frozen and chilled food, by means of reducing the inflow of air, without compromising thermal Comfort. The final results showed that the reduction of the amount of air to be inflated did not compromise the thermal comfort of the occupants. The Computational Fluid Dynamics (CFD) methodology allowed the creation of comfort maps, albeit for a single zone due to computational limitations. According to the results, the most comfortable zone was located right below the air insufflation with the summer being a more comfortable season. In winter, the main problem detected was the cold located near the floor.

Keywords: Thermal comfort · Supermarket · Computational Fluid Dynamics

1 Introduction

At the present time, the European Union (EU) faces an increasing energy demand, with volatile prices. The EU is the largest energy importer in the world, corresponding to about 53% of its energy supply and is dependent on a limited number of countries to fulfill their requirements of energy [1]. In this sequence, the European Union is focused on developing a policy that will ensure smart, sustainable and inclusive growth for the

© Springer Nature Switzerland AG 2020
O. Gervasi et al. (Eds.): ICCSA 2020, LNCS 12254, pp. 214–227, 2020.
https://doi.org/10.1007/978-3-030-58817-5_17

next decades, giving particular attention to the construction sector with significant energy consumption [2].

Allied to this environmental need and knowing that in industrialized countries Humans spend 90% of their time on enclosed spaces [3], the existence of an appropriate thermal environment is one of the determining factors for productivity, prolonged health and well-being [4]. In retail buildings, providing a comfortable environment is essential. When people are comfortable, they tend to spend more time inside the store and are more prone to purchase [5]. In order to provide a comfortable thermal environment, Heat Ventilation and Air Conditioning (HVAC) systems are installed. The managing of these systems is mostly related to the heat balance between the supermarket and the external thermal environment, changing mostly during the extreme seasons, namely, Winter and Summer.

While the indoor environment of Supermarkets is mostly the same, the freezing section presents a challenge while managing the HVAC systems. On one side there is the need to ensure the thermal environment, on the other side, these systems need special configuration to deal with the cold felt due to the freezers. The low temperatures are essential to preserve the food and ensure its quality. However, the cold that they cause must be balanced by the HVAC systems which generally translates in increased use of energy [6]. Finding the balance point where thermal comfort is available to the costumers and at the same time spending the lowest amount of energy is the objective of the HVAC management [7].

Thermal environment can be assessed using the thermal balance principle for which, the heat gained and generated by the human body is lost in the same amount to the environment. In a situation of thermal comfort, it is assumed that the human body is in thermal balance, which means that the heat flux produced and received by the organism is equal to the heat flux given by the organism to the surrounding environment. However this condition of thermal neutrality is not sufficient by itself since localized thermal discomfort phenomena such radiation asymmetry, draught or thermal gradients between head and ankle greater than 3 °C can occur [8]. When thermal comfort is not assured problems may occur to the individual, like poor interpersonal relationships, absenteeism, demotivation and low productivity [9]. In order to translate the thermal balance to an understandable scale, several thermal indices which correlate thermal variables and sensation were created. Among those, Fanger numerical index has been widely applied, by combining different environmental parameters, which can be divided into personal and environmental [4, 10]. The former consist of the metabolic rate and thermal insulation while the latter consist of air velocity, air temperature, relative humidity, and radiant temperature. The numerical index has significance in a scale of 7 points, ranging from −3 to +3, which can be related to the ASHRAE thermal sensation scale [11]. Accurately assessment of thermal comfort is not a simple task and in the case of supermarkets, Lindberg et al. (2017), pointed out that there are no recommendations on the indoor environment for the supermarket costumers [12]. Their study, performed in Sweden, presented measured and perceived comfort information on supermarkets, which can be used to prescribe suitable thermal environments for customers. The study measurements were carried out in functioning supermarkets, at summer and winter in front of twelve display cabinets, containing cold products, with over 1 100 questionnaires. Regarding the assessment of thermal comfort, the authors concluded that the Predicted Mean Vote (PMV) index can be used to prescribe a suitable thermal environment for customers. Additionally, it was observed that the environmental temperature surrounding a person has more influence on the thermal comfort than the vertical gradient of temperatures.

Alfano et al. (2019) studied the thermal comfort in supermarket refrigerated areas in central Italy [13]. The authors used the PMV index along with the Insulation Required (IREQ) and surveys to assess the thermal comfort of this section. In this study, the gradient temperatures showed a greater effect in the thermal environment, with women feeling generally more uncomfortable. Authors pointed out the difference in using clothing with less insulating, like open lady shoes. The difference in the obtained results is mainly due that the stratification in the cold areas, which are the focus of the study. Regarding the costumers PMV value, both in summer and winter was below −2 (Cold). The IREQ index pointed out the risk of cold exposure for the costumers in two zones, for exposition duration of about 40 min in summer and above 1 h in autumn. Since the costumers do not stay very long in the refrigerated areas, their safety is not at risk.

Accurately mapping the indoor environment is an exhaustive task. The area of study can be wide and have thermal contributions from different sources, such as the freezers. These types of equipment operate by removing heat from their chambers and moving it to the environment through an Inverted Carnot cycle. In this way, they work as a source of heat in the compressor and localized cold in the products' chamber. The latter cannot have good insulation since the products have to be in the costumers' field of view to ease the access and stimulate purchase. This leads to the mixture of cold air with the environment, reducing its temperature. Knowing the thermal environment for this situation is especially useful to achieve a balance between an attractive display of products and a thermal efficient refrigeration system.

Mukhopadhyay and Haberl (2014), studied the energy consumption in grocery stores located in hot humid climate by implementing Energy Efficiency Measures (EEM) [14]. The authors focused on four categories, which include the building envelope; lighting and daylighting; HVAC; Service Hot Water (SHW) systems; and refrigeration systems, performing a whole-building energy simulation. Regarding the HVAC category, the savings for site energy were between 0.2% to 12.1%, making it the second point with biggest savings, surpassed only by the savings in the refrigeration systems with for site energy savings between 0.1% to 16.9%. The results show that these two categories have great potential to promote energy savings. The overall site energy savings were of 57.9% when implementing different EEM.

Ideally, the thermal environment assessment should be performed prior to the construction phase, which allows applying constructive measures, avoiding several costs. On the other side, without a physical medium, the assessment of the thermal environment is inadequate. A recent review study performed by Lindberg (2020), showed the complexity of the thermal assessment in supermarkets, pointing out that multiple studies are necessary as a single study cannot provide a complete set of data [15].

In this regard, predictive methods, such as computer simulation are a crucial tool because it allows a rigorous analysis of the place to be studied, with the possibility of correcting risk factors and thermal discomfort. These methods have proven to be a great tool for studying in detail the thermal environment [16–18]. In this perspective, computational energy simulation of buildings is an important tool nowadays. Regarding the supermarkets case, Raimondo et al. (2015) used the Energy Plus, a simulation Software, to create a model of a retail floor ventilation system and micro-climate. The authors used simulation to delineate improvements for the building control systems, monitoring the results, which showed good agreement. The average energy saving that this methodology offered for the year of 2013 was of 24% [19].

Parpas et al. (2017) conducted a study of the air temperature distribution for chilled food processing areas using numerical simulation [20]. The authors verified a difference of only 5.3% between the experimental and the numerical data for the hourly energy consumption. A numerical simulation was also used in the assessment of the thermal environment for the chilled food manufacturing unit by Parpas, Amaris, and Tassou (2017) [21]. Al-Saadi and Zhai (2018) used CFD to evaluate the impact of three air distribution scenarios for supermarket display cases. The authors aimed to assess the energy efficiency of the different cases, considering the effects on costumers' thermal comfort. The computational simulations allowed the determination of the air flow pattern and temperatures. It was verified that the displacement ventilation, located on the supermarkets' aisle side, offered enhanced thermal comfort for the occupants, with improved energy performance for the vertical displays [22].

Numerical simulation is a tool that allows the numerical reproduction of a real case and to evaluate its thermal behavior. With this tool it is possible to consider several parameters such as environmental factors, occupancy rate, characteristics of the materials used in the building construction, air conditioning systems, etc. Also provides a way to change several thermal parameters and assess their influence on thermal comfort, without the costs of physical experimentation. Additionally, numerical simulation also allows the detailed mapping of the environmental variables. The combination of these advantages makes the simulation a great tool to assess the supermarket refrigerated area, giving insight into the thermal conditions, allowing a better understanding and management of the thermal environment.

2   Case Study

The study objective was to evaluate the thermal environment in the cold zone of a supermarket, by applying a numerical simulation methodology. With the simulation, the authors intended to assess the thermal comfort of the users and to reduce the energy consumption in this area. The chosen method, due to its ease of implementation, was to reduce the input of air flow. The developed model was accomplished using ANSYS Fluent with a CFD simulation.

2.1   Building Description

The building in the study is located in the district of Aveiro, Portugal. At the time of the study, it is still under construction and it will be a supermarket. The building comprises of three floors (Fig. 1). The Floor −1, below ground level, will have a technical space and a parking area. The second floor, identified as Floor 0, consists of the spaces

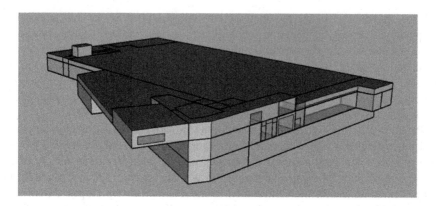

Fig. 1. Exterior view of the 3D modeling of the building.

affected by the commercial/sales area, where customers access the services authorized by the Supermarket policies. Also, this floor will have technical spaces, warehouses, toilets, a coordination room and a garage. The third floor, defined as Floor 1, will consist of a training room, a break room, changing rooms, toilets and technical spaces.

2.2 Simulation Study

The assessment of the thermal environment in the supermarket was performed with ANSYS Fluent. However, due to hardware resources limitations, some simplifications were necessary, such as in the geometry details and zone size. Since the cold section presented the most complex environment, the study was focused on that specific sector. Due to its size and symmetry, the simulation was performed on a fraction of the area, allowing to greatly decrease the computational time. The created geometry is a simplification of the real cold zone. The two parallelepipedal geometries represent two refrigerated murals and the external faces are symmetries, defining a fictional wall that separates a portion of the cold zone. Fig. 2 (a) shows the 3D modelling of this zone, including a diffuser to blow air at the top and an exhaust grid at the corner. For the volume discretization, the domain was divided into smaller and simpler geometries that allowed the creation of a hexahedral mesh. Once performed the mesh independency test, the obtained discretization is represented in Fig. 2 (b) with a total of 2 217 324 elements. The mesh aspect ratio was 1.0755 with the value of 1 being ideal, and a skewness near 0, which is ideal.

Setup. The mass continuity equation and the Navier-Stokes equations for the fluid flow were solved by the Realizable k-ε turbulence model. Additionally, since the focus was the simulation of thermal comfort, the energy equation and the surface to surface (S2S) radiation models were added. The former equation included the simulation of temperature while the S2S model was used to simulate the heat transfer through radiation. The final environmental parameter, the relative humidity, was simulated through the use of the species transport for multiphase flow where the air was defined as a mixture of nitrogen, oxygen and water vapor.

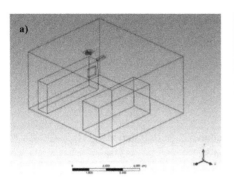 

Fig. 2. CAD design of CFD model (a) and mesh of CFD model for simulation (b).

Boundary Conditions. The conditions that define the thermal environment are mostly governed by outside environmental conditions. For this reason, two sets of boundary conditions, one for summer (22nd August), and other for winter (21st January) were defined, differing in the conditions of air insufflation and gains/losses across the boundaries. The objective of CFD was to optimize the insufflation conditions and thus the energy consumption of the sales area, adopting a strategy of evaluating thermal comfort only in an area of interest. In other words, an attempt was made to establish a trade off that would guarantee a reduction in the insufflation flow and thus a reduction in the thermal power of the rooftops, but that would not compromise the thermal comfort in locations with human presence. The area of established interest corresponds to an area limited horizontally by the refrigerated murals and vertically by a horizontal plane that has a height of 1.85 m from the ground, in the area that is affected by human presence. Table 1 and Table 2 represent, respectively, the different types of boundaries used in the model to be simulated, for both winter and summer conditions. In these simulations, the air insufflation was defined as 15% lower than the initial projected and with a minimum insufflation rate of 855 m^3/h. The values presented on in the tables were estimated based on the common characteristics for the materials and data from other supermarkets.

Table 1. Boundary conditions used in the CFD model for January 21.

Location	Boundary condition	Physical property		Material
Lamp	Wall	Heat flow	8.0 W/m^2	Glass
Roof	Wall	Heat flow	−5.3 W/m^2	Sheet metal
Floor	Wall	Heat flow	−5.1 W/m^2	Ceramic
Exterior wall	Wall	Exterior temperature	10.0 °C	Plaster
		Heat transfer coefficient (convection)	25.0 W/m.K	

(continued)

Table 1. (*continued*)

Location	Boundary condition	Physical property		Material
Fictitious wall	Symmetry	–	–	–
Mural refrigerated	Wall	Temperature	5.0 °C	Glass
Extraction grid	Outflow	–	–	–
Insufflation diffuser	Inlet Velocity	Velocity magnitude	6.6 m/s	–
		Turbulent intensity	4.33%	
		Temperature	33.0 °C	
		Fin angle	33.0°	
		Relative humidity	30.0%	
		Hydraulic diameter	0.08 m	

Table 2. Boundary conditions used in the CFD model on August 22.

Location	Boundary condition	Physical property		Material
Lamp	Wall	Heat flow	8.0 W/m²	Glass
Roof	Wall	Heat flow	4.7 W/m²	Sheet metal
Floor	Wall	Heat flow	4.4 W/m²	Ceramic
Exterior wall	Wall	Exterior temperature	32.0 °C	Plaster
		Heat transfer coefficient (convection)	25.0 W/m.K	
Fictitious wall	Symmetry	–	–	–
Mural refrigerated	Wall	Temperature	5.0°C	Glass
Extraction grid	Outflow	–	–	–
Insufflation diffuser	Inlet Velocity	Velocity magnitude	6.6 m/s	–
		Turbulence intensity	4.33%	
		Temperature	16.0°C	
		Fin angle	33.0°	
		Relative humidity	50.0%	
		Hydraulic diameter	0.08 m	

Regarding the materials used to define the boundary conditions, their properties are identified in Table 3.

Table 3. Characteristics of the thermal properties of the materials considered in the definition of the CFD model.

Material	Specific heat capacity (J/kg.K)	Thermal conductivity (W/m.K)	Density (kg/m³)	Emissivity
Stainless steel	500	15.0	8 000	0.70
Aluminum	871	202.4	2 719	0.15
Ceramic	1 000	1.3	2 300	0.90
Micro perforated sheet metal	1 000	78.0	4 000	0.20
Plaster	1 000	1.3	2 000	0.91
Glass	750	1.1	2 600	0.93

Numerical Solution. The standard algorithm SIMPLE (Semi-Implicit Method for Pressure Linked Equations) was selected to define the pressure and velocity coupling. Additionally, second-order interpolations were used. The transient regime was simulated, defining a fixed timestep of 0.5 s and to achieve convergence conditions, a maximum number of iterations per step of 105 has shown to be appropriated. To guarantee the convergence, maximum residues of $1E{-}4$ were defined for continuity, k, ε and for the species H_2O and O_2. Regarding the energy equation, the default value of $1E{-}6$ was maintained.

PMV Calculation. To assess the PMV and Predicted Percentage of Dissatisfied (PPD) index, an analysis was initially made of the spatial distribution of environmental variables (air temperature, air speed and relative humidity). Then, as these two indexes are not a direct output from ANSYS, a routine programmed in Phyton language was used. The algorithm is referred in ISO 7730:2005 and in its definition it was necessary to manually enter the average values for the thermal resistance of the clothing and the metabolic rate of the occupants.

3   Numerical Results

Figure 3 records the distribution for the temperature values in the three plans, for the zone of interest, on January 21. It is possible to verify that the inlet airflow follows a jet-like pattern. This behavior, promoted by the inlet grill, is necessary since the insufflation air temperature is higher than the surrounding air. This kind of insufflation gives the inlet flow enough kinetic energy to surpass the temperature stratification tendency and reach the bottom volume for better mixing of the air. The results also show that the higher air temperature provided by the insufflation is mostly located in the center plane, which will influence thermal comfort. In Fig. 4, is observed that the values of PMV show a tendency towards negative values, whose the most negative value is close to -2. In some regions of the middle plane, namely, next to the floor and away from the diffuser, as well as in the middle of the right plane the PMV value is 0. Additionally, the middle plane also registers the highest values of the PMV, given that it is also the region whose temperature is the highest due to the action of the diffuser, with an average value of −0.5 for the PMV. As we move away from the middle plane and approach the other planes, the PMV value slightly decreases, reaching average values of −0.8. This average value, according with ISO 7730:2005, is slightly over the limit of comfort of −0.7. However, there is also the matter of thermal asymmetries and discomfort by cold floor, which fall within the limits specified for comfort. Nevertheless, the local PMV near the floor has a lower value and should be addressed to improve the overall comfort. In this regard, the easiest parameter to change is the temperature. An increase in temperature near the floor could be achieved either by placing heated tiles or by adding an inlet of hot air near the floor. However, it should be addressed that this source of heat right near the freezers could affect their thermal efficiency.

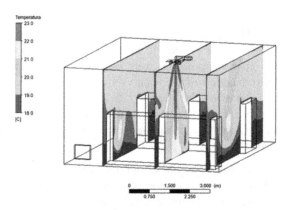

Fig. 3. Analysis of the temperature's distribution in the CFD model, on January 21.

The values of the PPD index, shown in Fig. 5, are a direct consequence of the PMV values. In the regions where the PMV values are close to zero, the number of dissatisfied people is smaller, corresponding to 5% of dissatisfied people. As the PMV value deviates from 0, the percentage of people dissatisfied increases. This way, the intermediate plane presents more favorable values in terms of thermal comfort than the other planes, with an overall PMV closer to 0 and an average PPD value of 10%. This is a value considered as comfortable according to ISO 7730:2005. In the plane next to the extraction grid, the average PPD value increases to 19% and in the other plane, at the opposite end, the average PPD is 18%.

Through the observation of Fig. 6, it is possible to verify that in the summer the insufflation tendency is inverted. In this case, the environment temperature is generally higher, and the insufflation air is used to lower the overall temperature. The insufflation air together with the temperatures set for the refrigerated murals can maintain a lower temperature near the floor. Additionally, the temperatures at this location are more uniform with localized colder zones near the murals. One important information is that the simulation allowed to verify the presence of air stratification with hot air near the ceiling, which can lead to inefficiency in cooling the area. If the issue is not addressed, this air will mix with the input air and act as a source of radiant heat. Fig. 7 records the

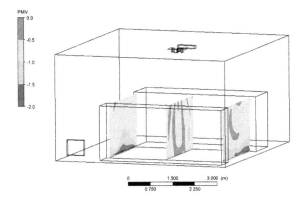

Fig. 4. Analysis of the PMV distribution in the CFD model, on January 21.

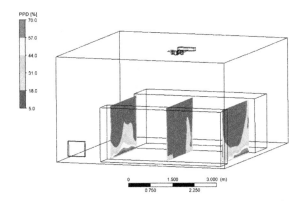

Fig. 5. Analysis of the PPD in the CFD model, on January 21.

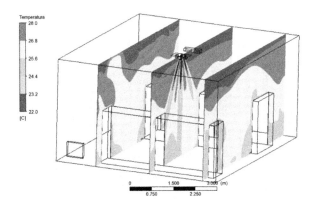

Fig. 6. Analysis of the temperature's distribution in the CFD model, on August 22.

values calculated for the PMV, on August 22. In this simulation, the trend is to obtain values in the range between −0.5 and 0.5. In the intermediate plane, because of the movement of the inflated air at a reduced temperature, there is a region with values close to −1. However, the average value in this plan is −0.1, which translates into an ideal PMV value for obtaining thermal comfort. In the extreme plane, close to the extraction grid, the average value of this index is 0.2, whereas in the opposite extreme plane, the average PMV is 0.1.

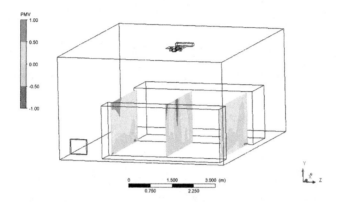

Fig. 7. Analysis of the PMV in the CFD model, on August 22.

As for the PPD index shown in Fig. 8 appears that the PPD values are very close to the minimum value of 5%, allowing occupants to feel thermally comfortable. The intermediate plan and the extreme plan next to the extraction grid present an average value of 6%, of dissatisfied people, whereas the rest plan registers a value of 5%.

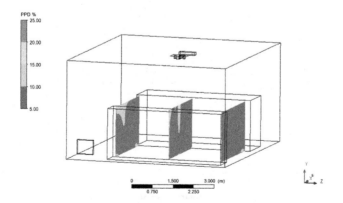

Fig. 8. Analysis of the PPD in the CFD model, on August 22.

Overall, the thermal comfort for the summer was not problematic. However, the simulation showed an accumulation of hot air near the ceiling. Providing a system that extracts this hot air from the ceiling and preventing its accumulation could lead to improvements in the HVAC energetic efficiency.

4 Conclusions

The objective of calculating PMV and PPD, seeking to adopt energy efficiency measures, was successfully met through Ansys Fluent.

In order to promote energy efficiency, but also to ensure thermal comfort in a supermarket, the sales area (the most consuming area in the building) was simulated in ANSYS Fluent. With the definition of a zone of interest and a reduction in flow by 15%, for the 21st of January, the average values are close to the lower limit value (−0.7) that the ISO 7730:2005 stipulates for thermal comfort. In the three planes, the average PMV varies between −0.5 and −0.8, with a PPD between 10 and 19%. However, in this case, there are values of local PMV that are lower than the limit. This issue could be addressed by providing localized heating such as heated tiles or air inlets. As for the August 22 simulation, the values are closer to thermal neutrality, with average values of PMV in the three planes between −0.1 and 0.2 and PPD of 5 to 6%. In short, very acceptable values of thermal comfort were guaranteed with the reduction in flow achieved, allowing to reduce energy consumption without compromising the well-being of individuals. However, the concentration of hot air near the ceiling showed that there is further potential for the energy optimization in the summer.

The CFD methodology, although restrictive in terms of computation power, allowed the assessment of the space and the creation of detailed comfort maps, otherwise hardly obtainable with traditional assessment methods. However, in the created CFD model the process of evaluating the average radiant temperature should be improved in future work, in order to better evaluate this variable contribution in the overall comfort index. In the current study, the model used only accounts for radiant heat exchanged between opaque surfaces. However, since the PMV is being calculated for each cell of the domain, an averaged value for the radiant temperature was used instead. Additionally, the effects of the number of occupants in the studied zone should be added for a more accurate simulation. Although the metabolic input is implemented in the PMV index calculation, if the zone has a great number of people, this may cause a raise in the surrounding temperature.

Acknowledgements. The authors would like to express their gratitude for the support given by FCT within the R&D Units Project Scope UIDB/00319/2020 (ALGORITMI) and R&D Units Project Scope UIDP/04077/2020 (MEtRICs).

References

1. Official Journal of the European Union A UE e a união de energia e a ação climática. Bruxelas, p 4 (2017)
2. Comini, R., Clement, F., Beirão, D., et al.: Eficiência Energética Nos Edifícios Residenciais Manual do Consumidor. Lisboa, Portugal (2017)
3. Höppe, P., Martinac, I.: Indoor climate and air quality. Review of current and future topics in the field of ISB study group 10. Int. J. Biometeorol. **42**, 1–7 (1998)
4. Parsons, K.C.: Human Thermal Environments: The Effects of Hot, Moderate, and Cold Environments on Human Health, Comfort, and Performance, 3rd edn. Taylor & Francis, London (2014)
5. Lindberg, U., Fahlén, P., Axell, M., Fransson, N.: Thermal comfort in the supermarket environment – multiple enquiry methods and simultaneous measurements of the thermal environment. Int. J. Refrig. **82**, 426–435 (2017). https://doi.org/10.1016/J.IJREFRIG.2017.06.020
6. Gowreesunker, B.L., Tassou, S.A.: Approaches for modelling the energy flow in food chains. Energy Sustain. Soc. **5**(1), 1–18 (2015). https://doi.org/10.1186/s13705-015-0035-y
7. ASHRAE ASHRAE Handbook - HVAC Applications (2011)
8. ISO 7730 Ergonomics of the thermal environment – Analytical determination and interpretation of thermal comfort using calculation of the PMV and PPD indices and local thermal comfort criteria (2005)
9. Dias AAC Avaliação da perceção da influência do conforto térmico na produtividade. Universidade do Minho (2013)
10. Miguel, A.S.: Manual de Higiene e Segurança do Trabalho, 13th edn. Porto Editora, Portugal (2014)
11. ASHRAE Standard 55P Thermal Environmental Conditions for Human Occupancy. ASHRAE Stand (2003)
12. Lindberg, U., Fahlén, P., Axell, M., Fransson, N.: Thermal comfort in the supermarket environment – multiple enquiry methods and simultaneous measurements of the thermal environment. Int. J. Refrig **82**, 426–435 (2017). https://doi.org/10.1016/j.ijrefrig.2017.06.020
13. d'Ambrosio Alfano, F.R., Dell'Isola, M., Ficco, G., et al.: Thermal comfort in supermarket's refrigerated areas: an integrated survey in central Italy. Build. Environ. **166**, 106410 (2019). https://doi.org/10.1016/j.buildenv.2019.106410
14. Mukhopadhyay, J., Haberl, J.: Reducing energy consumption in grocery stores: evaluation of energy efficiency measures. ASHRAE Trans. **120**, 416 (2014)
15. Lindberg, U.: Research for the retail grocery context: a systematic review on display cabinets. Trends Food Sci. Technol. **100**, 19–34 (2020). https://doi.org/10.1016/j.tifs.2020.03.027
16. Buratti, C., Palladino, D., Moretti, E.: Prediction of indoor conditions and thermal comfort using CFD simulations: a case study based on experimental data. Energy Procedia **126**, 115–122 (2017). https://doi.org/10.1016/j.egypro.2017.08.130
17. Rodrigues, N.J.O., Oliveira, R.F., Teixeira, S.F.C.F., et al.: Thermal comfort assessment of a surgical room through computational fluid dynamics using local PMV index. Work **51**(3), 445–456 (2015). https://doi.org/10.3233/WOR-141882
18. Nielsen, P.V.: Fifty years of CFD for room air distribution. Build. Environ. **91**, 78–90 (2015). https://doi.org/10.1016/j.buildenv.2015.02.035

19. Daniela, R., Anna, B., Paolo, C.S., Alena, T.: Energy consumption and thermal comfort assessment in retail stores: monitoring and dynamic simulation applied to a case study in Turin. Energy Procedia **78**, 1015–1020 (2015). https://doi.org/10.1016/j.egypro.2015.11.049
20. Parpas, D., Amaris, C., Sun, J., et al.: Numerical study of air temperature distribution and refrigeration systems coupling for chilled food processing facilities. Energy Procedia **123**, 156–163 (2017). https://doi.org/10.1016/j.egypro.2017.07.247
21. Parpas, D., Amaris, C., Tassou, S.A.: Experimental investigation and modelling of thermal environment control of air distribution systems for chilled food manufacturing facilities. Appl. Therm. Eng. **127**, 1326–1339 (2017). https://doi.org/10.1016/j.applthermaleng.2017.08.134
22. Al-Saadi, SNJ., Zhai, Z.: Impact of air distribution systems on thermal performance of supermarket. In: International Conference on Urban and Rural Energy and Environment. Jilin, China (2018)

International Symposium on Software Engineering Processes and Applications (SEPA 2020)

A Language for the Specification
of Administrative Workflow Processes
with Emphasis on Actors' Views

Milliam Maxime Zekeng Ndadji[1,2]([⊠]) [ID], Maurice Tchoupé Tchendji[1,2] [ID],
Clémentin Tayou Djamegni[1] [ID], and Didier Parigot[3]

[1] Departement of Mathematics and Computer Science, University of Dschang,
PO Box 67, Dschang, Cameroon
{ndadji.maxime,maurice.tchoupe}@univ-dschang.org, dtayou@yahoo.com
[2] FUCHSIA Research Associated Team, Rennes, France
[3] Inria, Sophia Antipolis, France
didier.parigot@inria.fr
https://project.inria.fr/fuchsia/

Abstract. Administrative workflows refer to variable business processes in
which all cases are known; tasks are predictable and their sequencing rules are
simple and clearly defined. When such processes are collaboratively executed by
several actors, it may be desirable, for security reasons (confidentiality), that each
of them has at all times, only a partial perception (this is what we call "actor's
view") of the current process state. This concern seems sufficiently important to
be considered when specifying such workflows. However, traditional workflow
specification languages (BPMN, BPEL, YAWL) only partially address it. This
is why we present in this paper, a new language for specifying administrative
workflows that allows us not only to simply model all of the processes tasks and
their sequence, but also and especially to explicitly express the rights of the various actors with respect to each of them, in order to guarantee a certain degree
of security. The proposed model is an executable grammatical specification that
allows to express using decorated productions, the different types of basic flows
(sequential, parallel, alternative and iterative) that are found in workflow specification languages; moreover, it also allows to specify the rights of each actor
in each process and on its data in a formalism similar to that used in UNIX-like
operating systems.

Keywords: Business process · Workflow language · Grammatical model
of workflow · Artifact · Accreditation · View

1 Introduction

Workflow technology is concerned with automating business processes. Since its emergence in the early 80s, it has continued to prove its worth in the computer-aided production industry by allowing companies to reduce the costs of their production, to
quickly and easily develop new products and services, and thus to be more competitive [3]. Technically, workflow technology provides a clear technological framework,

© Springer Nature Switzerland AG 2020
O. Gervasi et al. (Eds.): ICCSA 2020, LNCS 12254, pp. 231–245, 2020.
https://doi.org/10.1007/978-3-030-58817-5_18

composed of two major entities: (1) a *process specification language* or *workflow language* which allows the description of such processes in a (graphical and/or textual) format that can be interpreted by (2) an autonomous system called *Workflow Management System* (WfMS); the role of the latter is to facilitate collaboration and coordination between various actors involved in the (generally distributed) execution of processes, as well as to facilitate their ability to execute the tasks under their responsibility [2]: In this way, workflow technology reduces the automation of business processes to their specifications in *workflow languages*.

The growing reputation of workflow led to the creation, in 1993, of the *Workflow Management Coalition*[1] (WfMC) as the organization responsible for developing standards in this field. Since then, standards have been adopted, particularly for workflow languages. Through its standard *XML Process Definition Language* (XPDL), WfMC supports BPMN (*Business Process Model and Notation*[2]) [6] as a business process modelling standard. In addition to BPMN, several other process specification languages have been developed. Examples include YAWL (*Yet Another Workflow Language*) [7,8] which allows processes to be represented using a formalism derived from that of *Petri Nets*, and BPEL (*Business Process Execution Language*) [4] which allows to formalize the behaviour of business processes by choreographing web services.

Motivations of this Work: One of the inherent characteristics of business processes is, the confidentiality that must sometimes be guaranteed on data and/or tasks that are executed. It is indeed easy to imagine administrative processes in which, various actors at any given time, have only a potentially partial perception of all the activities that have already and/or must be carried out: the perception that an actor has on the current state of a process is called his "view on the process". For example, in a peer-review process, a reviewer does not necessarily need to know if another reviewer has been contacted for the expertise of the article entrusted to him; and even if so, he should not necessarily know if the latter has already returned his report, etc. Similarly, when organising a journey for a Head of State, not all actors (secret services, civil office, doctor, presidential guard, etc.) have access to the same information which may include for example, tasks to be executed, their dates and states of execution, etc.

Administrative workflows are characterized by the fact that all cases (tasks and their sequences), all actors and the permissions they have on tasks, etc. are known in advance. When specifying such processes, it should also be possible to model confidentiality constraints; for example, it should be possible to explicitly express the permissions - called in the following *accreditations* - which each actor has on each task. Unfortunately, traditional worflow languages (BPMN, BPEL, YAWL, etc.), although well developed and very expressive (very high expressiveness), do not allow to simply address this problem by providing formalisms (notations) to model them. Indeed, the formalisms they offer generally only allow to specify tasks, their sequencing and their allocation to actors; they delegate the detailed management of possible accreditations to the WfMS [4].

Another important aspect of administrative processes is that they are inherently distributed. It is therefore natural to consider specifying them for execution on truly

---

[1] Official website of the WfMC: https://www.wfmc.org/.

[2] BPMN was initiated by the *Business Process Management Initiative* (BPMI) which merged with *Object Management Group* (OMG) in 2005.

distributed architectures in order to take full advantage of the benefits (better fault tolerance, better performance, absence of congestion points, etc. [10]) that the latter provide over centralized architectures. On this aspect specifically, it can be noted that traditional workflow languages have been designed to write specifications to be executed on (distributed) WfMS built in the centralized architectural style standardized by the WfMC [9].

Paper Contribution: Considering the above-mentioned shortcomings of traditional workflow languages, we propose in this paper a new *Language for the Specification of Administrative Workflow Processes* (LSAWfP) allowing to simply express the standard characteristics (tasks, scheduling, etc.) of business processes as we would do with its predecessors. However, unlike these, LSAWfP makes it possible to specify the accreditations of the various actors of the process. With LSAWfP, the model of an administrative process is an executable grammatical specification given by a triplet $\mathbb{W}_f = \left(\mathbb{G}, \mathcal{L}_{P_k}, \mathcal{L}_{\mathcal{A}_k}\right)$ in which:

- $\mathbb{G}$ is the *Grammatical Model of Workflow* (GMWf - a grammar -): its sorts (symbols) represent all tasks and its productions (decorated by sequencing operators) express their ordering;
- $\mathcal{L}_{P_k}$ is the list of actors involved in the process;
- $\mathcal{L}_{\mathcal{A}_k}$ is the list of accreditations: it allows to define the *view of each actor* in a formalism inspired by the one used to specify user rights in UNIX-like systems.

Manuscript Organization: After reminding some basic definitions and notions on workflows in Sect. 2, we present more formally the proposed language (Sect. 3.1) followed by an illustration of its use for modelling a peer-review process (Sect. 3.2). A discussion on its expressiveness is conducted in Sect. 3.3. Section 3.4 gives an overview of the recommended WfMS architecture on which instances of LSAWfP (ie. specifications made in LSAWfP) must be executed. Finally, Sect. 4 is devoted to the conclusion.

2   Preliminaries

Workflow technology is full of many concepts. The presentation of some of them in this section aims at facilitating their understanding and especially, at motivating some of the choices made in this paper.

Definitions. A *business process* is a set of tasks that follow a specific pattern and are executed to achieve a specific goal [3]. When such processes are managed electronically, they are called *workflows*. The WfMC [9] defines *workflow management* as the modelling and computer management of all the tasks and different actors involved in executing a business process. The peer-review validation [1] of an article in a scientific journal is a common example of business process.

Workflow Typology. In the literature, there are several approaches to workflow classification. However, it is the approach that classifies them by the nature and the behaviour of automated processes that is most commonly used. According to the latter, workflows are divided into three groups: production workflows, administrative workflows and ad-hoc workflows [7]. Production workflows are those automating highly structured processes that experience very little (or no) change over time. Administrative workflows apply to variable processes of which all cases are known; that means that tasks are predictable and their sequencing are simple and clearly defined (these are the ones that are of particular interest to the work we are doing). Ad-hoc workflows are more general; they automate occasional processes for which it is not always possible to define all the rules in advance.

Business Process Specification. In the literature, the specification of a business process is commonly referred to as a *workflow model*. According to [2], a workflow model consists of three main conceptual models: the *organizational*, *informational* and *process* models.

The *organizational model* is used to express and classify the resources responsible for executing the tasks of the studied process. Generally, these are classified into *roles* to which tasks are assigned.

The *informational model* is used to describe the structure of consumed and produced data during processes execution.

Finally, the *process model* is used to describe the structure of each task, the coordination between them and consequently, the coordination between the various actors involved in their execution. The process model is generally expressed using a language and allows the expression of basic control flows (*sequential, parallel, alternative* and *iterative*) between tasks.

Ideally, a workflow language should be able to allow workflow model designers to express these three conceptual models.

3   A Language for the Specification of Administrative Workflow Processes (LSAWfP)

In this section, we present the language LSAWfP. It is a new language that allows to specify administrative workflow processes with a particular emphasis on the consideration of accreditations.

3.1   Language Definition

In LSAWfP, each administrative process is specified using a triplet composed of: a grammatical model (called *Grammatical Model of Workflow* - GMWf - thereafter), a list of actors and a list of accreditations. The GMWf is used to describe all the tasks of the studied process and the precedence of execution between them, while the list of accreditations provides information on the role played by each actor involved in the process execution.

In the rest of this manuscript, any specification of a business process produced using the language LSAWfP will be called *a Grammatical Model of Administrative Workflow Process* (GMAWfP). A GMAWfP is therefore a triplet formally defined as follows:

Definition 1. *A **Grammatical Model of Administrative Workflow Process** (GMAWfP)* $\mathbb{W}_f$ *for a given business process, is a triplet* $\mathbb{W}_f = \left(\mathbb{G}, \mathcal{L}_{P_k}, \mathcal{L}_{\mathcal{A}_k} \right)$ *wherein* $\mathbb{G}$ *is the studied process (global) GMWf,* $\mathcal{L}_{P_k}$ *is the set of k actors taking part in its execution and* $\mathcal{L}_{\mathcal{A}_k}$ *represents the set of these actors accreditations.*

Concept of GMWf. For a given process, the GMWf is the mathematical instrument that allows to specify all the tasks to be executed as well as the control flow (also called *routing*) that allows to schedule them. It is a grammatical model based on the observation that: the set of tasks of a given administrative process and their execution precedence orders can be described using a (finite) set of annotated trees (see Fig. 1). Each of these trees, called *target artifact*, is a task graph representing one of the possible execution scenarios of the studied process. In fact, it is sufficient to consider in each target artifact that, nodes represent the different tasks to be executed and each hierarchical decomposition (a node and its sons) represents an ordering.

For a given set of tasks $\{X_0, X_{s1}, \ldots, X_{sn}\}$, we consider two types of ordering simply specified using two types of decorated productions[3]: (1) *sequential ordering*, noted $X_0 \rightarrow X_{s1} \, ; X_{s2} \, ; \ldots ; X_{sn}$, which specifies that task X_0 precedes (ie. must be executed before all) tasks $X_{s1}, \ldots, X_{sn}$ which are to be executed in sequence (X_{s1} must precede $X_{s2}, \ldots$) and, (2) *parallel ordering*, noted $X_0 \rightarrow X_{p1} \parallel X_{p2} \parallel \ldots \parallel X_{pn}$, which specifies that task X_0 must be executed before tasks $X_{p1}, X_{p2}, \ldots, X_{pn}$ which can be executed concurrently.

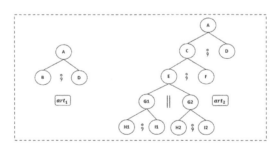

Fig. 1. Example of target artifacts for a given process (peer-review process)

From the above observations, it is easy to deduce that all the target artifacts of a given administrative process, form an algebraic tree language. It can therefore be defined by a grammar $\mathbb{G}$ (a GMWf) in which, each symbol (sort) corresponds to a task of the studied process and, each production (p) is of one of the two following forms:

---

[3] Decorations are made using the operators "$;$" (*is sequential to*) for sequential ordering and "$\parallel$" (*is parallel to*) for parallel ordering.

$p : X_0 \to X_1 \, \text{\textdagger} \ldots \text{\textdagger} X_n$ or $p : X_0 \to X_1 \parallel \ldots \parallel X_n$. Each target artifact t_i is *conform to* $\mathbb{G}$ and we note $t_i : \cdot \; \mathbb{G}$. We can thus define a GMWf more formally in the following way:

Definition 2. *A **Grammatical Model of Workflow** (GMWf) is defined by $\mathbb{G} = (S, \mathcal{P}, \mathcal{A})$ where S is a finite set of **grammatical symbols** or **sorts** corresponding to various **tasks** to be executed in the studied business process; $\mathcal{A} \subset S$ is a finite set of particular symbols called **axioms**, representing tasks that can start an execution scenario, and $\mathcal{P} \subseteq S \times S^*$ is a finite set of **productions** decorated by the operators "$\text{\textdagger}$" (is sequential to) and "$\parallel$" (is parallel to): they are **precedence rules**. A production $P = (X_{P(0)}, X_{P(1)} \cdots X_{P(|P|)})$ is either of the form $P : X_0 \to X_1 \, \text{\textdagger} \ldots \text{\textdagger} X_{|P|}$, or of the form $P : X_0 \to X_1 \parallel \ldots \parallel X_{|P|}$ and $|P|$ designates the length of P right-hand side. Each grammatical symbol $X \in S$ is associated with an attribute called **status**, that can be updated when task X is executed; **X.status** provides access (read and write) to its content. A production with the symbol X as left-hand side is called a X-production.*

For some business processes, there may be particular cases where it would be impossible to strictly order all tasks using the (only) two retained production forms for GMWf. This is for example the case of a process with four tasks A, B, C and D such that: task A precedes all the others, tasks B and C can be executed concurrently and precede D. In these cases, the introduction of a given number of new symbols known as *(re)structuring* ones (not associated with tasks), can make it possible to produce a correct ordering that respects the form imposed on productions. For the previous example, introducing a new symbol S allows us to obtain the following productions: $p_1 : A \to S \, \text{\textdagger} D$, $p_2 : S \to B \parallel C$, $p_3 : B \to \varepsilon$, $p_4 : C \to \varepsilon$ and $p_5 : D \to \varepsilon$ that model the proper ordering required for this process. To deal with such cases, we adjust the previously given definition of GMWf (Definition 2) by integrating *(re)structuring symbols* into it; the resulting definition is as follows:

Definition 3. *A **Grammatical Model of Workflow** (GMWf) is defined by $\mathbb{G} = (S, \mathcal{P}, \mathcal{A})$ wherein $\mathcal{P}$ and $\mathcal{A}$ refer to the same purpose as in Definition 2, $S = \mathcal{T} \cup \mathcal{T}_{Struc}$ is a finite set of **grammatical symbols** or **sorts** in which, those of $\mathcal{T}$ correspond to **tasks** of the studied business process, while those of $\mathcal{T}_{Struc}$ are (re)structuring symbols.*

Defined in this way, GMWf allow basic control flows (*sequential, parallel, alternative* and *iterative*) to be expressed between tasks as illustrated in Sect. 3.3.

Concept of Accreditation of an Actor. As business processes are generally executed collectively, it is necessary to set up mechanisms to ensure better coordination between the various actors and to guarantee the confidentiality of certain actions and data: this is the purpose of accreditation. With it, we propose to take these aspects into account during the workflow system design phase. The accreditation of a given actor provides information on its rights (permissions) relatively to each sort (task) of the studied process's GMWf. The nomenclature of rights that we handle and that we want simple, is inspired by the one used in UNIX-like operating systems. Three types of accreditation are therefore defined: accreditation in reading *(r)*, writing *(w)* and execution *(x)*.

1. *The accreditation in reading (r)*: an actor accredited in reading on sort X must be informed of the execution of the associated task; he must also have free access to

its execution state (data generated during its execution). An actor's *view* is the set of sorts on which he is accredited in reading.

2. *The accreditation in writing (w)*: an actor accredited in writing on sort X can execute/realize the associated task. To be simple, any actor accredited in writing on a sort must necessarily be accredited in reading on it.

3. *The accreditation in execution (x)*: an actor accredited in execution on sort X is allowed to ask the actor who is accredited in writing in it, to execute it (realization of the associated task).

More formally, an accreditation is defined as follows:

Definition 4. *An **accreditation** $\mathcal{A}_{A_i}$ defined on the set S of grammatical symbols for an actor A_i, is a triplet $\mathcal{A}_{A_i} = \left(\mathcal{A}_{A_i(r)}, \mathcal{A}_{A_i(w)}, \mathcal{A}_{A_i(x)} \right)$ such that, $\mathcal{A}_{A_i(r)} \subseteq S$ also called **view** of actor A_i, is the set of symbols on which A_i is accredited in reading, $\mathcal{A}_{A_i(w)} \subseteq \mathcal{A}_{A_i(r)}$ is the set of symbols on which A_i is accredited in writing and $\mathcal{A}_{A_i(x)} \subseteq S$ is the set of symbols on which A_i is accredited in execution.*

3.2 Example of Specification Using LSAWfP

As an illustrative example, consider the process of validating an article in a peer-reviewed scientific journal commonly referred to as peer-review process. The latter can be briefly described as follows:

- The process is triggered when the editor in chief receives a paper for validation submitted by one of the authors who participated in its drafting;
- After receipt, the editor in chief performs a pre-validation after which he can accept or reject the submission for various reasons (subject of minor interest, submission not within the journal scope, non-compliant format, etc.);
- If the submission is rejected, he writes a report then notifies the corresponding author and the process ends;
- In the other case, he chooses an associated editor and sends him the paper for the continuation of the validation;
- The associated editor prepares the manuscript, forms a referees committee (two members in our case) and then triggers the peer-review process;
- Each referee reads, seriously evaluates the paper and sends back a message and a report to the associated editor;
- After receiving reports from all referees, the associated editor takes a decision and informs the editor in chief who sends the final decision to the corresponding author.

Figure 2 shows the BPMN orchestration diagram corresponding to the graphical description of this peer-review process.

To specify this process using our language, we will proceed in four distinct steps during which we will produce each of the components of the triplet $\mathbb{W}_f = \left(\mathbb{G}, \mathcal{L}_{P_k}, \mathcal{L}_{\mathcal{A}_k} \right)$.

Step 1: *Identification and Ordering of Process Tasks.* From the description of the peer-review process made previously, it is easy to identify all the tasks to be executed, all the actors involved as well as the tasks assigned to them. A summary of this assignment is presented in Table 1.

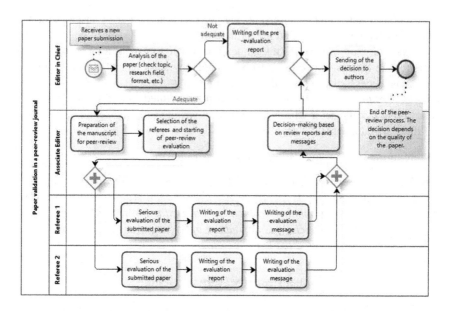

Fig. 2. BPMN orchestration diagram of the peer-review process.

Table 1. Exhaustive tasks list of a paper validation process in a scientific journal and their respective performers.

Tasks	Associated symbols	Executors
Receipt, pre-validation of a submitted paper and possible choice of an associated editor to lead peer-review evaluation	A	EC
Drafting of a pre-validation report informing on the reasons for the immediate rejection of the paper	B	EC
Sending the final decision (acceptance or rejection of the paper) to the author	D	EC
Study, eventually formatting of the paper for the examination by a committee	C	AE
Constitution of the reading committee (selection of referees) and triggering the peer-review evaluation	E	AE
Decision making (paper accepted or rejected) from referees evaluations	F	AE
Evaluation of the manuscript by the first (resp. second) referee	G1 (resp. G2)	R1 (resp. R2)
Drafting of the after evaluation report by the first (resp. second) referee	H1 (resp. H2)	R1 (resp. R2)
Writing the message according to evaluation by the first (resp. second) referee	I1 (resp. I2)	R1 (resp. R2)

From the analysis of the execution precedence constraints that exist between the highlighted tasks (see Table 1), we obtain the target artifacts art_1 and art_2 of Fig. 1. For example, the target artifact art_1 in Fig. 1 shows how the "*Receipt and pre-validation of a submitted article*" task, executed by the editor in chief (EC) and to which sort A has been associated (for readability purposes - see Table 1), must be executed before the two sequential tasks associated respectively to sorts B and D. This target artifact represents the scenario where the article received by the editor in chief is immediately rejected for form issues, research domain incompatibility, etc.

Step 2: *Deduction of the Grammatical Model of Workflow* ($\mathbb{G} = (\mathcal{S}, \mathcal{P}, \mathcal{A})$). When analyzing this example's target artifacts, we deduce that the set of grammatical symbols $\mathcal{S}$ is: $\mathcal{S} = \{A, B, C, D, E, F, G1, G2, H1, H2, I1, I2\}$ (see Table 1); the only initial task (axiom) is A (hence $\mathcal{A} = \{A\}$) and the set $\mathcal{P}$ of productions is:

$$
\begin{array}{llll}
P_1 : A \to B \, \substack{\circ \\ 9} \, D & P_2 : A \to C \, \substack{\circ \\ 9} \, D & P_3 : C \to E \, \substack{\circ \\ 9} \, F & P_4 : E \to G1 \parallel G2 \\
P_5 : G1 \to H1 \, \substack{\circ \\ 9} \, I1 & P_6 : G2 \to H2 \, \substack{\circ \\ 9} \, I2 & P_7 : B \to \varepsilon & P_8 : D \to \varepsilon \\
P_9 : F \to \varepsilon & P_{10} : H1 \to \varepsilon & P_{11} : I1 \to \varepsilon & P_{12} : H2 \to \varepsilon \\
P_{13} : I2 \to \varepsilon
\end{array}
$$

Step 3: *Actors Involved in the Execution of the Process* ($\mathcal{L}_{P_k}$). According to our description of the peer-review process, four ($k = 4$) actors participate in its execution: an editor in chief (EC), an associated editor (AE) and two referees ($R1$ and $R2$). So we deduce that $\mathcal{L}_{P_k} = \{EC, AE, R1, R2\}$. It should be noted that the notion of actor here does not necessarily refer to a specific natural person; it refers more precisely to a role that can be assumed by several natural persons with the same skills.

Step 4: *The Accreditation of Each Participant* ($\mathcal{L}_{\mathcal{A}_k}$). From the assignment of tasks to actors (see Table 1), it follows that the accreditation in writing of the editor in chief is $\mathcal{A}_{EC(w)} = \{A, B, D\}$, the one of the associated editor is $\mathcal{A}_{AE(w)} = \{C, E, F\}$ and that of the first (resp. the second) referee is $\mathcal{A}_{R_1(w)} = \{G1, H1, I1\}$ (resp. $\mathcal{A}_{R_2(w)} = \{G2, H2, I2\}$). Moreover, since the editor in chief can only execute task D if task C is already executed (see artifacts art_1 and art_2, Fig. 1), for the editor in chief to be able to request this task execution from the associated editor, he must be accredited in execution on it; therefore, we have $\mathcal{A}_{EC(x)} = \{C\}$. In addition, in order to be able to access all the information on the progress of the peer-review evaluation (task C) and synthesize the right decision to be sent to the author, the editor in chief must be able to consult reports (tasks $I1$ and $I2$) and messages (tasks $H1$ and $H2$) of the various referees, as well as the final decision made by the associated editor (task F). These tasks, in addition to $\mathcal{A}_{EC(w)}$[4] constitute the set $\mathcal{A}_{EC(r)} = \mathcal{V}_{EC} = \{A, B, C, D, H1, H2, I1, I2, F\}$ of tasks on which he is accredited in reading. Doing so for each of the other actors leads to the deductions of the accreditations represented in the Table 2 and we have $\mathcal{L}_{\mathcal{A}_k} = \{\mathcal{A}_{EC}, \mathcal{A}_{AE}, \mathcal{A}_{R1}, \mathcal{A}_{R2}\}$.

---

[4] Remember that in our case we can only execute what we see.

Table 2. Accreditations of the different actors taking part in the peer-review process.

Actor	Accreditation
Editor in Chief *(EC)*	$\mathcal{A}_{EC} = (\{A,B,C,D,H1,H2,I1,I2,F\}, \{A,B,D\}, \{C\})$
Associated Editor *(AE)*	$\mathcal{A}_{AE} = (\{A,C,E,F,H1,H2,I1,I2\}, \{C,E,F\}, \{G1,G2\})$
First referee *(R1)*	$\mathcal{A}_{R1} = (\{C,G1,H1,I1\}, \{G1,H1,I1\}, \emptyset)$
Second referee *(R2)*	$\mathcal{A}_{R2} = (\{C,G2,H2,I2\}, \{G2,H2,I2\}, \emptyset)$

3.3 On the Expressiveness of LSAWfP

In this subsection, we want to show that LSAWfP has all the expected characteristics of a workflow language. In particular, we show that each of its instances (i.e. a specification of a business process in this language) contains both an organizational model, an informational model and a process model.

Let's consider a specification $\mathbb{W}_f = \left(\mathbb{G}, \mathcal{L}_{P_k}, \mathcal{L}_{\mathcal{A}_k}\right)$ of a given business process $\mathcal{P}_{op}$. The organizational model of $\mathcal{P}_{op}$ that expresses and classifies/assigns the resources that must execute its tasks is given by the couple $\left(\mathcal{L}_{P_k}, \mathcal{L}_{\mathcal{A}_k}\right)$ of $\mathbb{W}_f$. Its informational model that describes the data structure being manipulated is given by the type of the attribute *status*[5]. LSAWfP does not impose any constraints on the type of this attribute and leaves the responsibility to the designer to specify it; by default it is a string type. The process model of $\mathcal{P}_{op}$ that provides information on the tasks and their sequencing (coordination) is then given by the GMWf $\mathbb{G}$ of $\mathbb{W}_f$.

Let's take a moment to look at the process model contained in a specification made in LSAWfP, to show that it effectively allows the designers to specify all the basic control flows (sequential, parallel, alternative and iterative) that they can find in traditional workflow languages. Figure 3 gives for each type of control flow its BPMN notation and the corresponding notations (tree and associated productions) in LSAWfP as described below:

- the sequential flow between two tasks A and B can be expressed either by a production p of the form $p : A \rightarrow B$, or by a production q of the form $q : S \rightarrow A \, \S \, B$ in which S is a (re)structuring symbol (see Fig. 3(a));
- the parallel flow between two tasks A and B is expressed using a production p of the form $p : S \rightarrow A \parallel B$ (see Fig. 3(b));
- the alternative flow (choice) between two tasks $A1$ and $A2$ is expressed using two productions $p1$ and $p2$ such that $p1 : S \rightarrow A1$ and $p2 : S \rightarrow A2$; S is a (re)structuring symbol expressing the fact that after "execution" of S, one must execute either task $A1$ or task $A2$ (see Fig. 3(c)).
- iterative routing (repetition) is expressed using recursive symbols. Thus the productions $p1 : A \rightarrow B$, $p2 : B \rightarrow C$ and $p3 : B \rightarrow A$ express a potentially iterative flow on the task A (see Fig. 3(d)).

---

[5] Reminder: each task is represented by a grammatical symbol with an attribute named *status* (see Definition 2).

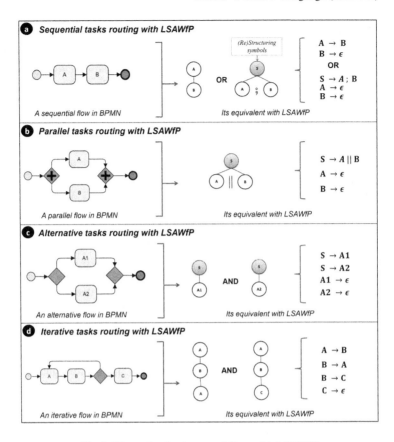

Fig. 3. Illustrating basic control flow with LSAWfP.

Note that, when the process to be specified contains an iterative routing (modeled by a cycle in the task graph according to the BPMN notation (see Fig. 3(d))), it is impossible to list exhaustively all the set of its target artifacts (execution scenarios) because the latter is infinite. In this case, we propose to represent it by all its generators: generators are a finite and minimal set of artifacts allowing to represent each artifact as a combination/juxtaposition of generators; each artifact is therefore decomposable into a set of sub-artifacts all belonging to the set of generators. A generator is a target artifact for which each of its branches (from the root to a leaf) contains a given symbol only twice at most. Operationally, when designing the target artifacts of a given process, the designer must prune each branch as soon as he encounters a symbol for the second time. This will provide a finite set of target artifacts (generators) whose elements, combined with each other, represent the set of possible execution scenarios for the studied process. That is what was done to obtain the two target artifacts shown in Fig. 3(d).

3.4 Privileged WfMS Architecture that Must Execute Instances of LSAWfP

Process specifications in LSAWfP (GMAWfP) can be easily executed in a distributed way, by fully decentralized WfMS, offering an artifact-centric execution of business processes. It is this type of WfMS, later called *P2P-WfMS-View*[6], that we describe in this section.

A *P2P-WfMS-View* is a set of components distributed on all the sites where various workflow actors operate. These different components (hereinafter referred to as *peers*) have the same architecture, execute the same protocols, communicate by service calls and cooperate in P2P to execute a GMAWfP. On each peer, a set of three (03) software components that manage the entire lifecycle (creation, storage, execution) of work-flows is executed. These are (see Fig. 4): a *local workflow engine* (LWfE), a *specialized graphic editor* and a *storage device*. The *local workflow engine* (LWfE) manages the life cycle of incoming requests on a given site. It communicates with engines of other peers via its communication interface which exposes four services: two input services or *pro-vided services* (*returnTo* and *forwardTo* for processing requests/responses) connected to two corresponding output services or *required service* (*returnTo* and *forwardTo* for sending requests/responses) (see Fig. 4). The *storage device* is a database (DB) of doc-uments (a JSON[7] database for example) used by the LWfE to store the state of each workflow that it manages. The *specialized editor* allows the local actor to access pro-cess data, access and execute tasks assigned to him. It is important to note that on a given site, the specialized editor only gives access to information relevant to the local actor; i.e. those for which he has sufficient accreditation. It therefore guarantees that each actor has only a potentially partial perception of the executed processes.

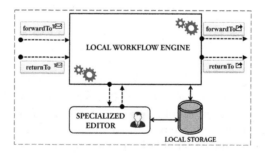

Fig. 4. Simplified peer architecture.

During the execution of a given GMAWfP, each peer keeps locally a copy of the (global) artifact representing the current execution state of the considered process. It is also the latter that serves as a medium for communication and coordination between actors: it is in this sense that the execution is *artifact-centric*.

The (global) artifact is in conformity with the GMWf of the considered GMAWfP and provides information on already executed tasks, on those ready to be immediately

---

[6] Peer to Peer Workflow Management Systems with emphasis on actor's Views.

[7] JavaScript Object Notation, http://www.json.org, https://www.mongodb.com.

executed as well as on their executors. In fact, when a given actor acts on the workflow (by executing his tasks through the specialized editor for example), his local copy of the (global) artifact is updated accordingly. In order to synchronize, actors exchange (through service invocations) their local copies of the (global) artifact and these are merged each time, to obtain a coherent state of process execution before it is continued. In this way, we succeed in using the unique and simple artifact formalism, as a mechanism for the specification of process models and as a model of the exchange and coordination between actors mediums. It should be noted that existing solutions generally use at least two formalisms for the same needs.

For experimentation purposes, we have produced a P2P-WfMS-View prototype called *P2PTinyWfMS*[8] through which we can simulate the completely decentralized execution of processes. In accordance with P2P-SGWf-View architecture (see Fig. 4), *P2PTinyWfMS* has a front-end for displaying and graphically editing artifacts handled when executing a business process (see Fig. 5 and 6), as well as a communication module built using SON[9] (Shared-data Overlay Network) [5]; SON is a middleware offering several DSL (Domain Specific Language) to facilitate the implementation of P2P systems whose components communicate by services invocations.

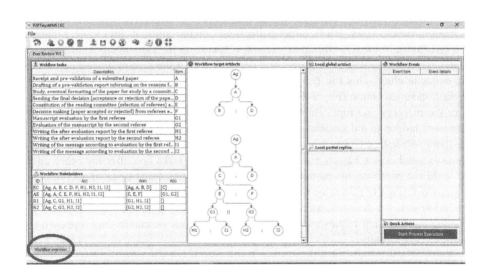

Fig. 5. P2pTinyWfMS on the editor in chief's site: presentation of the GMAWfP (tasks and their relationships, actors and their accreditations).

In order to execute our running example (the peer-review process), we deployed four instances of *P2PTinyWfMS* respectively identified by *EC*, *AE*, *R*1 and *R*2. Figures 5 and 6 are screenshots showing some highlights of the workflow's distributed execution. For example, on Fig. 5, the tab *"Workflow overview"* presents at the beginning of the

---

[8] *P2PTinyWfMS* is a tool developed in Java under Eclipse (https://www.eclipse.org).
[9] SON is available under Eclipse from SmartTools plugin family.

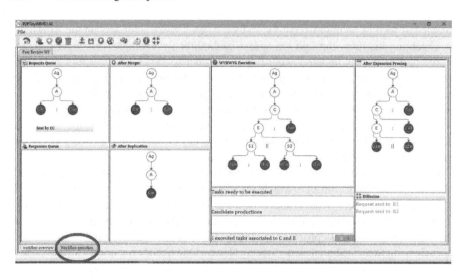

Fig. 6. Simulation of the execution of the peer-review process using P2PTinyWfMS.

execution, various tasks, actors, target artifacts etc., on the editor in chief's site. Figure 6 is a screenshot of the tab *"Workflow execution"* made on the associated editor's site; it shows artifacts resulting from processing performed after the receipt of a request from the editor in chief. This Fig. 6 actually reveals that: the associated editor received an artifact under execution (Fig. 6 (Requests Queue)) from the editor in chief's site; then, after the merging and replication operations performed by the LWfE, task D and its data were hidden to the associated editor (he does not have sufficient accreditations on the latter) while task C was proposed to him for execution. With the specialized editor, the associated editor has accessed and executed ready tasks one after the other until he could not continue; his partial copy of the global artifact was updated accordingly (Fig. 6 (WYSIWYG Execution)). Finally, the LWfE has calculated the overall process execution state on the associated editor's site through an operation called *expansion-pruning* and has sent requests to referees' sites on which execution was supposed to continue concurrently.

4   Conclusion

In this paper, we have proposed a new workflow language called LSAWfP which allows, through a simple grammar-based formalism, to specify business processes. Like any workflow language, LSAWfP allows to specify basic flows (sequential, parallel, alternative and iterative) that are generally found in workflow models; particularly, it allows (unlike other languages) to address certain security aspects of administrative workflows. In fact, LSAWfP allows the workflow models designers, to simply express each actor's accreditations for each task in a process, by the means of a formalism inspired by that used in UNIX-like operating systems for the expression of users' rights.

The utility and usability of LSAWfP has been satisfactorily tested through an experiment of its use for the implementation of a distributed environment to execute a peer-review process; this environment has been briefly presented in this paper. However, this experiment suggested that it would certainly be easier to handle LSAWfP if we had a (graphical) tool to assist in the design and validation of its instances. Moreover, it seems equally important to more precisely describe the model for executing business processes specified in LSAWfP. In our opinion, this is just a few of the many studies that must be carried out following the one presented in this paper.

References

1. Badouel, E., Hélouët, L., Kouamou, G.E., Morvan, C.: A Grammatical approach to data-centric case management in a distributed collaborative environment. CoRR abs/1405.3223 (2014). http://arxiv.org/abs/1405.3223
2. Divitini, M., Hanachi, C., Sibertin-Blanc, C.: Inter-organizational workflows for enterprise coordination. In: Omicini, A., Zambonelli, F., Klusch, M., Tolksdorf, R. (eds.) Coordination of Internet Agents, pp. 369–398. Springer, Heidelberg (2001). https://doi.org/10.1007/978-3-662-04401-8_15
3. Georgakopoulos, D., Hornick, M.F., Sheth, A.P.: An overview of workflow management: from process modeling to workflow automation infrastructure. Distrib. Parallel Databases **3**(2), 119–153 (1995). https://doi.org/10.1007/BF01277643
4. Jordan, D., et al.: Web services business process execution language version 2.0. OASIS Stand. **11**(120), 5 (2007)
5. Lahcen, A.A., Parigot, D.: A lightweight middleware for developing P2P applications with component and service-based principles. In: 15th IEEE International Conference on Computational Science and Engineering, CSE 2012, Paphos, Cyprus, 5–7 December 2012, pp. 9–16 (2012). https://doi.org/10.1109/ICCSE.2012.12
6. Model, B.P.: Notation (BPMN) version 2.0. OMG Specification, Object Management Group, pp. 22–31 (2011)
7. Van Der Aalst, W.M.P.: The application of Petri Nets to workflow management. J. Circuits Syst. Comput. **8**(1), 21–66 (1998). https://doi.org/10.1142/S0218126698000043
8. Van Der Aalst, W.M.P., Ter Hofstede, A.H.: Yawl: yet another workflow language. Inf. Syst. **30**(4), 245–275 (2005)
9. WfMC: Wfmc Standards: the Workflow Reference Model, Version 1.1 (1995). http://www.aiim.org/wfmc/mainframe.htm
10. Yan, J., Yang, Y., Raikundalia, G.K.: SwinDeW-a P2P-based decentralized workflow management system. IEEE Trans. Syst. Man Cybern. Part A **36**(5), 922–935 (2006). https://doi.org/10.1109/TSMCA.2005.855789

Risk Management Framework to Improve Associated Risk of Information Exchange Between Users of Health Information Systems in Resource-Constrained Hospitals

Amarendar Rao Thangeda[1(✉)] and Alfred Coleman[2]

[1] Faculty of Computing, Botho University, Gaborone, Botswana
amarendar.thangeda@bothouniversity.ac.bw
[2] Department of Computer Science, University of South Africa,
Pretoria, South Africa
colema@unica.ac.za

Abstract. Information exchange, privacy and security in the healthcare sector is a problem of greater significance. Healthcare Information frameworks capture, store, handle and transmit information identified with the health of the patient. However, risk management in a hospital is complex, as it includes assessing, identifying and averting risks in essentially each area of the healthcare system. In this paper, Octave Allegro based Deep Learning algorithm for a risk management framework to improve the associated risk of information exchange between users of health information systems in resource-constrained hospitals has been proposed. The experimental results show that the proposed algorithm OADLA has potential benefits for patients, organizations, health care providers, and the public during secure information exchange. The proposed Octave Allegro based Deep Learning algorithm which has higher performance when compared with existing Fuzzy based Healthcare Risk Management (FHRM).

Keywords: Risk management · Security · Privacy · Healthcare information system · Octave Allegro method · Deep learning

1 Introduction

The information Nowadays, the healthcare sector is multidimensional and competitive as any industry in the country. Risk Management in medical services involves the clinical and management frameworks, procedures, and reports utilized to identify, monitor, evaluate, mitigate, and prevent risks [1]. For utilizing Risk Management, healthcare associations proactively and methodical defend patient security just as the association's assets, brand worth, market share, accreditation, repayment levels and network standing [2, 3].

The role of risk management over hospitals, healthcare, and any other organizations is taking the approach called Enterprise Risk Management (ERM) [4]. ERM involves and encompasses eight risk domains human capital, financial, patient safety,

© Springer Nature Switzerland AG 2020
O. Gervasi et al. (Eds.): ICCSA 2020, LNCS 12254, pp. 246–260, 2020.
https://doi.org/10.1007/978-3-030-58817-5_19

operational, strategic, regulatory, technical and hazard, Fig. 1 shows the basic risk management framework [5].

Fig. 1. Basic risk management framework.

The health information system is a framework of capture, transmit data, store the data and manage the patient's data or activities [6]. These systems are utilized to gather, process, utilize and report health data, which is used to make decisions and drive policy, research and to produce highly health outputs [7]. The key components of the HIS; resources, the management, legislation, and planning system required for framework usefulness. This incorporates workforce, financing, logistics support, information, and communication technology (ICT) [8, 9]. Markers – a total arrangement of pointers and relevant targets, including data sources, yields, and results, determinants of health, and health status indicators. Information sources – including both population-based and organization-based information sources [10, 11]. Information the board – gathering and capacity, quality assurance, preparing and streamlining, compilation and analysis [12]. Data products – information which has been investigated and displayed as actionable data scattering and use – the way toward settling on information accessible to decision-makers and encouraging the utilization of that data [13, 14].

The OCTAVE (Operationally Critical Threat, Asset, and Vulnerability Evaluation) is a security structure for deciding the risk factors and arranging verses against cyber-attacks. The system characterizes an approach to enable hospitals or health care to limit risk to likely threats, decide the possible results of an assault and manage assaults that succeed.

The OCTAVE Allegro approach gives the best quality of analysis and estimate of security information risks of a hospital. The OCTAVE approach allows to evaluate more accurately and accordingly better to decrease the risk of data security for an organization.

The correlated state of art Octave Allegro based Deep Learning algorithm (OADLA) for a risk management framework to improve the associated risk of information exchange between users of health information systems in resource-constrained hospitals and proposed algorithm explained respectively in Sect. 3 and Sect. 4. Finally, the experimental results and conclusion discussed in Sect. 5 and Sect. 6 correspondingly.

2 Literature Survey

Richard Heeks et al. [15] introduced the Design Reality Gap Model (DRGM) for addressing the issues of health information system. They used case analysis and pilot testing of an improved model to reduce the risk and failure in the health information system. The risk assessment and mitigation on health information system is done using the design reality gap model. Determining the risk constraint in hospital and healthcare organization to predict the risk factors using the reality gap model.

WB Runciman et al. [16] suggested the method called Quadruple-loop learning (QLL) to improve the quality and safety measurements to handle the hospital and healthcare organization. They used an integrated framework for the universal patient safety classification by store, analyze and manage the data of the healthcare sector. The QLL framework can collect information from being restricted by the statement about the type of event or environment in hospital and able to be utilized by management, providers, care takers, patients, funders, and other users.

Mohamed Abomhara et al. [17] proposed the Work-Based Access Control (WBAC) model of sensitive safeguarding patient data and incorporating a risk assessment process. The access request of the risk associates identified using WBAC model and risk threshold, risk appetite against the risk of weighting to access the information or else the data will be negligible.

Claude Sicotte et al. [18] introduced the risk management system implementation using Interorganizational Clinical Information System (ICIS). The major challenges of risk associated with clinicians, IT specialists, managers, and patients or users was implemented using ICIS. The proposed taxonomy approach is to identify the risk factor or a large amount of information system security-related problem in a meaningful way to solve.

Longhua Zhang et al. [19] proposed the Role-Based Delegation Framework (RBDF) for information sharing in hospital. To reduce the risks in the healthcare sector selective information sharing is done on the basis of a role-based system. They established the feasibility of the RBDF framework through policy specification. The delegation framework includes the RDM2000 and RBAC gives a solution to the issues of handling complex access control rule set.

To overcome the above issues, in this paper, OADLA algorithm has been proposed for improving the information exchange between the health information systems in resource-constrained hospitals. The OCTAVE Allegro approach gives the best quality of analysis and estimate of security information risks of a hospital.

3 Proposed System

The Octave (Operationally Critical Threat, Asset and Vulnerability Evaluation) Allegro approach streamline improves the way towards surveying data security chances, so a healthcare sector can acquire adequate outcomes with a minimum capital in time for patients and other constrained assets. It has three main phases: (i) Create Asset and Threat based Profile (ii) Technical Vulnerabilities and assessment and (iii) Plan and Strategy Development. In phase 1, the investigation group distinguishes significant data-related resources and the present security system for the assets. The group at that point identify which of the distinguished resources are most important to the association's success, reports their protection requirement, and distinguishes threats that can interrupt with gathering requirements. In phase 2, the examination group plays out an assessment of the data framework to enhance the risk examination performed on stage 1 and in phase 3, the mitigation plan and protection strategy of the risk is being informed. The analysis group performs to recognize the actions and creates a mitigation plan for important resources. The Octave Allegro method is reducing the cost implication in the resource constrain hospital. The proposed framework that is expected to be easy to use, decreases the resource strain on the organizations, decrease training and awareness preconditions for members and the framework should fit for all sizes of the organizations(Hospitals/Healthcare institution).

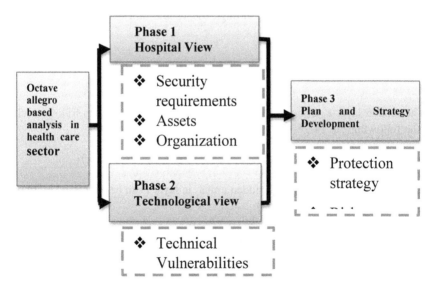

Fig. 2. The proposed Octave Allegro three-phase framework for the healthcare sector

A. Octave Allegro based on Deep Learning network algorithm

The deep learning is assisting the healthcare sector to determine the hidden information and serve better in the relating field. To make medical decisions using deep learning in healthcare provides doctors the analysis of any disease accurately and helps them to treat the patients better.

Octave Allegro based deep learning algorithm, the distribution of probability over inputs and constrained visible units and hidden units are completely connected. The higher-order visible unit denoted by u and hidden unit k_j. To reduces the overall energy in the training process the distribution data can be expressed as the following Eq. (1),

$$L(u, k) = \sum_{j=1}^{m} \sum_{i=1}^{n} E_{j,i} k_j u_i - \sum_{i=1}^{n} a_i u_i - \sum_{j=1}^{m} d_j k_j, \tag{1}$$

The model parameters indicated by $\theta = E, a, d$ and n, m are the hidden unit and visible units. The distribution of probability is stated through energy function the following Eq. (2) as,

$$S(u, k; \theta) = \frac{1}{Y(\theta)} \exp(-L(u, k; \theta)), \tag{2}$$

As shown in the Eq. (2) where $Y(\theta)$ denoted as partition function or normalized function.

The data distribution of margin through the visible unit as expressed as the following Eq. (3) is,

$$s(u, \theta) = \frac{1}{Y(\theta)} \sum_{k} \exp(-L(u, k; \theta)), \tag{3}$$

The hidden layer k_r bottom-up inference to determined attributes follows a chain rule the following Eq. (4),

$$s(k_o, k_{o-1}, \ldots, k_o | u) = s(k_o | k_{o-1}) s(k_{o-1} | k_{o-2}) \ldots s(k_1 | u) \tag{4}$$

The distribution conditional of hidden unit k_t in layer t can be expressed by m units in layer r-1 as the following Eq. (5)

$$s(k_t | k_{t-1}) = \rho(a_i^t + \sum_{j=1}^{m} E_{ji}^t k_j^{t-1}) \tag{5}$$

The bottom-up and top-down inference system are equal.

$$s(k_{t-1} | k_t) = \rho(b_i^{t-1} + \sum_{i=1}^{m} E_{ji}^t k_i^{t-1}) \tag{6}$$

Let's consider input y, an auto encoder builds the hidden layer illustration x via definitive mapping the following Eq. (7) is,

$$x = \rho(Ez + a) \tag{7}$$

Hidden layer x is mapped back into latent illustration to rebuild y with decoder the following Eq. (8) is,

$$y = \rho(E'x + a') \tag{8}$$

Using encoder and decoder function to minimize the error between x and y. The error can be measured by cross-entropy,

$$H_L(z, y) = -\sum\nolimits_{t=1}^{v}[z_t log y_t + (1 - z_t)\log(1 - y_t)], \tag{9}$$

The data training process reduces the error reconstruction utilizes gradient decent. Therefore, the gradient descent backpropagation based on latent feature the following Eq. (10) is,

$$\varphi_{ji} = \varphi_{j,i} + \delta\frac{\partial W}{\partial \varphi_{ji}}, \tag{10}$$

As shown in the Eq. (10) where φ_{ji} is the weight, W is the weight function assess the error between prediction and target.

Chain rule has been used to calculate the loss function as expressed as the following Eq. (11) is,

$$\frac{\partial W}{\partial \varphi_{ji}} = \frac{\partial W}{\partial k_i}\frac{\partial k_i}{\partial u_j}\frac{\partial u_j}{\partial \varphi_{ji}} \tag{11}$$

The gradient descent between two layers calculates the relationship between hidden and visible layer. It is expressed basis of employing derivative on k_t

$$\frac{\partial k_i}{\partial u_j} = k_i(1 - k_i)\varphi_{ji} \tag{12}$$

As shown in the Eq. (12) where $\frac{\partial k_i}{\partial u_j}$ is a gradient function. The contribution of the hidden layer expressed as the following Eq. (13),

$$\frac{\partial q_t}{\partial u_j} = \sum_i \frac{\partial q_t}{\partial u_i}\frac{\partial k_i}{\partial u_j} = \sum_i q_t(1 - q_t)\varphi_{ti}k_i(1 - k_i)\varphi_{ji} \tag{13}$$

The latent attributes learned by deep learning to classify the performance of the deep neural network. The entropy is calculated for hidden units in one layer and evaluate the purity of the critical attributes for the nodes,

$$entrophy = \sum_j^M \sum_i^{D_j} \frac{B_{ji}}{B_j} log \frac{B_{ji}}{B_j},\tag{14}$$

As shown in the Eq. (14) where M is the hidden units, the impurity can be measured using entropy for network node purity system.

Using this derivation and theory, the risk management framework is improved to reduce the associated risk of information exchange between users of health information system.

For the secure information exchange, need to identify associated risk during each stage of information exchange between the users of the hospital. The stages could be e.g. reception, medical laboratory, doctors, medical stores, one hospital to another, etc. in this paper, the proposed Octave Allegro based on deep learning algorithm illustrates the risk assessment and Fig. 3 is explained about the secure information system for healthcare divided into eight parts Authentication, Authorization, Auditing, cryptographic protection, De-identification, User Interaction, Dispute Resolution, Security Metrics.

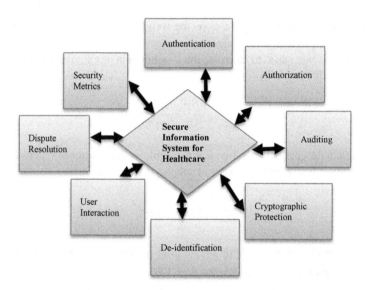

Fig. 3. Basic structure of information security system for healthcare

Algorithm: Octave Allegro Based Deep Learning Algorithm for risk factors
Input: Hidden layer, Visible layer

Output: Entropy

The training process of a deep learning algorithm

for every hidden layer k_j **do**

for every input k_o **do**

calculate $\dfrac{\partial k_i}{\partial u_j} = k_i(1 - k_i)\varphi_{ji}$ or

$$\frac{\partial q_t}{\partial u_j} = \sum_i \frac{\partial q_t}{\partial u_i}\frac{\partial k_i}{\partial u_j} = \sum_i q_t(1 - q_t)\varphi_{ti}k_i(1 - k_i)\varphi_{ji}$$

find k_j

end for

Imagine the score vector of all attributes

identify the characteristics of essential attributes

end for

estimate latent feature

For each hidden layer utilizing Eq. (12) or (13), a significant score vector with the goal that can rank all the potential risks. The system of testing latent attributes is explained in Octave Allegro Based Deep Learning Algorithm. One of the upsides of utilizing OCTAVE Allegro is that it tends to be performed in a workshop-style, community-oriented setting and is reinforced with all the required direction, work-sheets, and surveys. The technique is additionally proper for use by clients who need to perform risk investigation without broad administration inclusion, control, or information.

Algorithm 2 : Deep learning rule-based algorithm
Input : S, target
Output: Decision Rule
rule = {{rule Id},{rule name},{target}},
for (j rule) do
if Decision Rule = not found
else
if (j rule Eff= false) then
Decision Rule = false
end if
Decision Rule = true
end if
end for
else
not found
repeat
end if

In a hospital or healthcare sector transferring data of a patient's health report securely, the deep learning rule-based algorithm is a very useful technical tool to classify the information. The rule-based deep learning methodologies incorporate learning classifier systems, affiliation rule learning, artificial immune systems and whatever other strategies that depend on a lot of rules, each covering relevant information. These systems are utilized to gather, process, utilize and report health data and also used to make decisions and drive policy, research and highly health outputs. Data product information which has been investigated and displayed as actionable data scattering and use the way toward settling on information accessible to decision-makers and encouraging the utilization of that data. The patient Id, name and description of the diseases and classify the specific data to decide the deep learning rule-based algorithm has been used.

4 Experimental Results

4.1 Performance Ratio

Deep learning is subset of the machine learning, it is a complex procedure used to improve data analysis performance. Utilizing the Octave Allegro based deep learning algorithm (OADLA) in analytic procedures provides healthcare sector risks to predict reliably. The Proposed Octave Allegro based deep learning algorithm for a risk management framework to improve associated risk of information exchange between users of health information systems in resource-constrained hospitals, performance is high when compared to the other existing methods Design Reality Gap Model (DRGM), Quadruple-loop learning (QLL), Work-Based Access Control (WBAC),

Interorganizational Clinical Information System (ICIS), Role-Based Delegation Framework (RBDF). The performance analysis is illustrated in Fig. 4.

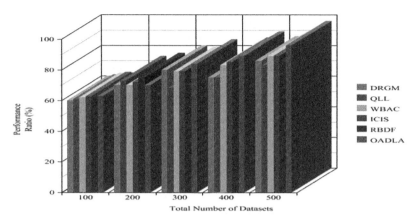

Fig. 4. Performance ratio

4.2   Accuracy Ratio

The accuracy and quality of the healthcare information security system to be identified using Octave Allegro based on deep learning algorithm (OADLA). The accuracy analysis of risk management framework to improve associated risk of information exchange between users of health information systems is high when compared to the other existing methods Design Reality Gap Model (DRGM), Quadruple-loop learning (QLL), Work-Based Access Control (WBAC), Interorganizational Clinical Information System (ICIS), Role-Based Delegation Framework (RBDF). The accuracy analysis is illustrated in Fig. 5.

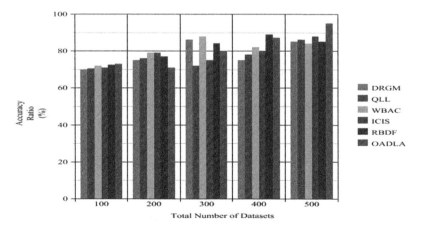

Fig. 5. Accuracy ratio

4.3   Risk Identification Ratio

Risk identification is the process of listing potential project risks and characteristics of the information security system. The Proposed Octave Allegro based deep learning algorithm (OADLA) for a risk management framework to improve associated risk of information exchange between users of health information systems in resource-constrained hospitals. Risk identification is high when compared to the other existing methods: Design Reality Gap Model (DRGM), Quadruple-loop learning (QLL), Work-Based Access Control (WBAC), Interorganizational Clinical Information System (ICIS), Role-Based Delegation Framework (RBDF). Risk Identification analysis is illustrated in Fig. 6.

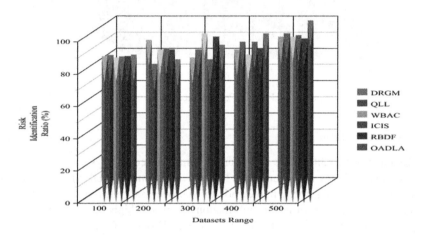

Fig. 6.   Risk identification ratio

4.4   Precision Ratio

The precision rate of the proposed approach Octave Allegro based deep learning algorithm (OADLA) for a risk management framework to improve associated risk of information exchange between users of health information systems in resource-constrained hospitals precision ratio is high when compared to the other existing methods Design Reality Gap Model (DRGM), Quadruple-loop learning (QLL), Work-Based Access Control (WBAC), Interorganizational Clinical Information System (ICIS), Role-Based Delegation Framework (RBDF). The Precision ratio analysis is illustrated in Fig. 7.

4.5   Error Rate

The information exchange between the user and the healthcare sector error ratio is very complex. To decrease the error rate the proposed Octave Allegro based deep learning algorithm (OADLA) for a risk management framework to improve associated risk of information exchange between users of health information systems in resource-

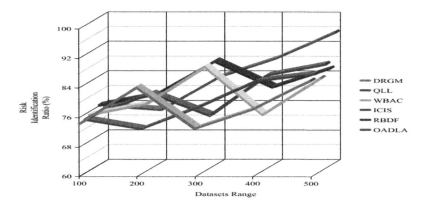

Fig. 7. Precision rate

constrained hospitals error rate is low when compared to the other existing methods Design Reality Gap Model (DRGM), Quadruple-loop learning (QLL), Work-Based Access Control (WBAC), Interorganizational Clinical Information System (ICIS), Role-Based Delegation Framework (RBDF). The error rate analysis is illustrated in Fig. 8.

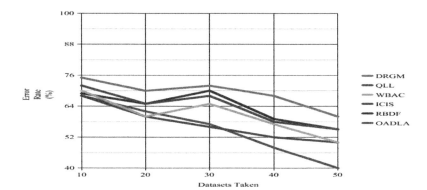

Fig. 8. Error rate

5   Comparative Analysis Between Octave Allegro Based Deep Learning Algorithm (OADLA) and Fuzzy Based Healthcare Risk Management (FHRM)

The Fig. 9 shows the Comparative Analysis between Octave Allegro based deep learning algorithm (OADLA) and Fuzzy based Healthcare Risk Management (FHRM). The OADLA algorithm which have 96% accuracy, 97% risk identification ratio, 95% precision and 98% performance ratio when compared to FHRM method.

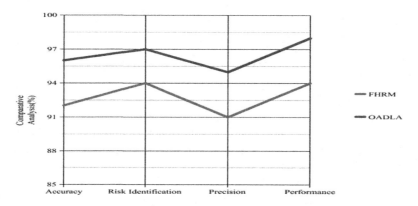

Fig. 9. Comparative analysis between OADLA and FHRM

6   Conclusion

In this paper, Octave Allegro based deep learning algorithm (OADLA) is proposed for a risk management framework to improve the associated risk of information exchange between users of health information systems in resource-constrained hospitals. Using the OCTAVE Allegro approach gives the best quality of analysis and estimate of security information risks of a hospital. The OCTAVE approach allows to evaluate more accurately and accordingly helps to decrease the risk of data security for an organization and also reducing the cost implication in the resource constrain hospital when compared to other existing methods (DRGM, QLL, WBAC, ICIS, RBDF). The experimental results and discussion section show the proposed OADLA which has better performance when compared to existing FHRM method.

References

1. Thibaud, M., Chi, H., Zhou, W., Piramuthu, S.: Internet of Things (IoT) in high-risk Environment, Health, and Safety (EHS) industries: a comprehensive review. Decis. Support Syst. **108**, 79–95 (2018)

2. Thota, C., Sundarasekar, R., Manogaran, G., Varatharajan, R., Priyan, M.K.: Centralized fog computing security platform for IoT and cloud in the healthcare system. In: Fog Computing: Breakthroughs in Research and Practice, pp. 365–378. IGI Global, Hershey (2018)

3. Zhang, X., Liu, S., Chen, X., Wang, L., Gao, B., Zhu, Q.: Health information privacy concerns, antecedents, and information disclosure intention in online health communities. Inf. Manag. **55**(4), 482–493 (2018)

4. Aloini, D., Cannavacciuolo, L., Gitto, S., Lettieri, E., Malighetti, P., Visintin, F.: Evidence-based management for performance improvement in healthcare. Manag. Decis. **56**(10), 2063–2068 (2018)

5. Kalid, N., Zaidan, A.A., Zaidan, B.B., Salman, O.H., Hashim, M., Muzammil, H.: Based on real-time remote health monitoring systems: a review on patients prioritization and related "big data" using body sensors information and communication technology. J. Med. Syst. **42** (2), 30 (2018). https://doi.org/10.1007/s10916-017-0883-4

6. Schnitter, R., et al.: An assessment of climate change and health vulnerability and adaptation in Dominica. Int. J. Environ. Res. Public Health **16**(1), 70 (2019)

7. Hignett, S., et al.: More holes than cheese. What prevents the delivery of effective, high quality and safe health care in England? Ergonomics **61**(1), 5–14 (2018)

8. Cresswell, K.M., Mozaffar, H., Lee, L., Williams, R., Sheikh, A.: Safety risks associated with the lack of integration and interfacing of hospital health information technologies: a qualitative study of hospital electronic prescribing systems in England. BMJ Qual. Saf. **26** (7), 530–541 (2017)

9. Sittig, D.F., Singh, H.: A new socio-technical model for studying health information technology in complex adaptive healthcare systems. In: Patel, V.L., Kannampallil, T.G., Kaufman, D.R. (eds.) Cognitive Informatics for Biomedicine. HI, pp. 59–80. Springer, Cham (2015). https://doi.org/10.1007/978-3-319-17272-9_4

10. Stenberg, K., et al.: Financing transformative health systems towards the achievement of the health sustainable development goals: a model for projected resource needs in 67 low-income and middle-income countries. Lancet Global Health **5**(9), e875–e887 (2017)

11. Liu, S., Wang, L.: Influence of managerial control on performance in medical information system projects: the moderating role of the organizational environment and team risks. Int. J. Project Manage. **34**(1), 102–116 (2016)

12. Mao, H., Liu, S., Zhang, J., Deng, Z.: Information technology resource, knowledge management capability, and competitive advantage: the moderating role of resource commitment. Int. J. Inf. Manage. **36**(6), 1062–1074 (2016)

13. Madon, S., Krishna, S.: The Digital Challenge: Information Technology in the Development Context. Routledge, New York (2018)

14. Funk, E., Riddell, J., Ankel, F., Cabrera, D.: Blockchain technology: a data framework to improve validity, trust, and accountability of information exchange in health professions education. Acad. Med. **93**(12), 1791–1794 (2018)

15. Heeks, R.: Health information systems: failure, success, and improvisation. Int. J. Med. Informatics **75**(2), 125–137 (2006)

16. Runciman, W.B., Williamson, J.A.H., Deakin, A., Benveniste, K.A., Bannon, K., Hibbert, P. D.: An integrated framework for safety, quality and risk management: an information and incident management system based on a universal patient safety classification. BMJ Qual. Saf. **15**(suppl 1), i82–i90 (2006)

17. Abomhara, M., Køien, G.M., Oleshchuk, V.A., Hamid, M.: Towards risk-aware access control framework for healthcare information sharing. In: ICISSP, pp. 312–321 (2018)

18. Sicotte, C., Paré, G., Moreault, M.P., Paccioni, A.: A risk assessment of two inter-organizational clinical information systems. J. Am. Med. Inform. Assoc. **13**(5), 557–566 (2006)
19. Zhang, L., Ahn, G.J., Chu, B.T.: A role-based delegation framework for healthcare information systems. In: Proceedings of the Seventh ACM Symposium on Access Control Models and Technologies, pp. 125–134. ACM, June 2002

Parameter Tuning Using Adaptive Moment Estimation in Deep Learning Neural Networks

Emmanuel Okewu[1]($\boxtimes$), Sanjay Misra[2], and Fernandez-Sanz Lius[3]

[1] Centre for Information Technology and Systems, University of Lagos,
Lagos, Nigeria
eokewu@unilag.edu.ng
[2] Department of Electrical and Information Engineering, Covenant University,
Ota, Nigeria
sanjaymisra@covenantuniversity.edu.ng
[3] Department of Computer Sciences, University of Alcala,
Alcalá de Henares, Spain
luis.fernandez.sanz@uah.es

Abstract. The twin issues of loss quality (accuracy) and training time are critical in choosing a stochastic optimizer for training deep neural networks. Optimization methods for machine learning include gradient descent, simulated annealing, genetic algorithm and second order techniques like Newton's method. However, the popular method for optimizing neural networks is gradient descent. Overtime, researchers have made gradient descent more responsive to the requirements of improved quality loss (accuracy) and reduced training time by progressing from using simple learning rate to using adaptive moment estimation technique for parameter tuning. In this work, we investigate the performances of established stochastic gradient descent algorithms like Adam, RMSProp, Adagrad, and Adadelta in terms of training time and loss quality. We show practically, using series of stochastic experiments, that adaptive moment estimation has improved the gradient descent optimization method. Based on the empirical outcomes, we recommend further improvement of the method by using higher moments of gradient for parameter tuning (weight update). The output of our experiments also indicate that neural network is a stochastic algorithm.

Keywords: Adaptive moment estimation · Deep learning · Neural networks · Error function · Parameter tuning

1 Introduction

Deep learning is an intelligent software process for extracting features of data using multiple layers of computational neurons [1]. Deep learning (DL) uses deep neural networks (DNN) as its main architecture [2]. Others include DL architectures are deep belief network, deep random forests [3], neural processes [4], deep gaussian processes [5].

The training process of DNN involves nonlinear transformation of input data which creates a statistical model (output) and improvement of the model using partial

© Springer Nature Switzerland AG 2020
O. Gervasi et al. (Eds.): ICCSA 2020, LNCS 12254, pp. 261–272, 2020.
https://doi.org/10.1007/978-3-030-58817-5_20

derivative (mathematical method). DNN training is characterized by forward transfer of input information and backward transfer of error. In forward transfer process of information, the input data is transferred layer by layer from the input level to the output level. The data reaching the output layer is compared with the expected (actual) data to ascertain if the error is within acceptable limits. Else, the error is transferred backward. The forward pass and backward pass are illustrated in Fig. 1.

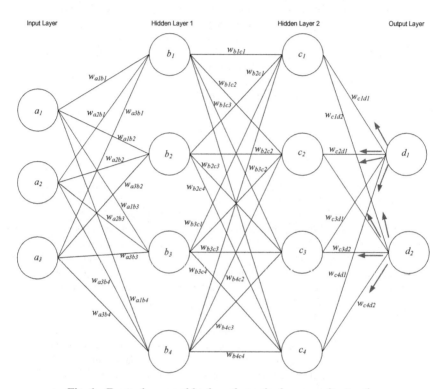

Fig. 1. Forward pass and backward pass in deep neural networks

The forward pass can be vectorized and matrix operations applied as neural network operations are largely matrix operations [6]. During the backward process, the error signal is transferred layer by layer from the output layer to the input layer. The error is distributed to neurons of each layer proportionate to the contributing parameter (weight) values, producing the error signal of each-layer neurons.

Refining and updating link weights, otherwise referred to as parameter tuning, requires a mathematical relationship between the parameters (weights) and errors so that changes made to one entity bring about a change in the other. The aim is to minimize the neural network's error and refine the parameter which is the neural network link weights. One of the commonly used optimization algorithms for achieving the task is Gradient Descent [1]. Gradient descent is an iterative optimization algorithm for finding the minimum of a function. To find a local minimum of a function using gradient descent, steps proportional to the negative of the gradient of the function at the current point are taken.

Given a simple neural network as shown in Fig. 2,

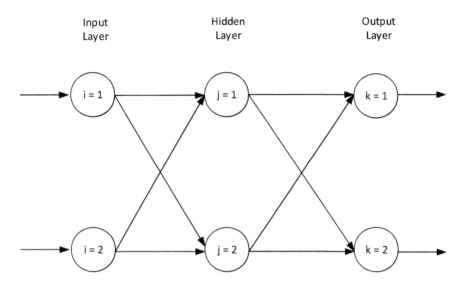

Fig. 2. A simple neural network

the task is to find how error E changes as the weight changes (the slope of the error function) towards a minimum. Mathematically, it is represented as:

$$\frac{\partial E}{\partial w_{jk}}$$

where E = error and W_{jk} = the link weight between layers.

Using activation function (say sigmoid), the slope of the error for link weights (parameters) between the hidden and the output layers as shown in Fig. 2 above is represented as [6]:

$$\frac{\partial E}{\partial w_{jk}} = -(t_k - O_k).\text{sigmoid}\left(\sum jW_{jk}.O_j\right)\left(1 - \text{sigmoid}\left(\sum jW_{jk}.O_j\right)\right).O_j$$

The slope of the error function for any other weights is:

$$\frac{\partial E}{\partial w_{ij}} = -(e_j).\text{sigmoid}\left(\sum jW_{ij}.O_i\right)\left(1 - \text{sigmoid}\left(\sum jW_{ij}.O_i\right)\right).O_i$$

where e_j = recombined back propagated error out of the hidden nodes
W_{ij} = weights into a hidden node j
W_{jk} = weights into an output node k
O_k = output from a node k
O_i = output from a node i

Parameter tuning (refinement of weight) is done using the formula:

$$\text{New } w_{jk} = \text{old } w_{jk} - \eta \cdot \frac{\partial E}{\partial w_{jk}}$$

where η is the learning rate, a factor that moderates the strength of the changes so that loss function does not overshoot the minimum.

For weights between hidden and output layer, the update is as follows:

$$\text{New } w_{jk} = \text{old } w_{jk} - \eta \cdot \frac{\partial E}{\partial w_{jk}}$$

While parameter tuning for weights between input and hidden layer is as follows:

$$\text{New } w_{ij} = \text{old } w_{ij} - \eta \cdot \frac{\partial E}{\partial w_{ij}}$$

However, some challenges of parameter tuning (weight update) which adversely impact on quality loss and training time are: (1) the step size (learning rate) for increasing weight could be very small, making learning slow and in extreme cases, learning is halted [7, 8]; (2) changes in weights alter the loss function towards the local minimum but in some instances, the movement could be impeded by paths of slow convergence surrounding saddle points [9]; (3) the presence of cost (weight) plateau resulting in the presence of many poor local minima [10]; (4) frequent weight update could lead to fluctuations in loss function which prolongs learning time [11]; (5) some weights are less frequently and scantily updated, resulting in sparse gradient – gradient that approaches slope slowly [12]; and (6) some parameter tuning (weight updates) may not be in the direction of local minimum.

2   Background and Related Work

2.1   State of Optimizers

Deep neural network optimizers like Adam, RMSProp, SGD, Momentum share the common goal of helping DNN models to learn and optimize network parameters like weights and bias after so many iterations. The optimizers also help to minimize errors. This implies that saving the state of an optimizer tantamount to saving the values of learnt network parameters [13]. Also, saving a model means saving the parameters' values which the model has learnt. In addition, saving a model translates into saving the entire network's architecture and the units in every layer (input, output and hidden), and also the results (loss and accuracy scores of models).

2.2 Moving Averages of Gradients and Learning Rate Adaptability in Deep Neural Networks

One of the strategies for aligning parameter updates with direction of gradient descent (local minimum) is the use of moving averages of gradients. Momentum changes in per-parameter updates as outlined in [14] was used in Adam stochastic optimization algorithm with first and second moments of gradients. The first moment connotes exponentially decreasing mean of past gradients and second moment refers to exponentially decreasing average of past squared gradients. The use of moving averages of gradients by popular deep learning algorithms like RMSProp and Adam has confirmed that the strategy enhances convergence rate and speeds up network training [15].

Moving average is a statistical concept also known as rolling average or running average relevant in deep learning optimization [16, 17]. It is a computation that focuses on analyzing data points through the creation of range of means of different subsets of complete dataset. It is equally known as rolling mean or moving mean (MM). On the other hand, the term 'moment' emanates from physics where the moment of a system of point masses is calculated using a formula to find the center of mass of the points. Also, in statistics, moments measure something relative to the center of the values though the values may not be masses. Moments in mathematical statistics involve basic calculations which are useful in finding probability distribution's mean, variance, and skewness [17].

Given a set of past gradients $g_1, g_2, g_3, \ldots, g_n$, as data points, the sth moment is given by the formula:

$$Sth = \left(g_1^s + g_2^s + g_3^s + \ldots + g_n^s \right) / n$$

Hence, first, second, third, fourth and even higher moments of gradients generated during neural network training can be calculated and used for updating individual parameters using momentum changes [19]. This facilitates convergence rate and speeds up neural network training.

2.3 Decay Rates for Deep Neural Networks

Stochastic gradient descent with a simple decay is not suitable for training deep neural networks [20]. This is because aligning parameter updates with the direction of gradient descent (local minimum) takes prolonged time and in extreme cases, the updates may tend in different direction. As a result, convergence may be a mirage. The tactics of gradient descent as a stochastic optimization technique revolves around obtaining optimal parameter values from initial random parameter values that guarantees minimal loss function. To prevent parameters from languishing on cost plateaus, there has been shift from updating parameters with constant and simple decay rate to parameter update adaptation to slope of loss function as in Momentum and Nesterov, adapting updates to individual parameter by calculating individual learning rates as in Adagrad, AdaDelta, RMSProp, and adapting updates to individual parameter by calculating individual parameter momentum changes as in Adam [14]. The proposed Adum-Aiona algorithm in this study uses higher order exponential decay rates for per parameter updates in a bid to tackle challenges faced by other optimization techniques like vanishing learning rate, parameters languishing on cost plateaus, high variance in parameter updates, sparse gradients, presence of many poor local optima, and saddle points.

2.4 Extensions and Variants of Stochastic Gradient Descent

Gradient descent is used for obtaining the minimum of a loss function. In a bid to obtain the local minimum, steps proportional to approximate gradient (or the gradient's negative) at the present point are taken. Conversely, gradient ascent refers to taking steps proportional to the gradient's positive which leads to the function's local maximum.

Though gradient descent is equally referred to as steepest descent, it is not the same as the steepest descent method which approximates integrals. Since optimization of the error function in DNN is a minimization problem, we use gradient descent.

There have been several proposals on the improvement of the basic gradient descent algorithm with particular focus on learning rate annealing and robust parameter updates for faster convergence. In machine learning specifically, setting a learning rate (step size) is a difficult task as setting the configuration parameter (learning rate) very high makes the algorithm not to converge while a very low learning rate ensures slow convergence.

For an iteration number t, the learning rate is essentially made its decreasing function η_t in order to fast-track convergence. This has been the focus of extensions of stochastic gradient descent. Hence, learning rate schedule should ensure first set of iterations cause large changes in the parameters just as fine-tuning is done by later set of iterations until the local minima and optimal parameter values are attained [21].

2.5 Per-Parameter Tuning Using Adaptive Moment Estimation

Per-parameter tuning using adaptive learning rate has proven to be beneficial for improved loss quality and training time. To further enhance convergence rate and network training speed, algorithms like Adam and RMSProp use adaptive moment estimation for updating parameters. The compute and separately store per parameter momentum changes. While RMSProp uses first moment of gradient, Adam uses first and second moments of gradient [8, 14].

Based on the outcome of software simulation conducted in the course of this study, we confirm that both adaptive moment estimation techniques (RMSProp and Adam) offer completive results in terms of loss quality (accuracy) and training time.

2.6 Related Works

Previous works on parameter tuning (weight update) in neural networks and adaptive moment estimation in deep learning are as follows.

In the work of Kim and Fessler [11], discussion centered on first-order iterative methods like gradient descent. The authors stressed that first-order techniques usually escape saddle points by following gradient direction (negative curvature). However, there are instances where plateaus surrounding saddle points known as regions of small curvature slow down first order methods, creating false impression of local minimum. In a bid to solve the problem of saddle point, some researchers have suggested a second order method that tackles the issue with Newton's method. Nonetheless, owing to computational requirements, second order methods are unfit for the training of large-scale models like DNNs. As a result, this study does not consider these approaches but focuses on first order methods which rely solely on gradient information.

Mei [22] focused on the development of stochastic gradient descent (SGD) as a variant of gradient descent for solving the issue of delayed training time synonymous with basic gradient descent. Prior to executing parameter update, basic (or batched) gradient descent computes gradient for entire training examples. This accounts in part for prolonged training time which incremental gradient descent or SGD was designed to address. In essence, gradient descent optimization is stochastically approximated. Because data instances are chosen at random or shuffled, it is referred to as stochastic. This is in contrast to standard gradient descent in which samples constitute single group or better still, according to their arrangement in training dataset. Parameter is tuned (updated) for each training instance. SGD is faster than standard gradient descent owing to the fact that it performs update per training instance. However, frequent updates exhibit high variance, stimulating fluctuation to different intensities by the loss function. Also, due to frequent updates, it can overshoot local minimum. Therefore, a technique like adaptive moment estimation that aligns parameter tuning (update) in the direction of gradient is required.

As part of efforts to align parameter tuning in the direction of gradient and tackle the problem of dropping learning rates for improved loss quality (accuracy) and training time, Tieleman and Hinton [8] developed RMSProp. The algorithm is an extension of SGD that focuses on per parameter learning. It uses momentum on rescaled gradient to compute parameter updates. The mean of past values of gradients is used to adapt the learning rate. This process involves calculating the running mean of recent gradient for a parameter and dividing the parameter's learning rate by the running mean. In many applications, the algorithm has demonstrated good adaptation of learning rate. It also works well on non-stationary and online problems like noisy problems on account of how fast it is changing. However, there is no bias-correction term in RMSProp.

Adam stochastic algorithm was proposed by Kingma and Ba [14]. The method is guided by the realization that the usefulness of computing per parameter learning rate as demonstrated in the SDG algorithms examined above is an eye opener that the computation and separate storage of per parameter momentum changes could be helpful in the further improvement of quality loss and training time of neural network. The meaning of Adam is Adaptive Moment Estimation. A popular algorithm for training DNN, it incorporates the merits of RMSProp and Adagrad. Its strategy involves using running mean of previous gradients in determining descent's direction (direction of local minimum) while simultaneously modifying learning rate using the moving average of previously squared gradients. Adam is an improvement on the

RMSProp optimizer. Whereas RMSProp uses only the first moment, Adam utilizes moving averages of second and first moments. Also, its bias-correction term helps it to outperform RMSProp tending towards the end of optimization when gradients get smaller. However, there is room for further improvement [15].

3 Methodology

Though optimization methods for machine learning include gradient descent, simulated annealing, genetic algorithm and second order techniques like Newton's method, we focused on gradient descent algorithms which have been adjudged as best suitable for deep neural networks [14]. We primarily investigated deep neural networks as a popular machine learning technique. Also, the availability of deep learning libraries is a motivating factor.

Our problem focus is ascertaining the performances of existing stochastic optimizers in terms of loss quality and training time. Additionally, we intend to verify if those that use adaptive moment estimation (such as Adam and RMSProp) for parameter tuning have gains over others. Our motivation is to leverage on our findings to propose a new stochastic gradient descent algorithm which outperforms existing ones.

Series of experiments were conducted using selected deep learning neural network optimizers such as Adam, RMSProp, [23]. Python deep learning libraries (Keras and TensorFlow) were used while the MNIST database of images of handwritten digits was used as dataset. The model (architecture) used is convolutional neural networks (CNN). For the purpose of the experiments, the database was broken into two datasets – training dataset and testing dataset. While the training data was used to fit (train) the model, the testing dataset was used to evaluate the model. Further analysis of the MNIST database as used for our experiments is as follows:

Training Data

Total examples (images) = 60,000 (images of handwritten digits)
Pixels per image = 28 x 28 = 784
Size (shape) of training (image) data = [60000,784]

Testing Data

Total instances (images) = 10,000
Pixels per image = 28 x 28 = 784
Size (shape) of training data = [10000, 784]

Label Data

Total examples (images) = 60,000
Total values in label = 60,000
Size (shape) of label data = [60,000]

4   Results and Interpretations

A total of seven experiments were performed using Python deep learning libraries (Keras API and Tensorflow). In experiments 1 and 7, the optimizer tested was Adam, a stochastic optimization method that uses adaptive moment estimation. In experiments 2 and 3, same optimizer (Adagrad) was tested. In experiment 4, we examined Adadelta while experiment 5 focused on RMSProp, another stochastic method that uses adaptive moment estimation. In experiment 6, sgd was examined. The essence of testing some optimizers twice was to empirically verify the stochastic (non-deterministic) behaviour of gradient descent algorithms. Though the output showed metrices like loss, accuracy and training, our major metric focus is accuracy. Each experiment is considered to be a study case and below is a case-by-case analysis.

Experiment 1

Optimizer = Adam
Training data shape (dimension) = (60000, 28,28,1)
Number of images in training dataset = 60,000
Number of images in testing dataset = 10,000
Number of epochs (iterations) = 10
Mean Accuracy = 0.98209 = 98.2%

Experiment 2

Optimizer = Adagrad
Training data shape (dimension) = (60000, 28,28,1)
Number of images in training dataset = 60,000
Number of images in testing dataset = 10,000
Number of epochs (iterations) = 10
Mean Accuracy = 0.97599 = 97.6%

Experiment 3

Optimizer = Adagrad
Training data shape (dimension) = (60000, 28,28,1)
Number of images in training dataset = 60,000
Number of images in testing dataset = 10,000
Number of epochs (iterations) = 10
Mean Accuracy = 0.97739 = 97.7%

Experiment 4

Optimizer = Adadelta
Training data shape (dimension) = (60000, 28,28,1)
Number of images in training dataset = 60,000
Number of images in testing dataset = 10,000
Number of epochs (iterations) = 10
Mean Accuracy = 0.98363 = 98.4%

Experiment 5

Optimizer = RMSProp
Training data shape (dimension) = (60000, 28,28,1)
Number of images in training dataset = 60,000
Number of images in testing dataset = 10,000
Number of epochs (iterations) = 10
Mean Accuracy = 0.98199 = 98.2%

Experiment 6

Optimizer = sgd
Training data shape (dimension) = (60000, 28,28,1)
Number of images in training dataset = 60,000
Number of images in testing dataset = 10,000
Number of epochs (iterations) = 10
Mean Accuracy = 0.94943 = 94.9%

Experiment 7

Optimizer = Adam
Training data shape (dimension) = (60000, 28,28,1)
Number of images in training dataset = 60,000
Number of images in testing dataset = 10,000
Number of epochs (iterations) = 10
Mean Accuracy = 0.98286 = 98.3%

Experiments 2 and 3 confirmed that deep learning is a stochastic (non-deterministic) optimization process in the sense that for the two different experiments, same optimizer (Adagrad) was used on the same dataset of MNIST handwritten images, yet different accuracy outcomes (97.6% and 97.7%) were obtained. In the same vein, experiments 1 and 7 that used Adam as sole optimizer produced different results (98.2% and 98.3%) even with the same dataset. Conversely, deterministic optimizers produce same outputs regardless of the number of times the experiment is performed using same dataset.

Also, though all the variants and extensions of gradient descent as the main optimization method for deep learning neural networks have steadily contributed to improved loss quality (accuracy) and reduced training time, the results in experiments 1,5 and 7 indicate that methods that incorporate adaptive moment estimation like RMSProp and Adam posted impressive and competitive outcomes. This indicates that adaptive moment estimation could be further explored in enhancing the loss quality (accuracy) and training time of deep learning.

5   Conclusion

In this study, neural network algorithms for deep learning were identified and experimentally evaluated using Python deep learning libraries and the MNIST database of handwritten images. Though these extensions of gradient descent as the cardinal optimization method for deep learning neural networks have shown significant improvement in loss quality and training time overtime, there is room for further improvement [15]. In particular, experimental outcomes showed that optimizers like RMSProp and Adam that use adaptive moment estimation are posting improved results.

In future work, we shall propose a fresh stochastic optimization algorithm called Adum-Aiona that uses adaptive moment estimation but with higher (four) moments of gradients for per-parameter tuning (update). Adum-Aiona shall be simulated and benchmarked against established optimizers evaluated in this work to ascertain any gains in terms of loss quality (accuracy) and training time.

References

1. Brownlee, J.: How to choose loss functions when training deep learning neural networks. In: Deep Learning Performance (2019)
2. Shridhar, K.: A beginners guide to deep learning (2017)
3. Zhou, Z., Feng, J.: Deep forest: towards an alternative to deep neural networks. In: Proceedings of the 26th International Joint Conference on Artificial Intelligence, pp. 3553–3559. AAAI Press (2017)
4. Garnelo, M., Schwarz, J., Rosenbaum, D., Rezende, V.F., Eslami, S.M., Teh, Y.W.: Neural processes, arXiv preprint arXiv:1807.01622 (2018)
5. Damianou, A., Lawrence, N.: Deep Gaussian processes. In: Artificial Intelligence and Statistics, pp. 207–215 (2013)
6. Pandey, P.: Demystifying neural networks: a mathematical approach (Part 2) (2018)
7. Zeiler, M.D.: Adadelta: an adaptive learning rate method, arXiv preprint arXiv:1212.5701 (2012)
8. Tieleman, T., Hinton, G.: Lecture 6.5-rmsprop: divide the gradient by a running average of its recent magnitude. COURSERA Neural Netw. Mach. Learn. **4**(2), 26–31 (2012)
9. Dauphin, Y.N., Pascanu, R., Caglar, G., Kyunghyun, C., Ganguli, S., Bengio, Y.: Identifying and attacking the saddle point problem in high-dimensional non-convex optimization. In: Advances in Neural Information Processing Systems, pp. 2933–2941 (2014)
10. Kawaguchi, K.: Deep learning without poor local minima. In: Advances in Neural Information Processing Systems (NIPS) (2016)
11. Kim, D., Fessler, J.A.: Optimized first-order methods for smooth convex minimization. Math. Prog. **151**, 8–107 (2016)
12. Aji, A.F., Heafield, K.: Combining global sparse gradients with local gradients. In: ICLR Conference (2019)
13. Walia, A.S.: Types of optimization algorithms used in neural networks and ways to optimize gradient descent (2017)
14. Kingma, D.P., Ba, J.L.: Adam: a method for stochastic optimization. In: International Conference on Learning Representations (2015)
15. Koushik, J., Hayashi, H.: Improving stochastic gradient descent with feedback. In: Conference Paper at ICLR (2017)
16. Polyak, B.T., Juditsky, A.B.: Acceleration of stochastic approximation by averaging (PDF). SIAM J. Control Optim. **30**(4), 838–855 (1992)

17. Zhang, S., Choromanska, A., LeCun, Y.: Deep learning with elastic averaging SGD. In: Neural Information Processing Systems Conference (NIPS) (2015)
18. Davies, C., Dembinska, A.: Computing moments of discrete order statistics from non-identical distributions. J. Comput. Appl. Math. **328**(15), 340–354 (2018)
19. Qian, N.: On the momentum term in gradient descent learning algorithms. Neural Netw. Official J. Int. Neural Netw. Soc. **12**(1), 145–151 (1999)
20. Lockett, A.: What is the most popular learning rate decay formula in machine learning? The University of Texas at Austin (2012)
21. Darken, C., Chang, J., Moody, J.: Learning rate schedules for faster stochastic gradient search. In: Neural Networks for Signal Processing II Proceedings of the 1992 IEEE Workshop (1992)
22. Mei, S.: A mean field view of the landscape of two-layer neural networks. In: Proceedings of the National Academy of Sciences (2018)
23. Okewu, E., Adewole, P., Sennaike, O.: Experimental comparison of stochastic optimizers in deep learning. In: Misra, S., et al. (eds.) ICCSA 2019. LNCS, vol. 11623, pp. 704–715. Springer, Cham (2019). https://doi.org/10.1007/978-3-030-24308-1_55

A Software Engineering Approach to Implementation of SDG 6 in Adum-Aiona Community of Nigeria

Emmanuel Okewu[1]([✉]), Sanjay Misra[2], and Fernandez-Sanz Lius[3]

[1] Centre for Information Technology and Systems, University of Lagos,
Lagos, Nigeria
eokewu@unilag.edu.ng
[2] Department of Electrical and Information Engineering, Covenant University,
Ota, Nigeria
sanjaymisra@covenantuniversity.edu.ng
[3] Department of Computer Sciences, University of Alcala, Henares, Spain
luis.fernandez.sanz@uah.es

Abstract. In this work, we adopt an engineering problem-solving approach to the open-air defecation health problem. We model social and behaviour change communication intervention among other components of a water-sanitation-hygiene (WASH) system in response to the menace of open defecation in rural and urban communities globally. We also used experimental outcomes to show empirically that patterns in data captured in the WASH process could be learnt for effective decision making using deep learning neural networks as an intelligent software engineering technique. Eradicating open defecation is one of the indicators used for measuring progress made towards the attainment of Sustainable Development Goal 6 (SDG 6). We use the Adum-Aiona community in Nigeria as case study in designing community-based total sanitation programs using software model-driven engineering approaches with the aim of promoting their implementation. This is because even when toilets and other sanitary infrastructure are available, behavior and social change efforts are needed to promote their large-scale use. Also, we demonstrate that besides being used to model software systems, computational models (software architecture) are useful in documenting and promoting understanding of concepts in virtually all fields of human endeavour. Our motivation is that enhancing understanding of open defecation through software modelling would help SDG 6 implementors and actors attain set sanitation goals in both rural and urban communities towards the SDGs target year 2030.

Keywords: Adum-Aiona · Behaviour change · Open defecation · Sustainable Development Goal 6 · Software models · Water-sanitation-hygiene

1 Introduction

Open defecation is an age-long concern which researchers and health practitioners have intensified efforts to curb. This work uses software architecture to proffer solution to the open defecation problem, a public health event of global concern. Software architecture

© Springer Nature Switzerland AG 2020
O. Gervasi et al. (Eds.): ICCSA 2020, LNCS 12254, pp. 273–288, 2020.
https://doi.org/10.1007/978-3-030-58817-5_21

does not only enhance documentation of system requirements but promote understanding of concepts among stakeholders for enhanced collaboration and participation in projects. A community-led total sanitation programme aimed at ending open defecation is a comprehensive water-sanitation-hygiene system whose interactive components need to be properly documented and understood by Sustainable Development Goals (SDGs) actors and implementors even at the rural settings for success attainment of SDG 6 by the year 2030.

Open defecation remains a public health event of international concerns as many urban and rural areas particularly in developing economies are battling to curb the menace [1]. Studies have shown that the provision of toilets and other sanitation ware by government, non-state actors and public-spirited individuals may not solve the problem as there is the challenge of social and behaviour change [2]. This implies that community-based water-sanitation-hygiene (WASH) system needs to be comprehensive and adaptive. WASH doubles as a public health foundation and galvanizer of several aspects of development. Though SDG 6 aims high, each step geared at better WASH services is crucial. It would help greater number of people to eradicate severe poverty just as it improves health and well-being of all.

In this study, we examine the open defecation problem in Adum-Aiona community of Nigeria and model a WASH system in response using software architecture. Our aim is to promote understanding of the problem among stakeholders so as to facilitate the implementation of a community-led response system. Adum-Aiona is a rural setting [3]. Particularly, we identify viable SDG actors and implementors in Adum-Aiona to include individuals, religious bodies, traditional institutions, health facility whose actions within the WASH framework could significantly impact on the open defecation free campaign and drastically reduce associated health risks. These stakeholders are their roles are captured in Fig. 1.

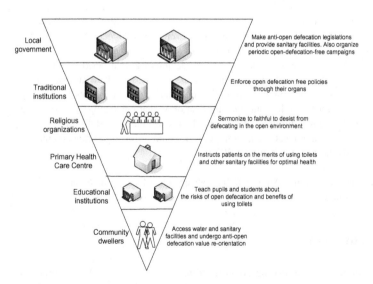

Fig. 1. Community-led WASH System actors and implementors

The model-driven Adum-Aiona WASH system would complement government's efforts towards eradicating open defecation by year 2025 as contained in the Nigeria's national open defecation-free plan [4]. Peculiar natural features of Adum-Aiona that need to harnessed for the availability and sustainable management of water and sanitation in line with SDG 6 are its lush vegetation and several bodies of water, otherwise called streams. These streams are natural spring waters which are clean, cool and pure. Hence, water purification as a functional requirement in some other climes, would be absent in Adum-Aiona's WASH system.

Studies carried out in other low-income communities in Indonesia, India, Malawi [5–7] corroborate the fact that social and behaviour change [2] are key to ensuring that no one is left behind in the global fight against open defecation and the realization of SDG 6 by target year 2030. Findings revealed that mere provision of sanitary infrastructure like toilets does not dissuade people's disposition towards open defecation. Rather, infrastructure provision needs to be complimented by comprehensive sensitization and mobilization strategies against the age-long practice. The anti-open defecation campaigns should be adaptive, taking into cognizance the peculiarities of the locals.

2   Background and Related Work

2.1   Software Architecture and Concept Understanding

Like mathematical models, the use of computational models for documenting and understanding concepts is gaining ground. The use of software architecture offers incisive and in-depth analysis of concept. Thereby enhancing stakeholders understanding and cooperation for sustainable project implementation.

We show in this work that software architecture as a model for providing incisive and in-depth analysis of concept is not the exclusive preserve of software projects but is applicable in enhancing implementation of projects in all fields of endeavor by providing clear-cut and intuitive designs.

2.2   Open Defecation and Sustainable Development Goal 6 (SDG 6)

The SDG 6 aims at ensuring availability and sustainable management of water and sanitation for all by the year 2030. One of the targets is to ensure all have access to sufficient and fair sanitation and hygiene and eradicate open defecation with priority attention given to women, girls and vulnerable people [8]. This is to be measured by proportion of the populace that use safely managed sanitation services such as handwashing facility along with soap and water. Clearly, in many rural and urban communities in developing economies, this index is failing as the widespread practice of open defecation negates these best practices. This often degenerates in to public health emergencies, fueling epidemics and high mortality rate. As observed by [9], achieving open-defecation-free-society requires more than the provision of sanitation and hygiene facilities. There is need for massive campaign and public advocacy against the practice which has assumed the dimension of a culture in many communities in developing countries [10]. This is why behavioural and social change management becomes a critical component of any successful WASH system. In modelling the WASH system for the Adum-Aiona community using component-based n-tier architecture, prominent attention is given to the Behaviour/Social Change component with a view to sensitizing all SDG 6 stakeholders on the importance of behaviour change in the anti-open defecation drive.

2.3 WASH System and Open Defecation in Adum-Aiona Community

Adum-Aiona residents have equitable access to safe and affordable drinking water in line with SDG 6.1. This is because of the prevalence of several streams within the community that naturally produce cool, pure and clean spring water. However, this is being threatened by the widespread practice of open defecation in the community. An effective and efficient WASH system that is anti-open defecation needs infrastructure such as water, toilets, among others. The community-based approach to the menace as advocated in this study examines water resources in Adum-Aiona viz-a-viz the open defecation problem. Using ontological analysis, the streams and the various settlements in Adum-Aiona community that patronize them are illustrated in Fig. 2 below.

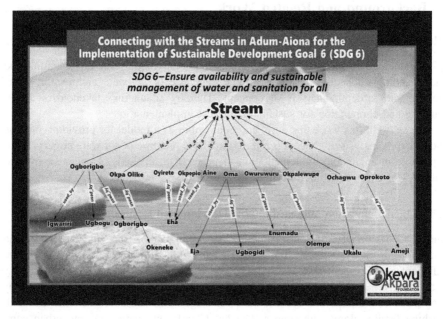

Fig. 2. Bodies of water in Adum-Aiona and patronizing settlements (Source: Okewu Akpara Foundation)

The verification, validation and documentation of these bodies of water in Adum-Aiona, a clan of Orokam in Benue State of Nigeria is to correct the wrongly held notion in the literature and among Orokam indigenes that Enumabia is the only body of water in Orokam district of Benue State [11]. Our study revealed that patronage is largely based on nearness of households in each settlement to a particular stream. Water is fetched from these streams majorly for cooking, agricultural activities, and for personal and environmental hygiene practices such as bathing, washing of cooking/food utensils. The use of water for toileting is still very unpopular as open defecation has assumed the status of a culture. This is the problem this study set out to address. Even with the provision of toilet facilities and hand-washing stations, value re-orientation through massive enlightenment on the health risks of open defecation is required. Beside the fact that open-air defecation does not encourage hand-wasting after excretion, human waste can be washed into the streams, making the community prone to diseases.

2.4 Related Works

Previous works on the implementation of software systems for global WASH initiatives are as follows.

In [4], it was stated that the Nigerian Federal Ministry of Water Resources is working with communities, development agencies, civil society, government at subnational levels and private sector to curb the scourge of open defecation. The work revealed that Nigeria has about 46 million people practicing open defecation, one of the nations in the world with the highest number of people engaged in the practice. Besides its negative impact on health and education of the populace, it contributed to the inability of the country to meet the Millennium Development Goal (MDG) target. In tandem with the global campaign for ending open defecation by the United Nation, an initiative was launched tagged "Making Nigeria Open Defecation Free by 2025: A National Roadmap". The Roadmap advocates different approaches such as Community-Led Total Sanitation; capacity development; provision of sanitation facilities in public places; promotion of improved technology options through sanitation marketing; creating enabling environment and coordination mechanism; and promotional and media campaigns, Among others, a multi-sectoral partnership between government, development partners and the private sector would be established empower rural dwellers such as Adum-Aiona dwellers in the provision of adequate water supply and sanitation services. However, the work did not explore the possibility of using software models to document and promoting understanding among stakeholders as advocated in our present study.

The authors in [12] focused on low sanitation coverage figures in the developing world. They argued that only sanitation hardware is not sufficient but needs to be complemented by sanitation software. While toilets and washing facilities constitute hardware, they refer to their acceptance by communities and proper usage as software. The work emphasized that except there is proper hygiene practices in homes and community at large, the expected impact of water and sanitation services remains a mirage. Hence, efforts are being made by health practitioners to reduce both the number of people without access to toilet as well as reduce the large number who don't use available facilities hygienically. The software approach targets change in behaviour and creation of service demands for the hardware sanitary facilities. The critical stakeholder targeted for open-defecation-free society include households, individuals, communities, organizations and institutions who are engaged in development programmes for social/behavioural change. In any case, the work did not specify how software engineering models (software architecture) could be used for documenting and enhancing understanding of SDG 6 actors and implementors about WASH system components as done in this paper.

In [13], it noted that Informationa and Communications Technology (ICT) could be used to bridge the information gap in the WASH sector and there solve several of the problems confronting it. The authors specifically observed that mobile phones are common in developing countries and could be harnessed for this purpose, thus promoting the mWASH concept. The study identified the challenges in the WASH sector to include lack of education on safe hygiene behaviours, inability of the poor to access basic water and sanitation services, as well as education about safe hygiene behaviors, high failur e rate of water and sanitation projects, unreliabe and poor quality of water and sanitation services, challenges of over-extraction, urbanization, pollution and climate change facing water systems sustainability globally. With better use of information by stakeholders, these challenges could be addressed. Actors such as the populace, non-state actors, governments need information for better management of water supply and enthrenching good sanitation/hygiene practices. The mWASH initiative through mobile phones with mobile software applications makes the collection, aggregation, and analysis of data WASH-related data from remote regions easy. Hence ICTs can address existing information gap in the WASH sector by the transformation of the process of data generation, communication, and sharing. Already, mobile phones are handy tools for data collection and dissemination in verticlas like health, agriculture, socio-economic development, disaster relief, and natural resource management. Though the paper stressed how software simulation (mobile application) is used to enhance WASH sector, it did not emphasized the role of software model-driven engineering in documenting and promoting understanding of concepts among stakeholders, the primary focus of our present study.

The study by [14] explored the use of Internet of Things (IoT) as one of the new development in ICT in the WASH sector of South Africa. The researchers opined that IoT could be used to address disease burden and improve quality of life since it aids the management of water, sanitation and hygiene. The technology integrates both digital and physical worlds, culminating in new services that could useful in various sectors, WASH inclusive. Already, the use of IoT in WASH context has been demonstrated by a system that uses accelerometers in water lever hand pumps to measure both the status and level of utilization a hand pump. This offers near-real time insight into the device operational status for prompt and better maintenance. The work however observed that there is limited deployment of the technology for rendering WASH services in South Africa. It was established that IoT could enhance the provision, monitoring and evaluation of WASH services just as it is useful in regulation and enforcement. Nonetheless, the report did not emphasize the role of model-driven engineering in the WASH sector as we do in this current study.

The paper of [15] emphasized the use of computer software for enhancing the sanitation component of WASH. The study proposed a sustainable sanitation management tool for decision making after reviewing ecological alternatives of small and isolated communities in Brazil. The authors opined that household-based worldwide range of technical sanitation guidelines could be connected using software with database to generate a single reference. This would promote resource-oriented decision making with respect to sanitation. A sanitation management tool was therefore developed whose outcome indicates that decision making process could be enhanced to choose sustainable sanitation solutions. The improved decision making also enhances sustainable maintenance and operational options of the systems. Other uses of the proposed tool include assisting local technicians, designers, engineering students, environmental licensing agencies, and elaboration of municipal sanitation plans. The software is applicable to other management tool. Nonetheless, the work is not based on demonstrating how model-driven engineering aids the documentation of concept, and promotes understanding among stakeholders for participatory implementation.

3   Methodology

Our study focused on the open defecation problem in rural settings. Though a public health emergency of international concern, the phenomenon is more prevalent in rural and urban communities in low-income countries [16]. We reviewed literature on open defecation, water-sanitation-hygiene (WASH) and SDG 6 implementation, used Adum-Aiona community as a case study, gathered requirements of a comprehensive and adaptive WASH system, and model WASH system using software models (Use Case Diagram and N-tier Layered Architecture). We aim at leveraging on the power of software architecture for not just documentation of processes and procedures within a system but promoting understanding among the stakeholders for maximum cooperation and collaboration towards optimal system implementation [17]. We also performed experiments to show that intelligent software engineering techniques like deep learning neural networks could be used to detect patterns in existing health-related image data so as to predict future occurrences of health emergencies with high degree of accuracy for proactive management of imminent water-and-hygiene-related disease burden. For our experiments, we used the MNIST database of images of handwritten digits.

The Adum-Aiona community is endowed with bodies of water referred to as natural streams which are also natural springs. Spring water is clean, pure and cool and therefore the safest form of water [18]. Though springs are used for a range of human needs such as drinking water, irrigation, domestic water supply, mills, electricity generation, and navigation, the main uses in the rural community of Adum-Aiona are drinking, bathing, washing, cooking and agricultural production, In other climes, modern uses of springs include water for livestock, therapy, supply for bottled mineral water, fish hatcheries, and for recreational activities like swimming, fishing and floating [19].

3.1 Requirements Analysis

To build an adaptive and comprehensive WASH system that adequately respond to the anti-open defecation needs of the Adum-Aiona people, we used interview and observation as requirements engineering tools [20]. The requirements gathering process culminated in a list of functional and non-functional (quality) requirements of the proposed WASH system.

The functional requirements of the SDG 6 actors and implementor vis-à-vis open defecation free community include Water Sources Services, Sanitary Container Services, Toilet Infrastructure Services, Behaviour/Social Change Services, Monitoring/Evaluation Services shown as use cases in the Use Case diagram in Fig. 3 and actions in the Class diagram in Fig. 4.

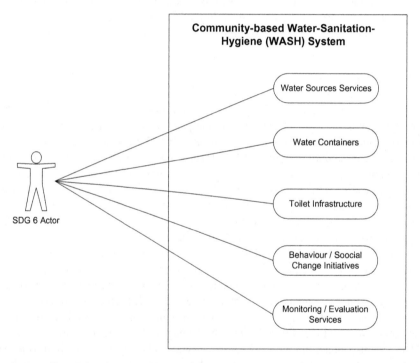

Fig. 3. Use Case Diagram showing functional requirements of proposed WASH system in Adum-Aiona

The SDG 6 actor is any of rural dwellers, primary healthcare centre, religious organization, educational institution, traditional institution and local government who have stake in the implementation of WASH in the Adum-Aiona community using available water and sanitary resources. They interrogate the WASH system with a view to getting vital and robust information for the performance of their statutory roles in the community-led sanitation and hygiene system directly targeted at combatting open defecation.

We model the actions of the SDG 6 actors and implementors in the rural community of Adum-Aiona using Class Diagram as illustrated in Fig. 4 below.

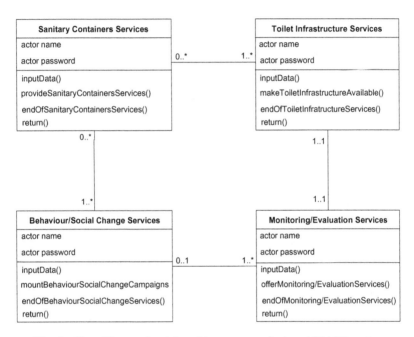

Fig. 4. Class Diagram for Adum-Aiona community-based WASH system

In the software analogy of the Adum-Aiona community-based WASH system shown in Fig. 3 above, there is need to keep track of SDG 6 actors and their actions. This is done by uniquely identifying each actor expressed as identity features (actor name and actor password). Practical services rendered by the open defecation free WASH system as denoted by use cases in Fig. 3 and actions/methods in Fig. 4 are outlined as follows:

Water Sources Services, Sanitary Container Services, Toilet Infrastructure Services, Behaviour/Social Change Services, Monitoring/Evaluation Services.

Water Sources Services () – every local in Adum-Aiona needs information on the various bodies of water available in the community for accessibility and usage for the purposes of sanitation and hygiene, among other uses.

Sanitary Container Services() – the system should offer services such as provision of water containers and accessories for enhancing preservation of water for sanitation and hygiene. Actors such as public-spirited individuals, the local government, schools and churches can assist in this area.

Toilet Infrastructure Services () – the proposed WASH system would provide toilet facilities such as well-maintained pit toilet (latrine), water system-based toilet, and hand-washing station.

Behaviour/Social Change Services () – Periodic anti-open defecation campaigns by the local government, religious organizations and primary healthcare centre in Adum-Aiona would go a long way in value re-orientation and advocacy for use of toilets.

Monitoring/Evaluation Services () – Traditional institutions should periodically review compliance with open defecation free policies and strengthen compliance enforcement.

[17] outlines the non-functional requirements (quality attributes) of systems such as WASH as including service availability, reliability, modifiability, adaptability, performance, scalability and portability.

3.2 System Design

Our computational metaphor of the community-led sanitation initiative uses an n-tier layered architecture to promote understanding of the components of an adaptive WASH system in a rural setting like Adum-Aiona. As shown in Fig. 5 below, the system is expected to hand-shake with components of external systems such as sources of water and people in neighbouring communities.

The three layers of the WASH system are Water Layer, Sanitation Layer and Hygiene Layer (Fig. 5). The water layer has two compartments – bodies of water in the Adum-Aiona community and water management services. The components of the Bodies of Water compartment are largely streams which are natural springs which are characterized in the literature as clean, pure and cool water [18]. They include ogborigbo, oprokoto, oma, okpalewupe, okpa-olike, okpepio, owururu, okpecho, ochagwu, Oyirete, Idiri, and Aine. The streams and their names are a cultural heritage that need to be preserved for a sustainable community in line with the ideals of Sustainable Development Goal 11 (SDG 11). The Water Management Services compartment accommodates two components - Purification and Accessibility. Although purification of water is a necessity especially for sanitary and hygiene purposes, the

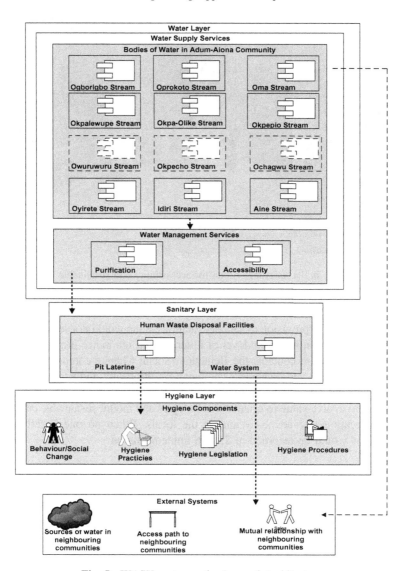

Fig. 5. WASH system n-tier Layered Architecture

spring water in Adum-Aiona may not need the purification process. However, for the purpose of applying the model in other climes whose sources of water may differ, water purification particularly in a rural setting involves among others, boiling, use of chemical and filtering. The Accessibility component offers sustainable management and access to water in line with SDG 6. It ensures that access to the bodies of water is guaranteed and the water beds adequately catered for. In Adum-Aiona, locals periodically clear bush paths leading to the streams while the Oprokoto stream has a bridge across it linking the neighbouring community of Okpoga as shown in Fig. 6 below despite the challenges of infrastructure financing and development in Nigeria [21, 22].

Fig. 6. The Oprokoto bridge in Adum-Aiona for accessibility and sustainable management of water

As posited by [10], provision of sanitary facilities alone would not suffice in the war against open defecation, given the level of illiteracy and ignorance in rural areas. The Hygiene Layer therefore contains the Behaviour/Social Change component that handles mass mobilization and awareness campaign on the health and economic risks of open-air defecation. This makes it incumbent on SDG 6 actors and implementors in Adum-Aiona to evolve value re-orientation strategies and mount sustainable campaigns for open defecation free advocacy among the locals. When no one is left behind, greater success would be recorded in SDG 6 implementation.

3.3   Experimentation

Besides using the power of software architecture to model a water-sanitation-hygiene system for a rural community, we performed software simulation using image and deep learning libraries. The essence of the software engineering modelling is for sharing knowledge among SDG 6 stakeholders and promoting understanding of what it takes for successful anti-open defecation campaign while the software simulation is to enable policy makers and health practitioners know the importance of applying predictive analytics to existing water-and-hygiene-related data for robust and reliable decision making. We applied deep neural networks (convolutional neural networks) to MNIST dataset using Python deep learning libraries (Keras and Tensorflow). The neural network algorithm used for the 2 separate experiments is Adam, a popular algorithm for training deep neural networks [23]. Our choice of Adam is hinged on the fact that it is an efficient stochastic gradient descent algorithm that offers good results in a vast range of problems; also, it tunes itself automatically [23]. The dataset was partitioned into training data and testing data, respectively containing 60,000 and 10,000 images. Each image is represented by 784 pixels. In each experiment, 10 iterations were observed.

4   Results and Interpretations

The results of the experiments are outlined in Table 1 as follows:

Table 1. Results of experiments

	Experiment 1	Experiment 2
Optimizer	Adam	Adam
Training data shape (dimension)	(60000, 28, 28, 1)	(60000, 28, 28, 1)
Number of images in training dataset	60,000	60,000
Number of images in testing dataset	10,000	10,000
Number of epochs (iterations)	10	10
Mean Accuracy	98.2%	98.3%

Though the Python code generated other metrics such as Loss in the output of the experiments, our major concern was the Accuracy metrics. This metrics shows the extent our model was able to map the inputs into output.

Since the accuracy output differs from one iteration to another, we calculated the average accuracy which is shown above as 'Mean Accuracy'. While experiment 1 has mean accuracy of 98.2%, that of experiment 2 is 98.3%. The empirical implication is that our neural network model has above 98% accurate prediction capacity. In other words, above 98% of all instances of health-related issues that require forecasting for proactive management would be predicted correctly. This is an encouraging result that can enhance efficient utilization of resources for the attainment of the SDG 6 goal by target year 2030.

The experiments also proved that Neural network is a stochastic algorithm. This means that when the same algorithm is applied to same dataset in different experiments, different results are obtained as a result of the application of different skill any time the code is run. This is not a bug but a feature of neural networks [24]. We observed that while both experiments used the same MNIST dataset with Adam stochastic algorithm as the only optimizer, the outcomes were different for corresponding iterations in both experiments.

5   Implications of a Community-Based WASH System and Predictive Analytics for Implementation of SDG 6

The SDGs aim at carrying everyone along for a future we desire. Poor health means low productivity. Studies have shown that open defecation increases global burden of diseases. However, efficient and effective sanitation and hygiene practices could be used to solve the problem of open defecation. As a result, water and sanitation are articulated in SDG 6 for the purpose of addressing this global health risk.

Even though we think water and sanitation as global solution, the strategies adopted have to be community-based for inclusivity. The bottom-up approach involves water-sanitation-hygiene strategies that take into cognizance the peculiar water and sanitation needs of every community. There is also need to assess the social and behavioural disposition of locals to the phenomenon of open-air defecation in every community. For instance, while in developed climes many see open defecation as anti-social and anti-health, many in developing economies believe it is a normal lifestyle that does not need to be challenged.

Hence, this study used software architecture to document and promote understanding of strategic components of a community-led anti-open defecation WASH system. Also, the experiments revealed that applying predictive analytics to WASH-related data could generate robust information for proactive decision-making during health emergencies. The adaptive WASH system took into cognizance the Adum-Aiona community of Nigeria as a template for other communities. Among others, the proposed system integrated a behaviour/social change component in its n-tier layered architecture to underscore the complimentary role of value re-orientation in the fight against open defecation. Therefore, SDG 6 actors and implementors are sensitized on the need to focus on both physical infrastructure and social/behavioural rebirth for a comprehensive solution to the global health challenge and attainment of SDG 6 by the target year 2030.

6   Conclusion

Participatory implementation of SDG 6 is required and a software engineering modelling approach that documents, promotes understanding and elicit cooperation and collaboration among stakeholders is key. In this vision paper, we examined open defecation as an indicator of progress made towards the actualization of SDG 6. Our proposed system particularly draws attention to the significance of behaviour/social change as a vital component of any viable WASH system as provision of sanitary facilities alone is not sufficient.

Our study proved that software models are not only useful for developing software systems but are invaluable in documenting activities and enhancing stakeholders understanding of operations in any human field of endeavor. If implemented, the proposed WASH system would go a long way in addressing the global problem of open defecation as well as facilitating the actualization of SDG 6 by the target date of 2030.

Regrettably, even with the provision of sanitary facilities and availability of water, community-led sanitation and hygiene is suffering set setbacks as poverty, illiteracy and ignorance have made people to accept open defecation as a norm rather than exception [1, 10]. In future works, researchers should explore and close this gap by evolving adaptive and strategic value re-orientation strategies and interventions that help everyone internalize the fact that open defecation poses serious health risks and could reduce global productivity as diseases deplete human productive capacity.

References

1. Mara, D.: The elimination of open defecation and its adverse health effects: a moral imperative for governments and development professionals. J. Water Sanitation Hyg. Dev. **7**, 1–12 (2017)
2. Ngwu, U.: The practice of open defecation in rural communities in Nigeria: a call for social and behaviour change communication intervention. Int. J. Commun. Res. **7**, 201–206 (2017)
3. Okewu, E., Misra, S., Okewu, J.: Model-driven engineering and creative arts approach to designing climate change response system for rural Africa: a case study of Adum-Aiona community in Nigeria. Problemy Ekorozwoju – Prob. Sustain. Dev. **12**(1), 101–116 (2017)
4. Adamu, S.H.: Making Nigeria Open-Defecation-Free By 2025-A National Road Map (2019)
5. Kumwenda, S., Msefula, C., Kadewa, W., Ngwira, B., Morse, T.: Estimating the health risk associated with the use of ecological sanitation toilets in Malawi. J. Environ. Public Health (2017)
6. Sumedh, M.K.: Community-based approaches to tackle open defecation in rural India: theory, evidence and policies, Occasional Paper No. 178, Observer Research Foundation, December 2018
7. Odagiri, M., et al.: Enabling factors for sustaining open defecation-free communities in rural Indonesia: a cross-sectional study. Int. J. Environ. Res. **14**, 1572 (2017)
8. Report of the Inter-Agency and Expert Group on Sustainable Development Goal Indicators (E/CN.3/2016/2/Rev.1)
9. United Nations: Implementing Water, Sanitation and Hygiene (WASH), UN-Water Decade Programme on Advocacy and Communication (UNW-DPAC), Information brief (2015)
10. UNICEF: Strategy for Water, Sanitation and Hygiene 2016–2030. Water, Sanitation and Hygiene (WASH) Section Programme Division, UNICEF, New York, August 2016
11. Ejembi, S.: Historical Background of Orokam (2017)
12. Peal, A., Evans, B., Voorden, C.: Hygience and Sanitation Software: An Overview of Approaches, March 2010
13. Hutchings, M.T., Dev, A., Palaniappan, M., Srinivasan, V., Ramanathan, N., Taylor, J.: mWASH: Mobile Phone Applications for the Water, Sanitation, and Hygiene Sector, April 2012
14. Coetzee, L., Kotzé, P.: The Internet of Things: opportunities for water, sanitation and hygiene (WASH) Management, WRC Report No. TT 757/18, August 2018
15. Fernando, J.C., Filho, M., de Queiroz, A.A.F.S.L., Machado, B.S., Paulo, P.L.: Sustainable sanitation management tool for decision making in isolated areas in Brazil. Int. J. Environ. Res. Public Health **16**, 1118 (2019)
16. O'Connell, K.: Scaling up rural sanitation what influences open defecation and latrine ownership in rural households? Findings from a global review, August 2014. The Water and Sanitation Program, World Bank Group (2014)
17. Gorton, I.: Essential Software Architecture (2011)
18. Brown, C.: National Systems to Support Drinking-Water, Sanitation and Hygiene: Global Status Report 2019, UN-Water Global Analysis and Assessment of Sanitation and Drinking-Water (GLASS) 2019 Report (2019)
19. Akpabio, E.M.: Water supply and sanitation services sector in Nigeria: the policy trend and practice constraints, ZEF Working Paper Series, No. 96, University of Bonn, Center for Development Research (ZEF), Bonn (2012)
20. Okewu, E.: Requirements engineering in an emerging market. In: Gervasi, O., et al. (eds.) ICCSA 2015. LNCS, vol. 9158, pp. 476–491. Springer, Cham (2015). https://doi.org/10.1007/978-3-319-21410-8_37

21. CIBN 2019: Infrastructure Development and Growth in Nigeria: Prospects and Challenges, 2019 CIBN Annual Lecture, The Chartered Institute of Bankers of Nigeria (2019)
22. Fatai, O.O., Omolara, Y.J., Taiwo, A.B.: Infrastructure finance and development in Nigeria. Arab. J. Bus. Manag. Rev. (Nigerian Chap.) **3**(12), 1–11 (2016)
23. Kingma, D., Ba, J.: Adam: a method for stochastic optimization, Published as a conference paper at ICLR (2015)
24. Brownlee, J.: Your First Deep Learning Project in Python with Keras Step-by-Step, 24 July 2019 in Deep Learning (2019)

A Survey on the Effects of Working Conditions on Programming Efficiency in an Educational Environment

Mariia Charikova, Ananga Thapaliya, Susanna Gimaeva,
Alexandr Grichshenko, Selina Varouqa, Luiz Jonatã Pires de Araújo$^{(\boxtimes)}$,
and Giancarlo Succi

Innopolis University, Innopolis 420500, Russia
l.araujo@innopolis.university

Abstract. A recurrent concern of instructors and managers in learning and industrial sectors is how to organise the working environment to increase the productivity in tasks such as programming and software testing. Evidence of the increasing interest from different domains in this topic is the growing amount of research that has been published on physical factors (e.g., product, personnel, project and process), programming tasks (e.g., tests, questionnaires, programming, testing and debugging), and assessment methods (e.g., time, software metrics and academic grading). The objective of this paper is to survey the literature and to enable one to gain valuable insights into the relevance of physical factors to improve programming efficiency, especially in a learning environment. This study also makes recommendations on the techniques that can provide further experience for learners before joining the industrial sector. Finally, this survey suggests research directions, including an analysis of the correlation between physical factors and measurable productivity.

Keywords: Programming efficiency · Academic environment · Physical conditions · Productivity factors · Evaluation of productivity

1 Introduction

The term "working conditions" is often used to refer to the environment and surrounding circumstances in which employees or students work. Such conditions include a wide range of aspects, from physical components of the workspace or study space to the methodologies that the institution implements, which can influence the developer's behaviour and productivity. Working conditions can be divided into product, personnel, project and process related circumstances [1]. Examples of these factors include elements in the work or the study space such as light, noise, music, company culture, job satisfaction, satisfaction of the study process, relationship with colleagues or other students, technical training, different coding practices such as pair programming, and the complexity of a task.

O. Gervasi et al. (Eds.): ICCSA 2020, LNCS 12254, pp. 289–300, 2020.
https://doi.org/10.1007/978-3-030-58817-5_22

This topic plays an essential part in educational processes for students enrolled in university-level courses of programming and industrial companies providing internal training. A careful study of the working conditions' impact on programming efficiency can increase the effectiveness of learning activities, leading to higher standards of education and skilful specialists. This paper surveys the existing literature concerning the effects of working or learning conditions on developers' efficiency in the educational process, focusing on the main investigated physical factors, programming tasks and assessment methods. Moreover, by analysing the trends and gaps in the literature, this study enables better decision making regarding the surroundings for students and practitioners in the academia and the industrial sector.

The methodology for collecting relevant literature consists of data acquisition from scientific journals and conferences using search keywords and sentences including "working conditions", "programming efficiency", "physical factors". This was followed by an analysis of the relevance of individual studies, resulting in a summary covering papers published between 1984 and 2018 addressing different working and academic conditions' effects.

The remaining of this paper is organised as follows. Section 2 outlines the existing research on physical factors, typical programming tasks and methods for performance assessment. It also categorises the current body of study and introduces a taxonomy for such factors. In Sect. 3, we discuss the trends and the gaps in the literature and this analysis constitutes a useful resource for researchers and software project managers willing to improve the work environment in their companies. Section 4 presents overall observations and suggestions for further research.

2   State-of-the-Art

2.1   On the Physical Factors

Physical factors can be divided into four different categories according to their characteristics: product, personnel, project and process factors. Product factors refer to software qualities that are established throughout the stages of software development. They concern to artefacts (e.g. software code, specifications, documents) and system characteristics (e.g. complexity, scalability, instability) [1]. Product factors also include the application type, programming language, database management system, development model (agile/waterfall), hardware platform, graphical user interface and operating system [2]. An example of a study on product factors is presented by Delorey et al. [3], which explained how the choice of programming language affects productivity and the outcome. In another study, Mohapatra et al. [4] showed that product factors such as code reusability and convenient document management system could significantly impact productivity while maintaining high quality.

Personnel factors comprise developers' attributes that impact the productivity of the whole team during the development process. This type of factor is often related to the expertise level of individuals and their roles in the project.

For example, the study by Trendowicz et al. [1] investigated how skills of development team members (e.g. analysts, architects, engineers, project managers), programming suppliers, clients, maintainers and subcontractors affect the overall performance. It is possible to see that age and gender influence the quality of the code and the productivity of the development team [5]. Moreover, personnel factors like pair programming [6], the role of a participant in the project [7] and compatible soft skills [8] also affect the programmers' efficiency. A common limitation of the aforementioned studies is that they ignore the relationship between developers in a team, which is an important personnel factor.

Project factors include various aspects of setup and maintenance, such as the high turnover rate of the staff. Examples of project factors that impact developers' productivity are customer participation, development environment adequacy, staff availability, use standards, methods, tools, software's logical complexity, requirements volatility, quality requirements, efficiency requirements, installation requirements, staff's soft skills and domain knowledge [2]. Raziq et al. [9] also discussed how satisfaction and relationship with colleagues or classmates during a project could affect productivity.

Process factors are related to the characteristics of software processes including techniques, apparatuses and innovations that are implemented during the product life-cycle. These factors also include quality of evaluations, consistency of examinations, quality of the tools, nature of the executive procedures, or degree of customer cooperation [1]. As described by Sudhakar [10], different software engineering tools and techniques such as rapid prototyping, software testing, e-mail, document management systems, programming languages, and configuration management systems are examples of process factors that affect efficiency.

2.2   On the Programming Tasks

In this section, we consider tasks which can be used for evaluation of the programming efficiency in an educational context. They can be grouped in four macro-categories: tests, questionnaires and exams; implementing data structures and algorithms; working on a project; testing and debugging.

This survey focuses on programming tasks in an educational process, which are mostly assessed through exams and tests. For example, Hu et al. [11] investigated the impact of such evaluation techniques on productivity. There were no special assignments to estimate students' productivity; instead, they studied in different physical conditions and took general exams and tests. Other studies focused on the task of learning an extracurricular topic, with outcomes being evaluated according to questionnaires for participants [12]. Wiedenbeck et al. [13] proposed a different approach for assessing students' progress by providing them with simple tasks for approximately 1.5 min. Such a method stands as an alternative method for evaluating the learning outcome since short tasks can assess knowledge but not ingenuity nor the ability to produce a creative solution quickly.

Another type of activity which is important for computer science students is the implementation of algorithms and data structures. Nanz and Furia [7], and Bergersen et al. [14] mention simple tasks for algorithms implementation. The development of basic algorithms allows researchers to consider the minimum number of internal human factors and focus on the implementation. Another approach outlined by Darcy and Ma [15] is to provide a coding task as an exercise. Different difficulty levels of the proposed tasks help researchers to evaluate the influence of physical factors on the programmer's productivity. Not only standard algorithms can be used in the evaluation as indicated by Sprigle and Schaefer [16], who used tasks in LOGO programming language for drawing.

Although this survey focuses on the academic environment, it is noteworthy to mention studies that focus on programming tasks in industrial projects. For example, Raziq and Maulabakhsh [9] used different types of tasks from those commonly used in academia. The advantage of using industrial tasks is that they can be studied over a long time, as indicated in [3] and [10]. For instance, in [2], the employees of a large company were observed during the software project, and researchers investigated how different factors affect productivity. It is worth emphasizing that, unlike academic tasks, industrial ones are more narrowly focused. For example, Sullivan and Umashi Bers [5] discussed software development and robotics tasks. There are many projects in industry that are dependent on the specific domain, which complicates the process of evaluating the productivity of programmers.

Testing and debugging are here considered separately, although both are part of industrial and academic projects. Chaparro et al. [6] mentioned different tasks which are related to debugging, re-factoring and program comprehension. When evaluating productivity, the debugging skill can be critical since small errors or problems with external services can cause the inability to present a working code. Khan et al. [17] organized multiple-choice questionnaires to measure a programmer's performance on recognizing debugging problems. Such an approach is one of the simplest ways to give objective feedback on the productivity of testers and programmers. A more comprehensive method is presented in [18], where the project manager assigned to programmers a set of modules for testing in model-based development. Khan et al. [19] proposed a special system of providing tasks for evaluating the productivity of programmers. The training session consisted of watching a video clip, followed by a series of debugging questions that had to be answered within a fixed time. After completing the training session, participants continued with the actual test, which consisted of two cycles of watching clips and debugging test.

2.3 Constraints and Performance Assessment of Programming Tasks

This section examines two important elements related to programming tasks: the constraints and evaluation methods for assessing programming performance. Most of the literature focuses on combining time constraint and completeness evaluation, using software development metrics and academic grading.

One of the simplest methods for evaluating programming performance which has been employed is to assess whether the task was finished in its entirety. In this type of evaluation, the time to solve a task is used as a performance metric. The literature contains several examples of research in this direction [3,6,7,14,20]. However, most of the research addresses programming in the workplace with limited research being done in an educational context [21].

Using software metrics is a practical way to evaluate not only students' performance but also the quality of the generated code. Some metrics have been commonly used by the industry sector and can offer a good benchmark. For example, Mohapatra [22] uses function points and a person's monthly effort to estimate individual productivity. Sudhakar et al. [10] employed a more comprehensive set of metrics to evaluate programming performance: use function, use case, object and feature points. The literature also contains examples of not conventional software metrics for programming quality assessment, including the number of lines of code (LOC) [7,10] and memory usage [7]. Darcy and Ma [15] extended LOC by considering blank, comment and executable lines. Vihavainen [23] employed an alternative measurement by counting indentation errors. It is noteworthy that LOC cannot be the only one measure because it partially depends on the choice of programming language.

Several studies have used academic grading for assessing programming quality [11,13,17]. For example, Raschs et al. [12] surveyed developers to compare his or her overall performance with peers at the same level and speciality area. A nine-point scale was used, with labels ranging from "very inferior, the very worst" to "very superior, the very best". Mohapatra [22] focused on evaluating team productivity and demonstrated that there exists a strong relationship between programming quality and following a systematic project management plan. It is also important to consider the fact of possible subjectivity of people who put such evaluation, which affects academic grading as a metric.

3   Discussion

As evident in the analyzed studies, working conditions play an essential role in software developers' performance. For example, Malik et al. [24] conducted a study to demonstrate that the physical environment has a significant positive effect on employees' productivity. The study used multiple regression analysis to emphasize that the performance mostly depends on physical working conditions, training and development, and communication practices. In another study, Srivastava [25] demonstrated that there is a dependence between the working environment and the employees' behaviour by examining the resultant organizational effectiveness and performance.

Several studies have also confirmed that environmental conditions affect the emotional and psychological health of employees. A job usually occupies a considerable portion of a person's day, which makes relevant any discussions about the impact of a job on the emotional health [26]. According to McCraty et al. [27], there is a strong relationship between emotional and physical health and the work-related indicators of workplace satisfaction as well as the perception of individual contribution. The study enabled an overall reduction of the blood pressure, improved emotional health and workplace-related measures of the employees by enhancing the work environment.

Working conditions have a significant effect not only on the emotional health of employees but also on their physical health [28]. One of the essential components of the workspace is its shape or design. Open workspaces might lead to different work collaboration and efficiency compared to small closed individual office design. The design of the workspace may influence the surrounding noise and have an impact on the employee's performance. One important aspect of choosing the office design is the type of work that is being done, whether it requires collaboration and teamwork, or it is an individual task. Danielsson and Bodin [29] showed that the lowest health status for employees was found in medium-sized and small open-plan offices, while the best health rates were found among employees in cell and flex offices.

A study by Estácio et al. [30] revealed that the work environment could also be affected by the style of work: individual, team-based, or pair-based, with collaborative practices outperforming solo programming with regard to acquiring programming skills. Furthermore, it was shown that enhancing the learning outcomes, improving students' satisfaction and reducing frustration in assignments could be achieved with pair programming [31] and more interactive learning environments [32]. Flor and Hutchins [33] noted that the "solutions space", i.e. all possible solutions for a problem, is maximized when two programmers concentrate on a task. There are other factors which may influence the effectiveness of collaborative learning. A study performed by Chaparro et al. [6] on postgraduate students reported that close skill level and personality compatibility are among the main elements that positively affect the success of pair programming. Another finding of the research is that collaborative programming can boost or undermine the performance depending on the type of task. According to the study, software design and implementation were demonstrated to be more efficient, while debugging was not significantly faster nor easier with this practice.

There has been a considerable increase in the number of publications on working conditions in the last decades. Appendix in Sect. 4 represents the summary of considered literature, namely physical factors, programming tasks and performance measure chosen for each study. Figure 1 shows an increasing amount of research on personnel physical factors and programmers' productivity. This growth is more noticeable on the number of studies about project and process factors such as satisfaction and relationship with colleagues. This interest is caused, among other factors, by an increasing concern with creating a comfortable atmosphere in offices and educational centres to improve the productivity of employees and students.

Regarding the number of publications on job-specific problems, there has been a considerable increase over the years (see Fig. 2a). This can be explained in part by the acknowledged relationship between profit and employees'

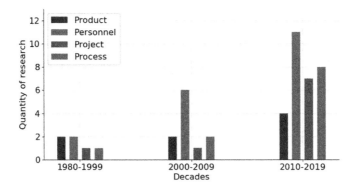

Fig. 1. Research of physical factors impacting performance in the last decades.

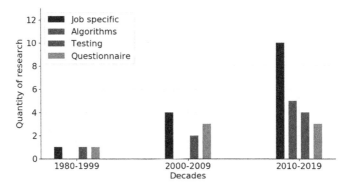

Research of programming tasks impacting performance.

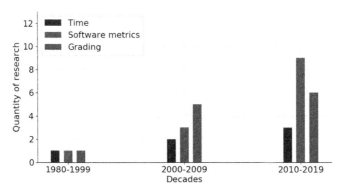

Research of measures evaluating performance.

Fig. 2. Research of programming tasks impacting performance.

productivity. Moreover, the number of papers considering debugging and testing tasks, as well as exams and questionnaires has also increased. Interestingly, there has been no significant amount of research on programming tasks related to algorithms, to the best of the authors' knowledge. It is also possible to notice that most of the research has focused on performance assessment using software metrics such as source lines of code (SLOC) and software function points (SFP), as shown in Fig. 2b.

It is noteworthy that most of the conducted research has focused on the physical factors in an isolated manner. In other words, the effects of the synergy between different factors are often ignored. Future research should focus simultaneously on several factors as their interaction can impact the results of the software project. Moreover, the majority of studies has used software metrics for assessing programming productivity addressing the industrial environment [7,10,22]. Such an approach might bring additional complexities and a steeper learning curve to students compared to the usual academic grading evaluation. However, the use of software metrics in a learning environment can also provide practical experience which might be useful for future industrial jobs [11,13].

4   Conclusion and Future Research

The research on working conditions is relevant not only for corporations aiming to maximise the productivity of their employees but also for educational institutions interested in improving their curricula and improving students' overall qualification before they enter the job market. A deeper understanding of concepts like physical factors, programming tasks and methods of evaluating performance can enable better decision making. The body of research is, therefore, a useful resource for professors and university managers to improve the academic environment.

This survey is meant to serve as a guideline to future researchers, software project managers and specifically university faculty members. Moreover, a taxonomy for physical and programming factors has been introduced to assist the stakeholders to quickly recognise and solve potential issues that might affect the performance. The review of the extensive literature on programming metrics can be applied to evaluate the existing model of performance in a company or the educational institution, identifying the need for improvements in their processes.

One possible research direction is the study on the potential synergy between different working conditions, and how their combination affects the performance. Such an approach could provide more comprehensive insight into the operation and management of the entire project or the curriculum. Any conclusions that might emerge from the integration of industry and academia will provide a better understanding of factors impacting performance and consequently benefit both fields.

Appendix

References	Physical factors	Programming tasks	Performance measure
Thadhani (1984)	Programming experience, task complexity, a fraction of time spent directly working on the task	Industrial project	Time (constraint) and lines of code
Rasch and Tosi (1992)	Goal difficulty and clarity, high-achievement needs, self-esteem	Job-specific tasks	Self-evaluation, relative performance
Maxwell and Forselius (2000)	Application type, programming language, database management system, development model, hardware platform	Regular development work	Customers' participation, development environment adequacy, staff availability, standards use, methods use, tools use, software's logical complexity, requirements volatility
Hu and Kuh (2003)	College environment, the estimated effort put into study	Usual tests and exams in university	System of points of the university
Wiedenbeck et al. (2004)	Programming experience, self-efficacy, ability to construct mental models	Time specific simple and complex tasks	Course grading system
Chaparro et al. (2005)	Pair Programming	Debugging, refactoring and program comprehension	Amount of finished exercises
Darcy and Ma (2005)	GPA and age	Individual coding task (Simple payroll system)	Specification conformance, code structure complexity
Del (2007)	Programming language	Job specific tasks (working on project)	Speed
Khan et al. (2007)	Programmers' mood and emotions	Various debugging exercises	Completion of the debugging test
Trendowicz and Mnch (2009)	Product, process, personnel and project factors	Industrial level tasks	Overall development productivity
Paiva et al. (2010)	Commitment, communication, benefits, consistent requirements, experience, motivation, location, project and team size	Job specific tasks	Questionnaire with developers
Bergersen et al. (2011)	Individual expertise and skills	Simple programming tasks	Time and quality
Khan (2011)	Programmer's current mood and emotions	Actual test, which consisted of two cycles of the movie and debugging test	Completion of the debugging test

References	Physical factors	Programming tasks	Performance measure
Mohapatra (2011)	Application complexity, client support, availability of modules and testing tools, document management system and computational performance	Software project development	Following systematic steps as laid down in the project management plan
Mohapatra (2011)	Effective training, availability of skilled manpower in the technology domain, well-documented procedure	Software development, maintenance and testing industrial projects	Function points, number of defects
Sudhakar et al. (2012)	Size of the team, computing infrastructure and software engineering tools	Software project	Lines of code
Watson et al. (2013)	Logs of compilation errors and code snapshots across the semester	Coding tasks in an introductory programming course	Overall coursework mark
Kamma and Jalote (2013)	Techniques used by programmers to organise their work	Set of modules for testing in model-based development	Actual effort spent by the programmer in a task and the software size of that task
Vihavainen (2013)	Students' programming behaviour (eagerness to start new exercises, the time required to complete an exercise)	Regular assignments in an introductory programming course	Course grade
Dagiene et al. (2014)	Prior coding experience	Algorithmic thinking contest tasks	Grades
Mohapatra and Sreejesh (2014)	Application complexity, training, client support, reusing existing code and quality of document management system	Software projects	Cost estimation model
Nanz and Furia (2015)	Roles of participants	Algorithm Implementation and other 745 simple tasks	Lines of code, memory usage
Raziq and Maulabakhsh (2015)	Relationship with team members	Job specific tasks	Job satisfaction
Sullivan and Umashi Bers (2017)	Age and Gender	IT and Robotic tasks	Function points, object points, use case points and feature points
Busechian et al. (2018)	Pair Programming	Job specific tasks	Topological brain maps
Wagner and Ruhe (2018)	Organisational cultural factors, Team Culture factors, experience and work environment factors	Industrial level tasks	Effort per SLOC (source lines of code), function points

References

1. Trendowicz, A., Münch, J.: Factors influencing software development productivity - state-of-the-art and industrial experiences. Adv. Comput. **77**, 185–241 (2009)
2. Maxwell, K.D., Forselius, P.: Benchmarking software development productivity. IEEE Softw. **17**(1), 80–88 (2000)
3. Delorey, D.P., Knutson, C.D., Chun, S.: Do programming languages affect productivity? A case study using data from open source projects. In: First International Workshop on Emerging Trends in FLOSS Research and Development, FLOSS 2007, p. 4 (2007)
4. Mohapatra, S., Sreejesh, S.: Model for improving productivity without impacting quality of deliverables in it projects. Int. J. Inf. Technol. Project Manage. (IJITPM) **5**(2), 14–29 (2014)
5. Sullivan, A., Bers, M.U.: Girls, boys, and bots: gender differences in young children's performance on robotics and programming tasks. J. Inf. Technol. Educ. Innov. Pract. **15**, 145–165 (2017)
6. Chaparro, E.A., Yuksel, A., Romero, P., Bryant, S.: Factors affecting the perceived effectiveness of pair programming in higher education. In: 17th Workshop of the Psychology of Programming Interest Group, June 2005, pp. 5–18 (2005)
7. Nanz, S., Furia, C.A.: A comparative study of programming languages in rosetta code. In: Proceedings - International Conference on Software Engineering, vol. 1, pp. 778–788 (2015)
8. Fernández-Sanz, L., Villalba, M.T., Medina, J.A., Misra, S.: A study on the key soft skills for successful participation of students in multinational engineering education. Int. J. Eng. Educ. **33**(6), 2061–2070 (2017)
9. Raziq, A., Maulabakhsh, R.: Impact of working environment on job satisfaction. Procedia Econ. Financ. **23**, 717–725 (2015)
10. Sudhakar, P., Farooq, A., Patnaik, S.: Measuring productivity of software development teams. Serb. J. Manage. **7**(1), 65–75 (2012)
11. Hu, S., Kuh, G.D.: Maximizing what students get out of college: testing a learning productivity model. J. Coll. Student Dev. **44**(2), 185–203 (2003)
12. Rasch, R.H., Tosi, H.L.: Factors affecting software developers' performance: an integrated approach. MIS Q. **16**, 395–413 (1992)
13. Wiedenbeck, S., Labelle, D., Kain, V.N.: Factors affecting course outcomes in introductory programming. In: 16th Workshop of the Psychology of Programming Interest Group, pp. 97–110 (2004)
14. Bergersen, G.R., Hannay, J.E., Sjoberg, D.I., Dyba, T., Karahasanovic, A.: Inferring skill from tests of programming performance: combining time and quality. In: 2011 International Symposium on Empirical Software Engineering and Measurement, April 2014, pp. 305–314 (2011)
15. Darcy, D.P., Ma, M.: Exploring individual characteristics and programming performance: implications for programmer selection. In: Proceedings of the 38th Annual Hawaii International Conference on System Sciences, p. 314a. IEEE (2005)
16. Sprigle, J.E., Schaefer, L.: Age, gender, and spatial knowledge influences on preschoolers' computer programming ability. Early Child Dev. Care **14**(3–4), 243–250 (1984)
17. Khan, I.A., Hierons, R.M., Brinkman, W.P.: Moods and programmers' performance. In: PPIG, p. 2 (2007)
18. Kamma, D., Jalote, P.: Effect of task processes on programmer productivity in model-based testing. In Proceedings of the 6th India Software Engineering Conference, pp. 23–28. ACM (2013)

19. Khan, I.A., Brinkman, W., Hierons, R.M.: Do moods affect programmers' debug performance? Cogn. Technol. Work **13**(4), 245–258 (2011). https://doi.org/10. 1007/s10111-010-0164-1

20. Thadhani, A.J.: Factors affecting programmer productivity during application development. IBM Syst. J. **23**(1), 19–35 (1984)

21. Watson, C., Li, F.W.B., Godwin, J.L.: Predicting performance in an introductory programming course by logging and analyzing student programming behavior. In: 2013 IEEE 13th International Conference on Advanced Learning Technologies, pp. 319–323. IEEE (2013)

22. Mohapatra, S.: Maximising productivity by controlling influencing factors in commercial software development. Int. J. Inf. Commun. Technol. **3**(2), 160–179 (2011)

23. Vihavainen, A.: Predicting students' performance in an introductory programming course using data from students' own programming process. In: 2013 IEEE 13th International Conference on Advanced Learning Technologies, pp. 498–499. IEEE (2013)

24. Malik, M.I., Ahmad, A., Gomez, S.F., Ali, M.: A study of work environment and employees' performance in Pakistan. Afr. J. Bus. Manage. **5**(34), 13227 (2011)

25. Srivastava, A.K.: Effect of perceived work environment on employees' job behaviour and organizational effectiveness. J. Indian Acad. Appl. Psychol. **34**(1), 47–55 (2008)

26. Robone, S., Jones, A.M., Rice, N.: Contractual conditions, working conditions and their impact on health and well-being. Eur. J. Health Econ. **12**(5), 429–444 (2011). https://doi.org/10.1007/s10198-010-0256-0

27. McCraty, R., Atkinson, M., Tomasino, D.: Impact of a workplace stress reduction program on blood pressure and emotional health in hypertensive employees. J. Altern. Complement. Med. **9**(3), 355–369 (2003)

28. Arnold, K.A., Dupré, K.E.: Perceived organizational support, employee health and emotions. Int. J. Workplace Health Manage. **5**(2), 139–152 (2012)

29. Danielsson, C.B., Bodin, L.: Office type in relation to health, well-being, and job satisfaction among employees. Environ. Behav. **40**(5), 636–668 (2008)

30. Estácio, B., et al.: Evaluating collaborative practices in acquiring programming skills: findings of a controlled experiment. In: 2015 29th Brazilian Symposium on Software Engineering, pp. 150–159. IEEE (2015)

31. Nagappan, N., et al.: Improving the cs1 experience with pair programming. ACM SIGCSE Bull. **35**(1), 359–362 (2003)

32. Oyesiku, D., Adewumi, A., Misra, S., Ahuja, R., Damasevicius, R., Maskeliunas, R.: An educational math game for high school students in Sub-Saharan Africa. In: Florez, H., Diaz, C., Chavarriaga, J. (eds.) ICAI 2018. CCIS, vol. 942, pp. 228–238. Springer, Cham (2018). https://doi.org/10.1007/978-3-030-01535-0_17

33. Flor, N.V., Hutchins, E.L.: A case study of team programming during perfective software maintenance. In: Empirical Studies of Programmers: Fourth Workshop, p. 36. Intellect Books (1991)

Calibration of Empirical Models for Path Loss Prediction in Urban Environment

Robert O. Abolade[1], Dare J. Akintade[2], Segun I. Popoola[3,4($\boxtimes$)],
Folasade A. Semire[1], Aderemi A. Atayero[3], and Sanjay Misra[3]

[1] Department of Electronic and Electrical Engineering,
Ladoke Akintola University of Technology, Ogbomoso, Nigeria
[2] Department of Electronic and Computer Engineering,
Lagos State University, Epe, Nigeria
[3] IoT-Enabled Smart and Connected Communities (SmartCU) Cluster,
Covenant University, Ota, Nigeria
[4] Department of Engineering, Manchester Metropolitan University,
M1 5GD Manchester, UK
segun.popoola@covenantuniversity.edu.ng

Abstract. The reliability and accuracy of radio propagation models depends on the unique localized features in the area under study. In this paper, we calibrate empirical radio propagation models for 1800 MHz cellular network planning in Lagos Metropolis, Nigeria. Drive test are conducted to obtain measured data within suburban and dense urban propagation environment. Received Signal Strength (RSS) and path loss values of radio signals in 1800 MHz cellular networks are recorded for model calibration and evaluation. COST 231–Hata model achieved the closest prediction results relative to the field measurement. Mean Error (ME), Standard Deviation (SD) and Root Mean Square (RMS) results are 11.004 dB, 12.194 dB and 16.43 dB respectively in dense suburban, while the corresponding results are 9.151 dB, 8.151 dB and 12.254 dB in dense urban. ME of all the calibrated propagation prediction models reduced to nearly zero (≈ 0 dB). Also, the SD and the RMS fall within the calibration quality target with ME as less than 1 dB and SD is less than 8.5 dB for each of the calibrated models. In conclusion, the proposed calibrated path loss models achieved minimum mean error and standard deviation. Prediction results improved when terrain type and clutter data were taken into account during path loss calculations.

Keywords: Path loss · Empirical model · Radio propagation · Radio network planning · Mobile communication

1 Introduction

Wireless channel is faced with some technical challenges. The wireless channel suffers multipath propagation problem which resulted in fading [1, 2]. The channel is also prone to noise, distortion and signal attenuation [3]. The need to access network without wire connection makes the channel less secure. Thus,

© Springer Nature Switzerland AG 2020
O. Gervasi et al. (Eds.): ICCSA 2020, LNCS 12254, pp. 301–310, 2020.
https://doi.org/10.1007/978-3-030-58817-5_23

it requires a stronger security mechanism to protect data and/or bandwidth. Consequently, the susceptibility of the radio channel to fading necessitate good network planning the study location [3]. There is a need for efficient network and good quality of service (QoS) for better radio network design by network operators. This has brought mobile network planning and signal optimization into a sharp focus.

Path loss (PL) analysis is paramount to network design in wireless communication systems. The success of mobile radio depends largely on how adequately the network is planned to provide good coverage the selected area. The empirical propagation models were developed using extensive measurement of path loss (PL) data obtained from different observations in an environment [4]. The empirical models are widely used for PL estimation due to their simplicity, but they are not usually accurate especially when deployed in other environment. The authors in [4–9] confirmed that empirical models are not consistent without proper tuning.

PL models are used to predict Received Signal Strength (RSS) at a particular environment in the channel. These models depend heavily on key features of the wireless channel for their development. Hence, adequate knowledge of height of the transmitting and receiving antenna, operational frequency and other physical or human-interactive elements in the propagation environment is a necessary prerequisite in developing these models [10,11]. The predictive abilities of path loss models, which guides mobile network operators in base station location, ensure that signal coverage is maximized, and the costs expended on network resources are minimized. This is of paramount importance as proportional increase in the number of base stations within a geographical area and mobile subscriber is equivalent to better QoS and greater signal coverage [12,13]. Path loss models will help in determining where to position base stations out of possible set of different location options. They serve as functional tools in radio network planning and radio optimization procedures [6,14,15].

As the number of mobile subscribers reaches an unprecedented level an increase in capacity of mobile radio network would be of absolute necessity to accommodate these demands [10]. Increase in mobile radio network capacity, will demand more installations of base stations which in the long-run becomes a more difficult task, in deciding the best location that maximizes coverage and minimizes the expenditures on network infrastructure. In this paper, we investigate the existing propagation prediction models with the view of working on calibration of empirical radio propagation models for GSM 1800 MHz cellular network planning in Lagos Metropolis, Nigeria. The main contributions of this paper are as follows:

(a) We conduct drive test measurements within the dense sub-urban and urban areas of Lagos, Nigeria and record RSS and PL values of radio signals in 1800 MHz GSM cellular networks;
(b) Accuracy of Okumura-Hata, COST 231, and SPM models is evaluated for PL predictions in cellular networks within dense suburban and dense urban propagation environments in Lagos Metropolis, Nigeria;

(c) Okumura-Hata, COST-231, and SPM PL models are calibrated with the field measurement data in ATOLL radio network planning tool so as to adapt the unique localized features of the selected propagation environments;

(d) Standard correction factors and model coefficients are generated for the formulation of modified Okumura-Hata, modified COST-231, and modified SPM PL models.

2   Materials and Method

Radio signal data was collected on a live network of different Base Transceiver Stations (BTS) within a cluster network in Lagos using TEMS Investigation software produced by Ericsson Company. TEMS has the capability of data collection, data analysis and post-processing. TEMS software package is a tool that was used to interfaces phones and other devices to collect data and records same in log files. The log files are thereafter imported in appropriate format (.txt) for further data processing. Eight (8) BTSs were considered in each clutter class for the purpose of propagation model calibration. The number of BTS selected depends on the terrain of the study area. Ten (10) BTS in each clutter class was adopted. During the selection exercise, the stations were ensured to have a good RF clearance to avoid signal obstruction in all direction. The height of the antennas varies between 20 m to 50 m. This study takes into considered the dense sub-urban and dense-urban clutter terrain of Lagos metropolis.

Long-distance routes were selected during drive test to reach the noise level of the receiver. Typically, the distance of 2 km was selected for sub-urban environment whereas 1 km was planned and used for the urban centers. The routes were planned to have equal number of samples for near and far station in all directions. These routes were planned to avoid crossing of forest and rivers for smooth data collection. Global Positioning System (GPS) of the drive test equipment was configured to match that of the mapping data. When planning the drive test measurement survey, the area to be covered was scanned to confirm is no interference.

A single frequency channel known as Broadcast Control Channel (BCCH) was measured during each survey. There are two contiguous unused channels of a clearance of 200 kHz on both sides of the measured signal so as to ensure that the measured frequency is clean. The Lee criterion in terms of sampling rate was satisfied to overcome fading effects. Over a distance of 40λ at least 36 samples were collected. The measured signals were averaged and the mean signal being the one stored. The maximum distance between the measured data is approximately equal to one and a half of the resolution of the clutter. In ATOLL, the drive test data files were imported as ASCII files with TXT extensions. The data files must contain the position of measured data and measured received signal levels for ATOLL to use the imported data files. The files imported also contain BCCH, Serving Cell BCCH, Radio Frequency Channel Number (RFCN), Base Station Identity Code, and Cell Identity (CI).

During the actual received signal strength prediction, one of the existing radio propagation models is selected and used as the prototype. The drive test data obtained from a live network on the local radio propagation environment is imported into the radio planning tool software (ATOLL). The coefficients of the existing propagation model formula are tuned such that the resulting calibrated propagation prediction model can accurately produce the actual prediction that at least approximately fits the field measured data.

3   Results and Discussion

The propagation coverage predictions were obtained from the existing radio propagation prediction models in-built in the ATOLL network planning tool. Figure 1 shows the predictions of SPM, Okumura-Hata and COST-231 models compared with the field measured data in dense suburban clutter of Lagos Metropolis. Field measured data obtained in the Dense Suburban clutter class has Mean Received Signal Strength (MRSS) of −71.3 dBm. The Okumura-Hata, COST-231 and SPM Models gave Mean Received Signal strength of −49.38 dBm, −64.28 dBm and −58 84 dBm respectively. The mean measured PL in Dense Suburban was 138.51 dB. The mean PL predicted by Okumura- Hata, COST-231 and SPM Models were 117.04 dB, 131.48 dB and 126.03 dB respectively.

Figure 2 compares the propagation coverage predictions of SPM, Okumura-Hata and COST-231 Models with the PL measured data at different points in the dense urban clutter of Lagos, Nigeria. Mean Received Signal Strength (MRSS) of the mobile station in Dense Urban terrain was −73.51 dBm. Okumura-Hata, COST-231 and SPM predicted MRSS of −62.76 dBm, −64.67 dBm and −58.63 dBm. The mean measured path loss in Dense Urban was 140.71 dB. The mean path losses predicted by Okumura – Hata, COST 231 and SPM were 129.96 dB, 131.87 dB and 125.83 dB, respectively.

Figure 3 shows the prediction results of the calibrated radio propagation models in Dense Suburban terrain. The field measured data obtained in the Dense Suburban clutter class has Mean Received Signal strength of −71.3 dBm. The Calibrated Okumura – Hata, Calibrated COST-231-Hata and Calibrated SPM have MRSS of −73.75 dBm, −73.75 dBm and −73.48 dBm respectively. The mean measured path loss in Dense Suburban was 138.51 dB. The mean path losses predicted by Calibrated Okumura – Hata, Calibrated COST 231-Hata and Calibrated SPM were 140.95 dB, 140.95 dB and 140.68 dB respectively.

Figure 4 shows the results of the calibrated radio propagation models in Dense Urban clutter class. The MRSS of the Mobile Station in Dense Urban terrain was −73.51 dBm. Calibrated Okumura-Hata, Calibrated COST-231 and Calibrated SPM predicted gave MRSS of −74.65 dBm, −74.61 dBm and −74.96 dBm. The mean measured path loss in Dense Urban was 140.71 dB. The mean path losses predicted by Okumura-Hata, COST-231 and SPM were 141.85 dB, 141.81 dB and 142.16 dB respectively. Mostly, the RSSL diminishes as the distance between the BTS and the MS increases, as anticipated. The RSSL varies randomly between −43 dBm and −100 dBm.

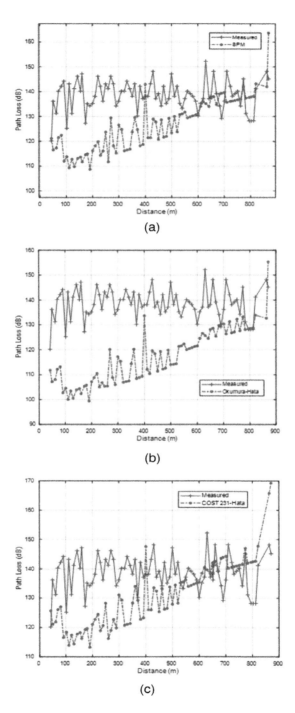

Fig. 1. PL predictions of (a) SPM (b) Okumura-Hata (c) COST 231-Hata models in dense suburban environment

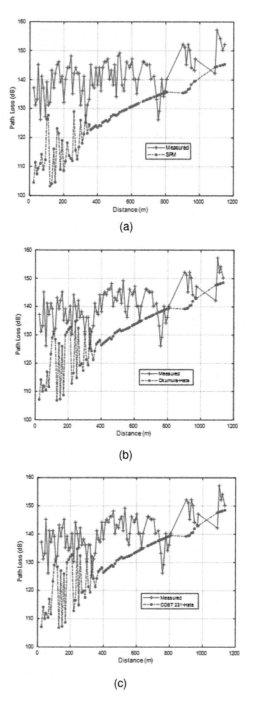

Fig. 2. PL predictions of (a) SPM (b) Okumura-Hata (c) COST 231-Hata models in dense urban environment

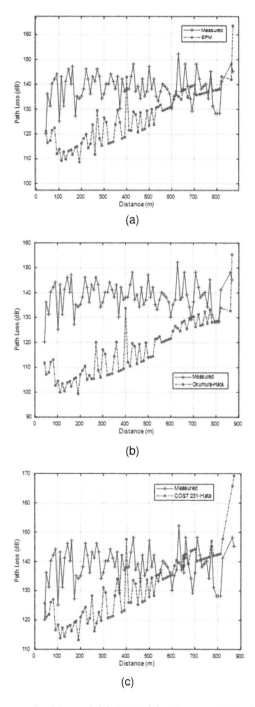

Fig. 3. PL predictions of calibrated (a) SPM (b) Okumura-Hata (c) COST 231-Hata models in dense suburban environment

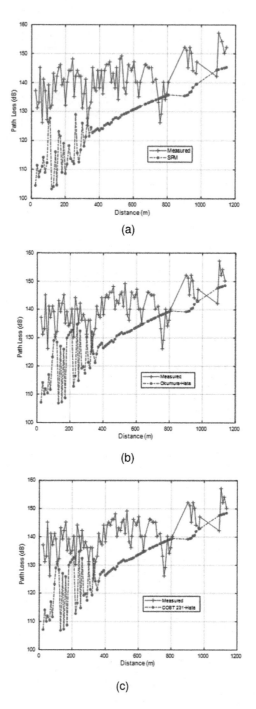

Fig. 4. PL predictions of calibrated (a) SPM (b) Okumura-Hata (c) COST 231-Hata models in dense urban environment

4   Conclusion

In this paper, we investigated the existing propagation prediction models with the view of working on calibration of empirical radio propagation models for GSM 1800 MHz cellular network planning in Lagos Metropolis, Nigeria. The performance evaluation of the existing empirical model namely: Okumura–Hata, COST-231-Hata and SPM under-estimate the PL at different locations away from the BTS. Consequently, the path losses in both the dense sub-urban clutter and the dense urban clutter of Lagos Metropolis were underestimated by the existing PL models.

In all, COST-231-Hata had the closest prediction results relative to the field measured data in both the Dense Sub-urban and Dense Urban clutter of Lagos. Whereas, the Okumura-Hata gave the widest deviation from the field measured data in the Dense Suburban clutter, while the Standard Propagation Model (SPM) gave the widest deviated results relative to the data obtained in the Dense Urban terrain of Lagos Metropolis. At the end of the calibration process, the mean errors of all the calibrated propagation prediction models have reduced to zero (0 dB). Also, the standard deviations and the root mean squares are now within the calibration quality target of each of the calibrated models. In the Dense Suburban clutter, the Calibrated Okumura – Hata Model gave SD and RME error of 9.083 dB. Calibrated COST 231-Hata model gave SD and RMS error of 9.083 dB. Calibrated Standard Propagation Model gave SD and RMS error of 9.428 dB. In the Dense Urban clutter, the Calibrated Okumura – Hata Model gave SD and RMS error of 7.459 dB. Calibrated COST 231-Hata model gave a standard deviation and root mean square of 7.459 dB. Calibrated Standard Propagation Model gave SD and RMS error of 6.745 dB.

Acknowledgement. This work was carried out under the IoT-Enabled Smart and Connected Communities (*SmartCU*) research cluster of the Department of Electrical and Information Engineering, Covenant University, Ota, Nigeria. The research was fully sponsored by Covenant University Centre for Research, Innovation and Development (CUCRID), Covenant University, Ota, Nigeria.

References

1. Popoola, S.I., Oseni, O.F.: Empirical path loss models for GSM network deployment in Makurdi, Nigeria. Int. Refereed J. Eng. Sci. **3**(6), 85–94 (2014)
2. Oseni, O.F., et al.: Comparative analysis of received signal strength prediction models for radio network planning of GSM 900 MHz in Ilorin, Nigeria. Int. J. Innov. Technol. Exploring Eng. **4**(3), 45–50 (2014)
3. Bhushan, N., et al.: Network densification: the dominant theme for wireless evolution into 5G. IEEE Commun. Mag. **52**(2), 82–89 (2014)
4. Chen, M., et al.: Body area networks: a survey. Mobile Netw. Appl. **16**(2), 171–193 (2011)
5. Negra, R., Jemili, I., Belghith, A.: Wireless body area networks: applications and technologies. Procedia Comput. Sci. **83**, 1274–1281 (2016)

6. Latré, B., et al.: A survey on wireless body area networks. Wireless Netw. **17**(1), 1–18 (2011)
7. Gondara, M.K., Kadam, S.: Requirements of vertical handoff mechanism in 4G wireless networks. arXiv preprint arXiv:1105.0043 (2011)
8. Dotche, K.A., Sekyere, F., Banuenumah, W.: LPC for signal analysis in cellular network coverage. Open Access Libr. J. **3**(07), 1 (2016)
9. Vegni, A.M., et al. A combined vertical handover decision metric for QoS enhancement in next generation networks. In: 2009 IEEE International Conference on Wireless and Mobile Computing, Networking and Communications. IEEE (2009)
10. Parmar, K.J., Nimavat, V.: Comparative analysis of path loss propagation models in radio communication. Int. J. Innov. Res. Comput. Commun. Eng. **3**(2), 840–844 (2015)
11. Luebbers, R.: Propagation prediction for hilly terrain using GTD wedge diffraction. IEEE Trans. Antennas Propag. **32**(9), 951–955 (1984)
12. Mohtashami, V., Shishegar, A.: Modified wavefront decomposition method for fast and accurate ray-tracing simulation. IET Microwaves Antennas Propag. **6**(3), 295–304 (2012)
13. Hufford, G.A.: An integral equation approach to the problem of wave propagation over an irregular surface. Q. Appl. Math. **9**(4), 391–404 (1952)
14. Zelley, C.A., Constantinou, C.C.: A three-dimensional parabolic equation applied to VHF/UHF propagation over irregular terrain. IEEE Trans. Antennas Propag. **47**(10), 1586–1596 (1999)
15. Popoola, S.I., Oseni, O.F.: Performance evaluation of radio propagation models on GSM network in urban area of Lagos, Nigeria. Int. J. Sci. Eng. Res. **5**(6), 1212–1217 (2014)

Investigating the Roles of Effective Communication Among Stakeholders in Collaborative Software Development Projects

Joseph Bamidele Awotunde[1] (ID), Femi Emmanuel Ayo[2] (ID),
Roseline Oluwaseun Ogundokun[3(✉)] (ID),
Opeyemi Emmanuel Matiluko[3], and Emmanuel Abidemi Adeniyi[3] (ID)

[1] Department of Computer Science, University of Ilorin, Ilorin, Nigeria
awotunde.jb@unilorin.edu.ng
[2] Department of Physical and Computer Science, Mcpherson University,
Seriki-Sotayo, Abeokuta, Nigeria
ayofe@mcu.edu.ng
[3] Department of Computer Science, Landmark University, Omu-Aran, Nigeria
{ogundokun.roseline, matiluko.opeyemi,
adeniyi.emmanuel}@lmu.edu.ng

Abstract. The development of software includes multiple stakeholders since it is a multidisciplinary collaboration. Processes in software development demonstrate many problems relating to multidisciplinary collaboration. Communication has been recognized as an important factor for success in software development projects because previous researches on stakeholder analysis and collaboration has demonstrated the importance of communication. Hence, this study investigated and analyzed communication between stakeholders in collaborative software development projects with references to team activities as a social and intellectual practice. The objective of the study was to define factors that would influence and recognize the process of collaboration during software development. The study focused on communication between the software developers (Students) and project managers (lecturers) during the software requirements phase, interdisciplinary collaboration, team process, and inter-team, particularly between software engineers and technical communicators. First, a survey questionnaire was developed to gather data and analyze the effects and sources of communication among the involved stakeholders in software development projects. An experimental analysis was also performed to further test the supporting impact of client documents on requirements gathering. An experimental study was conducted to further test the supporting effect on requirement gathering of client documents. The results revealed that project managers are vital to software development progress, because they are the one that will provide the team with documents that support requirements gathering, thus improving team productivity and efficiency. Finally, software teams ensured that participants from all professional backgrounds were actively involved in the projects with a relatively centralized team structure.

© Springer Nature Switzerland AG 2020
O. Gervasi et al. (Eds.): ICCSA 2020, LNCS 12254, pp. 311–319, 2020.
https://doi.org/10.1007/978-3-030-58817-5_24

Keywords: Collaborative software development · Effective communication · Stakeholders · Empirical

1 Introduction

Software development is a discovery and communication driven approach [1]. There is nothing in promoting inspiration but people's ideas, contact colleagues and the machine about those concepts and ideas [1, 2]. In complex circumstances, where multiple teams and integrated stakeholders are involved, the key drivers to projecting success are communication efficiency and the skills of team members [1, 3]. A communication breakdown within software project development teams can affect the outcome of the project if not properly managed [3]. Communication is very paramount to see clearly what needs to be done, thus bringing more self-confidence about what need not be done [2, 3]. Communication, skills, and community attention enables the project to be active and more responsive than focusing on the software process [1, 7]. Effective communication and teamwork are essential to achieving success in software development projects, especially in a collaborative environment. Effective communication and coordination between people in a software development project are enormous as workplace and resources [1]. The introduction of distributed software development as a substitute for standalone software development has increased demands for quality software products and services [24–26, 30]. The location and time limitations in distributed software development should be well managed to ensure knowledge management [27–31].

Software development is a team-up process inspired by various stakeholders from different disciplines [4–6, 8]. Software product planning marks the beginning of technical work and continues from requirement gathering until the software is no more functional [9–12]. The gathering of requirements from project managers is done by development teams and is based on the specifications design of the interface and implementation the project [12]. The implemented product undergoes an iterative process of usability testing before the final deployment. The collaborating stakeholders working together are organizations or people that may be impacted or influenced by a project [12–15]. The performance of software application development is based on the cooperation of stakeholders from different disciplines. However, this has created difficulties in interdisciplinary collaboration. The barrier of communication across disciplines was identified as the cause of many of the challenges.

The creation of software includes various individuals and departments and their respective knowledge and expertise. It's a labor-intensive and complex process [16, 17, 23, 31]. Therefore, new knowledge gathered in software development projects is crucial to handle the software output effectively, and it should be agreed that knowledge (i.e. know-how) should be successfully managed through the reconfiguration and exploitation of existing knowledge and project-related risks [18, 19]. Several scholars have stated and emphasized that project performance relates not only to the information stock or existing knowledge assets that members of the software development project team have [20–22] but also to their collective ability to understand how to evaluate the various multiple realities of key project-related issues. Also, how to critically, honestly, essentially, and beautifully apply both their experience and knowledge [23]. It is therefore important to gather collective wisdom through a software development project team to summarize all the expertise and come out with a strong and critical decision, insight, and aesthetic skill, thus becoming fully successful during software development efforts [21, 23]. The rest of this paper is organized as follows: Sect. 2 discusses the methodology and research questions. Section 3 presents results and discussion. Section 4 concludes the paper and discusses future research directions for the realization of efficient Collaborative Software Development Projects.

2 Methodology

2.1 Study Background

Communication between software development teams and project managers were identified as an important factor for successful software development projects. This study supported literatures on more teams in a fully placed framework with focus on teamwork performance. The framework of this study was a computer science project supervised by a team of lecturers. The goal of the project was to develop an Android application and website for both students and lecturers in the virtual classroom, allowing anyone to use it to collect data and information for E-library and computer use. The final year students from the University of Ilorin worked as a team to develop the apps and websites for E-library and computer use. The study was based on supervising their 2019 development processes. This collaboration required students to have both skillful collaborative attitudes and task-relevant specialized skills by involving stakeholders with many disciplinary backgrounds and working with teammates from other departments. Questionnaire, semi-structured interviews, WhatsApp, and notes meeting were used for the analysis.

2.2 Research Questions

The study investigation focused on the effective communication and project manager participation of diverse development teams. The two research questions to be answered are:

Question 1: What are the main communication channels or methods that influence the software development process?
Question 2: How can we improve efficient communication in software development?
Hypothesis 1: The communication between software developers and project managers can predict the success of requirement gathering.
Hypothesis 2: The quantity and quality of communication between software developers and project managers can positively impact team performance during the development process.

2.3   General Methods

The study used a questionnaire approach to acquire the types and effects of communication and their importance during software development. Seventy-five copies of this questionnaire were distributed mainly to project students involved in the software development, one of the students served as the team leader and the lecturers as the project managers in the same university where the work was carried out. A total of the seventy-three questionnaire was completed and returned making a 97% response rate. The study focused on communication because it is a general belief that communication would be a key factor that would bring about improvements and efficiency.

3   Discussion and Results

The questionnaires were distributed to the team members during and after the project, to understand the communication within the team throughout the software development process. To better investigate the communication process, WhatsApp and meeting notes were used to collect information because the team members were spread out, and semi-structure interviews were also conducted with members of each team. The participants were to mention the communication process adopted by their team leaders and lecturers as well as answer questions such as how many meetings they had with the leaders and lecturers of their teams and what methods were adopted. To test the first hypothesis, the evaluation posed four different questions and assessed the amount of communication in all media. In the study, questions like "how many times do you meet with your lecturers within a month?" were asked and the response could range from" once a month"," twice a month"," thrice a month" and" four-time a month". The number of meetings held using the WhatsApp platform was calculated based on the discussions on the group and chatting. The documents the team received from lecturers and students assumed to be used for the application were also studied and their effectiveness and contribution to the design of the app were determined. Due to the number of meetings and communication with team leaders and lecturers, attention was focused on four groups, thus helping their software correctness and usability tests. To determine the records of the correspondence, the analysis of both content and pattern was exploited.

As shown in Table 1 and Fig. 1, a total of 23 (7.6%) of the respondents meet their lecturers once per month, 38 (12.7%) meet their lecturers twice per month, 73 (24.3%) meet their lecturers thrice per month and 166 (55.4%) meet their lecturers four times per month. This showed that 55.4% of the students meet their lecturers to discuss the progress of their projects and how to improve project development. The two projects were studies (App and website), the projects covered seven (7) months of the final year students and the projects were completed.

Table 2 and Fig. 2, showed that WhatsApp chatting is the most commonly used communication medium. The evidence showed that group 2 team had more communication, while group 1 and group 3 had the least. This was used to estimate the frequency of communication in the survey at the end of the project. Therefore, this allowed us to better understand the overall level of coordination within each team. To

Table 1. Distribution of respondents by meeting times per month

Chat type	Once a month	Twice a month	Thrice a month	Four-time a month
Group one	7	10	19	45
Group two	3	5	25	46
Group three	10	15	10	37
Group four	3	8	19	38
Total	**23**	**38**	**73**	**166**

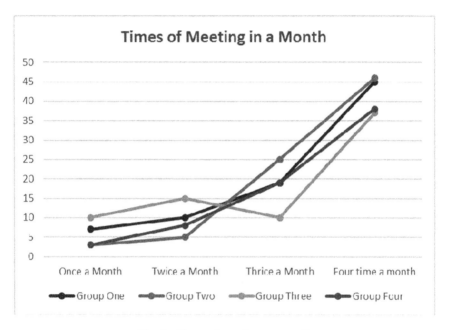

Fig. 1. Times of meeting per month

assess the frequencies of communication, the WhatsApp chat records were considered for the four teams between the students and lecturers during the four-month development of the app. It was found that the total number of WhatsApp group chat was 130. Table 2 summarizes the number of WhatsApp group chat, 130 agreeing to subject matter for each team. The group 2 team had 43 WhatsApp group chat in all, while no other team had less than 25 WhatsApp group chat. This number of WhatsApp group chat tested what students have appraised in the assessment, Table 2 and Fig. 2 showed that group 2 teams had more chats than other teams. In general, most of the chat wer about requirement gathering (39.5%) and project evaluations (34.8%).

Table 3 and Fig. 3, shows the WhatsApp group chat by quantities categories. From the table and figure, group 2 had 39.5% which was the highest in requirement gathering, group 1 had the highest percent of 17.3% for system design and coding, group 4 had 48.1% thereby making it the highest in project evaluations category and group 3

Table 2. Distribution of respondents by communication methods

Communication method	Group 1	Group 2	Group 3	Group 4
In-person	17	10	9	25
Phone	25	18	22	15
WhatsApp group	25	25	25	25
Texting	25	25	25	25
Skype	10	21	7	5

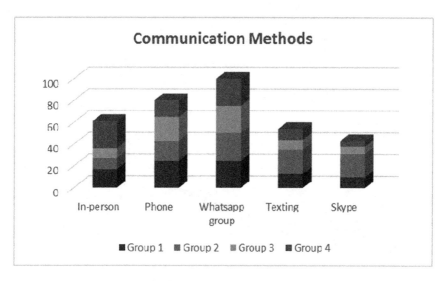

Fig. 2. Communication methods

had 12.9% making it the highest in task negotiation category. But in all, group 2 had the highest chat with 33.1%. The results showed that communication among the teams helped in requirement gathering and project evaluation processes.

Table 3. Distribution of respondents by summary of chat by quantities type

Chat type	Group 1	Group 2	Group 3	Group 4
Requirement gathering	6 (20.7%)	17 (39.5%)	12 (38.7%)	9 (33.3%)
System design and coding	5 (17.3%)	7 (16.3%)	5 (16.1%)	4 (14.9%)
Project evaluations	15 (51.7%)	15 (34.8%)	10 (32.3%)	13 (48.1%)
Task negotiation	3 (10.3%)	4 (9.4%)	4 (12.9%)	1 (3.7%)
Total	**29 (100%)**	**43 (100%)**	**31 (100%)**	**27 (100%)**

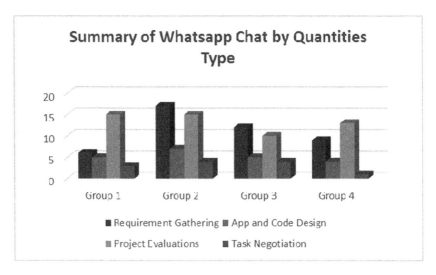

Fig. 3. Summary of chat by quantities type

The result of the questionnaire showed that group 2 chats more than the three other groups and their lecturers always responded by joining the group chat, responding during chats, scheduling meetings within the appointed time, and responding to chats on request within a short time. The responses of the other teams were slow, especially on requirement gathering and coding. Considering the number of meetings between lecturers and students, group 2 team had more group chat than other teams, therefore it suggested that the WhatsApp group chats were effective in arranging meetings for the group 2 team and that the group 2 scientists were available. The slip in requirement gathering from group 2 team indicates that group chat was a successful tool for collecting requirements, but not for project evaluations.

It was hypothesized that the communication between software teams and lecturers can forecast better requirement gathering. From the study, group 2 team showed that communication is critical to the requirement gathering phase. The delay in gathering requirements may be due to ineffective communication between software developers and clients. We also hypothesized that the quantity and quality of communication can impact team outcomes. The results showed that team performance did not depend on more communication among other team members and doesn't necessarily bring better team performance, thus it is quality, not the quantity of communication that positively influences team outcomes.

4 Conclusion

In software development, communication is a major factor that accelerates the developers' work. Communication has been proven to ensure quality, productivity, and facilitate the software development process. Communication is a vital process in sharing knowledge between the team members and coordinating a software development project. The study examined the importance of communication in software development projects by describing factors that help good communication between developers and clients especially during requirement gathering and project developments. The result showed that communication between software teams and project managers can lead to improved requirement gathering. Also, team performance is not always necessarily dependent on more communication but the quality of communication positively influences team results. The general belief is that more communication might lead to better team performance. However, this is not always true as in the case of these teams, group 2 team communicated with their lecturers much more than the other three groups, but this doesn't produce a better team performance as expected compared to group 3. Also, the communication methods used were WhatsApp chat, e-mail, and group discussion, but WhatsApp chat was discovered to be more effective and suited for better software performance.

References

1. Mishra, D., Mishra, A.: Effective communication, collaboration, and coordination in eXtreme programming: human-centric perspective in a small organization. Hum. Factors Ergon. Manufact. Serv. Ind. **19**(5), 438–456 (2009)
2. Ruano-Mayoral, M., Casado-Lumbreras, C., Garbarino-Alberti, H., Misra, S.: Methodological framework for the allocation of work packages in global software development. J. Soft. Evol. Process **26**(5), 476–487 (2014)
3. Misra, S., Fernandez-Sanz, L.: Quality issues in global software development. In: ICSEA 2011: The Sixth International Conference on Software Engineering Advances, pp. 325–330, October 2011
4. Brhel, M., Meth, H., Maedche, A., Werder, K.: Exploring principles of user-centered agile software development: a literature review. Inf. Softw. Technol. **61**, 163–181 (2015)
5. Bogers, M., Horst, W.: Collaborative prototyping: cross-fertilization of knowledge in prototype-driven problem-solving. J. Prod. Innov. Manag. **31**(4), 744–764 (2014)
6. Misra, S., Colomo-Palacios, R., Pusatlı, T., Soto-Acosta, P.: A discussion on the role of people in global software development. Tech. Gaz. **20**(3), 525–531 (2013). hrcak.srce. hr/file/153032
7. Colomo-Palacios, R., Casado-Lumbreras, C., Soto-Acosta, P., Misra, S., García-Peñalvo, F. J.: Analyzing human resource management practices within the GSD context. J. Glob. Inf. Technol. Manag. **15**(3), 30–54 (2012)
8. Borsato, M., Peruzzini, M.: Collaborative engineering. In Concurrent Engineering in the 21st Century, pp. 165–196. Springer, Cham (2015). https://doi.org/10.1007/978-3-319-13776-6_7
9. Bass, J.M.: How product owner teams scale agile methods to large distributed enterprises. Empirical Softw. Eng. **20**(6), 1525–1557 (2014). https://doi.org/10.1007/s10664-014-9322-z
10. Wiegers, K., Beatty, J.: Software Requirements. Pearson Education, London (2013)
11. Leffingwell, D.: Agile Software Requirements: Lean Requirements Practices for Teams, Programs, and the Enterprise. Addison-Wesley Professional, Boston (2010)
12. Zhang, W.: An analysis of stakeholders' communication in collaborative software development projects (2016)
13. Eskerod, P., Huemann, M., Savage, G.: Project stakeholder management—past and present. Proj. Manage. J. **46**(6), 6–14 (2015)

14. Majava, J., Haapasalo, H.: The roles of stakeholders in an NPD project: a case study. In: Proceedings MakeLearn TIIM Joint International Conference, pp. 199–205 (2015)
15. Davis, K.: An empirical investigation into different stakeholder groups' perception of project success. Int. J. Project Manage. **35**(4), 604–617 (2017)
16. Ghobadi, S.: What drives knowledge sharing in software development teams: a literature review and classification framework. Inf. Manag. **52**(1), 82–97 (2015)
17. Vasconcelos, J.B., Kimble, C., Carreteiro, P., Rocha, A.: The application of knowledge management to software evolution. Int. J. Inf. Manage. **37**(1), 1499–1506 (2017)
18. Akgun, A.E., Keskin, H., Cebecioglu, A.Y., Dogan, D.: Antecedents and consequences of collective empathy in software development project teams. Inf. Manage. **52**(2), 247–259 (2015)
19. Aurum, A., Daneshgar, F., Ward, J.: Investigating knowledge management practices in software development organizations – an Australian experience. Inf. Softw. Technol. **50**(6), 511–533 (2008)
20. Coakes, E.W., Coakes, J.M., Rosenberg, D.: Co-operative work practices and knowledge sharing issues: a comparison of viewpoints. Int. J. Inf. Manage. **28**(1), 12–25 (2008)
21. Dalal, N., Pauleen, D.J.: The wisdom nexus: guiding information systems research, practice, and education. Inf. Syst. J. **29**(1), 224–244 (2019)
22. Akgun, A.E., Keskin, H., Kircovali, S.Y.: Organizational wisdom practices and firm product innovativeness. RMS **13**(1), 57–91 (2019)
23. Akgün, A.E.: Team wisdom in software development projects and their impact on project performance. Int. J. Inf. Manage. **50**, 228–243 (2020)
24. Ayo, F.E., Awotunde, J.B., Taofeek-IBRAHIM, F.A., Fatokun, O.M.: A location-based expert system for software collaboration network using extended kruskal algorithm. Int. J. Inf. Process. Commun. (IJIPC) **6**(1), 87–100 (2018)
25. Abrahamsson, P., Salo, O., Ronkainen, J., Warsta, J.: Agile software development methods: review and analysis. arXiv preprint arXiv:1709.08439 (2017)
26. Šmite, D., Moe, N.B., Šāblis, A., Wohlin, C.: Software teams and their knowledge networks in large-scale software development. Inf. Softw. Technol. **86**, 71–86 (2017)
27. Kwahk, K.Y., Park, D.H.: The effects of network sharing on knowledge-sharing activities and job performance in enterprise social media environments. Comput. Hum. Behav. **55**, 826–839 (2016)
28. Marchewka, J.T.: Information Technology Project Management: Providing Measurable Organizational Value. John Wiley & Sons, Hoboken (2016)
29. Adewumi, A.O., Misra, S., Omoregbe, N.A.: A review of models for evaluating quality in open-source software. IERI Procedia **4**, 88–92 (2013)
30. Fernández-Sanz, L., Misra, S.: Influence of human factors in software quality and productivity. In: Murgante, B., Gervasi, O., Iglesias, A., Taniar, D., Apduhan, B.O. (eds.) ICCSA 2011. LNCS, vol. 6786, pp. 257–269. Springer, Heidelberg (2011). https://doi.org/10.1007/978-3-642-21934-4_22
31. Misra, S., Akman, I.: A model for measuring cognitive complexity of software. In: Lovrek, I., Howlett, R.J., Jain, L.C. (eds.) KES 2008. LNCS (LNAI), vol. 5178, pp. 879–886. Springer, Heidelberg (2008). https://doi.org/10.1007/978-3-540-85565-1_109

Severe Acne Skin Disease: A Fuzzy-Based Method for Diagnosis

Femi Emmanuel Ayo[1] 📵, Roseline Oluwaseun Ogundokun[2](✉) 📵,
Joseph Bamidele Awotunde[3] 📵, Marion Olubunmi Adebiyi[2],
and Abidemi Emmanuel Adeniyi[2] 📵

[1] Department of Physical and Computer Sciences, Mcpherson University,
Seriki-Sotayo, Abeokuta, Nigeria
[2] Department of Computer Science, Landmark University, Omu-Aran, Nigeria
ogundokun.roseline@lmu.edu.ng
[3] Department of Computer Science, University of Ilorin, Ilorin, Nigeria

Abstract. Dermis ailments are disorders that hurt or damage the dermis that has an enormous impact on the everyday life of a person. People's tight schedule has significantly impacted their accessibility for repetitive examinations, thereby preventing individuals from consulting a medical practitioner. Network-centered medicinal schemes' popularity is increasingly becoming a model for helping individuals recognize how crucial the level of an ailment is. Acne dermis ailment is one of the extremely well-known dermis sicknesses that troubles the sebaceous glands, thus repetitive diagnosis could assist to avoid blisters. Fuzzy based approach for diagnosing acne skin disease was proposed in this paper. It was suggested that the approach assisted solving the shortcomings of previous expert system methods. Expert machine reasoning is related to literary ambiguity. The proposed system of used fuzzy rules to address inaccuracy in the expert system's analysis. It was proven that the scheme was 82% accurate, indicating good performance. The Fuzzy expert system built had shown an extreme level of guidance, medical care recommendations and demonstrated the degree of seriousness of acne dermis state in patients.

Keywords: Expert system · Diagnosis · Skin disease · Fuzzy logic · Medical system

1 Introduction

Skin disease is a skin-exasperating condition which causes signs such as pain, bumping, sweltering and inflammation [1–3]. This can result in complex inferiority and dejection, besides the side effects caused by skin disease. People's schedule has been extremely tight that it affects their ability to perform regular routine check-up with their medical practitioners. An expert system is defined as an artificial intelligence competency that imitates human expert's reasoning ability [4] and has become an alternative to identifying different diseases on the basis of its credibility [5]. Combined with the inability to reveal their health status, the busy schedule for most people has prompted the implementation of a web-based medical system to replace 343 human specialists.

© Springer Nature Switzerland AG 2020
O. Gervasi et al. (Eds.): ICCSA 2020, LNCS 12254, pp. 320–334, 2020.
https://doi.org/10.1007/978-3-030-58817-5_25

The widespread adoption of this web-based diagnostic program has required a change from anthropoid meeting to computer meeting. The diagnostic scheme is a device which could classify infections on the basis of the symptoms and their severity [6]. A network-centered diagnostic system is a smart device in rule form [7, 8], with the expertise of some specialist. The software applies these rules to make wise and expert decisions based on some methods for inference [9, 10].

More so, using computer-based devices can go a long way to helping human experts discharge quality healthcare services. Artificial Intelligence (AI) also refers to an intelligent computing, it also refers to designing and implementing machines that act at a human expert level [5]. Compared with other machine learning methods, expert systems have established themselves a niche in AI. In the field of health care [11, 12] is intrinsic the most accepted area of application of expert systems for disease detection and control. As the most commonly used tool, they've been given the benefit of problem solving by the pleasant customer interface and description services provided by expert schemes. The system of experts is known for providing explanations, concluding derivatives and emerging from the fire of composite rules [13].

Acne is an illness which irritates the sebaceous glands. Acne happened to be reported as one of the utmost common dermis diseases; at one point or the other, an estimated 80 out of a hundred people have acne. Therefore, the safest way to avoid burns is believed to take early preventive measures [14, 15]. Several approaches have been used to assess the harshness of acne dermis sickness but most of these methods still lack the ability to accurately categorize the acne frequency [16].

This paper proposed a fuzzy based approach to diagnose acne dermis infection. A fuzzy scheme is an assembly of fuzzy set [16, 17] and linguistic variables established on some association purpose described on a certain fluctuating value range. The postulated structure incorporates fuzzy rules, as the administration of improbability in an intrinsically authoritative interest in designing and implementing expert scheme since considerable amount of the datasets available in the comprehension-centered expert scheme is inaccurate, and not entirely reliable [18]. Fuzzy logic is a group of analytical policies for apprehending the interim rates amid the Boolean drastic rates [19, 20]. Fuzzy logic is prepared with regards to accuracy in the representation of reasonable condition, improbability and unsteady structure, ensuing planning and execution of smart schemes [21, 22]. Consequently, the projected scheme of experts entrenched in fuzzy logic would contribute to accuracy, comprehensiveness and accurate endorsements.

The remainder of this manuscript is structured as thus: Sect. 2 describes the related works. Methodology is outlined in Sect. 3 and Sect. 4 outlines the process for implementing and reviewing the proposed method. Section 5 details the conclusion and the future work.

2   Literature Review

2.1   Acne Skin Disease

Acne Dermis infection is a long-term dermis condition that happens when hair follicles are obstructed by insensitive dermis cells and dermis oil [23]. It has spots or pustules, oily dermis and likely scratching. Known factors affecting sebum production are a number of Propionibacterium acnes, under the influence of natural circulating Dehydro-Epiandrosterone (DHEA), often activates AV during puberty. Patients seldom, if continuously, grumble concerning decreased sebum creation. However, increased sebum creation, instigating oily dermis which may be an antecedent to acne, is a usual criticism [1]. It is a very popular dermis syndrome that can occur mainly with provocative and non-inflammatory lacerations on the look as well as on the upper arms, the trunk and back. Gender, in particular, has a major and well-known impact, as sebum levels are usually low in infancy, rise in mid-to-late teen years, and remain stable in the seventh and eighth decades before endogenous androgen synthesis fades [1].

Acne can cause emotional distress, and depending on its severity, stain the skin. Acne can cause scarring to the skin but usually does not cause long-term health problems. In the self-corporate image other parts of the body like face play an important role. Even a minor lesion in this portion can be painful to the patient and appear large. This picture can cause mental disorders such as depression and anxiety, low self-esteem and reduced social relationships [1].

Acne mostly appears on the look but is also common on the knees, back and upper arms. Normally, the use of anabolic steroid leads to acne on the shoulders and upper back. The levels of acne severity are four [16]: mild, moderate, moderately extreme and severe (Figs. 1, 2, 3 and 4). Yet even mild acne can be distressing, especially for teenagers who see every pimple as a big cosmetic challenge.

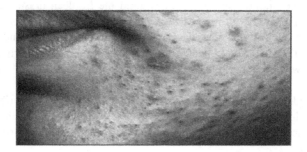

Fig. 1. Minor acne

Fig. 2. Average acne

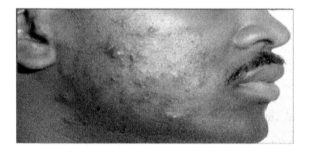

Fig. 3. Averagely harsh acne

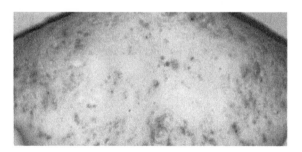

Fig. 4. Harsh acne

Acne severity (Table 1) is mostly considered by the number, size, and dissemination of lacerations (regions with A = {blackhead, pimples, pustules, comedones} (1) wound) [16].

Table 1. Severity of acne evaluation

Severity	Lesions distribution
Mild	0–10
Moderate	10–40
Moderately severe	40–100
Severe	100-above

2.2 Fuzzy Logic

Fuzzy reasoning has proven to be common in control systems. Fuzzy reasoning is designed to apprehend the interim standards amid in the intense Boolean standards [0 or 1]. Fuzzy logic is therefore best suited to regulate instability in an unstable system [16, 19, 24]. The University of California at Berkeley first proposed Fuzzy logic [25, 26], also called fuzzy sets, illustrated on his personal beliefs of semantic variables. Fuzzy logic comprises of constituents that includes fuzzy sets, association function, fuzzification, range uncertainty, engine deduction and defuzzification [19, 24].

2.3 Rule Based Device

The rule-based systems are employed as an information handling device in computer science [27]. Intellectuals often deploy them in the domain of machine-learning. A perfect instance of a rule-based structure is the knowledge-narrowed, knowledgeable decision-making method. For example, an expert system could improve a human doctor's ability to recommend. Rule-based methods may likewise be intended to run scanners for compiling PC programs, or in natural linguistic procedure [27]. Rule-based programming aims to extract instructions for execution from starting data and rules.

2.4 Related Works

[28] developed a system for diagnosing and classifying Acne Lesions in acne patients. The authors introduced numerous image separation techniques for detecting acne lacerations and machine-learning procedures for classifying acne lesions. With good performance accuracy, the designed system had proven to be a good method of detection and classification.

[29] suggested an expert system based on scientific criteria, severity assessment, diagnosis and chronic acne skin disease assessment. The results indicated the capacity of the developed method to diagnose, assess the extent of acne skin disease, and make a distinction between types of acne skin disease.

[30] developed an online expert rule-based structure for the detection and management of skin syndromes. The expert rules were embedded in the warning sign of every kind of dermis syndrome, and introduced employing tree diagram together with deduction exploiting depth-first search approach for forward chaining. The rule-based online expert program showed good results in identification and proved timely for diagnosing thirteen plus skin diseases.

[31] Fuzzy inferencing system designed and implemented to diagnose skin disease in infants. The writers dealt with selected infectious disorders, such as measles, German measles and chicken pox. The reason selected diseases were chosen was due to their infection resemblances and symptoms such as rash and fever. The authors based their Fuzzy inference system design on rules developed from the knowledge and literature of experts. The system's implementation had shown the ability to diagnose skin diseases correctly in infants.

[32] presented a mobile medical aid system to diagnose skin diseases by using case-based reasoning to deduce a new rule in the database and image processing technique to determine symptoms based on a newly captured picture of an infected skin. The work was designed to provide patients with infected skin with pre-examination assistance and increase awareness of skin diseases and their effects. This method was found to be effective in the early detection and treatment of problems with skin diseases.

[33] developed a novel spontaneous diagnostic approach for facial acne vulgaris, rooted in convolutionary neural networks for extraction and classification of features. The aim was to resolve the shortcomings of previous approaches of mostly expert systems which lack the ability to distinguish enough types of acne vulgaris due to the inaccuracy nature of the design of the expert system. The results showed that the neural network is operational to eliminate features from the images of facial acne vulgaris and to strengthen classifiers for proper classification.

3   Materials and Method

3.1   Datasets

For this work, the data set used was originally generated in accordance with expert guidelines and literature regulations.

3.2   Methodology

The Fuzzy logic was used in this study to develop a specialist scheme based on some identified symptoms to diagnose the gravity of acne dermis infection. Expert methodological detections and thoughts were filled with improbability from the literature, which is why the authors used fuzzy logic to propose solutions to these uncertainties.

3.3   Proposed Architecture Model

Figure 5 illustrates the projected system architecture for the detection of severity of acne dermis infection. The architectural model generates acne-related symptoms from the sufferer by means of the user interface and established on the sufferer feedbacks, the system converts the feedbacks to fuzzy valves and then employs its inference device established on the rules within the expert system to decide on the gravity of the acne dermis infection.

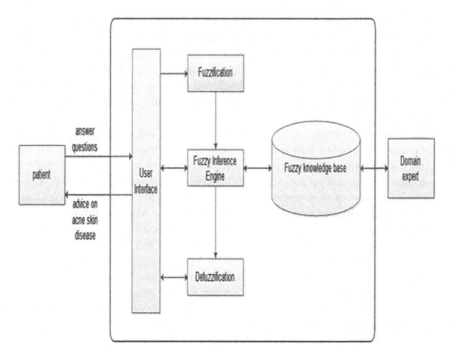

Fig. 5. System architecture

Table 2 reflects the procedures in the postulated fuzzy knowledge centred scheme, utilizing their corresponding etymological variables (small, medium, big, and very large). Within the knowledge base of the program, expert expertise in the area were used to shape the rules.

Table 2. Sample rule based

#no	Blackhead	Pimples	Pustules	Comedones	Conclude
1	Very large	Very large	Very large	Very large	Severe
2	Medium	Large	Large	Large	Moderately severe
3	Medium	Medium	Medium	Medium	Moderate
4	Small	Small	Small	Small	Mild

As shown in Fig. 6, the knowledge centred for the projected fuzzy network of experts (Table stores the details, laws and guidelines on the symptoms).

Blackhead/whiteheads
Pimples
Pustules
Comedones

Fig. 6. Acne symptoms

Accordingly, a modest clarification for rule 2 of Table 2 was: IF blackhead is medium together with pimples being large as well as pustules being large, THEN acne is moderate (comedones therefore are large). For the detection of intensity of the acne dermis infection, the illustrative rule in Table 2 above were a depiction of the knowledge centred system which comprises of rules in the projected fuzzy specialist scheme. The fuzzy varying rate amid the interval [0, 1] for the language variables of the postulated fuzzy sets is shown in Table 3. Likewise, Table 3 also indicates the severity spectrum of the lesions being distributed.

Table 3. Fuzzy range value

Linguistic variables	Linguistic range	Lesions	Lesions range
Small	$0.1 \leq x < 0.3$	Mild	0–10
Medium	$0.3 \leq x < 0.6$	Moderate	10–40
Large	$0.6 \leq x < 0.8$	Moderately severe	40–100
Very large	$0.8 \leq x < 0.1$	Severe	100-above

4   Result and Discussion

This study employed java programming language for the implementation of the proposed system. and Mysql database for storage. A login feature was introduced to the fuzzy expert structure developed for detecting acne dermis infection and this was illustrated in the Fig. 7. Java programming language was employed for the front end of the proposed scheme whereas Mysql was employed for the back end and this involves the user login feature introduced.

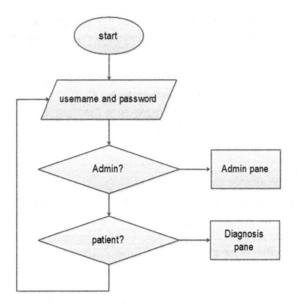

Fig. 7. Login flowchart

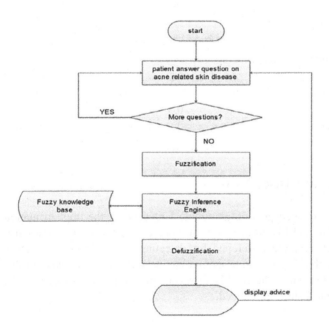

Fig. 8. System flowchart

Figure 8 shows the flowchart of the proposed system.

The Fuzzy expert program introduced assisted in establishing if an individual has acne dermis infection and categorize the acne intensity as mild, moderate or extreme and this was established on the amount and nature of the indications. The system was implemented with Intel Dual core 2.20 GHz processor on a PC workstation. An interface for the machine login pane is shown in Fig. 9. The device users (sufferers) were necessitated to validate their authorization into the system with their username and password information via the LOGIN button. A first timer can as well sign-up for future authentication in the system via the REGISTER button.

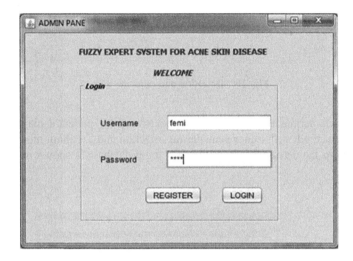

Fig. 9. Login interface

Figure 10 shows the Fuzzy Expert System detection and outcome pane. After a successful login the user was taken to this pane. The program elicits user-related acne-associated sickness problems. An individual is required to select answers and a variety of ambiguous linguistic alternatives that the program can employ to interpret, and to make suggestion in form of management. The outcome was revealed in the system's RESULT section, once a DIAGNOSE button was clicked.

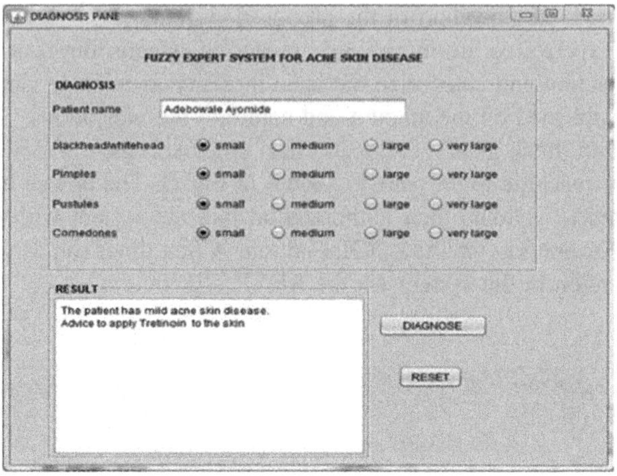

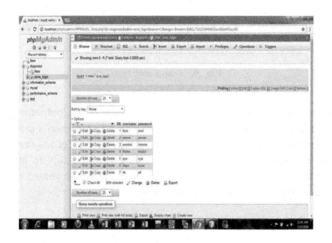

Fig. 10. Detection and outcome pane

The chosen permutation in Fig. 10 demonstrated the patient's diagnosis of the fuzzy expert method, with minor acne dermis infection and Tretinoin medication to be administered to the dermis infected. The user login database is shown in Fig. 11.

Fig. 11. Login database

5 Performance Evaluation

For the severity of the acne dermis syndrome, this paper adopted the following modelling process to validate the analysis precision of the projected fuzzy expert scheme. A confusion matrix which contained information that is needed for a classification system assessment. Table 4 presents a typical confusion matrix metrics. The system's prediction of acne severity was evaluated using those metrics. Therefore, severity had to be classified by lesion distribution. The information in Table 5 indicated the classification results, as the program predicted. For machine results, the uncertainty matrix is as shown in Table 6.

Table 4. Confusion matrix metrics

True class			
	Positive	Negative	Total
Predictive class	True Positive Count (TP) or Severe	False Positive Count (FP) or Moderately Severe	TP + FP
	False Negative Count (FN) or Moderate	True Negative Count (TN) or Mild	FN + TN
Total	TP + FN	FP + TN	TP + FN + FP + FN

Table 5. The results of system grading for 100 Cases

Lesions	Classification	Count
0–10	True negative or mild	36
10–40	False negative or moderate	16
40–100	False positive or moderately severe	2
100-above	True positive or severe	46

Table 6. Confusion matrix for 100 cases

	Observation class		Total
Positive	TP 46	FP 2	48
Negative	FN 16	TN 36	52
Total	62	38	100

With the confusion matrix in Table 6, the probability of true positive rate, true negative rate and accuracy rate were computed as follows:
Probability of true positive rate

$$TP/(TP + FN) = 46/(46 + 16) = 0.7419$$

Probability of true negative rate

$$TN/(TN + FP) = 36/(36 + 2) = 0.9474$$

Probability of Accuracy rate

$$(TP + TN)/(TP + TN + FP + FN) = 46 + 36/(46 + 36 + 2 + 16) = 0.82$$

6 Conclusion

The purpose of this paper was to improve people's check-up habits by designing a friendly and interactive fuzzy skin disease diagnostic expert system. Users can use the service provided by the designed fuzzy expert system to diagnose and get an idea of the severity of the disease that affects them. Using the evaluation results of Table 6, which includes the confusion matrix for 100 system classification cases, we can then deduce that the designed system showed a true positive rate, true negative rate, and accuracy rate of 0.7419, 0.9474, and 0.82 respectively. The conclusion taken from this result is that the device obtained an accuracy rate of 82% after the confusion matrix assessment process. This indicated a substantial good rating for the fuzzy expert method, and an indicator of its usefulness to help the mission of predicting the extent of acne skin disease, as well as providing advice on care.

7 Future Work

In the future, the authors will implement the use of adaptive neuro-fuzzy inference method for the same mission and then will compare the results.

References

1. Ak, M.: A comprehensive review of acne vulgaris. J. Clin. Pharm. **1**(1), 17–45 (2019)
2. Pereira, M.P., Kremer, A.E., Mettang, T., Ständer, S.: Chronic pruritus in the absence of skin disease: pathophysiology, diagnosis and treatment. Am. J. Clin. Dermatol. 1–12. Clerk Maxwell, J.: A Treatise on Electricity and Magnetism, 3rd edn., vol. 2. Oxford: Clarendon, 1892, 2016, pp. 68–73
3. Adeyinka, A.A., Adebiyi, M.O., Akande, N.O., Ogundokun, R.O., Kayode, A.A., Oladele, T.O.: A deep convolutional encoder-decoder architecture for retinal blood vessels segmentation. In: Misra, S., et al. (eds.) ICCSA 2019. LNCS, vol. 11623, pp. 180–189. Springer, Cham (2019). https://doi.org/10.1007/978-3-030-24308-1_15

4. Habif, T.P., Chapman, M.S., Campbell Jr., J.L., Dinulos, J.G., Zug, K.A.: Skin disease: diagnosis and treatment. Elsevier Health Sciences, pp. 201–214 (2011)
5. Yadav, G., Pandey, G.N.: Development of intelligent decision and prediction system using cyber-enabled. NESS Technology for oil availability and yield prediction. RIET-IJSET: Int. J. Sci. Eng. Technol. 2(1), 41–52 (2015)
6. Amarathunga, A.A.L.C., Ellawala, E.P.W.C., Abeysekara, G.N., Amalraj, C.R.J.: Expert system for diagnosis of skin diseases. Int. J. Sci. Technol. Res. 4(1), 456–472 (2015)
7. Lingiardi, V., McWilliams, N., Bornstein, R.F., Gazzillo, F., Gordon, R.M.: The psychodynamic diagnostic manual version 2 (PDM-2): assessing patients for improved clinical practice and research. Psychoanalytic Psychol. 32(1), 94 (2015)
8. Moses, D.: A survey of data mining algorithms used in cardiovascular disease diagnosis from multi-lead ECG data. Kuwait J. Sci. 42(2) (2015)
9. Adegun, A.A., Akande, N.O., Ogundokun, R.O., Asani, E.O.: Image segmentation and classification of large scale satellite imagery for land use: a review of the state of the arts. Int. J. Civil Eng.Technol. 9(11) (2018)
10. Ajala, F.A., Akande, N.O., Adeyemo, I.A., Ogundokun, R.O.: Smallest univalue segment assimilating nucleus approach to brain MRI image segmentation using fuzzy C-means and fuzzy K-means algorithms. Int. J. Comput. Technol. 16(7), 7065–7076 (2017)
11. Ayo, F.E., Awotunde, J.B., Ogundokun, R.O., Folorunso, S.O., Adekunle, A.O.: A decision support system for multi-target disease diagnosis: a bioinformatics approach. Heliyon 6(3), e03657 (2020)
12. McPherson, R.A., Pincus, M.R.: Henry's clinical diagnosis and management by laboratory methods. Elsevier Health Sciences (2016)
13. Jimoh, R.G., Awotunde, J.B., Babatunde, A.O., Ameen, A.O, James, T.R., Fatai, O.W.: Simulation of medical diagnosis system for malaria using fuzzy logic. Int. J. Inf. Process. Commun. (IJIPC) 2(1) (2014). Published by Faculty of Communication and Information Sciences, University of Ilorin, Ilorin
14. Horvitz, E.J., Breese, J.S., Henrion, M.: Decision theory in expert systems and artificial intelligence. Int. J. Approximate Reasoning 2(3), 247–302 (1988)
15. Constantinou, A.C., Fenton, N., Marsh, W., Radlinski, L.: From complex questionnaire and interviewing data to intelligent Bayesian network models for medical decision support. Artif. Intell. Med. 67, 75–93 (2016)
16. Ayo, F.E., et al.: A fuzzy based method for diagnosis of acne skin disease severity. i-manager's. J. Pattern Recogn. 5(2), 10 (2018)
17. Adebayo, O., Asani, E.O., Ogundokun, R.O., Ananti, E.C., Adegun, A.: A neuro-fuzzy based system for the classification of cells as cancerous of non-cancerous. Int. J. Med. Res. Health Sci. 7(5), 155–166 (2018)
18. Thompson, T., Sowunmi, O., Misra, S., Fernandez-Sanz, L., Crawford, B., Soto, R.: An expert system for the diagnosis of sexually transmitted diseases–ESSTD. J. Intell. Fuzzy Syst. 33(4), 2007–2017 (2017)
19. Jimoh, R.G., Afolayan, A.A., Awotunde, J.B., Matiluko, E.O.: Fuzzy logic based expert system in the diagnosis of ebola virus. Ilorin J. Comput. Sci. Inf. Technol. 2(1), 73–94 (2017). Published by Computer Science Department, University of Ilorin, Ilorin, Nigeria
20. Azeez, N.A., Towolawi, T., Van der Vyver, C., Misra, S., Adewumi, A., Damaševičius, R., Ahuja, R.: A fuzzy expert system for diagnosing and analyzing human diseases. In: Abraham, A., Gandhi, N., Pant, M. (eds.) IBICA 2018. AISC, vol. 939, pp. 474–484. Springer, Cham (2019). https://doi.org/10.1007/978-3-030-16681-6_47

21. Lawanya Shri, M., Ganga Devi, E., Balusamy, B., Kadry, S., Misra, S., Odusami, M.: A fuzzy based hybrid firefly optimization technique for load balancing in cloud datacenters. In: Abraham, A., Gandhi, N., Pant, M. (eds.) IBICA 2018. AISC, vol. 939, pp. 463–473. Springer, Cham (2019). https://doi.org/10.1007/978-3-030-16681-6_46

22. Alhassan, J.K., Misra, S., Umar, A., Maskeliūnas, R., Damaševičius, R., Adewumi, A.: A fuzzy classifier-based penetration testing for web applications. In: Rocha, Á., Guarda, T. (eds.) ICITS 2018. AISC, vol. 721, pp. 95–104. Springer, Cham (2018). https://doi.org/10. 1007/978-3-319-73450-7_10

23. Adegun, A.A., Ogundokun, R.O., Adebiyi, M.O., Asani, E.O.: CAD-based machine learning project for reducing human-factor-related errors in medical image analysis. In: Misra, S., Adewumi, A. (eds.) Handbook of Research on the Role of Human Factors in IT Project Management, pp. 164–172. IGI Global, Hershey (2020). https://doi.org/10.4018/978-1-7998-1279-1.ch011

24. Awotunde, J.B., Matiluko, O.E., Fatai, O.W.: Medical diagnosis system using fuzzy logic. Afr. J. Comput. ICT 7(2), 99–106 (2014). Published by IEEE Computer Society, Nigeria Section

25. Jang, J.S.: Neuro-Fuzzy Modeling: Architectures, Analyses, and Applications. University of California, Berkeley (1992)

26. Bo, Y. (ed.): Fuzzy Sets, Fuzzy Logic, and Fuzzy Systems: Selected Papers by Lotfi A Zadeh, vol. 6. World Scientific (1996)

27. Hachaj, T., Ogiela, M.R.: Rule-based approach to recognizing human body poses and gestures in real time. Multimedia Syst. 20(1), 81–99 (2013). https://doi.org/10.1007/s00530-013-0332-2

28. Alamdari, N., Tavakolian, K., Alhashim, M., Fazel-Rezai, R.: Detection and classification of acne lesions in acne patients: a mobile application. In: 2016 IEEE International Conference on Electro Information Technology (EIT), pp. 0739–0743. IEEE, May 2016

29. Zouboulis, C.C., Del Marmol, V., Mrowietz, U., Prens, E.P., Tzellos, T., Jemec, G.B.: Hidradenitis suppurativa/acne inversa: criteria for diagnosis, severity assessment, classification and disease evaluation. Dermatology 231(2), 184–190 (2015)

30. Asghar, M.Z., Asghar, M.J., Saqib, S.M., Ahmad, B., Ahmad, S., Ahmad, H.: Diagnosis of skin diseases using online expert system. Int. J. Comput. Sci. Inf. Secur. 9(6), 323 (2011)

31. Putra, A.A., Munir, R.: Implementation of fuzzy inference system in children skin disease diagnosis application. In: 2015 International Conference on Electrical Engineering and Informatics (ICEEI), pp. 365–370. IEEE, August 2015

32. Aruta, C.L., Calaguas, C.R., Gameng, J.K., Prudentino, M.V., Anthony, A., Lubaton, C.J.: Mobile-based medical assistance for diagnosing different types of skin diseases using case-based reasoning with image processing. IJ CI 3(3), 115–118 (2015)

33. Shen, X., Zhang, J., Yan, C., Zhou, H.: An automatic diagnosis method of facial acne vulgaris based on convolutional neural network. Sci. Rep. 8(1), 1–10 (2018)

Software Visualization Tool for Evaluating API Usage in the Context of Software Ecosystems: A Proof of Concept

Rodrigo Avancini[1,2]([✉]) (iD), Fábio Fagundes Silveira[1] (iD), Eduardo Martins Guerra[3] (iD), and Pedro R. Andrade[2] (iD)

[1] Federal University of São Paulo – UNIFESP, São José dos Campos, Brazil
avancinirodrigo@gmail.com, fsilveira@unifesp.br
[2] National Institute for Space Research – INPE, São José dos Campos, Brazil
pedro.andrade@inpe.br
[3] Free University of Bolzen-Bolzano – UNIBZ, Bozen-Bolzano, Italy
guerraem@gmail.com

Abstract. Software Ecosystem (SECO) is a consolidated research area in software engineering, emerging as a paradigm for understanding dynamics and relationships among software systems that collaborate with each other to achieve their goals. Understanding the ecosystem and how its elements interact is essential for software evolution, especially for those that provide functions and services for other systems, such as software APIs. Once an API is being used by different software, future changes need to be made in a systematic and appropriate manner, considering the whole ecosystem. However, there is a lack of formal and effective ways for APIs evaluation in the context of SECO. Thus, in this paper, we present Ecolyzer, a prototype tool that aims to support the analysis of API usage considering its ecosystem through interactive visualization. To demonstrate the feasibility of our tool, we conducted a proof of concept (PoC) using an open-source platform API. The results obtained with Ecolyzer are useful and show that the prototype meets the goals described for the accomplishment of this work.

Keywords: Software ecosystems · Software visualization · API usage

1 Introduction

Increasingly, software systems depend on other software to leverage their business. This fact occurs due to the vast availability of specialized software and components that have already established themselves in their respective domains. There are rare cases in which software is developed from scratch without reuse [25]. Nevertheless, the vast majority of analysis and development support tools do not consider the relationships among the systems and their software dependencies, having a limited view of the impacts caused by the inevitable software evolution [9].

© Springer Nature Switzerland AG 2020
O. Gervasi et al. (Eds.): ICCSA 2020, LNCS 12254, pp. 335–350, 2020.
https://doi.org/10.1007/978-3-030-58817-5_26

From the perspective of software that provides functions and services, guaranteeing permanence in the market does not depend only on its correct internal functioning, but also on a constant balance among software that use it [24]. This concern led to the study of software systems in a broader context, involving everyone that somehow influence their survival.

To investigate the relationship among software products and their dependencies, the term software ecosystems (SECO) emerged in 2003 [3], referring to a set of software that has some degree of symbiosis among them [20]. Several studies have emerged to model and represent a software ecosystem [21]. Despite the advances achieved so far, there is still no consensus between both academia and industry on the best way to present software ecosystem entities [22]. Also, the lack of formalism and tools to support the modeling and visualization of SECO is hampering the advance of knowledge in the area [15].

An API is a particular type of software that is intrinsically designed to deal with ecosystems. Useful APIs increase the productivity of developers who use them, the quality of the software they produce, as well as the corporate bottom line [5]. However, its evolution represents a high risk for its users since its changes might propagate other changes in the entire ecosystem, requiring additional maintenance by the software that uses the API. In the worst case scenario, the entire API is replaced by a more satisfactory solution. Thus, the evolution of an API needs to be strategically geared toward meeting the goals of its users. Unfortunately, there is a lack of effective ways to analyze APIs considering their ecosystem, which makes it difficult to devise a better design strategy for their evolution [11].

This article presents *Ecolyzer*, a tool that aims to explore the dependencies of software components considering its ecosystem. The novelty of our approach consists of the employment of visualizations, making it possible to analyze and explore an API that provides functions and services for other software, taking into account all software that use it, thus contributing to its development and evolution. To achieve our goals, we developed a tool that gathers the main ideas proposed in the literature on the visualization of software ecosystems. We adapted them to evaluate the API usage by other software through a proof of concept by using a real software.

The remainder of this paper is structured as follows: Sect. 2 presents the background notions related to software ecosystems and an overview of current work involving visualization tools. Section 3 describes our approach for analyzing API usage, considering its ecosystem through an interactive visualization tool. Section 4 presents a proof of concept to demonstrate the feasibility of our approach. Finally, Sect. 5 presents our final remarks and plans for future works.

2   Software Ecosystems and Tools

There are many definitions related to software ecosystems. Some of them are more focused on technical aspects of software engineering and software development, while others are more focused on business, encompassing the software product and services, organizations, markets, vendors, and all actors involved [14,21]. Although both distinctions are important, in this article, we limit our review to solutions available in the literature of software engineering applied to ecosystems.

2.1 Software Ecosystem

The term ecosystem was originated from ecology, which in short consists of a set of actors, connected to other actors with connections among them, interacting as a system [6]. In the context of software ecosystems, actors are represented by software systems, and the connections are the dependencies among them.

According to Barbosa and Alves [3], the term software ecosystem appeared in 2003, referring to a set of software that has some degree of symbiosis among them [20]. In turn, Lungu [17] defined it as a collection of software projects that belong to an organization and are developed in parallel with it. Later, this definition was refined for a collection of software projects that are developed and evolve together in the same environment [18]. As reported by Goeminne and Mens [9], SECO consists of the source code together with the communities of users and developers that surround a software. In consonance to Bosch [6], SECO consists of a central platform with products and applications built using this platform, developed by external developers.

These definitions of SECO seem more appropriate when it comes to the software engineering area. They were merged or reformulated as new work emerged, always referring to a collection of software projects, which: (1) evolve together and are maintained by the same developer community [22], (2) are dependent on each other linked through project artifacts, common contributors, and support communities [25], and (3) base their relationships on a common interest in a central software technology [12,21].

Despite the considerable number of definitions, the essence of software ecosystems remains the same as that of ecology: a set of actors and their relationships, where actors are represented by software products, developers, and users communities, and the relationships are the links and dependencies among the actors.

In this work, we define software ecosystem, from the point of view of software engineering, as a set of software projects, which use a common (or central) software platform that provides resources for other software, through functions and services. These functions and services may be symbiosis or not, disregarding actors and relationships that can not be obtained in a computationally way, that is, restricted to systems. This definition allows us to study an API considering the entire ecosystem, using a single tool that extracts data, analyzes and presents the central software, all in an automated way, helping in its maintenance, improvements, evolution, and insights about the system, besides helping the evolution in the area of SECO.

2.2   Ecosystem Visualization Tools

Despite several studies exploring the characteristics and relationships among software ecosystem entities, there are still few approaches dealing with software ecosystem analysis and visualization tools. This situation is even worse when it comes to automatized tools that lead the entire process from data extraction and analysis to presentation.

Basically, a software ecosystem at a lower level is comprised of systems and their relationships. From a business perspective, it can involve internal and external actors, organizations, companies, and other stakeholders [21]. Given these elements, models are created, showing how they are interconnected and how these connections are. Therefore, the relationship is an essential entity in an ecosystem, and it can mean dependencies among components, trade relationships, and collaborations [15].

There are benefits provided by the modeling and visualization of a software ecosystem, such as a way to understand it, enabling analysis, formalization, and providing insights about it [15]. These advantages contribute technically not only at the software level, in its maintenance, improvements, and evolution, but also at the project level, helping in economic and strategic decision-making process [4]. However, most of the SECO visualization tools currently proposed to outline the relationships among the elements of the ecosystem are composed of tailored tools designed for one or a few scientific experiments [9]. Thus, software engineering becomes fundamental to enable the advance in this area [8,19].

Lungu [18] can be considered one of the pioneers in the development of tools that support the analysis of software ecosystems, enabling visualization and exploration of an ecosystem through an interactive web interface, named Small Project Observatory (SPO). Developed as a web application, SPO extracts information about the ecosystem from data available in the versioning repositories of the projects. The authors call those repositories of an ecosystem as the super-repository. The architecture of SPO is depicted in Fig. 1.

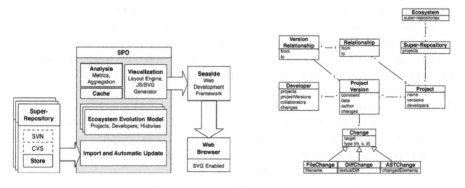

Fig. 1. The architecture and the ecosystem meta-model of SPO [18].

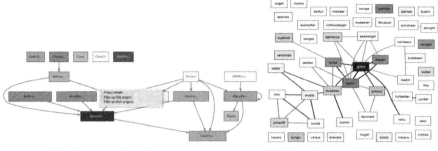

(a) Projects dependencies view.   (b) Developers collaboration view.

Fig. 2. Views of SPO [18].

Regarding visualization, SPO presents information taking into account all the super-repository, such as projects, developers, and inter-project relationships. The views are presented in Fig. 2.

Also, in their work, Lungu [18] present a usability study of the tool, showing that the main problems regard to the slowness of the system and the lack of scalability when many components are presented. It was pointed out the low interactivity on the visual elements, the lack of support for users to create their own views, and the impossibility for navigation to check relationships at a lower level, such as calls to methods between software.

Although SPO has a simple architecture and limited views and resources, their work shows elements and concerns to be considered when building a tool for analyzing and visualizing software ecosystems. Here, it can be cited the data extraction from version control systems, the statistical analysis of the code, statistics and metrics, and the representation of relevant elements of the ecosystem at lower level [18].

Following a slightly different approach, the tool presented by Goeminne and Mens [9] concerns not only with the relationships that can be extracted from the repositories but also from other data sources, such as mailing lists and bug tracking. For this, they created a generic multi-layer framework that is divided into three layers in which each layer processes and makes information available to the upper layers from the data sources to the application layer. The lowest layer is called the mining layer, which extracts information according to the data source. The middle layer is called the analysis layer, which extracts metrics under the data extracted from the mining layer. Finally, the upper one is called the application layer, which is responsible for presenting the data.

Goeminne and Mens [9] provide a resource to evaluate metrics commit to commit, making it possible to analyze in a straightforward way the evolution of the ecosystem. Although the tool proposed by the authors was designed to help understanding the evolution of software ecosystems by providing visualization of metrics through charts, it does not present ways of representing the relationships and dependencies among the systems.

Another important work presents a software ecosystem visualization and analysis dashboard tool named SECONDA [22]. It is similar to the Goeminne and Mens's [9] framework and follows the same approach regarding architecture, having modules for reporting, visualization, static analysis, metrics computing, and identity matching. In addition, the tool offers a dashboard with a variety of charts with metrics and statistics, both for projects and developers individually, as well as for analyzing them together. Despite that, SECONDA has not improved the representation of entities and their relationships within the software ecosystem, as its visualization presents only charts with metrics.

The work described by Santana and Werner [25] depicts a software ecosystem by visualizing the relationships of related software projects, providing views of relationships among project members, and relationships at the component level of the systems, such as method calls and object declaration between the systems. For that purpose, a procedure that consists of data extracting, data processing, and SECO visualization was built.

Other approaches have also been proposed in the literature for SECO modeling and visualization, but either they are not considered specific tools for data extraction and visualization or do not present the ecosystem entities and their relationships. Among the modeling techniques proposed to visualize software ecosystems, the most common are: ad hoc notations, tabular representations, conceptual maps, class diagrams, network graphs, software supply network (SSN), meta-models, and i* modeling [21].

Different from the solutions proposed by other researchers related to the visualization of ecosystems, our proposal focuses on a central system as the main software. We explore its components not in isolation as usual, but considering the software that use them.

3   Software Visualization Approach for API Usage

The approaches proposed in previous works to create modeling and visualization of software ecosystems are powerful and supportive of SECO analysis, but as noted by Jansen et al. [15], there are still opportunities for enhancements. This section presents a tool for analyzing central software, such as an application programming interface (API), a software development kit (SDK), a library, or any software that provides services to other software, considering its ecosystem. From now on, the term API always refers to the central system of our approach.

3.1   Overview

Common requirements need to be observed in the software ecosystem visualization tools, such as concerns about system modularity, data extraction in version control systems, and other data sources such as bug tracking and mailing list. Besides, features as static analysis, calculation of statistics and metrics, as well as the presentation of the ecosystem – its actors and relationships – must

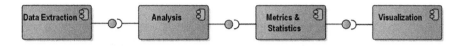

Fig. 3. Components of a SECO visualization tool.

be considered. Thus, a generic SECO visualization tool consists of component architecture, as shown in Fig. 3.

The first step in a SECO visualization system is related to data extraction from some data source. With the extracted data in hand, the second step consists of analyzing such data, which, in the context of SECO, refers to identify the relationships among the involved systems. The third step is responsible for extracting metrics and statistics from the mapped ecosystem. In this step, metrics and statistics should consider all software and their relationships within the ecosystem, and not only a software in isolation as in traditional approaches [16,25].

The novelty of our approach consists in SECO visualization that different from other works in which the concern is to show the entire ecosystem and their relationships, our tool provides API-centric visualization and all its components, taking into account all the systems that use this API. The advantage of this visualization is to enable the analysis in-depth of the API quickly and intuitively, as shown in the following sections.

3.2 Data Extraction, Analysis, and Metrics

Although it seems complex at first [25], data extraction can be done by software repository mining (MSR) techniques, which makes the task feasible. There are currently some MSR APIs available depending on the type of data source [26]. Among data that are possible to obtain from repositories, we highlight the source code and metadata of commits, such as developers, changes in the source code, date of the changes, among others. The metadata of commits makes it possible to study the evolution of systems [9]. Besides, data can be extracted directly from the software's directory structure regardless of a version control system. This data is enough to identify relationships among the software.

In the analysis process, relationships are created from the elements of the source code using functions (or methods) or some other resource made available by the components of the central API and calls (or invoking) for these functions coming from other software. The feasibility of this step depends on the source code analysis APIs, which build an abstract syntax tree (AST), providing the code elements, allowing the static analysis of the source code. The challenge of the analysis consists in identifying, for each call of a function from other software, whether it belongs to some component of the central API. Moreover, the relationships can contain information about data provided by version control systems such as authors, code elements creation, and modification dates.

After the analysis step, some metrics and statistics in the context of SECO can be determined, such as: (1) the most-used components, the least used ones,

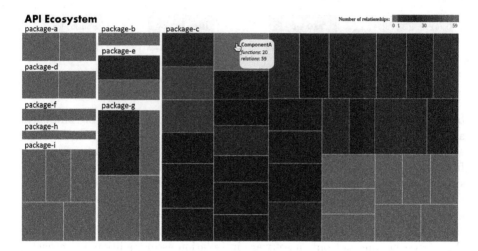

Fig. 4. Central system view of Ecolyzer.

and those not used by other software; (2) the software that use a specific API component; (3) the components of other software that use a specific API component; (4) which API functions are used by other software; (5) the number of functions used by other software over the number of functions available within an API component; and (6) the number of different functions used by a component of another software over the total number of functions used by the component. These metrics and statistics are better explained through our proposed visualization approach.

3.3 Software Ecosystem Visualization

Our approach provides a way to analyze an API as a whole, not only in an isolated way. The visualization considers other software and the relationships among its components at the level of elements of the source code, such as functions (or methods), function calls, and other shared resources. For this purpose, the visualization consists of a treemap combined with a heatmap. This strategy provides more dimensions for analysis through visual elements. Figure 4 depicts an example of visualizing an API.

In this view, each component is a rectangle grouped by system modules or packages. The area of each rectangle represents the number of operations provided by the given component. The colors inform the number of relationships that the respective component has with other software. The legend on upper right describes the number of relationships. Also, the rectangles have a tooltip for checking the component name and other additional information relevant to SECO.

By selecting an API component, it is possible to view the software that use this component and the software components that have some relationship with the selected API component. As can be seen in Fig. 5, this view differs slightly

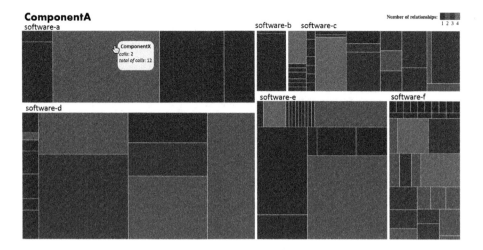

Fig. 5. Component view of Ecolyzer.

from the API view (Fig. 4). The areas of the rectangles represent the total number of calls to operations of some API component, and the colors represent the number of different called operations, disregarding calls to the same operation more than once.

If it is necessary to go deeper into the source code, selecting a software component makes it possible to view the code of the API component, side by side, with the code of the component that uses it. Also, this view provides a way to navigate among components by selecting common code elements between the source codes, as shown in Fig. 6.

3.4 The Ecolyzer

Aiming to achieve our goals, we developed a multi-tiered software system for data extraction, analysis, and visualization of the API's components, considering its ecosystem, named Ecolyzer. Its architecture, along with the main modules, is presented in Fig. 7.

Ecolyzer was developed as a client-server application and its architecture is based on RESTful web services. The main motivations that led to this architectural decision were simplicity, popularity, and the ease of developing RESTful applications due to the available frameworks [23]. The layers of Ecolyzer are briefly described here since it is beyond the scope of this paper to go deeper into architecture style.

The API layer is responsible for extracting data from the repositories, analyzing, and calculating metrics and statistics over the ecosystem. This layer provides

(a) Souce codes information.

(b) Navigation.

Fig. 6. Source codes side by side view.

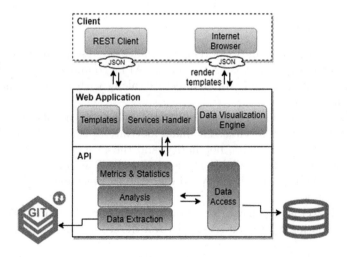

Fig. 7. *Ecolyzer* architecture.

database services for data access and storage. Currently, the API layer supports only Git[1] repositories and the Lua[2] programming language. The web application tier (or the back-end) is a web service for data handling and visualization. It is responsible for handling requests and responses from the clients and interacting with the API layer. The provided services can be accessed either by RESTful services or by web templates.

Finally, the client tier can be either an internet browser or a specific application that consumes REST services. This layer provides the visualization to the end-users by the web templates, which are HTML files that contain static data and placeholders for dynamic data rendering on the browser [10]. The graphs are provided by the data visualization engine D3.js [27].

4   Evaluating API Usage for TerraME

To demonstrate the feasibility of our approach, we conducted an exploration of the relationships of a SECO. The main purpose of this Proof of Concept (PoC) was to highlight the usage of the proposed visualizations in a real case project. We expected that the visualizations would aid in analyzing the API usage considering its ecosystem.

4.1   TerraME

TerraME (Terra Modeling Environment) is an open-source platform API to develop and simulate spatially explicit dynamic models based on cellular automata, agents, and network models [7]. TerraME provides a Lua code interpreter [13], as well as functions that ease the development of multi-scale and multi-paradigm models for environmental applications. Contributions to TerraME can be encapsulated in packages and might extend its functionalities or provide new resources and concepts through its API.

TerraME is part of the National Institute for Space Research (INPE) software ecosystem, which develops and provides a set of systems in the geoprocessing area. In addition to being part of an ecosystem, TerraME has its own ecosystem, specifically focused on environmental modeling.

All software of the TerraME ecosystem are publicly available on GitHub, consisting of ten packages developed by third parties and two software that only uses its functions. Among the software, we highlight INPE-EM (INPE - Emission Model), that produces annual estimates of greenhouse gas (GHG) emissions due to changes in land cover in Brazil [2], and LuccME, an open-source framework for spatially explicit land use and cover change (LUCC) modeling [1].

---

[1] https://git-scm.com.
[2] https://www.lua.org.

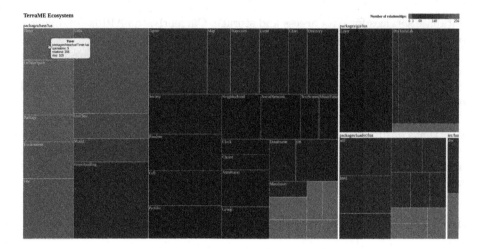

Fig. 8. TerraME heatmap. (Color figure online)

4.2 Proof of Concept

The extraction process starts by cloning the repositories and setting TerraME as the central system. We cloned the master branches of all software on January 5, 2020. Then, Ecolyzer scans the repositories and creates all relationships. After that, the ecosystem is ready for visualization on an internet browser. Figure 8 shows the heatmap of TerraME components.

Unlike object-oriented languages, where functions (or methods) are usually defined within classes, TerraME source files can be seen as components in which functions can be defined without the use of a structure like a class. By convention, TerraME defines most of its functions within Lua tables, which work similarly to classes.

On the API heatmap view (Fig. 8), it is possible to observe that TerraME has four modules composed of 52 components, 520 public functions, and 3658 relationships with other systems. The minimum and the maximum number of relationships among components is one and 256, respectively, as shown in the legend on upper right. Besides, ten components have no relationship at all (gray), eight components have a large number of connections (red), and the remainder has a low or medium number of relationships (blue).

Also as a result of the experiment: (1) the component with the most relationships is Timer, used by 180 components from nine software; (2) the system with more components that uses Timer is LuccME, with 38 components and 181 relationships; (3) the system that uses less components is INPE-EM, with only one component and one function call; (4) the component that most uses the Timer functions is the MultipleRuns component of the calibration package, with 26 function calls; (5) most software use only one Timer function; (6) the LuccME software components use the most number of different Timer functions. Figure 9 shows the component with the most relationships and the software that uses it.

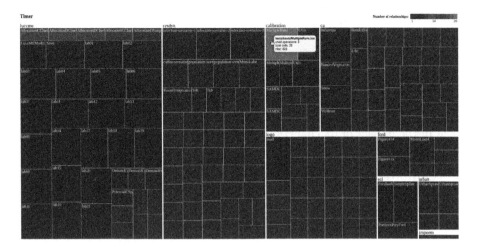

Fig. 9. Software with relationships on Timer component.

Our exploratory analysis through visualization has successfully provided important data about TerraME's usage, considering its ecosystem. Besides, we conducted an analysis together with the TerraME team in order to find out if our tool was able to provide more interesting feedback for the team involved in its development.

4.3   Insights for TerraME Ecosystem

To test the hypothesis that one of the main benefits provided by SECO visualization is to provide systematic insights, we introduced Ecolyzer to the TerraME development team and requested feedback on our tool. No protocol was followed, as we believe it would facilitate insights. We presented only some concepts of SECO, the tool, its functionalities, and how it works.

The team's first feedback reported that the TerraLib component, which is a facade for an API to access geographic data developed for the exclusive use of internal components, was strangely being used by two external packages. According to the development team, the functions of the facade is exposed through more specialized components in the most user-friendly way possible for end-users or other software that use TerraME, and should not be accessed directly by other software.

The TerraME's development team delivered other reports, such as: (1) *"the components supposed to be used a lot are, in fact, extensively used by other software"*; (2) *"some components in which we spent much work on them are not being used"*; (3) *"several new components with interesting functionalities have low usage, maybe we should publicize them better"*; (4) *"we could use this tool to measure the impact of changing any interface, which was not feasible so far"*; (5) *"we can use this tool to see how the functions are being used by other software"*;

(6) *"this tool might be helpful for new developers to understand how functions are used in practice"*.

This feedback allowed us to identify an important feature for those who analyze an API considering its ecosystem. It consisted of a filter on the functions provided by the components of the API. With this functionality, it would be possible to select a function provided by the component, and the heatmap would display only the software that uses this function, thus facilitating the measurement of the impact of its changes.

5   Conclusion and Future Work

There are several studies related to software ecosystems, and they can help the analysis and understanding of complex relationships among system dependencies. Furthermore, they come as an alternative to overcome challenges during the design, development, maintenance, and evolution of software, mainly on the ones that provide functions and services. However, there is still a lack of software tools to support software ecosystems analysis and visualization, thus making software engineering a critical research issue in the SECO domain.

This paper presented Ecolyzer, a software visualization tool for the visualization and analysis of API usage considering an ecosystem. A brief description of its architecture was presented, which was designed and implemented based on the directives proposed in the literature on SECO visualization tools.

The visualization provided by Ecolyzer was reported in detail. A proof of concept (PoC) in a real open-source platform API was conducted, demonstrating that the tool is useful for evaluating an API usage in the context of a SECO, allowing to quantify by who and how the API is actually used. Also, Ecolyzer proved to be useful for measuring the impacts of changes in API functions, providing insights on its usage, thus helping the organization that maintains the API to plan its evolution strategically.

As future work, we intend to (1) add a new feature to the tool that enables it to analyze the historical evolution of an API and its ecosystem using the commits metadata, (2) implement support for other programming languages to carry out studies in other ecosystems, and (3) investigate new metrics of API usage in the context of SECO. Finally, we plan to conduct a systematic usability evaluation of Ecolyzer.

Acknowledgment. The authors would like to thank the World Bank (grant #P143185) and FAPESP (grant 2018/22064-4) for financial support.

References

1. Aguiar, A., Carneiro, T., Andrade, P., Assis, T.: Luccme-terrame: an opensource framework for spatially explicit land use change modelling. GLP News **8**, 21–23 (2012)

2. Aguiar, A., et al.: Modeling the spatial and temporal heterogeneity of deforestation-driven carbon emissions: the INPE-EM framework applied to the Brazilian Amazon. Global Change Biol. **18** (2012). https://doi.org/10.1111/j.1365-2486.2012.02782.x
3. Barbosa, O., Alves, C.: A systematic mapping study on software ecosystems. In: Proceedings of International Workshop on Software Ecosystems (2011)
4. Berger, T., et al.: Variability mechanisms in software ecosystems. Inf. Softw. Technol. **56** (2014). https://doi.org/10.1016/j.infsof.2014.05.005
5. Bloch, J.: How to design a good API and why it matters. In: Companion to the 21st ACM SIGPLAN Symposium on Object-Oriented Programming Systems, Languages, and Applications, OOPSLA 2006, pp. 506–507. Association for Computing Machinery, New York (2006). https://doi.org/10.1145/1176617.1176622
6. Bosch, J.: From software product lines to software ecosystems. In: Proceedings of the 13th International Software Product Line Conference, SPLC 2009, pp. 111–119. Carnegie Mellon University, USA (2009)
7. Carneiro, T.G.d.S., de Andrade, P.R., Câmara, G., Monteiro, A.M.V., Pereira, R.R.P.: An extensible toolbox for modeling nature-society interactions. Environ. Model. Softw. **46**, 104–117 (2013). https://doi.org/10.1016/j.envsoft.2013.03.002
8. García-Holgado, A., García-Peñalvo, F.J.: Mapping the systematic literature studies about software ecosystems. In: Proceedings of the Sixth International Conference on Technological Ecosystems for Enhancing Multiculturality, TEEM 2018, pp. 910–918. Association for Computing Machinery, New York (2018). https://doi.org/10.1145/3284179.3284330
9. Goeminne, M., Mens, T.: A framework for analysing and visualising open source software ecosystems. In: Proceedings of the Joint ERCIM Workshop on Software Evolution (EVOL) and International Workshop on Principles of Software Evolution (IWPSE), IWPSE-EVOL 2010, pp. 42–47. Association for Computing Machinery, New York (2010). https://doi.org/10.1145/1862372.1862384
10. Grinberg, M.: Flask Web Development: Developing Web Applications with Python. O'Reilly Media, Inc. (2018)
11. Hammouda, I., Knauss, E., Costantini, L.: Continuous API design for software ecosystems. In: 2015 IEEE/ACM 2nd International Workshop on Rapid Continuous Software Engineering, pp. 30–33, May 2015. https://doi.org/10.1109/RCoSE.2015.13
12. Hanssen, G.K.: A longitudinal case study of an emerging software ecosystem: implications for practice and theory. J. Syst. Softw. **85**(7), 1455–1466 (2012). https://doi.org/10.1016/j.jss.2011.04.020. Software Ecosystems
13. Ierusalimschy, R., de Figueiredo, L.H., Filho, W.C.: Lua - an extensible extension language. Softw. Pract. Exper. **26**(6), 635–652 (1996). https://doi.org/10.1002/(SICI)1097-024X(199606)26:6⟨635::AID-SPE26⟩3.0.CO;2-P
14. Jansen, S., Finkelstein, A., Brinkkemper, S.: A sense of community: a research agenda for software ecosystems. In: 2009 31st International Conference on Software Engineering - Companion Volume, pp. 187–190, May 2009. https://doi.org/10.1109/ICSE-COMPANION.2009.5070978
15. Jansen, S., Handoyo, E., Alves, C.: Scientists' needs in modelling software ecosystems. In: Proceedings of the 2015 European Conference on Software Architecture Workshops. ECSAW 2015. Association for Computing Machinery, New York (2015). https://doi.org/10.1145/2797433.2797479
16. Knodel, J., Manikas, K.: Towards a typification of software ecosystems. In: Fernandes, J.M., Machado, R.J., Wnuk, K. (eds.) ICSOB 2015. LNBIP, vol. 210, pp. 60–65. Springer, Cham (2015). https://doi.org/10.1007/978-3-319-19593-3_5

17. Lungu, M.: Towards reverse engineering software ecosystems. In: 2008 IEEE International Conference on Software Maintenance, pp. 428–431, September 2008. https://doi.org/10.1109/ICSM.2008.4658096

18. Lungu, M., Lanza, M., Gîrba, T., Robbes, R.: The small project observatory: visualizing software ecosystems. Sci. Comput. Program. **75**(4), 264–275 (2010). https://doi.org/10.1016/j.scico.2009.09.004

19. Manikas, K.: Revisiting software ecosystems research: a longitudinal literature study. J. Syst. Softw. **117**, 84–103 (2016). https://doi.org/10.1016/j.jss.2016.02.003

20. Messerschmitt, D., Szyperski, C.: Software Ecosystem: Understanding an Indispensable Technology and Industry. MIT Press, Cambridge (2003). https://doi.org/10.7551/mitpress/6323.001.0001

21. Oscar, F.B., Ameller, D., Costal, D., Franch, X.: Open source software ecosystems: a systematic mapping. Inf. Softw. Technol. (2017). https://doi.org/10.1016/j.infsof.2017.07.007

22. Pérez, J., Deshayes, R., Goeminne, M., Mens, T.: Seconda: software ecosystem analysis dashboard. In: 2012 16th European Conference on Software Maintenance and Reengineering, pp. 527–530. IEEE, March 2012. https://doi.org/10.1109/CSMR.2012.69

23. Richardson, L., Amundsen, M., Amundsen, M., Ruby, S.: RESTful Web APIs: Services for a Changing World. O'Reilly Media, Inc. (2013)

24. da Silva Amorim, S., McGregor, J.D., de Almeida, E.S., von Flach, G.C.C.: Software ecosystems' architectural health: another view. In: 2017 IEEE/ACM Joint 5th International Workshop on Software Engineering for Systems-of-Systems and 11th Workshop on Distributed Software Development, Software Ecosystems and Systems-of-Systems (JSOS), pp. 66–69, May 2017. https://doi.org/10.1109/JSOS.2017.15

25. Santana, F.W., Werner, C.M.: Towards the analysis of software projects dependencies: an exploratory visual study of software ecosystems. In: International Workshop on Software Ecosystems (IWSECO), vol. 987, pp. 7–18. Citeseer (2013)

26. Spadini, D., Aniche, M., Bacchelli, A.: PyDriller: python framework for mining software repositories. In: Proceedings of the 2018 26th ACM Joint Meeting on European Software Engineering Conference and Symposium on the Foundations of Software Engineering - ESEC/FSE 2018, pp. 908–911. ACM Press, New York (2018). https://doi.org/10.1145/3236024.3264598

27. Zhu, N.Q.: Data Visualization with D3.js Cookbook. Packt Publishing Ltd (2013)

Temperature Controller Using the Takagi-Sugeno-Kang Fuzzy Inference System for an Industrial Heat Treatment Furnace

Jorge Buele[1,3]($\boxtimes$) ![ORCID], Paulina Ríos-Cando[2], Geovanni Brito[3], Rodrigo Moreno-P.[2], and Franklin W. Salazar[3] ![ORCID]

[1] SISAu Research Group,
Universidad Tecnológica Indoamérica, 180212 Ambato, Ecuador
jorgebuele@uti.edu.ec
[2] Escuela Superior Politécnica de Chimborazo, Riobamba 060155, Ecuador
i.paulina.rios.c@hotmail.com,
rodrigo.moreno@espoch.edu.ec
[3] Universidad Técnica de Ambato, Ambato 180103, Ecuador
{geovannidbrito,fw.salazar}@uta.edu.ec

Abstract. The industrial welding industry has a high energy consumption due to the heating processes carried out. The heat treatment furnaces used for reheating equipment made of steel require a good regulator to control the temperature at each stage of the process, thereby optimizing resources. Considering dynamic and variable temperature behavior inside the oven, this paper proposes the design of a temperature controller based on a Takagi-Sugeno-Kang (TSK) fuzzy inference system of zero order. Considering the reaction curve of the temperature process, the plant model has been identified with the Miller method and a subsequent optimization based on the descending gradient algorithm. Using the conventional plant model, a TSK fuzzy model optimized by the recursive least square's algorithm is obtained. The TSK fuzzy controller is initialized from the conventional controller and is optimized by descending gradient and a cost function. Applying this controller to a real heat treatment system achieves an approximate minimization of 15 min with respect to the time spent with a conventional controller. Improving the process and integrated systems of quality management of the service provided.

Keywords: Fuzzy logic controller · Gradient descent algorithm · Heat treatment · Temperature control

1 Introduction

The metalworking industry has considerable participation and growth in the world economy [1]. The most important sectors are oil, energy, industrial, mining, infrastructure, among others, being a strategic axis for its contribution in local and regional production chains [2, 3]. In traditional industries it can still be found that processes are controlled manually by an operator, which depending on their experience and competence may not show optimal results. Within the quality policies, the improvement of

© Springer Nature Switzerland AG 2020
O. Gervasi et al. (Eds.): ICCSA 2020, LNCS 12254, pp. 351–366, 2020.
https://doi.org/10.1007/978-3-030-58817-5_27

the production processes is proposed and thus reach higher levels of competitiveness and productivity required by nowadays market [4, 5]. That is why the need arises to implement technological solutions that minimize operation times in each process. Among the most popular automatic controllers in the industrial sector, the proportional, integral and derivative (PID) and their respective modifications stand out, which have taken a dominant position due to the simplicity of their structure and design [6]. However, this type of conventional control has deficiencies when used in processes that exhibit strongly non-linear and unexpected behaviors [7].

As a case study, there is a post-welding heat treatment furnace for stress relief in steel. Although it is a first-order system, when tuning the current controller, actuators fail to perform the necessary control actions to increase the response speed of the system and therefore it is necessary to look for more advanced control proposals, such as the fuzzy controller. This is based on the decision of a set of rules that determine the desired behavior of the system, through its three stages fuzzification, inference and defuzzification [8, 9]. Fuzzy set operations called membership functions are values assigned to system inputs and outputs and the controller design considers the error and the error change (derived value) [10]. The setup of the rules and gains in this controller is usually based on the experience of the designer, so determining the values of the mathematical model of the system allows predicting its behavior in a more exact way [11]. That is why intelligent evolutionary algorithms have now been developed, which establish these values by considering the system's behavior, reducing the complex mathematical calculations that controllers cannot perform [12]. Using artificial intelligence, optimization methods can be implemented, such as the descending gradient algorithm (AGD), an iterative optimization algorithm that allows to find minimum values of convex and differentiable functions throughout its domain [13].

The development of better controllers and their implementation in the industrial sector is a research topic that remains latent in the search to improve processes. In the work of [14] IAE tuning equations are used to optimize a PID controller, since controlling the temperature deviation is critical for the final product quality in the paper industry. The results show that the controlled variable deviation from the setpoint can be minimized, so that the value of IAE decreases. Similarly, in the manuscript of [15] the design of a fuzzy PD + I controller applied to control the temperature of a non-linear chemical process. To adjust and obtain the best parameters of the controller, optimization is performed using the evolutionary algorithm PSO (Particles Swarm Optimization), and its comparison with other controllers is carried out by simulation of a mixing tank with variable dead time. In [16] the behavioral model of a vehicle driver is presented using Takagi-Sugeno Fuzzy Control Systems (FCSs) based on gradient descent (GD) and having great results. For its part in [17], the GD and the Extended Kalman Filter (EKF) estimation is compared to improve the control performance of Fuzzy PID (FPID) controllers, it allows to enhance the reference tracking and disturbance rejection performance.

The need to control the temperature level at each stage of the proposed process and reduce the time spent have motivated the present investigation. In this document it is proposed to describe the design of a zero-order Takagi-Sugeno-Kang fuzzy controller identifying the plant model previously. The TSK fuzzy controller is made from a conventional controller and is optimized by descending gradient and a cost function. It is intended to demonstrate the advantages of controllers designed under the artificial intelligence technique compared to classical controllers in an industrial environment. In addition, reduce the operation time of the process, decrease in costs, man hours. Based on the described bibliography, GD optimization is used, focused clearly on the manufacturing sector, demonstrating its variability of applications and good industrial performance.

This paper is organized as follows: the introduction in Sect. 1 and the case study in Sect. 2, which describes the characteristics and identification of the furnace for the heat treatment process, temperatures and operating times. In Sect. 3 the design of the conventional controller is presented. In Sect. 4 the design of the TSK fuzzy controller is presented. The analysis of the tests performed and conclusions are described in Sect. 4 and Sect. 5 respectively.

2 Study Case

The Heat Treatment process for the relief of welding stresses is part of the production chain of the metalworking sector. Equipment made of carbon steel, such as: boilers, external boiler piping, pressure vessels and part of them are placed in a furnace where it is necessary to handle the temperature and the application of controlled heat on the steel to change or alter its properties. The furnace used works with gas and it has dimensions: 14000(L) × 4000(H) × 6000(W) mm. It has a thermal insulation of glass wool, two burners and Liquified Petroleum Gas (LPG) is used as fuel. The heat treatment starts when the equipment or steel pieces enter the furnace; thermocouples are welded into the welding joints and burners are ignited. This process is divided into 5 stages and in each of them a temperature monitoring is required at a defined speed and time, as shown in Table 1.

Table 1. Heat treatment process parameters for each stage.

Parameters	Preheating	Heating	Sustenance	Cooling	Ending
Starting Temp. (°F)	50	800	1150	1150	800
Final Temp. (°F)	800	1150	1150	800	50
Time	1:36	1:22	1:14	1:07	2:01
Speed	500 °F/h	320 °F/h	N/A	400 °F/h	375 °F/h

The heat treatment is carried out in an intermittent oven. Most ovens are non-commercial construction and manual operation. Temperature measurement is acquired by thermocouples which are welded directly to the welding joints of the equipment or part to be subjected to the treatment. The control of the process depends on a human operator who visualizes both temperature of the welding joints and required time of the process. Based on these variables, the intensity of the burner flame is regulated by adjusting the LPG air control valve. Temperature variations are recorded and a report is issued at the end of the process. Said process demands a high consumption of resources and man hours as a result of the lack of automation causing high operating times in the process. The level of automation and instrumentation in the heat treatment furnace is minimal, so the implementation of a system that allows automatic control of this industrial process is proposed.

3   Conventional Controller Design

3.1   Mathematical Model

To identify the plant, a dynamic model has been made. Said model is tested by the response to a step input. The reaction curve corresponds to the transfer function presented in (1), for a first order system and represents the conventional plant model.

$$G_p(s) = \frac{12.4007241995804}{1975.09828967136s + 1} \tag{1}$$

Consequently, throughout a linear transformation, the conventional model of the plant becomes a fuzzy model of TSK type. When designing the conventional controller, the characteristic closed loop polynomial and the plant was used in order to find its equivalent to the denominator of the transfer function of a second order system. Temporary characteristics were established such as settling time $t_s = 4\tau$, overshoot $M_p = 1\%$, in order to find the damping factor ξ and the undamped natural frequency Wn. Using the calculated parameters, the transfer function of a second order system is acquired, the same as defined in (2). In addition, the structure of the PI + D controller is shown in Fig. 1.

$$G(s) = \frac{3.33e^{-7}}{s^2 + 9.54e^{-4}s + 3.336e^{-7}} \tag{2}$$

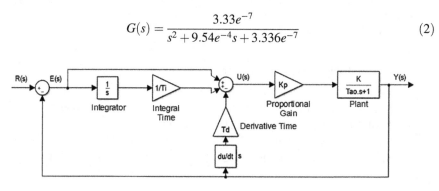

Fig. 1. PI + D controller structure.

To apply the pole assignment tuning method, the non-interacting conventional PID structure is used. By reducing the diagram blocks, the transfer function of the controller in closed loop with the plant is obtained, shown in (3). The denominator of the closed loop transfer function of the system is the characteristic polynomial $P(s)$ presented in (4).

$$\frac{Y(s)}{R(s)} = \frac{(T_i s + 1)(K_p K)}{T_i s(\tau s + 1 + K_p K T_d s) + (T_i s + 1)(K_p K)} \tag{3}$$

$$P(s) = s^2(T_i \tau + K_p K T_d T_i) + s(T_i + T_i K_p K) + K_p K \tag{4}$$

In (4) it is equal to zero to find the term-to-term equivalences with respect to the denominator of a second order system (2). Equivalences are defined and the three parameters of the controller are cleared: proportional gain K_p in (5); integral time T_i in (6) and derivative time T_d in (7).

$$K_p K = Wn^2 \rightarrow K_p = \frac{Wn^2}{K} \tag{5}$$

$$T_i + T_i K_p K = 2\xi Wn \rightarrow T_i = \frac{2\xi Wn}{1 + K_p K} \tag{6}$$

$$T_i \tau + K_p K T_d T_i = 1 \rightarrow T_d = \frac{1 - T_i \tau}{K_p K T_i} \tag{7}$$

3.2   Setpoint Tracking Controller

The designed controller objective is to follow a temperature curve that varies over time. Once the tuning gains have been found, considering that the Kp gain is zero, the PI + D is modified, remaining as an ID type controller. Its block diagram representation is shown in Fig. 2 and is presented in (8) the transfer function of the control signal $U(s)$ with respect to the error E(s).

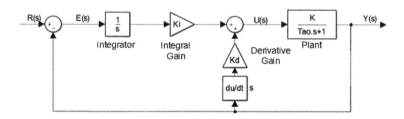

Fig. 2. ID controller structure.

$$\frac{U(s)}{E(s)} = \frac{(K_I/s)}{1 - \frac{KK_D s}{\tau s + 1}} \tag{8}$$

As a design part, the controller simulation is carried out in the MATLAB software, but for its real implementation the respective programming is carried out in a PLC, therefore, its discretization has been made through the Euler method and after executing an algebraic operation it is obtained the difference equation. It should be mentioned that sampling time selection T for a first order system is $T = \tau/10$, where τ is the plant time constant. The u_k variable defined as the control signal at the instant of time is cleared and the result is described in (9). To simplify this equation, the assignments shown in (10), (11), (12) and (13) are made.

$$u_k = \frac{(K_I T^2/\tau + K_I T)e_k - K_I T e_{k-1} - (-2 + 2KK_D/\tau - T/\tau)u_{k-1} - (1 - KK_D/\tau)u_{k-2}}{1 + T/\tau - KK_D/\tau} \tag{9}$$

$$\lambda_1 = \frac{K_I T^2/\tau + K_I T}{1 + T/\tau - KK_D/\tau} = \frac{K_I T \tau + K_I T^2}{\tau + T - KK_D} \tag{10}$$

$$\lambda_2 = \frac{K_I T}{1 + T/\tau - KK_D/\tau} = \frac{K_I T \tau}{\tau + T - KK_D} \tag{11}$$

$$\lambda_3 = \frac{-2 + 2KK_D/\tau - T/\tau}{1 + T/\tau - KK_D/\tau} = \frac{\tau - KK_D}{\tau + T - KK_D} \tag{12}$$

$$\lambda_4 = \frac{1 - KK_D/\tau}{1 + T/\tau - KK_D/\tau} = \frac{2KK_D - T - 2\tau}{\tau + T - KK_D} \tag{13}$$

The λ values found depend on the parameters of the first order model K, τ, the tuning gains of the controller KI, KD and the sampling time $T = 210$. By previous assignments, the equation is reduced and therefore (14) is obtained. The structure of the discrete conventional controller and the fuzzy plant is shown in Fig. 3. Subsequently, the respective simulation is carried out, which allows to evaluate the operation of the controller. The output of the u_k controller depends directly of these 4 inputs: e_k = Error in the instant of time; e_{k-1} = Error in previous time; u_{k-1} = Control signal in the previous time and u_{k-2} = Control signal in the previous time -1.

$$u_k = \lambda_1 e_k + \lambda_2 e_{k-1} + \lambda_3 u_{k-1} + \lambda_4 u_{k-2} \tag{14}$$

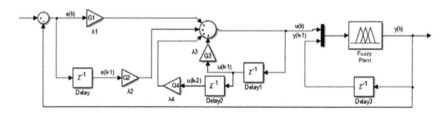

Fig. 3. Conventional discrete controller structure.

4 TSK Fuzzy Controller Design

Once the conventional setpoint tracking controller is tuned, the fuzzy controller is tuned and optimized to evaluate their performance and compare them. Similar to obtaining the fuzzy plant model, the discrete transfer function and its respective difference equation is required, it is described in (15). The structure, inputs and outputs of the fuzzy controller are defined in here for its design and simulation; where the inference system used is a zero order Takagi-Sugeno-Kang type. In a fuzzy model, the number of inputs have a serious role, since at the merger time the more inputs there are, the algorithms become more complex; this is why in (15) errors and control signals were grouped for get only two variables. Final difference equation, which defines the structure of the controller is presented mathematically in (16) and in a block diagram in Fig. 4. Where: u_k = Controller signal at the instant of time; ΔE_k = Error signal variation; ΔU_k = Variation of the control signal and λ_2, λ_4 = Constant values.

$$u_k = \lambda_2 \left(\frac{\lambda_1}{\lambda_2} e_k + e_{k-1} \right) + \lambda_3 \left(\frac{\lambda_3}{\lambda_4} u_{k-1} + u_{k-2} \right) \tag{15}$$

$$u_k = \lambda_2 \Delta E_k + \lambda_4 \Delta U_k \tag{16}$$

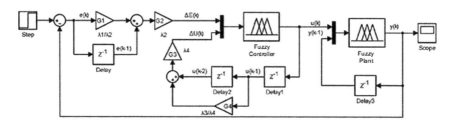

Fig. 4. Structure of the TSK fuzzy controller.

The inputs of the fuzzy controller are defined by the error variation and the control signal variation. The output is the control signal at a defined time instant. The 5 membership functions of the entries are triangular, which will facilitate the calculations in the optimization process, since they comply with the overlapping law, resulting in 25 system rules. The consequent of the controller is singleton or solitary type and represent a constant value, they are defined in (17). Where: E_p is the value of the speech universe of the error variation when $\mu_C(E_p) = 1$ and U_q is the value of the speech universe of the controller variation when the $\mu_D(U_q) = 1$, of the $p, q - ths$ rules and C and D are the fuzzy sets. The controller output is shown in (18). Where ψ_{ij} depends on the error variation signals and the burner variation, expressed in (19).

$$\theta_{pq} = \lambda_2 \Delta E_p + \lambda_4 \Delta U_q \tag{17}$$

$$u = \sum_{p,q=1}^{r,s} \psi_{pq} \cdot \theta_{pq} \tag{18}$$

$$\psi_{pq}(\Delta E_k, \Delta U_k) = \mu_{Cq}(\Delta E_k) \cdot \mu_{Dq}(\Delta U_k) \tag{19}$$

In this design, the singletons of each system rule were obtained and the optimization of them was carried out by the algorithm of the decreasing gradient. This algorithm evaluates a cost function that indicates how learning evolves in the tuning process. The cost function J to evaluate the performance of the TSK fuzzy controller is the mean square error described in (20). Where: y_r = Values of the Heat Treatment Curve (Set Point) and y_d = Temperature value when the fuzzy controller and fuzzy plant react.

$$J = \frac{1}{2}(y_r - y_d)^2 \tag{20}$$

Controller output shown in (18) is replaced in (20). Additionally, J is derived with respect to θ_{pq} and the optimization values, therefore the function gradient is obtained in order to iterate the learning algorithm shown in (21). To decrease the number of iterations, the conjugate descending gradient must be used, obtaining the second derivative of the cost function called the gradient address defined in (22).

$$\nabla \theta_{pq} = (y_r - y_d) \left[-\sum_{i,j=1}^{n,m} \mu_{Ai} \left(\sum_{p,q=1}^{r,s} \mu_{Cp}(\Delta E_k) \cdot \mu_{Dp}(\Delta U_k) \right) \cdot \mu_{Bj}(y_{k-1}) \cdot \beta_{ij} \right] \tag{21}$$

$$\nabla^2 \theta_{pq} = (y_r - y_d) \left[y_r - \sum_{i,j=1}^{n,m} \mu_{Ai} \left(\sum_{p,q=1}^{r,s} \mu_{Cp}(\Delta E_k) \cdot \mu_{Dp}(\Delta U_k) \right) \cdot \mu_{Bj}(y_{k-1}) \cdot \beta_{ij} \right] *$$
$$\left[-\sum_{i,j=1}^{n,m} \mu_{Ai} \left(\sum_{p,q=1}^{r,s} \mu_{Cp}(\Delta E_k) \cdot \mu_{Dp}(\Delta U_k) \right) \cdot \mu_{Bj}(y_{k-1}) \cdot \beta_{ij} \right] \tag{22}$$

Once the cost function is defined to use the optimization algorithm, the learning periods are evaluated by (23), to determine the modification of the controller singletons.

$$\theta_{pq+1} = \theta_{pq} - \alpha \nabla \theta_{pq} \cdot \nabla^2 \theta_{pq} \tag{23}$$

Where: θ_{pq+1} = Optimized controller singletons; θ_{pq} = Singletons from the previous driver; α = Learning Value; $\nabla \theta_{pq}$ = Cost function Gradient and $\nabla^2 \theta_{pq}$ = Gradient Address of the Cost Function.

5   Results Analysis

5.1   Conventional Controller

By (5), (6), (7) equivalences of the characteristic polynomial and the second order denominator of the transfer equation described in (2), it is obtained that parameters of the conventional controller found are the following:

$$K_P = 2.685011299244543e^{-8} \cong 0$$

$$K_I = 2.816403801927200e^{-5}$$

$$K_D = 284.586581456506408$$

The obtained control is an ID type since the proportional gain has a value that tends to zero, without this affecting the control algorithm. The integral gain K_I allows to reach the required setpoint and increase the response speed, while the derivative gain K_D takes care of the system stability. Controller transfer function and closed loop plant are presented in (24). Figure 5 shows the response of the ID controller when establishing an 800 °F setpoint, complying with the established M_P.

$$G_{LS}(s) = \frac{3.174e^{-10}s + 3.33e^{-7}}{s^2 + 0.0009533s + 3.33e^{-7}} \tag{24}$$

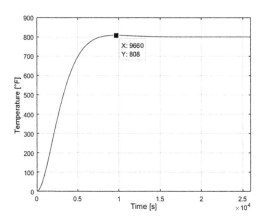

Fig. 5. Response in close loop of the ID controller.

5.2   Conventional Setpoint Tracking Controller

Conventional setpoint tracking controller is programmed based on (14) in a MATLAB script, so that it reacts with fuzzy plant. The lambda values are determined by (10), (11), (12) and (13), depending on the first order model parameters K, τ, tuning gains of the controller K_I, K_D and sampling time $T = 210s$ and are presented below:

$$\lambda_1 = 0.046916426094189$$

$$\lambda_2 = -0.042647360777619$$

$$\lambda_3 = 1.671907802716536$$

$$\lambda_4 = -0.671907802716536$$

Replacing lambda values found in Eq. (14), the control signal for simulation shown in (25) is obtained.

$$u_k = 0.0470e_k - 0.0427e_{k-1} + 1.672u_{k-1} - 0.6719u_{k-2} \tag{25}$$

According to the response of the controller, gains K_I, K_D are modified manually to improve the monitoring of the Heat Treatment Curve and at the same time verifying that the output of the controller is not saturated. The new values found are:

$$K_I = 6.196088364239840e^{-5}$$

$$K_D = 134.4926645158452$$

It is observed that in the setpoint tracking controller, the integral effect was increased so that it reaches the desired temperature values and also the derivative effect to eliminate the response overshooting, generated by integral gain. These values are the maximum allowed for this controller avoiding its saturation and possible damage to the actuators. With the recalculated values, the response of the ID controller with the conventional plant follows the heat treatment curve defined in each of its stages, complying with the established speeds and times, as observed in Fig. 6 (a). The reaction of the designed conventional controller is shown in Fig. 6 (b). In the heating and sustaining stage, the regulation of the control valve increases over time to a maximum value of 99.64% of opening. For the subsequent stages, a proportional closure of the valve is shown at the output of the controller. Both actions are signals achievable by the actuator.

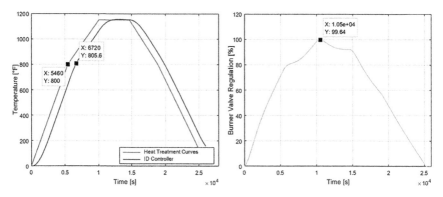

Fig. 6. Response curves: (a) Setpoint tracking during the process stages. (b) ID controller reaction with the plant.

5.3 TSK Fuzzy Controller

The speech universes for the fuzzy controller inputs are:

Error variation $= \begin{bmatrix} -1.5e^4 & 1.5e^4 \end{bmatrix}$

Control signal variation $= \begin{bmatrix} -250 & 100 \end{bmatrix}$

For each of the discourse universes, the sample space is divided with five membership functions (MF). The initial or subsequent singletons of the rules were found by (17) and are observed in Table 2.

Table 2. Initial consequences of the controller (singletons).

		Error Variation				
		MF1	MF2	MF3	MF4	MF5
Controller variation	MF 1	748.9884	690.3930	631.7977	573.2023	514.6069
	MF 2	458.0896	399.4942	340.8988	282.3034	223.7080
	MF 3	167.1908	108.5954	50.0000	−8.5954	−67.1908
	MF 4	−123.7080	−182.3034	−240.8988	−299.4942	−358.0896
	MF 5	−414.6069	−473.2023	−531.7977	−590.3930	−648.9884

The clear output of the controller is calculated by (21). One of the problems of fuzzy controllers is to set the tuning parameters based on manual test and error methods. For this case the design of the fuzzy controller starts from the differential equations of the conventional controller described in (15). The response of the TSK controller is identical and linear to the conventional one and its surface is flat. For the fuzzy control response to be superior to that of the conventional one, optimization of the consequent rules is required (singletons).

5.4 TSK Fuzzy Controller Optimization

Once the descending gradient algorithm was programmed in MATLAB, for the optimization of consequent rules, new values of the singletons were obtained as shown in Table 3.

Table 3. Consequent optimized for the controller (singletons)

		Error Variation				
		FP1	FP2	FP3	FP4	FP5
Controller variation	FP1	748.9884	690.3930	631.7977	573.2023	514.6069
	FP2	458.0896	2655.1274	3482.7209	353.4964	223.7080
	FP3	167.1908	110.1294	50.5570	−10.5127	−67.1908
	FP4	−123.7080	−4973.4768	−6344.0090	−362.8041	−358.0896
	FP5	−414.6069	−473.2023	−531.7977	−590.3930	−648.9884

The algorithm starts with the twenty-five singletons obtained with (17) and the evolution of the optimization algorithm is shown in Fig. 7. The initial value of the defined cost function is:

$$J = 1304.008698812647$$

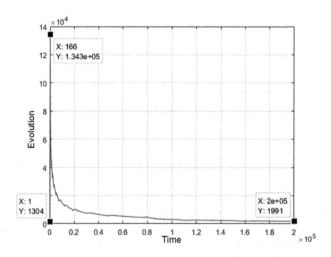

Fig. 7. Evolution curve of the controller optimization algorithm.

While the learning algorithm is running, in the first 166 iterations the cost function begins to increase until the correct optimization direction is found.

$$J_{i166} = 134253.56280e^4$$

From this iteration, the function decreases to 200000 iterations and reaches a final value of:

$$J_{op} = 1961.488335210303$$

The new singletons found with the descending gradient algorithm show a notable increase in four specific rules. In the most notable case, said variation reaches approximately twenty-seven times its initial value as seen in Fig. 8. With the variation of the singletons, the rules of the controller were also modified, resulting in a control surface that presents nonlinearities which is evidenced in Fig. 9.

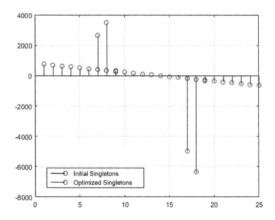

Fig. 8. Singletons controller variations.

With the optimized fuzzy controller, temperature curve monitoring is superior to the conventional one in each of the stages of the heat treatment process, achieving all required times and speeds. Figure 10 (a) shows that TSK fuzzy controller has a higher temperature tracking speed compared to the conventional controller. The ID controller got lower temperature values than those required in the holding stage, but they are accepted since the procedure allows a tolerance of $\pm$ 50°F. Figure 10 (b) shows that controller reaction is achievable in both types of controllers and although the optimized controller output is irregular compared to the conventional controller, it provides better results when tracking the setpoint.

It is notable that the regulation of the TSK fuzzy controller is more responsive in the heating and sustaining stages of the heat treatment process. Finally, in Fig. 11 it is observed that, by learning, the fuzzy TSK controller is able to follow any temperature curve at different times unlike the conventional controller, which does not reach the desired temperature.

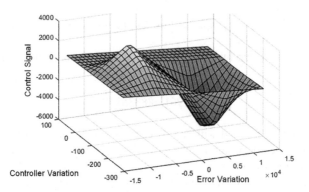

Fig. 9. Optimized controller surface.

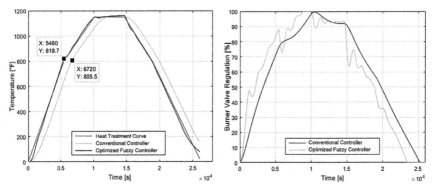

Fig. 10. Response Curves: (a) Controller comparison when tracking a setpoint. (b) Comparison of the controller reaction.

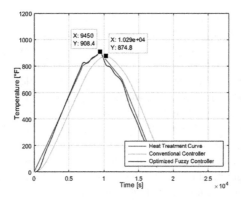

Fig. 11. Comparison of the monitoring curves of the controller setpoint at different times.

6 Conclusions

The structure of the PI + D controller designed for this first-order plant is equivalent to an ID type controller, where the integral constant (Ki) allows to reach the required setpoint and increase the response speed and the derivative constant (Kd) contributes in system stability. On the other hand, the TSK Fuzzy controller is initialized from the correctly tuned conventional controller, so both have the same dynamics, but by optimizing the fuzzy controller singletons with the descending gradient technique and a defined cost function, a better performance in response time and an output that can be achieved by the final actuator is obtained.

Manual process control takes 45% longer than the set time, depending on the steel thickness. Applying the conventional controller, this time decreases to 9% and with the optimized TSK fuzzy controller, it achieves a 4% minimization. The reduction of the time obtained in the welding process carried out by the heat treatment furnace implies a reduction in the consumption of LPG and other resources associated with the process letting the owner minimizes costs for the company. In addition, CO_2 emissions into the atmosphere are reduced, which makes this proposal an ecological solution for industrial processes. As part of the process of continuous improvement, this proposal has been developed to motivate the development of a culture of quality management and environmental management.

Obtaining positive results motivates the authors of this research to emulate the dynamics of an advance-delay compensator, to analyze its performance and to compare it with the controller designed in this proposal as a future work. In addition, it is proposed to focus this optimization process on other industrial processes, since its economic and ecological advantages for the productive sector have been evidenced.

References

1. Leme, R.D., Nunes, A.O., Message Costa, L.B., Silva, D.A.L.: Creating value with less impact: lean, green and eco-efficiency in a metalworking industry towards a cleaner production. J. Clean. Prod. (2018)
2. Mufarroha, F.A., Utaminingrum, F.: Hand gesture recognition using adaptive network based fuzzy inference system and K-nearest neighbor. Int. J. Technol. (2017). https://doi.org/10.14716/ijtech.v8i3.3146
3. Tamilselvan, G.M., Aarthy, P.: Online tuning of fuzzy logic controller using Kalman algorithm for conical tank system. J. Appl. Res. Technol. (2017). https://doi.org/10.1016/j.jart.2017.05.004
4. Rajesh Jesudoss Hynes, N., Kumar, R., Shenbaga Velu, P., Angela Jennifa Sujana, J.: Optimization of friction stud welding process parameters by integrated Grey-Fuzzy logic approach. J. Appl. Res. Technol. (2018). https://doi.org/10.22201/icat.16656423.2018.16.4.724
5. Garcia, C.A., et al.: MPC under IEC-61499 using low-cost devices for oil pipeline system. In: Proceedings - IEEE 16th International Conference on Industrial Informatics, INDIN 2018, pp. 659–664 (2018). https://doi.org/10.1109/INDIN.2018.8472094

6. Zimit, A.Y., Yap, H.J., Hamza, M.F., Siradjuddin, I., Hendrik, B., Herawan, T.: Modelling and experimental analysis two-wheeled self balance robot using PID controller. In: Gervasi, O., et al. (eds.) ICCSA 2018. LNCS, vol. 10961, pp. 683–698. Springer, Cham (2018). https://doi.org/10.1007/978-3-319-95165-2_48

7. Ortiz, J.P., Minchala, L.I., Reinoso, M.J.: Nonlinear robust H-infinity PID controller for the multivariable system quadrotor. IEEE Lat. Am. Trans. (2016). https://doi.org/10.1109/TLA. 2016.7459596

8. Buele, J., et al.: Interactive system for monitoring and control of a flow station using LabVIEW. In: Rocha, Á., Guarda, T. (eds.) ICITS 2018. AISC, vol. 721, pp. 583–592. Springer, Cham (2018). https://doi.org/10.1007/978-3-319-73450-7_55

9. García, C.A., et al.: Fuzzy control implementation in low cost CPPS devices. In: IEEE International Conference on Multisensor Fusion and Integration for Intelligent Systems, pp. 162–167 (2017). https://doi.org/10.1109/MFI.2017.8170423

10. Buele, J., Varela-Aldás, J., Santamaría, M., Soria, A., Espinoza, J.: Comparison between fuzzy control and MPC algorithms implemented in low-cost embedded devices. In: Rocha, Á., Ferrás, C., Montenegro Marin, C.E., Medina García, V.H. (eds.) ICITS 2020. AISC, vol. 1137, pp. 429–438. Springer, Cham (2020). https://doi.org/10.1007/978-3-030-40690-5_42

11. Wei, G., Alsaadi, F.E., Hayat, T., Alsaedi, A.: A linear assignment method for multiple criteria decision analysis with hesitant fuzzy sets based on fuzzy measure. Int. J. Fuzzy Syst. 19(3), 607–614 (2016). https://doi.org/10.1007/s40815-016-0177-x

12. Salem, M., Mora, A.M., Merelo, J.J., García-Sánchez, P.: Evolving a TORCS modular fuzzy driver using genetic algorithms. In: Sim, K., Kaufmann, P. (eds.) EvoApplications 2018. LNCS, vol. 10784, pp. 342–357. Springer, Cham (2018). https://doi.org/10.1007/978-3-319-77538-8_24

13. Ansari, Z., Ghazizadeh, R., Shokhmzan, Z.: Gradient descent approach to secure localization for underwater wireless sensor networks. In: 2016 24th Iranian Conference on Electrical Engineering, ICEE 2016 (2016). https://doi.org/10.1109/IranianCEE.2016.7585498

14. Duarte, J., Orozco, W.: Optimización de sintonización de controladores PID bajo el criterio IAE aplicados a procesos térmicos. Rev. Fac. Ing. 5, 35–45 (2015)

15. Campos, J., Jaramillo, S., Morales, L., Camacho, O., Chavez, D.: PD + i Fuzzy Controller optimized by PSO applied to a variable dead time process. In: 2018 IEEE 3rd Ecuador Technical Chapters Meeting, ETCM 2018 (2018). https://doi.org/10.1109/ETCM.2018. 8580277

16. Díaz-Álvarez, A., Serradilla-García, F., Jiménez-Alonso, F., Talavera-Muñoz, E., Olaverri-Monreal, C.: Fuzzy controller inference via gradient descent to model the longitudinal behavior on real drivers. In: IEEE Intelligent Vehicles Symposium, Proceedings (2019). https://doi.org/10.1109/IVS.2019.8814180

17. Sakalli, A., Beke, A., Kumbasar, T.: Gradient descent and extended kalman filter based self-tuning interval type-2 fuzzy PID controllers. In: 2016 IEEE International Conference on Fuzzy Systems, FUZZ-IEEE 2016 (2016)

Prototype System of Geolocation Educational Public Transport Through Google Maps API

Franklin W. Salazar[1] , Hernán Naranjo-Ávalos[1],
Jorge Buele[1,2(✉)] , Marco J. Pintag[1], Édgar R. Buenaño[3] ,
Cristina Reinoso[1] , Pilar Urrutia-Urrutia[1] ,
and José Varela-Aldás[2]

[1] Universidad Técnica de Ambato, Ambato 180103, Ecuador
{fw.salazar,hf.naranjo,ci.reinoso,
elsapurrutia}@uta.edu.ec, jorgebuele@uti.edu.ec,
jhofre.pintag@gmail.com
[2] SISAu Research Group, Universidad Tecnológica Indoamérica,
Ambato 180212, Ecuador
{jorgebuele,josevarela}@uti.edu.ec
[3] Escuela Superior Politécnica de Chimborazo, Riobamba 060155, Ecuador
edgarbl7l@gmail.com

Abstract. Urban traffic complications in most underdeveloped countries and congestion in all metropolitan areas has become a daily problem with a difficult solution. Disorganized mobility of drivers and pedestrians along with the increase in travel time, non-compliance with schedules, air pollution and intolerable sound levels, have harmful effects on human health. Therefore, this research describes a geolocation system of urban transport through a mobile application developed on the Xamarin platform. Drivers send the latitude and longitude points when starting a route, this data will be sent to the SQL SERVER online database server, using the SmarterASP.NET platform. By developing the geolocation system in ASP.NET, the coordinates are available to users in an interval of 5 s. The developed interface shows a location map, where the route in real time is presented. It also shows the administration of users, drivers, buses, assignment of routes, assignment of buses and registration of static routes. Being a prototype system, the university transport system has been taken as an object of study to corroborate its correct operation with the respective experimental tests. Satisfaction surveys have also been carried out on a group of 300 people, among students and university teachers and their validation is carried out through the Technological Acceptance Model (TAM). To interpret the results, Kendall Tau-b correlation analysis was used, obtaining positive correlation values with a high significance value.

Keywords: Public transport · Cloud computing · Databases · Global positioning system · Smart cities

© Springer Nature Switzerland AG 2020
O. Gervasi et al. (Eds.): ICCSA 2020, LNCS 12254, pp. 367–382, 2020.
https://doi.org/10.1007/978-3-030-58817-5_28

1 Introduction

Throughout history, the imbalance between developed and developing countries has been latent, as well as corruption and lack of government measures [1–3]. In addition, it must be added the excessive population increase in the poorest regions and the gradual aging that represents a deficient technological growth [4]. All this stuff has caused the increase in inequality in Latin America, the quality of life reduction and a deficient economic and social development, with serious consequences in cultural and environmental aspects [5]. Population growth expectations predict an accelerated increase in the urban population, so by 2020 it is expected to exceed 500 million[1]. That is why world governments seek to have a prospective vision of the situation and carry out future planning on sustainable models of citizen mobility [6–8].

People daily movement and the development of their activities are facilitated by using public transport [7, 9, 10]. Therefore, it is expected that such transport is ready for use when necessary and is in good condition on the journey from the point of origin to the destination. Given human needs, several types of land, sea and air transport have been developed which have evolved according to the social and economic conditions of the environment [9]. Within the metropolis, most common transport is the bus, a vehicle that makes a preset route through defined stops and can transport a large number of passengers [11]. Thanks to new technologies and advances in computing, transport administration is easier by using management programs, office applications or geolocation applications, as well as online geolocation which is a term that has gained great importance since the appearance of the Internet and has become a service that can be offered for various applications [12–14]. The Global Positioning System (GPS) was developed last century for military uses, although it was later used for civil use, which combined with the use of internet represents an important current tool [15].

2 Related Works

Problems in the efficient administration of urban transport have affected several cities of the terrestrial globe. It has led to the development of several studies in this regard. Creating efficient public transport systems that attract users is a challenging task in contexts where public transport control is divided between several actors. [16] presents a systematic review of several works with a focus on the development of understanding, on how to improve conditions for public transport. These articles allow us to understand the critical challenges in planning and implementation of measures to increase travel in public transport, how to face the latent problematic and, advantages and disadvantages of different labor practices.

The study of [15] presents the city reality of Dhaka, one of the largest and most overpopulated in the world, where most people depend on public transport for internal mobilization. Bus is the main public transport but the gap between supply and demand is large, since the number of buses is low compared to the number of passengers.

---

[1] https://population.un.org/wup/Publications/Files/WUP2018-Report.pdf.

In addition, there is no respect for preference seats such as those for pregnant women, older adults and people with disabilities, since passengers compete to get into the units. That is why the initiative of the Indian government is described, to generate a culture of respect and friendly attitude between passengers and bus staff, as well as the attachment to morality to solve their inconveniences when using the public transport. Another factor to consider is the definition of schedules in public transport, so in [16] a heuristic approach is shown to improve this condition and maximize passenger service while respecting an operating cost budget. The results of this case study in The Netherlands indicate that including line planning modifications allows to obtain schedules with a higher passenger service compared to the use of schedule modifications.

The management of public transport through technological platforms has been applied in several environments, as can be seen in [17]. Here we briefly describe the implementation of a new cooperative system for the location of buses with BLE devices (Bluetooth low energy). BLE devices are on a bus and have a GPS receiver, the developed applications are compatible with the participants' smartphones and a cloud service is established. This interactive bus location system is a demo version and therefore does not present relevant results. For its part in [18], a bus location system is developed, to eliminate user concerns about the arrival time of the units at the various stops in the city of Nonoichi. In this study it has been proposed to use Wi-SUN and LoRa; the first with a short transmission distance and requires many repeaters, while the second reduces the number of repeaters by 75%. Connectivity tests are carried out to support this proposal, demonstrating that LoRa offers better benefits at a lower economic cost.

Considering the importance and applicability of the use of online geolocation in transport management, the objective of this paper is to show the evaluation results of the tracking different routes of a bus line belonging to a state university. This allows users to know the location of buses in real time and to better organize their time when performing their school and social activities. Tests carried out allow us to demonstrate the usefulness of this system and, through surveys, know the user satisfaction. To measure the acceptance of this proposal and the impact produced at social level, a quantitative evaluation is performed using TAM. This work is composed of five sections and as an opening is the introduction to the subject in the first section. Section 2 presents related works and Sect. 3 the implementation of the proposal. The analysis of results and conclusions are described in Sects. 4 and 5 respectively.

3   Implementation

Technology development in smartphones (main hardware components of the system) and the good features they offer, allow greater interaction with the final user, better performance and the expansion of this proposal. Once identification, selection and acquisition stage of the main elements is completed, the design of the software architecture used is presented. As shown in Fig. 1, the process begins with online coordinate storage, where routes can be viewed in real time. On the other hand, there is the system administration, which includes: selection of users, drivers, buses, route assignment, bus assignment and registration of static routes and their design, all of which can be seen in Fig. 2.

Once the driver enters the application through an authentication process, he will start the assigned route. The bus positioning points will be sent to the server every 5 s. This time interval is established in the mobile application and can be parameterized. At the same time, users who use the application with said profile will be able to visualize in real time the route of the transport units that are active at that time, clearly identifying the route of their interest.

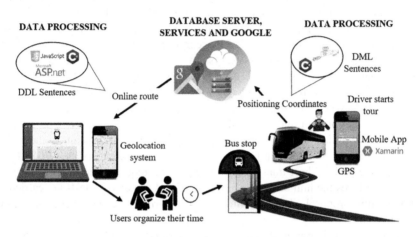

Fig. 1. General system diagram.

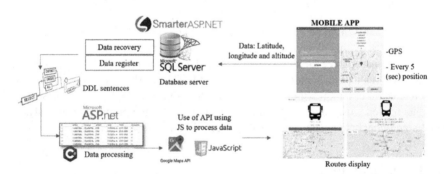

Fig. 2. Architecture used for online coordinate storage and visualization of routes in real time.

3.1   Database Model

The logical structure of the relational model that will be used is described in Fig. 3, including the relationships and limitations that allow determining the way of storing data and how it is accessed. By defining this model, the assignment of different profiles according to the user is enabled, facilitating the management and control of the information and the generation of reports on the routes offered.

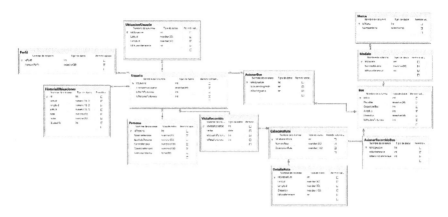

Fig. 3. Relational model of system database.

3.2   Web System Development

The architecture developed for this application is presented in Fig. 4, where the separation of the presentation, business, messaging and data layers is visualized. The purpose of the model developed is to achieve code reuse, ease of standardization, data transport, dependency between layers, decoupled code and ease of application maintenance.

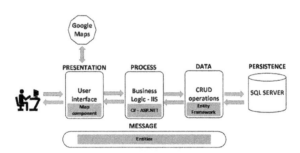

Fig. 4. Layered architecture.

The presentation layer is responsible for interacting with the client or end user, i.e. the interface in which all control and display options are presented. This layer communicates with the business or intermediate layer, responsible for implementing all business rules and dictates the application management guidelines. It also will maintain a dialogue with the data layer, which will handle the data persistence towards the engine and provide the response data towards the presentation layer. In this interface simple and intuitive forms have been developed, which allow the handling of several profiles, transport units, routes and reports, as show in Program code 1.

The main window contains all the established routes so; the user can choose the one of his convenience. In each case, a new window is displayed where the main parameters of this route are detailed, as can be seen in Fig. 5 (a). Routes shown are obtained from database server through DDL sentences, whose manipulation depends on the layer architecture described previously. In order to view the routes online, the user must enter the route of interest, which will be presented if it is active. Figure 5 (b) shows the complete route made by a conductor through an interface designed, as well as the assigned transport unit. One marker is located at the starting point and another at the arrival point. These data define positioning points in both latitude and longitude, thus managing to trace the entire path through the streets in which it is mobilized. Bus location is shown on a map with a marker and within 5 s its position will change as the bus moves. With this information the user can organize better their mobilization time in order to reach the transport at a desired time and fulfill their academic and social activities.

Program code 1. Management of Google Maps API within the Forms through JavaScript.

```
<script type="text/javascript">
function initialize() {
      var primeraposicion =<%=RecuperarValoresPrimerPosicion() %>;
   // Map settings
   var mapProp = {
      zoom: 15,
      center: primeraposicion,   };
   // Adding the map to the Google Map id tag
   var map = new google.maps.Map(document.getElementById("map_canvas"), mapProp);
   // Route coordinates
      var flightPlanCoordinates = <%=RecuperarValores() %>;
      var ultimaposicion =<%=RecuperarUltimaPosicion() %>;
      var marker = new google.maps.Marker({
        position: ultimaposicion,
          map: map      });
      var marker1 = new google.maps.Marker({
        position: primeraposicion,
          map: map      });
   // Route settings (coordinates, line color, etc.)
   var flightPath = new google.maps.Polyline({
   path: flightPlanCoordinates,
   geodesic: true,
   strokeColor: '#FF0000',
   strokeOpacity: 1.0,
   strokeWeight: 2,
   travelMode: google.maps.TravelMode.DRIVING});
   // Creating the route on the map
   flightPath.setMap(map);   }
   // Initializing the map when the page loads
   google.maps.event.addDomListener(window, 'load', initialize);
   </script>
```

(a)   (b)

Fig. 5. (a) Form for viewing an established route. (b) Form for viewing a route in real time.

Google Maps API was used within the forms where the management of maps is indicated, data recovered from business layer is used through the JavaScript by following the process:

- Obtain a key from the Google Maps API in: https://cloud.google.com/maps-platform/maps/?hl=es
- Load the JavaScript library from the Google Maps API.
- Management of the methods offered by the API through JavaScript.

The API provides functions that help to manipulate the data obtained from database server and after a conversion of the information, it can be displayed on a map or in a table. Within the forms where the sending or retrieval of data is planned, methods that interact with the presentation layer were performed, as shown in Program code 2.

Program code 2. Method for registering a new user, sending and retrieving data from the Business layer.

```
private void registrarNuevoUsuario()
  { // Register Person
    Persona personaNueva = new Persona();
    personaNueva.NombrePersona = TextBoxNombre.Text;
    personaNueva.ApellidoPersona = TextBoxApellido.Text;
    personaNueva.CorreoPersona = TextBoxCorreo.Text;
    personaNueva.TelefonoPersona = TextBoxTelefono.Text;
    personaNueva.DireccionPersona = TextBoxDireccion.Text;
    personaNueva = PersonaNegocio.GuardarPersonaNegocio(personaNueva);
    persona = personaNueva;
    // Register User
    Perfil perfil = new Perfil();
    perfil = PerfilNegocio. devolverPersonaxNombre (DropDownListPer-
fil.SelectedItem.ToString());
    nuevo.IdPerfilPertenece = perfil.IdPerfil;
    nuevo.ContraseniaUsuario = TextBoxContrasenia.Text;
    nuevo.IdUsuarioPertenece = persona.IdPersona;
    nuevo = UsuarioNegocio.GuardarUsuarioNegocio(nuevo);
    ClientScript.RegisterStartupScript(GetType(), "mostrarmensaje", "usuarioRegistrado();",
    true);
  }
```

The business layer is responsible for the logical processing of the application. In this layer the user's requirements are received and the responses are sent after the process while all the rules that must be followed are established. Therefore, methods were developed that communicate with both the presentation layer and data layer. Such methods are called from the presentation layer to transport data from forms, so this layer is the responsible to do the call to methods belonging to the data layer with which it wants to communicate.

The data layer is responsible for accessing, storing and retrieving all system information. It is here that connections to the database server are implemented, stored procedures are invoked and information persistence is managed from the business layer. Therefore, methods were developed that contribute to the connection of DML or DLL with the server located on the SmartASPNET platform, as shown in Program code 3.

The entity layer allows the transport of custom classes through all layers that are part of the architecture. This layer benefits data mobility, maintaining the same communication criteria in the project, regardless of the system's data access technology.

Program code 3. Method in data layer for user profile storage.

```
public static Persona GuardarPersonaDatos(Persona personaNueva)
{ try {
    SqlConnection connection = new SqlConnection(Settings1.Default.Conexion);
    connection.Open();
    SqlCommand cmd = new SqlCommand();
    cmd.Connection = connection;
    cmd.CommandType = System.Data.CommandType.Text;
    // DML statement to register a person on the database server
    cmd.CommandText = @"INSERT INTO [dbo].[Persona]
    ([NombrePersona]
    ,[ApellidoPersona]
    ,[CorreoPersona]
    ,[DireccionPersona]
    ,[TelefonoPersona])
    VALUES
    (@NombrePersona,@ApellidoPersona,@CorreoPersona,@DireccionPersona,@TelefonoPer
sona);SELECT SCOPE_IDENTITY()";
    cmd.Parameters.AddWithValue("@NombrePersona", personaNueva.NombrePersona);
    cmd.Parameters.AddWithValue("@ApellidoPersona", personaNueva.ApellidoPersona);
    cmd.Parameters.AddWithValue("@CorreoPersona", personaNueva.CorreoPersona);
    cmd.Parameters.AddWithValue("@DireccionPersona", personaNueva.DireccionPersona);
    cmd.Parameters.AddWithValue("@TelefonoPersona", personaNueva.TelefonoPersona);
    var idpersona = Convert.ToInt32(cmd.ExecuteScalar());
    personaNueva.IdPersona = idpersona;
    return personaNueva; }
  catch (SqlException ex) { var error = ex.Message; }
  return personaNueva; }
```

3.3 Mobile Application Development

Due to the advantages that current smart devices have and the ease of using the built-in GPS, a mobile application is developed using Xamarin[2] [19]. This mobile application was developed based on the model presented in Fig. 6, using ASP.NET with the programming language C #. Bootstrap was used to design the interface, allowing to work with CSS and JavaScript together.

The main screen can be seen in Fig. 7 (a), where the user can choose between creating a new account or registering with an existing account. If a new record is selected, it is directed to a form for entering information and selecting a profile. (Figure 7 (b)). If the user has a registered account, it will be validated through an authentication process by sending a security code to the user's email, and once registered, the application will be deployed based on the profiles associated with this account (administrator, driver or user). The option for password recovery is also presented, when user does not remember it.

Fig. 6. Model of the mobile application.

(a)   (b)

Fig. 7. Application screens: (a) Main window. (b) Registration form.

To save the positioning online, the driver will use the mobile application, with a procedure similar to the one followed in the web application, i.e. profile validation will be done with a previously registered email and password. The Program code 4 allows the acquisition of bus positioning data (latitude and longitude), time and date belonging

---

[2] https://dotnet.microsoft.com/apps/xamarin.

to a specific driver, to be sent to the storage method. Through this data the user can view the route online through the web system and the mobile application. Based on the Program code 5 you can obtain the real-time tour, as well as the positioning coordinates. All this data will be stored in the database that is hosted on the SmartASPNET server. To achieve this process the Xam.Plugin.Geolocator library was used, which is available in the package manager: NuGet.

Program code 4. Management of Google Maps API within the Forms through JavaScript.

```
public static HistorialUbicacionEntidad GuardarHistorialUbica-
cion(HistorialUbicacionEntidad historialUbicacion)
    { try {
        SqlConnection connection = new SqlConnection(url);
        connection.Open();
        SqlCommand cmd = new SqlCommand();
        cmd.Connection = connection;
// DML statement to register the coordinates on the database server
        cmd.CommandText = @"INSERT INTO [dbo].[HistorialUbicaciones]
                    ([latitud]
                    ,[longitud]
                    ,[altitud]
                    ,[hora]
                    ,[fecha]
                    ,[id_usuario])
                    VALUES
                    (@latitud
                    ,@longitud
                    ,@altitud
                    ,@hora
                    ,@fecha
                    ,@id_usuario);SELECT SCOPE_IDENTITY()";
        cmd.Parameters.AddWithValue("@latitud", historialUbicacion.Latitud);
        cmd.Parameters.AddWithValue("@longitud", historialUbicacion.Longitud);
        cmd.Parameters.AddWithValue("@altitud", historialUbicacion.Altitud);
        cmd.Parameters.AddWithValue("@hora", historialUbicacion.Hora);
        cmd.Parameters.AddWithValue("@fecha", historialUbicacion.Fecha);
        cmd.Parameters.AddWithValue("@id_usuario", historialUbicacion.IdUsuario);
        cmd.CommandType = System.Data.CommandType.Text;
        var id = Convert.ToInt32(cmd.ExecuteScalar());
        historialUbicacion.Id = id;
        connection.Close();
        return historialUbicacion;
    } catch (SqlException ex)
    { Console.Write("" + ex);
        return null;    } }
```

Program code 5. Method for obtaining real-time coordinates in an interval of 5 seconds

```
private async void IniciarLocalizacion()
{  // Instantiate position variable
   var locator = CrossGeolocator.Current;
   locator.DesiredAccuracy = 100;
   if (locator.IsGeolocationAvailable)
   {  if (locator.IsGeolocationEnabled)
      {  if (!locator.IsListening)
         {  // Set time to obtain coordinates
            await locator.StartListeningAsync(new TimeSpan(0, 0, 5), 0.30);  }
            locator.PositionChanged += (cambio, arg) =>
      {  // Get the coordinates
         var loc = arg.Position;
         lat.Text = loc.Latitude.ToString();
         lon.Text = loc.Longitude.ToString();
         altura.Text = loc.Altitude.ToString();
         // Instantiate the method of saving position in the database
         CambiarDePosicionMapa(loc.Latitude, loc.Longitude);
         GuardarHistorialUbicacion(loc);  };  }
      else{
         await DisplayAlert("Aviso", "Por favor active el  GPS", "Ok");  }  }  }
```

4   Result Analysis

Once the implementation is finished, this prototype system is used by users belonging to a university campus. When a user enters the web platform or mobile application to visualize a specific route, the server counts this information by the use of an accumulator and presents it in a tabulated way as can be seen in Fig. 8. In the same way, the analysis of the concurrence points between routes made by drivers was carried out, thus determining the busiest road traveled. This result was performed through the use of heat maps, which is offered by the Google Maps API as shown in Fig. 9.

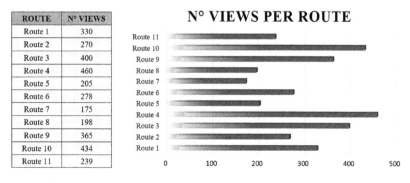

ROUTE	N° VIEWS
Route 1	330
Route 2	270
Route 3	400
Route 4	460
Route 5	205
Route 6	278
Route 7	175
Route 8	198
Route 9	365
Route 10	434
Route 11	239

N° VIEWS PER ROUTE

Fig. 8. Statistical data obtained from the route most viewed by users.

In Fig. 10, it is shown a screen developed with the purpose of displaying reports based on an analysis of the crowdest points by drivers when making the established routes, this data allows a better administration of the geolocation system. With these reports the usability of the system and the exact number of users who have used the platform can be determined, differentiating their profile: driver, administrator or normal user.

The quantitative acceptance assessment (surveys) has been applied to 300 users and has allowed us to obtain relevant information about this experiment. 51% of the participants are female, 95% are students and 86% do not have their own or family vehicle for mobilization. 76% live in urban sectors and the remaining 24% in rural areas and other surrounding towns; 89% live in areas greater than 10 km away from the establishment of higher education. From an ethnic perspective, 79% of the surveyed group is considered of mixed race.

Fig. 9. Heat map obtained from the routes performed.

To measure the acceptance of the application, it was proposed to carry out a quantitative evaluation. In this sense, the Technological Acceptance Model (TAM) was developed by Davis and has become one of the most popular models for predicting the use and acceptance of technology and information systems [20]. According to Davis, the fundamental objective of TAM is to identify the factors that determine the use of Information and Communication Technologies (ICT) from the user's perspective. TAM suggests that perceived utility and perceived ease of use are determining factors in an individual's intention when using a system. The relevance and impact of the TAM results, in the aforementioned studies, support the relevance and effectiveness of this methodology [21–23].

Based on the criteria of the TAM model [24], it can be defined the level of acceptance that this proposal has by users, its description is made below.

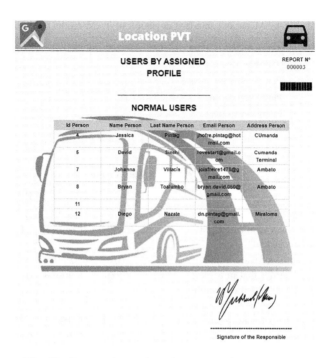

Fig. 10. Report of users issued by the Geolocation System

- The perceived ease of use when using the tool positively affects the attitude of use of the application.
- The application ease of use promotes its implementation as part of the information management of an efficient transport service.
- The feedback of the application information is strongly correlated with the optimization of the users' time with respect to the transport service routes. The user-friendly of the map allows intuitive access to georeferenced information.
- The interactive map is a fundamental component of the proposal and promotes the future use of the tool in the analyzed segment.

The values of the criteria in correspondence with their means and standard deviations are shown in Table 1. Considering a Likert scale with values from 1 to 5, its approval has been corroborated.

Using a Kolmogorov-Smirnov normality test it was shown that results of the technological acceptance criteria do not follow a normal distribution, with a p-value of 0.00. Therefore, the data analysis was based on a non-parametric correlation using Kendall's Tau-b. The resulting correlation between the elements was significantly positive as recorded in Table 2.

Table 1. Mean and standard deviation of TAM model criteria

TAM model criteria	Mean	Standard deviation
Attitude towards use	4.62	0.32
Perceived ease of use	4.38	0.61
Perceived profit	4.45	0.58
Intention to use	4.36	0.57

Table 2. Kendall's Tau-b table

N = 300		P1	P2	P3	P4
1. Do you think that when using the app for recovery information about transport units would you be satisfied?	CC	,527**	,203**	,190**	,244**
	AS	0,000	0,000	0,000	0,000
2. When analyzing the software prototype proposed, do you consider that in a short time you can become an expert user in this app?	CC	0,070	,227**	,124*	,173**
	AS	0,200	0,000	0,023	0,002
3. When analyzing the software prototype proposed, do you think that its design facilitates its use?	CC	,233**	0,084	,386**	,276**
	AS	0,000	0,104	0,000	0,000
4. Is the access to information through the map easy for you?	CC	,212**	0,087	,278**	,307**
	AS	0,000	0,094	0,000	0,000
5. Does the map component highlight the value of the information that is managed in the application?	CC	,244**	,205**	,314**	1,000
	AS	0,000	0,000	0,000	
6. Do the generated reports highlight the value of the information that is managed in the application?	CC	,239**	0,075	,408**	,130*
	AS	0,000	0,140	0,000	0,014
7. Is the usefulness of the map significantly high?	CC	,203**	,155**	,316**	,397**
	AS	0,000	0,003	0,000	0,000
8. Would you suggest the use of the application for the management of transport service information?	CC	,154**	,426**	,302**	,378**
	AS	0,004	0,000	0,000	0,000
9. Would you use the application for better time management with respect to the transport service?	CC	,204**	0,076	,609**	,299**
	AS	0,000	0,142	0,000	0,000

Abbreviations: P1: Software prototype considers this to be easy to use. P2: Prototype does not require much effort to use. P3: Access to information in an easy way. P4: The map component helps to understand the information. CC: Correlation coefficient. AS: Asymptotic Significance (Bilateral)

5   Conclusions

The prototype system that has been developed has a high functionality since it allows users to reduce waiting periods with uncertainty, organize their time more efficiently, access to information reports and interactive map presentation. Based on the results obtained, it has been possible to show that there are routes with greater concurrence than others, which demonstrates the need to take actions, such as planning to incorporate other transport units on these routes due to the large number of passengers. By using heat maps, points with the highest traffic can be established and thus suggest a possible change of streets when making the route, reducing the time taken to complete the entire route and improving the traffic congestion of the city.

The study shows quantitatively that university users (teachers and students) agree with the use of this type of applications. In this way, transport service routes and reporting to the authorities are better managed. TAM evaluation results allowed to confirm that the ease of use, the intention of use and the utility are highly correlated with the tool handling. Although this application has been tested with a state university, it is a pilot, for its good performance it has been included as part of the metropolitan management system, which will allow obtaining new results as a future job and being the basis of future research in Latin America.

References

1. Barragán-Ocaña, A., del Carmen del-Valle-Rivera, M.: Rural development and environmental protection through the use of biofertilizers in agriculture: an alternative for underdeveloped countries? Technol. Soc. (2016). https://doi.org/10.1016/j.techsoc.2016.06.001
2. Sankowska, P.J.: Smart government: an European approach toward building sustainable and secure cities of tomorrow. Int. J. Technol. (2018). https://doi.org/10.14716/ijtech.v9i7.2517
3. Buele, Jorge, et al.: Interactive system for monitoring and control of a flow station using LabVIEW. In: Rocha, Álvaro, Guarda, Teresa (eds.) ICITS 2018. AISC, vol. 721, pp. 583–592. Springer, Cham (2018). https://doi.org/10.1007/978-3-319-73450-7_55
4. Schmidt, K., Sandner, P.: Solving Challenges in Developing Countries with Blockchain Technology. FSBC Work. Pap. (2017)
5. Senra, H., et al.: Health-related quality of life and depression in a sample of Latin American adults with rheumatoid arthritis. Int. J. Rheum. Dis. (2017). https://doi.org/10.1111/1756-185X.12412
6. Jiang, S., Ferreira, J., Gonzalez, M.C.: Activity-based human mobility patterns inferred from mobile phone data: a case study of Singapore. IEEE Trans. Big Data (2016). https://doi.org/10.1109/tbdata.2016.2631141
7. Jiang, S., Guan, W., Zhang, W., Chen, X., Yang, L.: Human mobility in space from three modes of public transportation. Phys. A Stat. Mech. Appl. (2017)
8. Abayomi-Alli, Olusola, et al.: Smart ticketing for academic campus shuttle transportation system based on RFID. In: Jain, V., Chaudhary, G., Taplamacioglu, M.C., Agarwal, M.S. (eds.) Advances in Data Sciences, Security and Applications. LNEE, vol. 612, pp. 237–252. Springer, Singapore (2020). https://doi.org/10.1007/978-981-15-0372-6_18

9. Song, X., Hiroshi, K., Ryosuke, S.: DeepTransport: prediction and simulation of human mobility and transportation mode at a citywide level. In: IJCAI International Joint Conference on Artificial Intelligence (2016)
10. Hansen, S., Too, E., Le, T.: Lessons learned from a cancelled urban transport project in a developing country: The importance of the front-end planning phase. Int. J. Technol. 9, 898–909 (2018). https://doi.org/10.14716/ijtech.v9i5.1559
11. Bilgin, B.E., Baktir, S., Gungor, V.C.: A novel data collection mechanism for smart grids using public transportation buses. Comput. Stand. Interfaces (2016). https://doi.org/10.1016/j.csi.2016.04.003
12. García González, J.: El resurgir de los mapas. La importancia del « dónde » y del pensamiento espacial. Ería Rev. Cuatrimest. Geogr. (2017)
13. Buele, J., Franklin Salazar, L., Altamirano, S., Abigail Aldás, R., Urrutia-Urrutia, P.: Platform and mobile application to provide information on public transport using a low-cost embedded device. RISTI - Rev. Iber. Sist. e Tecnol. Inf. 476–489 (2019)
14. Abigail Aldás, R., Buele, J., Franklin Salazar, L., Soria, A., Manzano, S.: Integrated information system for urban public transport. Int. J. Eng. Adv. Technol. 8, 97–102 (2019)
15. Soe, N.C., Thein, T.L.L., Aung, T.: GPS tracking and traffic monitoring system in urban transportation. In: 2018 IEEE 7th Global Conference on Consumer Electronics, GCCE 2018 (2018). https://doi.org/10.1109/GCCE.2018.8574509
16. Hrelja, R., Khan, J., Pettersson, F.: How to create efficient public transport systems? A systematic review of critical problems and approaches for addressing the problems. Transp. Policy (2019). https://doi.org/10.1016/j.tranpol.2019.10.012
17. Tanaka, K., Naito, K.: Demo: implementation of cooperative bus location system with BLE devices and smartphones. In: 2017 14th IEEE Annual Consumer Communications and Networking Conference, CCNC 2017 (2017). https://doi.org/10.1109/CCNC.2017.7983180
18. Tanaka, M.S., Miyanishi, Y., Toyota, M., Murakami, T., Hirazakura, R., Itou, T.: A study of bus location system using LoRa: Bus location system for community bus "notty." In: 2017 IEEE 6th Global Conference on Consumer Electronics, GCCE 2017 (2017). https://doi.org/10.1109/GCCE.2017.8229279
19. Hermes, D., Hermes, D.: Mobile development using Xamarin. In: Xamarin Mobile Application Development (2015). https://doi.org/10.1007/978-1-4842-0214-2_1
20. Park, E., Baek, S., Ohm, J., Chang, H.J.: Determinants of player acceptance of mobile social network games: an application of extended technology acceptance model. Telemat. Inform. 31, 3–15 (2014). https://doi.org/10.1016/j.tele.2013.07.001
21. Alenazy, W.M., Mugahed Al-Rahmi, W., Khan, M.S.: Validation of TAM model on social media use for collaborative learning to enhance collaborative authoring. IEEE Access 7, 71550–71562 (2019). https://doi.org/10.1109/ACCESS.2019.2920242
22. Sari, R.Y., Budi, I., Sandhyaduhita, P.I.: Factors influencing users' intention to use E-budgeting in ministry of public works and housing using technology acceptance (TAM) approach. In: Proceedings - 2018 International Conference on Applied Science and Technology, iCAST 2018, pp. 680–686 (2018). https://doi.org/10.1109/iCAST1.2018.8751615
23. Syarifudin, G., Abbas, B.S., Heriyati, P.: TAM approach on E-commerce of aircraft ticket sales on consumer purchase intention. In: 2018 6th International Conference on Cyber and IT Service Management, CITSM 2018 (2019). https://doi.org/10.1109/CITSM.2018.8674357
24. Davis, F.D.: Perceived usefulness, perceived ease of use, and user acceptance of information technology. MIS Q. Manag. Inf. Syst. (1989). https://doi.org/10.2307/249008

Smartcitysysml: A SysML Profile for Smart Cities Applications

Layse Santos Souza[1]([✉])(iD), Sanjay Misra[2]([✉])(iD), and Michel S. Soares[1]([✉])(iD)

[1] Computing Department, Federal University of Sergipe, São Cristóvão, Brazil
laysesantossouza@gmail.com, michel@dcomp.ufs.br
[2] Center of ICT/ICE Research, Covenant University, Ota, Nigeria
sanjay.misra@covenantuniversity.edu.ng

Abstract. Current infrastructures in modern cities are highly dependent on complex software-intensive systems, which are composed of many elements, including software, sensors, actuators, and processes. Citizens and managers are also important stakeholders in these systems, as they provide data, provide and retrieve information and also manage the many systems that control the city infrastructures'. UML has been often considered for designing these types of systems, mostly with focus only on designing the software elements of the system. However, these infrastructures systems are composed of many more elements than software, including processes, constraints, sensors, networks, laws and further documents. SysML is a UML profile that has gained attention in past years, as SysML also models systems elements that are not software. In this paper, the main idea is to describe a SysML profile for modeling smart cities applications, which is useful as it specifies common elements of a city as native elements of system design. The profile, named SmartCitySysML, extended from SysML Requirements, Sequence and Block Definition diagrams in order to model system and software elements for smart cities. Design of a road traffic control system regarding a group of intersections is used as a case study. As a result, SmartCitySysML facilitates the use of common elements in smart city infrastructures and provides a visual representation to assess quality of diagrams from a practical point of view.

Keywords: Smart cities · SysML · Road traffic control system

1 Introduction

Modern life in cities is highly dependent on infrastructures such as road, rail and air traffic, energy, water and waste supply. These infrastructures are highly demanded by citizens and organizations, and their design and maintenance are crucial for our daily activities. These infrastructures present high complexity and demand, which leads to the necessity of applying Information and Communication Technologies and Processes for their design, control and management.

© Springer Nature Switzerland AG 2020
O. Gervasi et al. (Eds.): ICCSA 2020, LNCS 12254, pp. 383–397, 2020.
https://doi.org/10.1007/978-3-030-58817-5_29

The term smart city generally refers to the search and identification of smart solutions that allow modern cities to improve the quality of services provided to citizens. Giffinger et al. [7] state that a smart city has a good prospective performance in the economy, improves governance and mobility, and provides better life for citizens.

Currently, a large number of modeling languages are used for modeling software systems that are responsible for controlling cities infrastructures'. For instance, UML has been applied in [10] for developing a sewerage system using UML Activity diagrams and then converting them into Non-deterministic Finite Automata (NFA) in which a junction is represented by a state, and flow of water is represented as a transition. The proposed UML and automata-based models are then transformed into a formal model using TLA+ which has effective model checking capability. In another example, in Bouazza et al. [4], interconnected sensing and actuating devices modeled with Petri Nets are configured to provide users with comfort and energy-saving functionality.

Another example of modeling language used for software-intensive systems is SysML, which is considered a potential modeling language for smart cities, as a specific modeling language for systems engineering projects. Munuva et al. [13] presents a holistic SysML model in which a smart city works as an intelligent system and shows how the smart subsystems of a city system collect data from different sources, process it and share information on an integrated platform.

The proposal in this article is to extend SysML to include elements of smart cities as native components of SysML, tailoring the language to represent elements related to smart cities. The reason to chose SysML is twofold. First, SysML is an extension of UML, which means that designers who use UML already have basic knowledge about SysML. In addition, as UML is widely used for software development, there is a smooth learning curve related to designers who will use SysML. Finally, infrastructure systems for smart cities are a union of software but also systems elements, which means that it makes sense to integrate UML and SysML for modeling software-intensive systems [14,15].

The proposed approach has three main steps in this article: i) to identify and describe the decision-makers in a city, ii) to model the structure of a road traffic control system, and iii) to model the behavior of scenarios of a road traffic control system. For all these steps, the profile SmartCitySysML, which extends from SysML Requirements and Block Definition diagrams, is used for creating a design of a road traffic control system regarding a group of intersections.

2   Background

2.1   Smart Cities

Smart Cities are cities with computerized software-intensive systems composed of processes sensitive to the context of Big Data, cloud networks, and standalone communication across multiple distributed devices. These processes are used in a more efficient urban planning paradigm through predictions, which allow decision-making before problems and/or emergencies occur, as well as making urban activities more economic and sustainable [17].

Batty et al. [2] declare that smart cities are often pictured as constellations of instruments across many scales that are connected through multiple networks. These networks provide continuous data regarding the movements of people and materials in terms of the flow of decisions about the physical and social form of the city. Cities, however, can only be smart if there are intelligent functions that can integrate and synthesize these data to some purpose, ways of improving the equity, efficiency, sustainability and quality of life in cities [3].

According to Albino et al. [1], there are four most common characteristics of emerging smart cities. First, the network infrastructure of a city that allows political and social efficiency and cultural development. Second, an emphasis on urban development led by companies and creative activities for promoting urban growth. Third, social inclusion of various urban residents and social capital in urban development. Finally, the natural environment as a strategic component for the future.

2.2 Brief Introduction to SysML

SysML is a UML profile that supports the specification, analysis, design, verification, and validation of complex systems [5]. SysML has a focus on Systems Engineering, different from UML, which is a software engineering modeling language. Therefore, some UML diagrams and elements are used in SysML from the systems point of view, and software elements such as classes and objects are not present in SysML.

A full description of all SysML diagrams can be found in [21]. In this paper, only the SysML Requirements and Block diagrams are briefly introduced in this section, due to shortage of space, and also because they are the most important diagrams for the proposed profile.

The SysML Requirements diagram is a useful way to organize requirements by showing the types of relationships between each requirement. Another characteristic of using the SysML Requirements diagram is to standardize the way of specifying requirements through a defined semantics [19].

SysML can be combined with UML, and the requirements constructs provided by SysML fills the gap between user requirements specification, which are most often written in natural language, and Use Case diagrams, used as an initial specification of scenarios of system requirements [21].

Each individual SysML Requirement is represented with attributes Id and Name, but additional attributes can be considered by extending the basic SysML Requirement model. The SysML Requirements diagram represents relationships between requirements, through relationships hierarchy, derive, master/slave, satisfy, verify, refine and trace [21]. The meaning of each of these relationships is, respectively:

- **Hierarchy:** to represent hierarchy between requirements, providing a hierarchy of different levels of abstraction for requirements.

- **Derive:** derive relationship relates a derived requirement to its source requirement.
- **Satisfy:** the satisfy requirement describes how a model satisfies one or more requirements.
- **Verify:** the verify relationship defines how a test case can verify a requirement.
- **Refine:** this relationship is typically used to refine a text-based requirement with a model.
- **Trace:** this relationship provides a general-purpose relationship between a requirement and any other model element. Its semantics has no real constraints and is not as well-defined as the other relationships.

SysML Blocks are based on UML Classes extended by UML Composite Structures [21]. The SysML blocks are, respectively:

- **Block Definition Diagram:** defines resources and relationships between blocks, such as associations, generalizations, and dependencies. The Block Definition diagram specifies blocks in terms of properties, operations and relationships as a system hierarchy.
- **Internal Block Diagram:** captures the internal structure of a block in terms of properties and connectors between properties. A block can include elements, properties, values, parts, and references to other blocks.

3   The SmartCitySysML Profile

The SmartCitySysML profile can be used to meet the needs of management, operation and decision making, as well as the basis for designing software solutions for smart cities through urban data modeling so that various information services are related and provided to different users. Thus, this profile allows the realization of a successful system and is a good option for the design of complex systems, for example, real-time systems that are used to control a city infrastructure.

It is worth mentioning that the structure of a digital urban space is not static, that is, with the continuous improvement of theory and practice related to urban management and operations, urban components and their systems can be dynamically optimized and adjusted so that they can better cover all areas of the city. This structure can be changed according to big data that will carry out the self-optimization of a digital urban space driven by data [11].

Initially, the profile is organized into 5 main elements, named Stakeholders, Requirements, Solutions, Processes and Dimensions which are explained as follows.

By definition, a **Stakeholder** is a person or group that can affect the organization and management behavior adopted in response to these groups and individuals [6]. The person interested in **SmartCitySysML** can be the citizen, the manager or an employee, as depicted in Fig. 1. Managers can be the mayor, secretaries or councilors. Citizens can be class entities or residents' associations.

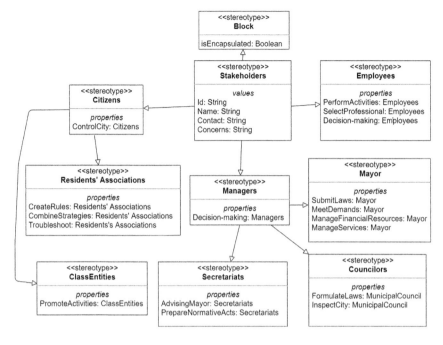

Fig. 1. Types of stakeholders

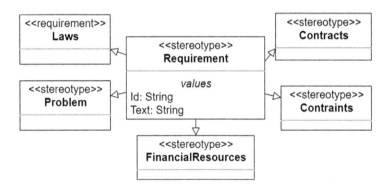

Fig. 2. Types of requirements and needs

By definition, **Requirements** illustrated in Fig. 2 describes functions and restrictions in detail that should address the needs and identify the possible benefits of a city. The types of requirements proposed here are economic resources, laws, problems, contracts and restrictions. These requirements are essential for the development of a sustainable city with good governance.

By definition, **Solutions** illustrated in Fig. 3 are possible solutions for a city that can be related to transformations for the well-being of the popula-

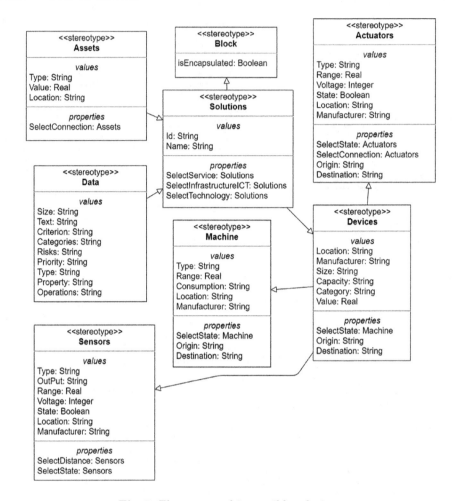

Fig. 3. Elements used in possible solutions

tion, so they need elements such as *data, assets, devices, sensors, actuators, and machines* to be used for designing possible solutions to the identified problems.

By definition, a **Process** illustrated in Fig. 4 is composed of tasks, for example, managing the city, managing taxes, organizing services, obeying laws, developing social functions, and activities, such as consulting and projects related to health, education, safety, transportation, among others.

Dimensions illustrated in Fig. 5 were identified by Giffinger et al. [7]. Staffans et al. [20] argue that *governance* refers to strategies and policies, including expanded urban planning, which enables the co-production of public services, *economy* refers to holistic economic transactions, *environment* refers to the care of natural resources and planetary culture, *mobility* refers to sustainable and innovative transport, logistics and communication systems, *people* refers to social

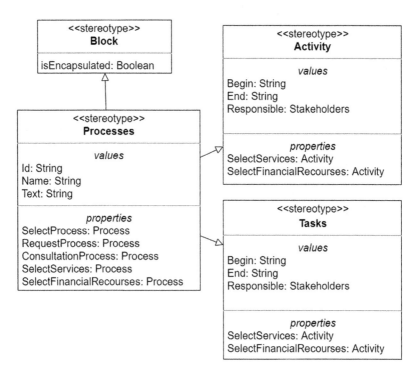

Fig. 4. Types of processes

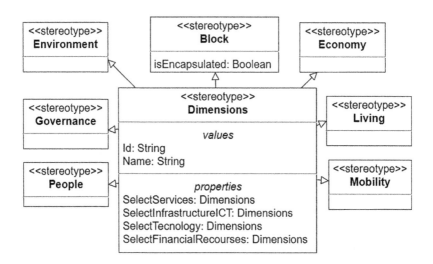

Fig. 5. Dimensions of interest in a smart city

capital and the level of qualification of people, and *living* refers to health, quality of life inhabitable and safe environments.

4 Case Study: Road Traffic Signal Control

The main objective of this section is to detail an application of the **SmartCitySysML** profile for modeling a road traffic signal control software system. For a better understanding of the case study, this section is divided into the specification of characteristics related to the control of traffic signals for a better understanding of the problem and description of the use of SysML extensions to model the problem. For this case study, software requirements for the intersection controller are inspired by examples in [9] and [18].

The traffic signal at intersections are control provisions applied to urban traffic and their objective is to optimize the flow of vehicles, allowing safe, efficient and appropriate crossing possible. When these signals are properly installed and operated, they provide safe crossing for vehicles, reducing the frequency and severity of accidents, and interruptions in heavy flows. However, when improperly installed and operated, these traffic signals can cause delays, an increase in the number of accidents, violation of red light and redirection of drivers who wish to avoid these signals [18].

The implementation of traffic signals for vehicles or pedestrians at an intersection is complex, as it is necessary to make decisions, that is, to establish rules to control the right of way, both for vehicles and pedestrians. Thus, it is necessary to establish new rules of priority between approaches to the intersection to allow crossing or prohibiting movement at the intersection, which could lead to accidents.

At an intersection between two or more roads, some movements cannot be performed simultaneously, as they conflict with each other. Traffic flow at the intersection changes constantly, depending on weather conditions, day of the week and time of year, in addition to road work and accidents that influence even more complexity and performance. Thus, a definition of priority time for traffic signals is considered, since the priority time deals with events that may occur in traffic based on the difference in traffic flow each day.

To solve this situation, a good solution is to establish a "green wave", that is, two or more traffic signals on a road or intersection are open for a period, allowing traffic to flow more efficiently. A traffic signal controller can provide fixed-time, actuated or adaptive time policies. The fixed-time controller uses simple timers with fixed-time and follows a canned cycle regardless of demand [12]. The actuated controller uses flexible, pre-established plans, where the displacement and phase duration at the intersections can be changed in response to perceived changes in traffic [8]. The adaptive controller uses distributed systems, that run at local intersections, advanced controllers that recalculate predictions, and optimizations for real-time traffic flow [12]. Most traffic signals use a fixed time controller.

Fig. 6. Specific region of urban network controlled by traffic signals

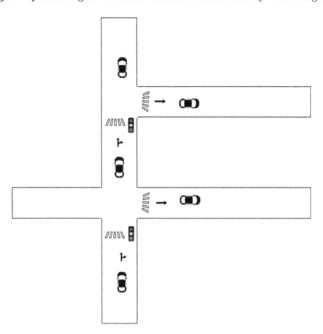

Fig. 7. Specific region of the urban network with visualization of traffic signals

Figure 6 shows a region with a high flow of vehicles in a city in northeastern Brazil. At this intersection, the driver can move forward or turn right at either of the two intersections. In this work, the two chosen intersections are controlled by traffic signals, limiting the conversion to the left on any of the roads. Figure 7 illustrates the same region highlighting the traffic signals that are considered for modeling this case study.

4.1   User Requirements

The following user requirements are used to model the system. Main users in **SmartCitySysML** are *Citizens* of the stereotype *Stakeholders*. Functional user requirements are presented below, at a high degree of abstraction, to solve the problem.

- FR01: The system should control the vehicle traffic pattern at the intersection.
- FR02: The system should control the pedestrian traffic pattern at the intersection.
- FR03: The system should store the vehicle flow on the roads.
- FR04: The system should control the traffic pattern related to each road.
- FR05: The system should allow a fixed traffic management policy.
- FR06: The system should allow a managed traffic management policy.
- FR07: The system should allow adaptive traffic management policy.
- FR08: The system should allow the synchronization of traffic signals.
- FR09: The system should allow choosing a priority route.
- FR10: The system should allow detection of the presence of pedestrians.
- FR11: The system should allow for in-person maintenance.
- FR12: The system should allow remote maintenance.
- FR13: The system should maintain the vehicle traffic history of the roads.
- FR14: The system should maintain the history of traffic policies in the periods of the year.
- FR15: The system must be able to implement new traffic policies.
- FR16: The system should store incidents at the intersection.
- FR17: The system should allow automatic operation of traffic signals.
- FR18: The system should store the incidents that occurred in software and hardware.

4.2   Case Study Models

Model of the SysML Block, Requirements, and Sequence diagrams illustrated below use the **SmartCitySysML** profile and are intended to help in understanding the system and offer a different view of the elements that make up that system.

Figure 8 illustrates a SmartCitySysML Block Definition diagram which includes the elements needed to solve the problem listed in this section. At this point, it is important to mention that in the proposed approach, concurrent behavior is modeled by synchronizing multiple Block Definition Diagrams via events.

The SmartCitySysML Requirements model constructs are intended to provide a bridge between traditional requirements management tools and the other

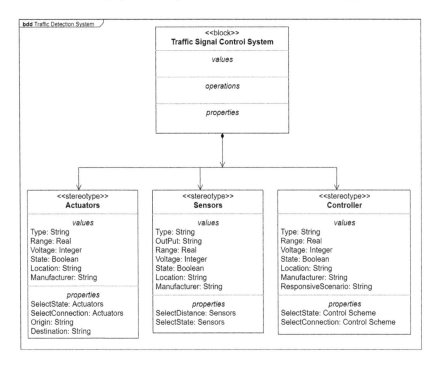

Fig. 8. SysML block diagram for traffic signal control system

SmartCitySysML models [21]. Figure 9 illustrates the SmartCitySysML Requirements diagram, considering the user requirements described previously and the **SmartCitySysML** profile using the *Problem* stereotype. With this stereotype, the system must control traffic on roads, manage traffic, synchronize traffic signals and detect the presence of pedestrians.

Figure 10 illustrates a SmartCitySysML Sequence diagram with a stakeholder (vehicle) that initiates the behavior by sending a message to a sensor. The sensor sends a message to the traffic controller. After evaluating the traffic, the controller assigns a response scenario (morning rush hour, afternoon rush hour, friday, sunday or quiet hour), that is, it will send the command (green, red or yellow signal) to the actuator (traffic signal).

5   Discussion

A smart city is an urban center that integrates a variety of solutions to improve infrastructure performance and achieve sustainable urban development. A smart city includes a collection of urban infrastructure with a common goal of enabling certain goals, for example, energy, transportation and municipal infrastructure, which represents the backbone of a city's efficient, livable and sustainable operations [16].

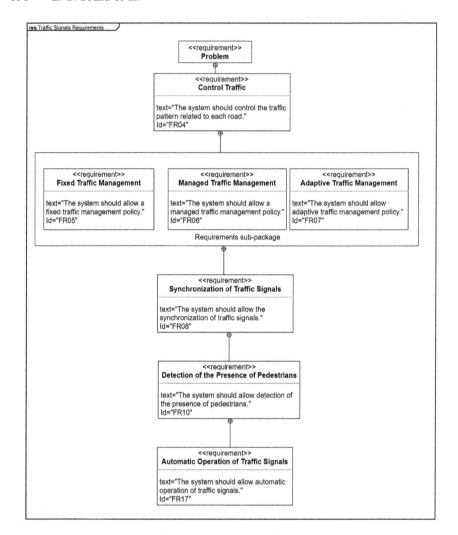

Fig. 9. SysML requirements diagram for traffic signals requirements

Thus, a city needs to be modeled as a system and transformed into a system due to the process of technological transformation, that is, the transformation of the city into a smart city system consists of uniting technology in infrastructures that allow intelligent operations, for example, road traffic signal control. In addition, it is essential to guarantee quality of life of citizens in a safe and healthy environment.

Traffic signal control is an important and challenging problem in the real world. Traffic signals need to operate in a synchronized manner and yet react to unexpected events such as a pedestrian pressing a button on the crosswalk or

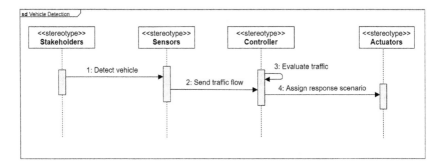

Fig. 10. Sequence diagram for representing vehicle detection

crossing the road at an inappropriate moment. Failure to operate properly can result in automobile accidents and even fatalities.

The profile proposed in this article extended SysML to include elements of smart cities as native components of SysML, adapting the language to represent elements related to smart cities. The profile facilitates the use of common elements found in smart city infrastructures, as they are native elements to be used to build system models. SmartCitySysML extended from the SysML Requirements, Sequence and Block Definition diagrams to model system and software elements for smart cities.

The SysML Requirements, Sequence and Block Definition diagrams are used because they are the most important diagrams considered for the SmartCitySysML profile. These diagrams are used for the design of a road traffic control system. During the elaboration of the design, some challenges arose related to formalism and consistency between the diagrams, mainly due to the lack of software tools that can fully implement all SysML resources.

6   Conclusion

Modeling real-time systems controlling infrastructures of a modern city is a complex activity, so there is no single standard to be used, as there are many modeling languages. This article proposed the *SmartCitySysML* profile to model elements useful for modeling software for smart cities using the SysML Requirements, Block and Sequence diagrams. The purpose of this article is to apply a new SysML profile to model a distributed system in real-time for the control of road traffic, more specifically, the control of interconnected traffic signals.

The proposed profile *SmartCitySysML* is applied to model the road traffic control system for a group of intersections, providing a visual representation of a smart city system. For that, the SysML Sequence diagrams and the SysML Block and Requirements and diagrams were used. Within SysML, it is possible to create other profiles or stereotypes to add to any profile or resources created. A first attempt to validate the *SmartCitySysML* profile is shown in this article through the case study.

Future work will focus on formal modeling using Petri nets and deploy the proposed case study in a simulated environment. In this way, it is possible to provide software developers with real-time modeling using SysML and evaluate the quality of diagrams from a practical point of view. In addition, it is possible to perform software modeling of other case studies, for example, in the domain of health information systems.

Acknowledgments. This study was financed in part by FAPITEC and the Coordenação de Aperfeiçoamento de Pessoal de Nível Superior - Brasil (CAPES) - Finance Code 001.

References

1. Albino, V., Berardi, U., Dangelico, R.M.: Smart cities: definitions, dimensions, performance, and initiatives. J. Urban Technol. **22**(1), 3–21 (2015)
2. Batty, M., et al.: Smart cities of the future. Eur. Phys. J. Spec. Top. **214**(1), 481–518 (2012)
3. Bibri, S.E.: On the sustainability of smart and smarter cities in the era of big data: an interdisciplinary and trans disciplinary literature review. J. Big Data **6**(1), 25 (2019)
4. Bouazza, K.E., Deabes, W.: Smart petri nets temperature control framework for reducing building energy consumption. Sensors **19**(11), 2441 (2019)
5. Friedenthal, S., Moore, A., Steiner, R.: A Practical Guide to SysML: The Systems Modeling Language. Morgan Kaufmann (2014)
6. Frooman, J.: Stakeholder influence strategies. Acad. Manag. Rev. **24**(2), 191–205 (1999)
7. Giffinger, R., Fertner, C., Kramar, H., Meijers, E., et al.: City-ranking of European Medium-Sized Cities. Cent. Reg. Sci. Vienna UT, pp. 1–12 (2007)
8. Klein, L.A., Mills, M.K., Gibson, D.R.: Traffic Detector Handbook, vol. I, 3rd edn. U.S, Department of Transportation (2006)
9. Laplante, P.A.: Real-Time Systems Design and Analysis. Wiley Online Library (2004)
10. Latif, S., Rehman, A., Zafar, N.A.: Modeling of sewerage system linking UML, automata and TLA+. In: 2018 International Conference on Computing, Electronic and Electrical Engineering (ICE Cube), pp. 1–6. IEEE (2018)
11. Ma, Y., Li, G., Xie, H., Zhang, H.: City profile: using smart data to create digital urban spaces. ISPRS Ann. Photogram. Remote Sens. Spatial Inf. Sci. 4 (2018)
12. McShane, W.R., Roess, R.P., Prassas, E.S.: Traffic Engineering. Pearson (2010)
13. Muvuna, J., Boutaleb, T., Mickovski, S., Baker, K.: Systems engineering approach to design and modelling of smart cities. In: 2016 International Conference for Students on Applied Engineering (ICSAE), pp. 437–440. IEEE (2016)
14. Ribeiro, F.G.C., Pereira, C.E., Rettberg, A., Soares, M.S.: Model-based requirements specification of real-time systems with UML, SysML and MARTE. Softw. Syst. Model. **17**(1), 343–361 (2018)
15. Ribeiro, F.G.C., Reuberg, A., Pereira, C.E., Soares, M.S.: An approach for architectural design of automotive systems using MARTE and SysML. In: 14th IEEE International Conference on Automation Science and Engineering, CASE 2018, Munich, Germany, August 20–24, 2018, pp. 1574–1580. IEEE (2018)

16. Shahidehpour, M., Li, Z., Ganji, M.: Smart cities for a sustainable urbanization: illuminating the need for establishing smart urban infrastructures. IEEE Electrif. Mag. **6**(2), 16–33 (2018)

17. Silva, M., Signoretti, G., Oliveira, J., Silva, I., Costa, D.: A crowdsensing platform for monitoring of vehicular emissions: a smart city perspective. Future Internet **11**, 13 (2019)

18. Silvestre, E.A., dos Santos Soares, M.: Modeling road traffic signals control using UML and the MARTE profile. In: Murgante, B., et al. (eds.) ICCSA 2012. LNCS, vol. 7336, pp. 1–15. Springer, Heidelberg (2012). https://doi.org/10.1007/978-3-642-31128-4_1

19. Soares, M.S., Vrancken, J., Verbraeck, A.: User requirements modeling and analysis of software-intensive systems. J. Syst. Softw. **84**(2), 328–339 (2011)

20. Staffans, A., Horelli, L.: Expanded urban planning as a vehicle for understanding and shaping smart, liveable cities. J. Community Inform. **10**(3) (2014) Kindly provide the page range for Ref. [20], if possible.

21. SysML, O.: Systems Modeling Language (SysML) Version 1.5 (2016)

Architecture Conceptualization for Health Information Systems Using ISO/IEC/IEEE 42020

Valdicélio Mendes Santos[1](✉) ⓘ, Sanjay Misra[2](✉) ⓘ,
and Michel S. Soares[1](✉) ⓘ

[1] Federal University of Sergipe, São Cristóãvo, Brazil
valdiceliomendes@gmail.com, michel@dcomp.ufs.br
[2] Center of ICT/ICE Research, Covenant University, Ota, Nigeria
sanjay.misra@covenantuniversity.edu.ng

Abstract. Health Information Systems (HIS) are complex systems which present many difficulties in their development. From the software engineering point of view, among the difficulties for HIS development are the necessity of managing and controlling data that must be held for decades, even considering the evolution of technology in the following years, as well as the necessity of cooperating with legacy systems and describing the needs and concerns of a variety of stakeholders. Considering the domain, HIS deal with human life, and errors during software development, management and operation can be catastrophic. These concerns are relevant from the software architecture point of view. Therefore, developing HIS based on a solid software architecture is a success factor that cannot be neglected. However, the processes related to the software architecture of HIS are often considered only from low level of abstraction, even for software architecture description. The ISO/IEC/IEEE 42020 defines 6 clauses for architecture process, among them the Architecture Conceptualization process is the subject of this paper. Given the importance of establishing a well-defined software architecture, and considering the difficulties of understanding an architectural standard, and also considering that ISO/IEC/IEEE 42020 has only recently been published, we propose a framework for using the Architecture Conceptualization clause, which leverages high level concepts and elements of software architecture. A case study on a HIS is described.

Keywords: Architecture conceptualization · ISO/IEC/IEEE 42020 · Health information system

1 Introduction

A variety of processes, methods, languages, frameworks and architectures have been proposed in order to deal with the challenge of developing complex software-intensive systems. Activities related to each one of these software engineering

© Springer Nature Switzerland AG 2020
O. Gervasi et al. (Eds.): ICCSA 2020, LNCS 12254, pp. 398–411, 2020.
https://doi.org/10.1007/978-3-030-58817-5_30

elements have been proposed in the past decades. However, processes related to software architecture are often neglected [2,9,10,16], even though it is well-known in industry and academia that software architecture processes are considered a critical success factor [5], and even for agile software development, software architecture processes and activities have been considered important [1].

Given the importance of Software Architecture processes, a family set of architecture standards was proposed under reference number 420X0. For instance, ISO/IEC/IEEE 42010 [6] was proposed in 2011 with the main objective of being a recommended practice for creating a description of software architecture. Recently, a new standard, the ISO/IEC/IEEE 42020 [8], was set in a document with the purpose of addressing a standard for governance management, conceptualization, evaluation and elaboration of architectures, and activities that enable these processes. Another standard in the family, the ISO/IEC/IEEE 42030, is about means to organize and record architecture evaluations for enterprise, systems and software fields of application. ISO/IEC/IEEE 42020 is the main subject of study in this paper.

Each architecture process described in ISO/IEC/IEEE 42020 is organized in terms of purpose, desired outcomes and a list of activities for achieving those outcomes. There are 6 architect processes in ISO/IEC/IEEE 42020: Architecture Governance, Architecture Management, Architecture Conceptualization, Architecture Evaluation, Architecture Elaboration and Architecture Enablement.

The proposal in this paper is to describe a software architecture for a Health Information System in accordance with the ISO/IEC/IEEE 42020 regarding the Architecture Conceptualization process, which leverages high level concepts and elements of software architecture. Given this proposal, we identified the main aspects for the clause Architecture Conceptualization of ISO/IEC/IEEE 42020 and described a simple framework for its use in practice. This article addresses the process Architecture Conceptualization for a Health Information Systems product line, given that our purpose here is to understand stakeholders needs, including their main concerns, requirements, purposes, processes and objectives, before dealing with the architecture description using, for instance, ISO/IEC/IEEE 42010. Further processes are planned for future research.

2   Background

Some basic concepts are necessary in order to read this paper, which are briefly introduced in this section.

2.1   Health Information System

Health Information Systems (HIS) can help in a variety of operations that are needed in every healthcare organization, such as data acquisition and presentation, communication and integration of information, surveillance, information storage and retrieval, data analysis, decision support and education [14].

In a broad view, HIS also includes systems that handle data related to the activities of caregivers and healthcare organizations. As an integrated effort, they can be leveraged to improve patient outcomes, improve research and influence decision-making. A variety of health stakeholders present demands for HIS, including patients, clinicians and public health officials. These stakeholders are responsible for collecting data and compiling it in a way that can be used to improve healthcare decisions and benefit everyone.

HIS are most commonly composed of software and system elements, as well as sensors, actuators, and medical machines. Examples of constituents systems elements of a HIS are wearable biomedical sensors, activity detection systems, sleep monitoring systems, environment monitoring systems, home security systems, energy management systems, home automation systems, and companion robots [12]. Integrating the many software systems and components of HIS has been subject of research, as existing HIS systems often do not contemplate inter operation with other systems running inside home provided by different companies. For instance, Losavio et al. [11] established guidelines to integrate heterogeneous, independent, and distributed Healthcare Information Systems, allowing the creation of software products for those systems. Considering the radiology domain, with many HIS to be integrated, the authors of article [15] developed a novel technology that integrates multiple HISs.

For the healthcare domain, there are guidelines to construct HIS that provide support to chronic disease management of patients at home. As HIS deal with human life, they have to be designed to achieve non-functional requirements including interoperability, security, safety, performance and reliability, which confirms the necessity of software architecture.

2.2   Standard ISO/IEC/IEEE 42020

Standard ISO/IEC/IEEE 42020 establishes a set of process descriptions for governance and management of a collection of architectures, as well as describe processes to architect entities. These processes are applicable both for a single project as well as for multiple projects and product lines. In addition, the standard is useful throughout the life span of an architecture of software systems [8].

Six architecture processes are proposed in ISO/IEC/IEEE 42020, named Architecture Governance, Architecture Management, Architecture Conceptualization, Architecture Evaluation, Architecture Elaboration, and Architecture Enablement. Each one of these processes is described in terms of purpose, desired outcomes, and a list of activities and tasks for achieving those outcomes. Tasks are recommended for implementing those activities. As the focus in this paper is on the Architecture Conceptualization Process, it is briefly introduced in the following subsection.

2.3 Architecture Conceptualization Process

The purpose of the Architecture Conceptualization process is to characterize the problem space and determine suitable solutions that address stakeholder concerns, achieve architecture objectives and meet relevant requirements. Conceptualization is the process responsible of establishing and maintaining alignment of architectures in the architecture collection with enterprise goals, policies and strategies and with related architectures. The focus is on identifying solutions, with an emphasis on fully understanding the complete problem space. This also entails the definition and establishment of architecture objectives, as well as negotiation with key stakeholders on prioritization of their concerns [8].

Outcomes of the Architecture Conceptualization are the definition of the problem being addressed, establishment of architectural objectives that address the key stakeholder concerns, definition of key architecture's concepts and properties, and the principles guiding its application and evolution. Besides these outcomes, the Architecture Conceptualization process addresses key tradeoffs, as well as identifies possible limitations. Finally, within this process the candidate solutions are clearly defined and understood.

There are 10 activities related to the Architecture Conceptualization Process. Each activity is composed of a number of tasks which implement the activity, in a total of 100 tasks. For instance, the activity "Relate the architecture to other architectures and to relevant affected entities" is composed of 6 tasks, one of them is to "Formulate principles and precepts expected to be used during execution of the life cycle processes".

The ten activities in Architecture Conceptualization Process are:

1. Prepare for and plan the architecture conceptualization effort.
2. Monitor, assess and control the architecture conceptualization activities.
3. Characterize problem space.
4. Establish architecture objectives and critical success criteria.
5. Synthesize potential solution(s) in the solution space.
6. Characterize solutions and the tradespace.
7. Formulate candidate architecture(s).
8. Capture architecture concepts and properties.
9. Relate the architecture to other architectures and to relevant affected entities.
10. Coordinate use of conceptualized architecture by intended users.

Due to shortage of space, and also because the idea here is to deal with high abstraction level elements related to first activities in order to establish a software architecture, in this paper only activities 1, 3, 4, 6, 8 and 10 are considered, and the other activities are subject of future works.

Work products of the Architecture Conceptualization Process are an architecture conceptualization plan, an architecture conceptualization status report, a problem space definition report, architecture objectives, a quality model, and architecture views and models.

Implementation of Conceptualization Process produces the following outcomes.

- The problem being addressed.

Stakeholders vary across projects when considered in the context of first activities of software development, as for instance, those related to Requirements Engineering, which includes requirements elicitation and prioritization. A minimum set of stakeholders consists of users and acquirers, who may not be the same, and even the number of users is most often higher than acquirers.

Complex projects can impact many users and many acquirers, each with different concerns. Project requirements can necessitate to include two other groups as part of the minimum set of stakeholders. First, the organization when developing, maintaining, or operating the system or software has a legitimate interest in benefiting from the system. Second, regulatory authorities can have statutory, industry, or other external requirements demanding careful analysis.

User requirements are then transformed into system requirements for the system-of-interest. Consistent practice has shown that this process requires iterative and recursive steps in parallel with other life cycle processes through the system design hierarchy. The recursive application of these processes will generate lower-level system element requirements [7].

- Architecture objectives that address the key stakeholder concerns.

First, activities are established to clarify stakeholders needs and concerns. After that, it should be established architecture objectives to meet those planned requirements. Architecture entities are used to compose an architecture objective that deals with issues of the problem space which can be used in other aspects of the solution. A generic example of an objective to take advantage of an opportunity is for the architecture of interest to support reuse of an entity across various technologies, protocols, platforms, operational venues, and market segments [8].

- The architecture's key concepts and properties.

These concepts and properties could be expressed in the form of information and communication technology constructions and models such as information flows, control flows, data structures, operational rules, event/trace diagrams, state transition diagrams, timelines, and roadmaps. Also, they could be expressed in other forms such as risk models, financial models, economic models, simulation models, sensitivity models, queuing models (as well as other kinds of continuous and discrete event simulation models), geospatial models, management models, business models, social-and environmental-impact models, value stream models, among others.

- Key tradeoffs are understood with respect to the problem being addressed and the relevant stakeholder concerns.

The solution might not be addressing the entire problem or all aspects of the problem. Therefore, it is important to understand where the solutions fall short and the tradeoffs that are to be considered when choosing among alternative solutions.

If needs, wants or expectations drive proposed solutions, then negotiations should be necessary with those stakeholders to determine which of the needs, wants or expectations are to be translated into requirements, as well as the relative priority of each one.

3   A Proposed Framework for Architecture Conceptualization

In order to create an Architecture Conceptualization, the organization should implement the relevant tasks (identified as list items under 8.4.N activity) as appropriate to the situation, according to Clause 8 of ISO/IEC/IEEE 42020 [8].

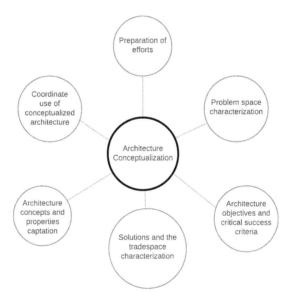

Fig. 1. Activities for architecture conceptualization framework

Figure 1 depicts the activities adopted by the Architecture Conceptualization framework, which are briefly described as follows.

Figure 2 depicts, as a work product, an architecture conceptualization plan proposed by the framework.

3.1   Preparing for and Planning the Architecture Conceptualization Effort

These are the first steps towards conceptualizing the software architecture, which occurs through accomplishment of some tasks. These tasks are concerned with

1.	Introduction

1. Introduction
2. Purpose
3. Scope
4. Objectives
5. Level of detail of the architecture conceptualization effort.
6. Architecture framework
7. Architecture strategies and approach
8. Architecture conceptualization schedule and defined associated milestones
9. References

Fig. 2. An architecture conceptualization plan outline.

identifying the general area of the problem, defining purpose, objectives and level of detail, deciding which architecture description framework will be used, the architecture strategies and approaches, developing architecture conceptualization techniques, methods and tools, and planning the architecture conceptualization effort. All these tasks need to be approved by related stakeholders, which means that they are responsible for the decisions. In the future, once a previous decision is questioned by a stakeholder, then the rationale for each decision can be retrieved. In addition, the team responsible to deal with each one of these tasks need to be assigned.

3.2   Characterizing the Problem Space

Software architects need to understand the basic situation that they will have to deal with for developing and managing all the software systems which they are responsible. Therefore, some important tasks are to identify the problem space and determining most important requirements of the interested parties. After that, the architects need to identify the solution space, which means they have to describe all the products, frameworks, patterns, services and technologies that will address these stakeholder problems and needs.

It is important to adopt a systematic approach to identify the most effective solution given a number of possibilities. An evaluation of alternative solutions should be provided by developers and the architecture team, and each possible solution should be documented in such a way that important architectural decisions can be retrieved whenever it is necessary. Thus, once a decision is documented, even if in the future the decision is classified as a bad one, at least it is created knowledge about the whole situation, providing additional experience for architects, developers and other stakeholders.

3.3 Establishing Architecture Objectives and Critical Success Criteria

In this activity, architectural objectives are identified and defined to address stakeholders' concerns, requirements, risks, constraints or quality attributes, which were previously identified. Critical success criteria are defined to assess whether the problem has been solved, checking whether the final objectives have been achieved. Even if the problem is not completely solved, a degree of success can be identified. It is also relevant to establish a quality model that considers the adopted quality measures as well as relationships between them.

Relevant scenarios are identified for each problem and opportunity regarding boundary conditions, root causes and drives. It is necessary to check if there are gaps, shortfalls of current or planned solution in dealing with respective problems and opportunities. After all these tasks, architectural objectives are identified and defined to address stakeholders' concerns, requirements or quality attributes. Critical success criteria are defined to assess whether the problem has been solved, checking whether the final objectives have been achieved.

3.4 Characterize Solutions and the Tradespace

When determining key criteria for system quality, it is commonly known that stakeholders will identify a number of quality characteristics expected for the final solution. Stakeholders will try to provide their feeling of what they need. For instance, an application needs to provide means to be secure, and also provide a minimum performance. Then, developers understand these restrictions, needs and constraints and establish non-functional requirements in structured documents. According to ISO/IEC/IEEE 29128, non-functional requirements have to be written in such a way that they can be verified, i.e., there are means to identify if the expected quality characteristics of a system are fulfilled.

Given the possible solutions, developers need to analyse tradeoffs between all possibilities. For each architectural relevant solution, an analysis should provide a full evaluation of pros and cons of each solution. For instance, as soon as developers understand the necessity of using a framework, criteria of evaluation are established and the candidates are evaluated. Typically, quality characteristics need to be prioritized. For instance, for most software systems, as long as they do not need to provide strict timing constraints, performance is not as important as maintainability, or even it is better to improve easiness of using instead of performance.

3.5 Capturing Architecture Concepts and Properties

Architecture Conceptualization only needs to describe the architecture to the level of specificity and granularity that is suitable for its intended users, which in many cases does not require significant elaboration [8]. The Elaboration Process deals with description, views and models that captures architecture concepts and properties.

This activity is related to capture architecture concepts in terms of views and models. This is possible through identification of relevant stakeholders, key aspects, and definition of the purpose, scope, breadth and depth of the architecture views and models. Nevertheless, Architecture Conceptualization only needs to describe the architecture to the level of specificity and granularity that is suitable for its intended users, which in many cases does not require significant elaboration [8].

This activity also provides registry of architectural concepts, rationales, properties, decisions, guidelines and characteristics. Achievement of architecture and solution characteristics is provided from the identified processes, activities and tasks in this stage. Besides, the architecture components, their interdependence and interactions are captured.

The ISO/IEC/IEEE 42010 [6] Standard should be used to describe relevant viewpoints, views and models. These artifacts are explored further in clause 10, Architecture Elaboration process of standard ISO/IEC/IEEE 42020.

3.6 Coordinating Use of Conceptualized Architecture by Intended Users

Key stakeholders should validate the conceptualized architecture through feedback of the description, views and models. Besides, there are other users of architecture conceptualization information who are responsible for evaluation or description of the architecture, as well as reviewing, managing, and designing the software architecture.

There are many ways that can be considered for validation. For instance, workshops in which each stakeholder can express its opinions about relevant aspects of the architecture described so far. Other possibilities are evaluation of technical manuals by stakeholders. Each item that can be improved is identified and documented for future reference, which improves architectural knowledge for the organization, and also improves software development processes.

After all the efforts to accomplish the previous tasks and activities, it is equally important to communicate the work products to the interest parties. Key stakeholders should validate the conceptualized architecture through feedback of the description, views and models. Besides, there are other users of architecture conceptualization information who are responsible for evaluation or elaboration of the architecture, review, management, design engineering, and so on.

Each item that can be improved is identified and documented for future reference. It is also required to monitor the use of architecture conceptualization information with the interested parties to make sure that all stakeholders have received it and are registering feedback on the contents of architecture work products. These feedback should be incorporated into architectural work products such as views, models and further descriptions.

When the conceptualized architecture is not clear, mature or complete enough to the stakeholders, it could be necessary to review current architectural products, and maybe refine or prepare a more complete set of architecture views and models.

4   An Example of Architecture Conceptualization for HIS

Work products of the Architecture Conceptualization Process are an architecture conceptualization plan, architecture conceptualization status report, a problem space definition report, architecture objectives, a quality model, and architecture views and models. From all of these work products, status report is not considered in this paper, as it refers to Activity Monitor, which is not addressed in this paper.

Regarding item 3.1 and relating to the architecture conceptualization plan in Fig. 2, the general nature of the problem area is a Health Information System product line capable of dealing with interoperability between legacy systems. The purpose is to define a conceptualization architecture which meet requirements of key stakeholders and capture early decisions about high-level design. These stakeholders have a special role to play in the architecture development effort because they will deal with the resulting solution for years to come.

> 1. Introduction
> 2. Potential problem area
> 3. Relevant aspects of the identified situation
> 4. Stakeholders and their concerns corresponding to each of these problems and opportunities.
> 5. Quality measures
> 6. References

Fig. 3. A problem space definition report outline.

Concerning item 3.2, characterization of the problem space, the problem space definition report is outlined in Fig. 3. Patients may need reminders or help to take their medications, and often need assistance with ambulation (walking) and transferring from a bed to a chair or wheelchair, or getting in and out of the shower. Many patients have adaptive equipment, such as walkers, wheelchairs, canes, and prosthetic devices, which assist them in moving around their home [13].

Existing HIS are sometimes proprietary, monolithic, present high coupling between modules, and expensive solutions for patients and their relatives. Most of such systems do not consider their inter-operation with existing, distributed, and external systems, such as Electronic Health Records (EHR), Patient Health Records (PHR), emergency systems (e.g., ambulances, fire departments), and other HIS.

For the healthcare domain, there are guidelines to construct HIS that provide support to chronic disease management of patients at home. As HIS deal with human life, they have to be designed considering important non-functional requirements including interoperability, security, safety, performance and reliability.

Patients are key stakeholders of HIS. An example of key patient user requirements, described at high level of abstraction, are as follows:

- Patients shall have all the relevant information needed to allow the management of their own health and their interaction with the health system.
- Patients shall be recognised when they access the system and can quickly see relevant health details.
- Patients shall access their own health records and maintain a health diary.
- Patients shall have high levels of trust in the security and confidentiality of services they are using.
- Patients shall have the ability to access services while traveling and on the move.

Care Providers are also key stakeholders. An example of key user requirements, described at high level of abstraction, are as follows:

- Care providers shall have the ability to constantly monitor and interact with patients despite distance and mobility of either party.
- The healthcare delivery environment shall be safe and supportive of patient-care.
- Care providers shall access information from other systems to support their decision.
- Care providers shall be able to interact with patients regardless their electronic devices.

Considering these two important stakeholders, related concerns for each one is as follows:

- Patients: Affordability, Availability, Dependability, Reliability and Usability.
- Care providers: Availability, Flexibility, Maintainability, Reliability, Usability, Resilience.

According to item 3.3 and as a work product, some architecture objectives and architectural significant requirements are described as follows.

- Domain requirements. The reference architecture must enable the development of HIS that, remotely, estimate and provide the patient physical status at any time, e.g., informing the status of patient through the analysis of his/her physiological functions and body systems (e.g., cardiovascular, nervous, respiratory) signs and symptoms.
- Interoperability and integration requirements. The architecture must enable the development of HIS that allow interoperable communication between legacy systems.
- Reliability requirements. The reference architecture must enable the development of HIS that offer fault-tolerant mechanisms for constituent systems interactions.

Another work product is a quality model. SOA Quality Model (SOAQM) [3,4] will be adopted. This model is based on ISO/IEC/IEEE 25010 and has quality attributes that are considered relevant during development of SOA applications. According to HIS objectives, the following characteristics of SOAQM will be measured:

- Compatibility.
- Usability.
- Reliability.
- Security.

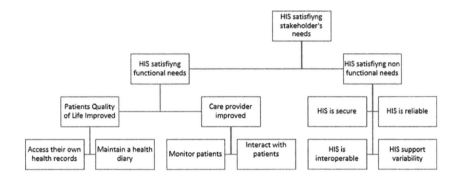

Fig. 4. High level mission view of HIS.

Concerning item 3.5 and the architecture views and models as a work product, Fig. 4 describes a high level mission view of HIS.

Regarding item 3.6, it is available to users an online form to register feedback on the architecture and on the contents of the architectural work products.

5   Discussion and Conclusion

Although the architecture processes can be executed simultaneously with the interactions between them and the iteration over time, as with the Core Processes of ISO/IEC/IEEE 42020 (Architecture Conceptualization, Architecture Evaluation and Architecture Elaboration), this document deals with Conceptualization Activities of a software architecture for a HIS product line. Following the activities and tasks in Clause 8 is helpful for starting the architectural effort.

However, some of the tasks seem to be repeated. For example, task "a) Identify the general nature of the problem area(s) that needs to be addressed" of activity "8.4.1 Prepare for and plan the architecture conceptualization effort", and the task "a) Identify the potential problem area(s) that needs to be addressed" of activity "8.4.3 Characterize problem space". This is likely because the processes are interrelated, which means that the software architecture team needs to be aware of these situations.

In addition, considering the high number of tasks (100), and their high level of abstraction, understanding and using the Architecture Conceptualization clause in practice, in industry, seems to be a challenge. Considering the novelty of the ISO/IEC/IEEE 42020 standard, this is subject for future work.

ISO/IEC/IEEE 42020 presents 6 Architecture processes with high level of abstraction in many of their Activities. It offers possible integration with related standards such as ISO/IEC/IEEE 42010, which presents a way to create an Architecture Description. ISO/IEC/IEEE 42010 proposes the system software architecture as a product composed of models, views, viewpoints, decisions and other architecture elements, representing important entities of a software architecture, but are at a lower level of abstraction when compared to the framework proposed in this paper. For instance, task "1) Develop an architecture description consisting of relevant viewpoints, views, models, model correspondences and express them in the specified form with a level of detail, correctness and completeness suitable for their intended use" of activity "8.4.8 Capture architecture concepts and properties". In other words, ISO/IEC/IEEE 42020 provides processes for application of Architecture Description defined by ISO/IEC/IEEE 42010 [8].

The work carried out concluded the activities and tasks proposed by Clause 8 of ISO/IEC/IEEE 42020, leading to a mature characterization of the solution proposed by the architecture. In a real situation, there would be many solutions, and the interested parties could decide the best one according to their needs.

A more complete form of architecture description, using more specific elements including views and models is subject of the Architecture Elaboration process, as presented in the ISO/IEC/IEEE 42020 standard [8]. Activities 1, 3, 4, 6, 8 and 10 from Architecture Conceptualization are considered in this paper, and the other activities (2, 5, 7 and 9) are subject of future works.

Acknowledgments. This study was financed in part by FAPITEC and the Coordenação de Aperfeiçoamento de Pessoal de Nível Superior - Brasil (CAPES) - Finance Code 001.

References

1. Abrahamsson, P., Babar, M.A., Kruchten, P.: Agility and architecture: can they coexist? IEEE Softw. **27**(2), 16–22 (2010)
2. Dasanayake, S., Aaramaa, S., Markkula, J., Oivo, M.: Impact of requirements volatility on software architecture: how do software teams keep up with ever-changing requirements? J. Softw. Evol. Process. **31**(6), 1–21 (2019)
3. França, J., Soares, M.S.: SOAQM: quality model for SOA applications based on ISO 25010. In: ICEIS 2017–Proceedings of the 19th International Conference on Enterprise Information Systems, vol. 2, April 2015

4. França, J., de Souza Lima, J., Soares, M.S.: Development of an electronic health record application using a multiple view service oriented architecture. In: ICEIS 2017–Proceedings of the 19th International Conference on Enterprise Information Systems, pp. 308–315, January 2017

5. Garlan, D.: Software architecture: a travelogue. In: Herbsleb, J.D., Dwyer, M.B. (eds.) Proceedings of the on Future of Software Engineering, FOSE 2014, Hyderabad, India, 31 May–7 June 2014, pp. 29–39. ACM (2014)

6. ISO/IEC/IEEE: Systems and Software Engineering - Architecture description. ISO/IEC/IEEE 42010:2011(E) (Revision of ISO/IEC 42010:2007 and IEEE Std. 1471-2000), pp. 1–46, December 2011

7. ISO/IEC/IEEE: ISO/IEC/IEEE International Standard - Systems and software engineering-vocabulary. 24765:2017(E), pp. 1–541, August 2017

8. ISO/IEC/IEEE: ISO/IEC/IEEE International Standard - Software, systems and enterprise - Architecture processes. 42020:2019(E), pp. 1–126, July 2019

9. Júnior, A.A.C., Misra, S., Soares, M.S.: A systematic mapping study on software architectures description based on ISO/IEC/IEEE 42010:2011. In: Misra, S., et al. (eds.) ICCSA 2019. LNCS, vol. 11623, pp. 17–30. Springer, Cham (2019). https://doi.org/10.1007/978-3-030-24308-1_2

10. Júnior, A.A.C., Misra, S., Soares, M.S.: ArchCaMO - a maturity model for software architecture description based on ISO/IEC/IEEE 42010:2011. In: Misra, S., et al. (eds.) ICCSA 2019. LNCS, vol. 11623, pp. 31–42. Springer, Cham (2019). https://doi.org/10.1007/978-3-030-24308-1_3

11. Losavio, F., Ordaz, O., Esteller, V.: Quality-based bottom-up design of reference architecture spplied to healthcare integrated information systems. In: 9th IEEE International Conference on Research Challenges in Information Science, RCIS 2015, Athens, Greece, 13–15 May 2015, pp. 70–75. IEEE (2015)

12. Majumder, S., et al.: Smart homes for elderly healthcare - recent advances and research challenges. Sensors **17**(11), 2496 (2017)

13. Mclain, K.B., O'Hara-Leslie, E.K., Wade, A.C.: Foundations for Assisting in Home Care. Open Suny Textbooks (2016). https://milnepublishing.geneseo.edu/home-health-aide

14. Teixeira, J.G., de Pinho, N.F., Patrício, L.: Bringing service design to the development of health information systems: the case of the Portuguese national electronic health record. Int. J. Med. Inform. **132**, 813–817 (2019)

15. Wang, K., Wellnitz, C., Zwart, C., Li, J., Wu, T.: Integration of multiple health information systems for quality improvement of radiologic care. IISE Trans. Healthc. Syst. Eng. **7**(3), 169–180 (2016)

16. Woods, E.: Software architecture in a changing world. IEEE Softw. **33**, 94–97 (2016)

Development of an Audio Steganography System Using Discrete Cosine Transform and Spread Spectrum Techniques

Olawale Timothy Adeboje, Arome Junior Gabriel$^{(\boxtimes)}$ ⓘ,
and Adebayo Olusola Adetunmbi ⓘ

Federal University of Technology, P.M.B. 704, Akure, Nigeria
{adebojeot, ajgabriel, aoadetunmbi}@futa.edu.ng

Abstract. In today's electronic society, security of information is an issue of major concern especially in the communication domain. Indeed, there is a very serious need for schemes that guarantee security of information exchanged between entities, over public networks. Several techniques such as cryptography and/or steganography have been proposed in existing literature. Audio steganography has certain advantages over conventional steganography. Existing audio steganography systems suffer from limitations that includes, their inability to embed information in multiple audio file formats, high distortion rate and low level of robustness of their resultant stego-files. To overcome these limitations, this current research focused on the development of an efficient and robust audio steganography system for the security of information whether in store or on transit across the Internet. This is achieved by first encrypting a given secret information, compressing the resultant cipher-text, then embedding the compressed file in a suitable cover (audio file) using frequency hopping spread spectrum technique, to yield as output, an audio stego file which is not distinguishable from the original audio cover file. To allow for the embedding of the secret compressed file, the selected audio cover file is first broken into frames using one dimensional Discrete Cosine Transform (DCT). Results of performance evaluation of this developed system shows that it has very low level of distortion as revealed by the Signal to Noise Ratio (SNR). The compression ratio obtained is also equal to one (1), which shows that the cover audio file is identical to the resultant stego-file.

Keywords: Cryptography · Cyber security · Encryption · Information security · Steganography

1 Introduction

Over the years, there have been significant growth in computer networks and more specifically, the Internet. Fundamentally, computers (or Information Technology) finds application in communications [1], health [2], electoral decision making (voting), governance and human resource management [3–5], crime control [6], prediction of weather/climate conditions [7], Web Services Security [8], and other facets of human existence. All these, coupled with the exponential increase of computer performance,

© Springer Nature Switzerland AG 2020
O. Gervasi et al. (Eds.): ICCSA 2020, LNCS 12254, pp. 412–427, 2020.
https://doi.org/10.1007/978-3-030-58817-5_31

has expedited the distribution of multimedia data such as images, audio, video etc. Data transmission has been made very simple, fast and accurate using the internet. However, one of the main problems associated with transmission of data over the internet is that it may pose a security threat, that is, personal or confidential data can be stolen or hacked in many ways. Users may be reluctant to distribute data over the internet due to lack of security. One of the ways to conceal information is Cryptography. In cryptography, the structure of a message is scrambled to make it meaningless and unintelligible unless the decryption key is available. Unfortunately, it is sometimes not enough to keep the contents of a message secret, it may also be necessary to keep the existence of the message secret [3, 9, 10]. A method referred to as steganography is used for achieving these. Steganography is defined as the art and science of writing concealed messages in a manner that no one, except the owner/sender as well as the intended recipient, suspects the presence of any embedded secret message. The major objective of steganography is to allow for secure information exchange in an absolutely imperceptible fashion and to avoid drawing suspicion to the transmission of a hidden data. This research work combined both Cryptography and Steganography to hide text file into an audio signal. The use of Huffman algorithm and Lempel-Ziv-Welch algorithm was adopted for text compression in order to reduce the distortion in the audio file and Frequency Hopping Spread Spectrum technique to increase the robustness of the stego file.

The remainder of this paper is organized in a way that, Sect. 2 contains review of related existing research works. The design of the new system is reported in Sect. 3. Then Sect. 4 presents results and findings of the experiment conducted. Section 5 presents performance evaluation of the system. Section 6 contains the conclusion.

2   Related Works

Although Information hiding techniques like watermarking and steganography have shown some qualities as promising solutions towards addressing security concerns, they still exhibit some teething problems or shortcomings. The research work presented by [11] and [12] for instance, has a shortcoming of yielding distorted stego-files, which arouses suspicion of attackers. The work titled, "Increasing the Hiding Capacity of Low-Bit Encoding Audio Steganography Using a Novel Embedding Technique" in [13], presented LSB technique as an efficient strategy for concealing information in sound signals. Be that as it may, as the size of the secret message increases, the embedding process gets complex or complicated.

Another novel method for embedding data in the audio stream was suggested in the paper presented in [12]. This method/system however could only embed information in dot-wav audio file. Other file formats were not considered for suitability as cover-image at all.

In a bid to combine encryption and steganography techniques so as to provide a more powerful message concealing technique, and to improve the quality of the resultant stego-file, towards completely eliminating suspicion of covert communication, the authors of the work reported in [14] developed a tool for encrypting a message and hiding the resultant cipher-text in a digital object. The encrypted message is embedded in the homogenous frames of mp3 audio file. The limitations of this research work are in two fold; first, the fact that the quality of the final output (stego-file) is dependent on file size and message length, has undesirable implications. Secondly, aside the mp3 audio file format, other audio file formats were not considered.

The authors of [15] in their work, "*analysis and design of three LSB techniques for secure audio steganography*" presented an audio steganography solution that uses encrypted image. The objectives were to embed image file in an audio file using 3rd LSB technique, and to analyze the quality of the resultant stego file after the embedding process is completed. Least significant bit (LSB) method was used. The limitation of the research work is that there was a big difference in the quality of the audio before and after embedding of information. This implies low robustness, and arouses a lot of suspicion on the part of their steganography system. The limitations of the research work are: the audio file used in the research is less (952 KB) and the research was only limited to .wav audio file.

The authors of the research paper in [18] carried out a survey of audio steganography techniques for secure data transmission. They opined that LSB is the simplest of steganography techniques, but spread spectrum technique offers more robustness to attacks.

The authors of the research work in [19] went further in their work to develop a more efficient audio steganography system that has increased robustness against attack, and is able to embed text messages in both MP3 and MP4 audio file formats, with impressive efficiency

In fact, other authors proposed the idea of more robust information systems that combine post quantum cryptography with steganography. Such systems can be used to protect information against common classical and even quantum attacks on information in the cloud [10], and even electronic voting systems [3].

In order to achieve improvement in the properties of images with embedded secrets and at the same time eliminate the propensity of high computational complexity in steganography systems, the authors of [20] adopted the use of particle swarm optimisation algorithm as well as AVX instructions available in modern CPUs. These as they claimed, accelerates data parallel operations required in image steganography with advanced optimizations.

The authors of the work in [21] proposed an Optical Character Recognition (OCR) based Steganography technique where, messages, in their feature forms, are embedded in a cover image. Character level features were extracted from images which contain the textual messages, and embedded in the cover image, thus strengthening the data hiding objective of steganography. They reported impressive results.

In the study titled "Image Steganography and Steganalysis based on LSB" as presented in [22], the authors proposed a new LSB steganography method which is an improvement on the 1-byte least significance method. The results they presented showed impressive performance of their model. This work however considered images alone, and could require some extension to be able to handle audio files as cover media.

3 The Proposed Audio Steganography System

Audio file format is a container format for storing audio data and metadata on a computer system. This format is divided into three major groups namely: the uncompressed audio formats, (e.g., WAV), formats with lossless compression, (e.g., WMA) and formats with lossy compression (e.g., MP3). In this research work, the selected cover media which is the audio signal undergoes different stages; the selected audio file irrespective of its format will be converted into .wav (Wave File Audio) format using a function in MATLAB.

Many types of audio file are available, such as Windows Audio Visual (WAV), Windows Media Audio (WMA), and MPEG (MP3) exist. The type used in this study is WAV file format of type Pulse Code Modulation (PCM), because it is an uncompressed audio format, which gives more flexibility for data hiding. A stego-object (WAV file) with high sampling rate and sampling resolution may draw suspicion, because of its large size, especially if its subjective quality is not high. Usually, it is easy to hide more secret data in the high quality audio data (for example, the use of least significant bit encoding to embed one bit in each sample, consist of 16 bits, sample has less effect on the stego object than adding one bit in a sample consist of 8 bits). In the developed system the wave files, with 8-bit samples resolution, are used as cover media for hosting the secret data.

There are some basic parameters to understand when discussing on digital audio files. This parameter includes:

A. **Sampling rate** (f_s) is the number of samples of audio carried per seconds. It is measures in Hertz. In this research, 44100 Hz is used in wav audio format.
B. **Frame size:** The frame size is the amount of bits in each frame.

$$\text{Frame Size} = \frac{1}{\textit{Partitioned frame size}} \tag{1}$$

C. **Frequency Resolution** (k_s): It is the scaling factor, which ensures the cover medium is embedded below the audibility threshold. It is measured in Hertz. Human Auditory System (HAS) works dynamically in a wide range of frequencies between 20 Hz–20000 Hz. It is calculated using Eq. 2;

$$k_s = \frac{f_s}{2 \times \frac{N}{2}} \tag{2}$$

where f_s is the sampling rate and N is the total number of frames.

The proposed/developed audio steganography system is broadly divided into two modules which are: the Embedding Module and the Extraction Module.

A. The Embedding Module

Embedding module is a module at which the secret message (text file) is embedded into the selected cover medium (audio Signal). This is depicted in the Fig. 1.

416   O. T. Adeboje et al.

Private Key

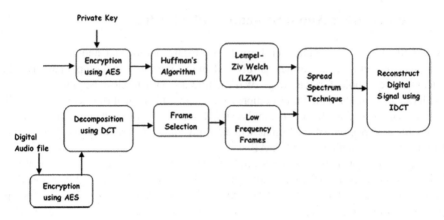

Fig. 1. The embedding module

The embedding module involves three processes which include: plain text (secret message) encryption and compression, audio signal decomposition as well as combined signal construction processes.

The secret message which is in plain text is encrypted in order to enhance the security of the secret message from the intruders by using a public key and private key to avoid unauthorized access of the text. This research work makes use of Advanced Encryption Standard (AES) over other encryption algorithms because it uses higher length key sizes such as 128, 192 and 256 bits for encryption, it uses 128-bit block size and also has 10, 12 or 14 rounds of bits depending on the key size used. Hence it makes AES algorithm more robust against hacking. The general encryption procedure is mathematically represented in Eq. 3;

$$E(K, M) = \{C\}K \tag{3}$$

where E represents the Encryption function, M denotes the Plain text (Secret message), K stands for Encryption Key, and C is the cipher text.

The encrypted text will be compressed using a two stage compression technique that uses the Huffman algorithm as well as the Lempel-Ziv Welch (LZW). The Huffman encoding algorithm starts by constructing a list of all the alphabet symbols in descending order of their probabilities. It then constructs, from the bottom up, a binary tree with a symbol at every leaf. This is done in steps, where at each step two symbols with the smallest probabilities are selected, added to the top of the partial tree, deleted from the list, and replaced with an auxiliary symbol representing the two original symbols. When the list is reduced to just one auxiliary symbol (representing the entire alphabet), the tree is complete. The tree is then traversed to determine the code words of the symbols. The C (Cipher text) in Eq. 5 would be subjected to compression using Huffman algorithm presented in equation.

The Lempel Ziv Welch algorithm is one of the many algorithms used for compression. It is typically used to compress certain text files, image files command among others. It relies on reoccurring pattern to save data space. Lempel ziv welch compression was adopted over Huffman lossless data compression because its construct its dictionary on the fly, going through the data once that is when reading through the data for compression it goes through it once unlike Huffman that goes through it data twice. The Lempel-Ziv algorithm compresses by building a dictionary of previously seen string. It codes groups of characters of varying length.

Data compression is a method of encoding rules that allows substantial reduction in the total number of bits to store or transmit a file and this will help to reduce distortion in the stego file. The feature of both LZW (Lempel-Ziv-Welch) and Huffman algorithms are combined to improve the compression ratio. The Huffman algorithms is represented as;

$$b_{Huff} = \sum_{a=1}^{n} f(a_i)L(\{C\}) \tag{4}$$

where $L(\{C\})$ denotes the length of the cipher text, $f(a_i)$ is the word character and n is the number of bit.

Lempel-Ziv Welch is represented as;

$$c_{lzw} = b_{Huff}(\log_2 b + \log_2 N + 2) \tag{5}$$

where b_{Huff} represents the compressed cipher text using Huffman model, N denotes the fixed codes and c_{lzw} denotes the LZW compression.

The main advantage of this combined algorithm is that the percentage of data reduction increases more compared to the existing text compression techniques.

The audio format irrespective of its audio file format is converted into .wav format. This is achieved using an audio write function in MATLAB. The reason for this is that it will be easier to decompose the digital audio signal into analog signal using the One Dimensional Discrete Cosine Transform (DCT).

The DCT is one of the powerful compact transforms. It relocates most of the signal energy into the first transform coefficients, lesser energy or information is relocated into other (i.e., high frequency) coefficients. The frames thus created are queued based on the energies of the frames. DCT is applied on the voiced blocks that have power less than the predefined second threshold value (T'). The block size was taken small to avoid the high computational complexity of DCT calculations which makes the system slow. Thereafter, selection of low frequency frames was carried out. The selection of the low frequency frames from other frames is in order to ensure the secret message to be embedded does not introduce audible distortion in the audio signal;

$$f_{dct}(x) = \sum_{u=1}^{N-1} \alpha(u)c(u) \cos\left[\frac{\pi(2x+1)u}{2N}\right] \tag{6}$$

for $x = 0, 1, \ldots\ldots\ldots N - 1$

where;

$$\alpha(u) = \begin{cases} \sqrt{\frac{1}{N}} \, for \; u = 0 \\ \sqrt{\frac{2}{N}} \, for \; u \neq 0 \end{cases} \tag{7}$$

where $f_{dct}(x)$ represents the original sequence of the audio signal, N denotes the Last frame in the audio file, x is the Number of frames in an audio file and u denotes the frame size.

Spread Spectrum technique was used to hide the encrypted and compressed secret message (Text file) into the digital Audio signal. Spread spectrum is a method by which energy generated in particular bandwidth is deliberately spread in the frequency domain, resulting in a signal with a wider bandwidth. Spread spectrum ($s_{sprectrum}$) systems encode data as a binary sequence which sounds like noise but which can be recognized by a receiver with the correct key. There are two types of spread spectrum techniques which are: Direct Sequence Spread Spectrum (DSSS) and Frequency Hopping Spread Spectrum (FHSS). In Direct Sequence Spread Spectrum, data to be transmitted is divided into small pieces and each piece is allocated to a frequency channel across the spectrum. In this research work, Frequency Hopping Spread Spectrum is used. In Frequency-Hopping Spread Spectrum, the audio file's frequency spectrum is altered so that it hops rapidly between frequencies. Spread spectrum combined the compressed text file with the low frequencies of the audio signal using;

$$s_{sprectrum} = c_{lzw} \cdot f_{dct}(low) \tag{8}$$

The embedded signal is added to the other frames of high frequency using:

$$f_{frame}(t) = s_{sprectrum} + f_{dct}(high) \tag{9}$$

The analog signal generated is then converted into digital signal using the Inverse Discrete Cosine Transform (IDCT) as given in Eq. 10;

$$c_{dct}(u) = \alpha(u) \sum_{x=1}^{N-1} f_{frame}(t) \cos\left[\frac{\pi(x+1)u}{2N}\right] \tag{10}$$

where $c_{dct}(u)$ is the new audio signal (stego file).

B. The Extraction Module

This is the reverse of embedding module. At this stage, the secret message is extracted from the stego file (the embedded audio file). The stages to accomplish this are depicted in Fig. 2.

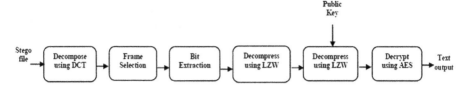

Fig. 2. The extraction module

The audio format irrespective of its audio file format is converted into .wav format. The reason for this is that it will be easier to decompose the wave file using the Discrete Cosine Transform (DCT) using the header of .wav file format. This is achieved using an audio write function in MATLAB.

At this stage, the stego file which is the embedded audio file is decomposed in to frames using one dimensional Discrete Cosine Transform (DCT).

$$c_{dct}(u) = \alpha(u) \sum_{x=1}^{N-1} f_{frame}(t) \cos\left[\frac{\pi(x+1)u}{2N}\right] \tag{11}$$

for $x = 0, 1, \ldots\ldots, N - 1$
where;

$$\alpha(u) = \begin{cases} \sqrt{\frac{1}{N}} \, for \, u = 0 \\ \sqrt{\frac{2}{N}} \, for \, u \neq 0 \end{cases} \tag{12}$$

where;
$f_{dct}(x)$ represents the original sequence of the audio signal, N denotes the last frame in the audio file, x stands for the number of frames in an audio file while, u denotes the frame size.

The decryption process is the process of converting the cipher text back to plain text. In addition, it has an edge over static compression methods because no dictionary or other pre-existing information is necessary for the decoding algorithm. Both encoding and decoding programs must start with same initial dictionary, in this scenario, all the 256 ASCII characters.

Here's how it works; The LZW decoder first reads in an index, looks up the index in the dictionary, and returns the substring associated with the index. The first character of this substring is appended to the current working string. This new concatenation is added to the dictionary. The decoded string then becomes the current working string (the current index, that is the substring, is remembered), and the process repeats.

For decomposition by Huffman Algorithm, this is the inverse of Huffman encoding module. To decode the encoded data, we require the Huffman tree. We iterate through the binary encoded data to find character corresponding to current bits, the following steps is used:

a. Start from the root and do the following until a leaf is found
b. If current bit is 0, we move to left node of the tree.

c. If the bit is 1, move to right node of the tree.
d. If during transversal, we encounter a leaf node, we print character of that particular leaf node and then again continue the iteration of the encoded data starting from step 1.

4 Results and Discussion

Implementation was done using MATLAB programming language on Windows 8.1 Operating System platform with hardware configuration of 3 GB RAM, 1.6 Hz Intel processor speed and 250 GB of hard disk.

In this developed system, three (3) different digital audio file formats were used as the cover media and different ranges of secret text were hidden into them for evaluation. The three different audio file formats used in the experiment include; .wav, .oga, and .m4a.

The stego files (embedded audio file) were evaluated. The stego file (audio file) retains its initial size after evaluating the proposed approach and the amount of information that the developed system can hide is very high (500 KB).

In order to cater for the evaluation of the research work, standard performance metrics as highlighted in Sect. 4.1 were used.

4.1 System Performance Evaluation Metrics

The proposed/developed system was evaluated based on the following metrics; *computational time, bit per character, compression ratio* and *signal to noise ratio*. These metrics are further highlighted as follows;

A. Compression Ratio

This is the ratio of the cover medium before and after the secret message is embedded into it to its ratio when the secret message is embedded into it.

$$\text{Compression Ratio} = \frac{output\ file\ size}{input\ file\ size} \tag{13}$$

From the result of experiment carried out in this research work, the system has a compression ratio of 1, which means the size of the audio file before the secret message is embedded into it is still the same size after the secret message is embedded into it.

B. Signal to Noise Ratio

Signal to noise ratio is a parameter used to know the amount by which the signal is corrupted by the noise. It is defined as the ratio of the signal power to the noise power.

Alternatively, it represents the ratio of desired signal (say a music file) to the background noise level. It is measured in decibel (db). SNR can be calculated by Eq. 14.

$$\text{SNR (db)} = 10 \log \frac{\sum_n I_n}{\sum n(E_n - I_n)^2} \tag{14}$$

where E_n = Stego file and I_n = Original Audio Signal

C. Computation Time

This is the time taken for the system to execute its function.

This times were recorded for the three (3) audio files used as cover-media in this experiment.

The columns of all table of records in this sub-section are labeled with letters A to J. This is to allow enough space for the tables to be captured. A = Plaintext Size (in kb), B = Audio cover file size (in mb), C = Length of Audio cover file (in minutes), D = Compressed Plaintext Size (in kb), E = Compression Ratio (in %), F = Entire System Operation time (in seconds), G = Signal-to-Noise ratio (in db), H = Bit Per Character, I = Stego Audio file size after embedding (in mb), and J = Extraction time.

4.2   System Performance Evaluation Results

The columns of all table of records in this sub-section are labeled with letters A to J. This is to allow enough space for the tables to be captured. A = Plaintext Size (in kb), B = Audio cover file size (in mb), C = Length of Audio cover file (in minutes), D = Compressed Plaintext Size (in kb), E = Compression Ratio (in %), F = Entire System Operation time (in seconds), G = Signal-to-Noise ratio (in db), H = Bit Per Character, I = Stego Audio file size after embedding (in mb), and J = Extraction time.

A. Using .Wav Audio Format as Cover File

For wav file, an audio size of 50.5 Mb and the length of 5 min were used for the evaluation. Table 1 shows the result of the evaluation using .wav file format.

Table 1. Results of experiment when .Wav audio file was used as cover

A	B	C	D	E	F	G	H	I	J
50	50.5	5	41	82.7	3	59.8	8	50.5	2
100	50.5	5	82	81.7	3	57.8	8	50.5	2
150	50.5	5	123	81.7	3	55.7	8	50.5	2
200	50.5	5	180	89.8	3	52.8	8	50.5	2
250	50.5	5	212	84.8	3	46.5	8	50.5	2
300	50.5	5	245	81.7	3	40.5	8	50.5	2
350	50.5	5	297	84.8	3	33.9	8	50.5	2
400	50.5	5	355	88.9	3	27.9	8	50.5	2
450	50.5	5	386	85.8	3	22.7	8	50.5	2
500	50.5	5	439	87.8	3	17.1	8	50.5	2

From Table 1, the values of the SNR are more than 50 db when the size of the text file to be embedded ranges from 50 kb to 200 kb, and this indicates that there will be no distortion in the stego file. But from 250 kb to 500 kb, the values of the SNR began to decrease; making the values to be less than 50 db and this shows that there will be distortion as the value decreases from 50 db. This can be represented graphically in Fig. 3 and Table 4.

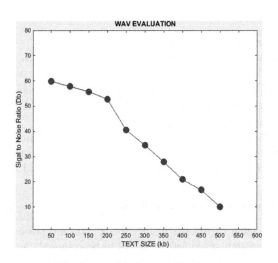

Fig. 3. Graph of WAV file format

B. Using the .OGA Audio Format as Cover

.OGA file format, with size 8.10 Mb and a length of 5 min was used as an experiment to perform the performance metrics. Table 2 shows the result of the evaluation.

Table 2. Results of experiment when OGA audio file was used as cover

A	B	C	D	E	F	G	H	I	J
50	8.10	5	45	89.8	6	56.4	8	8.10	4
100	8.10	5	83	82.7	6	54.7	8	8.10	4
150	8.10	5	132	87.8	6	51.5	8	8.10	4
200	8.10	5	168	83.8	5	44.1	8	8.10	4
250	8.10	5	227	90.8	6	39.6	8	8.10	4
300	8.10	5	272	90.9	6	31.0	8	8.10	4
350	8.10	5	290	82.7	6	28.8	8	8.10	4
400	8.10	5	364	91	6	19.5	8	8.10	4
450	8.10	5	409	90.9	6	13.9	8	8.10	4
500	8.10	5	450	89.8	6	8.8	8	8.10	4

From Table 2, the values of the Signal to Noise ratio are more than 50 db when the size of the text file to be embedded ranges from 50 kb to 100 kb, but the value of SNR for 150 kb is 48.5 which van be approximately to 50 db can also be accepted as good SNR vale. This indicates that there will be no distortion in the audio with a secrete message that's up to 150 kb. But from 200 kb to 500 kb, the values of the Signal to Noise Ratio began to decrease; making the values to be less than 50 db and this implicates that there will be distortion as the value decreases from 50 db. This can be represented graphically in Fig. 4.

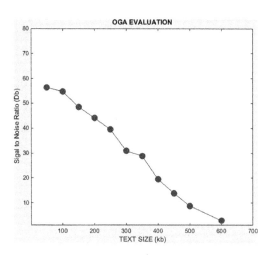

Fig. 4. Graph of OGA file format

C. Using the .M4A Audio Format as Cover

.M4A file format, with size 4.81 Mb and a length of 5 min was used in this experiment to evaluate the performance of the proposed system. The results of the evaluation are shown in Table 3.

Table 3. Results of experiment when M4A audio file was used as cover

A	B	C	D	E	F	G	H	I	J
50	4.81	5	43	14.2	9	59.7	8	4.81	7
100	4.81	5	89	11.1	8	55.9	8	4.81	6
150	4.81	5	132	12.2	8	51.6	8	4.81	6
200	4.81	5	163	18.3	8	49.8	8	4.81	6
250	4.81	5	225	10.1	8	42.6	8	4.81	6
300	4.81	5	273	9.1	8	37.6	8	4.81	6
350	4.81	5	307	12.2	8	31.7	8	4.81	6
400	4.81	5	355	11.2	8	28.7	8	4.81	6
450	4.81	5	400	11.1	8	22.0	8	4.81	6
500	4.81	5	424	15.2	8	18.6	8	4.81	6

From Table 3, the values of the Signal to Noise ratio goes beyond 50 db when the size of the text file to be embedded ranges from 50 kb to 100 kb, but the value of SNR for 150 kb is 48.6 which is approximately 50 db can also be accepted as good SNR value. This indicates that there will be no distortion in the audio with a secrete message that's up to 150 kb. But from 200 kb to 500 kb, the values of the Signal to Noise Ratio began to decrease; making the values to be less than 50 db and this implicates that there will be distortion as the value decreases from 50 db. This can be represented graphically in Fig. 5.

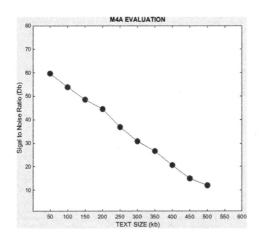

Fig. 5. Graph of M4A file format

Table 4. Results of the evaluated audio formats

Digital audio format	Maximum text sizewithout distortion (KB)	Average SNR (DB)	Average computation time (seconds)	Compression ratio
WAV	200	58.7	3	1
M4A	150	54.1	6	1
OGA	150	54.5	6	1

5 Performance of the New System Versus Existing Related Works

In this sub-section, we compared the performance of the current research work with other existing related ones in literature. Table 5 presents the details of this comparison.

As shown in Table 5 is the comparison of the developed model with some existing works in terms *Computation time, number of file formats, signal to noise ratio, compression ratio*, and *maximum text file that can be embedded without causing distortion in the cover media*. From Table 5, it is obvious that the current developed model supports five (5) different audio file formats as compared to other existing systems on the table that support one (1) audio format. Besides, the developed model has better computational time per file size. The compression ratio of the developed model is one (1) making stego-files difficult to be discerned. It makes the quality of stego-file can be maintained and reduces the suspicion towards the stego-file. The developed model has minimal distortion at an average signal to noise ratio of 59.8 db at 200 kb text file size.

Table 5. General performance comparison with some existing works

Name and year of research	Average computational time (sec)	Maximum number of file format	Average signal to noise ratio (DB)	Compression ratio	Maximum text file size before distortion begins (KB)
Current Research work	2.2	5	59.8	1	200
[13]	–	1	54.5	1	12.2
[16]	0.3	1	52	>1	8.2
[17]	–	1	–	>1	27.5
[15]	–	1	56	–	40

6 Conclusion and Recommendation

There are a number of proven methods for applying steganography to hide information within audio data. In this research work, an audio steganography system that uses Discrete Cosine Transform (DCT) and spread spectrum techniques was developed. It was shown through implementation and subjective experimentation that the proposed audio steganography system supports three different digital audio formats (WAV, OGA, and M4A). The system developed has the ability to embed a secret message of size that is up to 200 kb with respect to any digital audio length or size without any distortion and has the ability to retain the same size after embedding text into it.

Furthermore, the Wav, and M4A files have the SNR ratio that's greater than or approximately equal to 50 db at 200 kb. This implies that large file of size up to about 200 kb can be hidden without causing audible distortion in the cover medium.

However, the SNR value of OGA audio file format exceeds 50 db once the payload (secret text to be hidden) gets above 150 kb in size. This means that the highest text file that can be embedded into these files without any distortion is 150 kb.

This current work have been able to develop a robust stenographic system that would be very useful in securing and sharing large amount of sensitive data or information without arousing suspicion. The developed system is therefore recommended for security agencies and other organization that consider information security as being of uttermost priority. This system is a useful means for transmitting covert battlefield information via an innocuous cover audio signal.

For future work, the use of post-quantum crypto schemes to strengthen audio steganography systems could be considered.

References

1. Kuboye, B.M., Gabriel, A.J., Thompson, A.F., Joseph, V.O.: Analysis of algorithms in long term evolution (LTE) network. J. Comput. Sci. Appl. **25**(2), 59–71 (2018)
2. Alabi, O., Thompson, A.F., Alese, B.K., Gabriel, A.J.: Cloud application security using hybrid encryption. Commun. Appl. Electron. **7**(33), 25–31 (2020)
3. Gabriel, A.J., Alese, B.K., Adetunmbi, A.O., Adewale, O.S., Sarumi, O.A.: Post-quantum crystography system for secure electronic voting. Open Comput. Sci. **9**, 292–298 (2019)
4. Gabriel, A.J., Egwuche, S.O.: Modelling the employees' activities of public service sector using production rules. Anale. Seria Informatică **13**(2), 65–68 (2015). Vol. XIII fasc. 2 – 2015 Annals. Computer Science Series, University of Timisoara, Romania
5. Iwasokun, G.B., Egwuche, O.S., Gabriel, A.J.: Neural network-based health personnel monitoring system. Afr. J. Comput. ICT **8**(1), 79–87 (2015)
6. Alese, B.K., Gabriel, A.J., Olukayode, O., Daramola, O.A.: Modelling of risk management procedures for cybercrime control systems. In: Proceedings of the World Congress on Engineering (WCE 2014), London, United Kingdom (2014). ISBN 978-988-19252-7-5
7. Agboola, A.H., Gabriel, A.J., Aliyu, E.O., Alese, B.K.: Development of a fuzzy logic based rainfall prediction model. Int. J. Eng. Technol. **3**(4), 427–435 (2013). ISSN 2049-3444
8. Daodu, M.N., Gabriel, A.J., Alese, B.K., Adetunmbi, A.O.: A data encryption standard (DES) based web services security architecture. Ann. Comput. Sci. Ser. **14**(2), 53–58 (2016)
9. Gabriel, A.J. Alese, B.K., Adetunmbi, A.O., Adewale, O.S.: Post-quantum crystography; a combination of post-quantum cryptography and steganography. In: The 8th International Conference for Internet Technology and Secured Transactions (ICITST-2013), Technically Co-Sponsored by IEEE UK/RI Computer Chapter, London, UK, 9–12 December 2013, pp. 454–457 (2013)
10. Gabriel, A.J., Alese, B.K., Adetunmbi, A.O., Adewale, O.S.: Post-quantum crystography based security framework for cloud computing. J. Internet Technol. Secur. Trans. (JITST) **4** (1), 351–357 (2015)
11. Wheeler, D. Johnson, D., Yuan, B., Lutz, P.: Audio steganography using high frequency noise introduction. Thomas Golisano College of Computing & Information Sciences Rochester Institute of Technology, Rochester, NY, RIT Scholar Works (2012). http://scholarworks.rit.edu/other/302. Accessed 14 Sept 2018
12. Ghanwat, D., Rajan, R.S.: Spread spectrum-based audio steganography in the transformation domain. Glob. J. Adv. Eng. Technol. **2**(4), 66–77 (2013)
13. Olanrewaju, R.F., Othman-Khalifa, H.A., Suliman, R.: Increasing the hiding capacity of low-bit encoding audio steganography using a novel embedding technique. World Appl. Sci. J. **21**(26), 79–83 (2013)
14. Kresnha, P.E., Mukaromah, A.: A robust method of encryption and steganography using ElGamal and spread spectrum technique on MP3 audio file. In: Proceeding of Conference on Application of Electromagnetic Technology, vol. 3, no. 9, pp. 11–15 (2014)
15. Kumari, L., Goyal, D., Gyan, S.: Analysis and design of three LSB techniques for secure audio steganography. Int. J. Adv. Res. Comput. Eng. Technol. (IJARCET) **2**(2), 44–55 (2013)
16. Pratibha, A.N., Belagali, P.P.: Data concealing using speech steganography. Int. Res. J. Eng. Technol. (IRJET) **3**(11), 55–66 (2016)
17. Sakthisudhan, K., Prabhu, P., Thangaraj, P.: Secure audio steganography for hiding secret information. Int. J. Comput. Appl. **7**(8), 55–87 (2012)

18. Balgurgi, P.P., Jagtap, S.K.: Audio steganography used for secure data transmission. In: Aswatha Kumar, M., Selvarani, R., Suresh Kumar, T.V. (eds.) Proceedings of International Conference on Advances in Computing. AISC, vol. 174, pp. 699–706. (2013). https://doi.org/10.1007/978-81-322-0740-5_83

19. Adeboje, O.T., Adetunmbi, A.O., Gabriel, A.J.: Embedding text in audio steganography system using advanced encryption standard and spread spectrum. Int. J. Comput. Appl. **177** (41), 46–51 (2020). https://doi.org/10.5120/ijca2020919. (0975-8887)

20. Snasel, V., Kromer, P., Safarik, J., Platos, J.: JPEG steganography with particle swarm optimization accelerated by AVX (2019). https://doi.org/10.1002/cpe.544. Wiley: https://onlinelibrary.wiley.com

21. Chatterjee, A., Ghosal, S.K., Sarkar, R.: LSB based steganography with OCR: an intelligent amalgamation. Multimed. Tools Appl. **79**, 11747–11765 (2020). https://doi.org/10.1007/s11042-019-08472-6

22. Rachael, O., Misra, S., Ahuja, R., Adewumi, A., Ayeni, F., Mmaskeliunas, R.: Image steganography and steganalysis based on least significant bit (LSB). In: Singh, P.K., Panigrahi, B.K., Suryadevara, N.K., Sharma, S.K., Singh, A.P. (eds.) Proceedings of ICETIT 2019. LNEE, vol. 605, pp. 1100–1111. Springer, Cham (2020). https://doi.org/10.1007/978-3-030-30577-2_97

Diagmal: A Malaria Coactive Neuro-Fuzzy Expert System

Tinuke Omolewa Oladele[1], Roseline Oluwaseun Ogundokun[2(✉)] ⓘ,
Joseph Bamidele Awotunde[1] ⓘ, Marion Olubunmi Adebiyi[2] ⓘ,
and Jide Kehinde Adeniyi[2]

[1] Department of Computer Science, University of Ilorin,
Ilorin, Kwara State, Nigeria
[2] Department of Computer Science, Landmark University Omu Aran,
Omu Aran, Kwara State, Nigeria
ogundokun.roseline@lmu.edu.ng

Abstract. In the process of clarifying whether a patient or patients is suffering from a disease or not, diagnosis plays a significant role. The procedure is quite slow and cumbersome, and some patients may not be able to pursue the final test results and diagnosis. The method in this paper comprises many fact-finding and data-mining methods. Artificial Intelligence techniques such as Neural Networks and Fuzzy Logic were fussed together in emerging the Coactive Neuro-Fuzzy Expert System diagnostic tool. The authors conducted oral interviews with the medical practitioners whose knowledge were captured into the knowledge based of the Fuzzy Expert System. Neuro-Fuzzy expert system diagnostic software was implemented with Microsoft Visual C# (C Sharp) programming language and Microsoft SQL Server 2012 to manage the database. Questionnaires were administered to the patients and filled by the medical practitioners on behalf of the patients to capture the prevailing symptoms. The study demonstrated the practical application of neuro-fuzzy method in diagnosis of malaria. The hybrid learning rule has greatly enhanced the proposed system performance when compared with existing systems where only the back-propagation learning rule were used for implementation. It was concluded that the diagnostic expert system developed is as accurate as that of the medical experts in decision making. DIAGMAL is hereby recommended to medical practitioners as a diagnostic tool for malaria.

Keywords: Fuzzy inference system · Diagnosis · Expert system · Neuro-fuzzy modeling · Malaria

1 Introduction

Information and Communication Technology (ICT) based diagnostic tools were used in the diagnosis of specific illnesses such as malaria. Malaria is an extremely transmissible malady brought about by plasmodium, a gore organism [1, 2]. It is presently one of the foremost transmissible humid sicknesses that unpleasantly affect people's well-being and many developing countries' financial advancement, especially the sub-Saharan Africa (SSA).

© Springer Nature Switzerland AG 2020
O. Gervasi et al. (Eds.): ICCSA 2020, LNCS 12254, pp. 428–441, 2020.
https://doi.org/10.1007/978-3-030-58817-5_32

Malaria has been epidemic in our society since the dawn of history [3]. About 40% of the ecosphere's populace resides in rampant areas of malaria. Furthermore, 90% of instances and the bulk of mortalities occur in tropical Africa. Three million mortalities and 500 million medical instances were estimated yearly [4]. One of the major activities of W.H.O. is to make health care facilities available and accessible to all at all times and at various locations, but the current situation is the contrary. Most of the people who are to access these facilities are far removed from these facilities and resides farther from them or these facilities are too expensive to be accessed. In view of the foregoing, there is a necessity to provide a computerized system that is a knowledge-based system that will provide complementary medical services.

Several studies have shown that manual microscopy is not a reliable screening method unlike automated diagnosis [5–8]. An automated diagnosis system can be designed by understanding the diagnostic expertise [9, 10] for identifying malaria when prevailing symptoms are specified. An automated system aims at performing this task without human intervention and also provides an objective, reliable, and efficient tool to do so. Hence, Artificial Intelligence (AI) techniques based on neural network, fuzzy logic [11–17] and expert systems were applied in the diagnosis of malaria. These AI methods were used in place of the clinical laboratory in diagnosing malaria in patients.

This research was meant to showcase the prowess of the ICT approach to medical diagnosis. It will promote early diagonalization of malaria by making the diagnostic tool available and accessible to all even at the grass-root level. The ICT-based Neuro-Fuzzy Expert System diagnostic tool will optimize the activities of medical practitioners in the area of diagnosis of malaria. It will also assist academic institutions and the industry for the purpose of research.

In this research, the Coactive Neuro-Fuzzy Expert System diagnostic tool called DIAGMAL was designed and implemented. The diagnosis given by DIAGMAL is based on the prevailing symptoms given by the patients. Statistical Investigation of the datasets acquired after the administration of the questionnaires was also conveyed in order to establish the accuracy of the tool.

2   Literature Review

In the literature, ICT-based malaria diagnosis and some other diseases have been reported. In [18], fuzzy logic was employed and they developed a fuzzy expert malaria management system. Online system identification and management malaria was documented in [19], where a rule-based knowledgeable scheme was developed with the ability to interact with the scheme in real-time and via mobile devices based on the global mobile communication system (GSM) technology. Researchers [20] reported diamaltycin for malaria diagnosis and typhoid fever; a decision support system for medical application, a case-based decision support system for malaria and typhoid diagnosis. The study didn't apply the use of neural network and fuzzy logic algorithms. There was no precise method of distinguishing between malaria and typhoid. Decision support system model for diagnostic of tropical diseases using fuzzy logic was documented in [21], where fuzzy logic was used to diagnose tropical diseases such as malaria, typhoid, tuberculosis, sexually transmitted diseases, yellow fever, hepatitis B, leprosy and chickenpox. The confidence interval to give the assurance that the diagnosis given was actually for the specified disease was not computed.

[22] proposed a medical expert system for managing tropical diseases. In the proposed Medical Expert System (MES) the inference engine used a forward-looking chaining method to search the expert system for symptoms of a disease and it associate therapy which matches the query supplied by the patient.

[23] developed a flippant rule-based framework for tropical disease management. While assessing the extent of the tropical disease, fuzzy logic was employed. A fluffy expert system for hypertension management [9] was used to diagnose high blood pressure.

[24] provided a systematic empirical analysis of existing medical expert systems used to diagnose various diseases based on the increasing demand for human expert support systems. The study provided a descriptive overview of the different techniques used, such as rule-based, fuzzy, artificial neural networks, and smart hybrid models. The rule-based techniques were not too efficient based on its inability to learn. This required powerful search strategies for its knowledge-base. The fuzzy or ANN models are less efficient when compared to the hybrid models that can give a more accurate result.

[25] proposed an Adaptive Neuro Fuzzy Inference System (ANFIS) for malaria diagnosis. The system was designed to use the triangular membership function and as its learning algorithm used back propagation technique as well as the least square mean. The authors used the design of tagaki sugeno fuzzy inference to provide the system's rules base. The program result provided 98 percent accuracy in the identification of patients with malaria.

A decision support system centered on fuzzy logic was employed to diagnose tuberculosis [20]. In [26], a hybrid neuro-fuzzy expert scheme for the testing and forecast of thyroid disorders was conveyed in order to diagnose thyroid disorder. The system could be used for cases defined in the knowledge-based system since it was not an adaptive hybrid system.

This proposed system was therefore projected to develop a coactive neuro-fuzzy malaria diagnostic system tool, based on an adaptive neuro-fuzzy system model.

3   Methodology

3.1   Questionnaire

Questionnaire was designed for patients to capture their prevailing symptoms so as to be able to determine the presence or absence of malaria in their body system.

Questionnaire Design
The questionnaire designed for the diagnosis of malaria was subdivided into 3 sections.

i. Section A: Demographic and Socio-Economic characteristics of the respondents, such as; Age, sex, place of residence and so on was captured.

ii. Section B: Symptoms of malaria, such as; fever, headache, Body pain, Catarrh, cough, nausea, chills, sweating, bitter taste, vomiting, jaundice, diarrhea, body weakness, sore throat were specified.

iii. Section C: Treatment of malaria. This section is meant to capture the preferred treatment measure by the respondent such as self-medication, use of herbs, or orthodox medical treatment and so on.

Population and Sample size

The target population for this study included the staff and students of the University of Ilorin Health Centre as well as the patients at the Civil Service Clinic in Ilorin, Kwara State, Nigeria. 180 respondents were the sample size used for this study and this includes 100 respondents from University of Ilorin Health Center (Staff and students inclusive) and 80 respondents from Civil Service Clinic Ilorin, Kwara State, Nigeria.

Procedure for Questionnaire Administration

Atotal number of 100 questionnaires were administered at the University of Ilorin Health Centre, while 80 copies were administered at the Civil Service Clinic in Ilorin. Out of the 100 copies of the questionnaire administered at the University of Ilorin Health Centre, 85 copies were returned while 23 copies were returned out of the 80 copies administered at the Civil Service Clinic, giving a total of 108 returned copies of the questionnaire.

4 Results and Discussion

Neuro-Fuzzy measures were adopted in the CANFES model which was used in the implementation of the proposed system DIAGMAL, the diagnostic tool for malaria disease. This section offers an in-depth analysis and interpretation of the results and discussion of the findings.

4.1 Implementation of the Coactive Neuro-Fuzzy Expert System

In this paper, the developed Coactive Neuro-Fuzzy Expert System tool for diagnosis of malaria was called DIAGMAL. Screenshots capturing all the interfaces representing the modules in the expert system are displayed in this section. The stages involved in entering the signs, symptoms and historical data, and the diagnosis being made were also captured.

Splash Screen

Figure 1 shows the splash screen for the expert system. The splash screen is a slide show of DIAGMAL logo.

Patient Registration Page

The patient record page captures the biodata of each patient as displayed in Fig. 2.

Figure 2 displays the registered patient records. When new users registered by inputting their data into the system, it is stored in a database and this page shows sample of some of the patients' records already stored in the application.

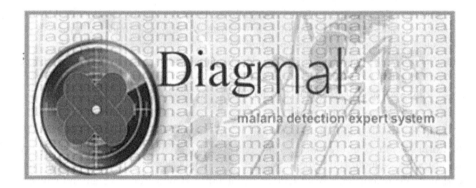

Fig. 1. DIAGMAL splash screen

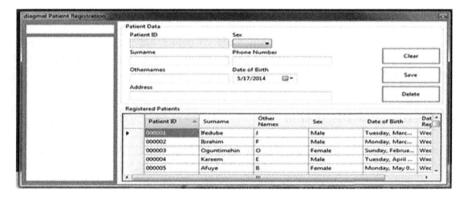

Fig. 2. Patient's registration form

Expert System Initial Test

This module captures the patient's historical and demographic data to a certain extent. The expert system then gives an assessment of the patient as being exposed to malaria based on the selected and entered data.

Figure 3 shows the expert system initial test. After the development of the application, the first implementation performed on the system is shown in this figure.

Expert System General Test

This module is divided into two columns, which are variable symptoms and selective symptoms. The variable symptoms are selected between a range of mild and high, while the selective symptoms are clicked as it applies to the patient.

Figure 4 shows the general test page. This is the page showing the general test which involves the variable symptoms.

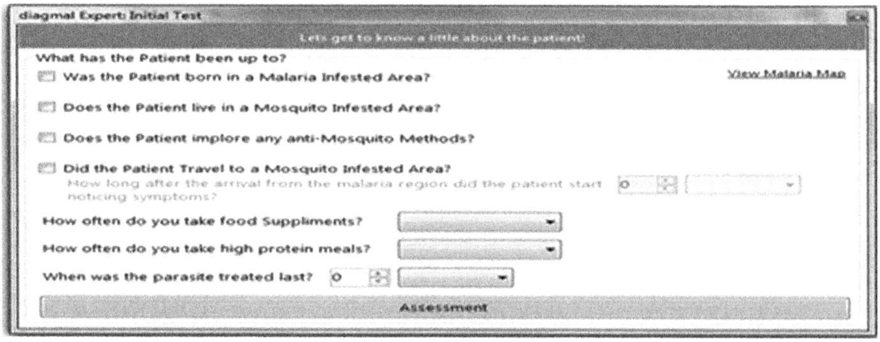

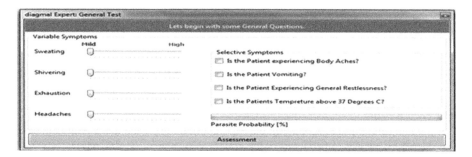

Fig. 3. Expert initial test

Fig. 4. General test

Expert System Secondary Test

This module contains variable symptoms where, body ache, extended cramps, and dizziness are captured between the range of mild and high. Respiratory rate is captured between normal and abnormal and lip texture is captured between normal and dry.

Figure 5 shows the secondary test which involves the variable symptoms but these symptoms are different from the ones in the general test page.

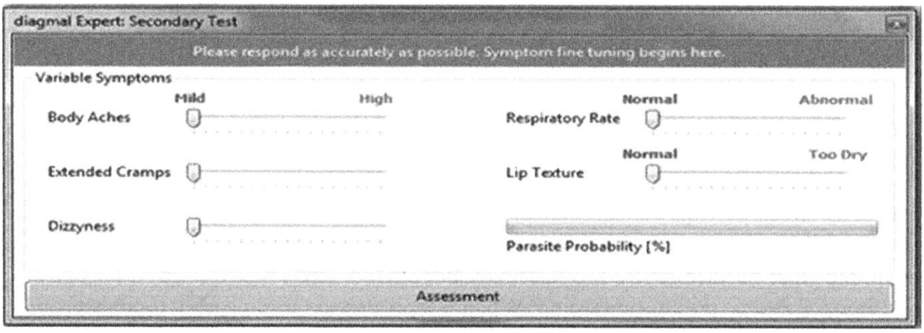

Fig. 5. Secondary test

Expert Final Test

This module contains variable symptoms which are intended to capture all the possible signs and symptoms that are exhibited by the patient.

Figure 6 shows the final test page and this is the final test module for the application developed. These also contains different variables from the two initial pages.

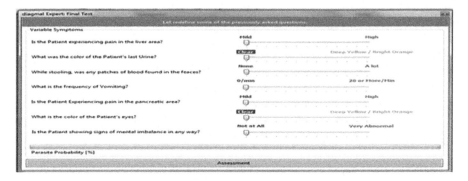

Fig. 6. Final test

Inference Result

This module serves as a link between the expert system result and the patient's biodata. The degree or intensity of malaria in the patient is displayed on this page.

Figure 7 shows the inference result. The inference setting was done and implementation was executed and Fig. 7 shows the outcome of the execution.

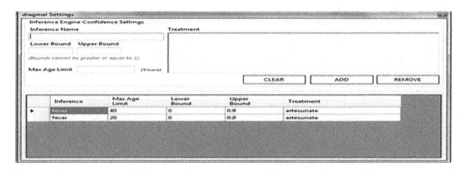

Fig. 7. Inference result

Report Engine

This module generates the patient's details with their respective diagnosis result. The result can then be printed by the administrator or the user.

Figure 8 shows the report engine. When a report scope is clicked, it displays reports about patients.

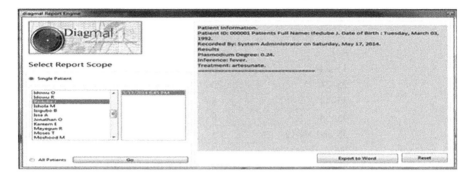

Fig. 8. Report engine

4.2   Questionnaire Data Analysis and Interpretation

The Demographic and Socio-economic Characteristics of the Respondents is shown in Table 1.

Table 2 shows that the average age of the respondents was 27.08 years (27 years). Also, it is obvious from the same table that expected monthly income of the respondents was 58,300 Naira. 37.3 °C was estimated to be the average body temperature of the respondents as at the time of investigation. With respect to the question relating to the frequency of malaria per year, most of the respondents claimed that they had malaria three times per year. A respondent affirmed that he/she has not had malaria before, whereas someone said that he/she had malaria ten times in a year.

Table 3 shows that almost all of the respondents had been diagnosed for malaria fever before survey (99.1%). Only one respondent (0.9%) said that he/she had never been a patient of malaria. One – fourth of those who claimed that they had been diagnosed for malaria before (26.9%) were still having malaria as at the time of survey. Almost four out of every five respondents (76.9%) asserted that their malaria cases were seldom. Nearly one – fifth of the respondents (18.5%) claimed that they had malaria fever frequently. The distribution of respondents according to the symptoms of malaria shows that two out of every five respondents (39.8%) said that headache was the most severe symptom of malaria. This is followed by those who claimed that body pain and fever were the major symptoms of malaria (18.5% and 17.5% respectively). Vomiting and Jaundice had the least representations (0.9%). This implies that both vomiting and jaundice were not the main symptoms of malaria. Only 4.6% of the respondents did not respond to the question relating to most severe symptoms of malaria at all. This is evident by the following bar chart depicted in Fig. 9.

It is evident by the following bar chart depicted by Fig. 9 that 15.7% of respondents have fever as their own symptoms of malaria, 39.8% have headache as their own symptoms, 16.7% have body pain as their own symptoms of malaria, 7.4% have catarrh as their own symptoms of malaria, 1.9% have chill as their own symptoms of malaria, 0.9% symptoms is vomiting and jaundice as their own symptoms of malaria, 1.9% have diarrhea as their own symptoms of malaria, 8.3% have body weakness as their own

Table 1. Demographic and socio-economic characteristics of the respondents

Characteristics	Number	Percentage
Age		
15–24	66	61.1
25–34	23	21.3
35–44	4	3.7
45–54	8	7.4
55 and above	5	4.6
No response	2	1.9
Total	**108**	**100.0**
Sex		
Male	60	55.6
Female	47	43.5
No response	1	0.9
Total	**108**	**100.0**
Marital status		
Single	83	76.9
Ever married	25	23.1
Total	**108**	**100.0**
Education		
Primary	3	2.8
Secondary	13	12.0
First degree	72	66.7
Higher degree	7	6.5
Undergraduate	8	7.4
No response	5	4.6
Total	**108**	**100.0**
Place of residence		
Urban	96	88.9
Rural	12	11.1
Total	**108**	**100.0**
Occupation		
Civil/public servant	12	11.1
Private salary employee	3	2.8
Self-employed	13	12.0
Artisan	2	1.9
Student	66	61.1
No response	12	11.1
Total	**108**	**100.0**
Hospitals used		
Unilorin health services	85	78.7
Civil service clinic	23	21.3
Total	**108**	**100.0**

Source: Survey, 2019.

Table 2. Summary of quantitative data

Characteristics	Minimum	Maximum	Mean
Age	16	89	27.08
Income	1000	699000	58300
Body temp	23 °C	42 °C	37.3 °C
Malaria per year	N/A	10	3.0

Source: Survey, 2019.

symptoms of malaria, 1.9% have sore throat as their own symptoms of malaria and lastly 4.6% respondents didn't give any response.

According to doctor's reports, more than three out of every five respondents (72.2%) were diagnosed for malaria fever at the time of the investigation. This is followed by those who were diagnosed with plasmodiasis (3.2%). Exactly one – fourth of the doctors (25.0%) did not indicate the current diagnosis of their patients. Only one patient was diagnosed with hypertension. The distribution of respondents according to hospital attendance for malaria treatment indicates that more than three out of every five respondents (63.0%) claimed that they attended hospital for malaria treatment while 31.5% of the respondents did not attend hospital for malaria treatment. Table 3 also shows that approximately one out of every five respondents (18.5%) preferred self-medication to attend the hospital. This is followed by those who said that they preferred orthodox medication (17.6%). More than the average of the respondents (57.4%) did not indicate their preference at all. It is obvious from the table that two out of every five respondents (41.7%) indicated tablets as what they used to treat malaria, while one – fifth of the respondents (21.3%) claimed that they used injections to cure malaria. But one - fourth of the respondents (25.9%) combined tablets with injections for malaria treatment.

5   Discussion of Results

5.1   Implementation of the Coactive Neuro-Fuzzy Expert System

The identification given by the expert system named DIAGMAL showed the exact diagnosis given by the doctor. This specifies that computer application can accurately determine the diagnosis of malaria. The essence of this research is to determine the extent to which neuro-fuzzy methodology represents the exact diagnosis of patients compared to that of physicians. Accuracy of the system was tested by observations made from the various populations which were assessed on the field. Based on the assessment, it was found that DIAGMAL gave accurate diagnostic predictions.

There are two platforms on which this application can be implemented. It can be implemented as a web-based application or as a desktop application. The expert system was developed as a desktop application that can be implemented on any personal

Table 3. Symptoms of malaria

Characteristics	Number	Percentage (%)
Ever diagnosed for malaria		
Yes	107	99.1
No	1	0.9
Total	**108**	**100.0**
Currently diagnosed for malaria		
Yes	29	26.9
No	74	68.5
No response	5	4.6
Total	**108**	**100.0**
Frequency of malaria		
Seldom	83	76.9
Frequently	20	18.5
Very frequently	2	1.9
No response	3	2.8
Total	**108**	**100.0**
Most severe symptoms of malaria		
Fever	17	15.7
Headache	43	39.8
Body pain	18	16.7
Catarrh	8	7.4
Chill	2	1.9
Vomiting	1	0.9
Jaundice	1	0.9
Diarrhea	2	1.9
Body weakness	9	8.3
Sore throat	2	1.9
No response	5	4.6
Total	**108**	**100.0**
Doctors' current diagnosis		
Malaria fever	78	72.2
Plasmadiasis	4	3.7
Hypertension	1	0.9
No response	25	23.1
Total	**108**	**100.0**
Hospital's attendance for malaria treatment		
Yes	107	63.0
No	34	31.5
No response	6	5.6
Total	**108**	**100.0**

(*continued*)

Table 3. (*continued*)

Characteristics	Number	Percentage (%)
Malaria treatment methods		
Self-medication	20	18.5
Herbs	6	5.6
Orthodox medical treatment	19	17.6
Other treatments	1	0.9
No response	62	57.4
Total	**108**	**100.0**
Malaria treatments preference		
Tablets	45	41.7
Injections	23	21.3
Tablets and injections combined	28	25.9
Herbs	4	3.7
No response	8	7.4
Total	**108**	**100.0**

Source: Survey, 2019.

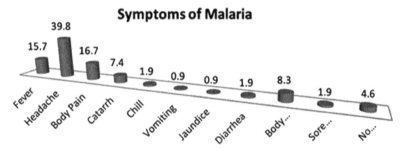

Fig. 9. Symptoms of Malaria

computer. Hence, the problem of internet connectivity has been overcome. This also specifies that the neuro-fuzzy expert system diagnostic tool can be truly deployed and made accessible at the grass-root level.

5.2 Summary of Findings

a. Design and implementation of a Coactive Neuro-Fuzzy Expert System diagnostic tool called DIAGMAL.
b. Empirically, the symptoms of malaria were identified;
c. The most severe symptoms of malaria were identified; and
d. It was deduced that even though headache, body pain, fever and other symptoms identified by the respondents (that is, patients) are symptoms of malaria, they are also symptoms of other diseases.

6 Conclusion

The need to develop a system that would assist physicians in the diagnosis of malaria cannot be over emphasized. This paper demonstrated the practical application of information and communication technology in the medical domain. It has employed the use of a coactive neuro-fuzzy expert system that can help in the diagnosis of malaria. The system is an interactive system that predicts the intensity of malaria in a patient.

The hybrid learning rule enhances the performance of the system. Based on these results, the study shows that the ICT-based Neuro-Fuzzy Expert System for diagnosis of malaria produces accurate results. DIAGMAL is hereby recommended to the world of academia and the industry for the purpose of research and to assist medical practitioners as a diagnostic tool for malaria.

Availability of Data and Material
The datasets used in this study were gotten from a survey and deposited in Zenodo Database repository [27].

References

1. Adebiyi, M., et al.: Computational investigation of consistency and performance of the biochemical network of the malaria parasite, *plasmodium falciparum*. In: Misra, S., et al. (eds.) ICCSA 2019. LNCS, vol. 11623, pp. 231–241. Springer, Cham (2019). https://doi.org/10.1007/978-3-030-24308-1_19
2. Carter, R., Mendes, K.N.: Evolutionary and historical aspects of the burden of malaria. Clin. Microbiol. Rev. **15**, 564–594 (2002)
3. White, N.J.: Antimalarial drug resistance. J. Clin. Invest. **113**, 1084–1092 (2004)
4. Kettelhut, M.M., Chiodini, P.L., Edwards, H., Moody, A.: External quality assessment schemes raise standards: evidence from UKNEQAS parasitology subschemes. J. Clin. Pathol. **56**, 927–932 (2003)
5. Coleman, R.E., et al.: Comparison of field and expert laboratory microscopy for active surveillance for asymptomatic Plasmodium falaparum and Plasmodium vivax in western Thailand. Am. J. Trop. Med. Hyg. **67**, 144–154 (2002)
6. Bates, I., Bekoe, V., Asamoa-Adu, A.: Improving the accuracy of malaria-related laboratory tests in Ghana. Malar. J. **3** (2004). Article number: 38. https://doi.org/10.1186/1475-2875-3-38
7. Mitiku, K., Mengistu, G., Gelaw, B.: The reliability of blood film examination for malaria at the peripheral health unit. Ethiop. J. Health Dev. **17**, 197–204 (2003)
8. Adebayo, O., Asani, E.O., Ogundokun, R.O., Ananti, E.C., Adegun, A.: A neuro-fuzzy based system for the classification of cells as cancerous of non-cancerous. Int. J. Med. Res. Health Sci. **7**(5), 155–166 (2018)
9. Djam, X.Y., Kimbi, Y.H.: Fuzzy expert system for the management of hypertension. Pac. J. Sci. Technol. **12**(1), 390–402 (2011)
10. Donfack, A.F., Abdullahi, M., Ezugwu, A.E., Alkali, S.A.: Online system for diagnosis and treatment of malaria (2009)

11. Lala, O.G., Emuoyibofarhe, O.J., Fajuyigbe, O., Onaolapo, S.O.: Diamaltycin for the diagnosis of malaria and typhoid fever: a decision support system for medical application. In: Proceedings of the First International Conference on Mobile Computing, Wireless Communication, E-Health, M-Health & Telemedicine (MWEMTem 2008), Held at Ladoke Akintola University of Technology (LAUTECH), Ogbomosho (2008)
12. Olabiyisi, S.O., Omidiora, E.O., Olaniyan, M.O., Dorikoma, O.: A decision support system model for diagnosing tropical diseases using fuzzy logic. Afr. J. Comput. ICT **4**(2), 1–6 (2011)
13. Adekoya, A.F., Akinwale, A.T., Oke, O.E.: A medical expert system for managing tropical diseases. In: Proceedings of the Third Conference on Science and National Development, pp. 74–86 (2008)
14. Obot, O.U., Uzoka, F.M.E.: Fuzzy rule-based framework for the management of tropical diseases. Int. J. Eng. Inform. **1**(1), 7–17 (2008)
15. Imhanlahimi, R.E., John-Otumu, A.M.: Application of expert system for diagnosing medical conditions: a methodological review. Eur. J. Comput. Sci. Inf. Technol. **7**(2), 12–25 (2019)
16. Osubor and Chiemeke: An adaptive neuro fuzzy inference system for the diagnosis of malaria. NISEB J. **14**(4), 212–222 (2015)
17. Agboizebeta, I.A., Chukwuyeni, O.J.: Application of neuro-fuzzy expert system for the probe and prognosis of thyroid disoder. Int. J. Fuzzy Log. Syst. (IJFLS) **2**(2), 1–11 (2012)
18. Ayo, F.E., et al.: A fuzzy based method for diagnosis of acne skin disease severity. i-Manager's J. Pattern Recogn. **5**(2), 10 (2018)
19. Awotunde, J.B., Matiluko, O.E., Fatai, O.W.: Medical diagnosis system using fuzzy logic. Afr. J. Comput. ICT **7**(2), 99–106 (2014)
20. Jimoh, R.G., Afolayan, A.A., Awotunde, J.B., Matiluko, E.O.: Fuzzy logic based expert system in the diagnosis of Ebola virus. Ilorin J. Comput. Sci. Inf. Technol. **2**(1), 73–94 (2017)
21. Thompson, T., Sowunmi, O., Misra, S., Fernandez-Sanz, L., Crawford, B., Soto, R.: An expert system for the diagnosis of sexually transmitted diseases–ESSTD. J. Intell. Fuzzy Syst. **33**(4), 2007–2017 (2017)
22. Azeez, N.A., et al.: A fuzzy expert system for diagnosing and analyzing human diseases. In: Abraham, A., Gandhi, N., Pant, M. (eds.) IBICA 2018. AISC, vol. 939, pp. 474–484. Springer, Cham (2019). https://doi.org/10.1007/978-3-030-16681-6_47
23. Lawanya Shri, M., Ganga Devi, E., Balusamy, B., Kadry, S., Misra, S., Odusami, M.: A fuzzy based hybrid firefly optimization technique for load balancing in cloud datacenters. In: Abraham, A., Gandhi, N., Pant, M. (eds.) IBICA 2018. AISC, vol. 939, pp. 463–473. Springer, Cham (2019). https://doi.org/10.1007/978-3-030-16681-6_46
24. Alhassan, J.K., Misra, S., Umar, A., Maskeliūnas, R., Damaševičius, R., Adewumi, A.: A fuzzy classifier-based penetration testing for web applications. In: Rocha, Á., Guarda, T. (eds.) ICITS 2018. AISC, vol. 721, pp. 95–104. Springer, Cham (2018). https://doi.org/10.1007/978-3-319-73450-7_10
25. Ayo, F.E., Awotunde, J.B., Ogundokun, R.O., Folorunso, S.O., Adekunle, A.O.: A decision support system for multi-target disease diagnosis: a bioinformatics approach. Heliyon **6**(3), e03657 (2020)
26. Jimoh, R.G., Awotunde, J.B., Babatunde, A.O., Ameen, A.O, James, T.R., Fatai, O.W.: Simulation of medical diagnosis system for malaria using fuzzy logic. Int. J. Inf. Process. Commun. (IJIPC) **2**(1) (2014)
27. Oladele, T.O., Ogundokun, R.O., Adebiyi, M.O.: Datasets on malaria disease [data set]. Zenodo (2019). http://doi.org/10.5281/zenodo.3592442

NatVi - A Framework for Agile Software Development, Service-Oriented Architecture and Quality Assurance

James Taylor Faria Chaves[(✉)] and Sergio Antônio Andrade de Freitas[(✉)]

University of Brasilia, Darcy Ribeiro Campus, Brasôlia, DF, Brazil
jameschaves@gmail.com, sergiofreitas@unb.br

Abstract. This research presents the NatVi Framework for Agile Software Development, Service-Oriented Architecture (SOA), and Quality Assurance (QA). The research took place in a context of profound and rapid changes in business environments that affect the software development environment. Our previous work did a Systematic Literature Review trying to find articles dealing with SOA and Agile and the challenges inherent in this combination of solutions. In order to build the Framework, this work took the shortcomings found in the solutions presented in the papers and further incorporated the necessary QA concept. In this context, the Framework attempts to provide an answer to how to develop software with quality and rapid deliveries in an ever-changing environment, where the traditional forms of software development may not handle it. Background research identified trade-offs among SOA, QA, and Agile, e.g., formality, documentation, and planning. The background research also identified strengths, weaknesses, and gaps in papers that addressed solutions to problems that arise in software development in the presented context. The results of the background research were assessed and exploited in Framework construction. In a single life-cycle, the NatVi Framework combines Agile, SOA, and QA and addresses the values and principles that guide them in 13 phases distributed in four layers. Each phase is carried out by people who perform specific roles, expressed in terms of inputs, tasks, and outputs. As a Framework, it is not exhaustive, and its main concepts may change and adapt to each environment. The Framework validation is underway, and a forthcoming paper will present the results.

Keywords: Service-oriented-architecture · SOA · Agile Software Development · Quality Assurance · QA · Software engineering

1 Introduction

Since the beginning of the 21st century, organizations must respond flexibly, rapidly, and dynamically to the demands of ever-changing customers, market opportunities, and external threats. This context arose with the increase in

© Springer Nature Switzerland AG 2020
O. Gervasi et al. (Eds.): ICCSA 2020, LNCS 12254, pp. 442–458, 2020.
https://doi.org/10.1007/978-3-030-58817-5_33

technology that allowed people and organizations to seek improvements that fit their needs. In this context, traditional forms of software development can present some disadvantages, such as reduced integration, delays in deliveries, and problems in sharing information among stakeholders [25]. These problems can compromise the quality of the process as a whole. Then, how to develop software with quality and rapid deliveries in an ever-changing environment?

This paper presents the NatVi Framework for Agile, Service-Oriented Architecture (SOA), and Quality Assurance (QA). It is a study for a software engineering solution to deal with the presented context, using concepts in terms of architectural design and development methods that are capable of maintaining or improving Quality Assurance (QA).

The Framework was the result of background research, including our previous work, a Systematic Literature Review (SLR) [8] that identified articles dealing with SOA and Agile and the challenges inherent in this combination of solutions. The SLR identified papers that addressed solutions for problems that arise in the presented context, and this work took the shortcomings found in those solutions and incorporated the necessary QA concept.

The Framework construction used the solutions found in the background research. It tried to take advantage of the strength and address the weakness and gaps of those solutions. It also sought to deal with the trade-offs among the central concepts identified in the studies, e.g., degree of formality, documentation, and planning.

The NatVi Framework does not merely combine agile development and SOA. It works as a single life-cycle with the necessary phases to implement services solutions in an Agile way. The NatVi Framework addresses in its four layers and 13 phases the values and principles of Agile and SOA. Likewise, it allows people to execute a well-planned and structured process that continually seeks to QA. The people involved in the development process perform specific roles in each phase, e.g., sponsor, end-user, developer, QA manager, and tester. Each phase of the Framework presents inputs, tasks, and outputs. As a Framework, it is not exhaustive, and its concepts, inputs, tasks, and outputs can change and adapt to each environment.

From the requirements' elicitation to the system monitoring, the Framework seeks to balance the principles and values of the three central concepts, Agile, SOA, and QA, putting them together in a well-constructed process. This balance sometimes seems to break some principles and values in some phases, e.g., initial phases can present more planning and documentation than in a normal Agile process, but, less documentation than an SOA process. This apparent breakdown of concepts is just enough to maintain balance, trying not to lose the essence of the concepts.

The Framework appears to be suitable for environments that experience rapid changes in business needs, reflecting the requirements of software systems. In a governmental setting, the Framework can help adapt systems to changes in the law and the interest of the citizen. In a service industry scenario, it can help organizations find end-user satisfaction. Nevertheless, all scenarios in which business changes occur quickly can exploit the use of the Framework.

As a theoretical work, the Framework requires validation. To that end, a case study will be carried out and presented in future work. The evolution of QA in the use of the Framework will be evaluated through the monitoring of error metrics in the source code, the involvement of the development team and customer satisfaction with the new development process.

Section 2 provides an overview of Agile, SOA, and QA. Section 3 discusses some previous solutions that helped to build the NatVi Framework. Section 4 presents the NatVi Framework, and Sect. 5 presents the conclusions.

2   Background

This section presents some background about Service-Oriented Architecture (SOA), Agile Software Development, and Quality Assurance (QA). The values and principles introduced are suitable for understanding these concepts and how they are essential in the Framework, but they are not exhaustible.

2.1   Service-Oriented Architecture (SOA)

Building new functionalities and reusing existing systems, all integrated, can be an issue. This context worsens by adding the expectation of a large number of stakeholders with different goals that can change at any given moment. In this context, at the end of the 20th century, the concept of services appeared. A new way of thinking about systems architecture, breaking complex structures into small parts of functionality [4,11,24]. Service-Oriented Architecture (SOA) arose as a solution to handle this context, integrating and uniforming old and new solutions, and simplifying business processes.

SOA is an architectural pattern that presents service providers and service consumers, kept together by elements of Information Technology (IT) [4,5,11]. It aims to enhance the efficiency, agility, and productivity of an enterprise [1]. To achieve these aims, it works in eight services principles [13]: Standardized Service Contract; Service Loose Coupling; Service Abstraction; Service Reusability; Service Autonomy; Service Statelessness; Service Discoverability; and Service Composability.

SOA also can be seen as a system development process [24,29]. However, the complexity of implementing SOA presents some challenges. Its flexibility represents a complex integration of many different resources, which can exhibit a large number of critical interdependencies across many of the resources. This complexity can also bring issues to its deployment, mainly in reliability [5,30]. Stakeholder interests also may be an issue while they can demand conflicting requirements that have to be rightly managed [7]. Performance is also a concern. If the processes present an undetermined number of requests, SOA may generate bottlenecks in peaks of a request [27]. Service providers may present various issues in an SOA environment, e.g., reusability, interoperability, and scalability [6,30].

2.2   Agile Software Development

In the 1990s and early 2000s, many writers were looking for a lightweight method for software development. They wrote articles where they were concerned with problems in the software development processes that were heavy and oriented to vast documentation [7]. These concerns led to Agile Software Development that came in the form of the Agile Manifesto, published in 2001 [2]. According to [36], 'Agile methods are the solution to the problems that can be caused by traditional methodologies'.

This software development method is rapid, flexible, and stakeholders' goals-driven. The Agile manifesto [2] values are as follows: '(1) individuals and interactions over processes and tools, (2) working software over comprehensive documentation, (3) customer collaboration over contract negotiation and (4) responding to changes over following a plan'. 'That is, while there is value in the items on the right, we value the items on the left more'.

This software development method is rapid, flexible, and stakeholders' goals-driven. Agile methods value the integration and collaboration between self-organized and multifunctional teams. It also values informal communication among stakeholders. It also emphasizes tacit knowledge over explicit knowledge and promotes the teams' improvement in the software process [3].

Among the main advantages of Agile are quick responses to changes in requirements, customer satisfaction with the fast and continuous delivery of useful software [18], lower error rates, and a shorter development cycle [36]. It has to be iterative, incremental, cooperative, and adaptable to changes in environments and requirements. To achieve the necessary flexibility, Agile is formal documentation-less and uses informal communication [1,9,14].

These properties of Agile also can be seen as a disadvantage of the method regarding the bureaucratic organization, critical systems, and maintainability [31]. Another disadvantage is the difficulty of assessing the effort required at the beginning of the software development life cycle [18].

Regardless of this disadvantage, Agile Software Development makes use of good programming practices that are considered one of the pillars of quality assurance [15]. Some advocate that agile development is oriented to a higher quality compared to plan-driven development [26].

2.3   Quality Assurance (QA)

High-quality delivery is expected in any software engineering process, agile or otherwise, so Quality Assurance (QA) is itself a necessity. Software quality is one critical criterion used to measure the success of a software development project [22]. QA, for software engineering, means that the requirements need to be met, and the final product needs to be appropriate for the use [32].

QA is a process to guarantee quality in a software development process, which leads to quality in the final product, and it is also a process to evaluate the development itself [16,20,32]. There are many descriptions in the literature of QA [26] and some other concepts that share the same description, such as

Software Assurance [33], Quality Attributes [12], and Software Quality [23]. In a broad concept, QA represents the degree to which a product or process meets established requirements. This definition may refer to the ability to meet functional requirements, but it may also refer to non-functional requirements, i.e., performance, reliability, availability, portability, and maintainability [26].

Hence, Quality Assurance (QA) is at the same time a planned and systematic process to provide adequate confidence that software conforms to requirements [16] and a set of activities designed to evaluate the process by which the software is developed. As a planned and systematic process, it is possible to list from literature some activities that help ensure the quality: demonstration of the software, test-driven development, automated acceptance testing, daily builds with Testing, pair programming, coding standard, refactoring, peer review, defect analysis, defect reporting, unit testing, test automation, continuous integration, testing level, defect prevention and static analysis [17,34]. For each activity, a set of features must be defined according to each environment: guidelines, benefits, processes, best practices, templates, and customization [17].

QA depends upon the degree to which those established requirements accurately represent stakeholder needs, wants, and expectations [20]. It depends on a good plan and documentation. It depends on a good process and a proper evaluation of this process. In other words, the entire process of software engineering is committed to QA [26].

3   Related Work

While Service-Oriented Architecture (SOA) and Quality Assurance (QA) follow more traditional concepts, e.g., comprehensive documentation and up-front design, Agile Software Development strongly refutes these concepts and aims a light way of developing software, mainly valuing people, arising a trade-off. Once Agile Software Development is a trend, the papers presented in this subsection aim to find a solution to this trade-off.

Our previous work, the Systematic Literature Review (SLR) in [8], presents papers that deal with Agile and SOA, and in [15], the authors show papers that deal with Agile and QA. In the preparation of this paper, the researchers did not find an article that deals straightforwardly with the three concepts together, Agile, SOA, and QA.

[28] exhibits a Service-Oriented Framework of Interface Prototype Driven Development that deals rapidly with changes in requirements and improves the quality and efficiency of analysis and design for a data-centered application system.

[35] shows the 'SOA based Model-driven Rapid Development Architecture - SMRDA'. The authors performed a combination of SOA, Model-driven Architecture (MDA), proposed by Object Management Group (OMG), and agile methods. They concluded that this combination is the "main trend of modern software development in enterprise applications. The key of which is modeling services correctly and applying agile development techniques".

In [9], authors present a platform called FraSCAti to be used with their proposed framework, the FASOAD, a Framework for Agile Service-Oriented Architectures Development.

[10] shows the Agile and Service-Oriented Software Development Method (ASOSDeM) that aims to overcome web-based development projects' complexity by dividing it into sub-projects to allow the application of agile methods' practices. It defines how a self-organizing team should execute an SOA agile development project. It describes the concepts that may be used in an SOA project such as 'Artifacts', 'Tasks', and 'Roles'. It addresses: 'development, analysis, architecture elaboration, granularity identification, components assembling, deployment, integration tests, and business processes assembling'.

From [15], is highlighted some papers that deal with Agile and QA. [18] presents the scope of the ISO 9126 quality attributes (Correctness, Maintainability, variability, efficiency, availability, portability, testability, and reliability)through agile practices derived from XP.

In [19], the authors present Agile practices responsible for quality assurance: test-driven development, acceptance testing, code inspection, pair programming, refactoring, continuous integration, collaborative work, system metaphor, continuous feedback, and coding best practices.

[21] presents 3C approach, in which the authors achieved quality assurance from an improvement of the practice of continuous integration, continuous measurement, and continuous improvement.

[22] the author identifies some practices that promote quality assurance in the Scrum framework and continuous collaboration, integration testing, continuous feedback and development, knowledge sharing, retrospective, and daily meetings.

4 The Framework

The Background, Sect. 2, presents some paper for dealing with Agile, Service-Oriented Architecture (SOA), and Quality Assurance (QA). Nevertheless, none of the work presents a substantial solution for the entire Software Development Life-Cycle (SDLC) with these three concepts. Few of the papers deal directly with the principles of SOA and Agile. None of them present a complete process for QA. The NatVi Framework proposes to address these gaps not covered by the other solutions.

In this way, the NatVi Framework came to seek to improve Quality Assurance (QA) while dealing with Service-Oriented Architecture (SOA) and Agile during the Software Development Life-Cycle. As a framework, it is not exhaustive and presents a flexible set of phases. In this way, people responsible for a new project need to assess the phases in front of their reality and decide whether to use it. Furthermore, they can decide to customize some phase or create a new one and aggregate it to the Framework.

The NatVi Framework is composed of four layers with respective phases. The 'Stakeholder Support' is an extra layer that permeates all other layers and exists only to remember that the integration of each system stakeholders, whether

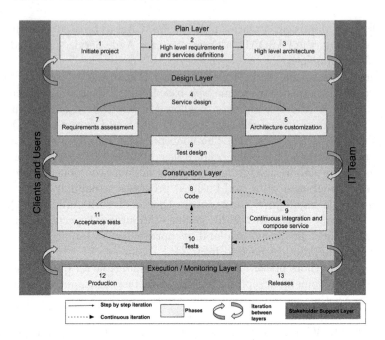

Fig. 1. NatVi Framework for Agile, SOA and QA - Figure created by the authors in the scope of this work.

clients, users and IT teams is critical to the success of the software project. The layers' position indicates they work sequentially, but the 'Iteration between layers' is indicated in the point of contact. In this way, if the development is facing problems in some layers, the work can jump virtually to any other layer to fix it (Fig. 1).

The Framework seeks to keep present the essential concepts of Agile, SOA, and QA throughout the process. From Agile, the values and principles (background Sect. 2.2). From SOA, the eight principles (background Sect. 2.1). From QA, the planning, and the process execution. Despite this, in some phases, some are highlighted, indicating that special attention is needed.

Phases of the Framework. As a framework, each iteration may need adjustments depending on the environment. Therefore, the terms used here are examples. In other environments, these terms may change and may extend. At each phase, a set of roles should be present, people who should be involved with the tasks of the phase. Each environment will be its own set of roles, defined by the environment according to their needs and organizational structure. Table 1 depicts examples of leading roles for each phase.

Table 1. Leading roles acting in each phase of the Framework.

Roles/phases	1	2	3	4	5	6	7	8	9	10	11	12
Sponsor	X										X	
Client	X	X		X		X	X			X		
End-user		X		X		X	X			X		
Business analyst	X	X	X	X		X	X					
Software designer		X	X	X	X							
Database administrator			X									
Developer						X	X	X	X	X		
Tester		X				X						
IT operator								X	X			X
QA manager			X	X	X	X	X	X	X	X	X	X

Table 2 depicts examples of a tool-set that may be present in each phase of the Framework. These tools can be electronic or not and include techniques that assist the execution, control, and documentation of tasks or the whole process.

The following subsections describe each phase of the Framework in terms of name, intention, inputs, tasks, and outputs. The items presented here are not exhaustive. For each environment, people responsible for roles may add new items and may exclude others, adapting these concepts to their reality. Inputs are all available material that can help people develop the tasks of the phase, e.g., the results of the previous phases, documents by the organization, and even outside documents. Tasks are specific actions that the roles need to do to achieve the phase objective. Outputs are the material result of the phase, e.g., report of elicited requirements, use cases, test cases, records in a control tool, developed code committed, ready system.

Table 2. Main tools used in each phase of the framework.

Tools/phases	1	2	3	4	5	6	7	8	9	10	11	12
Project management tools	X	X	X	X	X	X	X	X	X	X	X	X
Version control tool	X	X	X	X	X	X	X	X	X	X	X	X
Communication tool	X	X	X	X	X	X	X	X	X	X	X	X
Design tool		X	X	X	X	X	X					
Test tool		X					X	X	X	X	X	X
SOA management tools		X		X		X						
SOA building tool			X		X		X					
Development tool								X		X		
Continuous integration tool								X	X			X
Documenting tool	X	X	X	X	X	X	X	X	X	X	X	X

Phase 1 - Initiate Project. *Intention:* This phase is composed of a set of tasks that allow for a general understanding of the project. At this stage, people document the origin of the demand and its main concerns. The resulting document does not need a more precise technical definition. Stakeholders and the technical team must carry out this phase in conjunction. The phase can follow a standardized protocol. Here, stakeholders can be free to expose all their thoughts and concerns without much interference from the technical team. The technical team will make technical adjustments to subsequent tasks.

In this phase, the Agile values 'Individuals and interactions' and 'Customer collaboration' should receive special attention to guarantee QA since the beginning of the project.

Inputs: Relation of business goals. The organization's strategic plan. Industry contracts and regulations. Deadlines and available budget. Relation of stakeholders who will participate in the project.

Tasks: Formalize demand in a control system. Create initial documentation. Register the project in a specific project control tool. Grant access to project information to all stakeholders.

Outputs: The formalized project. The documentation with the key characteristics recorded, e.g., people involved, schedules, budget, the main concern with business objectives, problems to be resolved, expectations about the possible new system. Possible, because the solution may be other than developing a new system. In this phase is the time to decide whether to make a whole new system, adapt the functionality of an existing system, or purchase a Commercial off-the-shelf (COTS). The formalities of this document depend on the level of formalization required by the organization. It can be a record in an information system, or it can be a record in the project management tool 'read-me' file.

Phase 2 - High-Level Requirements and Service Definition. *Intention:* In this phase, people who perform roles elicit requirements and break them down into concrete business needs, meaning that they identify the problems and concerns of the clients and end-users. The main concern of people is to identify the problem domain and not the solution to those problems. They need to identify and extract information from the business needs and interpret, analyze, validate, and gather together to compose the services. In this phase, people who perform roles identify all stakeholders and technical teams. They also initiate a more precise technical definition of the requirements. All stakeholders need to understand the goals and divide them as much as possible. Each of these parts defines a service. Thus, each service represents a specific functionality that explicitly maps to a step in a business process.

Inputs: The outputs generated in Phase 1 - Initiate project. Business process mapping, if any, or detailed description of the phases of how the work is done. Other documents that support business objectives. Some information from Phase 1 - Initiate project is vital for all next phases and should appear as input for all of them, e.g., schedule and budget.

Tasks: Elicit requirements for services. Design the initial tests. Link requirements, services, and tests.

Outputs: Relation of requirements. Record of backlogs, stories, and use cases. Draft of the architectural views of the services. Draft of the case tests.

Phase 3 - High-Level Architecture. *Intention:* In this phase, people who perform roles elaborate on high-level architecture as SOA as an architectural pattern does not have a fixed way to be implemented. In this phase, if SOA is new, the technical team should elaborate on the whole architecture. If SOA is a well-established environment, the work here will probably be simplified, and the technical team should do only a few setups.

Many of the SOA principles are planed in this phase, but two principles need more attention, 'Service Reusability' and 'Service Discoverability' (see background Sect. 2.1 about SOA). Because, if other services already achieve the goal of some new service, these other services must be discovered and reused, even with some level of adaptation.

Inputs: The outputs generated in previous phases. Information from Phase 2 - High-level requirements and Service definition, e.g., drafts of the architectural views and other infrastructure information, including information about external clouds, if they exist.

Tasks: Design the architecture for building the SOA. If SOA already exists, design the customization for the project. Decide between developing a new service or using or adapting an existing service.

Outputs: The built architecture. The documentation registered in the project management tool.

Phase 4 - Service Design. *Intention:* In this phase, people design the services (Consumer and Provider) and address the solutions to the SOA issues. This phase represents the beginning of the first loop, or iteration, in NatVi Framework. This iteration will repeat until the service design is considered good enough to go to the next iteration, the construction layer. Even if the process is already in the next layers, people can assess the requirements at any time, and the process can return to that layer.

All the eight SOA principles must be addressed in this phase (see background Sect. 2.1), but if someone needs to prioritize one, it will be 'Standardized Service Contract', because this principle can drive the final service to high-level quality, mainly in the security aspect.

Inputs: The outputs generated in previous phases, mainly the high-level requirements and the drafts of the architectural views from Phase 2 - High-level requirements and Service definition and the blueprint of the high-level architecture from Phase 3 - High-level Architecture.

Tasks: Refine elicited requirements. Identify the business objectives in their smallest parts. Design the services. Find alternative treatments if a principle cannot be achieved.

Outputs: All the necessary documentation to built the services, e.g., service design and refined requirements. Information about architecture customization needed. All documentation recorded in a specific tool.

Phase 5 - Architecture Customization. *Intention:* At this phase, people who perform roles evaluate adjustments in the architecture. Because SOA is a design pattern, not a whole architecture, people may need to do some customization in architecture, e.g., a new interface or a new term in the standardized service contract.

Inputs: The outputs generated in previous phases, mainly the documentation of service design from Phase 4 - Service design and the blueprint of the high-level architecture from Phase 3 - High-level Architecture.

Tasks: Refine the architecture. Update the architecture documentation. Implement the architectural changes.

Outputs: The built architecture and the documentation registered in the project management tool.

Phase 6 - Test Design (Test First). *Intention:* At this phase, before the Construction phase (code), people create the tests. The technical team uses information gathered in the previous phases to create these tests. Creating the test first can help developers make the code closer to service needs, that is, close the business goals.

Inputs: The outputs generated in previous phases, mainly the high-level requirements, use cases, and draft of the case tests from Phase 2 - High-level requirements and Service definition. The refined requirements and the documentation of the design services from Phase 4 - Service design.

Tasks: Refine the drafts of the case tests. Elaborate the unit tests, integration tests, system tests, and acceptance tests. Select a metric to guarantee the QA. Document and register the tests in a specific tool.

Outputs: Tests designed and registered in specific tools and tests documented in the project management tool.

Phase 7 - Requirements Assessment. *Intention:* This phase is the bottom of the first loop, the end of the first iteration and a control point. After the previous phases, the technical team has more understanding of the needs of the services. The clients, end-users, and the technical team evaluate the elicited requirements and all the done work until here. If they decide to make changes, they restart the loop. Otherwise, it is time to pass to the construction layer.

Inputs: All the inputs and outputs of the previous phases.

Tasks: Evaluate all the work done. Make decisions and document what will be done.

Outputs: A document with the assessment of the work. Record of the decision made.

Phase 8 - Code. *Intention:* This phase is the beginning of the construction layer of the framework. Although phases 8, 9, and 10 are in sequence, they are in a continuous iteration. A dotted line indicates the continuous iteration.

This phase is where the developers, technical team members, make the code itself, that is, build the service. All the artifacts generated in the previous iteration 'Analysis and design' are used in this phase as input to create the service. This 'Construction' layer phase is the first one of a new loop or iteration. This iteration will repeat until the service passes acceptance tests, made by clients and users.

Inputs: The outputs generated in previous phases, mainly the documentation from Phase 4 - Service design, e.g., service design, and refined requirements. The test design from Phase 6 - Test design (test first).

Tasks: Build the code of the services. Build the code of the unit tests. Evaluate unit tests. Daily deploy code, i.e., commit, pushing, build, and release in a development environment. Document and register the code in a specific tool.

Outputs: the source code and test code recorded in a version control tool, available to the pipeline of continuous integration tools.

Phase 9 - Continuous Integration and Compose Service. *Intention:* As already seen, the phases 8, 9, and 10 of the construction layer work almost at the same time. In this phase, people set tools that are responsible for continuous integration. These tools receive the new code, compile it, test it, e.g., unit test and integration test, build the software, and release in a development environment.

In this phase, the services are composed according to the designed architecture and the customization, if one. Composing services means putting the service in the right place into the SOA and accessible for the other services, even the external ones.

Inputs: The outputs generated in previous phases, mainly source code and the test code from Phase 8 - Code and test design from Phase 6 - Test design (test first).

Tasks: Set the continuous integration tools for build and test. Release the software in a testing/staging environment. Evaluate the tests. Give feedback to developers. Document the results.

Outputs: The services composed and released in a testing/staging environment. Testing report result.

Phase 10 - Test. *Intention:* This phase in the framework is more about giving special attention to the tests. As seen in the previous phases, the concern about tests is constant, before and after coding. So this test phase, in particular, has an academic meaning. In fact, in the real world, these three phases, Phase 8 - Code, Phase 9 - Continuous integration and compose service and Phase 10 - Test are implemented at the same time, in a constant iteration.

At these three phases, the testers make and test the services based on the tests designed in Phase 6 - Test design (test first). The developers make the unit tests, and they execute these tests in their machine to identify the errors of the first before committing to the code. The unit tests will be executed again, in Phase 9 - Continuous integration and compose service.

The testers, QA manager, and operator still make the integration and system tests in this phase. The operators' participation is fundamental because they can think in a set of services and consider the SOA. These tests will be executed only in Phase 9 - Continuous integration and compose service, where is expected a more significant number of errors than the unit tests.

Phase 11 - Acceptance Test. *Intention:* The end of the loop or iteration of the construction layer. The services are already composed and tested by clients and end-users, according to the definitions of Phase 6 - Test design (test first). These tests can be done manually or using specific tools for this.

Inputs: The software released in a testing/staging environment. The acceptance tests design in Phase 6 - Test design (test first).

Tasks: Evaluate the software against the acceptance tests. Give feedback to the technical team. Do formal approval or disapproval. Document the results and decisions.

Outputs: Testing report result. Feedback report. Formal approval or disapproval for the services to go into production.

Phase 12 - Production. *Intention:* In this phase, the services are finalized and approved. The built services are ready to release in a production environment, preferably in an automatic way.

Inputs: The source code from Phase 8 - Code. The documentation of the architecture, from Phase 3 - High-level Architecture and Phase 5 - Architecture Customization. The formal approval from Phase 11 - Acceptance test.

Tasks: Adjust the architecture. Set the production environment, Make automatic pipelines for production. Release services in the production environment. Document the activities.

Outputs: The adjusted or the new SOA ready. the services composed and ready for a production environment. The documentation up to date.

Phase 13 - Release. *Intention:* The service is released in the production environment to end-users. These two phases, 12 and 13, represented the framework's monitoring layer, where services are already in a production environment and need to be tracked to identify problems in their execution.

5   Conclusion

This work carried out research to seek a solution to better deal with developing software with quality and rapid deliveries in a software environment that tries to follow business objectives in constant change. The solution appears in the form of a Framework that deals with Agile Software Development, Service-Oriented Architecture (SOA), and Quality Assurance (QA).

The construction of the Framework made use of previous works found in background research and assessed the strengths, weaknesses, and gaps in the found solutions. The background research did not find studies that deal straight with the concepts of SOA, Agile, and QA together. However, it found studies that deal with these concepts in pairs: SOA and Agile, SOA and QA and Agile and QA. We made an effort to join those works made in pairs and fit our purpose, that is, a greater understanding of the three concepts working together.

Background research also identified trade-offs that generally arise when working with these concepts, but also in pairs, mainly the principles and values of SOA and QA versus the principles and values of Agile. These trade-offs were also a concern in the Framework construction that tried to address them.

The NatVi Framework presented in this paper is composed of four layers and 13 phases that combine in one life-cycle Agile, SOA, and QA. It concatenates each of its 13 phases through the outputs and inputs and defines specific roles and tasks for each phase. The fundamental of the Framework is continuously, in all phase, pay attention to values and principles of the three concepts.

In conclusion, the NatVi Framework is suitable for building a well-structured process to deal with the software development scenario with quality and fast deliveries in an ever-changing environment. The process created from the Framework can act on essential factors for fast delivery with quality of the final product: sufficient initial plan; adequate software architecture; business objectives divided into small pieces and directed to functional parts of the software; iterative development capable of absorbing changes instantly; code and integration tests to find errors during development; monitoring to detect problems while running the system.

However, there is a need to implement the Framework in real-world scenarios and gather empirical evidence to validate and improve on it. The authors are preparing a case study to expose the NatVi Framework to a real development environment, assessing its application, employing some measures before and after the use, and appraise the acceptance by stakeholders.

References

1. Abdelouhab, K.A., Idoughi, D., Kolski, C.: Agile & user centric SOA based service design framework applied in disaster management. In: 2014 1st International Conference on Information and Communication Technologies for Disaster Management (ICT-DM), pp. 1–8 (2014). https://doi.org/10.1109/ICT-DM.2014.6917792
2. Agile Alliance: Agile manifesto, **6**(1) (2001). http://www.agilemanifesto.org
3. de la Barra, C.L., Crawford, B., Soto, R., Misra, S., Monfroy, E.: Agile software development: it is about knowledge management and creativity. In: Murgante, B., et al. (eds.) ICCSA 2013. LNCS, vol. 7973, pp. 98–113. Springer, Heidelberg (2013). https://doi.org/10.1007/978-3-642-39646-5_8
4. Bass, L.: Software Architecture in Practice. Pearson Education India, Delhi (2007)
5. Bianco, P., Kotermanski, R., Merson, P.F.: Evaluating a service-oriented architecture. Research Showcase @ CMU, 1 September 2007. http://repository.cmu.edu/sei
6. Bianco, P., Lewis, G.A., Merson, P., Simanta, S.: Architecting service-oriented systems. Technical report, Carnegie-Mellon Univ Pittsburgh Pa Software Engineering Inst., August 2011
7. Carvalho, F., Azevedo, L.G.: Service agile development using XP. In: 2013 Proceedings of the IEEE 7th International Symposium on Service-Oriented System Engineering, SOSE 2013, pp. 254–259 (2013). https://doi.org/10.1109/SOSE.2013.25
8. Chaves, J.T.F., de Freitas, S.A.A.: A systematic literature review for service-oriented architecture and agile development. In: Misra, S., et al. (eds.) ICCSA 2019. LNCS, vol. 11623, pp. 120–135. Springer, Cham (2019). https://doi.org/10.1007/978-3-030-24308-1_11
9. Chehili, H., Seinturier, L., Boufaida, M.: FASOAD: a framework for agile service-oriented architectures development. In: Proceedings of the International Workshop on Database and Expert Systems Applications, DEXA, pp. 222–226 (2013). https://doi.org/10.1109/DEXA.2013.28
10. Chehili, H., Seinturier, L., Boufaida, M.: An evolutive component-based method for agile development of service oriented architectures. Int. J. Inf. Syst. Serv. Sect. (IJISSS) **9**(3), 37–57 (2017)
11. Demchak, B., Farcas, C., Farcas, E., Krüger, I.H.: The treasure map for Rich Services. In: 2007 IEEE International Conference on Information Reuse and Integration, IEEE IRI-2007, pp. 400–405 (2007). https://doi.org/10.1109/IRI.2007.4296653
12. Dutil, D., Rose, J., Suryn, W.: Software quality engineering in the new ISO standard: ISO/IEC 24748 - systems and software engineering—guide for life cycle management, pp. 89–96 (2010). https://doi.org/10.1145/1822327.1822339
13. Erl, T.: SOA: Principles of Service Design, vol. 1. Prentice Hall, Upper Saddle River (2008)
14. Farroha, D., Farroha, B.: Developing corporate services in an agile environment. In: Proceedings of the IEEE Military Communications Conference MILCOM, pp. 1535–1540 (2011). https://doi.org/10.1109/MILCOM.2011.6127525
15. Fortunato, C.A., Furtado, F., Selleri, F., de Farias Junior, I., Leitão Júnior, N.: Quality assurance in agile software development: a systematic review. In: Silva da Silva, T., Estácio, B., Kroll, J., Mantovani Fontana, R. (eds.) WBMA 2016. CCIS, vol. 680, pp. 142–148. Springer, Cham (2017). https://doi.org/10.1007/978-3-319-55907-0_14

16. Galin, D.: Software Quality Assurance: From Theory to Implementation. Pearson Education India, Delhi (2004)
17. Hongying, G., Cheng, Y.: A customizable agile software quality assurance model. In: The 5th International Conference on New Trends in Information Science and Service Science, vol. 2, no. 60803110, pp. 382–387 (2011)
18. Hossain, A., Kashem, A., Sultana, S.: Enhancing software quality using agile techniques. IOSR J. Comput. Eng. **10**(2), 2278–661 (2013). https://doi.org/10.9790/0661-01028793. www.iosrjournals.org
19. Huo, M., Verner, J., Zhu, L., Babar, M.A.: Software quality and agile methods. In: 2004 Proceedings of the 28th Annual International Computer Software and Applications Conference, COMPSAC 2004, pp. 520–525 (2004). https://doi.org/10.1109/CMPSAC.2004.1342889
20. IEEE Computer Society: IEEE standard for software quality assurance processes. IEEE Std. 730-2014 (Revision of IEEE Std. 730–2002), pp. 1–138 (2014). https://doi.org/10.1109/IEEESTD.2014.6835311
21. Janus, A., Dumke, R., Schmietendorf, A., Jäger, J.: The 3C approach for agile quality assurance. In: Proceedings of the 2012 3rd International Workshop on Emerging Trends in Software Metrics, WETSoM 2012, pp. 9–13 (2012). https://doi.org/10.1109/WETSoM.2012.6226998
22. Khalane, T., Tanner, M.: Software quality assurance in Scrum: the need for concrete guidance on SQA strategies in meeting user expectations. In: IEEE International Conference on Adaptive Science and Technology, ICAST (2013). https://doi.org/10.1109/ICASTech.2013.6707499
23. Kitchenham, B., Pfleeger, S.L.: Software quality: the elusive target. IEEE Softw. **13**(1), 12–21 (1996). https://doi.org/10.1109/52.476281
24. Krogdahl, P., Luef, G., Steindl, C.: Service-oriented agility: an initial analysis for the use of agile methods for SOA development. In: 2005 IEEE International Conference on Services Computing (SCC 2005) Volume 1, vol. 2, pp. 93–100 (2005). https://doi.org/10.1109/SCC.2005.86
25. Kumar, G., Bhatia, P.K.: Comparative analysis of software engineering models from traditional to modern methodologies. In: 2014 Fourth International Conference on Advanced Computing Communication Technologies, pp. 189–196 (2014). https://doi.org/10.1109/ACCT.2014.73
26. Mnkandla, E., Dwolatzky, B.: Defining agile software quality assurance. In: 2006 International Conference on Software Engineering Advances (ICSEA 2006), p. 36 (2006). https://doi.org/10.1109/ICSEA.2006.261292
27. Posadas, J.V.: Application of mixed distributed software architectures for social-productive projects management in Peru. In: 2017 IEEE XXIV International Conference on Electronics, Electrical Engineering and Computing (INTERCON), pp. 1–4 (2017). https://doi.org/10.1109/INTERCON.2017.8079698
28. Rong, H., Zhou, N., Jin, M., Wu, J.: Research on service-oriented framework of interface prototype driven development. In: 2008 International Conference on Computer Science and Software Engineering, vol. 2, pp. 552–557 (2008). https://doi.org/10.1109/CSSE.2008.362
29. Shahrbanoo, M.: An approach for agile SOA development using agile principals. Int. J. Comput. Sci. Inf. Technol. **4**(1), 237–244 (2012). https://doi.org/10.5121/ijcsit.2012.4118

30. Sloane, E., Beck, R., Metzger, S.: AGSOA - agile governance for service oriented architecture (SOA) systems: a methodology to deliver 21st century military net-centric systems of systems. In: 2008 IEEE International Systems Conference Proceedings, SysCon 2008, pp. 106–109 (2008). https://doi.org/10.1109/SYSTEMS.2008.4518995

31. Sommerville, I., et al.: Software Engineering. Addison-Wesley, Boston (2007)

32. Sowunmi, O.Y., Misra, S., Fernandez-Sanz, L., Crawford, B., Soto, R.: An empirical evaluation of software quality assurance practices and challenges in a developing country: a comparison of Nigeria and Turkey. SpringerPlus 5(1), 1–13 (2016). https://doi.org/10.1186/s40064-016-3575-5

33. Sullivan, K., Yang, J., Coppit, D., Khurshid, S., Jackson, D.: Software assurance by bounded exhaustive testing. ACM SIGSOFT Softw. Eng. Notes **29**, 133–142 (2004)

34. Timperi, O.: An overview of quality assurance practices in agile methodologies. Soberit. Hut.Fi 650 (2004)

35. Wang, B., Wen, C., Sheng, J.: A SOA based model driven rapid development architecture - SMRDA. In: ICETC 2010–2010 2nd International Conference on Education Technology and Computer, vol. 1, pp. 421–425 (2010). https://doi.org/10.1109/ICETC.2010.5529218

36. Zamudio, L., Aguilar, J.A., Tripp, C., Misra, S.: A requirements engineering techniques review in agile software development methods. In: Gervasi, O., et al. (eds.) ICCSA 2017. LNCS, vol. 10408, pp. 683–698. Springer, Cham (2017). https://doi.org/10.1007/978-3-319-62404-4_50

A Two-Layer Image-Steganography System for Covert Communication Over Enterprise Network

Arome Junior Gabriel$^{(\boxtimes)}$ (iD), Adebayo Olusola Adetunmbi (iD), and Preye Obaila

Federal University of Technology, P.M.B. 704 Akure, Nigeria
{ajgabriel,aoadetunmbi}@futa.edu.ng,
preyeobaila@gmail.com

Abstract. Computers find application in virtually all aspect of human existence, especially in today's modern world. Although this comes with a lot of benefits, it also comes with a number of undesirable consequences. Chief among these consequences is the rising concerns for security of information and even loss of privacy. Steganography, an Information hiding technique could be a fitting solution to these security issues. This paper presents an improved Steganography technique for ensuring the security of the widely spread and used internet materials or information that are shared globally with risk of vulnerability of attack. In this current research work, Elliptic Curve Cryptography (ECC) and Discrete Cosine Transform (DCT) Steganography were combined together to achieve effective security in the proposed system. A given plain text or secret message is first converted to a cipher text using ECC. The resultant encrypted text is then hidden under a cover-image using DCT-based image steganography technique to produce a final output called stego-image. To the Human Visual System (HVS), the stego-image remains the same as the original cover image. This ensures that the hidden secret message gets delivered to the target recipient without any suspicion. Standard metrics such as Peak Signal to Noise Ratio (PSNR) and Mean Square Error (MSE), as well as average computation time, were used to evaluate the performance of the proposed steganography system. The results indicate better performance compared to the conventional steganography systems. Thus the proposed system is a 2-level steganography system effective for storing sensitive data and even for securely transferring information over an open/enterprise network.

Keywords: Cryptography · Cyber security · Information-Hiding · Information security · Steganography

1 Introduction

The world has in recent times witnessed an explosive upsurge in technological advancement. Indeed, in today's electronic or modern world, computers and other forms of information technology finds application in so many, if not all aspects of human lives as reported in literature [1–10]. It must be said that computers and their

© Springer Nature Switzerland AG 2020
O. Gervasi et al. (Eds.): ICCSA 2020, LNCS 12254, pp. 459–470, 2020.
https://doi.org/10.1007/978-3-030-58817-5_34

networks are here to stay, and they offer a wide range of benefits for users. All these come with several other concerns among which is security (privacy, confidentiality, integrity, non-repudiation and authentication) of information and/or individuals. In today's electronic world, access and exchange of all kinds of information ranging from text, audio, video and even images, is quite easy via the Internet [10]. The serious concern however, is that, sharing information over enterprise or open networks exposes such information to all sorts of internet-based attacks [9]. There is a serious need to have a mechanism for ensuring that the protection of sensitive/secret information is guaranteed. Data hiding (information hiding) which plays an important role in information security over the internet can be a viable solution to this problem. Data hiding involves embedding secret data subtly in a cover-media by marginally adjusting the elements of the cover-media. Cryptography method does not conceal the presence of information but rather, it changes a text to a cipher-text which is more like gibberish that cannot be understood. In contrast, steganography deals with hiding the mere existence of a secret communication [11]. So a steganographic system embeds secret information or messages in a text, audio, video or image file so that its existence is not detected by unauthorized persons.

The organization of the rest of this paper is such that, a review of related research works is presented in Sect. 2. In Sect. 3, a vivid discussion on the design of the proposed 2-layer steganography system is presented. Section 4 presents the discussion of experiments' results or findings. Finally, the conclusion of the paper is presented in Sect. 5.

2   Related Works

Quite a number of related works can be found online in other repositories. A summary of the most related ones is presented in this section.

In [12], the authors presented a research on text-based steganography. They used as cover-media, texts written in Malayalam local language. This cover-media was used for hiding secret messages towards ensuring enhanced information secrecy or security. Their research made use of use of two matrices for indexing the alphabets in the common language. These matrices were laden with the alphabet letter and their indices in increasing order. A method for Unicode extraction was designed towards finding the Malayalam text that is corresponding to a given English text. The indexes were selected diagonally. However, the limitation of their work lies in the fact that the hidden word is subject to breach from a cryptanalyst.

In [13], a steganography scheme based on adaptive circular queue image steganography plus RSA cryptosystem is proposed. The objectives was to use both cryptography and steganography to achieve the security of information. For the text to be encrypted RSA cryptography was used, while the resultant cipher-text is embedded in a randomly chosen grey image using a circular queue Least Significant Bit (LSB) steganography technique. RSA is characterized by a very slow key generation procedure. Besides, there is considerable difficulty in the choice of either large prime numbers or small prime numbers.

A research that adopted Genetic Algorithm and cryptography for the development of an image steganography architecture was carried out in [14]. The objective was to develop a secure communication mechanism using a combination of Advanced Encryption Standard (AES) cryptography scheme and a Genetic Algorithm-LSB steganography scheme. A given secret message or text was encrypted AES and then the resultant cipher-text is embedded in a selected cover-image using the steganography scheme. The AES scheme used however presents a limitation in that, there is problem of how to securely exchange the encryption key between a sender and a receiver. Besides, the LSB method can result in much alteration or distortion of the cover-image. This leads to easy detection or attack from attackers. Indeed, since the genetic algorithm competed for space, it is most likely for every information to compete just for a single pixel space which will make the stego different from the cover image.

In [15], a steganography graphical password scheme is proposed for Near Field Communication (NFC) smartphone access control system. The objectives was to create a novel and secured NFC ESGP smartphones security system to ensure convenient and secure use of these smartphone by their owners, as a key access to control systems. They extended the boundary of the capabilities of the technology via the creation of a new and secured NFC ESGP smartphones security system. The combination of both the NFC and the ESGP was in order to achieve higher security compared to the existing one. The work was however exclusively meant for smartphone users only.

The authors in [16] studied the embedding efficiency of LSB steganography technique in spatial and transform domains. Their major goal was to embed a large secret message in a given image using different LSB techniques such as $\pm$ embedding, F5 algorithm with or without matrix embedding. The LSB technique was combined with matrix embedding and F5 algorithm which is applied on both spatial and frequency domain of a given image. If LSB occurs on distortion, it can easily be altered, and wasted by more filtering, compression or a smaller than the original format or size transformation, which gave a very serious limitation to the work.

While working towards improving the properties of images with embedded secrets as well as eliminating the tendency of huge computational complexity in steganography systems, the papers in [17] used particle swarm optimisation algorithm as well as AVX instructions available in modern CPUs. These allow for parallel operations that are vital in image steganography.

An Optical Character Recognition (OCR) based Steganography technique where, messages, in their feature forms, are embedded in a cover image was proposed in [18]. Character level features were extracted from images which contain the textual messages, and embedded in the cover image, thus strengthening the data hiding objective of steganography. They reported impressive results.

In the study titled "Image Steganography and Steganalysis based on LSB", as reported in [19], Olomo et al. in [19] proposed a new LSB steganography method towards improving on the 1-byte least significance method. The results they presented showed remarkable performance of their model. This work however considered images, and requires some extension to be able to handle audio files as cover media.

An important angle to research in steganography is the audio steganography which uses audio files as cover media for hiding the existence of secret messages. Some authors have carried out studies in audio steganography. For instance, a survey of audio steganography methods for transmitting data securely was carried out in [20]. The authors posited that LSB is the simplest steganography method, but that when it comes to robustness against attacks, spread spectrum method offers more. Another research effort in the direction of audio steganography is that reported in [21]. The authors developed an efficient audio steganography system that has increased robustness against attack. Their proposed system is reportedly able to embed text messages in both MP3 and MP4 audio file formats, with remarkable effectiveness. As a drawback, audio steganography systems seem to have far more complexities, hence incur more computational overheads than simple-image based ones.

The need for more robust information security systems, especially those that are capable of providing resistance to common classical and quantum attacks has led other researchers to proposing the idea of combining post quantum cryptography with steganography. Such systems were reported in the research papers in [6, 9]. A Quantum image Least Significant Qubit information hiding algorithm that uses a novel enhanced quantum representation (the NEQR) was presented in [22]. The authors demonstrated the algorithm hides the message in the frequency spectrum of an image thereby improving the security of the message.

3 The Proposed 2-Layer Image Steganography System

In order to handle the shortcomings observed in the existing works and provide an improved solution, this current research work (paper) proposes a steganography model that will be used to hide a text (information)'M' in an image, in a way that, to the HVS, no visible difference between the cover-image (i.e. image without information) and stego-image (i.e. image with information) will be noticed. The proposed system is made of two (2) modules – The Cryptography (ECC) as well as the Steganography (using DCT on images) modules.

The ECC module makes use of prime Elliptic curve cryptography to provide for a high level of security with smaller key size compared to RSA cryptographic scheme that work based on the difficulty of solving Integer Factorisation Problem. In elliptic curve mathematics operations are carried out on the coordinate points of an elliptic curve using the formula in Eq. 1.

$$E : y^2 + a_2 x_y + a_3 y = x^3 + a_2 x^2 + a_4 x + a_6. \tag{1}$$

The general expression can then be simplified to yield;

$$y^2 = x^3 + Ax + B \tag{2}$$

when $a_2 = a_3 = 0$, x ranges from 0 to arbitrary selected number- 1,while A and B are integer constants.

The encryption procedure is formalised as in Eq. 3 and 4:

$$E_1 = \gamma c \tag{3}$$

$$E_2 = M + (\beta + \gamma)A_1 - \gamma A_2 + A_B \tag{4}$$

where E_1 and E_2 are cipher points which transform to a code table where the cipher text will be derived from. The communication is done between two parties. α is the first party's private key_1, β is second party's private key_1, Υ stands for a point selected on the elliptic curve, A_1 is the first party general public key_1, A_2 is the first party specific public key, B is the second party private key_2, B_1 is the second party general public key_1, A_B is first party public key for the second party, B_A is the second party specific public key for the first party, c is an agreed point on the elliptic curve.

The decryption process makes use of the Eq. (5)

$$M = E_2 - (\propto E_1 + \propto B_1 + B_A) \tag{5}$$

where M is the plain message after decryption

Discrete Cosine Transform offers a way for hiding large amount of data. It provides high security, a good invisibility and prevents loss of secret message. In DCT the choice of replaceable pixels is based on whether a given pixel has DCT coefficient below threshold are considered as potential pixels. The threshold value here is taken as zero. Hence, the pixels with DCT coefficient value below zero are used for data hiding. The general formula for DCT is:

$$c(u,v) = \propto (u) \propto (v) \sum_{x=0}^{N-1} \sum_{y=0}^{M-1} f(x,y) \cos\left[\pi \frac{(2x+1)u}{2N}\right] \cos \pi \frac{(2y+1)v}{2M} \tag{6}$$

For Embedding, a cover-image is chosen. Then, the DCT coefficient of carrier image is determined. Then traverse through each pixel in the cover-image to the end of the secret image. If the DCT coefficient value is below a stipulated threshold then, replace LSB(s) with MBS(s) of pixels in secret image. Insert 1 at the location in the key matrix, to retrieve the information back get the stego image, traverse through each pixel in the stego image till end. Check the key matrix for the location if it is 1, then extract LSBs from stego image otherwise move on to next pixel get estimate of secret image (Fig. 1).

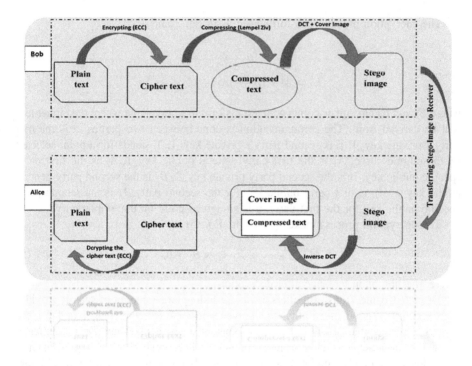

Fig. 1. Conceptual architecture of the proposed system

4   Results and Discussion

The developed system was implemented using MATLAB (R2017a version) programming language on Windows 10 Operating System platform with hardware configuration of 4 GB RAM, 2.0 GHz processor speed and 500 GB of hard disk.

In this research three different images were used as cover images, but any other image can also be used. These images are used to hide different ranges of secret text. To test the result, different sizes of the secret text files (37 KB, 122 KB, 140 KB, 143 KB, and 918 KB) were gotten and then hidden under an image and the quality of the image is tested using PSNR and also a steganalysis software to determine if the image can easily be detected by hackers. The images used for testing are presented in Fig. 2:

Fig. 2. Images used as cover files in this experiment

4.1   System Performance Evaluation Metrics

The proposed/developed system was evaluated based on the following metrics; *Peak Signal-to-Noise (PSNR)*, and *Mean Square Error (MSE)*. These metrics are further highlighted as follows;

A Peak Signal-to-Noise Ratio (PSNR) and Mean Square Error (MSE)
The Peak Signal-to-Noise Ratio (PSNR) is the metric that was used to access the quality of the resultant stego-image. If the PSNR value is greater than the Mean Square Error (MSE) value then the image has a very good quality. Otherwise, the resultant stego-image is regarded as not of good quality, which implies that the steganography system that produced that stego-image is inefficient.

Results obtained from our experiment shows that the PSNR obtained in all cases have higher values when compared to the corresponding MSE values. This indicates that the proposed system yields good stego-images (Table 1).

The mathematical formula or relations used is for computing the Peak Signal-to-Noise Ratio (PSNR) and the Mean Square Error (MSE) is as defined in Eqs. 7 and 8;

$$PSNR = 10log_{10}MSE \tag{7}$$

$$MSE = \left(\frac{1}{N}\right)^2 \sum \sum_N \left(x(i,j) - \bar{x}(i,j)^2\right) \tag{8}$$

Table 1. PSNR and MSE measurements

Cover-image Size (Kb)	Image_1		Image_2		Image_3	
	PSNR	MSE	PSNR	MSE	PSNR	MSE
37	39.6566	7.0375	38.8870	8.4163	35.1439	9.8925
122	39.7091	6.9530	39.0197	8.1491	35.1700	9.7733
140	39.6940	6.9772	38.9815	8.2211	35.1625	9.8074
143	39.6930	6.9787	38.9796	8.2246	35.1622	9.8089
918	39.6533	7.0429	38.8796	8.4163	35.1423	9.8997

$$T \propto S \tag{9}$$

B Steganalysis Testing

Ben 4D steganalysis software was used to carry out the system performance evaluation with respect to its resistance to steganalysis. Three different cover-images (see Fig. 2) were checked to determine the maximum size of test secret file they can contain/embed conveniently before their level of distortion becomes visible to the HSV. These images were also passed through the Ben4D software to determine their maximum embedding capacity just before a steganalysis software is able to detect such distortions. Table 2 shows the highest KB of test secret file each cover-image can take before distortions becomes detectable. Results as shown in Table 2 reveals that, image_1 starts experiencing a little decrease in its luminance component when a large size of 917 KB test file was hidden under it.

Table 2. Result of Ben 4D steganalysis on output of the proposed system.

	Image_1	Image_2	Image_3
Maximum text size before distortion (Kb)	917	917	528
Cover-image characteristics	YCC[1089, 0, 0] RGB[255, 255, 255]	YCC[1056, -26, 31] RGB[255, 254, 247]	YCC[1057, -10, 20] RGB[255, 255, 255]
Stego-image characteristics	YCC[1075, 0, 0] RGB[255, 255, 255]	YCC[1056, -26, 31] RGB[255, 255, 255]	YCC[1056, -26, 31] RGB[255, 254, 247]

Anyone who is interested in hiding a larger text file will be ready to take some form of trade-off time.

C Other Figures and Tables

This sub-section shows the effect of the LZW compression algorithm on some of our ciphertexts, as well as the computation time of the newly developed steganography system versus the existing RSA_DCT based steganography system.

The chart shown in Fig. 3 illustrates the impact of the LZW compression algorithm on the ciphertexts generated by the encryption sub-system of our proposed system. The algorithm obviously reduced the sizes of ciphertexts. The implication is that, the compression allows for more room in the selected cover-image, for the storage or embedding of more secret information. Another implication is that, the size of the

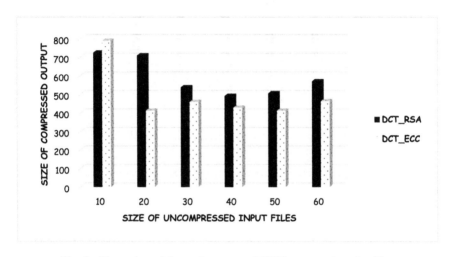

Fig. 3. Illustration of the performance of LZW compression algorithm

resultant output is greatly reduced compared to what is obtainable if compression was not involved. This means that the proposed system is also suitable for resource con-strained environments like those obtainable in Internet of Things (IoT).

A performance comparison of the newly developed DCT_ECC based system versus the existing traditional RSA based solutions in terms of the entire computation time was carried out, and the results are as presented in the diagram in Fig. 4. The computation time here refers to the time it takes to encrypt given secret message or data and embed the resultant cipher-text in a chosen cover-image.

These times it takes (in milliseconds), to encrypt and embed a given secret infor-mation (text) in a chosen cover-image to yield a stego-image, were recorded and plotted to yield the chart in Fig. 4. It can be clearly deduced that newly developed system

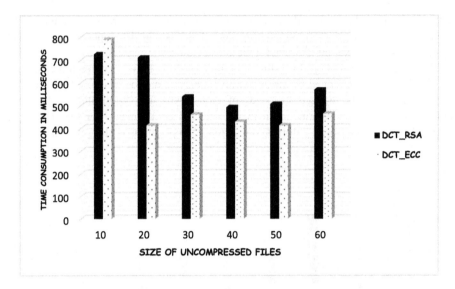

Fig. 4. Performance comparison of our system versus existing RSA-based

records lesser computation times, and therefore can be said to have outperformed the conventional RSA-based one.

5   Conclusion

Although a number of techniques for securing information whether in store or while being exchanged exist, there is a serious need for improvement, as individuals with malicious intents are growing in skills at circumventing existing security solutions. Steganography, an information hiding technique is effective for secure/covet communication, while not even arousing the suspicion of attackers.

In this paper, an improved image-based steganography system that uses Discrete Cosine Transform (DCT), Elliptic Curve Cryptography (ECC) and Lempel-Ziv techniques was developed. Results shows that this system has high capacity for hiding secret messages in cover images. This will enable confidential communications between entities even across enterprise networks. Due to the ECC used, small sized cipher texts are produced after encryption, as against what is obtainable when RSA crypto-system is used for encryption. This counts for robustness on the part of our technique.

Furthermore, the Lempel-Ziv algorithm also helps with compression. This reduces the eventual size of the cipher-text further before embedding same in a selected cover-image.

The performance analysis of the developed system as shown by the output of the Ben4D steganalysis software as well as the PSNR and MSE standard metrics, reveals the robustness of the proposed system for security of information whether in store or in transit across enterprise communication networks.

The work has been able to develop a robust 2-layer steganography system that would be very useful in securing and sharing large amount of sensitive data or information without arousing suspicion.

References

1. Alese, B.K., Gabriel, A.J., Olukayode, O., Daramola, O.A.: Modelling of risk management procedures for cybercrime control systems. In: Proceedings of the World Congress on Engineering (WCE 2014) London, United Kingdom. ISBN 978-988-19252-7-5
2. Daodu, M.N., Gabriel, A.J., Alese, B.K., Adetunmbi, A.O.: A Data Encryption Standard (DES) based web services security architecture. Ann. Comput. Sci. Ser. Tibiscus Univ. **14**(2), 53–58 (2016)
3. Kuboye, B.M., Gabriel, A.J., Thompson, A.F., Joseph, V.O.: Analysis of algorithms in Long Term Evolution (LTE) network. J. Comput. Sci. Appl. **25**(2), 59–71 (2018)
4. Gabriel, A.J., Egwuche, O.S.: Modelling the employees' activities of public service sector using production rules. Anale. Seria Informatică **13**(2), 65–68 (2015). Vol. XIII fasc. 2 – 2015 Annals. Computer Science Series, University of Timisoara, Romania
5. Iwasokun, G.B., Egwuche, O.S., Gabriel, A.J.: Neural network- based health personnel monitoring system. Afr. J. Comput. ICT IEEE **8**(1), 79–87 (2015)
6. Gabriel, A.J., Alese, B.K., Adetunmbi, A.O., Adewale, O.S., Sarumi, O.A.: Post-quantum crystography system for secure electronic voting, open computer science. DeGruyter **9**, 292–298 (2019)
7. Agboola, A.H., Gabriel, A.J., Aliyu, E.O., Alese, B.K.: Development of a fuzzy logic based rainfall prediction model. Int. J. Eng. Technol. **3**(4), 427–435 (2013). ISSN 2049-3444
8. Alabi, O., Thompson, A.F., Alese, B.K., Gabriel, A.J.: Cloud application security using hybrid encryption. Commun. Appl. Electron. **7**(33) (2020)
9. Gabriel, A.J., Alese, B.K., Adetunmbi, A.O., Adewale, O.S.: Post-quantum crystography; a combination of post-quantum cryptography and steganography. In: The 8th International Conference for Internet Technology and Secured Transactions (ICITST-2013), Technically Co-Sponsored by IEEE UK/RI Computer Chapter, London, UK, pp. 454–457, 9th–12th December 2013
10. Gabriel, A.J., Alese, B.K., Adetunmbi, A.O., Adewale, O.S.: Post-quantum crystography based security framework for cloud computing. J. Internet Technol. Secured Trans. (JITST) **4**(1), 351–357 (2015)
11. Malik, A., Sikka, G., Verma, H.K.: A high capacity text steganography scheme based on LZW compression and colour coding. Eng. Sci. Technol. Int. J. **4**–11 (2016)
12. Vidhya, P.M., Paul, V.: A method for text steganography using malayalam text. Proc. Int. J. Comput. Sci. **46**, 524–531 (2015)
13. Jain, M., Kumar, S.: Adaptive circular queue image steganography with RSA cryptosystem. Elsevier Perspect. Sci. **8**, 417–420 (2016)
14. Sethi, P., Kapoor, V.: A proposed novel architecture for information hiding in image steganography by using genetic algorithm and cryptography. Proc. Comput. Sci. **2016**(87), 61–66 (2016)
15. Cheong, S., Ling, H., Teh, P.: Encrypted steganography graphical password scheme for near field communication smartphone access control system. Elsevier Expert Syst. Appl. **41**(14), 3561–3568 (2014)
16. Malathi, P., Gireeshkumar, T.: Relating the embedding efficiency of LSB steganography. Elsevier Proc. Comput. **2016**(93), 878–885 (2016)

17. Snasel, V., Kromer, P., Safarik, J., Platos, J.: JPEG steganography with particle swarm optimization accelerated by AVX. Special Issue Paper (2019). https://doi.org/10.1002/cpe. 544. Wiley; https://onlinelibrary.wiley.com

18. Chatterjee, A., Ghosal, S.K., Sarkar, R.: LSB based steganography with OCR: an intelligent amalgamation. Multimed Tools Appl. **79**, 11747–11765 (2020). https://doi.org/10.1007/s11042-019-08472-6

19. Rachael, O., Misra, S., Ahuja, R., Adewumi, A., Ayeni, F., Mmaskeliunas, R.: Image steganography and steganalysis based on Least Significant Bit (LSB). In: Singh, P.K., Panigrahi, B.K., Suryadevara, N.K., Sharma, S.K., Singh, A.P. (eds.) Proceedings of ICETIT 2019. LNEE, vol. 605, pp. 1100–1111. Springer, Cham (2020). https://doi.org/10.1007/978-3-030-30577-2_97

20. Balgurgi, P.P., Jagtap, S.K.: Audio steganography used for secure data transmission. In: Kumar, M.A., Selvarani, R., Kumar, T. (eds.) Proceedings of International Conference on Advances in Computing. Advances in Intelligent Systems and Computing, vol. 174. Springer, Heidelberg (2013). https://doi.org/10.1007/978-81-322-0740-5_83

21. Adeboje, O.T., Adetunmbi, A.O., Gabriel, A.J.: Embedding text in audio steganography system using advanced encryption standard and spread spectrum. Int. J. Comput. Appl. (0975–8887) **177**(41), 46–51 (2020). https://doi.org/10.5120/ijca2020919

22. Wang, S., Sang, J., Song, X., Niu, X.: Least Significant Qubit (LSQb) information hiding algorithm for quantum for quantum image. Measurement **73**, 352–359 (2015)

Towards Explainable Direct Marketing in the Telecom Industry Through Hybrid Machine Learning

Russel Petersen and Olawande Daramola[(✉)]

Department of Information Technology,
Cape Peninsula University of Technology, Cape Town, South Africa
203132173@mycput.ac.za, daramolaj@cput.ac.za

Abstract. Direct marketing enables businesses to identify customers that could be interested in product offerings based on historical customer transactions data. Several machine learning (ML) tools are currently being used for direct marketing. However, the disadvantage of ML algorithmic models is that even though results could be accurate, they lack relevant explanations. The lack of detailed explanations that justify recommendations has led to reduced trust in ML-based recommendations for decision making in some critical real-world domains. The telecommunication domain has continued to witness a decline of revenue in core areas such as voice and text messaging services which make direct marketing useful to increase profit. This paper presents the conceptual design of a machine learning process framework that will enable telecom subscribers that should be targeted for direct marketing of new products to be identified, and also provide explanations for the recommendations. To do this, a hybrid framework that employs supervised learning, case-based reasoning and rule-based reasoning is proposed. The operational workflow of the framework is demonstrated with an example, while the plan of implementation and evaluation are also discussed.

Keywords: Machine learning · Direct marketing · Explainable AI · Telecommunication · Case-based reasoning

1 Introduction

Majority of industries today face greater challenges in selling the right product to the right customer and at the right time. With the vast amounts of data available through big data technologies, a direct marketing campaign can be constructed to analyse customer characteristics to recommend the right product offering to a customer at the right time [1, 2].

Machine learning (ML) is a substantially better way of making predictions using complex sets of data from data sources to derive results. It utilises specially designed algorithms to identify customer patterns from large data sources, which are more difficult to handle for traditional statistical methods, expert systems-based approaches, or manual approaches [3].

© Springer Nature Switzerland AG 2020
O. Gervasi et al. (Eds.): ICCSA 2020, LNCS 12254, pp. 471–486, 2020.
https://doi.org/10.1007/978-3-030-58817-5_35

The disadvantage of ML algorithms is that they are typically black-boxes that produce results without explanations. Often, the user must be an expert to interpret the result to utilise it [4]. This lack of explanation reduces the level of confidence in ML predictions, and adoption by the management of many organizations, particularly in critical sectors. [4, 5]. This problem makes it necessary to have highly skilled personnel to interpret the results produced by ML algorithms. This increases capital and operational expenditure of organisations on personnel significantly [4, 6].

The generally poor explanation attribute of ML systems has led to increased interests in the field of Explainable AI (XAI) [6]. The information available on product review websites such as *Softwareadvice* (www.softwareadvice.com), *capterra* (www.capterra.com), and *goto crowd* (www.g2crowd.com) revealed that most ML-based direct-marketing tools lack the capability to provide a detailed explanation. ML predictions accompanied by detailed explanations would allow for valuable insight into understanding customer behaviour [7].

The telecommunication (telecom) industry has seen a continuous decline in revenue in core areas such as voice and text messaging [8]. At the same time, the domain has also absorbed a variety of disruptive technologies, message services and over-the-top streaming services. These factors have resulted in the high need to continuously increase product sales within the domain. With the rich customer data available, a data-driven direct marketing strategy enables the right product to be offered to the right customer and at the right time [8]. This makes the concept of direct-marketing with explanations quite relevant to the telecom industry.

This paper presents the design of a process framework that explores a hybrid approach that is able to combine supervised machine learning, and an intelligent reasoning model (IRM) that consist of case-based reasoning, and a set of expert defined knowledge rules to generate explanations for direct marketing predictions. This type of framework facilitates the use of experience from previous use case scenarios, and domain knowledge to create the basis for rich explanations that justifies ML predictions. As a contribution, an adaptable process framework that enables effective direct-marketing with explanations in the telecom industry is proposed, which will be an improvement on previous approaches for direct marketing in the telecom domain that lack explanations.

The remaining part of this paper is described as follows. Section 2 presents an overview of the background and related work. Section 3 presents the description of the process framework, while an example was used to describe how the framework can be applied is presented in Sect. 4. Section 5 discusses the plan for implementation and evaluation, while the paper is concluded in Sect. 6 with a brief note.

2 Background and Related Work

This section provides an overview of important topics that are relevant to this paper. It reviews the subject of data-driven direct product marketing, machine learning, rule-based reasoning, and case-based reasoning. It also presents an overview of previous work on ML-based direct marketing.

2.1   Data-Driven Direct Marketing

Direct marketing is a method whereby customer features such as spending, geographical details and past product purchases are used to offer a product directly to a specific customer. Across industries, this method has been proven to increase sales significantly [1, 9]. The technological advancement in data processing and storage has allowed organisations to store large datasets. A larger set of data allows an organisation to know more about a customer and execute a more accurate prediction. The right data allows customers to be segmented accurately and products can be marketed to identified customer segmentations [2].

Over time technological advancements have enabled the use of data-driven direct marketing. Various data analytics technologies can be used to build customer characteristics and identifying customer patterns from data. It is now possible to predict the probability that a customer would respond to a specific product offering [10, 11]. Studies have shown that top-performing companies rely more on large detailed datasets and data analytics than low performing companies [9, 10].

2.2   Machine Learning

Machine learning (ML) is a computer-based method which looks at existing data as input and produces a prediction as output by applying an algorithmic model. An algorithmic model is a sequence of instructions used to convert the input into the output [12]. At a high level, ML consists of two phases. The first phase is applying an algorithmic model to a dataset to train the model on a dataset. The second phase is to take a dataset and make a prediction of future occurrences.

ML has proven to be very effective in direct marketing. It allows a company to take a large dataset, and then establish detailed customer characteristics based on the dataset, and apply an algorithmic model to make a probabilistic prediction [3]. The most accurate ML models are usually in a nested non-linear structure. Nested non-linear models such as Artificial Networks (ANN), Random Forest (RF) are mostly applied in a black-box manner where no explanation is provided on how the model arrived at a particular prediction. This lack of explanation makes it difficult to identify flaws in ML models and biases in the data [4].

2.3   Case-Based Reasoning

Case-based reasoning (CBR) uses the record of past occurrences to provide the solution to a new occurrence. The approach has been found to have strong explanation mechanisms because it derives its explanations from similar previous cases [13, 14]. Typically the CBR problem-solving process entails case retrieval, case reuse, case adaptation, and case retention. CBR can be applied to address the lack of explanation and simplify the interpretation of results. CBR can be used to substantiate the predictions made, which can complement a machine learning model in a good way. CBR examines past occurrences with similar output and provides a detailed explanation of why the current output occurred. Real evidence is used from a set of relevant cases to explain the task at hand. CBR Explanations are simplistic regardless of the complexity of the current problem [14].

2.4   Related Work

A number of efforts that focussed on the use of machine learning techniques to improve direct marketing have been reported in the literature. Of these efforts, the banking sector, and telecommunication appears significantly, hence they have been considered for review.

In [15], an attempt was made to determine the best classification technique for data-driven direct marketing. Four commonly used classification techniques were selected and evaluated. The results showed that decision trees produced a reasonably high sensitivity, specificity and accuracy. In [16] a similar attempt was made with respect to the banking sector where four different machine learning (ML) algorithms were compared to investigate the effectiveness in predicting potential customers for banking products. The results showed that the use of ML algorithms allows the processing of large amounts of data and gathering a greater historical view of customer spending patterns. The emphasis was on accuracy of results and no explanation. In [17] banking data was applied to the SVM and Random Forest (RF) Regression model to predict potential banking customers. Both models produced a good performance for classification but the RF Regression showed slightly improved results for accuracy and sensitivity. The study also noted that both models lacked explanation that can enable the understanding of results. In [18] the Naive Bayes and RF Regression model were compared by using a large banking dataset to determine customers for long term deposits. The RF Regression model performed better in terms of accuracy, specificity and sensitivity, but offered no explanation.

The authors in [19] showed that data classification techniques are effective in determining which customers will subscribe to term deposits in the banking industry. A banking dataset was labelled with relevant attributes, and customers grouped by region. Decision tree and Naïve Bayes classification techniques were used to categorise the customers. The decision tree was found to have a higher level of accuracy but offered no explanation.

In [20], it was found that the application of ML models improves overall marketing significantly. This was tested by applying a ML models to customer dataset containing various customer features to obtain predictions. In [21] a study to identify customers for upselling of products within the telecommunication industry using a ML was conducted. A Support Vector Machine (SVM) model was applied to a customer dataset to classify the customers as either a churner or a non-churner. The classification was then used to determine the probability to upsell or not. The prediction had high accuracy with minimal errors but no explanation was provided to justify the classification.

In [22] a deep learning model was applied to a telecommunication dataset to determine customer churn. The findings indicated that accurate predictions were made but the lack of explanation prohibited a greater understanding of customer behaviour to reduce the rate of churners in the long term proactively. A study by [23] recommended that extraction of data from the resource, service and customer layers within a telecommunication company could provide an accurate and insightful customer profile.

In addition to this, customer billing information which includes consumption, spend limit and usage data were found to be valuable in predicting product offerings. There is a relationship between a customer's past spending pattern and current consumption. This relationship can be exploited to recommend meaningful products to a customer at the right time. This paper extends the recommendation made by [23] by adding billing data as an extra dimension for generating prediction on customer choices, also focusses on providing explanations. A study by [24] revealed that combining a CBR system with a ML model can enhance the predictive accuracy as it enabled domain expert knowledge to be used to formulate cases in the case base. The hybridized system was applied to predict prices for internet domain names and it produced a better prediction. In [25] a CBR module was used to select the specific ML model that should be used to solve a problem. The CBR-ANN hybrid system showed improved results when compared to a situation when a basic ANN model is used. The aim of the CBR-ANN is not to improve explanation of results. A study to predict skin disease by using a real life skin disease dataset was reported in [26]. The CBR-ANN was adjudged to be of acceptable performance but the primary objective of the hybrid system was not explanation. In [27] a hybrid CBR-ANN system that can be used for different types of classification problems was presented. A trained ANN model was used to extract feature weights that were used to improve the performance of the CBR module within the hybrid system. use in case-based reasoning (CBR) system. The focus of the hybrid system is not explanation. In [28] a study that compared the performance and usability of a hybrid CBR-ANN system, a CBR system, and a ANN system for the prediction of the valuation of residential properties was presented. The hybrid CBR-ANN system was found to have better performance and usability. The emphasis of the CBR-ANN system was not primarily on explanation. Generally, although some hybrid systems have been proposed, and the concept of explainable machine learning is currently attracting increasing attention of researchers, so far, this has not been applied to the telecommunication domain, which makes the intended contribution of this paper to be unique [14, 29].

3 Methodology

In this section, the requirements and conceptual design of the proposed process framework for direct marketing with explanation are presented.

3.1 Requirements

In order to identify the requirements that the proposed approach must satisfy, the Joint Application Development (JAD) technique was used. JAD allows the inclusion of all project stakeholders, developers and users so that the requirements are scrutinized by all participants [30]. Requirements were derived from all functional and non-functional aspects that pertain to the system and all the identified use cases. Sessions were held over four days in scheduled daily sessions until all issues have been discussed and information collected [31]. The JAD session included 9 participants described as follows:

- Specialist in Predictive Analytics (2 persons)
- Customer Care End User (3 persons)
- Specialist in Customer Experience Management (2 persons)
- Customer Care Supervisor (1 person)
- Specialist in Business Intelligence (1 person)

During the JAD sessions, participants were given the opportunity to mention different types of interactions with customer data whether it is with the front-end resources or back-end resources. They were also asked to identify how a customer's purchasing pattern can be influenced in a positive way. They were also tasked to list any problem which they think might be a challenge in customer interaction or influence a customer's purchasing pattern. By using a brainstorming technique involving all participants, solutions were identified for all the problems, which were then converted to system requirements. At the end of the JAD sessions, the following requirements of the system were derived (Table 1):

Table 1. List of requirements

Req. No.	Description
1	The system shall predict customers that are most likely to be interested in a product and provide explanation of why the customers were selected
2	The system shall predict which products can be used to upsell specific customers
3	The system shall predict the customers that should not be considered for a particular product, with an explanation of why the customer were selected
4	The system shall produce its recommendations in a speedy and reliable manner
5	The system shall be able to classify customers into low and high spending customers based on the amount they spend per month
6	The system shall be able classify customers into low and high usage subscribers based on the amount they use per month
7	The system shall generate explanations that are easy to understand and of a high quality
8	The system shall enable use of specific computational operations in different scenarios through APIs or web services
9	The system shall ensure that customer data is protected through adequate security measures such as user authentication and user login access functions to disallow unauthorised users
10	The system shall display a list of available operations to enable the user to select an operation of choice or which prediction is required
11	The system shall display prediction results and explanation to the user
12	The system shall allow the user to load products to be sold to customers onto the system
13	The system shall allow a user accounts to be created and deleted

3.2 A Hybrid ML Approach for Explainable Direct Marketing

Based on the identified requirements, a hybrid ML approach that will enable direct marketing with explanation was conceived. The approach will enable data collection from 4 different layers of a telecommunication organisation, which are the resource, service, customer and billing layers, and to discover customers that should be targeted for direct marketing by using a hybrid ML approach (see Fig. 1). The resource layer includes subscriber and device data to verify the technologies available to the subscriber. The service layer includes the voice, data and video services utilized by the subscriber during a specific period of time. The customer layer includes the service provisioning data and any interaction the subscriber had with the organization; while the billing layer includes data on spending and user consumption data. After the data collection is complete, the data is passed to the hybridized machine learning system that does the prediction and generates an explanation.

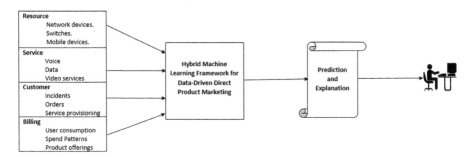

Fig. 1. An overview of the Hybrid ML approach for explainable direct marketing

3.3 A Process Framework for Explainable Direct Marketing (PROFEDIM)

We have formulated the process framework for explainable direct marketing (PRO-FEDIM), which consists of two phases. PROFEDIM is composed of a hybrid framework that integrates supervised machine learning (ML) and case-based reasoning (CBR). The activities of PROFEDIM, which can be classified into two phases are depicted in their sequential order of (1) – (15) in Fig. 2. The first phase consists of activities of data gathering – (1), data wrangling – (2), data labelling – (3), and data selection and model training – (4) which are all mostly semi-automated, and offline procedures. Data selection entails identifying the specific attributes that are required for the direct product marketing task at hand, while model training is the process of using supervised learning – (5) to train a nested non-linear ML model such as ANN, SVM, or RF on the selected dataset. Model training is an offline activity that is separated from the prediction task.

The second phase entails the generation of a prediction and an explanation in response to a query. For prediction, when data of new query case/instance – (6) are passed into the PROFEDIM, feature selection – (7) takes place so that relevant data are extracted from the new query case. To do this, case matching and case retrieval from the case base – (8) takes place to determine if the new case is similar to some old cases if the new query case is significantly similar to some old cases, then the CBR module– (9) by using the predefined rules by domain experts – (10) is used to generate a prediction and a relevant explanation – (11).

When significant similarity with cases in the case base cannot be established, the ML-based prediction module – (12) performs the prediction. This offers three possibilities, which are to determine if customers could be interested in a new product, not interested in a new product, and to determine if a customer can be a candidate for upselling. After the prediction by the supervised ML model – (13) the case-based reasoning module – (15) will search the case base – (14) for cases that have somewhat similar attributes to the current case, and use them to construct a relevant explanation for the new prediction – (11) by relying on the predefined rules by domain experts that are stored in the repository – (11). The two alternate paths of computation that can be explored in the course of operation of PROFEDIM is shown in Fig. 3.

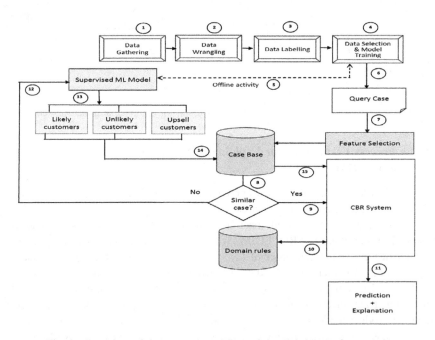

Fig. 2. Overview of the process workflow of the Hybrid ML framework

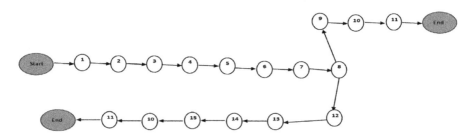

Fig. 3. Alternative computational paths of Hybrid ML framework

4   An Illustrative Example

In this section, we present a scenario example that deals with identifying subscribers that should be targeted for direct marketing for a new YouTube data product by a Telecom company (herein referred to as XC). The task is to select the subset of customers of XC that should be targeted for direct marketing from a large pool of subscribers. We shall use demo subscriber data that is derived based on data attributes that emulate the schema of an unnamed Telecom company.

i. Data Gathering Process
The data gathering activity will involve extracting data from various sources at the different layers of XC organization, which are pooled into a central database. The database will include the following:

- Subscriber Profile (A1) – the subscriber's main offering and any data package.
- Device Profile (A2) – the details of the device which was used by the subscriber this will include the device capability, streaming functionality and the technology supported by the device (2G, 3G, or 4G).
- Data Add-on Service (A3) – any other additional services such as a video streaming, WhatsApp or YouTube service that the customer uses.
- Billing Profile (A4) – the subscriber's billing data from the billing management system. This will include the total amount spent for the month, the monetary products attached to the profile and the billing cycle.
- Data Allocation (A5) – the amount of data allocated to the subscriber through purchase during a particular time period.
- Data Usage (A6) – the amount of data used by the subscriber during a particular time period.
- Transfer Activity (A7) – the amount of data received by the subscriber and the amount of data sent to other subscribers during a particular time period.
- Streaming Application Usage (A8) –This is the amount of data used on the 3 most used applications by the subscriber on these applications during a particular time period.
- Total Spend (A9) – the total amount spent by the subscribers during a particular time period based on the billing system (Table 2).

Table 2. Sample data on subscribers

Subscriber ID	A1	A2	A3	A4	A5	A6	A7	A8	A9
CUST9581111	Select + Package	iPhone 11	1 GB	2000 MB	19500	0 MB	500 MB	WhatsApp (300); Youtube (100); Facebook (450)	850.00
CUST9581001	Smart XL	Samsung S9	250 MB	250 MB	500	0 MB	0 MB	Youtube (100);	600.00
CUST9781011	Smart L	Samsung A1	1 GB	0 MB	1200	0 MB	0 MB	WhatsApp (300)	300.00
CUST3561221	Prepaid	Vodacom T1	0 MB	0 MB	200	0 MB	0 MB	WhatsApp (300)	110.00
CUST6481215	Smart Red	iPhone 10	2 GB	1000 MB	10500	500 MB	500 MB	Facebook (200)	1100.00
CUST4591101	Red VIP	iPhone 11	5 GB	1000 MB	2000	0 MB	0 MB	Youtube (100)	950.00

ii. Data Wrangling Process

Data wrangling process will entail cleaning the data and removing duplicate, and null values, and missing data that affects good data quality.

iii. Data Labelling Process

The data labelling process will allow the gathered data to be categorized and used as a basis to derive relevant data attributes that could be used as a basis for prediction (see Table 3). For this example case, the data attributes that were derived are the following:

- Spending Category (L1) – This is categorised as High, Medium, and Low based on A7, and A9 according to a predefined threshold (e.g. High $\geq$ R150; Medium R50 $\leq$ R149); or Low < R50)
- Data usage category (L2) – This will be categorised as High, Medium and Low based on A5, A6, and A7 according to a predefined threshold (e.g. High $\geq$ 300 MB; Medium $\geq$ 100 $\leq$ 299 MB; or Low < 100 MB).
- Period of connection (L3) – this is the measure of the period of years when the subscriber is connected to the network. This number of days will be divided by 365 days to convert it to years. This is derived based on A3.
- Spend rate per day (L4) – this is the ratio of the total monthly spend divided by the number of days in the month(s). This is derived based on A9
- Data usage rate per day (L5) – this is the ratio of the total amount of data used in the month divided by the number of days. This is derived based on A6
- Data add-on usage rate per day (L6) – the total monthly data add-on utilized divided the number of days in the month. This is derived based on A3.
- Device capability (L7) – This is categorized into 2G (Low), 3G (Medium) or 4G (High). This is derived based on A2.
- Streaming capability (L8) – This classified as streaming (1) or non-streaming (0) to indicate if a subscriber's device has the streaming capability or not.
- Streaming usage per day (L9) – This classified as Low, Medium, or High based on A8, and according to a predefined threshold.

Table 3. Subscriber profile after the data labelling process

Subscriber ID	L1	L2	L3	L4	L5	L6	L7	L8	L9
CUST9581111	Medium	Medium	28,33	66,66	33,33	10,33	High	1	High
CUST9581001	High	Medium	1,36	20,00	1,36	1,36	High	1	Medium
CUST9781011	High	Medium	3,28	10,00	33,33	0	High	1	Low

iv. Data Selection and Model Training

This activity involves selecting labelled data attributes that are relevant to the prediction task at hand from Table 3. For the current task L1, L2, L6, L7, L8, L9 are the most important to predict whether a customer would be interested in a new YouTube product or not. L4 and L5 are less important because their effects are subsumed by L1 and L2, which captures the total amount spent, and the total data usage by subscribers hence they were excluded. The selected attributes lead to a regression problem that seeks to predict the likelihood (True/False) that a customer would be interested in a new YouTube product as follows:

$$Y = a + L_1x_1 + L_2x_2 + L_6x_6 + L_7x_7 + L_8x_8 + L_9x_9 + e \qquad (1)$$

Where Y is the dependent variable to be predicted, a is the intercept, L is the slope, X is the observed score on the independent variable, and e is an error value. This regression task can be solved by using a supervised learning model such as ANN, Support Vector Regression (SVR) or Random forest (RF). A dataset K consisting of normalized vectors can be used to train the RF regression model.

$$K = \left\{ L_1^*, L_2^*, L_6^*, L_7^*, L_8^*, L_9^*, Y^* \right\} \qquad (2)$$

Where L_i^* and Y^* are the normalised values of L_i and $Y \in K$

In a scenario where RF is selected as the ML model to use, then a RF model can estimate the value of Y for every vectorized data of L_i that is presented to it. The most discriminant attributes that are found to be critical for the prediction by the RF model are also stored in the case base. For example after training and testing of the RF, the attributes L_1 – Spending category, L_2 – Data usage category, and L_9 – streaming usage per day could have been found to be the most significant attributes for the prediction made. These attributes are then stored in the case base for subsequent reuse in order to generate explanation in future prediction scenarios.

v. Random Forest (RF) Regression

Random Forest (RF) Regression performs prediction by using an ensemble learning approaches that returns the mean of the predictions of several decision trees to produce its prediction. The decision trees are made up of questions which branches the learning sample into smaller and smaller parts. The regression algorithm will search all possible variables and values to find the best available branch which would be returned as the prediction [32]. Studies have shown that RF Regression is an ideal technique in handling both categorical and numerical data because it produces a high level of accuracy of predictions and uses minimal overheads to perform predictions. The procedure the RF prediction will typically entail the following:

i) Import appropriate RF libraries, and load the dataset for training
ii) Split the dataset into a training set and test set (the 80/20 or 70/30 or 65/35 rules are options to consider depending on the nature of data)
iii) Create a RF regression model and fit it to the dataset.
iv) Experimentally adjust hyperparameters to obtain a good-fit of the training and validation data set.
v) Visualize the results.

vi. Prediction and Explanation via the CBR Module
The CBR module will work by comparing features extracted from a new case with existing cases in the case base. The retrieval of similar cases to a query (new) case will be done by using a K-Nearest Neighbour algorithm that fetches the set of most similar cases to the new case [13]. For our example, a similarity threshold in the upper percentile of 0.8 and above is considered significant. This is to ensure that case adaptation by the CBR module is based on the solution parts of existing cases that are significantly similar to a new case. The case adaptation process is used to generate a prediction for a current case. The predefined rules by domain experts are used together with the case attributes of the most similar cases to generate an explanation to justify the prediction. On the contrary, if similarity of less than 0.8 is established, the RF model will be used to generate the prediction because of its superior predictive ability compared to CBR when there are no significantly similar cases in the case base.

vii. Prediction and Explanation via the RF Model
When the set similarity threshold between a new case and existing cases is not met (< 0.8) then the pre-trained RF regression model is used to generate a prediction. After obtaining a prediction, the CBR module will use the knowledge contained in the case base to construct an explanation for the new prediction. To do this, the identified most discriminant attributes for the RF prediction are used as a basis to identify the existing cases that are most similar to the current case and retrieve them from the case base. The basis for this retrieval will normally be based on a lower similarity threshold so as to retrieve sufficient multiple cases. By using a heuristic search operation, individual discriminant attributes of these multiple cases are examined to find instances that are similar to those of the query case. These are then used together with the predefined domain rules to generate an explanation for the prediction obtained from the RF model for the query case. The examples of predefined rules to aid the generation of meaningful explanations to support the predictions made by the RF model are shown in Table 4.

Table 4. Sample domain rules that can influence explanation generation.

Rule No	Condition	Offer
1	If low spender and high data receiver and streaming capability	YouTube product
2	If medium spender and high data consumption and WhatsApp user	WhatsApp product
3	If low spender and long-time user	Data product
4	If high spender and high data consumption and streaming capability	Data product
5	If high spender and high data consumption and high streaming	Video streaming product
6	If high spender and medium data consumption and high streaming	Offer YouTube product
7	If low consumer and low spender and short-time user	No offering
8	If high spender and high data sender	Data product
9	If high spender and high streaming	Video streaming product
10	If low spender and high data consumption and streaming capability	Video streaming product

5   Implementation Plan

The recent advancement in the fields of machine learning (ML), and the existence of reliable software development frameworks for case-based reasoning (CBR) makes the actual implementation of process framework that can facilitate explainable direct marketing plausible. We intend to develop an integrated system that will be able to support the full scope of activities that spans the 2 phases of the process framework for explainable direct marketing (PROFEDIM) as outlined in Sect. 3. We plan to leverage Scikit-learn a Python-based ML framework to realise the supervised learning capabilities for prediction such as Artificial Neural Networks (ANN), Random Forest (RF), and Support Vector Machines (SVM). The myCBR Restful API [33] will be used as the building block to realise all case-based reasoning functionalities. The two development frameworks will be integrated within a single hybrid system architecture that can support end-to-end activities of PROFEDIM. A prototype software will be developed with distinct interfaces that support all forms of user activity such as selecting a specific direct marketing task of interest, pre-processing, the specific type of computation by using appropriate middleware algorithms, obtaining predictions, and obtaining explanations by relying on appropriate knowledge resources. The outlook of the components of the integrated hybrid ML system architecture is shown in Fig. 4.

From Fig. 4, it is obvious that data selection and feature selection can be invoked from both the Scikit-learn component and the myCBR component, while prediction and explanation capabilities are also enabled by these middleware components.

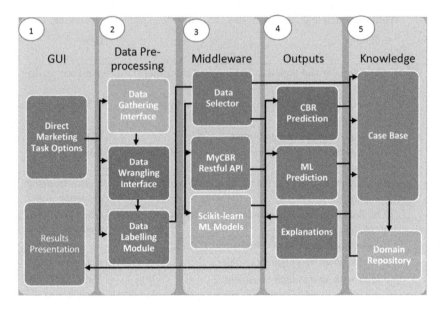

Fig. 4. Components of the Hybrid ML system architecture

Post-implementation, the evaluation of PROFEDIM will be done from two perspectives. First will be to assess the performance of the framework in terms of the accuracy of its predictions and the quality of its explanations. The process framework allows either of ANN, RF, and SVM to be selected as the ML model for generating a prediction, hence standard regression metrics will be used to do this. The quality of explanations that are generated to justify predictions will also be evaluated in terms of its understandability. The second perspective will be to assess the usability of PROFEDIM as it fits into the operational workflow of a Telecom company. These two evaluation perspectives will be essential in order to derive a valid conclusion of the plausibility of the proposed framework.

6   Conclusion

In this paper, the description of a process framework for explainable direct marketing (PROFEDIM) is presented. PROFEDIM is based on a hybrid architecture that integrated both supervised machine learning and CBR. The sequence of activities of the process framework, and its capabilities, and plan of implementation and evaluation was discussed. This is further demonstrated by using an illustrative example of how the process framework can be applied in a real problem scenario. The contribution of this paper is that it offers a new perspective on direct marketing in the telecom domain through the use of a hybrid AI architecture. This is because existing direct marketing tools   mostly   lack   explanation   capability   that   is   able   to   justify   their predictions/recommendations. In further work, we shall take steps to implement the proposed framework, and also conduct an evaluation.

References

1. Alanen, A.: Efficient direct marketing: Case: Valtapinnoite Oy (2016)
2. Yu, C., Zhang, Z., Lin, C., Wu, Y.J.: Can data-driven precision marketing promote user ad clicks? Evidence from advertising in WeChat moments. Ind. Mark. Manage. (2019). https://doi.org/10.1016/j.indmarman.2019.05.001
3. Erel, I., Stern, L.H., Tan, C., Weisbach, M.S.: Selecting directors using machine learning (No. w24435). National Bureau of Economic Research (2018)
4. Guidotti, R., Monreale, A., Ruggieri, S., Turini, F., Giannotti, F., Pedreschi, D.: A survey of methods for explaining black box models. ACM Comput. Surv. (CSUR) **51**(5), 1–42 (2018)
5. Gordon, J., Perrey, J., Spillecke, D.: Big data, analytics and the future of marketing and sales. Digital Advantage, McKinsey (2013)
6. Bonacina, M.: Automated reasoning for explainable artificial intelligence. In The First International ARCADE (Automated Reasoning: Challenges, Applications, Directions, Exemplary Achievements) Workshop (in association with CADE-26), Gothenburg, Sweden (2017)
7. Goebel, R., et al.: Explainable AI: the new 42? In: Holzinger, A., Kieseberg, P., Tjoa, A.M., Weippl, E. (eds.) CD-MAKE 2018. LNCS, vol. 11015, pp. 295–303. Springer, Cham (2018). https://doi.org/10.1007/978-3-319-99740-7_21
8. Vantara, H., Kalakota, R., Partner, LiquidHub: Transform Telecom: A Data-Driven Strategy for Digital Transformation, White Paper, Hitachi Vantara (2019)
9. Beheshtian-Ardakani, A., Fathian, M., Gholamian, M.: A novel model for product bundling and direct marketing in e-commerce based on market segmentation. Decis. Sci. Lett. **7**(1), 39–54 (2018)
10. Flici, A.: A conceptual framework for the direct marketing process using business intelligence (Doctoral dissertation, Brunel University Brunel Business School Ph.D. theses) (2011)
11. Buttle, F., Maklan, S.: Customer Relationship Management: Concepts and Technologies. Routledge, Abingdon (2019)
12. Pereira, F.C., Borysov, S.S.: Machine learning fundamentals. In: Mobility Patterns, Big Data and Transport Analytics, pp. 9–29. Elsevier (2019)
13. Daramola, O., Stålhane, T., Omoronyia, I., Sindre, G.: Using ontologies and machine learning for hazard identification and safety analysis. In: Maalej, W., Thurimella, A. (eds.) Managing requirements knowledge, pp. 117–141. Springer, Heidelberg (2013). https://doi.org/10.1007/978-3-642-34419-0_6
14. Vásquez-Morales, G., Martínez-Monterrubio, S., Moreno-Ger, P., Recio-García, J.: Explainable prediction of chronic renal disease in the colombian population using neural networks and case-based reasoning. IEEE Access **7**, 152900–152910 (2019)
15. Wisaeng, K.: A comparison of different classification techniques for bank direct marketing. Int. J. Soft Comput. Eng. (IJSCE) **3**(4), 116–119 (2013)
16. Nachev, A.: Application of data mining techniques for direct marketing. In: Computational Models for Business and Engineering Domains, pp. 86–95 (2015)
17. Lawi, A., Velayaty, A.A., Zainuddin, Z.: On identifying potential direct marketing consumers using adaptive boosted support vector machine. In: 2017 4th International Conference on Computer Applications and Information Processing Technology (CAIPT), pp. 1–4. IEEE (2017)
18. Ruangthong, P., Jaiyen, S.: Bank direct marketing analysis of asymmetric information based on machine learning. In: 2015 12th International Joint Conference on Computer Science and Software Engineering (JCSSE), pp. 93–96. IEEE (2015)

19. Karim, M., Rahman, R.: Decision tree and Naïve Bayes algorithm for classification and generation of actionable knowledge for direct marketing. J. Softw. Eng. Appl. **6**, 196–206 (2013)
20. Bayoude, K., Ouassit, Y., Ardchir, S., Azouazi, M.: How machine learning potentials are transforming the practice of digital marketing: state of the art. Period. Eng. Nat. Sci. **6**(2), 373–379 (2018)
21. Lian-Ying, Z., Amoh, D.M., Boateng, L.K., Okine, A.A.: Combined appetency and upselling prediction scheme in telecommunication sector using support vector machines. Int. J. Mod. Educ. Comput. Sci. **11**(6), 1 (2019)
22. Castanedo, F., Valverde, G., Zaratiegui, J., Vazquez, A.: Using deep learning to predict customer churn in a mobile telecommunication network (2014)
23. Chen, C.: Use cases and challenges in telecom big data analytics. APSIPA Trans. Sig. Inf. Process. **5**, e19 (2016)
24. Dieterle, S., Bergmann, R.: A hybrid CBR-ANN approach to the appraisal of internet domain names. In: Lamontagne, L., Plaza, E. (eds.) ICCBR 2014. LNCS (LNAI), vol. 8765, pp. 95–109. Springer, Cham (2014). https://doi.org/10.1007/978-3-319-11209-1_8
25. Hegdal, S.S., Kofod-Petersen, A.: A CBR-ANN hybrid for dynamic environments. In: CEUR Workshop Proceedings (2019)
26. Dabowsa, N.I.A., Amaitik, N.M., Maatuk, A.M., Aljawarneh, S.A.: A hybrid intelligent system for skin disease diagnosis. In: 2017 International Conference on Engineering and Technology (ICET), pp. 1–6. IEEE (2017)
27. Biswas, S.K., Sinha, N., Purakayastha, B., Marbaniang, L.: Hybrid expert system using case based reasoning and neural network for classification. Biol. Inspired Cognit. Archit. **9**, 57–70 (2014)
28. Musa, A.G., Daramola, O., Owoloko, E.A., Olugbara, O.O.: A neural-CBR system for real property valuation. J. Emerg. Trends Comput. Inf. Sci. **4**(8), 611–622 (2013)
29. Du, M., Liu, N., Hu, X.: Techniques for interpretable machine learning. Commun. ACM **63**(1), 68–77 (2019)
30. Hyseni, L., Dika, Z.: An integrated framework of conceptual modelling for performance improvement of the information systems. In: 2017 Seventh International Conference on Innovative Computing Technology (INTECH), pp. 174–180. IEEE (2017)
31. Couronné, R., Probst, P., Boulesteix, A.: Random forest versus logistic regression: a large-scale benchmark experiment. BMC Bioinform. **19**(1), 270 (2018). https://doi.org/10.1186/s12859-018-2264-5
32. Ouedraogo, I., Defourny, P., Vanclooster, M.: Application of random forest regression and comparison of its performance to multiple linear regression in modelling groundwater nitrate concentration at the African continent scale. Hydrogeol. J. **27**(3), 1081–1098 (2019). https://doi.org/10.1007/s10040-018-1900-5
33. Bach, K., Mathisen, B.M., Jaiswal, A. Demonstrating the myCBR Rest API. https://iccbr2019.com/wp-content/uploads/2019/09/01_paper_Demonstrating_the_myCBR_REST_API.pdf

A Dynamic Round Triple Data Encryption Standard Cryptographic Technique for Data Security

Oluwatobi Noah Akande[1]($\boxtimes$) (iD), Oluwakemi Christiana Abikoye[2] (iD),
Aderonke Anthonia Kayode[1] (iD), Oladele Taye Aro[3],
and Oluwaseun Roseline Ogundokun[1] (iD)

[1] Department of Computer Science, Landmark Univeristy, Omu-Aran, Kwara,
Nigeria
akande.noah@lmu.edu.ng
[2] Department of Computer Science, University of Ilorin, Ilorin, Kwara, Nigeria
[3] Department of Mathematical and Computing Sciences, Kola Daisi University,
Ibadan, Nigeria

Abstract. Cryptographic techniques have been widely employed to protect sensitive data from unauthorized access and manipulation. Among these cryptographic techniques, Data Encryption Standard (DES) has been widely employed, however, it suffers from key and differential attacks. To overcome these attacks, several DES modifications have been proposed in literatures. Most modifications have focused on enhancing DES encryption key; however, the strength of a cryptographic technique is determined by the encryption key used and the number of encryption rounds. It is a known fact that Advanced Encryption Standard (AES) cryptographic technique with 14 encryption rounds is stronger than AES with 12 rounds while AES with 12 rounds is stronger than AES with 10 rounds. Therefore, this study proposed a DES cryptographic technique whose number of rounds is dynamic. Users are expected to specify the number of encryption and decryption rounds to be employed at run time. Moreover, a predefined number of shifting operations which is left circular shift 2 was chosen for each encryption round. As, a trade-off in complexity, the number of Substitution box (S-box) was also reduced to 4, so that the input to the S-boxes would be arranged in four 12-bit blocks for the X-OR operation and not six 8-bit blocks as in the traditional DES. Finally, three keys were used to encrypt, decrypt and encrypt the plaintext ciphertext as in triple DES. The modified DES yielded a better avalanche effect for rounds greater than 16 though its encryption and decryption time were greater than that of the traditional DES.

Keywords: Data Encryption Standard (DES) · Modified DES · Electronic medical information · Data and information security

© Springer Nature Switzerland AG 2020
O. Gervasi et al. (Eds.): ICCSA 2020, LNCS 12254, pp. 487–499, 2020.
https://doi.org/10.1007/978-3-030-58817-5_36

1 Introduction

The huge volume of data available on the internet has made data and information security a topmost issue of concern for 21st century researchers. With an internet user increase of 50.3%, 15.9% and 11.5% in Asia, Europe and Africa respectively for the first quarter of 2020, the amount of data available on the internet is enormous [1]. Besides data available on the internet, it is estimated that 88% of businesses in US have over 1 million folders that are unprotected and freely accessible to employers [2]. Statista submitted that data breaches in the US have been increasing annually from 783 instances in 2014 to 781 cases in 2015; 1093 instances in 2016 to 1579 cases in 2017; 1244 instances in 2018 to more than 3800 cases in 2019 [3]. These have put US at the index position when it comes to data breaches. Furthermore, the frequency and complexity of data and cybersecurity breaches are on the increase, with 8% of government parastatals, 29.2% of medical and healthcare institutions and 45.9% of businesses being affected in 2018 alone [4]. Every data and cybersecurity breaches come with a cost. The global average cost of data breach in 2019 was put at $3.92 million in contrast to $3.86 million recorded in 2018 and $3.62 recorded in 2017 [5]. With these statistics, regardless of how simple it may be, organizations need to implement at least one security technique to ensure the confidentiality, maintain the integrity and guarantee the availability of their sensitive data and information from unauthorized access, manipulation or theft.

Cryptographic techniques have been widely used to achieve these. Cryptography makes data unreadable and unmeaningful to a third party, thereby making them unsusceptible to threats or attacks. Majorly, cryptography intends to maintain privacy of data so that only intended recipients will be able to read the messages; it can also be used to verify the identity of senders or recipients (Authentication), prove that a particular message has not been read or tampered with therefore assuring that the received message is the same with the original message (integrity). Furthermore, cryptographic techniques can be used to affirm the source of the received message (Non-repudiation). Generally, cryptographic techniques require a secret key for encrypting or decrypting sensitive messages. This could be used to categorize them to symmetric or asymmetric cryptographic techniques. Symmetric cryptographic techniques are also called secret key cryptography while asymmetric cryptographic techniques are called public key cryptography. While symmetric uses the same key for encryption and decryption, asymmetric uses different keys for encryption and decryption. Therefore, symmetric cryptography guarantees the privacy and maintain the confidentiality of messages. In the same vein, asymmetric cryptography enforces authentication and maintain non-repudiation of messages. In addition to symmetric and asymmetric cryptographic techniques, hash function is another category where data are mathematically transformed into an irreversible cipher text; this connotes that the plain text cannot be retrieved from the cipher text. They are majorly used to maintain the integrity of messages sent.

Symmetric cryptography could further be categorized as a stream or block ciphers. Stream ciphers work on a single bit per time but uses a feedback mechanism to constantly change the key. However, a block cipher converts a plaintext into a block of data and carries out the encryption one block per time without changing the key used on each block. The same plaintext in a block cipher will produce the same ciphertext whereas different ciphertext will be generated from the same plaintext in a stream cipher [11]. Block ciphers could be implemented in several modes such as: cipher feedback mode, output feedback mode, counter mode, cipher block chaining mode, counter mode and electronic codebook mode being the simplest. As illustrated in Fig. 1, several symmetric and asymmetric cryptographic techniques have been proposed and employed for various security applications over the years [6–8]. However, this article focuses on Data Encryption Standard (DES) cryptographic technique.

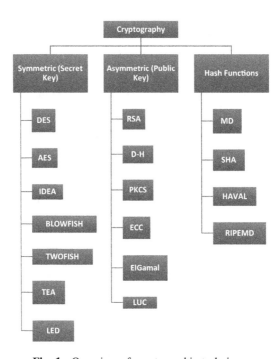

Fig. 1. Overview of cryptographic techniques

Where IDEA is International Data Encryption Algorithm, TEA is Tiny Encryption Algorithm, LED is Light Encryption Device, RSA was named after its inventors' authors Ronald Rivest, Adi Shamir, and Leonard Adleman, D-H is Diffie-Hellman, DSA is Digital Signature Algorithm (DSA), ECC is Elliptic Curve Cryptography, PKCS is Public Key Cryptography Standards, MD is Message Digest, SHA is Secure Hash Algorithm, RIPEMD is RACE Integrity Primitives Evaluation Message Digest, HAVAL is HAsh of VAriable Length. The next section of this article explains the encryption process of DES and Triple DES algorithm. An overview of several modifications to DES that have been reported in literature is provided under the related works section while the detailed steps taken to achieve the proposed DES modification is provided in the methodology section. The proposed modification was evaluated on an electronic medical database as explained in the results and discussion section. Processing time and Avalanche effects were used as performance evaluation metrics. Conclusion and recommendation for future studies were provided in the concluding part of the article.

2 DES/Triple DES Algorithm

DES is a 64-bit block cipher symmetric cryptographic algorithm that uses 56-bit key for encryption and decryption. As a 64 bits block cipher, DES divides input data into blocks of data and encrypts 64 bits of data at a time. DES is flexible in nature therefore it can operate in any of the cryptographic modes. Like other cryptographic algorithms, DES uses permutation and substitution operations for its encryption and decryption process. Substitution entails replacing a value with another while permutation reorders the positions of the bits in the input data. These processes are repeated in a number of times called rounds and it is generally believed that the more the number of rounds the higher the strength of the algorithm. DES encryption process goes thus:

Step 1: convert the input plaintext and the key into decimal and hexadecimal form using the ASCII character table

Step 2: afterwards, convert the decimal and hexadecimal form into binary bits

Step 3: divide the binary bits into 64 bits block size

Step 4: use the Initial Permutation (IP) table to randomize the bits in plaintext data block to yield E0

Step 5: substitute the key bits using permuted Choice 1 (PC - 1) table.

Step 6: divide the resulting bits into two; represent the leftmost 28 bits by L0 and the rightmost 28 bits by R0.

Step 7: using the cipher F function, shift Li and Ri to the left with "i" being the encryption round.

Step 8: combine Li and Ri from every round to produce a 56 bits LiRi

Step 9: using permuted Choice 2 (PC – 2) table, randomize LiRi to produce variable Ki

Step 10: starting with E0, use the expansion table to expand 32bits of the data to produce a new 48bits data Ei where i = i – 1.

Step 11: Perform modular X-OR of Ei and Ki to produce a 48bits Ai

Step 12: divide Ai into eight blocks data of six bits each.

Step 13: replace each of the eight blocks in step 12 with corresponding value in the substitution block to give a new variable Ni

Step 14: using the P – Box table, permutate each bit of Ni for i = 0 to 15

Step 15: XOR Ni and Ei-1 to produce a 32bits variable Ci

Step 16: after completing the 16 rounds, merge C_{16} and E_{16} to produce 64 bits $C_{16}E_{16}$

Step 17: Reverse positions of $C_{16}E_{16}$ to produce $E_{16}C_{16}$

Step 18: using Inverse Initial Permutation table, permutate $E_{16}C_{16}$ to produce the expected 64 bits Ciphertext

Steps 5 to 16 will be iterated 16 times where i indicates the current round number. To decrypt the ciphertext, steps 18 to step 1 will be performed backwards. A graphical representation of the encryption process is provided in Fig. 2.

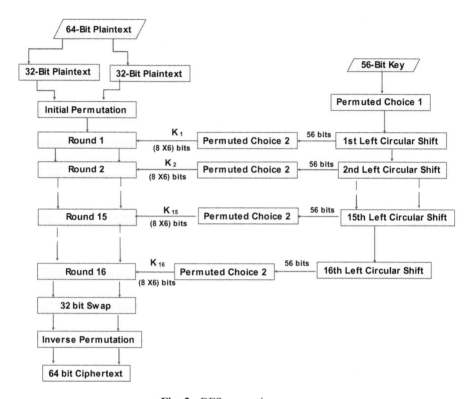

Fig. 2. DES encryption process

DES is vulnerable to key attack therefore its strength is dependent on the type of key used. To make DES more resistive to key attack, triple DES was introduced. It uses three different keys to encrypt, decrypt and encrypt each block of data. This means that the total length of keys used for the first encryption, decryption and the final encryption is 168 bits. These sub-keys can be used in three ways as opined in [14]. The three sub-keys can have the same combination or different combinations and the first and second key can have different combination while the first and third key can have the same combination. However, when the three sub-keys have different combinations then the effective key length is 168 bits but when the three sub-keys have the same combination, the effective key length is 56 bits (which is considered as the weakest combination). The second option where the first and third key have the same combination has an effective key length of 112 bits which is still preferable.

3 Related Works

The major strength of DES is its weak 58 bit encryption key which has made it susceptible to diverse forms of attack. The high computational power of 21st century computers has also favour most of these attacks. Therefore, several works aimed at improving the key generation process of DES has been proposed in the literature. For instance, a two-stage dynamic key generation approach was proposed in [10]. Linear Feedback Shift Register (LFSR) was used to generate the first key while chaotic encryption was used to generate the second key. LFSR uses a linear feedback function and a shift register for its key generation process while chaotic encryption uses a One-dimensional Logistic map for its key generation. Furthermore, two variants of DES: Dynamic DES (DDES) and Hashed DES (HDES) were proposed in [13]. DDES uses seed generator, Pseudo-Random Generator (PRG), boxes generator, seed filter and seed distributor to organize the relationship between the S-boxes and the generated P-box arrangements during each round of the encryption and decryption process. The seed generator uses three encryption keys to generate an initial seed that is used by the PRG to produce random numbers. These numbers are used as input into the boxes generator that produces the S-boxes and P-box arrangements dynamically for each round. After the 16 encryption rounds, the final seed generated is inserted into the ciphertext by the seed distributer. For the decryption process, the seed filter is used to extract the seed embedded in the ciphertext. On the contrary, a hash function is used by HDES to generate a random fingerprint for each blocks of data. The seeds produced by the fingerprint are then used to securely select S-boxes for each encryption and decryption rounds. The degree of randomness of the proposed techniques as measured by chi-square revealed that DDES with 93.7% has the best degree of randomness followed by 3DES with 95.9%, HDES with 97.7% and DES with 98.3%. Furthermore, hamming distance was used to measure the degree of randomness of the proposed encryption techniques. Results obtained revealed that DDES has the highest hamming, followed by HDES, then DES and 3DES. Nevertheless, 3DES has the highest encryption processing time while DDES has the highest encryption time.

The F-function of DES encryption is used to carry out XOR operation between the encryption key and the input plaintext. However, this function was replaced with striding and filtering techniques in [9]. After, the expansion process, a 48bit filter in form of a matrix is divided into four 3 by 4 matrices. The output of the expansion process was then XORed with the first filter. The result was then XORed with the second, third and fourth filter sequentially. The final result was then fed into the substitution box for the next encryption stage. An avalanche effect of 55% was recorded by the proposed modification. To introduce an additional degree of confusion to DES, authors in [16] integrated odd-even substitution process into the encryption process. After converting the plaintext into binary value, the even positions are replaced by 1 while the odd positions are replaced by 0. The modified DES recorded an encryption time of 365.2 ms while the traditional DES achieved an encryption time of 355.8 ms. Similarly, authors in [14] proposed a DES and 3DES cryptographic technique for securing data stored in smartcards. Simulation results revealed that data writing using DES encryption is faster than that of 3DES while data reading using DES decryption is also faster than 3DES decryption. Also, the execution time of the encryption process is faster than that of the decryption process. Towards increasing the performance of 3DES cryptographic algorithm implemented in ECB mode, a 48-stage pipelined depth design was proposed in [15]. Traditional DES is known to employ two permutations and 16 rounds of Feistel functions for its encryption and decryption process. So, to pipeline the DES, extra registers were added to the Feistel function rounds, the key bank and the key scheduler. Also, right rotations were integrated into the decryption key scheduler and finally a key bank was used to buffer the keys used for the 15 and 31 cycles. A high throughput of 3.2 Gbps at 50 MHz clock was recorded, however, a high cost was incurred due to the extra registers added to each DES component. Similarly, time variable sub-keys was combined with a 16 stage pipelining design in [12]. Different sub-keys that are dynamically generated by the permutation choice 1 box are used to encrypt the plaintext at each round. It is believed that the time variant behavior of the key will make the proposed technique difficult to break by hackers. The proposed design achieved a higher throughput value when compared to similar pipelining designs.

Towards further strengthening DES, its key length and substitution box was enhanced in [17]. DES key length and block size were increased from 64 to 128 bits while S-box values were increased from 64 to 256. In addition, if a computer with high computational power is programmed to decrypt a cipher at 50 billion keys per second, then it will take 400 days to break traditional DES, 800 days for a 112 bits 3DES and 5 × 1021 years for AES as well as the proposed DES. The proposed DES also yielded a higher avalanche effect when compared to the traditional DES. In wireless telecommunications system, it has been observed that the higher the signal to noise ratio of a wireless channel the lower the higher the accuracy of the received ciphertext. However, low SNR will always lead to loss of the ciphertext bits. Therefore, authors in [18] proposed a modification to DES that is aimed at minimizing its bit error rate in wireless applications. To achieve this, a new round with a new 80-bit key was added to the S-boxes. Also, the modified algorithm accepts 64 bits plaintext like the traditional DES but 128 bits ciphertext is produced instead of 64 bits in traditional DES. The modified DES also uses 136 bits key for encryption and decryption instead of 64 bits used by the traditional DES. This made it more secured to brute force and differential cryptanalysis attacks. To evaluate the performance of the proposed technique, several bits of errors were introduced into the input blocks of data. When 7 bits of error was introduced, a bit error rate of 0.22 was recorded as against 0.5 recorded with the traditional DES. However, when the complexity of the modified DES was measured in terms of clock cycles needed to encrypt each block, it was observed that traditional DES requires 160 byte-wise OR operations, 176 byte-wise shift operation, and 320 byte-wise AND operations to encrypt each block. This connotes that 8136 clock cycles were needed by traditional DES to encrypt each block while the modified DES requires 8944 clock cycles. Furthermore, though the encryption time of both algorithms increases with an increase in file size, the encryption time of the modified DES is higher.

4   Methodology

The strength of cryptographic algorithms is dependent on the encryption key used and the number of rounds required during its encryption process. It is generally believed that the more the encryption rounds the stronger the cryptographic algorithm. For instance, 128, 192- and 256-bits AES algorithm require 10, 12 and 14 encryption rounds respectively while DES algorithm requires 16 encryption rounds. Therefore, to further strengthening DES algorithm, a dynamic round DES algorithm is presented. Here, the number of rounds for the encryption and decryption will be specified at runtime by the user. However, a predefined number of shifting operations which is left circular shift 2 was chosen; this would be utilized for each round. Also, as a trade-off in complexity, the number of s-boxes used was reduced to 4, so that the input to the 4s-boxes would be arranged in four 12-bit blocks for the X-OR operation. Finally, three keys were used to encrypt, decrypt and encrypt the plaintext ciphertext as in triple DES. A graphical illustration of the modified DES is provided in Fig. 3 while the corresponding pseudocode goes thus:

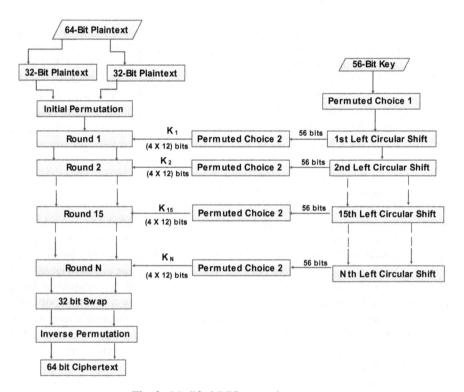

Fig. 3. Modified DES encryption process

Step 1: Input data is divided into 64 bits block size

Step 2: Permute with IP-1 table

Step 3: Divide into two 32 bits left and right half

Step 4: Initialize 'N' round operations applying cipher F function (with reduced number of s-boxes) with auto-generated key on right half.

Step 5: Perform modular X-OR of left half 32 bits with result from step 4 which be comes new right half 32bits.

Step 6: Initial right half 32 bits becomes new left half bits

Step 7: Combine the 32bits from step 5 and step 6

Step 8: Perform inverse permutation to obtain cipher text.

Step 9: For decryption, perform backwards from step 8 to step 1 to obtain plain text

Step 10: Repeat step 1–8 twice with same key as input and step 8 to step 1 backwards with separate key to perform the triple DES encryption. i.e. EncK1 (DecrK2) EncK1

5   Results and Discussion

5.1   The Developed Electronic Medical Information (EMI) System

An Electronic Medical Information (EMI) system was developed to evaluate the encryption and decryption capability of the proposed cryptographic technique. The medical database keeps sensitive textual and graphical information of patients in a hospital. After entering the needed patient information as shown in Fig. 4, the medical personnel are expected to choose an encryption round which is expected to be known to other legitimate users of the EMI system.

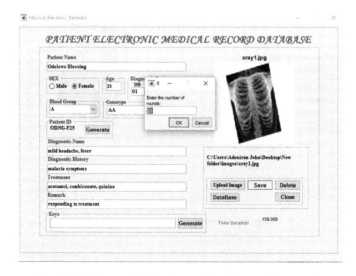

Fig. 4. EMI requesting for the number of encryption rounds

For the decryption process, the user is expected to automatically generate the encryption key and provide the correct number of encryption rounds. Should a wrong number of encryption round be supplied, a scrambled information will be displayed as shown in Fig. 5. A correct number of round will decrypt the encrypted information as displayed in Fig. 6.

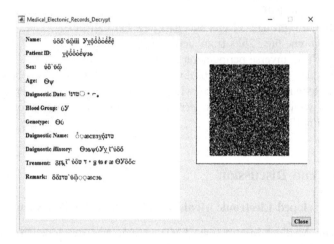

Fig. 5. Output due to wrong number of rounds or decryption key

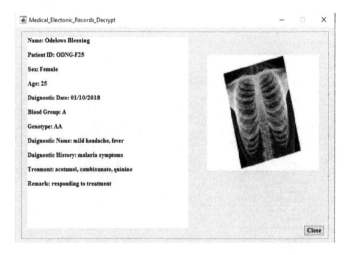

Fig. 6. Decrypted patient information

Table 1. Processing time of the modified triple DES

Number of rounds	Encryption time (sec)	Decryption time (sec)
10	57.4009	49.0655
11	62.8198	58.4639
12	66.8347	62.0624
13	73.0785	70.5850
14	72.3833	70.4269
15	77.5545	76.1033
16	80.8605	77.1530
17	89.7312	87.7793
18	96.2235	87.8725
19	95.8044	91.9472
20	102.217	96.3151

Table 2. Avalanche effects of modified triple DES

No of rounds	Plain text	Cipher text	Avalanche effects (%)
15	97157A6FC8E4BBE4	AB17796FC2E4240C	8(50)
	97157A6FC8F4BBE4	A710386FCAF407A0	
16	50ED00C48388EA9B	BCD0C1F84644BE33	14(87.5)
	50ED00C48388EA9A	62E5C2560F22B464	
17	0FB7C204C2C12D39	3BBC0214C0C1A1E5	15(93.75)
	0FB6C204C2C12D39	CB6A207C271225D8	

5.2 Performance Evaluation

To measure the performance of the proposed technique, the processing time of the system was measured in terms of encryption and decryption time. This was done on a 64 bit, dual core HP laptop with 4 GB RAM. The number of rounds was varied in steps of one from 10 to 20 as presented in Table 1. It was observed that the encryption and decryption time increased with an increase in number of rounds. Also, with 16 rounds, the processing time of the traditional DES is lower than that of the modified DES. But in real life scenario, processing time could be traded off for security. People are interested in securing their sensitive documents regardless of the time it takes to secure the documents.

Furthermore, the avalanche effect of the proposed technique was measured as documented in Table 2. This measured the degree of diffusion of a cryptographic technique. It is used to guarantee that any little change in the input plain text will have a corresponding huge change in the cipher text. The avalanche effect increased with an increase in the number of rounds. This connotes that the degree of confusion increased with an increase in the number of rounds. This is actually a good result. However, the avalanche effect of the modified DES with 16 rounds was evaluated with the traditional DES with 16 rounds. A higher avalanche effect of 90.43% was recorded by traditional DES against 87.50% achieved by the modified DES. However, higher rounds yielded a higher avalanche effect as presented in Table 2.

6   Conclusion

Our increasing sensitive data and information need to be protected from unauthorized access, manipulation and alteration. The effect of a small breach of data could cost an organization a huge amount of money and undermine the confidence reposed in their services. It is advisable for organization to implement at least one cryptographic technique to protect their sensitive data. This article has presented a modified DES cryptographic algorithm that could be used to secure sensitive data and information. Several literatures have reported modifications to the encryption key of traditional DES; however, this article explored the possibility of making the encryption rounds of DES user dependent. With this arrangement, users are expected to choose the encryption rounds desired. This encryption is expected to be greater than the default 16 rounds. Though the modification leads to an increase in encryption and decryption time, the performance evaluation results carried out revealed that the technique's avalanche effect increases with an increase in encryption rounds. The higher the avalanche effect, the greater the assurance that any small modification to the plaintext will have a huge noticeable difference in the ciphertext.

References

1. Internet Users Distribution in the World -2020 Q1. http://www.internetworldstats.com. Accessed 24 Mar 2020
2. Data under Attack: 2018 Global Data Risk Report from the Varonis Data Lab. https://info. varonis.com/hubfs. Accessed 24 Mar 2020
3. Cybercrime: number of breaches and records exposed 2005–2019. https://www.statista.com/ statistics/273550/data-breaches-recorded-in-the-united-states-by-number-of-breaches-and-records-exposed/. Accessed 24 Mar 2020
4. Biggest Data Breach Statistics. https://www.digitalinformationworld.com/2019/08/biggest-data-breach-statistics.html. Accessed 24 Mar 2020
5. Cost of a Data Breach Report https://securityintelligence.com/posts/whats-new-in-the-2019-cost-of-a-data-breach-report/. Accessed 24 Mar 2020
6. Abikoye, O.C., Adeshola, G.Q., Akande, N.O.: Implementation of textual information encryption using 128, 192 and 256 bits advanced encryption standard algorithm. Ann. Comput. Sci. Ser. **15**(2), 153–159 (2017)
7. Abikoye, O.C., Haruna, A.D., Abubakar, A., Akande, O., Asani, E.O.: Modified advanced encryption standard algorithm for information security. Symmetry **11**(1484), 1–17 (2019). https://doi.org/10.3390/sym11121484
8. Akande, N.O., Abikoye, C.O., Adebiyi, M.O., Kayode, A.A., Adegun, A.A., Ogundokun, R. O.: Electronic medical information encryption using modified blowfish algorithm. In: Misra, S., et al. (eds.) ICCSA 2019. LNCS, vol. 11623, pp. 166–179. Springer, Cham (2019). https://doi.org/10.1007/978-3-030-24308-1_14
9. Amorado, R.V, Sison, A.M., Medina, R.: Enhanced data encryption standard (DES) algorithm based on filtering and striding techniques. In: 2nd International Conference on Information Science and Systems, pp. 252–256 (2019)
10. Gautam, A.: FPGA Implementation of dynamic key generation to enhance des algorithm securities **4**(01), 673–677 (2015)

11. Kessler, G.C.: An overview of cryptography. http://Www.Garykessler.Net/Library/Crypto. Html. Accessed 20 Mar 2020
12. Oukili, S., Bri, S.: High throughput FPGA implementation of data encryption standard with time variable sub-keys **6**(1), 298–306 (2016)
13. Qasaimeh, M., Al-qassas, R.S.: Randomness analysis of DES ciphers produced with various dynamic arrangements. J. Comput. Sci. Original **13**(12), 735–747 (2017). https://doi.org/10. 3844/jcssp.2017.735.747
14. Ratnadewi, B., Roy, P.A., Yonatan, H., Saleh, A., Setiawan, M.I.: Implementation cryptography data encryption standard (DES) and triple data encryption standard (3DES) method in communication system based near field communication (NFC). J. Phys: Conf. Ser. **954**, 1–9 (2018)
15. Rosal, E.D., Kumar, S.: A fast FPGA implementation for triple DES encryption scheme. Circ. Syst. **8**, 237–246 (2017). https://doi.org/10.4236/cs.2017.89016
16. Sison, A.M., Tanguilig, B.T., Gerardo, B.D., Byun, Y.-C.: Implementation of Improved DES Algorithm in Securing Smart Card Data. In: Kim, T., Ramos, C., Kim, H.-K., Kiumi, A., Mohammed, S., Ślęzak, D. (eds.) ASEA 2012. CCIS, vol. 340, pp. 252–263. Springer, Heidelberg (2012). https://doi.org/10.1007/978-3-642-35267-6_33
17. Sivakumar, T.K., Sheela, T., Kumar, R., Ganesan, K.: Enhanced secure data encryption standard (ES-DES) algorithm using extended substitution box (S-Box). Int. J. Appl. Eng. Res. **12**(21), 11365–11373 (2017)
18. Zibideh, W.Y., Matalgah, M.M.: Modified data encryption standard encryption algorithm with improved error performance and enhanced security in wireless fading channels, pp. 565–573 (2015)

Lean UX: A Systematic Literature Review

David Aarlien and Ricardo Colomo-Palacios$^{(\boxtimes)}$ (iD)

Østfold University College, BRA Veien. 4, 1757 Halden, Norway
{david.aarlien,ricardo.colomo-palacios}@hiof.no

Abstract. The software industries often look for ways to remain competitive in terms of cost and time to market. Lean UX is a methodology aiming to achieve this. In this paper, by means of a Systematic Literature Review, authors outline the evolution of Lean UX since its origins, its challenges and benefits, and its definition by means of a systematic literature review. Results showed similarities of the definition of Lean UX, challenges and benefits regarding communication, user testing, team collaboration and the adoption of the concept.

Keywords: Systematic literature review · Lean UX · Lean User Experience

1 Introduction

Many software companies have started looking for newer and more effective methods to make software development more efficient [1] in order to preserve their competitive advantage [2]. Thus, organizations worldwide have keenly accepted agile development methods such as extreme programming (XP), SCRUM and lean software development [3–5]. Focusing on the later, the concept of "Lean" dates back to the manufacturing environments and is described with different synonyms such as: Lean Manufacturing, Lean Production, or Toyota Production System [6]. Ebert et al. [1] cite from [7] that Lean was first used in manufacturing to empower teams, reduce waste, optimize work streams, and keep the market and customer needs as the main source of decision-making.

In the software industry, further adaptations to lean methodologies have also appeared in recent years, and Lean UX is one of these adaptations. According to the Jeff Gothelf [8], the author of the seminal book "Lean UX: Applying Lean Principles to Improve User Experience", Lean UX consists of a combination of three fundamentals: Lean startup, Design Thinking and Agile Development philosophies. Lean Startup, the first pillar is presented in the book as a method for reducing project risk, by means of rapid development and learning using the feedback loop called "build-measure-learn". Like the lean principles, Lean startup focus on reducing wasteful innovations by solving problems for the real users with user-centered methodologies. The core concept of lean startup is that, in order to develop an efficient product, there must be a demand for it from the potential users [9]. To achieve this in Lean UX, the teams builds Minimum Viable Products (MVP) to answer hypothesis about the customer needs then learn from the feedback by the users testing the MVP [8]. Gothelf [8] describes Design Thinking, the second pillar, as a discipline in designers can use to design technologically feasible products based on direct observations of what the users want or need in

© Springer Nature Switzerland AG 2020
O. Gervasi et al. (Eds.): ICCSA 2020, LNCS 12254, pp. 500–510, 2020.
https://doi.org/10.1007/978-3-030-58817-5_37

their lives. Another description by Brown et al. [10] define design thinking as a method for designing solutions to problems by relying on the human minds capabilities to identify patterns, and the ability to form ideas with meaning and functionality. Gothelf [8] outlines the importance of Design Thinking in Lean UX, as this discipline encourages designers and non-designers to investigate every aspect, instead of a constrained environment. Furthermore, Gothelf [8] describes in his book that agile software development is a method for delivering working software continuously to the customers. He also explains that Lean UX applies four core principles of Agile development to product design. These principles are as follows:

- Individuals and interactions over process and tools: generate solutions rapidly by conversing and exchanging ideas with colleagues.
- Working software over comprehensive documentation: build solutions early and asses the solution for market fit and viability.
- Customer collaboration over contract negotiation: collaborate with colleagues and customers to build a shared understanding of the product. Reducing documentation, as team members have participated in the decisions.
- Responding to change over following a plan: Once developers discovers what's working or not, adjustments are made to test again with the market, keeping the development agile as market feedback pivot development in the right direction.

The goal of Lean UX is to produce products fitted for the consumer market, as fast and cheap as possible. This seems to be more important than ever, as the consumer market increasingly expects higher standards of user experience, and traditional development practices often won't fulfil these demands [11].

Lean UX is, taking all these aspects into account, a relevant concept for software workers. Moreover, to the best of authors' knowledge, there has not been conducted a systematic literature review (SLR) on Lean UX. In order to fill this gap, in this paper authors present a SLR to investigate the current definition and evolution of the Lean UX methodology, its challenges and reported benefits.

The rest of the paper is presented as follows: in Sect. 2, the authors present the methods for research. In what follows, the authors present and discuss the results or the tertiary study. Lastly, the authors conclude and present suggestions for future work in Sect. 4.

2 Research Methodology

2.1 Systematic Literature Review

To obtain an overview of the current literature, a SLR will be performed and presented in this paper. A SLR involves several activities for systematically extracting information about a chosen topic, and is defined as three stages, namely: Planning review, Conducting the Review, and Reporting the Review [12]. These stages will be presented more thoroughly in this section. According to the literature, before starting a SLR, it is a prerequisite to identify if there is a need for such a literature review, by investigating if it has been previously conducted [12]. As mentioned in the Introduction section, to the best of our knowledge there are not previous SLRs in the topic.

2.2 Review Protocol

A review protocol is a set of specified methods which is necessary for a literature review to reduce bias [12]. This subsection will present a review plan protocol based on the guidelines of "Procedures for performing systematic reviews" [12].

2.3 Research Questions

Four research questions are defined to investigate Lean UX. These are as follows:

- **Research question 1:** How is Lean UX defined in the literature?
- **Research question 2:** What are the reported benefits of Lean UX?
- **Research question 3:** What are the reported challenges of Lean UX?
- **Research question 4:** How has Lean UX evolved overtime?

2.4 Study Selection

This section describes the steps applied to find the literature in this study, such as which online databases are used in the search for literature, the search strategy, and the inclusion and exclusion criteria used to find the most relevant literature to this review.

Databases: The following databases were selected by recommendations of the library of Østfold University College for relevant databases in computing. The following databases were used to identify the current literature:

- ACM
- IEEE
- Springer
- Science Direct
- Google Scholar

As the first four listed above are large databases, they were used as main source of studies retrieved. But in order to identify other relevant studies conducted in the topic, Google Scholar was used to cross-examine.

Search Terms: To specify the relevance of each study to the research question, a specified search term was created. After a few trial runs, it was discovered "Lean UX" was defined differently such as "Lean UX", "LeanUX" and "Lean User Experience". Therefore, all these were included in the search term. The rest of the search string includes keywords relevant to the research questions and is presented as following: ("Lean UX" OR "LeanUX" OR "Lean User Experience") AND ("Definition" OR "Challenges" OR "Benefits" OR "Limitations" OR "Advantages").

Inclusion and Exclusion Criteria: After the search results were retrieved, a list of specified inclusion and exclusion criteria were applied to filter the most relevant studies. These are the following:

Inclusion Criteria:

- Literature that specifically discuss Lean UX at a theoretical or practical level.
- Literature that discuss advantages/benefits of Lean UX.
- Literature that discuss challenges/limitations of Lean UX.
- Literature that provide a definition of Lean UX.
- Literature only retrieved from the first 15 pages of google scholar.

Exclusion Criteria:

- Papers that are inaccessible.
- Books.
- Duplicates found in Google Scholar.
- Literature not written in English.

2.5 Literature Retrieval

In order to search and retrieve the relevant literature in an efficient and structured way, four stages were defined: The first stage was documenting the number of papers found in each database and google scholar. In the second stage authors retrieved the relevant articles based on the exclusion and inclusion criteria (accessible, not books, English written papers and matched with keyword Lean UX). In the third stage, authors read the title, abstract and keywords of each paper and selected the relevant papers. In the fourth and last stage, authors selected the primary studies after reading full text.

2.6 Data Storage

The retrieved literature was systematically organized in the program Zotero (reference manager). Furthermore, a table with a list of the retrieved literature was used to highlight the importance of each paper with color codes.

3   Results

In this section, the results from the review protocol will be presented and discussed to answer the research questions previously defined.

3.1 Studies Retrieved

In Table 1, the number of papers retrieved are displayed from the different stages of literature retrieval. Stage 1 displays how many results appeared in the search results, stage 2 is the number of results when excluding books, and locked articles. Stage 3 are the number of selected papers based on title, abstract, keywords and conclusion, and stage 4 is the number of selected papers after a full text read had been conducted. 11 papers were left to present in the results from the literature relevant to this systematic literature review. The literature review was performed in the first quarter of 2020.

Table 1. Number of papers considered per round

Source	1	2	3	4
ACM	83	35	9	4
IEEE	35	20	6	5
Springer	73	14	2	1
Science Direct	30	5	1	0
Google Scholar	820	25	11	2
Total	**1041**	**99**	**29**	**12**

3.2   RQ1: How Is Lean UX Defined in the Literature?

In the reviewed literature [9, 13–16], the contextual background of Lean UX are mostly taken from the definition of Lean UX from the seminal book [8] by Jeff Gothelf. The content of this book will not be presented as this book not part of the primary studies. Instead, to answer this research question, this paper will present the most presented and described aspects of Lean UX retrieved from the literature.

Liikkanen et al. [14] state that Lean UX is defined as a fast user-centered approach for development, especially for startups. Furthermore, Liikkanen et al. add that the goal of Lean UX is to produce a product with minimal resources used as fast as possible, that will satisfy the customer needs. Tonkin et al. [16] provide a similar definition, in which Lean UX is a fast and cheap methodology, with less focus on detailed documents or long user studies, focusing rather on creating minimum viable product(MVP) prototypes to be rapidly and iteratively released and tested with the representative users, with hypothesis to validate the MVP created. This form of iterative deployment and feedback provide knowledge from the users to guide the design process. [17] also provides a description of the concept of the MVP cited from [18], as launching something smaller to start learning early instead of creating a product for months with an extensive number of features that the end user might not even want then launching. [14] also claims that the MVP is the core concept of Lean UX, where the idea is to build the most basic version of the product to test, and if the MVP gives no viable results, then the idea should pivot.

Other definitions are also provided by papers such as [14], in which the authors pointed to the community that has created a Lean UX manifesto [19], in the way of the Agile manifesto [20], where they present six key principles of Lean UX:

- "Early customer validation vs. releasing products with unknown end-user value,
- Collaborative cross-functional design vs. lonely hero design,
- Solving user problems vs. adding cool features,
- Measuring key performance indicators vs. undefined success metrics,
- Applying appropriate tools flexibly vs. following a rigid methodology,
- and Nimble design vs. heavy wireframes or specifications."

Even though the primary studies provide proper definitions of Lean UX, they still have most of its content extracted from the book [8] suggesting that the book is the main source of information regarding Lean UX in terms of its definition. Other sources, such as the Lean UX manifesto, also cited in one of the primary studies, suggests that other sources of information could be interesting to investigate to broaden the definition of the term.

3.3 RQ2: What Are the Benefits of Lean UX?

Better Market Fit: Beverley Cook and Philip Twidle state that applying Lean UX highlighted early assumptions about their game design and allowed for continuous changes throughout the development fitted for the user [21]. This form of continuous user-validation led to a mobile game achieving its goal by altering and validating the game-design according to the user feedback. Contrary, [22] reported that lack of testing resulted in loss of UX and challenging technology to work with. As a result, this project chose a technology stack three times expensive to develop and time to reach the market. [23] promotes Lean UX as beneficial for businesses to understand the product value as early as possible, and further states that traditional UX techniques often won't apply to rapid and iterative development, because of time limits to deliver UX paralleled with a developed product. The author further suggests applying Lean UX as an alternative to solve this issue, where the MVP model is a central part of this. [24] even states that the MVP and "build-measure-learn" cycles were invaluable to find unique Russian design elements, when they applied Lean UX principles to understand the emerging market, specifically to Russia. Further, they conclude that even resources were saved when trying to answer their hypothesis, as they would only develop a simple prototype, rather than completely developed pages, with large amounts of design elements. [16] discuss in their paper that the current human-robot-interaction literature lacks guidelines for user experience for social robots. In this paper, the authors present an HRI-adapted Lean UX design methodology specifically for commercially available social robots using the MVP model to validate and invalidate design hypothesis of user needs regarding their robot. This model proved to be successful, improving user experience of the social robot placed at an airport.

Improved Team Collaboration: [13] suggests applying Lean UX to interdisciplinary student teams. They claim Lean UX to be beneficial to eliminate uneven workload as the individuals felt more certain to their project and the group discussions were more focused on the important aspects of the project. [9] adds that [8] stated that Lean UX provides methods for teams to become more cross-functional rather than separating designers from the technical implementations and business needs. In [15], authors outline that it was challenging developing good quality UX in their project if the whole team was not part of the team throughout the project. They suggested that all the team members should be involved from the beginning to end of the project to prevent this problem. [9] also suggest that Lean UX is beneficial in teaching UX. They claim that Lean UX was useful to decide what type of activities and designs were necessary for the students' progression, and that Lean UX provides foundations for interdisciplinary teams to collaborate by letting the students work together across multiple disciplines, creating a shared understanding of the design problems and preparing them for the workplace.

It would seem that Lean UX provides a great method for developing products fitted for the consumer market. Based on the findings in this SLR user testing seem to be a central part of Lean UX which provides great benefits to the business, as this part of development provides insights for which direction the product should take. Examples of this could be understanding what type of technology to use, testing design alternatives, validating whether the concept is doable or not, or even small design choices as cheap and fast as possible in throughout development. Furthermore, the findings in this SLR suggest that not testing thoroughly in a Lean environment could lead to a series of problems to the product, which could be uncovered at early stages. Indicating that testing is crucial for successful Lean UX development. Furthermore, one could argue that Lean UX is very beneficial as the product is assessed across multiple disciplines (such as designers and non-designers) which in return might lead to a high-quality product. This is, however, not always the case, and it's seen as challenging producing the same quality work when team members are missing. Lean UX is also seen as beneficial in other types of scenarios such as educational, providing new ways of teaching and learning. Another scenario could be using Lean UX principles to create new methodologies. This suggests that the principles of Lean UX can be applied to a variety of different settings.

3.4   RQ3: What Are the Challenges of Lean UX?

Communication: [15] discuss the importance of clear communication in Lean/agile environments as each part of the project must be consistently aligned and coordinated during the project, and the longer it takes to transfer tasks or knowledge across the team, the more context is lost. [15] also stated that they learned that poor communication often led to misunderstanding the feature requirements or the user context resulting in the team not performing as agile as possible. [25] outlines that in large organizations, with engineering as a dominating field, applying Lean UX are often challenging. Like [15], [25] suggest communication is crucial because the rapid pace of Lean UX, with team members assuming the implementations are correctly implemented by other team members if they are not present in the meetings. The challenging part of communication described by [25] is that a common notion about Lean environments from UX people is that it doesn't require design documentation, which often leads to miscommunication, especially in large, complex teams. However, in [25] authors present four communication strategies to help team members to communicate more effectively. These strategies are coined in the paper as follows:

- Employ a design framework,
- Maintain multiple prototypes,
- Use communication methods that fit your audience,
- Leverage agile use cases.

The authors suggest that these communication strategies should help UX communication be more effective without complicating the organizational structure.

Adopting Lean UX: In [14], authors present their experience adopting Lean UX in their company, an organization which delivers enterprise-ready front-end solutions. They outline small challenges such as allocating enough people to all the roles of an optimal Lean UX team, when the current team isn't large enough. To fulfill this, investments in training current UI developers on dealing with customers must be faced. Furthermore [14] states that the distribution of decision-making processes is challenging when adopting Lean UX in the case of large client organizations. The closer the client organization reaches the core business model during development, the harder it is to apply the startup mentality and pivot the business model, as more stakeholders are involved in the process.

Communication is seen as an important aspect to achieve success in Lean UX, as the development progress rapidly. If the individuals have issues with reporting their work, this could lead to fractures in the development as the team is dependent on each other's work. In organizations in which their structures are built on agile methods, adopting Lean UX in these organizations seems to be challenging, as organizational structures and mindsets must adapt accordingly.

3.5 RQ4: How Has Lean UX Evolved?

In order to investigate the evolution of the interest of Lean UX in the primary studies, in Table 2, the number of papers published each year discussing Lean UX from this systematic literature review is presented.

Table 2. Number of papers published by year

Year	#
2011	0
2012	1
2013	1
2014	2
2015	0
2016	2
2017	1
2018	4
2019	1

The results in Table 2 indicate that the evolution of the concept Lean UX has been discussed moderately over the past years, but not extensively. The results also indicate that the concept is quite new, suggesting that most of the discussion regarding Lean UX originated after the release of the book written by Gothelf [8] in 2013. [22], however, discussed UX in Lean environments in 2012, but without the definition provided by Gothelf suggesting that UX in Lean Environments have been thought of before the book. Larger corporations such as PayPal has also integrated aspects of Lean UX to their agile processes when shifting from a waterfall process [26]. In any, case the evolution of the concept is quite moderate and apart from 2018 in which four papers were published in the topic, the rest of the years present zero, one or two papers published.

4 Conclusion

This paper presents the results coming from a SLR conducted on Lean UX, with the goal of giving an overview of how Lean UX is defined in the literature, what challenges and benefits of applying Lean UX, and its evolution in the literature since its beginning. Four literature databases (ACM, IEEE, Springer and Science Direct) and Google scholar were used to gather 12 primary studies. The origin of Lean UX was the book written by Gothelf [8], which was also the main source of reference in most of primary studies with regards to the definition of the concept. It was however apparent, that many of the primary studies provided a similar definition of Lean UX, such as it being a concept for reducing time and resources to reach the market as fast as possible, with the concept of the minimum viable product being a core aspect of achieving this, by continuously user-test the MVP with the respective user to answer design hypothesis until the product reaches its goal. It was also presented in one of the papers, that community made definitions have also been defined. Challenges and benefits of Lean UX are also presented in this paper, such as the importance of user-testing to create a product wanted by the market, the effects of team collaboration or how challenges regarding communication can affect the effectiveness of work and the challenges of adopting the concept in larger companies. It seems Lean UX is being increasingly discussed in the literature and adopted with companies such as PayPal adopting the concept.

For future work, it would be interesting to perform a multi vocal literature review, as the results of this paper are quite few, and indications for more documented definitions and guidelines of Lean UX on the internet (such as community made) are found in the results. It would also be interesting conducting case study comparing Lean UX to other methodologies, to investigate the effectiveness of Lean UX.

References

1. Ebert, C., Abrahamsson, P., Oza, N.: Lean software development. IEEE Softw. **29**, 22–25 (2012). https://doi.org/10.1109/MS.2012.116
2. Colomo-Palacios, R., Fernandes, E., Soto-Acosta, P., Larrucea, X.: A case analysis of enabling continuous software deployment through knowledge management. Int. J. Inf. Manag. **40**, 186–189 (2018). https://doi.org/10.1016/j.ijinfomgt.2017.11.005
3. Alahyari, H., Gorschek, T., Berntsson Svensson, R.: An exploratory study of waste in software development organizations using agile or lean approaches: a multiple case study at 14 organizations. Inf. Softw. Technol. **105**, 78–94 (2019). https://doi.org/10.1016/j.infsof.2018.08.006
4. Poth, A., Sasabe, S., Mas, A., Mesquida, A.-L.: Lean and agile software process improvement in traditional and agile environments. J. Softw.: Evol. Process **31**, e1986 (2019). https://doi.org/10.1002/smr.1986

5. Jovanović, M., Mesquida, A.-L., Mas, A., Colomo-Palacios, R.: Agile transition and adoption frameworks, issues and factors: a systematic mapping. IEEE Access **8**, 15711–15735 (2020). https://doi.org/10.1109/ACCESS.2020.2967839
6. Kilpatrick, J.: Lean Principles. http://mhc-net.com/whitepapers_presentations/LeanPrinciples.pdf. Accessed 13 Apr 2020
7. Womack, J.P., Jones, D.T., Roos, D.: The Machine That Changed the World: The Story of Lean Production– Toyota's Secret Weapon in the Global Car Wars That Is Now Revolutionizing World Industry. Simon and Schuster, New York (2007)
8. Gothelf, J.: Lean UX: Applying Lean Principles to Improve User Experience. O'Reilly Media, Inc., Newton (2013)
9. Batova, T.: Extended abstract: lean UX and innovation in teaching. In: 2016 IEEE International Professional Communication Conference (IPCC), pp. 1–3 (2016). https://doi.org/10.1109/IPCC.2016.7740500
10. Brown, T., Wyatt, J.: Design thinking for social innovation IDEO. 4 (2010)
11. Implementing Lean UX in the real world - UX Collective. https://uxdesign.cc/implementing-lean-ux-in-the-real-world-8aa7ca880e54. Accessed 13 Apr 2020
12. Kitchenham, B.A.: Procedures for Performing Systematic Reviews. https://www.semanticscholar.org/paper/Procedures-for-Performing-Systematic-Reviews-Kitchenham/29890a936639862f45cb9a987dd599dce9759bf5. Accessed 13 Apr 2020
13. Chang, T.-W., Lee, Y., Huang, H.-Y.: Visualizing design process by using lean UX to improve interdisciplinary team's effectiveness – a case study. In: 2018 22nd International Conference Information Visualisation (IV), pp. 434–437 (2018). https://doi.org/10.1109/iV.2018.00081
14. Liikkanen, L.A., Kilpiö, H., Svan, L., Hiltunen, M.: Lean UX: the next generation of user-centered agile development? In: Proceedings of the 8th Nordic Conference on Human-Computer Interaction: Fun, Fast, Foundational, pp. 1095–1100. Association for Computing Machinery, Helsinki (2014). https://doi.org/10.1145/2639189.2670285
15. Manwaring, E., Carter, J.N., Maynard, K.: Redesigning educational dashboards for shifting user contexts. In: Proceedings of the 35th ACM International Conference on the Design of Communication, pp. 1–7. Association for Computing Machinery, Halifax, Nova Scotia, Canada (2017). https://doi.org/10.1145/3121113.3121210
16. Tonkin, M., Vitale, J., Herse, S., Williams, M.-A., Judge, W., Wang, X.: Design methodology for the UX of HRI: a field study of a commercial social robot at an airport. In: Proceedings of the 2018 ACM/IEEE International Conference on Human-Robot Interaction, pp. 407–415. Association for Computing Machinery, Chicago (2018). https://doi.org/10.1145/3171221.3171270
17. Kikitamara, S., Noviyanti, A.A.: A conceptual model of user experience in scrum practice. In: 2018 10th International Conference on Information Technology and Electrical Engineering (ICITEE), pp. 581–586 (2018). https://doi.org/10.1109/ICITEED.2018.8534905
18. Federoff, M., Courage, C.: Successful user experience in an agile enterprise environment. In: Smith, M.J., Salvendy, G. (eds.) Human Interface 2009. LNCS, vol. 5617, pp. 233–242. Springer, Heidelberg (2009). https://doi.org/10.1007/978-3-642-02556-3_27
19. The Lean UX Manifesto: Principle-Driven Design. https://www.smashingmagazine.com/2014/01/lean-ux-manifesto-principle-driven-design/. Accessed 14 Apr 2020
20. Beck, K.M., et al.: Manifesto for agile software development. https://www.semanticscholar.org/paper/Manifesto-for-Agile-Software-Development-Beck-Beedle/3edabb96a07765704f9c6a1a5542e39ac2df640c. Accessed 13 Apr 2020
21. Cook, B., Twidle, P.: Increasing awareness of alzheimer's disease through a mobile game. In: 2016 International Conference on Interactive Technologies and Games (ITAG), pp. 55–60 (2016). https://doi.org/10.1109/iTAG.2016.16

22. May, B.: Applying lean startup: an experience report – lean & lean UX by a UX veteran: lessons learned in creating launching a complex consumer app. In: 2012 Agile Conference, pp. 141–147 (2012). https://doi.org/10.1109/Agile.2012.18
23. Madathil, K.C., et al.: How to succeed in industry (as a UX researcher): strategies and skills to maximize your impact. Proc. Hum. Factors Ergon. Soc. Annu. Meet. **63**, 377–380 (2019). https://doi.org/10.1177/1071181319631273
24. Chan, S., Chen, G., Fu, L.: Understanding emerging markets by applying lean UX. In: Rau, P.L.P. (ed.) CCD 2014. LNCS, vol. 8528, pp. 417–426. Springer, Cham (2014). https://doi.org/10.1007/978-3-319-07308-8_40
25. Nudelman, G.: Lean UX communication strategies for success in large organizations. Interactions **25**, 80–82 (2018). https://doi.org/10.1145/3236683
26. Meingast, M., Ballew, T., Edwards, R., Nordquist, E., Sader, C., Smith, D.: Agile and UX: the road to integration the challenges of the UX practitioner in an agile environment. Proc. Hum. Factors Ergon. Soc. Annu. Meet. **57**, 1002–1006 (2013). https://doi.org/10.1177/1541931213571224

Solving the 0/1 Knapsack Problem Using a Galactic Swarm Optimization with Data-Driven Binarization Approaches

Camilo Vásquez[1], José Lemus-Romani[1(✉)], Broderick Crawford[1],
Ricardo Soto[1], Gino Astorga[2], Wenceslao Palma[1], Sanjay Misra[3],
and Fernando Paredes[4]

[1] Pontificia Universidad Católica de Valparaíso, Valparaíso, Chile
{camilo.vasquez.e,jose.lemus.r}@mail.pucv.cl,
{broderick.crawford,ricardo.soto,wenceslao.palma}@pucv.cl
[2] Universidad de Valparaíso, Valparaíso, Chile
gino.astorga@uv.cl
[3] Covenant University, Ota, Nigeria
sanjay.misra@covenantuniversity.edu.ng
[4] Universidad Diego Portales, Santiago, Chile
fernando.paredes@udp.cl

Abstract. Metaheuristics are used to solve high complexity problems, where resolution by exact methods is not a viable option since the resolution time when using these exact methods is not acceptable. Most metaheuristics are defined to solve problems of continuous optimization, which forces these algorithms to adapt its work in the discrete domain using discretization techniques to solve complex problems. This paper proposes data-driven binarization approaches based on clustering techniques. We solve different instances of Knapsack Problems with Galactic Swarm Optimization algorithm using this machine learning techniques.

Keywords: Galactic Swarm Optimization · Metaheuristic · Knapsack problem · K-means · DBSCAN · Machine learning

1 Introduction

Solving Knapsack Problem (KP) using metaheuristics, we provide acceptable solutions in a reasonable time to solve large-scale science and engineering problems, this through an iterative generation process that guides a subordinate heuristic through the combination of different intelligent concepts to explore and exploit the search space, metaheuristics represent a part of the optimization techniques that can be grouped into complete or incomplete techniques. Exact or complete techniques are those in which we find an optimal result independently of the process time instead. On the other hand, incomplete strategies are

© Springer Nature Switzerland AG 2020
O. Gervasi et al. (Eds.): ICCSA 2020, LNCS 12254, pp. 511–526, 2020.
https://doi.org/10.1007/978-3-030-58817-5_38

those where, in a limited processing period, a successful answer (not necessarily the best) is sought. This approach is suited best to the actual circumstances of the problems as solutions to the problems are required in daily life at a certain point. We consider metaheuristics inside provisional or incomplete technologies. We will solve KP using Galactic Swarm Optimization (GSO) which must be adapted to work in discrete domain, using different combinations between transfer techniques and binarization methods, in addition to the K-means and DBScan binarization algorithm to solve complex problems as KP.

The Knapsack Problem, it can be applied modelling, for example, the use of containers in customs, the selection of projects, where each project can be as a container of different items such as: project selection [5], the distribution of resources [12], the problem of network interdiction [13], investment decision making [8], among others.

To solve the KP, the algorithm will be tested with different binarization schemes, the novelty of this work is that we use K-means and DBSCAN, as general mechanisms to binarize continuous metaheuristics. And finally, the results obtained in the tests will be commented.

The remainder of the essay includes the following, Sect. 2 gives a brief explanation on metaheuristics, Sect. 3 defines the problem to be solved, Sect. 4 details the operation of the GSO algorithm, Sect. 5 explains the binarization techniques to be implemented, while Sect. 6 presents the experimental results, ending Sect. 7 with the conclusions.

2   Metaheuristics

Metaheuristics is formally described as a method that guides a subordinate heuristic by intelligently combining different concepts to explore and use the space of quest, unlike exact methods, metaheuristics allow to address cases of important problems by offering satisfactory solutions in a reasonable time. There is no guarantee of finding global optimal solutions or even limited solutions. Its use in many applications shows its efficiency and effectiveness to solve large and complex problems. The application of metaheuristics is found in a large number of areas, some are:

- Engineering design, topology optimization and structural optimization in electronics and Very Large Scale Integration (VLSI), aerodynamics, fluid dynamics, telecommunications, automotive and robotics.
- Machine learning and data mining in bioinformatics and computational biology and finance.
- Modelling, simulation and identification of systems in chemistry, physics and biology; control, signal and image processing.
- Routing problem planning, robot planning, programming and production problems, logistics and transportation, supply chain management, environment.

Metaheuristics Classification

- Nature inspired vs. non-nature inspired: In general, metaheuristics may be graded because they are based on the algorithm origin. It considers whether their models were naturally inspired. There are bio-inspired algorithms, such as Crow Search Algorithm (CSA) [11] and Intelligent Water Drops (IWD) [2], and those not inspired by nature, for example Tabu Search (TS) and Local Iterate Search (ILS). This classification is not very significant after hybrid algorithms have been developed.
- Population-based vs. single-point search (trajectory): In such situations, the number of solutions used at the same time is the feature used for the classification. First of all, single-point search algorithms work on a single solution that describes a search space trajectory during the search process. They cover local search-based metaheuristics, like variable neighborhood searchh (VNS), tabu search (TS) and iterated local search (ILS). In the other hand, population-based approaches function on the so-called population-based approach.
- Static vs. dynamic objective function: The metaheuristics with static objective functions, preserve the objective function in the problem during the entire process. However, other algorithms, such as Guided Local Search (GLS) have complex objective features, which change fitness during quest and add data gathered during the quest to avoid local optimums.

GSO and many other metaheuristics are motivated in a vector space $\mathbb{R}^n$, they cannot solve discrete or binary optimization problems. There are a variety of methods proposed which allow the use in discreet or binary problems of meta-heuristic real optimization. The following methods are known as discretization if the method allows the real technique to resolve integer problems and is known as binarization if it resolves binaries [1].

3   The 0/1 Knapsack

The Knapsack problem is one of the classic NP-hard optimization problems and the decision problem belongs to the NP-complete class. The decision problem 0/1 knapsack can be defined as follows. Given a set of N objects. Each object O has a specific weight w_j and a specified value u_j. Given a capacity, which is the maximum total weight of the knapsack, and a fee, which is the minimum total value that one wishes to obtain. The decision problem 0–1 knapsack is to find a subset of the objects whose total weight is at most equal to the capacity. The problem is to optimize the objective function:

$$\max f(\chi) = \sum_{j=1}^{n} u_j \chi_j \tag{1}$$

Subject to:

$$\sum_{j=1}^{n} \omega_j \chi_j \leq C \tag{2}$$

$$\chi_j = \begin{cases} 1 & \text{if the article is included} \\ 0 & \text{otherwise} \end{cases} \tag{3}$$

Binary decision variables x_j are used to indicate whether item j is included in the knapsack or not. It can be assumed that all benefits and weights are positive, A weight w_i and a value χ_j for each item and an integer C (total knapsack capacity), find a subset knapsack with the highest possible value, but that the total weight does not exceed C.

Problem Example. Given a knapsack with a maximum capacity of w and *Values* items, each with its own value and weight, throw the items into the knapsack so that the final content has the maximum value (Fig. 1).

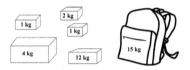

Fig. 1. Example Knapsack problem.

This is the general way in which the problem is explained: consider that a thief enters a house to steal and carries a knapsack. There is a fixed number of items in the home, each with its own weight and value, jewelry, with less weight and the highest value compared to the tables, with less value but much heavier. The thief has a limited capacity knapsack. Obviously, the selection of each item is given by 1/0 indicating whether to take it or leave it, that is:

$$w = (4, 1, 2, 1, 12) \tag{4}$$

Each object has a specific value, which is:

$$Value = (1, 3, 5, 1, 2) \tag{5}$$

The knapsack has a capacity C of 15 kg.

$$C = 15 \tag{6}$$

According to this notation and the formulation, the optimization problem is expressed as:

$$max = \chi_1 + 3\chi_2 + 5\chi_3 + \chi_4 + 2\chi_5 \tag{7}$$

Subject to:

$$4\chi_1 + \chi_2 + 2\chi_3 + \chi_4 + 12\chi_5 \leq 15 \tag{8}$$

where the valid solutions are those that exceed the capacity of the knapsack.

4   Galactic Swarm Optimization Algorithm

Galactic Swarm Optimization is proposed by Venkataraman Muthiah-Nakarajan in 2016 [7]. GSO simulates the movements of stars, galaxies and superclusters in the cosmos. Stars are not distributed evenly in the cosmos but grouped into galaxies that in turn are not evenly distributed. GSO simulates the motion of stars. The GSO algorithm emulates stars in a galaxy, massive masses, and galaxies to certain large masses as follows: individuals in any sub-population that are drawn to better PSO algorithm solutions in the sub-population, any sub-population is a better solution that sub-populations consider and view as superswarm. Each sub-population moving to the PSO algorithm includes super-swarm the best solutions.

The swarm and superswarm movement can be achieved since it is population-based, providing multiple exploration and exploitation cycles by dividing the search in terms of offers, providing the algorithm with more opportunities to accurately locate a local minimum, in the first level it is considered the exploratory phase where potential local minimums are identified, the second level of the GSO algorithm is the exploratory phase which uses the best solutions already calculated, by the sub swarms considering the information already calculated in the first level.

The swarm is a group of X D-Tuples that contains $(\mathrm{x}_j^{(i)} \in \mathbb{R}^D)$ that consists of M partitions, called subswarms X_i, each of size N, X is randomly initialized within the search space $[x_{min}, x_{max}]^D$, the full frame of the swarm is defined by:

$$X_i \subset X : i = 1, 2, ..., M \tag{9}$$

$$x_j^{(i)} \in X_i : j = 1, 2, ..., N \tag{10}$$

$$X_i \cap X_j : if \; \emptyset \; i \neq j \tag{11}$$

$$\cup_{i=1}^{M} X_i = X \tag{12}$$

X_i is a swarm of size N. The velocity and the best personal relationship with each particle $x_j^{(i)}$ are represented by $V_j^{(i)}$ and $P_j^{(i)}$, respectively. Each subswarm independently scans the search space, the declaration for updating the velocity and the position are:

$$v_j^{(i)} \leftarrow \omega_1 + c_1 r_1 (p_j^{(i)} - x_j^{(i)}) + c_2 r_2 (g^{(i)} - x_j^{(i)}) \tag{13}$$

$$x_j^{(i)} \leftarrow x_j^{(i)} + v_j^{(i)} \tag{14}$$

where the inertial weight ω_1, and the random numbers r_1 and r_2 are given by

$$\omega_1 = 1 - \frac{k}{L_1 + 1} \tag{15}$$

$$r_1 \sim \cup(-1, 1) \tag{16}$$

$$r_2 \sim \cup(-1, 1) \tag{17}$$

k is the current integer iteration number that varies from 0 to L1. The best solutions participate in the next stage of grouping creating a new superswarm X_i.

$$y^{(i)} \in Y : i = 1, 2, ..., M \tag{18}$$

$$y^{(i)} = g^{(i)} \tag{19}$$

In this second grouping stage the velocity $v^{(i)}$ and the position $y^{(i)}$ are updated according to the following expression:

$$v^{(i)} \leftarrow \omega_2 v^{(i)} + c_3 r_3 (p^{(i)} + y^{(i)}) + c_4 r_4 (g - y^{(i)}) \tag{20}$$

$$y^{(i)} \leftarrow y^{(i)} + v^{(i)} \tag{21}$$

$p^{(i)}$ is the best staff in relation to the vector $y^{(i)}$, is defined in relation to ω_2, r_3 and r_4 are similar way as it is done in the first level, g indicates us as the best global and is not updated unless the search finds us a better one and this is indicated as the best overall of the subswarm.

In two steps, the binarization performed according to the corresponding combination is performed in the highlighted segments:

Algorithm 1: GSO + Two steps

---

1 Level 1 Initialization: $x_j^{(i)}, v_j^{(i)}, p_j^{(i)}, g^{(i)}$ within $[x_{min}, x_{max}]^D$ randomly.

2 Level 2 Initialization: $v^{(i)}, p^{(i)}$, g within $[x_{min}, x_{max}]^D$ randomly.

3 **for** $EP \leftarrow 1$ to EP_{max} **do**

4   Begin PSO: Level 1

5   **for** $i \leftarrow 1$ to M **do**

6   **for** $k \leftarrow 0$ to L_1 **do**

7   **for** $j \leftarrow 1$ to N **do**

8   **for** $d \leftarrow 1$ to D **do**

9                     $v_{ij}^{(d)} \leftarrow \omega_1 v_{ij}^{(d)} + c_1 r_1 (p_{ij}^{(d)} - x_{ij}^{(d)}) + c_2 r_2 (g^{(i)} - x_{ij}^{(d)})$;

10                     $x_{ij}^{(d)} \leftarrow x_{ij}^{(d)} + v_{ij}^{(d)}$;

11   Apply binarization to, $x_{ij}^{(d)}$;

12   **end**

13   **if** $f(x_j^{(i)}) < f(p_j^{(i)})$ **then**

14                 $p_j^{(i)} \leftarrow x_j^{(i)}$

15   **if** $f(p_j^{(i)}) < f(g^{(i)})$ **then**

16                 $g^{(i)} \leftarrow p_j^{(i)}$;

17   **if** $f(g^{(i)}) < f(g)$ **then**

18                     $g \leftarrow g^{(i)}$;

19   **end**

20   **end**

21   **end**

22   **end**

23   **end**

24   **end**

25   Begin PSO: Level 2

26   Initialize Swarm $y^{(i)} = g^{(i)} : 1,2,...,M$;

27   **for** $k \leftarrow 0$ to L_2 **do**

28   **for** $i \leftarrow 1$ to M **do**

29   **for** $d \leftarrow 1$ to D **do**

30                 $v_i^{(d)} \leftarrow \omega_2 v_i^{(d)} + c_3 r_3 (p_i^{(d)} - y_i^{(d)}) + c_4 r_4 (g - y_i^{(d)})$;

31                 $y_i^{(d)} \leftarrow y_i^{(d)} + v_i^{(d)}$;

32   Apply binarization to, $y_i^{(d)}$;

33   **end**

34   **if** $f(y^{(i)}) < f(p^{(i)})$ **then**

35                 $p^{(i)} \leftarrow y^{(i)}$;

36   **if** $f(p^{(i)}) < f(g)$ **then**

37                 $g \leftarrow p^{(i)}$;

38   **end**

39   **end**

40   **end**

41 **end**

42 **end**

When designing and implementing the algorithms corresponding to the clustering technique, it is performed in the following outstanding segments:

Algorithm 2: GSO + Clustering techniques

---

1 - Level 1 Initialization: $x_j^{(i)}, v_j^{(i)}, p_j^{(i)}, g^{(i)}$ within $[x_{min}, x_{max}]^D$ randomly.

2 Level 2 Initialization: $v^{(i)}, p^{(i)}, g$ within $[x_{min}, x_{max}]^D$ randomly.

3 **for** $EP \leftarrow 1$ to EP_{max} **do**

4   Begin PSO: Level 1

5   **for** $i \leftarrow 1$ to M **do**

6   **for** $k \leftarrow 0$ to L_1 **do**

7   **for** $j \leftarrow 1$ to N **do**

8   **for** $d \leftarrow 1$ to D **do**

9                      $v_{ij}^{(d)} \leftarrow \omega_1 v_{ij}^{(d)} + c_1 r_1(p_{ij}^{(d)} - x_{ij}^{(d)}) + c_2 r_2(g^{(i)} - x_{ij}^{(d)});$

10                     $x_{ij}^{(d)} \leftarrow x_{ij}^{(d)} + v_{ij}^{(d)};$

11   **end**

12   **end**

13   Apply binarization to, x;

14   **if** $f(x^{(i)}) < f(p^{(i)})$ **then**

15             $p^{(i)} \leftarrow x^{(i)}$

16   **if** $f(p^{(i)}) < f(g^{(i)})$ **then**

17             $g^{(i)} \leftarrow p^{(i)};$

18   **if** $f(g^{(i)}) < f(g)$ **then**

19                 $g \leftarrow g^{(i)};$

20   **end**

21   **end**

22   **end**

23   **end**

24   **end**

25   Begin PSO: Level 2

26   Initialize Swarm $y^{(i)} = g^{(i)} : 1,2,...,M;$

27   **for** $k \leftarrow 0$ to L_2 **do**

28   **for** $i \leftarrow 1$ to M **do**

29   **for** $d \leftarrow 1$ to D **do**

30                 $v_i^{(d)} \leftarrow \omega_2 v_i^{(d)} + c_3 r_3(p_i^{(d)} - y_i^{(d)}) + c_4 r_4(g - y_i^{(d)});$

31                 $y_i^{(d)} \leftarrow y_i^{(d)} + v_i^{(d)};$

32   **end**

33   **end**

34   Apply binarization to, y;

35   **if** $f(y) < f(p)$ **then**

36             $p \leftarrow y;$

37   **if** $f(p) < f(g)$ **then**

38                 $g \leftarrow p;$

39   **end**

40   **end**

41 **end**

42 **end**

---

5 Binarizating Continuous Metaheuristics

When modifying GSO to adapt its work in the discrete domain, different binarization schemes are used, which are described in this section.

5.1 Classic Binarization Techniques

This method operates for continuous operators. In the process of binarisation, the first step refers to the normalization procedure and the second step relates to the binarization scheme, in which a binarization rule is used to turn the object into a binary.

Transfer Functions. Transfer functions define the probability of changing the elements of a position vector from 0 to 1 and vice versa. Transfer functions force particles to move in a binary space. When choosing a transfer function, it should be taken into account to give velocity values as follows:

- The range of a transfer function should be limited in the interval $[0,1]$, since they represent the probability that a particle changes its position.
- For a large absolute velocity evaluation a transfer function must provide a high probability to change the position. Components with strong absolute values of their speeds are definitely not the right way to swap their places in the next iteration.
- A transfer function should also have a small chance of changing the position for a small absolute velocity value.
- The return value of a transfer function should increase as the velocity increases. Particles that are moving away from the best solution should have their chance of changing their position vectors to return to their previous positions.
- The return value of a transfer function should decrease the velocity is reduced.

The 8 transfer functions corresponding to S-Shaped and V-Shaped are shown below (Table 1):

Table 1. S-Shape and V-Shape transfer functions.

S-Shape	V-Shape
$S1$: $\quad T(x_i^j) = \dfrac{1}{1+e^{-2x_i^j}}$	$V1$: $\quad T(x_i^j) = \left\| erf\left(\frac{\sqrt{\pi}}{2} x_i^j \right) \right\|$
$S2$: $\quad T(x_i^j) = \dfrac{1}{1+e^{2x_i^j}}$	$V2$: $\quad T(x_i^j) = \left\| tanh\left(x_i^j \right) \right\|$
$S3$: $\quad T(x_i^j) = \dfrac{1}{1+e^{\frac{-x_i^j}{2}}}$	$V3$: $\quad T(x_i^j) = \left\| \frac{x_i^j}{\sqrt{1+[x_i^j]^2}} \right\|$
$S4$: $\quad T(x_i^j) = \dfrac{1}{1+e^{\frac{-x_i^j}{3}}}$	$V4$: $\quad T(x_i^j) = \left\| \frac{2}{\pi} arctan\left(\frac{\pi}{2} x_i^j \right) \right\|$

Binarization Schemes. Together with the transfer techniques the experiments are carried out with 4 methods of binarization, which are shown below where:

- **Standard:** It is the most common method to assign a binary element, because a random variable is responsible for deciding whether its value will be 0 or 1.

$$x_i^j(t+1) = \begin{cases} 1 \text{ if } rand < T\left(x_i^j(t+1) \right) \\ 0 \text{ otherwise} \end{cases} \qquad (22)$$

– **Elitist:** In this equation, the value of the particle is assigned if the random value is contained in the probability of said variable, if not, it is assigned 0.

$$x_i^j(t+1) = \begin{cases} x_{best}^j & \text{if rand } < T\left(x_i^j(t+1)\right) \\ 0 & \text{otherwise} \end{cases} \tag{23}$$

– **Complement:** If the random value is in the range of the probability it is assigned the complement of the value of the particle, in another case, it is assigned zero.

$$x_i^j(t+1) = \begin{cases} \text{complement } \left(x_i^j(t)\right) & \text{if } rand < T\left(x_i^j(t+1)\right) \\ 0 & \text{otherwise} \end{cases} \tag{24}$$

– **Static Probability:** In this equation, the assignment of the particle variable is decided if the probability is less than, it is assigned the best particle until the moment, if the probability is in the range between and $1 = 2\ (1 +)$ it is assigns the best particle of the generation, in any other case, it is maintained.

$$x_i^j(t+1) = \begin{cases} x_i^j(t) & \text{if } 0 < T\left(x_i^j(t+1)\right) \leq \alpha \\ x_i^j(t+1) & \text{if } \alpha < T\left(x_i^j(t+1)\right) \leq \frac{1}{2}(1+\alpha) \\ x_{best}^j & \text{if } \frac{1}{2}(1+\alpha) < T\left(x_i^j(t+1)\right) \leq 1 \end{cases} \tag{25}$$

5.2 Binarization Techniques Inspired by Machine Learning

When comes to integrate machine learning and metaheuristics [9,10], two large groups can be mainly indicated. The first group, corresponds metaheuristic techniques improve the performance of machine learning algorithms. The second one covers machine learning algorithms enhance the metaheuristic algorithms quality. For the first group, we find four main areas of application: improving clustering algorithms, feature selection applications, improving classification algorithms and strengthening regression algorithms.

In the case of clustering, a variety of methods to solve it have been reported. One of the main problems that presents a greater algorithmic complexity, the centroid search is the same as the group of objects better studied. Since NP-hard is this problem, provisional methods for solving it have been suggested. There is a long list of studies in this area, however, in recent years the focus is to solve applied problems.

K-Means. A K-means Transition Ranking (KMTR) [3] as a general mechanism to binarize continuous Swarm Intelligence metaheuristics. This algorithm is composed of three operators. The main operator corresponds to the K-means transition operator. This operator translates the velocities obtained the continuous space to transition probabilities in binary spaces (Fig. 2).

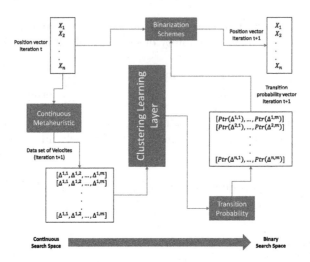

Fig. 2. Mapping the continuous search space to a discrete search space.

This translation is done by performing the clustering of solutions considering the solution velocity module in each dimension as metric. Because the clustering is executed at each iteration, the value of the transition probabilities of each solution is adapted depending on the clusters generated by the K-means Transition operator. In addition to the K-means transition operator, perturbation and repair operators are used.

DBSCAN. DBScan is an unsupervised learning technique that explores with the objective of using it in the binarization process of metaheuristic algorithms of continuous swarm intelligence. The objective of the binary db-scan operator is to group together the various solutions obtained by continuous metaheuristics. We must recognize the role of the particulate as a solution place in the quest space while considering solutions as particles. The velocity represents the vector for the transition from iteration to iteration of the particle $t + 1$.

DBScan utilizes the concept of density in the clustering: DBScan groups points with many close neighbors, given a set of S points in a metric space that marks outskirts those which are alone in low-density regions [4].

6   Experimental Results

To run the solution, instances are generated in Google Cloud Plaftform, which are configured with an Intel (R) Xeon (R) CPU @ 2.30GHz 3.5Gb RAM, 4gb of RAM, with Centos 7 distribution, for the development of the Solution uses Python language in its version 3 and Visual Studio Code and Spyder 3 tools (Fig. 3).

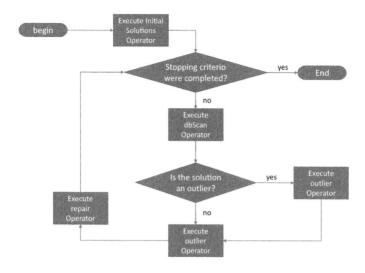

Fig. 3. General flow chart of the binary DBSCAN algorithm.

During the execution of the experiments, GSO has been executed with differ-ent two-step methods, K-means and DBSCAN, the instances performed in each problem are shown below.

The input parameters specified in the Table 3 were considered in the experi-ments conducted. The Table 2 shows the instances executed by the KP.

While the results obtained experimentally are divided in the following tables, Table 4 gives the results of the two-step binarization techniques, Table 5 the results obtained by K-means and Table 6 those corresponding to DBSCAN. The three tables have the same structure, in the first column the instance to be solved is presented, in the following two columns the transfer function and the discretization method that obtained the best performance are shown, in the following columns the optimal value of the instance, the minimum and maximum value found by the algorithm and the binarization technique, the average value and the Relative Percentage Deviation (RPD) defined in the EQ are shown. The average value and the relative percentage deviation (RPD) defined in the Eq. 26, as well as the computation time in seconds, are shown.

In addition, the violin graphs in Fig. 4 are presented, which help to identify the distribution of the data obtained.

$$\text{RPD} = \frac{100\,(Z_{min} - Z_{opt})}{Z_{opt}} \tag{26}$$

Table 2. Knapsack instances.

Instance	Vector	Parameters
f1	10	w = 95, 4, 60, 32, 23, 72, 80, 62, 65, 46; p = 55, 10, 47,5, 4, 50, 8, 61, 85, 87; b = 269
f2	20	w = 92, 4, 43, 83, 84, 68, 92, 82, 6, 44, 32, 18, 56, 83,25, 96, 70, 48, 14, 58; p = 44, 46, 90, 72, 91, 40, 75, 35,8, 54, 78, 40, 77, 15, 61, 17, 75, 29, 75, 63; b = 878
f3	4	w = 6, 5, 9, 7; p = 9, 11, 13, 15; b = 20
f4	4	w = 2, 4, 6, 7; p = 6, 10, 12, 13; b = 11
f5	15	w = 56.358531, 80.87405, 47.987304, 89.59624, 74.660482, 85.894345, 51.353496, 1.498459, 36.445204, 16.589862, 44.569231, 0.466933, 37.788018, 57.118442, 60.716575; p = 0.125126,19.330424, 58.500931, 35.029145, 82.284005, 17.41081, 71.050142, 30.399487, 9.140294, 14.731285, 98.852504, 11.908322, 0.89114, 53.166295, 60.176397; b = 75
f6	6	w = 30, 25, 20, 18, 17, 11, 5, 2, 1, 1; p = 20, 18, 17, 15,15, 10, 5, 3, 1, 1; b = 60
f7	7	w = 31, 10, 20, 19, 4, 3, 6; p = 70, 20, 39, 37, 7, 5,10; b = 50
f8	23	w = 983, 982, 981, 980, 979, 978, 488, 976, 972, 486, 486, 972, 972, 485, 485, 969, 966, 483, 964, 963, 961,958, 959; p = 81,980, 979, 978, 977, 976, 487, 974,970, 85, 485, 970, 970, 484, 484, 976, 974, 482, 962,961, 959, 958, 857; b = 10000
f9	5	w = 15, 20, 17, 8, 31; p = 33, 24, 36, 37, 12; b = 80
f10	20	w = 84, 83, 43, 4, 44, 6, 82, 92, 25, 83, 56, 18, 58, 14,48, 70, 96, 32, 68, 92; p = 91, 72, 90, 46, 55, 8, 35, 75,61, 15, 77, 40, 63, 75, 29, 75, 17, 78, 40, 44; b = 879

Table 3. Parameters used in GSO.

M	N	L1	L2	EPmax	c1 = c2 = c3 = c4
10	5	50	250	3	2,05

Table 4. KP - Two steps results

Instance	Step 1	Step 2	Optimo	Min	Max	Avg	RPD	Time
f1	sShape1	Elitist	295	284	295	293.06	0	0.69
f2	sShape1	Elitist	1024	894	1024	986.32	0.0	1.25
f3	sShape1	Complement	35	24	35	32.35	0	0.38
f4	sShape1	Complement	23	22	23	22.9	0	0.37
f5	sShape1	Elitist	481.069443	3.814.508	481.069.368	468.13	1,00E-07	1.0
f6	sShape1	Complement	52	39	52	47.32	0	0.7
f7	sShape1	Complement	107	90	107	105.9	0	0.57
f8	sShape1	Elitist	9767	9731	9756	9747.19	11	1.49
f9	sShape1	Complement	130	73	130	103.87	0	0.42
f10	sShape1	Elitist	1025	876	1025	989.74	0	1.28

Table 5. KP - K-means results

Instance	Optimo	Min	Max	Avg	RPD	Time
f1	295	295	295	295	0	422,51
f2	1024	1009	1024	1021,77	0	420,92
f3	35	35	35	35	0	286,95
f4	23	23	23	23	0	300,93
f5	481,0694	44,507,889	481,069,368	479,73	1,00E-07	420,86
f6	52	52	52	52	0	424,6
f7	107	107	107	107	0	413,62
f8	9767	9741	9756	9748,29	11	437
f9	130	130	130	130	0	349,82
f10	1025	1010	1025	1024,32	0	434,25

Table 6. KP - DBSCAN results

Instance	Optimo	Min	Max	Avg	RPD	Time
f1	295	295	295	295	0	108,52
f2	1024	933	1024	984,03	0	283
f3	35	35	35	35	0	35,68
f4	23	23	23	23	0	39,44
f5	481,0694	469,161,046	481,069,368	479,02	1,00E-07	183,49
f6	52	52	52	52	0	115,05
f7	107	107	107	107	0	70,84
f8	9767	9737	9755	9747,16	12	353,36
f9	130	130	130	130	0	46,86
f10	1025	935	1017	975,87	78	275,36

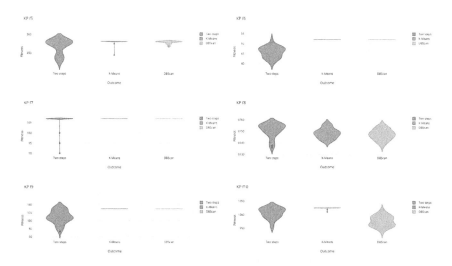

Fig. 4. Violin charts

6.1   KP Instance Distribution

It can be seen that in the figures corresponding to the instance distribution corresponding to KP, the great part of the experiments performed for the different instances shows promising results, K-means and DBScan have an identical behavior, obtaining in the majority good results.

Table 7. p-value Mann-Whitney-Wilcoxon test, KP - Two steps vs K-means.

Instance	Two steps vs K-means	K-means vs Two steps
f1	0.5	0.5
f2	1,0868E-03	1,0000E+00
f3	0.5	0.5
f4	0.5	0.5
f5	0.0231855071	0.976814493
f6	0.5	0.5
f7	0.5	0.5
f8	0.177609742	0.822390258
f9	0.5	0.5
f10	5,4801E-05	1,0000E+00

Table 8. p-value Mann-Whitney-Wilcoxon test, KP - Two steps vs DBSCAN.

Instance	Two steps vs DBSCAN	DBSCAN vs Two steps
f1	0.99967722	0.000322779755
f2	8,9637E+03	0.999910363
f3	0.999985704	1,43E+03
f4	0.841344746	0.158655254
f5	0.986436334	0.0135636663
f6	1,0000E+00	7,82E-05
f7	0.960840275	0.039159725
f8	0.000702254007	0.999297746
f9	0.999999997	2,95E-01
f10	0.999999892	1,08E+01

KP - Statical Test The general average of the 13,020 experiments performed to solve KP in Table 10.

A general comparison is made of the averages in Tables 7, 8 and 9 obtained in all the experiments performed, in this comparison all the experiments of the binarization schemes are included. KP corresponds to a maximization problem, in this case the average of the results obtained are similar and the best of them is DBScan, for both solved problems the best averages correspond to DBScan.

Table 9. p-value Mann-Whitney-Wilcoxon test, KP - K-means vs DBSCAN.

Instance	K-means vs DBSCAN	DBSCAN vs K-means
f1	0.99967722	0.000322779755
f2	0.999832952	0.000167047508
f3	0.999985704	1,4296E+03
f4	0.841344746	0.158655254
f5	0.999886089	0.000113910952
f6	1,0000E+00	7,8204E-05
f7	0.960840275	0.039159725
f8	0.00895109511	0.991048905
f9	0.999999997	2,9483E-01
f10	0.999999892	1,0812E+01

Table 10. Average results KP

Two steps	K-means	DbScan
1212,40	1291,60	1282,80

7   Conclusion

By modifying the GSO to solve the classical KP optimization problem using different binarization schemes considering two steps as well as new clustering techniques, different analyses and comparisons based on the results and statistical tests are obtained.

It can be seen that in the figures corresponding to the distribution of instances corresponding to KP, most of the experiments performed for the different instances show promising results, K-means and DBSCAN have an identical behavior, obtaining mostly good results. In addition, it should be considered that the use of K-means and DBSCAN allows to find viable solutions without the need to perform a large number of experiments as required by the two steps.

In addition to carrying out hypothesis testing in our report for the comparison in problem and solved instances, a general comparison of the averages obtained in all the experiments carried out in the different binarization schemes was made. Considering that KP corresponds to a maximization problem, in this case the average of the results obtained is similar and the best of them is the DBSCAN, for both solved problems the best averages based on proficiency correspond to the DBSCAN.

In a future work we want to investigate the behavior of other metaheuristics with the use of clustering techniques already used to solve NP-Hard problems and also include autonomous search that explore new variations between operators exploration and exploitation properties. Along with identifying metrics and quality indicators of the exploration and exploitation of the search space, which are fundamental for the correct functioning of the techniques [6].

Acknowledgements. Broderick Crawford is supported by Grant CONICYT/ FONDECYT/REGULAR/1171243, Ricardo Soto is supported by Grant CONICYT/ FONDECYT/REGULAR/1190129. José Lemus-Romani is supported by National Agency for Research and Development (ANID)/Scholarship Program/DOCTORADO NACIONAL / 2019 - 21191692.

References

1. Crawford, B., Soto, R., Astorga, G., García, J., Castro, C., Paredes, F.: Putting continuous metaheuristics to work in binary search spaces. Complexity **2017**(2), 1–19 (2017)
2. Crawford, B., Soto, R., Astorga, G., Lemus-Romani, J., Misra, S., Rubio, J.-M.: An adaptive intelligent water drops algorithm for set covering problem. In: 2019 19th International Conference on Computational Science and Its Applications (ICCSA), pp. 39–45. IEEE (2019)
3. García, J., Crawford, B., Soto, R., Astorga, G.: A clustering algorithm applied to the binarization of swarm intelligence continuous metaheuristics. Swarm Evol. Comput. **44**, 646–664 (2019)
4. García, J., et al.: A Db-scan binarization algorithm applied to matrix covering problems. Comput. Intell. Neurosci. **2019**, 3238516–3238572 (2019)
5. Mavrotas, G., Diakoulaki, D., Kourentzis, A.: Selection among ranked projects under segmentation, policy and logical constraints. Eur. J. Oper. Res. **187**(1), 177–192 (2008)
6. Morales-Castañeda, B., Zaldívar, D., Cuevas, E., Fausto, F., Rodríguez, A.: A better balance in metaheuristic algorithms: does it exist? Swarm Evol. Comput. **54**, 100671 (2020)
7. Muthiah-Nakarajan, V., Noel, M.M.: Galactic swarm optimization: a new global optimization metaheuristic inspired by galactic motion. Appl. Soft Comput. **38**, 771–787 (2016)
8. Peeta, S., Salman, F.S., Gunnec, D., Viswanath, K.: Pre-disaster investment decisions for strengthening a highway network. Comput. Oper. Res. **37**(10), 1708–1719 (2010)
9. Song, H., Triguero, I., Özcan, E.: A review on the self and dual interactions between machine learning and optimisation. Prog. Artif. Intell. **8**(2), 143–165 (2019). https://doi.org/10.1007/s13748-019-00185-z
10. Talbi, E.-G.: Machine learning into metaheuristics: a survey and taxonomy of data-driven metaheuristics, Working paper or preprint, June 2020
11. Valdivia, S., et al.: Bridges reinforcement through conversion of tied-arch using crow search algorithm. In: Misra, S., et al. (eds.) ICCSA 2019. LNCS, vol. 11623, pp. 525–535. Springer, Cham (2019). https://doi.org/10.1007/978-3-030-24308-1_42
12. Vanderster, D.C., Dimopoulos, N.J., Parra-Hernandez, R., Sobie, R.J.: Resource allocation on computational grids using a utility model and the knapsack problem. Future Gener. Comput. Syst. **25**(1), 35–50 (2009)
13. Yates, J., Lakshmanan, K.: A constrained binary knapsack approximation for shortest path network interdiction. Comput. Indu. Eng. **61**(4), 981–992 (2011)

Industry 4.0 CAMI: An Elastic Cloud Zynq UltraScale FPGA Metering Architecture

K. C. Okafor[1(✉)] and A. A. Obayi[2]

[1] Department of Mechatronics Engineering, Federal University of Technology, Owerri, Nigeria
kennedy.okafor@futo.edu.ng
[2] Department of Computer Science, University of Nigeria, Nsukka, Nigeria

Abstract. In the era of Industry 4.0, commoditized services (such as electricity, healthcare, etc.), require accuracy, availability, security and Quality of service (Qos) in the Cloud space. This paper presents cloud advanced metering infrastructure (CAMI) using Zynq UltraScale+ device field programmable gate array (FPGA). The architectural layout for energy tracking and profile measurement is discussed. Unlike existing systems with digital signal processors, it uses precision-based meter reading with encryption driven demand side management (DSM) to protect end-users. An energy service application with supporting hardware prototype is designed. Cryptographic algorithms, dynamic auto-scaling and predictive QoS provisioning are introduced as features of its backend cloud virtualization Infrastructure controller (CVIC). Process integration is achieved with CVIC synthesis for energy analytics and DSM. For the use case scenario, the CAMI prototype runs on Zynq UltraScale+ device with support for end-to-end dataset captures. The system provides on-demand visualization of energy consumption patterns for the end-users. In the experimental setup, two case scenarios demonstrate how the metering system executes fast edge computing profiling. Optimal performance is achieved for latency, utilization, and throughput under CVIC overhead constraint. It was observed that resource utilization responses for heterogeneous and non heterogeneous CVIC are 71.43% and 28.57% respectively. Latency profiles gave 71.43% and 28.57% respectively. With the VM controller, FPGA CAMI offered 47.36% while without VM controller, 52.63% throughput is observed. Consequently, the results highlights how FPGA hardware acceleration can significantly improve request distribution as well as workload processing for cloud based metering systems.

Keywords: Industry 4.0 · Cloud metering AMI · FPGA device · Demand side management · Cloud analytics

1 Introduction

1.1 Background

CAMI is the next digital future for energy management (EM) systems. In the domain of Cloud driven AMI, modern smart grid combines highly intelligent digital components

© Springer Nature Switzerland AG 2020
O. Gervasi et al. (Eds.): ICCSA 2020, LNCS 12254, pp. 527–543, 2020.
https://doi.org/10.1007/978-3-030-58817-5_39

with full duplex two-way communication to achieve seamlessness on- demand response [1, 2]. The essence is to create efficient monitoring and management of energy usage data efficiently. Precision-based sample captures, smart-consumption billing, intrusion alerts, negative-tampering feature, load isolation, on-line upgrades, DSM, and analytics, among others are desired features [3]. Developing countries like Nigeria will immensely benefit from the system looking at it from cost benefit and service delivery perspectives.

Unlike the legacy smart grid AMIs, an ultra-scaled AMI provides unbiased data profile in respect of instantaneous user consumptions. This simplifies billing automation with lower computational overhead. In most smart meters (SMs), metering and communication modules are the two most essential components. Both have specific controller units relating seamlessly during its operation. Also, these meters have load enable/disable switch, input-output (I/O) control interfaces with embedded power storage subsystems, among others. Modern designs are expected to enhance energy efficiency, reduces wastages and control usage pattern by consumers. The major difference between the recent smart metering systems and the legacy metering models is that the CAMI enforces active participation of consumers in energy conservation through real time feedback communication on their exact energy consumption profiles [4].

Various efforts on EM capabilities are mainly skewed towards embedded device architectures that support sequential rather than concurrent execution. The introduction of FPGA's into CAMI offers a disruptive strategy that have recently gained attention in today's energy industry. In the years ahead, smart metering designs with FPGA devices and digital inclusive technologies such as the Internet cloud will be relied on to provide new efficiency in energy metering and billing systems. This will obviously make CAMI to fully alter the way metering is carried out. In context, this will allow customers to participate fully in demand side management schemes [4].

Till date, most metering systems does not support low latency full duplex communication for real time energy feedback. Low latency/high speed processing capabilities is yet to be fully implemented and deployed leveraging bit stream encryption and decryption. This research presents low latency based CAMI which depends on high speed Zynq UltraScale+ FPGA processor (32/64bits compatibles). The major attraction of the proposed system is the secured computational executions running on the FPGA core with little power drain while having low delay real-time clock, signal conditional converter and other RF interfaces. For end users, the advantages of CAMI include overhead reduction in data gathering, improved reading precision, efficient billing processes, and significant increase in operational efficiency through real time metering activities. This paper presents CAMI implementation for distributed energy resources (DERs) in smart grid ecosystem. The 32 bit FPGA core design strategies, security and low latency implementations are discussed. Hardware acceleration via FPGA CAMI consumer workload is equally demonstrated as the most efficient scheme for smart grid DSM.

2 Related Works

In this Section, various efforts on advanced metering systems will be presented. Recently, the authors [4, 5] highlighted essential benefits of AMI for an energy driven society. These include: low latency energy data-stream updates; cumulative data-sets gathering from various home sources with passive backend data analytics; secured data privacy for users; bandwidth management of sensitive workloads in full duplex communication mode and trajectory data-mining and context-aware service provisioning. The work [3] presented an implementation of FPGA sigma delta architecture for the analog to digital conversion module in smart meters. The authors [6] presented a transceiver architecture that depicts resource estimations for application specific integrated circuit (ASIC) AMI. The work [7] presented a typical power measurement device whose computational units are embedded in an FPGA device. The authors [8] demonstrated a prototype implementation of smart metering utility networks using Altera's device. The authors [9] presented electric power measurement implementation in a three-phase power system by using an FPGA device architecture whose power calculation theory was verified with IEEE 1459-2010 Standard for power quality measurement methods [10]. In terms of FPGA processor architectures, various works have been carried out to address speed performance issues. For instance, the work [11] presented FPGA 32-bit extended arithmetic logic unit (ALU) architecture with Xilinx Vivado 14.4 tool and implemented on 28 nm Zynq 7000 FPGA board. The work in [12] presented a 32-bit MIPs FPGA-Based pipelined microprocessor with Very high speed hardware descriptive language (VHDL) [13]. The authors [14] presented an implementation of a 32-bit Microprocessor without Interlocked Pipeline Stage (MIPS) using rotation based algorithm. Other similar works on 32 bit FPGA designs have been studied and presented in [15]. With the FPGA device board [16], the design can be used create, implement, and test CAMI AMI design using programmable logic.

Considering FPGA based Cloud security designs, the work [17] proposed an FPGA Cloud which deals with privacy preservation and computing in the public Cloud domain. The authors [18], discussed a security pattern which supports the control-sharing and demarcation of FPGA accelerators in heterogeneous Cloud architectures. Similar work [19] focused on various advanced encryption security model at the FPGA layer without considering the latency profiles of these metering systems.

The research gaps in the existing Cloud based metering system involve ineffective DSM and the absence of concurrent hardware resource utilization due to unsatisfactory latency profiles. Also, FPGA Virtual machine provisioning for energy users has not been explored for scalability. From the literature carried out, the proposed CAMI offers a robust design with well-structured algorithm for security. Hardware acceleration using FPGA- Cloud service for optimal metering and billing has not been implemented in existing systems. In this work, CAMI is presented and it uses bit stream privacy while supporting energy traffic confidentiality with a deterministic load balancing.

3 FPGA Device Architecture

Clearly, the FPGA device architecture is perceived to have strong potential for optimal design of AMIs. This has been further buttressed in [20]. The authors identified the merits of using FPGA-ASIC namely:

- re-programmability for bug correction.
- FPGA development allows shorter time to market and reduces unnecessary costs.
- reduction in power drain.
- reduces component counts significantly.

Hence, using FPGA AMI with an isolated CPU chip often yield cost savings, miniaturized system, and reliability. Figure 1 shows the I/O ports highlighting the board layout with indications on the location and connections of various components. Quartus II IDE is used to configure the board alongside the downloaded USB blaster drivers.

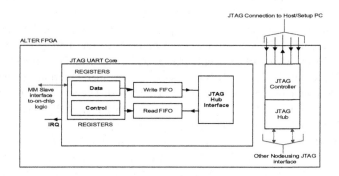

Fig. 1. Altera FPGA interface layout.

There are essential soft processor-core features in any commercial FPGAs. These include [21, 22]: gate count, clock frequency, data-path-width, pipeline- stages, register-files, instruction word, instruction cache, hardware ALUs among others. To achieve satisfactory CAMI, low latency FPGA design is absolutely needed. This can be achieved with electronic digital automation process (EDA) [23]. An earlier work in [4] shows the EDA process framework for CAMI on FPGA core processor (Zynq UltraScale+). The reason for selecting the processor in Fig. 1 (during system implementation) is as a result of cost and market availability considerations. The beneficial features of using the FPGA CAMI in the work include: workload tolerance, fair resource utilization, latency and throughput scaling supports, power efficient compared with CPUs/GPUs, output optimization. As such, the Zynq UltraScale+ Xilins MPSoC [24] was explored to achieve computational performance in the cloud domain. Section 4 introduces the CAMI context.

4   Cloud Metering Description

In this Section, a brief description of the CAMI is given. Now, Fig. 2 illustrates how the peripheral connectivity interface of the CAMI FPGA device that is mapped into a high speed 3-phase power micro-grid. The distributed energy resources (DER) earlier described served as the application context for deployment (i.e., Industry 4.0 domain). The various DERs connects to the CAMI which maps end users into the Cloud [4].

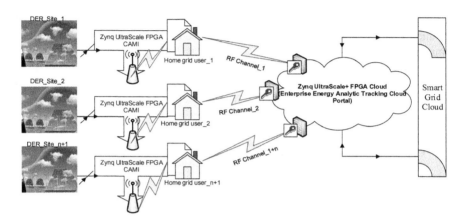

Fig. 2. Industry 4.0 framework for Smart Grid Cloud EMI.

Based on the consumption rate of end user $n+1$, the CAMI collects data locally and transmits into the cloud for analytics. For this to occur, the transmission happens as often as 1sec or as infrequently as daily, according to the usage of power. The collector retrieves the data, process in a full duplex mode for upstream processing. This is achieved in the analytics application which is represented as a Cloud service.

In this case, energy data is transmitted to the Cloud FPGA metering device for processing DSM. Such two way communications allow customers to participate in the smart grid scenario. The use of machine learning (ML) to achieve analytics was done with JAVA application program interface (API). This is based on massive online analysis (MOA). Data stream trajectory mining was achieved MOA using its JAVA ML classification for DSM audit logs. In wide-label classification, this can predict multiple output variables of DSM for every instantaneous input of the DER.

4.1   Advanced Metering Infrastructure

Let's further look at the AMI logic introduced in Fig. 2. In its operation, the metering filter (FPGA-ADC) was programmed with very high speed integrated circuit hardware descriptive language (VHDL) for Zynq UltraScale+ MPSoC device. This provided the desired System-On-a-Programmable Chip (SOPC) for CAMI. Specifically, 32-bit Cluster AMI device was built with eight Zynq UltraScale+ FPGA boards. This offers low latency profile in active state. The turning parameters used for the CAMI design is highlighted in the data sheet [24]. The CAMI design has TCP/IP interface for data stream interactions. The CAMI on a 32 bit Zynq UltraScale+ board while using its digital signal processor (DSP) for complex signal conditioning/processing functions especially for power quality measurement features. The system has an efficient multi-core processor (SOC) that runs on low latency shared peripheral and memory interface buses. Also, the method of interconnection of resources makes the system design modular and scalable. In the implementation phase, the CAMI satisfies the requirements of low energy measurement and security computational functions. This uses specialized Arm Cortex-A53 co-processor with additional peripherals for data exchange and communication handles this task. Also, the core supports sufficient flash and internal memory. Hence, this executes the embedded real time operating system for commercially available or open source protocol stacks (Wi-Fi, Modem/3G, TCP/IP, Zigbee, Bluetooth Peripherals, Wimax), among others. For the security of the AMI for Cloud processing, it is pertinent to discuss the cryptographic transactional function needed for operational cloud automation. In this case, 30 users were considered in the algorithm.

4.2 Cryptographic Transactional Function

Considering the Zynq UltraScale+ FPGA module, its security algorithm is described for end-to-end communication. This features the FPGA block clusters, encryption keys, message block, VM_map and likely- function. These are taken into considerations as depicted in Algorithm I and II. It uses 512 key length for selected addresses. The input and output variables are activated via loop algorithms and wait states to secure all data movements. The IoT-enabled Cloud AMI security is robust using strong key length. The Zynq acquisition module gathers data from end-user meters and transmit to the Cloud portal for analytics. It uses multiple security algorithm to encrypt data (512 key length). Overall, the cryptographic algorithm supports secure lookup DSM/energy consumption prediction, grid possible failure points, peak generation and consumption forecast on daily basis. Location identification, fault tracking and assignment of grid failure correction are securely shared with an active user remotely. For an address map of 30 users, below is the functional security algorithm used in the design.

Algorithm I:. FPGA CAMI_ AES-Encrypt (FPGA block clusters)

Input: Cust_trans, Crypt_Cipher-Key, Fun () memory block
              Crypt_mem_block size, bitstream map, likihood func ();
Output: FPGA_Cloud Domain, Cipher len, N Ran () Addresses (30);
While K_t = 512, $i\leftarrow0$;do
  Set Flag F = True/high (1);
  Function memory block = Curent_Mem_block;
  K Seed = Current Seed (time, ComputeID, addresses);

end while
Do
Repeat
K_t address (t) = model_memBlock (Mmb) ==.> 0;
Until i = 30;
  Repeat
    Set_Stage = Process (K_t address i)
  Until i =30
  While Set Stage k = 0
  Repeat
    If (i Ran 5 == 0) *Then*
    Encrypt_val (K_t address i) = key_length [L_k]
    Crypt_temp = Encrypt*(K_t address i)
    Encrypt_val[(K_t address i) = ObtainK block_value (tempt)
      L_k = L_k+1
    Else
      Encrypt_val[(K_t address i)]=Keylength [0:512]
    Endif
  Until i =30; Output ;
  End
Return *Input*

Algorithm II: FPGA CAMI_ Routine Cryptographic Analytics

Input: Cust_trans, Crypt_Cipher-Key, Fun () memory block
              Crypt_mem_block size, bitstream map, likihood func ();
Output: FPGA_Cloud Domain, Cipher len, N Ran () Addresses (30);
K_t = 512, K, J,M = 0; $i\leftarrow0$;
While (Crypt_round = 1) do
  Crypt_Seed = New_Seed (time, Proc_ID, Case_Address)
  Encrypt_Val(K_t address (0:30)) <==Encrypt_Val
  ([(K_t address [0: 30)XoR R_com(Round X5/Nk)]
  Repeat //redo
  K_t address(i * 6 + j) <== func () mem_block + RANDt ()
  % Crypt_mem_block_size;
  If (m= 0);
  Crypt_temp(K_t address(i * 6 + m)<==Crypt_temp
  (K_t address(i * 6 + m)XoRtempt
  Crypt_temp//Call output parameter
  State [k] [m-1] = State [k][m-1]XoRtempt
  Until m; k = 4; 3
    Until round =30;

  End
Return *Input*

5   System Implementation

Recall that the Cloud based FPGAs AMI has its bitstreams encrypted by AES on the client side as shown in Fig. 3. Also, the AES key is securely shared with Cloud driven FPGA core. At both the edge and Cloud, the bitstream protection on the FPGA cores facilitates advanced encryption standard (AES) key sharing for both encryption and decryption respectively. For high computational performance, the FPGA CAMIs leverages the low latency Xilinx FPGA ASIC processor for energy consumption computations. By acquiring data in real time from customer-side AMI (32 bit FPGA core) into the data-center server, this enabled the introduction of integrated OpenFlow load balancers (ISOLB) or Cloud virtual infrastructure controller (CVIC) for Cloud elasticity as shown in Fig. 3. Using ISOLB/CVIC algorithms III and IV, this handled the upward and downward scaling of compute resources considering end users.

For traffic workloads, Fig. 3 also allows on-demand power flexibility in terms of processing/computing power, storage and bandwidth. As a proof, discrete event data transfers is used to simulate the dynamic response characteristics of energy usage in the Cloud. By this approach of acquiring data, proactive management is introduced. The system sends frequent reports under stable QoS with impact on communication costs.

In terms of scalability, the FPGA elastic Cloud uses resilient engine which comes from the ISOLB/CVIC. The key benefit is on concurrent big data integration and security optimization. Overall, the cryptographic transform algorithm, predictor resource allocation and dynamic scaling are the novel features introduced to support Cloud and big data grid management. Clearly, the CVIC enables trusts on the Cloud servers thereby reducing exponential aggregation, storage, and processing. In the security activity, the joint collection points are secured thereby providing data availability always. Security history of huge datasets is computed and managed using weighted distributions for initial and posterior trends. The FPGA_cloud dynamic-scaling algorithm for is shown in Algorithm IV. AES key for the bitstream protection is securely shared between client and FPGA. The AES key is embedded in hardware bit stream and implemented in Fig. 4.

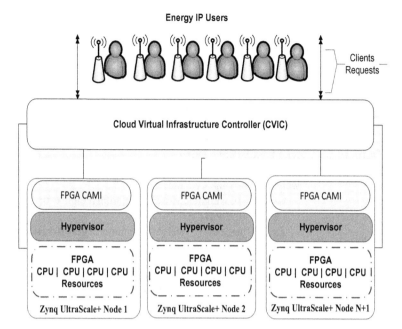

Fig. 3. Developed FPGA CAMI with Consumer loads (Energy IPs).

Algorithm III. FPGA Zynq UltraScale+ Predictor for QoS Allocation

Inputs: Bitstream_Control-CallSchedule for Zynq UltraScale i to $N+1$
History of CPS compute resources, QoS Provisioning and transactional workflow
$\prod \beta 1$ & $\prod \beta 2$// initialValue constant & trendPosteriorValue, respectively
pastValueForSubsytems, pastValueForSubsytems

Output: Zynq UltraScale+ _DES

Parameters: Zynq UltraScale+ _weight←Empty; // Zynq UltraScale+ weighted Moving Average
weight←0; weightedMoving←0; totalWeight←0;
fiboA←0; fiboB←1;
Zynq UltraScale+ _weight ContainerhistoryItem← null; // Resource Pattern

int i←0;

While i < Zynq UltraScale+ _monitorCallSchedule d **do**
   historyItem←HistoryList.get(HistoryList.size()–CPS_monitorCallSchedule – i)
   Zynq UltraScale+ _weight ←fiboA1 + fiboB2;
   Zynq UltraScale+ weightedMoving←CPSweightedMoving+ (ContainerhistoryItem * weight);
   total Zynq UltraScale+ _weight ←total Zynq UltraScale+ _weight + Zynq UltraScale+ weight;
   i ++;

end while

Zynq UltraScale+ _DES ← Zynq UltraScale+ weightedMoving / total Zynq UltraScale+ Weight;
// Calculate Dynamic Exponential Reliability
initialValue ←($\beta 1$ * Zynq UltraScale+ _weight) + (1 – $\beta 1$) * (pastInitialValue + trendPosteriorValue);
trendPosteriorValue←$\beta 2$ * (initialValue - pastInitialValue)+ ((1 – $\beta 2$) * pastTrendPosteriorValue);
Zynq UltraScale+_DES←initialValue+ trendPosteriorValue;
Return Zynq UltraScale+ _DES

Algorithm IV: FPGA_Cloud_Dynamic-Scaling algorithm

Elasticity   History of FPGA_Cloud Service provisioning for Zynq Ul
Container   traScale i to $N+1$
          Zynq UltraScale+_monitorCallSchedule
          QoS parameterStatus // Latency, Throughput & Service
          availability
          Zynq UltraScale+_decision←Empty;
          excessVM←Empty;
// Zynq UltraScale+_Monitor ( );
Redo every monitorCallPeriod Seconds
    // Analyzer
    if scalingParameterType is SLA-Aware **then**
    | parameterStatus←Predictor (history of Response Time)
    Elseif scalingParameterType is Resource-Aware **then**
    | parameterStatus←Predictor (history of QoS parameterStatus)
    end if
    // Zynq UltraScale+ Planner
    If parameterStatus is higher than Scale Up threshold **then**
    | decision←Scale Up (Zynq UltraScale+)
    Elseif parameterStatus is lower than Scale Down threshold **then**
    | decision←Scale Down (Zynq UltraScale+)
    End if
    // Zynq UltraScale+Executer
    If decision is Scale Up **then**
    | Scale Up (new On-Demand Zynq UltraScale+VM);
    Elseif decision is Scale Down **then**
    | excess Zynq UltraScale+VM←excessVM SelectionPolicy;
    | Scale Down (excess Zynq UltraScale+VM);
    end if
end return

6 Evaluation

6.1 Hardware and Software Integration

In this Section, the proposed Cloud based AMI for DSM and the hardware integration is discussed. To evaluate the application program interface (API) design built with service oriented programming approach (SOPA) in MoA, real-time captures was carried out for various cases. The implementation of the CAMI was completed with its API called enterprise energy tracking analytic cloud portal (EETACP) application. This was built with C++ engine and JAVA respectively. Similarly, the hardware environment provides supports for dynamic system-level integration using C++/VHDL code while targeting Zynq SoC device architecture. The integration includes software-to-hardware translation, device driver generation, and kernel creation. Also, its SoC platform allows for the specification of software functions for hardware translation. The FPGA Zynq SoC device explored C/C++ source code to realize the interface communications.

During the FPGA CAMI setup, the energy consumption patterns were monitored with low latency processing. Bit stream security was investigated for the workloads. In all cases, eight FPGA boards (ZCU102) were used in the configuration testbed. The individual modules contain Zynq UltraScale+ with Cortex-A53 quad-core processor (1.5 GHz, 4 GB DDR4 RAM), and has a number of programmable logic cells encapsulating the constructed 8-node cluster [24]. On the testbed, the eight nodes are connected through Ethernet via a high-end OpenFlow layer-3 switch [3]. In this regard, SDSoC 2016.4v [25] was introduced as an automation design tool from Xilinx and employed for the system code level implementation. As shown in Fig. 4, CAMI analytics application captures energy data from the CAMI for Cloud analytics. This event takes place every second based on 24-hour scale of daily energy supply. The API dynamically obtains the average power consumptions based on household loads. Case based observations was established via the metering system. In each case, AES bit-stream algorithm was invoked while showing the energy consumption for the CAMI processing. The demonstration setup revealed energy end user consumption profiles derived from the gathered load analytics.

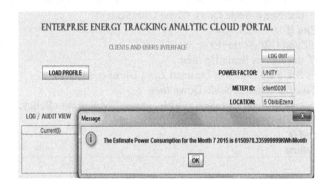

Fig. 4. Secured Cloud DSM Interface with history predictive load profiles.

6.2   Experimental Validations

In this Section, scheduling and resource allocation in the Cloud was done with Cloud Zynq UltraScale+ FPGA cores. To achieve scalability and security in CVIC, the work executed DSM (workload) in two basic instances namely: FPGA CAMI with hetero-geneous virtual machine (VM) controller (proposed) and FPGA CAMI without heterogeneous VM controller (legacy). In the former, CAMI node-level scheduling with optimized dynamic scaling (Cloud resource allocation) was combined as shown in Algorithm IV. In this case, complete vertical scaling and CPU utilization cycles exploits resources in Cloud VMs, thereby reducing power drain without compromising performance. Figure 5 shows how resource utilization under heterogeneous VM controller scales relative to the legacy model for similar transactional workload. In this case, the work varied the number of workloads per node which alters the workload intensity on the Cloud. Hence, the resource utilization responses are then observed. The CVIC actuates resources to the Cloud nodes based on CPU utilization cycles, and workload demands. About 71.43% utilization occurs due to the workload activities found in the proposed FPGA CAMI VM controller such as big data processing. Conversely, 28.57% utilization shows satisfactory performance with legacy workloads. The implication is that the resource usage of Algorithms I, II, III and IV are lowest in the Cloud without VM controllers. Though the proposed FPGA CAMI with VM offers very high resource utilization, but the impact of CVIC makes it to explore very minimal resources due to the optimal mapping on the control and management planes.

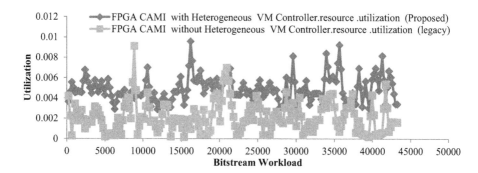

Fig. 5. Resource Utilization for FPGA CAMI transactional workload.

Figure 6 shows the latency response for FPGA CAMI transactional workload. It is the elapsed timeframe from the push-out of a service request to Cloud server for processing. To converge from Cloud failures, the latency times of both cases were observed. The plot shows that the latency profile of the proposed is higher (71.43%) when compared with the legacy FPGA CAMI scenario (28.57%) due to failure over-heads. The more workload or devices that fail, the more increase the latency becomes. Also, as the workloads increases, the latency response increases as well. Hence, service requests with the proposed FPGA CAMI scenario are optimal as result of the CVIC/ISOLB.

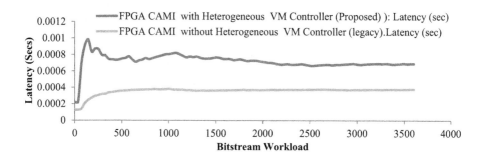

Fig. 6. Latency response for FPGA CAMI transactional workload.

Figure 7 shows the throughput response for FPGA CAMI transactional workload distribution. Clearly, he proposed algorithms suffer from overhead due to its close loop nature unlike the legacy FPGA CAMI without VM controller. From the results, the Open loop legacy algorithm is shown to provide a more reliable request distribution to the accurate Cloud servers.

However, due to dynamic auto-scaling in the proposed scheme, excess workloads and failures are reduced alongside the latency and utilization. With the VM controller, the FPGA CAMI offered 47.36% while without VM controller, 52.63% throughput was delivered. In this case, it was observed that the presence of heterogeneous VM controllers introduces overhead which deviated the latency, utilization and throughput metrics of the system. However, this is the tradeoff associated with FPGA scalability supports (and its ruggedness) necessary for high performance, security and flexibility characteristics.

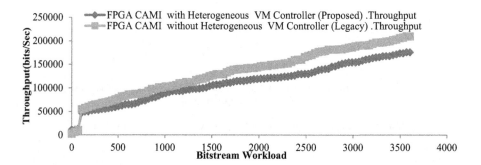

Fig. 7. Throughput response for FPGA CAMI transactional workload.

7   Challenges and Future Directions

Essentially, the author [26], highlighted that FPGAs with transition from about 10 million gates to about 50 million gates with internal logic clocks thereby creating massive opportunities for Cloud integrations. There are still issues regarding design time-market productivity, architectural scalabilities, power demands, flexibility among others. As its core density keeps evolving, the hardware-engines (logic element cores, LEC) and digital signal processors (DSP) data-paths becomes more complicated too.

Combining the LEC with soft-core and scaled embedded memories may present newer challenges for smart grid integration. First, the DSP-resource intensive constructs will need complicated arithmetic computations, massive memories, great bandwidth demands, and high-speed serial communications with dynamic reconfiguration. For mission critical services, the above specifications computationally will drain significant amount of power at peak performance states. Future direction of FPGA device architectures must focus on addressing these concerns with the least power consumption profiles. This should be done without degrading performance especially next generation networks (e.g., 5G/6G and SD-WAN). With the different construction blocks (e.g., transceivers, memories, and multipliers, for various designs), power consumption across its implementation must be optimized.

8 Conclusion

This paper has presented a use case of Industry 4.0 elastic Cloud AMI that leverages Zynq UltraScale+ FPGA cores. The system supports bi-directional communication for transactional workloads between customer meters and Cloud. Low latency FPGA ASIC implementation is developed to satisfy the requirements of smart grid architecture. The functionalities of CAMI are highlighted while enumerating the benefits. With the built analytics application, consumer energy frauds and other issues resulting from the existing metering model are addressed through DSM. Using an on-demand FPGA CAMI, the work discussed the functional algorithms for performance optimization. In terms of security, the FPGA CAMI, used 512 AES key length for metering data and also captured in the hardware design. In the evaluation, user's requests are mapped to the CVIC/ISOLB for workload optimizations. Low latency energy usage, predictive QoS allocation and dynamic-workload balancing are investigated in selected experiments. Despite the overhead introduced by the CVIC/ISOLB, the work showed that Cloud-based FPGAs provides optimal performance benefits. The results show that leveraging FPGA hardware acceleration has the potential to increase the attention on FPGA-assisted cloud systems. The proposed scheme can be applied in big-data applications as well as other security-constrained sectors such as Block chain. Future work will focus on CAMI reliability constraints in big data streaming applications and cyber-physical systems [27].

References

1. Song, Y., Kong, P.Y., Kim, Y., Baek, S., Choi, Y.: Cellular-assisted D2D communications for advanced metering infrastructure in smart grid. IEEE Syst. J. 1–12 (2019)
2. Kaveh, D., Yuxuan, Y., Zhaoyu, W., Fankun, B.: A game-theoretic data- driven approach for pseudo-measurement generation in distribution system state estimation. IEEE Trans. Smart Grid 1 (2019)
3. Padmaprabha, V.R., Divya, D.S., Jiju, K.: SOPC based sigma delta ADC IP core for smart energy meter. In: International Conference on Circuits & Systems (ICCS), pp. 140–144. IEEE Xplore, India (2017)
4. Okafor, K.C.: Development of a model for smart green energy management using distributed cloud computing network. Ph.D. thesis, University of Nigeria, Nsukka (2017)
5. Saroa, M.K., Aron, R.: Fog computing and its role in development of smart applications. In: IEEE International Conference on Parallel & Distributed Processing with Applications, Ubiquitous Computing & Communications, Big Data & Cloud Computing, Social Computing & Networking, Sustainable Computing & Communications (ISPA/IUCC/BDCloud/SocialCom/SustainCom), pp. 1120–1127. IEEE Xplore, Melbourne, Australia (2018)

6. Jessica, A.J., Oliveira, D., Augusto, F.R.Q., Lima, E.R.D., Mertes, J.: An MR-FSK transceiver compliant to IEEE802.15.4g for smart metering utility applications: FPGA implementation and ASIC resource estimation. In: Latin-American Conference on Communications (LATINCOM), pp. 1–4. IEEE Xplore, Peru (2015)
7. Luis, D.O.A., Guilherme, A.E.M., Carlos, A.C.: Power quantities calculation by using an FPGA device, applying IEEE 1459-2010 standard. In: IEEE Simposio Brasileiro de Sistemas Eletricos (SBSE), pp. 1–6. IEEE Xplore, Niteroi, Brazil (2018)
8. Augusto, F.R.Q., et al.: FPGA implementation of an IEEE802.15.4g MR-OFDM baseband modem for Smart metering utility networks. In: IEEE 4th Global Conference on Consumer Electronics (GCCE), pp. 125–126. IEEE Xplore, Japan (2015)
9. Luis, D.O.A., Guilherme, A.M., Carlos, A.C.: FPGA-based power meter implementation for three-phase three-wire and four-wire power systems, according to IEEE 1459-2010 standard. In: IEEE Brazilian Power Electronics Conference (COBEP), pp. 1–6. IEEE Xplore, Juiz de Fora, Brazil (2017)
10. Radek, S., Josef, V., Ján, T.: Wideband partial discharge meter using FPGA. In: IEEE 9th IEEE International Symposium on Diagnostics for Electric Machines, Power Electronics and Drives (SDEMPED), pp. 396–401. IEEE Xplore, Spain (2013)
11. Nidhi, G., Anu, M., Deepika, K., Devyani, T.: A novel implementation of 32 bit extended ALU Architecture at 28 nm FPGA. In: IEEE International Conference on Emerging Trends in Communication Technologies (ETCT), pp. 1–4. IEEE Xplore, India (2016)
12. Rohit, J., Raghavendra, M.: Implementation of 32-bit RISC processors without interlocked Pipelining on Artix-7 FPGA board. In: International Conference Circuits, Controls, and Communications (CCUBE), pp. 105–108. IEEE Xplore, Bangalore (2017)
13. Okafor, K.C., Guinevere, E.C., Akinyele, O.O.: Hardware description language (HDL): an efficient approach to device independent designs for VLSI market segments. In: Proceedings of the 3rd IEEE International Conference Adaptive Science and Technology (ICAST), pp. 262–267. IEEE Xplore, Abuja (2011)
14. Safaa, S.O., Ahmed, K.A.: Design and implementation of 32-Bits MIPS processor to Perform QRD based on FPGA. In: IEEE International Conference on Engineering Technology and their Appls, (IICETA), Iraq, pp. 36–41 (2018)
15. Omran, S.S., Ahmed, A.K.: Design of 32-bits RISC processor for hardware efficient QR decomposition. In: International Conference on Advance of Sustainable Engineering & its Application (ICASEA), pp. 69–73 (2018)
16. Ankita, G., Hamid, M.: Embedded System Design Flow, using ALTERA FPGA Development Board (DE2-115 T-Pad) (2020)
17. Xu, L., Shi, W., Suh, T.: PFC: privacy preserving FPGA cloud - a case study of map reduce. In: IEEE 7th International Conference on Cloud Computing, Anchorage, AK, pp. 280–287 (2014)
18. Hategekimana, F., Mandebi, J.M., Pantho, M.J.H., Bobda, C.: Secure hardware kernels execution in CPU+FPGA heterogeneous cloud. In: International Conference on Field-Programmable Technology (FPT), pp. 182–189. IEEE, Naha (2018)
19. Kim, H.-Y.: SafeDB: spark acceleration on FPGA clouds with enclaved data processing and bitstream protection. In: IEEE 12th International Conference on Cloud Computing (CLOUD), pp. 107–114. IEEE, Milan (2019)
20. McConnel, T.E.: ESC - Xilinx All Programmable System on a Chip combines best of serial and parallel processing (2010). https://www.eetimes.com/esc-xilinx-extensible-processing-platform-combines-best-of-serial-and-parallel-processing/. Accessed 15 Nov 2020
21. Hamblen, J.O.: Using system-on-a-programmable-chip technology to design embedded systems. IJCA 13(3) (2006)

22. Christophersen, H., Pickell, R., Neidhoefer, J., Koller, A., Kannan, S., Johnson, E.: A compact guidance, navigation, and control system for unmanned aerial vehicles. J. Aerospace Comput. Inf. Commun. ARC **3**, 187–213 (2006)

23. Jad, G.A.: EDA tools usage and tutorial authoring for basic electronic circuits education. In: IEEE 12th European Workshop on Microelectronics Education (EWME), pp. 51–54 (2018)

24. Xilinx. Zynq UltraScale+ MPSoC Data Sheet: Overview- DS891 (v1.8) (2019)

25. Kathail, V., Hwang, J., Sun, W., Chobe, Y., Shui, T., Carrillo, J.: SDSoC: a higher-level programming environment for Zynq SoC and Ultrascale+ MPSoC. In: Proceedings of the 2016 ACM/SIGDA, International Symposium, on Field-Programmable Gate Arrays, p. 4 (2016)

26. Bolsens, I.: Challenges and opportunities for FPGA platforms. In: Glesner, M., Zipf, P., Renovell, M. (eds.) FPL 2002. LNCS, vol. 2438, pp. 391–392. Springer, Heidelberg (2002). https://doi.org/10.1007/3-540-46117-5_41

27. Okafor, K.C.: Dynamic reliability modelling of cyber-physical edge computing network. Int. J. Comput. Appl. (IJCA), SI- Sustainable Comput. Intell. Syst. **40**(42), 1–10 (2019)

Midair: An Intermediate Representation for Multi-purpose Program Analysis

Maxim Menshikov$^{(\boxtimes)}$ ⓘ

Saint Petersburg State University, 7-9, Universitetskaya nab.,
St. Petersburg 199034, Russian Federation
info@menshikov.org

Abstract. The static analysis field had grown enough to be used not only for finding casual defects. In practice, it may be used to enforce the coding style and flag undesired syntax constructs, find logical mistakes, prove that the program satisfies its specification, apply domain-specific checks, or even verify cross-program compatibility. Those are all valid use cases that are required to be handled by the static analyzer, and the intermediate representation (IR) affects how can it be done.

A typical compiler or analyzer uses a number of IRs, each of them helps with a specific problem. For our static analyzer project, we found that existing IRs partially do not match our requirements, which led to the creation of Midair—an IR for multi-purpose program analysis. It is positioned right between IRs created primarily for the compilation (like LLVM, MLIR, GIMPLE) and verification IRs (such as Boogie) with the hope that it would be both close to a low level and suitable for verification while applying to practical analysis tools. The IR consists of 4 layers, allowing for a transparent transformation between forms saving time and space. A flexible type system supporting non-machinery types and an ability to augment the representation with external metadata provided by solvers had been added. The application of Midair to our analysis framework uncovered advantages and non-critical issues, which are planned to be worked around.

Keywords: Intermediate representation · Verification · Program analysis · Static analysis · Framework

1 Introduction

Decades ago intermediate representation became an industry-recognized way to separate concerns between parsing, analysis, optimization and code generation passes, yet to unify their input/output formats. Building efficient language-agnostic middle steps depends on it. Before LLVM [3], IRs were mostly considered an internal part of programming tools, unavailable from the outside. LLVM had presented its language and opened the framework for external tools. Many successful analyzers have built upon this universal, but a compiler-specific foundation.

© Springer Nature Switzerland AG 2020
O. Gervasi et al. (Eds.): ICCSA 2020, LNCS 12254, pp. 544–559, 2020.
https://doi.org/10.1007/978-3-030-58817-5_40

When the author was about to design an extensible static analysis framework [19], it was found that such universal IRs require a lot of extensions to be used efficiently. IR has to be wrapped to control flow graph nodes, own command wrappers; type system still has to be abstracted away for efficient conversion to solver formats (e.g. SMT-LIB for satisfiability modulo theories [6]), so it is essentially *separate* architecture and infrastructure side-by-side with the one provided by IR. Low-level IR adds overhead for most analyses, and high-level IR does not represent low-level primitives. What if they are combined and the redundant infrastructure is eliminated? Our hypothesis is that middle-level IR will still handle static analysis efficiently. That was the reason behind designing a new IR called Midair. Existing IRs are reviewed in Sect. 2, our requirements are shown in Sect. 3, and with all this insight our design solutions are judged in Sect. 4. A few notes on the used type system are in Sect. 5, a serialization mechanism is described in Sect. 6. The final evaluation results are presented in Sect. 7.

The project's *goal* is *to create an efficient middle-level intermediate representation, allowing for different analysis methods.* At least Abstract Syntax Tree analysis, control and data flow analyses, model checking and abstract interpretation are possible in that method and the author believes more analyses are necessarily suitable if the corresponding form is supported. At the moment of writing, there is no intention to support other purposes like compilation, code generation, etc. Therefore, these cases are not taken into account.

Novelty. The created IR has four representations with a simple "analyze & separate" transformation strategy, reducing the CPU and memory footprint between transformations. The built-in support for databases allows efficient resource loading. The IR suggests but does not enforce the cooperation between analysis passes by augmenting the IR with their results. To the knowledge of the author, no IR provides such features.

2   Related Work

Many sources [5,9] claim the following *classic* IR types. **Parse tree and Abstract Syntax Tree (AST)** serve the purpose of maintaining precise source mapping. In compilers and analyzers, this is the first structure that is often not considered an IR. In source-to-source systems, it is the first and the last representation. The AST and parse tree nodes might have duplicating children. **Directed Acyclic Graphs (DAG)** avoid the duplication introduced by AST. The DAG nodes might contain multi-parent children, so this IR is by definition smaller than AST. **The Control Flow Graph (CFG)** groups branch-free code. Such a technique helps determine control flow properties and is generally more applicable to other kinds of analysis.

There are five main linear forms. One and two address codes are now used too rarely, and **three-address code**, in which every command consists of two operands and the result, is still the foundation for many IRs. The **stack-machine code** is based on the concept of the stack: every parameter is pushed to stack or popped from it. This representation is very compact and still very popular. The **Static Single Assignment** form is different from the three-address code in the sense that variables are assigned only once.

Listed IRs are used in most projects, but complicated uses are all based on forks of these types. **SIMPLE** [12]—one of the first structured intermediate representations, employed in McCAT compiler. Effectively, it is not only SIMPLE but also FIRST and LAST representations, named by their actual appearance time during compilation.

GENERIC, **GIMPLE** [20], **RTL** (Registry Transfer Language) [2] are all different level intermediate representations used in GCC. GENERIC is a way to represent entire functions in trees. GIMPLE is influenced by SIMPLE, it is a simplified representation compared to GENERIC. RTL is a very low-level language limited to machine types. These IRs played a significant role in advancing compiler technologies, however, they are not widely used outside GCC community.

The **SUIF** [25] kernel features an intermediate representation, which is primarily used for optimization. This IR is of mixed-level: low-level operations are wrapped by high-level constructs, e.g. loops. That is ideologically close to our implementation. The **Soot** [24] started as an interprocedural Java bytecode analysis framework. It has four intermediate representations: Baf (a bytecode representation without complications), Jimple (3-address representation of byte code), Shimple (Single Static Assignment form of Jimple), and Grimp (unstructured representation of Java code). The difference compared to Midair is a focus on optimization, even though performing analysis is still possible. Also, Midair has more freely interpretable semantics with the intention of aggregating the results of different analyses. The **Byte Code Engineering Library (BCEL)** [1] is a byte code manipulation foundation for many language tools like FindBugs [13], AspectJ [14], etc.

Low Level Virtual Machine (LLVM) IR [3] is the language provided by LLVM. It is meant to be close to assembly and is created as the one IR for all analysis, compilation purposes. It features Static Single Assignment form, machine types, metadata support. The LLVM gradually changed the paradigm regarding the external usage of IRs. It is currently an industrial standard with many successful applications. **Multi-Level Intermediate Representation (MLIR)** [15] is a new language suggested by C. Lattner et al. It is built on top of the *dialect* concept. In some sense, it aims to be a superset of LLVM IR: the latter is considered just one of the possible MLIR dialects. For example, another existing dialect—**tf** from TensorFlow, a machine learning framework—adds tensors as the first-class types. The main focus is at more high-level optimization, i.e. let the compiler know some facts about the program that may help improve the output assembly.

C intermediate language (CIL) [21] is created specifically for program analysis and transformations. It comes with its parser and is said to support the most C features. It is not in active development at the moment of writing. **SAIL** [10]—static analysis intermediate language, suggested by I. Dillig,

T. Dillig and A. Aiken. It features high-level IR, which is close to Abstract Syntax Tree, and a low one, which is essentially a Control Flow Graph.

Boogie [16] is an intermediate verification language for other software verification tools to base on. Created by Microsoft Research, it provides a very comprehensive view of program analysis, combining both mathematics and programming foundations. Based on Racket, **Rosette** [23] is directed to be a programming language rather than IR. It provides a sufficient number of supported theories and data types, allowing for verification.

GraalVM [8] is a remarkable virtual machine for executing polyglot applications written in JVM-based, LLVM-based (e.g. via Sulong [22]) and other languages. It features the language implementation framework called Truffle [26], which provides means for creating AST-based interpreters. The Truffle AST partially covers the language-agnosticism required by our project, however, the described project requires additional flexibility. After all, GraalVM can be potentially used at the parsing stage as prerequisites before generating the Midair IR.

Also, it is worth mentioning **REIL** [11], a framework for static analysis of disassembled code, which is beyond the scope of this paper. Java [27] byte code is probably the most used IR in the world, and Microsoft's counterpart, MSIL or CIL [4], is the byte code for .NET technology. They both are based upon the concept of the stack machine code.

3   Requirements

We had the following set of requirements for the IR:

1. **Three-address code without Static Single Assignment (SSA) enforcement.**
   The SSA form is leaning towards code generation. It is still perfectly valid—not to say desirable—representation for analysis as well, yet a number of use cases imply more clear relations between variable versions:
   (a) Symbolic execution often does not require variable versions.
   (b) Detecting possible values for enumeration type variables.
   (c) The mapping between the source and the IR.
   Thus, the Midair does not enforce the single static assignment usage. LLVM and MLIR are both completely SSA, Boogie is on the other hand completely non-SSA.
2. **Ability to reuse Abstract Syntax Tree or Directed Acyclic Graph** for performance reasons.
   The performance is a major concern for any analysis, especially those associated with C-like languages which headers might inflate the global scope with thousands of unused objects. If it is possible to reuse AST/DAG, then a significant part of CPU cycles might be saved.
   LLVM language is completely unrelated to Clang or any other language AST, as well as Boogie is, so the mapping needs to be formed from scratch.

3. **Awareness of local and remote objects, possible reliance on the database.**
Objects have different scopes, might be obtained by different computational nodes. Some objects might be located remotely, so language should not enforce objects to be defined in place.
This requirement indirectly gives additional memory footprint reduction: e.g. C/C++ headers can have many possibly redundant cross-references. With the databases in mind, the analyzer might unload rarely used objects.

4. **The arbitrary type system, an ability to reuse short-lived interpretations.**
Each module using IR should contribute to the deep understanding of code, however, it is not trivial if command system enforces types, thus the types should only be suggested. Modules should be able to use the contributions of each other to a possible extent.
Of course, other IRs support omitting specific instructions, but for languages like LLVM IR it is not natural as only full program is supposed to be run. Recovering dependencies between over-simplified instructions might be a completely separate task.

While MLIR seems to have similar goals and even spelling, we believe it still mainly fitting for code generation. Unlike CIL, Midair was supposed to advance further by adopting a three-address code. Unlike Boogie and Rosette, it was supposed to leave mapping to the source (although it is harder in VM IR that we'll outline later). Based on these conclusions and existing IR overview, our intention was to set Midair right in the middle between verification and compilation to get the compilers' machine knowledge level, not sacrificing analysis quality.

The ultimate requirement is to have an architecture not narrowed to the specific analysis method. Compilation, optimization and code generation are not required at the current stage, so IR is not designed for them.

4   IR Overview

Midair consists of four representations (Fig. 1), ranging from DAG to designated virtual machine commands.

4.1   Plain Directed Acyclic Graph

First, we attacked defined problems by creating unified expression architecture [19]. The main idea is old: all language parsers create a unified representation (that is called *generalized syntax tree* in our implementation). Specific objects like structure declarations do not even have a direct equivalent in GST, they are saved directly to the type database. This GST consists of many C-like language constructs, the concepts of *statements, expressions*, and the notion of *resources*, as the objects including variables, functions, and implicit model objects.

The DAG helps find trivial issues with duplicate operands, unnecessary assignments, detects coding style violations.

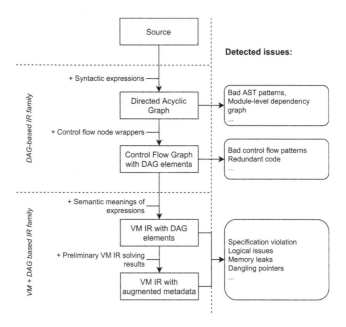

Fig. 1. Midair overview

4.2   Control Flow Graph with DAG Elements

The second step resembles the *Control Flow Graph* (CFG) construction. The DAG nodes are combined not only by the property of being branch-free but *any* property that may be considered worth differentiating by the analyzer. It is necessarily a syntax context, optionally a lockset, etc.

This representation is useful for the control flow checks, redundant code detection.

Transition to CFG. The transition from plain DAG is semantic-driven. The syntax traverse pass forms graph with linear, branch-free statements grouped within nodes. When a single statement is about to be added to some *active* graph node, it is verified against a predefined set of properties forming a *context*. If it operates in a different context, then it is saved to a separate CFG node. In this procedure, it is assumed that expressions are moved as is. The trivial scheme is shown in Fig. 2. This transition is reversible.

4.3   Virtual Machine Instructions

Our project uses a virtual machine [17] for performing data flow, model checking and abstract interpretation.

This level's intermediate representation is the only language for the virtual machine. It adds an understanding of what's happening within the DAG. All

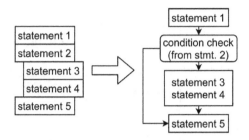

Fig. 2. Morphing between DAG and Control Flow Graph

the assignments, invocations, model checks are stated explicitly, so further verification passes do not have to look these facts up again.

Simplification Degrees. Two distinct simplification degrees exist in IRs. First, no simplification, just leaving DAG as it is in the source code. Second is over-simplifying: every operation essentially becomes an assignment in a three-address code.

We use a hybrid approach: all assigning, type-changing and some other operations are turned to assignments. All other operations remain as complex as they are in DAG. This has clear benefits for trivial operations. Approaching $x = a + b + c + d$ as the sequence of 4 loads and three sums is more computationally and memory expensive than just one command, yet reduced variance of commands is likely to benefit race condition analyses. If needed, a specific analysis pass may break the command to more instructions. Thus, with this approach, we are combining reduced search breadth with operations detailed enough for specific analysis type.

In our implementation, this process assumes *morphing*. Expressions do not get removed but are rather changed in place. This reduces the number of allocations required for analysis and positively improves performance.

Transition to VM Instructions. The transition from CFG to VM codes requires the knowledge of operational semantics of the target language. We will not cover it, but would rather show examples of conversion in Table 1.

if, do, for, while and other constructions are almost universally supported in imperative languages, so they form a basis of our language. This transition is the first to introduce the SSA form, and it is irreversible (Fig. 3).

Overview of VM Commands. The commands have the following syntax: [implicit] [dep] [property] *command* where **implicit** is set on commands created without clear user's request, **dep** signifies dependent commands made by diagnostic models, **property** determines the kind of information which can be retrieved by investigating the command, e.g. *safety*, *liveness*, etc. There are several big categories of *commands*:

1. Analysis-related commands.
   - **constraint** *expression* asserts an expression.

Table 1. The partial mapping between language constructs and VM IR

C construct	IR equivalent
type x	declare x:type
type f(args)	function f (args) → type end
if (cond)	branch *cond followup-kind* end branch -or- constraint *cond* -or- check *cond*
for (init; cond; inc)	assign *init* branch *cond* loop follows *inc* end branch
do; while (cond)	branch *cond* loop post end branch
while (cond)	branch *cond* loop end branch

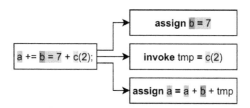

Fig. 3. Morphing between CFG/DAG and VM IR

- **check** *expression* indicates an always false expression that is still evaluated by the final computer/virtual machine.
- **annotate** (*annotation*) designates an ACSL [7] annotation for the next instruction.
2. Control flow altering commands.
    - **enter** [→ *var*] and **exit** signify block start and end, that defines variable visibility scopes.
    - **branch** *cond* [loop] [post] [*followup*]
      where *followup* can be *or continue* (signifies branch with else clause), *fallthrough* (signifies branch that must be exited, or it will enter the next clause), or *follows inc* (for incrementors)
    - **end branch** [*obj1, ..., objN*] ends the branch and signifies variables changed in a branch, which is immensely useful for variable elimination.

- **invoke** [*variable* =] *function*(*arg1*, ..., *argN*) calls the *function* and saves result to *variable*. The effect differs for intra- or interprocedural analyses.
- **return** *expression* acts as an assignment for the variable stated in **enter**. It is mapped to the **result** ACSL annotation variable.

3. Variable manipulation commands:
   - **declare** *resource* [= *expression*] adds a resource with a given ID to the current visibility list.
   - **load** *resource* prefetches a resource with a given ID, useful in case the variable is physically located on some other computational node.
   - **init** *variable* := *expression* sets the temporary variable to a specific value. It can be safely omitted if the command is processed on the computational node where simplification had been done as temporary variables are bound to values at that time.
   - **assign** *resource* = *expression* sets a resource to a given value.

4. Internal commands:
   - **system** *internal-expression* applies internal data to control or data flow. For example, we call it for replacing user-defined assert functions.
   - **augment** *name*: (*data*) adds an external object to the flow. This process is discussed in the next section.

4.4 Virtual Machine Instructions with Augmented Metadata

The last step feeds VM commands to passes each producing *augmentations* in their formats. For example, in our static analyzer project, we have SMT and Abstract Interpretation solver passes. SMT builds formulas in CVC4 terms and AI builds abstract domains approximating variables. The discovered facts are augmented back to IR (Fig. 4). Augmentation itself could not be helpful if passes did not have a possibility to reuse each other's results. For example, SMT solver may find abstract interpretation' insight about loop important for building better SMT models. A specific implementation might run passes again and again until all needed bits are retrieved, also it decides whether this data is permanent, i.e. saved to the index, or regenerated on demand.

4.5 An Example of a Function Computing Factorial

An example of a simple recursive function computing factorial is listed below. For CVC4 augmentation, we use a slightly modified syntax since the original one is verbose. For variables, we use the following naming schema: **NAME_N**, where NAME is the variable's name, and N is a revision number.

```
function factorial(n:int) -> int
enter -> res
  constraint n >= 0;
  branch n == 0 or continue
    | augment cvc4-sat-result:
      (indeterminate)
```

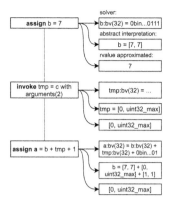

Fig. 4. IR with augmented solver's expressions

```
return 1
   | augment cvc4:
     (res_1 = 0bin0...01)
   | augment ai:
     (n == 0 => res_1 = 1)
   | augment ai-function:
     (n == 0 => return 1)
   | augment ai-approx:
     (n == 0 => (res_1 = 1))
end branch (res)
implicit branch (n != 0)
  | augment cvc4-sat-result:
    (indeterminate)
  invoke tmp = factorial(n - 1);
    | augment cvc4: (tmp = (<omitted
      due to size constraints>))
    | augment ai: (tmp =
      factorial(n - 1))
    | augment ai-approx:
      (tmp = [n - 1, inf])
  return n * tmp
    | augment cvc4:
      (res_2 = BVMUL(32, n, tmp))
    | augment ai:
      (n != 0 => res_2 = n * tmp)
    | augment ai-function:
      (n != 0 => return n * tmp)
    | augment ai-approx:
      (n != 0 => (res_2 = [n - 1, inf]
        * n = [n(n-1), inf]))
```

```
end branch
| augment cvc4-incompatible-branches:
  ((n == 0bin0...0) XOR
   NOT(n == 0bin0...0))
| augment cvc4:
  ((n == 0bin0...0 =>
     (res_3 = res_1)) AND
   (NOT(n == 0bin0...0) =>
     (res_3 = res_2)))
exit
| augment meta: (recursive,
  decreasing n, stops at n = 0)
| augment precond: (n >= 0)
| augment returns:
  (((n == 0) => return 1) XOR
   (n != 0) => return n *
     factorial(n - 1))
```

5   Type System

The type system [19] is made from scratch to allow for completely virtual
types, which are implemented as *unbounded* machine types. It provides a list
of integral machinery types of different endianness (e.g. **uint32_le**, **float80_be**,
float128_le, etc) with unambiguous patterns for cross-conversion, a set of
environments for well-known compilers, primarily GCC and Clang, and common CPU types including x86, x86_64, MIPS, private virtual processors. Every
expression has either fixed or a dynamic type. The type is fixed on explicit
or implicit casts, references, literals. A dynamic type is never saved and only
inferred using an internal inference mechanism taking language semantics into
account.

The type system provides API for all IR users. Type inference function is of
the most common use, the second most used function is a type trait retrieval
function, and the third is type conversion. With this API, all IR types get matching capabilities regarding handling complex types and type conversions.

A completely independent type system has the following benefits. First, it
adds fine-grained control of the supported features irrespective of CPU types,
used compiler or language semantics. Second, different level IRs can save space
by unifying the type system across them. Third, there is a better chance of
implementing support for conceptual languages, which is our goal in the long
run.

6   Serialization

In industry, it is expected that IR can be serialized and deserialized. Midair
supports two representations: textual and JSON. The textual representation is

useful for debugging, and that's what is presented in the paper. The deserialization from text is not that efficient as from JSON and it we tend to avoid in real code. JSON representation is suitable for parsing by external tools, for selected NoSQL databases like MongoDB. This is the primary use case, its scheme is presented in paper [18]. The binary serialization is being developed in the moment of writing for more performant indexing.

Why is serialization important? We pursue a few goals. First, program state space may be large, and it is highly probable that it will not fit the RAM. We unload global resources as soon as possible to avoid memory issues. Second, incremental analysis requires saving knowledge about the program to disk. The analyzer uses indices to find all missing yet required semantics and then loads it from disk. Third, we have a work-in-progress mechanism for searching within the state space using program query language, and compared to incremental analysis, it requires not just required semantics, but potentially all the semantics of a program.

The last important point is serializing target-independent binaries. When binary serialization is finished, it would be possible to pack IR to binary for distribution among cluster nodes. However, the input program target independence is not ensured at the moment of writing, thus after the IR is generated, it is not possible to relocate the program representation to another CPU architecture. It might be an interesting challenge for future versions.

7 Evaluation

Comparing IRs from a *practical* perspective is often impractical. The reason is that implementation drives the results, they are barely comparable. The efforts to build two distinct implementations—yet sufficiently optimized to ensure fair comparison—are too high. Instead, we prepared a study of practical implications of decisions made in Midair, and how they impact the real-world use in our extensible static analyzer [19].

7.1 Decisions and Their Impact

There were a few critical decisions made to comply with the requirements.

First, the arbitrary type system. The API supports type and transformation definitions, type inference, however, the actual type handling is on IR users. In result, the code directly related to type support makes 9.9% of CVC4-based analysis pass code base and 1% for abstract interpretation implementation. This difference is caused by the fact that Abstract Interpretation types map to internal type system more naturally.

Second, the static single assignment form choice. The abstract interpreter is based on a non-SSA version of IR, and CVC4 pass uses SSA. This difference requires efforts to bridge the gap between versioned and unversioned variables, allowing for the cooperation. In the project, the problem was fixed by essentially doing all computations in SSA form but removing versions when needed. That consideration reduced the need to save non-SSA IR.

Third, low-footprint morphing between IRs. In the testing, it gives significant savings. It was measured that IR preparation takes 10% of execution time while converting to SMT and verifying it requires up to 70% of the time.

Fourth, the database support. In practice, saving all objects to MongoDB increases execution time by the factor of 2–2.5, 1.5–2 for internal binary cache facility. However, when applied only to the global scope in headers, the increase for both facilities is only 1.1–1.2. The memory savings are more significant: it may cut memory usage by the factor of 2–3. The actual value depends on the data structure.

7.2   IR Properties

A few properties of the IR were evaluated:

- *Simple translation.* Considering that Midair is imperative, the conversion from LLVM and other "low-level" imperative IRs is trivial, however, not advantageous. The lack of knowledge of input program, e.g. loops, decreases the details the interpreter of Midair might take from it. So, at the moment of writing, the authors believe that evaluating the bidirectional translation requires further examination.
- *Hardware neutrality.* No types are pre-defined: they have to be supported by an interpreter. Thus, the language is completely hardware-neutral. To prove that statement, the authors apply it to several CPUs, including x86, ARM, MIPS (both big-endian and little-endian) and one private virtual machine.
- *Extensibility.* The language has a few "backdoors" for new functionality: first, a strict expression system is not provided. Second, the commands do not have a predefined storage format. With that, it is trivial to change commands and expressions when needed.
- *Semantic gap between source languages and the IR* is not big if only program semantics is considered. The transformation routine implies desugaring of syntax, so the issues arising from the syntax itself are not seen on Midair level.

8   Discussion

The main trade-off comes from a single command size. VM IR is not compact in the sense that it is not possible to use several bytes per command like it is in RISC assembly. A big command means fewer commands and less decoding, resulting in a higher level of abstraction. Also, IR is not serializable to just one representation. The advantage here is that more disk space is left for routine semantics. The disadvantage is that local and temporary variables consume the global symbol table. However, no changes are planned at the moment.

The other issue is a number of IRs to translate between. For C, it is Clang AST, GST or DAG, CFG with DAG elements, VM IR and augmented VM

IR. Even for intended cheap moving, running translation is costly. Our solution is that AST, GST, and CFG with DAG elements are not preserved as they are not required later. VM IR is what saved globally, and solver augmentation is volatile. The latter comes from the fact that not all deductions might be permanent. It has a performance effect since SMT conversion is by far the most expensive operation according to profiling data (40+% of Callgrind samples are taken when converting to SMT). This issue is being worked on. That profiling data also shows that translation from source to Clang AST and then to VM IR takes at most 5% of the time (this timing represents a subset of work done for IR preparation and transformations), which is acceptable.

We believe the development direction going forward would be to further discriminate between semantical actions (represented by complete VM IR commands) and syntactic constructions (represented by expressions). At the moment of writing, a big part of the syntax is passed to solvers as is, of course, not without extensive help for types and control flow management provided by the framework.

The foremost goal for the whole intermediate representation is to pursue more analysis features. For example, fusing variables in Static Single Assignment form is currently left entirely to the code, it is not a clearly defined command. There is no detection of loop transformations or even clear indication that the loop's body has independent iterations. It will all simplify solver passes, but we have to collect more experience to make such a generalization smooth.

The development started when MLIR did not exist. What can be interesting is representing Midair as MLIR dialect, making performant IR-to-native code compilation for faster analysis.

9 Conclusion

We presented Midair, a multi-purpose intermediate representation for program analysis. Its position among other IR was shown. We demonstrated how four representations of the IR materialize and transform: from Directed Acyclic Graph (DAG) to Control Flow Graph with DAG elements, and then to virtual machine (VM) IR and VM IR with augmented metadata. The important property of our IR is *morphing*: basic expressions are passed from DAG to CFG and VM IR as is without major modifications, saving time and RAM/disk space. The latter encourages cooperation between analysis passes. Another property is an ability to serialize any level IR to disk: thus it is possible to save intermediate results and continue later, allowing for incremental analysis. For VM IR, we presented a set of commands related to analysis, control flow and variable manipulation, and internal needs. The IR has its strong points in comparison to well-known IRs and we certainly look forward to its further development.

References

1. Apache Commons BCEL. https://commons.apache.org/proper/commons-bcel/
2. GNU Compiler Collection (GCC) internals: RTL. https://gcc.gnu.org/onlinedocs/gccint/RTL.html
3. LLVM Language Reference. https://llvm.org/docs/LangRef.html
4. Standard ECMA-335 - Common Language Infrastructure (CLI). http://www.ecma-international.org/publications/standards/Ecma-335.htm
5. Aho, A.: Compilers: Principles, Techniques, and Tools. Always Learning. Pearson, London (2014)
6. Barrett, C., Tinelli, C.: Satisfiability modulo theories. In: Clarke, E., Henzinger, T., Veith, H., Bloem, R. (eds.) Handbook of Model Checking, pp. 305–343. Springer, Cham (2018). https://doi.org/10.1007/978-3-319-10575-8_11
7. Baudin, P., Filliâtre, J.C., Marché, C., Monate, B., Moy, Y., Prevosto, V.: ACSL: ANSI C specification language (2008)
8. Bonetta, D.: GraalVM: metaprogramming inside a polyglot system (invited talk). In: Proceedings of the 3rd ACM SIGPLAN International Workshop on Meta-Programming Techniques and Reflection, pp. 3–4 (2018)
9. Cooper, K., Torczon, L.: Engineering a Compiler. Elsevier Science, Amsterdam (2011)
10. Dillig, I., Dillig, T., Aiken, A.: SAIL: static analysis intermediate language with a two-level representation. Technical report (2009)
11. Dullien, T., Porst, S.: REIL: a platform-independent intermediate representation of disassembled code for static code analysis (2009)
12. Hendren, L., Donawa, C., Emami, M., Gao, G., Sridharan, B.: Designing the McCAT compiler based on a family of structured intermediate representations. In: Banerjee, U., Gelernter, D., Nicolau, A., Padua, D. (eds.) LCPC 1992. LNCS, vol. 757, pp. 406–420. Springer, Heidelberg (1992). https://doi.org/10.1007/3-540-57502-2_61
13. Hovemeyer, D., Pugh, W.: Finding bugs is easy. ACM SIGPLAN Notices **39**(12), 92–106 (2004)
14. Kiczales, G., Hilsdale, E., Hugunin, J., Kersten, M., Palm, J., Griswold, W.G.: An overview of AspectJ. In: Knudsen, J.L. (ed.) ECOOP 2001. LNCS, vol. 2072, pp. 327–354. Springer, Heidelberg (2001). https://doi.org/10.1007/3-540-45337-7_18
15. Lattner, C., Pienaar, J.: MLIR Primer: A Compiler Infrastructure for the End of Moore's Law (2019)
16. Leino, K.R.M.: This is Boogie 2. Manuscr. KRML **178**(131), 9 (2008)
17. Menshchikov, M.: Scalable semantic virtual machine framework for language-agnostic static analysis. In: Distributed Computing and Grid-technologies in Science and Education, pp. 213–217 (2018)
18. Menshikov, M.: An approach to storing program semantics in static program analysis. In: Proceedings of The L Annual International Conference on Control Processes and Stability (CPS 2019), pp. 313–320 (2019)
19. Menshikov, M.: Equid—a static analysis framework for industrial applications. In: Misra, S., et al. (eds.) ICCSA 2019. LNCS, vol. 11619, pp. 677–692. Springer, Cham (2019). https://doi.org/10.1007/978-3-030-24289-3_50

20. Merrill, J.: GENERIC and GIMPLE: a new tree representation for entire functions. In: Proceedings of the 2003 GCC Developers' Summit, pp. 171–179. Citeseer (2003)
21. Necula, G.C., McPeak, S., Rahul, S.P., Weimer, W.: CIL: intermediate language and tools for analysis and transformation of C programs. In: Horspool, R.N. (ed.) CC 2002. LNCS, vol. 2304, pp. 213–228. Springer, Heidelberg (2002). https://doi.org/10.1007/3-540-45937-5_16
22. Rigger, M., Grimmer, M., Wimmer, C., Würthinger, T., Mössenböck, H.: Bringing low-level languages to the JVM: efficient execution of LLVM IR on Truffle. In: Proceedings of the 8th International Workshop on Virtual Machines and Intermediate Languages, pp. 6–15 (2016)
23. Torlak, E., Bodik, R.: Growing solver-aided languages with Rosette. In: Proceedings of the 2013 ACM International Symposium on New ideas, New Paradigms, and Reflections on Programming & Software, pp. 135–152 (2013)
24. Vallée-Rai, R. Co, P., Gagnon, E., Hendren, L., Lam, P., Sundaresan, V.: Soot - a java bytecode optimization framework. In: Proceedings of the 1999 Conference of the Centre for Advanced Studies on Collaborative Research, CASCON 1999, p. 13. IBM Press (1999)
25. Wilson, R.P., et al.: SUIF: an infrastructure for research on parallelizing and optimizing compilers. ACM SIGPLAN Notices 29(12), 31–37 (1994)
26. Wimmer, C., Würthinger, T.: Truffle: a self-optimizing runtime system. In: Proceedings of the 3rd Annual Conference on Systems, Programming, and Applications: Software for Humanity, pp. 13–14 (2012)
27. Yellin, F., Lindholm, T.: The Java virtual machine specification (1996)

Pasture Monitoring Applying Normalized Difference Vegetation Index (NDVI) Time Series with Sentinel-2 and Landsat 8 Images, to Improve Milk Production at Santa Mónica Farm, Imbabura, Ecuador

Garrido Fernando[✉] and Caranqui Víctor

Department of Software Engineering and Artificial Intelligence,
Faculty of Engineering in Applied Sciences, Technical University of the North,
Avenue 17 de Julio 5-21, Ibarra, Ecuador
{jfgarridos,vcaranqui}@utn.edu.ec

Abstract. The soils have had an increasing pressure due to the intensification of their use for agriculture, forestry, grazing and urbanization. In this way, the implementation of good practices for sustainable soil management are essential to reverse their tendency to degradation as preventive measures and so, guarantee food security and protect the provision of different ecosystem services associated with the soil. The advent of the Sentinel and Landsat satellite programs provide free data sets with good spatial and temporal resolution that can be a valuable source of information for monitoring pasture resources. In order to evaluate this type of techniques, a time series (TS) was generated with images of the Landsat 8 (L8) OLI (*Operational Land Imager*) sensor and a time series with images of the Sentinel-2 (S2), MSI (*Multispectral Imager*) sensor to determine the best results in the quantification of changes in the coverage of pastures at the Santa Mónica farm. In this study, pastures were analyzed using the normalized difference vegetation index (NDVI) time series obtained from median quarterly mosaics obtained in 2019. Different samples were drawn that represent the change trend throughout the time series and were classified according to their degree of change and persistence in the series. The results indicate that the densification of the time series allows to provide better results in the quantification of the changes and dynamics of the coverage. The established methodology represents a great advance on the generation of images and the monitoring and detection of changes in coverage through time series [22]. Hence, it is one the first studies carried out in the country that incorporate this type of process. It was concluded that the determination of spectral signatures with the index used together with the near infrared (NIR) and short wave infrared (SWIR 1) spectral bands, allow to extract values and intervals where the change produced by pastures is identified with an acceptable level of accuracy.

Keywords: Sentinel-2 · Landsat 8 · Pastures · Vegetation index · Livestock · Teledetection · Remote sensing · Time series

© Springer Nature Switzerland AG 2020
O. Gervasi et al. (Eds.): ICCSA 2020, LNCS 12254, pp. 560–575, 2020.
https://doi.org/10.1007/978-3-030-58817-5_41

1 Introduction

Livestock in Ecuador depends on grazing, in this scope pastures are more than the cheapest food available for livestock feed. They offer all the necessary nutrients for good animal performance. Therefore, everything that can be done to improve the pasture production technology will directly result in milk production. Pasture management, together with local climatic conditions will affect pasture productivity and quality, and therefore agricultural production.

Therefore, there is a need for regular forage monitoring and prediction of pasture growth rates, providing milk producers who practice controlled or rotary pasture grazing systems, which consists of rotating livestock within the Soil, to avoid compacting soils (especially in the rainy season), in this way the soil is allowed to rest and improves the regrowth of grasslands. The way grazing in which is managed has a major impact on the physical [2], chemical and biological properties of soils. If lawn quantity and quality can be determined from space (i.e. via satellite), with adequate precision and spatial/ temporal resolution. This opens up a number of possibilities for more efficient pasture management and a more profitable pasture farming [4].

The number of satellite Earth observation systems is increasing and therefore the information available to users is increasing. Higher resolution, cloud-free, imagery, such as captured by Landsat 8 (L8) and Sentinel-2 (S2) [6], provides excellent information on surface heterogeneity and vegetation extent, but it cannot provide adequate multi-angle observations to accurately capture the true effects of surface anisotropy [7].

The use of remote sensing for monitoring and predicting forage crops used for grazing or silage in animal and dairy production systems is not well established due to the fact that intensive grazing pastures are highly dynamic systems and grass need to be carefully kept at the optimum height to avoid overuse of grassland. Despite these limitations, there have been notable investigations mainly in the use of the time series Normalized *Difference Vegetation Index* (NDVI) [8].

The objective of this research is to determine to what extent L8 and S2 are compatible in the construction of time series of vegetation indexes for identification and monitoring of pastures and to present the results of the verification of robust algorithms that can be applied to a variety of pasture types and throughout the growing season in three parcel categories (occupied, rest, and dry) that differ in pasture types and management regimen in Area Of Interest (AOI). For this reason, the Determination of Spectral Signatures in Crops is used, these spectral traces depend on the optical properties of the plants, which are also a function of various factors such as radiation conditions, plant species, the thickness of the leaves, the structure of the leaf surface, the levels of the chlorophyll content and the internal structure of the leaves.

As is well known, solar radiation is the primary source of energy for numerous biological processes that the crop has. Much of the solar radiation is absorbed by the plants or rather the leaves and is converted into heat and used to maintain its temperature and processes of thermal effects [18, 19]. The leaves have a first contact with radiation, the value of the light that is absorbed or transmitted between the leaves depends on their wavelength and the absorption selectivity of the leaf pigments [9]. The analysis of spectral signatures of pasture crops is carried out with the help of geographic information system tools to obtain the characteristics of electromagnetic radiation with the structure of the pasture. The spectral signatures of pastures of the Regions of Interest (ROIs) or Training Areas are used.

2 Methods and Materials

2.1 Study Site

The present investigation was carried out at "Santa Mónica" farm, a property belonging to the Universidad Técnica del Norte, located 14 km from Ibarra city, in the area of Ilumán, in Imbabura province (0°17′N, 78°14′W). It has a perimeter of 106.7 hectares which is currently used for planting pastures and forage for around 300 dairy cows.

Its relief corresponds to an area mainly on slopes and extends in the central and southern part of the study area. The current use of the land is high with irrigation, exclusively for controlled or Intensive Rotary Beef Grazing. The frequency of permanence of the cattle in a single place depends on the existence and quality of the grass distributed in 96 hectares with 8 lots that oscillate between 0.5 and 3 hectares. The rest period is 20 days and the occupation period are 3 days. Additionally, 75% of the pastures at the farm are composed of Star grass (Cynodon nlemfuensis), the remaining 25% is found in Brachiarias species, such as decumbens and brizhanta (wire grass, bitter grass, hairy grass), in monoculture or mixed with Star. The predominance of pastoral use is found in the south west and south east of the study area, particularly in the lower parts and on slopes where important herds of cattle have been established. The study site is a combination with rest areas for grazing in the extreme south (named "reservorios" and "huertas"), where the cattle are grazed in pounding or folding (see Fig. 1).

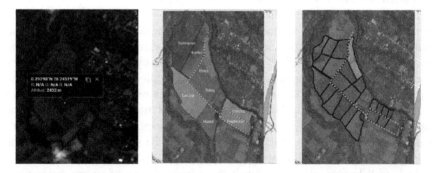

Fig. 1. Santa Mónica farm: Location, Lots and Plots. Source: own illustration.

The climate of the study site corresponds to equatorial semi-humid mesothermal, with extreme variations between day and night, whose average annual temperature is approximately 15 °C, the minimum average being 9 °C and the maximum being

20 °C. It receives a greater amount of solar energy than a similar surface located at sea level due to its geographical location and height [32].

It allows global solar irradiation to reach high values throughout the year due to its location at zero latitude with an annual average of 533 cal/cm^2/day. The average annual rainfall in this region is 852.8 mm, distributed in two rainy seasons (January to June and September to December), the dry months occur in July and August; relative humidity between 65 and 85%. However, there are also areas with low humidity. The average wind speed is 3 km/h. The driest month is July, with 16 mm of rain, and April is the warmest month of the year, and July is the coldest month of the year [33].

According to the study of the Agroecological Zoning of the study area between Pinsaquí and San Roque town, problems were identified, such as frost, hail, droughts, which hinder the development of crops, causing large losses, especially on the farm that requires grazing due to its dedication to milk production.

2.2   Controlled or Rotational Grazing

After a long period of pasture utilization, major changes in soil structure may occur such as compaction, which clogs the porous system, increases runoff and entrainment of particles, loss of organic matter, and decreased development of fine roots and, therefore, nutrient extraction [10].

Taking into account the economic and productive impact of degraded pastures on bovine production systems and the need to make decisions regarding the loss of pasture status and the absence of indicators that facilitate the implementation of the most relevant recovery practices, many milk producers use rotational grazing, where the interval or frequency of grazing (paddock rest) [1] is a function of the time the plant needs to regrow, recover organic reserves and complete the formation of green leaves. The density of the plant biomass makes it easier for cows to pluck the grass with their tongues to achieve large bite sizes and to facilitate the ingestion rate. On this subject Agnusdei [11], indicates that the consumption rates reach maximum values of 3.5–4 kg DM/h with heights greater than 18 cm; however, the consumption rates remained high (3 kg DM/h) in pastures of 15 cm and that the achievement of high intakes in dairy cows can be achieved both with high pastures (>15 cm) or with denser and lower pastures (<15 cm). The ideal meadow should have high availability and superior quality [12].

In order to establish a rotational grazing system, the systematic plan of rotations is established, that is, a regular sequence of periods of rest and periods of grazing or occupation of a series of grazing areas (set of plots or paddocks) is established in a cattle farm [13]. In this way it can be said that the number of paddocks and their formula to calculate it is given by Eq. (1):

$$Number\ of\ paddocks = \frac{\substack{Rest\ period \\ appropriate\ for\ the\ grass}}{\substack{Occupation\ period \\ of\ each\ group}} + number\ of\ grazing\ groups \quad (1)$$

The rest period is given by the optimal time required by the plant species to restore, through photosynthetic activity, the carbohydrate levels required to ensure good regrowth. The occupation time, that is, the total time in which a pasture is grazed (by one or several groups of animals) must be short enough so that the animals do not eat the sprouts of the plants eaten at the end. grazing. Ideally, the animals should be removed from the lot, leaving such a proportion of young and active leaves that it is possible to continue using solar radiation and the adequate movement of reserving carbohydrates from the base of the plant and the root, in addition to protect the reproductive organs.

The grazing period is recommended not to exceed 8 days, since longer times of permanence of the animals in the pasture would affect the emergence of regrowth's, since there is the possibility that a plant is grazed more than once, with which it is it affects the individual production of the plant and the grassland and this is detrimental to its persistence [14]. The grazing period also depends on the number of animals and the type of animal that is used, for example, for a cow producing 18 L of milk it is appropriate to use 1-day grazing times, for cows of 10-12 L 2-3 grazing days would be indicated, while for cows of 6-8 L, grazing times may be used 4 day grazing [15].

The factors that influence the state of the pastures, obtained by the association of indicators of condition and water erosion, on the one hand with variables related to pasture management (establishment, height of pasture, age of pasture, days of occupation and rest, fertilization, herbal cleansing, pest management and animal load) and on the other, with biophysical variables (slope and altitude), were the slope, amount of seed sown at the time of establishment, days of occupation and rest. As a general rule, it is admitted that, from the height of the pasture at the time of pasture, 2/3 parts can be eaten by animals, while 1/3 part must be reserved for regrowth [12].

Many dairy farmers who practice rotational grazing systems generally track pasture productivity through the "field walk," to visually estimate grass biomass by simply estimating grass height. Therefore, this empirical way of measuring can lead to an inaccurate prediction of available lawn biomass with a consequent reduction in utilization efficiency [16].

2.3   Multispectral Satellites

There are several satellites with different characteristics that acquire multispectral images of the Earth's surface, they are particularly useful for monitoring land cover because the images are provided free of charge and can be downloaded directly from various platforms.

Landsat Satellites. Landsat is a set of satellites developed by NASA (*National Aeronautics and Space Administration of USA*) and the USGS (*United States Geological Survey*) [10], since the early 1970's, the launch of ERTS-1 (Earth Resources Technology Satellite, later renamed Landsat 1) began the era from a series of satellites that have since acquired continuous form of land data obtained by space-based remote sensing. The latest Landsat series satellite, the Landsat Data Continuity Mission (LDCM), was launched on February 11, 2013. Now renamed Landsat 8, the data acquired by the satellite continues to expand the access for users from around the world [17].

The Operational Land Image (OLI) sensor and the Infrared Thermal Sensor (TIRS) presents the Landsat 8 satellite and the images consist of nine spectral bands with a 30-m spatial resolution of Bands 1 to 7 and 9. Ultra-blue band 1 is useful for cost and aerosol studies. Band 9 is useful for detecting cirrus clouds. The resolution of band 8 (panchromatic) is 15 m. Thermal Bands 10 and 11 are useful for providing the most accurate surface temperatures and are collected at 100 meters. The approximate size is 170 km scene from north to south by 183 km from east to west [6].

Sentinel-2 Satellite. The recent satellite program of the European Space Agency (ESA) [20, 21] of the Copernicus Sentinel-2 program comprises two satellites (2A, 2B) that ensure the continuity of the SPOT and LANDSAT programs and provide images with pixel size as fine as 10 m every five days (depending on latitude) [3]. The first Sentinel-2A satellite was launched on June 23rd, 2015, and the Sentinel-2B was launched on March 7th, 2017. The Sentinel-2B flies 180° opposite Sentinel-2A, with both spacecraft occupying synchronous orbits of the Sun at an altitude of approximately 786 km and covering Earth's land surfaces, large islands, inland and coastal waters of 84° N and 56° S [8]. It allows obtaining information on the two wavelengths, visible and infrared, allowing monitoring of changes in land and vegetation, as well as global monitoring of climate change [18]. It has an Multi Spectral Instrument (MSI) sensor that has 13 bands, of which four of them (in blue, green, red and near infrared) have 10 m of spatial resolution, six have 20 m of resolution that include bands on the red-edge and SWIR and the other three are 60 m for atmospheric correction and cloud detection.

The recent Sentinel-2 satellites in combination with Landsat (7 or 8), in both cases with freely available images [21], are ideal for monitoring pasture biomass availability on pasture farms and offer the opportunity to develop robust algorithms to exploit its potential in efficient and profitable pasture monitoring [5], and increase the possibilities of having time series data with higher spatial resolutions and denser, expanding the possibilities of its use in agriculture [19].

2.4   Classification of Land Cover

The objective of this study is to evaluate how different textural characteristics contribute to discriminate most types of vegetation and the state of pastures.

Vegetation Index. Vegetation analysis and detection of changes in vegetation patterns are key to the evaluation and monitoring of natural resources. So it is not surprising that the detection and quantitative evaluation of green vegetation is one of the main applications of remote sensing for natural resource management and decision making [22].

Chlorophyll is a pigment of plants, which gives them their green color and absorbs the light necessary for photosynthesis, energy strongly in the bands centered at 0.45 and 0.67 μm. That is why we perceive healthy green vegetation, due to the great absorption in blue and red by the leaves and the reflection in the green. When the vegetation is not healthy, the chlorophyll decreases, and the result is an increase in the spectral reflectance in the red, making the leaves appear yellowish (a mixture of green and red). In vegetation, the level of reflectance is mainly modified by factors such as: the types of pigments, the structure of the leaves and the moisture content. The first affects wavelengths of the visible spectrum (0.4–0.7 m) where 65% is absorbed by Chlorophyll, 29% by Xanthophyll and 6% by Carotenes [23].

Additionally, changes in vegetation vigor and infrared imaging have been valuable in detecting and mapping the presence, distribution, and extent of diseased crops and insect infestations. In addition, changes in leaf structure that accompany the natural maturity of crops are subject to detection with infrared imaging [24]. The spectral signature characteristic of healthy vegetation shows a clear behavior between the red bands (0.6 to 0.7 µm) and the near infrared (0.7 to 1.1 µm). There is a notable spectral contrast between the RED band of the spectrum and that of the NIR, which allows separating healthy vegetation from other covers [26].

Normalized Difference Vegetation Index – NDVI. It is an index used to measure the normalized difference between Red and Near Infrared (near IR) reflectance's, providing a measure of the quantity, quality and development of vegetation cover and vigor in large areas [25]. The frequent use of the **NDVI** for studies like the one here has been carried out, is that the active vegetation has a different behavior in the Red and near IR bands: in the visible region of the electromagnetic spectrum, the pigments of the leaves absorb most of the energy they receive by minimally reflecting the received solar energy, while in the near IR the absorption is very low and therefore the reflectivity is much higher than in Red.

For this reason, a spectral contrast is produced between these bands, which allows the vegetation to be clearly separated from other coverings [27]. For the S2 image, three NDVIs were used as a result of the combination of the bands: 6-4, 7-4 and 8-4, since bands 6 and 7 are specifically located in the spectral region of the red margin, whose purpose it is to detect changes in the biological state of the pastures [28], while band 8 is already considered in the near IR. For L8 the NDVI was performed between bands 5-4 since in this sensor band 5 is in the near IR. It can be seen in Fig. 2 that the adjustment lines obtained between sensors for the NDVI indexes are slightly above the 1: 1 line. This means that in a same pixel the value of the NDVI index in Landsat would be above the value in Sentinel [19].

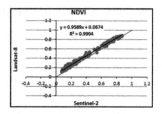

Fig. 2. NDVI relationship between Landsat-8 and Sentinel-2. Source: illustration based on [19].

The NDVI at L8 and S2 is calculated using the following expression [25]:

$$NDVI = (B5 - B4)/(B5 + B4) \, \text{Landsat 8}$$
$$NDVI = (B8A - B4)/(B8A + B4) \, \text{Sentinel - 2}$$

(2)

The range of the NDVI value varies between -1 and 1. Due to the strong relationship between this index and the photosynthetic activity of plants, this index is widely used to analyze the condition of vegetation, biomass, vegetation cover, among others.

Landsat 8 and Sentinel-2 Bands Color Composition. A band composition is an image made up of the combination of three different bands of the sensor and each arranged in the three projection channels on the screen: Red (R), Green (G) and Blue (B). The RGB scene results in a color image and they are: infrared, false color for urban detection, atmospheric penetration analysis, natural color, vegetation analysis, Normalized Differential Water Index (NDWI), Normalized Difference Snow Index (NDSI), Enhanced Vegetation Index (EVI).

Automatic Classification. The classification process, in the context of remote sensing, consists of assigning to each pixel of the original image a label corresponding to one of the classes that we either predefine prior to the classification process or, due to the similarity of the characteristics of the pixels of the image to classify, are automatically grouped in the process. For this, classifiers are used, defined as methods, criteria or algorithms that are used as a mechanism to assign these pixels or segments to each category [31].

Classes and Macro Classes. Land cover classes are identified with an arbitrary ID code (identifier). SCP (Semi-Automatic Classification Plugin) [30] allows creating ROIs defining the Classes and Macro classes. Each ROI is identified with a class ID (C) and each ROI is assigned to a land cover class through a macro class ID (MC). Macro classes are integrated of various materials that have different spectral signatures; to achieve good classification results, the spectral signatures of different materials must be separated, even if they belong to the same macro class. Therefore, multiple ROIs will be created for each macro class (setting the same MC macro class ID but assigning a different class ID (C) for each ROI). Table 1 shows the macro classes and classes created for this study.

Table 1. Macro Classes and classes of the AOI Santa Mónica farm.

Name Macro class	Macro class ID	Name class	Class ID
Pastures	1	Resting pastures	1
Pastures	1	Active pastures	2
Vegetation	2	Gully	4
Vegetation	2	Undergrowth	5
Pastures	1	Dry pasture	3

Source: own elaboration

Therefore, Classes are subsets of a Macro class, as shown in Fig. 3.

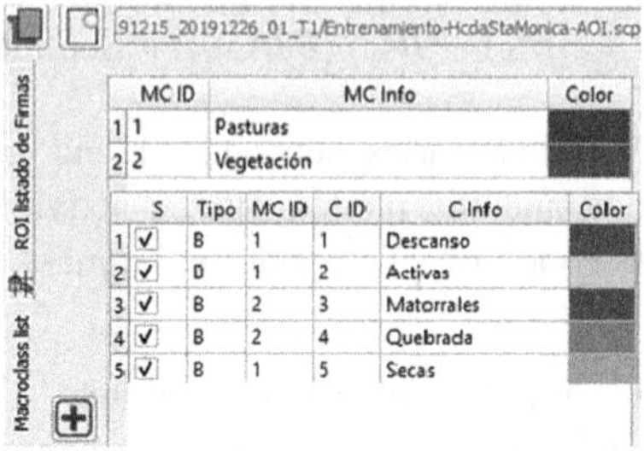

Fig. 3. List of signatures of the training areas at Santa Mónica farm; source: own study.

Spectral Signatures. Once electromagnetic energy reaches the earth's surface, it interacts with each type of material, either by reflection, absorption, or transmission, according to a spectral response pattern. This distinctive behavior of each type of material is exploited in image classification processes, and it is common to refer it as "spectral signature" [31].

If the spectral behavior of the plant canopy is analyzed, healthy vegetation offers low reflectivity in the red band of the spectrum (between 600 and 700 nm) and high in the near infrared (between 800 and 1000 nm), so that the higher the "vigor" the vegetation presents, the greater the contrast between the reflectance values captured in both bands [23].

Spectral Distance. It is useful to assess the spectral distance (or separability) between training signatures or pixels to assess whether different classes that are very similar to each other could cause classification errors. The Euclidean Distance has been used in this study, which is particularly useful for evaluating the results of the minimum distance classification. The Euclidean Distance is calculated from the center of the source cell to the center of each of the surrounding cells. Conceptually, the Euclidean algorithm works as follows: for each cell, the distance to each source cell is determined by calculating the hypotenuse with x_max and y_max as the other two sides of the triangle. This calculation derives the true Euclidean distance, rather than the cell distance. The shortest distance to an origin is determined, and if it is less than the specified maximum distance, the value is assigned to the location of the cell in the output raster (see Fig. 4).

	MC_ID = 1 MC_info = Pasturas C_ID = 1 C_info = Secas
	MC_ID = 1 MC_info = Pasturas C_ID = 2 C_info = Descanso
Jeffries-Matusita distance	n/a
Spectral angle	8.53773646251593e-07
Euclidean distance	3.644139862357838e-11
Bray-Curtis similarity [%]	99.9999973128634

Fig. 4. Spectral Distance between Dry Pastures and Rest Pastures of the AOI Santa Mónica farm. Source: own study.

2.5   Field Data Collection

The data of the study area were obtained during 2019 from the Sentinel-2 satellite [bands 2, 3, 4, 5, 6, 7, 8, 8A, 11.12] and from the Landsat 8 satellite [bands 2.3, 4,5,6,7], for this, Landviewer and Crop Monitoring satellite image platforms for remote sensing, applications developed by EOS DATA ANALYTICS, INC. [29]. With the images of the specified AOI (Area of Interest) it was possible to filter images by different criteria, mainly by year, month, percentage of cloudiness and solar elevation. Images with the highest spatial resolution ($\sim 0.5–1.5$ m/pxl) as a separate data source. They also have a period of frequent data review (≤ 1 day), which allowed controlling the conditions of the requested land surface.

The preliminary phase (cabinet) initially consisted of processing satellite images to identify: use, coverage, physiography of the terrain and access roads based on the following procedures.

Radiometric Correction. This procedure was performed to compensate for radiometric errors that may exist in the images. These errors are usually the result of defects in the operation of the sensors. Through radiometric correction, the image improved in its visual quality.

Resampling at 15 m. Landsat 8 images have the advantage of a panchromatic band with a spatial resolution of 15 m. This procedure allowed data from the multispectral reflection bands (1 to 5 and 7) with spatial resolution of 30 m to be resampled to 15 m.

Atmospheric Correction. Dark Object Subtraction (DOS), which is a family of image-based on atmospheric corrections [34], has been used for this study. Chavez [35] explains that "the basic assumption is that in the image some pixels are completely in shadow and, their radiation received from the satellite is due to atmospheric dispersion (haze effect). This assumption is combined with the fact that very few elements on the Earth's surface have an absolute black color. Therefore, an assumed reflectance of one percent is better than zero percent". The haze effect is given by Eq. (3) [36].

$$L_p = L_{min} - L_{DO1\%} \tag{3}$$

where:

L_{min} = "" radiance that corresponds to a digital value for which the sum of all pixels with digital values less than or equal to this value is equal to 0.01% of all pixels in the image under consideration" [37]. Therefore, the radiance obtained with that digital count value (DN_{min}).
$L_{DO1\%}$ = radiance of the dark object, with an assumed value of reflectance of 0.01.

In particular for Landsat images:

$$L_{min} = ML * DN_{min} + AL \tag{4}$$

Sentinel-2 images are converted to radiance before DOS1 calculation [30]. The Radiance of the Dark Object is given by Eq. (5):

$$L_{DO1\%} = 0,01 * [(ESUN_\lambda * \cos \theta_s * T_z) - E_{down}] * T_v / (\pi * d_2) \qquad (5)$$

Therefore, the haze effect is:

$$L_p = ML * DN_{min} + AL - 0,01 * [(ESUN_\lambda * \cos \theta_s * T_z) - E_{down}] * T_v / (\pi * d_2) \quad (6)$$

For Landsat 8, ESUN [38] can be calculated with Eq. (7):

$$ESUN = (\pi * d_2) * (RADIANCE_{MAXIMUM} / REFLECTANCE_{MAXIMUM}) \qquad (7)$$

where RADIANCE_MAXIMUM and REFLECTANCE_MAXIMUM is provided in the image metadata.

Figure 5 It shows the atmospheric correction made to images S2 and L8 of our study area, using the DOS1 algorithm.

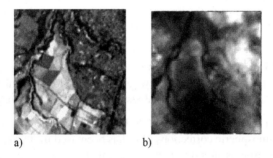

a)   b)

Fig. 5. a) Atmospheric Correction DOS1 in S2 b) Atmospheric Correction DOS1 in L8 of the AOI Santa Mónica farm. Source: study illustration.

Time Series Analysis. The time series graph for the study in 2019 was performed to show data based on the values of the NDVI spectral index of satellite images with a minimum percentage of cloud cover. This graph (see Fig. 6), which is determined by the types of surface registered in the field of view of the satellite sensor, and the peak values depend on the meteorological parameters (temperature, humidity, cloudiness, etc.). So, it allowed to have a better knowledge of the health of the pastures and to identify at an early stage the stressed or infected vegetation.

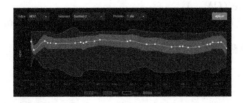

Fig. 6. Time series graph based on NDVI of the AOI in 2019. Source: own study.

Digital Classification of the Image. The image improved with the indices found was digitally classified, this process was started with the recognition of spatial patterns, later the training or supervised classification was performed to recognize the patterns detected in the rest of the image, the purpose was mainly to detect areas with occupied pastures and waste pastures (rest or dry) (see Fig. 7).

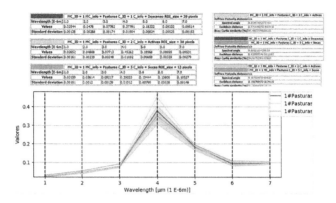

Fig. 7. Detail, distance, and spectral signature graph of the AOI Santa Mónica farm. Source: own study.

3   Results and Discussion

As observed in Fig. 7 which in the visible spectrum region has a low reflectance given the strong absorption by the foliar pigments. It is also observed that there is a change at the end of the wavelength of the red zone This characteristic is a spectral response of all vegetation, this is presented by the low reflectance of chlorophyll and the high reflectance in the near infrared, associated with the internal structure of each pasture and the water content. If the pastures in the study area were diseased, the carotenes and xanthophylls would be more dominant in the pastures, which could turn the pastures into a greater yellow influence since they absorb blue light and reflect green and red light. It does not happen in our spectral signatures. They are healthy pastures, they have a behaviour or pattern similar to the general spectral signature for vegetation. So, for instance in the near infrared zone the reflectance itself will reach remarkable values because the green leaves absorb the little energy of this region. However, in the mid infrared zone the spectral response will be dominated by the water of the plants and the high moisture content of green grasses, which give high absorption values and, therefore they lead to lower reflectance values, with this it is demonstrated how important is the determination of spectral signatures of crops.

In both satellites L8 and S2, the annual data of the NDVI was considered, the results shown in the dispersion graph (see Fig. 8) that the correlation analysis between the NDVI in active or occupied pastures indicates pastures healthy whereas for resting and dry pastures the correlation is weak because there is a high reflectance in the near infrared zone, which is basically associated with the internal structure of the pasture and the water content, which have a significant association in each ecosystem, and they are influenced by the degree of seasonality of rainfall. An important factor in dry pastures that predominates is the roughness since the reflectance tends to increase along the wavelength and they have larger thresholds, which means that this transfer zone has a high standard deviation. It is in large thresholds there will be a heterogeneity of pixels that make up the firm, where it verifies that the grasses are dry and are not absorbing water. So, there is no longer any absorption of energy, it has this behavior of increasing reflectance at along the wavelength.

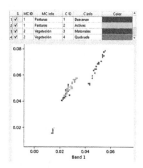

Fig. 8.   Dispersion graph of the spectral signature of the AOI Santa Mónica farm. Source: own study.

Therefore, it is recommended to also identify new pasture species that have a sensitive growth to changes in solar radiation to more accurately infer NDVI.

4   Conclusions

A significant improvement has been achieved with respect to the time of occupation and the time of rest, the map obtained from pastures at Santa Mónica farm, applying digital and visual techniques of interpretation of Landsat 8 and Sentinel-2 images, is quantitatively reliable in 90% accuracy when the location and distribution of the mentioned coverage is shown.

The condition of the pastures evaluated in the areas of the farm showed that 73.3% are in good conditions (occupied pastures), the remaining 26.7% was divided into conditions: 20.5% regular (rest pastures), 3.6% bad (dry pastures) and 2.6% very bad (thickets) to direct the pasture to an optimal condition according to the characteristics in the place and production expectations, indicators that explain the condition of the pasture in agreement with the slope, coverage, vigor, and the presence of laminar erosion.

In our country, the main tool to increase milk production per hectare is precisely the animal load with well-managed pastures in the valleys of the mountains. It can sustain 4 UB/ha. On the other hand, the milk production potential of temperate pastures (without supplementation) is about 15–18 L in contrast to 8–10 L in tropical pastures.

The proposal of this document groups and incorporates innovations to the best practices and spectral artifacts of the most evaluated methodologies, generating a considerable level of milk productivity. We can say that the Sentinel-2 data, combined with a semi-automatic classification model, can be used to monitor pastures at high space-time resolutions and with reliable precision.

References

1. Altieri, M., Nicholls, C.: Agroecología Teoría y práctica para una agricultura sostenible. Programa de las Naciones Unidas para el Medio Ambiente, México D.F (México). Primera edición (2000)
2. Abecia, J.: La "ganadería de precisión" en el sector de los pequeños rumiantes. Ganadería, Nº. 95, pp. 34–37 (2015). ISSN 1695-1123
3. Drusch, M., et al.: Sentinel-2: ESA's optical high-resolution mission for GMES operational services. Remote Sens. Environ. **120**, 25–36 (2012)
4. Granados, F.: Uso de Vehículos Aéreos no tripúlados (UAV) para la evaluación de la producción agraria. Instituto de Agricultura Sostenible-IAS/CSIC (2011)
5. Punalekar, S.M., Verhoef, A., Quaife, T.L., Bermingham, L., Reynolds, C.K.: Application of Sentinel-2A data for pasture biomass monitoring using a physically based radiative transfer model. Remote Sens. Environ. **218**, 207–220 (2018)
6. Mishra, N., Md, O.H., Leigh, L., Aaron, D., Helder, D., Markham, B.: Radiometric cross calibration of Landsat 8 operational land imager (OLI) and Landsat 7 enhanced thematic mapper plus (ETM+). Remote Sens. **6**, 12619–12638 (2014)
7. Aguilar, H., Mora, R., Vargas, Ch.: Centro Nacional de Alta Tecnología, Costa Rica: Metodología para la corrección atmosférica de imágenes aster, rapideye, spot 2 y landsat 8 con el módulo flaash del software ENVI. Revista Geográfica de América Central. **53**, 39–59 (2014)
8. Bravo, N.: Teledetección espacial Landsat, Sentinel2, Aster llt y Modis. 1ra. edición. Geomática Ambiental S.R.L., Huánuco, Perú (2017)
9. Benavides, M.F., Nieuwenhuyse, A., Villanueva, C., Ibrahim, M., Tobar, D., Robalino, J.: Capitulo 2 Evaluación de la condición de pasturas de Brachiaria Brizantha y su impacto económico en la producción ganadera en la cuenca media del río Jesús María, Costa Rica. Tesis Maestría de socio economía ambiental- CATIE (2017)
10. Avogadro, D., Padró, J.: Diferenciación de plantaciones forestales en entre ríos (Argentina): comparación de métodos de clasificación aplicados a imágenes Sentinel-2 y Landsat-8. Revista Internacional de Ciencia y Tecnología de la Información Geográfica. Departamento de Geografía, Universitat Autònoma de Barcelona Campus de Bellaterra, Cataluña, España (2019). http://dx.doi.org/10.21138/GF.652
11. Agnusdei, M.: Ecofisiología aplicada a pasturas. Unidad 1, Crecimiento de forraje. Grupo Producción y Utilización de Pasturas. Argentina: UI EEA INTA Balcarce, FCA UNM (2009)
12. León, R., Bonifaz, N., Gutiérrez, F.: Pastos y forrajes del Ecuador. Siembra y producción de pasturas. Editorial Universitaria Abya-Yala. Universidad Politécnica Salesiana. Quito - Ecuador (2018)
13. Godoy, P.: Desarrollo de un modelo espacial de riesgo de infección de fasciola hepatica en vacunos lecheros de la sierra central. Tesis para optar el grado de maestro magister Scientiae en Producción Animal, Lima, Perú (2018)

14. FAO. AGP - Praderas, pastizales y cultivos forrajeros. https://goo.gl/CsVaKw. Accessed 13 Aug 2019
15. Rincón, J.J.: Cuantas unidades animales por hectárea podemos manejar -PARTE 1 Conceptos básicos necesarios (2017) https://www.engormix.com/ganaderia-leche/articulos/cuantas-unidades-animales-hectarea-t41122.htm. 14 June 2019
16. Gebremedhin, A., Badenhorst, P., Wang, J., Spangenberg, G., Smith, K.: Prospects for Measurement of Dry Matter Yield in Forage Breeding Programs Using Sensor Technologies. Agronomy MDPI. (2019). https://doi.org/10.3390/agronomy9020065
17. ESA. Sentinel. S2 MPC Sen2Cor Software Release Note. Reference: S2-PDGS-MPC-L2A-SRN-V2.8.0 Issue: 02 (2019)
18. Díaz, J.: Estudio de Índices de vegetación a partir de imágenes aéreas tomadas desde UAS/RPAS y aplicaciones de estos a la agricultura de precisión. Trabajo fin de máster curso 2014–2015. Universidad Complutense de Madrid, Madrid, España (2015)
19. Tello, J., Gómez-Báguena, R., Casterad, M.A.: Comparación y ajuste en zonas agrícolas de índices de vegetación derivados de Landsat-8 y Sentinel-2. In: Ruiz, L.A., Estornell, J., Erena, M. (eds.) Nuevas plataformas y sensores de teledetección. XVII Congreso de la Asociación Española de Teledetección, pp. 81–84, Murcia, España (2017)
20. ESA (European Space Agency). http://www.esa.int/. Accessed 16 Feb 2020
21. USGS (U.S. Geological Survey). https://www.usgs.gov/. Accessed 10 Mar 2020
22. Zaraza, M.A., Manrique, L.M.: Generación de datos de cambio de coberturas vegetales en la sabana de Bogotá mediante el uso de series temporales con imágenes Landsat e imágenes sintéticas MODIS-Landsat entre los años 2007 y 2013. Revista de Teledetección Asociación Española de Teledetección (2019). https://doi.org/10.4995/raet.2019.12280
23. Hernández, H.: Procesamiento digital de imágenes. Universidad de Chile. (2011). ISBN 978-956-353-324-8
24. Chuvieco, E.: Teledetección Ambiental: La observación de la Tierra desde el Espacio, 3ra edición. Ariel Ciencia, Barcelona, España (2008)
25. Rouse, J., Haas, R., Schell, J., Deering, D.: Monitoring the vernal advancement and retrogradation (green wave effect) of natural vegetation. In: Fraden, S.C. (ed.) Third ERTS-1 Symposium, 10–14 December 1973, NASA SP-351, pp. 309-317. Goddard Space Flight Center Texas A&M University College Station, Texas (1974)
26. Maskova, Z., Zemek, F., Kvet, J.: Normalized difference vegetation index (NDVI) management of mountain meadows. Boreal Environ. Res. **13**, 417–432 (2008)
27. Soria, J., Granados, R.: Relación entre los índices de vegetación obtenidos de los sensores AVHRR del satélite NOAA y TM del Landsat. Ciencia Ergo Sum **12**(2), 167–174 (2005). Universidad Autónoma del Estado de México, México
28. Ju, C.H., Tian, Y.C., Yao, X., Cao, W.X., Zhu, Y., Hannaway, D.: Estimating leaf chlorophyll content using red edge parameters. Pedosphere **20**(5), 633–644 (2010)
29. LANDVIEWER. https://eos.com/lv/es/, https://eos.com/landviewer/?id=LE07_L1GT_010060_20200328_20200330_01_RT&b=Red,Green,Blue&anti&pansharpening&lat=-0.00195&lng=-77.26364&z=8. Accessed 03 Apr 2020
30. Congedo, L.: (SCP) Semi-Automatic Classification Plugin. Documentation. Versión 6.4.0.2 (2020). https://plugins.qgis.org/plugins/SemiAutomaticClassificationPlugin/
31. Carmelo, A., Moreno, A., Rodríguez, E.: Determinación experimental de la firma espectral de la vegetación. una sencilla práctica de introducción a la Teledetección. In: Avances y Aplicaciones. VIII Congreso Nacional de Teledetección, Albacete, España, pp. 429–432 (1999)
32. AccuWeather. https://www.accuweather.com/es/ec/national/satellite-wv. Accessed 24 Feb 2020
33. INAMHI. https://www.serviciometeorologico.gob.ec

34. Brizuela, A., Aguirre, C., Velasco, I.: Aplicación de métodos de corrección atmosférica de datos Landsat 5 para análisis multitemporal. Teledetección, Ed. Martin, UBA, Buenos Aires, Argentina (2007)
35. Chavez, J.: An improved dark-object subtraction technique for atmospheric scattering correction of multispectral data. Remote Sens. Environ. **24**, 459–479 (1988)
36. Tagestad, J.: Radiometric standardization of adjacent Landsat Thematic Mapper Image for multi-scene mosaics. Master of Science, Utah State University, Logan, Utah (2000)
37. Sobrino, J.A., Raissouni, N.: Toward remote sensing methods for land cover dynamic monitoring: application to Morocco. Int. J. Remote Sens. **21**, 353366 (2000)
38. GRASS GIS. https://grass.osgeo.org/, https://grass.osgeo.org/grass78/manuals/i.landsat.toar. html. Accessed 17 Sept 2019

Towards a New Perspective of Building Tools for Context-Aware Mobile Applications

Estevan Gomez-Torres[1,2(✉)] ⓘ, Cecilia Challiol[3,4] ⓘ,
and Silvia E. Gordillo[3,5] ⓘ

[1] Facultad de Ingeniería, Carrera de Ingeniería en Informática,
Universidad UTE, Quito, Ecuador
estevan.gomezt@info.unlp.edu.ar
[2] Facultad de Informática, UNLP, La Plata, Buenos Aires, Argentina
[3] LIFIA, Facultad de Informática, UNLP, La Plata, Buenos Aires, Argentina
{ceciliac,gordillo}@lifia.info.unlp.edu.ar
[4] CONICET, Buenos Aires, Argentina
[5] CICPBA, Buenos Aires, Argentina

Abstract. Technological growth has been exponential in relation to mobile devices (such as embedded sensors as GPS or accelerometer) that have allowed developing context-aware mobile applications for the market. This growth generates a new challenge about how to support the creation of this kind of application to adapt them to the current user's demand. Nowadays, there are several approaches that could be used to create context-aware mobile applications, but these approaches are not designed to support variability in the kind of generated applications. The aim of this paper is to propose a building tool that allows generating a wide variety of context-aware mobile applications. Our tool has been designed from scratch considering a taxonomy of variability concepts which help to identify the potential variability points to obtain more flexible building approaches. The first version of our tool is presented which is based on UML tools like Eclipse, Sirius Obeo, and JBoss. Finally, a discussion of different aspects is detailed to help designers to have guidelines to select the appropriate development environment for the design of building tools for context-aware mobile applications.

Keywords: Building tools · Context-aware mobile applications · Variability · UML tools · Eclipse

1 Introduction

Technological growth has been exponential in relation to mobile devices (such as embedded sensors as GPS or accelerometer) that have allowed to develop context-aware mobile applications for the market which are described in [1]. Moreover, it has emerged a new issue as is presented in [2], which consists of how to build context-aware mobile applications that are useful for users, something that is vital in today's market. This growth generates a new challenge about how to support the creation of this kind of application to adapt it to the current user's demand.

© Springer Nature Switzerland AG 2020
O. Gervasi et al. (Eds.): ICCSA 2020, LNCS 12254, pp. 576–586, 2020.
https://doi.org/10.1007/978-3-030-58817-5_42

Context-aware mobile applications are used in different domains, for example, traffic assistance, medical monitoring, tourism, etc. [1, 2]; but they could also be used in other potential scenarios, as mention in [3] for future mobile applications for education. Thus, building tools for this kind of applications should be designed to support new requirements. In [4], the authors identify two kinds of new requirements those that maintain the same goal of the application (associated with adaptation) and those that change the main goal of the application (related to evolution). According to [4], integrating runtime adaptation and evolution is crucial for the sustainability of software systems; and the building tools are not the exception.

There are currently several building tools that could be used to create context-aware mobile applications. However, there is not yet an agreed solution for this kind of application as it is mentioned in [5], so, it is an open area of research. There are building approaches for both non-expert users as is presented in [6]; and experts which require some technical knowledge for the modelling of features such as is detailed in [7]. Nevertheless, these tools are not designed to support variability in the kind of generated applications; for example, they only provide GPS as a location mechanism that is related to the available APIs. This limitation is one of the motivations of this paper.

When different building approaches for context-aware mobile applications are designed from scratch, the designer should identify the potential variability points in order to obtain more flexible tools. A possible way of handling some variability concept was exemplified in [8] for conceptual building approaches; however, it is not detailed from the building tool's perspective, so, this is the motivation for the research presented in this paper.

Therefore, the aim of this paper is to propose a building tool to support variability in while generating applications that have been designed using the taxonomy of variability concepts proposed in [8]. This tool is based on UML standards in order to have more interoperability with other existing tools.

In this paper, the first version of our tool is presented which is implemented following the UML specification described in [9]; and it integrates Eclipse, Sirius Obeo, and JBoss.

We hope that this paper helps designers to know a possible way of handling variability in building tools for context-aware mobile applications. To do so, a discussion in relation to this topic is presented, and details are presented on how to consider the variability in these tools to generate a wide variety of applications. This discussion could be used as guidelines to select the appropriate development environment for the design of these building tools.

The paper is structured as follows. Section 2 presents the methodology. Section 3 presents the first version of our building tool for context-aware mobile applications. Section 4 presents a discussion and the outlook of the paper. Finally, conclusions and future works are detailed in Sect. 5.

2   Methodology

Our building tool for context-aware mobile applications has been designed using the taxonomy of variability concepts described in [8]. This section describes a survey of the proposed taxonomy [8], in order to help the reader to better understand how our tool handles variability. In addition, our building tool is based on the UML standard to have more interoperability with other existing tools. Therefore, in this section, UML tools are also detailed to understand the interdependence with the tool.

2.1   Variability Concepts Used to Design Our Building Tool

We have been working on the topic of mobile applications for more than ten years. In the past, we have proposed in [10] a model approach to handling variability in context-aware mobile applications; which considers the separation between the aware-objects concept of its context-feature and in addition to the sensors (which assign values to these features).

We have been creating some authoring tools for this kind of application. For example, in [11] is presented an authoring tool to create in-situ location-based experiences; this tool has been extended in [12] in order to provide support for location-based educational activities. Besides, in [13] is presented an authoring tool to in-situ co-design location-based applications inside indoor spaces.

Based on our experience, an initial taxonomy version of variability concepts for building approaches for context-aware mobile applications has been presented in [14]. The taxonomy presented in [14] defines the following concepts: relevance, combination, categorization, precision and accuracy's margins, configuration type, and execution type. These concepts have been selected in order to help designers to identify the potential variability points to obtain more flexible building approaches. Only a brief description of each concept of this taxonomy is detailed in [14], without going into details on how should be handled in building approaches.

In [8] a possible way of handling each variability concept of [14] was exemplified for conceptual building approaches. In [8], each concept of the taxonomy is described using a pattern-based format, detailing how and what could be considered in the design phase of this kind of approach. However, in [8] is not detailed from the building tool's perspective, so, this is the motivation for the research presented in this paper.

Note that, when a building tool is designed from scratch considering the variability concepts presented in [8] and [14]; this eases the generation of a wide variety of context-aware mobile applications. Our previous works [8, 14] analyses variability concepts only describing them without the details of a concrete implementation.

The main contributions of this paper, in contrast with our previous works [8, 14], is to provide a building tool which handler variability concept to generate a wide variety of context-aware mobile applications.

A survey of the variability concepts presented in [8, 14] is presented below. This survey supports the reader to better understand the variability concepts handled by our building tool (which is presented in Sect. 3).

- *Relevance:* each context feature has its own relevance in each application; for some applications, some of them are critical and other optional. A building tool should provide a scale of relevance in order to choose, for example, the most important context-features to generate reduced versions of applications. In addition, it is required to handle the heuristics of what actions to take based on the selected context features. This last functionality can be complex to implement from a building tool.
- *Combination:* context-aware mobile applications could require the combination of various context-features to trigger some services or actions. The complexity of implementing this combination in a building tool is to define clear rules of how to react to each value that these context-features could take.
- *Precision and Accuracy's Margins:* each physical sensor used in context-aware mobile applications has its precision and accuracy's margin. When a tool generates an application, it should define how to react to each sensed value from these physical sensors; but also how to consider the precision and accuracy of them in order to trigger the correct action.
- *Categorization:* in context-aware mobile applications, there are different aware-objects, for example, the user or the environment. These aware-objects should have different treatment in the generated applications. Thus, the building tool should define the heuristics to handle the behavior based on each category of aware object.
- *Configuration Type:* the physical sensors used in context-aware mobile applications have default, passive or active configuration type, according to [8]. The building tool should handle each configuration type. The active configuration type is more complex to handle because it requires automatic learning.
- *Execution Type:* the physical sensors used in context-aware mobile applications have a passive or active execution type, according to [1]. The building tool should handle each execution type. The passive execution type is more complex to handle because it requires details of how the application will interact with the user; as well as, how it will react to each possible interaction.

Note that, the variability concepts described above are related to different aspects of the context-aware mobile application. Categorization is associated with aware-objects, Relevance and Combination are related to specific context-features of aware-objects; and the rest of the variability concepts (Precision and Accuracy's Margins, Configuration Type and Execution Type) are associated with physical sensors. A possible way to represent the variability concepts is presented in [8] which is based on the concepts presented in [10].

Using the representation presented in [8], in Fig. 1 are details the variability concepts used to design our building tool. The figure shows that some variability concepts are related to the concrete sensor, but others to the aware-objects or context-features as it has been mentioned.

2.2 Development Environment Used by Our Tool

In this section, the UML tools used by our tool are detailed in order to help the readers to understand why they have been chosen. Note that, there are lots of tools that could

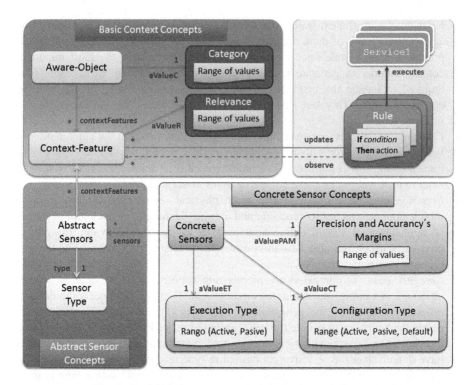

Fig. 1. Variability concepts used to design our building tool.

be used together to create context-aware mobile applications, but they have not been designed for this purpose. However, we have selected only UML tools to have more interoperability with other existing tools because they are based on the UML standard specification [9]. The selection of these UML tools has been focused on obtaining more flexibility in order to implement each variability concept described in Sect. 2.1.

There are two key points related to our selection; first, the tools should allow the possibility to represent information associated with each variability concept, and then they should allow a generation of applications using this information. We have considered these key points to choose which UML tools could be used together to design our tool.

The UML tools used to design our tool have been selected considering some research that compares different features of existing tools. For example, in [15] is reviewed the main features, potential advantages and current limitations of the main tools that exist for the development of graphical editors for visual Domain Specific Languages (DSL). In [16] is analysed the performance characteristics of the mobile applications developed with a number of common approaches and tools for mobile application development, including the native SDK's of Google Android and Apple iOS, and cross-platform tools of Apache Cordova, Microsoft Xamarin, and Appcelerator Titanium.

In addition, in Nueva [17] we had been analysed different UML development environment for the design of building tools for context-aware mobile applications; according to the variability concepts described in [8]. For each UML development environment, we had analysed, for example, the complexity to represent different concrete data, how could be generated mobile applications and the complexity of this, and what sensors could be used and how these could be integrated into the generated applications. In [17] had only analysed different UML development environment; but it had not presented a concrete solution, as it is the proposal in this paper.

Considering that mentioned above, we have chosen to use Eclipse [18] as a development environment combined with Sirius Obeo [19] in order to represent each concept using visual DSL's [20], and JBoss [21] to generate Android mobile applications. Thus, the meta-models are defined with Eclipse, and then these meta-models are used by Sirius Obeo to specify the visual DSLs. This allows specifying values related to each variability concept in a rapid and easy way.

In addition, Eclipse has a lot of plugins to access the device's sensors (such as GPS and Compass) that are compatible with JBoss; to generate mobile applications with sensor's functionalities. Moreover, JBoss allows creating new plugins to specify additional functionalities that are embedded inside the generated mobile applications.

Note that, JBoss works in conjunction with Hybrid Mobile tools [22] and extensive support Apache Cordova multiplatform [23] for the generation of hybrid applications; this lets using plugins for mobile device control and geolocation, among other features.

3 Results

The first version of our building tool is presented in this section which has been developed using Eclipse as the development environment combined with Sirius Obeo (to represent each concept using visual DSLs) and JBoss to generate Android mobile applications. Figure 2 shows how these technologies are integrated into our building tool. Note that, an Ecore Meta-Model [24] is created using Sirius Obeo and JBoss used both the Ecore Meta-Model and Sirius Obeo models in order to generate Android applications.

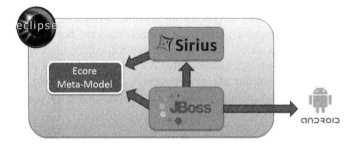

Fig. 2. Our building tool proposal.

The first step creates the Ecore meta-model with each concept described in Fig. 1. This offers the designers the possibility of using this meta-model to facilitate the task of creating concrete mobile applications because they could consume these concepts that have been defined. So, our building tool provides this meta-model as a baseline to generate mobile applications which are shown in Fig. 3.

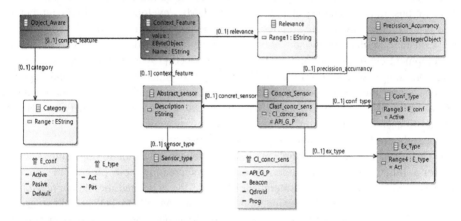

Fig. 3. Ecore meta-model with the basic context-aware and variability concepts.

Using the Ecore meta-model, we have created the visual DSL with Sirius Obeo as it is shown in Fig. 4. The main idea is that the designer gives specific values to the visual concept in a fast and easy way. Currently, we are working to improve the icons related to each concept and look for an easy way that designers could set the value of each concept. Figure 4 shows an aware-object classified as the user which has a location-feature (that is set by the GPS sensor and has a margin of precision) with a medium relevance. In this case, a rule could be to trigger services according to different location value.

When the visual DSL has been created three intermediate models are generated: cams model code (classes that represent the meta-model concepts), cams edit (classes associated with edition) and cams editor (classes associated with the visual editor). These intermediate models are shown in Fig. 5.

Currently, we are working on generating Android applications using JBoos integrated with its available sensor plugins. To do that, we have been researching some existing sensor tools, and we are working on an automatic derivation. Besides, we are defining a new plugin with this functionality. We have to emphasize that we want to obtain a version of our tool that allows designers to define and set the values to both basic context-aware and variability concepts in a rapid and easy way, but also to generate functional mobile applications.

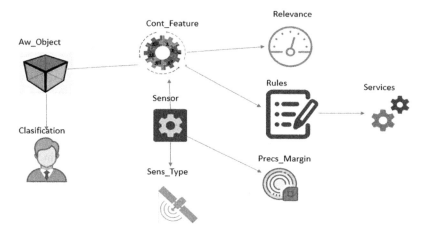

Fig. 4. A first scratch of the visual DSL of our tool.

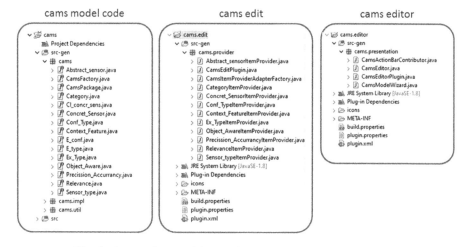

Fig. 5. Intermediate models associated with visual DSL of our tool.

4   Discussion

This section discusses different aspects of building tools for context-aware mobile applications to help designers to have guidelines in order to handle variability to facilitate them to choose the appropriate development environment.

Note that, this paper is focused on the variability concepts described in Sect. 2.1, but the variability is a feature of context-aware mobile applications which has been studied from different perspectives. For example, in [25] is analysed 36 different ways of modelling context-aware, which implies variability in the form of representation of this kind of application. In some cases, context-aware models allow variability not only at the design level, but also at execution time [10]. This allows, for example, to dynamically add context while the application is running without requiring to be compiled again. Therefore, to have this support, the modelling approach should be designed to consider variability. A taxonomy is presented in [26] which is useful to understand the differences and similarities in how variability is handled in context-aware software. Therefore, the researchers as [10, 25] and [26] could be used to enrich building tools for context-aware mobile applications with other variability concepts.

There are important key points related to select the appropriate development environment, in order to design building tools for context-aware mobile applications as is described below. First, the development environment should allow the possibility of represent information related at least to each variability concept described in Sect. 2.1, and it is important to mention that our tool provides visual DSLs to do this.

It should be considered that variability concepts are related to basic context-aware concepts. For example, precision and accuracy's margins, configuration type and execution type concepts are related to concrete physical sensors. The relevance and combination concepts are related to context-features and the classification concepts are associated with aware-objects. So, this requires representing basic context-aware concepts in a way that they are decoupled from each other's to allow reuse and extensibility. A possible representation to do that is presented in [10]. When decoupling basic concepts to be considered from a building approach, it allows the combination of different layers and thus, to handle the first level of variability. To do that, our tool provides meta-models with the basic context-aware concepts in order to have the first level of variability and based on this the designer could choose the value related to each variability concept using visual DSLs.

Another key point is that the development environment should generate applications using the information of basic context-aware and variability concepts. Sometimes, these development environments only bring support to embed physical sensors inside the generated applications such as JBoss. However, it is important to know that there are other ways to set context-feature values as described in [27]; the sensors could be of different types, for example, physical, virtual (using applications and services), direct user input, etc. Each of them has its own configuration and way of execution. So, the development environment should provide a way to represent these different sensors, for example, by using Eclipse and JBoss we could create plugins in order to handle each of them.

The combination variability concept implies to define the heuristics to specify how it behaves when the value of each combined context-features change. To do this, the development environment should allow the definition of these heuristics; in the case of Eclipse and JBoss, this could be done by creating a new plugin for each heuristic. Something similar occurs with the active configuration type because it requires an automatic learning program which in Eclipse and JBoss could be specified using a new plugin that implements the logic of this automatic configuration.

These discussion points are important when designers need to choose the appropriate development environment to design a building tool for context-aware mobile applications. We have considered these key points in the design of our tool in order to have the flexibility to implement the variability concepts.

5   Conclusions and Future Works

This paper has proposed a building tool to support variability for the generation of applications designed using the taxonomy of variability concepts proposed in [8]. This tool is based on UML standard tools like Eclipse, Sirius Obeo, and JBoss. The first version of our tool and some main features are presented in this paper.

In addition, a discussion and analysis are presented with recommendations that should be considered to select the appropriate development environment for the design of building tools for context-aware mobile applications.

We continue working to improve our tool to provide automatic generation of mobile applications. Besides, we will improve the tool with more plugins to increase functionalities for other sensors such as virtual sensors (using applications and services) and we will analyse how to define rules related to combined context-features easily.

In the future, we will analyse other variability features to enrich our building tool. For example, [26] to handler more variability in the generated mobile applications.

References

1. Alegre, U., Augusto, J.C., Clark, T.: Engineering context-aware systems and applications: a survey. J. Syst. Softw. **117**, 55–83 (2016)
2. Alegre-Ibarra, U., Augusto, J.C., Evans, C.: Perspectives on engineering more usable context-aware systems. J. Ambient Intell. Human. Comput. **9**(5), 1593–1609 (2018). https://doi.org/10.1007/s12652-018-0863-7
3. Chatterjee, S., Majumdar, D., Misra, S., Damaševičius, R.: Adoption of mobile applications for teaching-learning process in rural girls' schools in India: an empirical study. Educ. Inf. Technol. **25**, 4057–4076 (2020). https://doi.org/10.1007/s10639-020-10168-6
4. Weyns, D., Caporuscio, M., Vogel, B., Kurti, A.: Design for sustainability = runtime adaptation ∪ evolution. In: Proceedings of the 2015 European Conference on Software Architecture Workshops, pp. 1–7. ACM, New York (2015)
5. Bauer, C., Dey, A.K.: Considering context in the design of intelligent systems: current practices and suggestions for improvement. J. Syst. Softw. **112**, 26–47 (2016)
6. Bales, S.: Build Android Apps without Coding: Get started with Android Apps using Thunkable-MIT App Inventor. ACM, New York (2018). Independently Published
7. Hamdani, M., Butt, W.H., Anwar, M.W., Azam, F.: A systematic literature review on Interaction Flow Modeling Language (IFML). In: 2nd International Conference on Management Engineering, Software Engineering and Service Sciences, pp. 134–138. ACM, New York (2018)
8. Gómez-Torres, E., Challiol, C., Gordillo, S.E.: Variability features in building approaches for context-aware mobile applications. In: Fonseca C, E., Morales, G.R., Cordero, M.O., Botto-Tobar, M., Martínez, E.C., León, A.P. (eds.) TICEC 2019. AISC, vol. 1099, pp. 109–123. Springer, Cham (2020). https://doi.org/10.1007/978-3-030-35740-5_8
9. Rumbaugh, J.: Lenguaje Unificado De Modelado Manual De Referencia, 2nd edn. Addison-Wesley Iberoamerica (2007)
10. Fortier, A., Rossi, G., Gordillo, S.E., Challiol, C.: Dealing with variability in context-aware mobile software. J. Syst. Softw. **83**(6), 915–936 (2010)

11. Alconada Verzini, F.M., Tonelli, J.I., Challiol, C., Lliteras, A.B., Gordillo, S.E.: Authoring tool for location-aware experiences. In: 2015 Workshop on Narrative & Hypertext, pp. 21–25. ACM, New York (2015)

12. Zimbello, A.M., Alconada Verzini, F.M., Challiol, C., Lliteras, A.B., Gordillo, S.E.: Authoring tool for location-based learning experiences. In: 2017 IEEE/ACM 4th International Conference on Mobile Software Engineering and Systems (MOBILESoft), pp. 211–212. IEEE (2017)

13. Mendiburu, F.I., Challiol, C., Gordillo, S.E.: Herramienta de autor para co-diseñar in-situ Aplicaciones Móviles basadas en Posicionamiento. In: Simposio Argentino de Ingeniería de Software 2019 (ASSE) – JAIIO, pp. 29–42 (2019)

14. Gómez-Torres, E.R., Challiol, C., Gordillo, S.E.: Context-aware mobile applications: taxonomy of factors for building approaches. In: XXV International Conference on Electronics, Electrical Engineering and Computing, pp. 1–4. IEEE (2018)

15. Granada, D., Vara, J.M., Blanco, F.P., Marcos, E.: Model-based tool support for the development of visual editors- a systematic mapping study. In: 12th International Conference on Software Technologies (ICSOFT 2017). Science and Technology Publications, pp. 330–337 (2017)

16. Ebone, A., Tan, Y., Jia, X.: A performance evaluation of cross-platform mobile application development approaches. In: 2018 IEEE/ACM 5th International Conference on Mobile Software Engineering and Systems (MOBILESoft), pp. 92–93. IEEE (2018)

17. Gomez-Torres, E.R., Challiol, C., Gordillo, S.E.: Challenges in context-aware mobile applications building approaches. In: 2019 International Conference on Information Systems and Computer Science (INCISCOS), pp. 304–310. IEEE (2019)

18. Eclipse. https://www.eclipse.org. Accessed 14 Apr 2020

19. Obeo Sirius. https://www.obeodesigner.com/en/product. Accessed 14 Apr 2020

20. Viyović, V., Maksimović, M., Perisić, B.: Sirius: a rapid development of DSM graphical editor. In: IEEE 18th International Conference on Intelligent Engineering Systems INES 2014, pp. 233–238. IEEE (2014)

21. JBoss. https://docs.jboss.org. Accessed 14 Apr 2020

22. Hybrid Mobile tools. Description of Hybrid Mobile Tools and CordovaSim. https://docs.jboss.org/tools/4.1.x.Final/en/User_Guide/html/chap-Hybrid_Mobile_Tools_and_CordovaSim.html. Accessed 14 Apr 2020

23. Apache Cordova multiplatform. Description of Apache Cordova multiplatform. https://cordova.apache.org/plugins. Accessed 14 Apr 2020

24. EMF, ECore & Meta Model. https://www.eclipse.org/modeling/emft/search/concepts/subtopic.html. Accessed 08 Jun 2020

25. Bauer, C., Novotny, A.: A consolidated view of context for intelligent systems. J. Ambient Intell. Smart Environ. 9(4), 377–393 (2017)

26. Mens, K., Cardozo, N., Duhoux, B.: A context-oriented software architecture. In: 8th International Workshop on Context-Oriented Programming, pp. 7–12. ACM, New York (2016)

27. Rivero-Rodriguez, A., Pileggi, P., Nykänen, O.A.: Mobile context-aware systems: technologies, resources and applications. Int. J. Interact. Mobile Technol. 10(2), 25–32 (2016)

Smart Home Automation System Using ZigBee, Bluetooth and Arduino Technologies

Olutosin Taiwo[1], Absalom E. Ezugwu[2]([⊠]), Nadim Rana[3],
and Shafi'i M. Abdulhamid[4]

[1] School of Mathematics, Statistics and Computer Science, University of Kwazulu-Natal, Westville Campus, Private Bag X54001, Durban 4000, South Africa
219058760@stu.ukzn.ac.za

[2] School of Computer Science, University of KwaZulu-Natal, King Edward Road, Pietermaritzburg Campus, Pietermaritzburg 3201, KwaZulu-Natal, South Africa
Ezugwua@ukzn.ac.za

[3] College of Computer Science and Information Technology, Jazan University, Jazan, Kingdom of Saudi Arabia
nadimrana17@gmail.com

[4] Department of Cyber Security Science, Federal University of Technology, Minna, Niger State, Nigeria
shafii.abdulhamid@futminna.edu.ng

Abstract. The use of modern technologies for control and monitoring and accessing devices in domestic or industrial buildings with convenience, comfortable and easy access from any location is the primary aim of the internet of things (IoT) technology for smart home automation. Complete Smart home automation, with overall control from any place at any time is still not fully available. Nevertheless, this work proposes a mobile application system for smart homes, with the purpose of overall monitoring and control of home appliances and devices. The proposed method is based on Zigbee, Arduino and Bluetooth for wireless communication among devices in the home. At the same time, a mobile application is used for the control and monitoring of the devices or appliances. In this study, Zigbee and Bluetooth are combined in order to establish efficient communication either within or outside the home premises. A user scenario of the proposed work was simulated using Proteus Simulation software to validate the practicability of the new system.

Keywords: Smart home automation · Embedded systems · Zigbee · Bluetooth · Arduino

1 Introduction

A smart home is a residence incorporating communication networks that connect the major appliances and services and allows them to be remotely controlled, monitored, and accessed from both within and without the residence [1]. In a smart home, communication network links sensors, appliances, controls and other devices together to

O. Gervasi et al. (Eds.): ICCSA 2020, LNCS 12254, pp. 587–597, 2020.
https://doi.org/10.1007/978-3-030-58817-5_43

allow for remote monitoring and control by occupants or other uses to provide frequent and regular services to occupants. Smart home technology is a significant aspect of the internet of things (IoT), which is rapidly growing and being incorporated into daily activities, business, health, education and other aspects of life. Smart home technology is aimed at five major Cs; namely, convenience, comfort, consciousness, care and control. The ability to control ones' home from any location is highly convenient; for instance, in winter, making the house comfortably warm before even opening the door or switching on or off the sockets, lights, or appliances from an outside location.

Smart home technology not only benefits home users has an impact on the economy and lifestyle of the community it is being used. It reduces stress, and saves time, energy, and money by preventing wastage of resources and basic amenities. For an effective smart home, technology has to be automated. Smart home automation systems connect controlled devices in the home to a central hub through which a user can control lighting, climate, entertainment systems remotely with the assistance of ambient intelligence [2]. The use of smartphones for daily communication and interaction has enhanced the use of smart home technologies for controlling home appliances, devices and utilities, while the user is either at home or far away. Devices in a smart home establish a connection through communication, which is a major link for devices to transmit instructions to one another for automation. Such communication may be wired or wireless [3]. Wireless communication in smart home automation involves different types of protocols; examples from the literature include Bluetooth [4, 5], Zigbee [6], Wireless Fidelity (Wi-Fi) [7], GSM [8], and Z-wave [9].

This study proposes a method for control, monitoring and access to a home through the use of a smartphone. The home is controlled via an Android-based mobile application. The design of the proposed method is based on Bluetooth module, Arduino Uno Board, sensors for control of doors and gate, and a smartphone application. Communication between home appliances or devices is established through Bluetooth communication that is embedded in the smartphone Android-based mobile application. The primary function of the proposed system is to give the user convenience, ease of access and monitoring of home from any location. It is of particular value for assisting handicapped, elderly, frail or disabled persons in using home appliances with ease.

The remaining part of this paper is organized as follows: Sect. 2 gives a discussion on related work. Section 3 presents the system design and architectural framework of the proposed system. Implementation and simulation results are presented in Sect. 4. Finally, the concluding remarks and future work are discussed in Sect. 5.

2   Related Work

An IoT framework to control home appliances with the use of Digi Device Cloud was presented by Rajalekshmi and SivaSankari [10], which entailed a smart home system using a cloud-based network platform, a gateway and low-cost microcontrollers. The framework allows users to issue commands to turn on or off multiple appliances. However, the design and control of devices via mobile application were not explicitly described in their work. Ye and Huang [11] presented a framework for a cloud-based smart home that enables home automation, household mobility and interconnection.

Their cloud-based framework is expected to expand service scope in order to offer special and efficient home services for digital appliances. However, theirs is only a conceptual framework for a future intelligent household. Hence, there was no implementation.

Wahab et al. [12] presented the design and implementation of a smart home automation system for controlling all electrical home appliances via Wi-Fi, with the use of an Android-based smartphone, tablet, or laptop. The system also uses sensors to monitor environmental conditions such as temperature and humidity, and can control or monitor voltages. The technologies used in the system are Arduino, ESP8266 Wi-Fi module, as well as temperature, humidity, smoke and motion sensors. The remote control of electrical appliances in the designed system is also aimed at reducing energy consumption. Security of the home in case of intrusion into the house or breakage is ensured by the ability of the system to send alerts to the user's phone However, implementation of the system and performance were not discussed.

Another smart home automation system for monitoring and control through an Android application was presented by Hamzah et al. [13]. The system controls and monitors the temperature, humidity, gas flame, light, water and humidity level in the soil and detects motion. For example, room temperature is adjusted when it exceeds a set value; the kitchen is installed with a flame sensor and gas leakage sensor to forestall a fire accident and the homeowner's security is protected through a system alert notifying users of intruder in the building. The designed system is also capable of garden irrigation. The technologies used are Arduino, PIR motion sensor, ESP8266 microcontroller and Bluetooth. In this work, the designed system controls and monitors the home remotely and automatically, although exchange of data is limited to a short range due to Bluetooth being deployed in the system.

Soliman et al. [14], in their approach, presented a smart home automation system based on an Arduino microcontroller kit and LabView platform. The primary functions of the system are to control light, manage temperature and monitor home security through an ultrasonic security camera. Monitoring, access and control of the system are based on the signals received from the installed sensors in the system. For instance, temperature is measured by a sensor and, once it exceeds a set limit, a microcontroller in the system is capable of automatically turning on the fan. The system was evaluated based on object-sensor distance over which the sensor can detect changes and the auto-adjustment rate of temperature. The technologies involved are Arduino, temperature sensors and motion detectors.

A smart home energy management system proposed by Han et al. [15] detects use of energy based on wireless and wired networks. Power and energy from home appliances are transferred and measured through a low-power Zigbee communication network. Energy to run the system is generated through renewable energy sources (solar power and wind power); home energy usage is optimized based on power line communication. Light was installed as a means of energy and power measurement in a prototype system and was used for implementation with the home server of the proposed system. Results showed that the home server could achieve energy conservation and save energy costs.

Other research works [16, 17] have been conducted in the area of smart home automation for monitoring, control, and security, with the aim of making life more comfortable and easier. However, most systems are limited in terms of their technologies and the coverage range of communication between devices. This work intends to eliminate the short-range communication barrier by incorporating Zigbee with Bluetooth for on-site and off-site communication. It also provides for easy control and monitoring of home appliances from any location via a smartphone and using low-cost technologies that are capable of covering a more extensive communication range.

3   An Overview of the Proposed System

The proposed system consists of two major parts; specifically, the software and hardware. Components of the hardware are the Arduino board, Bluetooth module, Zigbee protocol and smartphone. In the proposed system Zigbee is combined with Bluetooth for off-site and on-site communication between devices. For instance, on the one hand, if one is at home, the gate, doors, or other appliances in the house can be controlled remotely via the Bluetooth link, without needing an internet connection. On the other hand, if one is off-site, the phone can communicate with the router using Wi-Fi communication to automatically open the door or gate through the internet, using the configured Zigbee stack in the router. The Bluetooth module is limited in communication range, hence the need for it being combined with Zigbee for wider communication coverage.

The software part of the proposed system consists of the mobile application, Arduino Uno Board configuration using the Arduino Integrated Development Environment, Bluetooth application for communication between smartphone and Arduino Board and Proteus for simulation.

3.1   Hardware Component

The primary hardware technologies used in the proposed system are Arduino Uno Board, Zigbee and Bluetooth module together with a Smartphone for communication, control and monitoring of the home. The hardware implementation is to be incorporated using the Arduino Board interfaced with Zigbee and the Bluetooth module.

Arduino Uno Board: Arduino boards have the ability to read inputs such as light on a sensor, a finger on a button, or a text message and turn it into an output – perhaps activating a motor, turning on a LED, publishing online and so on [18]. The Arduino Uno board was selected for this work because it has extensible hardware and it is a cross-platform program. The basic function of the board is to digitally read pins and the value of the given pin to set the input/output mode through the pin mode. The home is controlled remotely by Android smartphone using the Arduino board interfaced with Bluetooth. The board is configured using an open-source prototyping board formulated on easy-to-use hardware and software Arduino IDE (Integrated Development Environment) 1.8.10 windows version. Input and output signals are made available on the Arduino board using rows of conductors into which single inline connectors can be plugged. The Arduino development board has at least nine digital pins, which can be either input or output channels, four analog input channels and at least one serial port. The port may be used to download code to the Arduino board.

Bluetooth Module: An easy to use Bluetooth Module Serial Port Protocol was used for wireless communication and serial connection set up in the system. Bluetooth communication is serial, hence it is easy to interface with a board, microcontroller, or PC. In this work, the Bluetooth module is connected to the board for control of LEDs by sending commands. The Bluetooth is paired to the master device (smartphone) to establish connection between the home and the phone. In the proposed system the HC-06 Bluetooth module, which features a 2.4 GHz ISM band frequency, is used and controlled from the Arduino board. To power the Arduino board, the Smartphone's Bluetooth is turned on to search for nearby devices; once this is found, paring is required with a password and so connection is established. In our proposed work, Bluetooth has a dual-task (master-slave and slave-master). It communicates with the Android application and also with the Arduino board for home control. Bluetooth is known to cover only a short range and, to overcome this limitation, Zigbee is combined with Bluetooth for communication and connection in the proposed system.

Zigbee: ZigBee is a low power wireless mesh technology. It uses digital radios based on IEEE 802.15.4 standard for personal area networks with a focus on monitoring, control and sensor applications. It operates in mainly the 2.4 GHz ISM band [19]. A ZigBee network allows a set of devices to communicate wirelessly via one of several possible topologies. Packets of data can be sent between nodes and may be routed by intermediary devices to more distant nodes that would otherwise be out of range. Each device has both a MAC address and a ZigBee network address, the network as a whole has its own Private Area Network (PAN) ID shared by all devices. To secure communication with Zigbee, the IEEE 802.15.4 security model will be adopted. With the IEEE model, authentication, encryption and integrity of frames are ensured to avoid manipulation during network transmission and node communication in the home. In our work, sensors installed on home appliances such as doors, gates and lights and other sensors, such as those used for measuring ambient conditions like home temperature, are connected to Zigbee for communication with Arduino board and then home control through the smartphone.

3.2 Software Component

Functioning of the home automation system involves configuration of devices such as the Arduino board and development of applications such as an Android mobile app for smartphone. In this work, the software components are the Arduino Integrated Development Environment (IDE), Bluetooth terminal and the Android-based mobile application.

Mobile Application: An Android-based smartphone application is developed using Android Studio for the control of appliances in the proposed system. Android Studio is a recognized Integrated Development Environment (IDE) for Google's Android operating system. It is based on a Java integrated development environment for software development. The smartphone communicates wirelessly with the home appliances through Bluetooth, interfaced with the Arduino board for home control.

Arduino Integrated Development Environment IDE: Programming or coding of the Arduino Board for the proposed system is done using the Arduino IDE tool, which is a cross-platform application for Windows, Linux and macOS. The Arduino IDE is written in functions from C and C++ programing languages. Arduino IDE is used to write and upload programs to Arduino compatible boards. The command for receiving data serially from a smartphone is of the form "Serial.available()" while the command for transmitting data serially from an Arduino board to a smartphone is represented as follows:

```
int state;
If(serial.available() >0)          //check for serial input
{
}
```

Arduino IDE code is also used for turning ON and OFF appliances in the smart home system.

3.3   System Architecture

In order to address the issue of interoperability and scalability in the problem statement, the proposed home system is modelled to be a convenient, low-cost home controlling (activation and deactivation) and monitoring system. As shown in the architectural design illustrated in Fig. 1 below. The smart home system is divided into three major phases; viz, sensor-based appliances, non-sensor-based home appliances and IoT smart home automation technologies. The sensor-based home appliances include those which involve locks, such as gates, doors, etc. Non-sensor based appliances are basic home appliances such as microwave, fridge, fans, switches, electric cooker, television and so on. Technologies used are the Arduino board and microcontroller, Bluetooth module, Zigbee and sensors. The sensor-based appliances are interfaced with the Zigbee module for communication with the Arduino board, to enable better communication and control of the appliances. Other home appliances are connected to the Bluetooth module for wireless communication and interaction with the developed smartphone application. The set up for this module comprises integrating home devices to communicate simultaneously with one another and then communication between the homeowner (or user) and the home is through the mobile application. Zigbee is combined with Bluetooth in the developed system for both off-site and on-site communication of devices. The proposed methodology for the smart home mobile application system has two major modes or components. The user (home) and communication modes. For communication between the user and home appliances, Arduino Uno board, Zigbee and Bluetooth module are used and for home control, an Android Mobile application was developed. The smartphone communicates with the Bluetooth module through the developed mobile application; as such, the Bluetooth module sends a signal to the device, once they are connected, a signal is sent to the board for control of home devices.

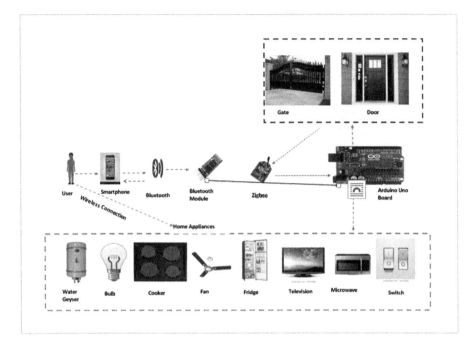

Fig. 1. Architecture of the proposed system

4 System Simulation and User's Scenario

The system proposed in this project was tested using Proteus Simulation Software to check its feasibility. The simulation output of the Arduino board and home appliances is shown in Fig. 2. For the simulation, the Arduino UNO board was used with LEDs (Red-Blue) connected to the pins; the LEDs were set to switch on and off with a delay of one second. A successful simulation makes the LEDs blink red and blue colors. The Arduino boards are designed for faster and easier building of electronics, and feature pins for inputs and outputs as well as a microcontroller. The code for the board was programmed using open-source Arduino IDE version 1.8.10. LEDs in Proteus were used to depict home appliances to be controlled by the board.

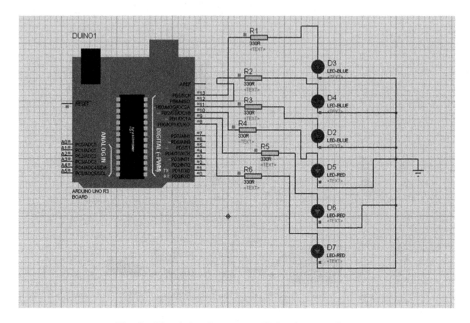

Fig. 2. Simulation in proteus (Color figure online)

Figures 3(a) to 3(e) shows the GUI of the developed mobile application for Bluetooth connection and communication with the home. Any mobile device that has the developed Android application installed can connect to the board via the Bluetooth module and the device thus controls home appliances such as fans, bulbs, sockets, fridge. For security, before access can be gained for control of the home appliances on the application the user creates login credentials. Also, a passcode is needed for establishing the Bluetooth connection and pairing of devices in the developed mobile application; (see Fig. 3a to 3c). After establishing successful communication, the user can then control home devices from the application (see Fig. 3d). In the developed application, the user can only gain access to establish communication with the Bluetooth module after a successful registration (see Fig. 3a). The passcode for set up would have been gotten during registration and the user is expected to use the passcode to gain access. Once the passcode is accepted (see Fig. 3(b)), a search is done for Bluetooth device and once it is paired, communication must be established with device is needed (see Fig. 3c). The home control module is initiated (see Fig. 3d), and lastly, control of devices can be initiated (see Fig. 3e).

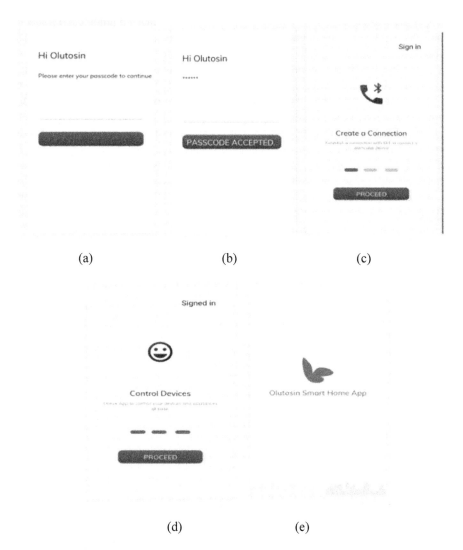

Fig. 3. User authentication and network connection establishment process

5 Conclusion and Future Work

In this paper, we have presented a system for controlling home devices or appliances from any location, with a hybrid technique based on an Android mobile application, Bluetooth, Zigbee and Arduino board. The main purpose of the work is to allow accessible communication between devices in the home and control of devices or appliances either from within or outside the house. The system has been tested using Proteus Simulation Software for feasibility. The next phase of the current study would be to establish a connection using actual hardware components required for building smart home automation. The simulation process shows that communication can be established between home appliances using the Arduino board, Bluetooth module and Zigbee. The mobile application should also be investigated for communication, control and monitoring of home from any location. In the future, closed circuit television (CCTV) installed in the home would also be connected to the system for monitoring of the house; thereby providing the security option of confirming a visitor's identity for whom the user may need to open the gate while not within the house. The home system is also intended to incorporate devices that could be useful for the elderly or handicapped. With the combination of both Zigbee and Bluetooth, the system seems to perform better in terms of communication range than with Bluetooth alone. Also, because the system accommodates a variety of sensors, the system could be extended for use in healthcare for monitoring and recording of a patient's vital health signs. Furthermore, to reduce costs, the system is intended to be used with an existing home appliances rather than the user needing to purchase new devices.

References

1. Nicola, K.: Smart Home - A Definition, September 2003. https://www.housinglin.org.uk/_assets/Resources/Housing/Housing_advice/Smart_Home_-_A_definition_September_2003.pdf. Accessed 5 Nov 2019
2. Lobaccaro, G., Carlucci, S., Löfström, E.: A review of systems and technologies for smart homes and smart grids. Energies 9(5), 348 (2016)
3. Carlsen, J.: A Guide to Home Automation Protocols, Future US Inc., 29 July 2014. https://www.toptenreviews.com/a-guide-to-home-automation-protocols. Accessed 5 Nov 2019
4. Asadullah, M., Ullah, K.: Smart home automation system using bluetooth technology. In: 2017 International Conference on Innovations in Electrical Engineering and Computational Technologies (ICIEECT). IEEE, pp. 1–6, April 2017
5. Singhal, H., Umrao, A., Faisal, A.: Android & bluetooth module based door automation system. Adv. Comput. Sci. Inf. Technol. (ACSIT) 2(12), 4–7 (2015)
6. Soliman, M., Abiodun, T., Hamouda, T., Zhou, J., Lung, C.H.: Smart home: integrating internet of things with web services and cloud computing. In: 2013 IEEE 5th International Conference on Cloud Computing Technology and Science, vol. 2, pp. 317–320. IEEE, December 2013
7. Sudharani, V., Siva, D., Vijaya Raju, M.: Smart home automation system using arduino and IOT. Int. J. Sci. Res. (IJSR) 7(9), 182–184 (2018)
8. Saxena, A., Saxena, S., Sharma, M., Maurya, A., Kumar, A.: Smart home automation using android application. Int. J. Sci. Res. Manag. Stud. (IJSRMS) 3, 326–329 (2017)
9. Yassein, M.B., Mardini, W., Khalil, A.: Smart homes automation using Z-wave protocol. In: 2016 International Conference on Engineering & MIS (ICEMIS). IEEE, pp. 1–6, September 2016
10. Rajaleksmi, J., SivaSankari, G.G.: IoT framework for smart home using cloud computing via open source mobile platform. Int. J. Comput. Eng. Appl. 64–70 (2016)
11. Ye, X., Huang, J.: A framework for cloud-based smart home. In: Proceedings of 2011 International Conference on Computer Science and Network Technology, vol. 2, pp. 894–897. IEEE, December 2011

12. Jabbar, W.A., Alsibai, M.H., Amran, N.S.S., Mahayadin, S.K.: Design and implementation of IoT-based automation system for smart home. In: 2018 International Symposium on Networks, Computers and Communications (ISNCC), pp. 1–6. IEEE, June 2018
13. Marhoon, H.M., Mahdi, M.I., Hussein, E.D., Ibrahim, A.R.: Designing and implementing applications of smart home appliances. Mod. Appl. Sci. **12**(12), 8–17 (2018)
14. Soliman, M.S., Alahmadi, A.A., Maash, A.A., Elhabib, M.O.: Design and implementation of a real-time smart home automation system based on arduino microcontroller kit and labview platform. Int. J. Appl. Eng. Res. **12**(18), 7259–7264 (2017)
15. Han, J., Choi, C.S., Park, W.K., Lee, I., Kim, S.H.: Smart home energy management system including renewable energy based on ZigBee and PLC. IEEE Trans. Consum. Electron. **60**(2), 198–202 (2014)
16. Poh, K.H., Tan, C.Y., Ruslan, N.S.M., Othman, W.A.F.W.: Design and implementation of simple IoT-based smart home system using arduino. Tech. J. Electr. Electron. Eng. Technol. **3**(1), 1–13 (2019)
17. Hoque, M.A., Davidson, C.: Design and implementation of an IoT-based smart home security system. Int. J. Netw. Distrib. Comput. **7**(2), 85–92 (2019). https://doi.org/10.2991/ijndc.k.190326.004
18. Singh, P: Common IoT Hardware Platforms, 8 May 2016. https://iotbytes.wordpress.com/popular-hardware-platforms-for-iot/. Accessed 19 Mar 2020
19. Samuel, S.S.I.: A review of connectivity challenges in IoT-smart home. In: 2016 3rd MEC International Conference on Big Data and Smart City (ICBDSC), pp. 1–4. IEEE, March 2016

Designing a Patient-Centric System for Secure Exchanges of Medical Data

Thais Webber⬤, Juan Mendoza Santana⬤, Andreas Francois Vermeulen⬤,
and Juliana K. F. Bowles⁽✉⁾⬤

School of Computer Science, University of St Andrews, St Andrews KY16 9SX, UK
{tcwds,jjm20,afv,jkfb}@st-andrews.ac.uk

Abstract. Designing patient-centric healthcare systems which consider the smart integration of distributed medical data is challenging. This includes handling numerous architectural dependencies and requirements as a result of blending a variety of future generation technologies. Examples of recent approaches are proposals of a unified format for medical records to facilitate efficient healthcare provision, transparent data access control using blockchain technology, and emergent authentication mechanisms and privacy-preserving techniques for data analytics. The Serums project proposes an innovative design for a Smart Health Centre System in a distributed development effort. The goal is a comprehensive solution for integration and access of transnational medical records. This paper focuses on the architectural design workflow as a way of delivering artefacts for development iterations and contribute towards module integration planning in the software development process. Our experience shows that in data integration projects for healthcare provision, system architects and developers can profit from the designed viewpoints as artefacts to reveal integration challenges and highlight quality attributes.

Keywords: Healthcare information systems · Patient health records · Architectural design

1 Introduction

The integration of Patient Health Records (PHRs) in a smart and secure environment for information retrieval can be an extensive challenge for researchers, system architects, healthcare providers and governments. Nonetheless, the vision of such an integration aims to enable, in the future, European-wide healthcare systems. In Europe, there is a clear trend towards patients becoming more empowered in healthcare processes and being increasingly aware of privacy and data ownership. For instance, patients may want to have more control over who has access to their data and to which parts of their data, whilst expecting the

This research is funded by the EU H2020 project Serums: Securing Medical Data in Smart Patient-Centric Healthcare Systems (grant code 826278).

O. Gervasi et al. (Eds.): ICCSA 2020, LNCS 12254, pp. 598–614, 2020.
https://doi.org/10.1007/978-3-030-58817-5_44

system to comply with the EU General Data Protection Regulation (GDPR)[1] and other legal and ethical regulations.

The EU Horizon 2020 project Serums[2] aims to combine next-generation technologies, such as blockchain and data lake principles, in a patient-centric toolchain for accessing, storing, communicating and analysing distributed medical records in a secure and privacy-preserving way [8]. It specifies the transformation and aggregation of PHRs from distributed data sources (e.g., from hospitals, medical practices, healthcare databases, health monitoring devices) into a unified and universal format for metadata storage named *Smart Patient Health Record* (SPHR). Complex access rules to SPHR are expected to be written by patients and healthcare professionals on a user-friendly front-end as *data sharing agreements*, which are stored as smart contracts over a blockchain network.

The challenge of designing an architecture like Serums for projects that employ diverse and emerging technologies is even bigger when teams are not co-located. Successful integration projects with dispersed teams rely on a system-level modular design with well-defined requirements and documentation about each module and their inter-dependencies [14]. The degree to which it is possible to reduce ambiguity and guarantee cohesion of requirements in a project is also dependent on how the architectural design workflow is conducted and documented from early stages of development [14].

In this paper, we discuss the *Smart Health Centre System* (SHCS) architectural design workflow within Serums and the contribution of each designed artefact (e.g. requirements specification, viewpoint diagrams, interaction diagrams, and several others) towards identifying development challenges. The discussions about the workflow outcomes are directed towards software engineering researchers, project managers and architectural analysts. We also point out the role of viewpoints in identifying the expected quality attributes (i.e., compliance, traceability, auditability, testability and interoperability) for the effective integration of systems such as SHCS.

This paper is structured as follows. In Sect. 2, we present related work regarding integrated healthcare records, emerging technologies and the Serums perspective. In Sect. 3, we introduce the *architectural design workflow* defined for Serums, and present an overview of its *architectural design* in Sect. 4. Sect. 5 discusses the design workflow outcome towards the desired quality attributes for a seamless integration, and further summarises considerable observations from applying the first iteration of the design process. We conclude with suggestions for further work in Sect. 6.

2   Recent Related Work

In recent years, sharing PHRs across healthcare institutions and countries has become an essential requirement of future-generation effective healthcare provision. To successfully achieve this goal, different integration solutions have been

---

[1] Information on GDPR can be found at https://gdpr-info.eu/.
[2] For more information see http://www.serums-h2020.org.

presented by researchers and software developers using different technologies such as Blockchain, Cloud Computing, IoT, Big Data, and so on [6,9,10,17]. In addition, prototypes have been developed to evaluate the design of such personalised and decentralised medical records systems. MedRec [5] is an example of a recent system developed with blockchain technology to deal with sensitive medical information. It is mostly focused on empowering patients and providers in the choice to release metadata and in engaging medical stakeholders to participate in the network as miners. The mining reward is to access and aggregate anonymised data to perform advanced analytics. By contrast, the Serums project applies the concept of distributed ledgers mostly to store and retrieve patient records, focusing on the development of a robust and secure authorisation mechanism that allows patients and healthcare organisations to create personalised access to medical records. Moreover, the goal of Serums is to establish a toolchain which is modular and integrates several next-generation technologies such as multi-factor user authentication schemes [2], and in the future, distributed privacy-preserving data analytics [11].

3   The Architectural Design Workflow

Serums follows an architectural design workflow in order to guarantee a clear integration process and adequate adherence to system requirements. An example of a basic design workflow for global software development (GSD) can be found in the work of Sangwan et al. [14].

The development of the Smart Health Centre System (SHCS) for Serums [8] can be classified as an example of a GSD project. The overall project assembles a total of 9 European partners within 7 countries including hospitals, academic and industrial partners. The coordinating team is responsible for the development and integration of the SHCS [8]. The *integration* task raises many challenges to the teams regarding sharing the understanding of system requirements, technological issues and various collaboration aspects such as exchanging concise technical reports to reduce design misalignment.

In addition, the project combines features of the *Rational Unified Process* (RUP) and incremental development models [15]. As described in [15], the development iterations are divided into four phases: *Inception, Elaboration, Construction* and *Transition*. The last is mainly concerned with the deployment of the system in the user community. In this paper, we focus on the *Elaboration* phase, aiming to include the integration task in the early stages of the design process. Figure 1 illustrates the Serums architectural design workflow.

3.1   Elaboration Phase

The *Elaboration* phase focuses on *architectural design* activities that enable a common understanding of the requirements and the establishment of an overall system architecture. It enables software architects to identify and describe the principal modules (aka subsystems) and their relationships [15]. For instance, the

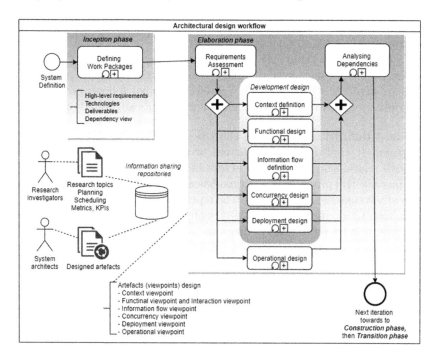

Fig. 1. Serums architectural design workflow

SHCS requires that only authorised users can access information from patient records which are usually distributed across multiple locations and may therefore present different privacy constraints that cannot be violated by the SHCS. Integrating both the requirements for the SHCS and the rules of each individual data source is an important integration challenge that must be addressed before reaching the *Construction* phase. This particular integration requirement can be refined on every development iteration assuming that for the first iteration only the rules of the SHCS are followed, whereas for the second iteration, the rules of each individual data source have to be integrated as well as part of the original requirement.

The SHCS architecture must be able to comply with this requirement that concerns not one but different scopes within the architecture such as the *security* modules and the *complex data storage and retrieval* modules. Thus, several artefacts need to be designed by each team to cope with this specification. Below, we describe each activity foreseen in the *Elaboration* phase of the architectural design workflow for Serums (see Fig. 1).

- *Requirements Assessment:* entails significant effort on the clear specification of system requirements and their coverage, generating a shared artefact called *Requirements Specification* (e.g., document). In practice, this document could also contain explicit remarks on how these requirements relate to the architecture towards supporting fundamental design decisions that impact non-functional aspects (i.e., quality attributes) [1].

- *Parallel design:* the listed activities in this workflow section could be partially performed in parallel, synchronously and/or asynchronously, even though they are depicted within a parallel gateway. In what follows, we give a brief description of each planned parallel activity and its suggested artefact.

- **Context definition:** the design effort begins delivering the system *Context viewpoint*. It captures the interaction of the system with its environment, through relationships with other actors such as people and external systems. Sommerville [15] proposes context models as an artefact to identify the boundaries of a system. These models can be represented through use case diagrams, UML interaction diagrams (typically sequence diagrams), and in our particular case using a more general diagram [13]. Use case diagrams can only be created when a system requirements specification is (at least partially) available. Preliminary architecture descriptions can focus on views that show the system's modules with their major internal processes and explicit dependencies.

- **Functional design:** aims to identify the functional blocks that will integrate the overall solution following the principles of high cohesion and low coupling [7]. In addition, this task includes the design of artefacts that describe the system's architectural elements that deliver the overall functionalities. Examples of artefacts generated from this activity are the functional and interaction viewpoints. These artefacts are needed to guide structural properties of the information, the concurrency, and the deployment whenever it is required. An incomplete system due to missing functional components can be a consequence of poor functional design. Additionally, modular development depends highly on this activity.

- **Information flow definition:** allows us to specify in a high-level manner how information is stored, manipulated, managed and transferred within the system. At the same time, this flow enables us to expand on the nature of the connections between components and modules identified in the functional design, for we agree that components interact with each other by passing information. This viewpoint is a high-level view of data elements and information flow, it can include some elements of the structure of the data and observations about static information (which is not transferred across components). A diagram can capture the sequence in which the information is passed and transformed through the modules of the system. The information flow is particularly relevant because it also allows architects to visualise the responsibilities of each module and their expected functionality, and define an initial design of the interfaces that will be provided.

- **Concurrency design:** aims to identify and describe the presence of concurrency within the system delivering a *Concurrency viewpoint* as artefact. A good concurrent design can help to identify bottlenecks and deadlocks generated by the interaction of different components. In addition, this design permits to identify convergence points in which the communication and the information flow can be synchronised.

- **Deployment design:** captures the environment in which the system will be deployed through the different stages of the development process. It is directly related to the infrastructure needed by each of the functional modules capturing the hardware requirements and runtime dependencies. This activity delivers a *Deployment viewpoint* that can be summarised into high-level diagrams containing visualisations of the mappings between logical and physical elements, processing components, network interconnections, and reflections on the storage facilities required.
- **Operational design:** captures how the system will be operated, administered, and supported when it is running in its production environment. It is a significant activity that must be considered and planned at design time to enable the definition of installation procedures, management, and normal operation of the system. Additionally, contingency plans can be introduced as means to mitigate problems resulting from unexpected functionality, which can be critical for healthcare systems.
- *Analysing dependencies:* marks the end of the *Elaboration* phase in terms of achieving a stable set of designed artefacts to follow up to the next phase of development cycle.

The parallel design activity above could also be named as *Development design*. The integration of these viewpoints entails an important step of architectural design, which will support the system development process. It aims to highlight the aspects of the architecture that are interesting to stakeholders involved in building, testing, maintaining, and enhancing the system. This perspective can be achieved by combining artefacts such as *Context viewpoint* to capture users and external agents, *Functional and Interaction viewpoints*, *Information flow viewpoint*, *Concurrency viewpoint* to define development units, dependencies and connections, and *Deployment design* to raise awareness about the system technical requirements. The *Operational viewpoint* will be evaluated towards the end of the *Construction phase* entering the *Transition phase*.

4 The Architectural Design for Serums

The architectural design plays a key role in system integration because its artefacts describe the responsibilities of each subsystem/module as well as the interfaces and steps required for their interaction [15]. The proposed SHCS architecture follows the workflow described in Sect. 3.

Context analysis: the *Context definition* within Serums' SHCS is shown in Fig. 2. There are three categories of users: hospital administrators, healthcare professionals, and patients. Each category can perform specific actions such as request a patient's SHPR and manage credentials or access rules. The diagram also shows that the system interacts with the data from three different hospitals (ZMC, FCRB and USTAN). Even though in a real scenario this interaction may

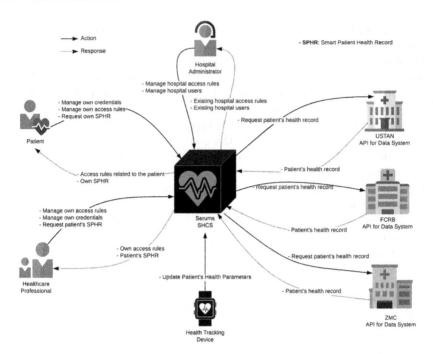

Fig. 2. SHCS context viewpoint

differ from hospital to hospital, for the current prototype we assume that it happens through standardised APIs for each data source. In addition, an interaction with personal health tracking devices is depicted. The context viewpoint allows us to place actors, functionalities and external connections in a perspective in which details of internal system features (e.g. front-end receiving requests for the security layer and for data retrieval processes) are abstracted in a black-box.

Functional design: the *Functional viewpoint* of SHCS is shown in Fig. 3. In this diagram, modules are explicitly divided following their main goals and interfaces with the integration module. The integration module has two sub-modules: the front-end dealing with user interface and users requests; and the back-end for interfacing and coordinating other modules to get responses. The functional viewpoint translates the requirements into implementation modules that will inter-operate via APIs. This diagram is the foundation for the information flow as well as for the deployment and interaction viewpoints, mostly because they all depend on the definition of functional modules to capture their different perspectives.

Information flow definition: the *Information Flow* within the SHCS is shown in the diagram of Fig. 4. It formalises the challenge of gathering the distributed medical records into a flexible infrastructure of data processing (acquisition, transformation, storage and retrieval). The data flow viewpoint enables the mapping of critical design decisions related to these operations. For instance,

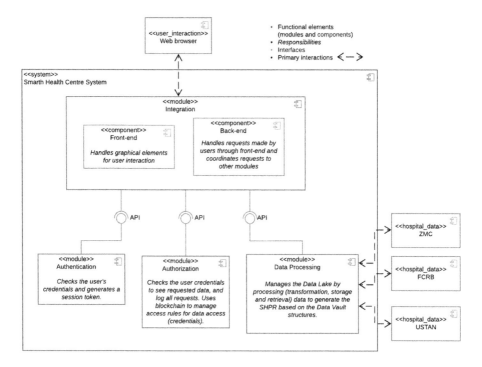

Fig. 3. SHCS functional viewpoint

the responsibilities of the integration module are detailed here and it depicts all needed handlers (*back-end*) and response flows to users (*front-end*).

Development design: the *Interaction viewpoint* is shown in Fig. 5. It represents the setup that will allow all the different modules to interact with each other. This viewpoint together with the *Information flow*, the *Functional viewpoint*, and the *Deployment viewpoint* (shown in Fig. 6) shape the development design. All perspectives combined enable developers to make relevant decisions for the modules implementations.

The modular approach proposed in the *Functional viewpoint* enables the SHCS to deal with different technologies, such as blockchain, distributed databases, and so on. Each high-tech solution has specific requirements that must be satisfied; our *Deployment viewpoint* shows the solutions for this issue by means of *containerisation* [16]. Furthermore, an additional level of interoperability has to do with the communication between modular subsystems, which is directly addressed in our *Interaction viewpoint*. *Concurrency design* is shown in a simplified manner through the *Interaction viewpoint* and the *Information flow viewpoint*. The *Operational design* is not included here because this is still a very early stage of the project in which operation modes have yet to be explored before being documented.

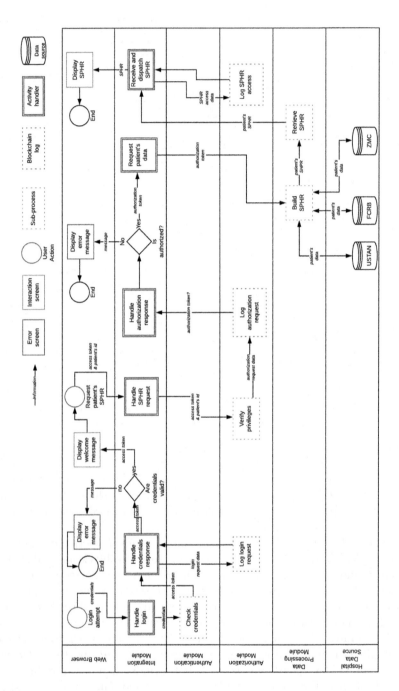

Fig. 4. SHCS information flow diagram

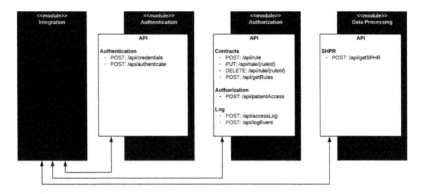

Fig. 5. SHCS interaction viewpoint

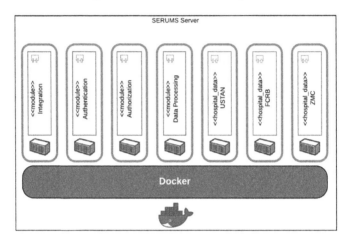

Fig. 6. SHCS deployment viewpoint

4.1 Architectural Design Overview

In the first software design iteration, we generated different viewpoints that can be aggregated in a high-level diagram showing the architectural overview, to gain an understanding of the required components of the SHCS. Figure 7 presents the Serums architectural overview that assembles four different perspectives (or layers) of integration.

Security layer: is responsible for handling privacy issues to guarantee confidentiality, integrity and availability when processing medical data. It is responsible for the generation of secure access tokens to be associated with user sessions, which will enable information exchange within the system components. It is also responsible for the synchronisation of two modules: (i) *Authentication* to make sure only individuals with credentials can access and visualise (fully or partially) the requested patient's health record and (ii) *Authorisation* which is managed

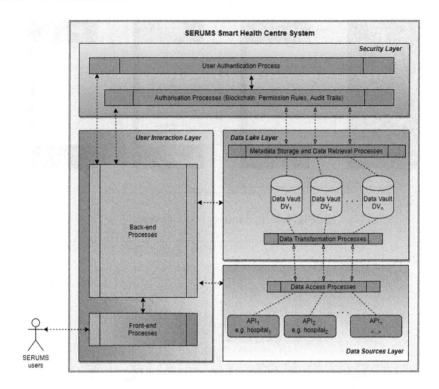

Fig. 7. SHCS architecture overview

by the Blockchain network to control the credentials and access rules for information retrieval. Role-based access permissions will be programmed as well as processes for maintaining records of the performed transactions for audit trail.

User Interaction layer: is responsible for building the system's front-end and back-end modules, which comprise the central integration layer for demonstrating the usage of Serums. It implements processes such as the interface graphical elements (front-end connection to users and its connection to the back-end processes), user access rules and credentials management (back-end connections to Security layer and Data Lake layer). Serums authorised users (individual, group or organisation) connect and interact with the system via the front-end, in it the authentication process has to be included as the first step of the navigation flow, subsequently the back-end will communicate with the *Authorisation* module to resolve the *Role-based permission rules* that are created, stored and updated in the Security Layer.

Data Lake layer (intermediate layer between the Serums SHCS and the data sources of medical organisations responsible for data storage and retrieval): integrates the module responsible for distributed medical data processing. It must be able to dispatch segments of a patient's health record based on the user's permission. This layer is responsible for assembling the *Smart Patient Health Record* (SPHR) as a unified format to represent medical data from multiple sources. The data lake will not store explicit medical information, instead it will store pointers to the real data, which will be retrieved on demand. The SPHR will be constructed based on the metadata extracted from the real data, the extraction of the metadata is also responsibility of this layer. The Data Lake layer depends directly on the Data Sources Layer, and provides services to the User Interaction Layer.

Data Sources layer: this layer can integrate modules, systems, subsystems or APIs responsible for creating a safe environment for data acquisition from organisations to integrate SPHR. It consolidates distributed data servers (i.e., from organisations such as hospitals, national databases, the patient's home environment), implicating in several trusted and untrusted network connections for the acquisition of PHR data. This layer, though depicted in our architectural overview, is not under the control of the Serums team, and as seen in the Context Viewpoint (Fig. 2) is external to the system.

Figure 7 is a valuable artefact delivered after a few iterations in the *Elaboration* phase of the design workflow. This output is the result of combining high-level requirements, preliminary design artefacts and several informal discussions between system architects of distributed teams.

5   Quality Attributes for SHCS Integration

The emphasis on non-functional requirements is usually orthogonal to functional design [4]. In this paper, we define quality attributes as non-functional requirements for SHCS integration. The design workflow should be able to produce artefacts that capture the desired quality attributes for the integrated SHCS: compliance, traceability, auditability, testability and interoperability. These properties are relevant for the project and they can, and should be, considered in the design of artefacts. The intersection between design viewpoints and quality attributes is summarised in Table 1.

Table 1. Desired quality attributes within integration perspective and major artefacts. Ticks indicate whether an artefact (viewpoint) is essential to inspect a quality attribute.

Artefact	Quality attributes for SHCS integration						
	Compliance	Traceability & Auditability	Testability V-model (testing approaches)				Interoperability
			Unit	Integration	System	Acceptance	
Requirements Specification	✓						
Context viewpoint	✓	✓			✓		✓
Functional viewpoint		✓	✓				✓
Information flow viewpoint	✓	✓		✓	✓	✓	✓
Interaction viewpoint				✓			✓
Concurrency viewpoint				✓			
Deployment viewpoint				✓			✓
Operational viewpoint							✓

Compliance determines that the integrated system is in accordance with established guidelines and specifications. From the collection of artefacts produced in the design workflow, compliance can be easily emphasised, for example, from the *Information flow viewpoint* refinement until it is thoroughly aligned with the requirements specification. In addition, compliance can be demonstrated with the help of the *Context viewpoint*, in which the actions and responses are described, thus enabling us to judge whether the system developed matches these actions. A more thorough analysis for compliance can be ultimately done with respect to the *Requirements Specification.*

Traceability in our context is defined as a quality attribute related to the ability to collect data regarding time records of transactions performed by users within the system. The *Information flow* and *Functional viewpoints* are valuable artefacts to ensure that this property will be fulfilled. In operation, the system should be able to produce transaction logs in the security layer that allow analysts to audit the system. Then, as a consequence of traceability, it is also possible to achieve Auditability, meaning that the integrated system can deliver information to verify if the requirements have been met and identify any non-conformance in the system operation. This can be achieved thanks to the security layer, in which a Blockchain implementation will automatically generate an entry into the ledger regarding information access. The *Information flow* diagram explicitly shows that the authorisation layer includes tasks related to the log entries in the Blockchain, just as it is mentioned in the *Functional viewpoint*. Complementary the *Context viewpoint* aids to capture what actions should be logged, hence strengthening traceability and auditability.

Testability is the degree to which a software artefact (module, requirements- or design document) supports testing in the test context. This quality attribute for Serums refers to the ability acquired through the viewpoints design to perform conclusive and reproducible testing. The *V-Model* [12] has been taken into consideration in order to align our architectural workflow and the generated artefacts to different stages of verification and validation according to that model. The context for *unit testing* can be related to the *Functional viewpoint*, in which individual components are responsible to perform specific tasks. *Integration testing* can be observed within the *Interaction viewpoint* in which all elements converge into the integration module. *System testing* can be placed within the *Deployment viewpoint* and the *Information flow*, that in conjunction provide a holistic perspective of the system. *Acceptance testing* can be done based on the actions and responses shown in the *Context viewpoint*. By enabling these testing stages related to the V-Model, our architectural workflow and artefacts contribute to develop testability as a feature of the integrated SHCS.

Interoperability is defined as the ability of systems to exchange and make use of information. SHCS has many challenges regarding module integration and how to define interfaces for secure data exchange. This quality attribute can be evaluated, for example, using the *Container viewpoint* to identify these interconnections. In our proposed architectural design, several other viewpoints (*Context, Functional, Information flow*) show the presence of external data sources related to hospital data. There is an evident demand for understanding interoperability, specially in the presence of dispersed data sources from partners and healthcare organisations. Irrespective of their specific implementations, the SHCS must be able to cope with each one of them seamlessly. It is at this point that standard protocols, such as *Health Level Seven* (HL7) [3] for delivering health information, can be considered.

Considering the five quality attributes highlighted as important in the context of the Serums project, we present a summary of observations gathered from the first iteration of the architectural design workflow.

1. Dispersed teams increase the challenges to specify and design modules because individual preconceptions have a greater weight in such project setup.
2. Sustaining informal discussions among dispersed teams often results in rework and misalignment of activities [14]. This is a challenge we have identified in our design workflow within the integration perspective.
3. Deriving formal specifications from high-level project requirements is not trivial because they focus on different aspects of the system.
4. Project requirements must be differentiated from system requirements and from individual requirements for each module.
5. *Requirements assessment* in the design workflow has the upmost relevance for acquiring all five quality attributes further in the remaining design activities.
6. There is a need for individual architectural design for each functional module besides the system's architectural design.
7. The relation between system architecture and module architecture must be clearly established to ease seamless integration.
8. *Functional viewpoint* granularity can vary depending on the perspective/responsibility of a development team.
9. The *Functional viewpoint* does not necessarily give a clear indication of all modules and operations involved in the overall architectural design. Several discussions in different communication channels were conducted during this modelling activity (not all captured in logs and documentation).
10. The *Functional viewpoint* and the *Information flow* are highly related to the SHCS desired quality attributes of traceability, auditability and testability.
11. *Information flow* is concerned with specific actions, thus there is no global description of the system's information flow.
12. The *Information flow viewpoint* is one of the richest artefacts to understand modules interfaces, data exchanges and security steps demanded by SHCS. It allows the module dependencies and internal processes to be further discussed and detailed amongst teams. Moreover, it could guide SHCS testing plan and expected system behaviour under user requests.
13. There are several approaches to interoperability, though we have proposed containerisation, we cannot guarantee at this stage that this will be sufficient for the entire system, additional development efforts are required to evaluate the effectiveness of containerisation.

14. Containerisation is being used instead of virtualisation, easing the deployment of modular components in a single shared unit of hardware.
15. Non-functional requirements and quality attributes have to be specified for the system as a whole and also for each individual module. The real contribution of each component to the success of quality attributes has to be reflected individually.

The architectural design workflow has been illustrated with artefacts to help the relevant stakeholders make design decisions that impact SHCS. These impacts are first understood in the *Elaboration phase* when the system architecture can still be prone to change. If these potential issues are detected and dealt with in this early stage, the *Construction* phase will follow a smooth development. For example, if the interaction between components is opportunely defined, then development teams can focus on satisfying the expected APIs, while the team responsible for the integration can handle the other modules as black boxes, and thus have no concerns regarding their actual implementation.

6   Conclusion

This paper addresses how the architectural design workflow of a system can be used as the means to uncover integration challenges, in our case the SHCS for Serums. It is natural to assume that modular decomposition of a system results in more focused artefacts across distributed teams. However this decomposition should be done taking into consideration the need for future integration at the centre of the architectural design. Early identification of module dependencies from architectural design artefacts and their derived models is a rich contribution to understand the challenges of Serums integration. For instance, the design viewpoints accompanied with several support diagrams help to identify integration factors needed to achieve desired quality attributes. In addition, these artefacts could help dispersed teams to share a common understanding of the integrated system in more effective ways to lead next development iterations.

Some challenges are still open for discussion regarding the architectural design workflow and the architectural design itself. Access to patient health records is granted on the basis of interaction rules between SHCS users. These interactions are rather complex, because they depend on time, geographical and other regulatory restrictions that might result in conflicting rules. These conflicts have to be identified and resolved first from a specification perspective, and then from an implementation one, that is, decisions have to be made by the stakeholders to define how these conflicts should be resolved.

This paper highlights that designing integrated healthcare systems can be less complex when following a proper design workflow. The proposed workflow emerged from the architectural and technological dependencies and challenges inherent in our project. Defining unambiguous requirements that can be concisely understood and documented is the first step to have teams sharing the same architectural vision from early stages of the software lifecycle. Moreover, reviewing the architectural design against desired quality attributes and business goals could be a key point for a future successful system integration.

References

1. Balsamo, S., Di Marco, A., Inverardi, P., Simeoni, M.: Model-based performance prediction in software development: a survey. IEEE Trans. Softw. Eng. **30**(5), 295–310 (2004)
2. Belk, M., Fidas, C., Pitsillides, A.: FlexPass: symbiosis of seamless user authentication schemes in IOT. In: Extended Abstracts of the 2019 CHI Conference on Human Factors in Computing Systems. ACM, New York (2019)
3. Benson, T., Grieve, G.: Principles of Health Interoperability: SNOMED CT, HL7 and FHIR. HITS. Springer, Cham (2016). https://doi.org/10.1007/978-3-319-30370-3
4. Blaine, J.D., Cleland-Huang, J.: Software quality requirements: how to balance competing priorities. IEEE Softw. **25**(2), 22–24 (2008)
5. Ekblaw, A., Azaria, A., Halamka, J.D., Lippman, A.: A case study for blockchain in healthcare: "MedRec" prototype for electronic health records and medical research data. In: Open & Big Data Conference, 22–24 August 2016. IEEE (2016)
6. Griggs, K.N., Ossipova, O., Kohlios, C.P., Baccarini, A.N., Howson, E.A., Hayajneh, T.: Healthcare blockchain system using smart contracts for secure automated remote patient monitoring. J. Med. Syst. **42**(7), 1–7 (2018). https://doi.org/10.1007/s10916-018-0982-x
7. ISO/IEC/IEEE: ISO/IEC/IEEE International Standard - systems and software engineering-vocabulary. ISO/IEC/IEEE 24765:2017(E), pp. 1–541, August 2017
8. Janic, V., Bowles, J., Vermeulen, A., et al.: The serums tool-chain: ensuring security and privacy of medical data in smart patient-centric healthcare systems. In: 2019 IEEE International Conference on Big Data (Big Data), Los Angeles, CA, USA, pp. 2726–2735 (2019)
9. Karimi, L., Joshi, J.: Multi-owner multi-stakeholder access control model for a healthcare environment. In: 2017 IEEE 3rd International Conference on Collaboration and Internet Computing (CIC), pp. 359–368. IEEE, October 2017
10. Khan, S.I., Hoque, A.S.M.L.: Health data integration with secured record linkage: a practical solution for Bangladesh and other developing countries. In: 2017 International Conference on Networking, Systems and Security (NSysS), pp. 156–161, January 2017
11. Kumar, M., Rossbory, M., Moser, B.A., Freudenthaler, B.: Deriving an optimal noise adding mechanism for privacy-preserving machine learning. In: Anderst-Kotsis, G., et al. (eds.) DEXA 2019. CCIS, vol. 1062, pp. 108–118. Springer, Cham (2019). https://doi.org/10.1007/978-3-030-27684-3_15
12. Mathur, S., Malik, S.: Advancements in the V-model. Int. J. Comput. Appl. **1**(12), 29–34 (2010)
13. Rumbaugh, J., Jacobson, I., Booch, G.: The Unified Modeling Language Reference Manual, 2nd edn. Pearson Higher Education, London (2004)
14. Sangwan, R., Bass, M., Mullick, N., Paulish, D.J., Kazmeier, J.: Global Software Development Handbook. Auerbach Series on Applied Software Engineering Series. Auerbach Publications, Routledge (2006)
15. Sommerville, I.: Software Engineering, 10th edn. Pearson, London (2015)

16. Syed, M., Fernandez, E.: A reference architecture for the container ecosystem. In: Proceedings of the 13th International Conference on Availability, Reliability and Security. ARES 2018. ACM, New York (2018)
17. Zhang, P., Schmidt, D., White, J., Lenz, G.: Chapter one - blockchain technology use cases in healthcare. In: Raj, P., Deka, G. (eds.) Blockchain Technology: Platforms, Tools and Use Cases. Advances on Computers, vol. 111, pp. 1–41. Elsevier, Amsterdam (2018)

SMOTE-Based Homogeneous Ensemble Methods for Software Defect Prediction

Abdullateef O. Balogun[1], Fatimah B. Lafenwa-Balogun[1],
Hammed A. Mojeed[1], Victor E. Adeyemo[2],
Oluwatobi N. Akande[3(✉)], Abimbola G. Akintola[1], Amos O. Bajeh[1],
and Fatimah E. Usman-Hamza[1]

[1] Department of Computer Science, University of Ilorin, Ilorin 1515, Nigeria
{balogun.aol,raji.fb,mojeed.ha,akintola.ag,bajehamos,
usman-hamza.fe}@unilorin.edu.ng
[2] School of Built Environment, Engineering and Computing, Leeds Beckett
University, Headingley Campus, Leeds LS6 3QS, UK
v.adeyemo5225@student.leedsbeckett.ac.uk
[3] Department of Computer Science, Landmark University, Omu-Aran,
Kwara State, Nigeria
akande.noah@lmu.edu.ng

Abstract. Class imbalance is a prevalent problem in machine learning which affects the prediction performance of classification algorithms. Software Defect Prediction (SDP) is no exception to this latent problem. Solutions such as data sampling and ensemble methods have been proposed to address the class imbalance problem in SDP. This study proposes a combination of Synthetic Minority Oversampling Technique (SMOTE) and homogeneous ensemble (Bagging and Boosting) methods for predicting software defects. The proposed approach was implemented using Decision Tree (DT) and Bayesian Network (BN) as base classifiers on defects datasets acquired from NASA software corpus. The experimental results showed that the proposed approach outperformed other experimental methods. High accuracy of 86.8% and area under operating receiver characteristics curve value of 0.93% achieved by the proposed technique affirmed its ability to differentiate between the defective and non-defective labels without bias.

Keywords: Software Defect Prediction · Class imbalance · Data sampling · Ensemble methods

1 Introduction

The rapid and continuous influence of software systems on human activities cannot be over-emphasized. This influence can be attributed to the comfort and pleasure derived from using these software systems [1, 2]. Developing quality and reliable software systems become imperative as the adverse effect of defective software systems may be disastrous. Aside from end-users' dissatisfaction, high over-head cost (human and capital) are some of the implications of defective software systems [3–6]. However, software quality assurance, a conventional process of ensuring quality software

© Springer Nature Switzerland AG 2020
O. Gervasi et al. (Eds.): ICCSA 2020, LNCS 12254, pp. 615–631, 2020.
https://doi.org/10.1007/978-3-030-58817-5_45

systems, is not adequate as modern software systems are implicitly large and inter-dependent as a result of periodic and continuous updates and upgrades [7–10]. Hence, sophisticated approaches such as software defect prediction are needed to complement conventional methods of software testing in building quality software systems.

Software Defect Prediction (SDP) is the deployment of Machine Learning (ML) methods for identifying defective software modules or components. SDP can assist software engineers to judiciously utilize available resources in software testing or maintenance by focusing on defective software modules or components before software release [11–14]. SDP models are built on details from software features such as source code complexity, software development history, software cohesion and coupling to predict defective modules in software systems. These software features are numerically quantified to determine the level of software systems quality and reliability [15–18].

Machine learning techniques are deployed for building SDP models using software features. Both supervised and unsupervised ML techniques have been used in building SDP models [3, 19–21]. The goal is to build an SDP model with high accuracy and precision on predicting defects in software systems. Nonetheless, the prediction performance of SDP models depends on the quality of software metric datasets used for developing the models. That is, software features used for building SDP models influence the prediction performance of SDP models [4, 9, 22, 23]. These software features are convoluted and distorted which can be traced to class imbalance problem. Class imbalance in SDP occurs when there is an unequal representation of class labels with non-defective instances as the majority and defective instances as a minority. It is a latent problem that occurs naturally in the software features and impedes the predictive performances of SDP models [21, 24].

Handling class imbalance has raised concerns and attention from researchers as many studies and methods have been proposed to address the imbalance problem [8, 11, 12, 21, 24–26]. From existing studies, it was observed that SDP models built with imbalanced datasets produces inaccurate results as the ensuing SDP models tend to over-fit. That is, SDP models built on imbalanced datasets recognize the majority class label more than the minority class label [12, 21, 24–26]. It is crucial to note that accurate prediction of the minority class label (defective class) is of utmost importance as a failure to predict a defective class may be detrimental. Consequently, researchers have employed methods such as data sampling, cost-sensitive learning and ensemble methods to address class imbalance problem in SDP [19, 25–28]. These methods had a good impact on SDP models; however, there is still a need for more solutions to address the class imbalance in SDP. Data sampling methods have been known to address class imbalance problem by increasing the minority class label (over-sampling) or decreasing the majority class label (under-sampling) [21, 24, 25]. Also, it has been established that class imbalance has little or no effect of ensemble methods [19, 26, 27]. Instigated by the preceding findings, this study proposes the combination of data sampling and ensemble methods to address class imbalance problem in SDP.

This study proposes a novel framework based on Synthetic Minority Oversampling Technique (SMOTE) and homogeneous (Bagging and Boosting) ensemble methods for SDP. SMOTE was used to balance the datasets while homogenous ensemble methods were used to amplify the prediction performances of SDP models. Bayesian Network (BN) and Decision Tree (DT) algorithms were implemented on the new preprocessed datasets to develop classifiers and the prediction performances of the proposed techniques were evaluated using accuracy, Area Under the Receiver Operating Characteristics (ROC) Curve (AUC) and f-measure.

In summary, the main contributions of this study are:

i. A novel software defect prediction framework based on homogeneous ensemble and SMOTE methods were presented.

ii. The effect of combining homogeneous ensemble and SMOTE data sampling methods on the prediction performances of SDP models was empirically validated.

The rest of the paper is outlined as follows. Section 2 presents a review of related works on class imbalance and high dimensionality in SDP. Section 3 describes the research approach employed in this study. Experimental results and analyses are discussed in Sect. 4. Section 5 concludes the study.

2   Related Work

Researchers have pointed out that the class imbalance problem negatively affects the prediction performance of SDP models. In most cases, class imbalance makes SDP models over-fits which make these models unreliable. Methods such as data sampling, ensemble methods and cost-sensitive analysis are the primary methods proposed by researchers to address class imbalance problem in

Singh, Misra and Sharma [29] conducted a study on the automation of bug (defect) severity prediction using summary extracted from bug metrics. Ensemble methods (voting and Bagging) were deployed to deal with the latent class imbalance problem from the generated bug dataset. Their results showed that ensemble methods had improved performance over single classifiers. This shows that ensemble methods work well with class imbalance.

El-Shorbagy, El-Gammal and Abdelmoez [30] in their study, combined SMOTE with a heterogeneous ensemble (stacking) method. They aimed to maximize the advantage of addressing the minority class labels by aggregating the performance of selected base classifiers. Their proposed method showed better prediction performance and outperformed other existing methods used on minority class labels. However, it is pertinent to note that stacking ensemble method consumes time in building models and requires several combinations of base classifiers to be effective [31, 32].

Balogun, Basri, Abdulkadir, Adeyemo, Imam and Bajeh [24] empirically validated the prediction performance stability of SDP models using data sampling methods. Both undersampling (Random Under-Sampling: RUS) and oversampling (SMOTE) were studied with varying imbalance ratio (IR). From their experimental results, it was observed that the presence of the class imbalance problem in SDP datasets affects the prediction performance of SDP models. Besides, they recommend the use of SMOTE technique for addressing the class imbalance problem in SDP. The findings from their study correlate positively with that of Yu, Jiang and Zhang [21].

Laradji, Alshayeb and Ghouti [33] investigated the effect of combining feature selection with ensemble methods for SDP. They aimed at addressing class imbalance problem with ensemble method and reduce feature redundancy via feature selection methods. Their results showed that carefully selected features improve the prediction performances of SDP models. Nonetheless, the effect of using ensemble methods to address class imbalance may not be as effective as using both data sampling and ensemble methods together.

Furthermore, Song, Guo and Shepperd [26] conducted an extensive empirical analysis on the effect of class imbalance on SDP models. Their experimental results showed that class imbalance affects the prediction performance of SDP models. Also, they opined that the right combination of data sampling methods and classifiers can yield good prediction performance. Goel, Sharma, Khatri and Damodaran [11] in their study also supported the claim of using the right data sampling technique for class imbalance problem in SDP.

Malhotra and Jain [34] empirically compared the prediction performances of seven (7) (boosting) ensemble methods. Their results indicated that data sampling technique should be applied before performing the boosting ensemble technique.

Similarly, Wang and Yao [35] carried out a comparative performance analysis of selected class imbalance problem solutions in SDP. They concluded that ensemble methods are superior to other methods such as data sampling and cost-sensitive methods. Findings from the preliminary studies of Rodriguez, Herraiz, Harrison, Dolado and Riquelme [25] also arrived at the same conclusion. Invariably, the combination of these methods may produce results better than any of the individual methods.

Kumar, Misra and Rath [36] used correlation analysis and multivariate linear regression feature selection method to select important source codes metrics for defect prediction. The culled datasets were trained by variants of neural network and ensemble methods. Their experimental results showed the effectiveness of ensemble methods in SDP specifically with feature selection.

Based on the preceding analysis, this study proposes the combination of data sampling (SMOTE) and homogeneous ensemble (Bagging and Boosting) to address class imbalance problem and subsequently improve the prediction performance of SDP models.

3   Methodology

In this section, the classification algorithms, data sampling method (SMOTE), homogeneous ensembles methods (Bagging & Boosting), and software defect datasets.

3.1   Classification Algorithms

Decision Tree (DT) and Bayesian Network (BN) algorithms are used as base-line prediction models in this study. DT and BN algorithms have been widely implemented in numerous SDP studies with good prediction performance. Besides, DT and BN have been reported to be stable with imbalance datasets [21, 24]. Table 1 presents DT and BN algorithms with their parameter setting as used in this study

Table 1. Classification algorithms

Classifier	Parameter setting
Decision Tree (DT)	ConfidenceFactor = 0.25; MinObj = 2
Bayesian Network (BN)	SimpleEstimator = alpha(0.25); SearchMethod = hillClimbing; MaxNoParents = 1

3.2 Synthetic Minority Over-Sampling Technique (SMOTE)

SMOTE is a statistical technique used for generating instances. Ideally, its implementation on a given dataset leads to the generation of synthetic instances belonging to the minority instances of the population without increasing the majority instances. This, therefore, increase the total population of the dataset by reducing the imbalance ratio between the minority and the majority class such that there exists no significant difference between the majority and minority instances. Software defect data are known to suffer from significant class imbalance [8, 21, 24, 35]. As SDP intends to predict defective instances, the developed classification model must be able to significantly discriminate between defective and non-defective instances without bias.

3.3 Homogeneous Ensemble Methods

Bagging Ensemble: Bagging is a homogeneous ensemble method used for amplifying the prediction performance of classification algorithms. The base classifiers of a bagging ensemble learn from a given dataset using different samples extracted from the original dataset. An aggregation of the classifiers' output is then carried out at prediction time [37]. Thus, this aggregation technique ensures that the variance of each classifier is reduced and each classifier bias does not also increase. In simple words, bagging algorithm randomly resamples the original datasets, trains multiple base classifiers using the resampled subsets, and finally makes a prediction by using the resulting classifications of multiple base learners [38]. Bagging ensemble is outlined in Algorithm 1.

Algorithm 1. The Bagging Algorithm

Input: training set S, Inducer I, integer N (number of bootstrap samples).

1.   for $i = 1$ to T {

2.   S' = bootstrap sample from S (sample with replacement)

3. $C_i = I(S')$

4.   }

5. $C^*(x) = \arg\max \sum_{i:C_i(x)=y} 1$ (the most frequently predicted label y)

Output: classifier C^*

Boosting Ensemble: Boosting ensemble method deploys a weak classifier in sequence, to train the re-weighted training data. In the end, it uses a majority vote mechanism for its final decision by integrating all weak hypotheses created by the weak classifiers into the final hypothesis [39]. Boosting uses weighted averages to transform weak classifiers into stronger classifiers with each model deciding what features the next iteration focuses on.

In this study, the AdaBoost.M1 algorithm [40] outlined in Algorithm 2 was implemented.

Algorithm 2. The AdaBoost.M1 Algorithm

Input: Training set $S = \{x_i, y_i\}, i = 1 \dots m, y_i \in Y, Y = \{c_1, c_2, \dots, c_k\}, c_k$ is the class label; The number of Iterations T; Weak classifier I.

1   Initializing weights distribution of $D_1(i) = 1/m$

2   for $t = 1$ to T

3   Train classifier $I(S, D_t)$, get a weak hypothesis

         $h_t = X \rightarrow \{c_1, c_2, \dots, c_k\}$

4   Compute the error rate of h_t, $\varepsilon_t \leftarrow \sum_{i=1}^{m} D_t(i)[y_i \neq h_t(x_i)]$.

5   If $\varepsilon_t > 0.5$ then

6          $T \leftarrow t - 1$

7   Continue

8   End if

9   Set $\beta_t = \dfrac{\varepsilon_t}{1 - \varepsilon_t}$

10   for $i = 1$ to m

11   Update weight $D_{t+1}(i) = D_t(i)\beta_t^{1-[y_i \neq h_t(x_i)]}$

12   End for i

13   End for t

Output: the final hypothesis $H(x) = \arg\max \left(\sum_{t=1}^{T} \ln\left(\frac{1}{\beta_t}\right) [Y \neq h_t(X)] \right)$

Similarly, Table 2 presents the homogeneous ensemble methods and their respective parameters as used in the experimentation stage of this study.

Table 2. Homogeneous ensemble

Homogeneous ensembles	Parameter setting
Bagging	Classifier = {BN, DT}, bagSizePercent = 100; numIteration = 10; seed = 1; calcOutOfBag = False; batchSize = 100
Boosting	Classifier = {BN, DT}, weightThreshold = 100; numIteration = 10; seed = 1; useResampling = True; batchSize = 100

3.4 Software Defect Datasets

In this study, software defect datasets from NASA repository were used for training and testing the SDP models. Shepperd, Song, Sun and Mair [41] cleaned version of NASA datasets was used in the experimentation. Table 3 presents a description of the selected datasets with their respective number of features, number of instances and imbalance ratio (IR). The IR is based on the ratio of defective instances to non-defective instances in each defect dataset. The diverse IR values of NASA datasets make it appropriate for this study. Also, NASA datasets have been widely used in existing related SDP studies [21, 24].

Table 3. Description of selected NASA software defect datasets

Datasets	# of Features	# of Modules	Imbalance Ratio (IR)
KC1	22	1162	3
KC3	40	194	4
MC2	40	124	2
PC3	38	1053	7
PC4	38	1270	6

3.5   Performance Evaluation Metrics

Existing studies have reported that the choice and selection of performance evaluation metrics is crucial in SDP [42, 43]. Using only accuracy value may be inaccurate due to the imbalance nature of the datasets used for training and testing the SDP models. Accuracy, F-Measure, and Area under Curve (AUC) were used to evaluate the prediction performances of the ensuing SDP models. These evaluation metrics have been widely used and proven to be reliable in SDP studies [4, 18, 21, 22, 27, 33].

i. Accuracy is the number or percentage of correctly classified instances to the total sum of instances.

$$Accuracy = \frac{TP + TN}{TP + FN + TN} \qquad (1)$$

ii. F-Measure is defined as the weighted harmonic mean of the test's precision and recall

$$F - Measure = 2X((PrecisionXRecall)/Precision + Recall) \qquad (2)$$

iii. The Area under Curve (AUC) shows the trade-off between TP and FP. It provides an aggregate measure of performance across all possible classification thresholds.

Where $Precision = \frac{TP}{TP+FP}$, $Recall = \frac{TP}{TP+FN}$, TP = Correct Classification, FP = Incorrect Classification, TN = Correct Misclassification, and FN = Incorrect Misclassification.

3.6   Experimental Framework

Figure 1 presents the experimental framework developed in this study. To empirically assess the efficacy of the proposed method on SDP models, the experimental framework is used on 5 defect datasets (See Table 3) with the base classifiers (DT and BN) (See Table 1) and homogeneous ensemble (Boosting and Bagging) (See Table 2). K-fold (where $k = 10$) cross-validation technique is used for the evaluation of the SDP models in this study. Our choice of 10-fold CV is in line with existing studies and its ability to build SDP models with low bias and variance [21, 22, 42, 43].

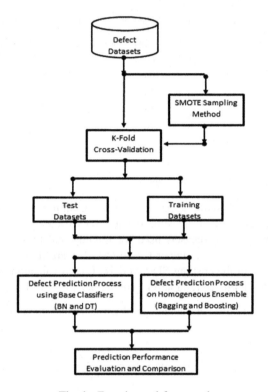

Fig. 1. Experimental framework

From the experimental framework, the majority and minority classes in each dataset are balanced using the SMOTE sampling technique. The balanced representation of the classes was based on 50% defective class and 50% non-defective class as used in existing studies [21, 24]. The essence of this is to ensure the resulting SDP models were trained with each class labels and to give credibility to the ensuing SDP models in predicting the appropriate class labels (defective or non-defective). Our choice of SMOTE as sampling technique is based on its performance and relevance in existing studies [11, 12, 24, 25, 30].

Thereafter, the homogeneous ensembles and the base classifiers are then applied on the original and balanced datasets based on 10-fold cross-validation (CV) technique. CV technique will ensure better usage of the datasets as each instance will be used for training and testing iteratively. Details on how CV works are reported and can be referenced in [44, 45]. Consequently, the prediction performance of the ensuing models will be evaluated using accuracy, f-measure and AUC.

Also, SDP models based on BN and DT classification algorithm with and without SMOTE and homogeneous ensemble (–i- BN, –ii- BN and SMOTE (BN + SMOTE), iii- Bagged BN, -iv- Boosted BN, -v- DT, -vi- DT and SMOTE (DT + SMOTE), -vii- Bagged DT, -viii- Boosted DT) were developed to create unprejudiced comparison and to measure the effect of SMOTE and ensemble on the prediction performance of the base classifiers. All experiments were carried out using the WEKA machine learning tool [46].

4   Results

The results obtained after evaluating the various developed models are presented and discussed in this section. It is important to showcase the significant impact of SMOTE sampling technique on SDP model development. More so, the efficacy of the ensemble methods over the base-line classifier is another focal point of this study. Thus, the results will be presented to reflect these impacts concerning each base-line classifiers.

Table 4 presents the prediction performances of base classifiers (BN and DT) on the original SDP datasets. The BN classifier, as seen in Table 4, yielded an average accuracy of 71.35%, average AUC of 0.69 and average F-measure of 0.73. Its accuracy scores range from 67.61% to 77.83%. Likewise, AUC scores ranged from 0.584 to 0.81, and F-measure scores from 0.693 to 0.775. The DT classifier also had good prediction performances with an average accuracy of 77.14%, average AUC of 0.65 and an average F-measure of 0.76. DT lowest (60.5%) and highest (86.93%) accuracy scores were from MC2 and PC4 datasets respectively.

Table 4. Prediction performance of BN and DT on the original datasets

Datasets	Original datasets					
	Accuracy (%)		AUC		F-Measure	
	BN	DT	BN	DT	BN	DT
KC1	68.33	74.18	0.681	0.604	0.698	0.717
KC3	77.83	79.4	0.584	0.653	0.775	0.783
MC2	70.16	60.5	0.614	0.589	0.693	0.608
PC3	67.61	84.71	0.779	0.591	0.731	0.839
PC4	72.83	86.93	0.81	0.789	0.767	0.869
Average	71.35	77.14	0.69	0.65	0.73	0.76

From the experimental results in Table 4, it is evident that the base classifiers (BN and DT) have good prediction performance on the original datasets (with class imbalance problem) with their respective average accuracy (BN:71.35%; DT:77.14%) and f-measure (BN:73%; DT:76%) values greater than 70% while there AUC (BN:69%; DT:65%) values are very close to 70%. The relative average prediction performances of BN and DT in this case although acceptable can be attributed to the occurrence of the latent class imbalance in the SDP datasets. Hence, the removal of the class imbalance problem by balancing the class labels may generate a better prediction performance for the base classifiers (BN and DT) [21, 24].

Table 5. Prediction performance of BN and DT on the balanced datasets

Datasets	Balanced datasets					
	Accuracy (%)		AUC		F-Measure	
	BN + SMOTE	DT + SMOTE	BN + SMOTE	DT + SMOTE	BN + SMOTE	DT + SMOTE
KC1	72.45	79.70	0.800	0.807	0.724	0.797
KC3	75.87	82.20	0.849	0.858	0.756	0.821
MC2	70.44	64.20	0.729	0.657	0.700	0.641
PC3	88.29	88.00	0.781	0.902	0.734	0.880
PC4	86.10	91.31	0.954	0.915	0.861	0.913
Average	78.63	81.08	0.820	0.830	0.760	0.810

Furthermore, Table 5 shows the prediction performances of BN and DT classifiers on the balanced datasets. This is to reveal the effect of data sampling (in this case SMOTE technique) on the prediction performance of SDP models. That is, to empirically validate if the removal of class-imbalance via SMOTE data sampling technique will positively improve the prediction performance of BN and DT classifiers.

It was observed that when BN was applied on the balanced datasets, an average accuracy of 78.63%, average AUC of 0.82 and an average f-measure of 0.76 was recorded. Besides, BN had its highest accuracy value (88.29%) on PC3 and its lowest accuracy value (70.44%) on MC2. On the other hand, when DT was applied on the balanced datasets, an average accuracy of 81.08%, average AUC of 0.83 and an average f-measure score of 0.81 was recorded. Also, DT had its peak (91.31%) and lowest accuracy (64.2%) values on PC4 and MC2 datasets respectively. It can be seen that both classifiers had their lowest accuracy values on MC2. This may be due to the high number of features in MC2 (40 features) (See Table 3).

Comparatively, the prediction performances of BN and DT on balanced datasets (See Table 5) were improved and better than their prediction performance with original datasets (See Table 4). Specifically, BN with balanced datasets (BN + SMOTE) had +10.2% increment in average accuracy, +18.8% increment in average AUC and +4% increment in f-measure values over BN with original datasets. The same trend was observed in DT on balanced datasets (DT +SMOTE). There was a percentage increase of +5.1% in the average accuracy, +27.7% in the average AUC and +6.6% in the average f-measure values of DT + SMOTE over DT. Consequently, the percentage increase observed in the prediction performance of BN + SMOTE and DT + SMOTE indicates that balancing via SMOTE technique has a positive effect on the prediction performances of BN and DT. Thus, our findings revealed that class imbalance impedes the performance of SDP models and can be resolved using data sampling technique (in this case SMOTE) [12, 21, 24, 25, 30, 34].

Tables 6 and 7 present the prediction performance of the homogeneous ensembles (Bagging and Boosting) respectively on the original SDP datasets. From Table 6, BaggedBN on the original datasets had an average accuracy of 71.50%, an average AUC of 0.73 and an average f-measure value of 0.74. Also, Bagged DT recorded an average accuracy of 80.66%, average AUC of 0.78 and average f-measure of 0.79 value across the studied datasets.

As presented in Table 7, BoostedBN had an average accuracy of 79.58%, average AUC of 0.7 and average f-measure 0.77 while BoostedDT had 78.68% average accuracy, 0.76 average AUC and 0.78 average f-measure value. From both tables (Table 6 and Table 7), there are no clear cut superior ensemble methods. That is, the prediction performance of both boosting and bagging ensemble methods depends on the choice of datasets and base classifiers. However, when compared with experimental results of the base classifiers on original datasets (See Table 4), the ensemble methods are superior in prediction performance.

Table 6. Prediction performance of bagging ensemble on original datasets

Datasets	Original datasets					
	Accuracy (%)		AUC		F-Measure	
	Bagged BN	Bagged DT	Bagged BN	Bagged DT	Bagged BN	Bagged DT
KC1	67.73	77.54	0.687	0.719	0.692	0.752
KC3	76.29	84.54	0.688	0.729	0.768	0.827
MC2	71.77	66.13	0.663	0.736	0.711	0.639
PC3	68.00	85.94	0.781	0.789	0.734	0.835
PC4	73.70	89.13	0.810	0.914	0.773	0.886
Average	71.50	80.66	0.730	0.780	0.740	0.790

Table 7. Prediction performance boosting ensemble on original datasets

Datasets	Original datasets					
	Accuracy (%)		AUC		F-Measure	
	Boosted BN	Boosted DT	Boosted BN	Boosted DT	Boosted BN	Boosted DT
KC1	74.01	73.24	0.670	0.691	0.680	0.721
KC3	81.44	79.38	0.590	0.712	0.799	0.777
MC2	70.16	66.94	0.596	0.701	0.693	0.668
PC3	85.66	85.66	0.785	0.788	0.820	0.846
PC4	86.61	88.19	0.868	0.893	0.855	0.879
Average	79.58	78.68	0.700	0.760	0.770	0.780

BaggedDT had a +4.56% increase of average accuracy values when compared with DT on original datasets. On the other hand, BaggedBN had an insignificant increment (+0.02) in its average accuracy value over BN on the original datasets. Also, BoostedBN had +11.4% increments in its average accuracy value over BN on the original datasets while BoostedDT had approximately +2% increments. The homogeneous (Bagging and Boosting) ensemble methods amplified the respective prediction performances of base classifiers BN and DT. Furthermore, the superiority of the homogeneous ensemble methods over the base classifiers can be attributed to its ability to cope with class imbalance. However, the prediction performances of the base classifiers (BN and DT) on the balanced datasets (BN + SMOTE and DT + SMOTE) were superior to the prediction performances of the homogeneous ensemble methods on original datasets. Hence, this study concludes that ensemble methods can amplify the prediction performances of base classifiers and accommodates class imbalance but ensemble methods are not as effective as data sampling methods in addressing the class imbalance in SDP.

The prediction performances of the homogeneous ensemble (Bagging and Boosting) methods on the balanced SDP datasets are presented in Table 8 and Table 9 respectively. BaggedBN + SMOTE had an average accuracy of 80.09%, an average AUC of 0.86 and an average f-measure value of 0.79. Also, BaggedDT + SMOTE recorded an average accuracy of 85.12%, average AUC of 0.79 and an average f-measure of 0.85 across the studied datasets.

Table 8. Prediction performance of bagging ensemble on balanced datasets

Datasets	Balanced datasets					
	Accuracy (%)		AUC		F-Measure	
	BaggedBN + SMOTE	BaggedDT + SMOTE	BaggedBN + SMOTE	BaggedDT + SMOTE	BaggedBN + SMOTE	BaggedDT + SMOTE
KC1	73.95	82.65	0.807	0.896	0.739	0.826
KC3	78.73	85.40	0.855	0.898	0.787	0.854
MC2	71.77	74.21	0.716	0.831	0.653	0.742
PC3	88.56	89.86	0.965	0.967	0.886	0.899
PC4	87.43	93.46	0.959	0.979	0.874	0.935
Average	80.09	85.12	0.860	0.910	0.790	0.850

Also, as presented in Table 9, BoostedBN + SMOTE had an average accuracy of 81.94%, average AUC of 0.88 and average f-measure of 0.82 while BoostedDT + SMOTE had had an average accuracy of 86.8%, an average AUC of 0.93 and an average f-measure value of 0.87. The results recorded revealed that BoostedBN + SMOTE and BoostedDT + SMOTE were superior to BaggedBN + SMOTE and BaggedDT + SMOTE. This may be due to boosting ensemble iterative nature of model building against the independent model building of the bagging method [31, 47].

As presented in Table 10, the prediction performances of the proposed approaches (BaggedBN + SMOTE, BaggedDT + SMOTE, BoostedBN + SMOTE and BoostedDT + SMOTE) were superior to the experimented methods (BN, BN + SMOTE, DT, DT + SMOTE, BaggedBN, BaggedDT, BoostedDT, BoostedBN). Specifically, BaggedBN + SMOTE recorded a significant positive increment of 12%, 17.8%, and 6.7% in average accuracy, average AUC and average f-measure values respectively while BaggedDT + SMOTE also recorded a significant positive increment of 5.5%, 16.67%, and 7.6% in average accuracy, average AUC and average f-measure values respectively over the prediction performance of BaggedBN and BaggedDT. BoostedBN + SMOTE achieved an increment of 2.96%, 25.7%, 6.49% in average accuracy, average AUC and average f-measure compared to an increment of 10.32%, 22.37% and 11.54% recorded by BoostedDT + SMOTE. From these analyses, it could be concluded that the prediction performances of homogeneous ensemble methods can also be amplified using the appropriate data sampling technique (in this case SMOTE technique).

Table 9. Prediction performance boosting ensemble on balanced datasets

| Datasets | Balanced datasets | | | | | |
| | Accuracy (%) | | AUC | | F-Measure | |
	Boosted BN + SMOTE	Boosted DT + SMOTE	Boosted BN + SMOTE	Boosted DT + SMOTE	Boosted BN + SMOTE	Boosted DT + SMOTE
KC1	74.41	80.46	0.816	0.880	0.744	0.805
KC3	82.22	86.35	0.904	0.926	0.822	0.863
MC2	70.44	80.50	0.732	0.877	0.700	0.805
PC3	91.38	91.65	0.965	0.970	0.914	0.917
PC4	91.27	95.02	0.976	0.985	0.913	0.950
Average	81.94	86.80	0.880	0.930	0.820	0.870

Table 10. Prediction performance comparison of the implemented SDP models

Prediction models	Average accuracy (%)	Average AUC	Average F-measure
BN	71.35	0.69	0.73
DT	77.14	0.65	0.76
BN + SMOTE	78.63	0.82	0.76
DT + SMOTE	81.08	0.83	0.81
BaggedBN	71.50	0.73	0.74
BoostedBN	79.58	0.70	0.77
BaggedDT	80.66	0.78	0.79
BoostedDT	78.68	0.76	0.78
*BaggedBN + SMOTE	80.09	0.86	0.79
*BoostedBN + SMOTE	81.94	0.88	0.82
*BaggedDT + SMOTE	85.12	0.91	0.85
*BoostedDT + SMOTE	86.80	0.93	0.87

(* indicates proposed methods)

5 Conclusions

This study has exhaustively discussed an SDP approach based on the combination of a homogeneous ensemble (Bagging and Boosting) and data sampling (SMOTE). The effects of data sampling and homogeneous ensemble methods are empirically validated. The experimental results showed that the SMOTE technique can improve the prediction performance of not only the base classifier (BN and DT) but the homogeneous ensemble methods inclusive. Also, the proposed approaches (BaggedBN + SMOTE, BaggedDT + SMOTE, BoostedBN + SMOTE and BoostedDT + SMOTE) significantly outperformed the base classifiers (BN and DT). This indicates that the combination of SMOTE and homogeneous ensemble does not only address the class imbalance problem but also positively increase the prediction performance of the base classifiers. Future work will attempt to optimize ensemble parameters and degree of data sampling on SDP approaches.

References

1. Basri, S., Almomani, M.A., Imam, A.A., Thangiah, M., Gilal, A.R., Balogun, A.O.: The organisational factors of software process improvement in small software industry: comparative study. In: Saeed, F., Mohammed, F., Gazem, N. (eds.) IRICT 2019. AISC, vol. 1073, pp. 1132–1143. Springer, Cham (2020). https://doi.org/10.1007/978-3-030-33582-3_106
2. Mojeed, H.A., Bajeh, A.O., Balogun, A.O., Adeleke, H.O.: Memetic approach for multi-objective overtime planning in software engineering projects. J. Eng. Sci. Technol. **14**, 3213–3233 (2019)
3. Balogun, A., Oladele, R., Mojeed, H., Amin-Balogun, B., Adeyemo, V.E., Aro, T.O.: Performance analysis of selected clustering techniques for software defects prediction. Afr. J. Comput. ICT **12**, 30–42 (2019)
4. Balogun, A.O., Basri, S., Abdulkadir, S.J., Hashim, A.S.: Performance analysis of feature selection methods in software defect prediction: a search method approach. Appl. Sci. **9**, 2764 (2019)
5. Bajeh, A.O., Oluwatosin, O.-J., Basri, S., Akintola, A.G., Balogun, A.O.: Object-oriented measures as testability indicators: an empirical study. J. Eng. Sci. Technol. **15**, 1092–1108 (2020)
6. Gupta, A., Suri, B., Kumar, V., Misra, S., Blažauskas, T., Damaševičius, R.: Software code smell prediction model using Shannon, Rényi and Tsallis entropies. Entropy **20**, 372 (2018)
7. Bashir, K., Li, T., Yohannese, C.W., Mahama, Y.: Enhancing software defect prediction using a supervised-learning based framework. In: 2017 12th International Conference on Intelligent Systems and Knowledge Engineering (ISKE), pp. 1–6. IEEE (2017)
8. Chen, L., Fang, B., Shang, Z., Tang, Y.: Tackling class overlap and imbalance problems in software defect prediction. Softw. Qual. J. **26**(1), 97–125 (2016). https://doi.org/10.1007/s11219-016-9342-6
9. Ghotra, B., McIntosh, S., Hassan, A.E.: A large-scale study of the impact of feature selection techniques on defect classification models. In: 2017 IEEE/ACM 14th International Conference on Mining Software Repositories (MSR), pp. 146–157. IEEE (2017)

10. Chaturvedi, K., Bedi, P., Misra, S., Singh, V.: An empirical validation of the complexity of code changes and bugs in predicting the release time of open-source software. In: 2013 IEEE 16th International Conference on Computational Science and Engineering, pp. 1201–1206. IEEE (2013)

11. Goel, L., Sharma, M., Khatri, S.K., Damodaran, D.: Implementation of data sampling in class imbalance learning for cross project defect prediction: an empirical study. In: 2018 Fifth International Symposium on Innovation in Information and Communication Technology (ISIICT), pp. 1–6. IEEE (2018)

12. Hamdy, A., El-Laithy, A.: SMOTE and Feature Selection for More Effective Bug Severity Prediction. Int. J. Softw. Eng. Knowl. Eng. **29**, 897–919 (2019)

13. Iqbal, A., Aftab, S.: A classification framework for software defect prediction using multi-filter feature selection technique and MLP. Int. J. Mod. Educ. Comput. Sci. **12**(1), 18–25 (2020). https://doi.org/10.5815/ijmecs.2020.01.03

14. Oluwagbemiga, B.A., Shuib, B., Abdulkadir, S.J., Sobri, A.: A hybrid multi-filter wrapper feature selection method for software defect predictors. Int. J Supply Chain Manag. **8**, 9–16 (2019)

15. Kamei, Y., Shihab, E.: Defect prediction: accomplishments and future challenges. In: IEEE 23rd International Conference on Software Analysis, Evolution, and Reengineering (SANER), vol. 5, pp. 33–45. IEEE (2016)

16. Kondo, M., Bezemer, C.-P., Kamei, Y., Hassan, A.E., Mizuno, O.: The impact of feature reduction techniques on defect prediction models. Empir. Softw. Eng. **24**(4), 1925–1963 (2019). https://doi.org/10.1007/s10664-018-9679-5

17. Li, Z., Jing, X.-Y., Zhu, X.: Progress on approaches to software defect prediction. IET Softw. **12**, 161–175 (2018)

18. Mabayoje, M.A., Balogun, A.O., Jibril, H.A., Atoyebi, J.O., Mojeed, H.A., Adeyemo, V.E.: Parameter tuning in KNN for software defect prediction: an empirical analysis. Jurnal Teknologi dan Sistem Komputer **7**, 121–126 (2019)

19. Tong, H., Liu, B., Wang, S.: Software defect prediction using stacked denoising autoencoders and two-stage ensemble learning. Inf. Softw. Technol. **96**, 94–111 (2018)

20. Usman-Hamza, F.E., Atte, A.F., Balogun, A.O., Mojeed, H.A., Bajeh, A.O., Adeyemo, V. E.: Impact of feature selection on classification via clustering techniques in software defect prediction. J. Comput. Sci. Appl. **26**(1), 73–88 (2019). https://doi.org/10.4314/jcsia.v26i1.8

21. Yu, Q., Jiang, S., Zhang, Y.: The performance stability of defect prediction models with class imbalance: An empirical study. IEICE Trans. Inf. Syst. **100**, 265–272 (2017)

22. Xu, Z., Liu, J., Yang, Z., An, G., Jia, X.: The impact of feature selection on defect prediction performance: an empirical comparison. In: 2016 IEEE 27th International Symposium on Software Reliability Engineering (ISSRE), pp. 309–320. IEEE (2016)

23. Gupta, A., Suri, B., Misra, S.: A systematic literature review: code bad smells in java source code. In: Gervasi, O., et al. (eds.) ICCSA 2017. LNCS, vol. 10408, pp. 665–682. Springer, Cham (2017). https://doi.org/10.1007/978-3-319-62404-4_49

24. Balogun, A.O., Basri, S., Abdulkadir, S.J., Adeyemo, V.E., Imam, A.A., Bajeh, A.O.: Software defect prediction: analysis of class imbalance and performance stability. J. Eng. Sci. Technol. **14**, 3294–3308 (2019)

25. Rodriguez, D., Herraiz, I., Harrison, R., Dolado, J., Riquelme, J.C.: Preliminary comparison of techniques for dealing with imbalance in software defect prediction. In: Proceedings of the 18th International Conference on Evaluation and Assessment in Software Engineering, pp. 1–10 (2014)

26. Song, Q., Guo, Y., Shepperd, M.: A comprehensive investigation of the role of imbalanced learning for software defect prediction. IEEE Trans. Softw. Eng. **45**, 1253–1269 (2018)
27. Yang, X., Lo, D., Xia, X., Sun, J.: TLEL: a two-layer ensemble learning approach for just-in-time defect prediction. Inf. Softw. Technol. **87**, 206–220 (2017)
28. Yohannese, C.W., Li, T.: A combined-learning based framework for improved software fault prediction. Int. J. Comput. Intell. Syst. **10**, 647–662 (2017)
29. Singh, V., Misra, S., Sharma, M.: Bug severity assessment in cross-project context and identifying training candidates. J. Inf. Knowl. Manag. **16**, 1750005 (2017)
30. El-Shorbagy, S.A., El-Gammal, W.M., Abdelmoez, W.M.: Using SMOTE and heterogeneous stacking in ensemble learning for software defect prediction. In: Proceedings of the 7th International Conference on Software and Information Engineering, pp. 44–47 (2018)
31. Zhou, Z.-H.: Ensemble Methods: Foundations and Algorithms. CRC Press, Boca Raton (2012)
32. Ardabili, S., Mosavi, A., Várkonyi-Kóczy, A.R.: Advances in machine learning modeling reviewing hybrid and ensemble methods. In: Várkonyi-Kóczy, A.R. (ed.) INTER-ACADEMIA 2019. LNNS, vol. 101, pp. 215–227. Springer, Cham (2020). https://doi.org/10.1007/978-3-030-36841-8_21
33. Laradji, I.H., Alshayeb, M., Ghouti, L.: Software defect prediction using ensemble learning on selected features. Inf. Softw. Technol. **58**, 388–402 (2015)
34. Malhotra, R., Jain, J.: Handling imbalanced data using ensemble learning in software defect prediction. In: 2020 10th International Conference on Cloud Computing, Data Science & Engineering (Confluence), pp. 300–304. IEEE (2020)
35. Wang, S., Yao, X.: Using class imbalance learning for software defect prediction. IEEE Trans. Reliab. **62**, 434–443 (2013)
36. Kumar, L., Misra, S., Rath, S.K.: An empirical analysis of the effectiveness of software metrics and fault prediction model for identifying faulty classes. Comput. Stand. Interfaces **53**, 1–32 (2017)
37. Collell, G., Prelec, D., Patil, K.R.: A simple plug-in bagging ensemble based on threshold moving for classifying binary and multiclass imbalanced data. Neurocomputing **275**, 330340 (2018)
38. Lee, S.-J., Xu, Z., Li, T., Yang, Y.: A novel bagging C4. 5 algorithm based on wrapper feature selection for supporting wise clinical decision making. J. Biomed. Inform. **78**, 144–155 (2018)
39. Sun, B., Chen, S., Wang, J., Chen, H.: A robust multi-class AdaBoost algorithm for mislabeled noisy data. Knowl.-Based Syst. **102**, 87–102 (2016)
40. Yijing, L., Haixiang, G., Xiao, L., Yanan, L., Jinling, L.: Adapted ensemble classification algorithm based on multiple classifier systems and feature selection for classifying multiclass imbalanced data. Knowl.-Based Syst. **94**, 88–104 (2016)
41. Shepperd, M., Song, Q., Sun, Z., Mair, C.: Data quality: some comments on the NASA software defect datasets. IEEE Trans. Softw. Eng. **39**, 1208–1215 (2013)
42. Balogun, A.O., Bajeh, A.O., Orie, V.A., Yusuf-Asaju, W.A.: Software defect prediction using ensemble learning: an ANP based evaluation method. FUOYE J. Eng. Technol. **3**, 50–55 (2018)
43. Jimoh, R., Balogun, A., Bajeh, A., Ajayi, S.: A PROMETHEE based evaluation of software defect predictors. J. Comput. Sci. Appl. **25**, 106–119 (2018)

44. Yadav, S., Shukla, S.: Analysis of k-fold cross-validation over hold-out validation on colossal datasets for quality classification. In: 2016 IEEE 6th International Conference on Advanced Computing (IACC), pp. 78–83. IEEE (2016)
45. Arlot, S., Lerasle, M.: Choice of V for V-fold cross-validation in least-squares density estimation. J. Mach. Learn. Res. **17**, 7256–7305 (2016)
46. Hall, M., Frank, E., Holmes, G., Pfahringer, B., Reutemann, P., Witten, I.H.: The WEKA data mining software: an update. ACM Sig. Exp. **11**, 10–18 (2009)
47. Singhal, Y., Jain, A., Batra, S., Varshney, Y., Rathi, M.: Review of bagging and boosting classification performance on unbalanced binary classification. In: 2018 IEEE 8th International Advance Computing Conference (IACC), pp. 338–343. IEEE (2018)

Analyzing the Impact of Assessing Requirements Specifications on the Software Development Life Cycle

Samah W. G. AbuSalim[1], Rosziati Ibrahim[1(✉)], Salama A. Mostafa[1],
and Jahari Abdul Wahab[2]

[1] Faculty of Computer Science and Information Technology,
Universiti Tun Hussein Onn Malaysia, 86400 Parit Raja, Johor, Malaysia
samahwgabusalim@gmail.com,
{rosziati,salama}@uthm.edu.my
[2] Department of Engineering R&D, SENA Traffic Systems Sdn. Bhd.,
Kuala Lumpur, Malaysia
jahari@senatraffic.com.my

Abstract. Developing an efficient and quality Software Requirements Specification (SRS) is based on software quality characteristics assessment such as completeness, consistency, feasibility and testability. These characteristics or attributes provide reasonably accurate predictions about system-free bias requirements and hidden assumptions and limit subsequent redesign. They additionally give realistic estimates for costs, risks, and timing of the product. This paper aims to identify possible rules and methods for measuring SRS quality in order to help the engineers to improve the quality of their SRS. The impact of these rules and methods on the software development lifecycle is also reviewed. In this paper, some methods of SRS quality assessment were analyzed from the literature and how to measure the impact of these SRS quality assessment methods on the software development lifecycle are also presented.

Keywords: Requirement Engineering · Software Requirements Specification (SRS) · SRS quality assessment

1 Introduction

Requirement Engineering (RE) is a process of organized and disciplined techniques to handle the identification and management of software products developments and achievement of goals. In SE, Software Requirement Specification (SRS) is considered as the most important factor and outcome of the RE process [1]. Without exception, the process of SRS development is considered a crucial process to get favorable results of a medium to large project [2]. SRS extraction and analysis are performed throughout the first stages of the software development life cycle. The SRS contains a group of activities that are gathering, analyzing, specifying and validating users' needs in a document that is written in a natural language [3]. Hence, the main goal of the SRS is to attempt to fully satisfy users' needs [4]. Therefore, several methods and techniques for SRS development have been used to extract these users' needs depending on the

© Springer Nature Switzerland AG 2020
O. Gervasi et al. (Eds.): ICCSA 2020, LNCS 12254, pp. 632–648, 2020.
https://doi.org/10.1007/978-3-030-58817-5_46

software complexity [5]. That is a set of documentation that captures the complete description of the features and properties of the software product. It has many advantages to the developers as it lays out the serviceable and no serviceable specification of the product, defines project scope, minimizes development effort and eliminates any confusion or misunderstanding on the initial stage [6]. An important role of difficulties for SRS is because of complex writing structures that describe the requirements that protect the features of good SRS [7]. A poor specification of software requirements can lead to failed quality of products because any product's quality depends on SRS quality itself.

Software Quality Assessment (SQA) used to protect the quality of software delivered by observing the methods and processes of software engineering that ultimately results, or at least gives confidence, in the quality of software products. SQA expands on whole SDLC which is depends on the design of software, coding, testing, and release management. SRS quality evaluation is very critical to evaluate the quality level and faults in very starting steps of the SDLC process [6, 7]. The standard features of SRS play an important role to create the software with respect to cost-effectiveness and users' real needs. Some major good features of SRS such as (1) Correctness. The software requirement specification is said to be correct if the software has the ability to perform tasks that are actually expected from the system as specified in the requirements. (2) Completeness implies that all the segments of software are completely presented and developed accordingly. (3) Consistency which means that the requirement should be understood in exactly the same way if they are read by more than one person. Requirements in SRS are said to be consistent if the features do not clash with one another or with main features and aims. (4) Feasibility which includes performance and practical satisfaction developed by system verification. An SRS is said to be feasible if the features are done in the context of benefits the life cycle and it will also extend the cost of the life cycle.

Further, the remaining sections are as follow; Sect. 2 represents overview of Software Development Life Cycle (SDLC). Section 3 presents the research methodology including the research questions and answered. Conclusion, as well as future work, is mentioned in Sect. 4.

2 Software Development Life Cycle (SDLC)

Software Development Life Cycle (SDLC) is a systematic process, used in the development or maintenance of any software product [8]. This process aims at detailing the procedures and methods used to guide the work of the software development team, which is an essential part of building any software project. The life cycle of software systems consists of a series of successive phases, where the system is built evolutionary, that is, the system evolves after each phase until it reaches the final system required. These phases include feasibility study, analysis, design, implementation, testing and maintenance. It also consists of models and methodologies used by the software development team that provides a framework for the entire development process to be designed and managed. The purpose of designing and building a software system is to carry out a variety of tasks. The collection of tasks the program can carry out also yields well-defined results based on complex calculations and manipulations. Therefore, overseeing the entire development cycle is a difficult and recurring challenge to ensure a high degree of quality and durability for the end product, as well as consumer acceptance. Therefore, to ensure the success of the system, it is necessary to use a comprehensive and systematic development process. At present, software developers are using two SDLC methodologies, namely conventional or traditional development and agile development. The following section will discuss and compare in detail these two methodologies and propose some improvements. [8, 9].

Traditional Software Development
This methodology is known as heavyweight because it relies on a set of heavy aspects which is to identify and record a complete set of requirements, followed by the development and examination of design and program performance. This methodology goes through four stages. The first stage is to determine the specifications and requirements of the project and specify the time needed to perform the different stages of the project development. After the requirements have been identified, the next step is to design and plan the program in the form of diagrams and models. From these things, we can anticipate the problems that the program may face during its development. The implementation process begins after the team approves the design and architectural plan of the project. The project continues in the development phase where the project is developed and built until the basic objectives are achieved. Sometimes, system development phases are divided into smaller tasks that are distributed between teams based on the skills of each team. Examples of this methodology include the Waterfall method, V-Model, and RUP. Sometimes the testing phase is performed in parallel with the development phase to ensure that problems are detected and resolved early. Once the project is completed and all the project requirements are implemented by the developers, the customer will engage in the project evaluation and feedback process and deliver the project after the client's satisfaction. The success of the project, which depends on the implementation of this method, depends on the identification of all requirements before the start of the project implementation, which means that any change during the development process can cause a problem. However, it is also easy to identify project costs and schedule resources and allocate them accordingly. It also helps to calculate project costs, schedule and allocate resources accordingly [7–10].

Agile Software Development
A set of steps through which to build software projects in several stages and short periods of time, where each stage generates a product distinct from the previous with additional characteristics. This process is often incremental and iterative until the entire project develops. This process focuses on the creation and formation of a team characterized by the process and intelligent accomplishment of the tasks, planning and continuous cooperation between team members. This helps to develop the project efficiently, deliver it on time and respond to any change. It is a conceptual framework that enhances the interactions expected during the development cycle. The key to the success of a software project is communication, flexibility and good analysis. that's why adopting agile approaches to software development. According to agile manifesto, the following four points are the main agile factors: (1) iterative development, (2) early customer involvement, (3) adaptation to change and (4) self-organizing teams.

There are currently six approaches known as agile methods of development, including crystal methodologies, dynamic software development method, feature-driven development, lean software development, scrum, and extreme programming [8–11].

Traditional Vs Agile Software Development
An important difference between agile and traditional development approaches is that in complex projects with unclear requirements, the former approach has the ability to deliver a result rapidly and cost-effectively. Agile approaches emphasize teams, work technology, customer interaction, and change response; whereas conventional methods emphasize agreements, schedules, procedures, records, and resources. Table 1 shows the differences in different aspects of agile and traditional approaches [7–12].

Table 1. Traditional vs agile software development [13]

Attribute	Agile	Traditional
User requirement	Iterative acquisition	Detailed user requirements are well defined before coding/implementation
Rework cost	Low	High
Development direction	Readily changeable	Fixed
Testing	On every iteration	After the coding phase completed
Customer involvement	High	Low
Extra quality required for developers	Interpersonal skills & basic business knowledge	Nothing in particular
Suitable Project scale	low to medium-scaled	Large-scaled

3   Research Methodology

The aim of this review paper is to analyze and discuss the quality assessments tools and methods used in SRS. The generic methodology used in this work consists of five main phases, which are research questions, literature review, filter papers, data extraction and result and discussion as shown in Fig. 1.

3.1   Definition of Research Questions

Software Requirements Specification is a way to gather and maintain user requirements. A good SRS should be clear and correct. There are a few approaches to go about ensuring your SRS is strong and complete and Some approaches are also not flexible in terms of usage but require background knowledge before using them. The research questions focus on the identification of the most recent methods and tools used for SRS

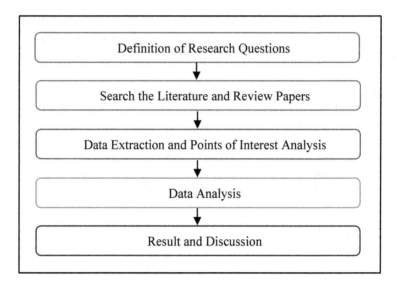

Fig. 1. Research methodology

quality assessment. Also, the impact of SRS quality on project success. Generally, this research aimed to answer the following questions:

1. What are the most recent SRS quality assessment methods?
2. What is the impact of SRS quality on project success?

3.2   Search the Literature and Review Papers

This research begins with conducting review on literature and previous research work regarding Requirement Engineering. Thus, we selected papers published in the ACM, IEEE, Science Direct, Springer, World Wide Web: Google Scholar and DBLP. In addition, other set of conferences and workshops were searched such as: ICSE, ICEET, AMCSE and ICIT. According to Brereton [14], these libraries are considered one of the most important resources and references in software engineering.

3.3   Data Extraction and Points of Interest Analysis

The goal of this phase is to design data extraction forms with which to accurately record the information obtained from the primary studies [5]. This paper aims at Investigate the current trends in SRS evaluation methods. The main points of interstate are identifying the used evaluation methods, the most used quality attributes and the main components of the related models. The data collected from 12 total papers was done by collating and summarizing the results of the primary studies.

3.4   Data Analysis

This section shows the answer of each research questions obtained after analysis the primary studies. The selected studies provided relevant evidence with which to satisfactorily answer the four RQs, as described below:

RQ1. What is the impact of SRS quality on project success?

During the practice of the software projects, these projects faced some problems and shortcomings and sometimes the failure of the application completely, resulting in significant delays and cost overruns. In fact, the software development life cycle of software systems has been plagued by exceeding budget, delayed or delayed deliveries and frustrated customers. In addition, the technology life cycle of software systems has been plagued by budget overrun, late or delayed delivery, and consumers have been frustrated. The Standish Group [8, 9] undertook a thorough investigation into this issue, they find that many projects do not deliver on time, do not deliver on budget, and do not deliver as planned or needed. The main reason for this is that the managers of the project do not smartly delegate the necessary number of staff and resources to the SDLC's different activities. For this reason, some phases of the SDLC are delayed and other phases are waiting for them to be completed without doing progress in the project. Thus, it creates a gap between the arrival and execution of projects, resulting in a failure to deliver a product on schedule, within the budget and at an acceptable quality level [9–12].

As mentioned earlier the basic task in a project begins with collection, analysis and definition of the requirements. In the requirements phase, a faulty requirement leads to specification errors and errors are induced from a requirement into the system specification. Then in the design phase, design errors occur which are induced from requirements and specification errors. These didn't stop here but in the implementation stage, program errors which in turn are induced errors from the requirement, specification and design occurs.

The worst part will happen however, in the testing and integration stage where known uncorrected errors and unknown errors happen and these leads to total failure of the system. This very showed clearly that failures can happen in each stage, mainly when the beginning starts with errors. Given the key role of specifications in the project life cycle and in assessing project success or failure, as a consequence, the overall quality of the software is directly associated with the requirements reliability. Project specifications should be of high quality to reduce failure of software products such as code and test cases [7, 12]. Arogundade et al. [15] examined and identified concepts that constitute a modeling technique for the safety risk assessment of the Information System (IS) and developed a conceptual model for the achievement of the safety risk assessment of the IS during the requirement analysis phase of the software process.

Ferguson and Lami [16] illustrate the value of quality in specifications for the occurrence of software development lifecycle deficiencies at later stages. Figure 2 uses information gathered by James Martin to highlight this argument, showing that over half of all defects are due to specification issues. Figure 3 shows that more than 80% of the rework effort can be traced to requirement-related defects.

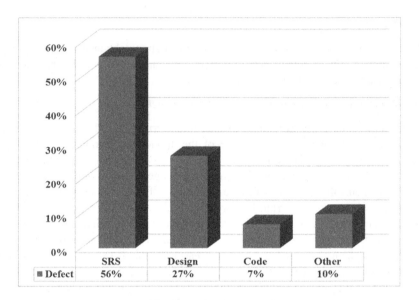

Fig. 2. Defects rate [17]

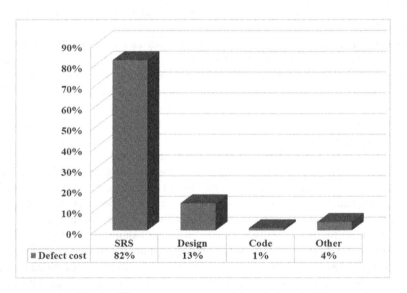

Fig. 3. Effort cost to repair the defects in Fig. 2 [17]

Wingers [18] discussed the need for quality requirements in order to minimize total project costs and mitigate risks that the project can face in the later stages of the software development life cycle. He shows the relative cost at various stages of the development process to fix a specification defect (Fig. 4). He says that issues with specifications can raise the cost of development by up to 50% and can add up to 80% to rework costs due to mistakes found after delivery. By improving the quality with detecting and correcting defects at the level of requirements rather than developing them later at other stages of project development, the cost will remain low and success will be greater.

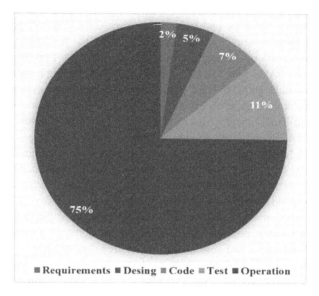

Fig. 4. The cost of correcting requirements defects [17]

RQ2. What are the most recent SRS quality assessment methods?

Several methods have been proposed to boost up the standard of SRS document. This paper analyzed some of the methods and tools used to evaluate SRS quality.

Antinyan and Staron [19] present an automated method to evaluate the understandability of the SRS document. Their method named (Rendex). Rendex assessed the understandability by using four indicators; complexity, Coupling, and size. The assessment results show that the Rendex achieved (73–80) % agreement compare with the manual result.

Nordin et al. [20] introduce a performance assessment tool for the SRS document based on two quality perspectives; Requirements Sentence Quality (RSQ) and Requirements Document Quality (RDQ) by developing the SRS Quality Checker tool as proof of the rules. Their paper concludes the methodology can be used as a framework and effort to measure the SRS quality.

Thitisathienkul and Prompoon [21] present an approach to how to analyses the use of common language in SRS, formation of documents, and overall standard of documents by making applicable the process evaluation model as a key tool for assessment of quality and standard of SRS also includes these two techniques to the evaluation process and measurement information. in this study, they conclude that only 3 features of specification requirement software are unambiguous, valid and changeable. Results of this study that faults in the standard can be removed by having a discussion which could be useful as a technique for future development and quality assessment of upcoming SRS.

Ali et al. [22] have developed a distinctive approach to increase the standard of the document. Their technique comprises of four processes i.e. Parsing Requirement (PR), Requirement Mapping using Matrix (RMM), Addition of demands in specification requirement software template and independent inspection. PR will get the required inputs from the Requirement Engineering Process after the implementation; requirements will be achieved by completing the rules of ontology. Stakeholders concerns could be saved by RMM that will be formed to decrease ambiguousness and errors. Previous results will be added to IEEE quality organize. Independent inspection will be done to cross-check the customers and SRS demands. Inspection model of SRS will be used to assigning Total Quality Score (TQS) the third party will submit a report in detail to a group of Requirement Engineers (RE).

Ahmad et al. [23] present an evaluation of a boilerplate technique with the assistance of a tool-based prototype to enhance the Software Requirements Specification (SRS) quality in terms of comprehensibility, correctness, and consistency. The value behind this boilerplate is to ease the process of discovering necessary specification for a common information management system and convert these specifications in SRS. Outcomes of this study present that tools based on common techniques enhance completeness, correctness, and consistency of requirements in SRS.

Stephen and Mit. [24] propose a platform to measure the quality of both structure and functional requirements in SRS. The SRS includes information to make it confirmed with the standard of software. Measurement proposed based on four quality properties namely preciseness, consistency, completeness, and correctness. The completeness properties used a minimum standard IEEE 830 to evaluate and measure the SRS. In the meantime, it is suggested to use the characteristics of consistency, correctness, and accuracy to measure the functional requirement in the document. The general SRS standard measurement calculated based on all standard characteristics. The rules and formula for computing the SRS quality are embedded in the proposed framework which is a basis for a platform for assessing the software quality.

Da Silva [25] proposes an automated validation strategy that can assist with sufficient tool support to alleviate some of these limitations and therefore improve the quality of the specifications of requirements, in particular, those are related to consistency, completeness and unambiguity. Their study extends the RSLingo strategy by considering that the demands in RSL-IL are automatically extracted from the specifications of the natural language or specifically generated by customers.

Yaremchuk et al. [26] mentioned ways to enhance the correct demands between the SRM frameworks. This also includes difficult method. To check the complexity of method RCM metric is used. It is handled by prioritizing the requirements and based on complexity. This method is more helpful as compared to check and verify the whole process. Defectiveness and correctness enhanced by applying the improved requirements. Table 2 shows a summary of the methods and tools used to evaluate the quality of the SRS document.

Aguilar et al. [27] enhance the Model-Driven tool, named the WebREd-Tool, in order to enable the web application designer with the NFR specification to make better

Table 2. Summary of the analyzed methods and tools.

Author	Quality attribute	Proposed method	Strength	Limitation
Antinyan and Staron [19]	Complexity Coupling Size	They introduce a new tool called Rendex. The tool is relying on four internal quality measures of the SRS document	Rendex tool produces to facilitate the readability and understandability of the requirement document.	Rendex requires more evaluation in order to grasp its generalization possibilities across different product sizes and domains.
Nordin *et al.* [20]	Requirements Sentence Quality (RSQ) Requirements Document Quality (RDQ)	The proposed tool can be used for demonstrating how the rules were implemented to measure SRS quality	Their tool benefit from the performance assessment of SRS for the attributes applied (1) requirements sentence quality (RSQ) (2) requirements document quality (RDQ) or even to be used in pre-review sessions	Their work is incomprehensive because it is not possible to automate certain quality attributes
Thitisathienkul and Prompoon [21]	Unambiguous Verifiable Modifiable	The suggested approach can be used to critically assess the quality of the SRS to use natural language in the document's overall quality to display the document's value and the defects that arise during the specification process	Measure and report the quality level and the document deficiency portion. SDLC documents identified metrics, validity requirements, performance standard and possible enhancement parts are registered and stored	The insistence on unambiguous and verifiable features due to the layout of the report is directly linked to the modifiable function. Other features are difficult to verify and require human judgment

(continued)

Table 2. (*continued*)

Author	Quality attribute	Proposed method	Strength	Limitation
Ali *et al.* [22]	Ambiguities Completeness Correctness Verification Validation and inspection	The proposed solution will reduce the negative factors which can affect the quality performance of software products directly or indirectly	Improves the reliability of the report, increases the number of times needed, ensures completeness of the requirements and tracks the incorrectness of the requirements and continues conditionally after correcting requirements	In the method presented, each step of the system presented functions within its own limitations
Ahmad *et al.* [23]	Comprehensibility Correctness Consistency	The proposed boilerplate technique can improve all three SRS quality attributes	Improves the SRS quality in comprehensibility due to guided sentence structure based on generic essential system functionality (information management system) which helps to reduce ambiguity	Their research is a focus on the second perspective as the boilerplate provides a guide to having essential requirements. And focuses only on internal consistency which is included in the SRS
Stephen and Mit [24]	Preciseness Consistency Completeness Correctness	The suggested framework demonstrates the flow of data and measured the structure and functional requirement	The completeness properties are evaluated on the basis of the structure and reliability, quality and accuracy of the report depending on the functional criterion	Their research focuses only on four quality properties that can be measured as early as the documentation stage of the specifications, which was preciseness, correctness, consistency, and completeness

(*continued*)

Table 2. (*continued*)

Author	Quality attribute	Proposed method	Strength	Limitation
Da Silva [25]	Consistency Completeness Unambiguousness	Their approach helps to mitigate some of the SRS documents limitations, particularly with regard to inconsistency, incompleteness, and ambiguousness	Their RSLingo approaches provide (1) a language for defining linguistic patterns that frequently occur in requirements specifications written in natural language (the RSL-PL language)	RSLingo does not provide yet any guarantees that the RSL-IL specifications have the required quality
Yaremchuk et al. [26]	Correctness	The proposed method makes it possible to boost the correctness of specifications by finding a greater number of resource-restricted defects	The approach allows the correctness and defectiveness of specifications to be improved and the achieved index of correctness and defectiveness to be evaluated	Their methodology allowed the quantity of observable actual and potential defects to be increased by 9% on average compared to the total verification of the complexity of the requirements
Aguilar et al. [27]	Non-Functional Requirements (NFRs)	Presented a Model-Driven tool, named WebREd-Tool, extending the requirements metamodel with a NFRs classification	The proposal offers several advantages such as including the specification of Non-Functional Requirements from the requirements analysis stage considering the design decisions from the initial stages of the Web application development process	The proposal supports an automatic derivation of Web conceptual models from a requirements model by means of a set of transformation rules, the derivation of the Web application source code is still in development

design decisions and also to use it to verify the consistency of the final web application. Their proposal promotes the automated derivation of web conceptual models from the requirements model by means of a set of transformation laws.

Table 2 shows that the most evaluated quality attributes are consistency, completeness and correctness. It for the shows that it is difficult to automating the quality attributes as they are written in natural languages and need human experts. The automation of quality attributes evaluation required advanced NLP algorithms such as Text Normalization, Stemming and Lemmatization, Topic modeling, TF-IDF algorithm and Naive Bayes algorithm.

3.5 Discussion and Remarks

The Natural Language (NL) is still the primary way to write the SRS document. The SRS document written by using the NL is considered simple and understood by the stakeholders and developers due to these document does not need specific knowledge and effort. However, the NL still poses different issues like ambiguity and imprecise. The requirements written in a poor way have a negative impact on the overall project. Ambiguous or incomplete requirements require an additional effort in the different stage of the project. Finally, bad requirements lead to misunderstanding and produce the wrong product. To overcome these problems many researchers, attempt to improve the quality of the SRS document, the researchers are scattered into three main ways to evaluate the quality of the requirements; fully automated, semi-automated and non-automated (expert) [28, 29]. Figure 5. Shows the SRS assessment architecture with different automation levels.

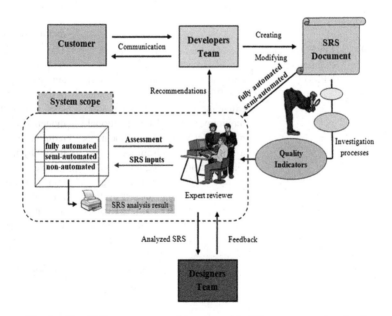

Fig. 5. The SRS assessment architecture with different automation levels

The fully automated way totally depends on the machine to complete whole steps of the assessment (without interacting by expert), the semi-automated the expert and machine are interacted between each other to produce the final assessment of the document, on the other hands, the non-automated is totally depends on the expert person to produce the final decision of the quality of the document. However, the expert still suffering from limited knowledge on the different domains, high cost, and consume time. For this reason, the researchers give more attention to produce an automated tool to solve the above-mentioned problems [10], [30–34]. Some of the advantages of the automated review are listed below:

The Automated Review Is Cheap and Fast: One of the main challenges that facing the projects is assessing the quality of the document by using manual review, this method has a high cost that derived thorough investigation. Consequently, the mechanism that delivers response with the free cost is a promising advantage as well as, the speed of response.

The Automatic Reviews are Consistent: Almost the expert reviewers are inconsistence because they effected by different private factors such; the state of his mind, or the current inputs of the reviewers. While the automated method is considered as a consistence.

Several methods and tools are used to assess the quality of SRS documents (in an automated manner) based on various quality SRS attributes and indicators like; consistency, completeness, complexity, and unambiguousness. These have been highlighted in Table 2. Since there are many resources for collecting knowledge and are used to identify requirements, there is no lack of knowledge and methods. But the problem is that many companies are unable to provide software products that satisfy the actual customer requirements due to flaws frequently found in SRS. Many studies concentrated on several quality characteristics. That can be evaluated as soon as the documentation phase of demands, which were preciseness, correctness, consistency, and completeness. Based from SRS, the system or software can be implemented. Once requirements are captured properly, the implementation is very straightforward. The SRS can also be used for formalization prior to implementing the system. Examples of research for formalization includes [35, 36].

4   Conclusion and Future Work

The project could be successfully completed if the required quality specification is clear to the team for development. Measuring the quality of SRS is based on software quality attributes like traceability, consistency, and completeness. This paper has analyzed several techniques and tools used to measure the SRS quality according to different quality attributes. Some researchers determined the SRS quality by examining different quality attributes such as accuracy, correctness and unambiguous. In the future, we can analyze and measure other quality attributes that have limited research coverage like cost. It will help to cost saving for persons that detection and correction of requirements failures.

Acknowledgement. This project is funded by the Ministry of Education Malaysia under the Malaysian Technical University Network (MTUN) grant scheme Vote K234 and SENA Traffic Systems Sdn. Bhd.

References

1. Aguilar, J.A., Zaldívar-Colado, A., Tripp-Barba, C., Misra, S., Bernal, R., Ocegueda, A.: An analysis of techniques and tools for requirements elicitation in model-driven web engineering methods. In: Gervasi, O., et al. (eds.) ICCSA 2015. LNCS, vol. 9158, pp. 518–527. Springer, Cham (2015). https://doi.org/10.1007/978-3-319-21410-8_40
2. Pekar, V., Felderer, M., Breu, R.: Improvement methods for software requirement specifications: a mapping study. In: 2014 9th International Conference on the Quality of Information and Communications Technology (2014)
3. Aguilar, J.A., Zaldívar-Colado, A., Tripp-Barba, C., Espinosa, R., Misra, S., Zurita, C.E.: A survey about the impact of requirements engineering practice in small-sized software factories in Sinaloa, Mexico. In: Gervasi, O., et al. (eds.) ICCSA 2018. LNCS, vol. 10963, pp. 331–340. Springer, Cham (2018). https://doi.org/10.1007/978-3-319-95171-3_26
4. Aguilar, J.A., Garrigo's, I., Mazo'n, J.N., Trujillo, J.: An MDA approach for goal-oriented requirement analysis in web engineering. J. UCS **16**(17), 2475–2494 (2010)
5. Zamudio, L., Aguilar, J.A., Tripp, C., Misra, S.: A requirements engineering techniques review in agile software development methods. In: Gervasi, O., et al. (eds.) ICCSA 2017. LNCS, vol. 10408, pp. 683–698. Springer, Cham (2017). https://doi.org/10.1007/978-3-319-62404-4_50
6. Souza, R.G.M., Stadzisz, P.C.: Problem-based software requirements specification. Revista Eletrônica de Sistemas de Informação **15**(2) (2016)
7. Jani, H.M., Mostafa, S.A.: Implementing case-based reasoning technique to software requirements specifications quality analysis. Int. J. Adv. Comput. Technol. **3**(1) (2011)
8. Leau, Y.B., Loo, W.K., Tham, W.Y., Tan, S.F.: Software development life cycle AGILE vs traditional approaches. In: International Conference on Information and Network Technology, vol. 37, no. 1, pp. 162–167 (2012)
9. Carlson, N., Laplante, P.: The NASA automated requirements measurement tool: a reconstruction. Innov. Syst. Softw. Eng. **10**(2), 77–91 (2013). https://doi.org/10.1007/s11334-013-0225-8
10. Jubair, M.A., Mostafa, S.A., Mustapha, A., Hannani, A., Hassan, M.H:. Fully automated quality assessment metrics for software requirement specifications, pp. 177–187 (2019)
11. Bassil, Y.: A simulation model for the waterfall software development life cycle. arXiv preprint arXiv:1205.6904 (2012)
12. Wallmuller, E.: Software Quality Assurance: A Practical Approach. Prentice-Hall BCS Practitioner. Prentice-Hall, Upper Saddle River (1994)
13. Stoica, M., Mircea, M., Ghilic-Micu, B.: Software development: agile vs. traditional. Informatica Economica **17**(4) (2013)
14. Brereton, P., Kitchenham, B.A., Budgen, D., Turner, M., Khalil, M.: Lessons from applying the systematic literature review process within the software engineering domain. J. Syst. Softw. **80**(4), 571–583 (2007)
15. Arogundade, O.T., Misra, S., Abayomi-Alli, O.O., Fernandez-Sanz, L.: Enhancing misuse cases with risk assessment for safety requirements. IEEE Access **8**, 12001–12014 (2020)

16. Ferguson, R., Goldenson, D., Fusani, M., Fabbrini, F., Gnesi, S.: Automated natural language analysis of requirements and specifications. In: INCOSE (International Council on System Engineering) International Symposium (2015)
17. Elcock, A., Laplante, P.: Testing software without requirements: using development artifacts to develop test cases. Innov. Syst. Softw. Eng. 2(3–4), 137–145 (2006). https://doi.org/10.1007/s11334-006-0009-5
18. Wiegers, K.E.: Software Requirements, Chapters 14-Appendix D
19. Antinyan, V., Staron, M.: Rendex: a method for automated reviews of textual requirements. J. Syst. Softw. 131, 63–77 (2017)
20. Nordin, A., Zaidi, N.H.A., Mazlan, N.A.: Measuring software requirements specification quality. J. Telecommun. Electron. Comput. Eng. 9(3–5), 123–128 (2017)
21. Thitisathienkul, P., Prompoon, N.: Quality assessment method for software requirements specifications based on document characteristics and its structure. In: 2015 Second International Conference on Trustworthy Systems and Their Applications (2015)
22. Ali, S.W., Ahmed, Q.A., Shafi, I.: Process to enhance the quality of software requirement specification document. In: 2018 International Conference on Engineering and Emerging Technologies (ICEET) (2018)
23. Ahmad, S., Anuar, U., Emran, N.A.: A tool-based boilerplate technique to improve SRS quality: an evaluation. J. Telecommun. Electron. Comput. Eng. 10(2–7), 111–114 (2018)
24. Stephen, E., Mit, E.: Framework for measuring the quality of software specification. J. Telecommun. Electron. Comput. Eng. 9(2–10) (2018)
25. da Silva, A.R.: Quality of requirements specifications: a preliminary overview of an automatic validation approach. In: Proceedings of the 29th Annual ACM Symposium on Applied Computing, pp. 1021–1022. ACM, March 2014
26. Yaremchuk, S., Bardis, N., Vyacheslav, K.: Metric-based method of software requirements correctness improvement. In: ITM Web of Conferences AMCSE (2016)
27. Aguilar, J.A., Misra, S., Zaldívar, A., Bernal, R.: Improving requirements specification in WebREd-Tool by using a NFR's classification. In: Murgante, B., et al. (eds.) ICCSA 2013. LNCS, vol. 7973, pp. 59–69. Springer, Heidelberg (2013). https://doi.org/10.1007/978-3-642-39646-5_5
28. Mostafa, S.A., Gunasekaran, S.S., Khaleefah, S.H., Mustapha, A., Jubair, M.A., Has-san, M.H.: A fuzzy case-based reasoning model for software requirements specifications quality assessment. Int. J. Adv. Sci. Eng. Inf. Technol. 9(6), 2134–2141 (2019)
29. Mostafa, S.A., Gunasekaran, S.S., Khaleefah, S.H.: Integrating fuzzy logic technique in case-based reasoning for improving the inspection quality of software requirements specifications. In: Khalaf, M.I., Al-Jumeily, D., Lisitsa, A. (eds.) ACRIT 2019. CCIS, vol. 1174, pp. 503–513. Springer, Cham (2020). https://doi.org/10.1007/978-3-030-38752-5_39
30. Ibrahim, R., Saringat, M.Z., Ibrahim, N., Ismail, N.: An automatic tool for generating test cases from system's requirements. In: CIT 2007: 7th IEEE International Conference on Computer and Information Technology, Article number 4385193, pp. 861–866 (2007)
31. Femmer, H.: Automatic requirements reviews - potentials, limitations and practical tool support. In: Felderer, M., Méndez Fernández, D., Turhan, B., Kalinowski, M., Sarro, F., Winkler, D. (eds.) PROFES 2017. LNCS, vol. 10611, pp. 617–620. Springer, Cham (2017). https://doi.org/10.1007/978-3-319-69926-4_53
32. Ashraf, S., Khan, R., Iqbal, K., Chohan, R.: Quality software requirement specification (SRS) and suitable SDLC leads to quality software. J. Appl. Environ. Biol. Sci. 6(4S), 137–146 (2016)
33. Sabriye, A.O.J.A., Zainon, W.M.N.W.: A framework for detecting ambiguity in software requirement specification. In: 2017 8th International Conference on Information Technology (ICIT), pp. 209–213. IEEE, May 2017

34. MacDonell, S.G., Min, K., Connor, A.M.: Autonomous requirements specification processing using natural language processing. arXiv preprint arXiv:1407.6099 (2014)
35. Aman, H., Ibrahim, R.: Formalization of transformation rules from XML schema to UML class diagram. Int. J. Softw. Eng. Appl. **8**(12), 75–90 (2014)
36. Aman, H., Ibrahim, R.: Formalization of versioning rules for XML schema using UML class diagram. J. Theoret. Appl. Inf. Technol. **95**(15), 3652–3661 (2017)

An Intelligent Machine Learning-Based Real-Time Public Transport System

Menzi Skhosana[1], Absalom E. Ezugwu[2(✉)], Nadim Rana[3],
and Shafi'i M. Abdulhamid[4]

[1] School of Mathematics, Statistics and Computer Science,
University of Kwazulu-Natal, Westville Campus,
Private Bag X54001, Durban 4000, South Africa
216032734@stu.ukzn.ac.za

[2] School of Computer Science, University of KwaZulu-Natal,
Pietermaritzburg Campus, King Edward Avenue, Pietermaritzburg 3201,
KwaZulu-Natal, South Africa
ezugwua@ukzn.ac.za

[3] College of Computer Science and Information Technology, Jazan University,
Jizan, Kingdom of Saudi Arabia
nadimrana17@gmail.com

[4] Department of Cyber Security Science, Federal University of Technology,
Minna, Niger, Nigeria
shafii.abdulhamid@futminna.edu.ng

Abstract. More often than not, commuters are left stranded at pick-up spots – clueless about the availability and proximity of public transport vehicles hence the stigma of public transport being unreliable, especially in developing countries. This is a result of poorly managed fleets, caused by varying demands and rigid schedules. In this paper, we present an intelligent real-time transport information system to keep commuters informed about the status of buses currently in transit, and also provide an insight to bus managers based on ridership data and commuter behavior. The system is composed of three sub-systems designed to cater for commuters, bus-drivers and bus managers respectively. This system is developed on the Backend-as-a-Service (BaaS) platform Firebase. Furthermore, a neural network is trained to provide predictions to bus managers on the expected ridership numbers per route. The trained model is integrated with a web application for bus managers. An Android application used by bus drivers collects the ridership data being fed to the network. The proposed system was evaluated with a real-world data set that contains the daily ridership on a per-route basis dating back to 2001. Evaluation results confirm the effectiveness of the new system in reducing the total mileage used to deliver commuters, reducing fuel costs, increasing the profit of bus operators, and increasing the percentage of satisfied ridership requests.

Keywords: Smart Irenbus · Bus location tracking · Mobile tracking · Short-term forecasting · Long-term forecasting

© Springer Nature Switzerland AG 2020
O. Gervasi et al. (Eds.): ICCSA 2020, LNCS 12254, pp. 649–665, 2020.
https://doi.org/10.1007/978-3-030-58817-5_47

1   Introduction

Public transport plays an integral role in the economy and sustainability of urban areas. Yet there are very little to no advancements being made in this sector in developing countries. Amongst many other benefits, public transportation is significantly afford- able, reduces traffic congestions, increases mobility and can lessen the carbon footprint of urban areas. The sizable capacity of public transport vehicles results in lesser trips and reduced fuel consumption. Statics South Africa (SSA) stated that more 76.7% of the South African population relies on public transport for daily commutes [1]. This again highlights the importance of public transport and why problems in this sector need to be addressed. With the recent trend and drive for more viable and eco-friendly environments through the construction of smart cities in developed countries around the world, modernising public transportation by integrating it with the latest tech- nologies could be an excellent way for developing countries like South Africa to also get started on this trend and potentially improve its economic state. Furthermore, it is noteworthy that approximately 55% of the world's population resides in urban areas, and this figure is expected to increase to 68% by the year 2050 [9]. The given statistics make it evident that the development of smart cities is needed to ensure sustainability and efficiency of urban areas, through the deployment and use of intelligent tech- nologies to render services to citizens and to manage and refurbish existing infras- tructures such as public transportation.

According to the Independent Communications Authority of South Africa (ICASA), smartphone usage has increased drastically over the last five years. As of 2018 September, 81.7% of the South African population owned a smartphone, which is nearly double the percentage of 2016. Also, according to ICASA's report on the state of the ICT sector in SA - March 2019, the national population coverage for 3G remained stable at 99.5% in 2018, and the coverage for 4G/LTE increased from 76.7% in 2017 to 85.7% in 2018 [10]. Given the widespread use of smartphones and good network coverage - the use of smartphones as a platform in implementing the public transport management system will allow for easy access to transit information, and lower implementation costs as almost all smartphones are equipped with Global Positioning System (GPS) technology and other position and orientation sensors.

The ability to predict future public transport demand could be revolutionary as it will allow for public transport vehicles to be scheduled based on forecasted demand. And this will, in turn, save the authorities a lot of money by reducing unnecessary trips, saving fuel, and mitigating the effects of global warming while ensuring that com- muters are transported efficiently.

This paper proposes the development of a holistic, dynamic real-time information system that keeps passengers informed about buses currently in transit and other rel- evant information such as vehicle arrival time. The system is composed of three subsystems that cater to commuters, bus drivers and bus managers, respectively. More so, a machine learning-based model is employed to predict ridership numbers that can be expected per route based on past ridership data, so that the buses are assigned by the bus managers accordingly. Summarily, the main goal of this paper is to build a dynamic transportation system which helps the traditional bus companies to become more competitive and productive in a typically challenging business environment. The system is called *Smart Irenbus*: an intelligent real-time public transport system and it is a software solution that assists bus companies in carrying out their logistic tasks by providing accessible communication between controllers and drivers and also serves as a data management tool to intelligently store and organize data collected on daily commutes and offer predictions and useful insights based on it. The proposed system differs from the previous Irenbus implementation presented in [29] because of the added intelligence and predictive capability that comes with the current system.

2   Related Work

Using GPS modules and embedded mini-computer systems, Sungur et al., developed a bus monitoring system that provided real-time information such as the estimated bus arrival time and the route name to commuters. This information was displayed on an LCD screen mounted at the bus stop [2]. Although this system is pretty solid and provides useful information to commuters it has a few shortfalls, such as being fixed at one place, i.e. it's not able to provide information to commuters who are not at the bus stop, and also implementing this system will be a costly operation since every bus stop has to have an LCD screen mounted on it.

In [23], the authors discussed how a machine learning approach could be used to implement and assess predictive services for the users of a bike-sharing system. The models used in this study were trained on real-world historical usage data comprising of more than 280 000 entries covering all hires in Pisa for two years. Seasonality manifests sharp changes in the usage patterns (e.g. bikes tend to be used more in spring compared to winter). These seasonal patterns were captured by the learning models through the appropriate encoding of the bike usage time, which explicitly models cyclic information such as weekday and holiday.

Manikandan et al. [12] used the Global System for Mobile Communication (GSM) Query Response System with GPS trackers to develop a real-time bus information system. Where a user has to send a request to the central server system using SMS, and a response is sent back to the user as an SMS with the information requested [12]. Implementing this system will be much easier as it uses mobile phones to provide real-time information to commuters. But the major drawback with this system is that the user has to send an SMS to request information of a specific bus - no information about all buses currently in transit is provided.

Shirisha et al. [5] designed a system that equipped a bus with GSM-based processor and a bus stop with a time data transmitter; this then allowed the commuters to identify at what time the bus reached its previous bus stop, and based on this information, the commuter can estimate the position of the bus [5]. The time data is transmitted continuously through IR led. And whenever the bus reaches a bus stop, the time data will be acquired through TSOP (IR sensor package) and it will be stored into the ROM of the main processing unit. The GSM module interfaced with the main processor can then send the time information along with the bus stop name to the caller (commuter) in the form of an SMS.

Othman and Tan [25] proposed a simulator supplied with predictive travel times through congestion prediction to evaluate and improve bus utilization through effective scheduling. Their model predicted correctly predicted the exact travel times 13% more accurately than the expected arrival times estimated by the Land Transport Authority (LTA) of Singapore.

In [26], Toqué et al. investigated the use of smart card data to forecast multimodal transport passenger flow with both long- and short-term forecasting time horizons. The study was deemed being challenging as it involved a major business district in the Paris Metropolitan Area (La Défense). Their results demonstrated the effectiveness of machine learning methods for such prediction tasks, as they obtained reliable results for all transport modes (train, tram, and bus). They aim at improving the results by investigating how anomalies could be considered in the prediction process.

Liu et al. in [27] proposed a system that uses a single inexpensive camera mounted overhead to count passengers by combining a Convolutional Neural Network detection model and a spatiotemporal context model to address the counting problem in the scenes of low resolution and with a variation of illumination, pose and scale. Experimental results showed better performance, and they plan to extend the current method with more deep learning algorithms. The only drawback to their system is that it may not work in a very dense and crowded scene, and for this case, they plan to explore crowd density map estimation for their future work.

A Web-based system was developed by Kumbhar et al. for tracking buses in transit using a GPS tracker installed on the bus. Users get real-time information straight to their mobile phones. Using Google Maps user can see the bus on the map as it moves [6]. Their system ensures punctuality - which has been proven to be an essential factor in making buses more reliable [4]. Their system also seems to be less expensive to implement compared to other previously done work but still lacks the ease of use - as it only offers a web application with no native mobile application. And doesn't give insight to public transport authorities about future demand and ridership patterns.

In [28], they explored options for using smart card data for performing simple analyses by using transport planning software. The data was converted to represent passengers per line and matrixes between stops. This matrix was then taken into the network to produce the measured passenger flows. Their method turned out to be valuable to operators to gain insights into small changes but was not able to give accurate insights into long-term changes.

According to our knowledge, there haven't been any published work that discusses how a holistic public transportation system can be designed and developed to relay useful transit information amongst commuters, drivers and bus operators while at the same time collecting and studying commuter boarding data to enable the prediction of future ridership patterns, hence allowing the development of better and more efficient bus schedules.

3 Smart Irenbus Design and Implementation

The primary objective of smart Irenbus is to provide transit information to commuters, but for commuters to get the bus transit information we have to be able to track the bus location, this then led to the incorporation of the driver component into Smart Irenbus. Again, the drivers need to be managed and assigned to specific buses; this then pointed out that a manager component will be needed for the system. After gathering all the system requirements, it was clear that the Smart Irenbus system will have to be divided into three subsystems. The Agile Software Development Methodology was employed as it is an adaptive approach that responds to changes favourably and allows for iterative development and continuous testing.

To take full advantage of the cloud, the system was mainly developed using Google's Firebase, which is Backend-as-a-Service platform. Firebase was chosen over other similar platforms such as the Amazon Web Service's EC2 because it allows both mobile and web applications access to shared data and computing infrastructures. Any changes made to the data are automatically synchronised with the Firebase cloud and with other clients within milliseconds [16]. As the mobile application was developed for Android devices, the integration of Firebase was seamless as both platforms are from Google.

A. Database Design

To handle frequent location updates and keep all devices connected in synchronization, a robust and dynamic database infrastructure is required. The Firebase Realtime Database is a non-structured query language (NoSQL) cloud-based database that synchronizes data across all clients in real-time and provides offline functionality. Data is stored in the Realtime database as JSON, and all connected clients share one instance, automatically receiving updates with the newest data [7]. In conventional database systems, the information is stored in tabular format. But for the NoSQL database, data or records are stored in a tree-like structure. Records are additionally prearranged in collections [11]. After several iterations of requirements gathering, the resulting database structure consisted of five nodes:

- *Buses* which stores basic bus information uniquely identified by a 16 character randomly generated id.
- *OnlineBus* which stores buses that are currently in-transit with both current location and current driver.
- *BusFares* which stores bus prices for different stages for both peak and off-peak times.
- *BusLines* which stores the bus line information like scheduled times and more.
- *Users* which stores basic user information.

The use of a NoSQL database was mainly chosen because of its dynamic schema - it provides the flexibility to change the data schema without modifying any of your existing data. While the traditional relational database management system relies on a static data structure, the best practices stipulate the establishment of a database schema before any coding even begins [15]. A lot of traditional databases use a locking mechanism to ensure data integrity, i.e. before a transaction starts, the relational database management system (RDMS) marks the data so that no other process can modify it until the transaction either succeeds or fails. This then can have a severe impact on the database performance when serving thousands of users concurrently. NoSQL makes a trade-off between consistency and performance by shunning the use of locked transactions. After taking all of these facts into consideration, the NoSQL database was an obvious choice to efficiently handle the dynamic data model of Smart Irenbus.

B. User Authentication

Mobile and web applications need to provide some form of authentication to identify users and control and protect user data. Without a way to differentiate one user from another, it would also be impossible for the application to know which data and settings belong to which user [7]. Furthermore, authentication allows users to set preferences, store data and helps provide personalized experiences that are consistent across all of the user's devices [8].

The Smart Irenbus mobile application can only be used by the commuter and the driver, and the web application (online dashboard) by the bus manager. The Smart Irenbus mobile application is mainly divided into two, based on the login credentials submitted the user interface for a commuter or a driver will be shown. When users are signing up, drivers are required to provide a bus code, which is a 16-character alphanumeric code, and this code can only be obtained by and from bus managers. The bus code ensures the integrity of the system and prevents bogus driver accounts from being created.

Commuter App

The following screenshots show some of the functionality of the Smart Irenbus commuter mobile application (Figs. 1, 2 and 3).

Fig. 1. Nearby fragment   **Fig. 2.** Map fragment   **Fig. 3.** Lines fragment

Nearby Fragment shows all nearby buses - which are buses within a 3 km radius from where the user (commuter) is currently located. The estimated distance and time it will take the bus to get to the user's location is shown along with the corresponding bus route/name. These estimates are calculated using the Google's Directions API, which is a service that calculates directions between locations, and it is accessed through an HTTP interface, with requests constructed as a URL string, and latitude/longitude coordinates to identify the locations [3]. Google also provides a similar API called the Distance Matrix API which provides access to travel distance and time for a matrix of origins and destinations, but the Directions API was chosen over this API because it offers more flexibility as it doesn't only calculate the shortest route but other alternate routes.

Map Fragment has the full map view which has all online buses' current locations, and these are updated in real-time as the buses move. The user can pan around, zoom in and zoom out to see the online buses. The map was created using the Maps SDK for Android API, which handles access to Google Maps servers, data downloading, map display, and response to map gestures.

Lines Fragment lists all bus lines schedule (timetables) - these are in a Portable Document Format. To minimize the amount of storage requirement of the mobile application on the user's device, these time-tables were uploaded to Cloud Storage for Firebase which is a powerful, simple, and a cost-effective object storage service that allows for file downloads regardless of the network quality. The PDF timetable of a bus line is then only downloaded when the user clicks on that bus line on the list.

Driver App
The following screenshots show some of the Smart Irenbus driver mobile application's functionality (Figs. 4, 5 and 6).

Fig. 4. Offline state

Fig. 5. Online state

Fig. 6. Bus change

Offline State has the bus driver as offline, which means that the current location of the bus that is driven by this driver will not be shown to Smart Irenbus users.

Online State has the bus driver as online, and the current bus location is updated in real-time as it moves around. And these location updates are set as visible Smart Irenbus users.

Bus Change option allows the currently logged in bus driver to change the bus they are presently driving. This is done by asking the bus driver to input the bus code, which is a 16-character alphanumeric code that uniquely identifies each bus in the Smart Irenbus system.

Online Dashboard

The online dashboard was developed to provide the bus manager with an overall view of the buses and drivers registered on the Smart Irenbus system. This dashboard is hosted using Firebase Hosting, which offers fast and secure hosting for web applications, static and dynamic content, and microservices.

Map Tab has a full map view of all buses currently in transit. The bus manager can interact with the map and click on any bus marker to see detailed information about that bus. The map also has Google Street View integrated into it, which enables users to view and navigate through 360 degrees horizontal and 290 degrees vertical panoramic street-level images of various cities.

Buses Tab shows a table of all registered buses. The bus manager can add more buses, edit, and update information about buses that already exist and search for buses using bus code, number plate, bus number and route name. And when a new bus is added the 16-character alphanumeric code is automatically generated. In this tab, the bus manager will see the predicted number of boardings per selected route, so that they can assign buses accordingly.

Drivers Tab shows a table of all registered bus drivers with the bus code of the bus they are currently driving. More than one driver can be assigned to one bus, but the system will not allow to online at the same time, because a bus only has one driver.

Data Collection and Further Training

The driver mobile application will be used to collect new data about daily ridership. The collected data will then be synchronized with the bus manager's web application and used to train the model further. The model will be retrained when enough data has been collected, every month or two.

Summary of Tools and Technologies Used

As mentioned in [14], the choice of tools used in the software development process can make or break a project. Hence, it is important to be aware of the types of tools that are available for use, and the benefits each can provide as well as the implications for using them. Given Smart Irenbu's requirements, the following were selected (Table 1 and Fig. 7).

Table 1. Selected tools and technologies

	Mobile application	Web application
Languages	Java	JavaScript
APIs	Firebase Storage	Firebase Storage
	Firebase Authentication	Firebase Authentication
	Firebase Database	Firebase Database
	Token Service API	Firebase Hosting
	Android Maps SDK	Token Service API
	Directions API	Maps JavaScript API
	Identity Toolkit API	Identity Toolkit API
Frameworks	Glide v4.8.0	Bootstrap v4.3.1
IDEs	Android Studio v3.4.2	Sublime Text v3.2.2
	Learning Models	
Languages	Python, JavaScript	
IDEs	PyCharm, Google Collab	
Frameworks & Libraries	TensorFlow + Keras, Pandas, Seaborn, Matplotlib	

Fig. 7. Map tab

Multiple tools were used to assess the quality of both the Smart Irenbus mobile and web applications. Firebase BaaS provides several testing tools, and we used three of those viz. Firebase Test Lab which is a cloud-based app-testing environment that allows you to test an Android or iOS app across a wide variety of devices and device configurations, and see the results which also include logs. Firebase Performance Monitoring helps you to gain insight into the performance characteristics of mobile and web applications. And Firebase Crashlytics, which is a crash reporter that enables you to track and fix stability issues that affect a mobile or web application's quality in real-time.

4   Machine Learning Integration

As mentioned earlier, the overall objective of this work is to demonstrate how a holistic real-time transport system can be assembled in the real world with technologies that are currently available to solve problems on the public transport sector within the South African context. Shown in Fig. 8 is how machine learning will be integrated into the system described in the previous sections through the use of an adaptive machine learning model. The model evolves as a result of being retrained periodically with both newly obtained and historical data collected through the Smart Irenbus mobile subsystem.

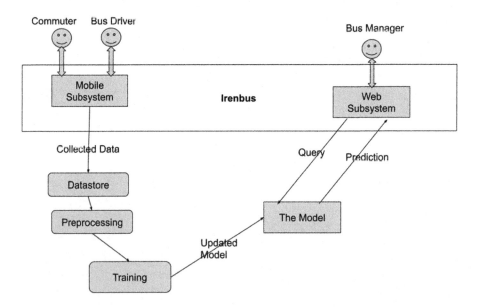

Fig. 8. Machine learning integration overview on the smart Irenbus system architecture

4.1   Dataset

The dataset for this study was obtained from the Chicago Data Portal, which is the City of Chicago's open data portal that lets you find city data and helps you find facts about the city's neighborhoods. Specifically, we used the Chicago Transit Authority's dataset [20], which is the operator of mass transit in Chicago, Illinois and some of its surrounding suburbs with a fleet of 1,879 buses and a 242.36 million annual bus ridership [21]. The dataset shows total daily ridership on a per-route basis dating back to 2001.

We filtered the dataset and only left relevant columns, namely boardings (daily), day type (working day or not), day of the month, day of week and route (number), which are self-explanatory. Shown in Fig. 9 is the distribution of data among these columns.

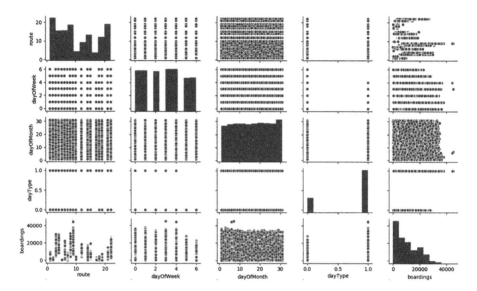

Fig. 9. The joint distribution of columns in the dataset

4.2   Machine Learning Model

Neural Networks can be trained to approximate virtually any nonlinear function to a required degree of accuracy [24]. The learning algorithm used in this study to adjust weights in the network is the Adaptive moment estimation (Adam) optimization algorithm, chosen because of its computational efficiency, little memory requirements and straightforward implementation.

A. Preprocessing

Because of the varying scale of values in the dataset in question, it is best practice to prepare the data before modelling it using a neural network model. Two methods were employed to rescale the attributes of the dataset viz, Normalization and Standardization. As mentioned in [22], unscaled input variables can result in slow or unstable learning, and unscaled target variables on regression problems can result in exploding gradients, causing the learning process to fail.

In normalization, the data is rescaled from the original range in such a way that all attributes have values within the range of 0 and 1. A normalized value of an attribute is calculated as follows: $y = \frac{x - min}{max - min}$.

Standardization is rescaling the distribution of values so that the mean of observed values is 0 with a standard deviation of 1. A standardized value is obtained using: $y = \frac{x - mean}{standard\_deviation}$.

B. Model Architecture

The model was built using Keras Sequential model with 4 densely connected hidden layers and a single output layer that returns one continuous value.

- The model expects rows of data with 4 variables
- The first hidden layer has 50 nodes and uses the ReLU activation function.
- The second hidden layer has 100 nodes and uses the ReLU activation function.
- The second hidden layer has 50 nodes and uses the ReLU activation function.
- The output layer has one node and uses the linear activation function (Fig. 10).

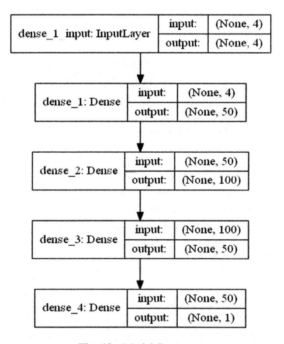

Fig. 10. Model Summary

C. Training

The training was done using three different alterations (standardized, normalized, and unscaled) of the dataset with 78 463 unique entries. This was done so we can observe the effect of preprocessing the dataset on the model's ability to learn. So ultimately there were three different resulting models. These models were trained concurrently on a Dell Personal Computer with 8 GB of Memory, Intel(R) Core (TM) i5-4310U CPU

@ 2.00 GHz, 2601 MHz, 2 Core(s), 4 Logical Processors. On average, each model took 2 h and 12 min to train. The training carried on for 500 epochs, which was found to be optimal. Each model used the Adam optimization algorithm, which automatically tunes itself to provide better results.

Validation loss is the same metric as training loss – it is calculated the same way, but it is not used to adjust the weights of the neural network. In neural networks, the validation set is typically used on every epoch, because training too long can cause overfitting, of which models do not recover from. And to prevent overfitting in a model the training curve in a loss graph should be similar to the validation curve (for most cases). The lower the loss, the better the model, unless the model has overfit the training data. But that will not be the case here, as the model is tested using unseen data.

To determine to the optimal number of epochs to be used in the training process, for each model we experimented with the number of epochs starting from 100 and increasing by 100 in each try while observing the amount of loss from each model. When we reached 400 the models trained with preprocessed dataset features showed some stability, we then increased the number of epochs by 100 again to make sure that the models were genuinely stable. As a result of the final training process (500 epochs), the loss calculated using the Mean Squared Error for each model was as shown in the Fig. 11.

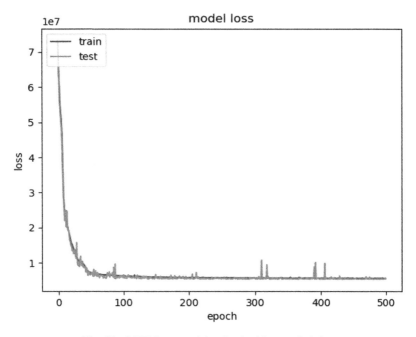

Fig. 11. MSE for a model trained with unscaled data

Training using raw dataset features results in a somewhat unstable model, as the model still has spikes of loss around the 400th epoch (Fig. 12).

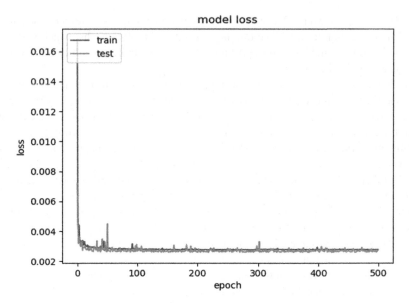

Fig. 12. MSE for a model trained with normalized data

Normalized dataset features significantly reduced the loss experienced when using raw features, as the last noticeable loss spike is around the 300th epoch (Fig. 13).

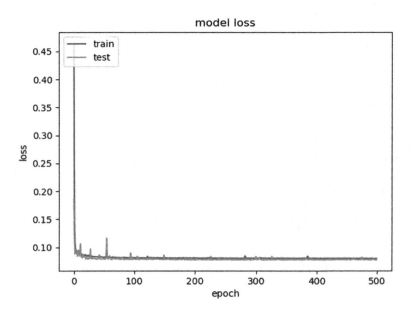

Fig. 13. MSE for a model trained with standardized data

With the standardized dataset features, the last noticeable model loss spike was around the 100th epoch, which is very good for a model trained on more than 70 000 instances and just 500 epochs. The standardization of the dataset features has dramatically improved the learning ability of the model in comparison with normalization. While training with raw dataset features shows greater loss compared to normalized dataset features, this then goes to show the importance of dataset preprocessing and how much it can affect the accuracy of a given model.

We can then save the model trained with standardized data as our best model. This model is then imported into the bus manager's web application using JavaScript and predicts the number of bus boardings that can be expected on a given day per route. This is an excellent deal for bus managers as they can now assign buses to routes based on demand (predicted by the model) and not stick to a static schedule. This will also help cut fuel costs and save the bus operator huge sums of money.

4.3   Discussion and Limitations

As the Smart Irenbus system mainly provides information based on the current user location, high accuracy is needed when tracking the device location. Android mainly offers two types of location permissions viz. ACCESS_COARSE_LOCATION, which report the device's current location with an accuracy equivalent to one city block, and ACCESS_FINE_LOCATION, which provides the highest possible location accuracy [13]. But the higher the accuracy, the higher the battery drain. This is as a result of the fact that the GPS receiver - a small chip and antennae located inside a smartphone - is always listening to cell towers, which give it a rough estimate of where the device is situated always geographically [17]. A lot of location tracking applications face the battery drainage problem, e.g. the popular cab-hailing app - Uber explains in [18] how they are attempting to solve this problem. The same issue will be faced by drivers when using the Smart Irenbus driver mobile application. But commuters with the Smart Irenbus commuter mobile application will not be affected as much since they will typically only use the app when they want to ride or track a bus. The Smart Irenbus mobile application only works on Android, for now, as the Android operating system makes up approximately 88 per cent of the mobile phone global market share [19].

5   Conclusion and Future Direction

With more than half of the world's population residing in urban areas, the need for reliable public transportation is more evident now than ever before. This solely depends on the availability of real-time information to commuters and useful in insights to bus operators. We developed an intelligent machine learning-based real-time transport system to address this. The system is composed of three subsystems to cater to passengers, drivers and bus managers. The new system mobile application is very lightweight, and after being subjected to several tests, it has proven to be efficient in terms of device resource consumption. And in comparison, with previous work done on this topic, this project took full advantage of cloud computing services while only requiring a smartphone to work - eliminating the need and costs of installing and maintaining separate GPS trackers on the vehicles. While additionally collecting daily ridership data and using it to offer useful insights to bus managers.

The proposed system can be improved by the incorporation of other modes of public transportation other than buses; automating the assignment of drivers through feeding the model's predictions to a driver assignment subsystem; and by additionally catering for iOS devices. Also, there have been discussions with the eThekwini municipality stakeholders about a possible implementation of the proposed system.

Appendix

Smart Irenbus GitHub repository with source code including raw and processed training data, https://github.com/m3n2ie/Irenbus.

References

1. Statistics South Africa. Measuring household expenditure on public transport (2015). http://www.statssa.gov.za/?p=5943
2. Sungur, C., Sungur, I., Babaoglu, A.: Smart bus station-passenger information system. In: 2015 2nd International Conference on Information Science and Control Engineering (2015)
3. Google Developers. Get started — directions api. https://developers.google.com/maps/documentation/directions/start?hl=enUS
4. Monchambert, G., De Palma, A.: Public transport reliability and commuter strategy. J. Urban Econ. **81**, 14–29 (2014)
5. Shirisha, K., Sivaprasad, T.: Acquire bus information using GSM technology. Int. J. Adv. Technol. (2016)
6. Kumbhar, M., Survase, M., Mastud, P., Salunke, A., Sirdeshpande, S.: Real time web based bus tracking system. Int. Res. J. Eng. Technol. (IRJET) **3**(02), 632–635 (2016)
7. Moroney, L.: The firebase realtime database (2017)
8. Moroney, L.: Using authentication in firebase. In: The Definitive Guide to Firebase. Apress, Berkeley (2017)
9. UN DESA — United Nations Department of Economic and Social Affairs. 68 per cent of the world population projected to live in urban areas by 2050, says un, 2018. https://www.un.org/development/desa/en/news/population/2018-revision-of-world-urbanization-prospects.html
10. Independent Communications Authority of South Africa. State of ICT sector in South Africa - 2019 report (2019). https://www.icasa.org.za/legislation-and-regulations/state-of-ict-sectorin-south-africa-2019-report
11. Lahudkar, P., Sawale, S., Deshmane, V., Bharambe, K.: NoSQL database-Google's firebase: a review. Int. J. Innov. Res. Sci. Eng. Technol. **7**(3), 243–250 (2018)
12. Manikandan, R., Niranjani, S.: Implementation on real time public transportation information using GSM query response system. Contemp. Eng. Sci. **7**(05), 2014 (2014)
13. Smaato. How to optimize your location data's accuracy (2019). https://www.smaato.com/blog/optimize-your-location-data-accuracy/
14. Smartdraw. Selecting the right software development tools for your developers. https://www.smartdraw.com/technology/right-softwaredevelopment-tools-for-developers.htm

15. WhiteSource Software. When to consider a NoSQL vs relational database. https://resources.whitesourcesoftware.com/blogwhitesource/when-to-consider-a-nosql-vs-relational-database
16. StackShare. Amazon EC2 vs firebase — what are the differences? https://stackshare.io/stackups/amazon-ec2-vs-firebase
17. The Verge. Why GPS-dependent apps deplete your smartphone battery (2018). https://www.theverge.com/2018/8/17/17630872/smartphonebattery-gps-location-services
18. Hameed, S., Chida, J.: Mastering Android Wear Application Development. Packt Publishing Ltd (2016). https://eng.uber.com/activity-service-dependency-android-architecture/
19. The Statistics Portal. Global market share held by the leading smartphone operating systems in sales to end users from 1st quarter 2009 to 2nd quarter 2018. Statistics Portal (2018). https://www.statista.com/statistics/266136/global-market-share-held-by-smartphone-operating-systems
20. CTA - Ridership - Bus Routes - Daily Totals by Route. https://data.cityofchicago.org/Transportation/CTA-Ridership-Bus-Routes-Daily-Totals-by-Route/jyb9-n7fm
21. Annual Ridership Report: Calendar Year 2018 (PDF). Transitchicago.com. https://www.transitchicago.com/assets/1/6/2018_Annual_Report_-_v3_04.03.2019.pdf
22. Machine Learning Mastery https://machinelearningmastery.com/how-to-improve-neural-network-stability-and-modeling-performance-with-data-scaling/
23. Bacciu, D., Carta, A., Gnesi, S., Semini, L.: An experience in using machine learning for short-term predictions in smart transportation systems. J. Log. Algebraic Methods Program. 1(87), 52–66 (2017)
24. Agarwal, P.K., Gurjar, J., Agarwal, A.K., Birla, R.: Application of artificial intelligence for development of intelligent transport system in smart cities. J. Traffic Transp. Eng. 1(1), 20–30 (2015)
25. Othman, M.S., Tan, G.: Machine learning aided simulation of public transport utilization. In: 2018 IEEE/ACM 22nd International Symposium on Distributed Simulation and Real Time Applications (DS-RT), 15 October 2018, pp. 1–2. IEEE (2018)
26. Toqué, F., Khouadjia, M., Come, E., Trepanier, M., Oukhellou, L.: Short & long term forecasting of multimodal transport passenger flows with machine learning methods. In: 2017 IEEE 20th International Conference on Intelligent Transportation Systems (ITSC), 16 October 2017, pp. 560–566. IEEE (2017)
27. Liu, G., Yin, Z., Jia, Y., Xie, Y.: Passenger flow estimation based on convolutional neural network in public transportation system. Knowl.-Based Syst. 123, 102–115 (2017)
28. Van Oort, N., Brands, T., de Romph, E.: Short term ridership prediction in public transport by processing smart card data. Transp. Res. Rec. (2015)
29. Skhosana, M., Ezugwu, A.E.: Irenbus: A real-time public transport management system. In: 2020 Conference on Information Communications Technology and Society (ICTAS), 11 March 2020, pp. 1–7. IEEE (2020). https://doi.org/10.1109/ictas47918.2020.234000

Telemetry and Video Surveillance System in a UAV for the Control and Monitoring of Long-Distance Missions

Jorge Buele[1,2,4,5]( ) , Estefanía Yánez-Arcos[1] ,
María Elena Moscoso[1] , Jordan S. Huilca[3] , Edisson P. Jordán[1] ,
Pilar Urrutia-Urrutia[1] , and Franklin W. Salazar[1]

[1] Universidad Técnica de Ambato, Ambato 180103, Ecuador
{eyanez0347,me.moscosoa,edissonpjordan,
elsapurrutia}@uta.edu.ec
[2] SISAu Research Group, Universidad Tecnológica Indoamérica,
Ambato 180212, Ecuador
jorgebuele@uti.edu.ec, fw.salazar@uta.edu.ec
[3] Escuela Superior Politécnica de Chimborazo, Riobamba 060155, Ecuador
hlcjdn94a08z605e@studenti.unical.it
[4] Universidad Internacional de la Rioja, 26006 Logroño, Spain
[5] Sociedad Nacional de la Cruz Roja Ecuatoriana, Quito 170403, Ecuador

Abstract. Unmanned aerial vehicles (UAVs) are multidisciplinary technological tools, which are used in the military area for surveillance, reconnaissance and intelligence tasks in conflict zones. Due to its versatility and performance, this manuscript describes the implementation of a telemetry and video surveillance system to develop long-range missions in a UAV prototype. Communications subsystems and a ground station are integrated, with which an unmanned aerial system (UAS) is formed, carrying out the necessary calibrations and configurations. After a set of tests and the necessary adjustments, a long-distance mission is carried out and its energy consumption, height reached and trajectory tracking are analyzed. In addition, the video signal level obtained and the percentage of telemetry signal in each of the tests are established, which managed to be 90% with a distance greater than 4 km. They have good benefits, with a low economic investment, representing an interesting proposal for developing countries with a limited budget for their improvement.

Keywords: Military missions · Monitoring · Telemetry · UAS · Video-surveillance system

1 Introduction

Continuous advances in technology in air field have allowed the development of mechanisms to make better applications [1–3]. Autonomous unmanned systems have provided researchers with an efficient means of controlling and monitoring sites that are difficult to access or that pose a danger to humans [4, 5]. Unmanned Aircraft Systems (UAS), commonly known as Unmanned Aerial Systems, are defined as a complete

© Springer Nature Switzerland AG 2020
O. Gervasi et al. (Eds.): ICCSA 2020, LNCS 12254, pp. 666–681, 2020.
https://doi.org/10.1007/978-3-030-58817-5_48

system that includes unmanned aerial vehicles (UAVs), ground operator stations, launch mechanisms, etc. [6] The UAS must consider within its design a command, a control and communication (C3) system and the personnel necessary to control the unmanned aircraft [7]. UAS systems have been integrated into applications in a wide variety of disciplines, such as geography, agriculture, archeology, planimetry, etc., due to their dynamism and flexibility [8] However, there has been a particular growth in the number of applications aimed at remote sensing, surveillance and monitoring, for data collection. Sometimes, the data obtained has a limited reliability which produces uncertainty in the effectiveness of their implementation, which has represented a limitation for their widespread use.

The main part of the system is the unmanned aerial vehicle (UAV), an aircraft which performs its function remotely [9–11]. Today they are mainly used for entertainment, although they have also played an important role in the military field [12, 13]. They represent one of the most promising tools for intelligence, surveillance and reconnaissance missions, due to their capabilities to achieve these objectives [14]. The need to develop these aircraft arises from the existence of illegal activities such as smuggling, cultivation, production, and drug trafficking that commonly affect various regions of the globe. In this way, air traffic control and the contribution of real-time information can be made for decision-making, both in military operations and for risk management and natural disasters [15]. The emergence of UAVs as a tool for surveillance and a means for providing services in an emergency, raises the need to establish ethical regulations. For this reason, the manuscript of [16] presents a study of how drones have become devices that require regulation. To carry out this procedure, 4 steps have been carried out that are detailed in order to formulate arguments regarding Latin American airspace.

Previous studies showing the implementation of surveillance systems in UAVs are of great relevance, as shown in [17]. In this work an electro-optical/infrared sensor is designed, developed and adapted in a mid-range UAV, for traffic detection, surveillance and recognition. Tests carried out at close range show the operation of the system through the acquisition of video in real time and its position in Google Earth. Similarly, in [18] the coupling of an electro-optical sensor in the Twin Otter DHC-6 aircraft is presented, for surveillance, reconnaissance and intelligence activities. To carry out this non-invasive and easy-to-assemble procedure, a previous study of affectation, aerodynamic, structural analysis, loads, weight and balance is considered. On the other hand, in the proposal of [19], the design and implementation of an ETL system (extraction, transformation and loading) is described, through which information is extracted, processed and shared from the UAV systems to the operator. The ETL system is developed on an integrated platform with the ability to perform multiple tasks, integrating signals with different communication protocols and high-speed information processing in real time. The development of this system facilitates the operation, control, monitoring and execution of information registration tasks of a mid-range UAV.

In response to the needs of the Ecuadorian Air Force, the initial study presented in [20] has been complemented. Using advanced technology, it is proposed to implement a UAS that allows long-range monitoring and surveillance tasks. From the ground station, you can control and receive video in real time, based on how the UAV performs the desired displacement. This prototype has good features and long-distance communication (range of kilometers) and with the possibility of storing this information. Through this research project, military control and patrolling activities can be carried out in tropical environments, where there is difficult access for the police personnel by land. Despite being a low-cost proposal, results obtained have demonstrated its efficient operation.

This document is distributed as follows: Sect. 1 describes a brief introduction and the respective state of the art. In Sect. 2 the selection of the elements that make up the Unmanned Aerial System (UAS) is described and Sect. 3 contains the software configuration and programming process for said equipment. The results of the experimental tests and the conclusions can be seen in Sect. 4 and Sect. 5 respectively.

2   Hardware

The UAS segments used for the project are shown in Fig. 1. The diagram consists of: 1) The air segment corresponds to the hummingbird aircraft, with all its instrumentation to develop manual and automatic flights; 2) The communications segment, which corresponds to the telemetry and video links; and 3) The land segment, which is made up of mechanisms for observing the mission and executing control processes. Table 1 details each of the mechanical characteristics with which the aircraft has been designed and built. These characteristics are of great importance since from them the proposed system is designed. For location of each of the components, certain restrictions must be considered, including the adequate distribution of the payload to achieve correct stability and control of the aircraft. Also, it should be considered that the physical structure with which the aircraft is built is made of carbon fiber, taking into account that this is a conductive material.

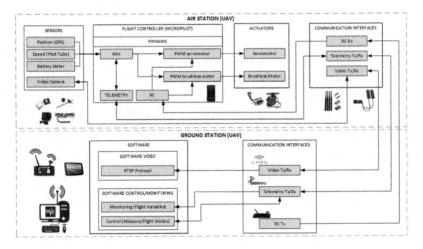

Fig. 1. General diagram of the proposal.

Table 1. Mechanical specifications of the UAV

Specification	Feature
Wingspan (m)	2.3
Weight (kg)	1.7
Stall speed (m/s)	9.29
Takeoff method	Manual launch
Landing method	Manual gathering
Payload (Kg)	1.5

In the air segment, the elements described in Table 2 are implemented, based on the mechanical specifications of the UAV. In the ground segment by means of a computer (personal computer) that has an interactive interface, the user can execute different processes, such as the programming of missions to the micropilot board (automatic navigation) and monitoring, where he/she can observe all data from telemetry as well as video on an auxiliary monitor. There is also the remote control (RC), which in conjunction with communication interfaces can take manual control of the aircraft at any time, either to take off, land or perform certain maneuvers. The communications segment is made up of two systems: one for data and the other for video, which works independently and is in charge of sending data from the flight controller to the ground station.

Table 2. Physical components of the system.

Function	Element
Flight controller or autopilot	Micropilot Pixhawk 2.1.
Sensorization	Positioning (GPS)
	Speed (Pitot Tube)
	Battery Measurer
	Image (Camera)
Actuators	Brushless Electric Motor
	Servo motors

3 Software

The software used in the earth station will be Mission Planner (MP) due to the ease of use it offers. It is worth mentioning that the video kit has a mission planner installed by default, which is QGround Control (QGC), where only the flight variables will be displayed; and additional mission information is obtained by doing added programming.

3.1 Initial Setup

The MP software version 1.3.64 is installed on the PC that acts as an earth station, its compatibility with the recommended versions of the micropilot used is verified and a wireless link is established between them, using the MAVLINK protocol. The MP software works with various types of UAV platforms, so it is necessary to install the firmware (software necessary to manage the information received from the outside, process it and transmit orders to the aircraft actuators) on the micropilot board, specifically for type platforms fixed wing.

For communication, the parameters of the transmission (TX) and reception (RX) modules of the RFD 900 radio modem are configured, with a minimum and maximum frequency of 915000 kHz and 928000 kHz respectively. The air transmission speed is established at 64 Kbps, considering that the higher the speed, the shorter the range and vice versa. However, the use of extremely low speeds due to loss of information by interference is not recommended in this application. As a security parameter against possible interference from other equipment of the same frequency that is operating in the area, the network identifier or Net ID is set to a value of 25 (in a range from 0 to 499). The transmission power is 20 dBm, denoting that all the modified parameters must be the same in both the TX and RX modules.

3.2 Sensor Calibration

Calibration of the aircraft sensors is performed using the MP and QGC software, in order to store these settings in the memory of the micropilot. Using MP, the pitot tube and battery monitor are generally calibrated on the Optional Hardware tab and the remaining sensors on the Initial Setup and Mandatory Hardware tabs. To calibrate the internal micropilot accelerometer, choose the Accel Calibration option, then place the aircraft on a horizontal plane and using the recommended configuration manager, follow the procedure indicated in Fig. 2 (left). For external GPS sensor, with the option Compas will open the recommended configuration manager, follow the movements in Fig. 2 (right) and when finished, restart the Pixhawk board.

In the case of the external Pitot Tube speed sensor, MP does not have the capacity to calibrate it, so QGC is used. To do this, start by covering the sensor, so that it measures a value of 0 and as the calibration process progresses, introduce air progressively until completing the procedure; battery capacity is 5000 mAh.

Fig. 2. Movements to be carried out for the calibration of: accelerometer (left). GPS (right).

3.3   Radio Control Setup and Calibration

The physical control joysticks need to be calibrated to capture the maximum and minimum ranges of PWM that will be obtained by executing a movement with these levers. The channels programmed in the physical control must be selected, as well as the Pitch, Yaw, Roll and Throttle axes and move the joysticks in all their directions (horizontal, vertical and circle). In this way the program captures the maximum and minimum ranges of PWM that are generated with the movements, i.e. the ranges in which the servos and the motor will operate. Figure 3 shows the results obtained from said process.

Fig. 3.   List of PWM ranges for each joystick.

3.4   Configuration of Flight Modes in Software

Flight modes establish how the aircraft should interact based on the needs of the operating missions and the degree of autonomy required. These modes are selected by the pilot through radio transmitter switches or buttons or commands from the earth station. The following flight modes were programmed for this project: Manual, Return to Launch (RTL), Auto, Autotune and Loiter, whose function is described in Table 3.

Table 3.   Flight modes description.

Mode	GPS usage	Description
Manual	No	The pilot has full control of the interfaces, the aircraft has no speed, height or position restrictions
Autotune	Yes	The assisted movement of the Pitch and Roll interfaces have limits of freedom, and the accelerator is controlled entirely by the pilot; uses manual changes to save values to the aircraft's Pitch and Roll control
Auto	Yes	Follow scheduled missions
Loiter	Yes	The aircraft rotates around the point where the mode was activated
949 (RTL)	Yes	Go back to the starting point and circle around

3.5   Video Equipment Configuration

The video system is a totally independent segment from the rest of the aircraft, because due to its high-power consumption, the pilot needs to have priority in telemetry data over video. The video kit is made up of a radio, called an aerial unit, which has two omnidirectional antennas with pin-type connections. One controller for the ground unit with an omnidirectional antenna and one directional with screw-type connector. A power supply to provide with energy the entire system and a GoPro camera. It is worth mentioning that the air unit and the controller have Full-Duplex communication.

The controller only supports QGC mission management software, since it can be installed on computers with an Android operating system, as is the case with this system. For the operation of the camera it is connected to one of the HDMI ports of the air unit and its resolution is modified to 1080p and a speed of 60fps. To view the video that the camera transmits, you have the screen of the controller, which through a video stream manager determines its source and the type of input (HDMI). In case you want to record in the internal memory of the controller or you want to stop recording, you have two buttons to carry it out. An auxiliary monitor (PC or smartphone) can also be used through the RTSP protocol, connecting to an enabled Hotspot network and thus running the player.

4   Tests and Experimental Results

After carrying out six operation tests at short distances as part of the initial phase of this project (one of them in mountainous locations), an overflight is carried out in the town of the South American Amazon order to verify the equipment operating efficiency over long distances. For this, a mission was carried out at a speed of 15 m/s, a maximum height of 350 m, a maximum distance of 5.02 km and a total perimeter traveled of 9.36 km. At the end of the mission, the information obtained is saved in a.log extension document for later analysis. The results obtained are presented below.

4.1   Height Analysis

The waypoints (WP) programmed for this mission with their respective heights are displayed in Fig. 4, where from a height of 100 m in RTL mode, the aircraft must climb to a maximum height of 350 m and descend again to 100 m during its flight in auto mode. During RTL mode it is required to maintain a constant height of 100 m.

In Fig. 5 the behavior of the UAV is observed throughout the mission, where it is verified that it reaches the values defined in each WP, as well as maintaining its height in a stable and constant way in the RTL mode (100 m). The summary of reached heights is detailed in Table 4; to reach the desired height between nearby points (WP1-WP2) it takes 1:24 min and for distant points (WP4-WP5) 2:27 min.

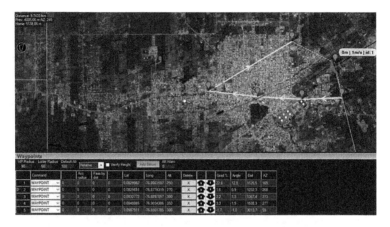

Fig. 4. Route established with their respective WayPoints.

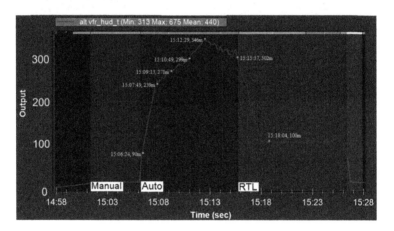

Fig. 5. Route taken by the UAV (various heights).

Table 4. Summary of reached heights.

Mode	Name	Position	Hour	Desired Height	Obtained Height
Manual	Home	0,091659; −76,86847	15:06:24	100	90.26
Auto	WP1	0,0829982; −76,8663597	15:07:49	250	239
Auto	WP2	0,0825691; −−6,8774319	15:09:13	270	271
Auto	WP3	0,0832772; −76,8897057	15:10:49	300	299
Auto	WP4	0,0848865; −76,9034386	15:12:29	350	346
Auto	WP5	0,0987911; −76,8801785	15:15:37	300	302
RTL	Home	0,091659; −76,86847	15:18:04	100	100

4.2 Speed Analysis

For this flight a constant speed of 15 m/s is required, since it allows the aircraft to capture the video adequately. This value has been used for all missions in Auto, RTL and Loiter mode. In Fig. 6 the speed behavior is analyzed, where a constant of 15 m/s is verified during all modes. However, at 15:15:37 a small acceleration peak of 20 m/s is observed, indicating mode change from Auto to RTL, when descending from 300 m to 100 m.

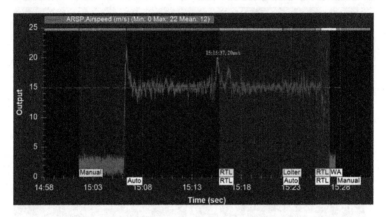

Fig. 6. Speed variations vs Time.

4.3 Energy Consumption Analysis

The variables analyzed are amps discharged per hour (mAh) and the voltage; the flight starts with a fully charged battery (16.5 V) and it is estimated that for 20:13 min the maximum consumption is 1700 mAh and a voltage discharge of less than 20%. It is worth mentioning that it is estimated a lower consumption than calculated by flying in a clear area with less height than the one reached in the mountain region. The graph in Fig. 7 describes the current consumption that aircraft has had throughout the flight, where maximum value reached is 860mAh, being less than expected. Similarly, it is identified that in Auto mode there is a higher consumption compared to RTL mode where it remains permanent.

Through Fig. 8, battery behavior (voltage discharge) during flight can be evidenced. It started with a voltage of 16.5 V and ends with an average of 14.8 V, which represents a discharge of 10.3%. The discharge is adequate throughout the flight, in small areas low voltage spikes are displayed, indicating high consumption on certain occasions, such as takeoff.

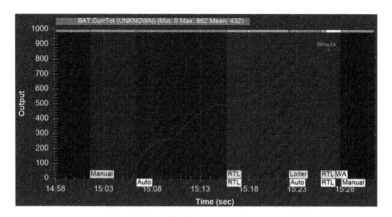

Fig. 7. Consumption of mAh vs Time.

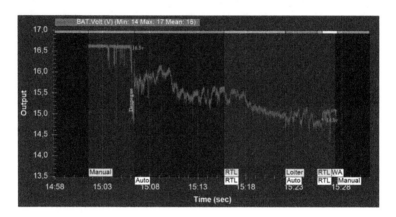

Fig. 8. Consumption of voltage vs Time.

4.4   Position Analysis

It is analyzed if the aircraft complied with the points programmed in an appropriate way, for this, in Fig. 9 the desired path is observed (black plane) and the executed path is shown (yellow plane). An optimal compliance of the trajectory without deviations is observed, satisfying each established WP.

Overall, in all tests carried out, it has been shown that the aerodynamics of the aircraft and its configurations were optimal considering the environmental conditions of the South American Amazon and the mountain region (in a previous test), registering a lower energy consumption than estimated. Due to the favorable conditions being a flight a few meters above sea level, it is identified that the battery consumption is 1.6 V for 20 min, an adequate proportion.

The telemetry link for a maximum height of 350 m was on average 94% of the signal, indicating that the aircraft can be sent over distances of 5 km without losing its monitoring and being able to execute remote control orders through of telemetry interfaces. In the video link at a distance of 3.58 km, a loss of information was obtained due to the controller equipment heating up and generating a restart. This is because proper precautions were not taken regarding the temperature to which the controller was exposed, with which this exceeded the manufacturer's recommended temperature. However, this design flaw was corrected. At a distance of 2.82 km, the link is recovered, obtaining a loss of information of 2:12 min.

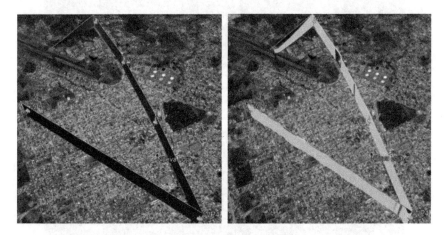

Fig. 9. Path Analysis: Programmed path (Left). Executed path by the aircraft (Right).

4.5   Analysis of Telemetry Signal Levels

Table 5 shows the signal levels obtained when performing the seven tests, although they are not all presented, as they are not of interest. The signal level of the link is displayed on the monitoring interface as a percentage as shown in Fig. 10, from which the data for each of the tests has been obtained according to the required distance.

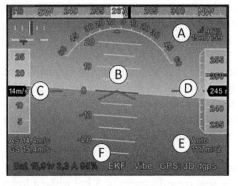

(A) Telemetry Signal Level and Time

(B) UAV Orientation

(C) Speed

(D) Height

(E) Flight Mode

(F) Battery Level

Fig. 10. Mission planner telemetry signal level.

Table 5. Analysis of telemetry signal levels.

Distance	Signal Percentage			
	Test 2	Test 5	Test 6	Test 7
Home	98%	95%	99%	99%
100	95%	92%	99%	99%
200	93%	92%	95%	99%
300	82%	88%	91%	99%
400	78%	60%	90%	98%
500	69%	54%	90%	98%
600	62%	60%	88%	98%
800	50%	85%	81%	97%
1000	49%	58%	89%	96%
1200	–	53%	89%	95%
1500	–	–	72%	95%
2000	–	–	68%	87%
2500	–	–	54%	92%
3000	–	–	–	98%
3500	–	–	–	93%
4000	–	–	–	91%
4500	–	–	–	90%

Tests 2 and 5 show considerable signal losses at distances not greater than 1 Km. This caused the data transmission to intermittent at certain points while in test 6 when antennas changed its position, the signal level increased considerably reaching a distance of close to 3 km. Finally, it can be seen that the levels in the operational test (Test 7) are efficient, after making certain corrections, since only at 2 km there was a percentage of less than 90%, recovering in a short time. These data confirm that, for environments with high vegetation and humidity, the telemetry transmission system works effectively and the navigation distance of the aircraft can be increased.

4.6 Analysis of Video Signal Levels

The signal spectrum is monitored in the video controller. Similar to the case of telemetry, the signal to noise ratio (SNR) data have been taken from the tests that were interest.

At a distance of 200 m from the base station, video transmission is good in all tests, although the quality of the captured image is better in tests 6 and 7 and can be confirmed with SNR levels that was obtained in each test. By setting a distance of 600 m from the base station, low SNR levels can be detected, and especially in Test 5 the image quality is lower because there are notable pixelations. For tests 6 and 7 you have high SNR levels and good image quality. Figure 11 demonstrates all said above.

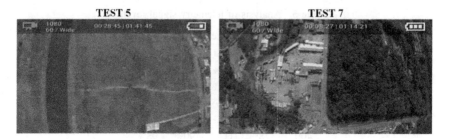

Fig. 11. Video SNR level at a distance of 600 m.

At a distance of 1000 m from the base station, tests 2 and 5 show extremely low SNR levels, so the images transmitted are of poor quality compared to the images in tests 6 and 7. These losses are attributed to a bad antennas location which allowed the absorption of the signal. Results can be seen in Fig. 12.

Fig. 12. Video SNR level at a distance of 1000 m.

Starting at 2000 m from the base station, only tests 6 and 7 are compared, since in the previous two missions the distance greater than 1 km were not met. Both tests have a stable video transmission, but when reaching a distance of 2.5 km in test 6 there is a link loss. The video recording of each test can be seen in Fig. 13.

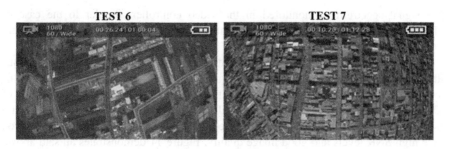

Fig. 13. Video SNR level at a distance of 2000 m.

At a distance of 3500 m from the base station, we only have the analysis in test 7, where it can be perceived that the SNR falls down completely as well as the video quality. The only test that was successful at this distance is presented in Fig. 14. With each of the results obtained, it has been determined that the transmission quality of the images is superior in tests 6 and 7 due to the modifications in the antennas positioning. In addition to these tests, the aircraft flew over to a maximum height of 3000 m, which did not happen in tests 2 and 5, this being another important factor to consider in the video link.

Fig. 14. Video SNR level at a distance of 3500 m.

As seen in references presented, there are several investigations where low-cost video surveillance systems (prototypes) are implemented in aircraft. In [17] and [18] the electro-optical sensor is presented as the tool to capture video in real time. However, in this proposal an own system based on a GO Pro camera is used. For its part [19], it presents a ETL system in a mid-range UAV but now, this work has now been done on a low-end aircraft. This represents a lower resource investment that can be exploited by developing countries, since long-distance results are highly efficient.

5   Conclusions

The UAV used for this project is medium-range, having a structure suitable for developing video surveillance missions at the borderline or in areas with difficult access. Despite having an efficient mechanical design and capable of executing stable flights, it has been detected that the systems for both mission control and monitoring are deficient, as they present a slow response and a maximum range of 800 m. For the hummingbird aircraft and its area of operation, specific requirements were established for each of the systems. A fast response control system with redundancy and a power system suitable for greater autonomy and long-range communication systems. For the latter, two different frequency bands were selected to avoid interferences between telemetry and video data; these were 915 MHz and 2.4 GHz respectively, since their characteristics are excellent for obtaining a greater range and penetration in areas whose climate is humid with high vegetation.

The hummingbird aircraft was converted into an operational aircraft as it performs long-range missions with constant monitoring of all telemetry or flight variables and live streaming of high-definition video. Through tests carried out in the operation area, communication ranges of 5 km for telemetry and 4 km for video have been reached but, it was detected by the levels of the telemetry signal that greater distances could be reached since only it shows a loss of 10%. Another aspect to note is that the aircraft was subjected to other tests with atmospheric difficulties where the same data quality was obtained, but with a slight decrease in distance. As future work, it is presented to expand this research, carrying out further tests in other geographical areas, with the possibility of carrying out a new prototype system.

Acknowledgments.   Special thanks to the support provided by CIDFAE Research Center of FAE, DIDE and SISAu Research Group.

References

1. Son, L., Adipta, K.F., Bur, M.: Analysis of the static behavior of a new landing gear model based on a four-bar linkage mechanism. Int. J. Technol. (2019). https://doi.org/10.14716/ijtech.v10i8.3486
2. Buele, J., et al.: Interactive system for monitoring and control of a flow station using LabVIEW. In: Rocha, Á., Guarda, T. (eds.) ICITS 2018. AISC, vol. 721, pp. 583–592. Springer, Cham (2018). https://doi.org/10.1007/978-3-319-73450-7_55
3. Berawi, M.A.: Managing artificial intelligence technology for added value. Int. J. Technol. (2020). https://doi.org/10.14716/ijtech.v11i1.3889
4. Shukla, A., Karki, H.: Application of robotics in offshore oil and gas industry-a review Part II. Rob. Auton. Syst. (2016). https://doi.org/10.1016/j.robot.2015.09.013
5. Solodov, A., Williams, A., Al Hanaei, S., Goddard, B.: Analyzing the threat of unmanned aerial vehicles (UAV) to nuclear facilities. Secur. J. (2018). https://doi.org/10.1057/s41284-017-0102-5
6. Pozniak, M., Ranganathan, P.: Counter UAS solutions through UAV swarm environments. In: IEEE International Conference on Electro Information Technology (2019). https://doi.org/10.1109/EIT.2019.8834140
7. Yasin, M.F.M., Zaidi, M.A., Nawi, M.N.M.: A review of Small Unmanned Aircraft System (UAS) advantages as a tool in condition survey works. In: MATEC Web of Conferences (2016). https://doi.org/10.1051/matecconf/20166600038
8. Singh, K.K., Frazier, A.E.: A meta-analysis and review of unmanned aircraft system (UAS) imagery for terrestrial applications. Int. J. Remote Sens. (2018). https://doi.org/10.1080/01431161.2017.1420941
9. Loya, H., Enríquez, V., Salazar, F.W., Sánchez, C., Urrutia, F., Buele, J.: Analysis and determination of minimum requirements of an autopilot for the control of unmanned aerial vehicles (UAV). In: Nummenmaa, J., Pérez-González, F., Domenech-Lega, B., Vaunat, J., Oscar Fernández-Peña, F. (eds.) CSEI 2019. AISC, vol. 1078, pp. 129–142. Springer, Cham (2020). https://doi.org/10.1007/978-3-030-33614-1_9
10. Saponaro, M., Tarantino, E., Fratino, U.: Geometric accuracy evaluation of geospatial data using low-cost sensors on small UAVs. In: Gervasi, O., et al. (eds.) ICCSA 2018. LNCS, vol. 10964, pp. 364–374. Springer, Cham (2018). https://doi.org/10.1007/978-3-319-95174-4_29

11. Barrile, V., Candela, G., Fotia, A., Bernardo, E.: UAV survey of bridges and viaduct: workflow and application. In: Misra, S., et al. (eds.) ICCSA 2019. LNCS, vol. 11622, pp. 269–284. Springer, Cham (2019). https://doi.org/10.1007/978-3-030-24305-0_21
12. De Marsico, M., Spagnoli, A.: Using hands as an easy UAV joystick for entertainment applications. In: ACM International Conference Proceeding Series (2019). https://doi.org/10. 1145/3351995.3352042
13. Orfanus, D., De Freitas, E.P., Eliassen, F.: Self-organization as a supporting paradigm for military UAV relay networks. IEEE Commun. Lett. (2016). https://doi.org/10.1109/ LCOMM.2016.2524405
14. Manyam, S.G., Rasmussen, S., Casbeer, D.W., Kalyanam, K., Manickam, S.: Multi-UAV routing for persistent intelligence surveillance & reconnaissance missions. In: 2017 International Conference on Unmanned Aircraft Systems, ICUAS 2017 (2017). https://doi. org/10.1109/ICUAS.2017.7991314
15. Brooks, J., Lodge, R., White, D.: Comparison of a head-mounted display and flat screen display during a micro-UAV target detection Task. In: Proceedings of the Human Factors and Ergonomics Society (2017). https://doi.org/10.1177/1541931213601863
16. Sandvik, K.B., Oliveira Martins, B.: Revisitando el espacio aéreo latinoamericano: una exploración de los drones como sujetos de regulación. Lat. Am. Law Rev. (2018). https:// doi.org/10.29263/lar01.2018.03
17. Jara-Olmedo, A., Medina-Pazmiño, W., Mesías, R., Araujo-Villaroel, B., Aguilar, W.G., Pardo, J.A.: Interface of optimal electro-optical/infrared for unmanned aerial vehicles. In: Rocha, Á., Guarda, T. (eds.) MICRADS 2018. SIST, vol. 94, pp. 372–380. Springer, Cham (2018). https://doi.org/10.1007/978-3-319-78605-6_32
18. León, G., Enríquez, V., Salazar, F.W., Guallo, J.F., Urrutia, F., Buele, J.: Implementation of an electro-optical sensor in the twin Otter FAE plane for the strengthening of the strategic surveillance capacity. RISTI - Rev. Iber. Sist. e Tecnol. Inf. **E29**, 1–12 (2020)
19. Medina-Pazmiño, W., Jara-Olmedo, A., Tasiguano-Pozo, C., Lavín, J.M.: Analysis and implementation of ETL system for unmanned aerial vehicles (UAV). In: Rocha, Á., Guarda, T. (eds.) ICITS 2018. AISC, vol. 721, pp. 653–662. Springer, Cham (2018). https://doi.org/ 10.1007/978-3-319-73450-7_62
20. Moscoso, M.E., et al.: Structural design of a telemetry and video surveillance system implemented in a UAV. RISTI - Rev. Iber. Sist. e Tecnol. Inf. **E29**, 451–464 (2020)

3D Object Reconstruction Using Concatenated Matrices with MS Kinect: A Contribution to Interiors Architecture

Jorge Buele[1,4(✉)] ⓘ, José Varela-Aldás[1] ⓘ,
Esteban X. Castellanos[2] ⓘ, Janio Jadán-Guerrero[1] ⓘ,
and Jeneffer Barberán[3] ⓘ

[1] SISAu Research Group, Universidad Tecnológica Indoamérica,
Ambato 180212, Ecuador
{jorgebuele,josevarela,janiojadan}@uti.edu.ec
[2] Universidad de las Fuerzas Armadas ESPE, Latacunga 050104, Ecuador
excastellanos@espe.edu.ec
[3] Instituto Superior Tecnológico Tsa'chila, Santo Domingo 230109, Ecuador
jbarberan@institutos.gob.ec
[4] Universidad Internacional de la Rioja, 26006 Logroño, Spain

Abstract. Interior architecture is part of the individual, social and business life of the human being; it allows structuring the spaces to inhabit, study or work. This document presents the design and implementation of a system that allows the three-dimensional reconstruction of objects with a reduced economic investment. The image acquisition process and treatment of the information with mathematical support that it entails are described. The system involves an MS Kinect as a tool to create a radar that operates with the structured light principle to capture objects at a distance of less than 2 meters. The development of the scripts is done in the MATLAB software and in the same way the graphical interface that is presented to the user. As part of the initial tests of this prototype, the digitization of geometric shape structures has been performed with an accuracy of over 98%. This validates its efficient operation, which serves as the basis for the development of modeling in interior architecture for future work.

Keywords: 3D object reconstruction · Combined matrix · Image processing · Interior architecture · Software applications

1 Introduction

The three-dimensional digitization of objects is one of the applications of technology that is currently of greatest interest [1–3]. Various methodologies, procedures and techniques have been developed in the last three decades in order to obtain better representations [3]. Three-dimensional reconstruction is the process that allows user to form digital models in a computer, acquiring information (shape, volume, dimensions) of real objects [4]. This is to develop an algorithm that allows the connection of the set of representative points of an object in the form of surface elements with a geometric shape, such as squares, triangles, etc. The quality of the final product depends on the

© Springer Nature Switzerland AG 2020
O. Gervasi et al. (Eds.): ICCSA 2020, LNCS 12254, pp. 682–697, 2020.
https://doi.org/10.1007/978-3-030-58817-5_49

systematic fulfillment of the stages that make up the process, as well as an efficient representation of the set of points.

Among the most widely used methods based on optimal principles for acquiring 3D images are: holography, moiré, interferometry, radar, depth of focus and diffraction [5]. The radar system adopts its name from the acronym Radio Detection and Ranging, whose objective is to discover the presence of objects at a certain distance thanks to electromagnetic radiation [6]. If the electromagnetic waves are reflected on a conductive surface, they return to the point of emission and it can be inferred that an obstacle is found in the propagation path [7]. The delay and characteristics of this reflected signal serve the radar to determine the position, speed and even morphological properties of the body found. Using the structured light principle, a laser pulse is emitted; the distance of the object is obtained according to the deformation of the pattern, which can be: frequency bands or coded light [8].

This model can be one-dimensional or two-dimensional, in the case of one-dimensional it is a line which is projected onto the object with a laser, while the two-dimensional model is a grid, where a series of parallel vertical laser lines are considered that sweep horizontally the object. It has the advantage of speed, since it scans multiple points instead of one at a time, managing to analyze the entire field immediately [9]. Depth cameras that use the structured light method are RGB-D cameras, an example is the Microsoft Kinect device. These devices, in charge of capturing the data, combine hardware and software to produce an image based on a real object [10]. These images receive various names depending on the context where they are, which includes: scope image, depth image, range image, 3D image, list of XYZ points, among others [11]. Applications of these systems have diversified and are used by meteorologists to detect storms, hurricanes, and tornadoes, air traffic controllers to order airport traffic, NASA to create topographic maps of planets, and police to determine the speed at circulating vehicles [12].

2   Related Work

Several investigations have been carried out evidencing the use of radars in different fields of knowledge. In [11] a low-cost proposal that tries to supplant Mobile Terrestrial Laser Scanners (MTLS) for characterizing the geometry and structure of plants and crops for technical and scientific purposes has been done. Using a Kinect v2 depth sensor, a real-time kinematic Global Navigation Satellite System (GNSS) and a review of theoretical foundations, some experimental results are presented that illustrate its performance and limitations. Despite having a low measurement speed, plants, crops and other objects reproduce accurately. In aviation, unmanned aerial vehicles (UAVs) are used to perform visual assessments of infrastructure in real time, and the use of additional technology is required to evade obstacles. In [13], a study of the main tools for evading objects is presented, among them are radar systems. This study highlights the limitations that are found, since data acquired by the sensor is seriously affected by material deterioration of the structures that are being inspected.

In the technological field, radar systems are used for objects detection or the three-dimensional mapping of internal structures, as in [14]. Using two servo motors, a Light

Detection and Ranging (LIDAR) is moved and controlled in such a way that it measures the distance and angles simultaneously. This prototype has a simple and economical design, which wants to compete with devices that use the photogrammetry technique. They are sophisticated but often slow and expensive. Despite limitations of its design, it has good performance in terms of precision, reliability and cost-effectiveness. Mapping of underwater objects can also be done as proposed [15]. This work proposes the possibility of three-dimensional reconstruction of the surface of an underwater object that is at a certain depth. Images quality degrades and lighting is not uniform on the objects surface, just as the presence of particles in the water produces Gaussian noise. As a result, there is the reconstruction of 3D objects under water, but making some visual compensations in order to have significant savings in computational costs.

Gesture recognition using a MS Kinect device allows the design of an interactive tourist guide application, as can be seen in [16]. The design of an interactive tourist guide for visitors that recognizes gesture commands to show important information about shopping centers, restaurants, hotels and places of interest has been carried out. A MS Kinect-based user interface allows tourists to control the tour guide with movements of their hands, to preview images, data, and maps. This is a prototype system that will be implemented in a real environment to reinforce local and international tourism. In the case of interior architecture, [17] describes methods for recording work data using Kinect sensors. Various types of movements are registered in a construction, thereby enhancing the architectural area by managing sensors and cameras of this technological device.

Although the use of these commercial devices is wide, their application in architecture could open doors for greater and better applications that facilitate the work of designers, with decreasing investments. Therefore, this work presents a prototype system that allows the three-dimensional reconstruction of objects in the field of low-cost interior architecture. The acquisition of images is carried out using the Kinect device, whose information is transferred to the MATLAB mathematical software. The mathematical process that must be considered before the development of the respective scripts that manage the subsequent digitization of the objects has been described. As well as the tests that demonstrate its operation and are used to determine its accuracy. This article is organized as follows: the introduction in Sect. 1, Sect. 2 shows the state of the art. In Sect. 3 the image acquisition is presented while in Sect. 4 the development of the proposal is detailed. The results of the experimental tests carried out and conclusions are described in Sect. 5 and Sect. 6 respectively.

3 Image Acquisition

3.1 Object Detection

The object is detected by emitting a signal from the Kinect's infrared sensor that manages to reflect itself after colliding with the object in question; this signal produces a modulation of a cosine function, as shown in (1). The wave is a function of time and the sampling frequency where (V_0) is the propagation speed, in which case it refers to the speed of light to be emitted from the Kinect's infrared sensor, (f) is the frequency of the transmitted signal, (t) the time and (φ_0) the phase angle. It must be taken into account that there is a time delay due to the emission and reflection of the wave, which in turn produces an offset, this generates Eq. (2) as a reference for the correct detection of the object.

$$V(t) = V_0 \cos(2\pi f_t + \varphi_0) \tag{1}$$

$$V_r(t) = V_0 K \cos(2\pi f(t - 2t_r) + \varphi_0)\, \mu(t - 2t_r) \tag{2}$$

3.2   Object Distance

Once the object is detected, it is necessary to know the distance at which it is located, so the Chirp signal that changes from low to high frequency or vice versa within a defined period of time is analyzed. The variant frequency in time $f(t)$ depends on the speed with which the frequency k changes, where the initial frequency of the wave f_0 and final frequency f_1 are taken into account for a duration T, thus obtaining (3) and (4) that by replacing data in (2), we finally obtain (5), where both the angle offset and the time delay of the signal are already considered. By using the Fast Fourier Transform (FFT) the distance at which the object was found is determined at the highest peak.

$$f(t) = \frac{k}{2}t + f_0 \tag{3}$$

$$k = \frac{f_1 - f_0}{T} \tag{4}$$

$$V_r(t) = V_0 K \cos\left(2\pi\left(\frac{k}{2}(t - 2t_r) + f_0\right)(t - 2t_r) + \varphi_0\right)\mu(t - 2t_r) \tag{5}$$

3.3   System Resolution

The resolution of the system is the ability to determine the minimum distance located between two objects whose characteristics are analogous; that is why the resolution is mathematically defined as the accuracy of the distance (e_d), shown in (6); whose value is found as a function of the wave propagation speed, defined as the speed of light (c) and the bandwidth (B) that is determined by the doubling of the maximum frequency of the system.

$$\Delta R = e_d = \frac{c}{B} = \frac{c}{2 * f_{\max}} \tag{6}$$

4 Development of the Proposal

4.1 Hardware

The proposal presented by the authors of the work is based on the interconnection of a personal computer (PC) with the MS Kinect device using software that expands compatibility, such as Open NI, for data extraction, and MATLAB for data processing. The minimum specifications of the PC lie in the possibility of processing images at high speeds without meaning a high economic cost, so in this proposal a PC with 8 GB of DDR4 RAM (Double Data Rate version 4), 4 GB of memory was used for a dedicated GDDR5 (Graphics Double Data Rate version 5) video card and a USB 3.0 port for obtaining data from the technology device as soon as possible.

Regarding the MS Kinect, the device with version 2.0 was used, which allows the detection of more objects with a better resolution. This translates into greater sensitivity in its CMOS emitters and receivers. The operation of the device is based on the emission of infrared signals that bounce off an object following a pattern of points that later return to the infrared CMOS receiver, as each signal bounces, the presence of an object or part of it is assumed. In Fig. 1 it can be seen the general scheme of the system that has a high portability index due to its low weight by the elements involved in it.

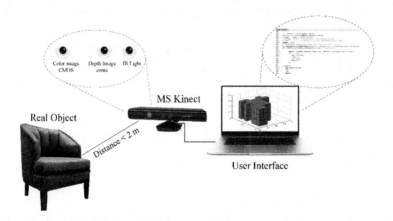

Fig. 1. General scheme of the system.

4.2 MATLAB Script

The initial part is the download and installation of the Open NI libraries, NITE PrimeSense and the MEX files that allow linking the Kinect device with the MATLAB software. The Open NI library provides a generic infrastructure based on open source APIs to access and control the Kinect accessories: camera, sensor and audio. The NITE library, whose code is not open, is used to access advanced device functionalities, such as tracking an object in real time. For the interaction between the device and the software, open source MEX files implemented by developers on the web have been used. These files are called Kinect-Mex and allow the necessary information to be obtained from the images regarding depth, RGB and infrared.

To establish the link, add the path of the folder where the MEX files are located, whose files allow to turn the device on and off, as well as access its operating modes. Through the "mxNiCreateContex" function, the SamplesConfig.xml operation mode is enabled, it allows to obtain both RGB and depth images at a resolution of 640 x 480 pixels (this structure will be kept by default from now on). The colour image information must be aligned with the depth image because the infrared camera is not in the same position as the RGB camera, so the images are offset from each other. RGB image information is stored in one variable and depth image information in another.

4.3   Selection of Information and Storage

The information obtained by default in Kinect is represented in pixels (u, v) for this reason the depth values must be transformed to units of length (mm). To obtain the distance of the object from the device, the depth image information is selected at a specific point. For this, coordinates that will select data location in the real_XYZ matrix are added, being of a special interest the central data of the image, as can be seen in Fig. 2. To store the information of each side face of the cube that covers the object, certain parameters are defined such as: height of the object (alt), distance that each measurement will be taken vertically (dlv), length of the horizontal edge (h) and the distance to which each measurement will be taken horizontally (dl). Its graphic representation can be seen in Fig. 2.

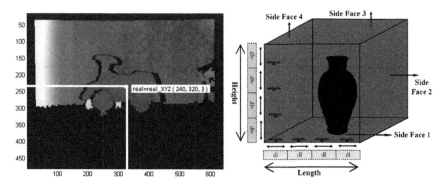

Fig. 2. Image Information of central data (Left). 3D Reconstruction parameters (Right).

The information stored in the variable real_XYZ is used each time the distance measurement is carried out for horizontal and vertical movements. To store all measurements made of one of the lateral faces in a vector, a repeating structure is used to cover the entire lateral face making a horizontal and vertical sweep. The distance at which the Kinect object is located is stored in the variable real_XYZ (240,320.3) in pixels and to obtain said distance in millimeters it is divided by 1000.

Real depth of an object is obtained with the difference between real_XYZ (240, 320, 3) and the length of the horizontal edge. On the other hand, if the horizontal edge length is less than the variable real_XYZ (240,320.3), the depth reminds to zero because no object is found for that location. This procedure is described in Algorithm 1.

Algorithm 1. Repetition structure used to cover the entire side face.

```
i=0;
base=0;
heightob=0;
range=h/dl; % Data number per row
rangealt=alt/dlv; % Row number
contalt=1;
cont=1;
while (base<= range && alturaob <= rangealt)
i=i+1;
real= (real_XYZ(240,320,3)/1000); %Profundity data
if (real<=h && real~=0)
   y(i)=h-real; % Distance data
   else
   y(i)=0;
end
    cont=cont+1;
    base=cont;
if (base>range && heightob<rangealt)
       cont=1;
       l=dl;
       base=0;
       contalt=contalt+1;
       heightob=contalt;
          end
   end
```

Once measurements are stored in the vector, said vector is converted into a matrix, for this the mathematical expressions described in (7) and (8) are used and thus dimensions of the matrix are determined. Where m = number of rows in the matrix, c = number of columns in the matrix, A = stored vector and M = information matrix.

$$m = \frac{alt}{dlv} \tag{7}$$

$$c = \frac{h}{dl} \tag{8}$$

4.4   Reconstruction of the 3D Object

Creation of Matrices 0's. Once matrices that store the depth measurements of the four lateral faces are obtained, four square matrices of 0's are created with a dimension equal to the number of columns that one of the stored matrices has, as expressed in (8). Thus, each data in a row of the depth matrix is related to a column of the 0's matrix, so that 1's is assigned in each column of the 0's matrix according to the value of the data in the row of the matrix of depth. The face 1 data matrix is presented in (9) and filled with zeros. Following the same principle, the matrices of the remaining faces (B (m × c), C (m × c) and D (m × c)) are defined.

$$A_{(mxc)} = \begin{pmatrix} a_{1,1} & a_{1,2} & a_{1,3} & \cdots & a_{1,c} \\ a_{2,1} & a_{2,2} & a_{2,3} & \cdots & a_{2,c} \\ a_{3,1} & a_{3,2} & a_{3,3} & \cdots & a_{3,c} \\ \vdots & \vdots & \vdots & \vdots & \vdots \\ a_{m,1} & a_{m,2} & a_{m,3} & \cdots & a_{m,c} \end{pmatrix} \tag{9}$$

Depth of an Object Represented in 1's. To assign 1's to the 0's matrices (10) is used, which determines the number of 1's that will be replaced in each column. This equation is used for all data in a row of the stored matrices. p1 is the number of 1 s representing the object distance from the Kinect location for matrix data A (1, j). Following the same principle, matrices 0's are defined for the other three remaining faces with data from matrices B (1, j) (p2), C (1, j) (p3) and D (1, j) (p4). Both p1 and p2, p3, and p4 must be integers. This process is described in Algorithm 2 and the respective 1's matrix is presented in (11).

$$p_1 = \frac{A(a_{1,j}) * c}{h} \tag{10}$$

$$\begin{cases} C1A_{i,j} = 1, \ i \geq p_1 \\ C1A_{i,j} = 0, \ i < p_1 \end{cases} \quad \forall i, j = 1, 2, \ldots, c$$

$$C1A_{(cxc)} = \begin{pmatrix} 1_{1,1} & 1_{1,2} & 1_{1,3} & \cdots & 1_{1,c} \\ 1_{2,1} & 1_{2,2} & 1_{2,3} & \cdots & 1_{2,c} \\ \vdots & \vdots & \vdots & \vdots & \vdots \\ 1_{(p),1} & 1_{(p),2} & 1_{(p),3} & \cdots & 1_{(p),c} \\ 0_{(p+1),1} & 0_{(p+1),2} & 0_{(p+1),3} & \cdots & 0_{(p+1),c} \\ \vdots & \vdots & \vdots & \ddots & \vdots \\ 0_{c,1} & 0_{c,2} & 0_{c,3} & \cdots & 0_{c,c} \end{pmatrix} \tag{11}$$

Algorithm 2. Definition of 0s matrices for whole four faces

```
cuad=(columns);
matcerosc1=zeros(cuad); %0's para Face 1
matcerosc2=zeros(cuad); %0's para Face 2
matcerosc3=zeros(cuad); %0's para Face 3
matcerosc4=zeros(cuad); %0's para Face 4
    for i=1:columns
    posc1= t1(controws,i); %Side Face 1
    posc11=((posc1*cuad)/h);
    posc111=round(posc11);
    posc2= t2(controws,i); %Side Face 2
    posc22=((posc2*cuad)/h);
    posc222=round(posc22);
    posc3=t3(controws,i); %Side Face 3
    posc33=((posc3*cuad)/h);
    posc333=round(posc33);
    posc4= t4(controws,i); %Side Face 4
    posc44=((posc4*cuad)/h);
    posc444=round(posc44);
        for j=1:posc111
        matzerosc1(j,i)=1;
        end
        for j=1:posc222
        matzerosc2(j,i)=1;
        end
        for j=1:posc333
        matzerosc3(j,i)=1;
        end
        for j=1:posc444
        matzerosc4(j,i)=1;
        end    end
```

Assigning 1's in the matrices of 0's for data of one of the rows of the matrices that keep the depth measurements. To continue with the process, rotations are made to the matrices of 1's according to the order of how depth measurements of the object are taken, which may be hourly or anti-hourly. Next, it should be performed the position by position multiplication type of the matrices 0's, obtaining as a result a matrix where the object is reconstructed in a flat way for row 1 of the matrices A, B, C and D. Finally, in order to obtain the object in 3D, the resulting matrix is graphed using the boxplot3 function. To reconstruct an object with n rows of information, a repeating structure must be followed to reuse matrices 0's and assign 1's for each row of information in matrices A, B, C and D, being m the number of rows which contains each information matrix stored as described in (12).

$$R_{(cxcxm)} = \text{ref}\left(\text{ref}\left(A(i.j)^T\right)\right)^T x\text{ref}\left(B(i.j)^T\right)xC(i.j)x(\text{ref}(D(i.j)))^T \qquad (12)$$

5 Result Analysis

5.1 Original Matrices

Based on technical features of the MS Kinect, it is recommended to locate the objects at a maximum distance of 2 m, without loss of information or confusion in the process. Several tests were carried out with rectangular geometric objects of different sizes, simulating the presence of typical objects from an architectural space. For the presentation of results, only one test has been taken as a reference, to test the correct operation and determine the parameters that must be considered. For this case, a horizontal displacement of 0.2 m, vertical displacement of 0.2 m and a height of 0.2 m have been established. In the reconstruction of objects, it is defined that each data with value "1" represents a fraction of the object that is located in an imaginary hexahedron or cube for the data set that contains the binary matrix.

Once matrices that store depth measurements of the four lateral faces are obtained, four 0's square matrices are created with a dimension equal to the number of columns that one of the stored matrices has. Once the system has determined the number of 1's that will be located in the 0's matrices and the result has been rounded, the Values of the stored data matrices are obtained as shown in Table 1 (row 1) and Table 2 (row 2). In Fig. 3 shows the matrices obtained and in Fig. 4 their reconstruction presented in the designed interface. In Fig. 4 the reconstruction of the same object from another point of view is evidenced.

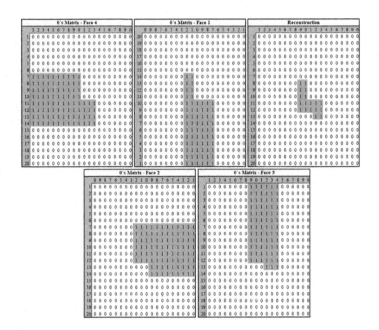

Fig. 3. 0's matrices (4 faces and reconstruction) with 1's assignment.

Table 1. 4-sided reconstruction matrix: Row 1

Item	Face 1 matrix			Face 2 matrix			Face 3 matrix			Face 4 matrix		
	M	R3	1's	M	R3	1's	M	R3	1's	M	R3	1's
(1.1)	0	0	0	0	0	0	0	0	0	0	0	0
(1.2)	0	0	0	0	0	0	0	0	0	0	0	0
(1.3)	0	0	0	0	0	0	0	0	0	0	0	0
(1.4)	0	0	0	0	0	0	0	0	0	0	0	0
(1.5)	0	0	0	0	0	0	0	0	0	0	0	0
(1.6)	0	0	0	0	0	0	0	0	0	0	0	0
(1.7)	0,993	9,93	10	1,181	11,81	12	0	0	0	1,309	13,09	13
(1.8)	0,994	9,94	10	1,181	11,81	12	0	0	0	1,309	13,09	13
(1.9)	0,993	9,93	10	1,179	11,79	12	1,182	11,82	12	1,31	13,1	13
(1.10)	0,994	9,94	10	1,18	11,8	12	1,188	11,88	12	1,301	13,01	13
(1.11)	1,313	13,13	13	1,181	11,81	12	1,181	11,81	12	1,017	10,17	10
(1.12)	1,309	13,09	13	1,18	11,8	12	1,181	11,81	12	1,017	10,17	10
(1.13)	0	0	0	0,884	8,84	9	1,317	13,17	13	1,012	10,12	10
(1.14)	0	0	6	0,88	8,8	9	1,318	13,18	13	1,012	10,12	10
(1.15)	0	0	0	0	0	0	0	0	0	0	0	0
(1.16)	0	0	0	0	0	0	0	0	0	0	0	0
(1.17)	0	0	0	0	0	0	0	0	0	0	0	0
(1.18)	0	0	0	0	0	0	0	0	0	0	0	0
(1.19)	0	0	0	0	0	0	0	0	0	0	0	0
(1.20)	0	0	0	0	0	0	0	0	0	0	0	0

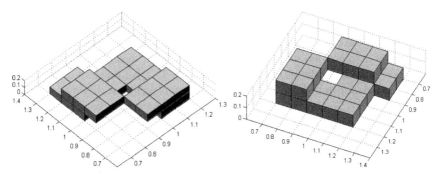

Fig. 4. Three-dimensional reconstruction of: First set of objects (Left). Other view (Right).

Table 2. 4-sided reconstruction matrix: Row 2

Item	Face 1 matrix			Face 2 matrix			Face 3 matrix			Face 4 matrix		
	M	R3	1's	M	R3	1's	M	R3	1's	M	R3	1's
(2.1)	0	0	0	0	0	0	0	0	0	0	0	0
(2.2)	0	0	0	0	0	0	0	0	0	0	0	0
(2.3)	0	0	0	0	0	0	0	0	0	0	0	0
(2.4)	0	0	0	0	0	0	0	0	0	0	0	0
(2.5)	0	0	0	0	0	0	0	0	0	0	0	0
(2.6)	0	0	0	0	0	0	0	0	0	0	0	0
(2.7)	0	0	0	1,208	12,08	12	0	0	0	0	0	0
(2.8)	1,138	11,81	11	1,208	12,08	12	0	0	0	0	0	0
(2.9)	1,138	11,81	11	1,21	12,1	12	0,85	8,5	9	1,288	12,88	13
(2.10)	1,35	9,94	13	0,912	9,12	9	0,85	8,5	9	1,287	12,87	13
(2.11)	1,35	13,13	13	0,912	9,12	9	0,85	8,5	9	1,287	12,87	13
(2.12)	1335	13,09	13	0,92	9,2	9	1,148	11,5	12	1,08	10,8	11
(2.13)	0	0	0	0	0	0	1,148	11,51	12	1,08	10,8	11
(2.14)	0	0	6	0	0	0	0	0	0	1,08	10,8	11
(2.15)	0	0	0	0	0	0	0	0	0	0	0	0
(2.16)	0	0	0	0	0	0	0	0	0	0	0	0
(2.17)	0	0	0	0	0	0	0	0	0	0	0	0
(2.18)	0	0	0	0	0	0	0	0	0	0	0	0
(2.19)	0	0	0	0	0	0	0	0	0	0	0	0
(2.20)	0	0	0	0	0	0	0	0	0	0	0	0

5.2 Concatenated Matrices

After obtaining the first results in previous works that were not completely satisfactory, the design of an algorithm is proposed in this research to dimension each data of the information matrices of the object lateral faces [18]. This is needed in order to obtain each dimensioned data to a sub-matrix of (5 * 5) by resizing the information matrices to (n * 5) × (m * 5). Resizing will allow curvilinear objects to be 3D reconstructed similarly to the real object. In (13) there is a normal matrix and in (14) the same matrix is obtained, but this time it is concatenated. To demonstrate the operation of the objects reconstruction in three-dimensional form with concatenated data from the measurements made on the lateral faces, the same objects previously tested were reconstructed exposing the results below. Figure 5 shows the results obtained.

$$A = \begin{pmatrix} aa_{1,1} & ab_{1,2} & \cdots & az_{1,m} \\ ba_{2,1} & bb_{2,2} & \cdots & bz_{2,m} \\ \vdots & \vdots & \ddots & \vdots \\ za_{n,1} & zb_{n,2} & \cdots & zz_{n,m} \end{pmatrix} \tag{13}$$

$$AC = \begin{pmatrix} \begin{pmatrix} aa_{1,1} & \cdots & aa_{1,5} \\ \vdots & \ddots & \vdots \\ aa_{5,1} & \cdots & aa_{5,5} \end{pmatrix}_{1,1} & \begin{pmatrix} ab_{1,1} & \cdots & ab_{1,5} \\ \vdots & \ddots & \vdots \\ ab_{5,1} & \cdots & ab_{5,5} \end{pmatrix}_{1,2} & \cdots & \begin{pmatrix} az_{1,1} & \cdots & az_{1,5} \\ \vdots & \ddots & \vdots \\ az_{5,1} & \cdots & az_{5,5} \end{pmatrix}_{1,m} \\ \begin{pmatrix} ba_{1,1} & \cdots & ba_{1,5} \\ \vdots & \ddots & \vdots \\ ba_{5,1} & \cdots & ba_{5,5} \end{pmatrix}_{2,1} & \begin{pmatrix} bb_{1,1} & \cdots & bb_{1,5} \\ \vdots & \ddots & \vdots \\ bb_{5,1} & \cdots & bb_{5,5} \end{pmatrix}_{2,2} & \cdots & \begin{pmatrix} bz_{1,1} & \cdots & bz_{1,5} \\ \vdots & \ddots & \vdots \\ bz_{5,1} & \cdots & bz_{5,5} \end{pmatrix}_{2,m} \\ \vdots & \vdots & \ddots & \vdots \\ \begin{pmatrix} za_{1,1} & \cdots & za_{1,5} \\ \vdots & \ddots & \vdots \\ za_{5,1} & \cdots & za_{5,5} \end{pmatrix}_{n,1} & \begin{pmatrix} zb_{1,1} & \cdots & zb_{1,5} \\ \vdots & \ddots & \vdots \\ zb_{5,1} & \cdots & zb_{5,5} \end{pmatrix}_{n,2} & \cdots & \begin{pmatrix} zz_{1,1} & \cdots & zz_{1,5} \\ \vdots & \ddots & \vdots \\ zz_{5,1} & \cdots & zz_{5,5} \end{pmatrix}_{n,m} \end{pmatrix}_{((n*5)x(m*5))} \tag{14}$$

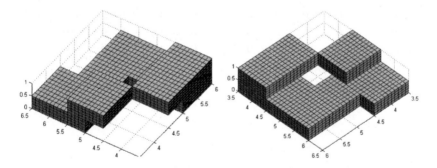

Fig. 5. 3D reconstruction of the object with concatenated data.

5.3   System Precision and Accuracy

To determine the depth data obtained accuracy, 20 experimental measurements were taken as a sample on an object located approximately 150 cm away. 10 ascending displacements with an interval of 20 cm and 10 descending displacements of the same value. All measures were taken to obtain the true error of each data and the mean of the relative percentage error of the data using (15). Where (Ev) is the true error and (Et) is the percentage relative error. Table 3 shows the actual depth data and those obtained in the measurements, expressed in millimeters and each of the previously mentioned errors.

$$\bar{Et} = \frac{Et_1 + Et_2 + Et_3 + \ldots + Et_n}{n} \tag{15}$$

Table 3. Depth errors.

Real	Measured	Ev	Et	Et(%)	Real	Measured	Ev	Et	Et(%)
1500	1517	17	0,011	1,13%	1480	1497	17	0,011	1,15%
1520	1538	18	0,012	1,18%	1460	1474	14	0,010	0,96%
1540	1557	17	0,011	1,10%	1440	1460	20	0,014	1,39%
1560	1578	18	0,012	1,15%	1420	1441	21	0,015	1,48%
1580	1598	18	0,011	1,14%	1400	1416	18	0,013	1,29%
1600	1617	17	0,011	1,06%	1380	1396	16	0,012	1,16%
1620	1641	21	0,013	1,30%	1360	1377	17	0,013	1,25%
1640	1667	27	0,016	1,65%	1340	1355	15	0,011	1,12%
1660	1685	25	0,015	1,51%	1320	1340	20	0,015	1,52%
1680	1711	31	0,018	1,85%	1300	1314	14	0,011	1,08%

Now, the accuracy is defined as how close is the measured value from the true value, so that for the measurements shown in Table 3, the accuracy with which a depth data is obtained is determined to be about 3 mm. Considering the mean of the relative percentage error (1.27%), it is determined that its difference expresses 98.73% of precision, for when the IR and RGB cameras are located at an angle parallel to the ground.

World current landscape involves digitization tasks, object reconstruction with high precision and task execution using gestures [14–16]. This proposal emphasizes a good content as well as less investment in resources. At this time, the economy in Latin America is not the most advantageous, so researchers are currently seeking to achieve great objectives by innovating methods that ensure functionality using low-cost tools. Thus, while [17] reconstruct an environment by mapping in 3D, it does not meet the precision needs for using the reconstructed model in design applications. Despite its reduced cost, it could not have an application that involves interior architecture as presented in this manuscript.

6 Conclusions

The applications presented by radar systems are multiple, as evidenced in the presented bibliography. The use of technology to establish new and better tools for interior space designers has motivated the development of this research as a low-cost proposal. The technical specifications of the Kinect applied to this application have determined that the angle of inclination of the infrared and photogrammetric camera is not more than 30° maximum down and up. The neutral position is when device is parallel to the ground, but 10 other different positions can also be programmed. Despite this, it has not been necessary to use them and the neutral position has been maintained with the intention of not accidentally modifying the data obtained. Tests carried out on previous prototypes were not satisfactory and after some modifications and considerations it has been determined that the minimum depth of an object is 89 cm and a maximum of 192 cm.

The initial object reconstruction presented results with insufficient definition and therefore it was necessary to apply concatenated matrices that allow better information processing to improve results. A sample of different measurements was taken while the experimental tests were carried out, and an accuracy of 98.73% was obtained when operating within the proposed depth range. Increasing this measurement, certain parts of the object were not properly reconstructed. During the experimental stage, geometric figures have been used, since they have facilitated the calibration and adjustment of the system. Feedback obtained during the development of this research will allow future improvements in the design of the third version of this prototype. In this way, it has been possible to demonstrate its correct operation and establish it as a valid technological tool to improve the interior environment design that professionals use to optimize their time at a low cost.

Authors propose as future work to improve this design and to carry out more detailed tests with other elements that are part of architectural interiors. Also test its application in other fields of science and be able to make a comparison of results obtained. This will allow to enrich the design of new technological instruments that seek to improve the quality of life of the human being.

Acknowledgments. A special thanks to the Universidad Tecnológica Indoamérica for supporting the development of this work.

References

1. Fernández-S, Á., Salazar-L, F., Jurado, M., Castellanos, E.X., Moreno-P, R., Buele, J.: Electronic system for the detection of chicken eggs suitable for incubation through image processing. In: Rocha, Á., Adeli, H., Reis, L.P., Costanzo, S. (eds.) WorldCIST'19 2019. AISC, vol. 931, pp. 208–218. Springer, Cham (2019). https://doi.org/10.1007/978-3-030-16184-2_21
2. Hugeng, H., Anggara, J., Gunawan, D.: Implementation of 3D HRTF interpolation in synthesizing virtual 3D moving sound. Int. J. Technol. (2017). https://doi.org/10.14716/ijtech.v8i1.6859

3. Elsayed, M., Soe, M.T., Kit, W.W., Abdalla, H.: An innovative approach to developing a 3D virtual map creator using an ultrasonic sensor array. Int. J. Technol. (2019). https://doi.org/10.14716/ijtech.v10i7.3245
4. Protasov, A.: Active infrared testing of composites using 3D computer simulation. Int. J. Technol. (2018). https://doi.org/10.14716/ijtech.v9i3.218
5. Taylor, M.: Lifshitz holography. Class. Quantum Gravity (2016). https://doi.org/10.1088/0264-9381/33/3/033001
6. Chiani, M., Giorgetti, A., Paolini, E.: Sensor Radar for object tracking (2018). https://doi.org/10.1109/JPROC.2018.2819697
7. Meinl, F., Stolz, M., Kunert, M., Blume, H.: An experimental high performance radar system for highly automated driving. In: 2017 IEEE MTT-S International Conference on Microwaves for Intelligent Mobility, ICMIM 2017 (2017). https://doi.org/10.1109/ICMIM.2017.7918859
8. Moreno Avilés, D., Mejía, J., Moreno, H.: Desarrollo de un algoritmo en MATLAB para la optimización de la resolución de una tarjeta USRP B210 para aplicaciones SDRadar. MASKAY (2017). https://doi.org/10.24133/maskay.v7i1.338
9. Iakushkin, O., Selivanov, D., Tazieva, L., Fatkina, A., Grishkin, V., Uteshev, A.: 3D reconstruction of landscape models and archaeological objects based on photo and video materials. In: Gervasi, O., et al. (eds.) ICCSA 2018. LNCS, vol. 10963, pp. 160–169. Springer, Cham (2018). https://doi.org/10.1007/978-3-319-95171-3_14
10. Capece, N., Erra, U., Romaniello, G.: A low-cost full body tracking system in virtual reality based on microsoft kinect. In: De Paolis, L.T., Bourdot, P. (eds.) AVR 2018. LNCS, vol. 10851, pp. 623–635. Springer, Cham (2018). https://doi.org/10.1007/978-3-319-95282-6_44
11. Rosell-Polo, J.R., et al..: Kinect v2 sensor-based mobile terrestrial laser scanner for agricultural outdoor applications. IEEE/ASME Trans. Mechatron. (2017). https://doi.org/10.1109/TMECH.2017.2663436
12. Pritchard, M.E., Yun, S.-H.: Satellite radar imaging and its application to natural hazards. In: Natural Hazards (2018). https://doi.org/10.1201/9781315166841-5
13. Jordan, S., et al.: State-of-the-art technologies for UAV inspections, (2018). https://doi.org/10.1049/iet-rsn.2017.0251
14. Riaz, M., Bukhari, S.A., Mukhtar, F., Kamal, T., Sarwar, H., Tahir, M.U.: 3D mapping using light detection and ranging. In: Proceedings of 2017 International Multi-Topic Conference, INMIC 2017 (2018). https://doi.org/10.1109/INMIC.2017.8289468
15. Anwer, A., Ali, S.S.A., Meriaudeau, F.: Underwater online 3D mapping and scene reconstruction using low cost kinect RGB-D sensor. In: International Conference on Intelligent and Advanced Systems, ICIAS 2016 (2017). https://doi.org/10.1109/ICIAS.2016.7824132
16. Minda Gilces, D., Matamoros Torres, K.: A kinect-based gesture recognition approach for the design of an interactive tourism guide application. In: Communications in Computer and Information Science (2018)
17. Ishida, K.: Construction progress management and interior work analysis using kinect 3D image sensors. In: ISARC 2016 - 33rd International Symposium on Automation and Robotics in Construction (2016)
18. Barberán, J., et al.: Radar system for the reconstruction of 3D objects: a preliminary study. In: Rocha, Á., Adeli, H., Reis, L.P., Costanzo, S., Orovic, I., Moreira, F. (eds.) WorldCIST 2020. AISC, vol. 1160, pp. 238–247. Springer, Cham (2020). https://doi.org/10.1007/978-3-030-45691-7_23

Bizdevops: A Multivocal Literature Review

Iraj Lohrasbinasab, Prameet Bhakta Acharya,
and Ricardo Colomo-Palacios$^{(\boxtimes)}$ ⓘ

Østfold University College, BRA veien. 4, 1757 Halden, Norway
{iraj.lohrasbinasab,prameet.acharya,
ricardo.colomo-palacios}@hiof.no

Abstract. BizDevOps as an extension of DevOps, reinforces the collaboration between business, development, and operation stakeholders in the organization in order to enhance the software cycle. While BizDevOps has not yet received much attention in academic circles, it has gained considerable prestige in the industry area. This situation reflects a gap between theory and practice in this context. In this work and by means of a Multivocal Literature Review authors gather visions from both academic and industry spheres on the topic. The result is a gathered image of BizDevOps, including definition, characteristics, related motivating issues, and potential challenges and benefits.

Keywords: BizDevOps · DevOps 2.0 · Multivocal literature review

1 Introduction

Software crisis is far from being solved. Although there are voices claiming that software crisis is exaggerated [1], software project failures are common [2]. One of the solutions to the problem frequently cited in the literature is the adoption of agile practices. With these practices, new values appear, like fast delivery, customer satisfaction, enhanced quality, cost of change reduction and decreased documentation [3]. In line with some of the agility achievements, and agreeing with [4], some of the problems in software delivery are embedded in the lack of connection among software development activities causing delays in software delivery. In this line, Continuous software engineering permits software features delivery at high paces [5]. It is based on the application of automation to the overall software development process by using means of tools and new practices [6]. Continuous software engineering is an umbrella covering several continuous activities: continuous integration that aims at integrating software continuously during development; continuous delivery, based on the previous and is about keeping the software in a releasable state and, finally, continuous deployment takes the final step in automation, where each change is built, tested and deployed to production in an automatic way, enabling in this way customers to use it [7].

These continuous practices expanded beyond software development boundaries to influence also the operational side. In this scenario, DevOps stands for a continuous integration between software development and its operational deployment. DevOps efficiently incorporates development, delivery, and operations, consequently easing a lean interaction of these conventionally detached silos [8]. Consequently, DevOps

O. Gervasi et al. (Eds.): ICCSA 2020, LNCS 12254, pp. 698–713, 2020.
https://doi.org/10.1007/978-3-030-58817-5_50

assimilates any aspect or process aiming to lessening the time between changing a system and transferring that change to production, including practices like continuous monitoring or continuous deployment [9]. This is crucial for developers and quality assurance professionals, benefiting from real data on the development of new products and features [10]. The concept of DevOps surfaced in 2009 and describes a process where software developers and operations work close together in order to release software features often and learn from the end users based on their experiences [11].

DevOps have also faced several evolutions. For instance, DevSecOps (known also as SecDevOps) is aimed to integrate security practices in the overall process [12]. Furthermore, another evolution is BizDevOps. Essentially, the idea behind BizDevOps is that, apart from Operations and Development, experts from the Business (Biz) world will join the team in order to develop user-centric products at a high pace. Although there are previous works in the field, including a Systematic Literature Review on the topic [13], to the best of authors' knowledge, a multivocal literature review (MVLR) on this topic has not yet been conducted. In order to fill this gap, in this paper authors carry out a MVLR to investigate BizDevOps. Given the novelty of the subject, searching in the scientific literature for academic papers that deal with specific aspects of BizDevOps does not yield many results. In the face of this, it is observed that the phenomenon has spread significantly among the communities of consultants and software developers. This observation led the need for a MVLR. Motivated by the target contribution to diminish the conceptual gap between the professional practices and the academic publications on this topic, this research aims to clarify the BizDevOps definition and scope to provide more scientific knowledge to support the investigation of its related issues. Besides, concerning the subject's associations with co-domain topics, especially DevOps, it has been attempted to limit the scope of discussion to proprietary aspects of the subject as much as possible to avoid unnecessary rework and prolongation of this research.

The remaining of the paper is presented as follows: in Sect. 2, authors present the methods for research. In what follows, the authors present and discuss the results. Lastly, authors conclude and present suggestions for future work in Sect. 4.

2   Research Methodology

2.1   Multivocal Literature Review

To obtain an overview of the current literature, including grey literature, a MVLR was performed and is presented in this paper. A MVLR is a form of Systematic Literature Review that encompasses the so-called gray literature in addition to published academic literature (e.g., articles published in scientific journals, or presented in scientific conferences). Gray literature refers to all available means of information, including tool vendors' websites, industry reports, white papers, blogs, and so on. A documented advantage of MVLR is its capacity to converge viewpoints and knowledge between researchers and practitioners, as well as providing an overview of state-of-the-art and latest practices in a given field [14]. In order to conduct the literature review, authors will follow the guidelines proposed by Garousi et al. [14]. The stages of the literature review will be presented in the following sections. With regards to the need for this literature review, as mentioned in Sect. 1, to the best of our knowledge, a MVLR in the topic does not exist, although there is a Systematic Literature Review on the topic [13]. The underlying nature of MVLR justifies the need to conduct the study, given the amount of material published as grey literature.

2.2   Research Questions

The purpose of this research is to collect, review, and report on existing literature regarding BizDevOps. We aim to delineate definitions, features, as well as foreseeable benefits and challenges in BizDevOps application. In this regard, we pursue the survey, bearing in mind the aforementioned goals in the form of four research questions [15]. These questions are as follows:

- RQ 1: What is the reported meaning of the term "BizDevOps"?
- RQ 2: What are the problems motivating the adoption of BizDevOps?
- RQ 3: What are the main characteristics associated with BizDevOps?
- RQ 4: What are the main potential benefits and challenges of adopting BizDevOps?
- RQ 5: How has BizDevOps evolved since its emergence?

2.3   Study Protocol

The study protocol describes the adopted systematic procedure, through which the surveyed literature in this research has been elicited from a mass of existing materials over the web.

Regarding procedures, authors performed a structured search out on Google and Google Scholar to find pertinent literature. The first step of the search process entails the identification of keywords. While compiling background information for this research, we found out that in some cases instead of the phrase "BizDevOps", or as an equivalent, the term "DevOps 2.0" is used. Consequently, in order to ensure that we do not miss the relevant items, we added the phrase "DevOps 2.0" to the search string. Thus, we chose the following string to acquire relevant materials:

("BizDevOps" OR "DevOps 2.0") AND ("motivations" OR "definition" OR "characteristics" OR "challenges" OR "benefits" OR "evolution")

Further, to access more relevant results, we relied on the snowballing technique to explore in some related domains such as DevOps and Agile.

Inclusion and Exclusion Criteria: After the search results were retrieved, a list of specified inclusion and exclusion criteria were applied to filter the most relevant studies. These criteria are as follows:

Inclusion Criteria:
- (I1): addressing the BizDevOps or "DevOps 2.0" term
- (I2): addressing the integration of business, development, and operation teams
- (I3): addressing the integration of "DevOps" and business
- (I4): Literature involving benefits, challenges, motivations, and characteristics in conjunction with BizDevOps or DevOps 2.0
- (I5): Literature published after 2014

Exclusion criteria:
- (E1): iterative sources and multi-quoted materials
- (E2): sources deemed as similar results by Google search
- (E3): sources published before 2014 when the term emerged
- (E4): material not written in English
- (E5): inaccessible sources
- (E6): Advertising materials
- (E7): Video and Audio files

This MVLR was performed by April 2020. Thereby, the search period was set from January 2014 - when the term "BizDev" was coined to April 2020. Moreover, considering that we are looking for those pieces of evidence containing the intended contents supporting RQs, the rest of the items that lack desired features, should be dropped. On the other hand, by Google's page ranking algorithm, we are facing a mass of results, of which only some first pages are connected to the subject. Thus, to restrict the search domain, we should cut off the search process at a specific point. Given the search criteria in this study, we decided to stop proceeding with more results once a page that did not bear relevant items was found [14].

2.4   Data Storage

We designed an Excel form to collect bibliographic information of each selected literature, as well as recording additional notes on how well it relates to RQs. Furthermore, color codes were used to highlight the importance of each paper.

2.5   Review Protocol

At the implementation stage, the structured search for gathering materials was performed by two researchers, via applying the aforementioned procedure. Essentially, the procedure consisted of the search process, followed by the analysis and sift of the preliminary results. Each process was carried out in parallel by both researchers. The primarily found items were stacked in an Excel form as a data pool. At the same time, authors controlled each other's collected results. Figure 1 depicts this procedure.

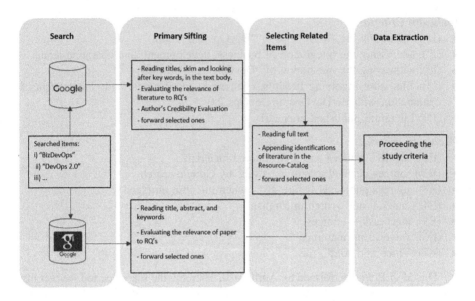

Fig. 1. Overview of the process adopted in the study (Adapted from [12])

3   Results

In this section, the results from the execution of the query will be presented and discussed to answer the research questions previously defined.

3.1   Retrieved Studies

In Table 1, the number of papers retrieved is displayed in each of the stages of the process. Stage 1 displays the number of studies that were retrieved by simply querying Google Scholar and Google Search. Stage 2 reflects the number of studies selected based on title, abstract, keywords and metadata, and stage 3 entails the number of selected studies after the full text has been read and analyzed.

Table 1. Number of search results elicited from databases

Engine	Initial results	Title, abstract, keywords, and metadata	Full text
Google Scholar	126	16	12
Google Search	150	103	50

3.2   RQ1: What is the Reported Meaning of the Term "BizDevOps"?

Terms like "culture", "movement", strategy", "method", "practice", "approach", "mindset", tools", and so on that come along with "BizDevOps" in the literature are often used with much tolerance. The most common definitions and descriptions provided in the grey literature on BizDevOps could be presented, in a high-level conceptual manner,, as follows: "BizDevOps incorporates business stakeholders into the Software Development Life Cycle (SDLC), creating a streamlined workflow from business strategy & planning to deployment and maintenance" [16]. In the purely research field, we find contributions as follows: BizDevOps, as an extension of DevOps in software development, is a combination of organizational strategies, approaches, and enabling technologies. It aims to strengthen cooperation and systematic interaction between business (Biz), development (Dev), and operations (Ops) [17], with emphasis on the active intervention of business stakeholders in the software development process [18, 19], providing continuous delivery Pipeline which establishes an end-to-end flow between customer demand and the fast delivery of a product or service [4].

The study conducted by Fitzgerald and Stol [4] is of utmost importance in terms of providing a comprehensive theoretical framework that explains the intellectual foundations of the subject and has been referenced broadly in later works. These authors introduce a general conceptual framework labeled as "Continuous *", divided into three main sub-phases: Business Strategy & Planning (Biz), Development (Dev), and Operations (Ops), that encompass various activities, with emphasis on being continuous, throughout the SDLC. Their proposed conceptual framework is derived from synthesizing Agile principles and Lean Philosophy and designed to establish a continuous flow of SDLC's activities that intends to realize the so-called continuous software engineering delivery pipeline.

3.3 RQ2: What are the Problems Motivating the Adoption of BizDevOps?

To ensure maintaining business value along the DevOps loops, a tighten alignment between people, processes, and technologies is essential. Nevertheless, the arduousness of translation and expressing desires and goals of the business domain into software engineering domain has always been a challenging issue, coupled with the lack of active participation of the business management team in the software development process [17, 20, 21] and [22] in the gray literature. This issue has been discussed as the requisition of convergence between business strategy and software development [4].

Summarizing what has been cited in various sources as motivations for using BizDevOps, the focus is on the need to facilitate the active participation of the business stakeholders in the software development. By doing so, it amplifies the feedback process, as well as ensures the maximum fulfillment of business goals and customer expectations. As a result, providing higher customer satisfaction and higher quality software, leads to maintaining the organization competitive and innovative [20].

3.4 RQ3: What are the Main Characteristics Associated with BizDevOps?

BizDevOps characteristics could be classified into some general layers, including values, principles, practices (theoretical and technical approaches), and toolchains. It is noteworthy that, despite its novelty, BizDevOps is rooted in some long-established topics across the evolution of the software industry. In fact, most of its principles and approaches have been widely discussed, particularly in the grounding domains, such as Agile methods and DevOps. In this context, integrating the infrastructural components under an umbrella concept like "Continuous *" by [4] provided a methodological model that is distinguishable in most of the subsequent researches, too.

For instance, Forbrig [23] has extended this framework by augmenting continuous requirements engineering, continuous business process modeling, and continuous human-centered design. In requirements engineering continuous compliance validation is a nascent need for a good set of current projects [24, 25]. Given the similarity and commonality of the principles, it should not be assumed that DevOps is trying to replace Agile. Rather, DevOps is trying to introduce areas where Agile can expand [26].

The approach adopted by most authors in describing the BizDevOps characteristics is to follow the hierarchical classification pattern of concepts in the Agile Manifesto and to recreate these concepts, in accordance to BizDevOps's specific facts and features. However, in some gray literature sources, this alignment is not very precise, and the boundaries seem to be blurred in the interpretation and use of terms such as "value", "principle", or "approach". Therefore, authors followed the scheme that is analyzed in what follows:

(i) VALUES

While some authors refer to the Agile Manifesto to outline the fundamental values of DevOps and BizDevOps, in other cases, the proposed manifestations are drawn on the CAMS (Culture, Automation, Measurement and Sharing) model, a term coined by Damon Edwards and John Willis back in 2010.

• *Culture*

There is consensus on the fact that BizDevOps and its predecessor DevOps, are above all, about changes in the culture of the organization [27–29]. DevOps is mostly focused on innovation and productivity. It replaces the traditional managerial habits and beliefs with a culture of collaboration and an "IT value stream" by merging trusted principles and practices from physical manufacturing to software arena [26, 27]

DevOps culture is strengthened by the practices it borrows from Agile and Lean principles, with a further concentration on service and quality [26]. That is, delivery of high-quality software to the end-user entails the cultural conversion in accepting joint responsibility [4].

Despite the wide range of BizDevOps commonalities with DevOps, the two differ in terms of the influenced area and involved stakeholders. Unlike DevOps, which focuses on development and operation functions and stakeholders, BizDevOps reinforces responsibility over the whole customer journey in one unified team, consisting of business management, development, and operation people [30] thoroughly. From this view, transforming the traditional relationship of business and IT from the employer-executive model to an interactive collaboration, with distributed responsibility, in the form of a unified team, is one of the significant cultural changes needed to become BizDevOps [31]. It is a critical prerequisite to enabling the company to execute end-to-end holistic experiments, building new features that stretch across product lines and improve the entire customer experience [30].

- *Automation*

A BizDevOps method offers an integrated and automated toolchain to allow as much automation and, as a consequence of this, development speed (the "Ops" in BizDevOps) as possible [17, 18]. It is based on orchestrating and automating business activities, and information into the DevOps lifecycle [32] and strongly advocates workflow automation and monitoring at all phases of software construction, including integration, testing, and releasing to deployment and infrastructure management [22].

- *Measurement*

Monitoring and getting feedback from the entire ecosystem of the process, including business-side metrics and end-user experience, as well as development, test, and operations metrics [33, 34] is a fundamental part of Agile [27], which ultimately maps to business outcomes. The risk across the value chain must be measured by a uniform mechanism [35]. Some of the key performance indicators (KPIs) [28, 35, 36], for BizDevOps, are :

- Deployment frequency
- Change volume
- Deployment time
- Lead time
- Customer tickets
- Automated test pass %
- Defect escape rate
- Availability
- Service level agreements
- Failed deployments
- Error rates
- Application usage and traffic
- Application performance
- Mean time to detection (MTTD)
- Mean time to recovery (MTTR)

- *Sharing*

Agile goals are achieved through the association between self-organizing and cross-functional teams, concentrating on bringing the highest business value in the shortest time [37]. Further, sharing points to a common vision, language, and knowledge, as well as sharing resources [35, 38].

(ii) PRINCIPLES

The cross-functional autonomous teams, i.e. the unified BizDevOps teams are composed of people with a variety of skills [39] from the business team and/or application owner, development, and operation sectors team members to effectively tackle the variety in their external environments [39]. Their focus could be a product company deliveries, or a business process, business component, or business service [40]. They have a higher degree of safety regarding planning [20, 41].

- *End-To-End Responsibility*: Unlike traditional organizations in which development responsibility ends up by handing over the product to operation team, in a DevOps environment teams are vertically organized such that they are fully accountable over the product's lifetime including performance support of products or services created and delivered by them [39].

- *Value stream and process mapping*: You have integrated business leaders, developers, and operations folks who all are working on a streamlined flow from your company's strategy to the deployment and ongoing operations of the product, service, or component. Organizations need to visualize as-is and to-be processes and how they feed higher-level value streams. These aspects are aimed to be used by business stakeholders without the need for training [32, 40].
- *Identifying and monitoring the key performance metrics*: requisition of key performance indicators, which include customer-centric metrics – e.g., user behavior and 'feature analytics', which in turn will enable gauging the value-add of specific features [4], to DevOps metrics such as time-to-business-impact and speed of remediation. It is essential for establishing continuous innovation [39, 40].
- *Automation toolchain*: BizDevOps leverages a range of automation platforms so-called "Toolchain", that allow to collaborate and automate across the different process and data items [40]. The toolchain is a combination of the most effective infrastructures for developing, delivering, and maintaining software according to agile principles [42]. It is essential to choose and leverage a proper set of tools in maintaining a healthy software development pipeline [34].
- *"Shift left" strategy*: that is, the need to identify and address the technical debt that accrues, at the time issues are first encountered, in order to prevent potentially problematic issues [4].

(iii) PRACTICES
The practices listed here are based on the "Continuous *" conceptual framework provided by Fitzgerald and Stol [4], appending the terms continuous requirements engineering, continuous business process modeling, and continuous human-centered design, proposed by Forbrig latter [23].

- *Business strategy and planning*: It implies in the form of Continuous Planning & Continuous Budgeting, that planning and budgeting become continuous activities, instead of the traditional annual approach hindering the fast response to the emergent needs and flexibility against changes in software projects.
- *Development*: This phase comprises Continuous Deployment/release, Continuous Delivery, Continuous Verification/Testing, all together incorporated in the Continuous Integration concept, which reflects the typical main activities in software development. It also includes two additional activities, namely that of continuous compliance and continuous security. With a slight difference in this grouping, Continuous Integration and Continuous delivery are widely cited in both scientific and grey literature as the two main drivers of DevOps, and consequently, BizDevOps.
- *Operation*: includes Continuous Use (refers to trading off trying to attract new customers versus focusing on retention of existing customers), Continuous Trust (satisfying customer demands without capitalizing on their vulnerabilities), and Continuous run-time Monitoring (being aware of all conceivable run-time behaviors in the context of continuous running cloud services).

- *Improvement and Innovation*: the activities mentioned within this category are not seen as a separate phase but implied as to the steady implicit endeavors across the software life cycle. These activities include Continuous Improvement (a concept rooted in Lean principles, that of data-driven decision making, and removing waste), Continuous Innovation (an endless process fed by monitoring metrics through SDLC, responding to the changing market conditions), and Continuous Experimentation (iterative cycles of Build-Measure-Learn, based on stakeholders experiments) [4].

(iv) TOOLCHAIN

Adopting a DevOps/BizDevOps model of software development in order to manage complex systems and scale workflows is strongly connected to effective tooling and choosing the proper technology. The toolchain in DevOps/BizDevOps is a categorization method that indicates what tools are used in which stages of the SDLC. The toolchain presented here is the most reported in the related grey literature [22, 34].

- *PLAN* –A set of continuous activities, including system requirements definition, metrics development, determining the transposition of new and improved features as well as security and release planning.
- *CREATE* –The tasks regarding code, namely, creation, release candidate, designing, building, test, and so on.
- *VERIFY* –Activities related to quality assurance, such as verification, various types of tests.
- *PACKAGE* –The required activities, before deploying new releases.
- *RELEASE* –The activities required for moving software into the product, including release and fallback/recovery.
- *CONFIGURE* –Preparing and configuration of hardware and software.
- *MONITOR* –Activities aimed at monitoring the fitness of production environments, including measuring the performance, availability, and other non-functional metrics. Further, observing the end-user experience and feedback from these activities is factored back into Planning activities.

The four upfront stages that comprise the Biz Loop:

- *ADAPT–* It refers to the consolidation of the latest feedbacks from the customer, business, and market, in order to define business initiatives, road map, and upfront plans [34].
- *DEFINE–* In this step, through a visual, well-understood solution model, visions of various stakeholders are defined. The solution is then parsed into functional components that determine the different activities over the toolchain. In defining a solution supporting the business needs, concerns from a variety of stakeholders are addressed.
- *ALIGN –* In this step, stakeholders across the organization can align by means of a shared model of what must be delivered, through visual models and automated workflows.
- *APPROVE –* At this step, stakeholders agree that the solution designed supports their business needs.

3.5   RQ4: What are the main potential benefits and challenges of adopting 'BizDevOps'?

With regards to the challenges, some of the challenges are derived from the ones in the implementation of continuous practices, as indicated by [4]. In the organizational sphere, literature reports the following challenges:

Prerequisite investments: in order to adopt BizDevOps, companies need to invest heavily in upgrading the required hardware and software infrastructure, as well as providing well-trained human resources. This issue is an essential inhibitory factor which can deter many organizations from using BizDevOps [16].

People's Behavioral Change: People's style of working is changing. This change introduces difficulties for the habits and culture of a large development organization that is deeply engrained [31]. Without a clear focus on the goal [43] along with motivation issues, it is an obvious reason for making such a change [31].

Lack of Skilled Product Owners in the Business Side: Transferring the traditional business-IT relationship, from the bureaucratic and inflexible employer-contractor framework, to a context of plenary interaction between these sectors and participation of business stakeholders in the SD process, is one of the cultural challenges ahead for moving to BizDevOps. Further, for such a change, business stakeholders in cross-functional teams, and business managers, are needed to be trained and familiar with technologies used in BizDevOps [31]. Due to the skill gap, selecting skilled employees is a challenging task [44]. Besides, for starting BizDevOps, the organization needs to improve its management process and application architecture [45].

Management Process: Teams need to be unified and collaborate with each other [37]. Collaboration sharing equal productivity, focusing on human touch is the major issue [46]. Due to the misunderstanding between the employees, what output needs to get at last was not clear [43]. Observation needs to be done on how the work is carried on [47]. Using the traditional approach for managing service will experience continued incident handling [48]. Thereby, it is essential to enabling communication between biz and DevOps [49].

However, it has been reported that it is hard for the business side to understand the programming code written by developers [50]. Due to this, biz are not able to adapt quickly into the application [51]. Difficulty in understanding what work is going on and what has been sent in the sprint has been noted [33]. Therefore, the business side needs to be integrated from the starting phase of the development process. Describing the new development process of application, which is fast enough for the customer side, was the main issue [44].

Inadequately addressing the business implications prevent DevOps from being the strategic IT capability business line [52]. To deliver enterprise-wide services, cost-effective shared services were necessary to be interfaced with team members [53]. In agile environments, the chance of releasing features every day is an unquestionable attractive. In contrast, it is needed for almost all business functions counting on with functionalities in a synchronized way as their processes change over time [54].

In reviewing the literature, what has excessively emphasized and repeated, as the benefit of BizDevOps, is the ability of this method to improve the various aspects of product or service and its capability to accelerate the value creation process, by removing the barriers between business, development, and operation teams. Authors in [17] impute three main achievements to BizDevOps approach:

- BizDevOps approach facilitates the exploration and review of requirements in a firsthand fashion. Hence, it catalyzes feedback cycling and reduces the need for knowledge-exchange between IT and Business (the "Biz" in BizDevOps).
- BizDevOps enables IT departments to have more control over the application development process, promising to guarantee the high quality of the software artifact (the "Dev" in BizDevOps).
- BizDevOps approach affords an assimilation of the automated and integrated toolchain to allow as much automation as possible and, consequently, accelerate development (the "Ops" in BizDevOps).

3.6   RQ5: How Has BizDevOps Evolved Since Its Emergence?

The increasing number of studies from 2015 indicates the growing rate of attraction to the subject. The number of studies per year are as follows:

- 2015: 3
- 2016: 8
- 2017: 17
- 2018: 29
- 2019:56
- 2020 (Not a full year): 13

4   Conclusion

In this research, authors attempted to provide a comprehensive and accurate portrait of the BizDevOps phenomenon. The research questions focus on recognizing the different dimensions of BizDevOps including definition, characteristics, motivating issues, potential challenges and benefits, and its evolution trend. We used Google Search and Google Scholar databases to find subject materials in both gray and scientific literature.
  Summarizing and analyzing the results shows that:

RQ1: there seem to be some disagreements over the exact definition, naming, and describing the term BizDevOps. However, it is a matter of consensus that BizDevOps is an extended model of DevOps and goes along with developing and generalizing it, in the scope of Agile software development. The transition flow of philosophy, principles, and methodologies used, from Agile methods to DevOps, and now to BizDevOps, indicates hierarchical originality and continuity, something like Russian Matryoshka dolls.
RQ2: the motivation for adopting BizDevOps could be expressed as follows: integration between the three sectors of business, development, and operations so that it establishes the active participation of business stakeholders in the software development process. It improves the continuous and efficient flow of

product/service, agility, quality, flexibility, which ultimately leads to the promotion of the organization's competitiveness.

RQ3: BizDevOps characteristics have been presented in terms of values, principles, practices, and toolchain.

RQ4: Some of the potential BizDevOps challenges and benefits are expressed in different aspects.

RQ5: The data collected in this study shows the rapid growth of this phenomenon in the industry. However, in the academic sphere, this paradigm has not received the attention it deserves.

Given the current high focus on the technological aspects of the subject, and considering that BizDevOps involves the mutual relationship between IT and business, affixing the business insight can help complete the picture in this discussion.

References

1. Emam, K.E., Koru, A.G.: A replicated survey of IT software project failures. IEEE Softw. **25**, 84–90 (2008). https://doi.org/10.1109/MS.2008.107
2. Lehtinen, T.O.A., Mäntylä, M.V., Vanhanen, J., Itkonen, J., Lassenius, C.: Perceived causes of software project failures – an analysis of their relationships. Inf. Softw. Technol. **56**, 623–643 (2014). https://doi.org/10.1016/j.infsof.2014.01.015
3. Jovanović, M., Mesquida, A.-L., Mas, A., Colomo-Palacios, R.: Agile transition and adoption frameworks, issues and factors: a systematic mapping. IEEE Access **8**, 15711–15735 (2020). https://doi.org/10.1109/ACCESS.2020.2967839
4. Fitzgerald, B., Stol, K.-J.: Continuous software engineering: a roadmap and agenda. J. Syst. Softw. **123**, 176–189 (2017). https://doi.org/10.1016/j.jss.2015.06.063
5. O'Connor, R.V., Elger, P., Clarke, P.M.: Continuous software engineering—a microservices architecture perspective. J. Softw. Evol. Proc. **29**, e1866 (2017). https://doi.org/10.1002/smr.1866
6. Colomo-Palacios, R., Fernandes, E., Soto-Acosta, P., Larrucea, X.: A case analysis of enabling continuous software deployment through knowledge management. Int. J. Inf. Manag. **40**, 186–189 (2018). https://doi.org/10.1016/j.ijinfomgt.2017.11.005
7. Dingsøyr, T., Lassenius, C.: Emerging themes in agile software development: Introduction to the special section on continuous value delivery. Inf. Softw. Technol. **77**, 56–60 (2016). https://doi.org/10.1016/j.infsof.2016.04.018
8. Ebert, C., Gallardo, G., Hernantes, J., Serrano, N.: DevOps. IEEE Softw. **33**, 94–100 (2016). https://doi.org/10.1109/MS.2016.68
9. Balalaie, A., Heydarnoori, A., Jamshidi, P.: Microservices architecture enables DevOps: migration to a cloud-native architecture. IEEE Softw. **33**, 42–52 (2016). https://doi.org/10.1109/MS.2016.64
10. Roche, J.: Adopting DevOps practices in quality assurance. Commun. ACM **56**, 38–43 (2013). https://doi.org/10.1145/2524713.2524721
11. Toh, M.Z., Sahibuddin, S., Mahrin, M.N.: Adoption issues in DevOps from the perspective of continuous delivery pipeline. In: Proceedings of the 2019 8th International Conference on Software and Computer Applications, pp. 173–177. Association for Computing Machinery, Penang, Malaysia (2019). https://doi.org/10.1145/3316615.3316619

12. Myrbakken, H., Colomo-Palacios, R.: DevSecOps: a multivocal literature review. In: Mas, A., Mesquida, A., O'Connor, R., Rout, T., Dorling, A. (eds.) Software Process Improvement and Capability Determination, pp. 17–29. Springer, Cham (2017). https://doi.org/10.1007/978-3-319-67383-7_2

13. Jäpel, L.M., Wedel, F.: BizDevOps: A Systematic Literature Review

14. Garousi, V., Felderer, M., Mäntylä, M.V.: Guidelines for including grey literature and conducting multivocal literature reviews in software engineering. Inf. Softw. Technol. **106**, 101–121 (2019). https://doi.org/10.1016/j.infsof.2018.09.006

15. de França, B.B.N., Jeronimo, H., Travassos, G.H.: Characterizing DevOps by hearing multiple voices. In: Proceedings of the 30th Brazilian Symposium on Software Engineering, pp. 53–62. Association for Computing Machinery, Maringá, Brazil (2016). https://doi.org/10.1145/2973839.2973845

16. Putano, B.: A Quick Guide to BizDevOps for Developers. https://stackify.com/bizdevops-guide/. Accessed 23 Apr 2020

17. Gruhn, V., Schäfer, C.: BizDevOps: because DevOps is not the end of the story. In: Fujita, H., Guizzi, G. (eds.) Intelligent Software Methodologies, Tools and Techniques, pp. 388–398. Springer, Cham (2015). https://doi.org/10.1007/978-3-319-22689-7_30

18. Forbrig, P.: BizDevOps and the role of S-BPM. In: Proceedings of the 10th International Conference on Subject-Oriented Business Process Management, pp. 1–8. Association for Computing Machinery, Linz (2018). https://doi.org/10.1145/3178248.3178250.

19. Forbrig, P.: Use cases, user stories and BizDevOps. In: REFSQ Workshops (2018)

20. Wiedemann, A., Wiesche, M., Gewald, H., Krcmar, H.: Implementing the planning process within DevOps teams to achieve continuous innovation. In: Proceedings of the 52nd Hawaii International Conference on System Sciences (2019)

21. Chasioti, K.: BizDevOps: A process model for the Alignment of DevOps with Business Goals (2019)

22. Blueprint: Agile and DevOps (and BizDevOps). https://www.blueprintsys.com/agile-development-101/agile-and-devops. Accessed 23 Apr 2020

23. Forbrig, P.: Continuous software engineering with special emphasis on continuous business-process modeling and human-centered design. In: Proceedings of the 8th International Conference on Subject-oriented Business Process Management, pp. 1–4. Association for Computing Machinery, Erlangen, Germany (2016). https://doi.org/10.1145/2882879.2882895

24. Aragon, G., Escalona, M., Hilera, J.R., Fernandez-Sanz, L., Misra, S.: Applying model-driven paradigm for the improvement of web requirement validation. Acta Polytechnica Hungarica **9**, 211–232 (2012)

25. Mustapha, A., Arogundade, O., Misra, S., Damasevicius, R., Maskeliunas, R.: A systematic literature review on compliance requirements management of business processes. Int. J. Syst. Assurance Eng. Manag. 1–16

26. Smartsheet: Support Your DevOps Practice with Tools for Success. https://www.smartsheet.com/devops-tools. Accessed 23 Apr 2020

27. MacSwain, D.: What is DevOps? A Complete History: Waterfall to DevOps 2.0. https://www.astadia.com/blog/what-is-devops-a-complete-history-waterfall-to-devops-2-0. Accessed 23 Apr 2020

28. Lowy, G.: Delivering Value with BizDevOps. https://www.appdynamics.com/blog/product/delivering-value-with-bizdevops/. Accessed 23 Apr 2020

29. Continuous: What is DevOps ? https://continuous.lu/devops/. Accessed 23 Apr 2020

30. Ward, C.: Do we need a DevOps 2.0? Yes, if you want to get back to "startup". https://searchsoftwarequality.techtarget.com/tip/Do-we-need-a-DevOps-20-Yes-if-you-want-to-get-back-to-startup. Accessed 23 Apr 2020

31. Systems, B.S.: The Complete Guide to Scaling Agile Software Development [eBook]. https://www.blueprintsys.com/content/complete-guide-to-scaling-agile-software-development. Accessed 23 Apr 2020

32. Ganpaul, A.: How to integrate business priorities into the DevOps process. https://appdevelopermagazine.com/how-to-integrate-business-priorities-into-the-devops-process/. Accessed 23 Apr 2020

33. StoryTeller: Business Alignment Through the DevOps Loop (2018). https://www.unifiedcompliance.com/wp-content/uploads/2017/04/Whitepaper-StorytellerBizDevOps.pdf

34. Smartsheet: The Way of DevOps: A Primer on DevOps Principles and Practices. https://www.smartsheet.com/devops. Accessed 23 Apr 2020

35. Talukdar, S., Ratneshwaran, S.: Connecting the Business, Development, and Operational dots in an enterprise [BizDevOps] - A TCS Approach (2013)

36. Watson, M.: 15 Metrics for DevOps Success. https://stackify.com/15-metrics-for-devops-success/. Accessed 23 Apr 2020

37. Van Langenhove, W.: How ING moves to real enterprise agility (2017). https://sai.be/UserContent/PSKXWMF62V72972ATPQR_SAI%20BizDevOps%20-%2020171114.pdf

38. Kulkarni, V.: Bringing Certainty and Speed to Decision Making with BizDevOps. http://sites.tcs.com/campaigns/framework-for-bringing-certainty-and-speedy-decision-making-retail/. Accessed 23 Apr 2020

39. DASA: DASA DevOps Principles. https://www.devopsagileskills.org/dasa-devops-principles/. Accessed 23 Apr 2020

40. Oehrlich, E.: What is BizDevOps? https://enterprisersproject.com/article/2019/9/devops-what-is-bizdevops. Accessed 23 Apr 2020

41. Drews, P., Schirmer, I., Horlach, B., Tekaat, C.: Bimodal enterprise architecture management: the emergence of a new EAM function for a BizDevOps-based fast IT. In: 2017 IEEE 21st International Enterprise Distributed Object Computing Workshop (EDOCW), pp. 57–64 (2017). https://doi.org/10.1109/EDOCW.2017.18

42. Watts, S.: What is a DevOps Toolchain?, https://www.bmc.com/blogs/devops-toolchain/. Accessed 23 Apr 2020

43. van der Graaff, A., Sequeira, V., Gatti, A.: Working together: BizDevOps for competitive advantage. https://www.digitalpulse.pwc.com.au/bizdevops-competitive-advantage/. Accessed 23 Apr 2020

44. Mullan, L.: Mendix: Redefining app development with a low-code approach | Cloud Computing | Gigabit Magazine. https://www.gigabitmagazine.com/cloud-computing/mendix-redefining-app-development-low-code-approach. Accessed 23 Apr 2020

45. Martynov, M.: DevOps 2.0 is here, and it's time to put end-to-end continuous delivery pipelines behind every project. https://blog.griddynamics.com/the-continuous-delivery-problem-has-been-solved-and-its-time-to-implement/. Accessed 23 Apr 2020

46. Yap, M.: BizDevOps Breaks Down Silos, Improves User Experience. https://indvstrvs.com/bizdevops-breaks-down-silos-improves-user-experience/. Accessed 23 Apr 2020

47. @Papa-fire: BizDevOps: business-first approach to DevOps. https://noti.st/leonfayer/AIVUSE/present. Accessed 23 Apr 2020

48. Bolash, J.: Modern Service Management For Azure (2017)

49. Baker, J.: What Does DevOps 2.0 Look Like? - DZone DevOps. https://dzone.com/articles/devops-20. Accessed 23 Apr 2020

50. Ismail, N.: Why DevOps must become BizDevOps for business and IT collaboration. https://www.information-age.com/devops-bizdevops-business-123471568/. Accessed 23 Apr 2020

51. Fregoni, S.: BizDevOps: Gaining a competitive advantage in an app-centric world. https://siliconangle.com/2020/01/29/bizdevops-gaining-competitive-advantage-app-centric-world-cleur/. Accessed 23 Apr 2020

52. Abdoulaye, P.A.: Why ignoring market responsiveness paves the way for Enterprise DevOps 2.0. https://www.cio.com/article/3013780/why-ignoring-market-responsiveness-paves-the-way-for-enterprise-devops-20.html. Accessed 23 Apr 2020
53. Regulski, T.: How CVP Puts the Biz in DevOps. https://www.cvpcorp.com/blog-BizDevOps-20170728/. Accessed 23 Apr 2020
54. Kadjani, S.: BizDevOps. Next level in your Enterprise Agile Maturity. https://www.linkedin.com/pulse/bizdevops-soheyl-kadjani-mba/. Accessed 23 Apr 2020

IT Project Management Critical Success Factors

António Trigo[1,2(✉)] ⓘ and João Varajão[2] ⓘ

[1] Polytechnic Institute of Coimbra, ISCAC, Quinta Agrícola, Bencanta,
3040-316 Coimbra, Portugal
antonio.trigo@gmail.com
[2] Centro ALGORITMI, University of Minho, 4804-533 Guimarães, Portugal
varajao@dsi.uminho.pt

Abstract. IT Project Management Critical Success Factors (CSFs) are the areas of an Information Technology (IT) project that are essential to its success, and that must be identified and followed throughout the life cycle of the project. The identification, definition and communication of CSFs help to ensure that the project manager and team maintain the focus on what is important while avoiding spending resources on other less important areas. Although each IT project is unique and therefore has a unique set of CFSs, in this article, we propose a framework based on a literature review, whose results provide researchers and project managers with a comprehensive understanding of current CSFs of IT projects.

Keywords: IT project · IT project management · IT project managers · Critical success factors

1 Introduction

Information Systems (IS) are critical to the proper functioning and development of virtually any human organization. By involving people, processes, Information Technology (IT), and other resources and organizational structures that facilitate the acquisition, storage, processing and availability of information in an organization, IS demands constant attention in order to properly fulfil its role and keep pace with the evolution of business needs [1]. As in other areas, organizational initiatives aimed at improving IT are typically configured as projects, which are fundamental to structuring the activities and resources required. IT projects are collective, collaborative, complex, creative, and knowledge-intensive efforts that involve people participating in different activities [2], coordinated to achieve a certain purpose.

According to ISO 21500 [3], a project consists of a single set of processes that encompass coordinated and controlled activities, which are executed in order to achieve the defined objectives, according to previously defined start and end dates. In this sense, a project is a temporary effort made to create one or several products, services or other results [4]. There are several types of IT projects executed to meet the different needs of organizations, and their nature may differ according to the nature of the organization and the scope of its action. Schwalbe [5] considers as examples of IT projects, activities that range from the simple replacement of computers in a company's finished department, or updating an organization's technological infrastructure to provide wireless network access, to projects for the development of new applications to increase sales force productivity or customer relationship management. Cadle & Yeates [6] classifies IT projects into eight categories: development of IT applications; implementation of IT application packages; improvement of IT systems; consulting and business analysis; migration of IT systems; implementation of infrastructure; outsourcing (and insourcing) projects; and disaster recovery.

According to ISO 21500 [3], "project management is the application of methods, tools, techniques and competencies to a project". Project management is carried out through processes and includes the integration of the various phases of the project life cycle. The processes selected to execute a project must be aligned according to a systemic vision, and each phase of the project life cycle must have specific deliverables and results, which should be regularly reviewed during the project life cycle to meet the requirements of the sponsor, customers, and other stakeholders.

Although IT projects are "famous" for their high failure rates, with the consequent overrun of costs and deadlines, there has been an improvement in the success of the projects [7], with organizations investing more in management good practices [8]. Due to this high rate of failures, researchers have acknowledged the need to investigate project management practices to identify critical success factors (CSFs) that contribute to the project final results [9].

In the context of this study, CSFs are the activities or areas essential for an IT project to achieve its objectives (e.g. production of deliverables, in software development projects), i.e., to be successful. CSFs management can anticipate problems like a lack of top management support, poor communication, or lack of resources [10]. CSFs highlight what the project needs to be successful, which helps to keep the project manager and team members focused. As far as IT projects are concerned, it is possible to see the suitability of CSFs in different areas such as the adoption of ITIL [11], agile software development [12] or continuous practices in DevOps context [13]. Although various studies exist regarding CSFs in IT Projects, there is no, to the best of our knowledge, a categorized summary to be effectively used by researchers and practitioners. This work presents the results of an effort to identify and organize current IT project management CSFs, so they can support research and be easily used in practice. From a theoretical, point of view, it provides a state-of-the-art framework on CSFs in IT project management.

The rest of the paper is structured as follows. Section two presents related work. Then in section three, it is presented the research method. In section four, the results obtained are presented and discussed. Finally, section five presents some final considerations and directions for future work.

2   Related Work

CSFs are the few variables that the manager must prioritize in order to achieve his goals. Effective and efficient management of CSFs is the basic requirement for project success. They must be systematically and quantitatively assessed, anticipating possible effects, in order to choose appropriate methods to deal with them [14]. The CSFs in the area of project management has been the target of many studies in the past, such as the Slevin & Pinto study [15], and are explored in the next sections.

2.1 CSFs in IT Project Management

IT projects have characteristics that make them different and more likely to fail than other projects, posing greater challenges to management [16]. The essence of this difficulty is the way information technologies are so closely linked to their organisational context, as opposed to, for example, construction projects. As a result, issues of organisational effectiveness and user involvement are more complex and more prominent in IT projects, which places too much emphasis on requirements-setting and customer involvement tasks than in other types of projects [17]. So, it is natural that there are specific CSFs for the management of IT projects and even for the different types of projects within IT projects.

Although there are some studies on IT/IS, like Rockart's [18], during the eighties, it is from the nineties onwards that the research around CSFs in the IT area and specifically in the field of IT project management starts. One of these studies that shows one of the facets that is different in IT projects is the study of Summer [19], in which there is clear concern about the relationship between the culture of the organization and the system to be implemented.

In the late nineties, many studies of CSFs emerged in the context of the implementation of ERP systems [20–22]. From the year 2000, the study of CSFs began to focus on another type of IT projects, the software development projects [23, 24]. From 2010 the focus shifted to the paradigm of agile software development [12, 25, 26]. It should be noted that many studies have been found on CSFs associated with software development projects [25, 27, 28].

In conclusion, the types of studies on CSFs in IT project management found are mainly of two types: literature review studies [27, 29, 30], which seek to identify which CSFs are most important; and surveys [28, 31–33], which seek to find out which CSFs are most important to the success of the project according to the participants in the study, which generally include IT project managers and other top managers in the organizations. In the results section, a summary is made of the CSFs, from the last five years, found in the review of literature carried out.

2.2 Categories of CSFs in IT Project Management

As the list of CSFs identified over the years is extensive it becomes important to classify them into categories so that it is easier for researchers and IT project managers to know what areas they are aimed at, for example, whether they are more focused on the internal team developing the project or factors associated with the client.

In the work of Belazi and Tukel [34] a first proposal is made to classify CSFs into categories, which the authors designated as a new framework for determining critical success/failure factors in projects. In this framework, the following categories were proposed: project; project manager and team members; organization; and external environment. Although this work was not focused on IT projects, the same served as inspiration for future CSF research in IT projects and software development.

In Adzmi's work [29] it is suggested the use of three categories, namely: project management competence; organization competence and project management methodologies, methods, tools and techniques. Ahimbisibwe [30], in his work on critical success factors for software development projects, suggests the use of five categories: organizational factors; team factors: customer factors; and project factors. These same factors are used in Garousi's work [28]. Nasir [35] proposes in his work the use of different categories from the previous authors, namely: people; process and technical.

In Cao's work [25] study of critical success factors in agile software projects, the following categories are used: organizational; people; process; and technical. These same categories were later used in Stankovic et al. [36]. Finally, in Warren's work [17] on CSFs Projects, IT Projects, and Enterprise Resource Planning Projects, the following categories are identified: organizational; process; social; technological.

There is, therefore, no consensus among the different authors in the literature as to the categories of CSFs. Thus, based on the previous works and considering the focus of our work, we propose a new classification, focused on the project, which allows having a more comprehensive perspective.

The proposed categories are: team factors related to the project team, which include factors related to the project manager and team members; process factors, which include all CSFs related to the way the project is managed, such as scope or risk management; organizational factors, which include all CSFs that depends on the organization, such as assuring top management support; and stakeholder relative factors, that refer to stakeholders external to the team. Some of these categories had already been identified in the literature but were not used with this classification scheme.

3 Method

The method used to conduct this research was a Literature Review, consisting of a methodologically rigorous review of search results [37]. Figure 1 presents the steps of the used search process.

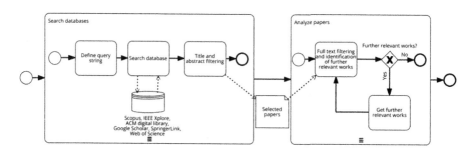

Fig. 1. Literature review search process.

The research question of this work is "*What are the current IT project management CSFs?*". The first step of the process was to define the research questions and the search terms to use. The following query string was used ("Critical Success Factors" OR "CSF") and ("IT Projects" or "Information Technology Projects"), with the initial year set for 2015. It was decided to focus the literature review on the last five years since the IT arena is always evolving, and the main objective was to identify the current CSFs.

Following the process defined in Kitcheman et al. [37], we searched the databases of articles that had in their title or abstract the terms identified above, having been discovered in SCOPUS 25 articles, in IEEE Xplorer 39 articles, ACM digital library nine articles, Google Scholar 39 articles (by title), Springer Link 34 articles, and Web of Science six articles. After integrating the results from the different searches, inspecting the titles and abstracts and removing the duplicates, a list of 22 papers was obtained.

The second step of the procedure consisted of reading each paper for compiling a list of CSFs. Every time a new relevant work was found in the full-text filtering, it was analysed in a snowball approach. This SLR process resulted in a final list of ten relevant papers.

4   Results

From the literature review, 25 unique CFSs were identified, as presented in Table 1.

In the work of Adzmi et al. [29], focused on the Malaysian public sector, the following success factors were identified: involvement of functional department in planning; involvement of the client in planning; authority of project managers; monitoring and feedback; client consultation; communication; monitoring and feedback; experience of the project manager; planning effort; team member experience; team member commitment; customer involvement; priorities of the project by team leader; training; project manager appropriate assignment; project manager involved in the planning stage; communication among project manager and organizations; project mission; support of top management; project schedule/plans; client agreement; a well-defined scope; all resource were defined; usage of WBS; usage of Gantt Chart; usage of CPM; usage of project management software; technical tasks; troubleshooting; and level and effectiveness planning. The factors were classified into five categories: project management; project manager; organization competence; and method and techniques.

In the work of Correa et al. [31], an empirical work conducted in small and medium enterprises of the IT sector in Bogota, 11 success factors were identified: project scope definition; planning; monitoring and control; manager empowerment; team skills; stakeholder management; effective communication; project management methodology; risk management; change control; and support from senior directors.

In a survey conducted in Pakistan by Fayaz et al. [32] to assess which identified CSFs had an effect on project success, were identified 15 CSFs: management support; effective communication; training; effective monitoring and control; leadership; clear goals; requirement specification; risk management; budget support; users involvement; project progress schedule; team capability; right team; project duration; and teamwork.

Table 1. IT project management critical success factors identified in the literature.

	Critical success factors/Papers	Adzmi et al. 2018	Correa et al. 2018	Fayaza et al. 2017	Gheni et al. 2017	Gumay et al. 2020	Saleem et al. 2019	Sarif et al. 2018	Vadhanasin et al. 2016	Wachnik 2017	Warren 2016	Total
Organizational	Top Management Support	x	x	x		x		x			x	6
	Organization culture (change management)								x		x	2
	Clear and realistic project goals		x	x	x	x	x				x	6
Stakeholders	Customer involvement	x	x	x	x	x		x			x	7
	Customer training			x						x	x	3
	Paying attention to customer needs		x		x			x	x			4
	Procurement management					x					x	2
	Communication and feedback (external stakeholders)	x	x	x		x	x		x			6
Process	Adequate use of resources (resource management)	x					x	x		x		4
	Appropriate use of methodologies and tools	x	x		x	x	x	x	x	x		8
	Clear and complete requirements specification	x		x		x	x			x	x	6
	Project complexity (duration, complexity, number of people involved, size)			x	x							2
	Project monitoring and controlling		x			x	x				x	5
	Project planning	x	x								x	3
	Quality management					x	x		x			3
	Realistic budgets (cost management)	x	x	x	x	x	x					6
	Risk management	x	x	x	x		x				x	6
	Realistic schedules (schedule management)			x			x			x	x	4
	Project changes (scope management)	x	x	x		x	x	x	x	x		8
Team	Project manager leadership	x	x		x	x	x	x			x	7
	Project manager capability (skills, expertise)		x			x	x		x		x	5
	Team commitment and motivation	x	x	x	x	x	x					6
	Team communication and collaboration	x								x		2
	Team composition (right people, multi-disciplinary)	x		x								2
	Team experience (skills, expertise, lessons learned)	x	x	x	x	x		x			x	7

Gheni et al. [33] also conducted an online survey among developers and IT managers to assess the CSFs for IT projects. In their study, they identify nine CSFs: committed and motivated team; internal communication; use of tools and infrastructures; goal and objectives; skilled project managers; skilled teams; risk analysis; project monitoring; and good estimation. According to the authors, the most important CSFs is to have a committed and motivated team.

Gumay et al. [38] conducted a survey in a Telco company in Indonesia and applied the analytical hierarchy process to identify CSFs. In their study they identified eight CSFs: top-level management and organizational culture; capability and leadership of the project manager; requirement management; project management and methodology; clear project objective; customer involvement and effective communication; capability and motivation of a team; and tools and infrastructures used. The three most important CSF were customer involvement and effective communication, capability and leadership of the project manager and project management and methodology.

In the work of Saleem et al. [27] were identified 14 CSFs: scope management; performance management; knowledge management; human resource management; feasibility; resource management; communication management; quality management; process management; complete requirements; stakeholders management; schedule management; budget management; and risk management.

Sarif et al. [39] conducted a survey among IT officers and staff of Malaysian government institutions involved in IT projects using nine CSFs, order by the importance attributed to them by the authors in their study: good user participation/involvement; good requirements and specifications; good of skills; complete requirements; good management and performance from vendor/contractor; good of project planning; realistic expectations; good of resources; good of executive support (top management).

Vadhanasin et al. [40] interviewed IT experts (executives and IT managers) from 12 leading Thai firms to discuss success factors and the measurement of IT project success. In their study they identified five CSFs: streamline of process and tools; emphasis on quality; scope control; change management; and platform for communication.

Wachnik [41] studied the importance of CSFs in 127 IT projects of five different types: standard implementation, upgrade, re-implementation, roll-out and implementation of a standard system with an add-on, analysing them using structural equation modelling. This study resulted in nine CSFs: effective process of establishing functional requirements for the implemented system; effective IT project management; credible estimation and agreement with the supplier regarding project parameters; competence and engagement of the client project group; choice and use of an IT implementation method; motivation of the client project group; added value brought by the supplier into the implemented system; information asymmetry between the supplier and the client; sharing knowledge about functionalities and technology of the implemented system.

Finally, in the study conducted by Warren [17], a literature review on CSFs in IT and ERP projects, were identified the following CSFs associated to IT Projects: user/client involvement; clear realistic objectives; support from senior management; skilled/suitably qualified/sufficient staff/team; proven/familiar technology; organisational adaptation/culture/structure; realistic schedule; project size (large)/level of complexity (high)/number of people involved (too many)/duration (over three years); sufficient/well allocated resources; good performance by suppliers/contractors/ consultants; strong detailed plan kept up-to-date; correct choice/past experience of project management; methodology/tools; differing viewpoints (appreciating); competent project manager; effective monitoring/control; environmental influences; good communication/feedback; training provision; adequate budget; good leadership; strong business case/sound basis for project; effective change management; political stability; past experience (learning from); and risks addressed/assessed/managed. The author of this study proposed a classification of the CSFs with the following categories: organisational; process; social; and technological.

5 Discussion and Conclusion

After the enumeration of the CSFs identified in the literature review, they were analysed in terms of similarity, i.e., it was verified if they represented the same concept, aiming at obtaining a unique set of factors. The factors were then ranked considering the number of references and classified according to the categories of factors previously mentioned in the related work section.

Figure 2 presents the framework that includes the most referenced factors. Each framework's factor has at least five references. Although this measure does not represent an absolute and definitive way for identifying the most important factors since it lacks statistical grounding, several authors use it to measure the importance [30, 35, 42]. In our study, using it was important since the focus of this paper is on the critical success factors (which are a subset of success factors, which cannot fail).

The obtained framework provides useful information for researchers, so they can focus their work in the areas of factors that are critical for the success of projects. It is also useful for practitioners, mainly IT project managers, in the sense that they can use it to identify significant contributors for project's success and to manage factors in their daily practice (for instance, by following factors with dashboards and associating each factor with Key Performance Indicators (KPIs) to monitor the evolution across the project lifecycle).

A limitation of this work is related to the selected measure for identifying the more relevant factors. The decision was to consider the 50% more referenced factors (corresponding to factors with five or more references). Future work should expand this perspective.

Each project is unique, thus having a unique set o CSFs. Project managers can use the framework (Fig. 2) as a checklist, for identifying the factors that are relevant in their own projects and to assure that they are duly considered. As further work, we propose the development of IT tools to support the management of CSFs in practice, integrating it with success management processes [43–45].

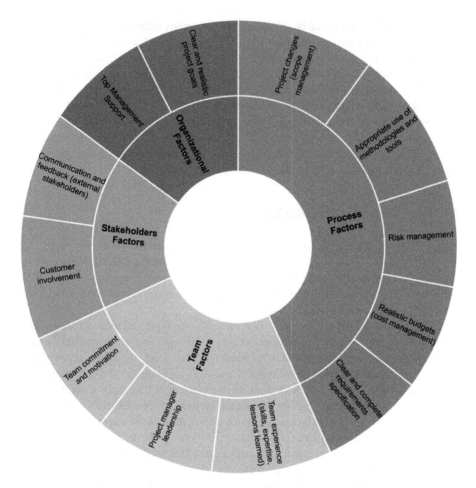

Fig. 2. Framework of current IT project management CSFs.

References

1. Varajão, J.: The many facets of information systems (+projects) success. Int. J. Inf. Syst. Proj. Manag. **6**(4), 5–13 (2018)
2. Alawneh, A.A., Aouf, R.: A proposed knowledge management framework for boosting the success of information systems projects. In: 2016 International Conference on Engineer-ing & MIS (ICEMIS), pp. 1–5 (2016)
3. ISO: ISO 21500:2012 - Guidance on project management (2012)
4. PMI: A Guide to the Project Management Body of Knowledge (PMBoK® Guide), 6th ed. Project Management Institute (2017)
5. Schwalbe, K.: Information Technology Project Management, 6th edn. Cengage Learning, Boston (2012)
6. Cadle, J., Yeates, D.: Project Management for Information Systems. Pearson Education Limited, London (2008)

7. Bezdrob, M., Brkić, S., Gram, M.: The pivotal factors of IT projects' success–insights for the case of organizations from the federation of bosnia and herzegovina. Int. J. Inf. Syst. Proj. Manag. **8**(1), 23–41 (2020)

8. PMI: Success in Disruptive Times—Pulse of the Profession (2018)

9. Ellerbe, C.Y.: Exploring cost and resources in information technology projects about project completion. Capella University (2020)

10. Pinto, J.K., Covin, J.G.: Critical factors in project implementation: a comparison of construction and R&D projects. Technovation **9**(1), 49–62 (1989)

11. Ahmad, N., Tarek Amer, N., Qutaifan, F., Alhilali, A.: Technology adoption model and a road map to successful implementation of ITIL. J. Enterp. Inf. Manag. **26**(5), 553–576 (2013)

12. Tam, C., da Costa Moura, E.J., Oliveira, T., Varajão, J.: The factors influencing the success of on-going agile software development projects. Int. J. Proj. Manag. **38**(3), 165–176 (2020)

13. Van Belzen, M., Kusters, R.: Critical success factors of continuous practices in a DevOps context. In: 28th International Conference on Information Systems Development (2019)

14. Frefer, A.A., Mahmoud, M., Haleema, H., Almamlook, R.: Overview success criteria and critical success factors in project management. Ind. Eng. Manag. **7**(1) (2018)

15. Slevin, D.P., Pinto, J.K.: The project implementation profile: new tool for project managers. Proj. Manag. J. **17**(4), 57–70 (1986)

16. Rodriguez-Repiso, L., Setchi, R., Salmeron, J.L.: Modelling IT projects success: emerging methodologies reviewed. Technovation **27**(10), 582–594 (2007)

17. Warren, A.M.: Increasing the value of research: a comparison of the literature on critical success factors for projects, IT projects and enterprise resource planning projects. Systems **4**(4), 33 (2016)

18. Rockart, J.F.: The changing role of the information systems executive: a critical success factors perspective (1980)

19. Sumner, M.: Critical success factors in enterprise wide information management systems projects. In: Proceedings of the 1999 ACM SIGCPR Conference on Computer Personnel Research, pp. 297–303 (1999)

20. Holland, C.R., Light, B.: A critical success factors model for ERP implementation. IEEE Softw. **16**(3), 30–36 (1999)

21. Pastor-Collado, J.E.S.J., Salgado, J.G.: Towards the unification of critical success factors for ERP implementations. In: Annual Business Information Technology (BIT) 2000 Conference, Manchester, UK, vol. 44 (2000)

22. Somers, T.M., Nelson, K.: The impact of critical success factors across the stages of enterprise resource planning implementations. In: Proceedings of the 34th Annual Hawaii International Conference on System Sciences, p. 10-pp (2001)

23. Niazi, M., Wilson, D., Zowghi, D.: Critical success factors for software process improvement implementation: an empirical study. Softw. Process Improv. Pract. **11**(2), 193–211 (2006)

24. Akman, I., Misra, S., Cafer, F.: The role of leadership cognitive complexity in software development projects: an empirical assessment for simple thinking. Hum. Factors Ergon. Manuf. Serv. Ind. **21**(5), 516–525 (2011)

25. Chow, T., Cao, D.-B.: A survey study of critical success factors in agile software projects. J. Syst. Softw. **81**(6), 961–971 (2008)

26. Pham, Q.T., Nguyen, A.V., Misra, S.: Apply agile method for improving the efficiency of software development project at VNG company. In: Murgante, B., et al. (eds.) ICCSA 2013. LNCS, vol. 7972, pp. 427–442. Springer, Heidelberg (2013). https://doi.org/10.1007/978-3-642-39643-4_31

27. Saleem, N., Mathrani, S., Taskin, N.: Investigating critical success factors of project management in global software development: a work in progress. In: CONF-IRM 2019 Proceedings, p. 3 (2019)

28. Garousi, V., Tarhan, A., Pfahl, D., Coşkunçay, A., Demirörs, O.: Correlation of critical success factors with success of software projects: an empirical investigation. Softw. Qual. J. **27**(1), 429–493 (2018). https://doi.org/10.1007/s11219-018-9419-5

29. Adzmi, R.M., Hassan, Z.: A theoretical framework of critical success factors on information technology project management during project planning. Int. J. Eng. Technol. (UAE) **7**(4), 650–655 (2018)

30. Ahimbisibwe, A., Cavana, R.Y., Daellenbach, U.: A contingency fit model of critical success factors for software development projects: a comparison of agile and traditional plan-based methodologies. J. Enterp. Inf. Manag. **28**(1), 7–33 (2015)

31. Correa, J.A.G., Castañeda, S.L.S., Quintero, D.A.V., Giraldo, G.E.: Identification and analysis of project management success factors in information technology SMEs. Int. J. Inf. Technol. Proj. Manag. **9**(4), 73–90 (2018)

32. Fayaz, A., Kamal, Y., Ul Amin, S., Khan, S.: Critical success factors in information technology projects. Manag. Sci. Lett. **7**(2), 73–80 (2017)

33. Gheni, A.Y., Jusoh, Y.Y., Jabar, M.A., Ali, N.M.: The critical success factors (CSFs) for IT projects. J. Telecommun. Electron. Comput. Eng. **9**(3-3), 13–17 (2017). Special Issue

34. Belassi, W., Tukel, O.I.: A new framework for determining critical success/failure factors in projects. Int. J. Proj. Manag. **14**(3), 141–151 (1996)

35. Nasir, M.H.N., Sahibuddin, S.: Critical success factors for software projects: a comparative study. Sci. Res. Essays **6**(10), 2174–2186 (2011)

36. Stankovic, D., Nikolic, V., Djordjevic, M., Cao, D.B.: A survey study of critical success factors in agile software projects in former Yugoslavia IT companies. J. Syst. Softw. **86**(6), 1663–1678 (2013)

37. Kitchenham, B., Pearl Brereton, O., Budgen, D., Turner, M., Bailey, J., Linkman, S.: Systematic literature reviews in software engineering – a systematic literature review. Inf. Softw. Technol. **51**(1), 7–15 (2009)

38. Gumay, L.A., Purwandari, B., Raharjo, T., Wahyudi, A., Purwaningsih, M.: Identifying critical success factors for information technology projects with an analytic hierarchy process. In: Proceedings of the 2020 2nd Asia Pacific Information Technology Conference, pp. 108–112 (2020)

39. Md Sarif, S., Ramly, S., Yusof, R., Fadzillah, N.A.A., Sulaiman, N.: Investigation of success and failure factors in IT project management. KEER 2018. AISC, vol. 739, pp. 671–682. Springer, Singapore (2018). https://doi.org/10.1007/978-981-10-8612-0_70

40. Wachnik, B.: Critical success factors in IT projects–from the practice of polish clients. In: Proceedings of Federated Conference on Computer Science and Information Systems, October, vol. 13, pp. 27–33 (2017)

41. Vadhanasin, V., Ratanakuakangwan, S., Santivejkul, K., Patanakul, P.: It project management effectiveness framework: a study in thai firms. J. Eng. Sci. Technol. **12**(Special Issue), 1–16 (2017)

42. Fortune, J., White, D.: Framing of project critical success factors by a systems model. Int. J. Proj. Manag. **24**, 53–65 (2006)

43. Varajão, J.: Success management as a PM knowledge area – work-in-progress. Procedia Comput. Sci. **100**, 1095–1102 (2016)

44. Varajão, J., Trigo, A.: Evaluation of is project success in InfSysMakers: an exploratory case study. In: 2016 International Conference on Information Systems. ICIS 2016 (2016)

45. Varajão, J.E.: A new process for success management–bringing order to a typically ad-hoc area. J. Mod. Proj. Manag. **5**(3), 94–99 (2018)

Embedded System to Support Skin Cancer Recognition

Gabriel de A. Batista[1]([✉]) [ID], Marcelo Nogueira[1,2] [ID],
Nuno Santos[2,3] [ID], and Ricardo J. Machado[2,3] [ID]

[1] Software Engineering Research Group, Paulista University, UNIP,
Campus Tatuapé, São Paulo, Brazil
[2] ALGORITMI Centre, School of Engineering, University of Minho,
Guimarães, Portugal
[3] CCG/ZGDV Institute, Guimarães, Portugal

Abstract. Skin cancer is the most common among all cancers and its early diagnosis increases the patient's chances of healing. One of the ways to make this diagnosis is through dermatoscopy. Dermatoscopy is a technique that consists of recognizing structures present in the skin, not visible to the naked eye. Therefore, for assisting the use of dermatoscopy by health professionals, this work presents a device to support skin cancer recognition using the histogram of oriented gradients and machine learning, based on the ABCDE rule.

Keywords: Machine learning · Skin cancer · Histogram of Oriented Gradients · Gaussian Naive Bayes · K Neighbors Classifier

1 Introduction

Nowadays, there are great technological advances, in which it is possible to count on the support of intelligent systems that are increasingly present in commerce, industry, medicine, finance, etc. One of the great advances is the computer vision that is related to image analysis, which has been developing a lot in recent years. This area deals with the extraction of information from images and the identification and classification of objects present in them. Computer vision systems have been used to recognize people, signatures and objects; inspection of parts on assembly lines; orientation of robot movements in automated industries etc. They involve image analysis and artificial intelligence or decision-making techniques, which allow the identification and classification of objects or images.

The technology has brought many health benefits, such as electronic devices (ultrasound, defibrillator, pulse oximeter, etc.), applications, expert systems to aid decision making and even artificial neural networks for pre-diagnosis of diseases such as breast cancer or skin cancer. Dermatologists use equipment that makes it possible to scan images of skin lesions, allowing for clinical skin evaluation and monitoring of the development of the disease. The advent of large collections of medical images brought with it the need to use computational techniques for efficient processing, analysis and retrieval of the information contained in the image.

© Springer Nature Switzerland AG 2020
O. Gervasi et al. (Eds.): ICCSA 2020, LNCS 12254, pp. 725–740, 2020.
https://doi.org/10.1007/978-3-030-58817-5_52

Skin cancer is by far the most common type of cancer, with basal cell carcinoma and squamous cell carcinoma being the most frequent [1], and melanoma the least frequent [2].

The world estimate shows that, in 2018, there were 287,723 new cases of melanoma skin cancer [3] and 1,042,056 non-melanoma skin cancer [4], totaling 1,329,779. There were 125,867 deaths, 65,155 from non-melanoma [4] and 60,712 from melanoma [3]. Male gender registered the highest number of occurrences, both in incidence and mortality (Fig. 1). In general, the highest incidence and mortality rates were observed in North America, Europe and Asia, and the lowest in Latin America, the Caribbean, Oceania and Africa (Fig. 2).

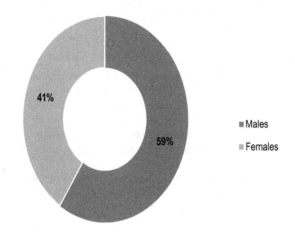

Fig. 1. Skin cancer occurrence rate.

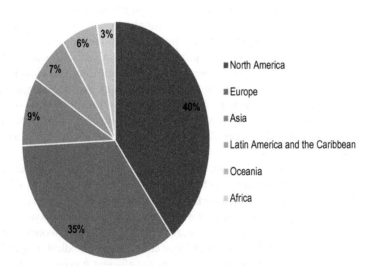

Fig. 2. Skin cancer incident and mortality rates, both sexes.

It is estimated that by the year 2040, incidents of melanoma skin cancer will increase by 62.3% and non-melanoma skin cancer will increase by 91.1%. The mortality rate will follow the same rate of increase, 74.4% for melanoma skin cancer and 83.8% for non-melanoma skin cancer (Fig. 3) [5].

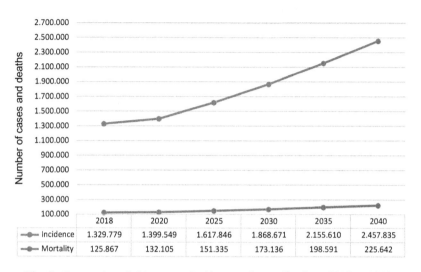

Fig. 3. Perspective of skin cancer incidents and mortality from 2018 to 2040.

The highest incidence rates worldwide are found in populations with a predominance of lighter skin color, such as Australia and New Zealand. Despite being the most frequent cancer, non-melanoma skin cancer is difficult to estimate, since not all cases are registered [6].

This work presents a device for supporting dermatoscopy by health professionals with the recognition of skin cancer using the histogram of oriented gradients and Gaussian Naive Bayes and K Neighbors classifiers, based on the ABCDE rule.

This paper is structured as follows: Sect. 2 presents the related work, encompassing topics from descriptors of characteristics, solutions for skin cancer treatments, BI-RADS and machine learning algorithms; Sect. 3 presents the methods applied for developing the device; Sect. 4 presents the results registered; Sect. 5 presents the research discussions; and Sect. 6 presents the conclusions.

2   Related Work

2.1   Descriptors of Characteristics

Most of the time, computer vision applications involve computationally complex tasks, i.e., object tracking, object identification, optical flow, among others. The first steps of all these applications are the detection, description and matching of the characteristics of high qualities, the descriptors being the most complicated and slow.

Descriptors focus on abstracting information from images that are associated with points of interest detected by the feature detector, however descriptors should avoid being complex or using too many math operations. A high-quality feature descriptor only describes a feature point, correctly identifying it in subsequent images [7].

The descriptor based on Histogram of Oriented Gradients (HOG) was proposed in 2005 by researchers Dalal and Triggs as part of a pedestrian detection algorithm in images. Generally used in pattern recognition and image processing to detect or recognize objects. This method aims to extract information regarding the orientation of the existing edges in an image, these edges being calculated through edge detection methods such as Sobel [8].

2.2   Treatments for Skin Cancer and the ABCDE Rule

Excessive and chronic exposure to the sun is the main risk factor for the onset of non-melanoma skin cancers, in relation to melanoma, in general, the greatest risk factor includes a personal or family history, in addition to sporadic and intense exposure in the sun with consequent sunburn in more than one episode. Other risk factors for all types of skin cancer include skin sensitivity to the sun and its color [9].

Surgery is the indicated treatment for melanoma skin cancer. Other forms of treatment that can be successful would be radiotherapy and chemotherapy depending on the stage of the cancer. When metastasis has already occurred (the cancer has already spread to other organs), melanoma is incurable in most of its cases. At this stage, a treatment strategy would only be to relieve symptoms and improve the patient's quality of life [10]. For non-melanoma skin cancer, surgery would be the most indicated treatment for both basal cell and epidermoid carcinoma. Basal cell carcinoma, when of low extent, can be treated with a topical medication (ointment) or radiation therapy, while epidermoid carcinoma, the usual treatment combines surgery and radiation therapy [11].

Skin spots or stains can be classified in a rule called ABCDE, which consists of evaluating five distinct characteristics. The same spot can have one or more of these characteristics and the higher the number, the greater the degree of suspicion of being a skin tumor. Some malignant skin tumors, however, escape this description and it is best to see a specialist if you suspect something different [12]. The ABCDE rule can be verified as in Table 1.

Table 1. ABCDE rule. [13]

ABCDE Rule	Benign	Malignant
A = Asymmetry, melanoma is suspected: the tumor is divided in half, and the halves are not similar.		
B = Irregular border, suspected melanoma: uneven or irregular borders.		
C = Color variation, suspected melanoma: there is more than one color of pigment.		
D = Diameter, suspected melanoma: if the diameter is greater than 6 mm.		

2.3   BI-RADS

The BI-RADS (Breast Imaging Reporting and Data System) is a system considered the greatest reference for standardization and uniformity of mammography. It was proposed by the American College of Radiology, with a focus on assisting and standardizing mammography so that the best approach can be defined, being defined in 6 levels, with zero being undetermined [14].

The annual hematological screening in women over 40 years old identifies 100 to 200 new cases of suspicious lesions in every 20,000 mammograms, with BI-RADS being a way to standardize and designate corresponding examinations [14].

2.4   Machine Learning

Machine learning is a field of study that gives computers the ability to learn without being explicitly programmed. Machine learning is the ability to improve performance in performing a task through experience [15]. It is an extremely important segment in artificial intelligence.

Informally, an algorithm is any well-defined computational procedure that takes some value or set of values as an input and produces some value or set of values as an output. Therefore, an algorithm is a sequence of computational steps that transform input into output.

There are several machine learning algorithms, but some were used in this work the MLP Classifier, Random Forest Classifier, AdaBoost Classifier, K Neighbors Classifier, Support Vector Machines, Gaussian Process Classifier, Quadratic Discriminant Analysis, Gaussian NB and Decision Tree Classifier.

During the process of creating a machine learning model, we need to measure its quality according to the objective of the task. There are mathematical functions that help us to evaluate the error and correctness of our models.

The metrics used in this work were ROC Curve, Confusion Matrix, Accuracy, Precision, Log Loss, Sensitivity and F1-Score. Since this research focused in using the Confusion Matrix, it is further detailed.

A confusion matrix is one of the easiest and most intuitive metrics to find the accuracy and precision of a model. It is used as a classification for problems where the output can be of two or more types of classes.

The confusion matrix has the following terms:

- TP (True Positives): the true positives are the cases where the true class is 1 (true) and the predicted also 1 (true). An example of a situation would be a patient having cancer (1) and the model classifies the case as cancer (1).
- TN (True Negatives): true negatives are the cases where the true class is 0 (false) and the predicted one is also 0 (false). A situation that applies to this case would be where a person does not have cancer (0) and the model classifies it as not being cancer (0).
- FP (False Positives): false positives are the cases where the true class is 0 (false) and the predicted is 1 (true). False being where the model predicted incorrectly and positively because the predicted class was positive (1). The case that applies situation where the person does not have cancer and the model classifies it as if it did.
- FN (False Negatives): False negatives are cases where the true class was defined as 1 (true) and the predicted one as 0 (false). False being where the model incorrectly predicted and negative because the predicted class was negative (0). An applicable situation would be where a person has cancer and the model defines it as if they did not have cancer.

3 Methods

The proposed system aims to provide support in decision making to diagnose melanoma skin cancer. For this purpose, some requirements were foreseen, which will be explained in the following sections.

3.1 Project Set-Up

Materials:
The components used in the project were a Raspberry Pi 3 model B, a 3.5" TFT LCD touch screen display, a V2 camera, a pair of sinks, a 16 GB SanDisk Class 10 card, a case and a 5V3A power supply (bivolt source). They were chosen after an abstraction of objects related to the constitution of the embedded system proposed in the planned architecture. An individual practical study was carried out of each component that played an important role in the functionality as a whole.

For each component that presents implementation complexity, practical tests were carried out separately, that is, one component was tested at a time, starting with the next only after having achieved a good result in the test of the previous one. Figure 4 shows the prototype.

Fig. 4. Protype.

Database:
The ISIC Archive project database was used for the development of the software and for carrying out the planned tests.

1642 (one thousand six hundred and forty-two) images with skin tumor and 1689 (one thousand six hundred and eighty-nine) images with benign skin spots/stains were removed, both with their metadata (diagnostics) from the database for the realization the training and validation of the algorithm. The training phase used 70% of the total base and 30% were used for tests.

3.2   Software Development and Management Methodology

For good management and software development, the Scrum agile management and development methodology was used in conjunction with the RUP, and the unified modeling language (UML).

The project was divided into thirteen iterations. Each iteration goes through the four phases of the software development process used (conception, elaboration, construction and transition).

At the beginning of the project, the team used the Kanban agile methodology together with the RUP, but with the increase in complexity, we changed to the Scrum agile methodology together with the RUP. In the beginning, Trello was used, later Azure DevOps from Microsoft, always working with sprints of fifteen days.

3.3   Image Processing

This step aims to improve the original image, removing any other elements that may be present in it, such as hair, skin and even some possible noise from the image environment.

The locked system resizes an image to a size of 204 pixels wide by 204 pixels high for reduced processing. After resizing, the system can apply a smoothing filter, aiming to reduce the number of derived images, such as hair. With a smoothed image, the system can create a grayscale copy for binaries in order to apply an opening morphological filter to reduce some noise that appear after binarization and pass an original to the YUV encoding system, with the purpose of equalizing and converting the RGB system to calculate the tone limit. With a morphological filter application, the system can use a copy of the image as a mask for an original image, resulting in an image with only one skin spot highlighted.

Figure 5 depicts the image processing structure.

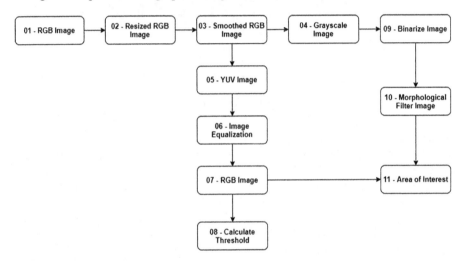

Fig. 5. Diagram of how image processing works.

Figure 6 shows an image of a spot before and after processing.

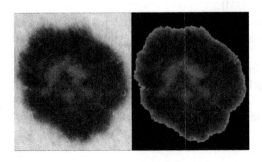

Fig. 6. Result of image processing.

Color Variation Analysis

To quantify the color variation of the skin spot, it is necessary to find the region of interest in the image resulting from the pre-processing in order to calculate the standard deviation and the number of points greater than the threshold of the histograms of each channel (RGB). This procedure represents rule C of the melanoma detection method. Figure 7 shows the steps that were taken to develop this stage.

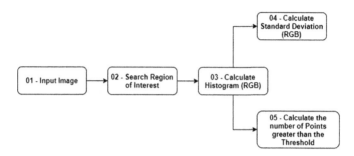

Fig. 7. Diagram of how color variation analysis works.

Table 2 lists the results found for each histogram belonging to a malignant and benign skin spot/stain.

Table 2. Standard deviation and points above the threshold in histograms

Channel	Standard deviation	Points above threshold
Benign		
Blue	353,48193	84
Green	464,20898	80
Red	145,35013	121
Malignant		
Blue	239,77455	64
Green	189,1244	78
Red	125,30375	129

If we look at the three histograms in each image and compare them, we will see that the histograms belonging to the malignant skin spot/stain are more "aggressive" than those of the benign skin spot/stain.

Edge Variation Analysis

To quantify the edge variation, it is necessary to find the region of interest in the image resulting from the processing, divide it into four parts, based on the center of the ROI, select the first part to calculate the edge in order to highlight the pixels brackets surrounded by darker pixels for a vector to result, where it will be calculated to identify the amount of local highs and lows contained in its vector from the horizontal and vertical histograms. This procedure represents rule B of the melanoma detection method.

Figure 8 shows the steps that were taken to develop this stage.

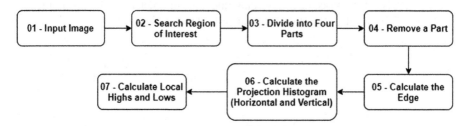

Fig. 8. Diagram of the operation of the edge variation analysis.

Table 3 lists the results obtained from each histogram belonging to a malignant and benign skin spot/stain.

Table 3. Maximum and minimum amounts of histograms

Quantities	Benign	Malignant
Maximum	236	189
Minimum	21984	22044

Diameter Analysis

For the extraction of the diameter of the skin stain, it is necessary to find the region of interest in the image resulting from the processing, so that it will be possible to find the contours of the ROI that will be used to extract the moments of the image, giving the ability to calculate some characteristics such as the center of the skin stain, the area, the radius and consequently the diameter. This procedure represents rule D of the melanoma detection method. Figure 9 shows the steps necessary to develop this step.

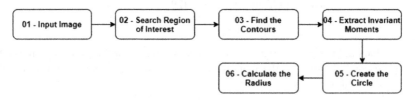

Fig. 9. Diameter analysis diagram.

Figure 10 shows the result obtained from the set of operations performed on the benign image, on the left side, and on the malignant image, on the right side.

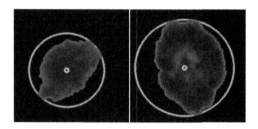

Fig. 10. Circumference of benign and malignant skin spot.

Table 4 lists the results obtained.

Table 4. Result of the diameter analysis

Benign (mm)	Malignant (mm)
5,1	6,7

Asymmetry Analysis

This step aims to compare two halves of the image, for this it is necessary to find the ROI and divide it in half, selecting the midpoint of the image width. This procedure represents rule A of the melanoma detection method.

Figure 11 shows the steps that were taken to develop this procedure.

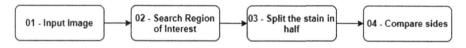

Fig. 11. Asymmetry analysis process.

These were the results obtained:

- **Benign:** 1,22036539; 0,76417758; −0,52827106; −0,16928178; 1,65588505; 0,07144739; −0,0779571;
- **Malignant:** −1,94320367; −1,24052967; −1,00843259; −1,6367098; −1,47681334; 0,72248248; −0,07596904;

The results described show us that the malignant skin spot/stain has more negative moments than the benign one and that the negatives of the benign skin spot/stain do not reach −1, while 5 of the 6 negative skin spots/malignant skin stain exceed −1.

Recognition of Standards

Standards are understood to mean properties that make it possible to group similar objects within a given class or category, through the interpretation of input data, which allow the extraction of the relevant characteristics of these objects.

This step aims to extract the characteristics of the image resulting from the processing. These characteristics are usually grouped into a scalar vector, called an image descriptor.

Figure 12 illustrates the steps that were necessary to develop the extraction of the patterns.

Fig. 12. HOG extraction process.

Figure 13 shows the result obtained in a malignant skin spot. The HOG managed to extract as many characteristics of the skin spots as possible, but the side effect was the increase in computational cost. However, the increase in confidence compensates for the loss of speed and the increase in cost.

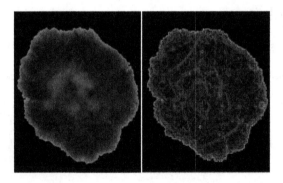

Fig. 13. HOG of the malignant spot.

Controlled Environment

The image acquisitions were performed in a controlled environment, so that a more accurate analysis of the risk scale classification algorithm for skin cancer tumor is possible.

Figure 14 shows the environment prepared for the tests.

Fig. 14. Test environment.

4 Results

With the result returned by the Oriented Gradients Histogram method, it was possible to obtain a vector that represents the necessary characteristics for the performance of the probabilistic calculation, image classification and the degree of risk of the skin spot/stain being a skin tumor. For the validation of the classification algorithms, the confusion matrix was used.

Table 5 shows the amounts of VP (True Positive), VN (True Negative), FP (False Positive) and FN (False Negative) of the nine classifiers.

Table 5. Confusion matrix classifiers

Classifier	VP	VN	FP	FN
Ada Boost Classifier	57%	70%	30%	43%
Decision Tree Classifier	64%	60%	40%	36%
Gaussian NB	74%	44%	56%	26%
Gaussian Process Classifier	60%	71%	29%	40%
KNeighbors Classifier	73%	50%	50%	27%
Quadratic Discriminant Analysis	17%	85%	15%	83%
MLPClassifier	70%	60%	40%	30%
Random Forest Classifier	61%	71%	29%	39%
SVC	67%	62%	38%	33%

As can be seen in Table 5, the classifiers that had the highest indexes of true positives (skin cancer patient and skin cancer model) with 74%, 73% and 70% were Gaussian NB, KNeighbors Classifier and MLPClassifier, respectively, but at the start they were the ones with the lowest cancer incidence rates (unused patient or skin cancer and model classified as not skin cancer) with 44%, 50% and 60%, respectively. This means that they were the best at identifying malignant skin spots, but were not as good at identifying benign skin spots.

The classifiers that had the highest rate of true negatives (patient does not have skin cancer and the model classifies it as not skin cancer) with 85%, 71% and 71% were Quadratic Discriminant Analysis, Random Forest Classifier and Gaussian Process

Classifier, respectively. Even though Quadratic Discriminant Analysis was the best at detecting benign skin spots, it was the worst, with 17%, at detecting malignant skin spots, and, consequently, having the highest balance of false negatives.

Decision Tree Classifier was the classifier that obtained the smallest difference between true positives and false positives with 4%, SVC was the second with 5% difference between VP and FP and the third parties were Random Forest Classifier and MLPClassifier with 10% difference, each. However, the classifiers that managed to reach or exceed 70% of VP or FP and maintain a small difference, between 10% and 11%, were the Random Forest Classifier, Gaussian Process Classifier and MLPClassifier classifiers.

5 Discussion

When we are working with health, what we should take into account in the confusion matrix is the FN column (patient has skin cancer and the model classifies it as not being skin cancer), because it is better to refer the patient who does not have skin cancer for a battery of tests that will prove the inexistence, than making the mistake and discharging a patient with skin cancer. Knowing this, the two algorithms that obtained the lowest false negative rates were the Gaussian NB and KNeighbors Classifier.

With the two classifiers, Gaussian NB and KNeighbors Classifier, implemented in the risk grade recognition and classification algorithm, it was possible to perform the classification of the spots.

The spots are classified into four levels, zero being indeterminate, based on the likelihood that the skin spot is melanoma. The levels were based on BI-RADS.

Table 6 shows the possible responses returned by the risk scale classification algorithm and recognition of melanoma skin cancer.

Table 6. Levels of the algorithm

Category	Classification	Probability	Conduct
1	Very low risk	≥ 0% and ≤ 25%	It is advisable for the patient to continue doing the monitoring annually
2	Low Risk	>25% and ≤ 50%	It is advisable that the patient be referred to dermatoscopy
3	Medium Risk	>50% and ≤ 75%	It is advisable that the patient is referred to the confocal microscopy
4	High Risk	>75% and ≤ 100%	It is advisable to collect a little of the patient's tissue for a biopsy

Table 7 shows the results obtained in each analysis, where the first column is the results of the image without the melanoma and the second the results of the image with the melanoma. The first line is the result of the Gaussian NB algorithm and the second is the result of the KNeighbors Classifier.

Table 7. Results of the analysis

Algorithm	Benign	Malignant
Gaussian NB	The skin spot analyzed has a low risk level with 49,086% veracity of being melanoma! Is advisable that the patient be forwarded to dermatoscopy	The analyzed spot has a medium risk degree with 69.38% veracity of being melanoma! Is advisable that the patient be referred for confocal microscopy
KNeighbors Classifier	The skin spot analyzed has a low risk level with 43,148% veracity of being melanoma! It is advisable that the patient be referred for dermatoscopy	The analyzed skin spot has a medium risk degree with 74.98% veracity of being melanoma! Is advisable that the patient be forwarded to confocal microscopy

As can be seen in Table 7, in addition to the algorithm returning to the user the degree of risk of and the percentage of veracity, the necessary exam is returned to prove that the tissue is cancerous. If the skin spot has a low degree of veracity, the device recommends an examination, as only a specialist has the ability to state this proposition.

6   Conclusions

In view of the large number of skin cancer cases, several researchers have been trying to develop techniques to improve and speed up the diagnosis, since, when detected early, the chances of curing this disease increase considerably. One of the ways to make the diagnosis is through dermatoscopy. In this technique, the doctor has the help of a dermatoscopy to analyze the lesions based on some characteristics. Despite analyzing the injury in a broader way, and the extracted characteristics are well-founded, this diagnosis is subjective, as it is affected by some factors. Thus, the utility of computational analysis has been researched in helping professionals to carry out this type of diagnosis.

In order to improve the accuracy of this diagnosis, the development of this study enabled the research and development of a device capable of providing statistical support to melanoma skin cancer specialists using a classification and recognition algorithm. In addition, it also allowed an analysis of how it can improve the reliability and accuracy of diagnoses performed in hospital environments, and an assessment of the data treatment process and of some classifiers available to perform such a task.

The initial proposal was to use one analysis, instead of two, in the classification and recognition algorithm. However, with studies and research it was found the need to use two analyzes and, consequently, two classifiers. In view of this modification, it was implemented, along with the ABCDE rule, an oriented gradient histogram technique, which aims to detect, describe and recognize patterns and characteristics.

When doing the tests in a controlled environment and with some images of the test base, it was found that the need for a good camera and capturing an image of the skin spot are fundamental for the performance of the processing and consequently of the analysis. However, even with a low-quality image, the device was able to analyze and classify it as expected. Thus, allowing the proposed objectives to be really achieved. The agile process was a key contributor to the completion of this MVP, because with the thirteen iterations, we are able to check every fifteen days if we were heading in the right direction and, otherwise, it is pivoting.

Acknowledgements. This research is sponsored by the Portugal Incentive System for Research and Technological Development PEst-UID/CEC/00319/2020 and University Paulista – Software Engineering Research Group by Brazil.

References

1. American Cancer Society. About Basal and Squamous Cell Skin Cancer. https://www.cancer.org/cancer/basal-and-squamous-cell-skin-cancer.html. Accessed 29 Feb 2020
2. American Cancer Society. About Melanoma Skin Cancer, https://www.cancer.org/cancer/melanoma-skin-cancer.html. Accessed 29 Feb 2020
3. Globo Can. Melanoma of Skin, International Agency for Research on Cancer, http://gco.iarc.fr/today/data/factsheets/cancers/16-Melanoma-of-skin-fact-sheet.pdf. Accessed 29 Feb 2020
4. Globo Can. Non-melanoma Skin Cancer. International Agency for Research on Cancer. http://gco.iarc.fr/today/data/factsheets/cancers/17-Non-melanoma-skin-cancer-fact-sheet.pdf. Accessed 29 Feb 2020
5. Globo Can. Cancer Tomorrow. International Agency for Research on Cancer. http://gco.iarc.fr/tomorrow/. Accessed 29 Feb 2020
6. Stewart, B.W., Wild, C.P.: World Cancer Report: 2014, 1st edn. IARC, Lyon (2014)
7. Desai, A., Lee, D.J., Wilson, C.: Using affine features for an efficient binary feature descriptor. In: 2014 Southwest Symposium on Image Analysis and Interpretation (SSIAI), pp. 49–52. IEEE, San Diego (2014)
8. Panceri, J.A.C., Pinto, L.A., Pereira, F.G., Cavalieri, D.C., Komati, K.S.: Facial recognition based on HOG and PCA: an invariance to illumination-based comparison. Ifes Ciência **1**, 41–62 (2015)
9. Costa, C.S.: Epidemiologia do câncer de pele no Brasil e evidências sobre sua prevenção. Diagn Tratamento **4**, 206–208 (2012)
10. José Alencar Gomes da Silva National Cancer Institute – INCA, Câncer de pele melanoma. https://www.inca.gov.br/tipos-de-cancer/cancer-de-pele-melanoma. Accessed 29 Feb 2020
11. José Alencar Gomes da Silva National Cancer Institute – INCA. Câncer pele não melanoma. https://www.inca.gov.br/tipos-de-cancer/cancer-de-pele-nao-melanoma. Accessed 29 Feb 2020
12. Oncoguia Institute. Sobre o Câncer de Pele Basocelular e Espinocelular. http://www.oncoguia.org.br/conteudo/sobre-o-cancer/751/146/. Accessed 29 Feb 2020
13. ISIC Archive. https://isic-archive.com/. Accessed 29 Feb 2020
14. Teixeira, M.B.R.: Avaliação dos achados mamográficos classificados na categoria 4 do sistema BI-RADS® e sua correlação histopatológica. Master's thesis, Botucatu Medical School (2011)
15. Mitchell, T.M.: Machine Learning, 1st edn. McGraw-Hill Science, New York (1997)

Does the Lean Inception Methodology Contribute to the Software Project Initiation Phase?

Igor Braga[1](✉), Marcelo Nogueira[1,2](✉) iD, Nuno Santos[2,3](✉) iD, and Ricardo J. Machado[2,3](✉) iD

[1] Software Engineering Research Group, Paulista University, UNIP, Campus Tatuapé, São Paulo, Brazil
marcelo@noginfo.com.br
[2] ALGORITMI Centre, School of Engineering, University of Minho, Guimarães, Portugal
[3] CCG/ZGDV Institute, Guimarães, Portugal

Abstract. This work aims to make a comparative analysis of the Lean Inception methodology and the Scrum methodology applied in the initiation phase of the embedded software project that consists of a small greenhouse for the indoor cultivation of sage, controlled by a cell phone application. The Lean Inception methodology is a combination of Lean Startup and Design Thinking that, at the end of the process, quickly obtains the Minimum Viable Product (MVP). Some of the questions explored in this paper were how much the Lean Inception methodology interferes in the agility of the production of MVP, how much it influences in the quality of the final product and depicting advantages in using this methodology in the project initiation phase.

Keywords: Lean Inception · Scrum · Project initiation · Minimum Viable Product

1 Introduction

Many software projects end up failing due to the lack of good planning, where most of the time they are one or more of the 3 main pillars affected: scope, time and cost.

The solution to this type of problem is a good survey of requirements with the user, the validation of the defined requirements and once every-thing is well defined, the initiation of modeling, because from it the scope, time and cost will be defined.

The importance of modeling is precisely the fact that it is the basis for the definition of the three pillars, and if there is a need for the user to make changes after the definition, we can see how much this change will influence the final delivery of the project.

For a better result, the Lean Inception methodology is applied in the initiation phase of the project, where the diagrams will already be developed through detailed requirements with the user and with that the time, cost and scope will already be

© Springer Nature Switzerland AG 2020
O. Gervasi et al. (Eds.): ICCSA 2020, LNCS 12254, pp. 741–752, 2020.
https://doi.org/10.1007/978-3-030-58817-5_53

defined culminating in a quality Minimum Viable Product (MVP) that serves the user and there is the possibility of adding value to the software developed over time.

The methodology also aims to develop people, improve work, have a different development change from the project, do until it is interpreted in a more relaxed way, many times this can generate a final product with a good quality.

To improve business results through Lean practice, it is necessary to change not only the processes, operations or include new technologies in the scope of work, but the mindset of the organization as a whole, guiding people to look at the internal factors that involve the company or product development. It is the ability to eliminate waste continuously and solve problems in a systematic way.

Software process it is a set of activities, actions and tasks performed in the creation of some artifact. The view of the activity is an objective without worrying about the difficulty and the effort generated, the action is the set of activities that result in a fundamental software artifact and the task focuses on a small, but well-defined objective. In general, the process is an adaptive approach that allows people to do the job in the best way by choosing the appropriate set of actions so that the software is delivered on time and of sufficient quality to satisfy the people who are sponsoring the development and those who are going to use it [1].

According to The Standish Group there are 4 main reasons for the significant improvement that has been happening over the years since 2010, with the application of agile methodologies being one of the main ones, the use of these processes grows at a rate of 22% CAGR (Compound annual growth rate), today this represents 9% of all IT projects and is adopted in 29% of new application development. The group concludes that the growth in the success rate is directly related to the increase in the adoption of agile methodologies [2].

Another reason is the cascade processes that consist of traditional methods and have already represented almost 50% of the number of new implementations, however, as they grow at 1% CAGR (Compound annual growth rate), their relative use has decreased, thus contributing positively to the success rate [2].

In the project that was chosen for the comparative analysis of this article, two different agile methodologies were applied, the first of which was scrum using simple Kanban and the second was Lean Inception.

The Scrum methodology do not have the part of people development and stimulus of creativity even though it is effective in the part of deliveries on time, however Lean Inception, on the other hand, promotes several techniques, such as people development, creativity stimulation work, through cycles passing through phases where there is the participation of everyone involved in the project, each phase has a different form of brainstorm until reaching a minimum viable product.

Based on studies, it has been proven that in terms of creativity for a minimum viable product for the user, the lean inception methodology has a faster result, mainly due to the fact that the idea is to develop the MVP as quickly as possible and over time add value to the product according to user requests and needs.

2   Background

2.1   Software Engineering

The basis for software engineering is the process layer. The software engineering process is the alloy that keeps the technology layers cohesive and makes it possible to develop software rationally and on time. The process defines a methodology that must be established for the effective delivery of software engineering technology. The software process forms the basis for controlling the management of software projects and establishes the context in which technical methods are applied, derivative products are produced (models, documents, data, reports, forms, etc.), milestones are established, quality is guaranteed and changes are managed appropriately [1].

Process is a set of activities, actions and tasks performed in the creation of some work product (work product). An activity striving to achieve a broad objective (for example, communicating with stakeholders) and is used to apply the field of application, the size of the project, the complexity of cuts or the degree of rigor with software engineering will be applied. An action (for example, architectural design) involves a set of tasks that result in a fundamental software artifact (for example, an architectural design model). A task focuses on a small but well-defined objective (for example, performing a unit test) and produces a tangible result [1].

In the context of software engineering, a process is not a strict prescription for how to develop software. Rather, it is an adaptable approach that allows people (a software team) to do the work of selecting and choosing the set of actions and tasks to be adjusted. The intention is always to offer software on time and with enough quality for the requirements that sponsor its creation and the requirements that will be used [1].

The basics for using any generic process methodology for software engineering comprises five activities:

- **Communication:** Before starting any technical work, it is vitally important to communicate and collaborate with the customer (and other interested parties). The intention is to understand the objectives of the stakeholders for the project and to survey the needs that will help to define the functions and characteristics of the software [1].
- **Planning:** This makes it easier for the team to better understand the progress of the steps. A software project has many steps, and the planning activity creates a "map" that helps guide the team. The software design plan defines the software engineering work, describing the technical tasks to be carried out, the probable risks, the resources that will be required, the resulting products to be produced and a work schedule [1].
- **Modeling:** An "outline" of the software project is created, so that one can get a general idea of the whole. Modeling is used to understand the needs of the software and the design that will meet those needs [1].
- **Construction:** This activity combines code generation and tests necessary to reveal errors in the coding [1].
- **Delivery:** The software is delivered to the customer, who evaluates the delivered product and provides feedback, based on the evaluation [1].

These five generic methodological activities can be used for the development of small and simple programs, for the creation of large applications for the Internet and for the engineering of large and complex computer-based systems. The details of the software process will be very different in each case, but the methodological activities will remain the same [1].

It is based on this information that the ideal methodology for a software project is defined, based on what is required by the project (term, scope and cost) that the ideal methodology to be used is chosen.

In this article, we will approach the two methodologies used in the same project to focus on the difference in modeling used in each of the methodologies, the objective is to make a comparative analysis between the models and the results of the project.

In the next chapters, a brief explanation of each of the two methodologies used in the project is defined.

2.2   Scrum

Scrum (the name is derived from an activity that occurs during a rugby match) is an agile software development method that was conceived by Jeff Sutherland and his development team in the early 1990s. In recent years, further development on the Scrum methods has been performed by Schwaber and Beedle [1].

Scrum principles are consistent with the agile manifesto and are used to guide development activities within a process that incorporates the following framework activities: requirements, analysis, design, evolution, and delivery. Within each framework activity, work tasks occur within a process pattern (discussed in the following paragraph) called a sprint. The work conducted within a sprint (the number of sprints required for each framework activity will vary depending on product complexity and size) is adapted to the problem at hand and is defined and often modified in real time by the Scrum team. The overall flow of the Scrum process is illustrated in Fig. 1.

Scrum focuses on using a set of software process standards that have proven to be effective for projects with tight deadlines, changing requirements, and business critical. Each of these process patterns defines a set of development actions:

The backlog is a prioritized list of project requirements or features that provide value to the customer. Items can be added to that record at any time (this is how changes are made). The product owner evaluates the record and updates priorities as required [1].

Backlog items consist of units of work requested to reach a requirement established in the backlog. Changes - for example, in backlog work items - are not introduced during sprints execution. Therefore, the sprint allows team members to work in a short-term but stable environment [1].

Scrum meetings - these are short meetings (typically 15 min), held daily by the Scrum team. Three key questions are asked and answered by all team members:

- What have you accomplished since the last team meeting?
- What obstacles are you encountering?
- What do you plan to accomplish by the next team meeting?

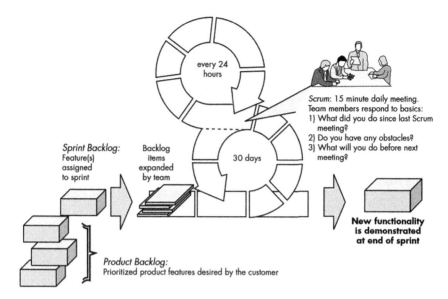

Fig. 1. Scrum process flow [1]

A team leader, called the Scrum master, conducts the meeting and evaluates the responses of each member. The Scrum meeting, held daily, helps the team to reveal potential problems as early as possible. It also leads to "knowledge socialization" and therefore promotes a self-organized team structure [1].

Delivery of the software increment to the customer is performed at the end of each sprint so that the implemented functionality can be demonstrated and evaluated by the customer. It is important to note that the demonstration may not have all the planned functionalities, but functions that can be delivered on time [1].

3   Lean Inception

A "Lean Inception" [4] is useful when the team needs to iteratively develop an MVP. Although the term is often misunderstood, the central property of an MVP is that it is something we build in order to learn whether it is worthwhile to continue building a product. Therefore, we choose features based on testing our assumptions of what is valuable to our users. For this, we need to understand who our users are, what activity they do that the product supports and how to measure if they find the product useful [4].

Lean Inception is valuable in two main circumstances:

- Large projects find a "Lean Inception" valuable to start quickly and be oriented to work in a "Lean" style. Such a start builds early iterations designed to discover and test what features are truly valued by their users [4].
- Smaller organizations (such as startups) use lean inceptions to take an idea that's been tested by some pre-software MVPs and evolve it into a software product [4].

MVP is the simplest version of a product that can be made available to validate a small set of assumptions on the business [4].

Basically, you don't want to waste time, money and effort building a product that won't meet your expectations. For that reason, you need to understand and validate your hypothesis about the business. MVP helps to validate and learn the fastest way [4].

Different from products created using traditional methods, usually taking too much time and effort for prototyping, analysis, and elaboration, the goal of MVP is only to validate the first step – the minimum product – which is far less developed than the final version. MVP focuses on the minimum but viable product to verify if the direction is correct. The initial set of functionalities needed for hypothesis validation and for learning more about the business [4] (Fig. 2).

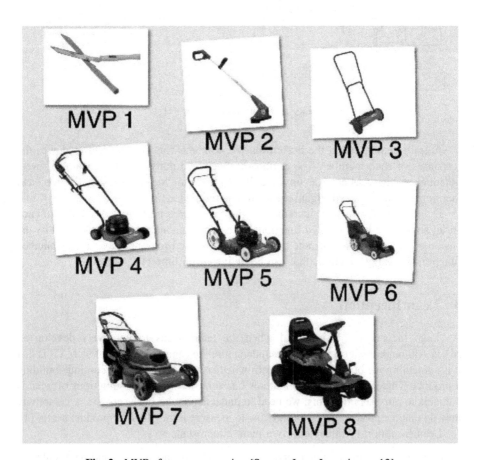

Fig. 2. MVPs for grass grooming [Source: Lean Inception p. 12]

The focus of lean inception is to create functionalities for an MVP based on the pains of personas with business-oriented modeling, always based on user experience.

4   Case Study

Anxiety disorders have become very common in people's daily lives, especially in Brazil where, according to WHO studies, about 9.3% of the population is affected with some type of anxiety disorder. This rate is considered the highest in the world, and from there we can imagine the weight of this scenario in our country. Some socioeconomic factors such as unemployment, poverty and lifestyles in big cities facilitate the opening to these disorders that can also trigger something more serious, such as depression, among other health problems [5].

Anxiety most often occurs at times considered to have a great emotional impact, which can be classified as "The Evil of the Century" and even as a public health problem, triggering difficulties in concentration, sleep problems and excessive worry [6].

Currently, there are few proven alternatives for the treatment or reduction of symptoms, some are psychotherapy, exercises and medicines, but there is still a lack of natural and usual means of daily life for those who have a running routine and little time for dedication.

The groundwork was created based on three methodological procedures:

- Bibliographic: which involves the analysis and interpretation of documents, articles, manuscripts, etc.
- Exploratory: it is the understanding of a subject little known by the group. At the end of this research, we will have a greater knowledge on the subject, therefore, we will be able to build new hypotheses.
- Experimental: Based on data from articles on existing research, the data regarding what the plant needs were manipulated for the best development of sage and applied this in the greenhouse to propose the exact climatic conditions and with the best quality in the development of the plant.

This was the human cause and the research methods that served as a basis for the development of the idea.

The general objective of the project was the development of a greenhouse with an embedded system in real time, fully adaptable for the best development of the medicinal plant called Salvia Officinalis.

One developed together with embedded software, which makes connection via bluetooth with a smartphone, making it possible to fully control and monitor all functions as the user synchronizes the application with the stove.

The specific objective is to allow the user to have control of the environment in which the salvia will grow, changing the temperature and monitoring according to parameters that will be presented in the application.

It was developed together with embedded software, which makes a Bluetooth connection with the smartphone, making it possible to modify and monitor the internal climate of the greenhouse as the user synchronizes the application, providing healthy development of sage, allowing the user to grow independently and food consumption to help treat anxiety.

The project parameters are:

- Air Humidity
- Temperature
- Water tank
- Ventilation
- Soil Moisture
- Water Pump Operation
- Lighting

The functioning of these parameters influences the internal climatic condition of the greenhouse and they work according to the temperature change, by the user on the smartphone, which is the trigger for the functioning of all components.

There is a manual temperature mode where the user sets the value and the stove works based on what has been defined and there is a default mode, for users who do not have an in-depth knowledge of cultivation, where the stove will operate with the standard settings defined in creation where the temperature value is set to 26° C.

4.1   Project Instance on Scrum

According to the requirements, two use cases were developed, one from an overview and the other from a detailed view for good modeling and understanding of the project (Figs. 3 and 4).

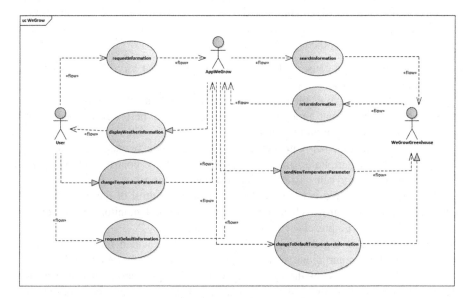

Fig. 3. General UseCase

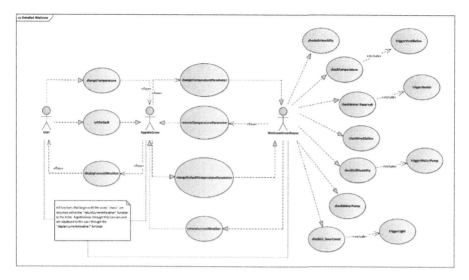

Fig. 4. Detailed UseCase

The methodology for the development of the project was Scrum, where the tasks were divided among the members of the group in such a way that each of them went through the review of all 4 members of the group to finish the sprint, culminating in the completion of each cycle was agile and quality.

In the agile Scrum world, instead of providing complete, detailed descriptions of how everything is to be done on a project, much of it is left up to the Scrum software development team. This is because the team will know best how to solve the problem they are presented [3].

That's why all team planning meetings were done quickly based on the desired outcome and focusing on features.

As the sprints progress, there is the possibility of extorting bugs, the task identified as a bug is in a kanban column specific to errors, where the programmers assume one by one for the correct correction and progress of the task.

4.2   Project Instance on Lean Inception

The objective of this project was to develop an MVP where the user could feel comfortable using the application and obtain a good result.

The result was a high speed in the delivery of the MVP where the initial result for the user was as expected.

It was identified through the survey of the user's pains primarily in the user's wish not to have healthy cultivation of sage in the external environment due to the interference of climatic variation of the environment.

Based on the project made in the scrum methodology, the idea was also raised that the user could have as an initial MVP an indoor sage cultivation greenhouse that did not have the functionality of modifying parameters manually because it was concluded that the minimum that the user needs to have a healthy plant is the greenhouse in operation according to the standard configurations, that is, an MVP where the greenhouse would work alone with its factory standards, with the settings and codes set inside the arduino, programmed to work as soon as there is electrical power in the hardware, without user intervention (Fig. 5).

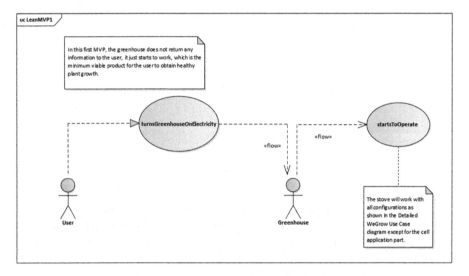

Fig. 5. First MVP UseCase

In a second MVP, the greenhouse would already communicate via Bluetooth with a smartphone, however, only for monitoring, that is, the user would only monitor the information of air humidity, temperature, water tank, ventilation, soil moisture, operation of the water pump and lighting and would not be able to change the temperature parameter (Fig. 6).

In a third MVP, the parameter modification functionality was already implemented, and the user could interact with the internal climate of the greenhouse (Fig. 7).

The next deliverables of the project were based on the user's experience, such as design and response performance.

The modeling using the Lean Inception methodology requires that the visualization is more focused on the business with less focus on the functionalities since the modeling already tells what should be done, the development team focuses on fulfilling the functionality so that it works.

In this type of modeling visualization, the client's understanding is better considering that the client's concern is focused on the functioning and not how it is created.

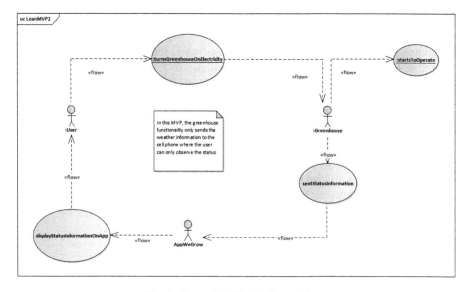

Fig. 6. Second MVP UseCase delivery

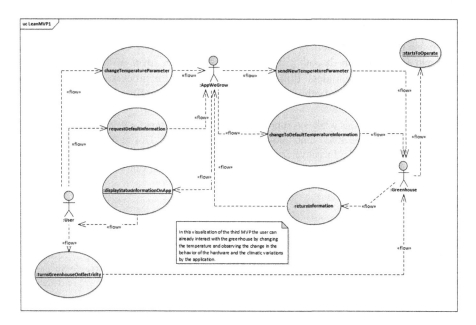

Fig. 7. Third MVP UseCase

5 Discussion

Depending on the methodology applied in a software, the project requires modeling with other levels of understanding and abstraction.

In the paper two agile methodologies that require different modeling methods and design dynamics were approached, where both have similar results but serve for different types of projects, the diagrams made in the same project but in different methodologies were highlighted in the article for a better visual understanding.

As discussed the focus of both methodologies are agile deliveries that bring a quality result to the client - lean inception with fractional deliveries of a MVP and Scrum with deliveries divided by sprints. The difference is the time the user will be able manipulate the application. When using lean inception the first delivery is already viable for the user. When using Scrum delivery will not necessarily be usual.

6 Conclusion

It is concluded that different development methodologies require different levels of abstraction in modeling and architecture, no matter how close they are, and their system requirements are the same, each method requires a different assessment.

Scrum for example, covers more with regard to the content of the system (whether functional or non-functional), the behavior of the application and how it will measure in the use of the final product.

Lean Inception, on the other hand, requires a higher level of abstraction, taking better care of the stakeholders' difficulties, evaluating all the processes involved so that there is satisfaction from both parties (development team and business owners).

Acknowledgments. This work was supported by FCT - Foundation for Science and Technology within the scope of the R&D units project: UIDB/00319/2020. This research is sponsored in collaboration between the Incentive System to Portugal for Technological Research and Development and Universidade Paulista UNIP - Research Group on Software Engineering in Brazil.

References

1. Pressman, R., Maxim, B.: Software Engineering: A practitioner's approach, 8th edn. McGraw-Hill Education, London (2015)
2. Bruno Adam Osiek. CHAOS Report (2011). Métodos Ágeis Aumentam Taxa de Sucesso de Projetos https://blog.myscrumhalf.com/metodos-ageis-impactam-positivamente-no-sucesso-de-projetos/. Accessed 26 Feb 2020
3. Mountain Goat Software. Scrum (2019). https://www.mountaingoatsoftware.com/agile/scrum . Accessed 5 Feb 2020
4. Caroli, P.: Lean Inception - How to Align People And Build The Right Product. Editora Caroli, Sao Paulo (2018)
5. OMS. Anxiety (2017). https://www.who.int/eportuguese/countries/bra/pt/. Accessed 20 Jan 2020
6. Palhares, I.: Brasil Tem a Maior Taxa de Transtorno de Ansiedade do Mundo, diz OMS (2017). https://saude.estadao.com.br/noticias/geral,brasil-tem-a-maior-taxa-de-transtorno-de-ansiedade-do-mundo-diz-oms,70001677247. Accessed 25 Feb 2020

A Novel Feature Extractor Based on the Modified Approach of Histogram of Oriented Gradient

Shaveta Malik[1]($\boxtimes$), Archana Mire[1]($\boxtimes$), Amit Kumar Tyagi[2]($\boxtimes$) (iD),
and Vasudha Arora[3]($\boxtimes$)

[1] Terna Engineering College, University of Mumbai, Mumbai, India
shavetamalik687@gmail.com, archanamire@ternaengg.ac.in
[2] School of Computer Science and Engineering, Vellore Institute of Technology,
Chennai Campus, Chennai 600 127, Tamil Nadu, India
amitkrtyagi025@gmail.com
[3] G.D Goenka, Gurugram, India
Vasudharora6@gmail.com

Abstract. In image processing, the goal of feature extraction is to extract a set of effective features from the raw data. Feature extraction starts from an initial set of measured data and builds derived values i.e. features intended to be informative and Non-redundant. The paper is based on the novel feature extraction approach for the detection of Epizootic Ulcerative Syndrome (EUS) fish disease which is misidentified among people. The EHOG (Enhanced Histogram of Oriented Gradient) which is a proposed feature Extractor to extract the features or information. The paper discuss its comparison with other existing techniques with different parameters. The Evaluation results shows that the EHOG is better in every parameters and also gives better accuracy and efficiency of the model which recognizes the disease.

Keywords: Epizootic ulcerative syndrome (EUS) · Histogram of oriented gradient (HOG) · Neural network · Fish disease

1 Introduction

The seasonal epizootic condition of great importance in wild and farmed fresh and brackish water fish is Epizootic Ulcerative Syndrome (EUS). It is considered as an indistinguishable now from red spot disease and it is observed first in eastern Australia [1]. The fungus *Aphanomyces* invader (A.piscicida in Japan) is the causative agent of EUS, when it invades the body, it causes intense liquefactive necrosis of muscle tissue in some cases the hyphae extend into the visceral organs. Often mass mortality is observed as an initial sign of distinct dermal lesions, including Ulcers. Fishes surviving from the diseases may get burn like marks, red-spots, blackish and deeper ulcers with red centres and white and it is usually have lesions of varying degree of severity. Especially in Asia-Pacific region and Africa due to spread of the disease has led to substantial damage to the livelihood of the fish farmers and fish resources [2]. It is hard to differentiate among fishes having EUS disease and ulcers. Red spot is not sufficient

© Springer Nature Switzerland AG 2020
O. Gervasi et al. (Eds.): ICCSA 2020, LNCS 12254, pp. 753–770, 2020.
https://doi.org/10.1007/978-3-030-58817-5_54

to differentiate [3–5]. Nevertheless by using image processing techniques and pattern recognition, it will be easy to recognize the EUS disease pattern of fish. Correct recognition will prevent the mortality of the fish. This paper proposed a new (modified) approach of feature extractor that is Enhanced Histogram of Oriented Gradient (EHOG) which extract the multiple features and provide more information and better accuracy by using the classification algorithm. The method of detecting the disease is divided into three steps i.e. pre-processing, resizing, normalization and then feature extraction to get the features after that classification will be done. After extracting the features it will be easy to classify the images. However The EHOG which is an enhanced feature extractor and it gives more enhanced and better results in every parameter.

1.1   Different Type of Features

The main task of feature extraction is to extract the relevant information. When the input data is too large and it takes too much time to process then it must have redundancy. It transform into reduced features that is named as feature vector. There are number of features as given below:-

Shape Features: For image content description shape is an important feature. The description of the size content cannot be defined exactly because it is difficult to measure the similarity between shapes. It has two parts one is contour based and another is region based. Here, Contour based is used for the boundary and region base is used for the whole image. As the dimensionality increases, the amount of training data increases. Moreover, there is an impetus to combine the features and to produce a feature vector as about shape & size and correlation between different features.

Edge and Boundary Features: It is a fundamental (basic) problem in image processing. In image processing, edges in the images have strong intensity and the quality of image is affected by the variations in intensity but the information will be preserved. The basic properties such as area, perimeter and shape can be measured easily only if the edges are identified accurately. In segmentation also the estimation of boundary edges are used.

Texture Feature: It is very significant (essential feature) property of image which helps in the process of retrieval. It maintains the information about the variation of the intensity, with the regular interval. The texture has the structure of the arrangement or repeated pattern of information. It is divided into two methods one is spatial and other is spectral texture. There are some pros and cons of it. In spatial it is easy to understand and can be extracted the information from any shape with losing the information but it is sensitive to noise. In spectral texture has less computational power and it is robust in nature but it need region of square image that can be of sufficient size.

The organisation of the paper is follows as: In Sect. 2, tells about the background and literature review of the related paper. Further, Sect. 3 discusses about the motivation why instant or correct detection of EUS disease is required today. Section 4, discusses about the basic algorithm of histogram of oriented gradient. Later, Sect. 5 discusses about the methodology which tells about general method of the process. Further, Sect. 6 discusses about the enhanced histogram of oriented gradient which is more efficient as compared to the basic Histogram of oriented gradient. In Sect. 7, discussion done about the classification with Neural Network algorithm and dataset. In Sect. 8 discussed about the analysis of our results. In last, this work is concluded with some interesting future scope.

2 Literature Review

The paper is based on the recognition [6] of the fish and it is a challenging task, it is based on the recognition of image using the coefficient correlation and then applied the HOG feature extractor then classified the fish images by using the SVM (Support Vector Machine). It is to detect the species of the fish on the boat of fishing. In which images were captured from boat cameras through various angles and that is to be used to prevent the endangered of fishing to fishes. The accuracy was 94% through the feature extractor which is HOG (Histogram of Oriented Gradient). The paper is based on the automated system [7] for the recognition of the images of color logo. In which color feature was used for recognition, for example, color moments and the feature extractor which had used Histogram of Oriented Gradients (HOG). In this, Classification of the logo images was done by using Support Vector Machine Classifier (SVM), i.e., the classifier used to recognize the logo image by Support Vector Machine (SVM). In which compared the HOG-SVM with other existing methods then the HOG-SVM approach was the fast in execution and easy in implementation and it gave 88.50% accuracy. In [8] authors focused the recognition of hand gesture using the different feature extraction techniques and classifier used is SVM. The proposed model was the hybrid of SIFT and HOG and classified through the SVM. In the age of computer the gesture of hand recognition is very important domain of the application of computer. The proposed model gave 97% of accuracy with the 10 gestures.

Further, in [9] authors proposed a method which automatically recognize the activity of human from the video stream using 'Histogram of Oriented Gradient (HOG) and classifier which is Probabilistic Neural network (PNN). The features of actions were extracted from input video frames. PCA was used for reduction of dimensionality. Experimentation was conducted on the KTH database and gave 89.8% accuracy for test set. The experimentation was implemented in MATLAB version 8.1.604 R2013a. The paper presented a novel method using PNN for action recognition and HOG features extractor [10] with PCA which for dimension reduction as the tool of feature extraction. This is for the applications of action recognition in fields like surveillance entertainment and healthcare systems. Further, in [11] authors presents a comparative study of the algorithm of matching, it define the efficiency level. In which FAST (Feature Accelerated Segment Test) algorithm is used and detects limited features and to the features was detected among the best one and detected features were with high contrast to the feature surroundings. The FAST algorithm works well with planar images and the fast too and the result came from the FAST in the matching efficiency 58.06%. Note that there are various attempts have been made in the previous decade with respect to this (discussed) problem, but none of approaches work efficiently. Further, some other mechanisms like Human Detection using Oriented

Gradients have been proposed [11, 12], also some other attempts have been made by many authors (in the past decade) in [10, 13–15].

In paper [16], author done an experimentation by ANN & SVM for the early detection of the lung cancer. In which ANN is ensemble with HOG for the prediction of lung cancer. Moreover it proposed a framework which has multiple biomarkers for the lung cancer and extracted the features from the Nucleosides sequences. HOG & LBP (Linear binary pattern) used to extract the features. ANN ensemble with ANN and gave 95.90% accuracy.

In paper [17] the author described the co-occurrence Histogram of oriented gradient (CO-HOG) that has been proposed to recognize the text in the scenes and compared with HOG (Histogram of oriented gradient). The weighted voting scheme has been used for character recognition in scene. The accuracy of proposed method was 80.6% and HOG with SVM classifier was 94.890%.

In summary, this section discuss about the performance or accuracy from different methods or techniques with different feature extractor and model. Now, next section will deal with the motivation why it is necessary to correct detection of EUS disease and what is the cause of increasing the mortality of the EUS fish disease.

3 Motivation

Fish is the livelihood of millions of people. Epizootic Ulcerative Syndrome (EUS) is one of the most serious aquatic diseases [18]. High mortality and fish rejection cause high losses to fish farmers and fishermen and the next concern is about the health due to the presence of ugly lesions and also abridged productivity of all susceptible fish species [19, 20]. The fish farmer's faced different restrictions when fish disease outbreaks occur in their farms.

There are number of factors which are the cause of fish mortality or outbreak, few reasons are listed here as:

- Lack of Knowledge on Treatment.
- Lack of Knowledge of fish disease.
- Lack of advisory services from government and non-government organization.
- Lack of Training Facility about fish disease treatment.

The above are the general factors for the mortality of fish.

4 Histogram of Oriented Gradient (HOG)

The Histogram of Oriented Gradients (HOG) is a feature extraction method which is used for the image classification [21], it computes the local gradient and magnitude with the overlapping of blocks. It focuses on the shape and size. It is for the application of the detection of person and it is focussed on where the feature in the image is quite large. Many methods or approaches believe on the Gaussian filtering methods but the HOG does not rely on the filtering Methods [22, 23].

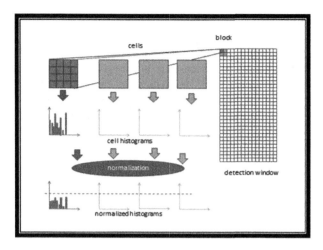

Fig. 1. Histogram feature extraction [16]

The Fig. 1 shows the image is divided into cells and then combine into block. The histogram shown in every block.

The algorithm works as follows:-

- Calculate the gradient of X and Y variable of each pixel of image.
- Divide the cell and after that combine it into the block.
- Calculate the gradient magnitude and direction with respect to the angle of each pixel of the image.
- Each cell is of specific dimension or cell size as it depending upon the gradient angle, allocate the gradient magnitude in predefined bin with the range of 20° only if the number of the bins will be 9.
- It should be as the range of 0 to 20, 20 to 40, 40 to 60, etc., and for those angles which are not in the centre of the bin, for example, 10, 30, 50, 70, etc. in the traditional approach HOG approach if the gradient with the angle 15° which is closer to the bin 1 and then 75% of its gradient will allocated to the bin 1 and 25% to the bin 2 [24, 25].
- In every cell of histogram of oriented gradient obtained with number of bins and the magnitude of every bin by calculate the magnitude of every bin by calculating the corresponding pixel of gradient and adding the interpolated gradient magnitude of all corresponding pixel.
- The cell can be group to form a block and the magnitudes of all histogram are normalized within the block.

Hence this section discuss about the basic algorithm of Histogram of oriented gradient, next section will discuss about the methodology about the general concept of classification.

5 Methodology

In methodology, the general concept of the classification is to extract the features from the feature Extractor after the pre-processing. In pre-processing, the number of the steps to be cover, i.e., binirization [26], Normalization etc. After that select the feature extractor which extract the features as useful information although the quality of the information depends on the feature extractor and then classify the EUS and Non-EUS through classification algorithm.

Fig. 2. Block diagram of methodology

The Fig. 2 shows the steps of methodology

Step 1: Extraction: The features from the feature extractor which extracts the features to extract the information after the pre-processing.
Step 2: Selection: After extracting the features then select the selected features from the feature extractor.
Step 3: Classification: Each object is represented by a feature vector for training and testing. In the problem of image classification, this feature vector is usually obtained using pixel-based method [27]. In the paper, have applied the feature extraction HOG from vector by applying the proposed feature extractor a feature vector V1 is obtained, then applied PCA (Principal Component Analysis) to the feature vector and form a new vector which is V2 as it has the lower dimensionality then apply the classification algorithm which is Neural Network.

Hence, this section discusses methodology. Next section discusses about modified feature extractor, i.e., Enhanced Histogram of Oriented Gradient (EHOG) in detail with a flow chart.

6 Proposed Feature Extractor (EHOG)

In the proposed methodology a modified approach which is Enhanced Histogram of Oriented Gradient as a new efficient feature extractor. It is expected to have better accuracy performance for EUS detection. It helps to enhance the features and improve the accuracy as compared to the other algorithms.

The flow chart of Modified Feature Extractor explain below:-

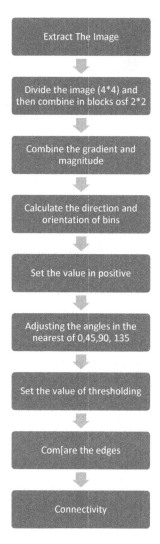

Fig. 3. Flow chart for enhanced histogram of gradient

The Fig. 3 explains the method to extract the features of EUS disease image through EHOG (Enhanced Histogram of Gradient).

Step 1: Divide the image into 4*4 for processing and then combine into 2*2 block with overlapping of blocks because in the paper taking the block size 2*2 and cell size 4*4 and it can be vary. Calculate the Block per image as showed in figure below.

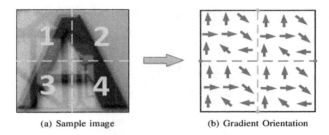

(a) Sample image   (b) Gradient Orientation

Fig. 4. a) Image divide into four parts [17] b) orientation of gradient [17]

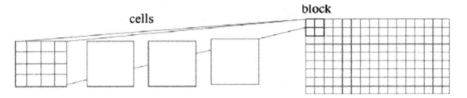

Fig. 5. Cell divided into blocks

In Fig. 4 and 5 Image is divided into four parts and cell is divided into blocks.

Calculation to find block per image: - Block per Image = Absolute value ((size (I)/cell size) Block size)/(Block size-block overlap) + 1).

The Fig. 3 explains the method to extract the features of EUS disease image through EHOG (Enhanced Histogram of Gradient)

e.g. B = Abs ((50*50)/4*4)2*2)/(2*2 − 1*1) + 1) (In case size of image is 50*50, then there will be 192 blocks per image) where I = Image.

Step 2:- After that calculate the magnitude and gradient while calculating the gradient in terms of X and Y direction, gradient will vary according to the values.

Step 3:- Calculate the orientation and direction of bins while calculating the theta. (Orientation is divided into bins).

Note:- If alpha $\geq$ 0 then Value is equal to Alpha if Alpha < 0 then Alpha = Alpha + 360, i.e., Alpha < 0 then b = 360 + Alpha where alpha is for angle then adjusting the angle into 0, 45, 90, 135°

Step 4:- Set the value of thresholding if the value less than T_{Low} then it is set to 0 and if the value greater than T_{high} then it is set to 1, all the values will be in the 0 and 1 after converting it into 0 and 1 according to the range then connect and compare the edges or corners.

6.1   Algorithm of Enhanced Histogram of Oriented Gradient (EHOG)

- Extract the EUS image.
- Divide the image into cells of size 4*4 and then combine into blocks 2*2

- After that compute the gradient and find the magnitude

$$\text{Gradient Magnitude} = \sqrt{g_x^2 + g_y^2} \tag{1}$$

$$\text{Gradient Direction} - \theta = tan^{-1}\left[\frac{g_y}{g_x}\right] \tag{2}$$

Derivate with respect to gradient in the X direction - Derivative with respect to gradient in the Y direction (refer Eq. 1 and 2)

- Calculate the directions and orientations of bins.
- For $[-180,180]$ to $[0,360]$ if alpha $\geq$ 0 then Value is equal to Alpha if Alpha < 0 then Alpha + 360, i.e., Alpha < 0 then b = 360 + Alpha
- Adjusting direction nearest to 0, 45, 95 and 135°, i.e., if the angle is nearer to 45 then it comes in the 45°. //**All the value should set in positive.**
- Set the value of thresholding, i.e., T_{Low}- 0.075, T_{high}- 0.175.
- Calculate the 8-Connected Blocks.
- Calculate the edges or corner

Hence this section discuss about the Modified feature extractor which is Enhanced Histogram of Oriented Gradient (EHOG). Next section will discuss about the Classification and Confusion Matrix.

7 Classification

For classification divide the dataset into two parts one is training set and another is testing data set then apply the neural network algorithm which classify the dataset into EUS fish image and Non-EUS fish image.

Neural Network
Neural Network is organized in layers all layers are connected with each other with neurons [28]. Input will be given to the input layer or patterns are recognize through the input layer but the actual processing is done through hidden layer with the weights and hidden layer is connected with output and output layer gives output.

Figure 6 shows that layer 1 is the input neurons, all the neurons are interconnected with hidden layer and then goes to the output.

Different feature extractor have been applied with Neural Network algorithm in the paper and calculate the values or analyse the value after classification.

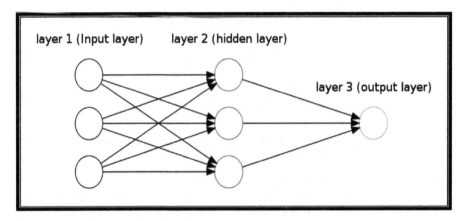

Fig. 6. Neural network

7.1 Sample of Training and Testing Dataset

The sample of "EUS (Epizootic Ulcerative Syndrome)" infected fish used in experimentation are the real images and collected from "(NBFGR, Lucknow) and ICAR-Central Inland Fisheries Research Institute (CIFRI), Kolkata".

Figure 7 shows the images of EUS (Epizotical Ulcerative syndrome) infected disease.

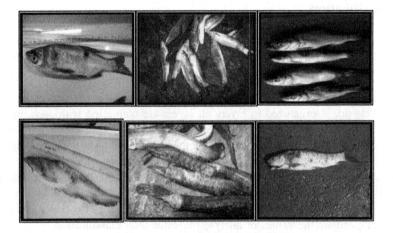

Fig. 7. Sample of training dataset (EUS Infected Fish) [16]

Classify the EUS and Non-EUS infected fishes through Neural network algorithm. The dataset is divided into training set which is Ttraining and testing set which is Ttesting. Portioning the data set into 70% training, 15% validation, and 15% testing. The data training set was used to train the network while the validation set was used to measure the error and the network training stops, when the error starts to increase for the validation dataset. Furthermore, to get the better results, train the neural network many times and get the average of classification accuracy. In which 10 cross validation has been used.

7.2 Confusion Matrix

Confusion Matrix gives the prediction results on classification. In data set, Total number of 80 images taken for training and testing of EUS and Non- EUS images. The images have been collected from CIFRI-Kolkata (research institute of fish) and NBFGR, Lucknow (research institute of fish disease). While classification the confusion matrix has created to find out the positive and negative results with respect to the actual and predicted class.

In Fig. 8 shows about the general confusion Matrix which help in to calculate number of parameter with respect to positive and negative values of True and False.

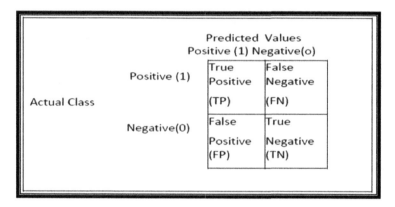

Fig. 8. Confusion matrix [27]

7.3 Confusion Matrix of EHOG with Neural Network Algorithm

Neural Network is used to classify the data and Enhanced Histogram of oriented gradient feature extraction has been used with PCA (principal of component analysis). It is used for the dimensionally reduction.

In Fig. 9 it is shown that how many images are correctly classified and how many are not correctly classified. It shows the accuracy also which is 98.8%. The first of the two diagonal cells which is in green color shows the number of correct classification by the trained model e.g. 39 fish images are correctly classified as EUS images that corresponds to 48.8% of total 80 images of fish. Similarly 40 fishes are correctly classified as Non-EUS image in diagonal opposite cell (green color in row 2). This corresponds to 50.0% of fishes. In fish column red colour cell one fish image which is Non-EUS, incorrectly classified as EUS and corresponds to 1.3% from total number of fishes images. In red color cell second column, zero number of the EUS images classified incorrectly as Non-EUS and this corresponds to 0.0% from total number of

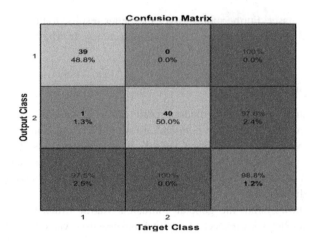

Fig. 9. Confusion matrix of EHOG-PCA-NN (Color figure online)

fish images. Out of 40 fish images in the first column EUS fish images prediction is 97.5% is correct and 2.5% is wrong. In second column last row out of 40 number of images. Non -EUS image prediction is 100% correct and 0.0% is wrong. In first row out of 39 EUS fish images 100% are correctly predicted as EUS and 0.0% is predicted as Non-EUS. In second row out of 41 Non-EUS images, 97.6% is correctly classified as Non-EUS and 2.4% is classified as EUS.

8   Performance Analysis

The Proposed feature extractor which is Enhanced Histogram of Oriented Gradient compared with the other feature extractor in terms of different parameters [29, 30] and it finds that the EHOG is better in every parameter as compared to the others according to analysis shows in the paper.

8.1   Analysis Performance Through Different Parameter

There are different parameters have been taken to compare the different feature extractor:

1) Accuracy
2) Precession
3) Recall
4) Specificity.

- **Calculation of Every Parameter**

1) **Accuracy:-** The accuracy rate can be calculated by the formula.

$$\text{Accuracy}: \quad \frac{TP + TN}{TP + FP + FN + TN} \tag{3}$$

Where TP = True Positive, TN = True Negative, FN = False Negative and FP = False Positive.

a) Positive (P): It observed that it is positive (e.g., it is a fish)
b) Negative (N): It observed that it is not positive (not a fish)
c) True Positive (TP): It is observed that it is positive, and it is predicted to be positive.
d) False Negative (FN): It is observed that it is positive, but it is predicted as negative.
e) True Negative (TN): It is observed that it is negative and it is predicted as negative.
f) False Positive (FP): It is observed that it is negative and it is predicted as positive.

   e.g. Taking the example of confusion matrix of EHOG-PCA-NN (Fig. 9) to find the accuracy refer formula no 3:

$$\text{Accuracy:-} \quad \frac{30 + 40}{80} = 98.8\% \tag{4}$$

2) **Precision:-** It is defined as the total number of correctly classified example of positives is divided by total number of positive predicted.

$$\text{Precision:-} \quad \frac{TP}{TP + FP} \tag{5}$$

   e.g. Taking the example of confusion matrix of EHOG-PCA-NN (Fig. 9) to find the Precision refer formula no 5:

$$\text{Precision:-} \quad \frac{39}{39 + 1} = 97.5\% \tag{6}$$

3) **Recall:-** It is defined as the correctly positive classified samples or examples is divided by True positive samples/examples

$$\text{Recall-} \quad \frac{TP}{TP + FN} \tag{7}$$

e.g. Taking the example of confusion matrix of EHOG-PCA-NN (Fig. 9) to find the Recall refer formula no 7:

$$\text{Recall-} \quad \frac{39}{39 + 0} = 100\% \tag{8}$$

Sensitivity/True Positive Rate: It is defined as the correctly positive Classified Samples/examples is divided by the True Positive Samples/examples.
The calculation is same as calculated in recall.

$$\text{Sensitivity-} \quad \frac{TP}{TP+FN} \tag{9}$$

4) **Specificity**: It is defined as the Specificity which is calculated as the number of correct negative predictions divided by the total number of negatives.

$$\text{Specificity-} \quad \frac{TN}{FP+TN} \tag{10}$$

$$1 - \text{specificity/False Positive Rate} \quad \frac{TN}{FP+TN} \tag{11}$$

e.g. Taking the example of confusion matrix of EHOG-PCA-NN (Fig. 9) to find the Specificity refer formula no 10:

$$\text{Specificity-} \quad \frac{40}{1+40} \quad = 97.5\% \tag{12}$$

While classification of dataset through different feature extractor with different parameters have been calculated with the help of confusion matrix.

• **Calculation of Error Rate**

It is defined as the "number of incorrect predictions" that is divided by the "total number of the dataset".

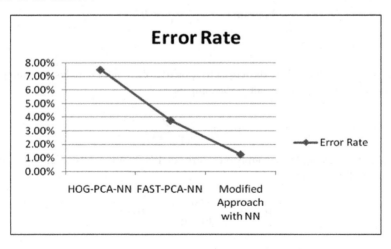

Fig. 10. Error rate between different techniques

In the above figure shows that the error rate in different Techniques with different Feature Extractor and that can be calculated by the Number of Incorrect Predictions divided by Total number of dataset.

$$\text{Error Rate:-} \quad \frac{FP + FN}{P + N} \tag{13}$$

Table 1. Error rate of different techniques

S. no	Technique/methods	Error rate
1	HOG-PCA-NN	7.5%
2	FAST-PCA-NN	3.75%
3	EHOG/modified approach with NN	1.25%

From the above Table 1 conclude that the EHOG/Modified Technique has less error rate as compared to other Techniques.

8.2 Analysis of Different Approaches with Different Parameters

In Table 1 shows the results analysis with different feature extractor with different parameters that have been calculated through confusion matrix. Confusion matrix will be vary with techniques. For classification neural network has been used with every feature extractor. However PCA (principal component analysis) has been used for dimensionality reduction.

Table 2. Analysis of Different Approaches with Different Parameters

Different approaches	Parameters				
	Accuracy	Specificity	Sensitivity	Precision	Recall
HOG-PCA-NN	92.5%	92.80%	92.10%	92.10%	92.10%
FAST-PCA-NN	96.3%	97.5%	97.3%	96.3%	94.3%
EHOG-PCA-NN	98.7%	100%	97.5%	100%	97.5%

Table 2 shows that the analysis of different parameters and the proposed feature extractor (EHOG) with the classifier which is Neural Network (NN) gives better result in every parameter. In terms of Accuracy (EHOG-PCA-NN) gives 98.7%, FAST-PCA-NN gives 96.3%, HOG-PCA-NN gives 92.5%. In precession (EHOG) gives 100%, FAST-PCA-NN gives 97.3%, HOG-PCA-NN gives 92.1%, In Recall (EHOGPCA-NN) gives 97.5%, FAST-PCA-NN gives 94.3%, HOGPCA-NN gives 92.5%, In Sensitivity(EHOG-PCA-NN) gives 97.5%, FAST-PCA-NN gives 97.3% and HOG-PCA-NN gives 92.10%. In specificity (EHOG-PCA-NN) gives 100%, FAST-PCA- NN gives 97.5%, HOG-PCA-NN gives 92.8%.

8.3   Analysis of F-Measure in Different Approaches

The F1 score measure the performance of the model and it is the harmonic average of the recall and the best value for the precision and recall is 1 and worst is 0.

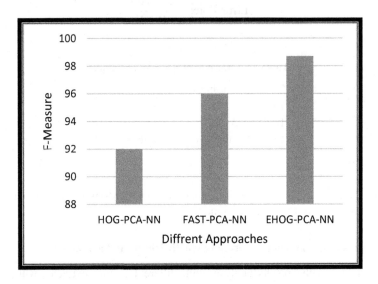

Fig. 11. Analysis of F-measure in different approaches

The Fig. 10 shows that the measure of a test's accuracy. It considers both the recall' r' and precision 'p' of the test to compute the test accuracy: p is the number of positive corrected results divided by the number of all positive results returned by the classifier, and r is the number of positive corrected results divided by the number of all relevant samples and sample should be considered as positive.

$$F1 = 2 * \frac{\text{Precision} * \text{recall}}{\text{Precision} + \text{recall}} \tag{14}$$

e.g. Taking the example of confusion matrix of EHOG-PCA-NN (Fig. 9) to find the F1 refer formula no. 14 (Table 2).

$$\text{Precision} = 97.5\% \qquad \text{Recall} = 100\%$$
$$F_1 = 2 * \frac{97.5 * 100}{97.5 + 100} = 98.73\% \tag{15}$$

Hence, this section discusses simulation results with our proposed algorithms (discussed in Sect. 8). Also, it discuss the comparison/performance of our proposed algorithm with other existing work. Next section will conclude this work in brief with some future enhancements.

9 Conclusion

In this work proposed an Enhanced Histogram of Oriented Gradient (EHOG) for extraction of EUS (Epizootic ulcerative syndrome) features. The performance comparison of proposed EHOG with Neural Network gives better result in detection of EUS disease as compared to other feature extractor with different parameters as experimentation done in the paper. In near future, Internet of Thing (IoT) will be used in automated fish farming, agriculture in many other sectors for increasing productivity. Moreover Blockchain can also be used for real-time surveillance in the farming of the fish. EHOG with Neural Network can also be applied on large number of dataset in future. However other techniques or algorithm of deep learning can be used.

Acknowledgment. The EUS disease images of fish have been collected from National Bureau of Fish Genetic Resources (NBFGR, Lucknow) and ICAR-Central Inland Fisheries Research Institute (CIFRI), Kolkata. Thanks to Dr. A.K Sahoo (CIFRI, Kolkata) and Dr. P.K Pradhan (NBFGR, Lucknow).

References

1. kumar Pagrut, N., Ganguly, S., Jaiswal, V., Singh, C.: An overview on epizootic ulcerative syndrome of fishes in India: a comprehensive report. J. Entomol. Zool. Stud. **11**(4), 1941–1943 (2017)
2. Suresh, A.J., Asha, P.: Human action recognition in video using histogram of oriented gradient (HOG) features and probabilistic neural network (PNN). Int. J. Innov. Res. Comput. Commun. Eng. **4**(7), 13255–13263 (2016)
3. Burge, C.A., et al.: Climate change influences on marine infectious diseases: implications for management and society. Ann. Rev. Mar. Sci. **6**, 249–277 (2014)
4. Lafferty, K.D., et al.: Infectious diseases affect marine fisheries and aquaculture economics. Ann. Rev. Mar. Sci. **7**, 471–496 (2015)
5. Malik, S., Kumar, T., Sahoo, A.K.: Image processing techniques for identification of fish disease. In: IEEE 2nd International Conference on Signal and Image Processing (ICSIP), pp. 55–59 (2017)
6. Antony Seba1, P., Rama Subbu Laskhmi, S., Umamaheswari, P.: Fish recognition based on HOG feature extraction using SVM prediction. Int. J. Adv. Res. Comput. Commun. Eng. **6** (5), 296–299 (2017)
7. Ansari, F.J.: Hand gesture recognition using fusion of SIFT and HoG with SVM as a classifier. Int. J. Eng. Technol. Sci. Res. IJETSR **4**(9), 206–210 (2017)
8. Maity, U., Mukherjee, J.: Automated color logo recognition technique using color and hog features. Int. J. Comput. Appl. **170**(2), 38–41 (2017)
9. Khan, H.A.: MCS HOG features and SVM based handwritten digit recognition system. J. Intell. Learn. Syst. Appl. **9**(2), 21–33 (2017)
10. Babri, U.M., Tanvir, M., Khurshid, K.: Feature based correspondence: a comparative study on image matching algorithms. Int. J. Adv. Comput. Sci. Appl. **7**(3), 206–210 (2016)
11. Dalal, N., Triggs, B., Schmid, C.: Human detection using oriented histograms of flow and appearance. In: ECCV 2006, pp. 428–441 (2010)

12. Dalal, N., Triggs, B.: Histograms of oriented gradients for human detection. In: Proceedings of the IEEE Computer Society Conference on Computer Vision and Pattern Recognition (CVPR 2005), pp. 886–893 (2005)

13. Fischler, M.A., Bolles, R.C.: Random sample consensus: a paradigm for model fitting with applications to image analysis and automated cartography. Commun. ACM **24**(6), 381–395 (1981)

14. Haiam, A., Abdul-Azim, H.A.: Human action recognition using trajectory based representation. Egypt. Inform. J. **16**(2), 187–198 (2015)

15. Pooja, G., Revansiddappa, S.K.: Abnormal activity detection using HOG features and SVM classifier. Int. J. Adv. Res. Electr. Electron. Instrum. Eng. **5**(4), 381–395 (2016)

16. Adetiba, E., Olugbara, O.O.: Lung cancer prediction using neural network ensemble with histogram of oriented gradient genomic features. Sci. J. **2015**, 1–17 (2015)

17. Tian, S., Lu, S., Su, B., Tan, C.L.: Scene text recognition using co-occurrence of histogram of oriented gradients. In: Proceedings of the 2013 12th International Conference on Document Analysis and Recognition, Washington, DC, USA, pp. 912–916 (2013)

18. Bagum, N., Monir, M.S.: Present status of fish disease and economic losses due to incidence of disease in rural freshwater aquaculture. J. Innov. Dev. Strateg. (JIDS) **7**(3), 48–53 (2013)

19. Lyubchenko, V., Matarneh, R., Kobylin, O.: Digital image processing techniques for detection and diagnosis of fish diseases. Int. J. Adv. Res. Comput. Sci. Softw. Eng. **6**(7), 79–83 (2016)

20. Kumar, V., Roy, S., Meena, D.K., Sarkar, U.K.: Application of probiotics in shrimp aquaculture: importance, mechanisms of action, and methods of administration. Rev. Fish. Sci. Aquac. **24**(4), 342–368 (2016)

21. Malik, S., Kumar, T., Sahoo, A.K.: A novel approach to fish disease diagnostic system based on machine learning. Adv. Image Video Process. **5**(1), 49–57 (2017)

22. ShavetaMalik, T.K.: Various edge detection techniques on different categories of fish. Int. J. Comput. Appl. **135**(7), 6–11 (2016)

23. Malik, S., Kumar, T., Sahoo, A.K.: Fish disease detection using HOG and FAST feature descriptor. Int. J. Comput. Sci. Inf. Secur. (IJCSIS) **15**(5), 216–221 (2017)

24. Cai, Z., Yu, P., Liang, Y., Lin, B., Huang, H.: SVM-KNN algorithm for image classification based on enhanced HOG feature. In: Proceedings of the International Conference on Intelligent systems and Image Processing (2016)

25. Stella, X.A., Sujatha, N.: Performance analysis of GFE, HOG and LBP feature extraction techniques using kNN classifier for oral cancer detection. J. Netw. Commun. Emerg. **6**(7), 50–56 (2016)

26. Niblack, W.: An Introduction to Digital Image Processing. Strandberg Publishing Company (1985)

27. Antony Seba, P., et al.: Fish recognition based on HOG feature extraction using SVM prediction. Int. J. Adv. Res. Comput. Commun. Eng. **6**(5), 296–299 (2017)

28. Santra, A.K., Christy, C.J.: Genetic algorithm and confusion matrix for document clustering. IJCSI Int. J. Comput. Sci. Issues **9**(1), 322 (2012)

29. Powers, D.M.W.: Evaluation: from precision, recall and F-measure to ROC: informedness, markendness & correlation. J. Mach. Learn. Technol. **2**(1), 37–63 (2011)

30. Lopes, J.N.S., Gonçalves, A.N.A., Fujimoto, R.Y., Carvalho, J.C.C.: Diagnosis of fish diseases using artificial neural networks. IJCSI Int. J. Comput. Sci. Issues **8**(6), 68–73 (2011)

Inspecting Data Using Natural Language Queries

Franscesca Bacci, Federico Maria Cau, and Lucio Davide Spano[(✉)]

Department of Mathematics and Computer Science,
University of Cagliari, Cagliari, Italy
davide.spano@unica.it

Abstract. In this paper, we discuss a simple architecture for supporting the inspection of a generic dataset using natural language queries.
We show how to integrate modern Artificial Intelligence libraries in the
system and how to derive chart visualization out of the user's intent. The
result is a lightweight architecture for supporting such natural language
queries in web-based visualization tools. Finally, we report on the user
evaluation of the interface, showing a good acceptance and effectiveness
of the proposed approach.

Keywords: Data visualization · Natural language interaction ·
Artificial Intelligence · Human computer interaction

1 Introduction

The interfaces for Information Visualization (InfoVis) usually exploit a direct
manipulation paradigm for selecting, filtering and inspecting data. The graphical
modality supports the trial and error and the user learns and drives conclusions
out the data during the inspection process. The paradigm applies also to the
visualization *construction*, supporting the user in selecting which attributes to
visualize and their layout. Such operations in the graphical modality are quite
tedious and repetitive, so the research focused on exploiting Natural Language
(NL) queries for building visualizations. Requests in NL are quick to express
and they proved quite easy to create for simple queries [6]. Different results
are available in the literature (see Sect. 2), but they all require complex NL
analysis techniques whose application effort often exceeds the benefits in most
visualization tools. In this paper, we propose a simple architecture for supporting
NL queries in visualization tools exploiting a standard chatbot API. Reducing
the development complexity we aim at a widespread inclusion of NL queries in
InfoVis tools.

The work has been founded by the AI4fit project (POR-FSER Sardegna 2014–2020,
CUP: F25D17000200008).

© Springer Nature Switzerland AG 2020
O. Gervasi et al. (Eds.): ICCSA 2020, LNCS 12254, pp. 771–782, 2020.
https://doi.org/10.1007/978-3-030-58817-5_55

2   Related Work

The quest for NL queries on databases has a history [6], difficult to summarise entirely here. We will focus on the work that most influenced our system design. Eviza [8] proposes a solution for enabling users to interact with existing visualizations using NL queries. Through open-ended questions, the user enhances the current visualization, tailoring it for specific purposes. The solution exploits a probabilistic grammar designed for the tool and finite state machines for driving the conversation. Evizeon [4] further develops the abilities of the previous system introducing multimodal conversations with the user. The system resolves the language ambiguities in the user's query through further questions and/or picking values in the current visualization. Once the system reaches a sufficient comprehension of the current request, creates or updates the visualization.

Recently, Setlur et al. [9] discussed a system for resolving partial utterances through syntactic and semantic constraints. They construct a heuristic for creating a manageable solution space and apply logical ranking for selecting the best candidate. Such inference allows the user to express the query in a much more natural way, including ambiguities and ellipsis that are managed by the system.

FlowSense [11] is a natural language interface that utilizes the latest natural language processing techniques to assist dataflow diagram construction. The system employs a semantic parser that expands the variables in the grammar to match the input query, exploiting special utterance tagging and placeholders to support progressive construction of dataflow diagrams that deal with various types of datasets.

Siwei Fu et al. propose Quda [3], a dataset which helps in the design of visualization-oriented natural language interfaces (V-NLIs). In this work, they present the design and implementation of a V-NLI prototype, called FreeNLI, that uses a language parser to process the query combined with a pool of design rules to provide useful charts and tables to the end-user.

Saktheeswaran et al. [7] conducted a qualitative user study in the context of a network visualization tool using a modified version of the Orko system [10], enhancing the multimodal aspect of the interface and types of interaction.

The system we propose leverages on different ideas proposed in this field. In opposition to more complex solutions, it exploits a general-purpose chatbot library for the natural language interpretation and relies on a partially automatic training, which simplifies the adoption of NL for performing queries. Besides, it splits complex requests into sub-queries, allowing the user to iteratively modify and delete them for obtaining the desired result. Finally, we combine the graphical and the NL modality for managing the data filtering.

3   System Architecture

In this section, we discuss the overall system architecture, describing the different components that cooperate for producing the chart visualization starting from an NL query. Figure 1 depicts the high-level solution components. The user, through

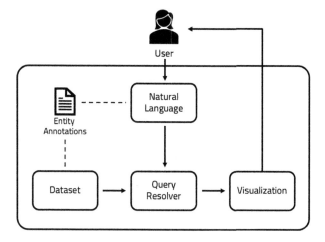

Fig. 1. Overall system architecture

a web user interface, inserts the query in a text field. The *Natural Language* component analyses the text for interpreting the user's intent. It takes as input the query and returns an object describing the entities involved and how the user wants to visualize them (the intent). This component relies on an Artificial Intelligence (AI) library for the natural language processing, Wit.ai[1]. The library requires training for understanding properly the specific queries in the current domain. In our case, the training has two levels of abstraction. At the higher level, we have the samples teaching the AI to recognize the intents for asking a specific visualization, such as *showing, ordering, correlating* etc. The wording used for requesting the visualization does not depend on the current domain or dataset, so they can be reused for different applications.

To build a proper visualization, the AI must recognize also the entities involved. Their names strongly depend on the considered dataset. Since seldom an entity identifier in a dataset is the name people would use for addressing it, we included an *Entity Annotation* file that maps the entities to one or more friendly names. It includes also other useful metadata, such as the abstract data type associated with each attribute (e.g., date, categorical, ordinal or quantitative) or human-readable labels for their values. We use the annotation file for generating some annotated queries in natural language for training the AI library on the four templates we introduce in Sect. 4. In this way, we have auto-generated samples exploiting the entities involved in a particular dataset, without requesting developers to manually perform the training. However, they can still add fine-tuned NL queries to the generated set. For instance, Wit.ai notifies developers when it is not able to correctly understand a user's sentence. In such a case, developers will need to enter the label manually.

---

[1] https://wit.ai/.

Fig. 2. Wit.ai training phase

At runtime, when the *Natural Language* component correctly identified the user's intent and the involved entities, the *Query Resolver* component reads, filters and sorts the required data from the *Dataset*, preparing them for the *Visualization* component, which generates the graphic rendering according to the user's intent. The current implementation exploits *Python* libraries for the data manipulation and D3.js[2] for the visualization.

3.1 Wit.ai Training

We will now see an example of how we can train Wit.ai to recognize the meaning of a sentence. Suppose we want to teach the Wit.ai engine how to interpret the clause *"Show me the best athletes"*: we will insert the latter in the *Understanding* tab of the engine making sure that it learns to associate the word *"best"* as a tag. Once this new behavior is learned, we will insert once more the sentence seen above and Wit.ai will return an intent with value *"best"* as shown in Fig. 2.

After the completion of the training step, we will query the tool through the Django framework via Python typing the previous sentence in the search bar. As a response, Wit.ai will return a JSON object whose structure is shown in Fig. 3.

On the Python side, we will check the *value* field of the intent object to understand what type of query to perform on the dataset. In this case, the behaviour of the Python code will create a query that will filter the dataset by selecting the athletes who have the highest average score and the corresponding unique code, ordering them in descending order. With the values obtained, we will draw through D3 the appropriate chart for the type of query, which in this case is the bar chart: we will insert the athlete code in the ordinates and the average of the marks of each in the abscissas, as shown in Fig. 4. Meanwhile, taking as an example the statement *"order the athletes' ratings"*, the training procedure will be slightly different: we will set the word "order" as intent and the word *"ratings"* as an entity to get the athletes ratings. So again we have only one intent in the JSON object and also an entity to check, with the resulting visualization shown in Fig. 6.

In general, the intent is controlled first and then the various entities in order.

---

[2] https://d3js.org/.

```
{
    '_text': 'mostra i migliori atleti',
    'outcomes': [
        {
            'confidence': None,
            'intent': 'default_intent',
            '_text': 'mostra i migliori atleti',
            'entities': {
                'intent': [
                    {
                        'confidence': 0.99984855184298,
                        'value': 'best'
                    }
                ]
            }
        }
    ]
}
```

Fig. 3. Resulting JSON file from the query.

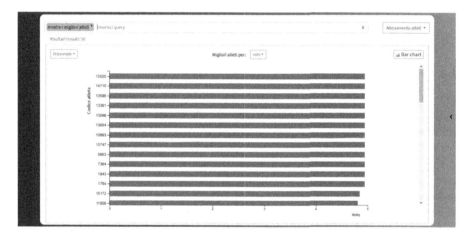

Fig. 4. Showing the best athletes ordered by ranking

4   Querying Datasets in Natural Language

In this section, we discuss different sample queries and how the proposed tool manages it. We use a running workout dataset, which contains different training sessions by both professional and amateur running athletes [2]. Each session includes the athlete's identifier, his/her age, the session date, the calories spent, the pace, the beats per minute and a 1 to 5 performance rating. A possible usage scenario for the following examples is that of a coach that inspects the athlete's performances for providing guidance.

At the beginning of the interaction, the interface shows a simple search bar waiting for the user's query. When the user confirms his/her input, the tool displays the generated visualization. Besides, it includes a button for showing and hiding the list of the data attributes in the dataset. The search bar is provided with an autocomplete function, which shows suggestions for the current query,

Fig. 5. Subqueries visualization

according to the templates used for training the AI component. As usual, the tool displays the autocompletion in a drop-down menu under the search bar. In addition, the tool splits the user's input into subqueries, i.e. parts of the same query that the user can interactively modify fir reaching the desired visualization. Subqueries separate the main user's intent (such as e.g., showing the athletes' rating) from aggregation and/or ordering functions. Figure 5 shows how the tool displays subqueries, using boxes grouping the input string. Each one has a button for removing the subquery and updating the visualization accordingly. In addition, the values of categorical attributes are displayed as drop-down menus for rapidly changing the ordering or grouping criterion.

4.1 Single Queries

The simplest query supported in the tool is a request for visualizing an entity in the dataset. The user requests such visualizations through a *show* intent, i.e. using the verb show or a synonym for expressing the command (e.g., display, draw etc.). Single queries may also include a request for ordering the values, both in the intent (*order* or synonyms) or as a subquery. A sample natural language query of a simple query is the *"Show me the ratings"* for displaying the rating of each workout in the dataset. The user can ask for ordering in two different ways: directly on the intent (e.g., *Order the athletes' ratings*) or through a subquery (e.g., *Show me the ratings in order*). In both cases, the tool will show the bar chart in Fig. 6, which is the default chart for numeric attributes. Categorical ones use the same chart, but they report the frequency distribution.

The visualization shows different interactive widgets that help the user in refining the initial query. On the top-left corner, the interface shows a button for changing the ordering (ascending or descending) and the orientation of the bar chart (vertical or horizontal). At the bottom, it shows a slider for filtering the bars according to the attribute value (in this case, the performance rating).

4.2 Grouping Queries

The second category of queries allows the user to aggregate the entries in the dataset according to the value of one attribute. Grouping queries work on categories, numerical and date attributes. In the latter case, the system requires the size of the discretization bucket, whose default are included in the annotation file.

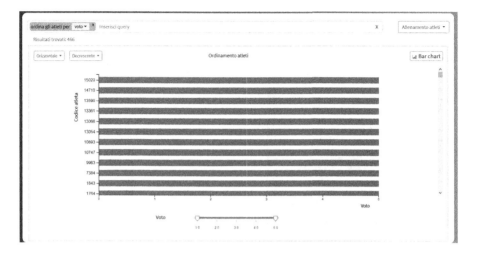

Fig. 6. A sample single query: ordering the athlete's ranking

There are two visualization templates for the grouping queries. The first one works for categorical or numerical attributes and allows the user to visualize the relative occurrence of a given category or the percentage of samples contained into a given bucket. A sample natural language query corresponding to this template is *"Group workouts by calories"*. The *group* intent and its synonyms request the aggregation, while the name of the involved entity bounds the considered query to the first template since calories are a numeric attribute in our dataset. Figure 7 shows the resulting pie chart, using buckets of 300 calories.

The second template for the grouping queries exploits a date (or time) attribute for the aggregation. In this case, the resulting visualization shows the trend of a numerical attribute over time. The user may set the interval directly in the query, or the system may use the default in the annotation file. A sample natural language query for this template is "Show me the login trend by month" or "Group the login by month". In this case, the user specifies an aggregation or a generic intent, but we recognize the request relying on the time unit (a month in our example, but it may be a day, week, year etc.). Figure 8 shows the resulting visualization for the sample query. The system uses a line plot for better displaying the overall trend. Besides, below the graph, the system displays the fields for filtering the plot by date.

4.3 Correlation Queries

Another category of queries available in the system shows the correlation between two attributes. As indicated by the name, a correlation query shows a possible relation between the two attributes through a scatterplot. A sample natural language query for this template is "Show me the workout distribution on calories and duration". In this case, the user specifies either an ordering or a generic

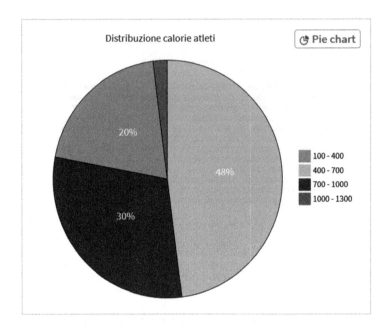

Fig. 7. Sample grouping query on a numeric attribute

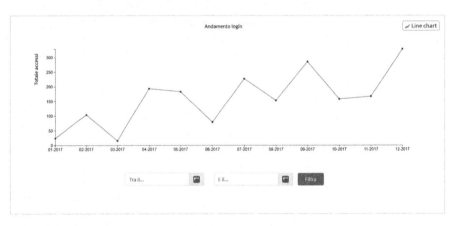

Fig. 8. Sample grouping query showing a trend over time

intent, but we recognize the correlation request relying on the specification of two different attributes for ordering the entries. Figure 9 shows the resulting plot.

4.4   Composite Queries

The tool supports the composition of the different query templates we discussed in the previous sections, resulting in multiple visualizations over the same data

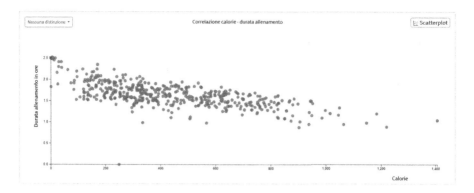

Fig. 9. Sample correlation query

attributes. In particular, the system supports the composition of up to three visualizations, requesting filtering, grouping and aggregation at the same time. A sample composite query is "Show me the duration of the workouts by athletes between 20 and 55 years old, grouped by calories and with their login trend by month". The resulting visualization is available in Fig. 10. It shows three different blocks: on the left, we have a column for the bar chart showing the workout duration and the line chart shows the login trend, while on the right we have the pie chart showing the grouping by calories. All the displayed entries satisfy the filtering condition on the athlete's age. The user can specify different composite queries combining only two intents (e.g., grouping and trend aggregation) or using different attributes.

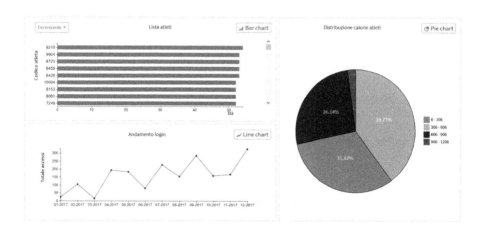

Fig. 10. Sample composite query

5   Evaluation

We evaluated the usability and the effectiveness of the proposed system through a user test, which included different data searching tasks on the athlete workout dataset. At the beginning of the session, we asked the participants to read a document explaining the test purposes, the organization of the dataset and an overall view of the requested tasks. After that, we asked each participant to fill out a demographic questionnaire and to complete the following five tasks through the application:

1. Sort the athlete workouts by ranking and filter out those lower than 2;
2. Inspect the relation between the calories spent and the duration of the workouts;
3. Find the best athletes and group them by calories spent;
4. Show the login trend in the last 12 months;
5. Filter the workouts of the athletes between 20 and 55 years old, group them by calories and analyse their login trend.

After each task, participants were requested to fill the Subjective Mental Effort Questionnaire (SMEQ) [12] for measuring the user's cognitive effort and the After-Scenario Questionnaire (ASQ) [5] for evaluating the ease of use and the supporting information. After completing the test, we requested the participants to fill out the System Usability Scale (SUS) [1] questionnaire for evaluating the overall usability, complemented by a set of questions on peculiar aspects of the application.

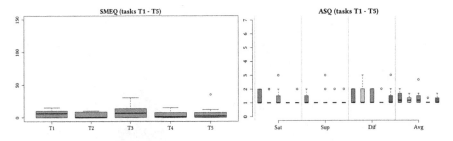

Fig. 11. User test results including the SMEQ [12] (left part) and ASQ [5] (right part) questionnaires.

Twelve people participated in the test. They had different education levels: 8 had a High School Degree, 3 a Bachelor, 3 a Master and one a PhD. They had a good experience with office applications ($\bar{x} = 5.5, s = 0.79$) in a 1 to 7 Likert scale) and they spend about 7 h ($\bar{x} = 7.2, s = 3, 1$) per day working or entraining themselves using the web.

They were all able to complete all the tasks. The ANOVA analysis for repeated measures on the SMEQ data shows that we do not have a significantly higher complexity ($p = .39$, $F(11, 44) = 1.05$, see Fig. 11 left part). Therefore, the cognitive effort requested to the users was comparable, but we noticed a slightly lower value for the tasks requesting to visualise only one chart (T1: $\bar{x} = 5.6$, $s = 5.3$, T2: $\bar{x} = 3.2$, $s = 4.6$) if compared against those requesting two (T3: $\bar{x} = 7.9$, $s = 9.3$) or three (T5: $\bar{x} = 5.9$, $s = 10.1$). All tasks require a cognitive effort below the *Not very hard to do* label in [12].

The ASQ questionnaire instead measures different perceived dimensions for each task: the satisfaction (*Sat*), the provided support (*Sup*), the difference between the time expected and spent (*Dif*), using a 1 to 7 Likert scale where 1 is positive and 7 is the negative end. All tasks received ratings between 1 and 2 and there was no significant difference among them (Fig. 11 right part).

The SUS post-test questionnaire [1] results show that the tool usability is very good ($\bar{x} = 93.8$, $s = 4.1$ in a 1–100 scale). In the post-test comments, the user highlighted some minor usability issues regarding the query suggestion feature when used through the keyboard. Overall, the users considered the approach very useful, especially for browsing online dataset when graphical elaboration is not available.

6   Conclusion and Future Work

In this paper, we discussed a simple solution for supporting natural language queries on a generic dataset. The approach exploits existing Artificial Intelligence libraries for natural language analysis and an annotation file for training query recognition. At runtime, a Python module executes the interpreted query while the visualization relies on a JavaScript library. We summarised the different types of queries supported in our system, describing how it extracts and presents the results. The user test results show that despite the simplicity of the approach, the usability results are very good, so we are positive that the integration of natural language queries will be more and more available in data exploration tools.

The proposed solution may be further developed in the future, adding a higher number of graphs. In particular, the tool is lacking support for geographical data (e.g., choropleth maps), which are both extremely useful and quite widespread on the web. In addition, we are working for going beyond the "one-shot" query interpretation model, where the user provides all his/her input at once and the system works on a single string. The next version of the tool will rely on a conversational interface, where the system will ask questions to the user for understanding which kind of visualization suits better the task, guiding him/her through the different option available. Considered the evolution of general-purpose conversational agents based on modern AI libraries, the technology is mature enough for studying its application in the information visualization field.

References

1. Brooke, J., et al.: SUS-a quick and dirty usability scale. Usability Eval. Ind. **189**(194), 4–7 (1996)
2. Cau, F.M., Mancosu, M.S., Mulas, F., Pilloni, P., Spano, L.D.: An intelligent interface for supporting coaches in providing running feedback. In: Proceedings of the 13th Biannual Conference of the Italian SIGCHI Chapter: Designing the Next Interaction, pp. 1–5 (2019)
3. Fu, S., Xiong, K., Ge, X., Tang, S., Chen, W., Wu, Y.: Quda: natural language queries for visual data analytics (2020)
4. Hoque, E., Setlur, V., Tory, M., Dykeman, I.: Applying pragmatics principles for interaction with visual analytics. IEEE Trans. Vis. Comput. Graph. **24**(1), 309–318 (2017)
5. Lewis, J.R.: Psychometric evaluation of an after-scenario questionnaire for computer usability studies: the ASQ. ACM Sigchi Bull. **23**(1), 78–81 (1991)
6. Popescu, A.M., Etzioni, O., Kautz, H.: Towards a theory of natural language interfaces to databases. In: Proceedings of the 8th International Conference on Intelligent User Interfaces, pp. 149–157 (2003)
7. Saktheeswaran, A., Srinivasan, A., Stasko, J.: Touch? speech? or touch and speech? investigating multimodal interaction for visual network exploration and analysis. IEEE Trans. Vis. Comput. Graph. **26**(6), 2168–2179 (2020). https://doi.org/10.1109/tvcg.2020.2970512, https://doi.org/10.1109/TVCG.2020.2970512
8. Setlur, V., Battersby, S.E., Tory, M., Gossweiler, R., Chang, A.X.: Eviza: a natural language interface for visual analysis. In: Proceedings of the 29th Annual Symposium on User Interface Software and Technology, pp. 365–377 (2016)
9. Setlur, V., Tory, M., Djalali, A.: Inferencing underspecified natural language utterances in visual analysis. In: Proceedings of CH 2019, Italy, pp. 40–51 (2019)
10. Srinivasan, A., Stasko, J.: Orko: facilitating multimodal interaction for visual exploration and analysis of networks. IEEE Trans. Vis. Comput. Graph. **24**(1), 511–521 (2018)
11. Yu, B., Silva, C.T.: Flowsense: a natural language interface for visual data exploration within a dataflow system. IEEE Trans. Vis. Comput. Graph. **26**(1), 1–11 (2020). https://doi.org/10.1109/tvcg.2019.2934668, https://doi.org/10.1109/TVCG.2019.2934668
12. Zijlstra, F.R.H., Van Doorn, L.: The construction of a scale to measure subjective effort. Delft, Netherlands, vol. 43, pp. 124–139 (1985)

P3 Block: Privacy Preserved, Trusted Smart Parking Allotment for Future Vehicles of Tomorrow

Amit Kumar Tyagi[1]([⊠]) ⓘ, Shabnam Kumari[2],
Terrance Frederick Fernandez[3]([⊠]) ⓘ, and C. Aravindan[3] ⓘ

[1] School of Computer Science and Engineering, Vellore Institute of Technology,
Chennai Campus, Chennai 600127, Tamilnadu, India
amitkrtyagi025@gmail.com
[2] Anumit Academy of Research and Innovation Network, NCR, Hapur, U.P,
India
shabnam.kt25@gmail.com
[3] Rajiv Gandhi College of Engineering and Technology, Puducherry, India
frederick@pec.edu, aravindan.c007@gmail.com

Abstract. As the urbanization is advancing day by day and demand of vehicles is being increased (or cheaper cost of vehicles), it made increased number of vehicles over the road, which faces several issues like traffic accidents, finding a parking spot, etc. Finding a car park slot has become one of the residents' key pain points. The key reason behind this is the restricted provision of parking lots and the struggle to spot vacant parking space during peak times. To overcome this restriction, one solution is to create smart allocation of free spaces that are easier to locate and use (i.e., trusted and privacy preserved for user or driver). In this work, we provide privacy preserved parking allotment (as a smart solution) to users (or vehicle users) who are willing to pay more charges when they require parking slot near to their destination (or urgent need). In this work (called as P3 Block: Privacy Preserving parking using Blockchain 2.0), one useful and different approach we used as "Incentive based smart parking". People will get cashback or reward for alerting or spreading genuine information among users. Also, miner will be rewarded for verifying users. Incentive feature will attract more users, also more trust and reputation of specific service provider matter a lot in providing efficient parking slot to vehicle user. Today world is moving towards automation, so automation will be available in all possible applications like manufacturing, finance, retail, food supply management, transportation, home appliances, etc.

Keywords: Automation industry · Privacy preserved paring · Smart parking · Vehicles of tomorrow

© Springer Nature Switzerland AG 2020
O. Gervasi et al. (Eds.): ICCSA 2020, LNCS 12254, pp. 783–796, 2020.
https://doi.org/10.1007/978-3-030-58817-5_56

1 Introduction

Smart parking schemes in a smart city typically strive to make it easier for car users to reserve available private parking spaces (just like time-sharing). Current day techniques are capable of verifying and supervising the parking spaces and automobiles without satisfying the privacy issues of the customers. This paper puts forth the underlying basis for an efficient parking system using Blockchain which is created with the aim of securing the privacy of the users by emitting the intervention of a third-party agency. The system which has been elucidated (i.e., P3-Block) incorporates the concepts of Blockchain and smart contract methods share parking spaces amidst drivers.

Note that in majority of the existing works, in general, parking systems are not designed to keep security and privacy issues in the respective work [2–4], but any system failure can leak private (sensitive) information from drivers/users.There are many threats (external, insider) that can affect the Internet of Things (IoTs) such as Eavesdropping, Sybil, Denial of Service or Controlling [14]. For the very same reason, Internet of Things (IoTs) or Internet Connected Things (ICT) or Smart Devices need to be tested and cross verified way before they're combined with Blockchain. They also need to be identified with respect to their locations and condensed in the perfect place to prevent any sort of physical modifications along with the inclusion of system crash detection methods each time they occur.

An Improved Parking System
Parking in densely populated, wealthy urban areas is a constant challenge for residents and drivers. Traffic jams and chaotic conditions on the road are majorly caused by drivers who hunt for empty parking lots. This indirectly leads to excessive petrol consumption and emissions of pollutants [1]. Drivers looking for available parking spaces used an additional 47,000 gal of fuel and 95,000 h of driving in 2017 [2]. These massive amounts indicate the necessity for an efficient parking program. Usually, parking systems depend on centralised control to manage the parking spaces which also include the private ones which provide reservation services. It's mandatory for the owners and customers of these parking lots to validate themselves with the supervisor of the parking station. Majority of the providers are local due to the difficulties they face from the logical perspective which consist of maintaining these in different cities and areas. In spite of the fact the parking systems aren't built for security and privacy reasons, a minute device crash can lead to data breaches of the users.

We implement a parking system based on Blockchain that securely stores user information and manages parking services. We select Blockchain in our work because it is transparent, immutable, distributed (without the need to involve a trusted third party), auditable (accessible anytime anywhere eon a public network by joined peers). Some popular success of Blockchain in previous decade are BitCoin [1], and Ethereum [12]. Today, we can use Blockchain revolution, Blockchain 2.0 or Smart Contract, in many applications for a transparent transition. Mark that the smart contracting allows owner to set rules and access controls. The system we architected implements smart contracts to procure the helping modules for registrations and transaction purposes, i.e. drivers and parking supervisors. Moreover, smart contracts aid to permit drivers to account for empty parking spaces which cater to ones needs. To protect the privacy of users, we selected a Blockchain consortium to verify that user information is readily available. In our work, the transactions are managed by privileged nodes which render information available or accessible only to union members in the chain. This program helps in overcoming the geographical limitations and permits the drivers to perform electronic transactions among each other. Eradicating the central control of the entire network can often result in reduces maintenance and overhead expenditure. Every individual node of the Blockchain contains system data for a system based on Blockchain which runs independent of a supervisor.

Hence, the organisation of this work is as follows: Sect. 2 discuses related work to our work. Section 3 discusses motivation behind our work, or our intention towards writing article on this critical problem of parking. Section 4 discusses our proposed work with discussing each and every module in detail. Further, system implementation is discussed in Sect. 5. And in the last section, this work is concluded with some remarks in brief.

2 Related Work

There are many attempts traced in previous years which provide efficient parking slot to drivers/users like ParkBid [9], ParkChain [11], etc. But, to best of our knowledge gained through our survey, till now no author has tried in preserving privacy of user's including building trust between service providers and drivers. In this section, we provide basic information about Blockchain, its types and its revolution in different applications [15].

State of the Art - Blockchain Basics

With the massive victory of Bitcoin, Blockchain has been implemented in it and in several other applications [4]. In simple words, Blockchain is a form of electronically dispatched ledger which is considered as a linear block series that can collect information like events and processes. Majority of the network nodes need to make use of consensus to validate the block (with its data). The details confined in the blocks are maintained in an orderly fashion while preserving their order. These blocks can join hands to form data chains, such that each block's head contains a hash from the previous block. When blocks are modified, every block succeeding it, shifts as well. In another sense, all validated alterations can be ignored. Blockchain can be classified as public, cooperative, or private. Every individual in a concerned network are treated equally in a public chain, such that they have equal access to the data in a Blockchain. However, this transparency and flexibility comes at an expense of the consumers' privacy. On the contrary, private chains are generally centralised form of Blockchain in which the creator alone has the rights to create information. Deployment architectures are in-built in this software. Though such a Blockchain proposes high level of privacy in comparison to public Blockchain methods, it's completely dependent on a reliable source for validating the information. The union, or gathering of super peers, choose the efficiency of the blocks and its' processes in a consortium chain. If a person prefers to join a chain, it has to be positively welcomed by most of the union committee members. The details in the chain can be either available (to the public) or accessible only to trade union leaders. Such a Blockchain, while implementing partial decentralization, can thus provide privacy to an extent.

State of the Art – Blockchain Integration
The thing to include in this chapter is related to the interactions between the Internet of Things (IoTs), i.e., the connectivity between the underlying Internet of Things (IoTs) infrastructures. Once Blockchain is implemented, it must be determined where those interactions will take place: within the IoT, a hybrid system involving IoT and Blockchain, or through Blockchain. Note that IoT- Cloud Computing was not that much valuable (or popular), but IoT- Fog (Edge) Computing integration can change the computing world (in terms of accessing services efficiently). Hence, integration of IoT can be discussed as:

Internet of Things - Internet of Things: This seems to be the solution which is the quickest with respect to latency and health because they can function offline too. A variety of methods for exploration and routing are of prime importance for the IoT systems to communicate with each other. Only a small portion of IoT data in gathered and collected in Blockchain when IoT interactions take place without the interference of Blockchain. This method is highly fruitful in scenarios with steady IoT data where there is reduced potential for IoT interactions.

Internet of Things –Blockchain: This method involves each and every interaction to parse through the Blockchain leading to unaltered interaction records [13, 16]. This process assures a traceable platform for all chosen communications as their data can be questioned in the Blockchain which in turn helps in increasing the autonomy of the IoT devices. All IoT applications which prefer to sell or lease (for example Slock) can adopt this approach. Moreover, keeping track of the Blockchain interactions would indirectly lead to increased bandwidth and data – one of the commonly known issues of Blockchain. On the contrary, Blockchain needs to store all IoT data which is linked with the concerned processes.

Hybrid approach: In the long run, a mixed or hybrid framework which permits only selected communications and data transfer to take place within the Blockchain works better as the remaining ones are directly exchanges with the IoT devices. Selection of experiences which must parse through the Blockchain is indeed a task. A victorious arrangement of this method/technique is the ideal way to holistically combine all technologies as it controls the benefits of Blockchain along with those of IoT communications in real time. Fog computing and even cloud computing, steps ahead here as they're capable of surpassing the drawbacks of Blockchain and IoT. In fact, fog computing calls for reduced number of devices which are restricted computationally (like gateways) and it has latency for mining repositories similar to other projects which implement IoT devices.

A general IoT application would utilize limited -Resource gadgets as end nodes which are capable of communicating with a gateway which is engaged in transferring the data from sensory apparatus to the cloud or the server. If the end nodes require communicating with the Blockchain during the process of integration, cryptographic operations provide a helping hand to the IoT gadgets. This is of grave seriousness as it plays a supreme role in identifying the IoT autonomy, which comes at the cost of highly sophisticated hardware and increased overhead expenditure (it is addressed in [14–16] an estimation of the cost of using Blockchain in IoT devices). It is also possible to incorporate gateways in these implementations, just as conventional applications do, though the advantages of using Blockchain in this way are less.

Today and Tomorrow Blockchain's Applications
Another popularly known application, apart from Bitcoin [4], based on Blockchain is Ethereum, which uniquely has its very own electro monetary system. However, peers in Ethereum can utilize smart contracts to produce anomalous dispersed implementations. Putting it in a nutshell, Bitcoin captures the financial processing while smart contracts provide more space for builders to venture into different applications, so as to exploit the use of Blockchain to its maximum. Smart contracts are basically chunks of code which can churn out random rules and norms. In other words, smart contracts are of the binary form and are situated in Blockchains as they can be executed by its virtual machine [6]. Similarly, in the parking-management system we have put forth calls for the capacity to create user validated smart contracts and parking lot sharing. Thus, we have decided to implement the usage of smart contracts to capture necessary and important details and data which can be made use of to control and supervise the system. Extensive explorations are being made in the field of Blockchain for numerous IoT related applications [7, 8]. Privacy preserving contracts have been elucidated in [5, 9] with the help of distributed Blockchain and zero-knowledge techniques. Chemical industries have implemented Blockchain to produce a Bitcoin-based electricity-sharing market [10], likewise Blockchain-based decentralized file-storage system and linkable ring signature have been used to implement privacy protection [11, 12]. Note that today Blockchain is used in many other applications like retail, finance, manufacturing, transportation, agriculture, supply chain management, logistics, etc. Hence, this section discusses related work regarding Blockchain, its types/variant, evolutions and used in many applications. Now, next section will discuss out motivation behind writing this article/doing this work.

3   Motivation

Due to the limited parking spaces available in the cities, parking has become one major problem for the people with the ongoing urbanization process. Parking is a constant struggle, especially in city areas, due to the acute space constraints. People have to travel long distances in a crowded locality searching for parking spaces. In our work, we provide a Blockchain based smart solution to all drivers to get a hassle free parking place. We use Blockchain in our work, because it is distributed ledger technology, immutable, transparent, auditable and does not require any intermediary (or central authority) for verifying the transactions. In this technology, trust among people is made through its consensus mechanism, i.e., proof of work and proof of stake. The parking system which we have put forth can be easily incorporated into the current day parking systems for granting parking pools to guarantee smart service to the clients along with which we can generate a transparent and flexible revenue model for their rental works.

By creating an unalterable audit trail in Blockchain, smart contracts would assure the acquiescence of logical terms such that the aspiring participants are secured from the legal complexities indulging in the process. In summary, our primary task in this proposed research is to provide revenue to parking service providers, and to protect privacy services to drivers/users in a minimum of time.

4   Our Proposed System Model – A Smart Parking Allotment System

The solution which we have thrown light on has an additional advantage of producing plush green surroundings and cities which have reduced pollutants, traffic blocks, decreased travel duration, healthy income production, better and fruitful lifestyle routines and healthy relations with landlords, authorities, tenants, etc. This paper puts forth a program with the help of non-fungible parking tokens to generate digital belongings which are compared to that of famished land to develop a smart parking pool. Blockchain techniques can provide trust, liability and ever-lasting traceability which are extremely important to rent out the unused parking lot. This work develops an audit-able system that uses smart contracts to ensure transparency in law and in financial matters. Now, every module of our proposed work is dealt with as:

Entities of the Proposed System
Majority of the modern and smart parking systems depend on a centrally controlled management to monitor the infrastructure and framework, clients, and information and this clearly doesn't provide any privacy to the users. We have put forward the technique of Blockchain which helps in uplifting the distance from the controlled version to a dispatched system by simultaneously assuring safety and security to users' (i.e. drivers and owners) data. Drivers can identify and lease out the vacant parking lots which meet their needs.

The owner of the parking lot has the rights to broadcast and modify the details related to their parking lots which include spot, timings, expenses, gate code, etc. It is to be noted that the users are free to retrieve and provide data to the network. In particular, users will need to provide the management layer with basic information to be authenticated. The Blockchain stores these kinds of private information and operations. Note that *Basic* Entities in Parking – Allotment (in our work) are: Service Provider (parking owner), vehicle users (who need free slot), and miners (who will verify transactions publicly).

The layer of management comprises trusted agencies including government departments and the certification authority. Such organizations are usually network issuers and authentication partners, and are represented as privileged members of a Blockchain consortium. The issuers own the smart contracts, and are solely responsible for the design, development, initialization and maintenance of the network. Issuers may also publish relevant details and allow customers asking to join the network. The authentication party mainly manages user authentication and ensures privacy for the users. In the case of a consumer conflict, the authentication party also serves as an arbitration body.

The Blockchain consortium acts as a distributed ledger within the storage layer. As the blocks are attached towards the end and linked to the preceding one with the help of hash, it grows and flourishes incessantly. Details pertaining to the users and their contract codes are collected and maintained in the chain which prevents any form of modification in the absence of detection. Transactions are implemented to handle data from the perspective of modifications, reviews, or work from the Blockchain server, and all the operations can be backtracked to assure transparency and flexibility through Blockchain.

Algorithm 1: Preserving Privacy in Smart Parking

Step 1: Service Provider will send Parking Slot to all users/drivers available in a public network
Step 2: Interested Driver/Vehicle User will approach to respective service provider for parking
Step 3: Among all existing users, one head will be elected
Step 4: Head will collect information from interested user and will provide to service provider for registration
Step 5: User's information is hidden from service provider, higher anonymity is maintained.

Algorithms 2: Building Trust during Allotment of Parking Slot

Step 1: Once Algorithm 1 process is completed
Step 2: Received Information is cross verified by peer users (or miners)
Step 3: Miners will validate authenticity of information
Step 4: Once Authenticity of information is done, information is stored in block and block become a part of Blockchain
Step 5: Once parking slot's use is over, payment will be done (automatically through smart contract, parking information will get updated) with a feedback mechanism (proceed by driver/user)

Hence in algorithm 2, higher trust is maintained through feedback and decentralized ledger technology.

Function Modules
The anticipated system has been created with Blockchain and smart contracts architecture (Fig. 1) and its functional module possesses registration, search and rent, waiving off expenses and rewarding modules.

In this work, Smart contracts handle the entire income cycle, as well as revenue sharing, and increase the ease with minimal differences of doing business. IoT related gadgets like On Board Unit (OBU) driven sensors and preceptors which are connected to the network monitor, track the parking frequency. The mobile application thus, proves to be the drivers' and parking owners' widgets.

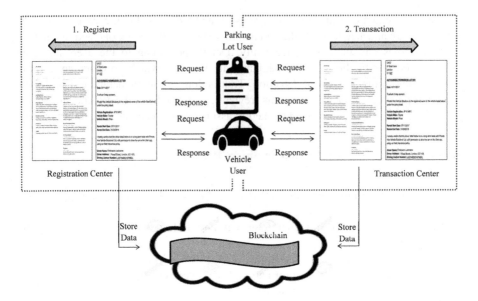

Fig. 1. Proposed model for privacy preserved, trusted smart parking

A. Registration Module

Each user is epitomised by a smart contract account which is based on Blockchain which is distinctly linked to different private keys. Users then provide their identities to the Blockchain consortium's privilege nodes at the time of registration so that each node can validate and authenticate the identities they are maintaining. For every novel transaction process, the user is likely to receive a different address which is to ensure that the fellow partners can't disclose the identity of the user by attempting to track their address. Once the user enters the network, they need to mandatorily submit the certification authority along with their basic details through smart contract; it's then stored in the Blockchain. Smart contracts are the basic underlying framework for controlling and managing the identities and records for the Blockchain. It can maintain the basic user records for sign up and then lock them into Blockchain. Vehicle users and parking lot owners have numerous types of data pertaining to the user along with a plethora of user inputs. These consist of the following fields: User ID, car ID, and user address. These further contain parking ID, location, and time of availability, price and owner's address for parking space owners. It's the users' responsibility to submit his/her user ID and parking ID at the time of sign up while the other fields are initialised to Null.

Along with that, smart contract provides a number of platforms which permit the user to scan, modify or extract details. The administrators can publish and alter their details with the help of smart contract after the successful registration. Consider this case as an example: Owners can alter the timings are cost of the parking lots. Each user's identity is secured under an array of address characters, such that, only the privileged workers in the management can retrieve the personal details. Other IoT applications can be found in [14].

Note that in this work, Smart Contracts provide on the Blockchain a decentralized, cheaper, safe and verifiable system for parking vehicles using private land area. In next module, IoT devices sense actual location/distance of driver/vehicle for providing efficient parking/nearby parking, i.e., with a minimum walking distance.

B. *Searching and Renting Module*

This module facilitates drivers and vehicle users to explore for available parking spaces which fulfil their needs by forwarding them to smart contract transactions which contain details consisting of location and time. If the administrator authenticates and validates the user, the contract is then passed on to the list of parking lots which would in turn return a number of suitable parking IDs. Each time the driver decides to reserve an empty parking space, he/she has to deposit an amount to the account linked with the contract (e.g., virtual or physical cash, a currency used in Counties). This deposit is later credited back into ones account after the user pays and leaves the parking space. Further, the status of the parking space will be updated to be locked or inaccessible accordingly as this would not allow chaotic scenarios like double booking which is similar to the value of double Bitcoins. Smart contract dependent on Blockchain are classified into external and client accounts. External accounts can be compared to Bitcoin accounts, while the latter is implemented for maintaining smart contracts. It's to be noted that though the contract account possesses the external account features, the amount is stored in the contract account. This account can only be accessed with a private key which belongs to the administrators. Smart contracts which are based on Blockchain also features the one-time pad function which is executed with a smart contract to allow the clients to disclose their identity. It calls for new addresses to be created by the users each time they prefer to process transactions with a different user or a contract.

C. *Payment Module*

The payment will be handled and accounted accordingly to invoke the transfer function. The vehicle user is required to form a transaction with a number of inputs and outputs to transfer the amount. Every input contains a public key pk_s for the sender and a secret key sk_s along with a public key pk_r for the receiver which is then topped up with some amount of virtual money. Sk_s is used for signing the contract while pk_r is used for encoding the transaction. Hence, only people who possess the right sk_s linked with the pk_r value can claim their charge. This is quite similar to that of Bitcoin, where in every input contains a reference to the previous output of the transaction. The outputs are of three types: payment recipient, shift charge and transaction fee. Transaction fee is to be waived off by the miner who publishes the transaction to the Blockchain. Money transfer modules are made use for the efficient performance of the rental and payment processes. Once the driver leaves the parking space during the payment process, he/she must transfer the sufficient amount of money to the respective address of the owner by virtual money transfer arrangements so as to return their deposit. Transaction sending is the root cause for performing the three featured modules with the help of the users' private key. So, each operation will cost a small amount of Virtual/Physical cash, payable to the Blockchain network miner. The process will be stored on the Blockchain to avoid fraud, forgery, or denial as each point in the chain network owns a copy of the full database.

D. *Incentive Module*

Numerous witnesses in this module authenticate and validate transaction signatures and time stamps by including them in blocks. Elections are performed with the help of opinion polls and are rewarded each time a witness creates a block successfully. This permits the delegates to set block dormancy within moments and validate transactions.

So, with the coming smart cities and the ever-increasing number of vehicles on the road, there will be demand for effective traffic management systems. For solving this critical problem of parking slots, this work provides a Blockchain based solution (or Blockchain based IoT powered transparent framework) Where parking pools can be built through the creation of a transparent network, where individuals can rent their unused land for a specified period. For the consistency of the entire system a non-fungible token system will be developed that reflects individual parking lots. Blockchain's public ledger process serves as the foundation of the framework for the management of unused land leasing. Note that if private owned unused land is available in each location, then some of these lands can be used to create smart parking slots, the vehicle congestion intensity on roads searching for a vacant lot can be mitigated or reduced. As a result, there may be fewer accidents over the road.

Hence, this section discusses our proposed work in detail with explaining each and every used module. Now, next section will provide details about our proposed system implementation.

5   System Implementation

We implement smart contracts based on Blockchain and this forms a chain that creates a number of peers of privilege (i.e., city and issuers). Smart contracts are standardised by solidarity. We also make use of Truffle [17] to compile and interpret binary codes for the smart contracts and post those contracts which are linked to Blockchain. In order to link it to the JSON-encoded remote call formality protocol for the implementation of Blockchain, we make use of JavaScript to develop an architecture which permits users to send and retrieve information in the smart contract which is based on Blockchain. The app enables users to sign up and modify the Blockchain records and also enables processes like scanning or reserving the available parking spaces which are compatible with the users' need. Further, the client also provides an interface for the easy transaction of money to the user. Until payment, some virtual/physical cash is prepaid by vehicle users as the deposit which is secured.

6 Blockchain Technology: A Way to Forward

As we know that merkle tree is the heart of Blockchain Technology, and mining is most important process/procedure for validating existing users in network (public or private). In near future, we see that Blockchain can be used for launching new cryptocurrencies by many nations that will be regulated or influenced by monetary policy. For example few nations like China, Russia, Venezuela, etc., have launched cryptocurrency for their nation. Few possibilities of Blockchain in near future are:

a. Decentralized Web
b. Decentralized Applications: for example, transportation – peer to driver to peer, in general, it needs to be peer to peer, provide by Blockchain Technology. It will remove fraud, bogus people in many applications with Saving time and money
c. Peer to Peer Economy
d. The Convergence of Blockchain, Machine Learning, Internet of Things and the Cloud
e. Retail/businesses: Find out sales per month for specific commodity
f. Smart Contact: Idea of smart contracts is its automatic execution when conditions are met. For instance, delivering goods after payment is received. However, other conditions of contracts should also be automatically regulated. Also, smart contract can be used to keep stakeholders documents, Distribution of funds, and KYC/AML utilities in a safe and secure way. In near future, we can use Smart contracts in Ethereum Blockchain. Also, we can solve the bug issue raised due to immutable systems. Bitcoin is a digital or cryptocurrency that verifies the number of digital currency a person has whereas, ethereum Blockchain mainly supports smart contracts. The programming language used in Ethereum Blockchain is complete during high level language called solidity. Ethereum Blockchain is not restricted only to currencies, ethereum protocol is not only visible to the parties involved in the smart contracts but also hundreds of people are witness and they validate the transactions. In near future, some possibilities of using smart contract in many applications are listed as:

- Internet of Things Networks: The smart contract can be used with some other technologies like the Internet of Things (IoT). Smart contracts and IoT can enable significant changes in industries, which help to develop new distributed applications.
- Agriculture: In agriculture, IoT sensors can be used which automatically initiate activities like irrigation or deployment of insecticide; this is being done with the help of programmed trigger values.
- Real estate: Internet enabled lock can be used for automatic locking of a house whenever the tenant is not paying the rent and then can unlock immediately after the completion of payment.
- Banking: Smart contract can be used significantly in banking sector which is an alternative to the traditional way of transactions. Smart contracts help to perform make payments, loans, and other transactions automatically.

- Supply Chain: In this area, smart contract can provide real-time visibility. Smart contracts guarantee inventory tracking which benefit supply chain financing and reduce the theft and fraud risks.
- Legal Issues: Smart contract can replace the traditional model of legal issues solving and document certification. If we use smart contracts, it removes the requirement of notarization, offering automated and cost-efficient solution. We can integrate Law into Smart Contracts for providing better services to users.
- Medical Records Management/e-healthcare: The medical reports associated to a person are one of the vital parameter of an individual's security, preserving this data is sole responsibility of the organization whosoever beholds it. While sharing the data among different platforms, the data may get leaked which may lead to some unavoidable circumstances. So in order to prevent this data to falling into dangerous hands, Blockchain Technology allows hospitals, other institutions/organizations and payers to split access to their networks without compromising or suspecting data security and integrity. Smart contract can be used to store sensitive personal health records, insurance related data. This also supports supervising drugs and other supplies, and also enables secure sharing of patient data for clinical trials and research
- Public Mobility: Due to increase in use of public transport of vehicles, it becomes difficult for government in cities to know the status of public transportation being used, so on implementing Blockchain Technology will help the cities to know and understand that how the public mobility is being used by their residents and how can they develop some different options for transportation.
- Charity: Using Blockchain Technology in charity institution or organization will help donators to track where their donations are going and who is going to use it. Blockchain will provide transparency and security to all the financial records and will give a greater visibility to the donors.

Hence, as mentioned above, there are many other similar industries that have great potential future with implementation of Blockchain in them like loyalty programs, natural resource management, education, advertisement, public assistance, publishing, gaming, travelling and even more. Moreover this, some other opportunities with Blockchain in near future are summarized here as:

- Improve social media functionalities
- Digital Ownership Revolution
- Keeping our ID (Identification) and Personal Information Secure
- Keep your identity safe and Location Privacy safe

Blockchain provides digital freedom by using smart contracts: It means that the system is not governed by any central authority so that any kind of manipulation cannot be done by them. Note that Blockchain is more popular in mortgage industry, i.e., with its transparent system, speed (when compared to the typical mortgage underwriting process), and immutability that will secure your home for as long as you own it. In near future, we can protect several important documents from several vulnerabilities by constructing smart contract for smart era's applications. Hence, this section discusses several possible applications of Blockchain (i.e., Blockchain 3.0) and for which smart contracts can be created and also discusses several opportunities to protect smart contract for the same/similar applications. Now, next section will conclude this work in brief.

7 Conclusion

Our work discussed a smart parking allotment system based on Blockchain including privacy preservation. We highlight the distributed pattern of paid parking spaces amidst the parking lot owners and the drivers/users. This work removed the need for a trusted third-party entity or an intermediary using Blockchain solution. Also, this approach provides incentives to all drivers who verify other drivers and inform about free parking slot to other user who is searching for a vacant parking slot. Notice that our proposed system is built on the smart contracts platform based on Blockchain, and its functional module includes modules for registration, search and rent, payment and rewards. We can use physical or virtual currency for payment, that is, according to the convenience of the user. An additional benefit of producing income from their usually unused property is indeed a striking feature. Smart Blockchain contracts implement the contractual agreement between the participants which ensures financial transparency in the system proposed. Gunning towards future work, given Blockchain's growth, it would make no sense to use it in many applications where databases have ample functionality, as high performance is expected. In many other applications that require functionality, we work on Blockchain scalability, 51% attacks, storage and eclipse attacks for efficient solution for future work.

References

1. Nakamoto, S., Bitcoin, A.: A peer-to-peer electronic cash system (2008)
2. Ni, J., Zhang, K., Yu, Y., Lin, X., Shen, X.S.: Privacy-preserving smart parking navigation supporting efficient driving guidance retrieval. IEEE Trans. Veh. Technol. **67**(7), 6504–6517 (2018)
3. Zhu, L., Li, M., Zhang, Z., Qin, Z.: ASAP: an anonymous smart-parking and payment scheme in vehicular networks. IEEE Trans. Dependable Secure Comput. (2018, in press)
4. Giuffrè, T., Siniscalchi, S.M., Tesoriere, G.: A novel architecture of parking management for smartcities. Procedia Soc. Behav. Sci. **53**, 16–28 (2012)
5. Wesam, A.A., Mohamed, B., Karim, B., Mohamed, M.: Privacy-preserving smart parking system using blockchain and private information retrieval. https://arxiv.org/pdf/1904.09703.pdf
6. Tyagi, A.K., Sreenath, N.: Vehicular Ad Hoc networks: new challenges in carpooling and parking services. CIC 2016, vol. 14. Special Issue Int. J. Comput. Sci. Inf. Secur. (IJCSIS). https://sites.google.com/site/ijcsis/. ISSN 1947-5500
7. Grazioli, A., Picone, M., Zanichelli, F., Amoretti, M.: Collaborative mobile application and advanced services for smart parking. In: Mobile Data Management, June 2013

8. Kopecký, J., Domingue, J.: ParkJamJAM: crowdsourcing parking availability information with linked data. In: Simperl, E., Norton, B., Mladenic, D., Della Valle, E., Fundulaki, I., Passant, A., Troncy, R. (eds.) ESWC 2012. LNCS, vol. 7540, pp. 381–386. Springer, Heidelberg (2015). https://doi.org/10.1007/978-3-662-46641-4_31

9. Al Noor, S., et al.: ParkBid: an incentive based crowdsourced bidding service for parking reservation. In: 2017 IEEE International Conference on Services Computing (SCC), pp. 60–67 (2017)

10. Tyagi, A., Niladhuri, S.: ISPAS: an intelligent, smart parking allotment system for travelling vehicles in Urban areas. Int. J. Secur. Appl. 11(12), 45–64 (2017). https://doi.org/10.14257/ijsia.2017.11.12.05

11. Jennath, H.S., Adarsh, S., Chandran, N.V., Ananthan, R., Sabir, A., Asharaf, S.: Parkchain: a blockchain powered parking solution for smart cities. Front. Blockchain 2, 6 (2019). https://doi.org/10.3389/fbloc.2019.00006

12. Ethereum, H.: Ethereum homestead documentation (2017). http://www.ethdocs.org/en/latest/

13. Mayra, S., Deters, R.: Blockchain as a service for IoT, In: Proceedings of the IEEE International Conference on Internet of Things, Proceedings of the IEEE Green Computing and Communications, Proceedings of the IEEE Cyber, Physical and Social Computing, and Proceedings of the IEEE Smart Data, pp. 433–436 (2016)

14. Tyagi, A.K.: Building a smart and sustainable environment using internet of things, 22 February 2019. Proceedings of International Conference on Sustainable Computing in Science, Technology and Management (SUSCOM), Amity University Rajasthan, Jaipur, India, 26–28 February 2019

15. Amit, K.T., Nair, M.M., Sreenath, N., Abraham, A.: Security, privacy research issues in various computing platforms: a survey and the road ahead. J. Inf. Assur. Secur. (JIAS) (2020). ISSN 1554-1010

16. Reyna, A., Martín, C., Chen, J., Soler, E., Díaz, M.: On blockchain and its integration with IoT. Challenges and opportunities. Future Gener. Comput. Syst. 88, 173–190 (2018)

17. Truffle, Truffle framework (2017). http://truffleframework.com/docs

Information Science-Knowledge Management-HCI-Project Management-CRM Models-Software Processes:

Implications To E-Commerce Open Design And Co-Design

Chien-Sing Lee$^{(\boxtimes)}$, Lee-Yin Yew, Pai-Lek Chew, Yew-Keong Chee,
Yit-Thang Hiew, and Jing-Pynn Wong

Department of Computing and Information Systems, Sunway University,
Subang Jaya, Malaysia
chiensingl@sunway.edu.my, yewleeyin93@gmail.com,
{14012264,13079959,13084058,
14031405}@imail.sunway.edu.my

Abstract. Information Science and Human-Computer Interaction (HCI) have often formed the fundamentals of Information Systems Analysis and Design (ISAD) aimed at creating better user experiences and addressing information overload. Data compression and information compression have thus become symbiotic disciplines. This paper investigates the efficacy of including Project Management (PM)-computational thinking as design considerations to Information Science-HCI and in the process, to investigate which of the customer relationship management models and software engineering processes are more suitable for open co-design. Three examples and user testing findings are presented as to how these three disciplines influence the design of navigational structures and creativity. The identified model for open co-design in our context is surprisingly, reflective of design thinking and agile methodology principles and values, and more specifically, Gartner's and the IDIC CRM models.

Keywords: Information Science · Knowledge management · Software engineering · Project management · Human-computer interaction · CRM models · Open co-design

1 Introduction

As competition increases in business-to-consumer e-commerce, customer loyalty and sustainability are challenging. Some have increased new customer support features such as assistive intelligent recommendations and chatbots. Correspondingly, the trends in project management [1] highlight the need for entrepreneurial project managers who think and decide not only quickly but also analytically and judiciously, by utilizing and managing frameworks and diverse decision support tools. This leads to application of agile project management as well as hybridization of project

© Springer Nature Switzerland AG 2020
O. Gervasi et al. (Eds.): ICCSA 2020, LNCS 12254, pp. 797–811, 2020.
https://doi.org/10.1007/978-3-030-58817-5_57

management methodologies from different industries to promote different ways to build things and enhance processes and outcomes [1, 2].

Another two trends which are increasingly gaining attention are open design collaboration and gamification. Europe's Open Innovation movement in 2016 sets off much interest. In parallel, Ikeda and Bernstein [3] suggest that open co-design and rewards would be a viable option especially when the economy is bad. Hence, if designed well, these can sustain motivation in e-commerce, supply chain and momentum in growth. Hence, there is a need to model and to use computational thinking to differentiate and generalize.

1.1 Objective

Information Science and Human-Computer Interaction (HCI) are key drivers underlying modern Information Systems Analysis and Design (ISAD). Both aim at addressing information overload and creating better user experiences. As such, data compression and information compression have become symbiotic. This paper contextualizes systemic modelling within an entrepreneurial framework. We investigate the efficacy of including Project Management (PM)-computational thinking as design considerations to Information Science-HCI in terms of the design of navigational structures and creativity. In the process, we investigate which of the customer relationship models and software engineering processes are more suitable for open co-design. User testing findings are positive and promising.

In the following section, we present sustainability-related work on user satisfaction and behaviors, Information Science, increasing choice through upsell and cross-sell, social media, gamification and the supply chain. Subsequently, three examples related to customer relationship management systems are presented and conclusions derived.

2   Related Work on Sustainable Systems

2.1   User Satisfaction and Behaviors

E-commerce enables sellers to access market segments of different demographics and buyers to access a wider variety of sellers [4]. In view of sustainability, understanding and predicting, online consumer behavior is key. Among the various factors influencing consumer behavior, user satisfaction is increasingly, the most important evaluation metric. [5] propose that e-satisfaction can be measured not only in terms of convenience, product offerings, and product information but also *site design*, and financial security.

[6] utilize [7]'s Technology Acceptance Model (TAM) and [8]'s TAM 2, TAM 3 models to understand customers' behavior. Though TAM models and [9]'s Theory of Reasoned Action (TRA) are influenced by social norms and perceived utility among diverse options, they differ in terms of foci. TAM models focus more on technological factors such as perceived usefulness and perceived ease of use as key contributors to

behavioral intention. TRA believes that intention towards a behavior will lead to actual behavior. Hence, motivation for an action is an aspect which proponents would analyze. This requires more in-depth knowledge and application of psychology, which we as information systems analysts, are not capable of, especially during adverse economic conditions.

In view of studies such as [5]'s, [6] suggest additional four predictors to the original TAM: expectations, process satisfaction, access average time and access total time, leading to satisfaction and eventually, traffic and return on investments. This increases the breadth and specificity in assessment compared to the original TAM. Interestingly, access average time and access total time, directly correlate with Search Engine Optimization (SEO) and user experience/user satisfaction.

2.2 Motivation: Increasing Choice Through Cross-Sell and Up-Sell

Customers expect new products. Choosing which products and related products to offer to which customers to increase sales is a challenge in e-commerce. Conventionally, past historical records are used to predict future purchases. According to [10], segmentation analysis, purchase acquisition trees and survival analyses are effective and can be applied in many contexts. Since it is possible to launch multiple campaigns through several distribution channels at different times such as through Salesforce, complexity in possible alternatives-actions can be transformed to positive opportunities.

2.3 Motivation: Increasing Choice Through Supply Chain

[11] highlights the critical role of third-party supply chain management systems to business to consumer (B2C) and business to business (B2B) companies. In B2B, each partner in the supply chain is variable and the choice of supplier at each stage in the chain depends on various factors, aimed at optimizing value creation. Besides choice of partner, modern logistics includes improving the efficiency of material flow, and reducing distribution costs. Consequently, the supply chain has transformed into an agile value chain with diverse partners and/or agents. Logistics acquisition, management and continuous re-evaluation of partnerships in the supply chain have become a necessity and a strength, to ensure sustainability. [12] echoes [11]'s proposition. He opines that not only will it lead to more environmentally friendly and sustainable transportation, but also create jobs.

2.4 Motivation: Social Media

Another means to promote sustainability and increasing *choice, cross-sell and up-sell* is by using social media as we can attract new customers, find out what customers think about the business, and build stronger relationships with existing customers. Influencers are also increasingly gaining leverage. For example, if a celebrity with many followers retweets a post, his/her post is more likely to be retweeted multiple times.

2.5   Motivation: Gamification

Gamification has transformed business models. Gamification, integrates game mechanics into non-game environments to motivate participation, engagement, and loyalty [13, 14]. It works because like social media, it recognizes that all of us are motivated by community, feedback, achievement and reward.

2.6   Some Recent Optimization Studies

The above contribute in part and in whole to Customer Relationship Management Systems [2]. Popular Customer Relationship Management Models are [15]'s strategic, operational, analytical and collaborative CRM, [16]'s competency model and [17]'s CRM value chain model. Each has a different focus and hence can be applied to different contexts based on needs.

Another important factor is optimization, for example, using association rules for online business process analytics based on confidence, support and lift in [18]'s study. [19]'s fast prediction of web user browsing behavior based on the most interesting browsing patterns using association rules reduces search time by more than 10. Association rules' confidence and support are utilized as part of interestingness measures along with lift, and average as well as conviction.

[20] address discovery of users' interests based on a three-layer model (TLM). This involves keyword extraction, analysis of semantic structures and ranking of interest words. The inclusion of semantic-structural analyses reflects how the underlying ontological associations and users' goals enables more efficient search compared to the existing hit rate methods.

Our approach is based on prior work [21, 22], which regard design as pre-processor to deeper analytics and that social factors such as in [8]'s TAMs are important besides technological factors. For this paper, we have extended to open co-design due to inspiration from [3].

3   Methodology

This research is influenced by Information theory and the first study in the series by [23]. In [23], self-organizing map (SOM)-principal component analysis (PCA) is simulated for adaptive e-learning in Matlab. SOM is used to identify significant clusters (k) and PCA to further confirm based on eigenvector/eigenvalues. For actual e-commerce, PCA-SOM concepts are applied, i.e., we need to first identify the gap in terms of market analyses through Project Management considerations and design/computational thinking aspects, e.g. patterns, with decomposition, abstraction and algorithmic thinking. Then, human-computer interaction [24] and information systems analysis, design and development principles are applied.

Incremental design prototyping is used for both systems but the second and third systems lean more heavily towards agile methodology's principles and values, as it involves more dynamic factors arising from high and direct degree of exposure to changes in market demands and trends. The user testing questionnaire is designed based on human-computer interaction (HCI) design principles [24].

4 Case Studies

4.1 Case Study 1: *Furnitize's* Systems Design and Development

The first Project Management consideration is *Project Integration Management* and the outcome is illustrated in Fig. 1a [25].

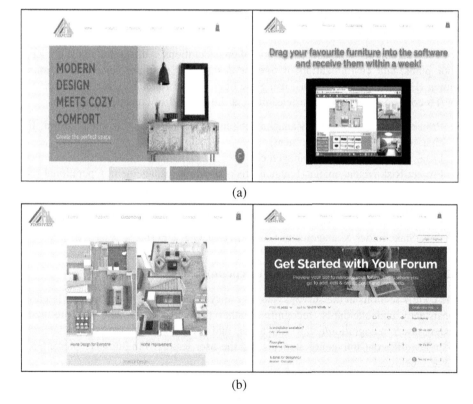

(a)

(b)

Fig. 1. a. *Furnitize* https://pailekchew963.wixsite.com/mysite, **b.** *Furnitize's* Customization System, Forum

Company Services

- Delivery system (Supply Chain Delivery System)
- Installation and renovation services
- Agent, to save cost and time

Company strategies

- Live chat, forum, instant reply to increase customers satisfaction and loyalty
- Joint venture with other companies to increase the variety of products
- Customize: to allow customers to have their own experiments with concepts and to increase customers' confidence in our company

Knowledge areas contributing to the above formulation are:

a. Project Scope Management (Marketing, Customers self-design, Customers transaction – PayPal payment gateway, Customer delivery system)
b. Project Time management, Project Cost Management
c. Project Quality Management

The outcome from this second round of considerations is illustrated in the choice of floor plans, and customization of interior design and furniture selection. Examples shown (Fig. 1b) are screenshots, using the open source *RoomSketcher* software.

To confirm implementation feasibility, a third round of considerations are:

a. Project Human Resource Management (customer feedback, customer forum, live chat support, Team development)
b. Project Communication Management
c. Project Risk Management (Financial risk-cashflow management, Operational risk-supply chain distribution, transport risk, Customer satisfaction risk and risk control and monitoring)
d. Project Procurement Management (Source selection (quality), contract administration, Stakeholder Management: CEO, CTO, COO, CFO)

4.2 *Furnitize's* Evaluation (User Perception)

There are 7 sections in the survey: visibility of system status, user control and freedom, consistency and standards, recognition rather than recall, aesthetic and minimalist design, users recognition/recall, diagnosis, and recovery from errors, and language [24]. Ten different university students did the user testing. Findings are presented in Table 1 below.

Table 1. *Furnitize's* user testing findings

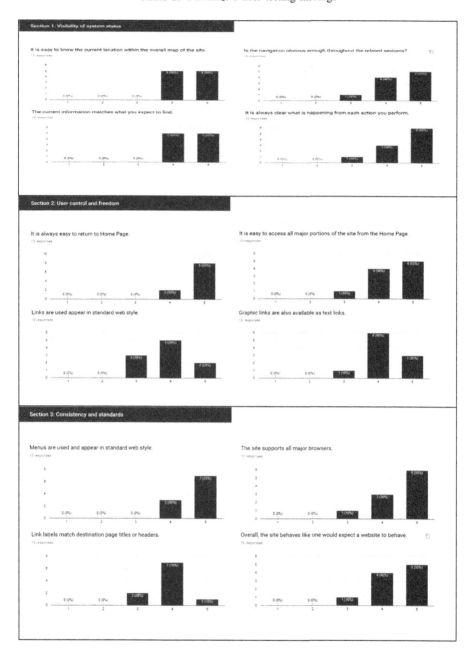

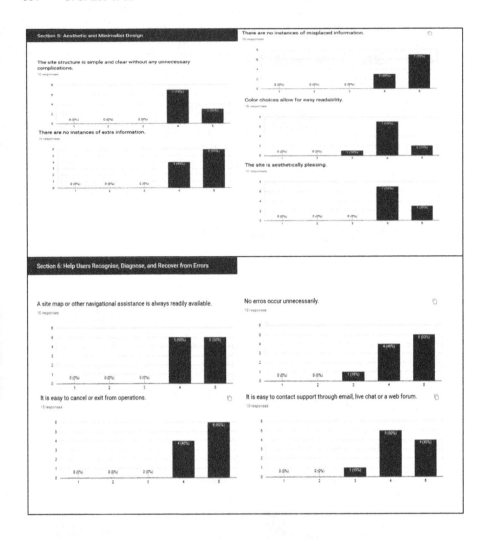

4.3   Case Study 2: *The Enchantress'* Systems Design-Development

The Enchantress [26], is a crowdsourcing platform which encourages the community to recycle and to imagine what these items can become, i.e., the user as designer with the challenge of enchanting buyers (Fig. 2).

Fig. 2. *The Enchantress*

4.4   *The Enchantress'* User Evaluation

Technology acceptance by users has also been positive. Figures 3a, b present some of the findings on 30 respondents.

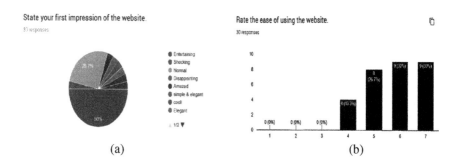

(a)   (b)

Fig. 3. a, b. *The Enchantress'* user testing findings

4.5   Case Study 3: *HerAll*

The *Enchantress* exemplifies business process reengineering, with gamification as the motivator. Yew and Lee [27] have further investigated the efficacy of three Knowledge Management approaches on a crowdsourced platform *HerAll* based on Shapira, Youtie, Yogeesvaran, and Jaafar's [28] propositions. Three hypotheses in the study (Fig. 4) are:

a)   A resource-based view approach (RBV) knowledge management approach will result in higher quality participatory design and have a positive and medium effect on customer satisfaction and in B2C e-commerce.

b)   A knowledge-based view approach (KBV) knowledge management approach will result in higher quality in participatory design and have a positive and low effect on customer satisfaction and in B2C e-commerce.

c)   A mixed (MBV) view knowledge management approach will result in higher quality in participatory design and have a positive and best effect on customer satisfaction and in B2C e-commerce.

The sample group are young Malaysian customers who are potential designers. The leader's design and leadership skills are instrumental to the number and quality of comments and likes, but the most important motivators are recognition and rewards. Some sample screenshots are presented in Figs. 5a, b, c.

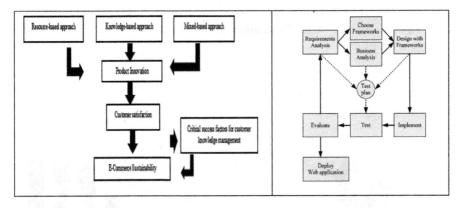

Fig. 4. [27]'s research model on Knowledge Management approaches in relation to product innovation, customer knowledge management and e-commerce sustainability (left) and the development methodology based on the SDLC (right)

(a)   (b)

(c)

Fig. 5. a. Top part of *HerAll's* [27] homepage, **b.** Upload and share at the Design Grid, **c.** Sample blog posts

In addition, among the three approaches, the Mixed Knowledge-Resource-based approach is the most successful approach compared to Knowledge-based and Resource-based approaches in developing more effective learning and higher customer satisfaction. The average customer satisfaction percentages based on the CSAT instrument for each approach are resource-based approach: 75.85%, knowledge-based approach: 71.40% and mixed approach: 81.35%. Some designers also improved over time (Fig. 6a). Blog posts also indicate increased interests and likes (Fig. 6b).

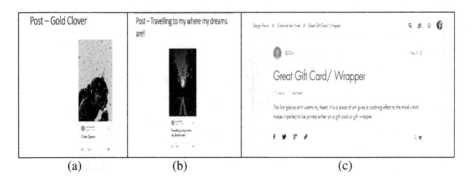

(a)   (b)   (c)

Fig. 6. a. A participant's card designs: Apr 5 (left), Apr 21 (centre), **b.** Sample blog posts on how to productize the designs

5 Discussion

Furnitize's design is more stable as the market and product items are predefined, though customization is allowed. *The Enchantress* and *HerAll's* degree of exposure to market demands and trends are higher, and designs are totally open. *HerAll* is especially sensitive as it caters to a niche market. Hence, we agree with CRMs with object-oriented architecture and agile-SCRUM/KANBAN design-work processes, integration and dashboards such as Salesforce's. Such model-driven architecture and work processes would enable more efficient and effective customization, monitoring and assessments. In addition, throwaway prototyping arising from the sharing of designs and comments greatly complements incremental rapid prototyping for all three systems.

These findings indicate the suitability of [16]'s yin-yang CRM model and [29]'s Identify, Differentiate, Interact, Customize (IDIC) model (Fig. 7) for open co-design. Both models emphasize tradeoffs/balancing and more importantly, design thinking's empathy at every stage. For instance, *identifying* customers as individuals and

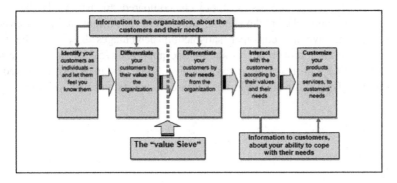

Fig. 7. IDIC CRM model: The identified model for agile open-co-design based on findings above Source: Medium (2020) [31]

subsequently, creating user experience and feelings of personalization at stage 1, *differentiating* based on customer's value to the organization (stage 2) and their needs from the organization (stage 3), *interacting* with customers based on their values and needs (stage 4) and finally, *customizing* to these needs (stage 5).

Findings also highlight the importance of social/humanistic factors such as in [8]'s TAM models and also [30]'s findings on design thinking-computational thinking and dispositions in the creative industries, transferred slightly, from computing.

The importance of the product innovation-supply chain is also supported by [32]'s product innovation-sustainable supply chain model. It extends the supply chain to environmental, operational, social and economic considerations in order to be sustainable. Moreover, since product innovation significantly influences sustainable supply chains upstream and downstream, strategic balancing between higher product margins arising from customization and total long-term supply chain costs, is critical. Due to varying different dimensions in dynamic market demands, agile supply chains take precedence. They also confirm the viability of socially responsible innovations towards social standing/reputation as well as green supply chains. Further investigation, however, are beyond our capacity and scope. Business process studies such as [33]'s series of studies, may play a bigger role in the future.

6 Conclusions

We have posited that ISAD-HCI and Project Management (PM) enable and enhance the product innovation model as well as the sustainable supply chain model concurrently. For instance, Information Systems Analysis and Design (ISAD) emphasize decomposition, loosely and tightly coupled relationships and methodologies. While human-computer-interaction has often been able to create more positive user experience, wider considerations influenced by the Technology Acceptance Model (TAM), highlights the importance of ease of use and usefulness and their influence towards intention and behavior. The integration would help modeling and simulation of what-if scenarios and in scoping user requirements, design and development in software engineering.

The three systems discussed in this paper started out as Information Systems Analysis and Design (ISAD)-Knowledge Management (KM)-Project Management (PM) projects. Hence, for all systems presented, informatics includes not only computational but also cognitive and social aspects. This integration has enabled us to better appreciate all Customer Relationship Management (CRM) models as the common thread across ISAD-KM-PM are retrieval, management, sustainability. Each captures the multifactorial facets influencing the possible degree of sustainability in open co-design. Furthermore, among these, information design, user experience, customer satisfaction metrics, diversity, and environmental support are the most important.

The design in our study is preliminary and involves a very small sample size. Findings confirm that sustainability should be multi-factorial even from the start and that Project Management-computational thinking as design considerations to Information Science-HCI and open co-design can be added strategic advantage to both product innovation and sustainable supply chains.

Acknowledgement. This paper is an extension of two group's Project Management course assignments and an extension of an undergraduate capstone project, in Sunway University. We thank Dr. K. Daniel Wong for introducing design thinking and computational thinking, Dr. Juan Carlos Aguilera for supporting the idea of hybridizing online product design in the past and thought leaders past and present who motivated us.

References

1. Pulse of the profession. Project Management Institute (2017). http://www.pmi.org
2. Valacich, J.S., Schneider, C.: Information systems today: managing in the digital world, 7th Global Edition, Pearson (2016)
3. Ikeda, K., Bernstein, M.S.: Pay it backward: per-task payments on crowdsourcing platforms reduce productivity. In: CHI Conference on Human Factors in Computing Systems, pp. 4111–4121 (2016)
4. Grandon, E., Pearson, J.: E-commerce adoption: perceptions of managers/owners of small and medium sized firms in Chile. Commun. Assoc. Inf. Syst. **13**, 80–102 (2004)
5. Szymanski, D.M., Hise, R.T.: E-satisfaction: an initial examination. J. Retail. **76**(3), 309–322 (2000)
6. Fayad, R., Paper, D.: The technology acceptance model e-commerce extension: a conceptual framework. Procedia Econ. Finan. **26**, 1000–1006 (2015)
7. Davis, F.D., Bagozzi, R.P., Warshaw, P.R.: User acceptance of computer technology: a comparison of two theoretical models. Manag. Sci. **35**(8), 982–1003 (1989)
8. Venkatesh, V., Morris, M.G., Davis, G.B., Davis, F.D.: User acceptance of information technology: towards a unified view. MIS Q. **27**, 425–478 (2003)
9. Azjen, I., Madden, T.: Prediction of goal-directed behavior: attitudes, intentions, and perceived behavioral control. J. Exp. Soc. Psychol. **22**(5), 453–474 (1986)
10. Salazar, M., Harrison, T., Ansell, J.: An approach for the identification of cross-sell and up-sell opportunities using a financial services customer database. J. Finan. Serv. Mark. **12**, 115–131 (2007)
11. Bolumole, Y.: The supply chain role of third-party logistics providers. Int. J. Logist. Manag. **12**(2), 87–102 (2001)
12. Nica, E.: Environmentally sustainable transport and e-commerce logistics. Econ. Manag. Finan. Mark. **1**, 86–92 (2015)
13. Mekler, E.D., Brühlmann, F., Tuch, A.N., Opwis, K.: Towards understanding the effects of individual gamification elements on intrinsic motivation and performance. Comput. Hum. Behav. **71**, 525–534 (2017)
14. Yang, Y., Asaad, Y., Dwivedi, Y.: Examining the impact of gamification on intention of engagement and brand attitude in the marketing context. Comput. Hum. Behav. **73**, 459–469 (2017)
15. Payne, A., Frow, P.: Customer relationship management: from strategy to implementation. J. Mark. Manag. **22**(1–2), 135–168 (2006)
16. Gartner's CRM competency model. https://www.gartner.com/en/documents/3637317/market-insight-the-five-competency-model-for-unifying-cu
17. Buttle, F.: Customer Relationship Management: Concepts and Technologies. Elsevier, Oxford (2009)
18. Lim, A.H.L., Lee, C.S.: Processing online analytics with classification and association rule mining. Knowl.-Based Syst. **23**(3), 248–255 (2010)

19. Sisodia, S., Khandal, V., Singhal, R.: Fast prediction of web user browsing behaviors using most interesting patterns. J. Inf. Sci. **44**(1), 74–90 (2018)
20. Yang, R., Xie, W., Chen, D.: A three-layer model on users' interests mining. J. Inf. Sci. **44** (1), 136–144 (2019)
21. Lee, C.S., Wong, K.D.: An entrepreneurial narrative media-model framework to knowledge building and open co-design. In: SAI Computing, pp. 1169–1175. Springer, London (2017)
22. Lee, C.S., Wong, K.D.: Design - computational thinking, transfer and flavors of reuse: scaffolds to information and data science for sustainable systems in smart cities. In: IEEE International Conference on Information Reuse and Integration, pp. 225–228, IEEE Computer Society, Salt Lake City (2018)
23. Lee, C.S., Singh, Y.P.: Student modelling using principal component analysis of SOM clusters. In: IEEE International Conference on Advanced Learning Technologies, pp. 480–484, Joensuu (2004)
24. Shneiderman, B., Plaisant, C., Cohen, M., Jacobs, S., Elmqvist, N., Diakopoulos, N.: Designing the user interface: strategies for effective human-computer interaction, 6th Edition (Global), Pearson (2017)
25. Chew, P.L, Chee, Y.K., Wong, J.P., Hiew, Y.T.: Furnitize. Project Management Assignment. Sunway University, Malaysia (2017)
26. Yew, L.Y., Lim, K.S., Sugumar, P.: The Enchantress. Project Management Assignment. Sunway University, Malaysia (2017)
27. Yew, L.Y., Lee, C.S.: Resource-knowledge-mixed knowledge management approaches to enhancing e-commerce sustainability: a comparative case study. In: International Conference on Engineering Technology, Sunway University undergraduate capstone project, 6–7 July 2019
28. Shapira, P., Youtie, J., Yogeesvaran, K., Jaafar, Z.: Knowledge economy measurement: methods, results and insights from the Malaysian knowledge content study. In: Triple Helix 5 Conference Panel Session on New Indicators for the Knowledge Economy (2005)
29. Peppers, D., Rogers, M.: Managing Customer Relationships: A Strategic Framework (2004)
30. Lee, C.S., Wong, K.D.: Developing a disposition for social innovations: an affective-socio-cognitive co-design model. In: IADIS International Conference on Cognition and Exploratory Learning in the Digital Age, pp. 180–186, Maynooth (2015)
31. The Customer Relationship Management Frameworks/Models, IDIC Model. https://medium. com/@saeee3d/the-customer-relationship-management-frameworks-models-idic-model-aaa649ffd29b
32. Golrizgashti, S., Piroozfar, S., Dehghanpoor, A.: Product innovation and supply chain sustainability. IEEE Eng. Manag. Rev. **47**(4), 128–136 (2019)
33. Dumas, M., La Rosa, M., Mendling, J., Reijers, H.A.: Business process management. Springer, Berlin (2007)

A Path for the Implementation of Best Practices for Software Requirements Management Process Using a Multimodel Environment

Gloria Piedad Gasca-Hurtado[1] and Mirna Muñoz[2(✉)]

[1] Ingeniería en Sistemas, Facultad de Ingenierías, Universidad de Medellín,
Carrera 87 no. 30-65, Medellín, Colombia
gpgasca@udem.edu.co
[2] Centro de Investigación en Matemáticas - Unidad Zacatecas, Parque Quantum,
Ciudad del Conocimiento Avenida Lassec, Andador Galileo Galilci, Manzana,
3 Lote 7, CP 98160 Zacatecas, Zac, Mexico
mirna.munoz@cimat.mx

Abstract. Continuous improvement is one of the topics of interest for organizations seeking positioning opportunities in the world market. However, software development organizations have high levels of difficulty to implement best practices that address continuous improvement. This paper presents a path to follow to facilitate the work of continuous improvement in a software development organization and that seeks to implement best practices in the software requirements management process. The path is drawn from an analysis of software process improvement models and standards related to software development best practices, under a multimodel environment. The path is structured with a set of techniques, tools, activities, and outputs associated with identified best practices, to facilitate the implementation of improvements in the software requirements management process. Besides, the established path is proposed as an alternative to facilitate the process improvement using a multimodel environment, this way allows establishing balance and instances of collaboration among best practices independent of the model or standard to be implemented.

Keywords: Requirements management · Standards · Models · Multimodel · Implementation path · Software development process

1 Introduction

Globally, the software industry is made up of Small and Medium (SMEs) sized companies in around 92% [1]. At the technology level and specifically for software development companies, efficient software engineering practices, which are tailored to the size, resources, and type of business, are needed. This need arises because of the high effort involved in the implementation of models and standards [2] such as CMMI-DEV v 1.3 [3], ISO 12207 [4], ISO 15504 [5] and ISO 9004:2009 [6].

© Springer Nature Switzerland AG 2020
O. Gervasi et al. (Eds.): ICCSA 2020, LNCS 12254, pp. 812–828, 2020.
https://doi.org/10.1007/978-3-030-58817-5_58

Research focused on determining the importance and difficulty of implementing models and standards for process improvements, confirms that they are oriented to large organizations, which represents less than 10% of the global software industry [7, 8]. Besides, these models and standards do not meet the needs of SMEs [7, 8]. Some of the causes that make difficult the implementation of these models and standards are the costs, the effort, and the return on investment (ROI) produced [9, 10].

The above mentioned, evidence mainly the Latin American context, in which not all software development organizations have the conditions to implement such models and standards. However, they need to stay in continuous improvement to achieve an adequate maturity level to produce quality software.

For SMEs starting in Software Process Improvement (SPI) initiatives represent a great investment and they often find that their improvement goals are not achieved in the short term, and sometimes with significant resource losses [11].

In this context, the process improvement based on multi-model environments aims to provide a harmonized and unified approach through the implementation of different models and/or standards within a SPI initiative [12] to get benefits [13] such as: a) unify a single improvement plan, b) focus the improvement proposal in the organization needs, instead of focusing it on the model or standard that will be implemented [14], and c) reduce the effort to implement a complete model or standard [14].

Because most researchers and the software industry define requirements management as a key process, and it is recognized as a key phase for successful project management [15, 16]. The goal of this paper is to provide a path to follow to facilitate the implementation of best practices in the requirements management process. The established path is proposed as an alternative to facilitate the process improvement using a multi-model environment being the main contribution of this paper.

This work is structured as follows: Sect. 2 establishes a baseline framework on requirements management and multi-model environments. Section 3 describes the research methodology that was applied to establish the implementation path based on the multi-model environment. Section 4 describes the structure of the path of implementation of best practices for the requirements management, and finally, Sect. 5 presents the conclusions and the future work.

2 Theoretical Framework

Requirements engineering can be understood as a process throughout the lifecycle of software development, even after the deployment of the project. However, requirements engineering can also be understood as an activity to manage changes in requirements [17].

The Requirements Management aims to capture, store, disseminate, and manage information [18]. In general, requirement management includes all activities related to version control and change control, as well as, the requirements tracking. Besides, indicators are highlighting that the failure of projects is the requirement management [17, 19].

This is not surprising given that the requirement management process has a great impact on the effectiveness of all software development processes [20]. A study in the

UK found that of 268 documented developmental problems, 48% represented problems related to software requirements [21]. Another study identified problems in software development organizations associated with requirements engineering activities [22]. This allows us to conclude that the phases associated with requirements engineering, such as requirement management are success factors in software development, having a high impact on the success of software development projects.

For these reasons, it is important to make proposals and research that will help improve the way organizations implement requirements engineering processes [15].

Around the best practices, some researchers focus on defining them, as well as the frameworks, standards, and models that contain them such as: CMMI-DEV v1.3 [3], PRINCE2 [23], ISO/IEC 15504 [5], IEEE 830 [24], IEEE 1233, ISO 12207 [4], ISO 9000:2000 [25], PMBOK [26].

There are research initiatives aimed at facilitating the implementation of best practices in software development organizations related to software requirements. Within these initiatives exist a guide generated through a research study in Malaysia. This research was aimed to document the experience of IT Managers to standardize a guide for software projects in the Public Sector in Malaysia [27]. This proposal is complemented with requirements management tools that incorporate the best practices in requirement management [28].

GlobReq is a framework for the requirements engineering process of global software development projects. This proposal focuses on adapting and customizing a framework of requirement practices defined by Sommerville, focused on global software development projects [29].

A case study on requirement practices in three open-source software projects is another of the initiatives associated with the implementation of requirement practices to achieve successful software development projects. The objective of this study was focused on understanding how each project manages requirements and identify research lines on requirements engineering by proposing a taxonomy to describe the spectrum of formal requirements practices [30].

Besides, there are hybrid approaches between agile methodologies and traditional methodologies that are proposed taking into account the importance of requirements engineering as fundamental elements for software development [31]. In the same orientation of the agile methodologies, there are studies related to the evaluation of the requirements engineering process and the aspects that seem to be ignored when using an agile environment. From this study, we can outline a path related to the essential requirements engineering practices and their possible adaptation in the context of agile ideas such as simplicity, short notes, continuous validation, and frequent refactoring, among others [32].

There are other studies related to requirements engineering where requirements management measures are proposed as efficient predictors of stability and volatility of requirements and management of change requests. This proposal has been validated using ten of the proposed measures and the generation of an industrial case where it is pretended to validate the efficiency of the proposed predictions [33].

Other important initiatives have been defined in terms of the need to generate requirements efficiently, eliminating ambiguity aspects. For the above, the process of generating requirements and its related activities are analyzed. It also focuses on methodologies, models, and requirements engineering techniques [34].

These studies not only demonstrate the interest of research and industry for the requirements engineering. It also shows that commercial software companies are looking for profits by actively exploiting viable business opportunities. To achieve and maintain a competitive advantage these companies face great challenges due to technological changes [35]. From the perspective of maximizing return on investment (ROI), Software development companies must focus on identifying and implementing the most cost-effective functionality, a goal that is strongly correlated with the identification of requirements that meet customer needs [36].

Unfortunately, this relationship seems to be underestimated: during the software engineering process, the requirements are not necessarily identified, qualified, or prioritized, which constitute weaknesses associated with the requirements management [15, 16, 37].

While these weaknesses can be solved implementing frameworks and standards such as CMMI-DEV v1.3, PRINCE2, ISO/IEC 15504, IEEE 830, IEEE 1233, ISO 12207, ISO 9000:2000, PMBOK, organizations increasingly tend to use a set of international standards and models to manage software development processes. They seek to increase customer satisfaction, achieve a competitive advantage, and benefit in process performance and normative compliance [38]. For this reason, a company probably prefers to implement a set with more than one software process improvement model, standard or normative [39]. This trend is known as a multimodel environment, an approach of the Software Engineering Institute (SEI) developed to harmonize the process improvement models [40]. However, there are difficulties in successfully implementing process improvement using multimodel environments, mostly due to the complexity of their implementation [41].

It is important to recognize that the implementation of a model or standard by itself or in a multi-model environment, according to the current trend of the organizations, it has an intrinsic complexity. For this reason, it is necessary to define a path to follow from the analysis of the needs of an organization and the process to be implemented.

3   Research Methodology

The design of activities is fundamental for applied disciplines. Design-oriented research has a long history in many fields, including architecture, engineering, education, psychology, and fine arts [42].

The area of Technology and Information Computing (TIC) has adopted many of the ideas, concepts, and methods of science based on the design that have originated in these other disciplines. This research paper has taken as a methodological basis the research paradigm proposed by Hevner [43]. This proposal consists of three cycles for scientific research based on design (See Fig. 1).

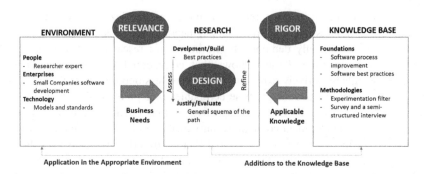

Fig. 1. General Scheme research paradigm proposed by Hevner [43].

The three cycles were followed to design the proposed path for implementing software development best practices for the RM process. Each one of these cycles was implemented as follows:

- In the *relevance cycle* the standards and models that will compose the multi-model environment, which will be used as a framework for the path, were identified. In this phase, the Models and Standards Similarity Study method (MSSS) [13] was used as a support strategy to establish a multimodel environment. As the method suggests, the models and standards were selected taking into account the application domain, and the problems and opportunities of the requirements management.
- In the *design cycle*, the base best practices, which are contained in the general schema of the implementation path, were selected. The selection of the best practices is based on the number of coincidences and relationships between the models and standards identified in the *relevance cycle*. A nomenclature was defined to identify relationships among different models and standards. Besides, the structure of the implementation path is established from the identified coincidences and relationships.
- In the *rigor cycle*, it is established the way to validate the implementation path. This validation was designed to be used by experts in process improvement. This cycle aims to establish a knowledge base that is suggested by the research paradigm.

4   A Path for Software Requirements Management

Next, the results obtained from the application research paradigm are shown.

4.1   Relevance Cycle

The MSSS method consists of a sequence of steps to determine how a reference model or standard is complemented by other models or standards.

Table 1 shows the steps of the MSSS method. Besides, it includes the adaptations done to the method and its justification.

Table 1. Adaptation of the MSSS method.

MSSS method steps	Adaptations	Justification
Select models and standards	Select the process to be compared	To focus the study on the process and select the best practices to be included in the implementation path
Select a reference model	Select models and standards	To focus on the selection of models and standards based on the focused process to define the implementation path
Select the process to be compared	Select a reference model or standard	A model or standard should be selected as a reference to integrate the multimodel environment based on specific criteria
Identify similarities between models		Without changes or adaptations from the original method
Create a matching template		
	Set the detail level	To facilitate the analysis of the information according to the recommendations of the MSSS method
Show obtained results		Without changes or adaptations from the original method

The results of the relevancy cycle allowed establishing the application domain, the problems, and the opportunities related to the requirement management. The following are the most relevant results found in this cycle:

1) The baseline for determining the similarity is the last level of reference model (CMMI-DEV), i.e. at the specific practice level. Making a comparative analysis at the specific practice level allows covering most of the structure of the reference model compared with other standards and models selected.
2) The correspondence template details the inputs, subpractices, and work products of the selected standards and models to complement the reference model [44].
3) Following the recommendations of the MSSS method, a glossary is established, which for this research is called nomenclature based on the initials of the model or standard, followed by a number as follows: CMMI-DEV v1.3 (C); IEEE 1233(I1); PRINCE2(P); ISO 12207 (IS1); ISO/IEC 15504 (IE1); ISO 9000:2000 (IS9); IEEE 830 (I8); PMBOK (PM)
4) The consolidated results describe how the evaluated elements of the models and standards complement the reference model. An example of the consolidated results is shown in Table 2 results table for the specific practice to establish the requirements for the product and the product components. The full analysis details the similarities, as well as the direct and indirect relationships established from the analytical study [44].

The similarity study performed allowed identifying the indirect relations of the elements of each standard and model analyzed, in Table 2 for this type of relations are used (α).

Table 2. Results table for the SP 2.1 Establish the requirements of the products and the product components.

SG 2 Develop the product requirements

SP 2.1 Establish the requirements for product and product components

Inputs	Tools and techniques	Work products
Customer Satisfaction (C) Business satisfaction (C) Project objectives and associated attributes (C) Production, operation and withdrawal requirements (C) Change requests (IE1) Customer petition (IE1) Customer requirements (IE1) Interaction that the software will have with people, hardware, other hardware, and other software (I8) (α) The speed, availability, response time, recovery time of various software functions, etc. (I8) (α) Portability, accuracy, maintenance, security requirements and other considerations (α) Standard requirements, application language, database integrity policies, resource limits, operating environment (I8) (α)	T2.1.1 Quality Function Deployment QFD (C) T2.1.2 Patterns of architecture (C) T2.1.3 Formal languages (IE1) T2.1.4 Traceability Matrices (IE1) T2.1.5 Prototypes (IE1) T2.3.1 Quality characteristics of the software described in the standard ISO/IEC 9126 (IE1) (α)	Derived requirements (C, IE1) Product requirements (C) Product component requirements (C) Architecture requirements, which specify or restrict the relationships between product components (C) Communication records (IE1) Change control records (IE1) System Requirements (IE1) Analysis report (IE1) Traceability records (IE1) Product functions (I8) (α) User characteristics (I8) (α) Restrictions that include regulatory policies, hardware limitations, interfaces to other applications, parallel operation, audit functions, control functions, language requirements, reliability requirements (I8)(α) Credibility of the application and security considerations (I8) (α) Specific requirements at a level of enough detail to facilitate design (I8) (α) Dependencies or statement of factors affecting the requirements stated in the SRS (I8) (α) Requirements not established by the customer but necessary for the specified use or intended use (IS9) (α)

Performing the similarity analysis, a complete coincidence is found between the models CMMI-DEV v1.3 and the ISO/IEC 15504 standard for inputs, tools, techniques, and work products. However, there are also indirect relationships (α) with the IEEE 830 and ISO 9000:2000 standards that can be identified by analyzing in detail their input and work product elements. Because they allow defining requirements expressed in technical terms that can be used for design decisions.

4.2 Design Cycle

This cycle is composed of two activities: 1) selection of best practices, and 2) structure the path. Each activity was developed to obtain the results expected in the design phase. That means the schematic design of an implementation path for best practices as next described:

Activity 1. Selection of Best Practices
To define and select the best practices, the following criteria were considered:

$$P > \, = 3 \rightarrow BP \in R^1 \tag{1}$$

$$P < 3 \rightarrow BP \notin R^1 \tag{2}$$

Where, P = relation established in the consolidated results tables, BP = best practice and R1 = Primary implementation path.

For each one of the best practices that were eliminated by criteria *(2)*, an analysis is performed. This analysis is carried out by a focus group of researchers who study each best practice regarding the model or standard to which the practice originally belongs. This study includes a comparison and identification of the elements that allows defining if the best practice is included in the path by criteria *(1)*, or it can be grouped as an activity or tool in R^1.

From this analysis, we obtain a first version of the implementation path, called the primary path (R^1), which the best practices base to implement and improve software requirements management, are identified. An example of a primary path for requirements management is shown in Fig. 2.

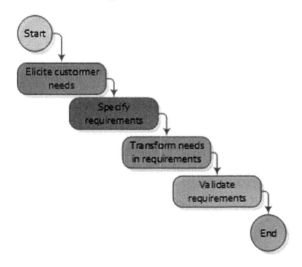

Fig. 2. General Scheme R^1 to implement best practices for requirement management.

The scheme shown in Fig. 2 corresponds to R^1. Up to this point, the scheme is sequential, indicating the start and end of the requirement management process. In the traced path, direct and indirect coincidences found in the similarity analysis are considered. These coincidences allow identifying both the standard and best practices according to the criteria for determining their membership in R^1. However, the objective of establishing a path for processes implementation, such as the requirement management, is to analyze and consolidate a multimodel environment, therefore the results were consolidated by applying the criteria (1) and (2). Table 3 shows the consolidation done by taking the reference model as a base.

Table 3. Consolidated results by applying the criteria (1) and (2).

CMMI-DEV v 1.3		P	IE1	I8	I1	PM	I9	IS12
Goal*	Practice							
DR	Eliciting needs	Y	Y	Y	Y	Y	Y	Y
	Transform needs into requirements	N	N	N	N	N	N	N
DPR	Establish products and components	N	Y	N	N	N	N	N
	Assign requirements to components	N	N	N	N	N	N	N
	Identify requirements interfaces	N	Y	N	N	N	N	N
AVR	Establish operating scenarios	N	N	N	N	N	N	N
	Establish a definition of quality and functionality	Y	N	N	N	Y	N	N
	Analyze requirements	N	N	Y	N	N	Y	Y
	Analyze requirements and balance	N	Y	N	N	N	N	Y
	Validate requirements	N	Y	Y	N	N	N	Y
RM	Understand	N	N	N	N	N	N	N
	Get commitment	N	N	N	N	N	N	N
	Manage changes	N	N	N	N	Y	Y	Y
	Maintain traceability	N	Y	Y	N	N	N	N
	Secure alignment	N	N	N	N	N	N	N

* DR: Develop requirement, DPR: Develop product requirement, AVR: Analyze and validate requirements and RM: Requirement Management.

As Table 3 shows, the reference model is CMMI-DEV v1.3 model, this model details the specific practices that must be considered to implement the requirements development (RD) and requirements management (REQM) processes. These processes have been grouped to select best practices in R^1. As shown in the table, it is recognized the existence of a direct relationship of all the standards and models to the practice of *eliciting needs*. This relation belongs to R^1 following the criteria (1). This is the only practice that has total coincidence among the analyzed models and standards.

With the direct relation analyzed in the first instance, it is also identified that the CMMI-DEV v 1.3 model and the ISO/IEC 15504 standard focus on improving the IT processes, and they define the specific practices to implement requirements management. Besides, they present at a high level of detail the inputs, tools, techniques, and work products. These relationships were excluded from R^1, but documented to perform an analysis in the later phases for structuring the path.

From Table 4, it can also be determined that the PRINCE2 and PMBOK define the requirements management in the definition and analysis phase of the project scope, in the definition of the functionality and the quality attributes, as well as in change management. For this reason, they were excluded from R^1.

Activity 2. Structuring the Best Practices Implementation Path
From the primary path defined in activity 1, the techniques and tools that will complement the scheme of the primary path (R^1) are analyzed. A new analysis is performed considering relationships documented in the relevance cycle. Moreover, a new structure of the best practices implementation path is defined. This new structure complements the linear scheme (R^1) becoming a scheme by quadrants.

The selected scheme allows visualizing the linear overview of the primary path including four essential characteristics to implement best practices in each quadrant, including: a) best practices, b) key activities, c) tools and techniques, and d) process outputs.

To identify each quadrant, four symbols are defined as shown in Table 4.

Table 4. Identifier Symbols and its description

Identifier Symbol	Identifier description
	Best practice: a sequential alphanumeric nomenclature established with the prefix BPi. Where i is a numerical value.
	Activity: a sequential alphanumeric nomenclature established with the prefix A followed by a dot and the identifier corresponding to the best practice, e.g. A.BPi.-j. Where j is a numerical value.
	Tool: a unique alphabetical nomenclature established for the quadrant that identifies the set of tools for the corresponding BP. This nomenclature is followed by the suffix corresponding to BP, e.g. H.BPi.
	Outputs: a unique alphabetical nomenclature established for the quadrant that identifies the set of outputs resulting from the implementation of the corresponding BP. This nomenclature is followed by the suffix corresponding to BP, e.g. S.BPi.

Each scheme represents the best practices associated with the analysis of the recommendations of the multimodel environment used to define the best practices implementation path. In the scheme of the BP1 (Fig. 3) each quadrant is represented with their corresponding identifier. Quadrants characterize each best practice as follows:

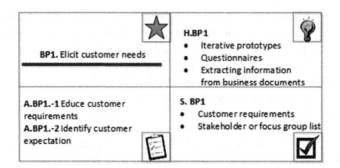

Fig. 3. Scheme for the practice (BP1) using the four essential characteristics.

Quadrant 1. Identified with the symbol of a yellow star. It corresponds to the name of the practice given from the multimodel environment.

Quadrant 2. Identified with the notepad symbol. It provides a set of activities that guides the implementation of the best practice provided in quadrant 1.

Quadrant 3. Identified with the bulb symbol. It provides a list of the tools that help in the implementation of the activities grouped in quadrant 2.

Quadrant 4. Identified with a tick square. It provides the outputs that represent the possible artifacts that are generated when executing the activities grouped in quadrant 2. Most of the time they are outputs resulting from the use of the techniques from quadrant 3.

Figure 4 shows the complete structure of the path by quadrants.

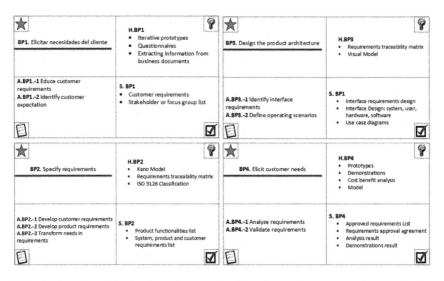

Fig. 4. Structure of the implementation path of requirement management by quadrants.

So far, these diagrams show activities, techniques, or methods and artifacts resulting from the implementation of best practices.

This proposal also includes a path in terms of flow diagram summarizing activities. This diagram is shown in Fig. 5. This path is defined with the identified activities in each one of the quadrants. Besides, the most important deliverables defined in the quadrants are included.

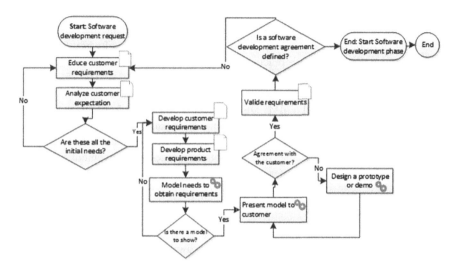

Fig. 5. Flow diagram for the implementation path.

4.3   Rigor Cycle

The validation process of the path was defined as an experimentation filter. This filter aims that researchers in the area present their opinion on the proposal. This phase was carried out using a survey and a semi-structured interview as an information collection technique.

Based on the similarities of the models and standards analyzed that address the requirements management process, the research team proposed the following recommendations:

- The requirements management process is the starting point in the implementation of process improvement for software development because it is the process that must be followed in detail to ensure an early quality.
- Software development organizations that implement best practices for software development focused on the specific practices of the RD and REQM process areas of the CMMI-DEV v1.3 model have complementary elements of other models, for example, techniques and tools. These complementary elements must be considered.
- The specific practices SP 1.1 and SP 3.2 of the RD process area, as well as the specific practice SP 1.3 of REQM, are critical in the process, therefore, they must be

implemented following in detail the recommendations of the CMMI-DEV v1.3 model. Besides, such criticality indicates that they are the first practices that must be implemented for the improvement of the software development process. Following some of the specific practices of greater criticality, contributes to reducing possible causes of failure associated with failures in definition, lack of participation from the user, incomplete requirements, and not properly managed changes [12].

- For the specific practices SP 2.1 and 2.3 of the RD process area of the CMMI-DEV v1.3 model, indirect relationships are identified $^{(\alpha)}$ relevant for the process improvement. These relationships reveal the importance of its implementation for each one of the analyzed models. Therefore, it is important that organizations seeking to implement improvements in processes related to software development requirements, consider such practices in the second instance.

- For specific practices SP 1.1, SP 2.2, SP 3.1, SP 3.3, SP 3.4, SP 3.5 of the RD process area and specific practices SP 1.1, SP 1.2, SP 1.4, SP 1.5 of the REQM process area of the model CMMI-DEV v1.3, it is concluded from the analyzes, that they are complementary practices because not all the analyzed models and standards are explicitly addressed them. However, the researchers' team considers it important to take into account that they are part of the process improvement and can be implemented in the medium-term.

4.4   Research Limitation

The experimentation filter conducted as a validation process can present threats to the results validation. Regarding to obtained results from the expert assessment can present threats associated with the experience and subjectivity of the experts in the study area, i.e. similarities of the models and standards analyzed that address the requirements management process.

To avoid the researcher bias during the validation process a supervised review process with a more experienced researcher was implemented. Moreover, we created a template format to register the semi-structured interview with the researchers, to obtain a baseline of the information from the interviewees.

Although, experts were chosen using the selection convenience technique, taking into account the experience of the experts in issues associated with the study area, such as: software engineering and software process improvement. For reducing the threats related to experience in the study area, we select the experts with high productivity in academy and research, using researchers databases.

In the future, we hope to collect results with a larger expert group, and compare the obtained results in a systematic literature review prepared for validation purposes. Such comparison will allow us to confirm the expert opinions and reduce the subjectivity of this validation.

5 Conclusions

An analysis of similarities between models and standards has been developed including CMMI-DEV v1.3, PRINCE2, ISO/IEC 15504, IEEE 830, IEEE 1233, PMBOK, ISO 9000:2000, and ISO 12207, all of them address the requirements management process.

The obtained results constitute a guide for the implementation of the best practices for the Requirements Management process. These best practices could be selected and implemented by small and medium-sized software development companies according to their needs, cost constraints, effort, and budget.

Besides, the result obtained allows determining the similarity or correspondence between the standards and models establishing the completeness, robustness, and detail for the implementation of standards and models widely accepted and adopted in small or medium organizations.

As a result of analyzing the coincidences and relations accomplished among the selected models and standards, it was possible to draw an implementation path. This path includes four basic practices for the development and management of project requirements. The implementation path was described in different charts such as, linear diagram for the basic path (see Fig. 2), four independent diagrams describing activities, methods or techniques, and outputs (see Fig. 4), and a flow diagram to explain the sequence of the path (see Fig. 5).

As future work, there has been identified that new lines of research associated with the design of best practices for other improvement processes. This would allow complementing the management path for software development requirements with intercommunicated processes that address the implementation of other software engineering processes.

The validation of this path is a line of work necessary to know results regarding the implementation of best practices grouped in the defined path and improvements that complement the design of the established implementation path.

References

1. Laporte, C.Y., Muñoz, M., Mejia, J., O'Connor, R.V.: Applying software engineering standards in very small entities-from startups to grownups. IEEE Softw. **35**(1), 99–103 (2017)
2. Kalinowski, M., et al.: Results of 10 years of software process improvement in Brazil based on the MPS-SW model. In: 2014 9th International Conference on the Quality of Information and Communications Technology (QUATIC), pp. 28–37 (2014)
3. Software Engineering Institute. CMMI for Development, Version 1.3 CMMI-DEV 1.3 (2010)
4. ISO/IEC. Systems and software engineering—Software life cycle processes, ISO/IEC 12207, ed. (2008)
5. ISO/IEC. International Standard ISO/IEC 15504 Software Process Improvement and Capability Determination, ed. (2004)
6. ISO/IEC. ISO 9004:2009, Managing for the sustained success of an organization – A quality management approach (2009)

7. Leung, H.K.N., Yuen, T.C.F.: A process framework for small projects. Softw. Process Improv. Pract. **6**(2), 67–83 (2001)
8. Staples, M., Niazi, M., Jeffery, R., Abrahams, A., Byatt, P., Murphy, R.: An exploratory study of why organizations do not adopt CMMI. J. Syst. Softw. **80**(6), 883–895 (2007)
9. Rico, D.F.: ROI of Software Process Improvement: For Project Portfolio Managers and PMO's (2004)
10. García, J., De Amescua, A., Velasco, M.: TOP 10 de factores que obstaculizan la mejora de los procesos de verificación y validación en organizaciones intensivas en software. Revista Española de Innovación, Calidad e Ingeniería del Software **2**, 18–28 (2006)
11. Zarour, M., Abran, A., Desharnais, J.-M., Alarifi, A.: An investigation into the best practices for the successful design and implementation of lightweight software process assessment methods: a systematic literature review. J. Syst. Softw. **101**, 180–192 (2015)
12. Srivastava, N., Singh, S., Dokken, T.: Assorted chocolates and cookies in a multi-model box. In: SEPG 2009 North America Conference. Software Engineering Institute, March 2019
13. Cuevas, G., Mejía, J., Muñoz, M., San Feliu, T.: Experiencia en la Mejora de Procesos de Gestión de Proyectos Utilizando un Entorno de Referencia Multimodelo. Revista Ibérica de Sistemas y Tecnologías de Información **1**, 87–100 (2010)
14. Muñoz, M., Mejía, J.: Establishing multi-model environments to improve organizational software processes. In: Rocha, Á., Correia, A., Wilson, T., Stroetmann, K. (eds.) Advances in Information Systems and Technologies, vol. 206, pp. 445–454. Springer, Heidelberg (2013). https://doi.org/10.1007/978-3-642-36981-0_41
15. Mustapha, A.M., Arogundade, O.T., Misra, S., Damasevicius, R., Maskeliunas, R.: A systematic literature review on compliance requirements management of business processes. Int. J. Syst. Assur. Eng. Manag. **11**(3), 561–576 (2020). https://doi.org/10.1007/s13198-020-00985-w
16. Aguilar, J.A., Zaldívar-Colado, A., Tripp-Barba, C., Espinosa, R., Misra, S., Zurita, C.E.: A survey about the impact of requirements engineering practice in small-sized software factories in Sinaloa, Mexico. In: Gervasi, O., et al. (eds.) ICCSA 2018. LNCS, vol. 10963, pp. 331–340. Springer, Cham (2018). https://doi.org/10.1007/978-3-319-95171-3_26
17. Xie, Y., Tang, T., Xu, T., Zhao, L.: Research on requirement management for complex systems. In: 2010 2nd International Conference on Computer Engineering and Technology, Chengdu, pp. V1-113–V1-116 (2010)
18. Paetsch, F., Eberlein, A., Maurer, F.: Requirements engineering and agile software development. In: WET ICE 2003. 2003 Proceedings of the Twelfth IEEE International Workshops on Enabling Technologies: Infrastructure for Collaborative Enterprises, Linz, Austria, pp. 308–313 (2003)
19. Oza, N.V., Hall, T.: Difficulties in managing offshore software outsourcing relationships: an empirical analysis of 18 high maturity Indian software companies. J. Inf. Technol. Case Appl. Res. **7**, 25–41 (2005)
20. Sommerville, I., Ransom, J.: An empirical study of industrial requirements engineering process assessment and improvement. ACM Trans. Softw. Eng. Methodol. **14**, 85–117 (2005)
21. Beecham, S., Hall, T., Rainer, A.: Software process improvement problems in twelve software companies: an empirical analysis. Empir. Softw. Eng. **8**, 7–42 (2003). https://doi.org/10.1023/A:1021764731148
22. Damian, D.E., Zowghi, D.: RE challenges in multi-site software development organizations. Requirements Eng. **8**, 149–160 (2003). https://doi.org/10.1007/s00766-003-0173-1
23. OGC: Managing Successful Projects with PRINCE2 (2005)
24. IEEE: IEEE 830, Recommended Practice for Software Requirements Specifications, ed. (1998)

25. International Organization for Standardization. (Enero 16, 2013). ISO 9000: 2005 -Basic concepts and language (2005)
26. IEEE: A Guide to the Project Management Body of Knowledge, IEEE Guide (2004)
27. Haron, M., Harun, M., Mahrim, N., Sahibuddin, S., Zakaria, N.H., Abdul Rahman, N.: Understanding the requirement engineering for organization: the challenges. In: 2012 8th International Conference on Computing Technology and Information Management (NCM and ICNIT), Seoul, pp. 561–567 (2012)
28. Zainol, A., Mansoor, S.: An investigation of a requirements management tool elements. In: 2011 IEEE Conference on Open Systems (ICOS), pp. 53–58 (2011)
29. Niazi, M., El-Attar, M., Usman, M., Ikram, N.: GlobReq: a framework for improving requirements engineering in global software development projects: preliminary results. In: 16th International Conference on Evaluation & Assessment in Software Engineering (EASE 2012), Ciudad Real, pp. 166–170 (2012)
30. Ernst, N.A., Murphy, G.C.: Case studies in just-in-time requirements analysis. In: 2012 Second IEEE International Workshop on Empirical Requirements Engineering (EmpiRE), Chicago, IL, pp. 25–32 (2012)
31. Kumar, M., Shukla, M., Argarwal, S.: A hybrid approach of requirement engineering in agile software development. In: 2013 International Conference on Machine Intelligence and Research Advancement (ICMIRA), pp. 515–519 (2013)
32. Eberlein, A., Leite, J.: Agile requirements definition: a view from requirements engineering. In: Proceedings of the International Workshop on Time-Constrained Requirements Engineering (TCRE 2002), pp. 4–8 (2002)
33. Loconsole, A.: Empirical studies on requirement management measures. In: Proceedings of the 26th International Conference on Software Engineering, pp. 42–44 (2004)
34. Dube, R.R., Dixit, S.K.: Process-oriented complete requirement engineering cycle for generic projects. Presented at the Proceedings of the International Conference and Workshop on Emerging Trends in Technology, Mumbai, Maharashtra, India (2010)
35. Wnuk, K., Pfahl, D., Callele, D., Karlsson, E.: How can open source software development help requirements management gain the potential of open innovation: an exploratory study. In: Proceedings of the 2012 ACM-IEEE International Symposium on Empirical Software Engineering and Measurement, Lund, pp. 271–279 (2012)
36. Aurum, A., Wohlin, C.: A value-based approach in requirements engineering: explaining some of the fundamental concepts. In: Sawyer, P., Paech, B., Heymans, P. (eds.) REFSQ 2007. LNCS, vol. 4542, pp. 109–115. Springer, Heidelberg (2007). https://doi.org/10.1007/978-3-540-73031-6_8
37. Biffl, S., Aurum, A., Boehm, B., Erdogmus, H., Grünbacher, P. (eds.): Value-Based Software Engineering. Springer, Heidelberg (2006). https://doi.org/10.1007/3-540-29263-2
38. Siviy, J., Patrick, K., Lisa, M., John, M.: The value of harmonization multiple improvement technologies: a process improvement professional's view, Software Engineering Institute (SEI), Carnegie Mellon University (2008)
39. Urs, et al.: A unified process improvement approach for multi-model improvement environments (2009)
40. Ferreira, A., Machado, R.: Software process improvement in multimodel environments. In: 2009 Fourth International Conference on Software Engineering Advances. IEEE (2009)
41. Gasca-Hurtado, G.P., Hincapié, J.A., Muñoz, M.: Software process improvement assessment for multimodel environment tool to diagnose an organization. In: 2017 12th Iberian Conference on Information Systems and Technologies (CISTI). IEEE (2017)
42. Cross, N.: Designerly ways of knowing: design discipline versus design science. Des. Issues 17, 49–55 (2001)

43. Hevner, A., Chatterjee, S.: Design science research in information systems. In: Hevner, A., Chatterjee, S. (eds.) Design Research in Information Systems, vol. 22, pp. 9–22. Springer, Boston (2010). https://doi.org/10.1007/978-1-4419-5653-8_2

44. Gasca-Hurtado, G.P., Muñoz, M., Mejia, J., Calvo-Manzano J.A.: Software requirements development: a path for improving software quality. In: Barafort, B., O'Connor, Rory V., Poth, A., Messnarz, R. (eds.) EuroSPI 2014. CCIS, vol. 425, pp. 194–205. Springer, Heidelberg (2014). https://doi.org/10.1007/978-3-662-43896-1_17

Educational Video Game Design Using Personalized Learning Scenarios

Boyan Bontchev$^{(\boxtimes)}$ ⓘ, Albena Antonova ⓘ, and Yavor Dankov ⓘ

Faculty of Mathematics and Informatics, Sofia University "St Kl. Ohridski",
Sofia, Bulgaria
{bbontchev,a_antonova,yavor.dankov}@fmi.uni-sofia.bg

Abstract. Educational video games are considered interactive, user-oriented, and motivating learning instruments, allowing delivery of tailored learning experiences. Designing and implementing adaptive and personalized educational video games can become a suitable tool for teachers in student-centric learning. In this context, the present research aims to outline how mini puzzle games adaptable to the individual learner and proactive learning scenarios can help teachers to adopt enhanced strategies for game-based learning, based on students' personalization and adaptation. The paper presents design approaches for adjusting educational video mazes to both individual and group student models, which are based on personalization and adaptation. It describes how basic learning scenarios can be personalized once at the level of the maze game by selecting puzzles appropriate for a given individual student and, next, inside each of the puzzles. While the personalization of the learning content and its structuring and presentation is realized statically, a dynamic adaptation of both the content difficulty and gameplay is suggested according to observable changes in student properties during playing the game. Both the personalization and adaptation of the maze containing puzzles are specified by XML descriptions, which are used by different software instruments for building the whole game and for analyzing the outcomes of its playing. There are discussed the design principles of personalized maze games allowing teachers and educators to create and apply their educational games.

Keywords: Game design · Personalization · Learning scenarios · Analytics

1 Introduction

Educational video games can support learning process adaptability and personalization, allowing teachers to design and adopt learner-oriented teaching strategies [1, 2]. Considering student needs, learning style, and preferences of each learner in the class [3], educational video games can assist teachers to apply flexible instruction scenarios. Thus, educational video games represent interactive platforms for innovative pedagogical practices, embracing learner-based and personalized teaching approaches [4]. In this way, by exploring different adaptation approaches, we would be able to identify how teachers can apply personalization and adaptability in game-based learning scenarios [5], based on adaptable mini-puzzle games in the class [6].

© Springer Nature Switzerland AG 2020
O. Gervasi et al. (Eds.): ICCSA 2020, LNCS 12254, pp. 829–845, 2020.
https://doi.org/10.1007/978-3-030-58817-5_59

Thus, the present research aims to outline how educational video games personalization and adaptation can be achieved via mini puzzle games and proactive learning scenarios, for supporting student-oriented and tailored learning. More specifically, the research determines the following approaches for educational video game adaptation and personalization, including:

(1) educational maze games generated automatically by the APOGEE (smArt adaPtive videO GamEs for Education) platform [7] and containing various mandatory and optional puzzle mini-games;
(2) learning objects embedded into the maze and the mini-games contained in the maze halls; and
(3) game-based learning scenarios designed for both the maze and embedded mini-games.

The present research will discover how the educational video-game platform-APOGEE will support adaptivity [8] and personalization [9], supporting teachers first to section puzzle mini-games for learners with a specific profile and, next, to link, structure and represent learning content inside mini-games by enhancing personalization of the overall game-based learning process. The selected puzzle mini-games and linked learning content inside each mini-game will be automatically presented to each learner having a specific profile. The learner profile includes static and dynamic properties about age, gender, learning goals, initial knowledge, learning/playing style, and others, determined before starting the game on the base of a self-report.

The paper is structured as follows: first, the authors outline the main approaches for learning adaptability and personalization, taking into consideration the learning scenarios for designing and implementing educational video games in the class [5]. Then, by investigating the common elements of various puzzle mini-games that can be embedded within the maze game generated by the APOGEE platform, there are identified common patterns and characteristics of these mini-games. Next, simplified tools and methods are identified to support personalization within every educational mini-game, reflecting as well for relevant pedagogical methodologies and in-class learning practices. Considering that one of the objectives of the APOGEE platform is to enable teachers to design and develop their own-generated educational games, new approaches for supporting them to apply learning personalization are proposed. In the conclusion section, the paper discusses the main challenges faced by teachers in the process of implementation personalization strategies in-class, combining adaptable educational video games and innovative teaching methods.

2 Related Works

Both interactive and reactive to learners, educational video games facilitate the inclusion of adaptation mechanisms in games and in the learning process as a whole. Even more, adaptation is one of the key features of educational video games. As discovered in [10, 11], adaptation affects the quality of the educational experience, allowing the learning environments to cater to students with different learning styles, different levels of initial knowledge, and different expectations and objectives. Further, personalized and adaptive educational video games can motivate usage, increasing user acceptance, and user identification within and outside of the game [11, 12]. Providing personalized experiences, educational video games facilitate achieving the targeted positive outcomes, allowing users to make progress in a motivating and rewarding manner.

Adaptability and personalization are often discussed interchangeably in-game literature [8, 11]. Discussing the main differences among the most popular terms, [12] determines that *adaptability* is the ability for changing some properties of the system to the needs of a user group or environmental context. The term *customization* reflects the act of changing the system (more often concerning appearance or content of the system) by explicit user intervention. *Personalization* explains how the system responds to specific user groups' demands depending on the user profile. Personalization can either be achieved manually or automatically by tailoring the content, appearance, or any other aspect of the system according to the needs and preferences of given user groups. Customization is often used interchangeably with the term personalization, but there is a subtle difference. In many cases where personalization relates to automatically individualized experiences, meaning that a system is configured or adjusted implicitly without interaction by the user, customization relates to manual, explicit adjustments and choices made by the users to optimize their experience. *Adaptivity*, on the other hand, means an automatic adjustment of the game features over time (e.g., changes in technical parameters or content level and presentation) conforming dynamic changes in the individual user model. In this context, the adaptivity of educational games content can mean the dynamic adjustment of learning paths, the dynamic creation of game content, or its adaptation to changes in the learner model observed while playing the game.

As stated in [12], adaptive games recognize and comprehend the players' interactions and intelligently alter themselves to adapt to the in-game goals of their players, improving the gameplay experience. Adaptive games typically require two-type methodology – player modeling and content generation (adaptation) [11]. The five components of personalized learning, as identified by Miliband [4], include personalized learning assessment, effective teaching, and learning strategies, curriculum entitlement and choice, school organization, and building a strong partnership beyond the school. Thus, the ultimate goal of an adaptive educational game is to support users to achieve progress towards individual learning goals.

2.1 Learning Scenarios for Educational Video Games

Learning scenarios represents a pedagogical method for developing a set of activities and their sequence (learning paths), enabling students to acquire skills and knowledge. There can be identified with different design guidelines that support the integration of adaptive games in online education environments [11, 13]. More specifically, learning scenarios define the main activities, roles, learning structure, and environment context–location, resources, tools, and services [12]. Learning scenarios define both the role of the students and what they have to accomplish as a set of learning activities to attain the expected learning outcomes. On their turn, learning outcomes usually are defined in terms of skills [14], knowledge, and competencies that learners will develop as a result of performing specific learning activities. Learning scenarios can support adaptability and personalization by adding/removing puzzles, changing which objects are in each room, adding/removing elements, skipping parts of the game, and others [8, 12].

Taking into consideration the three basic learning theories–behaviorism, cognitivism, and constructivism, Huo [15] proposes the following six categories of game scenarios. This way, the game scenarios related to the behaviorism theory cover *instruction*, or guidance of gameplay and knowledge acquisition, and *cultivation* – reinforcement of existing knowledge. The cognitivism theory supports *organization*-structured and interrelated knowledge, and *application* – assessment and application knowledge. And the constructivism theory discovers *experience*, or personalized experience-based learning and *adaptation*, or accommodation to the player individuality.

Considering that learning scenarios reflect the specific learning context, they have to define where and how specific learning activities and instruments will be integrated into the general learning process. Therefore, designing specific educational video game learning scenarios, teachers have to be able to structure several learning paths within the video games that will correspond to specific learning objectives. The six learning scenarios for adopting educational video games in class, as identified in [5] can combine six models (LS1-LS6). This way, the first scenario (LS1) explores an introduction game, where learners have to experience and get introduced to new learning content. Then, the second learning scenario is experiential game LS2, reflecting the experience-based learning cycle of Kolb [16]. The third learning scenario–LS3 involve students to gain an in-depth understanding of one specific knowledge domain by applying advanced cognitive models and strategies. Then, the testing game LS4 aims to facilitate students' learning process by designing dynamic and competitive testing experiences. Summary game scenario LS5 explores the overall knowledge domain, this time focusing on the most important contextual knowledge. Finally, interdisciplinary game scenario LS6 aims to connect the new knowledge domain to other disciplines, allowing learners to get a better understanding and perspectives of the links and connections within the learning content.

2.2   Design Approaches for Personalized Video Games for Education

The six learning scenarios defined in [5] for designing educational video games can be tailored according to specific characteristics of the individual student model. Concerning the nature of the student model properties, the tailoring process includes two important issues [16]:

A. Tailoring features of an educational video game based on some static properties of the group student profile such as age, gender, learning goals, special education needs, learning style, or personality traits. This type of tuning is known as a *macro-level adaptation* [17] and is accomplished before game starts;

B. Adjusting features of the video game according to some dynamic properties of the model of an individual student changing during the playing session, like effectiveness (shown learning outcomes as score and acquired knowledge or skills), efficiency (time and effort for achieving the score), and emotional state (recognized emotions and arousal during the play process). This type of tuning is known as a *micro-level adaptation* [17] and is implemented during the game-based learning process.

On the other hand, depending on the specifics of the game features tailored to the model of the student, two other main groups can be distinguished [18]:

I. Tailoring learning features of the educational game like the personalization of learning content incorporated into the game (including the degree of detailing and level of difficulty), content structuring and presentation at game levels, feedback to learners, and others;

II. Adjusting playing features of the game such as a dynamic difficulty of tasks; selection of specific mini-games, quests, and tasks; changes of audio-visual effects (i.e., sound volume or rate, illumination, and image contrast); adjustment of help and behavior of non-player characters (NPCs); tailoring of game mechanics, etc.

Personalized learning scenarios deal with tailoring learning features of the educational game (group I) aiming at better learnability of the game. The adjustment of a learning scenario can be implemented as a *static personalization* of learning content based on relatively constant properties of the student model (group A). For this purpose, static model properties are to be received from the student through self-report (usually before the playing session) or to be estimated during playing by methods like linear regression [18]. On the other hand, adjustment of a learning scenario can be realized as a *dynamic adaptation* of both the content difficulty and gameplay according to observable changes in some student properties during playing the game (group B). It this case, dynamic changes in student properties should be measured during the playing session (e.g., by measuring effectiveness and efficiency) or inferred through appropriate metrics (like emotion recognition based on facial analyses or psychophysiological measures [8]).

3 Personalized Learning Scenarios for Educational Mazes

3.1 Educational Maze Games with Puzzles

In the last decades, many video maze games were designed for free gaming for both fun gamers and learners. Thanks to their orientation on various activities involving interactions and assessments, playing with educational labyrinths and mazes were proven as an efficient game-based learning approach for developing problem-solving competencies [19], higher-order abilities (e.g., reasoning, evaluation, decision making) [20], and literacy skills [21].

The concept of rich educational video maze was coined in [22] as a 3D single-player maze video game able to provide didactic multimedia content presented inside each hall/room the maze not only on learning boards but as well within various mini-games. These mini-games represent puzzles of different types and are embedded into maze rooms or halls by the designer of the maze game simply by selecting the puzzle type and setting its position at a maze hall, learning content, and customization parameters. The game creators can define and customize the maze game and the puzzles embedded into it through predefined XML templates or using a graphic editor that generates an XML description of the whole game [23]. Next, this XML description is applied by the APOGEE platform to create automatically the rich educational video maze using the Unity environment.

The puzzle mini-games may have mandatory or optional completion. Mandatory puzzles available at a maze shall need to be completed for the player to advance to the next hall, while optional puzzles are played for fun and for gaining knowledge, skills, and points. Each puzzle belongs to one of the following groups [22]:

- Questioning puzzles – focused on solving a single problem for unlocking a door or answering a collection of questions (quiz);
- Searching puzzles – aiming at finding translucent or hidden objects, or matching identical or interrelated items in puzzles such as "word soup" or card-matching memory game;
- Arranging puzzles – asking for assembling a 2D image from parts having different shape or size, or for sorting/classifying objects according to specific criteria;
- Action puzzles – for example, shooting at flying balloons with attached 3D educational objects and, next, collecting the fallen objects.

Completing a puzzle mini-game means solving a learning task and adds some points to the player score. As well, it may bring to the player some game objects for being used further in the game. Next to puzzles, the rich educational maze provides intelligent virtual players (NPCs) able to help the player in solving the puzzles and to reply to questions about the learning domain [22].

3.2   Personalized Learning Scenarios for Maze Games with Puzzles

A rich educational video maze created through the APOGEE platform may contain various 2D or 3D puzzle mini-games of questing, searching, arranging, or action type, distributed at the maze halls according to the structure of the didactic material. The game creators (teachers or instructors) can adjust both the learning and playing features of a maze game according to the static and dynamic model properties of individual players, as explained in Sect. 2.2. Thus, a rich educational video maze may involve static personalization and dynamic adaptation of the learning content presented on the learning boards or in the puzzles embedded into the maze halls. In this way, each of the six learning scenarios for designing educational video games [5] (outlined in Sect. 2.1) can be tailored according to the specific characteristics of the individual student model. At *maze level*, the personalization may be achieved by the game designer simply by selecting types of puzzles suitable to the properties of specific learners such as age, gender, learning goal (introduction to the subject, a game with experiments, detailed study, assessment game, summarization, or intersectional game), or learning styles. The results of a representative online survey [23] revealed the level of appropriateness of each puzzle type according to the age, gender, and playing style of the students. As well, at the macro-level, the game designer can set some features of each maze hall, such as which are the mandatory puzzles for specific student properties, a threshold of the minimum total score for unlocking a door to the next hall, and others.

At *puzzle level*, the personalization may be accomplished by customizing the learning content and its structuring and presentation at all the levels for each puzzle game appropriate to the same student properties together with the initial knowledge (none, beginner, intermediate, or advance) of the individual player, with respect of the chosen learning scenario. Customization of learning content for each level (if any) of a puzzle game is possible by changing the default settings of the puzzle and adding specific textual, graphic and/or audio content to be presented in that puzzle. Different types of puzzles [22] may have common settings as didactic contents included in a puzzle or a threshold of the score for completing a given level and, on the other hand, different customization features depending on their specific context, for example:

- For questioning puzzles – customization of question type (open or closed), difficulty and complexity; the number of answers in a quiz; hints and feedback;
- For finding puzzles aiming at discovering something by exploration, thinking, or remembering – setting the number, criteria, positions, and type of objects/words/cards in finding objects/word soup/card-matching games;
- For arrangement puzzles involving ordering, classification, or association of items/objects/traits – customization of number, shape, and size of pieces, together with criteria for arranging/classifying them. Figure 1 presents a screenshot of such a puzzle game integrated into the maze and focused at an arranging of history pictures of Bulgarian kings in time order built on the years of their coronation;

Fig. 1. Screenshot of the "Arrange me!" puzzle game.

- For action puzzles requiring dynamic actions for matching/shooting/grabbing moving items, usually, for a limited time – setting the number, size, and type of objects for shooting, together with dynamics of the shooting process.

The personalization of the learning content and its structuring and presentation at the levels for each puzzle game is realized statically, by providing customization settings in the XML description for each puzzle game. Besides that, static personalization, the APOGEE platform is planned to provide a dynamic adaptation of both the content difficulty and gameplay according to observable changes in some student properties during playing the game, such as learning outcomes, efficiency, and emotional state. The dynamic adaptation will be achieved through machine learning or statistical analysis, however, its customization will be provided in the XML puzzle description.

4 Design of Personalized Educational Maze Games

4.1 Software Instruments for Educational Video Game Design

The conceptualization and development of the APOGEE instruments are based on previous research by the authors [23, 24]. Figure 2 presents the instruments and processes in the APOGEE software platform for the generation of educational video games. The platform consists of two main groups of instruments. These are *Assistive Instruments* and *Analytics Instruments*.

In the APOGEE platform, Analytics instruments enrich the platform with the ability to analyse data. This category includes *Learning Analytics*, *Gaming Analytics*, and *Analytics for users*. These tools provide stakeholders with a wide range of analytics capabilities that they can use. Analytics tools "*link what the user needs to what is available as data*" [25]. Thanks to Analytics, users can make various analyses of available data, visualize data results, extract valuable information and knowledge from data, and make informed strategic decisions. Analytics tools perform the analysis of all the available data on the platform and evaluate the design of the designed, generated, and played games by users. For that reason, the instruments in the Assistive instruments' category are directly related to Analytics instruments.

The software tools that help manage the design of personalized video games are those in the category "Assistive instruments". These include *Design Management Instruments* and *Game Design Validation and Generation instruments*. These tools manage the design, its validation, and subsequently the generation of a valid educational video game.

As shown in Fig. 2, users who intend to use the APOGEE platform for educational video games, must first go through "Registration, Authentication Process". The platform checks whether a given user has a registered account or not. If the user is not registered on the platform, it is necessary to create a personal profile for the user. The platform accounts are divided into three categories, each with its rights and limitations. These are *Student Profile*, *Game Creator Profile*, and *Admin Profile*.

If a user is logged in with a *Student profile* on the platform - he/she has three options to choose from. These are *Play Games*, *View Analytics*, or *Exit* the platform. In

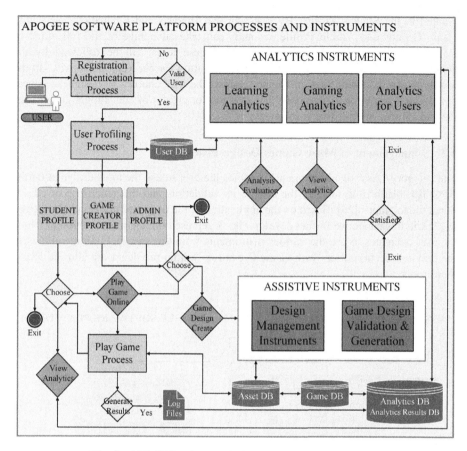

Fig. 2. APOGEE software platform process and instruments.

the Play Games process, the user plays a designed and generated game from the APOGEE platform. Upon completion of the game/learning process, data is generated in the form of log files for the various users' game sessions. These log files are stored in the Analytics database and are processed by tools in the Analytics Instruments category. In View Analytics, the user chooses to use Analytics capabilities to visualize data to the users. Thanks to this, the user can visually monitor the data about their results from game sessions played, statistics, personalized metrics, etc.

All available data is stored in the platform database. The main categories are *Asset DB, Game DB, Analytics DB and Analytics Results DB*. All data is interconnected and used by Analytics Instruments to process, analyse, and visualize data to the user.

Platform users who have *Game Creator* and *Admin* profiles can take advantage of the full range of capabilities provided by the APOGEE platform. They have the right to use both categories of Assistive and Analytics instruments. When logging in as a valid user with a Game Creator or Admin profile, he/she has the choice (depicted as diamonds on Fig. 2) of: 1) *Play Games*; 2) *View Analytics*; 3) *Analysis and Evaluation*; 4) *Game Design Create Processes*. Similarly, in (1) and (2) these users use the rights granted to the Student Profile. By selecting (3) Analysis and Evaluation, users with Game Creator and Admin Profile accounts can take advantage of the full range of features provided by Analytics Instruments. These tools will be followed by the completion of work and return to the starting position for choosing an activity. In the fourth choice (4) Game Design Create process, the user chooses to design an educational video game for its purposes. The designer or creator of educational games uses the capabilities of Assistive Instruments.

4.2 Management of Maze Games Design Process

The category "Assistive Instruments" enables the user to use the tools designed on the APOGEE platform to manage the design, its validation, and the generation of educational video games [24]. Based on the application of the proposed taxonomy developed in [24], in this paper, we further develop Fig. 3, representing the process through which the user navigates to use the various instruments from this category. As mentioned in the previous section, users with Game Creator or Admin privileges are allowed to use these tools.

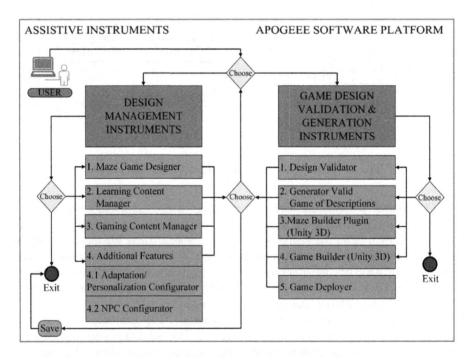

Fig. 3. Overview of the APOGEE software platform assistive instruments process.

Briefly, the process passes through several steps. The user intends to design and create an educational personalized video game. For this purpose, depending on his particular task, or the stage he has reached in designing a particular game, the user may choose to use the set of two categories of Assistive Instruments - *Design Management Instruments* and *Game Design Validation and Generation Instruments*. After making a choice, the user goes to the appropriate category. When the category Design Management Instruments is selected, the instruments available for use by the user are: 1) *Maze Game Designer*; 2) *Learning Content Manager*; 3) *Gaming Content Manager*; 4) Additional Features such as – *Adaptation/Personalisation Configurator* or *NPC Configurator*. After using these instruments and completing their work with them, the user returns to the starting position and can either go to the second category of tools and continue the process of creating and generating an educational personalized video game or to save its work and exit the platform.

When selecting the Game Design Validation and Generation Instruments category, the user similarly has the option to select the set of tools that are included in that category. These are: 1) *Design Validator*; 2) *Generator of Valid Game Descriptions*; 3) *Maze Builder Plugin (Unity 3D)*; 4) *Game Builder (Unity 3D)*; 5) *Game Deployer*. Once completed, the user can again save their changes and progress, exit the platform or return to the starting position and make changes to the design of their game using the Design Management Instruments.

4.3   Sample Customization of a Puzzle Game

The APOGEE platform allows teachers and educators to build video maze games enriched with puzzles of the four types described by the puzzle taxonomy in [22]. As explained in Sect. 3.2, these types of puzzles have both common settings and different customization features depending on the specific puzzle type and nature. The section presents an XML-based template for customization of both the personalization and adaptation of the APOGEE puzzle games. The template is going to be applied by the creators of educational mazes enriched with puzzles, through the APOGEE platform.

Each XML-based puzzle customization makes a part of the XML description of the whole puzzle game. The structure of the XML-based template for all the puzzle descriptions is presented by an XML Schema document, which is applied for both controlling an XSD-driven maze editor and for validation of XML description of each puzzle embedded into the maze. It follows a simplified version of an XML document for customization of one of a sample 2D puzzle, which is among the mini-games with relatively simpler customization.

```
<PuzzleGame>
  <Name>2D Puzzle</Name>
    <Settings>
    <General>
      <Audio>mysong.mp3</Audio>
      <AudioLoop>true</AudioLoop>
      <RelativeSize width="100" hight="100"></RelativeSize>
      <RelativePosition x="20" y="40" z="33"></RelativePosition>
    </General>
    <Level order="1">
      <Points>300</Points>
```

```
    <Time>120</Time>
    <NoOfItems>8</NoOfItems>
    <ShapeOfItems>rectangle</ShapeOfItems>
    <RotationOfItems>no</RotationOfItems>
  </Level>
  <Level order="2">
    <Points>700</Points>
    <Time>300</Time>
    <NoOfItems>24</NoOfItems>
    <ShapeOfItems>square</ShapeOfItems>
    <RotationOfItems>yes</RotationOfItems>
  </Level>
</Settings>
<Personalization schoolAge="primary, secondary"
        complexity="elementary"
        learningStyle="visual" playingStyle="dreamer">
  <GameElements>
    <GameElement level="1">
     <Text>What was the battle on this picture?</Text>
     <Image id="ID1">battle.jpg</Image>
    </GameElement>
    <GameElement level="2">
     <Text>
        Which was the Bulgarian capital in 12th century?
     </Text>
     <Image id="ID2">Tarnovo.png</Image>
    </GameElement>
  </GameElements>
</Personalization>
<Adaptation included="yes">
    <threshold    about="pixels    for    matching    two    items"
level="1">5</threshold>
    <threshold    about="pixels    for    matching    two    items"
level="2">3</threshold>
  </Adaptation>
</PuzzleGame>
```

The XML description given over makes a part of the whole XML document used for the automatic generation of the maze. It contains a general settings section, followed by settings for each level including points to gain, expected playing time, a number of items to be arranged, and their shape and rotation. The personalization settings specify the learning content by levels and the characteristics of students the game is appropriate for, such as age, complexity level, and learning and playing styles. The customization of adaptation here includes only values of thresholds for the matching distance between pictures.

Figure 4 presents a screenshot of playing an APOGEE 2D puzzle game at the first level. To complete the level, the two items that are not yet arranged should be moved over the white squares at the proper places.

Fig. 4. Screenshot of the APOGEE 2D puzzle game.

5 Discussion

The design of educational video games is a complex and demanding activity, as both learning and game objectives have to be taken into consideration. Ensuring that learners achieve the desired educational objective while experiencing an immersive video game scenario. Taking into account adaptation and personalization strategies, the APOGEE platform allows the creation of educational video mazes enriched with puzzle mini-games, providing support for both the personalization and adaptation approaches. The personalization is achieved in two ways:

(1) For each maze hall – by selecting puzzle games appropriate for a specific group student profile including static properties like age, gender, and learning/playing styles (achieved at the beginning of the game). The game creator should select the learning goal of the game, which determines the choice of a specific learning scenario for the game making it an introductory, experiment-based, detailed-study, assessment, summarization, or intersectional one;

(2) For each puzzle mini-game – by adjusting the learning content and its presentation according to the same static student properties plus the initial knowledge for the domain (all these found by self-report prior to the playing session).

On the other hand, the adaptivity is realized by dynamic adjustments of the complexity of learning content and/or some playing features like task difficulty, sound volume, visual effects, and game dynamics. The adaptation is a dynamic process during a playing session which depends on observed outcomes (i.e. effectiveness), efficiency, and emotional state of the individual student.

Customization of both the personalization and adaptivity is achieved by XML settings that are to be specified for the maze and all the puzzle mini-games embedded into it. Besides the customization settings, the XML documents include descriptions of all the multimedia assets needed for the generation of the maze game. Though the platform provides templates for the XML descriptions, such customization appears rather difficult for teachers and educationalists. This is the reason to add to the current platform new software modules such as the maze game designer and the adaptation/personalization configurator, which are under development and will help game creators to tailor their games much more easily. For facilitation of seamless integration of game content, these modules will be integrated with the managers of learning and playing content.

Finally, game creators need instruments for assessing both the personalization and adaptivity customized for a specific learning scenario. The software instruments for learning and gaming analytics are designed for providing them with various student metrics collected via log files during the playing sessions. These metrics include learning outcomes, gained points, efficiency, playing time, and other results achieved for each level of each puzzle. As well, the analytics tools will provide correlations of logged metrics and both the static and dynamic student properties. Thus, they will help the game creators in assessing the appropriateness of the chosen customization of the game and, hence the validation of the eventual improvements of learnability and playability [26].

6   Conclusions

The paper presented approaches for personalization and adaptation of educational video games achieved by tailored inclusion of mini puzzle games into video mazes. Both the personalization and adaptation are realized in a specific learning scenario aiming at flexible support of tailored, student-oriented game-based learning.

The flexibility of the creation of personalized and adapted educational games is achieved by customization of playing and learning features of the maze game and any of the puzzles included in its halls. The customized game descriptions, together with all needed game assets, next are used for an automatic generation of the maze game. The instruments of the APOGEE platform presented here support the processes of designing, managing, creating, analysing, and evaluating educational video games applying a student-centric approach. These instruments are directly interconnected and enrich the APOGEE platform with a wide range of capabilities. Using these tools in the design processes of adaptive and personalized educational video games allows teachers and pedagogues to apply different strategies for learning personalization and adaptation.

Depending on the characteristics of the user and, subsequently, the user's behaviour during the game, the APOGEE platform will be able to provide its users with personalization of the content and adaptation of the gameplay. This enables teachers and educators to create within the APOGEE platform personalized and adaptable learning scenarios to suit the needs of the individual student or student group. By creating such learning scenarios, educators will be able to dynamically respond to the different requirements of each of their students. Educational games with personalized and adaptive learning and gaming content can motivate usage, increasing user acceptance, and user identification within and outside of the game and the platform. Furthermore, educational video games provide a personalized experience, which is crucial to facilitate achieving the targeted positive outcomes, allowing users to make progress in a motivating and rewarding manner.

Future works on the APOGEE platform include finalization of all the assistive and analytics software instruments being under development, followed by their validation and assessment through controlled experiments. The experiments are going to involve practical usage of the platform for design, generation, and assessment of an education game through monitored game sessions. Two groups of students will play the same game – the first one will play it with personalization and adaptation of learning content and gameplay, and others (i.e., the control group) will play a game version without such customizations. After playing sessions, students will be asked to fill in questionnaires about the gaming experience, learning motivation, and game learnability [26]. By analysis of the self-reports and the playing and learning metrics measured during the game sessions with both the control and experimental groups, the effect of game personalization and adaptation will be estimated. Eventually, some machine learning methods will be applied for finding the most suitable adjustment of educational maze games with puzzles to both the static and dynamic properties of the student model.

Acknowledgements. The research leading to these results has received funding from the APOGEE project, funded by the Bulgarian National Science Fund, Grant Agreement No. DN12/7/2017.

References

1. Zagal, J.P.: Ludoliteracy: Defining Understanding and Supporting Games Education. ETC Press, Halifax (2010)
2. Göbel, S., Hardy, S., Wendel, V., Mehm, F., Steinmetz, R.: Serious games for health: personalized exergames. In: Proceedings of the 18th ACM International Conference on Multimedia, pp. 1663–1666. ACM (2010)
3. Jurado, F., Meza, R.E.: An exploratory study in the use of gamer profiles and learning styles to build educational videogames. Int. J. Eng. Educ. **33**(2), 1–10 (2017)
4. Miliband, D.: Personalised learning: building a new relationship with schools. In: Speech by the Minister of State for School Standards to the North of England Education Conference (2004)
5. Antonova, A., Bontchev, B.: Designing scenarios for personalized learning: enabling teachers to apply educational video games in class. Int. J. Educ. Learn. Syst. **4**, 20–26 (2019)
6. Paunova-Hubenova, E.: Are the school teachers ready to start using smart adaptive video games for education? In: Proceedings of the 13th International Technology, Education and Development Conference, Valencia, Spain, pp. 5191–5199 (2019). https://doi.org/10.21125/inted.2019.1294,
7. APOGEE Project. http://apogee.online/index-en.html. Accessed 26 May 2020

8. Bontchev, B.: Adaptation in affective video games: a literature review. Cybern. Inf. Technol. **16**(3), 3–34 (2016)
9. Terzieva, V.: Personalisation in educational games – a case study. In: Proceedings of 11th Annual International Conference on Education and New Learning Technologies, Palma de Mallorca, Spain, pp. 7036–7044 (2019). ISBN 978-84-09-12031-4
10. Moreno-Ger, P., Burgos, D., Martínez-Ortiz, I., Sierra, J.L., Fernández-Manjón, B.: Educational game design for online education. Comput. Hum. Behav. **24**(6), 2530–2540 (2008)
11. Streicher, A., Smeddinck, J.D.: Personalized and adaptive serious games. In: Dörner, R., Göbel, S., K-R, M., Masuch, M., Zweig, K. (eds.) Entertainment Computing and Serious Games. LNCS, vol. 9970, pp. 332–377. Springer, Cham (2016). https://doi.org/10.1007/978-3-319-46152-6_14
12. Lopes, R., Bidarra, R.: A semantic generation framework for enabling adaptive game worlds. In: Proceedings of 8th International Conference on Advances in Computer Entertainment Technology, pp. 1–8 (2011)
13. Ney, M., Emin, V., Earp, J.: Paving the way to game based learning: a question matrix for teacher reflection. Procedia Comput. Sci. **15**, 17–24 (2012)
14. Oyesiku, D., Adewumi, A., Misra, S., Ahuja, R., Damasevicius, R., Maskeliunas, R.: An educational math game for high school students in Sub-Saharan Africa. In: Florez, H., Diaz, C., Chavarriaga, J. (eds.) ICAI 2018. CCIS, vol. 942, pp. 228–238. Springer, Cham (2018). https://doi.org/10.1007/978-3-030-01535-0_17
15. Huo, Y.: A pedagogy-based framework for optimizing learning efficiency across multiple disciplines in educational games. Int. J. Inf. Educ. Technol. **9**(10), 704–709 (2019). https://doi.org/10.18178/ijiet.2019.9.10.1290
16. Kolb, D.A.: Experiential Learning: Experience as the Source of Learning and Development. FT Press, Upper Saddle River (2014)
17. Petrovica, S.: Multi-level adaptation of an educational game to individual student's gameplay, knowledge and emotions. In: Proceedings of 9th International Conference on Education and New Learning Technologies, IATED, pp. 2220–2230 (2017). https://doi.org/10.21125/edulearn.2017.1462
18. Bontchev, B., Georgieva, O.: Playing style recognition through an adaptive video game. Comput. Hum. Behav. **82**, 136–147 (2018). https://doi.org/10.1016/j.chb.2017.12.040
19. Eseryel, D., Law, V., Ifenthaler, D., Ge, X., Miller, R.: An investigation of the interrelationships between motivation, engagement, and complex problem solving in game-based learning. Educ. Technol. Soc. **17**(1), 42–53 (2014)
20. Norris, J.M., Davis, M.J., Timple-Laughlin, V.: Second Language Educational Experiences for Adult Learners (1). Routledge, New York (2017)
21. Kiliçkaya, F.: Infusing action mazes into language assessment class using quandary. In: Asutay, H. (ed.) Balkan Educational Studies – 2017, pp. 223–231 (2017)
22. Antonova, A., Bontchev, B.: Exploring puzzle-based learning for building effective and motivational maze video games for education. In: Proceedings of 11th Annual International Conference on Education and New Learning Technologies, pp. 2425–2434 (2019). ISBN 978-84-09-12031-4
23. Antonova, A., Dankov, Y., and Bontchev, B., Smart services for managing the design of personalized educational video games. In: Proceedings of ACM International 9th Balkan Conference in Informatics (BCI 2019). ACM (2019). https://doi.org/10.1145/3351556.3351574
24. Dankov, Y., Bontchev, B.: Towards a taxonomy of instruments for facilitated design and evaluation of video games for education. In: Proceedings of ACM International Conference on Computer Systems and Technologies (CompSysTech 2020). ACM (2020)

25. Dankov, Y., Birov, D.: General architectural framework for business visual analytics. In: Shishkov, B. (ed.) BMSD 2018. LNBIP, vol. 319, pp. 280–288. Springer, Cham (2018). https://doi.org/10.1007/978-3-319-94214-8_19

26. González Sánchez, J.L., Padilla Zea, N., Gutiérrez, F.L.: From usability to playability: introduction to player-centred video game development process. In: Kurosu, M. (ed.) HCD 2009. LNCS, vol. 5619, pp. 65–74. Springer, Heidelberg (2009). https://doi.org/10.1007/978-3-642-02806-9_9

System for Monitoring and Warning of the Ultraviolet Radiation Index: A Study Case in Ecuador Elementary Schools

Jorge Buele[1,2](✉) ⓘ, Francisco I. Chango[2] ⓘ,
María de Los Ángeles Chango[3] ⓘ, Marlon Santamaría[2] ⓘ,
and José Varela-Aldás[1] ⓘ

[1] SISAu Research Group, Universidad Tecnológica Indoamérica,
Ambato 180212, Ecuador
{jorgebuele,josevarela}@uti.edu.ec
[2] PGCH Research Group, Universidad Técnica de Ambato,
Ambato 180103, Ecuador
{fi.chango,ma.santamaria}@uta.edu.ec
[3] Hospital Regional Docente Ambato, Ambato 180105, Ecuador
angeles.chango@gmail.com

Abstract. Solar ultraviolet (UV) radiation has increased in recent years due to ozone layer depletion and in Ecuador in particular, due to its geographical position and the height of its cities. Prolonged sun exposures in childhood increase the risk of causing malignant effects on the skin and eyes, such as squamous cell carcinoma, melanoma and cataracts. For this reason, this document describes the design of a device based on UV optical sensors that allows determining the existing radiation index. As a processing unit there is the Raspberry Pi 3B+ embedded board and to display the data physically there are LED panels. The storage of information is done through a database managed by MySQL and also implemented on the board. The levels of the ultraviolet radiation index (UVI) are presented through a graphical user interface (GUI) in real time, which also allows generating a report in a .csv file. Functional tests were carried out in the central courtyard of two educational units, to raise awareness among parents and authorities on the adoption of preventive measures that avoid possible damage to the skin of children when carrying out outdoor activities.

Keywords: Web monitoring · Elementary schools · Skin cancer prevention · UV index · UV optical sensor

1 First Section

Ultraviolet radiation or UV radiation is part of the electromagnetic spectrum, its wavelength is between 100 and 400 nanometers (nm) and is invisible to the human eye as it is above the visible spectrum [1, 2]. It can be of natural (solar) or artificial origin, but in this investigation only the first one is evaluated, since it cannot be controlled by living organisms exposed to it. This radiation is an integral part of solar rays and causes

© Springer Nature Switzerland AG 2020
O. Gervasi et al. (Eds.): ICCSA 2020, LNCS 12254, pp. 846–861, 2020.
https://doi.org/10.1007/978-3-030-58817-5_60

various health effects as it is a radiation between ionizing and non-ionizing [3, 4]. The World Health Organization (WHO) mentions and warns about the possible effects of this radiation on human health, both due to insufficient exposure (at high latitudes during winter), and excessive exposure (during summer, especially at low latitudes) [5]. The risks of insufficient exposure include a higher incidence of certain bone diseases and perhaps some autoimmune diseases such as multiple sclerosis. On the other hand, exposure to sunlight in small doses, has a beneficial effect for a person, since it allows the synthesis of vitamin D and improves mood [6]. Increasing the doses also makes it dangerous, since they cause short-term effects such as sunburn (erythema), pigmentary diseases such as spots, melasma (pregnancy cloth) or vitiligo [7]. Other dermatological problems can appear such as photoimmunosuppression (cold sores), photodermatitis (benign solar flares), as well as other stranger types such as lupus, light urticaria or developing photosensitivity [8].

According to information of The Skin Cancer Foundation[1], one in three cancers that are diagnosed is skin; establishing more than 13 million cases of skin cancer annually and more than 65,000 people die each year from this disease. In Latin America the reliability of the measurement of solar irradiation is questionable, since it cannot be compared with those of neighboring countries, since they do not handle international measurement standards [9]. In some countries such as Mexico and Uruguay, according to the American Cancer Association, approximately 3 million non-melanoma skin cancers are diagnosed each year and 90% of these are associated with ultraviolet radiation [10]. At higher altitudes, there is less atmosphere and, therefore, less ozone that protects living beings from these rays. According to WHO1, for every 1000 m of altitude increase, there are 10% to 12% more UV rays and that is why, the geographical location of Ecuador is the factor that determines the high solar radiation it receives in summer. Being close to the equinoctial line, the rays fall perpendicularly and therefore the radiation is greater, as explained by the National Institute of Meteorology and Hydrology (INAMHI). The cities with the highest altitude (located in the Ecuadorian highlands) such as Quito (2,850 m), Ambato (2,550 m) and Cuenca (2,350) exceed 13 points of UVI, according to data recorded in recent years.

Variations in environmental conditions can cause serious health problems for people. That is why in [11] is presented a device that incorporates a portable network of sensors intended to monitor environmental conditions (CO_2, humidity, pressure and temperature) wirelessly (IoT). By means of a sensor node called WE-Safe, data is captured in real time and transmitted to a remote cloud server. Data can be displayed to users through a web-based application located on the cloud server. In particular, to determine the effects of UV radiation on the planet and its inhabitants, prototype non-scientific instruments are available on the market that measure different exposure parameters as presented in [12]. This study explores the ways in which UV radiation sensors can provide information about high sun exposure in playgrounds, tourist attractions, workplaces, and swimming pools. However, the risk of using personal meters that have not been validated as public health tools is specified. Another important study is described in [13], a comprehensive review of the use of smartphones

---

[1] https://cancerdepiel.org/quienes-somos/lider-en-la-Lucha-contra-el-cancer-de-piel.

in monitoring and predicting UV radiation. The practical aspects, limitations and general challenges are reviewed, specifically in relation to public education and its impact in geographical and social areas with low socioeconomic resources. Overall, the review shows that smartphones offer multiple opportunities in different ways to educate users about personal health regarding UV radiation.

Remote monitoring can be applied in various fields of science, obtaining exponential development thanks to continuous advances in computing and connectivity [14–19]. Semlali et al. [20] describes the development of a software that collects, processes, and displays environmental and pollution data. These data are used to build an environmental map and can be viewed from any location. Similarly in [21] is presented an independent system that allows you to store data on the climatic parameters of a city using IoT. This proposal allows access to information in real time, which can be viewed from a smartphone, PC or Tablet.

It is evident that performing remote monitoring tasks has contributed to improving human living conditions, as shown in the presented literature. By focusing these studies on skin care, you can prevent medium and extremely dangerous diseases [22]. In this context, it is proposed to implement a monitoring and alert system for the ultraviolet radiation index (UVI) inside two primary education units. This in order to support parents, teachers and school officials in taking protective measures for students from direct exposure to the sun, when performing outdoor school and entertainment activities. Schools are an essential means of getting the message across to young people. Teachers and the associations representing them should be encouraged to champion the cause and include UV radiation awareness and protection projects in the education system. This initiative seeks to demonstrate the risk that children suffer and to change people's thinking, attitudes and behavior regarding sun exposure from an early age and to prevent skin cancer in the future.

This work is made up of six sections: the introduction to the subject in Sect. 1 and the case study in Sect. 2. Section 3 shows the distribution of the hardware elements of the system and Sect. 4 respective software development. Analysis of results and conclusions are described in Sect. 5 and Sect. 6 respectively.

2   Study Case

In general, excessive exposure to the sun can cause damage to people's health, depending on the intensity and concentration. The majority of the inhabitants of the populations of the Ecuadorian highlands located over 2000 m are unaware that UV radiation is higher than in cities that are at sea level, despite being in the same country and having a reduced territorial extension[2]. It is important to consider that these quantities are much more sensitive to the state of the atmosphere and depend on multiple factors such as: clouds, aerosols, soil reflectivity (albedo), height of the place, thickness of the ozone layer, etc., making the study much more complex. These radiations have enough energy to produce damages in biological systems. Under

---

[2] https://twitter.com/inamhi/status/1032832578854764544/photo/1.

normal conditions, radiation with wavelengths shorter than 290 nm does not reach the Earth's surface. That is why, each species of living being, including different individuals of the same species, have a different response to solar radiation.

This research was carried out in the metropolitan district of Quito, the capital of Ecuador and better known as the half of the world, since it crosses the equator, which precisely gave its name to this nation and receives the sun's rays from perpendicular shape. In addition, tests have been carried out in the city of Ambato, given its geographical position and altitude similar to the first case. A prospective study was carried out on patients attending the consultation at the Society for the Fight Against Cancer of Ecuador (SOLCA), their cases and the type of skin cancer they had in the period 2017–2019 were analyzed, and thus was able to determine the incidence of skin cancer by city. According to the statistical data provided by SOLCA and the Ecuadorian Social Security Institute (IESS), the city of Ambato has the highest incidence of skin cancer in the country and then there is the city of Quito. Skin cancer or melanoma includes basal cell carcinoma and squamous cell carcinoma; they are the most common diseases in these cities. Risk factors include exposure to ultraviolet rays, having light hair and eyes, European descent, and living in tropical areas. The main factor has been identified as direct excessive exposure to sunlight without any protection.

3   Hardware

This proposal is based on the general scheme described in Fig. 1, where the services presented to the user can be seen. Regarding the prototype that is physically implemented, this section establishes the hardware components that are used to graphically display a numerical value that symbolizes the level of UV radiation available in that given time and space. Next, the parts that make up this system is explained.

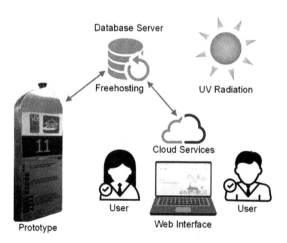

Fig. 1. General outline of the proposal presented.

3.1   Data Acquisition

Data acquisition is done using the Si1145 sensor, which has a calibrated light detection algorithm that can calculate UVI and is designed to operate directly with low-cost embedded boards such as Arduino or Raspberry Pi. This device is widely available in the market and has greater sensitivity, since it has a true ultraviolet radiation reader, at a reduced cost. Through the I2C protocol, this data is transferred to Raspberry Pi, using the 3.3 V, GND, SDA and SCL pins.

3.2   Information Processing

Its main component is the Raspberry Pi 3 model B + board, an integrated board with support for various peripherals of a common computer and that works with the Linux operating system (O.S.). It has GPIO (general purpose input/output) pins that can be used as digital inputs or digital outputs and different communication buses such as SPI and I2C. A micro SD card is incorporated to install the O.S. respective and for the storage of data from the previous stage. With this information, the conversion of bits to hexadecimal values is carried out and then to decimal numbers and other additional calculations.

3.3   Data Visualization

It is carried out in two ways: on a personal computer through a web application, which will be explained in more detail later and on the two prototypes physically implemented in the educational units. For the second case, a 64 × 32-pixel tricolor LED matrix screen 4 mm apart is used, where each pixel consists of a red and green LED (commonly called "1R1G"); For the dimensions, standards and budget were considered. In total there are 2,048 pixels and 4,096 individually directional LED elements, including shift register circuits, so all elements can be controlled with just 11 I/O lines from the controller.

3.4   Physic Structure

The structure was built using stainless steel, to protect the electrical and electronic devices that are part of the prototype, by making permanent measurements outdoors and supporting the different climatic environments that may arise. During the design, it was determined that the structure must allow the UVI sensor to protrude so that it captures the irradiation of the day and does not cover itself with any object. It should also be considered that the led panels have a significant height with respect to the ground, for better viewing and that a front door is incorporated to facilitate access to the devices in the event of a modification or failure. In addition, the protection measures that the user must have are visually incorporated, depending on the degree of exposure they are experiencing at that time.

4 Software

4.1 Initial Settings

The Raspbian OS is installed on the Raspberry Pi board, downloaded from the official website, whose image was saved on a 32 Gb micro SD memory card (recommended to be class 10). The Lite version of Raspbian (the "GUI"), is a "complete" version, which has resources that allow you to regulate the use of the Raspberry module for compiling the graphics part, preventing board overheating. In addition, it supports the configuration of the Wi-Fi connection, without having to connect to Ethernet first. The micro SD card is inserted into a PC, in order to access the directory: cd/Volumes/boot and there a file called wpa_supplicant.conf is created, where the necessary configurations are made. With this file in the directory, when the system starts, Raspbian will move it to:/etc./wpa_supplicant/. On the SD card to connect via SSH, you need to create an empty file called SSH to enable it. If this file exists, SSH will be enabled when the Raspberry Pi is started and with it you can enter the raspberry module remotely, without the need for a screen, keyboard or other peripherals. The wpa_supplicant.conf file automatically disappears from the micro SD boot directory, when Raspbian Lite first starts.

Once the card is switched on and connected to the network, the default username and password are set and the Matrix LED Adafruit software is downloaded from its official page. When installing and running it for the first time, you must choose the type of adapter used which is RGB Matrix HAT with RTC. Additionally, the drivers for the real-time clock must be installed and the image quality improvement of the LED matrix is managed. Please note that these settings could cause occasional flickering of the array and to correct this these plugins should be reinstalled or the image quality of the array slightly reduced.

4.2 Data Acquisition

Python is used as the programming language, whose scripts are simpler than C++, but can cause delays in animations if many pixel variations are required. On a Raspberry Pi you get a refresh rate of about 400 fps (85 fps for 5 strings) with a program developed in Python, while with C++ you can do the same with 3500 fps (700 fps for 5). In this project the SetPixel() function was used to incorporate static images without animation; SetImage() for animations; CreateFrameCanvas() to fill full off-screen boxes and SwapOnVSync() to make swaps. In addition, RGBMatrix for the management of led panels and for their use root privileges are required, therefore, all scripts are run as sudo.

To read the data from the Si1145 sensor, the I2C standard is enabled on the embedded board through the raspi-config interface, installing i2c support for the ARM kernel and for the Linux kernel. When checking the connected devices, it can be seen that two I2C addresses are in use: 0×40 and 0×70 by the Si1145 and Adafruit Matrix Hat. These values will be different depending on the modules that are connected to the Raspberry Pi I2C pins. As a last step, the complementary drivers of both devices are installed and the operation of the system is verified by running a preloaded example. The script allows converting the hexadecimal values of the transducer and taking the values of infrared proximity, UVI and ambient light, which allows the data to be accurate and for this purpose. This code must be saved in/home/intiuv.py.

4.3   Web Services

It allows the user to access IIS (Internet Information Services) through a website, it provides information about the radiation that is available in real time and the precautions that must be taken before going outside. It has a portal for the administrators of the measurement units, which consists of a presentation layer, which is responsible for interacting with the client or the end user, i.e., the interface in which all the display options are presented. This layer communicates with the productive or intermediate layer, responsible for implementing all the visual rules and dictating the application administration rules. It will also maintain a dialogue with the data layer, which will handle the switching of data to the engine and provide the response information to the presentation layer. This interface is easy to use and intuitive and allows the presentation of data and reports to the user. The architecture used is shown in Fig. 2.

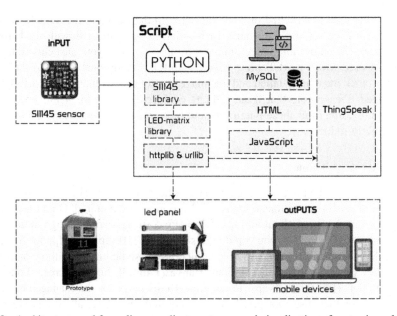

Fig. 2. Architecture used for online coordinates, storage and visualization of routes in real time.

For the development of the architecture the interactive web technique Ajax (Asinchrous JavaScript and Xml) is used, this application is executed in the client, which can be any web browser such as Chrome, Explorer, etc. In parallel, an asynchronous communication with the server is executed in the background through

ThingSpeak (IoT), which allows to collect and store data from the sensors in the cloud and update them when necessary, thus improving the speed of execution. It is a publish-subscribe architecture developed primarily to connect bandwidth-restricted and power-restricted devices over wireless networks. MQTT is a simple and lightweight protocol that runs on TCP/IP, WebSocket's, and SSL (Secure Socket Layer) sockets and has two components: agent and MQTT client. The first is a central point of communication; the broker is responsible for sending all messages between clients. While the second is any device (for example, a computer or a mobile phone) that connects to the corridor; a client who sends messages is a publisher and if he receives them, he is a subscriber. To receive a message, the customer must subscribe to the subject of that message. You can post and subscribe to MQTT messages using MQTT Publish and MQTT Subscribe blocks. These blocks support MQTT only through TCP/IP sockets. Algorithm 1 presents the connection between Python and ThinkSpeak.

Algorithm 1. connection between Python and ThinkSpeak

```
#!/usr/bin/python
import sys
import RPi.GPIO as GPIO
from time import sleep
import urllib2
import SI1145.SI1145 as SI1145
sensor = SI1145.SI1145()
baseURL= 'https://api.thingspeak.com/update?api_key=QO610ENLQWTUT3ES&field1=0'
uvIndex = 0
vis = 0
while( uvIndex < 1000):
    vis = sensor.readVisible()
    IR = sensor.readIR()
    UV = sensor.readUV()
    uvIndex = UV / 100.0
    print uvIndex
    f = urllib2.urlopen(baseURL + "&field1=%s&field2=%s" % (uvIndex, vis))
    f.read()
    f.close()
    print vis
    sleep(60)
print "Program has ended"
```

4.4   Data Storage and Visualization

The storage of the information is done through a database managed by MySQL, for its later presentation through the free software Grafana. MySQL is one of the most notorious relational database methods worldwide, it is a frequent inclusion in most LAMP stacks (Linux, Apache, MYSQL and PHP) and for PHP to access the database they must be installed mysql libraries. When connecting to the database, user and password are specified and when requested they must be modified for security. Default access to the MySQL server is through the primary IP address, which is disabled in the initial configuration. So, you must configure the local connection using commands or the internal socket connection. To grant access to a remote connection, a new user must be created to avoid using root and then set permissions for access from a fixed IP address.

To copy information from the database to/from a remote server, there are several methods, but being a low budget proposal, we worked with a method without cost, but which guarantees the quality of the data in a safe way. The command -ssl with mysqldump enables the connection through SSL, for domains without certificate configuration, so this option is only good if you have an SSL that is available. The database model used is ORM, the models.py file found in the respective folder is edited and the same is done with intibase.py. A file called intiuvser.py is created that allows data to be sent to the remote database.

Depending on the UVI variation that the sensors have captured throughout the day, week or month, this statistical information is expressed in a dynamic and user-friendly interface. This stage is made up of a server that, through Grafana (Apache, MySQL and PHP), provides web services that manage the database. The goal is to have real-time monitoring with access to history from anywhere with internet access. Figure 3 the historical ones presented.

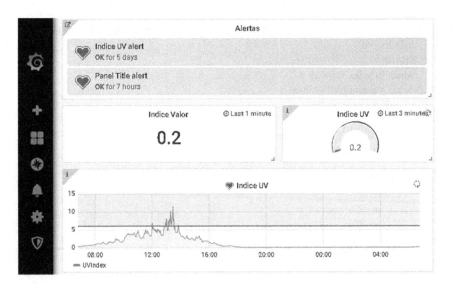

Fig. 3. Main board of the Grafana software presented to the user.

5 Tests and Experimental Results

Once the different elements of the UV measurement system were installed, the relevant tests were carried out to certify the validity of the system. On-site data acquisition is executed and sent to the central station, for further processing, storage, sending to the server and backup.

5.1 UV Sensor Validation

To validate the linearity of the Si1145 sensor, its configuration, working modes and tests were carried out under normal conditions based on its datasheet; electrical data assumes ambient light levels <1 klx (1000 lx). The sensor already integrated into the prototype measures the spectral and total intensity of UV radiation, in the range from 290 nm to 330 nm (includes UV-A and UV-B), with intervals of 0.4 nm. In addition, determine the total ozone column by examining the absorption of solar radiation at certain UV wavelengths. Based on all these parameters, the UVI is calculated. It should be considered that the proximity detection performance can be degraded, especially when there is high optical crosstalk, such as undesirable signals or adverse atmospheric conditions. This also produces variations in the power supply for the LED panels and for the controller, causing their saturation and the values to appear out of range, due to the fact that the sensor is optical and very sensitive to mishandling. As a reference, 32 klx are captured from sunlight on an average day at least and 100 klx at most, which has been proven to work properly to be used in subsequent tests.

5.2 Comparison with a Commercial Device

On August 12, 2019 (summer time) a period of quality control tests began, for which the operation of the prototype located in the city of Ambato was compared with a commercial device owned by the municipality. The procedure consisted of recording the level of UVI that these two instruments presented between 7:00 and 17:00 (- GTM 5) when exposed to UV-B radiation. Both were placed at a certain distance from each other relatively closely, with the intention of subjecting them to similar climatic conditions. For comparison, 4 samples were taken every 60 min for 3 weeks and the data obtained is described in Table 1. In Fig. 4 and Fig. 5, the daily and monthly results, respectively, are delivered to the user through the Web application.

The results of this comparison must have a discrepancy of less than 5%, to be considered a valid prototype according to local regulations established by the Ecuadorian Standardization Service (INEN). According to the information obtained, the comparison between the implemented prototype and the commercial device establishes an error margin that ranges between 5% and 1%, with an average error value of 2,28%, which is within the established range. The analysis is carried out in the Origin Lab software, which is in charge of regularizing the data and thus checking whether it is correct. Based on this, it can be indicated that the measuring device has a high fidelity, since the values are similar to those issued by a certified scientific team.

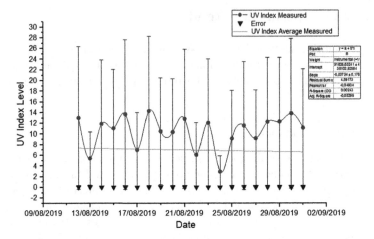

Fig. 4. Data measured with the prototype during August 2019 in Ambato.

Table 1. Data obtained when using the implemented device vs. a commercial nature device.

Date	UV Index Average	Commercial device - Ambato Municipality	Error	Error (%)
12/08/2019	13,33	13,00	0,33	2,54%
13/08/2019	5,41	5,00	0,41	8,20%
14/08/2019	11,87	12,00	0,13	1,08%
15/08/2019	11,06	11,00	0,06	0,55%
16/08/2019	13,68	14,00	0,32	2,29%
17/08/2019	7,03	7,00	0,03	0,43%
18/08/2019	14,27	14,00	0,27	1,93%
19/08/2019	10,50	10,00	0,5	5,00%
20/08/2019	10,34	10,00	0,34	3,40%
21/08/2019	12,81	13,00	0,19	1,46%
22/08/2019	6,10	6,00	0,1	1,67%
23/08/2019	12,06	12,00	0,06	0,50%
24/08/2019	2,93	3,00	0,07	2,33%
25/08/2019	9,15	9,00	0,15	1,67%
26/08/2019	11,57	12,00	0,43	3,58%
27/08/2019	9,18	9,00	0,18	2,00%
28/08/2019	12,26	12,00	0,26	2,17%
29/08/2019	12,28	12,00	0,28	2,33%
30/08/2019	13,83	14,00	0,17	1,21%
31/08/2019	11,14	11,00	0,14	1,27%
Average	**10,54**	**10,45**	**0,22**	**2,28%**

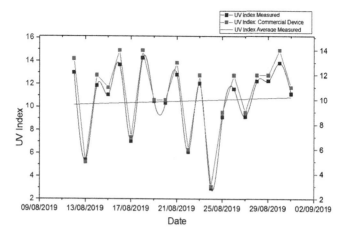

Fig. 5. Comparison of the data measured with the prototype and with a commercial device during August 2019 in Ambato city.

5.3   Comparison Between Cities

For the development of these tests, the prototypes have been located inside two state schools of primary education, in the cities of Quito and Ambato. Taking into account that environmental factors vary according to geographic position, a comparison has been made between these two populations to determine the level of UVI to which students are exposed during the month of August. Among the main atmospheric conditions to take into account is the time, height, climate and altitude. Table 2 shows the data obtained and Fig. 6 and Fig. 7 show the information collected graphically. Data for February (winter) have also been obtained and are being processed, but could not be included in this version of the blind peer review.

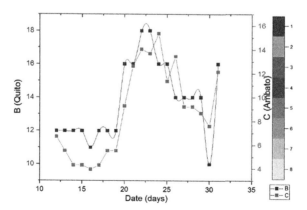

Fig. 6. Comparison of the data measured with the prototype in two educational units in Quito and Ambato respectively.

Table 2. Definition of parameters for tests.

Date	UVI - Quito	UVI - Ambato	Date	UVI - Quito	UVI - Ambato
12/08/2019	12,1	6,8	22/08/2019	17,9	14
13/08/2019	12,2	5,6	23/08/2019	18,2	13,8
14/08/2019	12,3	4,4	24/08/2019	15,9	15,3
15/08/2019	12,1	4,4	25/08/2019	16,1	11,4
16/08/2019	11,3	4,1	26/08/2019	13,1	12,6
17/08/2019	11,9	4,3	27/08/2019	13,2	8,7
18/08/2019	11,92	5,5	28/08/2019	14,3	9,4
19/08/2019	12,3	5,7	29/08/2019	14,1	8,7
20/08/2019	15,9	9,2	30/08/2019	10,1	7,7
21/08/2019	16,2	12,8	31/08/2019	15,7	11,9
...	...	...	Average	13,84	8,82

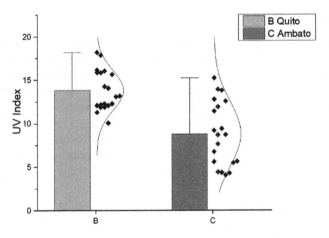

Fig. 7. Level of incidence of UVI in Quito and Ambato cities during August 2019.

In the month of August, the average level of the UVI for the city of Ambato during the test period was 23% lower compared to that of Quito. Comparable days are also analyzed, i.e. days totally clear in both places and the projection increases to a 53% difference. This shows that the Ecuadorian capital has higher levels of radiation and during longer intervals of time. The values obtained are explained by the existing altitude difference, since Ambato is 350 m below its torque. In addition, there is an attenuation coefficient due to the greater presence of suspended clouds in this area. These elements act as filters in the atmosphere and can scatter radiation. An-other important factor for which the project measurements may have a margin of error is related to the optics of the instrument. The neutral density filter does not have the same absorption for all wavelengths, as it happens in the optical fiber and the spectrometer, if there is any particle that prevents light from passing, it is scattered.

The UVI scale is endorsed by organizations such as the World Health Organization, the World Meteorological Organization, the UN Environment Program and the International Commission against Radiation. Thanks to it, the calculation methods of the index have been standardized, providing a color code and graphics to offer the information in a simple and practical way to the population about the care that must be taken. According to the data obtained on average, the level of UVI in the city of Quito is approximately 14 and that of Ambato is between 10 and 11, on a scale that goes up to 15 (but that could take even higher values). Considering that from number 11 it is considered that ultraviolet radiation is extremely high, residents should be made aware of the high potential for damage to the skin and eyes to which they are exposed. As suggested protection measures, a very high index (8, 9 and 10) is used: a hat or a cap, sunscreen with a high filter, sunglasses, care for children and an exposure of 11 to 34 min. maximum. For an extreme level it is recommended to avoid leaving the house, especially in the midday hours and in exceptional cases an exposure of 8 to 23 min maximum depending on skin tone.

6 Conclusions

The implementation of commercial devices that allow the ultraviolet radiation index to be measured has increased in large cities, given the increasing number of cases of people with skin cancer. Through wireless devices operating in the 2.4 GHz band, with hardware and free software platforms, a system was developed to collect data on solar radiation individually in two primary schools located in different cities. The prototypes have been designed with technologies and equipment that allow web development for multiplatform, the use of embedded systems reduces implementation costs, as well as the use of a host that is tailored to the needs. In this way a robust device can be presented to the general public that, using colored LED panels, expresses the appearance of a traffic light. Following the WHO recommendations, the display of information should use five colors (green, yellow, orange, red and violet) to denote the low, medium, high, very high or extreme degree of radiation. This device also shows informatively the minimum prevention measures that must be followed to protect yourself when you are in environments without a cover. When comparing this proposal with a commercial device, there was an uncertainty of less than 3%, demonstrating its validity as a detection tool for the level of UVI.

As a case study, two of the highest altitude cities in Ecuador have been chosen which, due to their geographical position, have the highest levels of radiation, which has been verified when using this system. The objective of this research has been to be able to provide primary education schools with a tool, since students can be exposed to high levels of radiation without knowing this reality. In the same way it happens with teachers and parents who do not provide the necessary protective equipment, since they are unaware of the subject. In Ecuador, in coordination with public health, the Department of the Environment and the municipalities, events are held that promote the development of a better culture of prevention in terms of prolonged exposure to sunlight. Part of their job is to manage a monitoring and alert network, which includes air quality, noise level reports, ultraviolet radiation, among others. Constituting an integral system that allows improving the quality of life of citizens and providing them with the necessary information channels.

The authors of this document have planned their implementation in parks and schools, where children and adults share moments of recreation without having knowledge of the latent danger. It is also planted to patent this proposal and through the support of private companies to obtain financial sustainability and be able to reach communities and villages with low economic resources that cannot invest in a commercial technological solution.

References

1. Young, A.R., Claveau, J., Rossi, A.B.: Ultraviolet radiation and the skin: photobiology and sunscreen photoprotection. J. Am. Acad. Dermatol. (2017). https://doi.org/10.1016/j.jaad.2016.09.038
2. Dietliker, K., Baro, J.: UV radiation sources and UV radiation measurement. In: Handbook of Industrial Inkjet Printing: A Full System Approach (2017). https://doi.org/10.1002/9783527687169.ch5
3. Premalatha, N., Valan Arasu, A.: Prediction of solar radiation for solar systems by using ANN models with different back propagation algorithms. J. Appl. Res. Technol. (2016). https://doi.org/10.1016/j.jart.2016.05.001
4. Acevedo-Luna, A., Bernal-Correa, R., Montes-Monsalve, J., Morales-Acevedo, A.: Design of thin film solar cells based on a unified simple analytical model. J. Appl. Res. Technol. (2017). https://doi.org/10.1016/j.jart.2017.08.002
5. Diffey, B.L.: Time and place as modifiers of personal UV exposure. Int. J. Environ. Re. Publ. Health (2018). https://doi.org/10.3390/ijerph15061112
6. Kechichian, E., Ezzedine, K.: Vitamin D and the skin: an update for dermatologists. Am. J. Clin. Dermatol. 19(2), 223–235 (2017). https://doi.org/10.1007/s40257-017-0323-8
7. Dessinioti, C., Katsambas, A.: Melasma. In: Hyperpigmentation (2017). https://doi.org/10.1201/9781315162478
8. Coffin, S.L., Turrentine, J.E., Cruz, P.D.: Photodermatitis for the allergist. Curr. Allergy Asthma Rep. 17(6), 1–7 (2017). https://doi.org/10.1007/s11882-017-0705-2
9. Pozzobon, F.C., Acosta, A.E.: Epidemiological profile of primary cutaneous melanoma over a 15-year period at a private skin cancer center in Colombia. Rev. Salud Publica (2018). https://doi.org/10.15446/rsap.v20n2.65616
10. García, J.A., Quinteros, C., Romero, A., Dutra, F.: Occurrence of squamous cell carcinoma in Milchschaf sheep in Uruguay. Ciência Rural (2017). https://doi.org/10.1590/0103-8478cr20170406
11. Wu, F., Redoute, J.M., Yuce, M.R.: WE-safe: a self-powered wearable IoT sensor network for safety applications based on LoRa. IEEE Access (2018). https://doi.org/10.1109/ACCESS.2018.2859383
12. Kanellis, V.G.: Ultraviolet radiation sensors: a review. Biophys. Rev. 11(6), 895–899 (2019). https://doi.org/10.1007/s12551-019-00556-9
13. Turner, J., Igoe, D., Parisi, A. V., McGonigle, A.J., Amar, A., Wainwright, L.: A review on the ability of smartphones to detect ultraviolet (UV) radiation and their potential to be used in UV research and for public education purposes (2020). https://doi.org/10.1016/j.scitotenv.2019.135873

14. Borgogno-Mondino, E., Sarvia, F., Gomarasca, M.A.: Supporting insurance strategies in agriculture by remote sensing: a possible approach at regional level. In: Misra, S., et al. (eds.) ICCSA 2019. LNCS, vol. 11622, pp. 186–199. Springer, Cham (2019). https://doi.org/10.1007/978-3-030-24305-0_15

15. García, C.A., et al.: Fuzzy control implementation in low cost CPPS devices. In: IEEE International Conference on Multisensor Fusion and Integration for Intelligent Systems, pp. 162–167 (2017). https://doi.org/10.1109/MFI.2017.8170423

16. Buele, J., et al.: Interactive system for monitoring and control of a flow station using LabVIEW. In: Rocha, Á., Guarda, T. (eds.) ICITS 2018. AISC, vol. 721, pp. 583–592. Springer, Cham (2018). https://doi.org/10.1007/978-3-319-73450-7_55

17. Kerdprasop, K., Kerdprasop, N.: Remote sensing based model induction for drought monitoring and rainfall estimation. In: Gervasi, O., et al. (eds.) ICCSA 2016. LNCS, vol. 9788, pp. 356–368. Springer, Cham (2016). https://doi.org/10.1007/978-3-319-42111-7_28

18. Buele, J., Varela-Aldás, J., Santamaría, M., Soria, A., Espinoza, J.: Comparison between fuzzy control and MPC algorithms implemented in low-cost embedded devices. In: Rocha, Á., Ferrás, C., Montenegro Marin, C.E., Medina García, V.H. (eds.) ICITS 2020. AISC, vol. 1137, pp. 429–438. Springer, Cham (2020). https://doi.org/10.1007/978-3-030-40690-5_42

19. Jonathan, O., Misra, S., Ibanga, E., Maskeliunas, R., Damasevicius, R., Ahuja, R.: Design and implementation of a mobile webcast application with google analytics and cloud messaging functionality. J. Phys. Conf. Ser. (2019). https://doi.org/10.1088/1742-6596/1235/1/012023

20. Semlali, B.E.B., El Amrani, C., Denys, S.: Development of a Java-based application for environmental remote sensing data processing. Int. J. Electr. Comput. Eng. 9, 1978–1986 (2019). https://doi.org/10.11591/ijece.v9i3.pp1978-1986

21. Shete, R., Agrawal, S.: IoT based urban climate monitoring using Raspberry Pi. In: International Conference on Communication and Signal Processing, ICCSP 2016, pp. 2008–2012 (2016). https://doi.org/10.1109/ICCSP.2016.7754526

22. Narayanamurthy, V., et al.: Skin cancer detection using non-invasive techniques. RSC Adv. 8, 28095–28130 (2018). https://doi.org/10.1039/c8ra04164d

Optimized DWT SVD Based Image Watermarking Scheme Using Particle Swarm Optimization

Megha Bansal[1](✉)(iD), Anurag Mishra[2], and Arpita Sharma[2]

[1] Department of Computer Science, University of Delhi, New Delhi, India
megha.cs.du@gmail.com
[2] Deen Dayal Upadhyaya College, University of Delhi, New Delhi, India
anurag_cse2003@yahoo.com, asharma@ddu.du.ac.in

Abstract. The robust watermarking techniques have gained popularity over last decade as more and more digital contents are being shared over Internet. This increase in data transmission also poses greater risk of various attacks which hamper data authenticity, integrity and quality. Therefore, efficient mechanisms are required that can handle robust transmission of digital data while honoring the Digital Right Management (DRM) protection measures of copyrighted content. In this paper, we explore an optimized Particle Swarm Optimization (PSO) based watermarking scheme on digital images in the hybrid Discrete wavelet transform (DWT) and Singular value decomposition (SVD) transform. The watermark is embedded in the host images by using both single scaling and multiple scaling factors for optimizing the visual quality of the signed images viz-a-viz robustness. Eight gray-scale and six colored images are used to carry out the experiments. Comparison of the proposed watermarking scheme with other techniques ascertain the proposed scheme outperforms others and it also fulfills all requisite conditions to be a robust and optimized watermarking scheme.

Keywords: Image watermarking · Transform domain · Discrete wavelet transform · Singular value decomposition

1 Introduction

In recent years, there is a vast increase in the amount of digital data communicated across the network. This has raised the security concerns related to authenticity and ownership of the data across Internet. Watermarking has emerged out as one of the solutions to above problems. Digital watermarking is a process for copyright protection and owner identification and verification in which a copyright data is embedded into the cover image as watermark in an invisible or visible manner that can be extracted later without much degradation of the cover signed image and the watermark [1, 2].

In this regard, visual quality of the signed images and robustness of the embedding scheme are two important parameters to quantify the performance of the watermarking scheme. Since both parameters are inversely related to each other, in lieu of this, watermarking can be visualized as an optimization problem. Cox et al. [1] proposed

© Springer Nature Switzerland AG 2020
O. Gervasi et al. (Eds.): ICCSA 2020, LNCS 12254, pp. 862–877, 2020.
https://doi.org/10.1007/978-3-030-58817-5_61

three groups to classify most commonly used watermarking schemes: Robust, Fragile, and Semi-fragile. Robust watermarking schemes are used for copyright protection and are resilient against compression, geometric and counterfeit attacks [3]. The fragile and semi fragile techniques are used when the focus is on image integrity and authenticity. The watermark is embedded in fragile framework in such manner that any attempt to modify signed image will result in complete distortion of the watermark. The semi fragile watermarks are developed to harness benefits of both robust and fragile framework. When the embedding process is carried out in the spatial domain of image, it leads to fragile watermarking. Such kind of watermarking results in directly changing the bits of the host image, thus, ease the implementation but compromises on the robustness of scheme against various attacks [3, 4]. On the other hand, watermarking in the transform domain results in embedding the watermark in the frequency domain coefficients of host image and has been found to be a more robust watermarking scheme. Out of various frequency domain techniques like Discrete Fourier Transform (DFT) [5, 6], Discrete Cosine Transform (DCT) [7, 8, 26] and Discrete Wavelet Transform (DWT) [9, 10, 25, 33], DWT has been found to achieve an imperceptible watermarking along with high robustness [1]. Xianghong et al. [29] proposed DWT in conjunction with vector transform as watermark embedding scheme. They have used single scaling factor for embedding the watermark in host image. These techniques have further been used in collaboration with other techniques like Singular value decomposition (SVD) [2, 11, 23, 27] for better watermarking efficiency.

The secure transmission of digital images has greatly evolved from the initial proposed algorithms like DFT, DCT to more sophisticated soft computing techniques like artificial neural networks, fuzzy logic systems, support vector machines along with HVS model [12–16, 24]. Mishra et al. [17] have proposed watermarking scheme based on characteristics of human visual model. They have exploited three HVS features and fed them into FIS. They have also integrated a single layer feed-forward neural network known as extreme machine learning to generate the watermark. They claimed that their scheme is capable to implement real time watermarking applications.

The last decade has seen numerous applications having origin in nature inspired techniques to efficiently solve optimization problems. Hybridization of different meta-heuristic techniques – Genetic Algorithm (GA), Ant Colony Optimization (ACO), Particle Swarm Optimization (PSO) and nature inspired algorithms like Spider monkey, Cuckoo search and Artificial Bee Colony optimization along with transform domain techniques have also been explored and reported. Lai et al. [18] presented tiny genetic algorithm in conjunction with the SVD transform domain. In their work, they used tiny-GA to compute the values of embedding scaling factors to optimize the parameters of watermarking algorithm. Agarwal et al. [19] proposed their watermarking scheme using cuckoo search algorithm. In their scheme, they have embedded the watermark in different coefficients of the host image using multiple scaling factors which they have optimized using CSA. Loukhaoukha et al. [30] have used multi-objective ant colony optimization technique in LWT-SVD domain while Ishtiaq et al. [32] have proposed the Particle Swarm Optimization technique to find the optimal values for multiple scaling factors. Mishra et al. [20] have presented their widely cited hybrid watermarking scheme in DWT domain using famous Firefly Optimization for gray-scale images. They have decomposed LL3 sub-band coefficients into singular values using SVD to embed the watermark. They have nicely analyzed the use of Multiple Scaling Factors (MSFs) for embedding the watermark in the images. The MSFs are generated through Firefly Algorithm by using an Objective Function (Obj) which is composed of the PSNR and all image processing operations they used to attack the signed images. Their results were superior to all other such schemes falling in the same category. Abdelhakim [31] have suggested a combination of DCT with Artificial Bee Colony for the optimization of watermarking scheme. They claimed that their proposed technique minimized the error between optimal and predicted solutions for watermark embedding. Kuppusamy et al. [21] have proposed a PSO based watermarking algorithm in daubechies4 transform domain. They employed various attacks over the signed images and claimed good results of their scheme using IQIM. Loukhaoukha et al. [22] have hybridized multi-objective particle swarm optimization technique with SVD in wavelet domain for watermarking. They showed significant improvement in their results with the use of MSFs for watermark embedding.

Image watermarking is performed by using embedding strength (α) which can be either single valued i.e. Single Scaling Factor (SSF) or there can be multiple values of the embedding strength i.e., Multiple Scaling Factors (MSFs). The SSF takes constant numerical value for every coefficient of the host image for watermarking purpose. Thus, it does not consider variations in the physical parameters like contrast and intensity of the host image. However, it has been seen that different regions of image vary in their structural and physical properties which disturbs the visibility of the signed image especially in the smoother regions [1, 4, 14]. Thus, MSF plays an important role in optimizing the results for an efficient watermarking scheme. The MSF considers different values for different coefficients of host image and thus, embedding the watermark with lesser strength in smoother areas as compared to the high intensity areas of the host image.

In this paper, we propose an optimized hybrid watermarking scheme using DWT-SVD based on PSO technique. We have carried out the watermark embedding using both the SSF and MSF in gray-scale and colored images for the sake of comparison. Our proposed scheme further examines the robustness parameter by employing various image process attacks which are also used in the Objective Function. This Objective Function happens to be a linear function of PSNR value of signed image and sum of Normalized Correlation (NC) values for attacked images. The research paper is organized as follows:

It presents the brief introduction of PSO along with its necessary mathematical inputs in Sect. 2. The Sect. 3 comprises of the proposed embedding and extraction schemes. Section 4 contains our experimental results and their analysis on the basis of its comparison with other hybrid schemes. Section 5 concludes the whole work.

2   Particle Swarm Optimization

PSO is a population-based global optimization technique modelled by Kennedy and Eberhart [28]. PSO is a meta-heuristic technique that is based on co-operative and social characteristics of evolution like flocking of birds, insects swarming as compared to other evolutionary strategies like genetic algorithms that use competitive aspects like survival of the fittest. PSO involves creating a diffuse population (known as swarm) of individuals (termed as particles) that tend to move in the search space and clustering in areas where local minima are located. In each iteration, particles learn from their surroundings and on that basis, update their positions and velocities which are based on the combination of best positions found by that particle (personal best, pbest) and also, the best position value achieved by entire swarm (global best, gbest).

```
Listing 1. Pseudo-Code of PSO
Input:  a)  An objective function obj(x),  x = [x₁,x₂,...,xₘ]ᵀ

        b)  A random population (swarms) of particles sᵢ,
            i = 1, 2, ..., n
        c)  Inertial weight: w = 1, acceleration constants:
            Ø₁ = 1, Ø₂ = 2
        d)  Uniformly distributed random vectors: r₁,r₂ =
            [0,1], maximum number of iterations: maxItr
Begin
  for each sᵢ
    generate a random position vector Pᵢ = U(low,high)
    if obj(pbestᵢ) > obj(gbest)
      gbest↑pbestᵢ
    end if
    generate a random velocity vector Vᵢ = U (−|high −
    low|,|high − low|)
  end for
  while (t < maxItr) or (StopCriterion)
    for each sᵢ
      Compute its velocity
```
$$V_i^{(t+1)} = wV_i^{(t)} + \emptyset_1 r_1\left(pbest_i - P_i^{(t)}\right) + \emptyset_2 r_2\left(gbest - P_i^{(t)}\right)$$
```
      Update its position
```
$$P_i^{(t+1)} = P_i^{(t)} + V_i^{(t+1)}$$
```
      if  obj(Pᵢ) > obj(pbestᵢ)
        pbestᵢ↑Pᵢ
      end if
      if  obj(pbestᵢ) > obj(gbest)
        gbest↑pbestᵢ
      end if
    end for
  end while
End
```

With each iteration, particles tend to move closer and converge towards a single point. The output generated by PSO largely depends on the values of parameters used like inertial weight *w*, maximum number of iterations used *maxItr* and the acceleration constants $\emptyset_1$ and $\emptyset_2$. As the process terminates, the best solution is denoted by gbest which provides the optimal solution.

3 Proposed Method

In the proposed scheme, host image (I) of 512 × 512 and binary watermark (W) of size 32 × 32 are used for embedding and extraction process. The embedding is carried out in the transform domain by partitioning the host image into sub-bands using 4 -level DWT and decomposing the coefficients using SVD as explained in Sect. 3.1. The extraction process is executed as the reverse procedure of embedding and is explained in Sect. 3.2 in detail.

3.1   Watermark Embedding

In the embedding process, the bits of the host image are altered according to the values of the coefficients of watermark to be inserted. Figure 1 represents the procedure through block diagram. A good embedding is determined by the visual quality of the signed images. The metric PSNR measures peak signal to noise ratio and determines the quality of embedding. Higher values of PSNR reflects higher visual quality of the signed images. It is given by the equation:

$$PSNR = 10 log_{10}\left(\frac{I_{max}^2}{MSE}\right) \tag{1}$$

where, I_{max} defines the maximum pixel intensity for image I and MSE denotes mean square error.

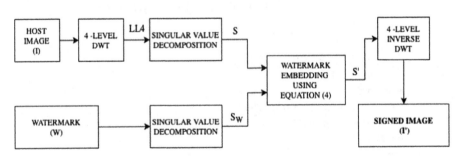

Fig. 1. Block diagram of watermark embedding

Listing 2. Embedding Process

- Decompose the host image using 4 -level DWT HAAR wavelet transform into four sub-bands: LL4, LH4, HH4, HL4.
- For good robustness, use LL4 sub-band for watermark embedding.

- For unique feature extraction, perform SVD on LL4 sub band of host image and obtain S using equation:

$$[USV] = SVD(LL4) \tag{2}$$

- Apply SVD on the watermark (W) used to achieve singular value matrix (S_w) using following equation:

$$[U_w S_w V_w] = SVD(W) \tag{3}$$

- Embed the watermark coefficients (S_w) into the obtained coefficients of host image (S) using equation:

$$S' = S + \propto . S_w \tag{4}$$

where, $\propto$ represents the embedding scaling factor that needs to be optimized.

- Obtain modified coefficients using equation given below:

$$LL4' = [US'V^T] \tag{5}$$

- Perform IDWT on the above modified coefficients resulting into signed image.

3.2 Watermark Extraction

This process recovers the extracted watermark from the signed image. The process is represented through the block diagram in Fig. 2. A good watermark extraction scheme should be robust to the image processing attacks. To measure the robustness of the scheme, NC (W, W') (normalized cross-correlation) coefficient is computed for the original watermark (W) from host image and the recovered watermark (W') from the signed image using the equation:

$$NC\left(W, W'\right) = \frac{\sum_{i=1}^{m} \sum_{j=1}^{n} \left[W(i,j) * W'(i,j)\right]}{\sum_{i=1}^{m} \sum_{j=1}^{n} \left[W(i,j)\right]^2} \tag{6}$$

The values closer to 1 indicate good recovery of the watermark from the signed image and hence, high robustness of the watermarking scheme.

Listing 3: Extraction Process

- For recovery, apply 4- level DWT on the host image and signed image.
- Retrieve LL4 and $LL4'$ sub band coefficients from both the images respectively.

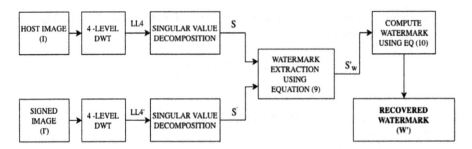

Fig. 2. Block diagram of watermark extraction.

- Apply SVD on above calculated coefficients and obtain corresponding singular values S and S' values using the following equations:

$$[USV] = SVD(LL4) \tag{7}$$

$$[U'S'V'] = SVD(LL4') \tag{8}$$

- Extract the singular values of the watermark (S'_w) through formula given by equation:

$$S'_w = (S' - S)/\propto \tag{9}$$

- Recover the watermark (W') using equation given below:

$$W' = \left[U_w S'_w V^T_w \right] \tag{10}$$

3.3 PSO Based Watermarking Algorithm for Scaling Factor Optimization

In this scheme, the watermark coefficients are embedded in the host image using the multiple scaling factor ($\propto$). This embedding is performed in the transform domain using discrete wavelet transform and singular value decomposition. The MSF ' $\propto'$ is optimized using PSO algorithm.

Listing 4: PSO based watermarking scheme

- Create an initial population of n swarms randomly, where each particle has position vector of size mxm. This corresponds to the size of binary watermark used.

- For each particle of swarm s_i:

  i) Perform watermark embedding in the host image using algorithm in Listing 2. MSF $'\propto'$ used in Eq. (4) is optimized by PSO algorithm given in Listing 1.

  ii) Generate T different attacked signed images by executing T image-processing attacks on obtained signed image I'.

  iii) Perform watermark extraction on all attacked signed images using the watermark extraction algorithm given in Listing 3.

  iv) Calculate the visual quality of signed image I' using PSNR by Eq. (1) and robustness of the watermarking scheme using $\text{NC}(W, W')$ values for the attacked signed images using Eq. (6).

  v) Finally, compute the value of objective function of the swarm using the function given by following equation:

$$\text{Obj} = \text{PSNR} + \delta * \left[\text{NC}\left(W, W'\right) + \sum_1^n \text{NC}\left(W, W'\right) \right] \tag{11}$$

where, δ is the weighting factor for NC (W, W') values. This factor is required to create balance in the equation since PSNR value largely outweighs NC (W, W') values.

- Update each swarm's global position with the best value according to the objective function value achieved above.
- Optimize the swarms using the algorithm given in Listing 1.
- Repeat the above steps till termination criteria are met.

4 Experimental Results

Experiments are performed on eight 512×512 gray scale host images: Baboon, Boat, Lena, Cameraman, Parrots, Tiger, Jumbo and Cosmological Cabbage. Embedding is done using 32×32 binary image as watermark. The PSO parameters: $w = 1$, $\varnothing_1 = 1, \varnothing_2 = 2$, maxItr $= 1\,0$ and swarm size (n) = 20 are set. MATLAB 2018 is used to perform the experiments on MacBook Air 1.6 GHz Intel Core i5 on macOS Catalina version 10.15.4.

4.1 Effect of SSF and MSF Over Visual Quality of Signed Images

The use of SSF results in embedding the watermark with same strength in the entire host image. Table 1 compiles the PSNR and NC (W, W') values of the four gray scale signed images used in the present work. These four test images are used by us as other researchers have used the same test images and this becomes a mandatory criterion to present a comparative assessment of various other schemes vis-à-vis the proposed one. Table 2 compiles the PSNR and NC (W, W') values of four additional gray scale signed images used in our work without any such comparison.

Table 1. Compilation and comparison of PSNR and NC (W, W') values of host image and signed image between proposed technique and existing state of art techniques of PSNR Values of Signed Images

Image	Algorithm	PSNR (DB)	NC (W,W')
Baboon	Suggested scheme (SSF)	56.8489	1.000
	Suggested scheme (MSF)	60.9734	1.000
	Loukhaoukha et al. (2011) (MSF)	52.379	1.000
	Ishtiaq et al. (2010) (MSF)	44.9624	NA
	Xianghong et al. (2004) (SSF)	49.075	0.999
Boat	Suggested scheme (SSF)	52.5321	1.000
	Suggested scheme (MSF)	56.6840	1.000
	Loukhaoukha et al. (2011) (MSF)	54.810	1.000
	Ishtiaq et al. (2010) (MSF)	50.1586	NA
	Xianghong et al. (2004) (SSF)	49.075	1.000
Lena	Suggested scheme (SSF)	55.8539	1.000
	Suggested scheme (MSF)	59.2610	1.000
	Loukhaoukha et al. (2011) (MSF)	47.718	1.000
	Ishtiaq et al. (2010) (MSF)	48.105	NA
	Xianghong et al. (2004) (SSF)	49.075	1.000
Cameraman	Suggested scheme (SSF)	54.4182	1.000
	Suggested scheme (MSF)	57.8539	1.000
	Loukhaoukha et al. (2011) (MSF)	48.902	1.000
	Ishtiaq et al. (2010) (MSF)	NA	NA
	Xianghong et al. (2004) (SSF)	49.075	1.000

A close observation of the data compiled in Table 1 reveals that embedding the watermark using the MSF strategy gives better results as compared to the SSF strategy in proposed scheme. We also compare our MSF and SSF results with the same of other schemes belonging to the similar category. Clearly, our results outperform the results presented by other state of art works. This is found true both the PSNR and NC (W, W') parameter of the signed images. Table 2 further compiles results of PSNR and

Table 2. Compilation of PSNR AND NC (W, W') values for four additional signed images

Image	PSNR (SSF scheme) (dB)	PSNR (MSF scheme) (dB)	NC (W,W') (SSF scheme)	NC (W,W') (MSF scheme)
Parrots	58.3182	61.3738	1.000	1.000
Tiger	57.2842	60.4191	1.000	1.000
Jumbo	54.5351	55.3924	1.000	1.000
CosmologicalCabbage	52.6182	54.0521	1.000	1.000

NC (W, W') parameters for four more gray scale images used in our work both for SSF and MSF strategies. In this case also, the MSF strategy outperforms the SSF strategy. The PSNR values for all four signed images are better placed for MSF while the NC (W, W') parameter is already found to be maximum (NC (W, W') = 1.000) both for SSF and MSF strategies. This again proves that MSF is better in comparison to SSF for all eight gray-scale images used in the proposed scheme.

4.2 Effect of SSF and MSF Over the Robustness of Watermarking Scheme

In the next part of this work, the next two tables compile the results for robustness studies carried out over these eight signed images by considering both SSF and MSF strategies. This is carried out to make an assessment of these embedding strategies over the robustness of the embedded watermark. Due to paucity of space and formatting issues, these results are divided into two tables – Table 3 and 4 respectively. The six image processing attacks being used in this work are - JPEG compression (with 10%, 20% and 30% compression ratios or QF = 0.9, 0.8 and 0.7 respectively), Noise addition (Salt & Pepper noise and Gaussian noise 5% each), Filtering (Gaussian filter and Median filter with Aperture size = 3), Cropping ((i) Crop the center of signed image with window size = 64 × 64 and replace it with the same window of the host image and (ii) Crop the corner of signed image with window size = 64 × 64 and replace it with the same window of the host image), Histogram Equalization, Scaling (reducing the signed image to half and then resizing it back to original size).

Table 3. Compilation of NC (W, W') values of gray scale signed images after various attacks

Image / Attacks	Baboon		Boat		Lena		Cameraman	
	SSF	MSF	SSF	MSF	SSF	MSF	SSF	MSF
JPEG (Q = 0.9)	0.9808	0.9841	0.9654	0.9759	0.9751	0.9818	0.9711	0.9897
JPEG (Q = 0.8)	0.9728	0.9795	0.9527	0.9727	0.9742	0.9769	0.9604	0.9778
JPEG (Q = 0.7)	0.9687	0.9724	0.9421	0.9614	0.9648	0.9702	0.9508	0.9622
Salt & Pepper Noise (5%)	0.9357	0.9672	0.8911	0.9238	0.9345	0.9601	0.9094	0.9274
Gaussian Noise (5%)	0.9489	0.9756	0.9032	0.9304	0.9387	0.9711	0.9105	0.9408
Gaussian Filtering (3x3)	0.9282	0.9576	0.9049	0.9304	0.9133	0.9416	0.9023	0.9404
Median Filtering (3x3)	0.9013	0.9453	0.8849	0.9131	0.8917	0.9379	0.8911	0.9299
Cropping (crop 64 x 64 center and replace with host image)	0.9557	0.9786	0.9297	0.9334	0.951	0.9617	0.9445	0.9531
Cropping (crop 64 x 64 corner and replace with host image)	0.9576	0.9733	0.9305	0.9417	0.9534	0.9687	0.947	0.9529
Histogram Equalization	0.9012	0.9107	0.8621	0.8859	0.8902	0.9074	0.8702	0.8913
Scaling (5 1 2 > 2 5 6 > 5 1 2	0.9939	0.9977	0.9912	0.9928	0.9930	0.9956	0.991	0.9929

A close observation of Table 3 and Table 4 clearly indicates that the NC (W, W') parameter values using MSF strategy for various image processing attacks are better as compared to SSF strategy. A high numerical value of the NC (W, W') parameter indicates that the watermark recovery out of the signed images is quite good which indicates a high robustness of the proposed scheme. Therefore, it can be deduced that our DWT-SVD hybrid transform based PSO watermarking scheme is suitable for optimizing the twin parameters of visual quality of signed grayscale images and the robustness of the watermark embedding scheme in the same. The use of the PSO based optimization of the Multiple Scaling Factors for embedding under DWT-SVD hybrid transform is primarily responsible for this outcome.

Table 4. Compilation of NC (W, W') values of gray scale signed images after various attacks (contd…)

Image / Attacks	Parrots		Tiger		Jumbo		CosmologicalCabbage	
	SSF	MSF	SSF	MSF	SSF	MSF	SSF	MSF
JPEG (Q = 0.9)	0.9711	0.9801	0.9586	0.9797	0.9692	0.9704	0.9439	0.9582
JPEG (Q = 0.8)	0.9613	0.9797	0.9492	0.9667	0.9544	0.9623	0.9296	0.9459
JPEG (Q = 0.7)	0.9405	0.9523	0.9073	0.9586	0.9070	0.9302	0.8921	0.9017
Salt & Pepper Noise (5%)	0.9181	0.9279	0.9216	0.9405	0.9086	0.9274	0.8867	0.9059
Gaussian Noise (5%)	0.9077	0.9488	0.9080	0.9416	0.9106	0.9311	0.9090	0.9393
Gaussian Filtering (3x3)	0.9434	0.9579	0.9181	0.9345	0.9075	0.9296	0.8987	0.9305
Median Filtering (3x3)	0.9374	0.9591	0.9096	0.9273	0.8933	0.9125	0.8809	0.9170
Cropping (crop 64 x 64 Center and replace with host image)	0.9602	0.9721	0.9591	0.9656	0.9426	0.9574	0.9371	0.9603
Cropping (crop 64 x 64 Corner and replace with host image)	0.9522	0.9678	0.9611	0.9703	0.9326	0.9420	0.9347	0.9534
Histogram Equalization	0.9032	0.9102	0.8993	0.9015	0.8785	0.8929	0.8020	0.8577
Scaling (5 1 2> 2 5 6> 5 1 2	0.9945	0.9981	0.9942	0.9977	0.9939	0.9969	0.9917	0.9957

4.3   Study of PSO Optimization Over Colored Images

In the previous sections, we have established that for eight different gray scale images, the PSO based optimization scheme operating under DWT-SVD hybrid transform is found comparatively better for watermark embedding. To further test the effectiveness of our proposed scheme, we extend our research work to six compressed colored images depicted in Fig. 3, working with SSF and MSF strategies. These images are – Parrot, Baboon, Tiger, Lena, Jumbo and Cosmological Cabbage, all compressed as Jpeg compression standard. It is important to note that the use of compressed copyright material is one of the major important requirements of Digital Rights Management (DRM). Therefore, we use these images in Jpeg compressed domain for testing our watermarking scheme. We tabulate the obtained results for PSNR and NC (W, W') in Table 5. Table 6 compiles the robustness studies data over the six colored images for SSF and MSF strategies. It is found that the results as obtained for the eight grayscale images reported in Sect. 4.2 and 4.3 above are repeated with MSF strategy out casting the SSF strategy in this case as well. Hence, it can be concluded that the PSO optimization has fairly performed well for colored images also. We conclude that the use of

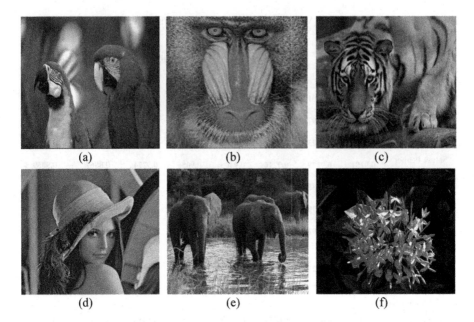

Fig. 3. Color host images a) Parrots.jpg, b) Baboon.jpg, c) Tiger.jpg, d) Lena.jpg, e) Jumbo.jpg and f) CosmologicalCabbage.jpg (Color figure online)

Table 5. Compilation of PSNR and NC (W, W') values of colored images under SSF and MSF strategies

Image	PSNR (SSF scheme) (dB)	PSNR (MSF scheme) (dB)	NC (W,W') (SSF scheme)	NC (W,W') (MSF scheme)
Parrots	60.7181	64.8534	1.000	1.000
Baboon	57.6204	63.6811	1.000	1.000
Tiger	59.8275	62.7539	1.000	1.000
Lena	60.0043	61.7653	1.000	1.000
Jumbo	55.2116	57.8201	1.000	1.000
Cosmological Cabbage	55.8022	58.4118	1.000	1.000

PSO optimization in DWT-SVD hybrid transform domain working with MSF embedding strategy is a good candidate for grayscale and compressed colored image watermarking. In the proposed scheme, all performance metrics have been verified and evaluated viz-a-viz., state of the art techniques and it has been found to outperform all of them.

Table 6. Compilation of NC (W, W') values over colored signed images after attacks under SSF and MSF strategies

Attacks/Image	Parrots		Baboon		Tiger		Lena		Jumbo		CosmologicalCabbage	
	SSF	MSF	SSF	MSF	SSF	MSF	SSF	MSF	SSF	MSF	SSF	MSF
JPEG (Q = 0.9)	0.9827	0.9915	0.9817	0.9908	0.9601	0.9841	0.9722	0.9869	0.9787	0.9821	0.9678	0.9765
JPEG (Q = 0.8)	0.9704	0.9844	0.9701	0.9802	0.9540	0.9713	0.9687	0.9742	0.9644	0.9706	0.9495	0.9634
JPEG (Q = 0.7)	0.9635	0.9736	0.9621	0.9742	0.9480	0.9673	0.9513	0.9681	0.9455	0.9703	0.9267	0.9356
Salt & Pepper Noise (5%)	0.9294	0.9493	0.9192	0.9472	0.9276	0.9511	0.9285	0.9605	0.9230	0.9521	0.9064	0.9330
Gaussian Noise (5%)	0.9335	0.9634	0.9264	0.9521	0.9474	0.9586	0.9384	0.9646	0.9453	0.9552	0.9195	0.9483
Gaussian Filtering (3x3)	0.9681	0.9829	0.9407	0.9643	0.9527	0.9814	0.9498	0.9785	0.9501	0.9792	0.9183	0.9571
Median Filtering (3x3)	0.9536	0.9663	0.9334	0.9575	0.9482	0.9710	0.9403	0.9648	0.9416	0.9702	0.9226	0.9536
Cropping (crop 64 x 64 center and replace with host image)	0.9723	0.9833	0.9636	0.9823	0.9661	0.9771	0.9628	0.9739	0.9523	0.9711	0.9498	0.9643
Cropping (crop 64 x 64 corner and replace with host image)	0.9766	0.9811	0.9688	0.9805	0.9584	0.9786	0.9604	0.9788	0.9566	0.9748	0.9512	0.9666
Histogram Equalization	0.9190	0.9279	0.9052	0.9197	0.9016	0.9172	0.9032	0.9204	0.8919	0.9110	0.8877	0.8990
Scaling (5 1 2 > 2 5 6 > 5 2)	0.9962	0.9992	0.9933	0.9956	0.9955	0.9984	0.9930	0.9965	0.9949	0.9978	0.9940	0.9966
Sharpening	0.9785	0.9910	0.9801	0.9908	0.9536	0.9708	0.9762	0.9899	0.9475	0.9628	0.9491	0.9652

We attribute better results obtained by us to the use of the hybrid objective function used to optimize the PSO technique. This objective function is a linear combination of the PSNR and the image processing attacks used in this work. This function has resulted in better optimization of the MSF for PSO based watermarking scheme.

5 Conclusion

The paper proposes an optimized PSO based watermarking scheme working in hybrid DWT-SVD transform domain. The PSO is used to determine the Multiple Scaling Factor (MSF) based embedding strength further used to embed the watermark in the image coefficients on the basis of its structural and physical properties. The experimentation is carried out over eight gray-scale and six colored images of the size 512×512. The Objective function proposed by Mishra et al. which is a linear combination of the PSNR and six different image processing attacks is used to run the PSO algorithm. The optimized value of the MSFs so generated by the PSO is used to embed the watermark in the selected low frequency coefficients of the host images. The signed images so obtained are found to exhibit very high visual quality and the watermark embedding scheme is also found to be quite robust. The proposed watermarking scheme outperforms several other identical schemes with the observed results. It is found that the PSO based scheme carried out in hybrid DWT-SVD transform domain is very successful to optimize the MSF parameters in accordance with various regions of the test images. Additionally, the visual quality of the signed images and the robustness parameter NC are also found to be well balanced due to its use. We attribute this exceling performance of our scheme to the use of particle swarm optimization technique in collaboration with the objective function used.

References

1. Cox, J., Kilian, J., Leighton, F.T., Shamoon, T.: Secure spread spectrum watermarking for multimedia. IEEE Trans. Image Process. **6**(12), 1673–1687 (1997)
2. Liu, R., Tan, T.: An SVD-based watermarking scheme for protecting rightful ownership. IEEE Trans. Multimed. **4**(1), 121–128 (2002)
3. Nikolaidis, N., Pitas, I.: Robust image watermarking in the spatial domain. Signal Process. **66**(3), 385–403 (1998)
4. Liu, J.-C., Chen, S.-Y.: Fast two-layer image watermarking without referring to the original image and watermark. Image Vis. Comput. **19**(14), 1083–1097 (2001)
5. Lin, C.-Y., Wu, M., Bloom, J.A., Cox, I.J., Miller, M.L., Lui, Y.M.: Rotation, scale, and translation resilient watermarking for images. IEEE Trans. Image Process. **10**(5), 767–782 (2001)
6. Solachidis, V., Pitas, L.: Circularly symmetric watermark embedding in 2-D DFT domain. IEEE Trans. Image Process. **10**(11), 1741–1753 (2001)
7. Hernandez, J.R., Amado, M., Perez-Gonzalez, F.: DCT-domain watermarking techniques for still images: detector performance analysis and a new structure. IEEE Trans. Image Process. **9**(1), 55–68 (2000)
8. Patra, J.C., Phua, J.E., Bornand, C.: A novel DCT domain CRT-based watermarking scheme for image authentication surviving JPEG compression. Digit. Signal Process.s **20**(6), 1597–1611 (2010)
9. Dawei, Z., Guanrong, C., Wenbo, L.: A chaos-based robust wavelet-domain watermarking algorithm. Chaos Solitons Fractals **22**(1), 47–54 (2004)
10. Meerwald, P., Uhl, A.: Survey of wavelet-domain watermarking algorithms. In: Security and Watermarking of Multimedia Contents III, pp. 505–516 (2001)
11. Liu, F., Liu, Y.: A Watermarking algorithm for digital image based on DCT and SVD. In: 2008 Congress on Image and Signal Processing, pp. 380–383 (2008)
12. Agarwal, C., Mishra, A., Sharma, A.: Gray-scale image watermarking using GA-BPN hybrid network. J. Vis. Commun. Image Represent. **24**(7), 1135–1146 (2013)
13. Mei, S.C., Li, R.-H., Dang, H.-M., Wang, Y.-K.: Decision of image watermarking strength based on artificial neural-networks. In: Proceedings of the 9th International Conference on Neural Information Processing (ICONIP 2002) (2002)
14. Li, Q., Yuan, C., Zhong, Y.-Z.: Adaptive DWT-SVD domain image watermarking using human visual model. In: 9th International Conference on Advanced Communication Technology (2007)
15. Mishra, A., Goel, A., Singh, R., Chetty, G., Singh, L.: A novel image watermarking scheme using extreme learning machine. In: 2012 International Joint Conference on Neural Networks (IJCNN) (2012)
16. Motwani, M. C., Motwani, R.C., Harris, F.C.: Wavelet based fuzzy perceptual mask for images. In: 2009 16th IEEE International Conference on Image Processing (ICIP) (2009)

17. Agarwal, C., Mishra, A., Sharma, A.: Digital image watermarking in DCT domain using fuzzy inference system. In: 2011 24th Canadian Conference on Electrical and Computer Engineering (CCECE) (2011)
18. Lai, C.C.: Corrigendum to 'A digital watermarking scheme based on singular value decomposition and tiny genetic algorithm'. Digit. Signal Process. **23**(4), 1333 (2013)
19. Mishra, A., Agarwal, C.: Toward optimal watermarking of grayscale images using the multiple scaling factor based cuckoo search technique. In: Bio-Inspired Computation and Applications in Image Processing, pp. 131–155. Elsevier (2016)
20. Mishra, A., Agarwal, C., Sharma, A., Bedi, P.: Optimized gray-scale image watermarking using DWT SVD and firefly algorithm. Exp. Syst. Appl. **41**(17), 7858–7867 (2014)
21. Kuppusamy, K., Thamodaran, K.: Optimized image watermarking scheme based on PSO. Proc. Eng. **38**, 493–503 (2012)
22. Loukhaoukha, K., Nabti, M., Zebbiche, K.: A robust SVD-based image watermarking using a multi-objective particle swarm optimization. Opto-Electron. Rev. **22**(1), 45–54 (2014). https://doi.org/10.2478/s11772-014-0177-z
23. Huang, F., Guan, Z.-H.: A hybrid SVD-DCT watermarking method based on LPSNR. Pattern Recogn. Lett. **25**(15), 1769–1775 (2004)
24. Agarwal, C., Mishra, A., Sharma, A.: A novel gray-scale image watermarking using hybrid Fuzzy-BPN architecture. Egypt. Inform. J. **16**(1), 83–102 (2015)
25. Ohnishi, J., Matsui, K.: Embedding a seal in to a picture under orthogonal wavelet transform. In: IEEE International Conference on Multimedia and Computing System, Hiroshima, Japan, pp. 514–521 (1996)
26. Bors, A.G., Pitas, I.: Image watermarking using DCT domain constraints. In: IEEE International Conference on Image Processing, pp. 231–234 (1996)
27. Araghi, T.K., Manaf, A.A.: An enhanced hybrid image watermarking scheme for security of medical and non-medical images based on DWT and 2-D SVD. Future Gener. Comput. Syst. **101**, 1223–1246 (2019)
28. Kennedy, J., Eberhart, R.: Particle swarm optimization. In: 1995 IEEE International Conference on Neural Networks, Perth, Australia, pp. 1942–1948. IEEE Service Center, Piscataway (1995)
29. Xianghong, T., Lu, L., Lianjie, Y., Yamei, N.: A digital watermarking scheme based on DWT and vector transform. In: Proceeding of International Symposium on Intelligent Multimedia, Video and Speech Processing, pp. 635–638 (2004)
30. Loukhaoukha, K., Chouinard, J.Y., Taieb, M.H.: Optimal image watermarking algorithm based on LWT–SVD via multi-objective ant colony optimization. J. Inf. Hiding Multimed. Signal Process. **2**(4), 303–319 (2011)
31. Abdelhakim, A.M., Abdelhakim, M.: A time-efficient optimization for robust image watermarking using machine learning. Exp. Syst. Appl. **100**, 197–210 (2018)
32. Ishtiaq, M., Sikandar, B., Jaffar, A., Khan, A.: Adaptive watermark strength selection using particle swarm optimization. ICIC Express Lett. **4**(5), 1–6 (2010)
33. Loukhaoukha, K., Refaey, A., Zebbiche, K.: Ambiguity attacks on robust blind image watermarking scheme based on redundant discrete wavelet transform and singular value decomposition. J. Electr. Syst. Inf. Technol. **4**(3), 359–368 (2017)

Smart Home Automation: Taxonomy, Composition, Challenges and Future Direction

Olutosin Taiwo[1], Lubna A. Gabralla[2,3], and Absalom E. Ezugwu[4(✉)]

[1] School of Mathematics, Statistics and Computer Science,
University of Kwazulu-Natal, Westville Campus, Private Bag X54001,
Durban 4000, South Africa
219058760@stu.ukzn.ac.za

[2] Department of Computer Science and Information Technology, Community
College, Princess Nourah Bint Abdulrahman University, Riyadh, Saudi Arabia
lagabralla@pnu.edu.sa

[3] Faculty of Mathematical Sciences, University of Khartoum, Khartoum, Sudan

[4] School of Computer Science, University of KwaZulu-Natal, King Edward
Avenue, Pietermaritzburg Campus, Pietermaritzburg, 3201 Kwazulu-Natal,
South Africa
ezugwua@ukzn.ac.za

Abstract. Smart home is an evolving technological innovation that originates from the numerous application areas of the Internet of Things (IoT). As the world is driving more and more closer to adopting smart cities based infrastructural environments, in which most activities involve innovative technological connectivity, smart home automation is one of the focused areas which has grown exponentially in the last few decades. The main objective of smart home automation is to make life easier and convenient for homeowners and users. The role of smart home automation is essential to healthcare and the social and economic well-being of all users through the provision of a convenient and conducive place of living. With the spontaneous evolution of new trends in smart home automation design, the various elements and functions of devices used in building smart home systems need to be explained as these technologies have significant benefits. They can assist traditional methods of controlling and monitoring home appliances, improve healthcare for the elderly and disabled, alert homeowners in case of potential risk and enable homes to be controlled even while the owner is far from home. Most importantly, smart home systems have great potential for reduction in energy loss. Furthermore, to provide valuable insights into these technological environments, we must clearly understand some of the available options and gaps in the area of smart home automation systems. This paper presents a taxonomy of IoT smart home automation systems with elaborate discussions on the technologies, trends and challenges in smart home automation system design. A constructive and detailed review of existing literature based on application areas of smart home automation is presented. Lastly, highlights of the approaches, technologies, and strength and weaknesses associated with the smart home automation systems are discussed.

Keywords: Internet of Things · Smart home automation · Home network · Smart home hardware platforms

© Springer Nature Switzerland AG 2020
O. Gervasi et al. (Eds.): ICCSA 2020, LNCS 12254, pp. 878–894, 2020.
https://doi.org/10.1007/978-3-030-58817-5_62

1   Introduction

With the emergence and swift growth of Internet of Things and smart home automation systems, people are interested in using convenient mechanisms through the internet to control and monitor appliances [1] remotely. A dynamic interaction and rapid response of smart devices to the needs of homeowners and environmental conditions makes a home smart and intelligent to operate. Some features and technologies are embedded into some of the essential devices we use at homes, namely, lighting, air conditioning, audio and video gadgets, heating control systems, security, and so on to make them intelligent [2]. Computing and connectivity are going beyond the desktop and other forms of traditional computing and moving towards wireless networking of environment and surrounding objects with the aid of Radio Frequency Identification (RFID), smart sensors and network technologies [3]. Transformation of things into appliances, data, connected by application of internet, create services usable in smart home automation [4]. Smart home automation has its background in the application of Internet of Things (IoT) technologies. The IoT technologies led to having smart appliances such as smart lighting control, smoke detectors, fire detectors, temperature monitoring, smart televisions, and so on deployed in smart homes. Some of these smart appliances have embedded sensors for monitoring conditions such as temperature and humidity. These chipped devices can capture, store and send information to the home controller, which enables the homeowner or user to control and monitor their homes remotely [5].

Smart home automation is a significant aspect of IoT, it is growing exponentially and is incorporated into our daily activities, business, health, education and other aspects of our day-to-day lifestyles. Smart home automation aims at five major characteristics, namely: Convenience, Comfort, Consciousness, Care and Control. The ability to control your home remotely from any location gives you convenience, making your house warm before opening the door during winter gives you comfort, and switching ON/OFF of sockets, lights and appliances from a location outside your home gives you convenience. Smart home, in other words, is the foundation for remotely accessible environments (that is, environments in which each appliance can be accessed from a distance and controlled using software such as android and web applications as an interface). As smart home acceptance, application and incorporation are on the rise globally, there are many areas of smart home application benefits that are yet to be discovered and implemented. For example, the smart home health system, which aims at providing basic care for the elderly, disabled and outpatients is one of the areas that is yet to be thoroughly considered.

Another perspective of the smart home shows that it enables homeowners and residents to incorporate communication networks that connect the major appliances and services utilized and allows these to be remotely controlled, monitored or accessed from both within and outside the residence [6]. In smart home, communication network link sensors, appliances and other devices work together to allow for remote monitoring and control by occupants and other verified users in order to provide them with the frequent and regular essential services they require. Smart home does not only benefit home users but also has an impact on the economy and lifestyle of communities in which it is being used. It reduces stress, saves time and money and avoids wastage of resources and basic amenities. However, to effectively utilize smart home, it has to be automated. Smart home automation system connects controlled devices in the home to a central hub that controls lighting, climate, entertainment systems and allows users to remotely control their home appliances and gadgets through the assistance of ambient intelligent mechanisms [7].

Despite the wide interest in smart home automation and its relevance to the design and implementation of our future smart cities, studies and researches in this area are very limited and scattered, as only a handful of research papers are available for referencing. Therefore, this paper provides a comprehensive explanation of the concept of smart home, its elements, application areas and services, review of related works, challenges and future direction. In summary, the technical contributions of this paper are as follows:

- Provides an extensive survey of methods and application areas in smart home automation from existing literature.
- Highlights some of the essential elements and technologies for smart home automation system based on the Internet of Things environment.
- Highlights key challenges that mitigate the design and implementation of smart home automation in the Internet of Things environment.
- Suggests future research directions aimed at facilitating the effective implementation of smart home automation.

The paper is organized as follows: Sect. 2 contains an extensive review of related literature pertaining to researches in the area of Internet of Things in smart home automation systems. Section 3 provides the elements for building smart home automation systems in Internet of Things. Application areas services of smart home automation i n Internet of Things are presented and discussed in Sect. 4; Sect. 5 explains the research trends, challenges and future research direction in smart home automation. Lastly, Sect. 6 concludes the paper.

2 Related Work

In application areas of smart home automation, several systems have been proposed, designed and developed through research projects with a focus on making life more convenient for homeowners and home users. The developed systems mostly aim at making home ubiquitous. In this Section, we review some literature related to smart home automation. The reviewed literatures are between 2010 and 2019 and are reviewed based on technologies used, application areas, and strength and weakness of the works. Figure 1 depicts a chart of existing studies carried out in smart home domain from 2010 to 2019 with the focus on application areas. The sources of all the publications identified in this paper were from Google scholar search engine and IEEE Explore databases with focus on ISI and Scopus indexed journals.

Several researches have been made to integrate IoT with Smart Home automation in different area of services. For instance, Muhammad and Ali [8] proposed an automation and control method for lighting, ventilation, air conditioning, heating and

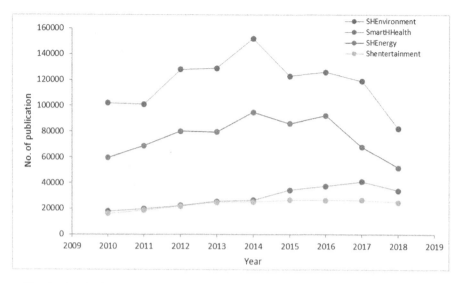

Fig. 1. Academic search trends of research in smart home automation application areas

security appliances in a smart building. The technologies used are Arduino UNO board, LEDs, and sensors which are controlled through a laptop in the building and an Android device when outside the building. The proposed method is implemented and evaluated using LEDs of different colors. The method should be verified using home appliances such as bulbs, fans and so on.

Majid, et al. [9], presented an IoT based sensing and monitoring system for energy efficiency in smart home appliances and monitoring to achieve maintenance of parameters within a certain range. The designed system uses EmonCMS platform for remote control of home appliances and devices. The platform is also used for collection and visualizing of monitored data. Technologies involved are Zigbee, Bluetooth, sensors, Arduino single board and ESP8266 microcontroller board.

Moreover, Shahram, et al. [10] presented a smart home automation tele-care system in conjunction with MEDeTIC. The system is designed to monitor and detect abnormalities in health situations of senior citizens, support medical consultations for the elderly from home and analyze activity patterns for unusual behavior in the system through Fuzzy Logic. Techniques of telemedicine and home automation were combined in the system. Technologies involved are sensors, Bluetooth and Zigbee. The system provides video conferencing and tele-consulting support between patient and doctor.

Waheb, et al. [11] presented a design and implementation of smart home automation system for controlling all electrical home appliances via WiFi with the use of an android-based smartphone, tablet or laptop. The system also monitors environmental conditions such as temperature and humidity with the use of sensors and has the ability to control or monitor voltage. The technologies used in the system are Arduino, ESP8266 WiFi module, temperature, humidity, and smoke and motion sensors. Remote control of electrical appliances in the designed system aims at reduction of energy consumption levels. The security of the home is also ensured with the ability of the system to send alerts to a user's phone in case of intrusion or breakage into the house.

Also, in [12], a smart home automation and energy management system for managing and power flow scheduling was presented. Home devices are controlled by mobile devices or systems through the internet for energy management in the system. The system was evaluated and tested with a prototype design using a controlled load bank to stimulate a scaled random real house consumption behavior. The technologies involved are Arduino Board, sensors (fire, gas, temperature, smoke, temperature and humidity), RFID and ESP8266 module.

Moreover, Abdulrahman, et al. [13] presented a design and model implementation of home automation system by application of Internet of Things. Seamless communication between individual applications and systems with a high level of security with use of robust web service protocol was ensured in the system through the deployment of Web Application Messaging Protocol (WAMP). Hardware development of the system was based on modular design for better functionality and reliability. Energy efficiency was ensured by the use of power actuators for control of home appliances. The system monitors ambient meteorological conditions and quantities such as temperature and light intensity. Environment and system interact and thus conditions are controlled based on the quantities measured.

Mohamed, et al. [14], in their approach, presented a smart home automation system based on Arduino microcontroller kit and LabView platform. The major functions of the system are to control light, manage temperature and monitor home security through an ultrasonic security camera. Temperature is measured by sensor, and Microcontroller in the system is capable of automatically turning on a fan once the temperature exceeds the set limit. Monitoring, access and control of the system are based on the signals received from the installed sensors in the system. The system was evaluated based on object distance, and range sensor is able to detect and automatically adjust the rate of temperature. Technologies involved are Arduino, temperature sensors and motion detectors.

A home healthcare system for recovery process, monitoring rehabilitation, studying daily activities and behavioral changes in patients was presented in [15]. The system is a Cloud-Based Smart Home Environment for home healthcare. Physiological data and body activity information are collected through non-invasive wearable sensors. Environmental sensors are deployed for collection of motion and activity information of humans. Data are stored in the cloud using a hybrid data storage model. The system proffers a solution to the provision of information about a patient at home to health caretakers. The limitation is the high level of energy consumption due to sensors and data transmission. Technologies used are environmental sensors and Zigbee protocol. Evaluation and experimental results showed that the system is effective in healthcare monitoring and assistance.

Himanshu, et al., in [16], proposed a smart home automation system for detection of presence or absence of a human or object in the house. The system aims at also providing information about levels of consumption of energy by sending a message to the homeowner, checking the status of gas cylinders to notify the homeowner if lower than a set threshold, and control of home appliances such as lights, fans and doors. The system uses technologies such as sensors for detection, MCU ESP8266 microcontroller and Arduino.

Smart home automation system for monitoring and control of different aspects of home through Android Application was designed by Hamzah, et al. [17]. The system controls and monitors temperature, humidity, gas, flame, light, measures water and humidity level in the soil, and detects motion. Temperature in the room is adjusted when it exceeds the set value. The kitchen is installed with a flame sensor and gas leakage sensor to forestall fire accidents. The designed system is also capable of garden irrigation. Security of homeowners is protected through an alert in the system to notify users of an intruder in the home/building. Technologies used are Arduino, PIR motion sensor, ESP8266 Microcontroller and Bluetooth. The designed system controls and monitors the home remotely and automatically, but exchange of data is limited to short range due to Bluetooth deployed in the system.

Zhuang, et al. [18] proposed an energy management system for smart home, based on optimal power scheduling method. The proposed system is for the home area network, based on smart grid and scheduling method for usage of power in the home. A genetic algorithm was adopted to optimize Operation Start Time of appliances, and Real Time Electricity Pricing was used for power scheduling in the home with the assistance of preference of residents. The system aims at optimizing power consumption for users and the pricing scheme also benefits utility companies.

A security system for smart home automation system was presented by Ajao, et al. [19]. The smart home automation system is for security of doors in order to safeguard access into the home. Entries into the home premises are authorized and authenticated before access is granted. A message is sent to the home user for security notification upon access or denial of access. Sensors are also embedded in the system for motion detection. Control of the home security system is through wireless IoT communication and Android mobile application. The presented system is easy and flexible to use but capturing of images of intruders is not included for surveillance.

Energy management in the home through distributed framework algorithm of appliance scheduling was proposed by Phani, et al. [20]. The proposed framework is demand response based on cost minimization. Scheduling of appliances in the system is based on knowledge of the price of electricity for the period. Greedy algorithm was proposed for cost minimization at the user's end, and to schedule appliances, a user needs to find an optimal start time and operating mode. Simulations and optimization methods show the proposed framework tends to yield lower costs for users, lower generation costs for utility companies and lower load fluctuations. The system was evaluated based on performance of the proposed algorithm.

Al-Ali, et al. [21] proposed a smart home Energy Management System that utilizes off-the-shelf Business Intelligence and Big data analytics software packages to manage energy consumption level and meet a consumer's demand. Home appliances are interfaced with IoT object (Data Acquisition module) with unique IP address leading to a large mesh network of devices in the system. Energy consumption data from each device in the system is collected by data acquisition system on chip module and then transmitted to a centralized server for processing and analysis. The system was tested and validated using a prototype built in laboratory to mimic heating, ventilation and air conditioning (HVAC) systems in a residential area.

Moreover, Jinsoo, et al. [22] proposed a smart home energy management system that generates energy based on wireless and wired networks. Power and energy from home appliances are transferred and measured through a low-power Zigbee communication network. Energy is generated through renewable energy sources (solar power and wind power) and home energy usage is optimized based on Power Line Communication. Light was installed as a means of energy and power measurement in a prototype system and was used for implementation with the home server of the proposed system. Results showed that the home server can achieve energy conservation and save energy costs.

An accident prevention subsystem for smart home automation was presented by Vasyl, et al. [23]. The system aims at sending signals to home users in case of potential danger/accident that may arise from fire outbreak in the home. Fire, gas and smoke sensors were used for detection of possible fire outbreak and a water leak detector for prevention of water leakage. In the proposed system, a neuro-controller interfaces the sensors with the appliances and alarms, and built models are based on Arduino microcontroller and programming model based on Artificial Neural network to test reliability and functionality. However, there is no implementation to show the installed home appliances and functionality.

Smart home control and monitoring system based on database replication method was proposed by Wibowo, et al. [24]. The user accesses the smart home through a single online master database through login (username and password). The system can control and monitor multiple systems online; however, implementation was not stated and system functionality depends solely on an online database, which implies that if there is problem with the online database, the system cannot function. A home mobile healthcare system for wheelchair users was developed by Lin, et al. [25]. The developed system and architecture are based on Wireless Body Sensor Networks (WSBN) and the system is used for measuring heart rate, ECG, and body pressure through nodes of the WSBN and ECG sensors. Apart from healthcare, this system is also capable of sensing a home environment and efficient monitoring of human activities in the home.

Also, Paul, et al. [26] proposed a smart home automation system based on voice control and Natural Language Processing (NLP). In the system, the user sends commands through speech to the mobile device, the message is interpreted and an appropriate command is then sent to a specific home appliance. NLP is used to interpret voice command in the mobile device. Home appliances are interfaced with Arduino board and programmed to interact with mobile devices. Better connection between user and devices is enhanced with NLP.

In addition, Radjeep, et al. [27] proposed a location detection system for smart home environment. The proposed system is intended to detect the location of a person in a home and to assist the medical caregiver to locate the patient in the home, provide healthcare, and keep track of the patient's daily living and medical condition from home. Technologies involved are Raspberry Pi, Arduino, and sensors. Voice recognition was embedded in the system to make the search for location easier and reduce the stress of the learning curve of new technologies for caregivers and family. The system is in progress and needs improvement for large scale implementation and reliability.

3   Elements of IoT Smart Home Automation

This Section presents a taxonomy of IoT Smart Home automation based on methods, technologies, application areas and other components involved in smart home automation systems. Furthermore, this Section also presents the taxonomy that will aid in defining the components required for the smart home automation from a high-level perspective as shown in Fig. 2.

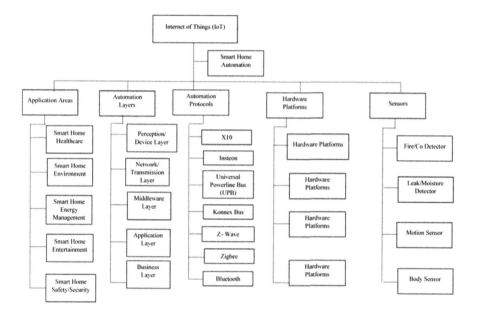

Fig. 2. Taxonomy of smart home automation system

Internet of things smart home automation involves a wide range of smart devices, appliances and sensors which are all interconnected and communicate with each other at anytime, anywhere and the communication is often wireless [28]. Elements of smart home are things and devices needed to make it smart and effectively communicate/interact with one another. These include mainly the home network, hardware platforms and home automation.

3.1   Internet of Things - Smart Home Automation Layers

IoT-Smart home can be divided into five layers namely: Perception, Network, Middleware, Application and Business layers. Higher-level layers are the Application and Business layers while lower level layers are Perception and Network layers and Middleware is the intermediate layer [29].

3.1.1   Perception Layer

The perception layer entails physical objects for collection of information from the smart home environment and is also referred to as the device layer. The overall management of devices such as identification and collection of specification information (location, humidity level, temperature level, etc.) by each type of sensor in the system are part of the responsibility of this layer. This layer consists of different types of sensors and environmental elements [28, 30].

3.1.2   Network Layer

The Network layer is responsible for secure transmission of information from sensor devices to the information processing system. This layer keeps sensitive information confidential from sensor devices to the central information processing system via RFID, WiFi and other transmission technologies [28]. Network layer is also referred to as transmission layer.

3.1.3   Middleware

Collection, transmission and processing of data in smart home automation are coordinated through a medium referred to as Middleware. The middleware layer is in charge of managing services in smart home and also acts as an intermediate layer to create an interface between lower level layers and higher level layers [30]. In smart home automation, communication passes through the middleware to other components involved in the system [31]. Middleware functions as a mechanism or software for hiding distribution of a home automation system from the user, and unification of different technologies through a single standardized API to the developer [32]. With middleware, products from different manufacturers but with the same technology can be used.

3.1.4   Application Layer

Based on processed information in middleware layer, application layer is responsible for general applications management. For instance, if there is an alert from the middleware layer, actions for control are taken in the application layer. Application layer is responsible for proper operation deployed application [30].

3.1.5   Business Layer

Management of the overall system, including application, sensors and other devices are the responsibility of business layer. The business layer is capable of creating practical graphs, business models, reports, and so on, based on the amount of accurate data received from the lower layer. Analysis of a report generated from this layer assists the functional manager in making more accurate predictions and decisions about business strategies [28].

3.2   Home Network

A network is a group of two or more devices that can communicate. Smart home involves integration of various devices to form a system. In a smart home, network makes use of a range of techniques such as computers, network communication protocols to communicate with objects and devices in the home. The two major levels of communication in smart home are connection between devices, objects and appliances in the home (internal network) and communication between the home and the internet world (external network).

Internal network is the network that makes appliances, devices, products and services inside the home communicate with themselves. Internal home network can be based on wire, cable or wireless connection, protocols and controllers. Local Area Network (LAN), Personal Area Network (PAN) and Body Area Network (BAN) are mostly used in indoor environments, into which home automation can be categorized. Local Area Network is the connection of several devices over a network in the same location and limited area, typically within a single building or home [33]. PAN is a communication between devices near a person. Examples include wireless keyboards, mouse, and barcode scanners. BANs are based on smart objects localized on the body of the user. They are a continuity of PAN but on a smaller scale [34]. Network communication in smart home involves protocols and controllers.

3.3   Hardware Platforms

Hardware platforms are an integral part of home automation technology in building a smart home. Platform in this context refers mainly to microcontrollers used in the development of home automation systems. ESP8266 Board, Intel Edison, Raspberry Pi and Arduino board are some of the major boards used in configuring IoT smart home systems. A sensor is an hardware device that detects certain external stimuli and responds in a distinctive manner. It is used to measure/monitor properties such as pressure, position, temperature or acceleration. With the development of Internet of Things, smart home sensors can help in the prevention of property damage. There are many types of sensors that are applicable in smart home automation [35]. These are environmental sensors (gas, water, smoke, lighting, movement, rain, wind, humidity, wind, temperature, and so on), multimedia sensors (microphones, cameras, and so on), physiological sensors (for measuring blood pressure, pulse rate, body temperature, respiration, and so on) and wearable sensors (sensors that are worn by the users by embedding in shoes, eye-glasses, ear-rings, clothes or directly placed on the body).

4   Smart Home Application Areas and Services

Smart home system was developed to make life convenient and reduce wastage of resources. To achieve these and many other aims, its applications are diverse but can still be monitored and controlled from any location for safety, care, and convenience. Smart home automation system renders services in areas such as healthcare for the elderly or aging, security, control and monitoring of home appliances and environmental conditions, improved energy efficiency and entertainment. Figure 3 presents an illustration of automation areas and services for smart home systems.

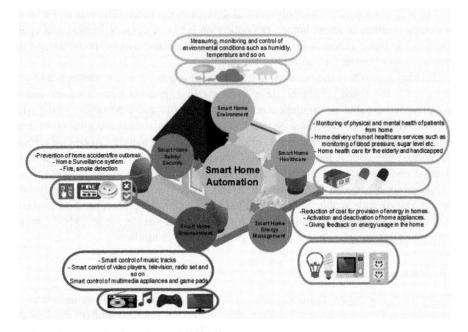

Fig. 3. Smart home application areas

4.1   Smart Home Healthcare

Health care is the prevention, treatment and management of illness or the preservation of mental and physical well-being through services offered by medical personnel. Smart home technology enables a better life quality with an independent and comfortable life for the elderly [36]. Automating a home will make it possible for doctors to monitor patients while at home and give patients the pleasure of having company at home. Also, smart home healthcare aims at catering for the needs of the disabled by making controlling appliances from devices such as phones, which are easily accessible to them. Other means of control and monitoring in home healthcare are the use of technologies such as sensors, wrist-straps and actuators. Some application areas of smart home healthcare include tracking of patients, data gathering, object sensing, monitoring and delivery of medical supplies online, administering drugs to patients while at home, and so on [4].

4.2   Smart Home Energy Efficiency

With technologies used in smart homes, there is reduction in energy. Heating, cooling, lights, water pumps and other electrical appliances in the home can be controlled by homeowners/users from any location through smart home technologies. Energy reduction is achieved with technologies such as automatic timers and motion detectors that automatically turn off lights when not in use and light dimmers to reduce wattage and output, thus saving energy [35]. Other areas are control of home appliances through smartphones as an automation system is also mobile application based.

4.3 Smart Home Entertainment

Social and lively environments are achieved in the home with convenience through IoT. Volume of music and changing tracks can be controlled without pressing buttons on the player. Smart home entertainment eliminates unnecessary remotes and makes life more convenient with control of different entertainment appliances from a smart phone. Interoperable communication in smart homes is obtainable through technologies such as WiFi, Bluetooth, Zigbee, for Plug-and Play services, Audio/Video remote control, Video Distribution Technology and High-Definition Television [37] for entertainment in the home thus making control of entertainment appliances possible.

4.4 Smart Home Safety

Quick detection and prevention of abnormal occurrences such as fires, flood, electricity leakage or unauthorized access in the home can be achieved with smart home technologies. For detection of unauthorized access and security violation signals can be sent from home to a user through smartphone application and there will be rapid response to control such situation. Smart homes are equipped with sub-systems for video surveillance, alarms, remote monitoring and emergency response [38].

5 Research Trends, Challenges and Future Direction

Smart home trends are increasing as deployment and application areas of smart home automation are opening up. In the previous sections, literature works have been reviewed and technologies in smart homes have been discussed and explained. In order to understand the direction of research in smart home automation, this Section aims at discussing research trends, challenges and possible solutions for future direction.

5.1 Research Trends

5.1.1 Energy Efficiency and Reduction in Consumption Level
Home energy management systems are for conservation of electricity costs, improvement of energy utilization through monitoring and scheduling of home appliances based on preferences of home users [39]; they tend to lower consumption rate of energy, increase the availability of energy to consumers and reduce or eliminate wastage. Current research trends favor demand-side management more than the supplier. But on the side of the supplier, research should be channeled towards developing energy efficient algorithms and systems that will deploy smart homes to balance efficiency, profitability and utility at both consumer and supplier's ends.

5.1.2   Privacy, Security and Trust in Smart Home

Security of data is currently under research for information generated in smart homes. Automation of various devices, users in the home and technologies generate lots of data, but preservation and integrity of these data needs to be worked on. Under security, authentication and authorization of users still needs to be considered in smart home system design and development. Current research shows proposed and prototype designs to address these issues.

5.1.3   Innovative Technology

As smart home automation systems are evolving and becoming acceptable in homes, new research is coming up with the discovery of innovative technologies that will be compatible in smart home automation systems and eliminate interoperability issues among devices so as to develop and implement systems that will enable efficient interaction and communication among devices in the system. From 2017, the research focus seems to have shifted from prototype and framework to development of real systems that are universal, scalable and have interoperability in smart homes. Trends are moving towards making devices from different manufacturers communicate reciprocally.

5.2   Challenges in Smart Home Automation

Challenges identified in smart home automation are security attacks, privacy concerns, incompatibility of devices and technologies in smart home automation system, and integrity of information sent and received. Smart home automation systems are designed for continuous monitoring of home, health, environment and to also give prompt notification to avert danger or accidents in the deployed area of application. Although a plethora of research appears to be regularly evolving on the subject of making smart home automation systems fully functional without danger or challenges, there are still areas of general challenges associated with smart home automation that need further development to improve performance of the system. These challenges are discussed in this Section.

5.2.1   Authentication, Authorization and Integrity of Users

Authentication and authorization of users in case of stolen control devices, are still a neglected part of smart home automation. Also, security applications to forestall unauthorized access into the home or developed system is another challenge in smart home automation system. Most of the developed systems do not focus on deployment and integration of security measures to check companion users of the system. A possible solution to this challenge is for developers, in conjunction with vendors/manufactures of devices involved in smart home automation of systems, to consider authorization and authentication while developing the system. Research effort should be intensified on possible solutions to authorization and authentication of people and devices involved in smart home automation systems. Moreover, use of authentication codes for access and gateway ensure data integrity and authenticity.

5.2.2 Privacy of Information/Data

Preservation of patients' data, privacy and authentication on the user's side to confirm if communicating with the right medical personnel in smart home healthcare system is another challenge attached to smart home health care area. Developers should ensure that the users' integrity and information are kept private and that they are communicating with the correct personnel at every instance of using the system.

5.2.3 High Cost and Incompatibility of Devices

Most technologies and devices used in smart homes are above average price levels; this makes full implementation and deployment of smart home systems slow. Efforts should be made towards making prices of devices and technologies lower than the current rate. Another challenge is incompatibility of devices; different manufacturers are involved in the supply of home automation devices and most of these devices do not communicate with each other because of differences in manufacturer. Manufacturers should reach high standards of production of smart home automation devices. A possible solution to incompatibility of devices is for developers of systems to design systems that will be built on compatible devices and development of gateways that will support communication of devices from different manufacturers.

5.2.4 Efficient Energy Management

Most smart home systems involve sensing devices for monitoring parameters and alarm systems, actuators and other devices that are electricity dependent for functionality. Connecting all these devices in smart home automation can lead to energy overload. Use of some appliances especially during electricity peak periods can also lead to high consumption of energy. All these contribute to challenges in energy efficiency in smart home automation. The use of solar energy supply or batteries can serve as possible solutions to the challenge of energy efficiency in smart home automation. Development of scheduling process in smart home automation systems can enhance their energy efficiency.

6 Conclusion

In this paper, we presented a review of IoT-smart home automation system. Smart home automation system aims to bring convenience and ease of access to home owners/users. A review of related literature in application areas of smart home automation systems was discussed with a highlight on technologies involved, design methodologies alongside their required implantation technologies, as well as strengths and weaknesses of the existing literatures published to date. Furthermore, the elements of smart home automation systems were discussed in detail, likewise properties of smart home automation technologies, sensors, automation layers, protocols and hardware platforms were also discussed to give prospective IoTs systems designers and developers of smart home automation system the necessary insight to those essential elements. Application areas of smart home automation were also discussed and lastly, trends and challenges were discussed and possible solutions to the identified challenges highlighted. Future opportunities for the smart home automation systems would involve interfacing them with intelligent enabled smart sensors such as motion sensors for security surveillance and light sensors that will assist in conserving energy wastage by ensuring efficient optimization of usage. Furthermore, the next step for smart home adoption is its extension and integration to smart city design and automation process.

References

1. Sadi, M., Safayet, A., Kawshik, S.: A smart home automation and metering system using Internet of Things (IoT). In: 2019 International Conference on Robotics, Electrical and Signal Processing Techniques (ICREST) (2019). https://doi.org/10.1109/icrest.2019. 8644232
2. Somayya, M., Ramaswamy, R.: Smart homes (conceptual views). In: 2014 2nd International Symposium on Computational and Business Intelligence (2014). https://doi.org/10.1109/ iscbi.2014.21
3. Jayavardhana, G., Rajkumar, B., Slaven, M., Marimuthu, P.: Internet of Things (IoT): a vision, architectural elements, and future directions. Future Gener. Comput. Syst. **29**(7), 1645–1660 (2012). https://doi.org/10.1016/j.future.2013.01.010
4. Saber, T., Miadreza, S.-K., Pierluigi, S., Vincenzo, L., Aurelio, T., João, P.S.C.: A review of smart cities based on the Internet of Things concept. Energies - MDPI J. **10**(421), 1–23 (2017). https://doi.org/10.3390/en10040421
5. Xu, L., Rongxing, L., Xiaohui, L., Xuemin, S.S., Jiming, C., Xiaodong, L.: Smart community: an Internet of Things application. IEEE Commun. Mag. **49**(11), 68–75 (2011). https://doi.org/10.1109/mcom.2011.6069711
6. King, N.: Smart Home- A Definition, September 2003. https://www.housinglin.org.uk/_ assets/Resources/Housing/Housing_advice/Smart_Home_-_A_definition_September_2003. pdf. Accessed 20 Jun 2019
7. Gabriele, L., Salvatore, C., Erica, L.: A review of systems and technologies for smart homes and smart grids. Energies **9**(5), 348 (2016)
8. Muhammad, A., Ali, R.C.: An effective approach to build smart building based on Internet of Things (IoT). J. Basic Appl. Sci. Res. **6**(5), 56–62 (2016)
9. Majid, A.-K., Abdulrhman, R., Yousef, I., Laith, A.-S., Adel, G., Mohieddine, B.: Smart-home automation using IoT-based sensing and monitoring platform. In: 2018 IEEE 12th International Conference on Compaitbility, Power Electronics and Power Engineering (CPE-POWERENG 2018), Doha Qatar, 2018. https://doi.org/10.1109/cpe.2018.8372548
10. Nourizadeh, S., Deroussent, C., Song, Y.Q., Thomesse, J.P.: Medical and home automation sensor networks for senior citizens telehomecare. In: 2009 IEEE International Conference on Communications Workshops, Dresden, 2009. https://doi.org/10.1109/iccw.2009.5208093
11. Waheb, A.J., Mohammed, H.A., Nur Syaira, S.A., Samiah, K.M.: Design and implementation of IoT - based automation system for smart home. In: 2018 International Symposium on Networks, Computers and Communications (ISNCC), Rome. Italy, 2018. https://doi.org/ 10.1109/ISNCC.2018.8531006
12. Hemalatha, G., Johnet, M.J., Arunkumar, N., Nitheesh, M.P.: Energy management system for smart home using IoT. Int. J. Adv. Res. Ideas Innov. Technol. **4**(2), 1867–1873 (2018)
13. Abdulrahman, T.A., Isiwekpeni, O.H., Surajudeen-Bakinde, N.T., Otuoze, A.O.: Design, specification and implementation of a distributed home automation system. In: 2nd International Workshop on Internet of Things: Networking, Applications and Technologies (IoTNAT 2016), 2016. https://doi.org/10.1016/j.procs.2016.08.073

14. Mohamed, S.S., Ahmad, A.A., Abdulwadoud, A.M., Mohamed, O.E.: Design and implementation of a real-time smart home automation system based on arduino microcontroller kit and LabVIEW platform. Int. J. Appl. Eng. Res. **12**(18), 7259–7264 (2017). ISSN 0973-4562

15. Minh, P., Yehenew, M., Ha, D., Weihua, S.: Delivering home healthcare through a cloud-based smart home environment (CoSHE). Future Gener. Comput. Syst. **81**, 129–140 (2018). https://doi.org/10.1016/j.future.2017.10.040

16. Himanshu, S., Vishal, P., Vedant, K., Venkanna, U.: IoT based smart home automation system using sensor node. In: 4th International Conference on Recent Advances in Information Technology (2018). https://doi.org/10.1109/rait.2018.8389037

17. Hamzah, M.M., Mohammed, I.M., Ehab, D.H., Ahmed, R.I.: Designing and implementing applications of smart home appliances. Mod. Appl. Sci. **12**(12), 8–17 (2018). https://doi.org/10.5539/mas.v12n12p8

18. Zhao, Z., Lee, W.C., Shin, Y., Song, K.B.: An optimal power scheduling method for demand response in home energy management system. IEEE Trans. Smart Grid **4**(3), 1391–1400 (2013). https://doi.org/10.1109/TSG.2013.2251018

19. Ajao, L.A., Kolo, J.G., Adedokun, E.A., Olaniyi, O.M., Inalegwu, O.C., Abolade, K.S.: A smart door security-based home automation system: an Internet of Things. SciFed J. Telecommun. **2**(2), 1–9 (2018)

20. Phani, C., Peng, Y., Arye, N.: A distributed algorithm of appliance scheduling for home energy management system. IEEE Trans. Smart Grid **5**(1), 282–290 (2014). https://doi.org/10.1109/TSG.2013.2291003

21. Al-Ali, A.R., Imran, A.Z., Mohammed, R., Ragini, G., Mazin, A.: A smart home energy management system using IoT and big data analytics approach. IEEE Trans. Consum. Electron. **63**(4), 426–434 (2017)

22. Jinsoo, H., Chang-Sic, C., Wan-Ki, P., Ilwoo, L., Sang-Ha, K.: Smart home energy management system including renewable energy based on Zigbee and PLC. In: IEEE International Conference on Consumer Electronics (ICCE) (2014). https://doi.org/10.1109/icce.2014.6776125

23. Vasyl, T., Vasyl, B., Pavlo, D., Taras, T., Andrii, L.: Development and implementation of the technical accident prevention subsystem for the smart home system. Int. J. Intell. Syst. Appl. **1** (2018). https://doi.org/10.5815/ijisa.2018.01.01

24. Wibowo, H.S., Muhammad, I.G., Alif, C.M.: Multiple smart home controlling system using database replication method. In: International Conference on Computer Science and Engineering Technology, Indonesia (2018). https://doi.org/10.4108/eai.24-10-2018.2280553

25. Lin, Y., Yanhong, G., Wenfeng, L., Wenbi, R., Weiming, S.: A home mobile healthcare system for wheelchair users. In: Proceedings of the 2014 IEEE 18th International Conference on Computer Supported Cooperative Work in Design (2014). https://doi.org/10.1109/cscwd.2014.6846914

26. Paul, J.R., Jason, B., Praveen, K.B., Praveen, K., Santhosh, K.: Voice controlled home automation system using natural language processing (NLP) and Internet of Things (IoT). In: Third International Conference on Science Technology Engineering & Management (ICONSTEM) (2017). https://doi.org/10.1109/iconstem.2017.8261311

27. Rajdeep, K.N., Rajnish, B., Himanshu, T.: IoT based indoor location detection system for smart home environment. In: 2018 IEEE International Conference on Consumer Electronics (ICCE), Las Vegas, USA (2018). https://doi.org/10.1109/icce.2018.8326225

28. Shivangi, V., Jyotsnamayee, R., Janit, M., Saurav, V., Chetana, P.: Internet of Things (IoT) a vision, architectural elements and security issues. In: International conference on I-SMAC (IoT in Social, Mobile, Analytics and Cloud) (I-SMAC 2017) (2017). https://doi.org/10.1109/i-smac.2017.8058399

29. Rafiullah, K., Sarmad, U.K., Rifaqat, Z., Shahid, K.: Future internet: the Internet of Things, architecture, possible applications and key challenges. In: 10th International Conference on Frontiers of Information Technology (2012). https://doi.org/10.1109/fit.2012.53

30. Sumathi, L., Valarmathi, M.L.: A survey on middleware for smart home application. Int. J. Latest Trends Eng. Technol. 8(1), 078–085 (2017). https://doi.org/10.21172/1.81.010

31. Wlodarczak, P.: Smart cities – enabling technologies for future living. In: Karakitsiou, A., Migdalas, A., Rassia, Stamatina Th., Pardalos, P.M. (eds.) City Networks. SOIA, vol. 128, pp. 1–16. Springer, Cham (2017). https://doi.org/10.1007/978-3-319-65338-9_1

32. Thibaut, L.G., Petur, O., Anders, P.R., Jesper, R., Arne, S.: HomePort: middleware for heterogeneous home automation networks. In: 2013 IEEE International Conference on Pervasive Computing and Communications Workshops (PERCOM Workshops 2013), San Dieg, California, USA (2013). https://doi.org/10.1109/percomw.2013.6529570

33. Gavin, B.: What is a Local Area Network (LAN), 12 July 2018. https://www.howtogeek.com/353283/what-is-a-local-area-network-lan/. Accessed 22 Jun 2019

34. Vincent, R., David, M., David, D., Bruno, M., Laurent, D., Christophe, L.: The smart home concept: our immediate future. In: 1st IEEE International Conference on E-Learning in Industrial Electronics, ICELIE (2007). https://doi.org/10.1109/icelie.2006.347206

35. Dann, A.: 6 Smart Detectors that Protect Your Family and Property from Harm, 5 June 2015. https://www.makeuseof.com/tag/6-smart-detectors-protect-family-property-harm/. Accessed 27 Jun 2019

36. George, D., et al.: Older adults' attitudes towards and perceptions of 'smart home' technologies: a pilot study. Med. Inform. Internet Med. 29(2), 87–94 (2004). https://doi.org/10.1080/14639230410001684387

37. Aragues, A., Martinez, I., Del Valle, P., Munoz, P., Escayola, J., Trigo, J.D.: Trends in entertainment, home automation and e-health: toward cross-domain integration. IEEE Commun. Mag. 50(6), 160–167 (2012). https://doi.org/10.1109/mcom.2012.6211501

38. Costin, B., Marius, B., Amelia, B.: An overview of smart home environments: architectures, technologies and applications. In: CEUR Workshop Proceedings, vol. 1036, pp. 78–85 (2013)

39. Zhang, P., Li, C., Bhatt, N.: Next-generation monitoring, analysis and control for the future smart control center. IEEE Trans. Smart Grid 1(2), 186–192 (2010). https://doi.org/10.1109/tsg.2010.2053855

Some Means Supporting Responsibility and Openness in Information and Control Systems

Michal Žemlička[1,2,3](✉) [iD] and Jaroslav Král[4] [iD]

[1] Faculty of Science, Jan Evangelista Purkyně University,
Pasteurova 1, 400 96 Ústí nad Labem, Czech Republic
michal.zemlicka@ujep.cz
[2] Faculty of Mathematics and Physics, Charles University,
Malostranské nám. 25, 118 00 Praha 1, Czech Republic
zemlicka@sisal.mff.cuni.cz
[3] AŽD Praha, Závod Technika,
Žirovnická 2/3146, 106 17 Praha 10, Czech Republic
zemlicka.michal@azd.cz
[4] Faculty of Informatics, Masaryk University,
Botanická 68a, 602 00 Brno, Czech Republic
kralq@seznam.cz

Abstract. The structure of many current systems is independent of related responsibility borders. It comes from the fact that they are designed by programmers that as a rule give more importance to efficient data moving than to reflecting existing business and control processes and to precise personal or organizational responsibility. It results in non-trivial issues when looking for reasons and responsibility for improper system behaviour and its overall quality. Another serious issue is that the requirements on the systems are changing during their development and use. Accommodation to the changes often introduces new serious issues to the systems. Proper support for responsibility and flexibility is a necessary precondition for solving the issues or for recovery from them. We cope with those issues by proposing software architecture simplifying alignment of software with responsibility domains. The solution is enabled by a proper application of specific software service types described here. The proposed solution significantly improves system and organizational flexibility and openness and brings many other interesting engineering advantages. The proposed solution is based on observations from human behaviour and roles within organizations and their cooperating groups.

Keywords: System flexibility · Organizational responsibility · Software architecture · System openness · Architectural patterns · Processes in SOA · Responsibilities of users · Middleware

© Springer Nature Switzerland AG 2020
O. Gervasi et al. (Eds.): ICCSA 2020, LNCS 12254, pp. 895–909, 2020.
https://doi.org/10.1007/978-3-030-58817-5_63

1   Introduction

Software parts covering logically closed functionalities of information and control systems (SPICS) grow and become continuously more complex. The requirements on their functions and services and quality grow. It is known that such systems cannot have a monolithic architecture if they should be developed in time and be maintainable (compare the consequences of software engineering metrics [4,5,25] and quality characteristics – see e.g. [15]).

SPICS must have a proper architecture also for further reasons. If a SPICS is very large, then its development, maintenance, and use are difficult tasks for many experts and users (e.g. user domain IT experts, managers, IT maintainers, users, or administrators).

It follows that such SPICS must have a service-oriented architecture. SPICS should have the structure of a network of autonomous units, services, exchanging understandable messages. The messages have a form similar to the form of digitalized documents or messages similar to inter-human communication used for cooperation and communication between corresponding real-world services.

The understandability, as well as usability, are crucial aspects of SPICS – see e.g. [23]. Understandability of messages implies that the messages used in communication of services are textual and gradually have more complex structure (given by a variant of syntax). It enables many system quality aspects and simplifies balancing them. Examples are aspects discussed below.

Understanding of the notion "service" used here is different from the proposals by W3C [35], Erl [9], and others. It comes from the origin of the different versions of service orientation – compare [26]. The proposed version of service-orientation combines experience collected by the authors mainly in the domain of structured systems [37,41] and control systems [17]. It could be used to handle current issues in the development of information and control systems. The applicability spans from e-government [19] to huge control systems like traffic management systems covering large areas [42]. It is possible to design a system so that it can implement important features Responsibility and Openness (see below).

The service orientation mentioned here can work in a specific way: The messages could be redirected to other service or to manual processing (if necessary). The message addressee(s) could be defined by sender or selected according the message body and according available potential processors (software services or human beings).

Human involvement enables the use of information available to people but not available to software (e.g. it could be hard to enter it or it is not programmed yet to handle such information). In some cases, human involvement is a necessity for successful solutions of many problems to which the owners of the systems could face. We will, therefore, focus on definition, control, and solving issues related to responsibility of individual users and their groups, as well as of other people.

Our proposal is based on structuring a class of software systems according functional and responsibility borders. The presented architecture is supported by specific services supporting and enforcing its policies.

The paper is structured as follows: Sect. 2 concerns responsibility and its selected aspects, Sect. 3 Openness. Security is discussed in Sect. 4. How these observations should influence information and control systems design and use is described in Sect. 5. Finally, Sect. 6 gives conclusions.

2 Responsibility

2.1 Responsibility Identification

It holds in many countries that a human being or an institution could bear responsibility only for that matters he, she, or it can influence. With the appearance of information and control systems, there appeared also situations when the decisions were not made by human beings but by computers. It raised a problem who is then responsible for such decisions: the owner of the computer, the owner of the software, the author of the software, or even someone else?

Structure of many contemporary systems do not lower insistency of this question: the decisions are made using so complex processes divided into many parts provided by various software artefacts created by different vendors. It is then very difficult (if not impossible) to determine, who or what part of the system is responsible for a given decision. The appearance of the cloud and to it related technologies make such task even more complicated. Often it can be a problem even to determine in what country the individual decisions have been made.

Responsibility is important not only in the sense of identification of criminal liability of individual parties, but especially in the context of (sense of) control over given service, opportunity to adapt it, and especially for the opportunity to understand it properly – many of contemporary systems do not allow to understand them and to influence how or what they (the systems) process.

2.2 Responsibility and System Comprehension

Full computerization of systems is extremely difficult to achieve (if the resulting product should be really of high quality) comparing to cooperational computerization where people and computers cooperate [15]: It must be estimated ahead what all could happen and tried to solve it – and all such situations must be not only analysed but also proper solutions must be developed and exhaustively tested for them.

The developers could work arbitrarily perfect but the world is so complex that for sufficiently large or complex systems it could always appear a situation what has not been expected or that even could not be expected (e.g. significant new developments or observations are often not expected). It, therefore, makes sense to allow properly trained and domain knowing people to influence the system, if necessary—or to take control over its parts or even over the entire system itself.

On behalf of fulfilling the functions of the system, the people should have opportunity to control and to influence run of the system (they can get to information important for a proper run of the system that could not be entered into the system) or to take control over the selected part of the system (bugs, accidents, or catastrophes could arise any time). We know from our experience that an opportunity to take over functions of selected modules could be advantageous also for system development, its incremental deployment, or its use under more difficult conditions [22].

It is advantageous to use the above-mentioned observation already during system development. Individual parts of the system should be therefore equipped by interface allowing supervision and conditionally also control over the given part. Individual parts should be similarly equipped by such interface that could provide communication with other parts of the system as well as with people providing the functionality of the others.

2.3   Responsibility Delegation

Responsibility is in the real world usually bound to institutions or their clearly defined parts, respective to given human beings – either due to their function in the organization or as individuals. Systems that respect this responsibility should have borders reflecting the corresponding responsibility borders.

Responsibility could be in some cases of hierarchical nature (for something it is responsible entire organization, for something its division, for something its department, and for something exact person). In such cases (and probably not only then) it makes sense to decompose system supporting such organization into parts corresponding to the organizational breakdown of the organization.

Contemporary information and control systems often do not follow such schema. They are usually structured according to layered architecture with a limited number of layers (the classic ones have 2–3 layers, the newer ones usually up to 9—compare e.g. [6, 29]).

2.4   Conditions for Responsibility Taking

Responsibility also requires that the one who should be responsible for some system should have an opportunity (either personally or using other people) to convince itself that given system works properly. In the opposite case, it would be no responsibility, it would be a hazard. Taking responsibility is easier if it is possible in an emergency or other unexpected or rare cases to take control of the entrusted task. It allows coping also with situations that have not been taken into account, whose solution would be too expensive, or that even could not be taken into account.

2.5   Responsibility Issues

Responsibility is in full extent a very general concept. Being aware of this we start with coping with some related issues and hoping for solving the others later. Responsibility of users is a very complex problem, compare rules related to security and responsibilities needed to use clouds in SOA processes.

3 Openness

Under the notion of openness, we understand an opportunity to extend the system easily by new parts or functions or to connect the system with other systems without a necessity to modify the system significantly. Different systems can be created using different methods, can be based on different approaches, and can use different communication protocols. Direct interconnection of such systems without their previous modification is as a rule not performable or is applicable only exceptionally. Sometimes it is even a very hard task to understand how the partner system works – not to speak of how to identify parts that must be involved in the required cooperation.

Real-world services, to what the systems serve, simply not only can cooperate but often must cooperate. There are often involved more than two services in such cooperation.

It is given by the fact that interfaces of real-world services are primarily problem-oriented instead of being implementation-oriented as it is by many information or control systems. Hence on the interface, it is specified what should be done, not how – not to speak about solving technical details. Such real-world interfaces are already in use for a very long time – years, decades, or even longer. We suppose that it makes sense to let ourselves to inspire by such interfaces when designing interfaces of software systems playing a similar role. Understandability of communication improves supervision of many aspects of quality especially security and safety.

4 Security

Security has many aspects. We focus here on restricting access only to agreed partners (mostly to their systems) and their reasonable behaviour at all system levels. Precise access control is here combined with natural borders of responsibility what also improves the chance that people will be more likely to respect other security measures. We suppose that reasonable access control could be based on the following principle: the access to the system should be by design limited to partners that are planned (e.g. if they have signed an agreement with the institution running the system).

It is, the access to the system must be controlled so that it could be efficiently blocked if necessary. It is also reasonable if the access of individual partners to the system could be controlled independently. Then if any of the partner systems starts to behave incorrectly (e.g. producing too much traffic), it is possible to block such communication without a necessity to restrict other partner systems. Communication in such structure could and should be authorized and protected by corresponding encryption methods.

Information and control systems face many security threats. Many papers are identifying at least some of them and trying to cope with them – compare e.g. [8, 27, 32]. Some authors tried to classify the threats. Let us mention at least Jouini et al. [16] or Gerić and Hutinsky [11].

5   Impacts

Let us look at how fulfilling the above quality aspects could reflect on the structure of the system.

5.1   Security

Cooperation with other systems must be under control. Required openness without support from the security side could be hazardous. Therefore both aspects must be solved side-by-side.

To control individual access from individual partners we can equip the system with special autonomous services – *access points* (AP). The situation is depicted in Fig. 1.

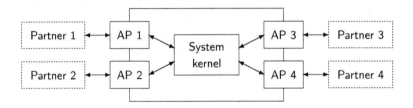

Fig. 1. System with distinguished access points

It makes sense to connect AP on both sides to different networks. The inner interface should be connected to the internal network of the company or its unit, the outer to a dedicated link between the partner and the AP or to an at least encrypted channel through a public network.

The AP's appear when necessary (e.g. after signing a cooperation contract between institutions) and disappear when it is not necessary or when the protected (sub)system gets under attack (e.g. when a system of the partner or the channel do not work as agreed). It is reasonable to have a separate AP for each contract as it allows precise control over the connection and forces the partner not to reveal the connection data to third parties.

Access points could be used also for precise control over a communication of individual parts of a system even within a single organization. It could then control explicit access to subnetworks of individual organizational subunits. Such a solution can improve the chance that attacking one part of the system does not affect the entire system.

It could happen that there will be established multiple access points for cooperation with the same partner. Such an approach could separate individual agreements between the cooperating organizations. It is also possible and could be reasonable to establish multiple AP by a single agreement. The individual AP's then can separate cooperation between the institution according to additional attributes like access rights on the partner side, communication style (e.g. stream vs. messaging), etc.

An access point could be treated as a smart plug: it allows to connect a partner and check the validity of the connection (the partner can establish the connection – e.g. using a proper key) and can establish a connection to its counterpart (to log to partner's system). Access points are expected to serve for a given period only – according to the time-span of the related agreement between partners. As the agreements could be renewed/extended, the time limitation of the access points should be also possible.

Access points are expected to separate connections to the partners from the inner network of the organization. They route the traffic from the partner only to desired parts of the organizational systems and support sending requests to the partner system if necessary.

The use of access points (and other architectural services described below) reduces the severity of many security threats. As there are multiple system access points (separate for individual partners), it is harder to block access to the system using distributed denial of service (DDoS) attacks. Moreover, using dedicated connections gives more responsibility to the partners for the systems connected to them.

The incoming communication is processed by relatively simple services. Taking control over them (or their disabling) still gives only very limited opportunity to make harm to the rest of the system as well as only very limited access to the processed data. The real processing and storing of data is in the system kernel (its services/applications) so there is a chance for system administrators to detect attacks on the outer services and take relevant measures sooner than the attack gets to the critical parts of the system.

So, systems described here could resist at least partially to most known security threats caused by external subjects. As individual agendas are usually handled by different parts of the system that could be also protected by access points, there is a chance that even insiders could have only limited impact.

5.2   Flexibility

The responsibility is usually taken for assurance of some service or task to be provided. Sometimes once, sometimes for a given number of iterations or for some period. The environment and other conditions could change during time.

Fulfilling the responsibility could be conditioned by a proper extent of flexibility of the task to be able to cope with the changes (and still fulfil for what the person or organization is responsible). It could happen that some subtask can be re-delegated to other partner or that partners' systems could change, etc. To simplify accommodation to the above-mentioned changes, it is possible to perform the cooperation with partners using some high-level stable interface—preferably the one that is understandable for professionals in a given domain, resp. topic.

Such interface need not be the same as the interface of the system supporting or providing the requested functionality. It is possible to translate an existing system interface to the interface made available for cooperation with partners. Moreover, it is possible and reasonable support partners with different needs using different interfaces. The interface translation could be provided by special autonomous services called *front-end gates* (FEG; introduced in [20]). Front-end gates could be developed using techniques developed for compilers (parsers, transducers, compiler back-ends [1,2,12,39]) or using XML transformation (XSLT [34], XPath [36]). The situation then can look like in Fig. 2.

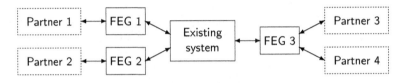

Fig. 2. Supporting flexibility by front-end gates (interface translators)

In practice, it makes sense to combine both flexibility and security provided by front-end gates and access points to support both tailored interfaces and tailored access—compare Fig. 3.

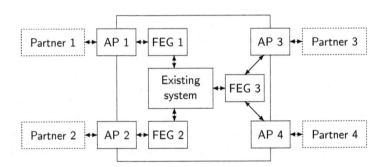

Fig. 3. Customized communication channels using front-end gates and access points

The access point(s) then ensure that only given partner is communicating given channel whereas front-end gate(s) support the partner-specific communication protocol. When multiple partners are using a very similar user interface provided by the same front-end gate, it is possible to let the access points restrict the supported interface (e.g. to inhibit the use of improper values). On the other hand, it could be possible to let one access point provide access to a single partner to multiple front-end gates.

5.3 System Decomposition and Composition

As stated above, the structure of the system should be able to follow a breakdown of the responsibility and organizational breakdown. The flexibility provided by front-end gates as well as partial security support provided by access points could be used at any level of decomposition.

To keep the system structure clean it is reasonable to treat parts at any level as black boxes. It is, all their outputs and inputs must go through a selected entry point.

A closed group of cooperating services having concentrated inputs and outputs to and from the services outside the group into single service we call *composite service* (CS) and the distinguished service *head of composite service* (HCS) or *head* for short. Composite services could look like the one on Fig. 4.

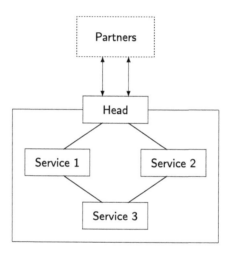

Fig. 4. Composite service – a simplified view; taken from [43]

HCS (its outer interface) behaves to related front-end gates like a primary gate in the case of simple services. The inner interface of an HCS behaves to services in the composite group as one of the partners – it is, it can be protected (as well as their front-end gates) by its access point(s). From the network point of view, the role of HCS is very similar to the role of a router in communication networks.

The composite service often conforms to an organizational subunit or another responsibility unit. It should, therefore, fulfil similar requirements as the system as a whole: it should be open (having flexible interfaces) and respect responsibility border (by supporting distinguished access control). The composite service could and should be then equipped by front-end gates as well as by access points. The same holds also for services forming the composite service. The resulting situation can look like in Fig. 5.

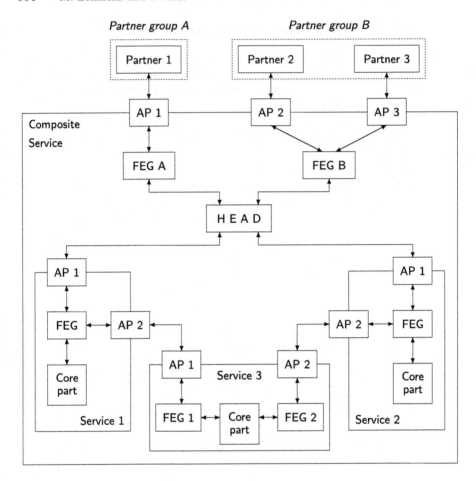

Fig. 5. More detailed view on the composite service from Fig. 4

Composite services can be composed of simple services as well as of other composite services. We can create or model this way hierarchical structure following organizational or responsibility structure of a supported organization. Let us note that even the single services are systems used to support the activity and could be still complex applications.

All services in the system could have (and often should have) user interfaces allowing to supervise their work or to take manual control or replacement over them. It is possible to do some work manually and the rest of the work could be let on the supporting applications. For details see [22].

5.4 Processes

In the real world, activities are performed in business or control processes. They control the cooperation of several actors to produce the desired output.

Business processes could be hard-coded in the services (they could know whom to ask to perform some subtask or whom to give the work to continue). It is possible in the case of very stable and already optimized business processes known ahead. The business processes must be described in detail as there is no chance to modify them or to make exceptional processing.

When the processes are not so stable, they should be driven more flexibly: by scripting, by a roadmap defined in an additional document, or by special services controlling the process run – *business process managers* (BPM; see [21,24]). Scripting adds an opportunity to change the business process a bit faster than when they are hardcoded. But scripts are programs and as such, they should not be modified when the business or control process is already running.

The attached document (forwarding bill) driven business process is quite popular in many institutions. The flexibility of so driven business process depends on the rights that the users have to the forwarding bill—who can modify it or how flexible the instructions stored in it could be interpreted (in some cases the requested signature from the boss could be replaced by some vice-bosses probably after consultation with the boss—if the boss is physically not available). This kind of handling of some business processes is used for many decades and many people can use them intuitively. Some practical experience of their application is described e.g. in [18].

There are multiple business process notations [3,7,14,31,38,40]. They were developed for various conditions. It is therefore reasonable if the services providing business process management could handle various business/control process notations. Such services should provide an interface to the responsible person – process owners. It is advantageous if the user interface is customizable—there is a bigger chance that it will be more intuitive for their users (process owners).

In some cases, the business process manager could play the role of head of composite service. In the case when a business process must be run across multiple organizational units, it is reasonable that the business processes could be partitioned according to organizational structure: individual sub-processes will be run in the organizational subunits and the overall part will be managed at the lowest common level. It could be often reasonable if the sub-process' managers report the process status to the upper business process manager.

5.5   System User Interfaces (Portals)

Complex systems usually support not only local interfaces to individual parts but also interface(s) to the system as a whole. The system is typically used by different user groups. It is therefore reasonable to equip the system with corresponding user interfaces fulfilling and matching the needs and rights of the user groups. Most systems distinguish at least between more trusted users (and support them by an intranet interface) and general users (supported by an extranet interface).

The services supporting such an interface (and playing to some extent also the role of access points) are called portals. As they can be based on web technology, their name could suggest usable technology.

5.6   Remarks

Services creating system structure like front-end gates, access points, or heads of composite services are important from the architectural point of view. They are therefore called *architectural services*. They are, as a rule, newly developed or customized for a given system. Moreover, as other services in the system, they can be equipped by user interface allowing responsible people to supervise them or to make some decisions manually. The supported activities could include also message redirection, transformation or even execution. It corresponds to forwarding improperly addressed requests or to transforming improperly formulated requests in human organizations. Such an opportunity is advantageous for debugging or in rare or emergency cases.

The combination of front-end gates and access points can someone remind on Façade [10]. The proposed pattern focuses on services instead of on objects, it is more restrictive in control over accessing the original interface and it could support human supervision if necessary.

It makes sense to structure the underlying networking so that the architecture services could fully play its role. It is, if an architectural service should be a unique connection to some part of the system, it should be so also from the networking point of view. It is especially important at the security borders originated from responsibility borders (like at borders between organizations) or where subsystems with different security or safety should cooperate.

Architectural services can be seen as special microservices [13,33] being glue for application services that could be large and complex services or again microservices.

6   Conclusions

Responsibility and its borders are significant for the structure of an information system. It is often neglected (yes, even now there are created standards ignoring and blocking it).

When we reflect the responsibility borders in the way described above, we can improve many interesting features like openness, flexibility, maintainability, or distributed development. It could be related to the fact that it corresponds to the recommendation of information hiding [30]. Moreover, the learning curve could be flattened as there is used language and formats understandable and intuitive to the users.

The proposed service-oriented architecture significantly differs from most service-oriented architectures described in the literature—compare [6,9,29] and others. The hierarchical system structure reflects the usual organization structure where managers control only a limited number of subordinates (people or organizational subunits). It simplifies understanding and utilizes already gained knowledge and skills of managers of various levels.

Such system structure to some sense reflects also observations of Miller [28] or information hiding recommendation of Parnas [30].

The impacts of user responsibility to system architecture must be further studied – especially in the frame of dependence between the development team and resulting system structure. It seems that clients' organizational structure should be reflected by the structure of the system and it should be reflected in the structure of the developer's team. It is a hypothesis that should be proven yet.

We believe that the problem of responsibility in processes can be solved gradually starting from current practices, standards, and patterns. Some practices must be used in parallel or combined with new solutions. It is not easy to do it as it has features of a new philosophy.

It appears to be reasonable to reflect the responsibility of user subunits or individuals into system structure and reflect it to the structure and responsibilities of the development team. The flexible interfaces provided by the combination of front-end gates handling protocol flexibility and access point handling access flexibility appear to be a good background for it.

Handling responsibility of end-users in their current roles is an important issue. There are strong security issues. The system design must solve the responsibilities of end-users (represented by their roles). It must be taken into account that the responsibilities of individual users vary in time. The responsibilities could be assigned and unassigned. There must be collected experience with end-user roles during the system lifetime (and reflected in system maintenance). There should be solved complex security issues enabled e.g. by human involvement. A reasonable solution is a topic of further research.

References

1. Aho, A.V., Ullman, J.D.: The Theory of Parsing, Translation and Compiling, Vol. I.: Parsing. Prentice-Hall, Englewood Cliffs (1972)
2. Aho, A.V., Ullman, J.D.: The Theory of Parsing, Translation and Compiling, Vol. II.: Compiling. Prentice-Hall, Englewood Cliffs (1973)
3. Andrews, T., et al.: Specification: Business process execution language for web services version 1.1 (2003). http://www-106.ibm.com/developerworks/library/ws-bpel/. Last Accessed Jan 2005
4. Boehm, B.W.: Software Engineering Economics. Prentice Hall, Upper Saddle River (1981)
5. Boehm, B.W., et al.: Software Cost Estimation With COCOMO II. Prentice Hall, Upper Saddle River (2000)
6. Brown, P., Estefan, J.A., Laskey, K., McCabe, F.G., Thornton, D.: Reference architecture foundation for service oriented architecture version 1.0, December 2012. http://docs.oasis-open.org/soa-rm/soa-ra/v1.0/cs01/soa-ra-v1.0-cs01.pdf
7. Business Process Management Initiative: Business process modelling notation (2004). http://www.bpmn.org/
8. Cîrnu, C.E., Rotună, C.I., Vevera, A.V., Boncea, R.: Measures to mitigate cybersecurity risks and vulnerabilities in service-oriented architecture. Stud. Inform. Control **27**(3), 359–368 (2018)
9. Erl, T.: Service-Oriented Architecture: Concepts, Technology, and Design. Prentice Hall, Upper Saddle River (2005)

10. Gamma, E., Helm, R., Johnson, R., Vlissides, J.: Design Patterns Elements of Reusable Object-Orieneted Software. Addison-Wesley, Boston (1993)
11. Gerić, S., Hutinski, Ž.: Information system security threats classifications. J. Inf. Organ. Sci. **31**(1), 51–61 (2007)
12. Grune, D., van Reeuwijk, K., Bal, H.E., Jacobs, C.J.H., Langendoen, K.: Modern Compiler Design, Second edn. Springer, New York (2012). https://doi.org/10.1007/978-1-4614-4699-6
13. Hasselbring, W., Steinacker, G.: Microservice architectures for scalability, agility and reliability in e-commerce. In: 2017 IEEE International Conference on Software Architecture Workshops (ICSAW), pp. 243–246 (2017). https://doi.org/10.1109/ICSAW.2017.11
14. IDS Scheer: Aris process platform. http://www.ids-scheer.com/international/english/products/31207
15. International Organization for Standardization, International Electrotechnical Commission: ISO/IEC 25010:2011 systems and software engineering - systems and software quality requirements and evaluation (SQuaRE) - system and software quality models (2011). https://www.iso.org/obp/ui/#iso:std:iso-iec:25010:ed-1:v1:en
16. Jouini, M., Rabai, L.B.A., Aissa, A.B.: Classification of security threats in information systems. In: The 5th International Conference on Ambient Systems, Networks and Technologies (ANT-2014), the 4th International Conference on Sustainable Energy Information Technology (SEIT-2014). Procedia Computer Science, vol. 32, pp. 489–496 (2014). https://doi.org/10.1016/j.procs.2014.05.452, http://www.sciencedirect.com/science/article/pii/S1877050914006528
17. Král, J., Demner, J.: Towards reliable real time software. In: Proceedings of IFIP Conference Construction of Quality Software, pp. 1–12. North Holland (1979)
18. Král, J., Novák, P., Žemlička, M.: A system based on intelligent documents. In: Gervasi, O., et al. (eds.) ICCSA 2017. LNCS, vol. 10409, pp. 176–187. Springer, Cham (2017). https://doi.org/10.1007/978-3-319-62407-5_12
19. Král, J., Žemlička, M.: Electronic government and software confederations. In: Tjoa, A.M., Wagner, R.R. (eds.) Twelfth International Workshop on Database and Experts System Application, pp. 383–387. IEEE Computer Society, Los Alamitos (2001). https://doi.org/10.1109/DEXA.2001.953091
20. Král, J., Žemlička, M.: Component types in software confederations. In: Hamza, M.H. (ed.) Applied Informatics, pp. 125–130. ACTA Press, Anaheim (2002)
21. Král, J., Žemlička, M.: Implementation of business processes in service-oriented systems. In: 2005 IEEE International Conference on Services Computing (SCC 2005), vol. 2, pp. 115–122. IEEE Computer Society (2005). https://doi.org/10.1109/SCC.2005.58
22. Král, J., Žemlička, M.: Software architecture for evolving environment. In: Kontogiannis, K., Zou, Y., Penta, M.D. (eds.) 13th IEEE International Workshop on Software Technology and Engineering Practice, pp. 49–58. IEEE Computer Society, Los Alamitos (2006). https://doi.org/10.1109/STEP.2005.25
23. Král, J., Žemlička, M.: Usability issues in service-oriented architecture. In: Cardoso, J., Cordeiro, J., Filipe, J. (eds.) ICEIS 2007: Proceedings of the Ninth International Conference on Enterprise Information Systems, vol. DISI, pp. 482–485. EST Setúbal, Setúbal (2007). https://doi.org/10.5220/0002387704820485
24. Král, J., Žemlička, M.: Implementation of business processes in service-oriented systems. Int. J. Bus. Process Integr. Manage. **3**(3), 208–219 (2008). https://doi.org/10.1504/IJBPIM.2008.023220

25. Král, J., Žemlička, M.: Inaccessible area and effort consumption dynamics. In: Dosch, W., Lee, R., Tuma, P., Coupaye, T. (eds.) Proceedings of 6th International Conference on Software Engineering Research, Management and Applications (SERA 2008), pp. 229–234. IEEE CS Press, Los Alamitos (2008). https:// doi.org/10.1109/SERA.2008.27

26. Quintela Varajão, J.E., Cruz-Cunha, M.M., Putnik, G.D., Trigo, A. (eds.): CEN-TERIS 2010. CCIS, vol. 110. Springer, Heidelberg (2010). https://doi.org/10.1007/ 978-3-642-16419-4

27. Li, Z., Liu, K.: An event based detection of internal threat to information system. In: Kim, J.H., Geem, Z.W., Jung, D., Yoo, D.G., Yadav, A. (eds.) ICHSA 2019. AISC, vol. 1063, pp. 44–53. Springer, Cham (2020). https://doi.org/10.1007/978-3-030-31967-0_5

28. Miller, G.A.: The magical number seven, plus or minus two: some limits on our capacity for processing information. Psychol. Rev. **63**, 81–97 (1956). https://doi. org/10.1037/h0043158

29. Open Group: Open Group standard SOA reference architecture, November 2011. https://www2.opengroup.org/ogsys/jsp/publications/PublicationDetails. jsp?publicationid=12490

30. Parnas, D.L.: Designing software for ease of extension and contraction. IEEE Trans. Softw. Eng. **5**(2), 128–138 (1979). https://doi.org/10.1109/TSE.1979.234169

31. Pokorný, J.: Workflow management systems: a survey of possibilities. In: Coelho, J.D., Jelassi, T., König, W., Krcmar, H., O'Callaghan, R., Sääksjärvi, M. (eds.) Proceedings of the Fourth EuropeanConference on Information Systems. ECIS1996, Lisbon, Portugal, pp. 253–264 (1996)

32. Safianu, O., Twum, F., Hayfron-Acquah, J.B.: Information system security threats and vulnerabilities: evaluating the human factor in data protection. Int. J. Comput. Appl. **143**(5), 8–14 (2016). https://doi.org/10.5120/ijca2016910160

33. Taibi, D., Lenarduzzi, V.: On the definition of microservice bad smells. IEEE Softw. **35**(3), 56–62 (2018)

34. W3 Consortium: XSL transformations (XSLT) version 2.0, January 2007. http:// www.w3.org/TR/xslt20

35. W3 Consortium: Web of services (2015). https://www.w3.org/standards/ webofservices/

36. W3 Consortium: XML path language (XPath) version 3.1, March 2017. https:// www.w3.org/TR/xpath/

37. Weinberg, V.: Structured analysis. Prentice-Hall software series, Prentice-Hall, Englewood Cliffs (1979)

38. WFMC: Workflow management coalition home page (1993). http://www.wfmc. org/

39. Wilhelm, R., Maurer, D.: Compiler Design. International Computer Science, Addison-Wesley, Wokingham (1995)

40. Workflow Management Coalition: Workflow specification (2004). http://www. wfmc.org/standards/docs/Wf-XML-11.pdf

41. Yourdon, E.: Modern Structured Analysis, 2nd edn. Prentice-Hall, Upper Saddle River (1988)

42. Zanella, G.L., Pinasco, M.: Deliverable d8.1: Requirements for the integration layer (Sep 2016). http://www.in2rail.eu/download.aspx?id=aef8ad3a-8581-4f56-be5c-77d6329dd7f4

43. Žemlička, M., Král, J.: Software architecture enabling effective control of selected quality aspects. In: Misra, S., et al. (eds.) ICCSA 2019. LNCS, vol. 11623, pp. 536–550. Springer, Cham (2019). https://doi.org/10.1007/978-3-030-24308-1_43

Investigating Innovative E-Commerce Practices During COVID-19 Movement Control Order: Lessons from 4 Examples

Chien-Sing Lee[1($\boxtimes$)] and K. Daniel Wong[2]

[1] Sunway University, Subang Jaya, Malaysia
chiensingl@sunway.edu.my
[2] Daniel Wireless Software, Singapore, Singapore
dwong@danielwireless.com

Abstract. The Movement Control Order (MCO) encourages mandatory stay-at-home and has resulted in much socio-economic-technical repercussions. As such, this study aims to identify lessons from innovative examples to quicken recovery for the tourism industry in Malaysia. We investigate two examples of global innovation and two examples of local innovation with regards to organizational/process/product (including innovative privacy and security protection) and marketing innovation during the COVID-19 MCO in Malaysia. Findings highlight the need for organizational innovation, (including careful privacy and security protection), followed by business model transformation through shifts in centrality in design, mediated by product/process/marketing innovation. A human-centred, crowd-sourcing (social-collaborative computing) use case is presented as an example. Another key contribution is confirmation of a Restorative Innovation framework's components and its adaptation post-COVID-19.

1 Introduction

Economic recovery from COVID-19 and its movement control order (MCO) would tax many countries not only in terms of healthcare, but also mentality, practices and market share. In an age when many are suggesting that we will most likely see more merger and acquisitions, decentralization enhanced by technology are thriving, such as food delivery systems. There are also many who share messages of hope and carry on with business with just a video camera, knowledge and skills such as the exercise industry and the entertainment industry.

Another example is contact tracing. One of the most challenging parts of contact tracing is to reconstruct where people have been, in order to discover when some people may have been near others. Initial contact tracing efforts have been through traditional means such as interviews, phone calls, tracking data on spreadsheets. As the number of COVID-19 cases increases, contract tracing workers start getting overloaded and spreadsheets become less efficient when matching contacts. The mobile phone is then utilized as citizens carry their mobile phones around with them most of the time. Furthermore, mobile apps can track a variety of variables, e.g. (a) GPS

© Springer Nature Switzerland AG 2020
O. Gervasi et al. (Eds.): ICCSA 2020, LNCS 12254, pp. 910–922, 2020.
https://doi.org/10.1007/978-3-030-58817-5_64

location; (b) presence at locations e.g. malls or stores in malls; or (c) proximity tracing when two Bluetooth devices running the contact tracing app come within ranges of proximity. China extends such sensor technologies, with color codes. This extension not only addresses the problem of contact tracing but also aids clear and simple communication; a very lean, multi-pronged effective solution.

With many countries implementing state surveillance, privacy and security are carefully considered. For instance, for GPS location to be useful for contact tracing, a continuous stream of GPS locations would have to be recorded by each running app, and possibly, passed back to a server to match locations with time. Such data can be misused in the wrong hands. Hence, it is critical to design and implement the system securely, so that no unauthorized person can a) access the GPS data of the app users, and b) leak/modify the data. A creative policy by Singapore [1] has data remaining encrypted on the device until and unless the user is confirmed to be a COVID-19 patient. If and only if the latter happens, then the data is passed to the Ministry of Health.

All these examples highlight that addressing concerns during MCO and post-COVID-19, requires well-planned, lean, multi-pronged, creative transformations and agility in technology design, development and management.

1.1 Objectives

We are interested to investigate:

1) two international case studies with regards to process/organizational/marketing/product innovations the tourism industry has evidenced during MCO, which can be adapted to the local context post-COVID-19,
2) two local case studies with regards to process/organizational/marketing/product innovations the tourism industry has evidenced during MCO, which can be enhanced post-COVID-19,
3) key factors which would enable faster recovery post-COVID-19 in line with [2]'s Innovation Diffusion theory,
4) the efficacy of [3]'s *Payitbackwards* framework and adaptation of [4]'s Restorative Innovation model. Considering the higher initial cost in the latter, we would like to investigate how we can adapt these economic-cum-restorative concepts to the Malaysian context and for bad economic times post-COVID-19.

1.2 Framework

With little or no revenue during MCO due to movement constraints, there is a need to increase creative use of technology to mitigate economic impacts as much as possible, while creating tangible and intangible benefits with lean costs and management. [5]'s studies on generative processing for education and healthcare builds on [6]'s cognitive load theory and suggests that germane cognitive load needs to be addressed first and then used to offset intrinsic and extraneous loads. Hence, we surmise that in economics, germane, intrinsic and extraneous loads are analogous to new directions, debts/constraints and external competition. Moreover, distributed cognition can offset the load of enactive and embedded cognition. This creates room for technologies such as Internet of Things (IoT). However, to be lean and sustainable begs the question how?

Two frameworks are applied for this research:

a) [3] 's *Payitbackward* framework identifies key tenets to open innovation/co-creation as collaborative-social human-centered computing mediated/motivated by diversified task-reward models (Fig. 1). They suggest that these can form the foundation for formulation of different business models, useful especially during economic downturns,

b) [4] 's Restorative Innovation framework (Fig. 2), an economic model, sheds further light on possible foci. In the framework, value capitalization focuses on three components, i.e., *health*, *humanity* and the *environment*. With mass acceptance/adoption, economy of scale would result.

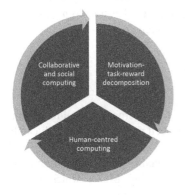

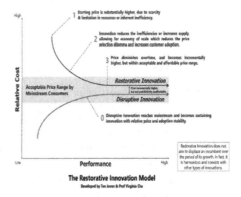

Fig. 1. Key tenets underlying [3]'s Crowdsourcing-HCI *PayItBackwards*

Fig. 2. [4]'s Restorative Innovation framework (used with permission)

Both frameworks are generative processing models and involve knowledge management. They also highlight the importance of human-centred computing and social/collaborative computing/engagement. However, we surmise that the success of any open innovation framework would depend much on human capital development as well as the establishment of a robust, lean yet equitable entrepreneurial ecosystem.

1.3 Hypothesis

We note that centrality of design [7] in model-driven architectures, shifts with the context, task, assessments [8] and specific needs of a demographic. This means that [4]'s Restorative Innovation is likely to result in disruptive innovation, by redefining opportunities to those which are needs-based, reusable and sustainable. In addition, [9] proposes that systematic reuse of software can be in different forms and is based on architecture, process and organization. This proposition is supported by [10, 11]'s series of studies on reuse in Malaysia.

We hope to identify business process re-engineering practices that would be restorative in the long run. Based on [7]'s centrality of design and [9]'s proposal that systematic reuse of software is based on architecture, process and organization, we hypothesise that shifting the centrality of design by pivoting and subsequently reusing/ refactoring/reengineering existing Service-Process System Innovation towards needs-based domains which share core services-processes are more likely to be pervasive and successful post-COVID.

1.4   Contributions

Our contributions are:

a) identification of e-commerce-based process/organizational/marketing/product innovations during Movement Control Order (MCO), which subsequently confirms the value of shifting centrality of design to result in creative transformation;
b) confirmation of [4] 's framework components/foci, i.e., health, humanity and the environment and adaptation of the framework to include fractal reverse engineering;
c) confirmation of the analogical efficacy of [6]'s cognitive load model and economics with regards to generative processing.

2   Related Work

The novel coronavirus has impacted industries beyond imagination due to the speed by which it spreads, the number of infections, fatalities and seriousness of after-effects. Global statistics indicate that the novel corona virus has resulted in a total of 9, 277, 214 confirmed cases of COVID-19, including 478, 691 deaths, reported to WHO [12].

Many countries have implemented nation-wide or partial lockdown, i.e., Movement Control Order (MCO). These restrictions have gravely impacted GDP and unemployment rates are rising. Malaysia is not spared. For instance, Malaysia's MCO [13] covers these measures:

a) no religious, social, cultural or sports activities or mass gathering;
b) self-quarantine of 14 days for Malaysians returning from overseas;
c) closure of borders and cancellation of flights resulting in no tourist inflows;
d) closure of kindergartens, government as well as private schools and universities;
e) closure of all government and private organizations, excluding utility, health, safety, banking, transport, retail.

Consequently, the Ministry of Tourism, Arts and Culture has announced that all over-the-counter and online new applications, renewal of travel and operating licenses for businesses, travel tourist guides, tourism training institute and registration of rated tourist accommodation premises are on hold [14]. Furthermore, hotel cancellations have challenged hoteliers to their wits ends. To highlights its gravity, Malaysian Association of Hotels CEO, Yap Lip Seng, laments that based on historical data, the first 14 days of MCO (from March 18 to 31) has resulted in an estimated RM560 million (US$127.3 million) loss in (hotel) business [15].

[16] therefore contend that to transform tourism, we need to change our focus from number of arrivals as the means by which success in tourism is measured. They add that though number of arrivals is the norm to UNWTO, ICAO, CLIA, WTTC and many other local organizations, fixating on volume may block our perspectives to hitherto hidden opportunities facilitated by technology.

For instance, for elderly Asian tourists, [17] point out that post-SARS, personal economic wellbeing and disposable income, changes in cost, perceived health risks, and changed capacities for consumption influences consumer behaviour. [18] see a silver lining from these past lessons. In a survey, they find that consumers in China, Italy, Spain, UK and the US are becoming more optimistic, having crossed the early stages of the issue-attention cycle [19]. In [20], they surprisingly, find that Chinese consumers are increasingly interested in environmentally friendly products. Hence, [20] suggest that with the uncertainties and global magnitude of the COVID-19 pandemic, we should not be in a hurry to revert back to what was. Instead, we should reconsider global economic value chains to align more closely to the Sustainable Development Goals. Only then, will tourism be sustainable.

Along similar lines, [21] opines that we need to consider the macro-and microeconomic principles and basic requirements for the development of strategic innovative activities. Such strategic innovations must aim at not only increasing resource potential but more importantly, to do so, without increasing the use of these resources. As such, the volume of resources may not be as important as their quality, structure, balance and rationality of use.

Similar to the above, [22–25] agree that the socio-economic system has innovation potential. These are often in terms of service innovation and its indicators, i.e., organizational, product, process, marketing innovations. If designed well, especially strategic marketing via technological advancement, well-trained service teams, transparent information sharing, on the newly discovered market, may emerge as and support innovations to promote long-term revenue growth, and accelerated industrial recovery.

So what is the way forward? [2]'s Diffusion of Innovation (DOI) Theory suggests that the innovation, communication channels, time, and a social system are key to the rate of technology adoption. The perception that the new idea, behavior, or product is new or innovative would increase the rate of diffusion.

This theory supports [26]'s propositions on the importance of customer engagement. This means that due to the uncertainties of how soon the economy will recover, government leaders as well as the market need to be even more sensitive to customer trends and needs. As such, many initiatives are aimed at focusing on the now with incremental plans for the future (Fig. 3). We conjecture that each company's capability maturity model would differentiate its ability to rise above disruption.

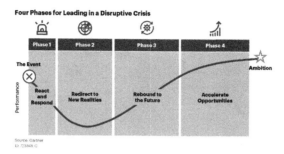

Fig. 3. [26]'s four phases to mitigate and lead during disruptive crises Source: McDonald/Gartner [26], April 2, 2020

Moreover, being agile, [26] further recommends mobilizing people and customers to a future vision without fully defining that vision." They stress that this requires communication to be not only engaging but also clear and transparent, creating trust and awareness; a sense of inclusiveness; to lead and to bind people amidst changing public policy, cost-saving measures and restrictive movement.

3   Case Studies

Many companies capitalize on object-oriented analysis and design (OOAD) and optimization of processes and outcomes. The following cases are exemplary of the use of OOAD and optimization. For instance, Alibaba is exemplary as a very successful *global supply chain* platform through its partnership with more than 22 global vendors. Such breadth in partnerships would enable anyone in the world to procure daily or niche items, in respective quantities without having to hunt high and low. Its supply chain is flexible based on tangible value e.g. ROI and intangible value perceived by users such as trust and diversity.

3.1   Buzz Travel: Organizational Innovation (OI) > Product Innovation (PIN) > Marketing Innovation (MI)/Process Innovation (PI)

Our main references for tourism are Buzz.travel and AirBnB websites. Buzz.travel in Europe (Fig. 4a, b, c) creates opportunities for B2B/B2C partnerships (organizational innovation). This in turn leads to marketing/process innovations for products such as family trips, community development and citizen journalism in video form where anyone can share their invaluable experiences. What sustains are not only the thriving social network but also *educational* opportunities such as webinars for members and the public which enables self-improvement and upward mobility across the network accessible at the marketplace (job opportunities) (Table 1).

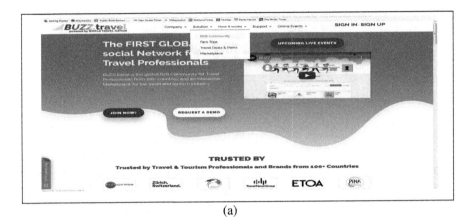

(a)

(b)   (c)

Fig. 4. a. Buzz's homepage. b, c. Buzz's homepage highlights
Source: Buzz.travel: https://buzz.travel/

Table 1. Buzz.travel's opportunities

Travel deals and perks	Marketplace	Community	Family Trips
Best rates in: •Hotels •Flights •Packages •Cruises •Tours	•Job Offers, Job Seek •Marketplace Ads •B2B Sales •Meetups •Webinars, Education •Exchange Programs	•Present a stunning profile •Interact with members in News Feed •Stay up to date with the latest Travel News, Forum	Post about family trips

3.2   AirBnB: Organizational Innovation (OI) > Product Innovation (PIN) > Marketing Innovation (MI)/Process Innovation (PI)

AirBnB's business model is also interesting. Organizational innovation shifts product/process and marketing innovation from physical rooms and services to hosting *experiences* online with attractive pricing; extending its reach to a wider global market. Furthermore, fun and education feature prominently. Anyone who signs up and design their experiences, share their ideas, submit their experiences, set up (including determine their own pricing) and start hosting. The highlights are presented in Table 2.

Table 2. AirBnB's online experience hosting analogical to music streaming

3.3   AirAsia: Organizational Innovation (OI) > Product Innovation (PIN) > Marketing Innovation (MI)/Process Innovation (PI)

AirAsia, Malaysia's local budget airline, shifts its business core to *emulate* e-commerce websites to what families would value during lockdown e.g. survival items, fresh mart, childcare relief, fashion and healthcare (Fig. 5). Experts in reuse of system processes, it reuses its current search, book and payment systems for the new products (Fig. 3) and links these to their reward systems. Hence, planes may not be flying much, but travel planning, and purchasing are still on-going.

Fig. 5. AirAsia's extended business model
Source: https://www.airasia.com

3.4   Tourism Malaysia: Organizational Innovation (OI) > Product Innovation > (PIN) > Process Innovation (PI)/Marketing Innovation (MI)

Tourism Malaysia serves as a search, planning and experience sharing website. The planner is visual, attractive and user-friendly. Interaction e.g. citizen journalism and that of buzz.travel would spice up their website, extending and enhancing user experience. Post-COVID, the Government is encouraging domestic travel. From personalization using a Trip Planner, the new Tourism Malaysia website has included *networking* opportunities to increase the global value chain and more *interactive* displays with short videos of diverse attractions, analogical to highlights from a modern trendy "filmstrip". The videos tell the story best.

4   Suggested Human-Centred Social-Collaborative Computing

Based on the above findings, it seems logical that Ikeda and Bernstein [3]'s human-centred and social-collaborating computing, inclusive of citizen journalism, may result in faster recovery for the tourism industry. An example use case supported by the IEEE Systems, Man and Cybernetics (Malaysia chapter) is presented in Fig. 6.

It emulates Buzz, AirBnB's citizen journalism/customer-to-customer synergies and Alibaba's global supply chain. This use case is formulated during MCO and at a time when the end of MCO is uncertain locally and globally. As such, the taking of pictures and changing of the background of dream destinations via software, is deemed to be part of encouraging potential tourists to dream/imagine what actually being there would be like and thus to desire to travel to the respective destinations/countries more. The component is not meant to replace actual travel as nothing can replace the actual experiences, sights, sounds, smells and memories of actual travel. This is the generative aspect.

We conjecture that post-COVID, the contents will still focus on the above examples, (which incidentally support the Restorative Innovation framework's components), i.e., health, humanity and the environment. The forms of the latter two are creative playgrounds. Essentially, we *reverse* the Restorative Innovation framework's direction and promote *refactoring* at the system and component levels.

For community-engagement and open co-design, based on past studies [27, 28], developing the users' dispositions is also important. Success would, however, depend on the opportunities identified and capability maturity level of each company.

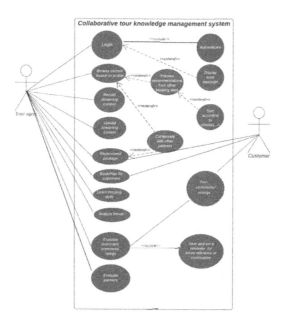

Fig. 6. Example of a human-centred social-collaborative computing use case

Recently, on June 23rd, 2020, Alibaba launched its online trade show, where vendors can stream live and interested buyers can chat directly with vendors. Similar to AirAsia, these are evidences of refactoring of its architecture and processes, made possible due to its existing Ali Cloud and very highly educated and tech savvy citizenry. The latent value is that of trending data analytics as a service (Analytics as a Service). This is a positive confirmation of refactoring and faith in human-socio-technical factors towards, improving economic resilience.

5   Conclusion

Transferring from researches, we have hypothesised that shifting the centrality of design by pivoting and subsequently reusing/extending existing Service-Process System Innovation towards needs-based domains, which inherently require similar core services-processes, are more likely to be pervasive and successful post-COVID. We have also hoped to extend [4]'s Restorative Innovative framework, highlighting the importance of business model transformations/adaptations with smart partnerships to create new value supply chains, for the shared economy to cope with environmental changes and customer trends in the new normal/post-COVID-19. We are not economists, but we believe that their framework can be applied in bad times, by *reversing* the framework's direction, while retaining all other aspects of the framework and while responsive to smaller fractal cycles arising from agile refactoring in architectures and business processes (improvements and reengineering).

From the above case studies, customer relationship management and event management (promoting, planning for different customer segments with different customized promotions) coupled with global value supply chain and citizen participation/journalism assisted by technology may be playground for further organizational/product/process/marketing innovations.

The above studies also suggest that for e-commerce-based organizational/product process/marketing innovations during Movement Control Order (MCO), centrality of design and transformative reuse within model-driven architectures, are critical, not only for inclusive design but also agility, extensibility and scalability. Correspondingly, SCRUM/KANBAN's user stories and sprints will feature more prominently in object-oriented design and development environments, adapted to different demographics to create attractive customer experiences.

Interestingly, the foci of innovations from these case studies, are evidently related to [4]'s health, humanity and the environment. Our contributions are thus a) confirmation of the value of shifting centrality of design to result in creative transformation during Movement Control Order (MCO), b) confirmation of [4]'s components and adaptation of [4]'s framework, c) confirmation of the analogical efficacy of the cognitive load model and economics. The findings also confirm [26]'s recommendations and [29]'s contention that web usability, playfulness, empowerment, and increasingly, storytelling beyond computational thinking, is important. How we think, influences our innovative capabilities.

Due to the small sample size, these preliminary findings need to be further supported and refined through more global and local examples. Hence, future work may involve more sampling, more analyses and categorization to derive deeper insights based on the Innovation Matrix, inspired by Prof. Hajo Reijers's research.

Acknowledgement. The first author would also like to specially thank the following for their support when she was a Faculty in these universities: Multimedia University for systems modelling, AI and e-commerce, Universiti Tunku Abdul Rahman (UTAR) for the epistemology, foundations and the opportunity to experiment with design, design thinking, computational thinking and sustainability, fun and reuse in the creative industries. These form the foundations for the paper. She would also like to thank Prof. John H. Hughes, Senior Fulbright, for past collaboration on healthcare, Prof. Bo Jiang forprior collaboration on analogical and fractal thinking, Assoc. Prof. Boon-Liat Cheng for earlier support on digital marketing, and deepest thanks to the IEEE SMC (M) and UTAR for their invaluable support towards the use case in an IEEE HAC development grant application.

References

1. Contact tracing device to be rolled out this month. New Straits Times, Singapore, 9 June 2020. https://www.straitstimes.com/singapore/contact-tracing-device-to-be-rolled-out-this-month
2. Rogers, E.M.: Diffusion of Innovations. Free Press, New York (2003)
3. Ikeda, K., Bernstein, M.S.: Pay it backward: per-task payments on crowdsourcing plat-forms reduce productivity. In: CHI 2016, 07–12 May 2016, San Jose, CA, USA (2016)
4. Tan, J., Cha, V.: Restorative innovation framework (2018)
5. Lee, C.S., Hughes, J.H.: Refocusing on cognitive load design through a meta-analysis on learnability, goal-based intentions and extensibility towards personalized cognitive-social-affective engagement among seniors. In: International Conference on Intelligent Software Methodologies, Tools, and Techniques (SOMET19), 23–25 September 2019, Kuching, Sarawak, Malaysia, pp. 456–469. Frontiers in Artificial Intelligence and Applications, IOS Publishing (2019)
6. Sweller, J.: Cognitive load during problem solving: effects on learning. Cogn. Sci. **12**, 257–285 (1988)
7. Giovannella, C., Spadavecchia, C., Camusi, A.: Educational complexity: centrality of design and monitoring of the experience. In: Leitner, G., Hitz, M., Holzinger, A. (eds.) USAB 2010. LNCS, vol. 6389, pp. 353–372. Springer, Heidelberg (2010). https://doi.org/10.1007/978-3-642-16607-5_24
8. Marini, A., Genereux R.: In: McKeough, A., Lupart, J., Marini, A. (eds.) Teaching for Transfer: Fostering Generalization in Learning, pp. 1–20. Lawrence Erlbaum Associates, Mahwah (1995)
9. Griss, M.: Systematic Software Reuse: Architecture, Process and Organization are Crucial (1996). http://martin.griss.com/pubs/fusion1.htm
10. Lee, C.S., Wong, K.D.: An entrepreneurial narrative media-model framework for knowledge building and open co-design. In: SAI Computing, 18–20 July 2017, London, UK, pp. 1169–1175 (2017)
11. Lee, C.S., Wong, K.D.: Design-computational thinking, transfer and flavors of reuse: scaffolds to information and data science for sustainable systems in smart cities. In: IEEE International Conference on Information Reuse and Integration, Salt Lake City, Utah, 6–9 July, pp. 225–228 (2018)
12. WHO Coronavirus Disease (COVID-19) Dashboard. https://covid19.who.int/

13. Foo, L.-P., Chin, M.-Y., Tan, K.-L., Phuah, K.-T.: The impact of COVID-19 on tourism industry in Malaysia. Curr. Issues Tourism (2020). https://doi.org/10.1080/13683500.2020. 1777951

14. Shukri, H.N.: Cancellation of Visit Malaysia 2020 (VM2020) Campaign and Guest Stay at Tourist Accommodation Premises throughout the Movement Control Order (MCO). Tourism Malaysia (2020). https://www.tourism.gov.my/media/view/cancellation-of-visit-malaysia-2020-vm2020-campaign-and-guest-stay-at-tourist-accommodation-premises-throughout-the-movement-control-order-mco

15. Puvaneswary, S: Malaysian hoteliers brace for further fallout from lockdown extension. https://www.ttgasia.com/2020/03/26/malaysian-hoteliers-brace-for-further-fallout-from-lockdown-extension/. Accessed 26 Mar 2020

16. Gössling, S., Scott, D., Hall, C.M.: Pandemics, tourism and global change: a rapid assessment of COVID-19. J. Sustain. Tourism (2020). https://doi.org/10.1080/09669582. 2020.1758708

17. Lee, C.C., Chen, C.J.: The reaction of elderly Asian tourists to avian influenza and SARS. Tourism Manag. 32(6), 1421–1422 (2011)

18. McKinsey and Company: Global surveys of consumer sentiment during the coronavirus crisis (2020a). https://www.mckinsey.com/business-functions/marketing-and-sales/our-insights/global-surveys-of-consumer-sentiment-during-the-coronavirus-crisis. Accessed 6 Apr 2020

19. Hall, C.M.: Degrowing tourism: décroissance, sustainable consumption and steady-state tourism. Anatolia 20(1), 46–61 (2009)

20. McKinsey and Company: Cautiously optimistic: Chinese consumer behavior post-COVID- (2020b). https://www.mckinsey.com/business-functions/marketing-and-sales/our-insights/global-surveys-of-consumer-sentiment-during-the-coronavirus-crisis. Accessed 6 Apr 2020

21. Sandybayev, A.: Strategic innovation in tourism. a conceptual and review approach. Int. J. Res. Tour. Hosp. 2(4), 5–10 (2016)

22. Cheng, B.L., Gan, C.C., Imrie, B.C., Mansori, S.: Service recovery, customer satisfaction and customer loyalty: evidence from Malaysia's hotel industry. Int. J. Qual. Serv. Sci. 11(2), 187–203 (2019)

23. Cheng, B.L., Mansori, S., Cham, T.H.: The associations between service quality, corporate image, customer satisfaction, and loyalty: evidence from the Malaysian hotel industry. J. Hosp. Mark. Manag. 23(3), 314–326 (2014)

24. Cheng, B.L.: The impact of service innovation on tourist satisfaction: evidence from the Malaysian tourism industry. Glob. J. Bus. Soc. Sci. Rev. 2(3), 93–106 (2014)

25. Lee, C.S.: Fluid structures and behavior in inculcating creative reasoning. In: Wong, S.L., et al. (eds.) Proceedings of the International Conference on Computers in Education. Asia-Pacific Society for Computers in Education, Putrajaya, Malaysia, pp. 785–787 (2010)

26. McDonald, M.: 4 Phases for Technology and Service Providers to Lead in the COVID-19 Environment, 2 April 2020

27. Lee, C.S., Wong, K.D.: Developing a disposition for social innovations: an affective-socio-cognitive co-design model. In: International Conference on Cognition and Exploratory Learning in Digital Age, Ireland, 24–26 October 2015, pp. 180–186 (2015)

28. Lee, C.S., Yew, L.Y., Chew P.L., Chee Y.K., Hiew, Y.T.: Information science-knowledge management-HCI-project management-CRM models-software processes: implications to e-commerce open design and co-design. In: SEPA Workshop, International Conference on Computational Science and Its Applications, 1–4 July (2020)

29. Tasso, S., Gervasi, O., Locchi, A., Sabbatini, F.: Hahai: computational thinking in primary schools. In: Misra, S., et al. (eds.) ICCSA 2019. LNCS, vol. 11620, pp. 287–298. Springer, Cham (2019). https://doi.org/10.1007/978-3-030-24296-1_24

Ambidextrous Socio-Cultural Algorithms

José Lemus-Romani[1]([✉]), Broderick Crawford[1], Ricardo Soto[1], Gino Astorga[2],
Sanjay Misra[3], Kathleen Crawford[1], Giancarla Foschino[2],
Agustín Salas-Fernández[1], and Fernando Paredes[4]

[1] Pontificia Universidad Católica de Valparaíso, Valparaso, Chile
{jose.lemus.r,juan.salas.f}@mail.pucv.cl, {broderick.crawford,
ricardo.soto}@pucv.cl, kathleen.cra@gmail.com
[2] Universidad de Valparaíso, Valparaso, Chile
gino.astorga@uv.cl, giancarla.fos@gmail.com
[3] Covenant University, Ota, Nigeria
sanjay.misra@covenantuniversity.edu.ng
[4] Universidad Diego Portales, Santiago, Chile
fernando.paredes@udp.cl

Abstract. Metaheuristics are a class of algorithms with some intelligence and self-learning capabilities to find solutions to difficult combinatorial problems. Although the promised solutions are not necessarily globally optimal, they are computationally economical. In general, these types of algorithms have been created by imitating intelligent processes and behaviors observed in nature, sociology, psychology and other disciplines. Metaheuristic-based search and optimization is currently widely used for decision making and problem solving in different contexts. The inspiration for metaheuristic algorithms are mainly based on nature's behaviour or biological behaviour. Designing a good metaheurisitcs is making a proper trade-off between two forces: Exploration and exploitation. It is one of the most basic dilemmas that both individuals and organizations constantly are facing. But there is a little researched branch, which corresponds to the techniques based on the social behavior of people or communities, which are called Social-inspired. In this paper we explain and compare two socio-inspired metaheuristics solving a benchmark combinatorial problem.

Keywords: Social-inspired metaheuristics · Socio-cultural inspired metaheuristics · Human-based algorithm · Teaching–learning-based optimization · Twitter optimization · Ambidextrous metaheuristics

1 Introduction

From time to time humanity is faced with various problems and within them is the scarcity of resources or problems of daily life that are difficult to solve by the human mind. In this context, optimization constitutes an alternative to give solution to these problems. In general the optimization methods allow to

© Springer Nature Switzerland AG 2020
O. Gervasi et al. (Eds.): ICCSA 2020, LNCS 12254, pp. 923–938, 2020.
https://doi.org/10.1007/978-3-030-58817-5_65

give solution to engineering problems for which exact or approximate methods can be used. Within the approximate methods we find the metaheuristics that are in charge of giving us good solutions, that eventually can be the optimal one in a limited time of process unlike the use of an exact method that can be non-efficient in computer time.

It cannot be ignored that throughout history there is a direct relationship between technological development and human societies. The human being carries out during his daily life a series of activities that he wants to optimize. Similarly, human societies become a source of inspiration for problem optimization algorithms. This inspiration can be based on the behaviour of societies in the face of external agents that affect them, such as natural phenomena or the same interaction between humans that causes changes in behaviour. Similarly, the human being can have psychological changes considering external agents, as it happens for example with pandemics.

Human behavior can be understood under three perspectives: personal, interpersonal and social. But in practice they are linked since to understand a person's behavior we must investigate his interpersonal relationships and social factors, as well as to understand social relationships we must understand the relationships between people and the differences or similarities with others. Therefore, individual and society are two inseparable worlds [24].

It is important to consider that social and human phenomena must be evaluated considering the cultural context of the moment. For example, wars, pandemics (as is COVID-19 today) or important revolutions like the industrial one or the current digital transformation [6,37,38]. There are various human and social behaviours that can be used as inspiration. One of them is the natural ambition to achieve a better life. Success in life can be different for each person and for this reason we work to achieve some specific objectives. The path they use to achieve success may be different, but these paths generally take into account the experience that some have over others, for that reason some have the intention of learning from the most experts with the aim of improving their skills. On the other hand, each person during their life contacts others and can use their experiences to improve their life [1].

An overview of various existing Metaheuristics is found in [36].

Metaheuristics have abilities both of exploration and exploitation, exploration is the process of visiting entirely new regions of a search space (Solutions), whilst exploitation is the process of visiting those regions within the neighborhood of previously visited solutions. In order to be successful, a search algorithm needs to establish a good ratio between exploration and exploitation. Moreover, designing a good metaheuristic is making a proper trade-off between these two "Forces" [39]. Unfortunately, there is no complete answer to this question up to now [40].

A general outline for a metaheuristic is presented in the Fig. 1 [34].

The trade-off between the exploration: A Multidisciplinary Dilemma. The trade-off between the exploration of new possibilities and the exploitation of old certainties constitutes one of the most basic dilemmas that both individuals and organizations constantly are facing. In [13] Duncan proposed the notion of Organizational Ambidexterity, it is understood as the ability of firms to do two different things at the same time, such as exploration and exploitation, efficiency and flexibility, and matching and adaptation.

Create one or several start solutions, randomly
While termination criterion not satisfied **do**
    If intensify **then**
        Create new solution by exploitation;
    Else
        Generate new solution by exploration;
    End
    Update best found solution (if necessary);
End
Return Best found solution;

Fig. 1. General skeleton of the metaheuristic.

In [10] was presented a short paper focusing in a psycological view of meta-heuristics in problem resolution. Problem solving from a creative perspective has two key aspects, from the point of view of psychology, as are convergent and divergent thinking. The first one, which corresponds to critical or convergent thinking, is the congenital processing of information around a common point, in other words, it is an attempt to bring thoughts from different conclusions to a common union or conclusion. Creative or divergent thinking, on the other hand, starts from a common point and moves to a variety of perspectives, thus generating a different idea that works as well or better than previous ideas.

Considering the source of inspiration we find an area little explored, such as those based on human and social relations, called socio-cultural inspired [20,21].

In this paper, an implementation of Teaching - Learning - Based Optimization [29] algorithm is presented, solving the Set Covering Problem. Together with this, its results are compared with another social-inspired algorithm, Twitter Optimization [8], in addition to other techniques present in the literature. The results of this type of technique are promising, besides being an interesting line of research, for the implementation of other social-inspired metaheuristics.

The work is structured in the following way, in Sect. 2 the works related to the social-inspired metaheuristics are detailed, in Sect. 3 the algorithm considered are presented, in Sect. 4 the combinatorial problems is presented, in Sect. 5 the results obtained are shown, and finally in Sect. 6 the conclusions and future works are presented.

2   Related Work

In this section the basic concepts to understand the structure and behavior of the metaheuristics will be given, in addition to giving a brief classification of them, to later give a brief review according to what was presented by Kumar and Anand [20], and thus be able to have a better context of the socio-inspired techniques.

2.1   Metaheuristics

The optimization methods can be classified into two large groups, the exact methods, with which we can obtain the optimal value for a given search space, having as main disadvantage that the computation times are increased in large combinatorial problems. While the other group are the approximate methods, which do not evaluate all the search space. Among the approximate methods are the metaheuristics, which have presented high quality results in reasonable computation times for various problems. Metaheuristics can be classified according to their way of operating, that is, based on population or on a single solution. The Fig. 2 below summarizes the classifications of the optimization methods.

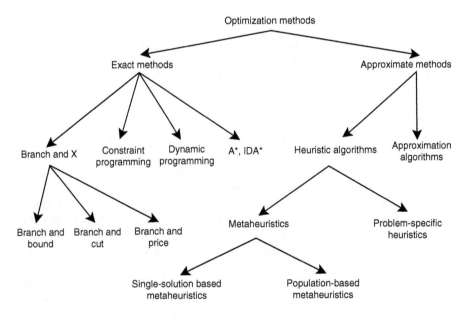

Fig. 2. Optimization methods [35].

Over the years, metaheuristics has become a real alternative solution for everyday problems, for this very reason it becomes an attractive focus for research using different sources of inspiration such as the processes of biological evolution and natural selection to give rise to Evolution-based, others based on collective behavior or swarming by some animals to give rise to Swarm-based, also others that imitate, there are also some based on physical processes called Physics-based. On the other hand, those inspired by human or social behaviour are called Human-based.

According to Blum and Roli [5], metaheuristics can be defined as an iterative process of generation that guides a subordinate heuristic, generating an efficient combination between exploitation and exploration of the search space, with strategies that structure the information to find almost optimal solutions.

The metaheuristics based on a single solution or also called trajectories, have an approach of exploitation of the search space, where at the level of iteration a solution candidate is evaluated, which was generated by its respective movement or disturbance. While population-based metaheuristics have an exploration approach, which at the iteration level evaluates a set of possible solutions.

2.2 Social-Inspired Algorithms

Social-inspired metaheuristics is a relatively new field, but there are reviews of literature that support its classification. One such review is the Kumar and Anand [20], where they present a classification of four sub-categories of Social-inspired. These categories are detailed in Fig. 3.

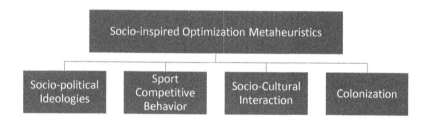

Fig. 3. Classification of socio-inspired algorithms [20].

The first category is Socio-Political Ideologies, among the metaheuristics that we can find this Ideology Algorithm (IA) [16], which is based on the interactions and behavior of individuals belonging to political parties, where each party has a certain political ideology. Election Algorithm (ELA) [14], which is inspired by the functioning of political elections, where this population technique is composed of voters and candidates for public office, these candidates belong to different electoral parties. Election Campaign Algorithm (ECO) [25,26], which bases its behavior on how voters choose the candidate with the best prestige (best quality of objective function).

Another category is Sports Competitive, where two techniques stand out, League Championship Algorithm (LCA) [18], which is based on the behavior formed in the matches of a league, where a team competes with each other to obtain the championship. Another variation is the Soccer League Competition Algorithm (SLC) [28], which is inspired by the relationships between players and teams in a soccer league, where the population represented by each team competes with each other for the best position in the ranking table, while as in real life, the players of each team compete with each other to define which individuals will belong to the starting team or to the substitutes' team.

The third category is those related to Socio-Cultural, where reference is made to techniques such as Teaching Learning Based Optimization (TLBO) [29], which abstracts the synergy that occurs in classroom teaching, where a teacher influences students and how they learn in community. Twitter Optimization (TO) [27], which is inspired by the behavior of the social network of the same name, where users generate tweets (Solutions), which are also followed among users, which generates celebrities and current users, to determine the operators to use. Cohort Intelligence (CI) [19], is based on the interaction of a group of people with similar qualities, who compete with each other to improve and evolve. Cultural Evolution Algorithm (CEA) [22] which seeks to obtain benefits and improve collectively, leaving individual improvement in the background, with the aim of evolving and surviving through social and multicultural influence. Social Learning Optimization (SLO) [23] is based on three co-spaces in how human intelligence evolves and improves, which are the genetic, cultural and belief levels, which are transmitted to future generations, gradually changing according to cultural changes. Socio-evolution and Learning Optimization Algorithm (SELO) [21], is based on the interaction of family nuclei composed of parents and children, which can improve through the interaction of Father and Son, as in the interaction of Sons with Sons, to obtain individual and collective improvements for each family nucleus. Social Group Optimization (SGO) [31] is based on the human need to overcome the problems for which positive and negative qualities are used, where each person has them in different measures, then it becomes necessary the relationship with other individuals to overcome the problems of life. Also used as a source of inspiration is human behavior that has a diverse variability of behaviors and interests, who try to improve and achieve success by their own knowledge and experience or try to learn from others in order to improve their own experience in life and that of their interest [1,32].

The fourth category corresponds to those based on Colonization, where we have the following techniques. Society and Civilization Algorithm (SCO) [30], which classifies individuals into societies that in turn make up civilization, as is typical of each group of individuals, there are leaders (better fitness), which guide that society, so that each individual tries to imitate their leader, in parallel the leaders of societies can migrate to other societies. Imperialist Competitive Algorithm (ICA) [3,15], which behaves imitating the idea of imperialism, where there are powerful nations that are called empires, while the weaker ones are called colonies, which belong to a certain empire. The determination of the empires and colonies are random at the beginning of the algorithm, but iteratively the colonies begin to be conquered by other empires, until all the nations are colonized by one great empire. Anarchic Society Optimization (ASO) [2] based on the anarchic behavior of individuals in a society, this algorithm randomly initiates the generation of solutions, which iteratively explores the search space based on three movement policies, which are related to the best value in comparison with the other solutions at the present time, in the best global and a third operator that depends on the fitness history of each individual, which is represented in that the movements will be more anarchic, that is random, when the solution is far from the best results.

3 Socio-Cultural: Teaching–Learning-Based Optimization and Twitter Optimization

This section explains the operation of the social-inspired Teaching-Learning-Based Optimization techniques [29] and Twitter Optimization [27], where the operators inspired by social interactions are described.

3.1 Teaching–Learning-Based Optimization

TLBO is a population method based on the knowledge that a teacher in a classroom that is shared with students improves the knowledge level of the class. Moreover, the students are evaluated by the value of the qualification average of the students in the class. Additionally, the results can be improved with learning that occurs with the interaction between students. The population is composed of a group of students, and the variables constitute the subjects offered; finally, the fitness corresponds to the learning results of the students. In the entire population, the best solution is considered the teacher. TLBO is composed of two phases, the Teacher Phase and the Learner Phase.

Teacher Phase. A random sample and orderly points are generated, which are the learners in the search space. A point considers the wisest person to be a teacher who shares his knowledge with students. It is the first part of the algorithm where the mean of a class increases from M_A to M_B depending upon the strength of the teacher. The teacher must guide the students in such a way that they reach their own level of knowledge. In practice, this is not possible, and a teacher can only move the mean of a class up to a certain extent depending on the capability of the class. This method follows a random process depending on many factors. Let M_i be the mean and T_i be the teacher at any iteration i. T_i will try to move M_i towards its own level; thus, the new mean will be T_i, designated M_{new}. The solution is updated according to the difference between the existing and the new mean given in Eq. (1):

$$DifferenceMean_i = rand(X_{new} - T_F M_i) \qquad (1)$$

Where T_F is a teaching factor that decides the value of the mean to be changed, and rand is a random value between 0 and 1. The value of T_F can be either 1 or 2, which is again a heuristic step and is randomly decided with equal probability using the following Eq. (2) [13]:

$$T_F = round[1 + rand\{2 - 1\}] \tag{2}$$

This difference modifies the existing solution by means of Eq. (3) [14]:

$$x_{new} = x_{old,i} + DifferenceMean_i \tag{3}$$

Learner Phase. The students increase their knowledge by interactions among themselves. A solution is randomly interacted to learn something new with other solutions in the population. A solution will learn new information if the other solutions have more knowledge than him or her. The learning phenomenon of this phase is expressed by Eq. (4):

$$
\begin{aligned}
x_{new}^d &= x_i^d + rand(x_j^d - x_i^d), \quad If \quad f(x_i) > f(x_j) \\
x_{new}^d &= x_i^d + rand(x_i^d - x_j^d), \quad If \quad f(x_i) < f(x_j)
\end{aligned} \tag{4}
$$

At any solution x, considering two different learners x_i and x_j, where $i \neq j$. Consequently, we accept x_{new} if it gives a better function value. After a number of sequential teaching learning cycles, the teacher passes on knowledge to the learners, and those levels increase towards his or her own level; the randomness distribution within the search space decreases, close to the point of being considered a teacher. The algorithm converges to a solution when the knowledge level of a class shows smoothness. The term criterion can be the number of evaluations or can reach a maximum number of iterations as previously established. The algorithm is shown in Fig. 4.

3.2   Twitter Optimization

Twitter Optimization is inspired by the interaction between people in the social network Twitter, where each tweet is a feasible solution to evaluate, while following corresponds to the relationship between users, where each user generates tweets which are retweetted by other users, which is reflected in the use of operators defined below. With this interaction between users, which correspond to a set of solutions, and the relationship between tweets and retweeting, the technique manages to explore and exploit the search space.

Therefore each Tweet represents a solution composed of a binary vector taking the value 0 and 1, of size n, as indicated in the Eq. 5

$$x = \{x1, x2, ..., xn\}, \forall i \in 1, 2, ..., n \wedge x_i \in \{0, 1\} \tag{5}$$

The algorithm when initialized generates a graph of the relationships between users. The process starts with each user generating a solution, i.e. a tweet, as indicated in the Eq. 6, then the users are followed at random for the first iteration, where each user can only follow F users. Then for each iteration, users update the list of people F that follows, retweeting the tweet with the best fitness and following its author, if it wasn't followed until this moment, after this the user removes the tweet with the worst fitness to keep F.

$$x_i^k = min_i + (max_i - min_i) \cdot rand(0, 1) \tag{6}$$

Algorithm 1: TLBO

1: Set k=1;
2: Objective Function $f(x)$, $x_i = (x^1, x^2 ..., x^d)^t$ d=*no. of design variables*
3: Generate initial students of the classroom randomly x^i, i=1,2...,n
   n=*no. of students*
4: Calculate objective function $f(x)$ for whole students of the classroom
5: **while** the termination conditions are not met **do**
6:    {teacher phase}
7:    Calculate the mean of each design variable x_{mean}
8:    Identify the best solution (teacher)
9:    **for** $i = 1 \rightarrow n$ **do**
10:       Calculate teaching factor $T_F^i = round[1 + rand\{2 - 1\}]$
11:       Modify solution based on best solution(teacher)
12:       $x_{new}^i = X^i + DifferenceMean_i^d$
13:       Calculate objective function for new mapped student $f(x_{new}^i)$
14:       **if** x_{new}^i is better than x_i , *i.e* $f(x_{new}^i) < f(x_i)$ **then**
15:          $x^i = x_{new}^i$
16:       **end if**
17:    {end of teacher phase}
18:    {student phase}
19:    {Randomly select another learner (x_j) , such that j≠i}
20:       **if** x^i *is better than* x^j , *i.e* $f(x^i) < f(x^j)$ **then**
21:          $x_{new}^i = x_i + rand(x_i - x_j)$
22:       **else**
23:          $x_{new}^i = x_i + rand(x_j - x_i)$
24:       **end if**
25:       **if** x_{new}^i *is better than* x_i , *i.e* $f(x_{new}^i) < f(x^i)$ **then**
26:          $x^i = x_{new}^i$
27:       **end if**
28:    {end of student phase}
29:    **end for**
30:    $k=k+1$
31: **end while**

Fig. 4. Classification of socio-inspired algorithms [20].

Where x_i^k is the value of the dimension i for the user k, besides that max_i and min_i represent the maximum and minimum values for the values of the dimension i.

Moreover, the Twitter Optimization algorithm adds two interaction operators, which are comments and participation, these are applied generating a perturbation at the moment of retweeting, that is, when the user k retweets to another user p, the user k has to choose randomly between the operators comments (Eq. 7) and participation (Eq. 8).

$$x_i^p = x_i^p + Character^k \cdot rand(-1, 1) \tag{7}$$

$$x_i^p = x_i^k \tag{8}$$

Another operator is the so-called publishing new tweet, which eliminates the tweet with the worst fitness after having generated a new tweet. On the other hand there is the classification of celebrities and current, which make a differentiation for the application of a specific operator for the 1% with better fitness in their tweet. This operator takes into consideration if his solution has not been updated during the last times W, where W corresponds to the number of followers of k in the current round. The behavior for the averages in each round, will be to generate a new tweet according to the Eq. 9. The celebrity will choose the tweet with the best aptitude and own it.

$$x_i^k = x_i^{best} + \delta \cdot rand(-1, 1) \tag{9}$$

Where x^{best} corresponds to the best solution found so far, δ is scanning radius. This operator generates solutions close to the best value, performing a local search.

The algorithm is summarized in the flow chart in Fig. 5.

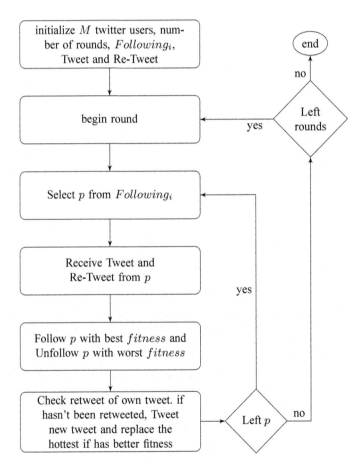

Fig. 5. Social media optimization workflow [8].

4   Combinatorial Problems

Combinatorial problems are in several areas of computer science and their application domains. These problems involve finding a grouping, ordering or assignment of a discrete and finite set of elements, in order to satisfy certain conditions. Candidate solutions do not necessarily have to meet all the conditions, but those that do become feasible, therefore evaluable solutions [5].

The application domains can be discrete, continuous or mixed, therefore they take interest since they can represent diverse problems of the real life, that can be simple to solve when the decision variables are limited, but at the moment of having a relatively great number of variables, the own combinatorial of these problems causes that the possible solutions increase of exponential way, which makes difficult its resolution in time of computation reasons under complete optimization techniques.

Among the classic examples of these problems we can find the Travelling Salesman Problem, Knapsack Problem, in addition to Karp's 21 famous problems [17].

4.1   Set Covering Problem

Set Covering Problem can be defined as follows, considering a A binary array of m-rows and n-columns size, where $a_{i,j} \in \{0,1\}$ corresponds to the value of the A binary matrix, while i and j are the size of rows m and columns n respectively (Eq. 10).

$$A = \begin{pmatrix} a_{1,1} & a_{1,2} & \dots & a_{1,n} \\ a_{2,1} & a_{2,2} & \dots & a_{2,n} \\ \dots & \dots & \dots & \dots \\ a_{m,1} & a_{m,2} & \dots & a_{m,n} \end{pmatrix} \tag{10}$$

If a_{ij} takes the value of 1, this means that the column j satisfies the row i, which is related to a cost $c_j \in C$, $C = \{c_1, c_2, ...c_n\}$, besides that $i = 1, 2, ..., m$ and $j = 1, 2, ..., n$.

SCP aims at minimizing the cost associated to the subset $S \subseteq J$, having as a constraints to satisfy all rows $i \in I$ with at least one column $j \in J$. Where $I = \{1, 2, ..., m\}$ and $J = \{1, 2, ..., n\}$ The columns j belonging to the subset S are that have value 1, while those with value 0 do not.

The SCP can be defined as follows:

$$\text{Min} \quad \sum_{j=1}^{n} c_j x_j \tag{11}$$

Subject to

$$\sum_{j=1}^{n} a_{ij} x_j \geq 1 \quad \forall i \in I \tag{12}$$

$$x_j \in \{0,1\} \quad \forall j \in J \tag{13}$$

Table 1. Instances group 4.

Instances	Zopt	TLBO	TO	BCSO	BFO	BSFLA	BELA	BABC
4.1	429	430	451	459	429	430	447	430
4.2	512	524	611	570	517	516	559	513
4.3	516	526	522	590	519	520	537	519
4.4	494	501	514	547	495	501	527	495
4.5	512	518	520	545	514	514	527	514
4.6	560	566	566	637	563	563	607	561
4.7	430	433	446	462	430	431	448	431
4.8	492	507	499	546	497	497	509	493
4.9	641	660	644	711	655	656	682	649
4.10	514	524	543	537	519	518	571	517
Avg	510	518.9	531.6	560.4	513.8	514.6	541.4	512.2

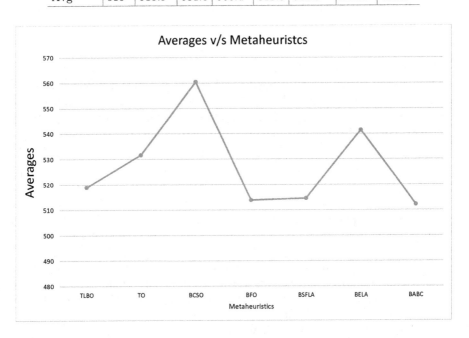

Fig. 6. Averages for metaheuristics.

5   Experiments and Results

The experiments were performed using a computer with a Windows 10 operating system, 16 GB of RAM, and an i7-6700 processor are used. The instances from Beasley's OR-Library are used in the experiments in this study [4]. For the instance group, the algorithm was executed 30 times to use the average of the results obtained. Each instance was pre-processed. In addition to being compared with different literature optimization techniques, such as Cat Swarm Optimization (BCSO) [7], Binary Firefly Optimization (BFO) [12], Binary Shuffled Frog Leaping Algorithm (BSFLA) [11], Binary Artificial Bee Colony (BABC) [9] and Binary Electromagnetism-Like Algorithm (BELA) [33]. The results are shown in Table 1 and Fig. 6.

6   Conclusion

In this paper we have made a brief review of the literature related to socio-inspired metaheuristic techniques, where we highlight the work in this area, specifically those related to socio-culture, which is inspired by the behavior of societies and groups of people, such as TLBO and TO techniques, which imitate the behavior of students and teachers in the classroom, as well as interactions in social networks such as Twitter.

Under the current and recurrent scenario, of having scarce resources to manage, it is necessary to use this type of techniques to solve the diverse combinatorial problems present in real life, where the socio-inspired techniques have proven to be participants in diverse implementations, besides being an attractive alternative at present.

In this work, after comparing the performance of TLBO and TO, in benchmark instances of OR-library, a clear superiority of TLBO solving Set Covering Problem is noticed, but at the same time comparing with other techniques of the literature, its results are not the best quality making a comparison of the averages obtained, however this does not mean that this kind of techniques are not a competitive alternative for the resolution of combinatorial problems.

Among the future works for this kind of socio-inspired problems, the use of hybridization techniques to improve the performance of these are denoted, in addition Autonomous Search techniques could be implemented, along with the use of techniques from Machine Learning to improve some of the operators.

Acknowledgements. Broderick Crawford is supported by Grant CONICYT/ FONDECYT/REGULAR/1171243, Ricardo Soto is supported by Grant CONICYT/FONDECYT/REGULAR/1190129. José Lemus-Romani is supported by National Agency for Research and Development (ANID)/Scholarship Program/ DOCTORADO NACIONAL/2019 - 21191692.

References

1. Ahmadi, S.-A.: Human behavior-based optimization: a novel metaheuristic approach to solve complex optimization problems. Neural Comput. Appl. **28**(1), 233–244 (2017)
2. Ahmadi-Javid, A.: Anarchic society optimization: a human-inspired method. In: 2011 IEEE Congress of Evolutionary Computation (CEC), pp. 2586–2592. IEEE (2011)

3. Atashpaz-Gargari, E., Lucas, C.: Imperialist competitive algorithm: an algorithm for optimization inspired by imperialistic competition. In: 2007 IEEE Congress on Evolutionary Computation, pp. 4661–4667. IEEE (2007)

4. Beasley, J.E., Chu, P.C.: A genetic algorithm for the set covering problem. Eur. J. Oper. Res. **94**(2), 392–404 (1996)

5. Blum, C., Roli, A.: Metaheuristics in combinatorial optimization: overview and conceptual comparison. ACM Comput. Surv. (CSUR) **35**(3), 268–308 (2003)

6. Crawford, B., Soto, R., Astorga, G., Lemus-Romani, J., Misra, S., Rubio, J.-M.: An adaptive intelligent water drops algorithm for set covering problem. In: 2019 19th International Conference on Computational Science and Its Applications (ICCSA), pp. 39–45. IEEE (2019)

7. Crawford, B., et al.: A binary cat swarm optimization algorithm for the non-unicost set covering problem. Math. Probl. Eng. (2015)

8. Crawford, B., Soto, R., Cabrera, G., Salas-Fernández, A., Paredes, F.: Using a social media inspired optimization algorithm to solve the set covering problem. In: Meiselwitz, G. (ed.) HCII 2019. LNCS, vol. 11578, pp. 43–52. Springer, Cham (2019). https://doi.org/10.1007/978-3-030-21902-4_4

9. Crawford, B., Soto, R., Cuesta, R., Paredes, F.: Using the bee colony optimization method to solve the weighted set covering problem. In: Stephanidis, C. (ed.) HCI 2014. CCIS, vol. 434, pp. 493–497. Springer, Cham (2014). https://doi.org/10.1007/978-3-319-07857-1_86

10. Crawford, B., Soto, R., de la Barra, C.L., Crawford, K., Paredes, F., Johnson, F.: A better understanding of the behaviour of metaheuristics: a psychological view. In: Stephanidis, C. (ed.) HCI 2014. CCIS, vol. 434, pp. 515–518. Springer, Cham (2014). https://doi.org/10.1007/978-3-319-07857-1_90

11. Crawford, B., Soto, R., Peña, C., Palma, W., Johnson, F., Paredes, F.: Solving the set covering problem with a shuffled frog leaping algorithm. In: Nguyen, N.T., Trawiński, B., Kosala, R. (eds.) ACIIDS 2015. LNCS (LNAI), vol. 9012, pp. 41–50. Springer, Cham (2015). https://doi.org/10.1007/978-3-319-15705-4_5

12. Crawford, B., Soto, R., Suárez, M.O., Paredes, F., Johnson, F.: Binary firefly algorithm for the set covering problem. In: 2014 9th Iberian Conference on Information Systems and Technologies (CISTI), pp. 1–5. IEEE (2014)

13. Duncan, R.B.: The ambidextrous organization: designing dual structures for innovation. Manag. Organ. **1**(1), 167–188 (1976)

14. Emami, H., Derakhshan, F.: Election algorithm: a new socio-politically inspired strategy. AI Commun. **28**(3), 591–603 (2015)

15. Hosseini, S., Al Khaled, A.: A survey on the imperialist competitive algorithm metaheuristic: implementation in engineering domain and directions for future research. Appl. Soft Comput. **24**, 1078–1094 (2014)

16. Huan, T.T., Kulkarni, A.J., Kanesan, J., Huang, C.J., Abraham, A.: Ideology algorithm: a socio-inspired optimization methodology. Neural Comput. Appl. **28**(1), 845–876 (2017)

17. Karp, R.M.: Reducibility among combinatorial problems (1972). https://people.eecs.berkeley.edu/~luca/cs172/karp.pdf

18. Kashan, A.H.: League championship algorithm: a new algorithm for numerical function optimization. In: 2009 International Conference of Soft Computing and Pattern Recognition, pp. 43–48. IEEE (2009)

19. Kulkarni, A.J., Durugkar, I.P., Kumar, M.: Cohort intelligence: a self supervised learning behavior. In: 2013 IEEE International Conference on Systems, Man, and Cybernetics, pp. 1396–1400. IEEE (2013)

20. Kumar, M., Kulkarni, A.J.: Socio-inspired optimization metaheuristics: a review. In: Kulkarni, A.J., Singh, P.K., Satapathy, S.C., Husseinzadeh Kashan, A., Tai, K. (eds.) Socio-cultural Inspired Metaheuristics. SCI, vol. 828, pp. 241–265. Springer, Singapore (2019). https://doi.org/10.1007/978-981-13-6569-0_12

21. Kumar, M., Kulkarni, A.J., Satapathy, S.C.: Socio evolution & learning optimization algorithm: a socio-inspired optimization methodology. Future Gen. Comput. Syst. **81**, 252–272 (2018)

22. Kuo, H., Lin, C.: Cultural evolution algorithm for global optimizations and its applications. J. Appl. Res. Technol. **11**(4), 510–522 (2013)

23. Liu, Z.-Z., Chu, D.-H., Song, C., Xue, X., Lu, B.-Y.: Social learning optimization (SLO) algorithm paradigm and its application in QoS-aware cloud service composition. Inf. Sci. **326**, 315–333 (2016)

24. Luque, A.G., Dorado, S.R., de Fátima Vieira Severiano, M., Burillo, F.J.: Fundamentos sociales del comportamiento humano. Editorial UOC (2013)

25. Lv, W., He, C., Li, D., Cheng, S., Luo, S., Zhang, X.: Election campaign optimization algorithm. Procedia Comput. Sci. **1**(1), 1377–1386 (2010)

26. Lv, W., et al.: Verifying election campaign optimization algorithm by several benchmarking functions. In: Tan, Y., Shi, Y., Tan, K.C. (eds.) ICSI 2010. LNCS, vol. 6146, pp. 582–587. Springer, Heidelberg (2010). https://doi.org/10.1007/978-3-642-13498-2_76

27. Lv, Z., Shen, F., Zhao, J., Zhu, T.: A swarm intelligence algorithm inspired by Twitter. In: Hirose, A., Ozawa, S., Doya, K., Ikeda, K., Lee, M., Liu, D. (eds.) ICONIP 2016. LNCS, vol. 9949, pp. 344–351. Springer, Cham (2016). https://doi.org/10.1007/978-3-319-46675-0_38

28. Moosavian, N., Roodsari, B.K., et al.: Soccer league competition algorithm, a new method for solving systems of nonlinear equations. Int. J. Intell. Sci. **4**(01), 7 (2013)

29. Rao, R.V., Savsani, V.J., Vakharia, D.: Teaching-learning-based optimization: a novel method for constrained mechanical design optimization problems. Comput.-Aided Des. **43**(3), 303–315 (2011)

30. Ray, T., Liew, K.-M.: Society and civilization: an optimization algorithm based on the simulation of social behavior. IEEE Trans. Evol. Comput. **7**(4), 386–396 (2003)

31. Satapathy, S., Naik, A.: Social group optimization (SGO): a new population evolutionary optimization technique. Complex Intell. Syst. **2**(3), 173–203 (2016)

32. Soto, R., Crawford, B., González, F., Vega, E., Castro, C., Paredes, F.: Solving the manufacturing cell design problem using human behavior-based algorithm supported by autonomous search. IEEE Access **7**, 132228–132239 (2019)

33. Soto, R., Crawford, B., Muñoz, A., Johnson, F., Paredes, F.: Pre-processing, repairing and transfer functions can help binary electromagnetism-like algorithms. In: Silhavy, R., Senkerik, R., Oplatkova, Z.K., Prokopova, Z., Silhavy, P. (eds.) Artificial Intelligence Perspectives and Applications. AISC, vol. 347, pp. 89–97. Springer, Cham (2015). https://doi.org/10.1007/978-3-319-18476-0_10

34. Sotoudeh-Anvari, A., Hafezalkotob, A.: A bibliography of metaheuristics-review from 2009 to 2015. Int. J. Knowl.-Based Intell. Eng. Syst. **22**(1), 83–95 (2018)

35. Talbi, E.-G.: Metaheuristics: from Design to Implementation, Chapter 1.3, vol. 74. Wiley, Hoboken (2009)

36. Tzanetos, A., Fister Jr., I., Dounias, G.: A comprehensive database of nature-inspired algorithms. In: Data in Brief, p. 105792 (2020)

37. Valdivia, S., et al.: Bridges reinforcement through conversion of tied-arch using crow search algorithm. In: Misra, S., et al. (eds.) ICCSA 2019. LNCS, vol. 11623, pp. 525–535. Springer, Cham (2019). https://doi.org/10.1007/978-3-030-24308-1_42

38. Vásquez, C., et al.: Galactic swarm optimization applied to reinforcement of bridges by conversion in cable-stayed arch. In: Misra, S., et al. (eds.) ICCSA 2019. LNCS, vol. 11623, pp. 108–119. Springer, Cham (2019). https://doi.org/10.1007/978-3-030-24308-1_10
39. Xu, J., Zhang, J.: Exploration-exploitation tradeoffs in metaheuristics: survey and analysis. In: Proceedings of the 33rd Chinese Control Conference, pp. 8633–8638. IEEE (2014)
40. Yang, X.-S.: Metaheuristic optimization: algorithm analysis and open problems. In: Pardalos, P.M., Rebennack, S. (eds.) SEA 2011. LNCS, vol. 6630, pp. 21–32. Springer, Heidelberg (2011). https://doi.org/10.1007/978-3-642-20662-7_2

Entropy Based Machine Learning Models for Software Bug Severity Assessment in Cross Project Context

Madhu Kumari[1], Ujjawal Kumar Singh[2], and Meera Sharma[3(✉)]

[1] Delhi College of Arts & Commerce, University of Delhi, Delhi, India
mesra.madhu@gmail.com
[2] Amity School of Engineering and Technology, GGSIP University, Delhi, India
ujjawalkumarsingh99@gmail.com
[3] Swami Shraddhanand College, University of Delhi, Delhi, India
meerakaushik@gmail.com

Abstract. There can be noise and uncertainty in the bug reports data as the bugs are reported by a heterogeneous group of users working across different countries. Bug description is an essential attribute that helps to predict other bug attributes, such as severity, priority, and time fixes. We need to consider the noise and confusion present in the text of the bug report, as it can impact the output of different machine learning techniques. Shannon entropy has been used in this paper to calculate summary uncertainty about the bug. Bug severity attribute tells about the type of impact the bug has on the functionality of the software. Correct bug severity estimation allows scheduling and repair bugs and hence help in resource and effort utilization. To predict the severity of the bug we need software project historical data to train the classifier. These training data are not always available in particular for new software projects. The solution which is called cross project prediction is to use the training data from other projects. Using bug priority, summary weight and summary entropy, we have proposed cross project bug severity assessment models. Results for proposed summary entropy based approach for bug severity prediction in cross project context show improved performance of the Accuracy and F-measure up to 70.23% and 93.72% respectively across all the machine learning techniques over existing work.

1 Introduction

In software development life cycle, bug reporting and fixing is a continuous and iterative activity [1]. A large number of bugs are reported on bug tracking systems by different users, developers and staff members located at different geographical locations in a distributed environment. Bug severity is one of the most important bug attributes which tells about its extent of impact on the functionality of the software. Bug severity is labeled in seven classes from 1 to 7, namely "Blocker", "Critical", "Major", "Normal", "Minor", "Trivial" and "Enhancement". The automated bug severity prediction is useful in resource allocation and bug fix scheduling. It also assists the priority assignment for the bug. Bug severity prediction needs training data, i.e. the history of

© Springer Nature Switzerland AG 2020
O. Gervasi et al. (Eds.): ICCSA 2020, LNCS 12254, pp. 939–953, 2020.
https://doi.org/10.1007/978-3-030-58817-5_66

the software to train the classifier. But it is not easy to get such data always as some projects may be new with very less of no history of bug data. In such situation, we can use history of bug data from other software projects for training purpose [2, 4–6]. Bugs are reported by users with different levels of understanding and knowledge about the software working which may result in noise and uncertainty in different bug attributes entered. This noise and uncertainty present in training data may degrade the performance of automated bug severity assessment and hence need to be considered during prediction process. Bug summary attribute (the brief description of the bug) has been used for bug severity prediction in this paper. No attempt has been made in literature to consider uncertainty in bug summary in cross project context for bug severity prediction. The contribution of this paper is cross project severity prediction models based on summary entropy in addition to priority and summary weight using "k-Nearest Neighbors (k-NN)", "Support Vector Machine (SVM)", and "Naïve Bayes (NB)". The proposed models result in improved performance when compared with summary based cross project bug severity assessment models [6].

The remaining paper is structured as follows: Sect. 2 describes the review of related work. Section 3 contains the brief of bug reports and its pre-processing. Section 4 deals with data collection and model building required to perform the analysis. Results have been documented in Sect. 5. The conclusion of the paper has given in Sect. 6.

2 Related Work

Bug severity prediction helps in assigning bug priority, fix time prediction and resources allocation. Many bug summary based severity assessment models have been proposed in literature [7–12]. Different authors compared the performance of different machine learning techniques for bug severity assessment [19–21].

An attempt has been made to propose bug summary based cross project severity prediction models using "SVM", "NB" and "k-NN" [6]. Authors also identified the best training candidates for a project. Bug summary based cross project priority prediction models have been proposed by [2, 4] using "SVM", "NB", "k-NN" and "NNET".

Entropy based measure has been used to predict the bugs lying dormant in the software [14, 15]. Recently entropy based measures have been used to handle the uncertainty during the prediction of priority and severity of the reported bug [3, 13].

To our knowledge, no work has been done for considering the uncertainty and noise present in bug summary data that can affect the performance of prediction models in cross project context. In this paper, we have measured the uncertainty in bug summary by using entropy based measures for cross project severity prediction. In addition to summary entropy, we have considered bug priority and summary weight to assess bug severity in cross project context. We have compared our proposed summary entropy based cross project bug severity assessment models with [6] and found improvement in the performance of the classifiers.

3   Bug Reports and Pre-processing

A bug report contains the information about bug in the form of different attributes reported by the users and the developers use this information to fix the bug. In this section we have discussed different bug attributes and two derived attributes summary weight and summary entropy used in bug severity prediction.

We have taken bug priority and two derived bug attributes: summary weight [4] and summary entropy to predict severity in cross project context.

Bug priority and severity are categorical attributes, whereas summary weight and summary entropy are continuous attributes. Bug priority determines the importance of a bug in the presence of others. Bugs are prioritized by P1 level, i.e. the most important to P5 level, i.e. the least important.

Bug severity tells about the extent of bug's impact on software functionality. Eclipse project define the seven levels of severity, namely "Blocker", "Critical", "Major", "Normal", "Minor", "Trivial" and "Enhancement". Throughout this analysis, we have not included bugs with "Normal" and "Enhancement" severity levels because "Normal" is the default standard stated in the reports submitted, and "Enhancement" does not reflect actual bug reports. The severity weights and levels as mentioned in Table 1 (IEEE std 92, 1989) have been defined by IEEE Standard Classification Levels [16]. "Blocker" and "Critical" are most severe severity levels, "Major" is medium severity level and "Minor", "Trivial" are minor severity levels.

Table 1.   Severity levels categories [16]

From the IEEE Standard Severity Classification Levels	Severity Weight	Severity Level
Blocker, Critical	10	Most Severe
Major	3	Medium
Minor, Trivial	1	Minor

Summary weight attribute is extracted from the bug summary provided by the numerous users. We pre-processed the bug summary in RapidMiner tool [18] to compute the summary weight of a reported bug, with the steps of text mining: "Tokenization", "Stop Word Removal", "Stemming to base stem", "Feature Reduction" and "Info Gain" [6].

We assume that the bug reports, i.e. different bug attributes, reported in software bug repositories are trustworthy during bug triaging process. In reality, the bug reports data is not trustworthy in terms of various aspects like integrity, authenticity and trusted origin as the bugs are reported by users who may or may not have proper knowledge of the software. It may result in uncertainty in reported bug data. Without proper handling of these uncertainties in different bug attributes, the performance of learning strategies used for different bug attributes prediction can be significantly reduced.

The validation of cross project is a key concern in empirical software engineering where we train the classifiers with historical data of projects other than the testing projects. In literature, researchers have made attempts for cross project bug summary based severity assessment [6]. But no attempt has been made to handle uncertainty in bug summary in cross project context for bug severity assessment.

We have proposed summary entropy based measure to build the classifier for bug severity prediction to handle uncertainty in cross project context. We have calculated the summary entropy for model building using Shannon's entropy [17]. Shannon's entropy, S is defined as:

$$S = -p_i \log_2 p_i$$

In the case of summary entropy, p is calculated as:

$$p_i = \frac{total\ number\ of\ occurences\ of\ terms\ in\ i^{th}\ bug\ report}{total\ number\ of\ terms}$$

To rationalize the effect of the severity, we multiplied entropy with 10 for "Blocker" and "Critical" severity level bugs, 3 for "Major" severity level bugs and 1 for "Minor" and "Trivial" severity level bugs as given in Table 1 [16].

The cross project bug severity model has been shown in Fig. 1.

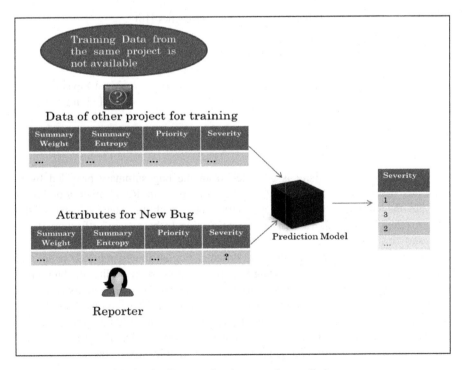

Fig. 1. Cross project bug severity prediction

4 Methodology

In this section, we briefly described the data collection and model building for summary entropy based cross project bug severity assessment.

4.1 Data Collection

The empirical validation has been conducted on different products, namely "CDTDebug (CD)", "EclipseDebug (Deb)", "EclipseJDTUI (TUI)", "EclipseSWT (SWT)", "EclipseUI (UI)", "IDEPlatform (IDE)", and "JDTUI (TUI2)" of Eclipse project (http://bugs.eclipse.org/bugs/) to assess cross project bug severity. Table 2 shows the severity level wise number of bug reports across different products.

Table 2. Severity wise Bug Reports in Eclipse Projects [6]

Projects	1 (Blocker)	2 (Critical)	3 (Major)	4 (Minor)	5 (Trivial)	Total
CD	25	25	122	53	8	233
Deb	23	97	213	72	39	444
TUI	23	81	282	281	81	748
SWT	71	161	298	64	36	630
UI	28	124	401	327	109	989
IDE	23	75	267	148	85	598
TUI2	1	24	118	204	56	403

4.2 Model Building and Experimental Setup

We have developed summary entropy based models using different classifiers, namely "k-NN", "SVM" and "NB" for cross project bug severity assessment by taking priority and summary weight. The empirical evaluation has been validated on 7 products of the Eclipse project. Number of cross fold validations is taken as 10 with stratified sampling for different classification techniques. We have validated our proposed approach and compared it with state of art [6] using performance measures, namely Accuracy and F-measure.

The experimental setup of severity prediction in cross project context developed in RapidMiner tool [18] has been shown in Fig. 2.

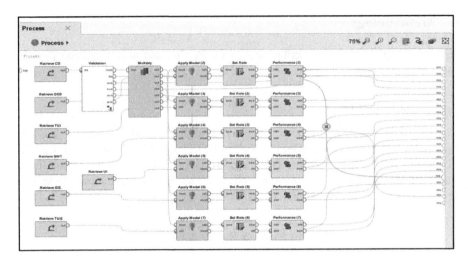

Fig. 2. Experimental Setup for Cross project bug severity prediction in RapidMiner

The parameter values used for tuning the classifier parameters, namely "k-Nearest Neighbor (k-NN)", "Support Vector Machine (SVM)" and "Naïve Bayes (NB)" have been shown in Table 3.

Table 3. Parameters Optimized for different Classifiers

Classifier	Parameters
NB	laplace_correction
k-NN	k
SVM	C (cost)
	G (gamma)

Using "Optimize Parameters (Grid)" operator in the RapidMiner tool, we obtained optimal parameter values. Table 4 shows the parameters optimized for each classifier.

Table 4. Optimal Parameter Values for Eclipse products

Eclipse products	NB laplace_correction	k-NN k	SVM C	G
CD	False	8	1	1
Deb	False	8	1	1
TUI	False	13	3	3
SWT	True	2	2	2
UI	True	6	4	4
IDE	True	20	1	1
TUI2	True	4	3	3

5 Results and Discussion

We have proposed summary entropy based models using different classifiers, namely, "k-Nearest Neighbors (k-NN)", "Support Vector Machine (SVM)" and "Naive Bayes (NB)" for cross project bug severity prediction. We have compared the proposed entropy based approach with Singh et al. [6]. We have taken the same datasets and techniques as taken by the authors in [6] to predict bug severity. Singh et al. [6] considered the F-measure performance of different classifiers only for "Major" severity class, since fewer bug reports for other severity class than the "Major" severity class. This results in low performance for these severity classes. In order to compare with state of art literature [6] we have also considered the F-measure performance for "Major" severity class. Tables 5, 6 and 7 show the F-measure performance for "Major" severity class for different classifiers, namely "k-NN", "SVM" and "NB" respectively. Tables 8, 9 and 10 show the Accuracy of different classifiers, namely "k-NN", "SVM" and "NB" for different testing projects. Across Tables 5, 6, 7, 8, 9 and 10 '–' indicates that no analysis was performed on this particular combination of testing and training dataset, since the training and testing data sets are similar.

Table 5. k-NN F-measure (%) for "Major" severity class

Training Projects	Testing Projects						
	CD	Deb	TUI	SWT	UI	IDE	TUI2
CD	–	93.63	55.65	51.54	49.00	77.15	69.70
Deb	96.27	–	49.39	33.10	33.33	64.45	89.06
TUI	91.21	89.54	–	88.16	91.20	93.72	71.67
SWT	61.87	53.69	86.21	–	90.25	91.04	31.40
UI	64.19	58.94	95.04	96.71	–	95.72	38.57
IDE	96.77	90.00	88.56	87.97	86.90	–	62.88
TUI2	91.27	97.25	54.88	27.71	40.95	58.71	–

Table 6. SVM F-measure (%) for "Major" severity class

Training Projects	Testing Projects						
	CD	Deb	TUI	SWT	UI	IDE	TUI2
CD	–	90.64	58.29	54.95	53.38	80.07	62.03
Deb	95.90	–	54.54	36.43	35.09	65.71	96.27
TUI	66.97	65.84	–	96.08	95.45	96.45	52.50
SWT	58.62	50.64	89.71	–	90.51	89.73	33.07
UI	43.86	23.26	97.39	98.50	–	97.21	22.94
IDE	87.60	84.34	91.79	94.35	90.73	–	57.30
TUI2	96.69	98.84	59.52	39.45	39.57	69.74	–

Table 7. NB F-measure (%) for "Major" severity class

Training Projects	Testing Projects						
	CD	Deb	TUI	SWT	UI	IDE	TUI2
CD	–	95.57	73.18	51.49	62.23	77.61	69.70
Deb	94.87	–	87.38	69.87	77.53	88.11	92.51
TUI	56.08	80.57	–	89.08	92.70	92.65	66.66
SWT	39.64	51.09	76.01	–	83.61	73.57	43.27
UI	41.32	67.15	95.43	92.77	–	89.34	50.42
IDE	71.43	89.04	96.27	85.90	91.63	–	77.39
TUI2	88.51	96.08	84.29	63.65	78.43	89.65	–

Table 8. k-NN accuracy (%) for different testing candidates

Training projects	Testing projects						
	CD	Deb	TUI	SWT	UI	IDE	TUI2
CD	–	68.24	57.35	39.37	51.16	62.04	63.52
Deb	80.69	–	50.27	31.11	37.92	54.85	80.89
TUI	76.82	76.58	–	72.70	78.97	77.42	64.52
SWT	46.78	49.32	73.26	–	76.95	74.58	27.05
UI	53.65	51.58	82.62	80.32	–	79.10	33.75
IDE	78.97	78.15	78.61	73.65	76.44	–	61.04
TUI2	72.53	82.43	54.14	24.44	45.20	50.84	–

Table 9. SVM accuracy (%) for different testing candidates

Training projects	Testing projects						
	CD	Deb	TUI	SWT	UI	IDE	TUI2
CD	–	67.34	58.56	42.54	53.49	65.22	55.33
Deb	81.55	–	58.69	34.44	47.02	56.86	83.37
TUI	57.94	56.98	–	78.57	81.70	78.76	50.12
SWT	46.78	47.52	80.08	–	80.08	76.25	33.75
UI	39.91	25.45	83.16	81.59	–	79.93	21.59
IDE	69.96	73.20	80.61	79.05	78.67	–	55.83
TUI2	73.39	83.78	55.35	38.73	45.40	61.20	–

Table 10. NB accuracy (%) for different testing candidates

Training projects	Testing projects						
	CD	Deb	TUI	SWT	UI	IDE	TUI2
CD	–	70.43	66.22	41.49	58.70	62.41	65.25
Deb	80.26	–	76.34	57.94	68.86	71.24	81.89
TUI	45.49	69.82	–	73.81	80.79	75.92	66.00
SWT	31.33	47.75	67.78	–	74.52	61.37	40.69
UI	33.05	57.66	82.22	77.46	–	76.42	49.63
IDE	55.79	77.48	81.15	72.06	79.17	–	72.95
TUI2	66.09	82.43	69.12	53.33	64.41	75.59	–

We have designed 7 cases for 7 training projects given below.

Case 1: F-measure of Major Severity Level and Accuracy improvement over Singh et al. (2017) for training project CD

The proposed approach improved the F-measure performance by 29.73%, 1.98%, 15.56% and 25.16% for testing projects "Deb", "TUI", "IDE" and "TUI2" respectively for KNN classifier. For SVM the F-measure performance improved by 20.70%, 2.70%, 12.26% and 62.03% for testing projects "Deb", "TUI", "IDE" and "TUI2" respectively. For testing projects "Deb", "TUI", "SWT", "UI", "IDE" and "TUI2", the F-measure performance improve by 62.24%, 64.29%, 35.16%, 52.01%, 64.47% and 25.16% respectively for NB classifier.

The entropy based proposed approach improved the Accuracy performance by 20.94%, 20.45%, 11.12%, 17.56% and 33% for testing projects "Deb", "TUI", "UI", "IDE" and "TUI2" respectively for KNN classifier. For SVM the Accuracy performance improved by 19.37%, 21.13%, 13.05%, 20.57% and 26.3% for testing projects "Deb", "TUI", "UI", "IDE" and "TUI2" respectively. For testing projects "Deb", "TUI", "SWT", "UI", "IDE" and "TUI2", the F-measure performance improved by 46.78%, 50.04%, 25.93%, 39.89%, 45.35% and 46.64% respectively for NB classifier.

Case 2: F-measure of Major Severity Level and Accuracy improvement over Singh et al. (2017) for training project Deb

In case of KNN and SVM classifiers, F-measure performance improved by 34.27%, 3.60%, 44.21% and 30.97%, 1.44%, 93.59% for testing projects "CD", "IDE" and "TUI2" respectively. Our approach improved the F-measure performance by 60.62%, 81.49%, 60.63%, 68.18%, 83% and 82.20% for testing projects "CD", "TUI", "SWT", "UI", "IDE" and "TUI2" respectively for NB classifier.

The proposed approach improved the Accuracy performance by 37.34%, 13.24%, 10.54% and 53.35% for testing projects "CD", "TUI", "IDE" and "TUI2" respectively for KNN classifier. For SVM the Accuracy performance improved by 28.33%, 21.93%, 6.58%, 12.21% and 55.08% for testing projects "CD", "TUI", "UI", "IDE" and "TUI2" respectively. For testing projects "CD", "TUI", "SWT", "UI", "IDE" and "TUI2", the Accuracy performance improved by 59.23%, 65.78%, 42.38%, 56.32%, 60.37% and 70.23% respectively for NB classifier.

Case 3: F-measure of Major Severity Level and Accuracy improvement over Singh et al. (2017) for training project TUI

In case of KNN and SVM classifiers, the proposed approach improved the F-measure performance by 25.64%, 24.93%, 29.41%, 30.64%, 93.72%, 28.29% and 12.39%, 12.01%, 41.82%, 42.43%, 42.83%, 49.81% for testing projects "CD", "Deb", "SWT", "UI", "IDE" and "TUI2" respectively. For testing projects "CD", "Deb", "SWT", "UI", "IDE" and "TUI2", the F-measure performance improved by 35.03%, 67.71%, 80.08%, 86.44%, 83.50% and 51.65% respectively for NB classifier.

The entropy based proposed approach improved the Accuracy performance by 28.32%, 30.41%, 31.59%, 26.49%, 37.62% and 4.22% for testing projects "CD", "Deb", "SWT", "UI", "IDE" and "TUI2" respectively for KNN classifier. For SVM the Accuracy performance improved by 21.03%, 17.57%, 37.62%, 39.74%, 37.62 and 13.15% for testing projects "CD", "Deb", "SWT", "UI", "IDE" and "TUI2" respectively. For testing projects "CD", "Deb", "SWT", "UI", "IDE" and "TUI2", the Accuracy performance improved by 33.04%, 57.43%, 59.68%, 67.95%, 65.22% and 47.14% respectively for NB classifier.

Case 4: F-measure of Major Severity Level and Accuracy improvement over Singh et al. (2017) for training project SWT

We observed that the F-measure performance of our approach has improved by 34.05%, 36.03% and 70.76% for testing projects "TUI", "UI" and "IDE" respectively in case of KNN classifier. In case of SVM, the F-measure performance improved by 28.99%, 28.33%, 25.33% and 32.41% for testing projects "TUI", "UI", "IDE" and "TUI2" respectively. For testing projects "CD", "Deb", "TUI", "UI", "IDE" and "TUI2", the F-measure performance improved by 18.39%, 38.41%, 69.26%, 76.40%, 61.45% and 27.67% respectively for NB classifier.

In case of KNN classifier, our approach improved the Accuracy performance by 1.29%, 7.2%, 38.23%, 39.94%, 34.11% and 0.5% for testing projects "CD", "Deb", "TUI", "UI", "IDE" and "TUI2 respectively. In case of Accuracy values of SVM classifier, our approach improved by 43.05%, 40.04%, 31.06% and 4.72% for testing projects "TUI", "UI", "IDE" and "TUI2" respectively. In case of NB classifier, for testing projects "CD", "Deb", "TUI", "UI", "IDE" and "TUI2", the Accuracy performance improved by 16.74%, 38.29%, 55.35%, 61.68%, 47.49% and 28.53% respectively.

Case 5: F-measure of Major Severity Level and Accuracy improvement over Singh et al. (2017) for training project UI

The proposed approach improved the F-measure performance by 34.25%, 35.41% and 39.41% for testing projects "TUI", "SWT" and "IDE" respectively for KNN classifier. For SVM the F-measure performance improved by 43.52%, 41.21 and 39.82% testing projects "TUI", "SWT" and "IDE" respectively. For testing projects "CD", "Deb", "TUI", "SWT", "IDE" and "TUI2", the F-measure performance improved by 19.18%, 49.22%, 89.42%, 79.73%, 79.94% and 30.30% respectively for NB classifier.

The entropy based proposed approach improved the Accuracy performance by 2.15%, 5.18%, 29.28%, 36.99%, and 35.96% for testing projects "CD", "Deb", "TUI", "SWT" and "IDE" respectively for KNN classifier. For SVM the Accuracy performance improved by 46.26%, 37.15% and 36.45% for testing projects "TUI", "SWT" and "IDE" respectively. For testing projects "CD", "Deb", "TUI", "SWT", "IDE" and "TUI2", the F-measure performance improved by 20.6%, 43.7%, 68.05%, 66.03%, 64.38% and 35.49% respectively for NB classifier.

Case 6: F-measure of Major Severity Level and Accuracy improvement over Singh et al. (2017) for training project IDE

In case of KNN, F-measure performance improved by 33.85%, 25.89%, 34.95% and 25.98%, 30.19% and 93.59% for testing projects "CD", "Deb", "TUI", "SWT", "UI" and "TUI2" respectively. For SVM, F-measure performance improved by 25.80%, 22.64%, 33.81%, 32.49%, 29.54% and 56.57% for testing projects "CD", "Deb", "TUI", "SWT", "UI" and "TUI2" respectively. The F-measure performance improved by 52.06%, 72.88%, 83.97%, 73.12%, 86.38% and 62.14% for testing projects "CD", "Deb", "TUI", "SWT", "UI" and "TUI2" respectively for NB classifier.

In case of KNN, the Accuracy performance improved by 33.05%, 31.53%, 41.71%, 29.68%, 35.69% and 30.77% for testing projects "CD", "Deb", "TUI", "SWT", "UI" and "TUI2" respectively. For SVM the Accuracy performance improved by 18.89%, 26.58%, 44.38%, 31.75%, 38.53% and 27.05% for testing projects "CD", "Deb", "TUI", "SWT", "UI" and "TUI2" respectively. For testing projects "CD", "Deb", "TUI", "SWT", "UI" and "TUI2", the Accuracy performance improved by 41.2%, 66.44%, 68.05%, 56.98%, 67.44% and 59.05% respectively for NB classifier.

Case 7: F-measure of Major Severity Level and Accuracy improvement over Singh et al. (2017) for training project TUI2

In case of F-measure performance of KNN classifier, our approach improved by 23.90% and 36.35% for testing projects "CD" and "Deb" respectively. In case of SVM, the F-measure performance improved by 51:90%, 54.56%, 22.80% and 66.83% for testing projects "CD", "Deb", "TUI" and "IDE" respectively. For testing projects "CD", "Deb", "TUI", "SWT", "UI" and "IDE", the F-measure performance improved by 70.98%, 82.83%, 71.43%, 47.40%, 71.29% and 78.46% respectively for NB.

The entropy based proposed approach improved the Accuracy performance by 21.89%, 39.86% and 10.87% for testing projects "CD", "Deb" and "IDE" respectively for KNN classifier. For SVM the Accuracy performance improved by 51.07%, 67.56%, 18.18%, 28.73%, 11.83 and 36.45% for testing projects "CD", "Deb", "TUI", "SWT", "UI" and "IDE" respectively. For testing projects "CD", "Deb", "TUI", "SWT", "UI" and "IDE", the F-measure performance improved by 55.36%, 62.16%, 46.53%, 37.46%, 40.04% and 57.53% respectively for NB.

Out of 42 cases, i.e. 7 training datasets * 6 testing datasets, the classifiers "k-NN", "SVM" and "NB" perform better in 27, 30 and 42 cases respectively in terms of F-measure performance for Major severity class in comparison with Singh et al. [6]. For Accuracy comparison the classifiers k-NN, SVM and NB perform better in 35, 35 and 42 cases respectively.

Figures 3, 4 and 5 show the F-measure performance comparison of "k-NN", "SVM" and "NB" techniques for proposed summary entropy based cross project severity prediction with Singh et al. [6].

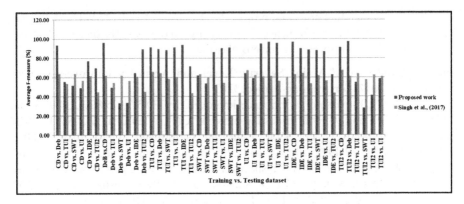

Fig. 3. k-NN F-measure comparison for "Major" severity level

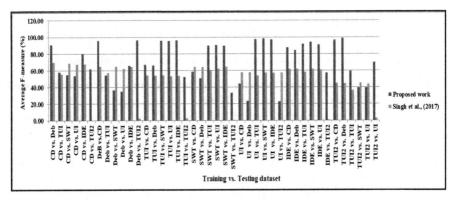

Fig. 4. SVM F-measure comparison for "Major" severity level

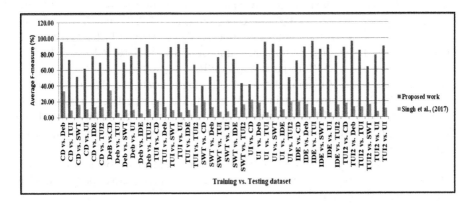

Fig. 5. NB F-measure comparison for "Major" severity level

The Accuracy comparison of the proposed entropy approach with Singh et al. [6] using k-NN, SVM and NB techniques for cross project severity prediction has been shown in Fig. 6, 7 and 8.

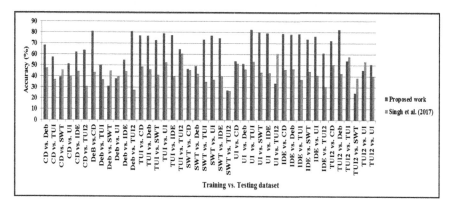

Fig. 6. k-NN accuracy comparison (proposed work vs. Singh et al. (2017))

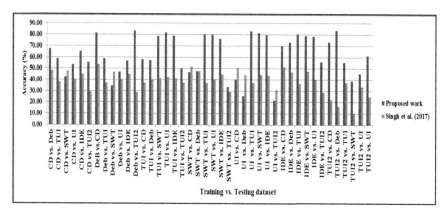

Fig. 7. SVM accuracy comparison (proposed work vs. Singh et al. (2017))

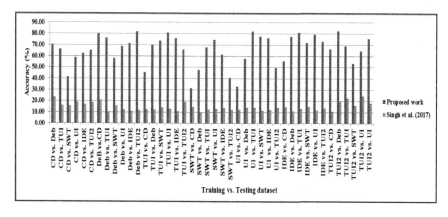

Fig. 8. NB accuracy comparison (proposed work vs. Singh et al. (2017))

6 Conclusion

In this paper, we have proposed an approach using bug priority, summary entropy and summary weight for cross project bug severity prediction. For taking care of uncertainty in bug summary attribute, we have derived an attribute termed as summary entropy using Shannon entropy. Summary weight is also derived by taking the sum of weights of summary terms using information gain criteria. We have used machine learning techniques, namely "k-Nearest Neighbors", "Support Vector Machine" and "Naïve Bayes" to build the classifiers. The empirical evaluation has been validated on seven products of Eclipse project. The built-in classifiers based on these techniques predicted the severity of bug reports in cross project context with significant Accuracy and F-measure. We have also optimized the parameters by using Grid Search. Our proposed approach outperform with the work available in the literature [6]. The proposed approach improved the F-measure for "k-NN", "SVM", "NB" by 1.98% to 93.72%, 1.44% to 93.59% and 18.39% to 89.42% respectively across all the 42 cases for cross project bug severity prediction in comparison with [6]. Our entropy based proposed approach improved the Accuracy from 0.5% to 53.35% for k-NN, 4.72% to 67.56% for SVM and 16.74% to 70.23% for NB across all the 42 cases. NB outperforms for bug severity prediction across all the 42 cases in terms of both F-measure and Accuracy performance. More analysis in the field of summary entropy based metric models may be performed in the future with other projects data. We can measure various forms of entropy and test the built in classifier with more techniques and data sets.

References

1. Singh, V.B., Chaturvedi, K.K.: Bug tracking and reliability assessment system. Int. J. Softw. Eng. Appl. **5**(4), 17–30 (2011)
2. Sharma, M., Bedi, P., Chaturvedi, K.K., Singh, V.B.: Predicting the priority of a reported bug using machine learning techniques and cross project validation. In: International Conference Intelligent Systems Design and Applications (ISDA), pp. 27–29. IEEE (2012)
3. Kumari, M., Sharma, M., Singh, V.B.: Severity assessment of a reported bug by considering its uncertainty and irregular state. Int. J. Open Source Softw. Process. (IJOSSP) **9**(4), 20–46 (2018)
4. Sharma, M., Bedi, P., Singh, V.B.: An empirical evaluation of cross project priority prediction. Int. J. Syst. Assurance Eng. Manage. **5**(4), 651–663 (2014). https://doi.org/10.1007/s13198-014-0219-4
5. Sharma, M., Kumari, M., Singh, R.K., Singh, V.B.: Multiattribute based machine learning models for severity prediction in cross project context. In: Murgante, B., et al. (eds.) ICCSA 2014. LNCS, vol. 8583, pp. 227–241. Springer, Cham (2014). https://doi.org/10.1007/978-3-319-09156-3_17
6. Singh, V.B., Misra, S., Sharma, M.: Bug severity assessment in cross project context and identifying training candidates. J. Inform. Knowl. Manage. **16**(1), 1750005 (2017)
7. Menzies, T., Marcus, A.: Automated severity assessment of software defect reports, pp. 346–355. Int. Conf. Softw. Maintenance, IEEE (2008)

8. Lamkanfi, A., Demeyer, S., Giger, E., Goethals, B.: Predicting the severity of a reported bug. In: Mining Software Repositories (MSR), pp. 1–10 (2010)
9. Lamkanfi, A., Demeyer, S., Soetens, Q.D., Verdonck, T.: Comparing mining algorithms for predicting the severity of a reported bug. In: CSMR, pp. 249–258 (2011)
10. Chaturvedi, K.K., Singh, V.B.: Determining bug severity using machine learning techniques. In: CSI-IEEE International Conference on Software Engineering (CONSEG), pp. 378–387 (2012)
11. Tian, Y., Lo, D., Sun, C.: Information retrieval based nearest neighbor classification for fine-grained bug severity prediction. In WCRE, Kingston, ON, Canada, pp. 215–224. IEEE, New York (2012)
12. Chaturvedi, K.K., Singh, V.B.: An empirical comparison of machine learning techniques in predicting the bug severity of open and close source projects. Int. J. Open Source Softw. Process. **4**(2), 32–59 (2013)
13. Kumari, M., Singh, V.B.: An Improved classifier based on entropy and deep learning for bug priority prediction. In: Abraham, A., Cherukuri, A.K., Melin, P., Gandhi, N. (eds.) ISDA 2018 2018. AISC, vol. 940, pp. 571–580. Springer, Cham (2020). https://doi.org/10.1007/978-3-030-16657-1_53
14. Singh, V.B., Sharma, M., Pham, H.: Entropy based software reliability analysis of multi-version open source software. IEEE Trans. Softw. Eng. **44**(12), 1207–1223 (2017)
15. Kumari, M., Misra, A., Misra, S., Fernandez Sanz, L., Damasevicius, R., Singh, V.B.: Quantitative quality evaluation of software products by considering summary and comments entropy of a reported bug. Entropy **21**(1), 91 (2019)
16. IEEE88: IEEE Standard Dictionary of Measures to Produce Reliable Software. IEEE Std 982.1-1988, Institute of Electrical and Electronics Engineers (1989)
17. Shannon, C.E.: A mathematical theory of communication. Bell System Tech. J., **27**, 379–423, 623–656 (1948)
18. Mierswa, I., Wurst, M., Klinkenberg, R., Scholz, M., Euler, T.: YALE: Rapid prototyping for complex data mining Tasks. In: Proceedings of the 12th ACM SIGKDD International Conference on Knowledge Discovery and Data Mining (KDD-06) (2006). http://www.rapid-i.com
19. Chaturvedi, K.K., Singh, V.B.: An empirical comparison of machine learning techniques in predicting the bug severity of open and closed source projects. Int. J. Open Source Softw. Process. (IJOSSP) **4**(2), 32–59 (2012)
20. Yang, C.Z., Hou, C.C., Kao, W.C., Chen, X.: An empirical study on improving severity prediction of bug reports using feature selection. In: Software Engineering Conference (APSEC), 19th Asia-Pacific, vol. 1, pp. 240–249. IEEE (2012)
21. Iliev, M., Karasneh, B., Chaudron, M. R., Essenius, E.: Automated prediction of bug severity based on codifying design knowledge using ontologies. In: Proceedings of the First International Workshop on Realizing AI Synergies in Software Engineering, pp. 7–11. IEEE Press (2012)

Empirical Framework for Tackling Recurring Project Management Challenges Using Knowledge Management Mechanisms

Abimbola Oluwamayowa[1]([✉]), Afolabi Adedeji[1], Misra Sanjay[2],
and Akinbo Faith[1]

[1] Department of Building Technology, Covenant University, Ota, Nigeria
mabimbola91@gmail.com, {adedeji.afolabi,
tomisin.akinbo}@covenantuniversity.edu.ng
[2] Department of Computer Engineering, Covenant University, Ota, Nigeria
sanjay.misra@covenantuniversity.edu.ng

Abstract. The construction industry is termed as a highly risky industry, considering the alarming rate of recurring challenges and its negative impact on the economy, man, and his environment. This study aimed to develop a framework using knowledge management in tackling recurring problems in the Nigerian construction industry. The data instrument was a well-designed questionnaire directed at construction professionals. Out of the 80 questionnaires distributed, the study used 78 (97.5%) questionnaires for analysis. The study identified corruption, inadequate planning measures, and reduced government policies as the main factors influencing recurring project management challenges in the Nigerian construction industry. The study revealed significant knowledge management strategies used by Nigerian construction professionals, which include the use of emails, face-to-face interactions, and brainstorming sessions. The knowledge management strategies are further classified into data mining based, traditional based, and mobile technology-based knowledge management strategies in the construction sector. The primary benefits associated with knowledge management mechanisms in the construction industry include high growth performance, aid decision making, and innovation in the construction sector. Further classification showed that these benefits are mainly performance-based and collaboration and learning-based benefits. The study proposed a knowledge management framework for tackling recurring challenges in the Nigerian construction industry. Some recommendations drawn from the findings and conclusions can be found in this study.

Keywords: Construction industry · Emails · Knowledge management · Recurring challenges · Nigeria

1 Introduction

The construction industry is an essential sector in an economy that seeks development. This industry affects all other areas of the economy ranging from the agricultural sector, transportation sector, energy sector, manufacturing sector, economic sector, among

© Springer Nature Switzerland AG 2020
O. Gervasi et al. (Eds.): ICCSA 2020, LNCS 12254, pp. 954–967, 2020.
https://doi.org/10.1007/978-3-030-58817-5_67

others. The construction industry plays a crucial role in the economic development of several countries [1, 2]. The continuous need for infrastructural development resulted in a large percent of Nigeria's working population been found in the construction sector either directly or indirectly. According to [3], the Nigerian construction industry gives employment to over 3 million of the 160 million population in the country. Over the years, the growing construction sector has successfully attracted both private and public stakeholders in the industry. The construction industry is a complex and expandable sector that has developed over the years to shelter and accommodate the rise in the country population [4]. However, the perception of the construction industry is that it is a high-risk industry. If the management of these risks is ineffective, there are probabilities of the sector having recurring challenges that can affect lives and properties concerned. [5] corroborated this assertion that in terms of occupation area in modern society, construction work is one of the popular high-risk occupations. The recurring challenges have affected every phase of the construction process in Nigeria [2].

Some of the highlighted recurring challenges in Nigeria construction industry are building collapse [6], faulty design [7], time overrun and cost overrun [8], poor health and safety track record [9], high construction waste [10] and high energy consumption [2]. The trigger for the recurring challenges facing the construction industry could also be corruption and ineffective communication challenges. An individual or a profession cannot solve specific recurring problems; the Nigerian construction industry must seek more knowledge collaboration in the construction industry.

The lack of effective communication (knowledge sharing) among professionals and professional bodies may consistently lead to an unsuccessful project in the Nigerian construction industry. As stated by [11], effective communication is a critical aspect of construction project success outcomes. This study posits that many of the recurring challenges identified in this study can be resolved or lessened using appropriate software and other ICT-based tools as a prerequisite in the potential expression of a sound knowledge management system. Therefore, this study intends to develop an empirical framework for tackling recurring project management challenges using knowledge management mechanisms in the Nigerian construction industry. The outlines of the contributions of the study are to;

- Identify the factors influencing recurring project management challenges in the construction sector.
- Examine the knowledge management strategies used by construction professionals in Nigeria.
- Evaluate the benefits associated with knowledge management mechanisms.
- Develop a knowledge management framework for tackling recurring challenges in the construction sector.

2   Literature Review

Knowledge management is the open and efficient process of managing knowledge as a resource for the advantage of the society or individual's use. This knowledge can be generated, stored, and shared to make informed decisions. This information required in knowledge management can be produced individually or collectively from a group of people. Practically, when organizations put this knowledge together, it can form information management, of which organizations can learn from them [12]. Knowledge management cuts across different disciplines as it improves the outcomes within various industries by learning from the use of knowledge created within the firm or industry. Knowledge management processes involve designing, implementing, and reviewing different activities that improve knowledge acquisition in a company's operation. Knowledge management encourages innovation because it fosters the use of tested smart processes; it is people-centered and compares past behaviors to reduce complexity and ambiguity through the knowledge networks and connections. To understand knowledge management further, Fig. 1 sheds more light on the three orientations in which knowledge management.

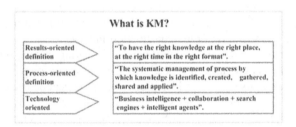

Fig. 1. Understanding knowledge management Source: [13]

Knowledge management is not a new managing concept. This managerial concept has been well established in other fields such as Accounting, Banking, Information technology, and other knowledge-based professions. To examine knowledge management strategies in Nigeria, this study evaluated previous studies, as shown in Table 1, the use of knowledge management in tackling issues in various industries across other countries.

Table 1. Previous studies on the use of knowledge management

S/n	Issues	Sector	Country	Author	Remarks
1	Fragmentation of data, data stored in different formats and traditional project processes	Civil Engineering	USA	[14]	Used Building Information models as an efficient and effective knowledge management tool
2	Unstructured ways in which construction defects data are stored	Architecture and Building Science	South Korea	[15]	Used Building Information Modelling (BIM) to link and share construction defect data to reduce search time and improve accuracy
3	Inefficient management of knowledge hampers growth within a firm	Building	Malaysia	[16]	Developed a framework that links knowledge management and the growth performance of construction firms
4	Inability to recognize, collect accurate data on safety risk, and disseminate promptly	Civil Engineering	Taiwan	[17]	They developed a safety risk recognition platform through the use of Building Information Modelling (BIM)
5	Construction activities involve high risk, which needs to be identified and prevented	Built Environment	China	[18]	Used Building Information Modelling (BIM) to develop a methodology that manages construction risks
6	The usefulness of knowledge management using BIM-based on social platforms	Civil Engineering	Canada	[19]	BIM-based social platforms can improve, perform, provide low-cost housing
7	Knowledge management is viewed as a critical success factor in the everyday business of the society	Environmental Planning	Kenya	[20]	To deepen and surpass the role of effective Knowledge management in the construction industry

3 Methodology

For this study, the research design adopted to answer the research question was a cross-sectional survey research design. The research design was used to draw from the population of the study. The population includes registered and unregistered construction professionals such as Architects, Builders, Civil Engineers, Estate surveyors, Land surveyors, Service Engineer, and Quantity Surveyors working in construction firms. The preferred study area was Lagos state in the south-west of Nigeria. This state currently has many ongoing construction projects and building professionals working within the construction industry. A convenience sampling technique, which is a non-probabilistic sampling technique, was adopted for the study, which helped select a total of eighty (80) construction practitioners who participated in the survey. The study utilized a survey questionnaire as the data instrument to obtain information from the research participants.

The questionnaire designed had four (4) sections, which includes the background information of research participants, factors influencing recurring challenges, knowledge management strategies, and the benefit of using knowledge management mechanisms in tackling recurring difficulties. The objectives in the questionnaire were represented using a 5-point Likert scale. A total of seventy-eight (78) survey instruments were retrieved and used in the data analysis, which represented a 97.5% retrieval rate. The analysis of the study was carried out using statistical package for social science (SPSS) version 23. This was presented using mean scores and principal component analysis (PCA).

4   Result and Discussion

This section in this research presented the analysis of the collected data and discussed the results, including background information of the respondents, factors affecting recurring challenges in the construction industry, knowledge management strategies used in the industry, and the benefit of knowledge management in the construction industry. Table 2 represents the summary of the background information of the participants in this study.

Table 2 showed the type of organization of the respondent, the highest academic qualification, year of work experience in the construction industry, and the profession of the respondent in the industry. In Table 2, most of the construction professionals worked in contracting organizations. Considering the highest educational qualification, most of the construction professionals had a bachelor' degree certificate. Most of the construction professionals had 1 to 10 years of work experience in the construction sector. Table 2 showed that there were 10 (12.8%) Architects, 38 (48.7%) Builders, 11 (14.1%) Civil Engineers, 11 (14.1%) Service Engineers, and 8 (10.3%) Quantity Surveyors. The distribution of the summary of the background information of the respondent showed that the construction professionals possess the required qualification in the industry to be able to contribute their quota effectively in the research.

Table 3 showed the factors influencing recurring challenges in the Nigeria Construction industry. Corruption with a mean score of 4.52 is the factor that impacts most of the recurring problems in the construction industry. It is followed by inadequate planning measures with a mean score rating of 4.22 and by government policies with a mean score rating of 4.18. Poor contract administration with a mean rating of 3.74 and poor weather conditions with a mean rating of 2.90 ranked as the least important factors influencing recurring challenges in the construction industry. Table 3 showed that Corruption, Poor planning measures, and Poor government policies ranked 1st, 2nd, and 3rd, respectively. The construction industry has been damaged by corruption at

Table 2. Background Information

General Information	Frequency	Percent
Type Of Organization		
Client Organization	20	25.64
Contracting Organization	36	46.15
Consulting Organization	22	28.21
Highest Academic Qualification		
Bachelor Degree	55	70.51
Masters Degree	17	21.79
Ph.D. Degree	2	2.56
OND/HND Degree	4	5.13
Work Experience in the Construction Sector		
1–10 years	71	91.03
11–20 years	4	5.13
21–30 years	3	3.85
Profession		
Architect	10	12.8
Builder	38	48.7
Civil Engineer	11	14.1
Service Engineer	11	14.1
Quantity Surveyor	8	10.3

multiple levels and results in underperformance and recurring challenges of a construction project such as quality defect and cost overrun [21]. [22] noted that up to 40% of the contract sum is most times expended on bribery of management officials in the process of contract award, execution, and payment issuance to contractors. [23] opined that the high level of corruption in the Nigerian construction industry would ultimately lead to building collapse, project abandonment, discrepancies between contract sum and final construction cost, project delay and poor building life-span. There has been a considerable economic loss in the industry caused by the corrupt activities practiced in the industry, which needs elimination to increase productivity in the construction sector.

Table 4 showed various strategies used for knowledge management in the Nigerian construction industry. Email with a mean score of 4.37 is the most used strategy for knowledge management in the Nigerian construction industry. It is followed by face-to-face interaction with a mean rating of 4.27 and by brainstorming with a mean rating of 3.97. Intranet with a mean score of 2.95 and cloud and drive services with a mean rating of 2.74 ranked as the least strategies for knowledge management used by Nigerian construction industries, as suggested by the respondents. In all, Table 4 showed that Emails, Face-to-face interactions, and Brainstorming ranked 1st, 2nd, and 3rd, respectively, as the most used knowledge management strategies in the construction industry. The study by [24] noted that emails had become an integral part of most organizations by providing essential communication and collaboration channels.

Table 3. Factors influencing recurring challenges in the construction industry

Factors	Mean score	Std. deviation	Ranking index
Corruption	4.52	.681	1st
Poor planning measures	4.22	.767	2nd
Poor government policies	4.18	.785	3rd
Inadequate techniques used during construction processes	4.13	.750	4th
Poor construction methodologies	4.00	.837	5th
Economic crunch	3.99	.974	6th
Poor communication among stakeholders	3.99	.814	6th
Inability to learn from past mistakes and experiences	3.97	.852	8th
Lack of construction standards	3.96	1.074	9th
Poor project financing	3.96	1.038	9th
Lack of adequate project information	3.91	.996	11th
Low managerial skills	3.87	.972	12th
Inadequacies in the training of project professionals	3.87	1.036	12th
Non-use of Information technologies	3.77	1.025	14th
Poor contract administration	3.74	.986	15th
Poor weather conditions	2.90	1.135	16th

In [25], they opined that emails had become a key component of knowledge management of most firms. Furthermore, [26] argued that using emails as a knowledge management strategy has a higher quality than face-to-face conversations. Whereas, [27] stated that the critical key in the use of emails is the informal knowledge flow among the firm's workers. While [28] noted that more than three-quarters of a company's email contains the best insight of a company's knowledge generation and storage. [29] identified the advantages of email as a knowledge management mechanism. One of the significant benefits is the ability to integrate email as a knowledge management tool in the everyday work practice of companies.

The study utilized Principal Component Analysis (PCA) to understand further the classification and characteristics of the strategies used in knowledge management by construction professionals. Table 5 showed the Principal Component Analysis of the knowledge management strategies. From Table 5, a cut-off point of 0.5 was used as the criteria for the selection of the components in the 3-dimension PCA. Examining the approach in three dimensions, the procedures that have a dimension figure report less than 0.5 is term insignificant during the analysis. Email and Brainstorming were termed irrelevant because they were less than 0.5. Table 5 further classified the strategies of knowledge management by characterizing each dimension by finding the frequent attribute in that dimension. Based on Table 5, there are three main classifications to the knowledge management strategies used in the construction industry.

The three primary groupings have been termed data mining based knowledge management strategy, traditional based knowledge management strategy, and mobile-based knowledge management strategy. The following characteristic component is a data mining based knowledge management strategy, which is a concern with the sourcing of data and information in the planning and execution of projects. Some of the analyzed strategies are in-house web-based systems, gathering of the report, post-project reviews, and cloud and drive services. The other characteristic component is a traditionally based knowledge management strategy. This characteristic focuses on the earlier method of knowledge storage and knowledge transfer. The procedures analyzed were face-to-face interaction and paper-based archiving. The final characteristic component determined was the mobile-based knowledge management strategy, which is an innovative and more efficient way of knowledge management. The analyzed strategy in the study was the WhatsApp mobile application.

Table 6 showed the various benefits of knowledge management in the Nigerian construction industry. High growth performance with a mean score of 4.53 is the most important benefit of knowledge management in the construction industry. It is followed by it helps for decision making, and development of strategies with a mean rating of 4.50 and knowledge management fosters innovation with a mean score of 4.43. High growth performance, it helps for decision making and development of strategies, and it fosters innovation ranked 1st, 2nd, and 3rd, respectively, as the primary benefits associated with the use of knowledge management. The study showed that when construction businesses implement the application of knowledge management, they record high growth performance.

Table 4. Strategies for knowledge management

Strategies for knowledge management	Mean score	Std. deviation	Ranking index
Emails	4.37	.791	1st
Face-to-face interactions	4.27	.715	2nd
Brainstorming	3.97	.967	3rd
Paper-based archiving	3.91	1.015	4th
Gathering of report	3.87	.9718	5th
Communities of practice	3.62	.886	6th
Mentoring and apprenticeship	3.60	.944	7th
Google browsers	3.60	1.036	8th
Post-project reviews	3.53	1.181	9th
Enterprise systems	3.38	.894	10th
Group WhatsApp	3.38	1.203	11th
Other social platforms	3.32	1.006	12th
In-house Web-based systems	2.96	1.129	13th
Intranet	2.95	1.075	14th
Cloud and drive services	2.74	1.140	15th

The study utilized Principal component analysis to understand further the classification and characteristics of the strategies used in knowledge management by construction professionals. Table 7 showed the Principal component analysis of the benefits of knowledge management strategies in the construction industry.

From Table 7, a cut-off point of 0.5 was used as the criteria for the selection of the components in the 2-dimension PCA. Table 7 presented the report of the principal component analysis carried out on the listed benefit of knowledge management in the Nigerian construction industry. It fosters innovation was termed insignificant because of less than 0.5. Table 7 further classified the benefit of knowledge management in the Nigerian construction Industry by characterizing each dimension by finding the prevalent attribute in that dimension. Based on Table 7, there are two categories of knowledge management benefits in this study. The classification of the benefits of knowledge management has been termed performance benefit and collaboration and learning benefit.

Lastly, the study developed a proposed framework of using knowledge management in tackling recurring challenges in the Nigerian construction industry. The study identified three (3) main routes through which construction professionals use knowledge management, as shown in Fig. 2. Either using the electronic or traditional based knowledge management system, the study showed that knowledge is generated and stored in the construction industry. The study noted that there is two (2) classification of benefits garnered from adopting knowledge management in the construction business. By using knowledge management, construction professionals consider the performance, collaboration, and learning benefits attributes in choosing knowledge management. The study proposed that by using knowledge management, the recurring challenges in the construction industry can be resolved.

Table 5. Principal component analysis on knowledge management strategies

Components	Knowledge management strategies	Dimension		
		1	2	3
Data mining based knowledge management strategy	In-house Web-based systems	.790		
	Gathering of report	.721		
	Post-project reviews	.705		
	Enterprise systems	.681		
	Cloud and drive services	.673		
	Communities of practice	.661		
	Other social platforms	.607		
	Mentoring and apprenticeship	.591		
	Intranet	.575		
	Google browsers	.544		
Traditional based knowledge management strategy	Face-to-face interactions		.708	
	Paper-based archiving		.519	
Mobile-based knowledge management strategy	Group WhatsApp			.714

Table 6. Benefit of knowledge management

Benefit of knowledge management	Mean score	Std. deviation	Ranking index
High growth performance	4.53	.528	1st
It helps for decision making and the development of strategies	4.50	.528	2nd
It fosters innovation	4.43	.498	3rd
Improves construction performances	4.43	.594	3th
Learning process and performance is improved	4.39	.542	5th
Risk occurrences are reduced on construction sites	4.38	.762	6th
Increases competitive advantage and swift response to client needs	4.35	.641	7th
Provides a common platform for collaboration	4.33	.574	8th
Simplifies ideas	4.33	.638	8th
Ease of searching for solutions in previously exchanged documents	4.29	.559	10th
Share ideas in real-time	4.26	.692	11th
It is a critical success factor	4.24	.687	12th

Table 7. Principal component analysis on the benefit of knowledge management in the Nigerian Construction Industry

Component	Benefit of knowledge management	Dimension	
		1	2
	It helps for decision making and the development of strategies	.947	
	Improves construction performances	.944	
Perfor-mance benefit	High growth performance	.938	
	Increases competitive advantage and swift response to client needs	.938	
	It is a critical success factor	.769	
	Risk occurrences are reduced on construction sites	.716	
	Ease of searching for solutions in previously exchanged documents	.594	
	Provides a common platform for collaboration	.	.848
Collabora-tion and learning benefit	Simplifies ideas		.788
	Share ideas in real time		.732
	Learning process and performance is improved		.680

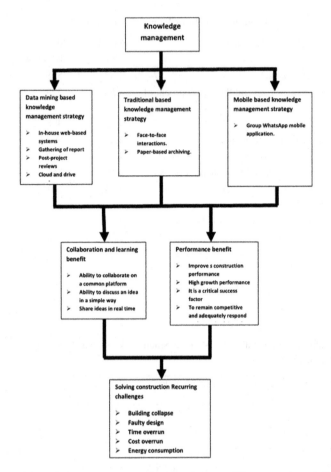

Fig. 2. Proposed knowledge management framework for tackling recurring challenges in the Nigerian construction

5   Conclusion

The prevailing of recurring problems in the Nigerian construction industry has a considerable impact on all major and minor project stakeholders in the industry. These actions can undermine the reputation of the Nigerian construction industry and to increase the expenses incurred by construction firms and the final construction cost. The identified corruption, inadequate planning measures, and poor government policies as the main factors influencing recurring project management challenges in the Nigerian construction industry. The main knowledge management strategies used by Nigerian construction professionals include the use of Emails, face-to-face interactions, and brainstorming sessions. Furthermore, knowledge management strategies were classified into data mining based, traditional based, and mobile technology-based knowledge management strategies in the construction sector. The significant benefits associated with knowledge management mechanisms in the construction industry include high growth performance, aid decision making, and innovation in the construction sector. Further classification showed that these benefits are mainly performance-based and collaboration and learning-based benefits. The study proposed a knowledge management framework for tackling recurring challenges in the Nigerian construction industry.

Based on the findings, the study showed that less information and communication technology-based knowledge management strategies are being used in the construction sector. In contrast, traditional based methods are being widely used. This research points out that the traditional based knowledge management strategies are prone to certain drawbacks that may inhibit archiving and storing of the information generated. The use of ICT-based knowledge management mechanisms can give superior benefits to traditional-based methods. The construction industry should have more awareness seminars and training on the use of knowledge management mechanisms, especially the use of ICT based tools. Therefore, the need for construction businesses to increase investment in ICT-tools can aid knowledge management within their firms. Furthermore, knowledge management from our findings gives both performance benefits and collective and learning benefits. For this reason, professional bodies and construction firms should seek knowledge exchange, data storage, and proper use of this information. Besides, knowledge management should be introduced and well developed into the curriculum of tertiary institutions and professional courses in the construction industry. Training and continuous education on knowledge management should be conducted for employers and employees periodically to maximize productivity and minimize recurring challenges in the Nigerian construction industry.

This study becomes necessary in tackling recurring issues in the Nigerian construction industry. This study suggests the need for construction firms to migrate their construction activities' knowledge creation, storage, and usage from a traditional-based mechanism to an ICT-based mechanism. The ICT-based tool is a major prerequisite for the effective and efficient expression of the needs of knowledge management systems in the Nigerian construction industry. This study showed the benefits which construction businesses can accrue from the use of knowledge management. For the construction business to be able to adapt to new and current trends, it needs to adapt quickly to the use of adequate and efficient knowledge management systems. Areas of further studies can be the development of a web-based knowledge management system for use in the Nigerian construction industry. Its performance, adoption, and benefits can be measured.

Acknowledgment. The authors appreciate the kind efforts of Covenant University through its Centre for Research, Innovation, and Discovery in paying for the article processing charge of this article.

References

1. Afolabi, A.O., Ojelabi, R.A., Bukola, A., Akinola, A., Afolabi, A.: Statistical exploration of dataset examining key indicators influencing housing and urban infrastructure investments in megacities. Data Brief **18**, 1725–1733 (2018)
2. Akadiri, P.O.: investigating factors influencing building materials selection in Nigerian construction industry. Am. J. Civil Eng. Archit. **6**(4), 154–157 (2018)
3. Osmani, M., Glass, J., Price, A.D.F.: Architects' perspectives on construction waste. Waste Manag. **28**, 1147–1158 (2008)
4. El-razek, M.E.A., Bassioni, H.A., Mobarak, A.M.: Causes of delay in building construction projects in Egypt. J. Constr. Eng. Manag. **134**(11), 831–841 (2009)
5. Udo, U.E., Usip, E.E., Asuquo, C.F.: Effect of lack of adequate attention to safety measures on construction sites in Akwa Ibom State, Nigeria. J. Earth Sci. Geotech. Eng. **6**(1), 113–121 (2016)
6. Ejeh, S.P.: Building collapse Phenomenon in Nigeria: the role of NBRRI. In: NBRRI Proceedings of Stakeholders' Forum, pp. 67–77 (2011)
7. Nigerian Building and Road Research Institute, NBRRI: Technical report on collapse of a 2-storey building at Mararaba, NBRRI Report (2011)
8. Hussin, J., Rahman, I.A., Memon, A.H.: The way forward in sustainable construction: issues and challenges. Int. J. Adv. Appl. Sci. **2**(1), 31–42 (2013)
9. Tunji-Olayeni, P.F., Afolabi, A.O., Okpalamoka, O.I.: Survey dataset on occupational hazards on construction sites. Data Brief **18**, 1365–1371 (2018)
10. Afolabi, A.O., Tunji-Olayeni, P.F., Ojelabi, R.A., Omuh, I.O.: Construction waste prevention as a sustainable tool in building mega cities: a theoretical framework. In: 2nd International Conference on Environmental and Energy Engineering (IC3E), IOP Conference Series: Earth and Environmental Science, pp. 1–7 (2018)
11. Gamil, Y., Abdul, I.: Identification of causes and effects of poor communication in construction industry: a theoretical review. Emerg. Sci. J. **1**(4), 239–247 (2017)
12. Serrat, O.: The SCAMPER technique (2009). https://digitalcommons.ilr.cornell.edu/intl. Accessed 18 Feb 2020
13. Benjamins, V.R., et al.: Skills management in knowledge-intensive organizations. In: Gómez-Pérez, A., Benjamins, V.R. (eds.) EKAW 2002. LNCS (LNAI), vol. 2473, pp. 80–95. Springer, Heidelberg (2002). https://doi.org/10.1007/3-540-45810-7_10
14. Abhiject, D., Salman, A.: A framework for a BIM-based knowledge management system. Procedia Eng. **2014**(85), 113–122 (2014). Creative Construction Conference
15. Lee, D., Chi, H., Wang, J., Wang, X., Park, C.: Automation in Construction a linked data system framework for sharing construction defect information using ontologies and BIM environments. Autom. Constr. **68**, 102–113 (2016)
16. Yusof, M.N., Hassan, A., Bakar, A.: Knowledge management and growth performance in construction companies: a framework. Procedia – Soc. Behav. Sci. **62**, 128–134 (2012)
17. Li, M., Yu, H., Liu, P.: An automated safety risk recognition mechanism for underground construction at the pre-construction stage based on BIM. Autom. Constr. **91**, 284–292 (2018)
18. Ding, L.Y., Zhong, B.T., Wu, S., Luo, H.B.: Construction risk knowledge management in BIM using ontology and semantic web technology. Saf. Sci. **87**, 202–213 (2016)
19. Grover, R., Froese, T.M.: Knowledge management in construction using a SocioBIM platform: a case study of AYO smart home project. Procedia Eng. **145**, 1283–1290 (2016)

20. Idris, K.M., Richard, K.A.: Environmental factors of knowledge management model for implementation and adaptation in the construction industry. J. Soc. Sci. Stud. **3**(1), 251–264 (2016)

21. Shan, M., Le, Y., Yiu, K.T.W.: Investigating the underlying factors of corruption in the public construction sector: evidence from China. Sci. Eng. Ethics **23**, 1643–1666 (2017)

22. Ayodele, E.O.: Bribery and corruption – threats to the Nigeria. Construction industry economy. Int. J. Eng. **4**(2), 257–262 (2010)

23. Olusegun, A.E., Ogunbode, A.B., Ariyo, I.E., Alabi, O.M.: Corruption in the construction industry of Nigeria: causes and solutions. J. Emerg. Trends Econ. Manag. Sci. **2**(3), 156–159 (2011)

24. Meta Group: 80% of users prefer E-Mail as business communication tool, says META Group'. Press Release, META Group (2003). http://domino.metagroup.com/pressHome.nsf/ (webPressRelease)/D279165CF57E398785256D10004C9B41?OpenDocument. Accessed 18 Feb 2020

25. Ducheneaut, N., Bellotti, V.: Email as a habitat: an exploration of embedded personal information management. Interactions **8**(5), 30–35 (2001)

26. Kock, N.: Sharing interdepartmental knowledge using collaboration technologies: action research study. J. Inf. Technol. Impact **2**(1), 1–6 (2000)

27. Lucas, W.: Effects of Email on the organization. Eur. Manag. J. **16**(1), 28–29 (1998)

28. CIO.com: From data to information to knowledge—to results. White Paper Library, CIO.com (2001). http://www.cio.com/sponsors/061501_data.html18 Feb 2020

29. Lichtenstein, S., Swatman, P.: Email and Knowledge Management. In: PACIS 2003 Proceedings, pp. 803–815 (2003)

Development of a Plastics and Paper Waste Management System for a University Community

Afolabi Adedeji[1(✉)], Afolabi Ibukun[2], Misra Sanjay[3],
and Akinbo Faith[1]

[1] Department of Building Technology, Covenant University, Ota, Nigeria
{adedeji.afolabi, tomisin.akinbo}@covenantuniversity.edu.ng
[2] Department of Computer and Information Sciences,
Covenant University, Ota, Nigeria
ibukun.fatudimu@covenantuniversity.edu.ng
[3] Department of Computer Engineering, Covenant University, Ota, Nigeria
sanjay.misra@covenantuniversity.edu.ng

Abstract. In Nigeria, poor waste management practices are evident in many urban centers. This study considered a University community as the model to explore the use of digital solutions in proper waste management. This study developed a web-based waste management system for the collection of plastics and paper in a University community. The framework developed utilized the use case and system block diagram. In this study, HTML, CSS, MySQL and Java programming language was used in the design of the web-based system. The result of this study was presented using screenshots. The web-based system had an interface to show profiles of the users, waste pickup information, incentive platform, and the admin dashboard to monitor and approve pickups and incentives. Past studies have indicated the success of using incentives to build sustainable behavioural change towards efficient waste disposal. Therefore, this study was able to introduce the incentive platform which converts weight of paper and plastics waste to points then to rewards for the users. The web-based waste management system for the collection of plastics and paper can be deployed for University communities to help reduce the number of paper and plastics that end up in landfills. Also, by picking the paper and plastics waste from source helps to prevent bin contamination.

Keywords: Paper · Plastics · University · Waste management · Web-based system

1 Introduction

Municipal waste is a challenge in most urban cities. This also the assertion in the study by [1], where it stated that most Nigerian towns and cities are confronted with the significant problems of poor solid waste management. The high level of urbanization and rural-urban migration has inhibited the ability of the appropriate waste management agencies' capacity to deal with the high levels of solid waste. The studies by [1–3]

© Springer Nature Switzerland AG 2020
O. Gervasi et al. (Eds.): ICCSA 2020, LNCS 12254, pp. 968–979, 2020.
https://doi.org/10.1007/978-3-030-58817-5_68

reported that the waste management crisis is evident with the presence of mountain of refuse on major roads and streets in Lagos, Kano, Ibadan, Enugu, Onitsha to mention a few. The sudden increase in the solid waste and its weak disposal system is becoming alarming and becoming a health hazard to communities. Health hazards such as cholera, typhoid, dysentery and so on have been linked to inadequate solid waste management [4]. In [5] it was noted that this is compounded with the high volume of plastics waste that has littered streets, drainages, and public premises. As far back as 1986, the report by [6] noted that the high volume of solid waste experienced in major cities in Nigeria has been due to the incomplete removal of the central refuse dump. In addition to the problem of poor collection and disposal system is the population explosion in urban cities, nonchalant attitude towards adequate waste disposal, and lack of environmental awareness [7].

This assertion is also supported by [8], that the major contributing factors to poor waste management in Nigerian communities is its inadequate collection methods, unsatisfactory coverage and inappropriate disposal systems. One of the ways that have been used in collection of solid waste such as scrap metals, bottles, plastics from dumpsite is the use of informal labour waste collectors [2]. By collecting these specific solid waste, recycling and reuse of these solid wastes is encouraged.

Most importantly, [2] found out that as population increases in urban centres, most of the solid waste generated are non-biodegradable which necessitates the need to recycle and reuse. Lack of necessary waste management infrastructure particularly improper coordination of waste collection and disposal is taking a toll on major cities in Nigeria. This study proposes that with the use of web-based systems and other digital technologies it will improve the coordination and planning of waste management units in door-to-door collection of waste thereby enhancing health and wellbeing of communities. As [9] noted, proper waste management should take effect from inception to the final disposal.

This study considered a University community as the model to explore the use of digital solutions in proper waste management. The studies by [10] and [11] stated that educational institutions, even though regarded as small communities, can actively and significantly impact their surrounding urban communities. The study by [12] supported the notion of proper solid waste management systems in educational institutions in that it can train students on the best practices which can be replicated in their communities when they leave the school premises. With the understanding of the need to carry out appropriate waste management practices within universities and outside, this study developed a web-based waste management system for the collection of plastics and paper in a University community.

2 Literature Review

Proper waste management strategies are gaining traction from most educational institutions [13]. Notably, since they are the citadel of learning, they should be at the forefront of best practices to protect the environment. [14] stated that Universities have the responsibility of ensuring that communities imbibe sustainable plans and policies, mainly as it deals with the environment. This is why there is an increased focus on institutions of higher learning on enhanced sustainability [15]. The study by [15] reported that Universities have a moral obligation towards fostering sustainability agendas due to its possession of academic staff and their comprehensive range engagement of various stakeholders in their community.

Studies by [12] and [16] opined that some are adopting the zero-waste policy. This involves a conscious and rigorous effort to recycle solid waste generated within the educational institution. The first step in this has been able to show the composition and characteristics of the solid waste generated within a community [11, 13]. The solid waste generated per location will differ due to the prevalent activities within the area [14]. This would also help identify the best and workable waste management strategy. A previous study carried out in the same location as this study showed that the waste generation rate was 0.3–0.4 kg/capita/day [14]. The composition of these wastes was organic waste and non-biodegradable, which were generated from halls of residence, residential premises, cafeterias, and other business and religious areas within the University community. The non-biodegradable solid waste is sorted at the dumpsite and sold off to waste scavengers [14].

Even though the University has dust bins specially marked to separate different types of solid waste, many students and staff still do not comply. [14] suggested the need to carry out intensive awareness programs that teach and foster best practices in solid waste management. In the area of recycling in a higher education institution, [15] noted that the significant barriers were lack of motivation to recycle, high levels of bin contamination, and lack of knowledge on recycling initiatives within the University. In Romania, [9] proposed an online platform for waste management of selected items within a university community. Their study examined the present waste management system used within the University community and the volume of waste generated per time. By using IT integrated with the existing waste management infrastructure, they were able to raise the level of waste collection and recycling. The online waste management system proposed by [9] aimed at increasing operational efficiencies and cutback waste generation from the source. However, only the system architecture was shown in this study without the actual online platform.

3   System Design and Implementation

This section showed the system requirement, design of the system and the step-by-step implementation of the web-based waste management system.

System Requirement:
1. Users should be able to register their profile and be able to indicate the need for the waste management unit to pick up paper and plastics waste from residential homes, offices and student hostels within the University community.
2. Waste Managers/administrators should have their own profile and be able to identify point for pick up for paper and plastics waste from residential homes, offices and student hostels within the University community.

3. Waste Managers/Administrator should be able to input the weight of either the paper or plastic waste in the system at the point of pick up from the residential homes, offices and student hostels.
4. The weight generated from each pick up location should be converted to points which would show on the Users' profile.
5. The points gathered on a User's profile should be able to amount to rewards on the user's page to encourage an incentive system for proper waste management.

The study developed a web-based system for plastics and paper waste management within a University community. In the system design, the study followed the patterns of the unified modeling language (UML) used in [18, 19]. The UML used user case diagrams and system-block diagram. The coding language included HTML for the interface, CSS, MySQL for the database, and Java programming language in the NetBeans IDE. In the use case diagram, shown in Fig. 1, it helped explain the actions/steps defining the interactions between the users and the system developed. Figure 1 indicates that there are two primary users- the user needing waste pickup and the administrator of the waste management platform. In this study, the users can be faculty, staff, and students within the University community. In Fig. 1, there are five primary interfaces the administrator can access, whereas the user can access six primary interfaces. In the UML diagram, the system block diagram in Fig. 2 showed the flow of the process in the web-based system.

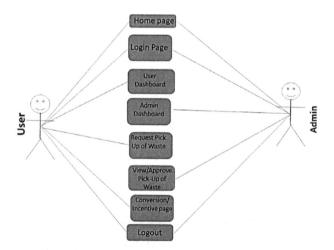

Fig. 1. Use case diagram of the plastics/paper waste management system. Source: Author's Design

The system block diagram showed the step by step activity pages the users can access via the URL of the web-based system. The URL of the waste management platform can be hosted as a link on the University community website. Users in need of a pickup of plastics and paper waste click on the URL and login to the platform. Figure 3 showed the homepage of the Plastics/Paper Waste Management System. Both

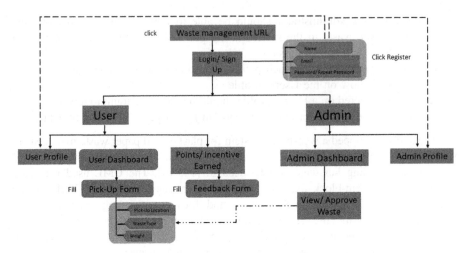

Fig. 2. System block diagram of the plastics/paper waste management system. Source: Author's Design

the users and admin supply their login details on the home page. Information about pickup times is displayed on the homepage in terms of the locations within the University community; hostels, residential homes, and offices. For new users, there is a sign-up page to create a profile on the Plastics/Paper Waste Management System, as shown in Fig. 4.

Fig. 3. Home page of the plastics/paper waste management system

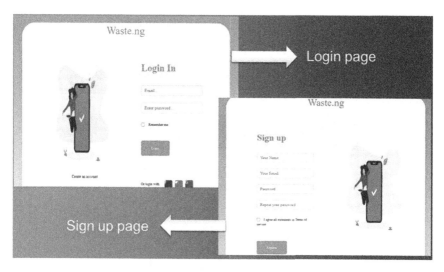

Fig. 4. Login page of the plastics/paper waste management system

Once each user has satisfactorily logged into the Plastics/Paper Waste Management System, a profile is created, which shows name and email, as shown in Fig. 5. The setting icon helps users to be able to supply other details associated with the user. Figure 6 showed the user dashboard of the Plastics/Paper Waste Management System. In the user dashboard, the total number of requests, location, number of times logged in, and points earned by the user is displayed. On the panel, there is also a recent pickup and request. Figure 7 showed the Pickup Form Page in Plastics/Paper Waste Management System. Users can fill the forms to indicate pickup location, waste type, and weight of waste. Figure 8 showed the Incentive Page of the Plastics/Paper Waste Management System. The study by [20] noted that ensuring waste reduction at landfills cannot be achieved solely based on a voluntary change in behavior by individuals; instead, they can be motivated using incentives. Figure 8 showed various incentives based on points that have been garnered. The score is generated from the weight of paper and plastics that have been put together for pick up over time. Incentives such as cash, toilet rolls, envelopes, and branded books are incorporated on the web-based platform. The incentive tool is in line with the previous study, such as the cash-for-trash program in Thailand [20].

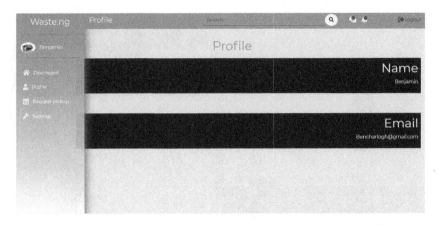

Fig. 5. User profile page of the plastics/paper waste management system

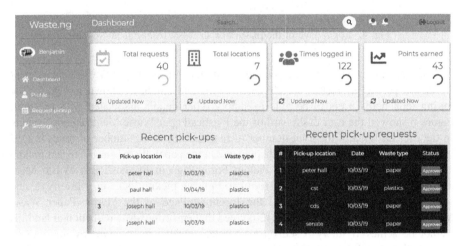

Fig. 6. User dashboard of the plastics/paper waste management system

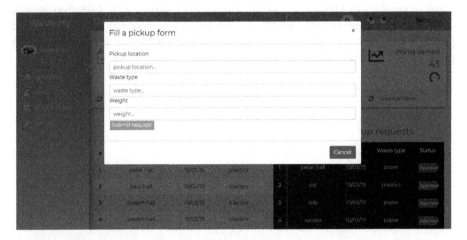

Fig. 7. Pick-up form page in plastics/paper waste management system

Fig. 8. Incentive page of the plastics/paper waste management system

Fig. 9. Admin login page of the plastics/paper waste management system

Figure 9 showed the admin login page of the plastics/paper waste management system. In Fig. 9, the admin supplies the email and password to access the web-based platform. The action from Fig. 9 takes the admin into the admin panel of the plastics/paper waste management system, as shown in Fig. 10. Figure 11 showed the view page of the plastics/paper waste management system. Displayed on the admin dashboard is all the pickup requests. Figure 12 presented the approval page of the plastics/paper waste management system. In this section, the admin approves the

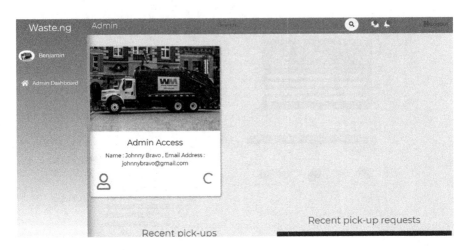

Fig. 10. Admin dashboard of the plastics/paper waste management system

Fig. 11. View page of the plastics/paper waste management system

pickup and confirms the weight of the paper/plastics waste. Figure 13 highlighted the feedback page of the plastics/paper waste management system. Users of the platform can provide messages to improve the platform and state challenges experienced in the use of the platform.

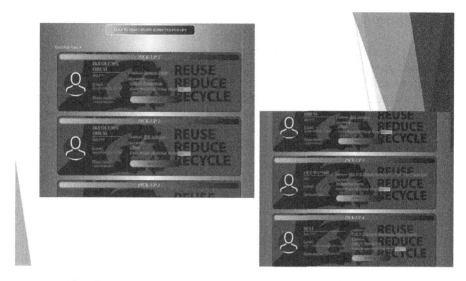

Fig. 12. Approve page of the plastics/paper waste management system

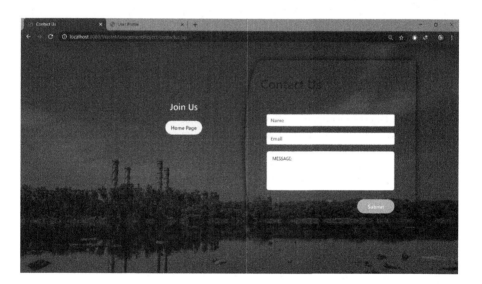

Fig. 13. Feedback page of the plastics/paper waste management system

4 Conclusion

This study developed a web-based waste management system for the collection of plastics and paper in a University community. The result presented were in screenshots. The web-based system had an interface to show profiles of the users, waste pickup information, incentive platform, and the admin dashboard to monitor and approve pickups and incentives. Past studies have indicated the success of using incentives to build sustainable behavioral change towards efficient waste disposal. Therefore, this study was able to introduce the incentive platform, which converts the weight of paper and plastics waste to points then to rewards for the users. The web-based waste management system for the collection of plastics and paper can be deployed for University communities to help reduce the number of paper and plastics that end up in landfills. Also, by picking the paper and plastics waste from source helps to prevent bin contamination. Areas of future studies should include the performance testing of a web-based management system in a controlled community. Also, the web-based waste management system can be extended for use in a State to understand the challenges and prospects in its use.

Acknowledgment. The authors appreciate the kind efforts of Covenant University through its Centre for Research, Innovation, and Discovery in paying for the article processing charge of this article.

References

1. Nwachukwu, M.U.: Solid waste generation and disposal in a nigerian city: an empirical analysis in Onitsha metropolis. J. Environ. Manag. Saf. **1**(1), 180–191 (2010)
2. Ogboi, K.C., Okosun, A.E.: The role of scavengers in urban solid waste management in nigeria. Environ. Stud. Res. J. **2**, 85–92 (2003)
3. Afolabi, A.O., Tunji-Olayeni, P.F., Ojelabi, R.A., Omuh, I.O.: Construction waste prevention as a sustainable tool in building mega cities: a theoretical framework. In: 2nd International Conference on Environmental and Energy Engineering (IC3E), IOP Conference Series: Earth and Environmental Science, pp. 1–7 (2018)
4. Ogbalu, A.I.: Refuse management: the role of health education. Environ. Stud. Res. J. **4**(2), 41–53 (2004)
5. Chukwu, A.O.: The effect of indiscriminate disposal of plastic waste in the environment: a case study of Enugu. An Unpublished BURP Dissertation of Department of Urban and Regional Planning, University of Nigeria, Enugu Campus (2002)
6. Adesanya, Y.O.: Constraints to solid waste management: a case study of Ibadan. An Unpublished MURP Degree Dissertation. University of Ibadan (1986)
7. Ugwunwa, F.A.: Indiscriminate disposal of solid waste in urban environment: cause and consequences: a case of Onitsha metropolis. An Unpublished BURP Degree Dissertation of Department of Urban and Regional Planning, University of Nigeria, Enugu Campus (2005)
8. Ogwueleka, T.C.: Municipal solid waste characteristics and management in Nigeria. Iran. J. Environ. Health Sci. Eng. **6**(3), 173–180 (2009)
9. Popescu, D.E., Bungau, C., Prada, M., Domuta, C., Bungau, S., Tit, D.M.: Waste management strategy at a public University in smart city context. J. Environ. Prot. Ecol. **17**(3), 1011–1020 (2016)

10. de Vega, C.A., Benitez, S., Ramirez-Barreto, M.: Mexican educational institutions and waste management programmes: a university case study. Resour. Conserv. Recycl. **39**, 283–296 (2003)
11. Taghizadeh, S., Ghassemzadeh, H., Vahed, M., Fellegari, R.: Solid waste characterization and management within university campuses case study: University of Tabriz. Elixir Pollut. **43**, 6650–6654 (2012)
12. Moqbel, S.: Solid waste management in educational institutions: the case of the University of Jordan. J. Environ. Res. Eng. Manag. **74**(2), 23–33 (2018)
13. Smyth, D., Fredeen, A., Booth, A.: Reducing solid waste in higher education: the first step towards 'greening' a university campus. Resour. Conserv. Recycl. **54**, 1007–1016 (2010)
14. Coker, A.O., Achi, C.G., Sridhar, M.K.C., Donnett, C.J.: Solid waste management practices at a private institution of higher learning in nigeria. Int. Conf. Solid Waste Manag. Procedia Environ. Sci. **35**, 28–39 (2016)
15. Zhang, N., Williams, I.D., Kemp, S., Smith, N.F.: Greening academia: developing sustainable waste management at higher education institutions. J. Waste Manag. **7**(31), 1606–1616 (2011)
16. Mason, I., Brooking, A., Oberender, A., Hardford, J., Horsley, P.: Implementation of a zero waste program at a university campus. Resour. Conser. Recycl. **38**, 257–269 (2003)
17. Bailey, J., Pena, M., Tudor, T.: Strategies for improving recycling at a higher education institution: a case study of the University of the West Indies, cave hill campus Barbados. Open Waste Manag. J. **8**, 1–11 (2015)
18. Afolabi, A., Afolabi, I., Eshofonie, E., Akinbo, F.: Improving employability skills through a web-based work integrated learning database for construction students. In: Misra, S., et al. (eds.) ICCSA 2019. LNCS, vol. 11623, pp. 372–382. Springer, Cham (2019). https://doi.org/10.1007/978-3-030-24308-1_31
19. Afolabi, A., Eshofonie, E., Akinbo, F.: Development of an alumni feedback system for curriculum improvement in building technology courses. In: Misra, S., et al. (eds.) ICCSA 2019. LNCS, vol. 11623, pp. 257–265. Springer, Cham (2019). https://doi.org/10.1007/978-3-030-24308-1_21
20. Tangwanichagapong, S., Nitivattananon, V., Mohanty, B., Visvanathan, C.: Greening of a campus through waste management initiatives: experience from a higher education institution in Thailand. Int. J. Sustain. High. Educ. **18**(2), 203–217 (2017)

Analysis of Bluetooth Low Energy RSSI Values for Use as a Real Time Link Quality Indicator for Indoor Location

Jay Pancham[1(✉)], Richard Millham[1(✉)], and Simon James Fong[2,3(✉)]

[1] Department of IT, Durban University of Technology, Durban, South Africa
{panchamj,richardml}@dut.ac.za
[2] Durban University of Technology, Durban, South Africa
ccfong@umac.mo
[3] Department of Computer and Information Science, University of Macau,
Taipa, Macau SAR

Abstract. Technologies that can be used for location outdoors are readily available using Global Positioning Systems (GPS) whilst technologies used for indoor location still prove to be a challenge. Technologies such as Radio Frequency Identification (RFID), Bluetooth, and Wi-Fi, together with location algorithms that include optimization, still require further research for large-scale deployments. This study adopts Bluetooth Low Energy technology and uses the Received Signal strength Indicator (RSSI) from messages as a data source. We then analyse the RSSI from Low Power Nodes, their calculated mean, median and mode values as a basis for further use in an indoor real time location system. Fingerprint databases have been used extensively as a reference to determine location. However, due to the changing indoor environment these may become outdated very quickly. Therefore, this study proposes the use of a Link Quality Indicator as a reference point for further calculation of the location of an asset or a person. The Nordic System on Chip (SOC) is used as the low power node together with a series of Raspberry Pi gateways. Results show that the mean and mode can be used in combination to filter and smooth RSSI values. These calculated RSSI values can then be used and as inputs for an indoor location engine for location determination.

Keywords: Real Time Location System · RTLS · RFID · Indoor positioning · Bluetooth low energy networks · Mean · Moving average · Mode · Link Quality Indicator

1 Introduction

For many decades, researchers have sought ways to track assets and people indoors. Recently technologies such as BLE [1], Ultra Wide Band (UWB) [2–4], visualization from video recordings [5], Wi-Fi [6], visible light positioning [7] are still being researched for implementation for indoor tracking. Furthermore, the availability of hardware has prompted new research in localization and navigation especially for indoor environments. Tracking both objects and the public outdoors is feasible using

© Springer Nature Switzerland AG 2020
O. Gervasi et al. (Eds.): ICCSA 2020, LNCS 12254, pp. 980–991, 2020.
https://doi.org/10.1007/978-3-030-58817-5_69

Global Navigation Satellite Systems (GNSS). Similarly, localization of both people and objects is a requirement for many indoor applications. This must be achieved with a reasonable degree of accuracy within indoor environmental constraints. There is also a need to locate the position of objects and people indoors at real time. Real time indoor positioning is not possible using GPS technology [8] as the tracking device requires a direct view to several positional satellites [9]. Therefore, alternative technologies for indoor location are required for implementation in real world applications. According to [10], a Real Time Location System (RTLS) can be defined as a "combination of hardware and software that is used to continuously determine and provide the real time location of assets and resources equipped with devices designed to operate with the system".

The results of any system often depends on its inputs. For indoor location, this means that the location determined by the designed system depends on the inputs obtained for the related hardware and software placed in the environment. Therefore, this research is to evaluate and establish a sound data source as input to such a system for the purpose of location determination within the system's theoretical, social, environmental constraints. This paper is organized as follows: literature review, methodology, and research findings.

2 Literature Review

2.1 Review of Indoor Positioning Technologies

A number of indoor positioning technologies have been researched and proposed over the decades with varying levels of successful implementations. Some of these indoor positioning technologies include (RFID), Near Field Communication (NFC), Bluetooth and Bluetooth Low Energy (BLE). [11] surveyed indoor localization systems and reported that technologies using vision and active /passive tags had weaknesses such as poor performance, high cost, and installation complexity.

The reason that Wi-Fi is proposed as a solution to RTLS is that most indoor environments already have Wi-Fi infrastructure installed. A Wi-Fi system entails a Wireless Access Point (WAP) and a Wi-Fi device. The Wi-Fi device contains a Wi-Fi radio that is used for connectivity. Wi-Fi being a popular technology for indoor usage provides connectivity for most devices. Therefore an indoor RTLS could use existing Wi-Fi infrastructure to relay messages from Wi-Fi tags [12]. However, to use Wi-Fi for RTLS, additional hardware such as Wi-Fi access points are required for reasonable accuracy for indoor positioning of objects or people. [11] investigated wireless technologies because of their high availability and concluded that the solutions could not deliver the performance level required by applications. The coverage provided by the WAP will impact on the reception of the devices that are required to connect to the network. Other constraints include form factor, battery life etc. These factors together with the fact that Wi-Fi was not designed for RTLS make this technology unsuitable for an indoor RTLS.

RFID is another technology based on active or passive tags. A tag constitutes a chip that stores a unique ID and an antennae that is used to transmit and receive data [13].

RFID tags are used in diversified applications including retail, food and restaurant, logistics, travel and tourism, health care etc. [13] identified two main technical issues with RFID systems. The first is where reader collisions occur when multiple readers read a single tag. The second is tag collision occur where a reader reads many tags at the same time. Both these types of collisions result in difficulty in determining the individual identities of tagged entities. Other issues identified include signal interference and privacy.

Despite the use of RFID systems for a number of years, a number of issues still need to be addressed. One of the problems highlighted by [13] is that models researched by academics are not implementable in real-world settings and eventually do not help the practitioner. Challenges experienced in implementation of these models prevent wide scale rollout. Three main difficulties in implementing RFID systems discussed by [14] are related to the high cost of infrastructure and tags and its uncertain return on investment; technical issues such as electromagnetic interference and distractions by metallic objects in reading tags; and security and privacy. The high cost of implementing solutions to mitigate these difficulties makes it unfeasible and hence not scalable.

A newer technology based on NFC is a passive one way identification technology for very short distances requiring no batteries for its tags as power is electromagnetically induced with an NFC reader in range [15]. This technology works well for transmission of data only for short distances i.e. a few centimeters. Therefore, it is unsuitable for use in an RTLS.

Another wireless technology for communication over short distances is Bluetooth. Signal interference and attenuation of Bluetooth classic signals poses serious drawbacks in crowded areas. Although Bluetooth classic can transmit large quantities of data, it does consume battery power quickly and is more costly than Bluetooth Low Energy or other indoor localizations technologies [16]. Furthermore, accuracy for RTLS differs at a cost in terms of form factor, power consumption, and other factors. In particular the smaller the form factor the smaller the battery size. This results in less power being available and hence consumption needs to be reduced. Development in the Bluetooth space resulted in Bluetooth Low Energy suitable to exchange smaller amounts of data while consuming lower energy and be available at a lower cost. However, BLE compared to Bluetooth (BT) and NFC offers several additional advantages such as lower cost, smaller form factor etc. When combined with beacon technology BLE can achieve coverage of distances of up to 50 m [17]. [18] identified that BLE nodes only has limited coverage over a short range when using point-to-point communication. They proposed using multiple nodes in a multi-hop network using a wireless mesh configuration. These nodes communicate with each other to enable routing of packets thereby extending the previous limited coverage range. Technologies and algorithms that are more efficient can be used to extend this distance.

BLE is more attractive due to its low power consumption and ease of deployment [1], and small form factor [9]. The advantage of using Bluetooth Low Energy tags is that consumes low energy and has a low cost [19] as well. However, an important issue to consider is that most wireless signals suffer from multipath fading (variation of the attenuation) and /or shadowing (deviation of the power received) during transmission [20]. Consequently, more solutions propose use a combination of multiple technologies to minimize the disadvantages experienced in using a single technology. [19] evaluated the reliability of detection and tracking of people with Bluetooth Low Energy tags. Their system consisted of a Tag that sends 2.4 GHz signals, a stationary anchor to receive signals and a local engine. The local engine collects received signal data and performs the calculations for the location of the tag based on this data. Their results were more reliable when tags were closer to the anchors, detection was unreliable for boundary conditions especially in penetrable walls, and hence more work was required to improve accuracy.

2.2 Location Determination

Different techniques such as trilateration [21] or finger printing, using Received Signal Strength Indication (RSSI) are used to determine locations [1] of objects or people. Trilateration uses multiple receivers to receive the messages from a transmitting node. Each of the receivers calculates the probable location using the received RSSI. In the case of finger printing a historic set of RSSI values are recorded by each receiver for each of the transmitting nodes. This database of RSSI values is referenced when a new set of RSSI values are obtained at real time. The closest match is found and their historic location is used as the probable location. RSSI is the most popular source of information from which distance estimation for wireless systems can be calculated with an average accuracy error of 1–2 m [22]. The use of the Kalman filter on Bluetooth RSSI values improves accuracy to 0.47 m. However, this use is at a cost of increased form factor (due to increased storage requirements) and increased power consumption [23].

Application of the Kalman filter is powerful technique but also requires a large number of RSSI measurements and calculations to enhance accuracy. Also processing and storage capacity is a limitation of this algorithm especially for Low Power Nodes (LPNs) [24]. Their simple prototype, with a rapid and dynamic approach and without detailed calibrations, delivered a fixed point positioning error of 0.47 m. As can be seen, the use of Kalman filter techniques applied to RSSI values increases energy consumption and increases the form factor for Bluetooth.

[25] used the Link Quality Index (LQI) in a ZigBee network for location both indoor and outdoor environment. This LQI is derived from the physical layer and is used from reference nodes in the network. For an indoor environment, the area is divided into zones and sub zones for further processing. Another popular technique to improve on RSSI as a source is to average the RSSI and then apply inter Ring Localization Algorithm (iRingLA) technique [26] for localization.

3 Methodology

This research focuses on establishing a reliable basis of RSSI values to be used as a LQI for indoor location. The intention is to establish a simple method in an initial phase for subsequent location determination. It is important for the basis of the data source to be reliable so that the error in the calculated position can be minimised. The hardware selected uses the latest technology available and the firmware has been customised specifically for this research. The research entails setup and capture of data from LPN's to a server for processing.

3.1   Hardware Selection and Software Configuration

In our study we used Skylab's SKB501 single chip solution shown in Fig. 1 as the Low Power Node (LPN). It is designed take advantage of the feature advancements of Bluetooth® 5. Also it takes advantage of Bluetooth 5's increased performance capabilities which include high throughput modes and long range. The Bluetooth 5 specification enables the NRF52840 and other similar SOC's to take advantage of the considerable performance improvements for BLE V5.

Fig. 1. SKB501 – LPN top view

The gateway used for this research is a Raspberry Pi 4 running Ubuntu server V18.04 forming the bridge between the LPN and the server. The gateways scan for Bluetooth messages from the LPNs, converts them and then pushes the data to a UDP server via a Wi-Fi network. The server runs an Ubuntu Operating System with a PostGreSql database. This high level architecture is depicted in Fig. 2.

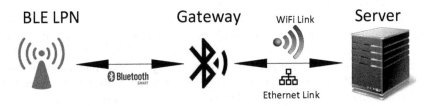

Fig. 2. Architecture

3.2   Data Collection

Firmware for the LPN was configured to broadcast the unique LPN identifier, transmit RSSI level and unique message identifier every 100 ms. The unique message identifier was used to analyse how each broadcast message was received at each of the gateways. The gateways named GW-001 to GW-004 were placed at the corners of a 2 m² area. LPN's named LPN001to LPN007 were placed at the positions depicted in Fig. 3. The LPNs 1, 3, 4 and 6 were placed adjacent to the gateways as well to establish the initial signal loss experienced. The LPNs 2, 5, and 7 were placed at equal distance between the gateways to determine the similarity in RSSI received by the gateways. Positions are labeled as x, y where x is the horizontal measurement whilst y is the vertical measurement in meters. This depicted in Fig. 3.

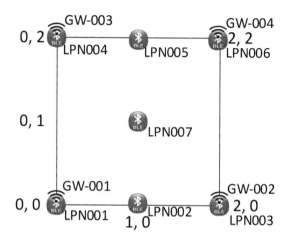

Fig. 3. LPN and gateway layout

Once the LPNs, gateways and server were setup the LPNs began broadcasting messages every 100 ms. These messages were received by the Gateways which converted them and uploaded them to the server. The time limit for capturing the messages used was 10 min and 30 min sessions.

To obtain the filtered mean the formulae (1) was used to calculate the mean RSSI using a value of 20 for n. This meant that for each calculation a window of 20 RSSI values were used. The principle of first in first out was used the manage the RSSI stream.

$$Mean\ RSSI = 1/n \sum\nolimits_{i=1}^{n} xi \tag{1}$$

The mode indicates the element that occurs most often in a data set. However, in this research in addition to calculating the mode, the count for each unique RSSI occurrence is computed. The number of occurrences of the RSSI values is studied to determine a possible pattern to be used for further calculation.

4   Results

In excess of 152 000 messages were recorded from the LPNs. Figures 4a to 4d depict the actual RSSI, mean, median and mode. The RSSIs measured at gateway and depicted in the graphs are used for illustration as similar results were calculated for the remaining data set.

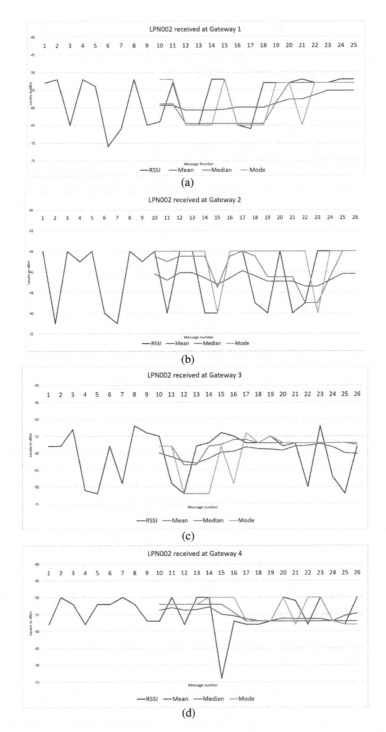

Fig. 4. a. LPN002 messages received at GW-001, b. LPN002 messages received at GW-002, c. LPN002 messages received at GW-003, d. LPN002 messages received at GW-004

Figure 5, which is used for illustrative purposes, shows the mode of the RSSI received at gateway 001 for messages received from LPN003. In addition, the graph also show the count of each of the unique RSSI values indicating the variation and distribution. In this case, this stability can be seen from the fact that the number of messages received are at levels −56 and −54 are 366 and 228 respectively.

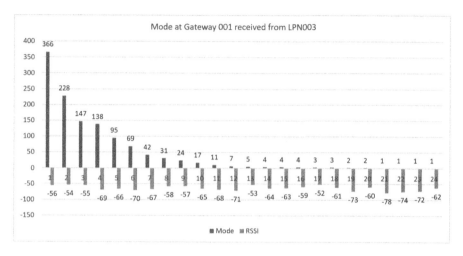

Fig. 5. Mode at GW-001 from LPN002

Figure 6 shows the mode of messages received at Gateway 2 from the LPN005. One hundred and forty one messages were received at level of −51 and 93 were received level −55. The graph also shows the count of unique RSSI values received. The RSSI count of remaining messages were much lower than the first two in both these examples. All readings were taken with the LPN and the Gateways fixed at the same positions as indicated in Fig. 3. This pattern has been identified generally across all of the data received and recorded. Therefore, one such sample is used for illustrative purpose.

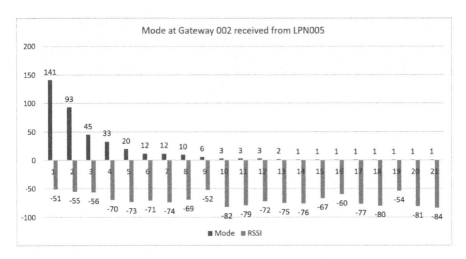

Fig. 6. Mode at GW-002 from LPN005

5 Discussion

The results obtained from this research, indicate that a reliable metric that is best suited for smoothing of the results is established. The moving average (mean) calculated from five RSSI values was not as reliable for the smoothing of the original RSSI for further use. After some detailed computation, it was found that the moving average (mean) calculated using ten RSSI values delivered a more reliable source for further computation. Hence, for the most reliable location calculations, a minimum of ten RSSI readings is recommended. The mean showed the best smoothing calculation followed by the median at each of the four gateways.

[27] improves the raw RSSI values by applying a factor between 0 and 1 to the current and previous RSSI values to obtain an improved RSSI value. This new RSSI value is therefore dependent on the previous and current RSSI values. They then apply a 20 value moving average to the newly obtained RSSI stream to calculate a smoothed RSSI. The RSSI values are then passed for further processing to determine the location. This has an additional step as compared to our proposed process. Is also uses twice the number of RSSI values to for the smoothing process adding to the complexity of the process of obtaining a data stream for further computation.

The mode calculated at each of the four gateways indicate that the RSSI stabilizes after a period and remains constant. A large percentage of the RSSI levels appear to be at the top three RSSI counts in most cases with the mode being more prominent when observed for a longer period. This pattern has been identified generally across the data recorded. Therefore, the combination of the mean, mode and RSSI values close to the mode proves to be a reliable basis to commence the calculation of the location. In this case, there is no need for a fingerprint to be captured, saved and referenced, as an indoor environment is a dynamic one. The changing indoor environment will result in different RSSI values reported each time. Also with the movement of people causing a changing environment, the location becomes more difficult to calculate accurately. Therefore, this will warrant a more dynamic LQI to be used to determine the location of an asset or a person.

6 Conclusion

Cost effective applications of RTLS solutions can deliver much needed value in various sectors, for example health care. RTLS have improved over time and tremendous benefits are realized in some use cases. However, there is opportunity for research to overcome the serious technical constraints to be successfully used in applications such as asset management [28]. Computation for indoor location systems has proven to be complex and resource intensive. This because the number of RSSI values captured must be large in order to perform a reasonable calculation of the location in real time. Furthermore, the dynamic nature of an indoor environment resulting from electromagnetic interferences and obstacles require that the calculations for location use a dynamic data set.

This research has established a useful pattern as a basis to determine location with dimension reduction of signals. Future research will include establishing and testing a reliable RSSI data set using a combination of the mean and mode, using machine learning to determine location through obstacles, balancing computational system requirements and minimizing battery power usage in delivering a reliable location. Also at present since messages are broadcast at 100 ms intervals there will be 10 messages per second. A higher frequency would result in more transmissions resulting in more computations. Therefore, the moving average for both mean and mode will be investigated when messages are broadcast at a higher frequency within the constraints of an indoor RTLS. The most suitable metrics were established using simple calculations, which we hope to use when calculating mobile-tagged entities in the future. Then, the use machine learning will be used for further calculations of locations of moving objects around obstacles.

References

1. Naghdi, S., O'Keefe, K.: Trilateration with BLE RSSI accounting for pathloss due to human obstacles. In: International Conference on Indoor Positioning and Indoor Navigation (IPIN), pp. 1–8. IEEE (2019)
2. Schroeer, G.: A real-time UWB multi-channel indoor positioning system for industrial scenarios. In: 2018 International Conference on Indoor Positioning and Indoor Navigation (IPIN), pp. 1–5. IEEE (2018)
3. Risset, T., Goursaud, C., Brun, X., Marquet, K., Meyer, F.: UWB ranging for rapid movements. In: 2018 International Conference on Indoor Positioning and Indoor Navigation (IPIN), pp. 1–8. IEEE (2018)
4. Martinelli, A., Jayousi, S., Caputo, S., Mucchi, L.: UWB positioning for industrial applications: the galvanic plating case study. In: International Conference on Indoor Positioning and Indoor Navigation (IPIN), pp. 1–7. IEEE (2019)

5. Kim, C., Bhatt, C., Patel, M., Kimber, D., Tjahjadi, Y.: InFo: indoor localization using fusion of visual information from static and dynamic cameras. In: International Conference on Indoor Positioning and Indoor Navigation (IPIN), pp. 1–8. IEEE (2019)

6. Moreira, A., Silva, I., Meneses, F., Nicolau, M.J., Pendao, C., Torres-Sospedra, J.: Multiple simultaneous Wi-Fi measurements in fingerprinting indoor positioning. In: International Conference on Indoor Positioning and Indoor Navigation (IPIN), pp. 1–8. IEEE (2017)

7. Liang, Q., Lin, J., Liu, M.: Towards robust visible light positioning under LED shortage by visual-inertial fusion. In: International Conference on Indoor Positioning and Indoor Navigation (IPIN), pp. 1–8. IEEE (2017)

8. Kim, S., Ha, S., Saad, A., Kim, J.: Indoor positioning system techniques and security. In: Fourth International Conference on e-Technologies and Networks for Development (ICeND), pp. 1–4. IEEE (2015)

9. Sato, A., Nakajima, M., Kohtake, N.: Rapid BLE beacon localization with range-only EKF-SLAM using beacon interval constraint. In: International Conference on Indoor Positioning and Indoor Navigation (IPIN), pp. 1–8. IEEE (2019)

10. International Standards Organization (ISO): Information technology - automatic identification and data capture (AIDC) techniques - harmonized vocabulary - part 5: locating systems. Vol. ISO/IEC 19762-5. ISO, Geneva (2007)

11. Basri, C., El Khadimi, A.: Survey on indoor localization system and recent advances of WIFI fingerprinting technique. In: 5th International Conference on Multimedia Computing and Systems (ICMCS), pp. 253–259. IEEE (2016)

12. Wang, B., Toobaei, M., Danskin, R., Ngarmnil, T., Pham, L., Pham, H.: Evaluation of RFID and Wi-Fi technologies for RTLS applications in healthcare centers. In: 2013 Proceedings of PICMET 2013 Technology Management in the IT-Driven Services (PICMET), pp. 2690–2703. IEEE (2013)

13. Zhu, X., Mukhopadhyay, S.K., Kurata, H.: A review of RFID technology and its managerial applications in different industries. J. Eng. Technol. Manag. 29, 152–167 (2012)

14. Yazici, H.J.: An exploratory analysis of hospital perspectives on real time information requirements and perceived benefits of RFID technology for future adoption. Int. J. Inf. Manag. 34, 603–621 (2014)

15. Narzt, W., Furtmüller, L., Rosenthaler, M.: Is bluetooth low energy an alternative to near field communication. J. Mob. Multimed. 12, 76–90 (2016)

16. Zaim, D., Bellafkih, M.: Bluetooth Low Energy (BLE) based geomarketing system. In: 11th International Conference on Intelligent Systems: Theories and Applications (SITA), pp. 1–6. IEEE (2016)

17. Cheng, R.S., Hong, W.J., Wang, J.S., Lin, KW.: Seamless guidance system combining GPS, BLE Beacon, and NFC technologies. Mobile Information Systems (2016)

18. Raza, S., Misra, P., He, Z., Voigt, T.: Building the Internet of Things with bluetooth smart. Ad Hoc Netw. 57, 19–31 (2016)

19. Han, G., Klinker, G.J., Ostler, D., Schneider, A.: Testing a proximity-based location tracking system with bluetooth low energy tags for future use in the OR. In: 17th International Conference on E-health Networking, Application & Services (HealthCom), pp. 17–21. IEEE (2015)

20. Stüber, G.L.: Principles of Mobile Communication. Springer, Cham (2017). https://doi.org/10.1007/978-3-319-55615-4

21. D'Aloia, M.C., Cortone, F., Cice, G., Russo, R., Rizzi, M., Longo, A.: Improving energy efficiency in building system using a novel people localization system. In: IEEE Workshop on Environmental, Energy, and Structural Monitoring Systems (EESMS), pp. 1–6. IEEE (2016)

22. Bal, M., Xue, H., Shen, W., Ghenniwa, H.: A 3-D indoor location tracking and visualization system based on wireless sensor networks. In: IEEE International Conference on Systems Man and Cybernetics (SMC), pp. 1584–1590. IEEE (2010)

23. Tsang, P., Wu, C., Ip, W., Ho, G., Tse, Y.: A bluetooth-based indoor positioning system: a simple and rapid approach. Ann. J. IIE (HK) **35**, 11–26 (2015)

24. Tsang, P., Wu, C., Ip, W., Ho, G., Tse, Y.: A bluetooth-based indoor positioning system: a simple and rapid approach. Ann. J. IIE (HK) **35**, 11–26 (2015)

25. Kuo, W.H., Chen, Y.S., Jen, G.T., Lu, T.-W.: An intelligent positioning approach: RSSI-based indoor and outdoor localization scheme in Zigbee networks. In: International Conference on Machine Learning and Cybernetics, pp. 2754–2759. IEEE (2010)

26. Thaljaoui, A., Val, T., Nasri, N., Brulin, D.: BLE localization using RSSI measurements and iRingLA. In: IEEE International Conference on Industrial Technology (ICIT), pp. 2178–2183. IEEE (2015)

27. Jayakody, J.A., Lokuliyana, S., Chathurangi, D., Vithana, D.: Indoor positioning: novel approach for bluetooth networks using RSSI smoothing. Int. J. Comput. Appl. **137**, 26–32 (2016)

28. Fisher, J.A., Monahan, T.: Evaluation of real-time location systems in their hospital contexts. Int. J. Med. Inform. **81**, 705–712 (2012)

Customer Relationship Management for Personalized Nutrition Service

Jitao Yang[(✉)]

School of Information Science, Beijing Language and Culture University,
Beijing 100083, China
yangjitao@blcu.edu.cn

Abstract. Sufficient food and nutrition supplement is very important for the health of our body. However, most of us do not know which food or nutrition is needed for our bodies, because we do not know our bodies' detail nutrition requirement. Each person's nutrition demand is different because of the differences of each person's genes, age, and life style. With the fast development of genomics, genetics, nutrigenomics, nutrigenetics, and nutrition science, we can now provide personalized nutrition service for customers. The service can provide personalized food supplement solutions based on the DNA genetic testing and the lifestyle evaluation. For the nutrients that can not be supplemented sufficiently from food, the service can provide dietary supplement solutions for customers. Since the dietary supplement products on the market are general products for all the people that can not meet the need of each person's unique nutrition requirement, therefore, our solution collaborates with nutrition product production factory to produce customized nutrition products for the customers. Personalized nutrition service needs to connect customers, genetic testing laboratories, and nutrition product production factory, therefore a customer relationship management (CRM) system is necessary to let customer read genetic report, order personalized nutrition products, place an order to nutrition factory to produce personalized nutrition products. In the paper, we give the technical design and deployment of a CRM system for supporting the personalized nutrition service. The CRM system has been delivered online and provides very successful service for customers, business partners, and intelligent nutrition factory.

Keywords: Nutrition · Genetic testing · Personalized service · Customer relationship management

1 Introduction

Sufficient proteins, carbohydrates, fats, vitamins, and minerals are very important to each person's body to maintain heath and strengthen immune ability. Proteins, carbohydrates, fats are easy to be obtained from our daily food and are required in large amounts for the development of body. Proteins could be obtained from fish, eggs, milk, and meats; carbohydrates could obtained from

© Springer Nature Switzerland AG 2020
O. Gervasi et al. (Eds.): ICCSA 2020, LNCS 12254, pp. 992–1002, 2020.
https://doi.org/10.1007/978-3-030-58817-5_70

bread and rice; fats could also obtained from meats. Vitamins including vitamin A, vitamin B2, vitamin B3, vitamin B6, folic acid, vitamin B12, vitamin C, vitamin D, vitamin E, and vitamin K are very important for disease prevention and immune strengthening. Minerals including calcium, zinc, iron, magnesium, selenium, phosphorus are also vital for the wellness of body. Vitamins, minerals and the other micronutrients can not be produced in body and must be absorbed from diet. Therefore, reasonable diet and nutrition supplement are very important to make our bodies work in good condition and far from diseases.

Each person's physical condition is different from others, due to the variations of genes and lifestyle, therefore, the nutrition supplement solutions should be personalized for each person.

The fast development of nutrigenomics [1], nutrigenetics [2,3] and nutrition science, makes personalized nutrition solution possible. Based on the analysis of DNA genetic testing and lifestyle evaluation data, we can provide food supplement solutions, and for the nutrients that can not be absorbed sufficiently from food, we give the diet supplement solution. Further, since the diet supplement products on market are general products for all the people, we therefore collaborate with nutrition products production factory to produce tailored diet supplement products to meet the nutrition requirement of each person.

We published a personalized nutrition service which requires the customer to have genetic testing first, and based on the electronic genetic interpretation report the customer can order personalized nutrition products online, then the nutrition factory will receive the customer's order and begin to produce the customized nutrition products for the customer. Therefore, a customer relationship management system is necessary to connect customers, genetic testing laboratory, and nutrition product production factory to let different parities to finish their tasks respectively and orderly. Without a CRM the personalized nutrition service can not be completed efficiently, especially when the factory needs to produce hundreds or thousands of personalized nutrition products in one day.

2   Related Works

CRM systems have been existed for many years, and there are very popular CRMs such as Salesforce [14], Oracle CRM [15] and etc. However, since the personalized nutrition service is very new, its business process is not supported by the existing CRMs, and the extension development of the existing commercial CRMs is very expensive. Therefore, in this paper we first describe the personalized nutrition business process, then we give the technical design and implementation of the CRM system for supporting the personalized nutrition service.

3   Personalized Nutrition Service

Figure 1 describes the business process of personalized nutrition service. The service platform is composed by multiple systems: E-commerce System, Customer Relation Management (CRM) System, Laboratory Information Management

System (LIMS), Bioinformatics Analysis System, Genetic Interpretation System, Business Partner's Systems, and Factory's Order System.

E-commerce system, supports the business to customer service, which has the similar shopping functions like Amazon.com, Alibaba Tmall.com and the other online shopping systems, however the system only sells genetic testing products and personalized nutrition products. Additionally, the e-commerce system has the functions of registering sample, viewing genetic testing report, viewing personalized nutrition supplement solutions, registering personalized nutrition product card.

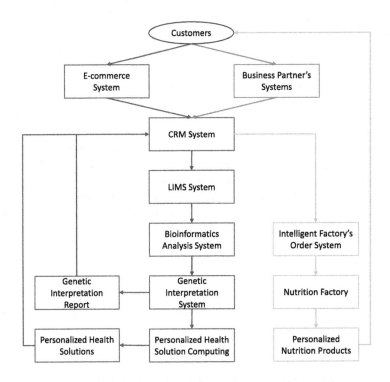

Fig. 1. The business process of personalized nutrition service.

Our customer relation management system, provides both the services of business to customer (B to C) and business to business (B to B).

– To support the business to customer service, the CRM system will communicate with the E-commerce system to receive product order information from customers. Then, the CRM system will notify warehouse operator to send the DNA (saliva) collection kit to customer. When the DNA collection kit has been posted back to the laboratory, the CRM system will synchronize the laboratory operation processes from LIMS and let the customer know the sample status. The CRM system also has an interface to transfer the genetic report from the genetic interpretation system to the e-commerce system.

– To support the business to business service, the CRM can provide services for multiple business partners through APIs or directly. For each business partner, the CRM system provides a customized service to support partner's business.

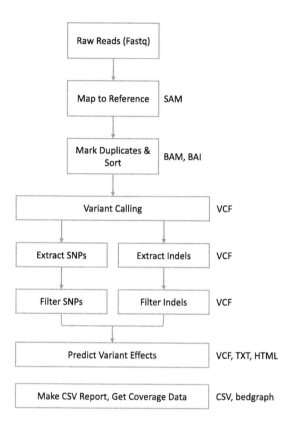

Fig. 2. The next generation sequencing data SNP calling pipeline workflow.

Laboratory Information Management System (LIMS), manages all the gene sequencing laboratory jobs, which include DNA extraction, quality control, DNA sequencing, and etc. DNA sequencing has multiple methods [10], the DNA sequencing-by-synthesis (SBS) technology has four basic steps: library preparation, cluster generation, sequencing, and data analysis. LIMS standardizes the experimental process, schedules experiment tasks, and monitors experiment progress in the laboratory. After laboratory experimental process, the DNA samples will get their sequencing data generated by DNA sequencing equipment such as HiSeq X Ten [11], NovaSeq [12], or iScan System[13], the DNA sequencing data (generally in FASTQ [16] format) will be stored in persistent data storage disks or the network attached storage (NAS) [17] system.

Bioinformatics Analysis System, supports the parallel running of multiple genetic data analysis pipelines to analyze the DNA sequencing data, such as the SNP (Single Nucleotide Polymorphisms) [8] calling analysis pipeline [4] and the DNA insertions and deletions (indels) [5] identifying pipeline can analyze thousands of DNA samples in parallel. The next generation sequencing data SNP calling pipeline workflow is described in Fig. 2 [9]. The SNP calling pipeline applies the Genome Analysis Toolkit 4 (GATK4) [6, 7] to perform variant calling, which includes the steps of map to reference, mark duplicates & sort, variant calling, and etc.

Genetic Interpretation System, interprets the SNPs and Indels based on the SNP calling and Indels identifying result. Genetic interpretation should follow standards and guidelines for the interpretation [18], using the interpretation database such as the Locus-Specific Mutation Databases for Neurodegenerative Brain Diseases [25], the Online Mendelian Inheritance in Man, an Online Catalog of Human Genes and Genetic Disorders (OMIM) [21,22], the AutDB [23], and the highly recognized published scientific papers such as Crider KS, Yang TP et al. [24]. The genetic interpretation should also employ polygenic algorithm model [19,20] to evaluate the impact of different genes on phenotypes, because many phenotypes are associated with multiple genes. Since the bioinformatics analysis can analyze thousands of DNA samples in parallel, therefore, the genetic interpretation system is required to have the ability to interpret thousands of DNA samples in parallel, and generate reports automatically in html or pdf format. At the same time, the genetic interpretation is required to interpret and generate multiple different types of genetic reports such as disease risks, nutrition, safe medication, monogenic hereditary disease, and so on to support different business requirements.

Factory's Order System, accepts the orders for producing customized nutritional products. The product orders are based on the analysis result of different people's genetic interpretation data, diet data, and sports data. The product order describes clearly which kind of product to be produced including the nutritional ingredients to be contained in the product, the nutrient contents of the product and so on. The packing of each product is also customized that, the name of the corresponding customer will be printed on the box of the product. The produced customized nutritional products will be posted to customers respectively from the factory, and the customers will be notified the production and posting status information through the e-commerce system.

4   Customer Relationship Management System Implementation

The CRM system supports both the:

- business to customer service, and
- business to business service.

The CRM connects with the E-commerce system to provide business to customer service, and connects with the business partner's business management systems to provide business to business service.

Additionally, not all the business partners (especially the small business partners such as a private mom and baby store) have their own business management system, therefore, the CRM system opens online accounts for different small business partners. Suppose Kidswant is one of the small business partners, then the CRM will open an online account for Kidswant; through the online CRM account, Kidswant can apply for DNA and nutrition products for sale, monitor Kidswant's customers' DNA testing status and customized nutrition product producing status.

The CRM system also supports sales management with the functions of:

- sales' channels management;
- business partner management;
- salesperson management;
- contract management;
- sales task management;
- sales accounting management;
- product inventory management;
- customer management.

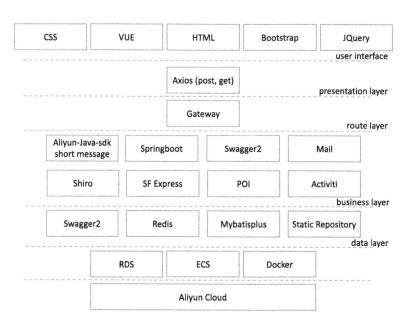

Fig. 3. The technical architecture of CRM system.

Figure 3 demonstrates the technical architecture of the CRM system. The CRM is implemented in Alibaba cloud [26] environment, using elastic compute service (ECS) [28] as system server and relational database service (RDS) [27] as database. Above the computing and storage layer:

- MyBatis-Plus [33] is a persistence database framework used to support for SQL, procedures and mappings, MyBatis-Plus provides enhanced and efficient operations for MyBatis;
- Redis [31] is used to cache the user login session and shopping cart;
- Swagger2 [32] is used to design and document the APIs, so that different layers of the system can communicate through standardized APIs;
- Activiti [39] is a lightweight workflow business management engine providing business process approval service;
- Shiro [38] is a security framework used to provide authentication, authorization, session management, and the other security services;
- SF express service is the API that provided by the express company SF, through which the customer can order express service from home or office online;
- Aliyun Java sdk short message is the API that provided by Aliyun, through which a company can call the API and send short messages to customers;
- Spring cloud [29] is used to host distributed microservices [37], and each microservice is implemented by Springboot [30];
- Spring cloud gateway [34] provides simple and effective way to route to the APIs provided by the business layer such as Activiti, Mail and etc, all of which provide external services through swagger standardized APIs;
- Axios [35] is used to provide Promise based HTTP client for the browser and Vue [36] javascript framework.

The user interface of the CRM is developed with Vue, BootStrap, JQuery, HTML and CSS, and the user interface can adjust to different equipment (mobile phones, pads, and computers).

Figure 4 describes the system architecture of the CRM system, which provides primarily the business service and the report service respectively:

- The business service focuses more on the CRM business part, such as the sales management, customized nutritional product orders. The CRM B to C business service primarily provides services, such as customized nutritional product order process to customers, sales management, customer management, business partner management to sales and product managers. The CRM B to B business service opens APIs to connect with business partner's business system to provide services, such as accept the customized nutritional product order from business partner, place order to the factory to produce the customized product, tell the posting status of the customized product.
- The report service focuses more on the genetic testing report and the corresponding nutritional solution report part. The CRM B to C report service transfers the genetic testing reports and the corresponding nutritional solution reports to E-commerce system and then to customers. The B to B

report service provides genetic testing reports and the corresponding nutritional solution reports to business partner's business systems.

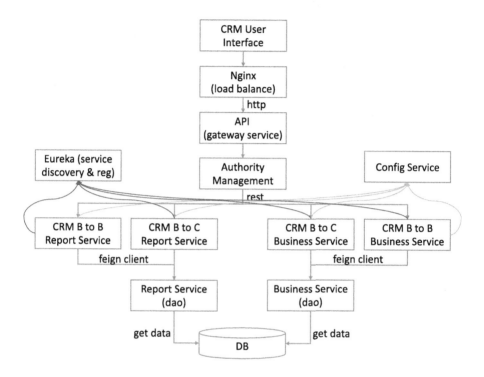

Fig. 4. The system architecture of CRM system.

All the services (such as CRM B to C business service) mentioned above are deployed as microservices which should be registered in Eureka (service discovery & register) so that to be discovered and used through port and IP address. Config service provides a properties configuration place for microservices-side and client-side across the whole system environments. Feign is used to write java http clients to exchange data. Nginx is in charge of the load balance service. The API (gateway service) distributes the business requests to different microservices. The Authority Management module makes sure the data access is authorized and secured.

The CRM system has been implemented and delivered online providing personalized nutrition services efficiently and successfully. For instance, to now the maximum one-day order number is 1008, under the management of the CRM, the nutrition factory has produced the 1008 personalized nutrition products and posted the products to customers in different areas in one day successfully.

5   Conclusions

People's nutrition demands differs from individual to individual due to the differences of DNA and lifestyle, therefore, in this paper, we first introduce the concept of personalized nutrition, then we describe the personalized nutrition service business process based on nutrigenomics, nutrigenetics and nutrition science. Finally, we give the technical solution and deployment of a customer relationship management system to support the personalized nutrition service.

The CRM system can provide both business to customer and business to business services, connecting with the customers, genetic testing laboratory, and nutrition factory to produce personalized nutrition products efficiently. The CRM system has been working online successfully and has provided services for tens hundreds of thousands of customers.

Concerning future work, the CRM will further provide more functions including monthly sales data statistics, personalized nutrition products consumption status forecast, customer data mining and etc.

Acknowledgment. This work was partially supported by the Science Foundation of Beijing Language and Culture University (supported by "the Fundamental Research Funds for the Central Universities") (20YJ040007, 19YJ040010, 17YJ0302).

References

1. Sales, N.M.R., Pelegrini, P.B., Goersch, M.C.: Nutrigenomics: definitions and advances of this new science. J. Nutr. Metab. **2014**, 202759 (2014)
2. Simopoulos, A.P.: The impact of the Bellagio report on healthy agriculture, healthy nutrition, healthy people: scientific and policy aspects and the international network of centers for genetics, nutrition and fitness for health. J. Nutrigenet Nutrigenomics **7**(4–6), 191–211 (2015)
3. Fenech, M., et al.: Nutrigenetics and nutrigenomics: viewpoints on the current status and applications in nutrition research and practice. J. Nutrigenet Nutrigenomics **4**(2), 69–89 (2011)
4. Nielsen, R., Paul, J.S., Albrechtsen, A., Song, Y.S.: Genotype and SNP calling from next-generation sequencing data. Nat. Rev. Genet. **12**(6), 443–451 (2011)
5. Mullaney, J.M., Mills, R.E., Pittard, W.S., Devine, S.E.: Small insertions and deletions (INDELs) in human genomes. Hum. Mol. Genet. **19**(R2), R131–R136 (2010)
6. McKenna, A., et al.: The genome analysis toolkit: a MapReduce framework for analyzing next-generation DNA sequencing data. Genome Res. **20**(9), 1297–1303 (2010)
7. Genome Analysis Toolkit. https://gatk.broadinstitute.org/. Accessed 2 May 2020
8. U.S. National Library of Health: What are single nucleotide polymorphisms (SNPs)? https://ghr.nlm.nih.gov/primer/genomicresearch/snp. Accessed 2 May 2020
9. Khalfan, M.: Variant Calling Pipeline using GATK4. https://gencore.bio.nyu.edu/variant-calling-pipeline-gatk4/. Accessed 2 May 2020
10. Illumina: DNA Sequencing Methods Collection. https://www.illumina.com/content/dam/illumina-marketing/documents/products/research_reviews/dna-sequencing-methods-review-web.pdf. Accessed 2 May 2020

11. HiSeq X Ten Sequencing System. https://www.illumina.com/systems/sequencing-platforms/hiseq-x.html. Accessed 2 May 2020
12. NovaSeq Sequencing System. https://www.illumina.com/systems/sequencing-platforms/novaseq.html. Accessed 2 May 2020
13. iScan System - Array scanner for extensive applications. https://www.illumina.com/systems/array-scanners/iscan.html. Accessed 2 May 2020
14. Salesforce. https://www.salesforce.com/. Accessed 2 May 2020
15. Oracle CRM. https://www.oracle.com/crmondemand/. Accessed 2 May 2020
16. Cock, P.J., Fields, C.J., Goto, N., Heuer, M.L., Rice, P.M.: The Sanger FASTQ file format for sequences with quality scores, and the Solexa/Illumina FASTQ variants. Nucleic Acids Res. **38**(6), 1767–1771 (2010)
17. Nagle, D.F., Ganger, G.R., Butler, J., Goodson, G., Sabol, C.: Network support for network-attached storage. In: Proceedings of Hot Interconnects, Stanford University, Stanford, California, USA, August 1999
18. Richards, S., et al.: Standards and guidelines for the interpretation of sequence variants: a joint consensus recommendation of the American College of Medical Genetics and Genomics and the Association for Molecular Pathology. Genet. Med. **17**(5), 405–423 (2015)
19. Lee, J.J., Wedow, R., Okbay, A., et al.: Gene discovery and polygenic prediction from a genome-wide association study of educational attainment in 1.1 million individuals. Nat. Genet. **50**, 1112–1121 (2018)
20. Sanchez-Roige, S., et al.: Genome-wide association studies of impulsive personality traits (BIS-11 and UPPS-P) and drug experimentation in up to 22,861 adult research participants identify loci in the CACNA1I and CADM2 genes. J. Neurosci. **39**(13), 2562–2572 (2019)
21. Hamosh, A., Scott, A.F., Amberger, J.S., Bocchini, C.A., McKusick, V.A.: Online mendelian inheritance in man (OMIM), a knowledgebase of human genes and genetic disorders. Nucleic Acids Res. **33**(Database issue), D514–D517 (2005)
22. OMIM - Online Mendelian Inheritance in Man, an Online Catalog of Human Genes and Genetic Disorders. https://www.omim.org/. Accessed 2 May 2020
23. Pereanu, W., et al.: AutDB: a platform to decode the genetic architecture of autism. Nucleic Acids Res. **46**(D1), D1049–D1054 (2018)
24. Crider, K.S., Yang, T.P., Berry, R.J., Bailey, L.B.: Folate and DNA methylation: a review of molecular mechanisms and the evidence for folate's role. Adv Nutr. **3**(1), 21–38 (2012)
25. Cruts, M., Theuns, J., Van Broeckhoven, C.: Locus-specific mutation databases for neurodegenerative brain diseases. Hum. Mutat. **33**(9), 1340–1344 (2012)
26. Alibaba Cloud. https://www.alibabacloud.com/. Accessed 3 May 2020
27. ApsaraDB RDS for MySQL. https://www.alibabacloud.com/product/apsaradb-for-rds-mysql. Accessed 3 May 2020
28. Elastic Compute Service. https://www.alibabacloud.com/product/ecs. Accessed 3 May 2020
29. Spring Cloud. https://spring.io/projects/spring-cloud. Accessed 2 May 2020
30. Spring Boot. https://spring.io/projects/spring-boot/. Accessed 2 May 2020
31. Redis. https://redis.io/. Accessed 3 May 2020
32. Swagger. https://swagger.io/. Accessed 3 May 2020
33. MyBatis-Plus. https://mybatis.plus/en/. Accessed 3 May 2020
34. Spring Cloud Gateway. https://spring.io/projects/spring-cloud-gateway. Accessed 3 May 2020
35. Axios. https://github.com/axios/axios. Accessed 3 May 2020

36. Vue - JavaScript Framework. https://vuejs.org/. Accessed 3 May 2020
37. Francesco, P.D., Malavolta, I., Lago, P.: Research on architecting microservices: trends, focus, and potential for industrial adoption. In: IEEE International Conference on Software Architecture (ICSA), Gothenburg, pp. 21–30 (2017)
38. Apache Shiro. http://shiro.apache.org/. Accessed 3 May 2020
39. Activiti. https://www.activiti.org/. Accessed 3 May 2020

ABDA: An Automated Behavioral Disorder Assessment Framework

Rahma Bouaziz[1,2(✉)], Gaida AL-Ahmadi[1], Anhar AL-Lehebi[1],
Walaa AL-Sehil[1], and Shoog AL-Jumadii[1]

[1] Computer Science Department, Taibah University, Medina, Saudi Arabia
rkammoun@taibahu.edu.sa,
smilyface1417@hotmail.com, anhar1417@yahoo.com,
Walaa-hssh@hotmail.com, Shoogy705@gmail.com
[2] Redcad, University of Sfax, Sfax, Tunisia

Abstract. In this paper, we investigate the problem of manual behavioral disorder assessments completion for the purposes of determining the early warning signs for patients with behavioral disorder symptoms. This study resides in the application domain of Autism Spectrum Disorder (ASD) as a motivating example. With the automation of behavioral disorder assessment, we seek to decrease the amount of time required for each diagnostic test and therefore increase the efficiency of diagnostic and number of diagnosed patient. We have evaluated our system with sufficient number of diagnostic tests and found that our system can perform almost quick and accurate Autism Spectrum Disorder diagnostic. In this work, we present the proposed framework and take advantages of the automation of the proposed solution in order to facilitate diagnostics.

Keywords: Behavioral disorder · Diagnostic tests · Automation · Assessment tool

1 Introduction

In this paper, we approach the problem of manual diagnoses intellectual and developmental children's disabilities to determine children with autistic disorder. This approach is based in particular on the collection of subjective data by means of a questionnaire as Gilliam Autism Rating Scale [1].

In the electronic world of today, we are moving towards fast adaptation of technology in every field of life including healthcare, financial, transportation and communication. This adaptation has allowed us to move from registers to computers and from offline systems to real time systems. Electronic data is not only timely and precise, it is also easy to store and access [2]. In healthcare field and especially Behavioral Disorder diagnostics, such adaptation is required to diagnoses intellectual and developmental disabilities [3]. The problem studied is a real-life problem occurring at the children department at Al Amal Mental Health center in AL Madinah Al Mounawara. Psychologists perform those assessments manually based on printed documents. The actual manual method is time consuming because they need special math calculations

© Springer Nature Switzerland AG 2020
O. Gervasi et al. (Eds.): ICCSA 2020, LNCS 12254, pp. 1003–1012, 2020.
https://doi.org/10.1007/978-3-030-58817-5_71

to get the result, which is difficult to process due to the lack of automated process tools for such type of documents. Moreover, it may sometimes lead to some error when calculating results. These behavioral tests are mostly proposed as printed documents and are normally processed by hand by psychologist. Manual assessments completion is extremely time-consuming. The time required to complete an assessment can range anywhere from one hour to two hour per survey, per child. The use of tests in diagnosing psychiatric diseases is an effective technique that was able to withstand the test of time. Gilliam Autism Rating Scale (GARE) aims to determine individuals with autistic disorder from 3 to 22 years. It can be used either by regular individuals at home, school environment or by professionals [5] or as Asperger Syndrome Test [4].

Automatically estimate person disabilities based on predefined standard scales can overcome those limitations [6]. The prevention of behavioral disorders requires an ergonomic approach, which aims to a quick diagnostic. In our proposed system, a psychologist can conduct a diagnostic test for a particular patient (child) electronically.

This automatization will save an immense amount of time. After accounting for many assessments completed by many psychologists, the number of diagnosis children will be improved. By decreasing the amount of time required to complete these assessments through eliminating the need to re-enter basic information each time, more assessments can be completed, and more children can be diagnosed. Our proposed system process the electronic document for answer evaluation. In the evaluation process, answers are detected and counted, for a result generation; the output of the diagnostic test will be shown as a percentage number and as average.

The organization of the paper is summarized as follows: Sect. 2 represents a brief review of related work. In Sect. 3, we gave a detail sketch of the computation framework of our proposed approach. Experimental results are presented in Sect. 4. In Sect. 3.2, we will present an evaluation study. Finally, Sect. 6 conclude this work and present future research directions.

2 Related Works

There are several applications, which are used to automate BDA. Those systems are not based on standard scale but we have found no such system, which automate DBA from manual pages to statistical results. In [7] authors proposes to automate the collection of quality of life data and a comparison of paper and computer touch screen questionnaires. This comparison was made between the paper test and the electronic test. The electronic tests got high scores and results. The data was better confidentially, were healthier and did not include spelling errors.

In [8] authors propose an automated system to handle and analyze surveys and convert them into electronic documents. The main advantage of the proposed approach was the high accuracy and the rapid analysis of documents. In [9], electronic surveys were used instead of manual surveys and making comparisons between them. It was concluded that transfer helps in efficient collection of the market by reducing time. The Asperger's Syndrome Test described in [10] is an application for self-diagnosis that can be used by anyone who suspects they may have Asperger's Syndrome. The test gives a standard of autistic properties in grownups. On the other hand, the Autism-Spectrum Quotient (AQ) [11] is a questionnaire designed by Baron Cohen to assess the attributes of the autism spectrum in mentally qualified adults in both the general population and the community and is designed to evaluate 5 different areas of performance: social skills, attention transfer, and attention to detail, communication and imagination.

In another work, [12] authors propose a tool named Q-global. The proposed tool is a web-based system for psychological assessment management. It provide above 50 assessments in different area of performances. It generate many sub-accounts, which is helpful in departments and examiners management. In addition, it Create comprehensive reports from the assessment records.

Based on the same principle as the previous work, PARiConnect [13] is an online assessment management platform that provides standardized assessments in deferent categories. It provide assigning assessment and generating reports following many assessments categories.

In [14] authors investigate how Machine Learning (ML) has been introduced into the medical field as a means to provide diagnostic tools capable of enhancing accuracy and precision while minimizing laborious tasks that require human intervention.

Regarding personality analysis, [15] propose a tool named Personality Match that conducts a free test of the personality by asking questions to the user to discover the type of personality and can invite friends to take this test.

Personality Test presented in [16] is another interesting automated survey that propose many questions to determine the type of personality once you have completed the test. Results obtained after the competition if the survey were very accurate.

Our research intends to propose an efficient framework in Arabic language to automate manual assessments of behavioral disorder by allowing a psychologist to conduct a diagnostic test for a particular patient electronically. Our proposed system estimate automatically patient disabilities based on predefined standard scales. This system makes diagnoses intellectual and developmental disabilities fast, easy and more accuracy and it may overcome the limitations of the existing manual diagnostics.

3   System Architecture and Design

The aim of this work is to develop an automated diagnostic test framework that involves carrying out the diagnostic test and producing diagnostic results. Using this framework diagnostic assessment can be done easily, quickly and accurately.

The proposed Automated Behavioral Disorder Assessment (ABDA) framework requires a sequential workflow of serval components. The combination of the components of the system constructs the system architecture (see Fig. 1).

In a first stage, data is received from the system. Once the data is received, it is associated with the appropriate process it belongs to. This is done by extracting the patient ID field from the data block. Once data is associated with the correct patient, the appropriate test that will be generated populated and associated with each process data block. Weights or predefined standard scales, used from the weighting schema proposed in this model are associated to different individual steps of processes, this aims to estimate automatically patient disabilities. Especially for each diagnostic test dimension. Then the data is transmitted to the evaluation module to generate results and reports. The flowchart of activities performed in this model is shown in Fig. 1.

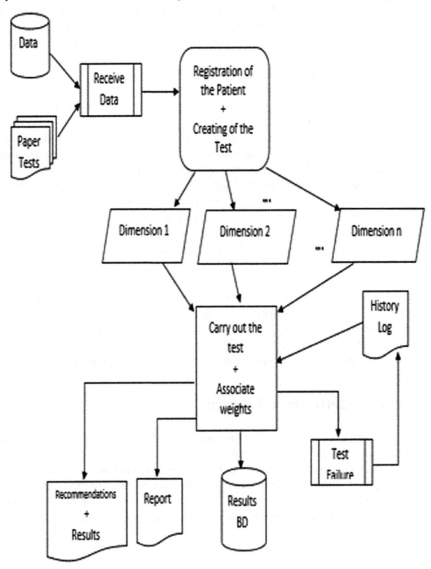

Fig. 1. Overall architecture of the automated BDA framework

3.1   Creating ABDA Test Module

At the beginning of the session, psychologist needs to create a Behavioral Disorder Assessment. So, it creates a unique identifier for a patient and store the test and dimension of each one into the corresponding tables in database tables. Figure 2 Shows the algorithm for dimension selection.

Algorithm: Select Dimension
Input: Patient Registration
1. **Begin**
2. **For** each Patient **do**
3. Count the number of dimensions the user had chosen
4. Insert the dimensions the user chosen according to their number
5. Compare the selection with stored data in data base
6. **If** section match **do**
7. display the dimension selection
8. **Else** return error :
9. **End**

Fig. 2. Algorithm of selecting dimesion

3.2   Answer Evaluation and Weight Association Module

Answers given by the psychologiste that matches with the option stored with the database are counted in this phase. This count and evaluation will be used to generate results. The used algorithm todo that is given in Fig. 3.

Algorithm: Calculate Autism Coefficient

Input: Psychologist Test answers

1. **Begin**
2. **Table** is a predefined standard table used to convert the total sum to an equivalent autism coefficient value depending on the number of dimension the user had chosen
3. Use Counter
4. Calculate total sum of each dimension
5. Generate autism coefficient
6. Call autismMeaning function giving autism coefficient as parameter
7. **End**

Fig. 3. Algorithm of calculating autism coefficient

The algorithm presented in Fig. 4 will generate the result of the test for the diagnostic patient.

Algorithm: autismMeaning

Input: autism coefficient

```
 7.  Begin
 8.  If coefficient >131 do
 9.  Print autism coefficient is " very high "
10.  Else if 121 <= coefficient <= 130 do
11.  Print autism coefficient is " high "
12.  Else if 111 <= coefficient <= 120 do
13.  Print autism coefficient is " above average "
14.  Else if  90 <= coefficient <= 110 do
15.  Print autism coefficient is " average "
16.  Else if 80 <= coefficient <= 89 do
17.  Print autism coefficient is " below average "
18.  Else if 70 <= coefficient <= 79 do
19.  Print autism coefficient is " low "
20.  Else if  coefficient <= 69 do
21.  Print autism coefficient is " very low "
22.  End
```

Fig. 4. Algorithm to give meaning for the autism coefficient

All algorithms described above that we used in our proposed framework are used for simplicity of coding and calculations and for acquiring a higher accuracy of the system. The flowchart of activities performed to generate a report and diagnostic for patient are shown in Fig. 5.

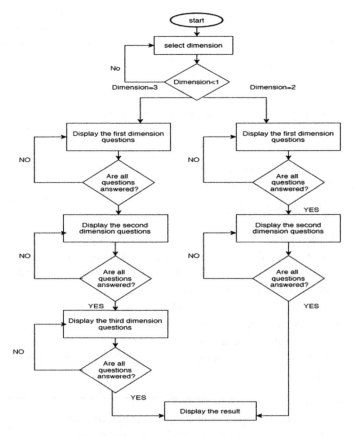

Fig. 5. Flowchart of the proposed system

4 Implementations and Experiments

In this section, we have provided the implementation procedure with necessary explanation that clearly describe the outcome of the system. We have also provided the experimental setup of our developed system.

The proposed framework has been developed with Visual studio was chosen using C# as a tool to achieve the required goals.

At the beginning of proposed system the psychologist provide patient's file number and then display the patient's information if the patient is already registered. In this interface, we show that if the patient is not registered in the system, the doctor will register a new patient as shown in Fig. 6.

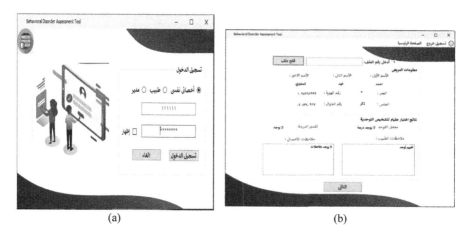

(a)   (b)

Fig. 6. (a) Start the BDA, (b) Display patient information

Here and in order to carry out the diagnostic test, the psychologist selects the test that he wants to perform on the patient. Here as an example the user choose Gilliam test. As we mentioned earlier that we convert the paper Gilliam test into an electronic test here showing the dimensions used in the Gilliam test the psychologist determines the dimensions that he wants to perform on the patient and then starts the test Fig. 7 (a).

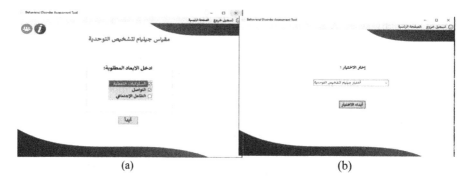

(a)   (b)

Fig. 7. (a) Perform the test for a patient. (b) Choose Gilliam test

In this step, after selecting the appropriate dimensions, the dimensions questions are presented to the psychologist and answers the appropriate way that suits the patient's condition (see Fig. 8.a). In this step, after the psychological specialist finishes answering all the dimensional questions, the test result will appear for the psychological specialist, and the psychologist can save the result or not to save it and return the home page and he can repeat the test for the patient. As shown by Fig. 8.b.

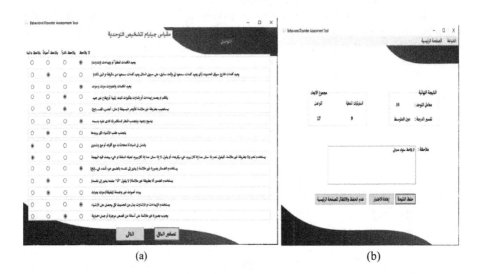

(a)   (b)

Fig. 8.   (a) List of dimensions questions. (b) Generate test result

5   Empirical Result and Discussion

In order to validate the proposed framework, we compare results proposed by the ABDA developed tool and the actual approach based on a manual performing and calculation of Guillum Test as example of behavior disorder Assessment to diagnose children Autism. Both methods use the same data as input. The comparison will be based on: 1) Number of patient to be diagnostic, 2) The paper waste generated by those manual tests and 3) The time required to determine the result and recommendation for a patient. Actually an example trial run consisting of twenty manual survey completions and twenty automated survey completions.

The time required is taken to be the mean of: firstly, the times required fill out the test and secondly, the time required to calculate the result, the recommendation and generate report to print. This computation time represent a very important parameter in a diagnostic process. Actually, it tacks from one to two hours using a manual method and also the manual calculation can lead to diagnostic errors. Using ABDA tool the process is instantly done. The research resulted in a large decrease in the amount of time required to complete each behavioral disorder Assessment. For the sample used of Gillum Test for Autism diagnostic used, the average amount of time required to complete the test was reduced. This trend is predicted to continue for all other behavior disorder tests, perhaps even reducing the percentage of time required by even more. The proposed technique save at least 90% of the time spent manually and reduces the number of steps by more than 50%.

In addition, the number of patient diagnostic per day is very important because it facilitate and anticipate treatment of the behavior disorder of the child. As the time required for each patient decreased the number of patient diagnoses per day decreased also and the total number of patient decrease. In the other hand, paper waste is a crucial point because it need storage strategies to facilitate patient record searching and finding. Using the proposed method.

6   Conclusion and Future Work

In this paper, we study the problem of manual completion of printed test documents for the aim of diagnoses the intellectual and developmental disabilities for patients. In many cases, child's behaviors are assessed manually using paper tests, which is costly in time, effort and sometimes lead to errors. These motivated us to develop a computational methodology for translating well-known BD tests into automated ones. The proposition could bridge domains like psychology and social science with computer science. Our work is to develop an automated diagnostic framework that completes tests and generates diagnostic results that will save time, get more accurate results and easily used and perform data analysis to show statistics. In the proposed system, we used documents with multiple-choice questions (MCQ) for Gillum Test as sample.

In the future, the proposed automation process can be improved in several ways. Currently, the phycologist can carry out one BDA has to begin the process themselves and click a button to automatically complete the test. This could be improved with further automation. The availability of tests' results to evaluate the program performance was a limitation because the limited number of patients with the time passing, more results will made available for estimation. Due to lake of time many other manual tests automation is left to the future. In addition, it could be more interesting if our future work also contains deeper data analysis and verity of statistics. These improvements would further increase the gains of automating surveys versus manual completion.

References

1. Robinson, J.: Gilliam Autism Rating Scale (GARS). In: Volkmar, F.R. (ed.) Encyclopedia of Autism Spectrum Disorders. Springer, New York (2013). https://doi.org/10.1007/978-1-4419-1698-3_879
2. Zahid, A.: Towards a continuous process auditing framework (Case study in Healthcare Auditing and Decision Support - Infection Regime Control Survey). Electronic Theses and Dissertations, University of Windsor (2012)
3. Sheibner, H.J., Spengler, S., Kanske, P., et al.: Behavioral assessment of mindfulness difficulties in borderline personality disorder. Mindfulness 7, 1316–1326 (2016)
4. Velikova, G., et al.: Automated collection of quality-of-life data: a comparison of paper and computer touch-screen questionnaires. J. Clin. Oncol. 17(3), 998 (1999)

5. Scott, F., Baron-Cohen, S., Bolton, P., Brayne, C.: The CAST (Childhood Asperger Syndrome Test): preliminary development of a UK screen for mainstream primary-school age children. Autism **6**(1), 9–31 (2002)
6. Brito, G.N., Pinto, R.C., Lins, M.F.: A behavioral assessment scale for attention deficit disorder in brazilian children based on DSM-IIIR criteria. J. Abnorm. Child Psychol. **23**(4), 509–520 (1995). https://doi.org/10.1007/BF01447211
7. Karren, B.C.: A test review: Gilliam, J.E. (2014). Gilliam Autism rating scale–third edition (GARS-3). J. Psychoeduc. Assess. **34**, 342–356 (2016)
8. Yasmin, F., Hossain, S.M.M., Arefin, M.S.: APSD: a framework for automated processing of survey documents. In: 2017 International Conference on Electrical, Computer and Communication Engineering (ECCE), pp. 411–416 (2017)
9. Davis, Z., Brill, C., Siddiqui, H., Olmsted, A.: Automating e-Surveys. In: 2016 International Conference on Information Society (i-Society), pp. 103–104 (2016)
10. https://apps.apple.com/us/app/aspergers-test-determine-your-autism-spectrum-quotient/id684261444
11. Baron Cohen. https://psychology-tools.com/test/autism-spectrum-quoient
12. Q-global tool. https://qglobal.pearsonclinical.com
13. Victor, E., Aghajan, Z.M., Sewart, A.R., Christian, R.: Detecting depression using a framework combining deep multimodal neural networks with a purpose-built automated evaluation. Psychol. Assess. **31**(8), 1019–1027 (2019)
14. https://www.pariconnect.com
15. https://apps.apple.com/sa/app/personalitymatch/id1098507017
16. https://play.google.com/store/apps/details?id=com.my.typepersonality

Detection of Obstacle Features Using Neural Networks with Attention in the Task of Autonomous Navigation of Mobile Robots

Kirill Sviatov[1]([✉]) [iD], Alexander Miheev[1] [iD], Sergey Sukhov[2],
Yuriy Lapshov[1] [iD], and Stefan Rapp[3]

[1] Ulyanovsk State Technical University, Ulyanovsk, Russia
{k.svyatov,y.lapshov}@ulstu.ru, a.miheev@simcase.ru
[2] Ulyanovsk Branch of the Institute of Radio Engineering and Electronics,
V. A. Kotelnikov of Russian Academy of Science, Moscow, Russia
s_sukhov@hotmail.com
[3] Darmstadt University of Applied Sciences, Darmstadt, Germany
stefan.rapp@h-da.de

Abstract. This article describes the design process of a software package for image recognition of a mobile robot camera using neural networks with attention, which allows to identify the probability of a robot colliding with obstacles standing in its way. A key feature of this software is using a dataset that is prepared without manual labeling of all obstacles and the probability of a collision.

Currently, an important task in mobile robotics is the need to use numerous heuristics and deterministic algorithms in control programs along with neural networks. The use of a single neural network that solves all the tasks of scene analysis (the so-called "end-to-end" solution) is impossible for several reasons: the high complexity of the training samples due to the large parameter space of the environment of the robot and the insufficient formalization of these parameters, as well as the computational complexity of machine learning algorithms, which is critical for mobile robots with strict energy requirements. Therefore, the development of a universal algorithm (end-to-end) is a laborious process.

The article describes a method that allows to use weakly formalized parameters of the robot environment for training convolutional neural networks with attention using the obstacle recognition task. At the same time, weak formalization reduces the time-consuming process of manual data labeling due to automatically generated datasets in the NVIDIA Isaac environment, and the attention mechanism allows increasing the interpretability of the analysis results.

Keywords: Artificial intelligence · Neural networks · Machine learning · Computer vision · Attention networks · Self-driving car

This work was supported by RFBR Grant 18-47-732004 p_MK and 18-07-00989 a

© Springer Nature Switzerland AG 2020
O. Gervasi et al. (Eds.): ICCSA 2020, LNCS 12254, pp. 1013–1026, 2020.
https://doi.org/10.1007/978-3-030-58817-5_72

1 Introduction

One of the first steps in the process of autonomous navigation of a mobile robot is to analyze the external environment in order to build a model. During the analysis, the location of obstacles on the path of the robot is determined. This can be done with deterministic algorithms using specialized, expensive sensors (e.g. lidars). But in the mass use of mobile robotics, it is preferable to use ordinary cheap video cameras. Also, navigation methods based on video cameras allow to use more information about the environment and reduce the integral error when building a map and localizing the robot in space. But in this case, there is no simple way to detect formalized features: dynamic and static obstacles on the robot path, for example, other mobile robots, the road itself, or the walls.

In this paper, we consider the solution of three tasks for identifying obstacles on the way of a mobile robot:

1. Development of a software tool for generating a special dataset: a method for generating synthetic data for training a neural network for recognizing obstacles at robot camera image in an NVIDIA Isaac environment.
2. Recognition of weakly formalized features of a scene. A weakly formalized feature is understood as a binary characteristic indicating the danger of collision with an obstacle on the current way of the robot or the absence of such a danger. In this case, a fully formalized attribute would contain complete information about obstacles: their location in the frame, their size, shape, and class of the object. The same object may be an obstacle if it is located on the way of the robot, or it may not be. In addition to the fact of the presence of an object, it is necessary to analyze its position relative to the robot and other characteristics. Analysis criteria can contain dynamic properties of objects, which affects the time and cost of labeling the training dataset in the case of using neural networks or the development of heuristic algorithms. Only static objects are considered in this article, moving objects will be considered in following papers. This paper describes an approach in which a weakly formalized binary feature is used as the target feature for the training sample, indicating whether there is an obstacle for the robot or not: the neural network tries to automatically search for patterns in the complex features of scene objects, in order to determine the presence of an obstacle. This will significantly reduce the cost of labeling complex data.
3. Neural network unsupervised training for localization of obstacles. It is shown that a convolutional neural network with "attention" can train to localize obstacles in a camera frame more accurately than a regular convolutional network. It also allows to localize an object in a camera frame without additional cost for labeling the dataset compared to the classification task. Moreover, the resulting model can be used to interpret the results of the neural network, i.e. to clarify the reasons for its decisions, which is extremely important in the tasks of autonomous control of mobile robots, when decisions are made related to the safety of people.

2 Literature Review

Despite the success of using neural networks in image processing, they usually perform only certain processing steps: object detection, localization in the image, and class prediction. It is also possible to determine all available objects in the image for subsequent analysis, for example, a geometric assessment of the relative position of objects, their size, and shape. From this a decision is made on the parameters of the control actions to achieve the robot's goals.

Recently, a large number of models and approaches have been developed for detecting objects in images. They result in a segmentation with a multi-channel mask at the output [1, 2] or a detection bounding rectangles. A number of modifications of these methods for quality and speed [3–5] have been reported.

Navigation of the robot is performed dynamically because the state of the robot and the environment is constantly changing. Therefore, the same objects may be obstacles, or they may not be. It depends on the position of this object. Generally, it is better to detect obstacles earlier. This effect is similar to the rewards in Reinforcement Learning. Within this type of training, there are several methods for solving the problem of training a model with rewards or predicting the occurrence of an obstacle. In some approaches, neural networks perform the entire cycle of scene analysis and decision making [6–9]. But this approach is not so popular due to the low interpretability of the results of the network, which is expressed in the fact that a person does not understand the reasons for decisions. In addition, the use of Reinforcement Learning is a difficult task to implement with a number of disadvantages (instability, long training, etc.). Therefore, in this paper, the main focus is on simple "end-to-end" approaches that are able to solve the problem.

The attention mechanism in neural networks [10] is more popular now among researchers [11], because it allows us to interpret the results of the models and perform selection according to positions of objects in feature maps. Despite the fact that the technology appeared only several years ago, the range of application is very wide [12].

3 Offered Approach

The work [17] describes the problem of recognizing the relationship between objects in the image. The authors note that the variability of relations between objects is too large, therefore it is very difficult to create a one-hot sample to solve a similar problem. They offer an approach based on the search for patterns in textual descriptions of images. Such a network output can be considered weakly formalized, because human speech also has great variability, although textual descriptions of images are much easier to find. The authors use a recursive network that iteratively analyzes objects in the scene and words in the text. However, to solve such a complex problem, the authors use the preliminary extraction of features from the image, namely, they select objects and spatial information between them. We solve a simpler problem and offer a weakly formalized end-to-end approach.

The paper [18], approaches to the analysis of scenes by mobile robots are considered in detail. These approaches imply a strong formalization of target labels. Objects are first recognized in the scene or the scene is classified (corridor, kitchen, bedroom, etc.). On the other hand, for the navigation task, it is necessary to distinguish one corridor from another for which visual signs are extracted from the images, for example, from hidden layers of the network, which allows to build a graph of the robot's movement. And although the vector of hidden signs is not interpretable and understandable for humans, the distance metric has been successfully used in the space of such vectors.

In the approach described in this paper, the detection of obstacles during movement of the robot can be performed discretely: at each iteration of the program control cycle, the robot detects the state around itself by an analysis of video camera frames and makes a small movement. In this case, the robot always moves co-directionally with the camera. Therefore, objects located in the center of the frame and close to the robot can be recognized as obstacles.

But these criteria for determining the obstacles are known only to the developers. The trained neural network model does not know these rules and assumptions and receives only binary labels "0" or "1" characterizing the absence or presence of an obstacle. The task of a neural network is to predict the presence of an obstacle taking into account its position, size, type of object, and all possible patterns that it can find in the dataset.

To solve the problem, it is necessary to select a random frame from the camera of the robot and a binary mask of the presence of an obstacle for the following cycles of the robot control program. Creating a suitable dataset is one of the main tasks in this research. For classification and segmentation, there are many open data sets, but there is, to the knowledge of the authors, no dataset for obstacle detection as described before. As part of the study, it was decided to create a synthetic dataset using the NVIDIA Issac robotic platform and the built-in simulation tools. Thus, the image from the robot's camera was replaced with a rendering of the virtual 3D world with photorealistic quality. Some papers show that the modern level of game graphics is a way to replace the real-world images for creating training samples [13].

But standard tools are not able to determine the likelihood of a risk of a movement for the robot, therefore, a software component was implemented for automatically labeling the sample based on segmentation masks for the scene, also obtained from the NVIDIA Isaac platform.

Two neural networks were trained in this research: a convolutional network with VGG architecture and a convolutional network with visual attention without a recurrent block in the style of [14].

Structure of the convolutional network (output of the model.summary() method):

```
Layer (type)                 Output Shape              Param #
=================================================================
input_1 (InputLayer)         [(None, 240, 420, 3)]     0

conv2d (Conv2D)              (None, 238, 418, 16)      448

max_pooling2d (MaxPooling2D) (None, 119, 209, 16)      0

conv2d_2 (Conv2D)            (None, 117, 207, 32)      4640

max_pooling2d_1 (MaxPooling2 (None, 58, 103, 32)       0

conv2d_4 (Conv2D)            (None, 56, 101, 32)       9248

max_pooling2d_2 (MaxPooling2 (None, 28, 50, 32)        0

conv2d_5 (Conv2D)            (None, 26, 48, 64)        18496

flatten (Flatten)            (None, 79872)             0

dense (Dense)                (None, 64)                5111872

dense_1 (Dense)              (None, 2)                 130
=================================================================
Total params: 5,144,834
Trainable params: 5,144,834
Non-trainable params: 0
```

Structure of the convolutional network with attention (output of the model.summary() method):

Layer (type)	Output Shape	Param #
input_1 (InputLayer)	[(None, 240, 420, 3)]	0
conv2d (Conv2D)	(None, 238, 418,32)	896
conv2d_1 (Conv2D)	(None, 236, 416, 32)	9248
max_pooling2d (MaxPooling2D)	(None, 118, 208, 32)	0
conv2d_2 (Conv2D)	(None, 116, 206, 64)	18496
conv2d_3 (Conv2D)	(None, 114, 204,64)	36928
max_pooling2d_1 (MaxPooling2	(None, 57, 102, 64)	0
conv2d_4 (Conv2D)	(None, 55, 100, 64)	36928
reshape (Reshape)	(None, 5500, 64)	0
lambda (Lambda)	(None, 5500, 64)	0
tf_op_layer_Sum_1 (TensorFlo	[(None, 5500)]	0
flatten (Flatten)	(None, 5500)	0
dense (Dense)	(None, 64)	352064
dense_1 (Dense)	(None, 2)	130

```
Total params: 454,690
Trainable params: 454,690
Non-trainable params: 0
```

4   Generation of the Dataset

To generate a training dataset, it was decided to use the NVIDIA Isaac robotics platform. The NVIDIA Isaac Developer Toolkit (SDK) contains software tools, libraries, GPU algorithms, and components designed to accelerate the development of software components for robots. NVIDIA Isaac can also be used to develop AI solutions optimized for deployment on the NVIDIA Jetson platform.

Other robotic frameworks such as V-Rep, ROS (with the Gazebo simulation environment) have similar functionality to NVIDIA Isaac, but the advantage of the Isaac SDK compared to them is the use of the Unity 3D framework for photorealistic simulation of the environment and robots (ISAAC SIM), as well as a rich set of libraries for solving problems of autonomous control, and the availability of pre-trained neural networks. Also, it contains software integrated with the Cuda SDK for calculating motion parameters and scene analysis. Due to this, a significant acceleration of such calculations can be realized.

The task of generating the training dataset was formulated as follows: it is necessary to develop a software component for generating pairs of images in a simulation environment: a picture frame from a color camera and an image with color semantic segmentation, in which each pixel of the segmentation mask is mapping a number from 1 to 5 into the value of the RGB tuple (red, green, blue), corresponding to one of five classes:

- Free space for movement (floor)
- Laneline
- Obstacle
- Wall
- Beam

To accomplish this task, the Isaac Sim environment used the "Medium Warehouse" scene and a standard script that allows us to randomly change the position of the camera, perform "teleportation" (changing the position, roll, pitch, yaw). In addition, a segmentation neural network with the UNet architecture (standard Isaac SDK component) was used.

Before launching the "teleportation" commands, it is necessary to launch the Unity 3D environment from the simulator directory. The following parameters of teleportation and camera rotation where use: roll 180 degrees, pitch 68.5 degrees, yaw 90 degrees, the frequency of "teleportation" 30 Hz.

After executing the commands, a window opens with a visualization of the storage scene (Fig. 1).

Fig. 1. Visualization of the scene (Medium Warehouse)

When the application (Codelet) is launched in the Isaac SDK environment, the WebSight server (standard visualization application) is launched on port 3000. It allows to display graphs, 2D and 3D scenes, the current state of the application (active nodes and connections), and also to update the configuration. When the "freespacednn" application is launched, images from the camera are displayed in the WebSight environment, as well as the result of the segmentation network with the UNet architecture (network model definition file - packages/freespace_dnn/apps/freespace_dnn_training_models.py).

Camera images and the results of the segmentation network are displayed in the WebSight environment through the channels "ColorCameraViewer/Color" and "Segmentation".

The target training sample should store files with the same names in the "image" and "seg" folders for the corresponding image and segmentation map. To save the camera image and the result of the segmentation network into files, it is necessary to develop an application in the Isaac SDK environment, using the capabilities of this platform.

The developed application consists of four files:

- __init__.py - service file required to run the software package, it may be empty
- BUILD - build file for the Bazel application, for compilation and launching of the software system.
- seg_dataset.app.json - application configuration file, designed in accordance with the requirements of the Isaac SDK.
- seg-dataset.py - application program code (Fig. 2).

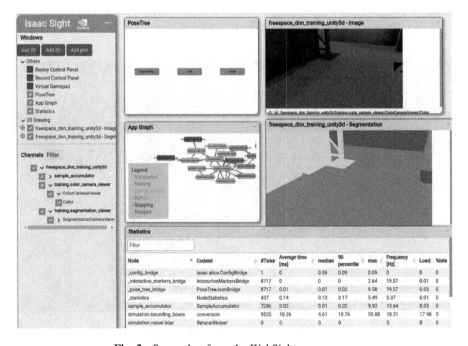

Fig. 2. Screenshot from the WebSight server page

The BUILD file contains parameters for the application launch and execution. The script seg_dataset.py implements the collection of messages from the robot camera, messages from the segmentation network, as well as the generation of a segmentation image, and the saving of all images in the target directory, taking into account the naming rules (the same file names for the corresponding images in the "seg" and "image" folders). To receive images from the camera and the segmentation network, it is necessary to create objects corresponding to the channels for the color image and segmentation data:

```
self.rgb_rx = self.isaac_proto_rx ("ColorCameraProto", "color")
self.seg_rx = self.isaac_proto_rx        ("SegmentationCameraProto",
"segmentation")
```

The entry point for the program is the "tick" method, which is automatically called by the Application type object when the developed application is registered in the Isaac SDK environment. Checking for the presence of an image in the data channel is carried out using the self.rgb_rx.available () method.

If the image is available for reading, then the reading is performed by the rgb_image_proto = self.rgb_rx.get_proto () code.

Saving is done using standard python language methods:

```
rgb_image = np.frombuffer (rgb_image_buffer, dtype = rgb_data_type)
rgb_image = rgb_image.reshape ((rgb_rows, rgb_cols, rgb_channels))
im = Image.fromarray (rgb_image)
im = im.resize ((420, 240), Image.ANTIALIAS)
im.save ("/images /color /robot_image _ {}. png".format (num))
```

A segmentation mask is generated similarly with the only difference that segmentation data is a matrix with scalar values corresponding to class numbers. It is necessary to transform them into a color segmentation image (3 RGB channels for each pixel) with some simple code:

```
width, height, channels = image.shape
out = np.empty ((width, height, 3), dtype = np.uint8)
image = np.stack (image, axis = -1)
image = np.stack (image, axis = -1)
# 1 = red 255 0 0
# 2 = blue 0 0 255
# 3 = green 0 255 0
# 4 = cyan 0 255 255
# 5 = yellow 255 255 0
red = lambda x: 255 if (x == 1) or (x == 5) else 0
green = lambda x: 255 if (x == 3) or (x == 4) or (x == 5) else 0
blue = lambda x: 255 if (x == 2) or (x == 4) else 0
out [:,:, 0] = np.vectorize (red) (image)
out [:,:, 1] = np.vectorize (green) (image)
out [:,:, 2] = np.vectorize (blue) (image)
```

As a result, a dataset of synthetic data is obtained, where x (features) is the rendering of the scene, that simulates the video camera data located on the mobile robot, and y (target) is the corresponding mask of scene objects. Each class of scene objects is represented in the mask by its color. In essence, this is an automatic segmentation of a scene (Fig. 3).

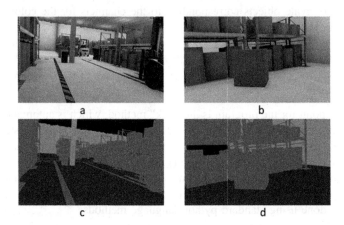

a   b

c   d

Fig. 3. In the upper part of the figure (a, b) examples of the virtual world renderings are presented. In the lower part of the figure (c, d) the mask of objects corresponding to these rendering are presented. It can be seen that each type (class) of objects in the scene has its own color.

5   Automatic Sample Labeling for the Classification Task

After obtaining the basic sample, it is necessary to change the target variable "y" so that it was is a scene mask, but a binary scalar value (0 or 1) indicating the presence of an obstacle that could be dangerous for the robot during the next program control cycle.

Before solving the dynamic problem, assumptions are made that the current robot path coincides with the center of the image from the robot camera. Such an assumption is typical for control tasks in mobile robotics.

For the binarization of the target parameter, a simple hypothesis is proposed: if objects are located in the central zone of the frame and occupy a sufficiently large area, then they are an obstacle, if they are in another place or occupy a small area, then they are not an obstacle. With a segmentation mask, this hypothesis can be implemented using the OpenCV library.

The algorithm can be represented by the following pseudo-code:

```
function calc_risk(segmentation_mask, triangle_points, area_thresh-
old):
        triangle_mask = draw_triangle_mask(triangle_points)
        roi = image_bitwise_and(segmentation_mask, triangle_mask)
        _, blocks_clr_mask = filter_non_blocks_colors(roi)
```

```
risk_area = count_nonzero(blocks_clr_mask)
risk_status = 0
if risk_area > area_threshold:
    risk_status = 1
return risk_status
```

As an intermediate stage in the execution of this algorithm, the following segmentation masks where obtained (Fig. 4). A simple threshold function based on the object position determines whether an object is an obstacle or not.

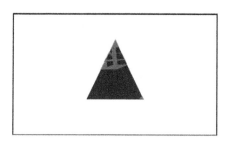 

Fig. 4. The appearance of the zone of interest (variable "roi" in pseudo-code) to assess the risk of movement. In this area, the area of potential barriers is estimated on the frame and a binary mark is calculated.

6 Experiments

Only a visual representation of the scene is provided as input for the neural networks without additional information about the objects. A flag characterizing the risk of further movement of the robot is expected as output.

Each model is run 10 times for statistical confidence in the results. The training is run with 15 epochs, after which the models are saturated, the batch size is 32, the total sample consists of 3511 images, 33% of which were validated. After each epoch, the training sample was shuffled (shuffle = True), and between each run (out of 15 iterations), the samples were randomly divided into training and validation subsets.

Table 1 shows that a convolutional neural network successfully finds a correlation between objects, their position in the frame, and risk. A convolutional network with attention works more accurately, also it allows to localize these objects without additional labeling of the training sample.

Table 1. Accuracy of motion risk recognition

Metric	CNN	ATT	P Value by Fisher's criterion
Train Accuracy, %	$\mu = 0.949$, $\sigma = 0.142$	$\mu = 0.981$, $\sigma = 0.005$	$0.22 > 0.05$
Valid Accuracy, %	$\mu = 0.939$, $\sigma = 0.145$	$\mu = 0.947$, $\sigma = 0.015$	$0.24 > 0.05$

A network with attention allows to not only get a class label but also an attention mask. After several epochs of training, visualization of attention masks shows high values on the desired objects. Figure 5 shows that if an object is located on the way of the robot, then it is classified as an obstacle (a, c), and when the object is located far from the center of the frame, then it is ignored (e, g). At the same time, attention covers potential obstacles regardless of their location, but the binary score is determined correctly. In several frames, potential obstacles are practically not visible. This is exactly the behavior that was expected from the system.

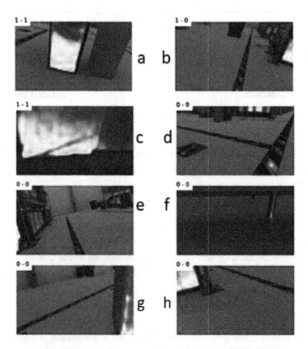

Fig. 5. Heat maps of attention. White signals potential obstacles in the frame.

Next, this mask was binarized using a threshold function and the contours of the proposed objects (obstacles) were selected. With sufficient accuracy of the model, one can localize objects in the frame and evaluate their parameters (area, specific object class, etc.). The whole process is implemented without manual labeling of segmentation masks for training of the network (Fig. 6).

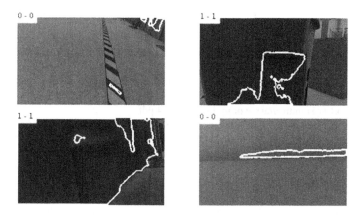

Fig. 6. Selecting objects using attention. The object is considered a connected area with a value of attention above 10% of the maximum level of the mask of attention. In the frame at the bottom left, one can see that the cabinets stand out quite accurately. The box in the upper right frame is fragmented.

In this paper, we do not measure the quality of the selection of the contours of objects (obstacles). This is the task for the next study. The approach itself turns out to be viable, but the accuracy of the result can be improved.

7   Conclusion

The article describes an approach for generating synthetic datasets with automatic marking using the NVIDIA Isaac robotic platform for scene analysis tasks for mobile robots. In the proposed approach, the obstacle detection problem is solved as a binary classification problem using the "end-to-end" convolutional neural network model with an accuracy of 93.9% without complex data labeling or development of additional heuristics.

Using the attention mechanism, the developed approach can be used to obtain additional information about obstacles, such as the location of objects in the frame and their size. The use of attention increases the accuracy of recognition of obstacles in a weakly formalized feature.

Further work can be aimed at improving the accuracy of localization and determining the spatial properties of obstacles (size, contours, distance to the object, etc.), as well as predicting situations of collisions with dynamic objects.

Weak formalizations of the target variable can be applied in a wide range of scene recognition and analysis tasks in addition to obstacle recognition for mobile robots. Attention mechanism allows to select the required objects with weakly formalized data sample.

References

1. Liu, X., Deng, Z., Yang, Y.: Recent progress in semantic image segmentation. https://arxiv.org/ftp/arxiv/papers/1809/1809.10198.pdf
2. Girshick, R., Donahue, J., Darrell, T., Malik, J.: Rich feature hierarchies for accurate object detection and semantic segmentation
3. Tech report (v5). https://arxiv.org/pdf/1311.2524.pdf
4. Redmon, J., Divvala, S., Girshick, R., Farhadi, A.: You only look once: unified, real-time object detection. https://arxiv.org/pdf/1506.02640.pdf
5. Girshick, R.: Fast R-CNN. https://arxiv.org/pdf/1504.08083.pdf
6. Zhao, Z.-Q., Zheng, P., Xu, S., Wu, X.: Object detection with deep learning: a review. https://arxiv.org/pdf/1807.05511.pdf
7. Gu, S., Holly, E., Lillicrap, T., Levine, S.: Deep reinforcement learning for robotic manipulation with asynchronous off-policy updates. https://arxiv.org/pdf/1610.00633.pdf
8. Singh, A., Yang, L., Hartikainen, K., Finn, C., Levine, S.: End-to-end robotic reinforcement learning without reward engineering. https://arxiv.org/pdf/1904.07854.pdf
9. Vezhnevets, A.S., Osindero, S., Schaul, T., Heess, N., Jaderberg, M., Silver, D., Kavukcuoglu, K.: https://arxiv.org/pdf/1703.01161.pdf
10. Srinivas, A., Laskin, M., Abbeel, P.: CURL: contrastive unsupervised representations for reinforcement learning. https://arxiv.org/pdf/2004.04136.pdf
11. Xu, K., et al.: Show, attend and tell: neural image caption generation with visual attention. https://arxiv.org/pdf/1502.03044.pdf
12. Wang, W., et al.: Learning Unsupervised Video Object Segmentation through Visual Attention. http://openaccess.thecvf.com/content_CVPR_2019/papers/Wang_Learning_Unsupervised_Video_Object_Segmentation_Through_Visual_Attention_CVPR_2019_paper.pdf
13. Saleh, F.S., Sadegh, M., Salzmann, M., Petersson, L., Alvarez, J.M.: Effective use of synthetic data for urban scene semantic segmentation. https://arxiv.org/pdf/1807.06132.pdf
14. Sun, J., Darbehani, F., Zaidi, M., Wang, B.L.: SAUNet: shape attentive U-Net for interpretable medical image segmentation. https://arxiv.org/pdf/2001.07645v3.pdf
15. Sviatov, K., Miheev, A., Kanin, D., Sukhov, S., Tronin, V.: Scenes segmentation in self-driving car navigation system using neural network models with attention. In: Misra, S., et al. (eds.) ICCSA 2019. LNCS, vol. 11623, pp. 278–289. Springer, Cham (2019). https://doi.org/10.1007/978-3-030-24308-1_23
16. Siam, M., Gamal, M., Abdel-Razek, M., Yogamani, S., Jagersand, M., Zhang, H.: A Comparative Study of Real-time Semantic Segmentation for Autonomous Driving. http://openaccess.thecvf.com/content_cvpr_2018_workshops/papers/w12/Siam_A_Comparative_Study_CVPR_2018_paper.pdf
17. Liao, W., Shuai, L., Rosenhahn, B., Yang, M.Y.: Natural language guided visual relationship detection. https://arxiv.org/pdf/1711.06032.pdf
18. Ortiz, J.C.R.: Scene Understanding for mobile robots exploiting Seep Learning Techniques. https://ridda2.utp.ac.pa/bitstream/handle/123456789/6473/tesis_jose_carlos_rangel_ortiz.pdf?sequence=1&isAllowed=y

Author Index

Printed in the United States
v Bookmasters